Handbook of Research on the Influence and Effectiveness of Gamification in Education

Oscar Bernardes
ISCAP, ISEP, Polytechnic Institute of Porto, Portugal & University of Aveiro, Portugal

Vanessa Amorim
ISCAP, Polytechnic Institute of Porto, Portugal

Antonio Carrizo Moreira
University of Aveiro, Portugal

IGI Global
PUBLISHER of TIMELY KNOWLEDGE

A volume in the Advances in Game-Based Learning (AGBL) Book Series

Published in the United States of America by
IGI Global
Information Science Reference (an imprint of IGI Global)
701 E. Chocolate Avenue
Hershey PA, USA 17033
Tel: 717-533-8845
Fax: 717-533-8661
E-mail: cust@igi-global.com
Web site: http://www.igi-global.com

Library of Congress Cataloging-in-Publication Data

Names: Bernardes, Oscar, 1978- editor. | Amorim, Vanessa, 1992- editor. | Moreira, Antonio Carrizo, 1961- editor.
Title: Handbook of research on the influence and effectiveness of gamification in education / Oscar Bernardes, Vanessa Amorim, and Antonio Carrizo Moreira, Editors.
Other titles: Research on the influence and effectiveness of gamification in education
Description: Hershey, PA : Information Science Reference, [2022] | Includes bibliographical references and index. | Summary: "This reference book considers the importance of gamification in the current learning environment and discusses the best practices, opportunities, and challenges of this innovative technology within an educational setting by covering a wide range of critical topics such as engagement, serious games, and escape rooms"-- Provided by publisher.
Identifiers: LCCN 2022014832 (print) | LCCN 2022014833 (ebook) | ISBN 9781668442876 (hardcover) | ISBN 9781668442883 (ebook)
Subjects: LCSH: Educational games--Research. | Gamification--Research. | Education--Computer-assisted instruction. | Teaching--Aids and devices. | Simulation games in education.
Classification: LCC LB1029.G3 H367 2022 (print) | LCC LB1029.G3 (ebook) | DDC 371.33/7--dc23
LC record available at https://lccn.loc.gov/2022014832
LC ebook record available at https://lccn.loc.gov/2022014833

This book is published in the IGI Global book series Advances in Game-Based Learning (AGBL) (ISSN: 2327-1825; eISSN: 2327-1833)

British Cataloguing in Publication Data
A Cataloguing in Publication record for this book is available from the British Library.

All work contributed to this book is new, previously-unpublished material. The views expressed in this book are those of the authors, but not necessarily of the publisher.

For electronic access to this publication, please contact: eresources@igi-global.com.

Advances in Game-Based Learning (AGBL) Book Series

Robert D. Tennyson
University of Minnesota, USA

ISSN:2327-1825
EISSN:2327-1833

Mission

The **Advances in Game-Based Learning (AGBL) Book Series** aims to cover all aspects of serious games applied to any area of education. The definition and concept of education has begun to morph significantly in the past decades and game-based learning has become a popular way to encourage more active learning in a creative and alternative manner for students in K-12 classrooms, higher education, and adult education. **AGBL** presents titles that address many applications, theories, and principles surrounding this growing area of educational theory and practice.

Coverage

- Curriculum Development Using Educational Games
- Digital Game-Based Learning
- Edutainment
- Electronic Educational Games
- Game Design and Development of Educational Games
- MMOs in Education
- Pedagogical Theory of Game-Based Learning
- Psychological Study of Students Involved in Game-Based Learning
- Role of instructors
- Virtual worlds and game-based learning

The Advances in Game-Based Learning (AGBL) Book Series (ISSN 2327-1825) is published by IGI Global, 701 E. Chocolate Avenue, Hershey, PA 17033-1240, USA, www.igi-global.com. This series is composed of titles available for purchase individually; each title is edited to be contextually exclusive from any other title within the series. For pricing and ordering information please visit http://www.igi-global.com/book-series/advances-game-based-learning/73680. Postmaster: Send all address changes to above address.

Titles in this Series

For a list of additional titles in this series, please visit: www.igi-global.com/book-series/advances-game-based-learning/73680

Handbook of Research on International Approaches and Practices for Gamifying Mathematics
Cristina A. Huertas-Abril (University of Córdoba, Spain) Elvira Fernández-Ahumada (University of Córdoba, Spain) and Natividad Adamuz-Povedano (University of Córdoba, pain)
Information Science Reference • © 2022 • 422pp • H/C (ISBN: 9781799896609) • US $270.00

Handbook of Research on Using Disruptive Methodologies and Game-Based Learning to Foster Transversal Skills
Irene Rivera-Trigueros (University of Granada, Spain) Abigail López-Alcarria (University of Granada, Spain) Diego-Pablo Ruiz-Padillo (University of Granada, Spain) María Dolores Olvera-Lobo (University of Granada, Spain) and José Gutiérrez-Pérez (University of Granada, pain)
Information Science Reference • © 2022 • 507pp • H/C (ISBN: 9781799886457) • US $285.00

Handbook of Research on Acquiring 21st Century Literacy Skills Through Game-Based Learning
Carol-Ann Lane (University of Toronto, Canada)
Information Science Reference • © 2022 • 958pp • H/C (ISBN: 9781799872719) • US $525.00

Esports Research and Its Integration in Education
Miles M. Harvey (University of New Mexico, USA) and Rick Marlatt (New Mexico State University, USA)
Information Science Reference • © 2021 • 313pp • H/C (ISBN: 9781799870692) • US $215.00

Exploring the Cognitive, Social, Cultural, and Psychological Aspects of Gaming and Simulations
Brock R. Dubbels (McMaster University, Canada)
Information Science Reference • © 2019 • 333pp • H/C (ISBN: 9781522574613) • US $190.00

Design, Motivation, and Frameworks in Game-Based Learning
Wee Hoe Tan (Sultan Idris Education University, Malaysia)
Information Science Reference • © 2019 • 306pp • H/C (ISBN: 9781522560265) • US $175.00

Handbook of Research on Collaborative Teaching Practice in Virtual Learning Environments
Gianni Panconesi (Esplica, Italy) and Maria Guida (National Institute for Documentation, Innovation, and Educational Research, Italy)
Information Science Reference • © 2017 • 637pp • H/C (ISBN: 9781522524267) • US $240.00

IGI Global
PUBLISHER of TIMELY KNOWLEDGE

701 East Chocolate Avenue, Hershey, PA 17033, USA
Tel: 717-533-8845 x100 • Fax: 717-533-8661
E-Mail: cust@igi-global.com • www.igi-global.com

Editorial Advisory Board

List of Contributors

Table of Contents

Detailed Table of Contents

Schools are pioneers of innovation in the process of teaching and learning. This study researches and analyzes new opportunities that modern information and communication technologies open up in the field of education and lifelong learning. It uncovers what place gamification in schooling holds, how it affects people, and what students take away from the progressive idea. Thus, it recognizes the possibilities and limits of its implementation in the education process. The author aims to understand better how gamification can be used in educational institutions, its function, and how to apply game principles in this context as successfully as possible. Gamification is often seen as one of the supports for student motivation. Concerning the design of teaching, teaching methods, and educational goals, the learning principles of games can be used innovatively as supplements to classroom teaching, where the curriculum is supported by game elements as important components of the teaching method. It is an inspiration for educators and designers in building gamified learning contexts.

Over the last decade, we have seen a large amount of research performed on technology-enhanced learning. Within this area, the use of games and gamification in education has gained popularity over the years. In this work, the author aim to identify the main topics in these areas within the last 10 years. The researchers propose a new methodology to conduct text analytics-driven topic analysis following a bibliometrics and text analytics-driven approach. The authors collected all the metadata from 7815 papers in these areas over the last 10 years. The author used it to find the main topics across the papers and hidden relationships between author and papers. The analysis in this work has focused on three main objectives: 1) discover the main topics in games and gamification in education based on paper keywords and topic modeling; 2) discover the evolution of said topics over the last ten years of research; and 3) discover how papers and authors from different communities have interacted over the years from a network's perspective.

The chapter investigates the ways of a distance communication channel with gamification elements created in the electronic educational environment of maritime higher education institutions. The example of the gamified educational electronic environment on LMS Moodle is presented in the chapter. The chapter also gives examples of gamified activities on LMS Moodle to form communicative competency of future maritime professionals. The distance communication channel presented in the chapter contains the use of a social virtual reality platform. The static 360-degree virtual environment with a 2D video stream for English classes was analyzed. According to the received results, the quality and success of training increased. The use of gamification proved useful and helpful in the distance education of future maritime specialists.

This chapter explores the intricate socio-political-cultural factors affecting Thai design students' learning and examines the potential of games and gamification in sustainability learning as an unconventional design pedagogical approach in Thai higher education. This chapter's heart is an extensive participatory action research case study from the sustainable design course of two universities in Bangkok. The project allows students to learn from game design to raise awareness of sustainability-related issues and use the games to enhance their sustainability learning through peer interactions. Games and gamification can assist Thai design students in obtaining skills essential to education for sustainable development while reducing power distance and uncertainty avoidance among classroom members. Research findings also reveal the complex relationships between game-based pedagogical practice and cultural characteristics, such as fun-pleasure orientation and interdependence orientation.

Higher education is currently experiencing a period of self-examination as tuition costs soar, academic relevance is being challenged, and institutions experience stagnant enrollment. This changing collegial landscape has prompted higher education faculty and administration to reexamine many of their current practices. One area that some faculty have begun to explore is their pedagogical approach to instruction. Having realized that the lecture format is no longer sufficient for delivering engaging education, faculty have started to embrace alternative pedagogies such as games or game elements to enhance assignments and increase student engagement. This chapter will explore gamification implementation as an alternative pedagogical method and examine various elements of a gamified class structure at the university level. Other key features discussed in this exploration include the design and evaluation of course assignments, the use of locks on assignments, and the relevance of competition within gamified courses.

Firstly, the authors introduce the concept of gamification design applied to various contexts. Then, they discuss how the gamification approach is used within the space sector to develop online and offline resources to foster passion and interest in STEM-related subjects. Indeed, a decreasing number of students nowadays decide to take up STEM-related studies and careers. Therefore, following an edutainment logic, it is essential to design more gamification activities to increase students' motivation and engagement with STEM topics. Given this, they consider the cases of the videogames Kerbal Space Program (KSP) and MinecraftEdu, the ESA Kids website, Mission X, CanSat Competition, Moon Camp, Climate Detectives, Astro-Pi Challenge, and the ESERO Project. They also carry out a netnographic study on some social media pages. Moreover, they discuss how gamification activities may promote the company's corporate brand for NASA and the European Space Agency (ESA). Finally, they focus on the digital divide, which might limit the gamification methodology in approaching disadvantaged socio-economic countries.

This chapter presents a collaborative autoethnography study whereby two academics at a medium-sized UK university explore their experiences of teaching entrepreneurship in different business and law school departments to combine expertise and resources to develop interdisciplinary gamification solutions. The combined experiential reflections have contributed to the generation of ideas that will prompt future interdisciplinary content to be created to bridge together fields such as business, social, legal, and technical studies. The chapter concludes that critical factors limiting developments in interdisciplinary entrepreneurship games include a lack of focus on entrepreneurial skills in departments within HEIs other than business schools and a lack of cross-departmental communication and collaboration. Although all the required expertise and resources are present within the university, a genuinely holistic approach can only be developed if innovative teaching tools combine multidisciplinary content from all faculties.

In this chapter, the authors describe a Star Wars scientific gamification experience, presented as a gymkhana with seven different activities to be carried out in the classroom. This proposal was designed to be done with prospective primary teachers during their science training studies. The prospective teachers have to observe, explore, experiment, and describe the different physical and chemical phenomena involved. The emotional response of prospective teachers was studied to describe their affective dimension after this "science fair." Such gamification promotes high rates of positive emotions (such as surprise or curiosity) and very low rates of negative emotions (such as boredom or rejection). The affective domain should be considered during teacher training, which is possible with this kind of experience.

Grabbing students' attention is becoming more challenging in the digital age, distance education, and increasing low literacy. This complex educational phenomenon needs to be mitigated to prevent negative social and economic consequences. This work presents the use of gamification in higher education to engage and motivate students in Calculus, a course that traditionally presents high failure and dropout rates. The main goal is to report an experience developing an RPG-style educational digital game to be used and tested in part of the course during one semester. The project applied concepts of gamification, educational digital games, digital game-based learning, and the theory of meaningful learning as a theoretical basis for the formulation of the game. The results showed positive acceptance of this approach by the students and an increase of interest in proceeding with using the game for learning purposes. According to the results, 73% of students declared the game contributes to the learning process, and 82% showed interest in using the game for the whole semester.

This contribution explores the connections between gameful elements, bodily interactions, and musical features in the context of three case studies of music learning applications, demonstrating the role of these components in accomplishing the application's task. The critical essential element common to the three case studies is engagement due to gameful elements and other design characteristics such as the choice of music materials and the link between their structural elements and full body/gestural interaction. Assessment and experimental results demonstrate that these characteristics deeply influence users' involvement, memory, and learning.

This chapter presents the Commercium & Cognitionis project, which aligns technology and playfulness, implementing DICTs and gamification as pedagogical tools that value didactic content and engagement, combining competition and collaboration in the search for knowledge to solve the proposed challenges. The proposal is aligned with the insertion of urban youth into a highly imagetic and technological

The more the technique's suitability, the better will be the results. Game-based learning is where game features and principles are implanted within learning activities. Game-based learning is also an effective learning technique in which games boost student learning. Game-based learning (GBL) brings advancement, experimentation, and disclosure of internal ability in learners. For the educators, it creates original thoughts and ways to deal with the teaching-learning process, allowing instructors to learn new methodologies lined up with research on how students learn. This chapter attempts to sort out the requirement for game-based learning as a creative educating approach. The significant finding of this chapter is a conceptual framework that will enable researchers to identify critical factors for the successful implementation of GBL.

This chapter describes a case study of the gamification of an educational technology graduate course at the University of Hawaii. The chapter will provide some background literature about chat apps, chat apps in education, and gamification. Next, the chapter will discuss how gamification design elements, framed by the curricula, were implemented in the Discord chat app server using roles, bots, and participation-based experience points. Finally, the chapter will discuss the benefits, challenges, and lessons from incorporating gamification in the Discord server for a graduate online asynchronous course. Recommendations will be provided for instructors who are considering gamifying their college courses.

Gamification and design thinking can be considered part of instructional design (ID) in the higher education (HE) context. Each of these fields has much to learn from the others. For example, although there is a lack of an agreed method to gamify learning, there are established models for ID. Furthermore, ID and gamified learning share limitations, notably a lack of reflection and empathy/systems approach in the processes used, that can be remedied by borrowing from design thinking. In the context of HE, it is appropriate to frame that empathy as student engagement to draw on the literature base. A gamification method is presented that incorporates reflection and student engagement to remedy these limitations. Although conceived to improve student engagement with formative assessment in UK HE, the process may be widely applied to other settings to support user engagement and enhance relevant outcomes (e.g., satisfaction) in different global locations.

Software project management is a multitask process that involves planning, organizing, monitoring, and controlling. And Scrum is an agile project management method based on self-organized teams; that is, the team members, although guided by a product owner and the Scrum master, evaluate the project's tasks and decide who will take care of them and the schedule. However, in academia, the Scrum method might not work as expected in a professional environment because of the commitment of the team members. Also, it seems more proper for the students to be motivated to take care of more diverse tasks, not just those they are comfortable with. By gamifying the Scrum dashboard for their final subject project, the motivation to take varied and challenging activities is expected. A study was conducted where the main results indicate that the teams under a gamified project in the academy context, have a greater tendency to complete the project.

Chapter 27
Understanding the Challenges of Game-Based Training: Recommendations for Moving Research Forward in Game-Based Learning.......... 541
Diana R. Sanchez, San Francisco State University, USA
Clifton A. Lee, San Francisco State University, USA

Substantial resources have been put towards game-based learning and the use of games in multidisciplinary research and practice. Despite this growing popularity, a definitive link has yet to be established between games and learning outcomes such as improved motor skills or recall of information. The problems researchers face are a series of challenges that prevent researchers from conducting research on game-based learning in a consistent and standardized way. Through reviewing and aggregating the literature, the authors describe five challenges currently facing the area of game-based learning and offer recommendations as to what future research could do to resolve these challenges moving forward. The primary purpose of this chapter is to provide a steppingstone in the game-based learning literature to help move the field away from conflicting research findings and toward a clearer understanding of game-based learning as an educational solution across disciplines.

Chapter 28
Solving a Crime in the Geology Lab: A Gamification Lesson Plan to Get Familiar With Common Rocks and Minerals.......... 579
Isaac Corbacho-Cuello, University of Extremadura, Spain
Rodrigo González-García, University of Extremadura, Spain
Miriam Andrea Hernández-Barco, University of Extremadura, Spain

This work shows an innovative and manipulative activity to learn about rocks and minerals using gamification and problem-based learning. This proposal was designed to be carried out with primary school prospective teachers during their training studies but can also be applied in either primary or secondary education levels. Students role-play aspirants who intend to enroll in a fictitious scientific police school. The admission test to that school consists of a practical case, where light has to be thrown on a death case. They need to determine if it could be a self-poisoning or murder case, deciphering some hints and using their basic geology knowledge and skills to show that they deserve a place in that school. This activity takes advantage of the popular TV dramas based on forensics to engage and motivate the students to work in the lab with minerals and rocks that the students could otherwise not have well received.

Preface

Gaming is increasingly present in our society and everyday lives as a form of leisure, so we play in different contexts and situations to gain pleasant and single experiences for ourselves and others (Robson et al., 2015; Rapp, 2020; Hassan & Hamari, 2020). The gamification concept and its operationalization in non-gaming contexts have become a growing practice (Yang et al., 2017), with particular emphasis on education.

Gamification is considered a concept whose origin is associated with the digital industry, and its first use was in 2008; however, it has only started to be widely used in 2010 (Deterding et al., 2011; Huotari & Hamari, 2012; Rapp, 2020; Bai et al., 2020). According to the authors Deterding et al. (2011), the gamification is represented by a set of specific criteria, identified through the concepts: gamefulness – which means the quality of experience and behavior; gameful interaction – resources that provide a certain quality; and gameful design – design of the elements presents in the games. It is then possible to define gamification as "the use of game design elements in non-game contexts" (Deterding et al., 2011).

According to Huotari and Hamari (2012), gamification is based on "a process of enhancing a service with affordances for gameful experiences in order to support user's overall value creation." The authors state that this definition highlights the aim of a gamified application or service, represented by the experiences it creates, not the methodologies used. This definition also stresses that gamification does not necessarily need to be successful and may only contribute to creating meaningful experiences for users, contributing to creating the same psychological experiences that games generally produce.

Hamari et al. (2014) complement that gamification is "a process of enhancing services with (motivational) affordances in order to invoke gameful experiences and further behavioral outcomes." It is further described in the literature that gamification represents a "process of applying elements of game design to a non-game context, where the interaction between the game mechanisms and personal disposition results in a fun and enjoyable experience" (Tobon et al., 2020).

Gamification uses numerous game elements to obtain a response or behavior from users within a specific context in which it is applied (Klock et al., 2020). Thus, one can consider that the process of designing gamified strategies is different from the design of a game structure, given that in gamification, the goal is to enhance the interaction of its users with a particular purpose or behavior, while in the gaming industry the aim is to create fun and entertainment for its players (Nasirzadeh & Fathian, 2020). According to Zainuddin et al. (2020), the gamification elements allow for an excellent way of learning because it enables a better orientation to individuals' objectives.

According to Xi and Hamari (2020), gamification represents one of the last decade's most significant technological tendencies, given organizations' interests. Gamification has slowly incorporated the new acceptance of executives in this area, so the value of the gamification market in 2016 was expected to increase to \$2.8 billion (Lucassen & Jansen, 2014), \$5.5 billion in 2018 (Conaway & Garay, 2014) and \$19.39 billion by 2023 (Xi & Hamari, 2019). However, Lucassen and Jansen (2014) state that the expected gamification concept adoption rate is not present in the literature despite the possibility of significant expected growth. This technological novelty is the basis for an innovative change in the any environment, and it is expected that until now, approximately 70% of the world's organizations seeking original methods will use gamification, according to Gartner's projections (2011) identified in the study of Hamid and Kuppusamy (2017).

Information systems enable learning and teaching to be successful for students. In this sense, gamification in the educational context draws on elements of game design to improve educational outcomes in order to make their activities and learning more engaging and enjoyable (Ofosu-Ampong, 2020). Several studies show that gamification is an innovative method of teaching and learning that encompasses various approaches, such as problem-based learning, design thinking, or competency-based learning, among others (Nadi-Ravandi & Batooli, 2022). The main purposes of gamification in education are to enhance learning ability, set goals that support learning, provide greater student engagement while enhancing their learning, induce positive behavioral changes, and foster their socialization skills (Smiderle et al., 2020).

This comprehensive and timely publication aims to be an essential reference source, building on existing literature in the field of gamification and education, while providing additional research opportunities in this dynamic and growing field. Thus, the book aims to reflect on this critical issue, increasing the understanding of the importance of the topics, and providing relevant academic work, empirical research findings, and an overview of this relevant field of study. It is hoped that this book will provide the resources necessary for academicians, interdisciplinary researchers, advanced-level students, technology developers, managers, and government officials to adopt and implement solutions for a more digital world. The book comprises 33 chapters, where every chapter explains different applications of gamification from an educational view.

The first chapter, "The Place of Gamification in the Educational Context," researches and analyzes new opportunities that modern information and communication technologies open up in education and lifelong learning. It also uncovers what place gamification in schooling holds, how it affects people, and what students take away from the progressive idea. Thus, it recognizes the possibilities and limits of its implementation in the education process. This chapter aims to inspire educators and designers in building gamified learning contexts.

Over the last decade, we have seen a large amount of research performed on technology. In Chapter 2, "A Bibliometrics and Text Analytics Review of Games and Gamification in Education," the authors aim to identify the main topics in these areas within the last ten years. The analysis in this work has focused on three main objectives: 1) Discover the main topics in games and gamification in education based on paper keywords and topic modeling; 2) Discover the evolution of said topics over the last ten years of research; and 3) Discover how papers and authors from different communities have interacted over the years from a network's perspective.

The next chapter, "Gamification in Healthcare Education: Demystifying a Trend," calls for reflection on one of the most promising technologies in healthcare education, the use of virtual patients and clinical virtual simulation as a pedagogical strategy to improve clinical decision-making and enhance clinical safety and healthcare quality. The chapter discusses the new challenges in healthcare education and the use of clinical virtual simulation in undergraduate healthcare education and lifelong learning, integrating gamification and serious games as strategies to increase intrinsic and extrinsic students' motivation.

"Gamification in Higher Education: Analysis of Your Strengths and Weaknesses" addresses the elements to consider for creating a gamified learning environment in Higher Education, specifically in the University classroom. It investigates various didactic proposals for gamification at the University by different authors in recent years, the variables they have addressed in their study, how they have been evaluated, and the most relevant findings.

The chapter "Gamified Learning Effectiveness Model" aims to evaluate the impact of online gamified learning among undergraduate medical students. The study developed a hypothetic model to investigate the effects of game characteristics, learning climate, and learners' self-efficacy on medical students' motivation, engagement, and improved learning process. Structural equation modeling examined the causal relationships between the observed and latent variables. The findings generated in this study indicate those game elements can positively influence students' performance and learning achievement through motivation and engagement.

Chapter 6, "The Efficacy of Gamification for the Involvement of Students in Distance Education," presents quantitative research that analyzes gamification's effectiveness in the distance learning undergraduate mathematics course. The research data suggest that gamification promoted students' engagement with learning. It is concluded that the categories presented in the study indicate that students perceive gamification as an alternative to create more dynamic classes and promote learning.

The following chapter, "The Game Pentade: A Design Model Proposal for Games for Education," considers the design of Games for Education, where players cultivate their knowledge and practice their skills by multiplying numerous hindrances during gaming. Educational elements are integrated into the gameplay, which players acquire while playing. The game's effectiveness depends on the players' ability to form a cheerful and encouraging environment to continue playing while increasing their interest in gameplay and improving academic performance.

"The Rise of Educational Escape Rooms: Designing Games as Formative Tasks" is the title of Chapter 8, highlighting the rise of escape rooms as a worldwide extended leisure activity is a reality. Such success has been achieved briefly and has motivated its use as a formative tool at various academic levels. Some authors have reported successful use of educational escape rooms in multiple topics. This chapter aims to provide background, information, case reports, and guidelines for using educational escape in various curricular disciplines.

Chapter 9, "Converting Course Material to Educational Escape Room Formats," considers that game-based learning and gamification concepts are growing as educators look to engage, motivate and create memorable learning experiences for their students. In this chapter, the authors provide a primer to bring teachers and academics up to date on developing educational escape rooms for their classrooms.

The escape rooms and breakouts are immersive games in which the participants are locked in a room and must solve a series of puzzles to escape. In virtuality, these games have also aroused interest in the educational field as a learning tool to transform students from passive spectators to active participants. Immersive learning allows students to learn about a topic while practicing teamwork and communication. In this context, the chapter "Escape Rooms and Breakouts: Novel Educational Strategies" aims to explain how these tools work and describe the implementation process using digital educational resources available on the Web.

"Development of Computer Games by Students," Chapter 11, describes practical tasks related to developing computer games in students' education. Game development uses modern platforms that provide ample opportunities. Students create 3D models, write scripts, and research interaction principles between different applications. Such tasks will help protect the younger generation from misuse of computer games, improve programming and modeling skills, and develop spatial thinking and creativity.

The next chapter, "Creation of Distance Communication Channel With Gamification Elements," investigates the ways of a distance communication channel with gamification elements created in the electronic educational environment of maritime higher education institutions. The example of the gamified educational electronic environment on LMS MOODLE is presented in the chapter. The chapter also gives examples of gamified activities on LMS MOODLE to form communicative competency of future maritime professionals.

"Games and Gamification in Sustainability Learning: A Peer-Based Approach for Thai Design Education" explores the intricate socio-political-cultural factors affecting Thai design students' learning and examines the potential of games and gamification in sustainability learning as an unconventional design pedagogical approach in Thai higher education. This chapter's heart is an extensive participatory action research case study from the Sustainable Design course of two universities in Bangkok. The project allows students to learn from game design to raise awareness of sustainability-related issues and use the games to enhance their sustainability learning through peer interactions.

Chapter 14, "Gamification 101: An Exploration of a Gamified Instructional Approach," explores gamification implementation as an alternative pedagogical method and examines various elements of a gamified class structure at the university level. Other key features discussed in this exploration include the design and evaluation of course assignments, the use of locks on assignments, and the relevance of competition within gamified courses.

The following chapter, "Gamification in the Space Sector: How Gamification Activities Can Foster the Passion and Interest for STEM-Related Studies," discusses how the gamification approach is used within the space sector to develop online and offline resources to foster passion and interest in STEM-related subjects. The chapter also focuses on how gamification activities may promote the company's corporate brand for NASA and the European Space Agency and the digital divide, which might limit the gamification methodology in approaching disadvantaged socio-economic countries.

"Interdisciplinary Communication: Paving the Way for Gamification in Entrepreneurship Education – A Case Study From a Medium-Sized UK University" is the title of Chapter 16. This chapter presents a collaborative autoethnography study whereby two academics at a medium-sized UK university explore their experiences teaching entrepreneurship in different business and law school departments to combine expertise and resources to develop interdisciplinary gamification solutions. The chapter concludes that critical factors limiting developments in interdisciplinary entrepreneurship games include a lack of focus on entrepreneurial skills in departments within HEIs other than business schools and a lack of cross-departmental communication and collaboration.

Chapter 17, "Science Fair Project in the Teacher Training Process: Its Emotional Response and Implications," describes a Star Wars scientific gamification experience, presented as a gymkhana with seven different activities to be carried out in the classroom. This proposal was designed to be done with prospective primary teachers during their science training studies. Future teachers have to observe, explore, experiment, and describe the different physical and chemical phenomena involved.

The next chapter, "The Use of an Educational Digital Game in Higher Education: Design and Application to Increase the Motivation in Calculus Learning," presents gamification in higher education to engage and motivate students in Calculus. This course traditionally offers high failure and dropout rates. The main goal is to report an experience developing an RPG-style educational digital game to be used and tested in part of the course during one semester. The project applied concepts of gamification, educational digital games, digital game-based learning, and the theory of meaningful learning as a theoretical basis for the formulation of the game.

"The Role of Gameful Elements, Bodily Interactions, and Musical Features in Fostering Engagement and Learning in Musical Serious Games" explores the connections between gameful elements, bodily interactions, and musical features in the context of three case studies of music learning applications, demonstrating the role of these components in accomplishing the application's task. The critical essential element common to the three case studies is engagement due to gameful elements and other design characteristics such as the choice of music materials and the link between their structural elements and full-body/gestural interaction.

Chapter 20, "Commercium and Cognitionis Project: A Gamification Experience in an Undergraduate Course," presents the Commercium and Cognitionis project, which aligns technology and playfulness, implementing DICTs and gamiðcation as pedagogical tools that value didactic content and engagement, combining competition and collaboration in the search for knowledge to solve the proposed challenges. The proposal is aligned with the insertion of urban youth into a highly imagetic and technological contemporary culture.

Digital game-based learning (DGBL) is a novel methodology implemented in many educational virtual settings to improve students' attention, motivation, and engagement while learning. The chapter "Educational Opportunities of Virtual Game-based Initiatives for Students with Disabilities" aims to provide insight into how game-based methods can enhance students' learning process with sensory, intellectual, and learning disabilities. Specifically, this chapter's key is to assess the possibilities offered by introducing DGBL in educational contexts from a theoretical perspective.

The following chapter, "Flow, Motivation, Social Interaction, and Design Issues of Serious Games in Education," discusses the flow, motivation, social interaction, and design issues in serious games in education from a theoretical perspective. Serious games in education aim to improve students' skills or provide them with knowledge while entertaining. The serious game design process and its challenges help create serious games that meet students' needs and expectations.

Chapter 23, "Gamification Framework Understanding the Critical Success Factors for Using Gamification as a Pedagogical Tool," attempts to sort out the requirement for Game-Based Learning as a creative educating approach. Game-based learning is where game features and principles are implanted within learning activities. Game-based learning is also an effective learning technique in which games boost student learning. For educators, it creates original thoughts and ways to deal with the teaching-learning process, allowing instructors to learn new methodologies lined up with research on how students learn.

"Gamification to Engage Students: Integrating the Use of Discord Chat App" describes a case study of the gamification of an educational technology graduate course at the University of Hawaii. The chapter provides some background literature about chat apps, chat apps in education, and gamification. Next, the chapter discusses how gamification design elements, framed by the curricula, were implemented in the Discord chat app server using roles, bots, and participation-based experience points. Finally, the chapter discusses the benefits, challenges, and lessons from incorporating gamification in the Discord server for a graduate online asynchronous course.

The following chapter, "Gamified Learning in Higher Education: An Instructional Design Method to Improve Engagement," highlights that Gamification and Design Thinking can be considered part of Instructional Design (ID) in the Higher Education (HE) context. Each of these fields has much to learn from the others. Furthermore, ID and Gamified Learning share limitations, notably a lack of reflection and empathy/ systems approach in the processes used, that can be remedied by borrowing from Design

Thinking. In the context of HE, it is appropriate to frame that empathy as student engagement to draw on the literature base.

Software project management is a multitask process that involves planning, organizing, monitoring, and controlling. Scrum is an agile project management method based on self-organized teams; that is, the team members, although guided by a product owner and the Scrum master, evaluate the project's tasks and decide who will take care of them and the schedule. The chapter "Scrumming: Gamifying a Dashboard for Undergraduate Students' Motivation" highlights that in academia, the Scrum method might not work as expected in a professional environment because of commitment to the team members. Therefore, the principal results indicate that the teams under a gamified project tend to complete the project.

In the chapter "Understanding the Challenges of Game-Based Training: Recommendations for Moving Research Forward in Games-Based Learning," reviewing and aggregating the literature describes five challenges currently facing the area of game-based learning, the authors offer recommendations as to what future research could do to resolve these challenges moving forward. The primary purpose of this chapter is to provide a stepping stone in the game-based learning literature to help move the field away from conflicting research findings and toward a clearer understanding of game-based learning as an educational solution across disciplines.

Chapter 28, "Solving a Crime in the Geology Lab: A Gamification Lesson Plan to Get Familiar With Common Rocks and Minerals," shows an innovative and manipulative activity to learn about rocks and minerals using gamification and problem-based learning. This was designed to be carried out with Primary School prospective teachers during their training studies but can also be applied in either, Primary or Secondary education levels.

The next chapter, "Entrepreneurial Competences Development Through Game Strategies: A Case Study of a Card Game Focused on Social Transformation With Health Students," discusses a Higher Education experience using an online tailor-made card game to develop entrepreneurial competencies within health students on an online course. The project counted 892 participants from 12 different health majors. The research is qualitative exploratory, based on a case study with a non-probabilistic sampling. The findings indicate the implemented strategies greatly enhanced the student's engagement and co-responsibility in their learning processes, along with the expansion of interaction and experimentation.

"Fostering Motivation to Learn Through Gamification: Understanding the Impact of Different Kinds of Rewards on Learner Motivation" aims to provide teachers with more guidance in the gamification design process, especially concerning the difficult task of planning a motivating reward system. To do so, the authors conducted a qualitative study of the gamified learning app Duolingo. The study focused on understanding how users respond to the different kinds of rewards the app provides and how rewards affect their motivation to learn by fulfilling their need for competence, relatedness, and autonomy, in the framework of Self-Determination Theory.

Chapter 31, "Gamifying the Refugee Classroom: Challenges and Potential," presents the design, implementation, and evaluation of a theory-driven educational scenario for students with a refugee background based on Gamification to support learning Greek as a Second Language. The scenario was implemented in an Educational Priority Zone (ZEP) classroom of a Greek primary school with eight refugee students aged 9 to 11 with a diverse linguistic background. The findings indicate that the game elements significantly impacted engagements were competition and collaboration and some immersion-related features like storytelling, which increased autonomy.

"Increasing Engagement Through Explicit and Implicit Gamification in Higher Education" provides specific definitions of these terms and acknowledges that such attempts to increase engagement often offer an additional layer of extrinsic motivators. The authors propose that this can lead to unexpected and undesirable effects if extrinsic motivators are not well aligned to the desired behavior. This chapter presents a taxonomy of engagement strategies regarding their implicit and explicit game attributes and their implicit and explicit teaching attributes.

The last chapter, "Merging Tangibles and Gamification to Teach Algorithmic Thinking to KG Children With Gamirithmic," presents the design, implementation, and evaluation of a new technique to improve children's algorithmic thinking skills that enable solving problems following clearly defined steps. Gamirithmic teaches children to codify ideas by coming up with solutions to problems in systematic and structured ways via its step-by-step procedure with the increasing complexity of commands in each step. Gamirithmic teaches technology-related concepts using a technology-independent medium that is less likely to induce behavioral problems associated with screen-based methods.

We hope that this book provides an enjoyable reading experience.

Óscar Bernardes
ISCAP, ISEP, Polytechnic Institute of Porto, Portugal & University of Aveiro, Portugal

Vanessa Amorim
ISCAP, Polytechnic Institute of Porto, Portugal

António Carrizo Moreira
University of Aveiro, Portugal

REFERENCES

Bai, S., Hew, K. F., & Huang, B. (2020). Does gamification improve student learning outcome? Evidence from a meta-analysis and synthesis of qualitative data in educational contexts. *Educational Research Review*, *30*, 100322. doi:10.1016/j.edurev.2020.100322

Conaway, R., & Garay, M. C. (2014). Gamification and service marketing. *SpringerPlus*, *3*(1), 1–11. doi:10.1186/2193-1801-3-653 PMID:25392812

Deterding, S., Dixon, D., Khaled, R., & Nacke, L. (2011). From Game Design Elements to Gamefulness: Defining "Gamification." *Proceedings of the 15th International Academic MindTrek Conference on Envisioning Future Media Environments - MindTrek '11*. 10.1145/2181037.2181040

Hamari, J., Koivisto, J., & Sarsa, H. (2014). Does gamification work? - A literature review of empirical studies on gamification. *Proceedings of the Annual Hawaii International Conference on System Sciences*, 3025–3034. 10.1109/HICSS.2014.377

Hamid, M., & Kuppusamy, M. (2017). Gamification Implementation in Service Marketing: A Literature Review. *Electronic Journal of Business & Management*, *2*(1), 38–50.

Hassan, L., & Hamari, J. (2020). Gameful civic engagement: A review of the literature on gamification of e-participation. *Government Information Quarterly*, *37*(3), 101461. doi:10.1016/j.giq.2020.101461

Huotari, K., & Hamari, J. (2012). Defining Gamification-A Service Marketing Perspective. *Proceeding of the 16th International Academic MindTrek Conference on - MindTrek '12*. 10.1145/2393132.2393137

Klock, A. C. T., Gasparini, I., Pimenta, M. S., & Hamari, J. (2020). Tailored gamification: A review of literature. *International Journal of Human-Computer Studies*, *144*, 102495. doi:10.1016/j.ijhcs.2020.102495

Lucassen, G., & Jansen, S. (2014). Gamiðcation in Consumer Marketing - Future or Fallacy? *Procedia: Social and Behavioral Sciences*, *148*, 194–202. doi:10.1016/j.sbspro.2014.07.034

Nadi-Ravandi, S., & Batooli, Z. (2022). Gamification in education: A scientometric, content and co-occurrence analysis of systematic review and meta-analysis articles. *Education and Information Technologies*, 1–32. doi:10.100710639-022-11048-x PMID:35431599

Nasirzadeh, E., & Fathian, M. (2020). Investigating the effect of gamification elements on bank customers to personalize gamified systems. *International Journal of Human-Computer Studies*, *143*, 102469. doi:10.1016/j.ijhcs.2020.102469

Ofosu-Ampong, K. (2020). The Shift to Gamification in Education: A Review on Dominant Issues. *Journal of Educational Technology Systems*, *49*(1), 113–137. doi:10.1177/0047239520917629

Rapp, A. (2020). An exploration of world of Warcraft for the gamification of virtual organizations. *Electronic Commerce Research and Applications*, *42*, 100985. doi:10.1016/j.elerap.2020.100985

Robson, K., Plangger, K., Kietzmann, J. H., McCarthy, I., & Pitt, L. (2015). Is it all a game? Understanding the principles of gamification. *Business Horizons*, *58*(4), 411–420. doi:10.1016/j.bushor.2015.03.006

Smiderle, R., Rigo, S. J., Marques, L. B., Peçanha de Miranda Coelho, J. A., & Jaques, P. A. (2020). The impact of gamification on students' learning, engagement and behavior based on their personality traits. *Smart Learning Environments*, *7*(1), 1–11. doi:10.118640561-019-0098-x

Tobon, S., Ruiz-Alba, J. L., & García-Madariaga, J. (2020). Gamification and online consumer decisions: Is the game over? *Decision Support Systems*, *128*, 113167. doi:10.1016/j.dss.2019.113167

Xi, N., & Hamari, J. (2019). Does gamification satisfy needs? A study on the relationship between gamification features and intrinsic need satisfaction. *International Journal of Information Management*, *46*, 210–221. doi:10.1016/j.ijinfomgt.2018.12.002

Xi, N., & Hamari, J. (2020). Does gamification affect brand engagement and equity? A study in online brand communities. *Journal of Business Research*, *109*, 449–460. doi:10.1016/j.jbusres.2019.11.058

Yang, Y., Asaad, Y., & Dwivedi, Y. (2017). Examining the impact of gamification on intention of engagement and brand attitude in the marketing context. *Computers in Human Behavior*, *73*, 459–469. doi:10.1016/j.chb.2017.03.066

Zainuddin, Z., Chu, S. K. W., Shujahat, M., & Perera, C. J. (2020). The impact of gamification on learning and instruction: A systematic review of empirical evidence. *Educational Research Review*, *30*, 100326. doi:10.1016/j.edurev.2020.100326

Chapter 1
The Place of Gamification in the Educational Context

Jan Miškov
Masaryk University, Czech Republic

ABSTRACT

Schools are pioneers of innovation in the process of teaching and learning. This study researches and analyzes new opportunities that modern information and communication technologies open up in the field of education and lifelong learning. It uncovers what place gamification in schooling holds, how it affects people, and what students take away from the progressive idea. Thus, it recognizes the possibilities and limits of its implementation in the education process. The author aims to understand better how gamification can be used in educational institutions, its function, and how to apply game principles in this context as successfully as possible. Gamification is often seen as one of the supports for student motivation. Concerning the design of teaching, teaching methods, and educational goals, the learning principles of games can be used innovatively as supplements to classroom teaching, where the curriculum is supported by game elements as important components of the teaching method. It is an inspiration for educators and designers in building gamified learning contexts.

INTRODUCTION

In the new millennium, there has been a remarkable boom in the use of badges, leaderboards, challenges, and other game elements in various software, applications and websites. Digital games are inherently fun and motivating to play without outside pressure. Increasing the performance, efficiency, motivation, and involvement of students in learning can allegedly be achieved through gamification, which uses elements from digital games (such as game mechanics and dynamics) in non-game applications. In connection with thinking about game mechanics in a non-game context, we are talking about so-called "gamifying."

Therefore, the experience of gamification in our lives is not new. It stems from the spread of offline and online games. People of all ages around the world spend hours playing games without being forced to do so. This concept seems to be permeating economic, political and social contexts due to the growing popularity of digital games among the general public.

DOI: 10.4018/978-1-6684-4287-6.ch001

Users' satisfaction depends on their good experience. Research on users of gamified learning environments focuses on understanding their behavior, needs, and motivation through interviews, analysis of surveys, and other methods of feedback. Studies of the motivational potential of educational game principles are still somewhat limited by the development of learning management systems. However, it is necessary to start gaining insight to the preferences and needs of key actors in the learning process, in order to contribute to the development of good gamification practices in education.

Tulloch (2014) argues that gamification is a product of a neglected history of pedagogical improvement, a history of training that is effective but largely ignored, namely the game process that teaches players how to play (so-called tutorial). The author questions the evolving concept of gamification - he does not conceptualize it as a simple set of techniques and mechanics, but as a pedagogical heritage and an alternative framework for training and shaping the participant's behavior, which at the core contains concepts of fun and engagement.

This contribution highlights a shift in the educational paradigm from an instructive (i.e., linear and passive) concept to teaching based on game principles. The purpose of this chapter is to provide a broader awareness of gamification and the possibilities of its use (not only) in schools. The text includes examples that inspire to work with educational game principles in class. The introduction deals with the educational potential of game principles in learning from the perspective of actors in the educational process. It explores how digital games can enter teaching and learning in school, whether educational game principles are compatible with the logic of the dominant educational paradigm, and what their advantages and disadvantages are. Studies on learning with game elements will help to grasp their possible benefits and pitfalls in education. Based on the discussion of the findings, the author recommends to teachers, organizations, and developers of gamified learning environments how they could improve their teaching design in accordance with students' needs and different learning styles.

Insight on gamification in education offers recommendations on how to use game elements in different contexts (e.g., in the classroom, during an excursion or on social media) (Morschheuser et al., 2018; Robson et al., 2015; Toda et al., 2019). The author will also mention examples of good practice and teaching experience simulating the professional training of graduates. After all, Conrad and Tucker (2019) pointed out that the type of player correlates with the performance of individuals in gamified applications, and that the rewards do not guarantee an increase in performance or motivation when playing games. According to the author, adapting gamification based on player types is the first step to personalizing learning.

Chapter Outline

The authors first define the working concepts and the theoretical basis framing the subsequent findings from the research that was conducted in the field of gamification. The interpretation focuses on self-determination theory and its key concept of motivation. The next section discusses the basic components of the gamification approach and the function of game elements in the educational context. It identifies key frameworks and structures of game design thinking. The following part deals directly with game elements in the school environment and illustrates examples of good practice.

The second half of the chapter seriously considers possible difficulties with the implementation of gamification in the educational context. It is necessary to keep in mind that side effects, undesirable behaviors and obstacles may occur. The authors offer recommendations on how to cope with such situations or directly prevent them from the outset. Future research and the personalization of the educational process with regard to the experience of users of gamified systems, their feedback, predispositions, preferences and learning styles can also contribute to that.

THEORETICAL BACKGROUND

Based on the theoretical basis of behavioral psychology, anthropology and game studies, the authors propose a model for the design and assessment of playful experiences in educational environments inspired by game design. The theoretical framework of the overview study stems from existing research and practices and underpins the interpretation of presented results, it would be problematic to select a suitable gamification structure without it or to distinguish which of the used game mechanics and principles are desirable to achieve learning objectives and learning outcomes.

According to Gee (2003), digital games convey learning experiences that show how learning and literacy change in the modern world. He names the learning principles of digital games, the application of which is understood by the author as a way of satisfying basic psychological needs according to the self-determination theory (SDT) (Deci & Ryan, 1985). Gamification is "the use of elements of game design to motivate users in nongame contexts" (Deterding et al., 2011, p. 9). Van Roy and Zaman (2017) proposed procedures for effective gamification implementation in online learning system. These heuristics aim to provide autonomous motivation. They propose the following points:

- Not to force users to use a gamified system, so that they feel in control.
- To choose between the offer of suitable options and their number.
- To prepare goals that are challenging, but manageable.
- To incorporate feedback mechanisms that positively inform students about their progress.
- To enable user interaction and foster a sense of belonging.
- To take into account other psychological needs when designing a specific element to support one of them.
- Gamification should facilitate the motivation to achieve goals.
- Students should perceive the online learning environment as open and the gamified system should take into account the personal differences of users and their preferences.

Köse et al. (2019) studied the moderating effects of the user's conception of the utilitarian-hedonistic purpose of the system on its continuous use. The author included user experience, usefulness, and ease of use of the system as variables. The results show that the concept of the user is an influential aspect determining the continuation of use of the system. Utility and hedonic value are important predictors of the intention to use it (Baptista & Oliveira, 2019). Self-study (online) usually requires stronger inner motivation. Especially in education, gamification techniques are being welcomed as a promising strategy to enhance motivation (Ramirez & Squire, 2015), which is found to be an important determinant of educational success (Abramovich et al., 2013; Buckley & Doyle, 2014; Taylor et al., 2014).

Other researchers believe that it is important to use an expanded inventory of techniques that balance external with internal motivators (Dichev et al., 2014) and to design a gamification system that can be adapted to ensure that all students in the classroom can enjoy the benefits of gamification (Eickhoff et al., 2012; Hamari, 2013; Hamari & Koivisto, 2013). How people perceive game elements is influenced by situational factors. Transferring a game element to a nongame context within the gamification process can fundamentally change its meaning. For example, in the context of a mobile gamified application, Featherstone and Habgood (2019) found that constructive competition can be achieved through careful game design, and that avatars and videogames provide virtual currency with meaning and value.

SDT is useful for understanding, researching, and designing gamification. According to van Roy and Zaman (2019), game elements can support or hinder the satisfaction of basic psychological needs. In their view, "the design practice of gamified systems generally shows excessive dependence on external motivational regulations" (p. 10). Gamified systems that provide feelings of autonomy, competence, and relatedness are likely to strengthen students' inner motivation, both by causing and explaining the pleasant, motivating, and engaging experiences gained within them (Deci & Ryan, 2008). Xi and Hamari (2019) examined the relationship between gamification and satisfaction of internal needs. Success and social gamification predicted the satisfaction of the needs of autonomy, competence, and relatedness. Instead, immersion in activity is only related to fulfilling the need for independence. For the same reason, any "future intervention effort that intends to capitalize on the motivational pull of video games should purposely include game features that have the potential to increase need satisfaction" (Peng et al., 2012, p. 192).

When originally external motivational stimuli appeal to the basic psychological needs of the actor, all the more so, external regulations are thoroughly internalized, which leads to autonomous motivation. External regulation, and, by broadening the scope, also the typical implementation of gamification, have the potential to intensify feelings of inner motivation, provided that people perceive them as desirable for their psychological needs. In the educational context, this is associated with various positive educational consequences, such as improved grades and a better understanding of the subject materials (Deci & Ryan, 2015; Ryan & Deci, 2009).

GAMIFICATION IN THE EDUCATIONAL SECTOR

Game Elements in a Learning Environment

Judicial, strategic, and appropriate use of game elements can lead to a learning situation with a high level of active involvement and motivation, which, in turn, creates positive results in the cognitive, emotional, and social areas. Experts appreciate the versatility of gamification used in a classroom lecture, as a homework assistant, as a final exam or as a main learning activity to motivate students to improve their abilities or maximize learning. (Faiella & Ricciardi, 2015, p. 15)

In this section, the author focuses on gamification in an educational context. The reader should gain a better comprehension of how interaction with the gamified system can develop in education before addressing the question of whether gamification works. As such, it provides guidance for researchers, educators, designers, and software developers in building a new generation of gamified educational contexts.

Gamification is identified as one of the technologies that will have a major impact on schools in the world's most technologically advanced countries (Johnson et al., 2014), and is considered as a new approach that can bridge the generation gap between teachers and students (Kapp, 2007). It is increasingly seen as a possible solution to the declining motivation observed in students. Gamified educational contexts require a user-centered approach, characterized by a focus on students' needs and wishes.

Gamification is an approach that uses the properties of games (e.g., their various elements, mechanics, frameworks, aesthetics, game thinking or metaphors) situated outside the virtual world of the game. Its application is recommended in areas of everyday life where boredom, passivity, and repetition predominate to support the desired behavior. Applications of the gamification approach in education aim to improve student motivation and involvement and maximize learning. They are based on the need to arouse students' interest in learning and engage them so that they can have fun, encouraging them to achieve more ambitious goals and comply with the rules.

According to Werbach and Hunter (2012), gamification scenarios can be divided into three categories (Figure 1):

1. **Dynamics:** It forms the highest conceptual level in a gamified system. It contains limitations, emotions, narration, progress, and relationships.
2. **Mechanics:** It is a set of rules dictating the outcome of interactions within a system, while dynamics is a response of users to a set of these mechanics. Mechanics refers to the game elements that drive action forward. These are challenges, chance, competition, cooperation, feedback, resource gathering and rewards.
3. **Components:** They form the basic level of the gamification process. They include achievements, avatars, badges, collections, content unlocks, progress bars, donations, leaderboards, levels, and virtual goods. For example, points (components) provide rewards (mechanics) and create the impression of progress (dynamics).

Apostol et al. (2013) identified eight elements of games that are used to gamify teaching, namely rules, goals and results, feedback and rewards, problem-solving, story, player(s), safe environment, and sense of mastery.

Kapp (2012) distinguished those qualities that can only lead to a superficial level of student involvement from those that are most valuable for education. The first group consists of qualities that can only serve as a source of external motivation, such as rewards, points, and badges. In addition, de Sousa Borges et al. (2014) noted that, "in gamification approaches, these elements are not the center of the system, but aim to motivate users to use it" (p. 217). Others form story, challenge, decision making, sense of control, and mastery. Kapp (2012) considered it acceptable to give students a sense of autonomy and competence, if they voluntarily perform tasks for their own improvement. In particular, Kapp considered that, "in order for a game to become an effective learning experience, a combination of several elements is needed which makes it an effective means of education" (p. 50).

Perrotta et al. (2013) combined game mechanics with processes involved in learning. They stated that the gamification of learning is:

- Intrinsically motivating because rules are inputs into a wide range of decision-making processes.
- Fun, because the goals allow the student to see the direct impact of their efforts.
- Authentic, because the imagination provides a compelling background that allows students to experiment with their abilities without suffering the consequences of failure in real life.
- Leading to self-sufficiency, as feedback to students leads to facilitation and correction of performance.
- Experiential, because the social element allows students to share experiences and build bonds.

Figure 1. Game design model of components, mechanics and dynamics (Werbach & Hunter, 2012)
Source: adapted from gamestudies.cz, 2013

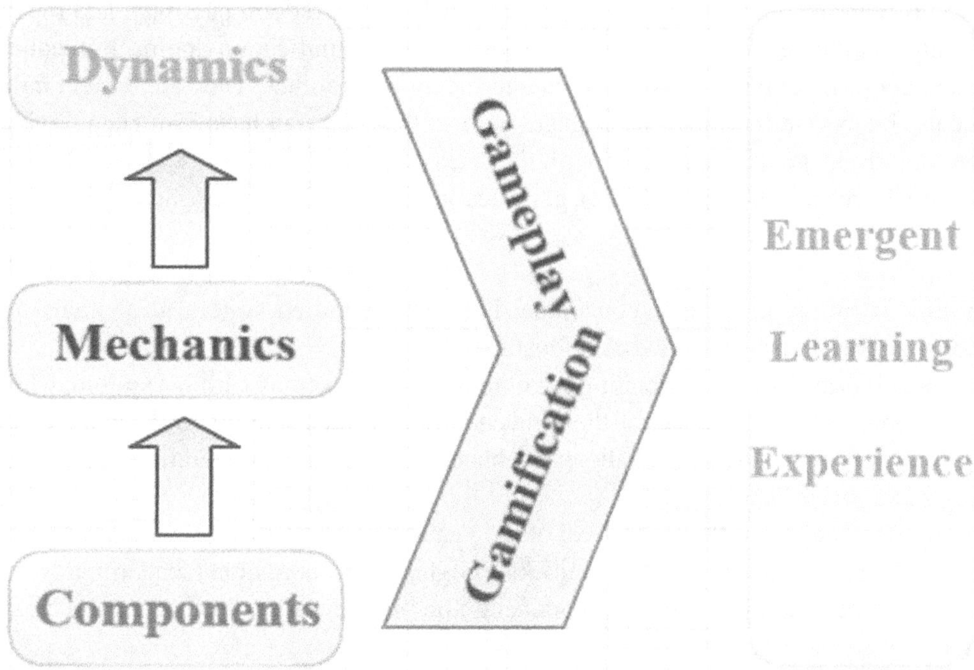

In addition to remuneration and feedback mechanics, gamified systems should provide a secure online learning environment where students can gain experience without being judged or punished for failure (Hakulinen et al., 2015; Lehtonen et al., 2015).

Apostol et al. (2013) sustained that "the best way for an educational designer or teacher to choose elements of the game is to consider the learning objectives and desired outcomes of the learning process" (pp. 68-69). They recommended it for a course design.

Games in a Classroom

From an early age, people are socially approaching the way they should act in different contexts according to their cultural norms (Giddens et al., 2013). In other words, they socialize or enculturate. Gamification is a guide for individuals to adjust their expectations of how they should behave, while transforming existing culture into gaming and games. However, it can be argued that, by introducing gamification, people are encouraged to start playing even in contexts where the game is culturally inappropriate (van Roy & Zaman, 2015).

In addition, when the typical game behavior "trial and error" (Buckley & Doyle, 2014, pp. 1–14) becomes part of the culture of society, people may also begin to believe that they would try again, if they failed on their first attempt, which may become problematic in sectors such as healthcare or the judiciary. For example, when simulating an operation, the consequences of failure are not fatal and the responsibility for human life is not so burdensome. Thus, the question arises of the compatibility of learning by trial and error with the teaching objectives of a particular field.

The new line of research develops the theory of educational gamification by combining motivational and learning theories to link gamification with practical education (Landers, 2015; Landers et al., 2015) or creating a framework for integrating gamification with pedagogy (Tulloch, 2014) or psychology of games (Lieberoth, 2015). According to Lieberoth (2015), it may not be the game itself that stimulates the individual, but rather the wrapping, that is the fact that the activity resembles a game. Simply framing an activity as a "game" can potentially change an individual's behavior. The outputs suggest that engagement and fun increased significantly due to the psychological effects of framing a task as a game but did not really increase any interest or amusement by adding game mechanics to the task once it was framed as a game. Only the wrapping of the activity as a game thus affects the students' engagement. Other studies report positive effects of gamification on student performance, for example in terms of better grades (Sua & Cheng, 2013) and learning behavior, or in terms of task effort (Barata et al., 2013). Denny (2013) found that adding badges to an online learning tool leads students to contribute more and be more involved than otherwise.

Research from the study of the text further shows that storytelling promotes learning and involvement. For example, compared to interpretive text or newspaper articles, stories are accompanied by better retention, generate more associations, and are more entertaining (Graesser et al., 1994). Another argument for adding a narrative to the game is that it can act as a support scaffold to solve problems during the game (Dickey, 2006). From a cognitive perspective, however, it can be argued that engaging narrative can distract students from the subject matter and, due to limited cognitive capacity, prevents cognitive activity that involves learning (Mayer et al., 2008). McQuiggan et al. (2008) found a negative narrative effect compared to the minimalist story of a digital game, and Cordova and Lepper (1996) reported a beneficial effect when a narrative component was included (specifically mentioning fantasy).

It is essential for students to verbalize their knowledge, as this allows them to integrate new knowledge with their previous knowledge, leading to better retention and higher learning transfer (Wouters et al., 2008). Complementary teaching methods (e.g., discussions and internships) allow students to engage in learning activities that further support the articulation of knowledge. One argument for learning together in digital games is that it supports students in creating knowledge that would otherwise remain intuitive (van der Meij et al., 2011), but research comparing collaboration and solo play is ambiguous. Inkpen et al.'s (1995) observation that team play resulted in significantly higher ratings of motivation and learning outcomes than individual play was not confirmed by van der Meij et al. (2011). Vogel et al.'s (2006) meta-analysis showed that both individual users and groups showed higher cognitive gains in interactive simulations and games than in conventional teaching methods, but the magnitude of the effect for individual users was much larger than for groups.

Positive outcome in the cognitive, emotional, and social areas should also ensure a positive effect on student performance and scores (Connolly et al., 2012; Kapp, 2012; Ke, 2009; Sitzmann, 2011). In particular, Domínguez et al. (2013) suggested that frequent, meaningful, and quick feedback can improve student outcomes as well as motivation. According to these authors, the experience of gamified learning should have timely, frequent, and meaningful feedback.

Lee and Hammer (2011) stated that the game develops problem-solving skills through a comprehensive system of rules that supports active exploration and discovery. They recognized the value of specific challenges that are tailored to the level of players' abilities and increase in difficulty as their abilities expand. They also emphasize the importance of the "emotional realm," which refers to all the strong emotions people feel during playtime–such as pride, joy, optimism, and curiosity, but also frustration at failure. From Lee and Hammer's point of view, games offer the possibility of "reframing failure as a necessary part of learning" (p. 3), as error becomes an opportunity to try, practice, and improve again. Gamification thus determines the emotional transformation, because there is not so much in the event of a failure at stake; on the contrary, repeated failure allows individuals to learn something more and new. Lee and Hammer also insisted on the social dimension of the gamified environment, which enables students to identify themselves publicly, strengthen social credibility, and gain recognition for achievements that might otherwise remain invisible. From a demographic perspective, it is interesting to find out how the perception of game elements in education differs between men and women, especially in connection with competition and cooperation.

Summary

The use of digital games' educational principles can make teaching more interesting, attractive and fun for students, but also improve the memorization of the studied material and its use in practice. The games are popular and widespread among students, allowing them to try out any learning scenarios and apply their own problem-solving ideas. Game principles have a positive effect on students' attitudes towards regular learning, but also towards school. They can affect classroom relationships, where play often encourages students to work together and solve problems together. The game reflects the level of students' self-concept, their own picture of their performance or the effectiveness of their efforts. It supports the skill of memorizing and learning facts. Their immediate feedback and evaluation, which is independent of the teacher, is very important. Learning the principles and contexts of causes and effects is key. Students gain space for an experiment that would not be feasible in a normal context. The game contains challenges, students have the opportunity to meet them, or make mistakes in them and learn from their own mistakes. Education-based on digital games also offers help to students with special needs, the development of more advanced skills, education in life in the information society (with digital technologies and media education) or the potential of educational games for the modernization of school systems.

CRITICAL POINTS

Lack of Internal Motivation

Students' own interest in learning and coordinating their studies is proving to be crucial. In his own investigation, the author spoke to a number of teachers, who mostly believe that people themselves must want to use new technological tools, which is associated with their motivation. In accordance with the basic need for belonging, the human factor of the mentor and fellow students has a positive effect on students' motivation. The author agrees that the implementation of game elements should pursue educational goals. The aim is to stimulate students to regular and continuous preparation by immersing themselves in and continuing their studies. Among the respondents, the presumption of internal motivation of students to actively engage in learning themselves was repeatedly voiced. In order to change their behavior, teachers, as educational designers, apply various strategies. Their statements suggest that they are a compromise of the ideal image of an internally motivated student and the real situation.

Only when game elements make boring activities interesting can they increase the level of inner motivation. When they increase external motivation, the level of internal motivation decreases significantly, which leads to less enthusiasm for work. These results are consistent with SDT (Deci & Ryan, 1985) and research on play (Caillois & Barash, 2001), according to which rewards and incentives reduce a person's intrinsic motivation to perform a task. There is an indirect relationship between rewards and internal motivation. Gamification focuses too much on external motivators, and its effects on motivation are not the same for all students in the class (van Roy & Zaman, 2017).

Van Roy and Zaman (2017) looked at gamification from the perspective of SDT–they show that different types of motivation lead people's behavior differently and point to the importance of satisfying the basic psychological needs of autonomy, competence, and relatedness. Their answers to the research questions "what is gamification" and "how it works" explain that adding game elements as external and unjustified regulations can quite possibly have a detrimental effect on students' internal motivation.

Hanus and Fox (2015) tested motivation by comparing students in two classes. The same curriculum was used in both classes, but only one of them included gamification elements. The results showed that students in the gamified class have a lower level of motivation and a lower score on the final exam. The researchers concluded that the low score in the final exams was affected by levels of intrinsic motivation and that negative effects on intrinsic motivation could be attributed to gamification. Empirical evidence from this longitudinal study is "consistent with the existing literature on the negative effects of rewards on motivation" (Hanus and Fox, 2015, p. 159) and suggests that "providing rewards in the form of badges and coins, as well as promoting competition and social comparison through digital rankings, harms motivation" (p. 159).

Social elements are essential for creating motivational learning with the game. An experiment performed on students of an e-course showed a negative effect of social comparison on motivation and especially that gamification is not an important motivating factor for all, because some students do not like to compete with their classmates (Domínguez et al., 2013). "Some motivational benefits (which otherwise received positive comments) were perceived as negative (such as those supporting competition) and supported the idea that different types of players experience the same benefits differently." (Hamari et al., 2014, p. 3030)

The effects of gamification are highly dependent on users who use gamified learning environments. Experience from practice emphasizes equal access for students and the possibility of adapting the teaching process to their learning style. Game elements are easy to implement, as they resemble the traditional classroom assessment model, which often leads to their overuse not justified by learning objectives. The goal is to increase student involvement. Engagement can be defined as student attention and immersion in the task. Studies indicate that gamification increases student engagement and course participation (Barata et al., 2013; Hamari et al., 2014). The impact of gamified interventions on involvement varies depending on whether the student is motivated internally or externally (Buckley & Doyle, 2014; Hamari et al., 2014).

Gamification enhances participation especially when students can choose between gamified and traditional teaching methods (Cheong et al., 2013; Domínguez et al., 2013; Mollick & Rothbard, 2014). However, the involvement decreases over time. Once the effect of novelty subsides, students' interest in gamification ceases (Koivisto & Hamari, 2014), and involvement is lost at an incredible rate, if all learning contexts have been gamified (Hanus & Fox, 2015). Some students may oppose "mandatory fun" and view the established reward system as binding (Mollick & Rothbard, 2014).

Side Effects

When designing gamification as an implementation of external regulation, SDT helps understand unwanted side effects. When students are forced to exert external leverage as a way of managing their learning behavior, they are more likely to feel diminished autonomy and perform study activities primarily to receive promised external rewards (e.g., bonus points). In such a situation, controlled motivation can undermine any preexisting autonomous motivation (Cameron & Dwyer, 2005; Filsecker & Hickey, 2014). Students can then begin to attribute their motivation to added external regulations that reduce or even eliminate any initial inner motivation. As a result, feelings of autonomy can be further reduced, which, at the same time, reduces any internal impulse, so that the student's motivation eventually changes from one's own to a controlled motivation (Glover, 2013; Tohidi & Jabbari, 2012).

Some authors point to mixed results (de-Marcos et al., 2014), including cases where no significant difference could be observed between the gamified and non gamified educational context. Although Hakulinen et al. (2013) found small differences in learning behavior between students who were rewarded with badges for doing exercises and those who were not, they found no difference in the marks the students obtained. Implementing gamification in education can even cause side effects. Some studies have found that students performed worse in circumstances involving badges, trophies, challenges, rankings, and levels compared to peers who were not exposed to these game elements (de-Marcos et al., 2014). Nongamified activities were also more motivating than those that became part of the game (Domínguez et al., 2013).

Competitiveness, one of the most used features of games (Vorderer et al., 2003) in gamification (Glover, 2013), as opposed to cooperation, encourages the struggle to be the best, even by cheating. If victory automatically means loss for someone else, it can promote a more self-centered society and selfishness (Simon et al., 2014), and discourage admirable qualities such as volunteering or doing good for people. Although losers may set higher goals for the future, research has shown that they will ultimately be systematically worse than their "winning" counterparts, regardless of their previous competencies (Buser, 2014). The example shows that gamification can obscure its goal and have far-reaching negative effects on those who perform the worst and on the least motivated. Christy and Fox (2014) concluded that the use of rankings in educational settings can lead to a stereotypical threat (i.e., the belief that someone can be judged on the basis of a negative stereotype). Thus, the use of leaderboards in an academic setting may, under certain circumstances, affect the academic performance of different demographic groups differently. Other results show that, although competition against peers is important (contrary to the prevailing understanding), the challenge of overcoming and cope with obstacles is what players value the most, regardless of the type of game (Dichev & Dicheva, 2017).

The importance of keeping students motivated is a long-term challenge for education. This explains the considerable attention that gamification has received due to its motivational potential of students in different teaching contexts. Overall, progress has been made in a student-centered study of the psychological effects of gamification, which can be summarized in the following question: How are students with different personalities, dispositions, and learning styles affected by game elements? For what/whom is gamification effective? However, the educational benefits of gamification in terms of increasing student motivation or linking motivation to learning outcomes are still not well understood.

Although gamification is promoted as a motivational tool, studies measuring its motivational effect are limited, and there is a lack of quality empirical evidence to support general claims about the impact of gamification on students' learning and motivation. Although the implementation of external motivation can encourage people in the short term, it also has the potential to deprive them of existing internal motivation (Deci et al., 2001; Tohidi & Jabbari, 2012) and teach users that they should only act if they are rewarded (Muntean, 2011). Most gamified systems rely on external incentives by rewarding activity with badges or encouraging competition. Replacing existing higher-order internal motivation with its external counterpart can potentially harm highly motivated people (Hanus & Fox, 2015).

In an effort to clarify these unconvincing conclusions, some authors have argued that the desired motivational effects are temporary in nature, accompanied by excitement from the newly introduced system, and that they can be attributed to the novelty effect caused by adding digital and/or game elements to the educational context (Attali & Arieli-Attali, 2015; Hanus & Fox, 2015; Koivisto & Hamari, 2014). The ubiquity of gamification can speed up the process, turn the novelty of the technique into mundane, and eliminate the initial excitement. As a result, users will turn away from already boring gamification, which will be the opposite of what it was implemented for (van Roy & Zaman, 2015).

Others report that side effects are more the result of flawed design (Domínguez et al., 2013; Rojas et al., 2013). By simply adding points and rankings to the system, according to this argument, gamification is limited to insignificant pointification without any or, conversely, adverse effects. Similarly, Domínguez et al. (2013) pointed to poor suggestions and the absence of "healthy pedagogy" (p. 9) as the cause of undesirable results. The designers overlooked motivation as a key prerequisite influencing student performance.

Most theoretical research on gamification believes that focusing on points and rewards rather than play and internal engagement may not always meet the goal of desired behavioral change by adapting to students' intrinsic values (Hansch et al., 2015; Songer & Miyata, 2014; Tomaselli et al., 2015). In their exploratory study, Hansch et al. (2015) explored the motivational potential of gamification in online learning. Through a review of ten platforms and in-depth analysis, they examined how the motivational potential of gamification mechanics and social and interactive elements in online learning can be effectively combined to build a community of students involved. Hansch et al. concluded that the starting point for gamifying online education should be students' needs, motivations, and goals, rather than a platform-centered approach that seeks to use technical features to achieve some predefined performance indicators.

For example, Pedro et al. (2015) stated that game mechanics implemented in a virtual learning environment had no effect on student motivation and performance. These findings are in line with the conclusions of Koivisto and Hamari (2014), who, in a more general context, showed that women experience a stronger effect when gamification includes social aspects, and men when it involves some kind of competition.

A limitation of gamification may be that it trivializes the subject. Besides, mental work in learning can only be considered a game; some games are more suitable for encouraging the student to deal with concepts, rather than absorbing them. Further, games alone are not enough to increase performance, and learning difficulties cannot be overcome with games alone (Apostol et al., 2013).

Wouters et al.'s (2013) meta-analysis is a contribution to the use and effectiveness of serious games. According to the authors, they are more motivating in education, compared to the study group receiving active instruction, which tries to involve them in teaching. In relation to traditional teaching methods, serious games are more motivating when they are not combined with other teaching methods. However, this does not correspond to the main finding that students learn more when serious games are supplemented by other teaching methods. Therefore, when using serious games, the educator should consider what his or her learning goal is, the students' motivation or how much to teach the students at the given time. There is some support for simulation games that acquired knowledge and skills are maintained over time (Pierfy, 1977; Sitzmann, 2011; van der Spek, 2011). So-called sustainable learning occurs when students are still able to properly apply the acquired knowledge and skills in the long run.

The premise that has become the basis for the motivational attractiveness of serious games is based on the high entertainment value of commercial digital games. The results of the meta-analysis did not confirm the hypothesis that serious games would be more motivating than the (so-called traditional) teaching methods used in the control group. The inference of an approach based on the SDT (Ryan et al., 2006) assumes that autonomy supports intrinsic motivation. As a result, conditions that restrict a sense of control or freedom of action can undermine intrinsic motivation (Deci et al., 1999). In serious games, the level of control is doubled: It is applicable to actions and decisions within the game, but also to the educational context, when it is necessary to decide on issues such as the type of game and when to play it. It is relevant to examine whether the variation in the level of student control moderates intrinsic motivation.

In terms of the level of control in the educational context, the fundamental difference between digital leisure games and serious games is that the choice of the type of game to play and how much time to spend is up to the player, as opposed to the learning context, while the game type and playing time are generally defined in the curriculum, in the case of serious games. Within the teaching, it is possible that the lack of control over these decisions weakens the motivational potential of serious games for students who are unable to influence the choice. From an educational point of view, if a designer uses a pop-up screen with a message that prompts the player to reflect on something, such a focus can bring learning, but it is also likely that the intervention will disrupt the flow of the game and subsequently undermine its fun nature. Several dimensions of this issue (e.g., the opposition of learning and acting or freedom vs. control) need to be addressed in order to create truly engaging serious games (de Castell & Jenson, 2003; Wouters et al., 2011).

Key Takeaway

When distributing bonus points and rewards, keep in mind that shortcuts may be created, and students may have false expectations or lose their notion of the meaning of the activity for which they are (arbitrarily) rewarded. Behind activity, they see only the reward, instead of reflecting on what it meant to them and where it moved them. Doubts then arise about the potential to safely simulate a real work environment for instance.

SOLUTIONS AND RECOMMENDATIONS

Personalization is the customization of content and services based on the prediction of what users want, which leads to their higher satisfaction. How would students react if teachers gave them control over the personalization of their studies? Such an approach allows them to choose their own technological tools, team roles, and methods of presenting the results of their work. They can choose from which sources to obtain their information and learn in a way that meets their needs. To a certain extent, students adjust what and how to learn. With the resources available, they have much more power to do what they want. The aim is to help them use (and enjoy) technology for learning. The role of the teacher is to guide students with the help of new tools. What tools they use to work depends on them. Students with specific learning styles use tools that meet their requirements and expectations.

Personalization could find support in artificial intelligence, making it easier for educators to discover specific patterns of behavior, serious mistakes, and traits of students' behavior in game-based learning. McGonigal (2003) further described "extreme networks" that benefit from the power of the collective intelligence of massive and diverse groups of people to solve real-world problems. Similarly, Web-based software can leverage education data to provide immediate feedback to students, recommending additional lessons, sites, and resources that they can use, based on what has helped other students learn. Such a program would analyze the student's learning style and suggest other references, whether to simulations, games, reading or drill concepts, simply what worked for the specific student. The electronic personal assistant can guide the user in the right way to the right information, remind him or her of an appointment in time or predict needs of the person. An educational assistant modeled on this concept would direct students to the activities that would be most beneficial for them at the moment. For example, if a student did well on a project-based learning basis, the software would recommend where to go for research according to his or her preferences. These preferences would arise from the analysis of (educational) data.

FUTURE RESEARCH DIRECTIONS

There is a need to adapt gamified learning and consider how it affects different students and what its effects on the different personality profiles that make up a class are (Barata et al., 2015; Hanus & Fox, 2015). Future research should isolate game elements and evaluate their effectiveness in the teaching/learning process as well as to better understand how they work in a given educational context. It should further clarify how individual game elements relate to behavioral and motivational outcomes, and how to design a gamification system to support and increase intrinsic motivation (Morris et al., 2013). In addition, it should set out the conditions under which gamification affects the performance and scores of individual course participants. The evidence supports the need to create an environment with clear goals, challenges, and authentic stories in which team spirit is strengthened through game mechanics, discussions, and debates. In addition, these gamified environments must meet the student's needs and also suggest that gamification must add an aspect of fun or novelty. Voluntary participation must also be ensured, as research has shown that the effectiveness of gamification is greater when a student can choose. Commitment affects the nature of gamified activity and reduces student motivation (Cheong et al., 2013; Mollick & Rothbard, 2014).

CONCLUSION

Gamification design requires a user-centered approach considerate of students' needs. Gamified systems also target education to create a framework that enables and guides students. Similar systems are automated, and the awarding of prizes takes place from derived indicators, which may not be accurate, lead to patterns of behavior that students would not otherwise replicate or even to a weakening of their autonomous motivation. Gamification thus obscures its goal and can have far-reaching negative effects on learners with the worst performances and on the least motivated (Hanus & Fox, 2015). The use of game elements affects the learning performance of different demographic groups differently, and it is up to the educator to consider the predispositions of individuals. Students' personality traits need to be considered in the gamification design and offer different learning styles. Teaching with game elements could be suitable for those with insufficient inner motivation who do not like traditional forms of teaching; it also suits competitive types, students with special educational needs, and those who self-study remotely. Others prefer cooperative game principles and team play. However, it may not be pleasant for introverts.

Although teachers believe that teaching with the help of educational game principles would benefit most students playful in nature, there is an opinion among them that it would be particularly suitable for weaker students who need to be attracted to study through play. This also applies to future educators in training who work with students in fields as special and inclusive pedagogy. On the contrary, it could be unsuitable for students who are gifted and exceptionally gifted, because for them the intrinsic motivation is the topic itself, which they enjoy because they understand it. Thus, students' character and their strengths should be taken into account in the course design and different learning or playing styles (e.g., competition, project teaching, simulation, role-playing) should be offered as well. In the hands of modern teachers acting as designers of the educational process lies new possibilities for how to effectively design learning experiences to achieve their teaching goals. Hopefully, some insight will be useful and transferable to other educational contexts for practical purposes and development of gamification.

ACKNOWLEDGMENT

This chapter is part of a specific research project *Current Challenges in the Teaching Profession of the 21st Century* supported by the Masaryk University [MUNI/A/1481/2020].

REFERENCES

Abramovich, S., Schunn, C., & Higashi, R. M. (2013). Are badges useful in education? It depends upon the type of badge and expertise of learner. *Educational Technology Research and Development*, *61*(2), 217–232. doi:10.100711423-013-9289-2

Apostol, S., Zaharescu, L., & Alexe, I. (2013). Gamification of learning and educational games. In *Proceedings of the 9th. International Scientific Conference eLearning and Software for Education* (pp. 67-72). Academic Press.

Attali, Y., & Arieli-Attali, M. (2015). Gamification in assessment: Do points affect test performance? *Computers & Education*, *83*, 57–63. doi:10.1016/j.compedu.2014.12.012

Baptista, G., & Oliveira, T. (2019). Gamification and serious games: A literature meta-analysis and integrative model. *Computers in Human Behavior*, *92*, 306–315. doi:10.1016/j.chb.2018.11.030

Barata, G., Gama, S., Jorge, J., & Gonçalves, D. (2013). Engaging engineering students with gamification. In *Proceedings of the fifth International Conference on Games and Virtual Worlds for Serious Applications* (pp. 24-31). Academic Press.

Barata, G., Gama, S., Jorge, J., & Gonçalves, D. (2015). Identifying student types in a gamified learning experience. In M. Khosrow-Pour (Ed.), *Gamification: Concepts, methodologies, tools, and applications* (pp. 541–558). IGI Global. doi:10.4018/978-1-4666-8200-9.ch026

Buckley, P., & Doyle, E. (2014). Gamification and student motivation. *Interactive Learning Environments, 22*(6), 1–14.

Buser, T. (2014). *The impact of losing in a competition on the willingness to seek further challenges.* Social Science Research Network. doi:10.2139srn.2479837

Caillois, R., & Barash, M. (2001). *Man, play, and games*. University of Illinois Press.

Cameron, B., & Dwyer, F. (2005). The effect of online gaming, cognition, and feedback type in facilitating delayed achievement of different learning objectives. *Journal of Interactive Learning Research, 16*, 243–258.

Cheong, C., Cheong, F., & Filippou, J. (2013). Quick quiz: A gamified approach for enhancing learning. In *Proceedings of PACIS 2013* (paper 206). Academic Press.

Christy, K. R., & Fox, J. (2014). Leaderboards in a virtual classroom: A test of stereotype threat and social comparison explanations for women's math performance. *Computers & Education, 78*, 66–77. doi:10.1016/j.compedu.2014.05.005

Connolly, T. M., Boyle, E. A., MacArthur, E., Hainey, T., & Boyle, J. (2012). A systematic literature review of empirical evidence on computer games and serious games. *Computer Education, 59*(2), 661–686. doi:10.1016/j.compedu.2012.03.004

Conrad, C. E., & Tucker, C. S. (2019). The effects of player type on performance: A gamification case study. *Computers in Human Behavior, 91*, 333–345. doi:10.1016/j.chb.2018.10.005

Cordova, D. L., & Lepper, M. R. (1996). Intrinsic motivation and the process of learning: Beneficial effects of contextualization, personalization, and choice. *Journal of Educational Psychology, 88*(4), 715–730. doi:10.1037/0022-0663.88.4.715

de Castell, S., & Jenson, J. (2003). Serious play. *Journal of Curriculum Studies, 35*(6), 649–665. doi:10.1080/0022027032000145552

de-Marcos, L., Domínguez, A., Saenz-de-Navarrete, J., & Pagés, C. (2014). An empirical study comparing gamification and social networking on e-learning. *Computers & Education, 75*, 82–91. doi:10.1016/j.compedu.2014.01.012

de Sousa Borges, S., Durelli, V. H. S., Macedo Reis, H., & Isotani, S. (2014). A systematic mapping on gamification applied to education. In *Proceedings of the 29th Annual ACM Symposium on Applied Computing* (pp. 216-222). 10.1145/2554850.2554956

Deci, E. L., Koestner, R., & Ryan, R. M. (1999). A meta-analytic review of experiments examining the effects of extrinsic rewards on intrinsic motivation. *Psychological Bulletin, 125*(6), 627–668. doi:10.1037/0033-2909.125.6.627 PMID:10589297

Deci, E. L., Koestner, R., & Ryan, R. M. (2001). Extrinsic Rewards and Intrinsic Motivation in Education: Reconsidered Once Again. *Review of Educational Research*, *71*(1), 1–27. doi:10.3102/00346543071001001

Deci, E. L., & Ryan, R. M. (1985). The general causality orientations scale: Self-determination in personality. *Journal of Research in Personality*, *19*(2), 109–134. doi:10.1016/0092-6566(85)90023-6

Deci, E. L., & Ryan, R. M. (2008). Self-determination theory: A macrotheory of human motivation, development, and health. *Canadian Psychology*, *49*(3), 182–185. doi:10.1037/a0012801

Deci, E. L., & Ryan, R. M. (2015). Self-determination theory. In J. D. Wright (Ed.), *International Encyclopedia of the Social & Behavioral Sciences* (2nd ed., Vol. 21, p. 486). Elsevier. doi:10.1016/B978-0-08-097086-8.26036-4

Denny, P. (2013). The effect of virtual achievements on student engagement. In *Proceedings of the SIGCHI Conference on Human Factors in Computing Systems* (pp. 763-772). ACM. 10.1145/2470654.2470763

Deterding, S., Dixon, D., Khaled, R., & Nacke, L. (2011). From game design elements to gamefulness: Defining gamification. In *Proceedings of the 15th International Academic MindTrek Conference: Envisioning Future Media Environments* (pp. 9-15). ACM. 10.1145/2181037.2181040

Dichev, C., & Dicheva, D. (2017). Gamifying education: What is known, what is believed and what remains uncertain: A critical review. *International Journal of Educational Technology in Higher Education*, *14*(9), 1–36. doi:10.118641239-017-0042-5

Dichev, C., Dicheva, D., Angelova, G., & Agre, G. (2014). From gamification to gameful design and gameful experience in learning. *Cybernetics and Information Technologies*, *14*(4), 80–100. doi:10.1515/cait-2014-0007

Dickey, M. D. (2006). Game design narrative for learning: Appropriating adventure game design narrative devices and techniques for the design of interactive learning environments. *Educational Technology Research and Development*, *54*(3), 245–263. doi:10.100711423-006-8806-y

Domínguez, A., Saenz-De-Navarrete, J., De-Marcos, L., Fernández-Sanz, L., Pages, C., & Martinez-Herráiz, J. J. (2013). Gamifying learning experiences: Practical implications and outcomes. *Computers & Education*, *63*, 380–392. doi:10.1016/j.compedu.2012.12.020

Eickhoff, C., Harris, C. G., & de Vries, A. P. (2012). Quality through flow and immersion: Gamifying crowdsourced relevance assessments. *Proceedings of SIGIR'12*. 10.1145/2348283.2348400

Faiella, F., & Ricciardi, M. (2015). Gamification and learning: A review of issues and research. *Journal of e-Learning and Knowledge Society, 11*(3), 13-21.

Featherstone, M., & Habgood, J. (2019). UniCraft: Exploring the impact of asynchronous multiplayer game elements in gamification. *International Journal of Human-Computer Studies*, *127*, 150–168. doi:10.1016/j.ijhcs.2018.05.006

Filsecker, M., & Hickey, D. T. (2014). A multilevel analysis of the effects of external rewards on elementary students' motivation, engagement, and learning in an educational game. *Computers & Education*, *75*, 136–148. doi:10.1016/j.compedu.2014.02.008

Gee, J. P. (2003). *What video games have to teach us about learning and literacy*. Palgrave. doi:10.1145/950566.950595

Giddens, A., Appelbaum, R. P., Duneier, M., & Carr, D. (2013). *Essentials of sociology*. W. W. Norton & Company.

Glover, I. (2013). Play as you learn: gamification as a technique for motivating learners. In J. Herrington, A. Couros, & V. Irvine (Eds.), *Proceedings of World Conference on Educational Multimedia, Hypermedia and Telecommunications 2013* (pp. 1999-2008). AACE.

Graesser, A. C., Singer, M., & Trabasso, T. (1994). Constructing inferences during narrative text comprehension. *Psychological Review*, *101*(3), 371–395. doi:10.1037/0033-295X.101.3.371 PMID:7938337

Hakulinen, L., Auvinen, T., & Korhonen, A. (2013). Empirical study on the effect of achievement badges in TRAKLA2 online learning environment. Learning and Teaching in Computing and Engineering (LaTiCE), 2013. doi:10.1109/LaTiCE.2013.34

Hakulinen, L., Auvinen, T., & Korhonen, A. (2015). The effect of achievement badges on students' behavior: An empirical study in a university-level computer science course. *International Journal of Emerging Technologies in Learning*, *10*(1), 18–29. doi:10.3991/ijet.v10i1.4221

Hamari, J. (2013). Transforming homo economicus into homo ludens: A field experiment on gamification in a utilitarian P2P trading service. *Electronic Commerce Research and Applications*, *12*(4), 236–245. doi:10.1016/j.elerap.2013.01.004

Hamari, J., & Koivisto, J. (2013). *Social motivations to use gamification: An empirical study of gamifying exercise* [Paper presentation]. 21st European Conference on Information Systems, Utrecht, The Netherlands.

Hamari, J., Koivisto, J., & Sarsa, H. (2014). Does gamification work? A literature review of empirical studies on gamification. In *Proceedings of the 47th Hawaii International Conference on System Science* (pp. 3025-3034). 10.1109/HICSS.2014.377

Hansch, A., Newman, C., & Schildhauer, T. (2015). *Fostering engagement with gamification: Review of current practices on online learning platforms*. HIIG Discussion Paper Series No. 2015–04, 23. 11.

Hanus, M. D., & Fox, J. (2015). Assessing the effects of gamification in the classroom: A longitudinal study on intrinsic motivation, social comparison, satisfaction, effort, and academic performance. *Computer Education*, *80*, 152–161. doi:10.1016/j.compedu.2014.08.019

Inkpen, K., Booth, K. S., Klawe, M., & Upitis, R. (1995). Playing together beats playing apart, especially for girls [Paper presentation]. The meeting of Computer Support for Collaborative Learning '95, Bloomington, IN.

Johnson, L., Adams Becker, S., Estrada, V., & Freeman, A. (2014). *NMC Horizon Report* K-12. The New Media Consortium.

Kapp, K. M. (2007). Tools and techniques for transferring know-how from boomers to gamers. *Global Business and Organizational Excellence*, *26*(5), 22–37. doi:10.1002/joe.20162

Kapp, K. M. (2012). *The gamification of learning and instruction: Game-based methods and strategies for training and education*. Pfeiffer.

Ke, F. (2009). A qualitative meta-analysis of computer games as learning tools. In R. E. Ferdig (Ed.), *Effective electronic gaming in education* (pp. 1–32). Information Science Reference. doi:10.4018/978-1-59904-808-6.ch001

Koivisto, J., & Hamari, J. (2014). Demographic differences in perceived benefit from gamification. *Computers in Human Behavior*, *35*, 179–188. doi:10.1016/j.chb.2014.03.007

Köse, D. B., Morschheuser, B., & Hamari, J. (2019). Is it a tool or a toy? How user's conception of a system's purpose affects their experience and use. *International Journal of Information Management*, *49*, 461–474. doi:10.1016/j.ijinfomgt.2019.07.016

Landers, R. N. (2015). Developing a theory of gamified learning: Linking serious games and gamification of learning. *Simulation & Gaming*, *45*(6), 752–768. doi:10.1177/1046878114563660

Landers, R. N., Bauer, K. N., Callan, R. C., & Armstrong, M. B. (2015). Psychological theory and the gamification of learning. In T. Reiners & L. Wood (Eds.), *Gamification in education and business* (pp. 165–186). Springer. doi:10.1007/978-3-319-10208-5_9

Lee, J., & Hammer, J. (2011). Gamification in education: What, how, why bother? *Academic Exchange Quarterly*, *15*(2), 3–4.

Lehtonen, T., Aho, T., Isohanni, E., & Mikkonen, T. (2015). On the role of gamification and localization in an open online learning environment: Javala experiences. In *Proceedings of the 15th Koli Calling Conference on Computing Education Research* (pp. 50-59). ACM. 10.1145/2828959.2828973

Lieberoth, A. (2015). Shallow gamification: Psychological effects of framing an activity as a game. *Games and Culture*, *10*(3), 249–268. doi:10.1177/1555412014559978

Mayer, R. E., Griffith, E., Naftaly, I., & Rothman, D. (2008). Increased interestingness of extraneous details leads to decreased learning. *Journal of Experimental Psychology. Applied*, *14*, 329–339. doi:10.1037/a0013835 PMID:19102616

McGonigal, J. (2003). This is not a game: Immersive aesthetics and collective play. In *Proceedings of the Melbourne DAC 2003 Streamingworlds Conference*. RMIT University.

McQuiggan, S., Rowe, J., Lee, S., & Lester, J. (2008). *Story-based learning: The impact of narrative on learning experiences and outcomes*. Springer.

Mollick, E. R., & Rothbard, N. (2014). *Mandatory fun: Consent, gamification, and the impact of games at work*. The Wharton School Research Paper Series.

Morris, B. J., Croker, S., Zimmerman, C., Gill, D., & Romig, C. (2013). Gaming science: The "Gamification" of scientific thinking. *Developmental Psychology*, *4*, 1–16. PMID:24058354

Morschheuser, B., Hassan, L., Werder, K., & Hamari, J. (2018). How to design gamification? A method for engineering gamified software. *Information and Software Technology*, *95*, 219–237. doi:10.1016/j.infsof.2017.10.015

Muntean, C. I. (2011). Raising engagement in e-learning through gamification. In *Proceedings of the 6th International Conference on Virtual Learning* (pp. 323-329). Academic Press.

Pedro, L. Z., Lopes, A. M. Z., Prates, B. G., Vassileva, J., & Isotani, S. (2015). Does gamification work for boys and girls? An exploratory study with a virtual learning environment. In *Proceedings of the 30th Annual ACM Symposium on Applied Computing* (pp. 214-219). 10.1145/2695664.2695752

Peng, W., Lin, J.-H., Pfeiffer, K. A., & Winn, B. (2012). Need satisfaction supportive game features as motivational determinants: An experimental study of a self-determination theory guided Exergame. *Media Psychology*, *15*(2), 192. doi:10.1080/15213269.2012.673850

Perrotta, C., Featherstone, G., Aston, H., & Houghton, E. (2013). *Game-based learning: Latest evidence and future directions*. NFER.

Pierfy, D. A. (1977). Comparative simulation game research: Stumbling blocks and stepping. *Simulation & Games*, *8*(2), 255–268. doi:10.1177/003755007782006

Ramirez, D., & Squire, K. (2015). Gamification and learning. In S. P. Walz & S. Deterding (Eds.), *The gameful world: Approaches, issues, applications* (pp. 629–652). The MIT Press.

Robson, K., Plangger, K., Kietzmann, J., McCarthy, I., & Pitt, L. (2015). Is it all a game? Understanding the principles of gamification. *Business Horizons*, *58*(4), 411–420. doi:10.1016/j.bushor.2015.03.006

Rojas, D., Kapralos, B., & Dubrowski, A. (2013). The missing piece in the gamification puzzle. In *Proceedings of the First International Conference on Gameful Design, Research, and Applications* (pp. 135-138). ACM. 10.1145/2583008.2583033

Ryan, R. M., & Deci, E. L. (2009). Promoting self-determined school engagement, motivation, learning, and well-being. In K. Wentzel, A. Wigfield, & D. Miele (Eds.), *Handbook of motivation at school* (pp. 171–196). Routledge.

Ryan, R. M., Rigby, C. S., & Przybylski, A. (2006). The motivational pull of video games: A self-determination theory approach. *Motivation and Emotion*, *30*(4), 347–365. doi:10.100711031-006-9051-8

Simon, R. L., Torres, C. R., & Hager, P. F. (2014). *Fair play: The ethics of sport*. Westview Press.

Sitzmann, T. (2011). A meta-analytic examination of the instructional effectiveness of computer-based simulation games. *Personnel Psychology*, *64*(2), 489–528. doi:10.1111/j.1744-6570.2011.01190.x

Songer, R. W., & Miyata, K. (2014). A playful affordances model for gameful learning. In *Proceedings of the TEEM '14 2nd International Conference on Technological Ecosystems for Enhancing Multiculturality* (pp. 205-213). 10.1145/2669711.2669901

Sua, C. H., & Cheng, C. H. (2013). A mobile game-based insect learning system for improving the learning achievements. *Procedia: Social and Behavioral Sciences*, *103*, 42–50. doi:10.1016/j.sbspro.2013.10.305

Taylor, G., Jungert, T., Mageau, G. A., Schattke, K., Dedic, H., Rosenfield, S., & Koestner, R. (2014). A self-determination theory approach to predicting school achievement over time: The unique role of intrinsic motivation. *Contemporary Educational Psychology*, *39*(4), 342–358. doi:10.1016/j.cedpsych.2014.08.002

Toda, A. M., do Carmo, R. M. C., da Silva, A. P., Bittencourt, I. I., & Isotani, S. (2019). An approach for planning and deploying gamification concepts with social networks within educational contexts. *International Journal of Information Management*, *46*, 294–303. doi:10.1016/j.ijinfomgt.2018.10.001

Tohidi, H., & Jabbari, M. M. (2012). The effects of motivation in education. *Procedia: Social and Behavioral Sciences*, *31*, 820–824. doi:10.1016/j.sbspro.2011.12.148

Tomaselli, F., Sanchez, O., & Brown, S. (2015). How to engage users through gamification: The prevalent effects of playing and mastering over competing. In *Proceedings of the Thirty Sixth International Conference on Information Systems* (pp. 1-16). Academic Press.

Tulloch, R. (2014). Reconceptualising gamification: Play and pedagogy. *Digital Culture & Education*, *6*(4), 317–333.

van der Meij, H., Albers, E., & Leemkuil, H. (2011). Learning from games: Does collaboration help? *British Journal of Educational Technology*, *42*(4), 655–664. doi:10.1111/j.1467-8535.2010.01067.x

van der Spek, E. D. (2011). *Experiments in serious game design: A cognitive approach* [Unpublished doctoral dissertation]. Universiteit Utrecht, The Netherlands.

van Roy, R., & Zaman, B. (2015). Moving beyond the effectiveness of gamification. In *Proceeding of CHI 2015 Workshop Gamifying Research*. ACM.

van Roy, R., & Zaman, B. (2017). Why gamification fails in education and how to make it successful: Introducing nine gamification heuristics based on self-determination theory. In M. Ma & A. Oikonomou (Eds.), Serious games and edutainment applications, volume II (pp. 485-509). Springer International Publishing AG.

van Roy, R., & Zaman, B. (2019). Unravelling the ambivalent motivational power of gamification: A basic psychological needs perspective. *International Journal of Human-Computer Studies*, *127*, 38–50. doi:10.1016/j.ijhcs.2018.04.009

Vogel, J. J., Vogel, D. S., Cannon-Bowers, J., Bowers, C. A., Muse, K., & Wright, M. (2006). Computer gaming and interactive simulations for learning: A meta-analysis. *Journal of Educational Computing Research*, *34*(3), 229–243. doi:10.2190/FLHV-K4WA-WPVQ-H0YM

Vorderer, P., Hartmann, T., & Klimmt, C. (2003). Explaining the enjoyment of playing video games: The role of competition. In *Proceedings of the Second International Conference on Entertainment Computing* (pp. 1-9). Carnegie Mellon University.

Werbach, K., & Hunter, D. (2012). *For the win: How game thinking can revolutionize your business*. Wharton Digital Press.

Wouters, P., Paas, F., & van Merriënboer, J. J. M. (2008). How to optimize learning from animated models: A review of guidelines base on cognitive load. *Review of Educational Research*, *78*(3), 645–675. doi:10.3102/0034654308320320

Wouters, P., van Nimwegen, C., van Oostendorp, H., & van der Spek, E. D. (2013). A meta-analysis of the cognitive and motivational effects of serious games. *Journal of Educational Psychology*, *105*(2), 249–265. doi:10.1037/a0031311

Wouters, P., van Oostendorp, H., Boonekamp, R., & van der Spek, E. D. (2011). The role of game discourse analysis and curiosity in creating engaging and effective serious games by implementing a back story and foreshadowing. *Interacting with Computers*, *23*(4), 329–336. doi:10.1016/j.intcom.2011.05.001

Xi, N., & Hamari, J. (2019). Does gamification satisfy needs? A study on the relationship between gamification features and intrinsic need satisfaction. *International Journal of Information Management*, *46*, 210–221. doi:10.1016/j.ijinfomgt.2018.12.002

ADDITIONAL READING

Aldrich, C. (2009). *Learning online with games, simulations, and virtual worlds: Strategies for online instruction*. Jossey-Bass.

Beavis, C., Dezuanni, M., & O'Mara, J. (2017). *Serious play: Literacy, learning, and digital games*. Routledge. doi:10.4324/9781315537658

Freitas, S. D., & Maharg, P. (2011). *Digital games and learning*. Continuum International Publishing Group.

Kapp, K. M., Blair, L., & Mesch, R. (2014). *The gamification of learning and instruction fieldbook: Ideas into practice*. Wiley.

Kowert, R., & Quandt, T. (2017). *New perspectives on the social aspects of digital gaming: Multiplayer 2*. Routledge. doi:10.4324/9781315629308

Steinkuehler, C., Squire, K., & Barab, S. A. (2012). *Games, learning, and society: Learning and meaning in the digital age*. Cambridge University Press. doi:10.1017/CBO9781139031127

Tekinbaş, K. S. (2004). *Rules of play: Game design fundamentals*. MIT.

Whitton, N., & Moseley, A. (2012). *Using games to enhance learning and teaching: A beginner's guide*. Routledge. doi:10.4324/9780203123775

KEY TERMS AND DEFINITIONS

Cognitive Apprenticeship: Any learning should be linked to the context in which learners can use the results of that learning. Students need authentic experience, they must test their knowledge in practice at the same time, and it is this practice that further teaches them.

Cone of Experience: The theory reflects the gradual arrangement of teaching methods from direct experiences such as simulations and role-playing to abstract verbal symbols while reading text or counting. Educationally, it is easier for the learners to remember a certain experience during which all their senses are involved.

Distributed Practice: Dividing the educational experience into shorter sections with a time span that will allow learners to think about new knowledge and understand it. The next sections give room to recap what the learners forgot between them. Repetition will make it easier to store new knowledge in the long-term memory.

Flow: A state of mind where the student is fully engaged in the activity, which must be fun and reasonably demanding. The key is that almost any task or work can be transformed into a flow experience by creating opportunities for feedback and setting achievable goals within the task.

Game-Based Learning: Digital game-based education that uses digital games as a resource to support an educator who uses a framework of game rules for a specific learning purpose.

Gamification: A relatively new educational technique that increases students' interest through the use of game resources, game designs, game thinking, and game principles in non-game areas.

Self-Determination Theory: It is not the amount of motivation, but the particular nature of distinct motivational types that holds the most predictive and explanatory power as to how people behave.

Chapter 2
A Bibliometrics and Text Analytics Review of Games and Gamification in Education

Jose A. Ruipérez Valiente
https://orcid.org/0000-0002-2304-6365
University of Murcia, Spain

ABSTRACT

Over the last decade, we have seen a large amount of research performed on technology-enhanced learning. Within this area, the use of games and gamification in education has gained popularity over the years. In this work, the author aim to identify the main topics in these areas within the last 10 years. The researchers propose a new methodology to conduct text analytics-driven topic analysis following a bibliometrics and text analytics-driven approach. The authors collected all the metadata from 7815 papers in these areas over the last 10 years. The author used it to find the main topics across the papers and hidden relationships between author and papers. The analysis in this work has focused on three main objectives: 1) discover the main topics in games and gamification in education based on paper keywords and topic modeling; 2) discover the evolution of said topics over the last ten years of research; and 3) discover how papers and authors from different communities have interacted over the years from a network's perspective.

INTRODUCTION

Nowadays, technology is changing and improving year after year, and this development is also making a significant impact on educational environments. Despite previous studies suggest that the use of games present some limitations that contribute to the still-limited applications of technology in education (such as finding the time for both the presenter/preceptor and student to learn the systems employed, the financial impacts on both parties, or technical limitations), research and interest in this area have been growing over the years (de Klerk & Kato, 2017; Eiland & Todd, 2019). Within this context, there have

DOI: 10.4018/978-1-6684-4287-6.ch002

been two mainstream trends that have gained an important influence in education, which has been the use of games and gamification in educational environments.

On the one side, gamification can be defined as the use of game design elements in a non-game context to encourage users to perform desired behaviors (Deterding et al., 2011; Patrício et al., 2021), and also to encourage users' motivation, enjoyment and engagement (Patrício et al., 2018). Usually, gamification approaches do not represent games in the proper meaning of the word. Instead, they make use of the possibilities of Information Technology (IT) to develop incentive concepts, which continuously engage users in using products, services and information systems (Blohm & Leimeister, 2013). Moreover, gamification techniques in education have been used broadly in the last years. The main reason to implement gamification elements in education is to improve the motivation and engagement of the student towards the learning goals (Hamari et al., 2014).

On the other side, one of the most prominent examples of technology in education is the use of digital games for learning (De Freitas, 2006). Playing video games is one of the most popular activities in the world. According to a survey from the Entertainment Software Association (ESA, 2019), the role of video games in the American family is changing: nearly three-quarters (74%) of parents believe video games can be educational for their children, and more than half (57%) enjoy playing games with their child at least weekly. This has prompted a rapidly increasing interest in using games in educational settings, not merely because "it is what kids are paying attention to," but because well-designed games are very closely aligned with the design of good educational experiences (Gee, 2008).

Therefore, motivated by the widespread use of both gamification and games in education, the authors would like to conduct a topic analysis of the main trends across the last ten years of research, considering the use of both digital and non-digital games. Usually, there are several approaches to do this type of analysis, such as systematic reviews or scoping reviews, among others. Unfortunately, these analyses are very time-consuming, especially when we have an extensive collection of documents or when they are performed by a small team of researchers (Kovačević et al., 2012).

With the explosive growth in the research literature production, the need for new approaches to structure knowledge emerged (Kokol et al., 2020). In this work, the authors explore some areas that could be useful to alleviate this workload and perform trends analysis in an easy and scalable way. Researchers aim to do so by taking a mixed approach of three different areas: the first area is text analytics, and specifically topic modeling, that will be used to extract the main topics using the papers' abstract; the second is the area of bibliometrics, in which authors will use the papers' keywords to find the most common ones as well as their evolution over time; finally, researchers will use network analysis to create one network using the papers' authors, and another one using the citations between publications. Thus, this work aims to analyze over 7500 publications indexed in Scopus, benefitting from all these techniques mentioned and obtaining helpful information, using an easy, quick, and scalable approach. More specifically, our main research questions (RQs) are as follow:

- **RQ1**: What are the main topics of the use of games and gamification in education based on keywords and topic modeling?
- **RQ2**: What has been the evolution of such topics over the last ten years of research?
- **RQ3**: What are the communities of authors and papers in this topic based on a network analysis perspective?

The rest of the chapter is organized as follows: next section explains the background behind this study focusing on the three methods applied: NLP, bibliometrics, and network analysis. Then, researchers will describe the methodology, including the data acquisition, data pre-processing, the final data collection, and then how each one of the three areas mentioned were applied in this research. Next, the results will be presented as well as a discussion of the main findings. Then, researchers will finish with the limitations, future work, and a brief conclusion.

BACKGROUND

In this research, the authors address a set of research areas in order to provide a novel methodology to conduct an interesting analysis on games and gamification in educational contexts, and one of these areas is bibliometrics. The term "bibliometrics" was first used, so far as can be ascertained, in the Journal of Documentation in 1969 (Burchfield, 1972). Since then, numerous definitions have emerged: "the application of mathematics and statistical methods to books and other media of communication," or "quantitative analyses of the bibliographic features of a body of literature" are only two of the existing definitions of this field (Broadus, 1987). One of its subfields is historical bibliometrics. Historical bibliometricians recognized that adding the dimension of time and space to bibliometric analysis can give new insight into the knowledge development and scholarly record (Kokol et al., 2020).

Thus, bibliometrics can measure, for example, an article's impact. Bibliometric methods can estimate how much influence or impact a selected research article has on future research, and it usually does this by counting the number of times the article is cited after it is published (Cooper, 2015). Authors also found several studies that aimed to perform bibliometric analysis in research papers: authors in (Lv et al., 2011) collected data about graphene research from 1991 to 2010 from the Science Citation Index database, Conference Proceeding Citation Index database, and Derwent Innovation Index database integrated by Thomson Reuters, and publications, subjects, collaborations, times cited, co-words, cluster analysis of the papers and patents were deeply examined. Furthermore, authors in (Miau & Yang, 2018) reviewed the literature growth and author productivity of Blockchain technology research from 2008 to March 2017. Eight hundred-one articles were retrieved from the Scopus database and analyzed with a bibliometrics approach using different perspective views.

As we have seen, bibliometric measures are commonly used to estimate the popularity and the impact of published research, and they provide "quantitative" indicators of how good a published paper is (Abu-Jbara et al., 2013). In this research, we also use Natural Language Processing (NLP) to add a "qualitative" but automatic nuance about the analyzed publications. NLP is defined as a theoretically motivated range of computational techniques for analyzing and representing naturally occurring texts at one or more levels of linguistic analysis for the purpose of achieving human-like language processing for a range of tasks or applications (Liddy, 2001). NLP has emerged as an interdisciplinary area, as it is a combination of computational linguistics and Artificial Intelligence (AI), and its main goal is to specify a language comprehension and production theory to such a level of detail that a person is able to write a computer program which can understand and produce natural language (E. Kumar, 2011). The principal difficulty in processing natural language is the pervasive ambiguity found at all levels, such as lexical, semantic, structural, or pragmatic ambiguity, among others. All these forms of ambiguity may interact and produce an extremely complex interpretation process (Allen, 2003).

The NLP field has recently gained much attention for representing and analyzing human language computationally due to its applications in many different fields such as machine translation, email spam detection, information extraction, summarization, medical, and question answering, among others (Khurana et al., 2017). Several works where authors used NLP and text mining to discover trends in many different research areas were found. These areas include Big Data (Amado et al., 2018), educational technologies (Chen et al., 2020), smart cities (Park & Lee, 2019), or even transportation (Sun & Yin, 2017).

Moreover, bibliometric information can be used to discover more complex information than if only quantitative measures are used. Moreover, network analysis is becoming increasingly popular as a general methodology for understanding complex patterns of interaction. It examines actors who are connected directly or indirectly by one or more different relationships, comprising graphical representations of the relationships (edges) between variables (nodes). Network analysis provides the capacity to estimate these complex patterns of relationships and the network structure can be analyzed to reveal the network's core features (Hevey, 2018). Social network analysis has been used in studies of kinship structure, social mobility, scientific citations, corporate power, international trade exploitation, class structure, and many other areas (Scott, 1988). Moreover, that use of NLP for mining scientific papers leads us to the research topic on "NLP-enhanced Bibliometrics", which aims to promote interdisciplinary research in bibliometrics, NLP, and computational linguistics in order to enhance the ways bibliometrics can benefit from large-scale text analytics and sense mining of papers (Atanassova et al., 2019).

Previous work using network analysis in research papers was found. For example, (Schmidt-Kraepelin et al., 2018) examined previous research on healthcare gamification to explore: 1) the evolution of the body of knowledge; and 2) the primary research foci of past research on the area and research gaps. With that purpose in mind, they conducted a structured literature review, followed by a citation network analysis, and a concept-centric content analysis of identified studies. We can see another example in (Zhang et al., 2021), where authors investigated three computer science education conferences (SIGCSE Technical Symposium, ITiCSE and ICER) by analyzing authorship and affiliation details for publications in the proceedings over the lifetime of the respective conferences, totaling over 4500 publications, and concluding that the community is open to newcomers, and both the number of authors, and the overall level of collaboration is growing.

Moreover, in this work the authors aim to use the previous areas to analyze two primary trends: games and gamification. On the one hand, gamification has rapidly emerged as one of the favorite persuasive technologies widely used with the aim of promoting a positive change in the user's behavior by means of including game like elements in non-game contexts (Trinidad et al., 2021). As a research discipline, gamification have been growing fast, especially in education, and this growth is an ideal motivation to perform a detailed analysis on current research in this area. Today's learners are digital natives and have different learning styles, new attitudes to the learning process and higher requirements for teaching and learning. Thus, teachers have to use different learning methods adapted to new students' requirements to be active with strong motivation and engagement, and one of these learning methods is gamification (Kiryakova et al., 2014). On the other hand, with the implementation of technology in the classroom, educational games have emerged as a powerful tool (Gordon, 1970): games that bring knowledge or skill to the student by removing traditional learning methods' rigidity. The combination of three factors has led to this explosion of games for learning (Van Eck, 2006): firstly, there is extensive related research that has given the field a robust scientific base. Secondly, there is the ease of acceptance of games and technology in general by the new generations born amid the technological era. Finally, we find the

Figure 1. Complete methodology followed to conduct the research

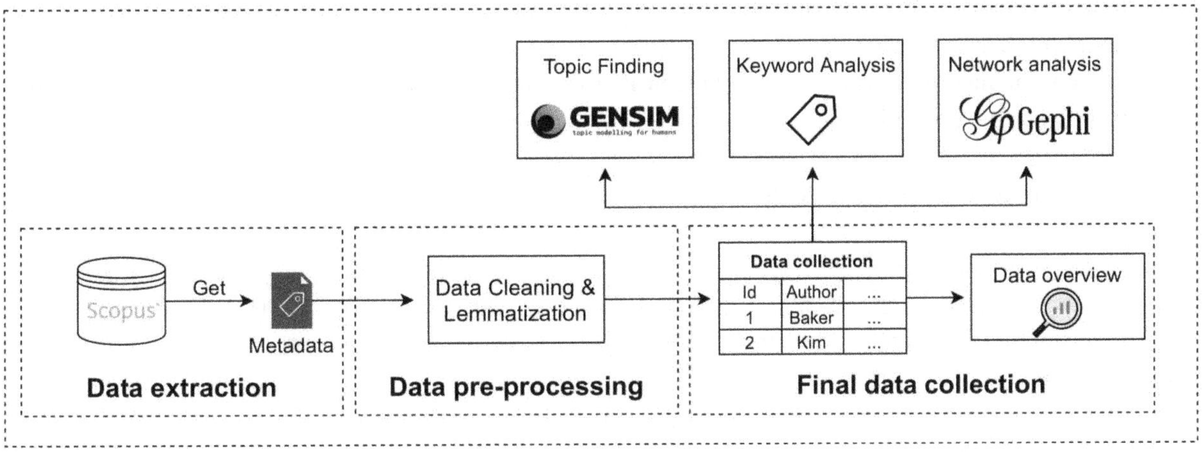

importance of video games today, which have captured the attention of the majority of the population across platforms and contexts (Ruipérez-Valiente et al., 2021).

The researchers also found previous work that applied the mentioned areas to games and gamification in education. For example, in (Martí-Parreño et al., 2016), authors noted that little research has focused on providing a comprehensive literature review on gamification in education. Thus, they performed a review using bibliometrics, social networks and text mining analysis in order to provide useful up-to-date information about the topic. With that purpose in mind, they collected 139 articles published in top journals over 2010 and 2014, allowing to identify relevant authors and institutions, key constructs and themes involved, and trends of knowledge development. Another example can be found in (Swacha, 2021), where authors tried to identify the main characteristics of gamification in education using a bibliometric approach. Their main analysis is performed on 2517 records retrieved from Scopus, and the main conclusions underlined the sustained growth of the area, as well as the effective research communication documented by the number of citations and a map of co-citations. Finally, we can see the work of (Chen et al., 2020), who conducted a structural topic modeling analysis of 3963 articles published in *Computers & Education* journal between 1976 and 2018, finding interesting topics, along with collaborations among the top 20 prolific institutions.

METHODOLOGY

To conduct the research, the authors divided their work in different stages: A) data extraction, B) data pre-processing, C) final data collection analysis, D) NLP analysis, E) network analysis. The entire methodology process is represented in Figure 1.

Data Extraction

The first step in our analysis was to get all the metadata necessary to begin the research. To limit the scope of the analysis we have added the following criteria:

- Papers that contain education and (gamification or game) in the title, abstract or keywords.
- Papers published during the last ten years (omitting 2021 because it was not a full year).
- Papers published in English.
- Papers published in journals, to guarantee that the studies that we include are quality research that went through peer-review process.

Then, the final query is the following one:

```
(TITLE-ABS-KEY (education) AND (TITLE-ABS-KEY (gamification) OR TITLE-ABS-KEY (game))) AND (LIMIT-TO (LANGUAGE, "English")) AND (LIMIT-TO (DOCTYPE, "ar")) AND (LIMIT-TO (PUBYEAR, 2020) OR LIMIT-TO (PUBYEAR, 2019) OR LIMIT-TO (PUBYEAR, 2018) OR LIMIT-TO (PUBYEAR, 2017) OR LIMIT-TO (PUB-YEAR, 2016) OR LIMIT-TO (PUBYEAR, 2015) OR LIMIT-TO (PUBYEAR, 2014) OR LIMIT-TO (PUBYEAR, 2013) OR LIMIT-TO (PUBYEAR, 2012) OR LIMIT-TO (PUB-YEAR, 2011))
```

Moreover, the downloaded metadata includes the title, keywords, abstract, source of publication, publication year, authors and so on.

Data Pre-processing

After collecting all the data, we had to pre-process and clean each paper's abstract. We performed cleaning actions by removing, for example, unnecessary URLs, numbers, or additional space characters. Moreover, to apply NLP techniques afterward, we needed to define a set of "stop words," which are not considered in the text analysis. In addition to the set of stop words defined by default, we added some more words after reviewing our data, such as "et," "al," "abstract," "table," or "figure," which are common words that appear in every document but do not provide helpful information to the analysis.

From now, we can start treating each abstract as a "document," since most of the cleaning process has ended. Once the text is cleaned, we lemmatized every document using *pywsd* library. The lemmatization is the process of converting a word to its base form (Plisson et al., 2004), and its implementation in *pywsd* works as follows:

- It tokenizes the string, dividing it in a set of tokens (words).
- It uses a Part-Of-Speech (POS) tagger to map each word to a POS tag (adverb, noun, adjective, and so on).
- It calls the lemmatizer with the token and the POS tag to get the base form of the word.

Final Data Collection

In this stage, the complete data collection is cleaned and ready to be used by further modeling algorithms. In order to explore the final data, descriptive statistics can be shown, such as such as the number of documents, the number of different sources (e.g., conferences, journals), the number of words or the number of unique words.

In this research, the final data collection contains a total of 7815 papers from 2698 different sources. The most important sources are shown in Table 1. The abstracts of these papers contain a total of 1696506 words, with 63378 unique words. In addition, the researchers present a word cloud model to describe the collection, which can be seen in Figure 2. A "word cloud" is a visual representation of word frequency derived from written text. The more often the word appears within the corpus being analyzed, the larger it appears in the image generated, providing a synopsis of the main themes contained within the text (Atenstaedt, 2017).

Table 1. Main sources where papers were published in

Source title	Number of publications
Computers and Education	208
Computers in Human Behavior	97
Simulation and Gaming	75
PLoS ONE	71
International Journal of Emerging Technologies in Learning	70
Sustainability (Switzerland)	68
International Journal of Environmental Research and Public Health	63
British Journal of Educational Technology	59
Physical Education and Sport Pedagogy	58
Journal of Chemical Education	57

Figure 2. Word cloud model

As we expected, the most frequent and important words are related with games and education, and include words such as "game", "learning," "student," "teacher," and "intervention." As we aimed with our selection of keywords in the search, we have gathered a myriad of papers revolving around the desired topics, and we further confirm that the studies found are relevant to our search.

NLP Analysis

To discover which are the main topics in this context, the authors have applied Latent Dirichlet Allocation (LDA) topic modeling to our data (Jelodar et al., 2019), using the abstract of each paper. LDA is usually used as an intuitive approach for a similarity calculation between source files and to obtain the respective distribution of topics across each document. Specifically, *gensim*, a pure Python library focused on unsupervised, semantic analysis of plain text in digital collections (Řehůřek & Sojka, 2011), and its *ldaMallet* model (Yao et al., 2009) have been used. Generally, in LDA each document can be described by a distribution of topics, and each topic can be described by a distribution of words; *ldaMallet* uses an optimized Gibbs sampling algorithm for LDA.

There are multiple metrics for evaluating the optimal number of topics. Recent studies have shown that the classic predictive likelihood metric (or equivalently, perplexity) and human judgment are often not correlated, and even sometimes slightly anti-correlated (O'callaghan et al., 2015). This has led to many studies that have focused upon the development of topic coherence measures. In this study, the authors use two of these coherence measures: *C_v* and *C_umass* (Röder et al., 2015):

- *C_v* measure is based on a sliding window, one-set segmentation of the top words and an indirect confirmation measure that uses normalized pointwise mutual information (NPMI) and the cosine similarity.
- *C_umass* is based on document co-occurrence counts, a one-preceding segmentation, and a logarithmic conditional probability as confirmation measure.

Then, to apply topic modelling, we followed the next steps:

1. **Step 1:** We created several models to decide the optimal number of topics based on the coherence measures specified previously. We determined 10 as the optimal number of topics, with a *C_v* score of 0.42 and a *C_umass* score of -1.5.
2. **Step 2:** We conducted an initial manual topic labeling based on the first five words of each topic.
3. **Step 3:** We reviewed ten random papers from each topic to delimit topics more precisely.
4. **Step 4:** We assigned the final label to each topic.

Moreover, to discover the main topics based on the papers' keywords, we applied to the keyword collection the same cleaning method that we previously applied to the abstracts, and then we inspected the data manually to merge similar keywords into a single one. That way, when we count the keywords, if we find, for example, "intelligent tutoring system" and "intelligent tutor systems,'' both keywords are merged, and their number of appearances are aggregated.

Network analysis

The next step in our work was to perform network analysis using the metadata from the collected papers. Specifically, we built two different networks:

- **Co-authorship network**: A co-authorship network in an undirected graph that describes the authors working together within a collection of documents. Each node in the graph represents an author in the collection, and each edge is connected from one author to another that have shared one or more papers. Co-authorship in research articles is considered a reliable proxy of research collaborations, bringing different talents together to give scientific credibility (S. Kumar, 2015).
- **Citation network**: A citation network is a directed graph that describes the citations within a collection of documents. Each node in the graph represents a document in the collection, and each edge is directed from one document toward another that it cites. Since citations of others papers are hand-picked by the authors as being related to their research, the citations can be considered to judge relatedness (Lu et al., 2007).

In this work, authors used the metadata to obtain the information from authors and citations of each paper, and then create both networks using *Gephi*, an open-source network analysis and visualization software package written in Java on the NetBeans platform (Bastian et al., 2009). Note that, in the citation network, researchers created an identifier for each paper, concatenating the first author's name with the first word of the paper title and the year of publication (e.g., if the paper is "Beyond the answer: Making sense of neuroprudence," the first author is "Kamalnath A.J.," and the year of publication is 2012, the identifier will be "KamalnathBeyond2012").

RESULTS

RQ1. Main Topics of the Use of Games and Gamification in Education Based on Keywords and Topic Modeling

As a preliminary output of the results, we found the following 10 predominant topics based on the NLP analysis, where each topic is identified by their most important words in terms of the Term Frequency-Inverse Document Frequency (TF-IDF). Each topic, along with its description and main terms, can be found in Table 2. As part of the analysis and results, we will discuss each one of these topics and the papers that have been assigned to them. Then, we will analyze the temporal evolution of these topics, to see if there are emerging trends or these have been quite constant over time

Based on these topics discovered, the authors evaluated each paper to get its topics associated (note that, in LDA, each document can be assigned to several topics with a certain weight), and calculated the proportion of each topic using the following equation:

$$Proportion\_topic_j = \frac{\sum_{i=1}^{N} weight\_topic_{ij}}{N} * 100$$

Then, the proportion of topic *j* would be the summation of each weight assigned to the topic *j* in each document from *i* to *N*, divided by the number of documents in the corpus (*N*). We can see the topic's distribution across the last ten years in Figure 3. As we can observe, the most frequent topics have been "Games in the classroom," "Games and behavioral addictions," and "Simulation games," as opposed to "Learning technologies" and "Games in medical settings," which have not been so popular.

Table 2. Main topics discovered by the model

Topic	Description	Main terms
Game-based learning	This topic is focused on using digital games for learning purposes	Game, learn, design, learning, educational, digital
Games in the classroom	This topic has a focus on the teacher side, using games and gamification with different groups to improve teaching and motivation	Student, teacher, study, game, motivation, group, gamification
Simulation games	This topic contains several studies using simulation games across different domains such as management, engineering, or science teaching.	Game, project, simulation, skill, management, engineering
Games, society and culture	This topic contains a number of studies on the interactions that game have with culture, policy, politics, discourse, and society in general.	Education, cultural, policy, culture, article, social
Games in medical settings	This topic agglutinates games that are used in medical settings either for patient recovery or for doctors' training.	Patient, medical, care, clinical, score, training, resident
Game issues regarding health	This topic involves papers that describe physical issues raised in children and adolescents and potential interventions.	Child, parent, adolescent, health, intervention, physical
Learning technologies	This topic involve article that utilize learning technologies to improve education processes, and games are notoriously used within these articles.	System, user, technology, application, robot, information, network
Children & games	This topic contains studies focused on children (pre-school or primary school) where games are used for different learning or educational purposes.	Child, cognitive, group, preschool, motor
Games & behavioral addictions	This topic involves addition risks generated by games like gambling, internet, alcohol and other behavioral and social problems.	Risk, gamble, internet, addiction, behavior, alcohol, social
Digital sports games	This topic is completely focused on sports games including those for entertainment, but also for training and injury recovery.	Sport, athlete, coach, physical, player, injury, football, basketball

Moreover, the authors also used paper keywords to conduct a similar analysis of the distribution, using the following equation:

$$Proportion\_keyword_j = \frac{n\_occurrences_j}{total\_occurrences} * 100$$

Then, the proportion of keyword *j* would be the number of occurrences of *j*, divided by the total number of occurrences of all keywords (*total_occurrences*). The top 20 keywords proportion across the last ten years were calculated. As we see in Figure 4, the most frequent keywords appearing are "education" (1.57%), "gamification" (1.5%) and "serious game" (1.25%).

Figure 3. Topic's distribution across all papers

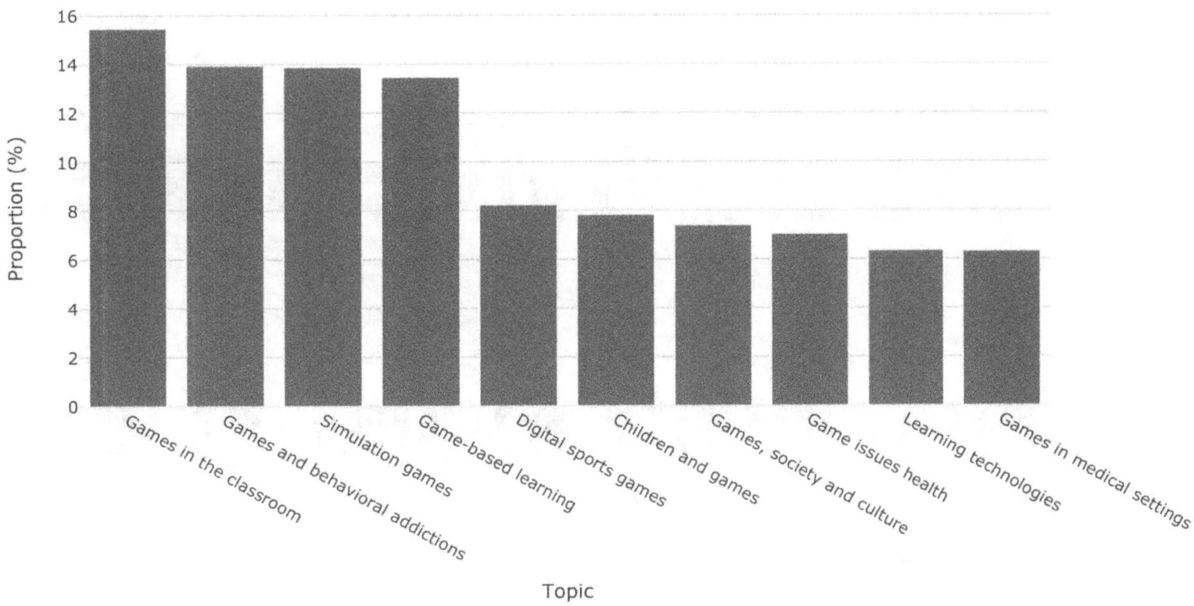

Figure 4. Keyword's distribution across all papers

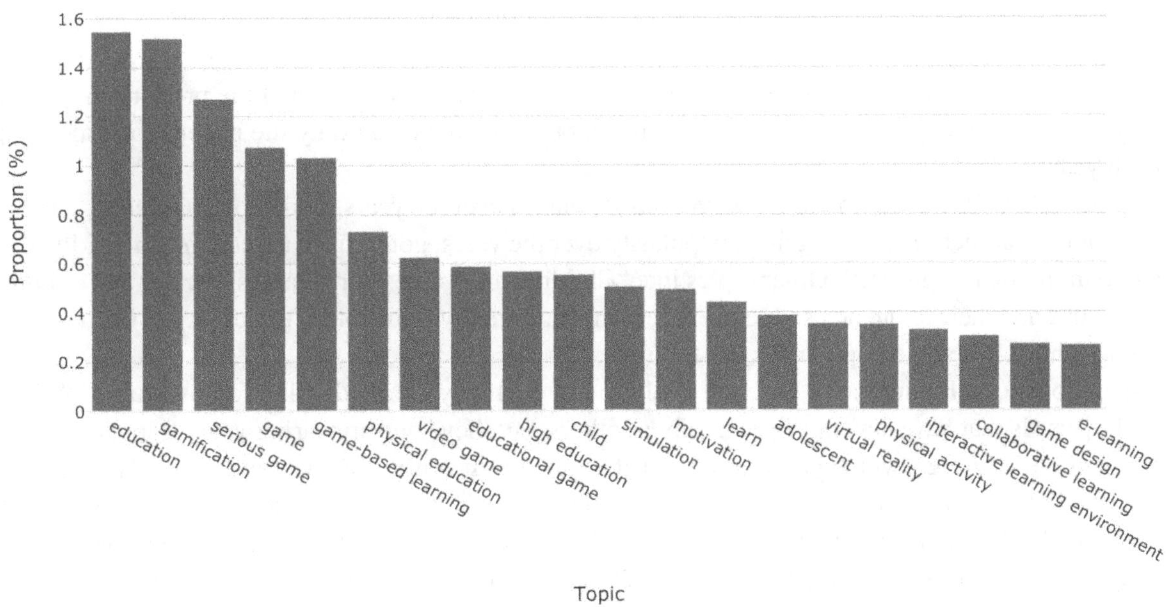

RQ2. Evolution of Topics Over the Last Ten Years of Research

Now that keywords and topics taking into account all ten years have been reviewed, researchers present

Figure 5. Topic's distribution by year

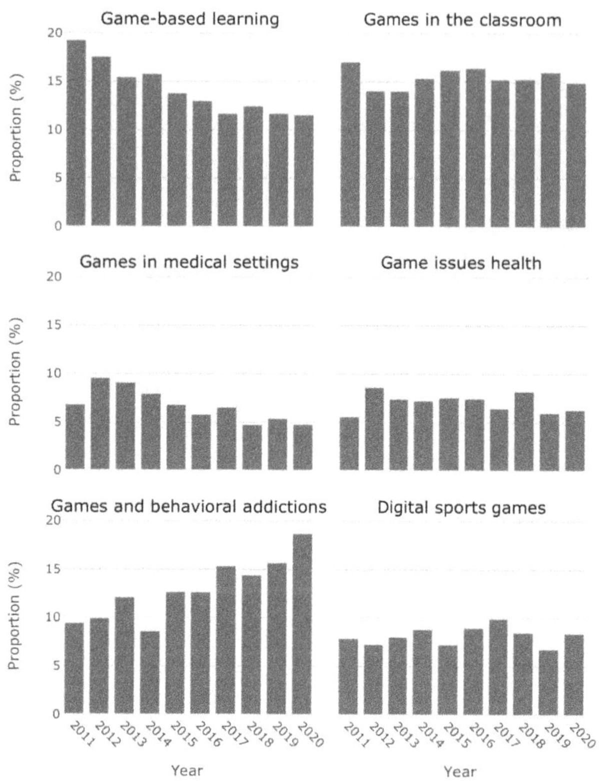

a second analysis, taking into account each year separately. Authors calculated the proportion of each topic in each year using the same formula as above, but this time using only the papers corresponding to each year.

Figure 5 shows the evolution of each topic's distribution over the years. Some topics, such as "Games and behavioral addictions," have gained popularity over the years, going from a frequency of 9% in 2011 to a maximum of 18% in 2020. Other topics like "Children and games" or "Games, society and culture" have maintained their frequency stable over the years, and finally, some other topics (e.g., "Game-based learning") have lost some popularity over time.

Analogously, in Figure 6, we have the evolution of each keyword's distribution over time. We see some keywords that have never been as trendy as others, but they keep appearing year after year. This is the case of "e-learning," which has a stable distribution almost every year. Moreover, we also see other keywords that have increased their frequency significantly, such as "gamification" (increasing from almost 0% in 2011 to a maximum of 2.45% in 2019). What we discover looking at Figure 6 is that most of the keywords have lost frequency from 2019 to 2020, which possibly means that 2020 was a year with new trends, or maybe papers' keywords are more diverse.

RQ3. Communities of Authors and Papers in this Topic Based on a Network Analysis Perspective

As said previously, authors created two different networks: a co-authorship network and a citation network.

Figure 6. Keyword's distribution by year

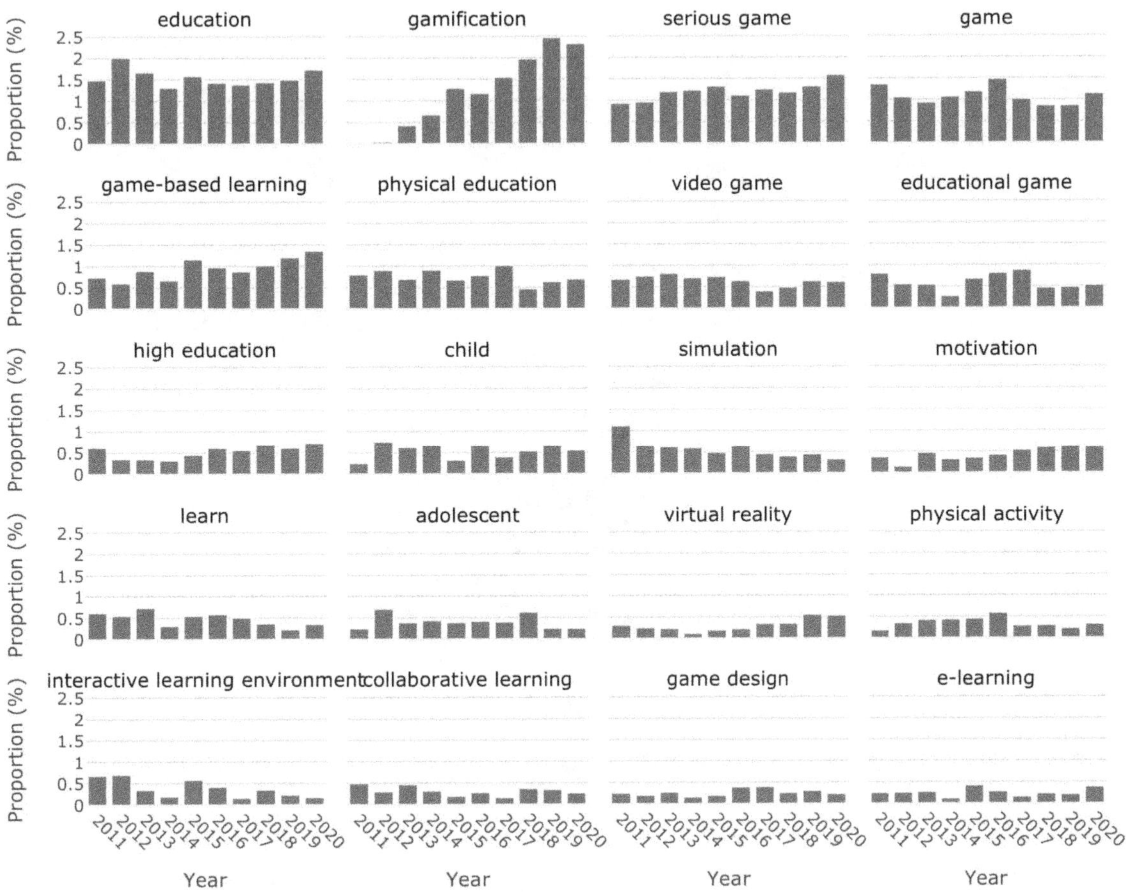

In Figure 7, we can see the co-authorship network built in the code and then streamed into *Gephi*, where each node represents an author. Note that, in the plot, only the giant component is shown (a giant component is a connected component of a network that contains a significant proportion of the entire nodes in the network).

There are 28052 author names across papers (an average of 3.6 authors per paper), and 23031 of those author names are unique. Furthermore, the top central authors are "Miguel-Berges M.L.," "Latomme J.," "Sánchez-Lopez M.," "Lobstein T.," and "Dorgelo A.," among others. Thus, we can see that these authors are the ones that collaborate with a large proportion of other authors that are also considered as central authors in the graph. This study also revealed the authors with a more significant proportion of published papers: "Harvey S." (0.28% of the papers), "Hwang G.-J." (0.24%), "Fernández-Manjón B." (0.19%), "Chen Y." (0.17%), and "Hong J.-C." (0.17%). Another interesting fact is that 0.17% of the papers do not provide the author's names in the metadata.

This giant component shown in the graph has 3969 nodes (17.2% of the authors), meaning that the rest of authors (82.8%) are not collaborating with the authors shown in the giant component, so they represent sub-communities within the games and gamification in education context. In general, we see a fragmented community that is weakly connected (overall density of only 0.001).

Figure 7. Co-authorship network built

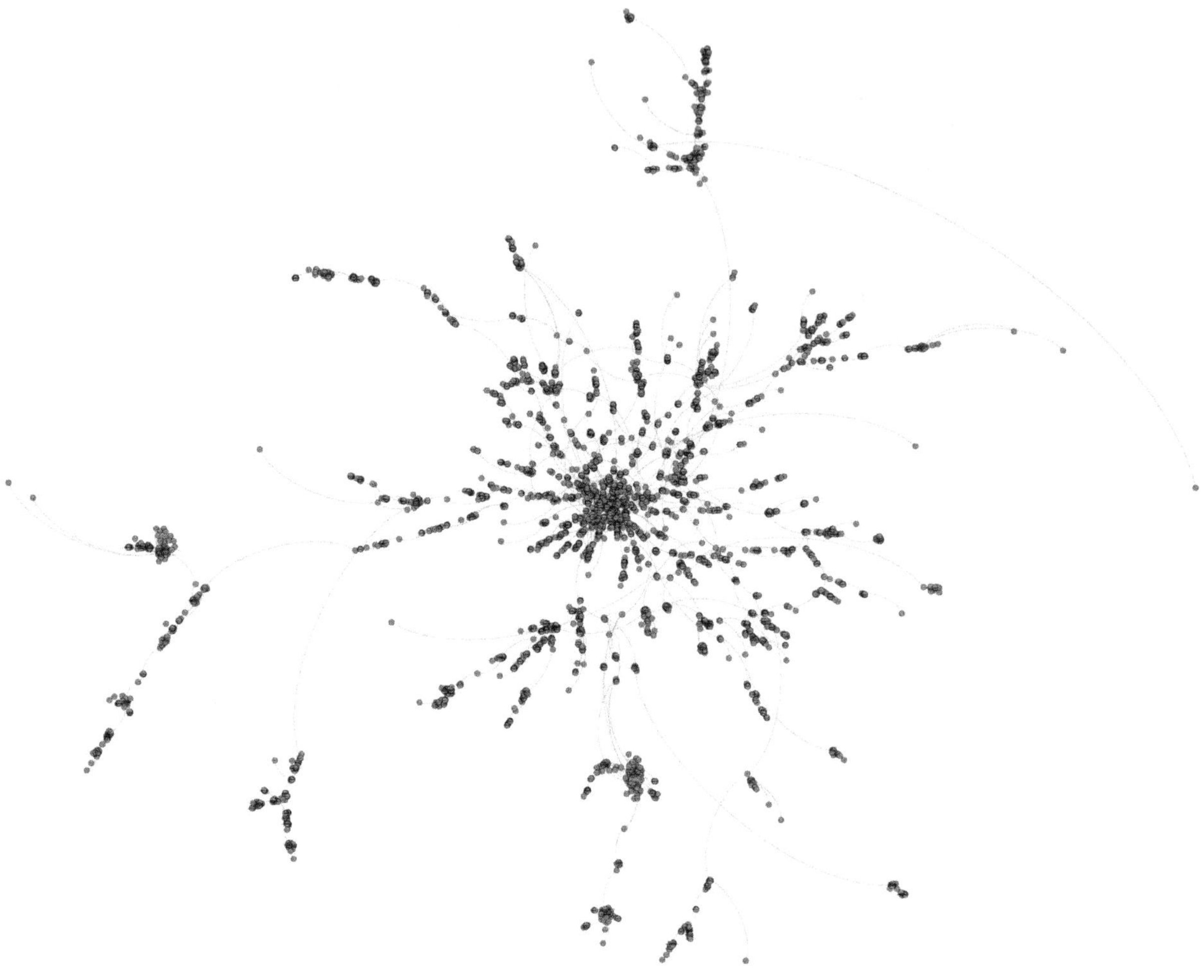

Moreover, in Figure 8, we can see the citation network built in the code and then streamed into Gephi. Each node represents a paper in the network, and each edge is a citation between the two papers (nodes). Note that, in our plot, only the giant component is shown. This giant component shown in the graph has 3533 nodes (45.59% of the papers), meaning that the rest of papers are not strongly connected (being cited or citing) with the rest of papers in the collection. Again, we see a fragmented community that is weakly connected (overall density of only 0.001).

The algorithm has found 9352 references between papers. The top central papers are "Game on" (Vasquez, 2019), "Gamification in education" (Medica Ružić & Dumančić, 2015), "A systematic literature review of empirical evidence on computer games and serious games" (Connolly et al., 2012), "Gamifying learning experiences: Practical implications and outcomes" (Domínguez et al., 2013) and "Gamification in education: A systematic mapping study" (Dicheva et al., 2015). Looking at the top central papers, we note that one of them was published in 2012, one in 2013, two of them in 2015, and another in 2019. Since these are the papers that have been most cited between them, we note that they are the ones having a major influence on the community being analyzed.

Figure 8. Co-citation network built

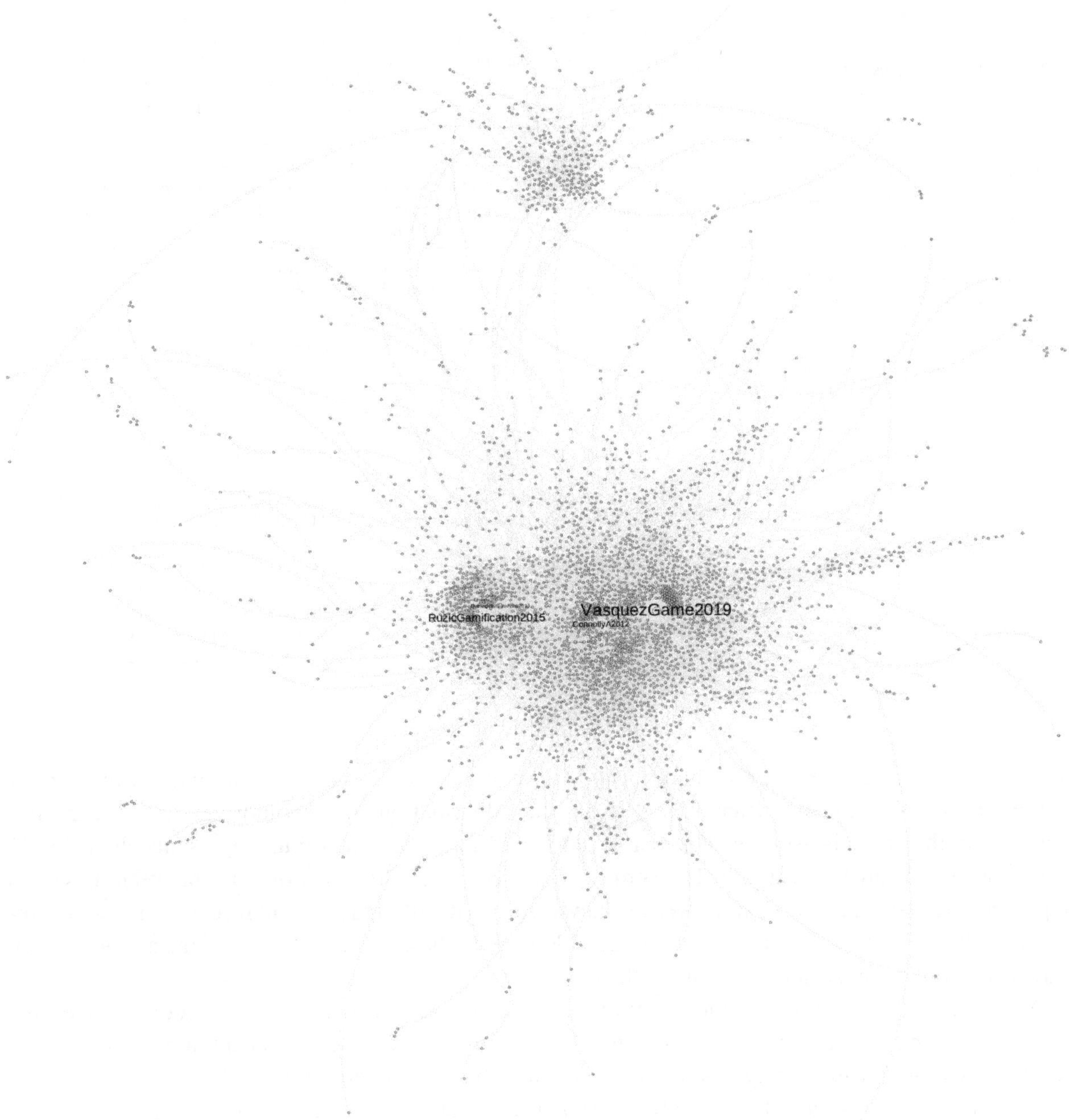

DISCUSSION

In this study, the authors automatically found the main trends during the last ten years in games and gamification in education, basing the analysis on two primary sources: the full manuscripts and the keywords. We can see a summary of the main findings in Table 3. Comparing both results, we note that

Table 3. Summary of the main findings

Question	Findings
What are the main topics of the use of games and gamification in education based on keywords?	The main topics found are "education," "gamification," "serious game," "game," "game-based learning," "physical education," "video game," "high education," "child," "simulation," "motivation," "learn," "adolescent," "virtual reality," "e-learning," "interactive learning environment," "game design," and "collaborative learning."
What are the main topics of the use of games and gamification in education based on topic modeling?	The main topics found are "game-based learning," "games in the classroom," "simulation games," "games, society and culture," "games in medical settings," "game issues health," "learning technologies," "children and games," "games and behavioral addictions," and "digital sports games."
What has been the evolution of such topics over the last ten years of research based on keywords?	The topic that has gained more popularity has been "gamification", while other topics such as "education," "game-based learning," "serious game," and "physical education" have kept a high popularity over time.
What has been the evolution of such topics over the last ten years of research based on topic modeling?	The topic that has gained more popularity has been "games and behavioral addictions," while other topics such as "game-based learning," "games in the classroom," and "simulation games" have kept a high popularity during those years.
What are the communities of authors and papers in this topic based on a network analysis perspective?	The most central authors are "Miguel-Berges M.L.," "Latomme J.," "Sánchez-Lopez M.," "Lobstein T.," and "Dorgelo A.". The most prolific authors are "Harvey S." (0.28% of the papers), "Hwang G.-J." (0.24%), "Fernández-Manjón B." (0.19%), "Chen Y." (0.17%), and "Hong J.-C." (0.17%). The most central papers are "Game on" (Vasquez, 2019), "Gamification in education" (Medica Ružić & Dumančić, 2015), "A systematic literature review of empirical evidence on computer games and serious games" (Connolly et al., 2012), "Gamifying learning experiences: Practical implications and outcomes" (Domínguez et al., 2013) and "Gamification in education: A systematic mapping study" (Dicheva et al., 2015).

some of the topics revealed are common, such as "Simulation games" and "Simulation." However, most of the topics discovered are different, and so are their distributions and evolution over the years. For example, in the analysis using the abstracts, the topic "Game-based learning" represents about 13.6% of the papers, meanwhile using the keywords, it represents 1%. The key difference between these two approaches is that the authors carefully select keywords to fit within the current research lines and communities. In contrast, topic modeling is finding hidden topics based on the abstract of the articles, which may reflect more realistically the topic of the paper.

Moreover, this current study found the most central authors and papers. If we take a look at the results, we see that being a central author does not imply that your paper will be also a central paper within the community, as we are measuring separately collaboration between authors, and citations between papers. We also see that publishing a large number of papers does not imply being a more central author, as the centrality measure depends on the relationship with other authors. In fact, no author appears in both central and large publishing top lists. We also noted that there were no authors with a really large proportion of papers within the collection, since the most prolific author appears in a 0.28% of the papers. In fact, 82% of the author names are unique, which means that only 18% of the authors appear in more than one paper. Furthermore, we see that almost no author that is highlighted in the results appears as a main author in the citation network. This fact is related to the continued debate on the relative importance of quality and quantity in scientific publications, since published works herald a movement to reemphasize quality research over quantity (Donaldson & Cooke, 2014; Fischer et al., 2012). Moreover, we see that there is not a huge difference in the percentage of publications between the top authors, indicating that the leadership is distributed and there might not be a single author leading this research area. In addition, as (Swacha, 2021) previously noted in his work, there are a small percentage of authors (17.9%) that have contributed with more than one paper, which also indicates that research in these areas can involve single sporadic research studies rather than an area of scientific specialization during all the career of a researcher. This also reveals the type of work that the analyzed communities are developing in these areas. Further research could explore the transfer of these trends to many other communities, to check the similarities and differences between communities in these aspects.

We can compare our work with other topic finding papers in terms of the methodology applied. For example, in (Choi et al., 2017), authors analyzed research trends in personal information privacy. For their research, they applied text mining to the abstract of each paper recovered, and then the optimal number of topics is determined by maximizing the log-likelihood of the topic model. In this research, the authors use two coherence measures to determine the number of topics. Those coherence measures show, in contrast to the likelihood of held-out data, a higher correlation with human topic ranking data, the gold standard for topic interpretability (Syed & Spruit, 2017). The authors also found studies that previously explored trends in the gamification in education field. For example, (Swacha, 2021) analyzed the most frequent keywords using 2517 records from Scopus, finding that most of the keywords also appear in this study (e.g., gamification, education, game design, game-based learning, simulation, motivation). They also built a citation network, also finding the most cited papers, such as "Gamifying learning experiences: Practical implications and outcomes" (Domínguez et al., 2013) and "Gamification in education: A systematic mapping study" (Dicheva et al., 2015), which also appear as the most central papers in our citation network. Moreover, (Martí-Parreño et al., 2016) noted that *Computers & Education* and *Computers in Human Behavior* were the top leading journals in their study. In our study, both journals are also the top leading journals, with 208 (2.66%) and 97 (1.24%) published papers, respectively.

Despite our study is mainly limited by the search query, we might be missing some existing publications that are using other keywords in their papers. However, this study is still larger than previous existing ones, and we believe that it can be helpful to discover current trends in the area easily and quickly. The use of the abstracts for determining the topics could also introduce some bias, since previous studies suggest that using full-text data provides better results, especially in a small corpus of documents (Syed & Spruit, 2017). Since our study uses a large corpus of papers, future research could explore if the use of full-text data provides similar or better results. Also, we made assumptions when labeling topics, as each topic identified by the model could refer to more than one area, and our own background can also influence that manual labeling in the inferred topics.

LIMITATIONS AND FUTURE WORK

Of course, this work also has some limitations. First, this research is limited by the search query, since other communities might be working in games and gamification in education but using slightly different terms to describe their work. Therefore, they might not be included in this research. However, the authors opted for this search query to analyze the core of games and gamification while also having a manageable selection of papers. Second, this research is focused on Scopus, the primary academic database, but there are many other databases, and also non-academic papers, technical or white reports that could be missed in the research. With respect to the keyword analysis, we are limited by author's keywords, expecting they cover all the possible topics addressed in each paper. However, usually, it is not like that. We are also limited by the number of topics selected to build the LDA model, since there might be some hidden topics that have not been discovered. Another limitation is related to the fact that some authors and organizations have different ways to present their names, and this can introduce some bias in the network analysis. Furthermore, this approach to discover trends and topics cannot provide as much in-depth information as other types of qualitative and manual reviews can, but it offers helpful information that can be enough for certain purposes, specially within bibliometrics field.

Since this methodology provides a novel approach to perform quick reviews, as part of our future work, the development of a framework that can be used with any corpus of papers, providing quick results automatically, will be explored. Previous studies (Syed & Spruit, 2017) have compared two options when performing topic modeling on research papers: using the full text or using only the abstract, concluding that using the full text produces higher number of topics with higher coherence, and therefore better results. Thus, researchers will also explore this approach using full-text papers.

CONCLUSION

This research stated three main research questions: to answer the first one related to the main topics of the use of games and gamification in education, researchers used two approaches, one of them using topic modelling on the papers' abstract, and another one using the complete keyword collection from the metadata. Then, for the second research question, the authors analyzed the evolution of the identified topics by both previous approaches by applying the same methodology to each year separately revealing how topics evolved over the years. Finally, to discover what are the communities, main authors, and main papers in this topic, the authors used network analysis to create two different representations: a co-authorship network and a citation network.

This study has used a bibliometrics and text mining approach to quickly discover trends and relationships in a large collection of papers corresponding to the games and gamification in education areas. Specifically, this work has used NLP, topic modeling, and network analysis, instead of a classic qualitative review that often requires a significant amount of time to be performed. The authors applied this approach to 7815 papers from 2698 different sources, collected from the Scopus database. Some of the most frequent topics discovered are "Simulation," "Game-based learning," or "Games in medical settings." Some of the topics have gained popularity over time (e.g., "Games and behavioral addictions"); meanwhile, others had been very popular, but their popularity has been decreasing over time (e.g., "Game-based learning"). This also shows common trends within research communities, since usually, when a topic is gaining popularity, this growth promotes more and more research in that topic, creating a bubble that can burst anytime. This is also affected by the impact that external funding can have, as well as the impact that press and public opinion have on each area, which can also encourage or discourage research. Moreover, the authors also found the most central and prolific authors, along with the most central papers in the collection. Researchers expect this study to shed some light on the latest trends and evolution of these fields using this novel bibliometrics and text mining approach.

REFERENCES

Abu-Jbara, A., Ezra, J., & Radev, D. (2013). Purpose and polarity of citation: Towards nlp-based bibliometrics. *Proceedings of the 2013 Conference of the North American Chapter of the Association for Computational Linguistics: Human Language Technologies*, 596–606.

Allen, J. F. (2003). Natural language processing. In Encyclopedia of computer science (pp. 1218–1222). Academic Press.

Amado, A., Cortez, P., Rita, P., & Moro, S. (2018). Research trends on Big Data in Marketing: A text mining and topic modeling based literature analysis. *European Research on Management and Business Economics*, *24*(1), 1–7. doi:10.1016/j.iedeen.2017.06.002

Atanassova, I., Bertin, M., & Mayr, P. (2019). Mining scientific papers: NLP-enhanced bibliometrics. *Frontiers in Research Metrics and Analytics*, *4*, 2. doi:10.3389/frma.2019.00002 PMID:33870034

Atenstaedt, R. (2017). Word cloud analysis of the BJGP: 5 years on. *The British Journal of General Practice*, *67*(658), 231–232. doi:10.3399/bjgp17X690833 PMID:28450341

Bastian, M., Heymann, S., & Jacomy, M. (2009). Gephi: an open source software for exploring and manipulating networks. *Third International AAAI Conference on Weblogs and Social Media*.

Blohm, I., & Leimeister, J. M. (2013). Gamification: Design of IT-based enhancing services for motivational support and behavioral change. *Business & Information Systems Engineering*, *5*(4), 275–278. doi:10.100712599-013-0273-5

Broadus, R. N. (1987). Toward a definition of "bibliometrics.". *Scientometrics*, *12*(5–6), 373–379. doi:10.1007/BF02016680

Burchfield, R. W. (1972). A supplement to the Oxford English dictionary. Academic Press.

Chen, X., Zou, D., Cheng, G., & Xie, H. (2020). Detecting latent topics and trends in educational technologies over four decades using structural topic modeling: A retrospective of all volumes of Computers & Education. *Computers & Education*, *151*, 103855. doi:10.1016/j.compedu.2020.103855

Choi, H. S., Lee, W. S., & Sohn, S. Y. (2017). Analyzing research trends in personal information privacy using topic modeling. *Computers & Security*, *67*, 244–253. doi:10.1016/j.cose.2017.03.007

Connolly, T. M., Boyle, E. A., MacArthur, E., Hainey, T., & Boyle, J. M. (2012). A systematic literature review of empirical evidence on computer games and serious games. *Computers & Education*, *59*(2), 661–686. doi:10.1016/j.compedu.2012.03.004

Cooper, I. D. (2015). Bibliometrics basics. *Journal of the Medical Library Association: JMLA*, *103*(4), 217–218. doi:10.3163/1536-5050.103.4.013 PMID:26512226

De Freitas, S. (2006). Learning in Immersive worlds A review of game-based learning. *JISC ELearning Innovation, 3.3*(October), 73. doi:10.1111/j.1467-8535.2009.01024.x

de Klerk, S., & Kato, P. M. (2017). The future value of serious games for assessment: Where do we go now? *Journal of Applied Testing Technology*, *18*(S1), 32–37.

Deterding, S., Khaled, R., Nacke, L. E., & Dixon, D. (2011). Gamification: Toward a Definition. Gamification Workshop. *CHI 2011 Gamification Workshop Proceedings,* 12–15.

Dicheva, D., Dichev, C., Agre, G., & Angelova, G. (2015). Gamification in education: A systematic mapping study. *Journal of Educational Technology & Society*, *18*(3), 75–88.

Domínguez, A., Saenz-de-Navarrete, J., De-Marcos, L., Fernández-Sanz, L., Pagés, C., & Martínez-Herráiz, J.-J. (2013). Gamifying learning experiences: Practical implications and outcomes. *Computers & Education*, *63*, 380–392. doi:10.1016/j.compedu.2012.12.020

Donaldson, M. R., & Cooke, S. J. (2014). Scientific publications: Moving beyond quality and quantity toward influence. *Bioscience*, *64*(1), 12–13. doi:10.1093/biosci/bit007

Eiland, L. S., & Todd, T. J. (2019). Considerations when incorporating technology into classroom and experiential teaching. *The Journal of Pediatric Pharmacology and Therapeutics: JPPT: the Official Journal of PPAG*, *24*(4), 270–275. doi:10.5863/1551-6776-24.4.270 PMID:31337989

ESA. (2019). *2019 Essential Facts About the Computer and Video Game Industry*. ESA.

Fischer, J., Ritchie, E. G., & Hanspach, J. (2012). Academia's obsession with quantity. *Trends in Ecology & Evolution*, *27*(9), 473–474. doi:10.1016/j.tree.2012.05.010 PMID:22727015

Gee, J. P. (2008). Learning and games. *The Ecology of Games: Connecting Youth, Games, and Learning*, 21–40. doi:10.1162/dmal.9780262693646.021

Gordon, A. K. (1970). *Games For Growth*. Educational Games in the Classroom.

Hamari, J., Koivisto, J., & Sarsa, H. (2014). Does Gamification Work? A Literature Review of Empirical Studies on Gamification. *2014 47th Hawaii International Conference on System Sciences*, 3025–3034. 10.1109/HICSS.2014.377

Hevey, D. (2018). Network analysis: A brief overview and tutorial. *Health Psychology and Behavioral Medicine*, *6*(1), 301–328. doi:10.1080/21642850.2018.1521283 PMID:34040834

Jelodar, H., Wang, Y., Yuan, C., Feng, X., Jiang, X., Li, Y., & Zhao, L. (2019). Latent Dirichlet allocation (LDA) and topic modeling: Models, applications, a survey. *Multimedia Tools and Applications*, *78*(11), 15169–15211. doi:10.100711042-018-6894-4

Khurana, D., Koli, A., Khatter, K., & Singh, S. (2017). *Natural language processing: State of the art, current trends and challenges.* ArXiv Preprint ArXiv:1708.05148.

Kiryakova, G., Angelova, N., & Yordanova, L. (2014). *Gamification in education*. Academic Press.

Kokol, P., Blažun Vošner, H., & Završnik, J. (2020). Application of bibliometrics in medicine: A historical bibliometrics analysis. *Health Information and Libraries Journal*. PMID:31995273

Kovačević, A., Konjović, Z., Milosavljević, B., & Nenadic, G. (2012). Mining methodologies from NLP publications: A case study in automatic terminology recognition. *Computer Speech & Language*, *26*(2), 105–126. doi:10.1016/j.csl.2011.09.001

Kumar, E. (2011). *Natural language processing*. IK International Pvt Ltd.

Kumar, S. (2015). Co-authorship networks: A review of the literature. *Aslib Journal of Information Management, 67*(1), 55–73. doi:10.1108/AJIM-09-2014-0116

Liddy, E. D. (2001). *Natural language processing*. Academic Press.

Lu, W., Janssen, J., Milios, E., Japkowicz, N., & Zhang, Y. (2007). Node similarity in the citation graph. *Knowledge and Information Systems, 11*(1), 105–129. doi:10.100710115-006-0023-9

Lv, P. H., Wang, G.-F., Wan, Y., Liu, J., Liu, Q., & Ma, F. (2011). Bibliometric trend analysis on global graphene research. *Scientometrics, 88*(2), 399–419. doi:10.100711192-011-0386-x

Martí-Parreño, J., Méndez-Ibáñez, E., & Alonso-Arroyo, A. (2016). The use of gamification in education: A bibliometric and text mining analysis. *Journal of Computer Assisted Learning, 32*(6), 663–676. doi:10.1111/jcal.12161

Medica Ružić, I., & Dumančić, M. (2015). Gamification in education. *Informatologia, 48*(3–4), 198–204.

Miau, S., & Yang, J.-M. (2018). Bibliometrics-based evaluation of the Blockchain research trend: 2008–March 2017. *Technology Analysis and Strategic Management, 30*(9), 1029–1045. doi:10.1080/09537325.2018.1434138

O'callaghan, D., Greene, D., Carthy, J., & Cunningham, P. (2015). An analysis of the coherence of descriptors in topic modeling. *Expert Systems with Applications, 42*(13), 5645–5657. doi:10.1016/j.eswa.2015.02.055

Park, K. C., & Lee, C. H. (2019). A study on the research trends for smart city using topic modeling. *Journal of Internet Computing and Services, 20*(3), 119–128.

Patrício, R., Moreira, A. C., & Zurlo, F. (2018). Gamification approaches to the early stage of innovation. *Creativity and Innovation Management, 27*(4), 499–511. doi:10.1111/caim.12284

Patrício, R., Moreira, A. C., & Zurlo, F. (2021). Enhancing design thinking approaches to innovation through gamification. *European Journal of Innovation Management, 24*(5), 1569–1594. doi:10.1108/EJIM-06-2020-0239

Plisson, J., Lavrac, N., & Mladenic, D. (2004). A rule based approach to word lemmatization. *Proceedings of IS, 3*, 83–86.

Řehůřek, R., & Sojka, P. (2011). *Gensim—statistical semantics in python*. Retrieved from Genism. Org.

Röder, M., Both, A., & Hinneburg, A. (2015). Exploring the space of topic coherence measures. *Proceedings of the Eighth ACM International Conference on Web Search and Data Mining*, 399–408. 10.1145/2684822.2685324

Ruipérez-Valiente, J. A., Gomez, M. J., Martínez, P. A., & Kim, Y. J. (2021). Ideating and Developing a Visualization Dashboard to Support Teachers Using Educational Games in the Classroom. *IEEE Access: Practical Innovations, Open Solutions, 9*, 83467–83481. doi:10.1109/ACCESS.2021.3086703

Schmidt-Kraepelin, M., Thiebes, S., Baumsteiger, D., & Sunyaev, A. (2018). *State of play: A citation network analysis of healthcare gamification studies*. Academic Press.

Scott, J. (1988). Social network analysis. *Sociology*, *22*(1), 109–127. doi:10.1177/0038038588022001007

Sun, L., & Yin, Y. (2017). Discovering themes and trends in transportation research using topic modeling. *Transportation Research Part C, Emerging Technologies*, *77*, 49–66. doi:10.1016/j.trc.2017.01.013

Swacha, J. (2021). State of research on gamification in education: A bibliometric survey. *Education Sciences*, *11*(2), 69. doi:10.3390/educsci11020069

Syed, S., & Spruit, M. (2017). Full-text or abstract? examining topic coherence scores using latent dirichlet allocation. *2017 IEEE International Conference on Data Science and Advanced Analytics (DSAA)*, 165–174. 10.1109/DSAA.2017.61

Trinidad, M., Ruiz, M., & Calderón, A. (2021). A bibliometric analysis of gamification research. *IEEE Access: Practical Innovations, Open Solutions*, *9*, 46505–46544. doi:10.1109/ACCESS.2021.3063986

Van Eck, R. (2006). Digital game-based learning: It's not just the digital natives who are restless. *EDUCAUSE Review*, *41*(2), 16.

Vasquez, V. M. (2019). Game on. *Curriculum Inquiry*, *49*(2), 173–190. doi:10.1080/03626784.2019.1593789

Yao, L., Mimno, D., & McCallum, A. (2009). Efficient methods for topic model inference on streaming document collections. *Proceedings of the 15th ACM SIGKDD International Conference on Knowledge Discovery and Data Mining*, 937–946. 10.1145/1557019.1557121

Zhang, J., Luxton-Reilly, A., Denny, P., & Whalley, J. (2021). Scientific Collaboration Network Analysis for Computing Education Conferences. *Proceedings of the 26th ACM Conference on Innovation and Technology in Computer Science Education*, 1, 582–588. 10.1145/3430665.3456385

ADDITIONAL READING

Allen, J. F. (2003). Natural language processing. In Encyclopedia of computer science (pp. 1218–1222). Academic Press.

Atanassova, I., Bertin, M., & Mayr, P. (2019). Mining scientific papers: NLP-enhanced bibliometrics. *Frontiers in Research Metrics and Analytics*, *4*, 2. doi:10.3389/frma.2019.00002 PMID:33870034

Dicheva, D., Dichev, C., Agre, G., & Angelova, G. (2015). Gamification in education: A systematic mapping study. *Journal of Educational Technology & Society*, *18*(3), 75–88.

Martí-Parreño, J., Méndez-Ibáñez, E., & Alonso-Arroyo, A. (2016). The use of gamification in education: A bibliometric and text mining analysis. *Journal of Computer Assisted Learning*, *32*(6), 663–676. doi:10.1111/jcal.12161

Scott, J. (1988). Social network analysis. *Sociology*, *22*(1), 109–127. doi:10.1177/0038038588022001007

Trinidad, M., Ruiz, M., & Calderón, A. (2021). A bibliometric analysis of gamification research. *IEEE Access: Practical Innovations, Open Solutions*, *9*, 46505–46544. doi:10.1109/ACCESS.2021.3063986

KEY TERMS AND DEFINITIONS

Bibliometrics: Bibliometrics is the use of statistical methods to analyze books, articles and other publications.

Corpus: A collection or body of knowledge or evidence.

Gamification: The use of game design elements in a non-game context.

Lemmatization: The algorithmic process of determining the lemma of a word based on its intended meaning.

Metadata: A set of data that describes and gives information about other data.

Natural Language Processing: Branch of computer science which aims to understand and produce language the same way as human beings can.

Network Analysis: Set of techniques which allow to depict relations among actors and to analyze the social structures emerging from those relations.

Text Analytics: Process of drawing meaning out of written communication.

Topic Modeling: A topic model is a type of statistical model for discovering the abstract "topics" that occur in a collection of documents.

Chapter 3
Gamification in Healthcare Education:
Demystifying a Trend

José Miguel Padilha
https://orcid.org/0000-0002-6631-776X
Tech4EduSim-CINTESIS, Nursing School of Porto, Portugal

João Frias Rosa
https://orcid.org/0000-0001-6328-9807
ICBAS, School of Medicine and Biomedical Sciences, Portugal

Daniel José Cunha
Higher School of Health of Santa Maria, Portugal

ABSTRACT

This chapter calls for reflection on one of the most promising technologies in healthcare education, the use of virtual patients and clinical virtual simulation as a pedagogical strategy to improve clinical decision-making and enhance clinical safety and healthcare quality. This chapter discusses the new challenges in healthcare education and the use of clinical virtual simulation in undergraduate healthcare education and lifelong learning, integrating gamification and serious games as strategies to increase intrinsic and extrinsic students' motivation. Considering the novelty of this topic, this chapter will be strategic for technology developers and healthcare educators, identifying emerging challenges and opportunities.

INTRODUCTION

Healthcare Education: New Challenges

Healthcare education is well recognised by the need to ensure high-quality standards to guarantee an effective and safer clinical practice (WHO, 2011a). Healthcare educators are constantly challenged by

DOI: 10.4018/978-1-6684-4287-6.ch003

healthcare students on different ways of learning, interests, technological literacy, availability, and use of information and communication technologies (ICT) (Guze, 2015; OECD, 2016). Over the last years, we have been witnessing a decrease in the young generation's interest in pursuing healthcare education. In addition, the availability of clinical practice internships - with the high standards required by the legal regulatory bodies to the accreditation of healthcare institutions as recognised learning environments, has been reduced. Furthermore, in the current global context, another significant challenge is posed by the restrictions imposed by the COVID-19 pandemic. Currently, developed countries are experiencing increasingly ageing populations and non-communicable diseases or chronic diseases. In addition, the financial constraints of education institutions resulting from lack of financing are noticeable (OECD, 2008, 2019; WHO, 2011b, 2020a).

Therefore, healthcare institutions and educators are urged to increase the attractiveness of the healthcare field education courses to the young generation of students. This requires the use and integration of disruptive new technologies and pedagogical methodologies as opposed to traditional health education by introducing constructivist strategies directed to enhancing active learning. Nowadays, the biggest challenge is finding ways to enhance the engagement and motivation of students to be active learners and providing them with tools to meet their goals. The aim is to empower these students to cope with the continuous changes in scientific knowledge and endless new techniques and technologies to enhance health outcomes and safety (OECD, 2016; WHO, 2013, 2020b).

The need to integrate new technologies to enhance engagement, quality and safety led institutions to first introduce simulation and, over the last year's, to an attempt to integrate gamification and serious games as strategies to increase intrinsic and extrinsic students' motivation (Kim et al., 2018).

Simulation in Healthcare Education

Over the last centuries, healthcare educators have been debating how to translate fundamental concepts and technics to clinical practice to ensure quality and safety in the provision of healthcare (Norman, 2009). Simulation emerged as an educational strategy allowing to recreate safe learning environments where healthcare students can master the translation of knowledge, skills or attitudes to clinical practice.

Simulation emerged in the 18th century with Madame Du Coudray (1712-1794) first attempts to recreate realistic learning environments where healthcare students had the opportunity to practice obstetrical procedures (Carty, 2010), applying and developing knowledge, skills and attitudes. Since Madame Du Coudray first achievements in recreating realistic learning environments, simulation was widely implemented in the health education field with well-recognised outcomes in knowledge retention, technical abilities, reflection on and about action, transfer of competencies, motivation and realism (Goldshtein et al., 2020; Hammoud et al., 2008; Hegland et al., 2017; Kneebone, 2005; Lapkin et al., 2010; Mcgaghie et al., 2010; Meakim et al., 2013)

Notwithstanding these outcomes, simulation as a pedagogical strategy has evolved to the current definition of a technique that recreates a situation or environment, allowing people to experience a representation of a real event for the purpose of practice, learning, evaluation, testing, or gaining an understanding of systems or human actions (Lioce et al., 2020).

Simulation uses programmed situations very similar to real clinical contexts. It allows the training of the necessary skills in a protected and controlled environment and the occurrence and correction of errors without its effects. Additionally, it enables the control of external factors, the standardization of the presented problems, immediate feedback, increased self-knowledge, and confidence in autonomous action within the actual context of action. Simulation also contributes to the transferability of competencies to clinical practice with significant improvement in morbidity and/or mortality outcomes (Goldshtein et al., 2019; Hegland et al., 2017; Lasater, 2007; Mcgaghie et al., 2010)

In recent decades, advancements in the technological field led to disruptive innovations and the widespread adoption of ICT applied to simulation in healthcare education. The improved features and developments in ICT allowed the development of different levels of fidelity in the simulation field. Fidelity is the degree to which the simulation replicates the real event or workplace, including the physical, psychological, and environmental elements (Lioce et al., 2020). Since the 1950s, fidelity has progressed from low to high-fidelity simulation. Nowadays, universities are implementing highly realistic scenarios, allowing high interactivity and realism, using humans, manikins, task trainers, and different virtual reality resources (Lioce et al., 2020).

Simulation was traditionally conceived without the need for game elements like a scoring system and a win/lose condition (Alessi, 1988). However, game-design techniques and solutions can be employed to create simulated reality and live experiences. Therefore, simulation is best seen as a learning activity that necessarily involves some game intention, but up to now, it has not included game elements (van Gaalen et al., 2021).

One of the most striking challenges in health education is how to develop clinical reasoning and clinical decision-making (Delany & Golding, 2014). Even high-fidelity simulators need dedicated spaces to be used and can only store a limited number of clinical cases. These obstacles reduce educators' options and availability for students to repeat simulations because training sessions need to be guaranteed for all students alike. The most up-to-date simulators are also limited in helping students master clinical reasoning and decision-making skills. These skills are intrinsically cognitive and can only be improved by using high realism and dynamic clinical scenarios that respond to each decision. Moreover, these clinical scenarios should be made available where and when students perceive the need to practice and learn (Dieckmann et al, 2012; Liaw et al, 2014)

Recent technological developments allowed the recreation of patients in virtual environments. As a result, virtual patients and virtual solutions are being widely adopted based on dynamic clinical virtual simulators, supported by physiological algorithms responsive to user decisions and interventions (Padilha et al. 2018, 2019, 2020).

Clinical Virtual Simulation in Healthcare Education

Clinical Virtual Simulation (CVS) is reality depicted on a computer screen involving real people operating simulated systems. It is a type of simulation that places people in a central role by exercising their decision-making, motor control, and communication skills (Mcgaghie et. al., 2010; Padilha et. al., 2019). CVS uses virtual patients in dynamic and immersive clinical scenarios, from prehospital to community environments. The concept is based on the virtual patient being accessed through a variety of multimedia, screen-based interactive and dynamic patient scenarios, supported by physiological algorithms (Berman et. al., 2016; Padilha et. al., 2019).

CVS simulators are available through ICT devices as laptops or smartphones. The availability through ICT devices allows students to use simulators when and where they need them, according to their interests and availability. In addition, simulators provide the opportunity to repeat scenarios and training to fulfil a purpose, goal or develop the intended perceived self-efficacy in clinical decision-making.

CVS technologies can help refocus healthcare students and professionals in their learning processes within a quasi-real clinical scenario by optimising the learning conditions (Padilha et al., 2018, 2019). The main goal is not to replace clinical experience or internship but rather to prepare healthcare students and professionals to engage in future real clinical scenarios helping them to anticipate intervention needs and ensure safety and healthcare quality. Thus, gamified learning environments using CVS in health education offer a wide range of opportunities for the learning processes, namely the improvement of knowledge retention, professional skills, satisfaction, critical thinking, decision–making and self-confidence (Padilha et al., 2019, 2020).

Although CVS is not a recent phenomenon, its constant evolution requires a continuous and current rationale to put it into practice (Foronda et al., 2020).

Notwithstanding the last developments of CVS use in healthcare education, some gaps are identified in the literature, mainly resulting from the scarcity and low quality of the available evidence. Recent research has identified gaps that prevent generalizability/establishing of trends in the use of CVS. These gaps include the time needed to use CVS to reach the expected learning outcomes, the relationship between researcher and participants (the researcher is often the teacher), sample size, debriefing practices, and age-related knowledge acquisition (academic training stage of the participants) (Foronda et al., 2020). In 2021, the evidence gaps related to CVS use emerge from using different strategies/tools, assessment methods, and resources to meet the targeted virtual clinical simulation. This fact hinders the generalizability of the findings, identification of practical guidelines, and CVS assessment.

Over the past year, the COVID-19 outbreak and the global shutdown, associated with the need to maintain healthcare professionals' education boosted the widespread use of CVS by universities. Nowadays, the question is no longer if we need or should use CVS, but how to develop and deepen the engagement and intrinsic motivation of healthcare students to master their decision skills before their evolvement in clinical practice using CVS.

Gamification Buzz in Healthcare Education

The use of games and their components in education have surfaced as a strategy to enhance students' engagement and motivation. Recently, teachers have been using commercial games as pedagogical games to achieve learning goals, and in some cases, introducing some game elements in simulation or no game environments (Kim et al., 2018). Pedagogical games are different from other knowledge transfer methods for incorporating playing features to enhance students' engagement and motivation.

As a learning strategy, gamification includes the use of gaming elements and practices in non-game contexts, such as the health context. In 2012, Reiners defined games as "mapping real-world problems into virtual environments in a simulated reality space for educational purposes" (Reiners, 2012, p. 94).

The Triad "Points, Reward and Ranking" (PBL - Points, Badges, Leaderboards) represents the most widely used method in gamification, adding a personal reward and the competitive element between the users. According to Borys and Laskowski (2013), PBL involves the following principles: to allow for the repetition of experiences until the intended goal is achieved; to provide immediate feedback and the increasing difficulty of the activities according to the individuals' performance, thus increasing motivation; to divide tasks into more effective activities, and therefore, decreasing their complexity; and to recognize the acquisition of knowledge by means of a reward or emblems.

In addition, Nicholson (2015) suggests that gamification can achieve its potential for learning by using the elements involved in game development. These elements include simulation, allowing for errors and failures in a monitored environment; the presentation of real situations allowing for player intervention; the use of information to promote knowledge retention through the game; the engagement to facilitate the resolution and collective learning; the reflection, which proposes the association between other interests and experiences and learning.

Games provide opportunities to explore the problematic situations that might appear in everyday practice, promoting the increase in autonomy and critical thinking concerning undergraduate training and future professional practice (Soares et al., 2015).

Patrício et al. (2020) suggest that the best strategy to create new solutions using gamification is by combining the participants' engagement and coordination while keeping them focused on the project's goals and thus reaching optimal solutions.

In health education, the use of game elements in non-game environments, defined as gamification, allowed enhancing engagement, motivation, learning performance, academic achievement, information recall and retention, providing instant feedback, catalysing behavioural change, allowing students to follow their progress and promoting collaborative skills (Kim et al., 2018; van Gaalen et al., 2021). Gamification is related to the use of goals, rules and interactions in environments not primarily developed for gaming. Gamification in health is applying game elements (set of activities or processes to solve problems) to clinical scenarios targeted at developing clinical skills (Kim et al., 2018).

The use of game elements added to CVS is crucial to enhance the learners' intrinsic motivation and increase enjoyability with the healthcare learning process. The most up-to-date CVS allows students to achieve goals, obtain scores, and compare scores between colleagues. However, little is known about cut-off points and their relationship with learning, clinical competencies, and safety.

Over the last few years, we have witnessed the rapid development and use of serious games. Serious Games are games developed to achieve learning outcomes. In the health education field, serious games are designed to develop competencies transferable to clinical practice. In addition, serious games are designed so that users learn while playing, and goals are achieved when they successfully complete the missions of the game (Kim et al., 2018).

Despite the low quality of available evidence, serious games used in the education of healthcare professionals have been shown to improve knowledge, skills, and satisfaction (Gentry et al., 2018; Wang et al., 2016).

CVS in Undergraduate Healthcare Education

In light of the current technological revolution, it is crucial to adapt the teaching-learning strategies of those involved in the care process. The use of ICT is now a reality in students' daily lives. Thus, teachers must apply innovative educational strategies to achieve active participation of students in the acquisition of knowledge, prioritising their understanding and adequate mobilisation.

One of these strategies is CVS, where an individual plays the leading role in training procedures, developing and practising instrumental skills, and exercising decision-making and communication. CVS is understood as the recreation of a reality, which is represented on a computer monitor, where real people perform to solve a clinical problem or situation.

Some advantages of introducing CVS in undergraduate training are already known, particularly the potential to improve knowledge acquisition and clinical reasoning (either initially or after its use) and increase satisfaction with learning among nursing students (Foronda et al., 2020; Padilha et al., 2019).

In addition to the previously mentioned, we can also add the perception of self-efficacy, improved performance (Foronda et al. 2020), development of critical thinking and decision-making (Macauley et al. 2017) as advantages associated with the use of clinical virtual simulation.

The use of this strategy aims to contribute to the demands of society, namely the provision of excellent healthcare. Furthermore, Keys and colleagues (2019) illustrate this topic in a study using a virtual simulation game, implying the mobilization of knowledge to appropriately respond (interventions to be implemented) to an individual who suffers a cardiac arrest. These learning strategies enable the earlier preparation of students and professionals while promoting quality performance.

Moreover, during the current pandemic, virtual education has been the primary option for continuing the transfer of knowledge. Therefore, while allowing unlimited access to information, it enables the use of this knowledge for patient care. Medical schools are urged to invest in technology and equipment/materials to maintain basic training and carry out the respective evaluation (Tabatai, 2020).

CVS in Healthcare Lifelong Learning

Lifelong learning is one of the most accessible and widely employed strategies to keep health professionals updated. This concept expresses a self-motivated and voluntary search for knowledge for professional or personal reasons. The overall goal of learning is to improve knowledge, skills, and competencies. Its early adoption is associated with in-service training, universities, and educational institutions (European Commission, 2017).

In healthcare, contemporary impositions demand the certification and updating of professionals in the core domains of clinical practice. This ensures high safety standards and the quality of the healthcare provided. In the era of globalization, access to high-quality certified digital lifelong learning education faces some constraints, such as family management, time and financial burden, among others.

Recently, the high technological literacy and massive use of ICT by young generations of healthcare providers contribute to a positive intention to adopt and perceived usefulness of new pedagogical approaches to facilitate lifelong learning education (Padilha et al., 2018, 2020).

This trend has boosted health education pedagogical tools using virtual worlds. In addition, this new generation of digital-native professionals is more tech-savvy and more likely to be comfortable learning through virtual simulation (Palfrey & Gasser, 2008; Shorey & Ng, 2020).

CVS technologies can help focus healthcare professionals on their learning processes in a near-real clinical setting, enhancing learning conditions (Padilha et al., 2018, 2020). The complementary use of this strategy does not overlap with clinical experience or internship. It aims to prepare health professionals by helping them respond to intervention needs in future real clinical settings to ensure the safety and delivery of quality healthcare. Gamified learning environments using CVS in health education are believed to be beneficial for the learning processes, namely in improving professional skills, knowledge retention, critical thinking, decision-making, satisfaction, and self-confidence (Foronda et al., 2020; Johnson et al., 2010; Marques, 2018; Padilha et al., 2019, 2020; Roh et al., 2013; Rosa, 2018; Tsai et al., 2008; Wilson-Sands et al. 2015)

For example, a recent study that used emergency nurses showed high results for perceived ease of use, usefulness, and intention to use CVS (Padilha et al., 2020). These data support the perceived need for a resource that supports the development of emergency nurses' clinical reasoning skills. These results may well indicate the readiness and willingness of current nurses to use virtual technology to enhance their lifelong learning education. The data collected attest to the ease of use and usefulness of the CVS as perceived by these professionals and their intention to access more user-friendly educational strategies as part of their lifelong learning. In addition, these results demonstrate that technological innovation is appealing and desirable regardless of age, professional experience, and academic level. These results allow us to merge knowledge in this field and show that this is not just a fashion trend related to technology features.

These findings are in line with a previous study conducted by Padilha et al. (2018) with nursing students, using the same simulator and questionnaire. The study proposes that CVS meets the expectations and requirements of both generations of nurses. A parallel can be drawn with previous studies showing that these professionals perceive usefulness and value simulated experiences within the professional practice (Liaw et al., 2015; Perkins, 2007; Roh et al., 2013). Similarly, an analogy can be made with recent evidence in medical education (Pottle, 2019).

Despite the positive results extracted from the recent application of CVS, the generalizability of the findings still needs further study. There is still little information on the real impact of introducing this digital strategy in the lifelong learning programs in the various health professional areas. Similarly, there is an urgent need to study the actual impact of this digital tool on quality indicators and health care outcomes.

The potential contributions and implications of providing digital training and educational content through digital devices were recently highlighted by the WHO, subsidizing the introduction of CVS as a pedagogical strategy to improve clinical reasoning skills in lifelong learning for health professionals, on the condition that it complements, rather than replaces, traditional methods of providing continuing health education and in-service training (WHO, 2019).

Overall, the consensus on the need to change and update the pedagogical strategies and tools in use, bridging the developing impositions of technological innovations, is underlined. In this context, CVS gains relevance, positioning itself as a strategy with great promise as a novel approach to lifelong learning for contemporary health careers.

MOOC's in Healthcare Education

Within this emerging paradigm, integrating digital strategies into professional education has increased the attractiveness of lifelong learning. Moreover, these strategies have enabled a tailored, unique and direct educational experience, with greater viability - by free online or offline access - and the possibility of updating content (BMJ Best Practice, 2020; Longhini et al., 2020).

Technology-enhanced teaching associated with ICT development has supported distance learning based on open educational resources, open courses and open access (Kesim & Altinpulluk, 2015; Koutropoulos et al., 2012).

In parallel, the increasing use of massive open online courses (MOOCs), described as an innovative teaching method capable of ensuring effective and convenient online learning compared to face-to-face education, is noticeable (Gitlin & Hodgson, 2016; Longhini et al., 2021).

The definition of MOOC emerged in 2008, resulting from the combination of several concepts, such as electronic learning (e-learning), massive communication, knowledge sharing, and openness. This explains a form of knowledge sharing using the digital channels of the internet (Aparício et al., 2019).

Since their beginnings, MOOCs aim to promote an educational community based on a thematic educational offer and the coherent systematization of contents according to a guiding thread. Thus, basic characteristics are defined, such as (1) openness, related to the freedom to enter and leave the course and place and remove content from it; (2) autonomy, allowing participants to pursue their own goals and assessments, cooperating with each other; (3) diversity, through the suitability for various time zones and learning styles; and (4) interactivity, where learning outcomes reflect the results of sharing among participants (Downes 2015, Longhini et al., 2021).

Scientific evidence highlights that MOOCs promote active learning based on different teaching methodologies, such as quizzes and multimedia. They also foster interactive, peer-to-peer education centred on participation in forums (Gitlin & Hodgson 2016; Wang et al. 2019).

The theoretical models that support MOOCs have constantly been evolving. According to the underlying pedagogical theory, we can identify two types: connectivist MOOCs (cMOOCS) grounded in connectivist theories, in which knowledge and learning are the result of networking of relationships; and extended MOOCs (xMOOCs) grounded in behaviorist theories, which emphasize the content built by the reference educational entities, user satisfaction, and engagement motivation (Aparício et al., 2019; Padilha et al., 2021).

Despite the opportunities associated with this pedagogical strategy, up to now, it was not possible to identify a structural model to evaluate its success (Aparicio et al., 2019). Indeed, questions linked to usefulness and feasibility arise when analysing the high rate of educational dropouts when using MOOCs (Aydin, 2018; Jordan, 2014). For developers, overcoming this gap has been one of the biggest challenges, using alternative strategies based on strengthening participants' internal and external motivation.

The recent introduction of gamified environments in MOOCs translates into a possible positive increment by increasing participants' motivation and course completion rates (Buckley & Doyle, 2014; Guillén-Nieto & Aleson-Carbonell, 2012; Khalil et al., 2018). Gamified learning environments use game elements to increase satisfaction and challenge and may include playful and ludic elements that evolve, in health-related content, to interact with virtual patients (Berman et al., 2017). Recent studies show that students' motivation and participation increase when gamified environments and serious games are used in association with MOOCs (Aparicio et al., 2019; Buckley & Doyle, 2014; Chau et al., 2013; Gentry et al., 2018; Guillén-Nieto & Aleson-Carbonell, 2012; Padilha et al., 2021).

This is consistent with another strategy used to increase the perception of the interest of these courses, which combines the most recent evidence on a given topic with technology (development of platforms, multimedia resources), creating learning scenarios as similar as possible to reality (Padilha et al., 2021).

Thus, MOOCs have a major role in education, particularly when associated with factors that increase the success of the courses and the participants' adherence. Despite few studies in the health area, it seems that MOOCs are very likely to increase due to their free, open, (Almeida et al., 2017) and easier access. Furthermore, the engagement of professionals from different areas contributes to the success of MOOCs implementation and dissemination.

The most significant disadvantage of MOOCs is the difficulty in assessing learning, particularly regarding the implementation of practices and procedures, that is, the development of experimental skills (Martinengo et al., 2019). Nevertheless, through this health promotion tool, knowledge is provided to all health professionals and the general public.

The topics of these courses can be more extensive or more specific, such as infection control and dissemination, as some of them have been developed in the current pandemic situation. The dissemination of knowledge has the major purpose of improving the health of the general population, while promoting the safety and quality of care (Longhini et al., 2021).

MOOCs are modifying health education because they involve trainees using, for example, "live chats" and videos, providing each participant with the opportunity to actively participate in the learning process. At the same time, they also offer a greater diversity in pedagogical and teaching-learning models (Maxwell et al., 2018).

MOOCs potential is also reaffirmed by the unrestricted number of participants. For example, research conducted by Barteit and colleagues (2019) evidenced the large number of individuals who joined MOOC`s in the poorest countries, demonstrating the relevance of access equality to quality knowledge.

In those countries, the role of these courses is dual: to enable and increase the training of health professionals in priority areas and as a resource for the general population. In the context of public health, in which the ultimate goal is for knowledge and information to reach the largest number of individuals, MOOCs are a resource or strategy to be used, especially in places where health education is hampered or inhibited, such as the lack of openness to discuss certain topics relating to sexual health, addictions or other communicable diseases (Liyanagunawardena & Aboshady, 2018).

In sum, it is possible to conclude that gamification embodies the use of MOOCs, with strong individual and organizational impact, influencing how users perceive the usefulness of courses, learning objectives, and individual progress (Looyestyn et al., 2017; Padilha et al., 2021). The importance of conducting further studies on the impact of these two strategies on health education is also emphasized. Unfortunately, the sparse existing evidence makes it impossible to properly associate these courses with improvements in safety, quality, and professional development in health.

SOLUTIONS AND RECOMMENDATIONS

Regarding the future developments in CVS technology, a special highlight is given to the need for developing new solutions for serious games based on virtual patients and clinical environments that allow follow-up and monitoring of patients over time. This will enable students to overcome learning tasks, achieve and develop competencies alongside their curriculum development. These developments should integrate multidisciplinary and multi-professional skills (Olszewski & Wolbrink, 2017), optimizing technological, educational and clinical skills to ensure the availability of resources that fit the needs of students and health teachers.

In this new globalization era, the availability of educational contents in the healthcare field available in e-learning format over massive educational platforms will boost accessibility to lifelong learning and reduce constraints with upskilling and reskilling, in line with the WHO (2020) view about how to strengthen education and training capacity of healthcare workers. The platforms should integrate gamified clinical virtual simulators or serious games to enhance intrinsic motivation and reduce dropouts.

FUTURE RESEARCH DIRECTIONS

Future research developments in simulation in the healthcare field should allow the integration between CVS features and physical simulators, using gamification elements to enhance realism, enjoyability and motivation. Developers are now faced with the unique challenge to ensure interoperability between operating systems.

The developments in virtual reality features, and consequent massification of the technology, will enable the recreation of learning environments related to exception situations and potentially enhance healthcare professionals' readiness for unpredicted situations.

Moreover, research should focus on the effectivity of CVS use in healthcare education and their impact over clinical safety, quality and patient outcomes, in line with the WHO – "Digital education for building health workforce capacity" (2020).

Research and developments are essential to make available learning management systems (LMS) that support and give learners guidance in the learning process and lifelong learning supporting up/reskilling. Artificial intelligence and intelligent tutoring systems need to be advanced to develop LMS capable of responding to challenges posed by new generations of health workers.

CONCLUSION

We are currently on the verge of the CVS massification in healthcare education propelled by the pandemic.

However, we need to begin preparing the technology, educational institutions, and educators for the next generation of highly computer-literate students. These should encourage educators and entrepreneurs to develop CVS as clinical games targeted at the acquisition of clinical reasoning and decision-making competencies based on scorings, user's enjoyability, and intrinsic challenges.

These new developments should use virtual worlds as a means to guarantee and facilitate the transferability of competencies to be later translated to the real world in clinical practice, students' assessment, and certification of students and healthcare professionals.

In order to successfully support the development and integration of CVS on healthcare education, some steps need to be taken:

- Long-term plans, closely aligned to the national and international health goals and needs;
- Governance models to coordinate developments and funding;
- Funding to support for new developments;
- Collaboration among different stakeholders from technology and health field;
- Academic and industry system involvement for accreditation and licensing processes;
- Standardization of the quality of curricula.

REFERENCES

Alessi, S. (1988). Fidelity in the design of instructional simulations. *Journal of Computer-Based Instruction*, *15*(2), 40–47.

Almeida, L., Canabarro, S., & Silva, H. (2017). Ferramenta de Ensino-Aprendizagem na área da saúde: Massive Open Online Courses. *EmRede - Revista de Educação à distância, 4*(1), 130-142. https://www.aunirede.org.br /revista/index.php/emrede/article/view/153

Aparício, M., Oliveira, T., Bacao, F., & Painho, M. (2019). Gamification: A Key Determinant of Massive Open Online Course (MOOC) Success. *Information & Management*, *56*(1), 39–54. Advance online publication. doi:10.1016/j.im.2018.06.003

Aydin, C. H. (2018). MOOCs as change agents. In D. Jansen & L. Konings (Eds.), *The 2018 OpenupEd Trend Report on MOOCs* (pp. 18–21). EADTU.

Barteit, S., Sié, A., Yé, M., Depoux, A., Louis, V. R., & Sauerborn, R. (2019). Lessons learned on teaching a global audience with massive open online courses (MOOCs) on health impacts of climate change: A commentary. *Globalization and Health, 15*(1), 52. doi:10.118612992-019-0494-6 PMID:31438984

Berman, A. H., Biguet, G., Stathakarou, N., Westin-Hägglöf, B., Jeding, K., McGrath, C., Zary, N., & Kononowicz, A. A. (2017). Virtual Patients in a Behavioral Medicine Massive Open Online Course (MOOC): A Qualitative and Quantitative Analysis of Participants' Perceptions. *Academic Psychiatry, 41*(5), 631–641. doi:10.100740596-017-0706-4 PMID:28390054

Berman, N. B., Durning, S. J., Fischer, M. R., Huwendiek, S., & Triola, M. M. (2016). The Role for Virtual Patients in the Future of Medical Education. *Academic Medicine, 91*(9), 1217–1222. doi:10.1097/ACM.0000000000001146 PMID:26959224

BMJ Best Practice. (2020, March 20). *Medical education during the COVID-19 out-break*. The BMJ. https://bestpractice.bmj.com/info/covid-19/

Borys, M., & Laskowski, M. (2013, June 19-21). *Implementing game elements into didactic process: A case study'* [Paper presentation]. Management, Knowledge and Learning International Conference. Zadar, Croatia. http://www.toknowpress.net/ISBN/978-961-6914-02-4/papers/ML13-326.pdf

Buckley, P., & Doyle, E. (2014). Gamification and student motivation. *Interactive Learning Environments, 24*(6), 1162–1175. doi:10.1080/10494820.2014.964263

Carty, E. (2010). Educating Midwives with the World's first simulator: Madame du Coudray's eighteenth century mannequin. *Revue Canadienne de la Recherche et de la Pratique Sage-femme, 9*(1). https://www.cjmrp.com/files/ v9n1_carty_ducou dray.pdf

Chau, M., Wong, A., Wang, M., Lai, S., Chan, K. W. Y., Li, T. M. H., Chu, D., Chan, I. K. W., & Sung, W. (2013). Using 3D virtual environments to facilitate students in constructivist learning. *Decision Support Systems, 56*, 115–121. doi:10.1016/j.dss.2013.05.009

Delany, C., & Golding, C. (2014). Teaching clinical reasoning by making thinking visible: An action research project with allied health clinical educators. *BMC Medical Education, 14*(1), 20. Advance online publication. doi:10.1186/1472-6920-14-20 PMID:24479414

Dieckmann, P., Friis, S. M., Lippert, A., & Østergaard, D. (2012). Goals, Success Factors, and Barriers for Simulation-Based Learning. *Simulation & Gaming, 43*(5), 627–647. doi:10.1177/1046878112439649

Downes, S. (2015). The Quality of Massive Open Online Courses. In B. H. Khan & M. Ally (Eds.), *International Handbook of E-Learning: Theoretical Perspectives and Research* (1st ed.). Routledge.

European Commission. (2017). *Glossary: Lifelong learning*. EUROSTAT - Statistics Explained. https://ec.europa.eu/Eurostat/statisticsexplained/index.php/Glossary:Lifelong_learning

Foronda, C. L., Fernandez-Burgos, M., Nadeau, C., Kelley, C., & Henry, M. (2020). Virtual simulation in nursing education: A systematic review spanning 1996 to 2018. *Simulation in Healthcare, 15*(1), 46–54. doi:10.1097/SIH.0000000000000411 PMID:32028447

Gentry, S., L'Estrade Ehrstrom, B., Gauthier, A., Alvarez, J., Wortley, D., van Rijswijk, J., Car, J., Lilienthal, A., Tudor Car, L., Nikolaou, C. K., & Zary, N. (2018). Serious Gaming and Gamification interventions for health professional education. *Cochrane Database of Systematic Reviews*. Advance online publication. doi:10.1002/14651858.CD012209.pub2

Gitlin, L. N., & Hodgson, N. (2016). Online training - can it prepare an eldercare workforce? *Generations (San Francisco, Calif.)*, *40*(1), 71–81.

Goldshtein, D., Krensky, C., Doshi, S., & Perelman, V. S. (2019). In situ simulation and its effects on patient outcomes: A systematic review. *BMJ Simulation & Technology Enhanced Learning*. Advance online publication. doi:10.1136/bmjstel-2018-000387 PMID:35514456

Guillén-Nieto, V., & Aleson-Carbonell, M. (2012). Serious games and learning effectiveness: the case of it's a deal! *Comput. Educ. 58*(1), 435–448. .compedu.2011.07.015 doi:10.1016/j

Guze, P. A. (2015). Using Technology to Meet the Challenges of Medical Education. *Transactions of the American Clinical and Climatological Association*, *126*, 260–270. PMID:26330687

Hammoud, M. M., Nuthalapaty, F. S., Goepfert, A. R., Casey, P. M., Emmons, S., Espey, E. L., & Peskin, E. G. (2008). To the point: Medical education review of the role of simulators in surgical training. *American Journal of Obstetrics and Gynecology*, *199*(4), 338–343. doi:10.1016/j.ajog.2008.05.002 PMID:18639203

Hegland, P. A., Aarlie, H., Strømme, H., & Jamtvedt, G. (2017). Simulation-based training for nurses: Systematic review and meta-analysis. *Nurse Education Today*, *54*, 6–20. doi:10.1016/j.nedt.2017.04.004 PMID:28456053

Johnson, D., Flagg, A., & Dremsa, T. L. (2010). Effects of using human patient simulator versus a CD-ROM on learning the management of patients exposed to chemical agents. *U.S. Army Medical Department Journal*, 9–16. PMID:21181669

Jordan, K. (2014). Initial trends in enrolment and completion of massive open online courses. *The International Review of Research in Open and Distributed Learning.*, *15*(1). Advance online publication. doi:10.19173/irrodl.v15i1.1651

Kessim, M., & Altinpulluk, H. (2015). A Theoretical Analysis of Moocs Types from a Perspective of Learning Theories. *Procedia: Social and Behavioral Sciences*, *186*, 15–19. doi:10.1016/j.sbspro.2015.04.056

Keys, E., Luctkar-Flude, M., Tyerman, J., Sears, K., & Woo, K. (2020). Developing a Virtual Simulation Game for Nursing Resuscitation Education. *Clinical Simulation in Nursing*, *39*, 51–54. doi:10.1016/j.ecns.2019.10.009

Khalil, M., Wong, J., de Koning, B., Ebner, M., & Paas, F. (2018). *Gamification in MOOCs: A review of the state of the art* [Paper presentation] IEEE Global Engineering Education Conference (EDUCON2018). 10.1109/EDUCON.2018.8363430

Kim, S., Song, K., Lockee, B., & Burton, J. (2018). *Gamification in Learning and education - Enjoy Learning Like Gaming*. Springer International Publishing AG. doi:10.1007/978-3-319-47283-6

Kneebone, R. (2005). Evaluating clinical simulations for learning procedural skills: A theory-based approach. *Academic Medicine*, *80*(6), 549–553. doi:10.1097/00001888-200506000-00006 PMID:15917357

Koutropoulos, A., Gallagher, M. S., Abajian, S. C., De Waard, I., Hogue, R. J., Keskin, N., & Rodriguez, C. O. (2012). Emotive Vocabulary in MOOCs: Context & Participant Retention. *European Journal of Open, Distance and E-Learning, 1*. https://www.eric.ed.gov/PDFS/EJ979609.pdf

Lapkin, S., Fernandez, R., Levett-Jones, T., & Bellchambers, H. (2010). The effectiveness of using human patient simulation manikins in the teaching of clinical reasoning skills to undergraduate nursing students: A systematic review. *JBI Library of Systematic Reviews*, *8*(16), 661–694. doi:10.11124/01938924-201008160-00001 PMID:27820553

Lasater, K. (2007). Clinical judgment development: Using simulation to create an assessment rubric. *The Journal of Nursing Education*, *46*(11), 496–503. doi:10.3928/01484834-20071101-04 PMID:18019107

Liaw, S. Y., Chan, S. W., Chen, F. G., Hooi, S. C., & Siau, C. (2014). Comparison of virtual patient simulation with mannequin-based simulation for improving clinical performances in assessing and managing clinical deterioration: Randomized controlled trial. *Journal of Medical Internet Research*, *16*(9), e214. doi:10.2196/jmir.3322 PMID:25230684

Liaw, S. Y., Wong, L. F., Chan, S. W., Ho, J. T., Mordiffi, S. Z., Ang, S. B., Goh, P. S., & Ang, E. N. (2015). Designing and evaluating an interactive multimedia Web-based simulation for developing nurses' competencies in acute nursing care: Randomized controlled trial. *Journal of Medical Internet Research*, *17*(1), e5. doi:10.2196/jmir.3853 PMID:25583029

Lioce, L., Lopreiato, J., Downing, D., Chang, T., Robertson, J., Anderson, M., Diaz, D., & Spain, A. E.Terminology and Concepts Working Group. (2020). *Healthcare Simulation Dictionary* (2nd ed.). Agency for Healthcare Research and Quality. doi:10.23970imulationv2

Liyanagunawardena, T. R., & Aboshady, O. A. (2018). Massive open online courses: A resource for health education in developing countries. *Global Health Promotion*, *25*(3), 74–76. doi:10.1177/1757975916680970 PMID:28134014

Longhini, J., Rossettini, G., & Palese, A. (2021). Massive open online courses for nurses' and healthcare professionals' continuous education: A scoping review. *International Nursing Review*, *68*(1), 108–121. doi:10.1111/inr.12649 PMID:33855697

Looyestyn, J., Kernot, J., Boshoff, K., Ryan, J., Edney, S., & Maher, C. (2017). Does gamification increase engagement with online programs? A systematic review. *PLoS One*, *12*(3), e0173403. doi:10.1371/journal.pone.0173403 PMID:28362821

Macauley, K., Brudvig, T. J., Kadakia, M., & Bonneville, M. (2017). Systematic Review of Assessments That Evaluate Clinical Decision Making, Clinical Reasoning, and Critical Thinking Changes After Simulation Participation. *Journal, Physical Therapy Education*, *31*(4), 64–75. doi:10.1097/JTE.0000000000000011

Marques, D. (2017). *Virtual immersive simulation in nursing continuous education: Study developed at a hospital from Minho* [Master's thesis, Nursing School of Porto, Portugal]. RCAAP – Repositório Comum. http://hdl.handle. net/10400.26/22508

Martinengo, L., Yeo, N., Tang, Z. Q., Markandran, K. D., Kyaw, B. M., & Tudor Car, L. (2019). Digital Education for the Management of Chronic Wounds in Health Care Professionals: Protocol for a Systematic Review by the Digital Health Education Collaboration. *JMIR Research Protocols*, *8*(3), e12488. doi:10.2196/12488 PMID:30907743

Maxwell, W. D., Fabel, P. H., Diaz, V., Walkow, J. C., Kwiek, N. C., Kanchanaraksa, S., Wamsley, M., Chen, A., & Bookstaver, P. B. (2018). Massive open online courses in U.S. healthcare education: Practical considerations and lessons learned from implementation. *Currents in Pharmacy Teaching & Learning*, *10*(6), 736–743. doi:10.1016/j.cptl.2018.03.013 PMID:30025774

McGaghie, W. C., Issenberg, S. B., Petrusa, E. R., & Scalese, R. J. (2010). A critical review of simulation-based medical education research: 2003-2009. *Medical Education*, *44*(1), 50–63. doi:10.1111/j.1365-2923.2009.03547.x PMID:20078756

Meakim, C., Boese, T., Decker, S., Franklin, A. E., Gloe, D., Lioce, L., Sando, C. R., & Borum, J. C. (2013). Standards of Best Practice: Simulation Standard I: Terminology. *Clinical Simulation in Nursing*, *9*(6), S3–S11. doi:10.1016/j.ecns.2013.04.001

Nicholson, S. A. (2015). A Recipe for Meaningful Gamification. T. In L. C. W. Reiners (Ed.), *Gamification in Education and Business*. Springer. doi:10.1007/978-3-319-10208-5_1

Norman, G. (2009). Teaching basic science to optimize transfer. *Medical Teacher*, *31*(9), 807–811. doi:10.1080/01421590903049814 PMID:19811185

Olszewski, A. E., & Wolbrink, T. A. (2017). Serious Gaming in Medical Education: A Proposed Structured Framework for Game Development. *Simulation in Healthcare: Journal of the Society for Simulation in Healthcare, 12*(4), 240–253. doi:10.1097/SIH.0000000000000212

Organisation for Economic Co-operation and Development. (2008). *The Looming Crisis in the Health Workforce: How can OECD countries respond?* OECD Publishing.https://www.who.int/hrh/migration/looming_crisis_health_workforce.pdf?ua=1

Organisation for Economic Co-operation and Development. (2016). *Innovating Education and Educating for Innovation: The Power of Digital Technologies and Skills*. OECD Publishing. https://www.oecd.org/education/ceri/GEIS2016-Backgr ound-document.pdf

Organisation for Economic Co-operation and Development. (2019). *Health at a Glance 2019: OECD Indicators*. OECD Publishing. c09-en doi:10.1787/4dd50

Padilha, J., Machado, P., Ribeiro, A., & Ramos, J. (2018). Clinical virtual simulation in nursing education. *Clinical Simulation in Nursing*, *15*(C), 13–18. doi:10.1016/j.ecns.2017.09.005

Padilha, J., Machado, P., Ribeiro, A., Ramos, J., & Costa, P. (2019). Clinical virtual simulation in nursing education: Randomized controlled trial. *Journal of Medical Internet Research*, *21*(3), e11529. doi:10.2196/11529 PMID:30882355

Padilha, J., Ribeiro, A., Rosa, J., Marques, D., & Machado, P. (2020). Clinical Virtual Simulation as Lifelong Learning Strategy—Nurse's Verdict. *Clinical Simulation in Nursing*, *47*, 1–5. doi:10.1016/j.ecns.2020.06.012

Padilha, J. M., Machado, P. P., Ribeiro, A. L., Ribeiro, R., Vieira, F., & Costa, P. (2021). Easiness, usefulness and intention to use a MOOC in nursing. *Nurse Education Today*, *97*, 104705. doi:10.1016/j.nedt.2020.104705

Palfrey, J., & Gasser, U. (2008). *Born Digital: Understanding the First Generation of Digital Natives*. Basic Books.

Patrício, R., Moreira, A., Zurlo, F., & Melazzini, M. (2020). Co-Creation of New Solutions Through Gamification: A Collaborative Innovation Practice. *Creativity and Innovation Management*, *29*(1), 146–160. doi:10.1111/caim.12356

Perkins, G. (2007). Simulation in resuscitation training. *Resuscitation*, *73*(2), 202–211. doi:10.1016/j.resuscitation.2007.01.005 PMID:17379380

Pottle, J. (2019). Virtual reality and the transformation of medical education. *Future Healthcare Journal*, *6*(3), 181–185. doi:10.7861/fhj.2019-0036 PMID:31660522

Reiners, T., Wood, L. C., Chang, V., Guetl, C., Herrington, J., Teräs, H., & Gregory, S. (2012). *Operationalising gamification in an educational authentic environment* [Paper presentation]. International Conference on Internet Technologies & Society 2012. https://researchrepository.murdoch.edu.au/id/eprint/13958/1/reiners_et_al_2012PostprintOperationalising_gamification_in_an_educati onal_authentic_environment.pdf

Roh, Y. S., Lee, W. S., Chung, H. S., & Park, Y. M. (2013). The effects of simulation-based resuscitation training on nurses' self-efficacy and satisfaction. *Nurse Education Today*, *33*(2), 123–128. doi:10.1016/j.nedt.2011.11.008 PMID:22153054

Rosa, J. (2017). *Virtual immersive simulation in nursing continuous education: Study developed at a hospital from Douro Litoral* [Master's thesis, Nursing School of Porto, Portugal]. RCAAP – Repositório Comum. http://hdl.handle.net/1040 0.26/22506

Shorey, S., & Ng, E. D. (2020). The use of virtual reality simulation among nursing students and registered nurses: A systematic review. *Nurse Education Today*, *104662*. Advance online publication. doi:10.1016/j.nedt.2020.104662 PMID:33203545

Soares, A., Gazzinelli, M., Souza, V. D., & Araújo, L. H. (2015). The Role Playing Game (RPG) as a pedagogical strategy in the training of the nurse: An experience report on the creation of a game. *Texto & Contexto Enfermagem*, *24*(2), 600–608. doi:10.1590/0104-07072015001072014

Tabatabai, S. (2020). Simulations and Virtual Learning Supporting Clinical Education During the COVID 19 Pandemic. *Advances in Medical Education and Practice*, *11*, 513–516. doi:10.2147/AMEP.S257750 PMID:32821192

Tsai, S. L., Chai, S. K., Hsieh, L. F., Lin, S., Taur, F. M., Sung, W. H., & Doong, J. L. (2008). The use of virtual reality computer simulation in learning Port-A cath injection. *Advances in Health Sciences Education: Theory and Practice*, *13*(1), 71–87. doi:10.100710459-006-9025-3 PMID:16944000 van Gaalen, A., Brouwer, J., Schönrock-Adema, J., Bouwkamp-Timmer, T., Jaarsma, A., & Georgiadis, J. R. (2021). Gamification of health professions education: A systematic review. *Advances in Health Sciences Education: Theory and Practice*, *26*(2), 683–711. doi:10.100710459-020-10000-3 PMID:33128662

Wang, R., DeMaria, S., Goldberg, A., & Katz, D. (2016). A Systematic Review of Serious Games in Training Health Care Professionals. *Simulation in Healthcare: The Journal of the Society for Simulation in Healthcare*, *11*(1), 41–51. doi:10.1097/SIH.0000000000000118 PMID:26536340

Wang, W., Guo, L., He, L., & Wu, Y. J. (2019). Effects of social-interactive engagement on the dropout ratio in online learning: Insights from MOOC. *Behaviour & Information Technology*, *38*(6), 621–636. doi:10.1080/0144929X.2018.1549595

Wilson-Sands, C., Brahn, P., & Graves, K. (2015). The Effect of Instructional Method on Cardiopulmonary Resuscitation Skill Performance: A Comparison Between Instructor-Led Basic Life Support and Computer-Based Basic Life Support With Voice-Activated Manikin. *Journal for Nurses in Professional Development*, *31*(5), E1–E7. doi:10.1097/NND.0000000000000203 PMID:26381346

World Health Organization. (2011b). *Global Health and Aging*. World Health Organization. https://www.who.int/ageing/publications/global_health.pdf

World Health Organization. (2013). *Transforming and scaling up health professionals' education and training: World Health Guidelines 2013*. World Health Organization. https://apps.who.int/iris/bitstream/handle/10665/ 93635/978 9241506502_eng.pdf

World Health Organization. (2019). *WHO guideline: Recommendations on digital interventions for health system strengthening*. World Health Organization. https://apps.who.int/iris/rest/bitstreams/1238054/retrieve

World Health Organization. (2020a). *WHO Global Code of Practice on the International Recruitment of Health Personnel*. World Health Organization. https://apps.who.int/gb/ebwha/pdf_files/WHA73/A73_9-en.pdf

World Health Organization. (2020b). *Digital education for building health workforce capacity*. World Health Organization. https://apps.who.int/iris/ bitstream/handle/10665/331524/9789240000476-eng.pdf?sequence=1&isAllowed=y

World Health Organization & WHO Patient Safety. (2011a). *Patient safety curriculum guide: multi-professional edition*. World Health Organization. https://apps.who.int/iris/handle/10665/44641

KEY TERMS AND DEFINITIONS

Clinical Virtual Simulation: Clinical virtual simulation (CVS) is a reality represented on a computer screen involving real people operating simulated systems. Using CVS, people can actively experience decision making, motor control and communication.

Gamification: Gamification in healthcare means the application of elements used to create games in settings different from these, looking for a more expressive engagement of students. The intention is to use the specificities and advantages of games for real concepts, processes, and real clinical situations, increasing the challenges and the fun of their participants.

Healthcare Simulation: Technique through which each participant can train, assess, investigate and integrate knowledge to ensure client safety. This provides a better understanding of human reactions to our decision-making and implemented interventions. Healthcare Simulation can be performed online, including the assessment, diagnosis, and treatment of virtual clients.

MOOC: Open online courses, accessible to everyone with access to internet. The great majority of such courses are free and require no previous conditions for its realization. Some of them consist of interdependent modules, creating a learning journey, which culminates in the achievement of a certificate.

Serious Games: Game designed for an educational purpose, making allow the training of the decision-making and interventions of a real-life case, in such a way as to solve the problems found, so that its ending is not just to be entertainment.

Simulation: A technique that produces a circumstance or scenario, allowing the individual to experiment with a reproduction of a real experience so they can practice, test and evaluate the effect of their choices or operations.

Simulation-Based Learning Experience: A group of structured activities representing real or possible situations, in training and in practice implementation. With this activity's participants increase knowledge and improve skills, providing a more appropriate solution to a clinical case, in a simulation context.

Virtual Reality Simulation: Use of immersive visual and 3D elements to recreate health conditions/situations and/or health procedures. It differs from computer-based simulation in that it includes other support tools such as the computer keyboard, mouse, voice recognizer, touching devices or mobility sensors.

Chapter 4
Gamification in Higher Education:
Analysis of Your Strengths and Weaknesses

Víctor Arufe Giráldez
https://orcid.org/0000-0002-6440-048X
University of A Coruña, Spain

Rubén Navarro-Patón
University of Santiago de Compostela, Spain

Alberto Sanmiguel-Rodríguez
https://orcid.org/0000-0001-5119-5141
University of Camilo José Cela, Spain

ABSTRACT

This chapter addresses the elements to consider for creating a gamified learning environment in higher education, specifically in the university classroom. It investigates various didactic proposals for gamification at the university made by different authors in recent years, the variables they have addressed in their study, how they have been evaluated, and the most relevant findings. It is intended to develop a text that will serve as a basis for many scholars in education and gamification, which casts its own light on gamification in higher education, presenting its strengths and weaknesses and offering clear ideas and strategies to get the maximum educational potential to gamification.

INTRODUCTION

Since the 80s and 90s, gamification has made an increasingly strong impact on the business world (Looyestyn et al., 2017; Morford, Witts, Killingsworth, & Alavosius, 2014; Rodrigues, Oliveira, & Costa, 2016). There have been many national and international companies that have incorporated this technique

DOI: 10.4018/978-1-6684-4287-6.ch004

into their philosophical and strategic planning, improving customer loyalty and favouring employee motivation, corporatism and trust towards the brand, as well as group cohesion (Kim, S., 2021; Miri & Macke, 2021; Sigala, 2015). Some authors (Patrício, Moreira, & Zurlo, 2021) even show that gamification has the power to improve and complement the design of thinking practices, organizing tasks and improving the coordination and commitment of employees in the innovation process, thus being associated with innovation (Patricio, Moreira, Zurlo, & Melazzini, 2020; Patrício, Moreira, & Zurlo, 2018).

In recent years, gamification has been timidly exported to the educational field (Hamari, Koivisto, & Sarsa, 2014; Prieto Andreu, 2020; Rivera & Garden, 2021; Wang, Song, Gao, & Tao, 2020). An area that demands motivated students and teachers committed to the teaching-learning process. The number of studies related to educational gamification has increased notably since its emergence in 2010, being able to consult in June 2021 about 3000 documents indexed in Web of Science and 3141 documents in Scopus, in both cases with the following equation search ["Gamification" AND "Education"].

Through this chapter, the authors address the elements to take into account for the creation of a Gamified Learning Environment (GLE) in Higher Education, specifically in the university classroom. It investigates various didactic proposals for gamification at the University made by different authors in recent years and the analysis of the variables they have addressed in their study, how they have been evaluated and the most relevant findings. It is intended to develop a text that will serve as a basis for many scholars in the field of education and gamification, which casts its own light on gamification in Higher Education, presenting its strengths and weaknesses and offering clear ideas and strategies to get the maximum educational potential from gamification.

GAMIFICATION AS AN ACTIVE METHODOLOGY IN EDUCATION

Gamification is part of the so-called active methodologies (Carrion Candel, 2019; Lopes et al., 2019), a type of methodologies that try to offer different results from those offered by "traditional" methodologies, such as direct control or lectures. Active methodologies focus mainly on the autonomous learning of students. Thus, the focus of interest lies with the students as the authentic protagonists of the teaching-learning process and less on the teacher, being the teacher's role to provide guidance for the students. (Gomez, Moron, Ferrandez, Saiz, & Garrido, 2017; Jimenez-Saez, Ramirez de la Piscina, Castellanos, & Palacios, 2019).

In addition, active methodologies promote greater motivation in students and a greater willingness to participate in different projects and tasks (Elena Parra-Gonzalez, Segura-Robles, & Rosa Gomez-Barajas, 2020; Vergara, Paredes-Velasco, Chivite, & Fernandez-Arias, 2020).

Other examples of active methodologies are: Flipped Classroom, Escape Room or Service Learning among others (López-Pernas, Gordillo, Barra, & Quemada, 2019, Ross & Bennett, 2020; Salam, Awang, Ibrahim, & Farooq, 2019; Schmitt, & Cequea, 2020) It is important to highlight the difference in some terms that are sometimes confused by the teaching community. Thus, gamification is different from Game Based Learning or serious games. The latter are a type of game designed to improve different skills in human beings, especially skills related to professions, having a professional training nature (Abt, 1970). Game-based learning consists of playing in class while learning, for this, classic board games or other types of games that promote fun in students while working on content of different subjects can be used as a medium (Pivec, Dziabenko, & Schinnerl, 2003). Aspects of Game-Based Learning.. Gamification, as we will see later, mainly uses the mechanics and dynamics of games in a non-playful environment to improve learning, being defined as; "Gamification" is the use of game design elements in non-game contexts (Deterding et al., 2011).

Some authors (Zolkina, Lomonosova, & Petrusevich, 2020) have confirmed a certain demand, by university students, for the implementation of gamification in Higher Education, establishing interactive learning environments based on games. A recent systematic review work (Subhash & Cudney, 2018) investigated how gamification can be very useful as a learning technique in Higher Education; the authors indicate that universities can employ and explore efficient gamified teaching and learning systems to improve student engagement, motivation and performance.

One of the purposes of gamification as an active methodology is to propose attractive activities that promote critical thinking, scientific thinking, teamwork, decision-making or autonomy, among other skills and competences in students (Ardila-Muñoz, 2019). Along the same lines are the results of a study (Martí-Parreño, Galbis-Córdova, & Currás-Pérez, 2021) carried out with a mapping approach in a sample of university faculty members. In this work, it was found that teachers believe that gamification can be positive for promoting teamwork, oral communication skills, critical thinking and the development of social skills. The authors encourage both university teachers and political leaders to promote the creation of gamified learning environments to work on students' multiple skills. An important aspect to note is that using gamification does not always guarantee success, since the results in terms of abandonment and interaction will depend on how it is carried out, as (de la Peña, Lizcano, & Martínez-Álvarez, 2021) claim, who worked in their study with a sample of 150 university students who participated in a well-designed gamified learning environment in contrast to another sample of students who did not perform gamification, observing a greater commitment to learning in the gamified group.

THE CONCEPT OF GAMIFIED LEARNING ENVIRONMENT CREATION

When the use of gamified systems or programs is transferred to the educational field, it is more correct to speak of the Gamified Learning Environment (GLE). A GLE is the intentional creation of a teaching-learning process in the formal environment, through which the teacher establishes learning objectives by planning different curricular elements, designing and organizing multiple elements of the game or video games and developing a mechanics and dynamics to be followed by students. This is based mainly on the interests of the students and the teacher's own knowledge about different subjects or fields of knowledge related to graphic design, narrative or the use of Information and Communication Technologies, among others, with the aim of favouring the motivation of students towards said process. Since the main purpose of bringing gamification to the educational field is to improve the teaching-learning processes in students.

A recent study (Luria et al., 2021) suggests that structuring learning and assessment to decrease failure and increase repeated opportunities for successful performance, such as in gamification, can generate effective learning that incorporates broad perspectives and memories positive. This can occur even in the absence of an intrinsic motivation to master a particular subject. The use of this information in instructional design can benefit many educational settings. For many students, most of the content in the standard curriculum is of little intrinsic interest. The Theory of Self-Determination points out that intrinsic motivation and autonomous regulation are the optimal bases for effective learning and growth (Ryan & Deci, 2020). But ... what happens if there is no intrinsic interest? From this point of view, gamification can be a solution. The perspective based on a neurobehavioral model of motivational

Figure 1. Creating a gamified learning environment

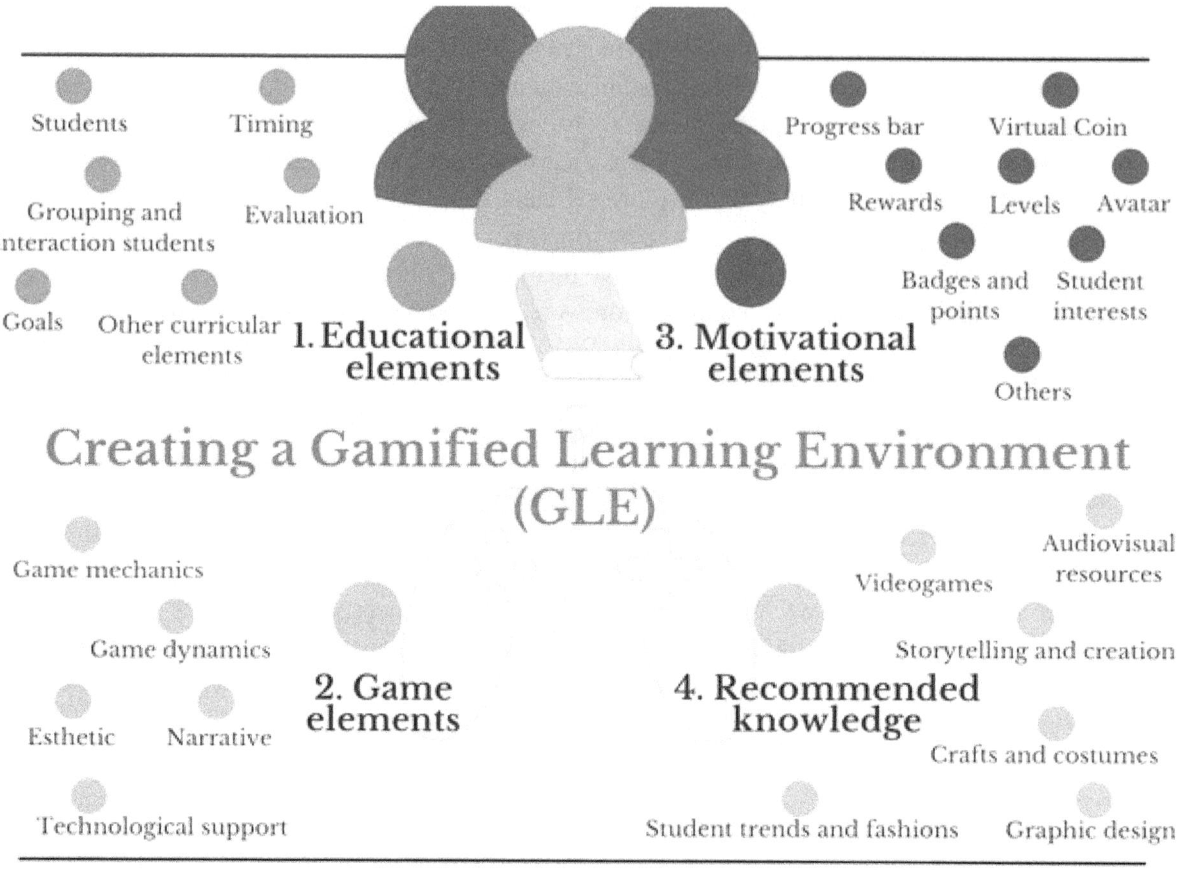

influence on MTL dependent memory (Murty & Adcock, 2017) presents a novel approach suggesting that reward-related goals support the formation of rich and relational memories that can then be more easily recalled (Luria et al., 2021).

Over the last few years, several models have emerged to contextualize and understand the processes that gamification entails. Some models that are explained below refer to the business field, but others, like the one presented in the first place, are limited to the educational field.

The model used for the creation of a GLE will provide a supportive approach to the challenges of game thinking, emotion building and motivational influences to improve student retention, engagement, motivation and problem solving (Costello & Lambert, 2019).

This first model proposed (figure 1) by Arufe Giráldez & Navarro Patón (2020) and focused on gamification in all educational stages, including Higher Education, conceptualizes the components to take into account when creating a GLE and involves an exhaustive analysis of the elements and / or parameters that can influence student motivation, in the gamified system and in the elements of the educational system.

In this way, the GLEs have to take into account up to 4 large blocks of elements:

Educational Elements

Educational elements are those of the educational system and are part of the teacher's programming. This group includes aspects related to evaluation, objectives, competences, student profile, timing, methodology, etc. The most important thing about this block is the need to link gamification to the different elements of the curriculum, A GLE will be better planned if the teacher takes into account the different elements of the educational curriculum, since it will involve a greater educational component. Gamification must enhance the skills of the students, meet the objectives programmed in the subject area, be evaluated through valid instruments that can allow the teacher to verify the effect caused by it and it must also detail the way to organize the class group. In addition, to specify the methods that will be used to generate learning and other aspects of teaching planning.. This block is what differentiates a gamified system within the educational context from a gamified system in the business environment.

It should be noted that in the literature reviews (Darina Dicheva, Christo Dichev, Gennady Agre, & Galia Angelova, 2015; Kalogiannakis, Papadakis, & Zourmpakis, 2021) that have been carried out on studies related to educational gamification, one of the greatest weaknesses is the lack of a correct evaluation of the gamification system. Evaluation is one of the most important elements to incorporate in creating a gamified learning environment (Cardinale Nunes Menezes & De Bortolli, 2016; Zainuddin, Shujahat, Haruna, & Chu, 2020) .

Game Elements

They refer to the parameters that configure gamification from its playful component. This second group includes the dynamics and mechanics of gamification, narrative forms used, aesthetics, technological support, etc. Sometimes gamified learning environments are observed that develop these elements very well while others do not go as deep. Some teachers have stated in different educational forums that they do not dare to use gamification because they are not "geeks". This concept has already been addressed by several authors (Lodi, 2017; McCartney et al., 2017) who have coined the term "geek gene" referring to people, both students and teachers interested in Information and Communication Technologies (ICTs).

Teachers who do not dare to use a narrative form inspired by the interests of the students, generally a famous television series, television programme, film, novel or even using as a support for the narrative some successful digital platforms or social networks used by the students, perceive that their introversion or shyness can be an obstacle to creating narratives or aesthetics of gamification that invite the students to participate. The truth is that the more the teacher takes care of all these elements of the game, the more students will experience a greater immersion in gamification, being able to attract their attention and participation even more, and therefore their commitment.

Some teachers carry out an important staging, such is the case of the Spanish university professor Victor Arufe awarded the International SIMO Education Award for the Best Innovative Experience in Higher Education 2020 (Arufe Giráldez & Navarro Patón, 2020). The teacher created an GLE inspired by the famous Netflix series Money Heist. On the first day of class, the teacher projected a trailer (see figure 2) where students were invited to participate in an important mission and encouraged to get health and experience points each week through the fulfilment of multiple volunteer tasks.

These tasks were linked to the competences, syllabus and contents of the subject area, so if the students did them they would be working and enhancing their learning in the contents of the subject. The students formed work groups, since gamification stimulated individual participation and involvement,

Figure 2. QR code with direct access to the trailer published on YouTube of the gamified project Money Heist. Access https://youtu.be/gMytLJmd0kg

but also group, cooperative and collaborative work. Each student was given a city name, as it happens in the series, and the teacher made a roll call in each class calling the students by the name of their city. The entire project was published on a specific website (https://victorarufe.es/proyectos/la-casa-del-papel/) so that students could access it and check the points they had, the way to get points and all the mechanics and dynamics of gamification. In the first sessions, a photographic session was held to enhance the involvement of students in the project, and the images of the student teams training were published on the project website and propagated on social networks so that students could share and encourage their followers.

Within this block it is important to also take care of the aspects related to the mechanics and dynamics of gamification, which are really the guidelines and rules to be followed by the players and the way in which they will interact with each other, with the teacher, and the subject area in general. It is worth highlighting here the importance that students know at all times the regulations of the gamified system itself, so the teacher must make an effort to synthesize key information and transmit it to students, making sure that it is correctly perceived by all students.

Motivational Elements

This group includes all the parameters related to the motivation of the gamification recipients. What reward systems will be used, which must be defined, some of them may be the establishment of badges, virtual currency, levels, personalization of avatars or points, among others. A study (Ćwil, 2020) carried out on a sample of 150 university students found that students prefer to see their scores in a leaderboard instead of a traditional table, since it increases their motivation when they can see how many classmates in their group obtain better and worse scores than them.

It should be noted that here the teacher must establish two important objectives. On the one hand, create a motivating climate that invites all students to participate and, on the other, keep the level of

Figure 3. Spanish university professor with a group of students who participated in a gamification inspired by the famous Netflix series Money Heist (Photo taken from the web www.victorarufe.com)

motivation stable throughout the duration of the GLE. If the gamification of a subject has been considered throughout the course, the teacher must correctly plan the motivational elements so that the student maintains such motivation. That is why there is a certain need to create attractive and interesting learning experiences through which students increase their motivation. This is important because when motivation is increased, effort and commitment towards a certain task also increases (Dweek, 1986).

A failure in the creation of the GLE would be, for example, for a student to achieve all the badges established in gamification in the first month of the course, leaving the rest of the months without any motivation to get more badges after having obtained them all. Another example of the failure of the gamified system can be found in the degree of difficulty to get a certain badge. If the effort made by the student is greater than the reward, a feeling of discouragement ensues that causes the student to abandon gamification. Therefore, planning the different motivational elements is very important in creating a gamified system.

Today, we can see how different companies, large hypermarket chains or companies linked to online sales, generate a gamified system that causes the customer to try to maintain their commitment to buy in a certain store throughout the year or website. In the educational field and within a GLE that is the objective, to ensure that our students do not diminish their commitment to the tasks proposed in gamification so that they continue to improve their skills and learning. From this business field we must transfer some elements that have been successful such as loyalty cards, points system, badges system, reward system or progress bars among other motivational elements. The use of PBL (Points, Badges and Leaderboards) improves motivation and is considered as an adequate combination of mechanics in the implementation of any gamification process in higher education (Prieto, 2020). All of them must be correctly planned and timed, as well as spread out. Students must be aware of the tasks they have to do to get these elements. You must know how to carry them out, when to carry them out and where to go to accomplish them or deliver them. Furthermore, we can apply here a premise from another field of knowledge, the field of advertising. Advertisers have two clear aspects when they begin to design the advertising of a new product or service. First, the product or service must be known in an attractive, creative and original way and second, most importantly, create a need for that product / service to the viewer. In the educational field, we must not only publicize the tasks that students must do to get points or rewards, but also create that need to want to do them.

Linked to this last aspect, (Zichermann & Cunningham, 2011) highlight the ambivalent nature of games and consequently gamification, by integrating these elements typical of games. Thus, when a person plays a certain video game or game, either they may have a feeling of motivation if the game is dosing its degree of difficulty based on the degree of involvement of the user, or a feeling of discouragement if the overcoming of a certain phase of the game or achieving a certain goal, requires a large amount of time invested, which can lead to abandonment. That is why we can observe people who get involved or play a certain game and others do not, which indicates the complexity of designing the motivational elements to get all the students to get involved with the same degree of involvement and motivation. This has already been addressed by different authors (Nasirzadeh & Fathian, 2020) who found unequal levels of commitment and motivation in their studies based on people's personalities.

It is also worth highlighting in this section the four player profiles that (Bartle, 2015) defined in his work establishing four main roles or interests that players have when they play a game: the role of the killer, socializer, achiever and explorer. Although this classification is focused on the types of players of online multiplayer games.

This must be taken into account in the design of a GLE to try to involve all types of student profiles. Thus, gamification should contain a certain social component so that those students who like to interact with other classmates can have that motivation in gamification. But it must also meet the most competitive profiles or those who like to explore and investigate, looking for clues, discovering new tasks or investigating progressively. If the teacher manages to integrate all these elements, he will be designing a very complete gamification that can arouse the interest of all the students.

Elements Linked to the Recommended Knowledge

Generally, the creation of GLEs requires certain multidisciplinary knowledge for a greater wealth of gamification. This knowledge includes: video games, audiovisual and multimedia resources, story creation and graphic design among others. Some studies (Ab. Rahman, Ahmad, & Hashim, 2018) have confirmed that university students are more motivated and more satisfied when using gamified systems in technological support, improving the attitude of students towards gamification.

Figure 4. The Octalysis gamification framework (Chou, 2015)

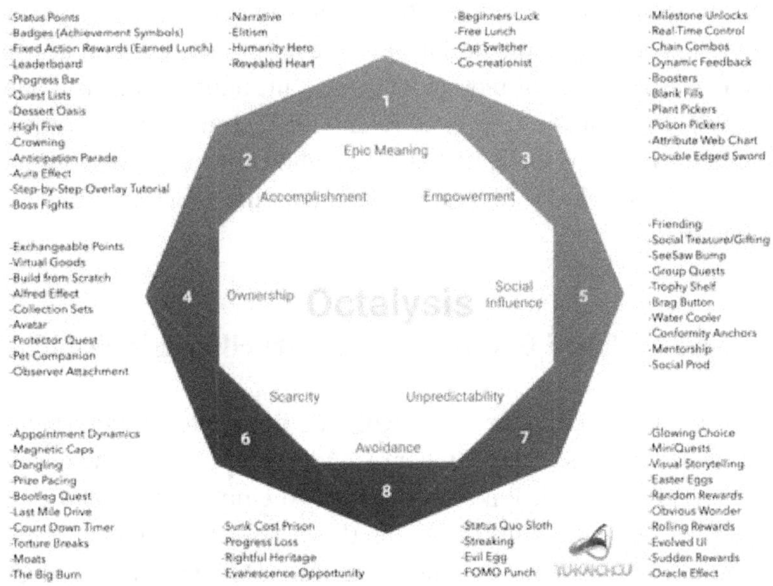

OTHER EXPLANATORY MODELS OF GAMIFICATION

Other authors, referenced below, propose other models that bring together the elements of gamified programs or systems. Although all these proposals are different, they present certain common elements that can be used in the design of gamified systems in the educational field (Kim, & Castelli, 2021), in order to enhance learning in students, favour their intrinsic and extrinsic motivation and promote desired behaviours that lead students towards the continuous updating and recycling of knowledge, improving the acquisition of skills both qualitatively and quantitatively.

This model of creating a GLE has been seen in the first place given its link to the educational field, but it is important to show other models that, not being typical of the educational field, can help to contextualize and design gamified systems.

The octalysis model (Chou, 2015) is one of the models that organises and analyses the different elements of a gamification. The author claims to create it after more than 17 years of work and research in the field of gamification and establishes 8 important nuclei related to gamification and human behaviour and motivation. Those located on the right side of the octahedron are the most related to intrinsic motivation and those located on the left side would be related to the reward system. In turn, in the upper part would be the elements most linked to the motivations or positive impulses of the human being, while in the lower part it would refer to more negative motivations, such as the fear of losing something or the uncertainty that a certain situation can generate.

Another model for understanding the processes involved in gamification is the kaleidoscope of effective gamification (Kappen & Nacke, 2013). This proposal arises to create motivating and creative game strategies with the aim of making gamification effective by encouraging people to interact. It is a proposal conceptualized in the business environment but with transfer to the educational field if the educational elements or components are incorporated. This model presents gamification as a set of interconnected layers that converge at a point called effective gamification. At the outermost part there is a layer of (perceived) fun that the user experiences, followed by a layer of game design process with principles, mechanics, models, patterns and interface as its elements, to later give way to a new layer that collects the gaming experience, including achievements, challenges and actions. The final layer that surrounds the nucleus is the layer of motivated behaviour, built on intrinsic and extrinsic motivation of the Theory of Self-determination (Deci & Ryan, 1985). Intrinsic motivation is represented by the combination of autonomy, competence, and affinity, while extrinsic motivation comprises badges, points, leaderboards, incentives and rewards. As can be seen, this model has many similarities with the model created by Chou (2015).

STRENGTHS OF THE USE OF GAMIFICATION IN HIGHER EDUCATION

The creation of GLEs does not undergo the same evolution in all educational stages. Thus, in the scientific literature there are differences in the number of studies addressed in the different stages (Blanco Fernández, 2017; Dominguez Alonso & Pino Juste, 2014). At University or Higher Education there are few studies that analyse the impact of gamification on the different variables related to the educational and motivational environment of students (Pegalajar Palomino, Ma del Carmen, 2021). However, if the number of scientific studies linked to gamification in Higher Education is compared with other educational stages, it is at the university stage where more studies are registered (Kalogiannakis et al., 2021). This may be due to the fact that university teachers have a more solid training in the field of research, which can trigger a greater interest and ease to investigate compared to other teachers of lower educational stages, such as Infant, Primary or Secondary Education teachers that sometimes lack knowledge related to the scientific field.

Generally, the creation of GLE in Higher Education arises from individual initiatives, not so much from groups or research projects, but rather from teachers who wish to take a further step in the use of active methodologies and incorporate, to a greater or lesser extent, for better or worse a gamified system on the subject area teaching at University.

Among the teachers who have this initiative, two groups can be distinguished, those who use gamification in the classroom and do not analyse the impact it produces, therefore, it is unknown at a scientific level if there are positive or negative effects or no effect at all on learning, and those who use gamification and design a system for measuring the impact or effect created in one or more variables involved in the educational process, such as knowledge assessment, motivation, enjoyment or the assessment of different competences.

The next few paragraphs present some of the recent studies carried out with solid research protocols in the field of Higher Education and based on the analysis of the impact of a gamified system. Several sections have been established depending on the objective of the study.

Improved Academic Performance and / or Learning

In a sample carried out with 132 students of macroeconomics (Murillo-Zamorano, Lopez Sanchez, Godoy-Caballero, & Bueno Munoz, 2021) taught at the Economic and Business Sciences Faculty and where a control group and an experimental group were established with gamified design, it was concluded that the generation of a co-creative and empowered game causes positive learning results without any

Figure 5. The kaleidoscope of effective gamification (Kappen and Nacke, 2013)

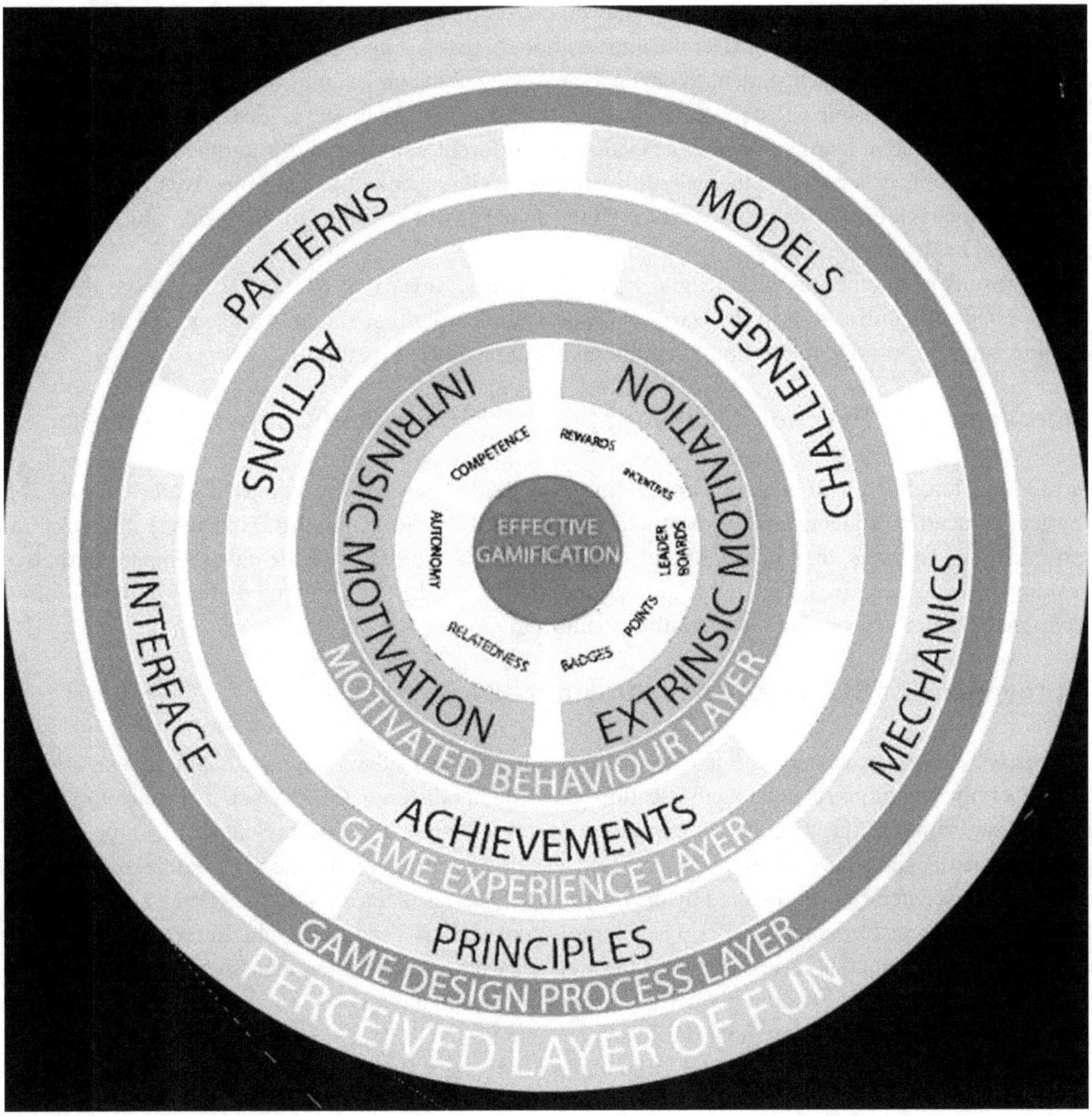

loss of academic performance, and they allow the development of a series of skills that are especially relevant for professionals in the 21st century.

In the Primary Education Degree studies and specifically in the field of Physical Activity in the natural environment, the study carried out by (Ferriz-Valero, Østerlie, Martínez, & García-Jaén, 2020) addressed a gamified environment using a control group and an experimental group over two academic years. The authors found an increase in external regulation only in the experimental group and significantly better academic performance, but did not confirm an increase in intrinsic motivation. The authors conclude that the creation of a GLE is beneficial for academic performance at the university stage, although the intrinsic motivation does not change. Furthermore, the nature of rewards or punishments, as a characteristic of this pedagogical approach, could play an important role in the expected results, since external regulation increased significantly after the intervention. In this last investigation, the Classcraft platform was used, which allows each student to create a personalized avatar in addition to choosing a character from among three possible ones: magician, warrior or healer. The platform is ideal for generating gamified and collaborative learning as well as evaluating different behaviours of the players. Through this gamification tool, it is possible to evaluate certain behaviours linked to the objectives of the subject area. These behaviours define progress through the achievement of points of different nature: points of experience, health, power, etc.

The results of another research (Signori, De Guimarães, Severo, & Rotta, 2018) showed the moderating effect of gamification in the learning process, indicating that students present a higher level of learning when exposed to the teaching method using the gamified method.

Improvement of Psychological Variables, Creativity, and Cooperative Work

Parra González, Segura Robles, & Gómez Barajas (2020) analysed the gamified experience in 255 Physical Education students and teachers using the GAMEX scale (Gameful Experience in Gamification). As main findings, they highlight that gamification is a facilitator of the development of creative thinking, reduces negative effect and improves cooperative work. The confirmed effect in the gamified experience occurs in a similar way in both students and teachers.

Improvement of Students' Commitment to the Subject

University degrees associated with teacher training and Physical Education have captured a significant number of investigations related to gamification, carrying out different GLEs teachers in various subject areas of the Primary Education Degree, Physical Activity Degree and Sports Sciences Degree.

University teachers have developed a gamified learning environment in one of the subjects they teach in the Sports Science Degree inspired by the famous HBO series Game of Thrones (Perez Lopez, Rivera Garcia, & Trigueros Cervantes, 2019). Their sample consisted of 57 students who immersed themselves in a narrative based on this series, verifying through daily records of the feelings, they found an increase in the students' motivation and a greater involvement towards the tasks of the subject area, enhancing the feeling of satisfaction throughout the semester.

Another experiment carried out in a sample of 47 university students of the Primary Education Degree on a gamified session based on the adaptation of the famous Fortnite video game to the Physical Education classroom confirms that didactic proposal improved the students' motivation towards sports practice and their adherence to it, and also favoured collaborative teamwork and promotion of values (Arufe-Giráldez, 2019; Arufe Giráldez, Vaquero Cristóbal, & Isorna Folgar, 2021). The system used for rewards was to earn badges per game won. The gamified experience addressed various contents of the official educational curriculum. The GLE implied the individual and group participation of the students, sometimes the students participated individually and in others in a group way, stimulating collaborative work. By winning a game, the student obtained a collectible badge, which was an object related to the subject area. At the time of delivery of this object, a debate was held with the students to promote the learning of contents related to the subject area.

In a qualitative study with a quasi-experimental design (Bilro, Loureiro, & Angelino, 2021) and carried out over a semester, it was confirmed that participants perceive gamification as a useful tool, revealing a positive feeling about the approach of gamification that helps increase participant engagement.

Another empirical work (Ahmad et al., 2020) carried out in the final computer science course, evaluated the effectiveness of gamification by measuring the effect of group size on the level of student satisfaction and also its impact throughout 6 months. The results indicate improvements in student satisfaction and commitment to the subject area.

On the other hand, some authors (Pinter, Čisar, Balogh, & Manojlović, 2020) suspect that the first year at university can produce discouragement, which is why they have considered using gamification as a technique to favour the commitment and motivation of students. For their study, they selected students assigned to a Faculty of Applied Sciences. The creation of GLE improved student engagement, motivation, attendance, and academic performance.

Improved Student Motivation

Campos Mesa, González Campos, & Castañeda Vázquez (2019) analysed the influence of an educational innovation process based on formative evaluation, including gamification techniques, on the motivation of university students towards a subject area in the Primary Education Degree. 91 university students participated in this study and the Motivated Strategies for Learning Questionnaire (CEAM II) was applied. The results confirm high levels of intrinsic and extrinsic motivation.

Another study carried out by Castaneda-Vazquez, Espejo-Garces, Zurita-Ortega, & Fernandez-Revelles (2019), Spanish university teachers, focused on increasing the levels of motivation and involvement of Primary Education Degree students in subject areas linked to Physical Education. They developed a gamification of the subject throughout the course, confirming the results: a high participation of the students in the gamified learning environment and a passing rate in the first call close to 90%. The study authors also observed high levels of student involvement throughout the course classes, as well as higher levels of intrinsic and extrinsic motivation.

Other authors (Perez-Lopez, Rivera Garcia, & Trigueros Cervantes, 2017) present another gamified experience called "The prophecy of the chosen ones" and applied to a sample of 69 students in the final year of Physical Activity and Sports Sciences Degree. They worked throughout the semester of the course and created a gamified learning environment focusing attention on the setting, challenges, points, levels and narrative. Once again, they used as an instrument to evaluate the experience, the narrations made by the students at the end of the experience using a questionnaire via Google drive. The authors confirm high motivation in the students and great active and collaborative participation, enhancing three

Improvement in the Evaluation Processes of the Subject

In university studies related to sports and recreation, another research (Botha-Ravyse, Lennox, & Jordaan, 2018) sought to evaluate the use of a mobile application in order to improve the preparation of university students in summative evaluation and improve their learning experience. The sample consisted of a total of 103 students who stated that they had improved their motivation after using the application based on learning activities through games, but pointed out some its disadvantages in order to make improvements.

WEAKNESSES IN THE USE OF GAMIFICATION IN HIGHER EDUCATION

Although gamification in Higher Education has multiple strengths, as seen in the previous section, it is necessary to carry out an exercise of reflection and criticism and also to analyse its weaknesses.

Lack of Standardized Research Protocols

One of the greatest weaknesses is the difficulty in using standardised protocols to compare studies, since each work uses a different approach to gamification and collects information through differentevaluation instruments used for the analysis of the variables studied (Darina Dicheva et al., 2015).

At the scientific level, there is still great difficulty in comparing the results of studies that have addressed gamification in education, due to the existence of incorrect protocols causing numerous biases. This is a mayor weakness since each study follows a different protocol and in some cases these protocols present different errors leading to certain biases.

Therefore, more studies are needed to solidly investigate the didactic experiences or pedagogical proposals based on the creation of gamified learning environments in Higher Education, in order to have an objective point of view of the effects of gamified systems on the education system linked to the university stage. This conclusion is also confirmed by (Broer, 2017) who, after completing his doctoral thesis, states that the analysis of empirical studies on gamification had two great results: research has to continue, to show that gamification has positive effectsand secondly, some studies report partial success of gamification, others are inconclusive, and others report negative results. A recent systematic review on gamification in the Spanish educational environment (Navarro, Pérez & Marzo, 2021) also confirms the weaknesses in the research protocol of the studies analysed.

The review work carried out by Metwally et al., (2021) that performs an analysis of a total of 46 review articles published between 2016 and 2020 concludes the need to establish rigorous methods that validate gamified proposals.

Little Training in Gamification of the Teaching Community

Another weakness in the use of gamification in Higher Education is the scarce training in gamification that teachers have, not only in relation to knowledge about gamification but in general about active methodologies (Martins et al., 2019) . In this sense, 3 large groups of teachers could be established, those who are completely unaware of what gamification is, a second group that includes teachers who have seen or read something about gamification and who, based on that, have made a gamified proposal with greater or lesser success and a third group of teachers who attend training sessions, update their knowledge annually and know in some depth what gamification is, being able to carry it out or not.

Incorrect or Inappropriate GLE Designs

Associated with this weakness is another threat to the success of gamification and this is the dissemination on multiple blogs and social networks of gamified proposals with deficiencies in their planning and design. The term gamify has been confused with that of playing or serious play. Some teachers publish on their social networks followed by other teacher's pedagogical proposals that are not really gamified systems but game-based learning, some only incorporate a playful component in the classroom and others even confuse gamify with a system of points, badges and leaderboards (PBL) (Navarro, Pérez, & Marzo, 2021)., which can cause great misunderstanding about what gamification really is.

Difficulty in Improving the Motivation of all Students

The difficulty of being able to motivate all students equally is another of the weaknesses of gamified learning environments. Previous pages have shown how important it is to deal with all the motivating elements for gamification to succeed. In some studies, highly varied levels of motivation have been found in students, due to the different profiles of interests and roles assumed by students. In a study (Denden et al., 2021) on a sample of 189 university students, the effect of gender and personality differences on students' perception of gamification was measured. Three online gamified formations were designed, based on the theory of self-determination, during two academic years. The results showed that gender and personality can affect students' perception of specific elements of the game. The authors note that women find feedback more useful than men. They also indicate that students with low levels of extraversion find a progress bar more useful than students with high extraversion. The results also showed that gender moderates the effect of personality on students' perception of the implemented game elements. For example, men with low extraversion are more likely to perceive more positively the usefulness of badges in gamified courses than men with high extraversion. Findings from this study can help designers and educators customize the design of their gamified courses based on personality and gender.

Another work (Martins et al., 2019) highlights that the motivation to participate in the proposed gamified tasks was higher at the beginning, and subsequently decreased. In this case, a PBL system and the use of a digital platform were established. The authors conclude that perhaps the novelty of the platform played a role. They also confirmed that a greater number of tasks does not improve academic performance, but rather, increased student attention on the task.

Mandatory Participation of Students in Gamification to the Detriment of Voluntariness

It has also been observed that most of the scientific works that deal with the evaluation of gamified proposals in Higher Education have addressed compulsory gamified systems for students. This causes some difficulty in actually measuring whether the student's motivation is intrinsic or extrinsic. If the teacher forces their participation, we may be facing a weakness in the scientific results. Evaluating gamified learning environments with the voluntary participation of the students would be a new line of work to verify the effects of gamification on the intrinsic motivation of the students.

Low Sample Size of Investigations

Linked to the research protocols, there is also another weakness, such as the low sample size with which the gamified pedagogical proposals are worked with in various studies. In some ways this can be difficult to improve gamification in various investigations.

Table 1. Strengths and weaknesses present in the creation of GLE

Strengths	Weaknesses
Improved academic performance and / or learning	Lack of standardised research protocols
Improvement of psychological variables, creativity and cooperative work	Little training in gamification by the teaching community
Improvement of students' commitment to the subject area	Incorrect or inappropriate EAG designs
Improved student motivation	Difficulty in improving the motivation of all students
Improvement in the evaluation processes of the subject area	Mandatory participation of students in gamification to the detriment of voluntariness
	Low sample size of research
	Absence of a control group in the research and pre & post-test design.
	Preferential use of self-reported evaluation over other data collection instruments

Absence of a Control Group in the Investigations and pre and Post-test Design

In the research design of some works, there is also another aspect to improve, such as the absence of a control group in the research. Sometimes the study of various variables in a single group of students has been approached without establishing a control group, something important to be able to evaluate the effects of gamification.

Preferential Use of Self-Reported Evaluation Over Other Data Collection Instruments

Finally, it should be noted that most of the research includes a self-reported evaluation of the measures of the variables instead of using other data collection systems that can better measure the effect caused, this is undoubtedly an aspect to improve to standardise the results (Darina Dicheva, Christo Dichev, Gennady Agre, & Galia Angelova, 2015; Kalogiannakis, Papadakis, & Zourmpakis, 2021) .

CONCLUSION

Throughout this chapter, the role of gamification in Higher Education has been analysed. The origins of gamification, its shaping elements and some of the main models proposed by various authors were investigated. Its impact on Higher Education, its strengths and weaknesses, as well as future lines of work to improve its effectiveness in the educational field have been analysed.

The following table summarizes the strengths and weaknesses previously exposed and that may be present in the creation of a GLE.

Gamification can be an effective learning technique in Higher Education, improving the motivation of students towards the contents worked on in the classroom, but for this it is necessary to correctly design gamified learning environments, establishing objectives to be achieved by the teacher and certain competences to work for the students. Attention should be paid to all the elements of the teaching-learning process, from aspects of group organization, up to the design of teaching materials and evaluation instruments and criteria, without forgetting the correct planning of gamification elements. Always with the aim of improving educational quality and excellence. In turn, more empirical studies are needed to continue measuring the effects of gamification used in education.

Certainly, creating a GLE in Higher Education is a real challenge for the teacher.

REFERENCES

Ab. Rahman, R., Ahmad, S., & Hashim, U. R. (2018). The effectiveness of gamification technique for higher education students engagement in polytechnic muadzam shah pahang, malaysia. *International Journal of Educational Technology in Higher Education, 15*(1). Advance online publication. doi:10.118641239-018-0123-0

Abt, C. C. (1970). *Serious games*. Viking Press.

Ahmad, A., Zeshan, F., Khan, M. S., Marriam, R., Ali, A., & Samreen, A. (2020). The impact of gamification on learning outcomes of computer science majors. *ACM Transactions on Computing Education, 20*(2), 1–25. Advance online publication. doi:10.1145/3383456

Ardila-Muñoz, J. Y. (2019). Theoretical assumptions for the gamification in the higher education [Supuestos teóricos para la gamificación de la educación superior]. *Magis, 12*(24), 71–84. doi:10.11144/Javeriana.m12-24.stge

Arufe-Giráldez, V. (2019). Fortnite EF un nuevo juego deportivo para el aula de educación física. propuesta de innovación y gamificación basada en el videojuego fortnite. *Sportis: Revista Técnico-Científica Del Deporte Escolar, Educación Física Y Psicomotricidad, 5*(2), 323-349.

Arufe Giráldez, V., & Navarro Patón, R. (2020). Creación de un entorno de aprendizaje gamificado inspirado en la casa de papel. In H. Morente Oria, F. T. González Fernández, & A. S. Sánchez Fernández (Eds.), (pp. 65–83). Ediciones Morata.

Arufe Giráldez, V., Vaquero Cristóbal, R., & Isorna Folgar, M. (2021). Can a didactic proposal for the Physical Education classroom inspired by the Fortnite video game develop the values and various psychological variables in children and adolescents? *Sport Science (Travnik), 14*(1), 68–78.

Bartle, R. A. (2015). MMOs from the inside out: The history, design, fun, and art of massively-multiplayer online role-playing games. In MMOs from the inside out: The history, design, fun, and art of massively-multiplayer online role-playing games (pp. 1-735) doi:10.1007/978-1-4842-1724-5

Bilro, R. G., Loureiro, S. M. C., & Angelino, F. J. D. A. (2021). The role of creative communications and gamification in student engagement in higher education: A sentiment analysis approach. *Journal of Creative Communications*. Advance online publication. doi:10.1177/0973258621992644

Blanco Fernández, J. (2017). *Evaluación de la motivación académica en niños de primer ciclo de educación infantil*. Available from DIALNET.

Botha-Ravyse, C., Lennox, A., & Jordaan, D. (2018). Lessons learned from gamification of a learning experience: A case study. *S.A. Journal for Research in Sport Physical Education and Recreation*, *40*(2), 23–40.

Broer, J. (2017). *The gamification inventory: An instrument for the qualitative evaluation of gamification and its application to learning management systems* Retrieved from https://9dok.org/document/6zkewnez-gamification-inventory-instrument-qualitative-evaluation-gamification-application-management.html

Cardinale Nunes Menezes, C., & De Bortolli, R. (2016). Potential of gamification as assessment tool. *Creative Education*, *7*(4), 561–566. doi:10.4236/ce.2016.74058

Carrion Candel, E. (2019). The use of the game and the cooperative Methodology in Highet Educatio: An alternative for creative teaching. *Artseduca*, (23), 70–97. doi:10.6035/Artseduca.2019.23.4

Castaneda-Vazquez, C., Espejo-Garces, T., Zurita-Ortega, F., & Fernandez-Revelles, A. B. (2019). Physical education's teacher training program through gaming, ict and continuous assessment. *Sport Tk-Revista Euroamericana De Ciencias Del Deporte*, *8*(2), 55–63. doi:10.6018portk.391751

Chou, Y. (2015). *Learn gamification — The cheat codes to win the game of life*. Retrieved from https://yukaichou.com/

Costello, R., & Lambert, M. (2019). Motivational influences for higher education (HE) students. *International Journal of Online Pedagogy and Course Design*, *9*(1), 38–50. doi:10.4018/IJOPCD.2019010103

Ćwil, M. (2020). *Leaderboards – A motivational tool in the process of business education* (M. Ma, B. Fletcher, S. Gobel, J. Baalsrud Hauge, & T. Marsh, Eds.). Springer Science and Business Media Deutschland GmbH. doi:10.1007/978-3-030-61814-8_15

de la Peña, D., Lizcano, D., & Martínez-Álvarez, I. (2021). Learning through play: Gamification model in university-level distance learning. *Entertainment Computing*, *39*, 100430. Advance online publication. doi:10.1016/j.entcom.2021.100430

Deci, E. L., & Ryan, R. M. (1985). *Intrinsic motivation and self-determination in human behavior*. Plenum Press. doi:10.1007/978-1-4899-2271-7

Denden, M., Tlili, A., Essalmi, F., Jemni, M., Chen, N., & Burgos, D. (2021). Effects of gender and personality differences on students' perception of game design elements in educational gamification. *International Journal of Human-Computer Studies*, *154*, 102674. Advance online publication. doi:10.1016/j.ijhcs.2021.102674

Deterding, S., Dixon, D., Khaled, R., & Nacke, L. (2011). From game design elements to gamefulness: Defining "gamification". *Proceedings of the 15th International Academic MindTrek Conference: Envisioning Future Media Environments, MindTrek 2011*, 9-15. doi:10.1145/2181037.2181040

Dicheva, D., Dichev, C., Agre, G., & Angelova, G. (2015). Gamification in education: A systematic mapping study. *Journal of Educational Technology & Society*, *18*(3), 75–88.

Dominguez Alonso, J., & Pino Juste, M. (2014). Motivación intrínseca y extrínseca. análisis en adolescentes gallegos. *International Journal of Developmental and Educational Psychology*, *1*(1), 349–358.

Dweek, C. S. (1986). Motivational processes affecting learning. *The American Psychologist*, *41*(10), 1040–1048. doi:10.1037/0003-066X.41.10.1040

Elena Parra-Gonzalez, M., Segura-Robles, A., & Rosa Gomez-Barajas, E. (2020). Assessing gamified experiences in physical education teachers and students. *Ijeri-International Journal of Educational Research and Innovation*, (13), 166–176.

Ferriz-Valero, A., Østerlie, O., Martínez, S. G., & García-Jaén, M. (2020). Gamification in physical education: Evaluation of impact on motivation and academic performance within higher education. *International Journal of Environmental Research and Public Health*, *17*(12), 1–16. doi:10.3390/ijerph17124465 PMID:32575919

Garcia-Iruela, M., Hijón-Neira, R., & Connolly, C. (2021). Analysis of three methodological approaches in the use of gamification in vocational training. *Information, 12*(8). doi:10.3390/info12080300

Gomez, T., Moron, C., Ferrandez, D., Saiz, P., & Garrido, R. (2017). Gamification in the education: The benefits of learning through play. *Inted2017: 11th International Technology, Education and Development Conference*, 1051-1060.

Hamari, J., Koivisto, J., & Sarsa, H. (2014). Does gamification work? - A literature review of empirical studies on gamification. *2014 47th Hawaii International Conference on System Sciences (Hicss),* 3025-3034. 10.1109/HICSS.2014.377

Jimenez-Saez, J. C., Ramirez de la Piscina, S., Castellanos, M., & Palacios, P. (2019). Trends in university teaching in physics: Interaction and gamification. *Edulearn19: 11th International Conference on Education and New Learning Technologies*, 2831-2836. 10.21125/edulearn.2019.0763

Kalogiannakis, M., Papadakis, S., & Zourmpakis, A. I. (2021). Gamification in science education. A systematic review of the literature. *Education Sciences*, *11*(1), 22. Advance online publication. doi:10.3390/educsci11010022

Kappen, D. L., & Nacke, L. E. The kaleidoscope of effective gamification: Deconstructing gamification in business applications. *Conference on Gameful Design*, 119-122. 10.1145/2583008.2583029

Kim, J., & Castelli, D. M. (2021). Effects of gamification on behavioral change in education: A meta-analysis. *International Journal of Environmental Research and Public Health*, *18*(7), 3550. Advance online publication. doi:10.3390/ijerph18073550 PMID:33805530

Kim, S. (2021). How a company's gamification strategy influences corporate learning: A study based on gamified MSLP (mobile social learning platform). *Telematics and Informatics*, *57*, 101505. doi:10.1016/j.tele.2020.101505

Lodi, M. Growth mindset in computational thinking teaching and teacher training. *13th ACM Conference on International Computing Education Research (ICER)*, 281-282. 10.1145/3105726.3105736

Looyestyn, J., Kernot, J., Boshoff, K., Ryan, J., Edney, S., & Maher, C. (2017). Does gamification increase engagement with online programs? A systematic review. *PLoS One*, *12*(3), e0173403. Advance online publication. doi:10.1371/journal.pone.0173403 PMID:28362821

Lopes, A. P., Soler, M., Cana, R., Cortes, L., Bentabol, M., Bentabol, A., ... Luna, M. J. (2019). Gamification in education and active methodologies at higher education. *Edulearn19: 11th International Conference on Education and New Learning Technologies*, 1633-1640. 10.21125/edulearn.2019.0480

López-Pernas, S., Gordillo, A., Barra, E., & Quemada, J. (2019). Examining the use of an educational escape room for teaching programming in a higher education setting. *IEEE Access: Practical Innovations, Open Solutions*, *7*, 31723–31737. doi:10.1109/ACCESS.2019.2902976

Luria, E., Shalom, M., & Levy, D. A. (2021). Cognitive Neuroscience Perspectives on Motivation and Learning: Revisiting Self-Determination Theory. *Mind, Brain, and Education, 15*(1), 5-17. https:// doi:10.1111/mbe.12275

Martí-Parreño, J., Galbis-Córdova, A., & Currás-Pérez, R. (2021). Teachers' beliefs about gamification and competencies development: A concept mapping approach. *Innovations in Education and Teaching International*, *58*(1), 84–94. doi:10.1080/14703297.2019.1683464

Martins, A. M. O., Coimbra, M. N., Oliveira, J. A., & Maturano, A. S. (2019). Metodologias ativas para a inovação e qualidade do ensino e aprendizagem no ensino superior. *Revista EDaPECI, 19*(3), 122-132. doi:10.29276/redapeci.2019.19.312147.122-132

McCartney, R., Boustedt, J., Eckerdal, A., Sanders, K., & Zander, C. (2017). *Folk pedagogy and the geek gene: Geekiness quotient.* Seattle, WA: Assoc Comp Machinery. doi:10.1145/3017680.3017746

Mesa, del Carmen, Campos, & Vázquez. (2019). Análisis de la motivación del estudiante de educación superior participante en una propuesta de evaluación formativa. *Sport TK: Revista Euroamericana De Ciencias Del Deporte, 8*(2), 53-58.

Metwally, A. H. S., Nacke, L. E., Chang, M., Wang, Y., & Yousef, A. M. F. (2021). Revealing the hotspots of educational gamification: An umbrella review. *International Journal of Educational Research, 109*. doi:10.1016/j.ijer.2021.101832

Miri, D. H., & Macke, J. (2021). Gamification, motivation, and engagement at work: A qualitative multiple case study. *European Business Review*. Advance online publication. doi:10.1108/EBR-04-2020-0106

Morford, Z. H., Witts, B. N., Killingsworth, K. J., & Alavosius, M. P. (2014). Gamification: The intersection between behavior analysis and game design technologies. *The Behavior Analyst*, *37*(1), 25–40. doi:10.100740614-014-0006-1 PMID:27274957

Murillo-Zamorano, L. R., Lopez Sanchez, J. A., Godoy-Caballero, A. L., & Bueno Munoz, C. (2021). Gamification and active learning in higher education: Is it possible to match digital society, academia and students' interests? *International Journal of Educational Technology in Higher Education*, *18*(1), 1–27. doi:10.118641239-021-00249-y

Murty, V. P., & Adcock, R. A. (2017). Distinct medial temporal lobe network states as neural contexts for motivated memory formation. In D. E. Hannula & M. C. Duff (Eds.), *The hippocampus from cells to systems* (pp. 467–501). Springer. doi:10.1007/978-3-319-50406-3_15

Nasirzadeh, E., & Fathian, M. (2020). Investigating the effect of gamification elements on bank customers to personalize gamified systems. *International Journal of Human-Computer Studies*, *143*, 102469. Advance online publication. doi:10.1016/j.ijhcs.2020.102469

Navarro Mateos, C., Pérez López, I., & Marzo, P. (2021). La gamificación en el ámbito educativo español: revisión sistemática (Gamification in the Spanish educational field: a systematic review). *Retos*, *42*, 507–516. doi:10.47197/retos.v42i0.87384

Palomino, P., & del Carmen, M. (2021). Implications of gamification in Higher Education: A systematic review of student perception. *Rie-Revista De Investigacion Educativa*, *39*(1), 169–188. doi:10.6018/rie.419481

Parra González, M. E., Segura Robles, A., & Gómez Barajas, E. R. (2020). Assessing gamified experiences in physical education teachers and students. *IJERI: International Journal of Educational Research and Innovation*, (13), 166–176.

Patricio, R., Moreira, A., Zurlo, F., & Melazzini, M. (2020). Co-creation of new solutions through gamification: A collaborative innovation practice. *Creativity and Innovation Management*, *29*(1), 149–160. doi:10.1111/caim.12356

Patrício, R., Moreira, A. C., & Zurlo, F. (2018). Gamification approaches to the early stage of innovation. *Creativity and Innovation Management*, *27*(4), 499–511. doi:10.1111/caim.12284

Patrício, R., Moreira, A. C., & Zurlo, F. (2021). Enhancing design thinking approaches to innovation through gamification. *European Journal of Innovation Management*, *24*(5), 1569–1594. doi:10.1108/EJIM-06-2020-0239

Perez Lopez, I., Rivera Garcia, E., & Trigueros Cervantes, C. (2019). 12+1. feelings of physical education college students towards a gamification proposal: "Game of thrones: The anger of the dragons. *Movimento*, *25*, e25038. doi:10.22456/1982-8918.88031

Perez-Lopez, I. J., Rivera Garcia, E., & Trigueros Cervantes, C. (2017). "The prophecy of the chosen ones": An example of gamification applied to university teaching. *Revista Internacional de Medicina y Ciencias de la Actividad Física y del Deporte*, *17*(66), 243–260. doi:10.15366/rimcafd2017.66.003

Pinter, R., Čisar, S. M., Balogh, Z., & Manojlović, H. (2020). Enhancing higher education student class attendance through gamification. *Acta Polytechnica Hungarica*, *17*(2), 13–33. doi:10.12700/APH.17.2.2020.2.2

Pivec, M., Dziabenko, O., & Schinnerl, I. (2003). *Aspects of Game-Based Learning*. Academic Press.

Prieto Andreu, J. M. (2020). A systematic review about gamification, motivation and learning in high school [Una revisiÓn sistemÁtica sobre gamificaciÓn, motivaciÓn y aprendizaje en universitarios]. *Teoría de la Educación*, *32*(1), 73–99. doi:10.14201/teri.20625

Rivera, E. S., & Garden, C. L. P. (2021). Gamification for student engagement: A framework. *Journal of Further and Higher Education*, *45*(7), 999–1012. Advance online publication. doi:10.1080/0309877X.2021.1875201

Rodrigues, L. F., Oliveira, A., & Costa, C. J. (2016). Does ease-of-use contributes to the perception of enjoyment? A case of gamification in e-banking. *Computers in Human Behavior*, *61*, 114–126. doi:10.1016/j.chb.2016.03.015

Ross & Bennett. (2020). Increasing Engagement with Engineering Escape Rooms. *IEEE Transactions on Games*. . doi:10.1109/TG.2020.3025003

Ryan, R. M., & Deci, E. L. (2020). Intrinsic and extrinsic motivation from a self-determination theory perspective: Definitions, theory, practices, and future directions. *Contemporary Educational Psychology*, *61*, 101860. doi:10.1016/j.cedpsych.2020.101860

Salam, M., Awang Iskandar, D. N., Ibrahim, D. H. A., & Farooq, M. S. (2019). Service learning in higher education: a systematic literature review. *Asia Pacific Education Review, 20*(4), 573-593. doi:10.1007/s12564-019-09580-6

Schmitt, V. G. H., & Cequea, M. M. (2020). Flipped classroom: A change in paradigms in higher education [Aula invertida: Uma mudança nos paradigmas no ensino superior; Clase invertida: Un cambio de paradigmas en la educación superior]. *Interciencia*, *45*(11), 501–507.

Sigala, M. (2015). The application and impact of gamification funware on trip planning and experiences: The case of TripAdvisor's funware. *Electronic Markets*, *25*(3), 189–209. doi:10.100712525-014-0179-1

Signori, G. G., De Guimarães, J. C. F., Severo, E. A., & Rotta, C. (2018). Gamification as an innovative method in the processes of learning in higher education institutions. *International Journal of Innovation and Learning*, *24*(2), 115–137. doi:10.1504/IJIL.2018.094066

Subhash, S., & Cudney, E. A. (2018). Gamified learning in higher education: A systematic review of the literature. *Computers in Human Behavior*, *87*, 192–206. doi:10.1016/j.chb.2018.05.028

Vergara, D., Paredes-Velasco, M., Chivite, C., & Fernandez-Arias, P. (2020). The challenge of increasing the effectiveness of learning by using active methodologies. *Sustainability*, *12*(20), 8702. doi:10.3390u12208702

Wang, J., Song, Q., Gao, S., & Tao, Y. (2020). *A systematic review of game learning research in China*. Retrieved from https://www.scopus.com/inward/record.uri?eid=2-s2.0-85088751792&doi=10.1007%2f978-3-030-50164-8_36&partnerID=40&md5=8eaa111998a526f90927667bbab3443a doi:10.1007/978-3-030-50164-8_36

Zainuddin, Z., Shujahat, M., Haruna, H., & Chu, S. K. W. (2020). The role of gamified e-quizzes on student learning and engagement: An interactive gamification solution for a formative assessment system. *Computers & Education*, *145*, 103729. Advance online publication. doi:10.1016/j.compedu.2019.103729

Zichermann, G., & Cunningham, C. (2011). *Gamification by design. Implementing game mechanics in web and mobile apps*. O'Reilly.

Zolkina, A. V., Lomonosova, N. V., & Petrusevich, D. A. (2020). Gamification as a tool of enhancing teaching and learning effectiveness in higher education: Needs analysis [Оценка востребованности применения геймификации как инструмента повышения эффективности образовательного процесса]. *Science for Education Today*, *10*(3), 127–143. doi:10.15293/2658-6762.2003.07

Chapter 5
Gamified Learning Effectiveness Model

May Honey Ohn
https://orcid.org/0000-0002-1951-6598
University Lewisham Hospital, UK

Khin Maung Ohn
Universiti Malaysia Sabah, Malaysia

Ng Pey Luen
University College London Hospital, UK

ABSTRACT

The increasing use of gamification in educational institutions may be attributed to its efficacy in enhancing learning. The objective of this study was to evaluate the impact of online gamified learning among undergraduate medical students. The study developed a hypothetic model to investigate the impact of game characteristics, learning climate, and learners' self-efficacy on medical students' motivation, engagement, and improved learning process. Structural equation modeling (SEM) examined the causal relationships between the observed and latent variables. This study showed that game characteristics positively influence learners' learning engagement and intrinsic motivation. However, the learning environment and self-efficacy did not influence the perceived satisfaction of users. The findings generated in this study indicate those game elements can positively influence students' performance and learning achievement through motivation and engagement.

INTRODUCTION

The incorporation of gamification technology into the medical education curriculum is a dynamic and innovative way to enhance preclinical and clinical learning outcomes (McCoy et al., 2016). Gamification can be used as a holistic teaching, learning and assessment intervention to maximise the learning opportunity for all learner (Buckley & Doyle, 2017). A quasi-experimental study conducted by Ohn MH

DOI: 10.4018/978-1-6684-4287-6.ch005

et al. (2019) revealed that digital online gamified learning is more effective than conventional electronic learning (e-learning) in undergraduate medical learning. It was found that the dropout rate of learning without gamification was 1.5 times higher than learning with game elements (Sousa-Vieira et al., 2021). Patrício et al. (2021) mentioned that gamification promotes achievement of specific goal directed learning intervention and idea development among learners in a structured and relaxed learning environment. Gamification also encourages teamwork spirit, knowledge transfer among team members, social character building, creativity, and productivity (Patricio et al., 2018). Campillo-Ferrer et al. (2020) highlighted that gamification encourages creativity, minimises distraction, and improves social, and Information and Communication Technology (ICT) competencies. Özdener (2018) also uncovered that gamification increases learner engagement and participation as it was found that learners view more pages if existing of gamification elements. According to Huang & Soman (2013), gamification is perceived to play a vital role in the motivation of students and the enhancement of positive learning attitudes and behaviors. As a result, there has been an increasing interest in the use of gamification technology in medical education. Gamification provides a learning environment that provides instant gratification as well as fosters motivation and engagement in learners. Furthermore, gamification eliminates the negative feelings (such as frustrations or cynicism) that are present in traditional learning environments. Based on the existing literature, gamified learning can be infused into the medical curricula to improve learning outcomes (Akl et al., 2010; Bateman et al., 2013; Courteille et al., 2008) and the level of engagement of learners (Freeman et al., 2014; Ortiz-Rojas et al., 2017; Pettit et al., 2014). However, there is little to no available evidence of how the use of gamification impacts learning achievement for medical students (Akl et al., 2013). Thus, there is a need to conduct further research studies to evaluate the effectiveness of gamification in medical education.

LITERATURE REVIEW

In a qualitative study conducted by Ohn MH et al. (2020) to evaluate gamified learning experience and acceptance among medical students, it was revealed that medical students perceived that game attributes encourage motivation and engagement which influences positive learning environment. Game characteristics (such as game mechanics and game elements) are important variables. However, there is a paucity of information on how the various game characteristics interact to enhance the level of engagement and motivation of medical students. The unavailability of this vital information has influenced the decision to recommend the infusion of gamification into the medical curricula (Shin, Sutherland, Norris, & Soloway, 2012). Game elements (such as points, badges, leader-boards, and achievements) are vaguely perceived to increase learner engagement (Landers, 2014). However, there is a need to determine how the interaction between various elements foster the engagement, motivation, and overall success of the learning process. An understanding of this interaction will enable researchers to predict the factors that may influence the learning behaviour and attitude of students toward the use of gamification. Furthermore, it is essential to assess the impact of gamified learning on students' engagement because such students are motivated to invest their time and efforts in learning and participating in study activities (Bakker et al., 2015). Wang and Eccles (2013) stated that it is important for learners to engage actively in learning in order to acquire the knowledge and skills required for a successful academic performance as well as their future careers. Hence, the investigation of game characteristics as a factor that influences student motivation and engagement may provide insights on the effectiveness of gamification in the improvement of the academic performance and perceived satisfaction of learners (Armstrong & Landers, 2014; Ortiz-Rojas et al., 2017). According to Toda et al. (2019), gamification in education contexts should have a systematic approach and take in consideration of elements like resources and stakeholders in order to achieve the desired behaviour.

Over the years, many researchers have demonstrated that there is a positive relationship between the gamification of learning and the motivation, engagement, and academic performance of students (Annetta et al., 2009; McCoy et al., 2016; Ortiz-Rojas et al., 2017; Shin et al., 2012). However, despite the conduction of several studies on the efficacy of the integration of gamification into medical education curricula, few studies have investigated the extent to which gamification elements influence the motivation, engagement and enhanced learning process of medical students (Shin et al., 2012). This research study aimed to investigate the predicting factors of learning achievement (i.e. learning attitude and behaviors) on learning achievement via the enhanced motivation and engagement and satisfaction of medical students. Therefore, the study developed a hypothetic model to investigate the impact of game characteristics, learning climate, and learners' self-efficacy on the motivation, engagement, and improved learning process of medical students.

Hypotheses

Badges are often used to influence suitable learning attitudes and behavior in learners. This game element is a form of reward that triggers strong desires in learners (Khaleel et al., 2016). Studies conducted by Aldemir et al. (2018) found that gamification with badges related to enhanced participant's confidence, enable self-assessment in a continuous and systematic way. Some of the important aspects of a gamification system include the actions of the players and the rules and rewards of the game. Thus, badges are used as a reward system to increase the level of motivation and engagement of users during the learning process. Consequently, these result in effective learning applications and improved learning outcomes (Heng, 2014; Ortiz-Rojas et al., 2017). Based on these aforementioned facts deduced from existing literature, hypothesis 1 was developed.

Hypothesis 1. The Badge (Game Element) has Positive Effect on Intrinsic Motivation

The badge is one of the game elements that positively impact learner's engagement. According to Gibson et al., (2015) a badge is "a representation of an accomplishment, interest or affiliation that is visual, available online, and contains metadata including links that help explain the context, meaning, process and result of an activity". This game element enables learners to engage in positive learning behaviors during the learning process. It also allows learners to their level of progress. Thus, many studies on gamification have focused on the relationship between badges and learner engagement in online environments (Chou, 2015; Looyestyn et al., 2017). Ding et al. (2018) proposed that badge has positive effect on learner's behavioural, cognitive and emotional engagement. Based on these aforementioned facts deduced from existing literature, hypothesis 2 was developed.

Hypothesis 2. The Badge (Game Element) has Positive Effect on Learning Engagement

Çakıroğlu et al. (2017) mentioned that leaderboard set up a controllable competition which could be an attractive experience for learner as gaining reputation. Previous studies on gamification have documented that leaderboards have a positive effect on the emotions of learners (Paas et al., 2005). The leaderboard evokes certain emotions that stir the intrinsic motivation and the level of engagement of learners. According to Khaleel et.al., (2016) the use of game elements increases motivation as well as the learning application of students. Based on these aforementioned facts deduced from existing literature, hypothesis 3 was developed.

Hypothesis 3. The Leader board (Game Element) has Positive Effect on Intrinsic Motivation

The study conducted by Tay (2010) documented that the extent to which the use of leaderboards create or increase learning behaviors and attitudes in students is unknown. However, Kapp (2012) stated that contextual learner engagement can be altered via the integration of gamification elements (such as leaderboards) into medical education. Thus, the purpose of the gamification of learning is to improve learning outcomes. Even though Zichermann and Cunningham (2011) argued that psychological engagement is only a tool to trigger behavioural change, gamification practitioners believe that the use of leaderboards can influence a learning-related behavior (Whitton & Moseley, 2014). Based on these aforementioned facts deduced from existing literature, hypothesis 4 was developed.

Hypothesis 4. The Leader board (Game Element) has a Positive Effect on Learning Engagement

Several studies have been conducted to investigate the effect of game points on the behavior and attitude of learners (Landers & Landers, 2014; Ortiz-Rojas et al., 2017; Tay, 2010). Wilson et al. (2009) proposed that the increased adaptation of game elements to the learner's ability improves the cognitive strategies (behaviour) of learners. The authors also documented that the use of game elements (such as points) may enhance the intrinsic motivation and learning attitude of learners. Based on the aforementioned facts deduced from existing literature, hypothesis 5 was developed.

Hypothesis 5. The Point (Game Element) has Positive Effect on Intrinsic Motivation

There is a need to develop an effective instructional content that facilitates the successful integration of game elements into learning. Game elements can be used to enhance the level of engagement of students. According to Tay (2010), points, leaderboard, and badges were used to increase learners' engagement at Indiana University. The author explained that these were designed to improve the pre-existing and core instructional components of the course. In addition, the use of points proved to be effective in the improvement of learner's engagement. Based on these aforementioned facts deduced from existing literature, hypothesis 6 was developed.

Hypothesis 6. The Point (Game Element) has Positive Effect on Learning Engagement

A case study conducted by Jurgelaitis et al. (2019) confirmed the hypothesis that gamification significantly promotes learners' intrinsic motivation. Gamified learning motive students to have a higher goal, complete more assignments or exercise, and promote learners to interact with each other (Huang & Hew, 2018). According to Bicen and Kocakoyun (2018), the inclusion of game elements positively influences motivation in students. The author further explained that gamification improved the level of understanding and academic performance of learners. These game elements also influence the perceived satisfaction of learners. Thus, motivation is an important factor that influences the perceived satisfaction of learners (Ortiz-Rojas et al., 2017; Sun et al., 2008). However, to what extent intrinsic motivation impacts on the perceived satisfaction of learners is unknown. Based on these aforementioned facts deduced from existing literature, hypothesis 7 was developed.

Hypothesis 7. Motivation has a Positive Effect on the Satisfaction of Learners Toward Gamified E-learning.

The gamification of learning provides a dynamic environment that motivates learners to participate in different study activities (Ortiz-Rojas et al., 2017). According to Pappas (2017), the learning environment provided by gamification is an effective tool that enhances motivation in learners. The author further explained that the game design principles (such as challenges, goals, customization, rapid feedback, visible status, freedom to fail or make choices and social engagement) increase motivation in students (Ortiz-Rojas et al., 2017; Pappas, 2017). Based on these aforementioned facts deduced from existing literature, hypothesis 8 was developed.

Hypothesis 8. Learning Climate of Gamified Learning has Positive Effect on Motivation

The gamification of courses creates an enjoyable and collaborative virtual environment that enhances the level of engagement of learners (Bicen & Kocakoyun, 2018). Gamified software not only creates opportunities for interactions and cooperative learning amongst learners, but it also eliminates the barriers in the constructive learning process. The gamification of learning eliminate restrictions to the space and time of learning. Thus, learners can communicate from any location at their convenience. Furthermore, game elements such as discussion boards enable students to ask questions and express their thoughts with other learners. The learning climate provided by gamified learning may enhance the level of participation of students (Bicen & Kocakoyun, 2018; Ortiz-Rojas et al., 2017; Pappas, 2017; Sun et al., 2008). Based on these aforementioned facts deduced from existing literature, hypothesis 9 was developed.

Hypothesis 9. Learning Climate has a Positive Effect on the Engagement of Students in Gamified E-learning

The different behaviors and attitudes of learners may contribute to variations in the learning process. However, the extent to which these attitudes and behaviors impact learning varies with the construct. For instance, learning effectiveness may reduce if the learners do not put enough cognitive effort into their learning (Paas et al., 2005). Learners who do not participate actively in the learning process will find it difficult to acquire the skills and knowledge required for a stellar academic performance (Zhao & Kuh, 2004). As a result, the academic performance of such students reduced because they did not engage fully in the learning process (Carini et al., 2006). According to Hattie et.al.,(1996) the learning behavior and attitude of students determine the effectiveness of the use of gamification. Furthermore, the authors further stated that the superior cognitive and meta-cognitive strategies (such as note-taking and reflection on material learned) improved learning outcomes and learners' engagement. Therefore, Baydas and Cicek (2019) emphasized that the use of game elements and dynamics help learners to control the frequency of meta-cognitive reminders, that influences the learning engagement, which in turn enhances learning process. Based on these aforementioned facts deduced from existing literature, hypothesis 10 was developed.

Hypothesis 10. Engagement Influences Learning Effectiveness

The perceived satisfaction of learners increases the efficiency and effectiveness of the learning process (Ortiz-Rojas et al., 2017). The game design and game elements used in gamified learning influence the level of engagement of learners and reinforce positive learning attitudes/behavior in students (Simões, Redondo, & Vilas, 2013). Furthermore, the perceived satisfaction of students motivates them to study more and make learners become more active (Bicen & Kocakoyun, 2018). A study conducted by Hanus and Fox (2015) documented the effect of motivation on the perceived satisfaction of learners toward gamified learning. The authors stated that low motivation resulted in the low satisfaction of learners while a high motivation resulted in the high satisfaction of learners toward gamified learning. The authors further stated that the gamification mechanics used determines the level of motivation of students, which results in an increase in the satisfaction of learners to gamified learning. Based on these aforementioned facts deduced from existing literature, hypothesis 11 was developed.

Hypothesis 11. The Satisfaction toward Gamified E-learning has a Positive Effect on Learning Effectiveness

Self-efficacy can be defined as an individual's belief in own ability to prepare and carry out the course of action required to produce certain accomplishments (Bandura, 1997). Thus, self-efficacy is considered to be an essential factor that influences learning outcomes. Learners who possess a high level of self-efficacy are persistent and confident about their capability to grasp the concepts of a particular topic (Compeau et al., 2006; Johnson & Marakas, 2000; Yi & Davis, 2003). According to Bandura (1997), various sources of information influence the development of self-efficacy beliefs in various individuals. The author further explained that the mastery of the past experiences derived from a learner's performance accomplishments are the strongest source of self-efficacy because they provide genuine proof of the learner's abilities. In online gamified learning, the performance of fellow trainees may be an important source of information about self-efficacy because vicarious experiences are noticeable when comparison targets are similar to the experiences of other individuals. Comparing the performances of peers who participated in a gameful competition makes it easier to determine their learning capabilities (Compeau et al., 2006; Ortiz-Rojas et al., 2017). According to Bandura (1997), social comparisons can be used to determine the self-efficacy of learners. For instance, a low relative performance indicates a low efficacy while a high relative performance indicates a high efficacy. Based on these aforementioned facts deduced from existing literature, hypothesis 12 was developed.

Hypothesis 12. Self-efficacy of Learning has a Positive Effect on the Satisfaction of Learners.

METHODOLOGY

Sampling

A total number of 142 undergraduate medical students (academic years 1-5) were randomly selected from a local university in East Malaysia. After traditional Electrocardiogram (ECG) classroom teaching, a combination of online and blended learning approaches was used to assess the impact of online gamified learning. The GaMED ECG@™ platform is a novel prototype which incorporates game-based techniques (competition, level, leader-board, badge, social interaction, time, and challenge) as a gamified strategy to deliver specified learning outcomes according to the curriculum (Ohn MH et al., 2018). The outcome variables of gamified learning include learning achievement and satisfaction; these variables were assessed. There was no attrition upon evaluation after two weeks of online gamified learning. The participation of each participant was voluntary. Informed consent forms were completed by the participants. The use of the random sampling method restricted the researcher from having control over the representativeness, irrespective of their characteristics (Chang et al., 2009). Ethic approval was taken from the ethic board committee of Universiti Malaysia Sabah (JKEtika 1/17 (5)).

Data Collection Instrument

The survey questionnaire was divided into three sections. The first section was comprised of questions related to the demographic and academic profile of the students (such as gender, age, academic year, academic achievement, and mean hours of weekly playtime); the responses of participants were coded accordingly. The second section consisted of five main constructs: game characteristics dimension (point, badge & leader-board), learner dimension (self-efficacy), learning environment dimension (learning climate), attitude & behaviour change (motivation and engagement), and satisfaction as shown in Table 1. These constructs were investigated using several items that measured the different latent variables in the proposed research model. The items used to measure the learning climate were adapted from (Chou & Liu, 2005). The perceived self-efficacy of learning and performance items were adopted from the study conducted by Bandura (1997). The items for game characteristics were derived from the study conducted by Codish and Ravid. (2014). Measures of student engagement included the absorption construct, which was adopted from the Utrecht Work Engagement Scale for Students (UWES-S) developed by Schaufeli et al. (2002). The intrinsic motivation of students was measured via the academic motivation scale developed by Vallerand et al. (1989). Perceived satisfaction of learners with the course, instructor, and learning activities were measured using the academic satisfaction scale developed by Gunawardena and Zittle (1997). The third part of the questionnaire involved the objective assessment of learning achievement via close supervision. The learning achievement of students was assessed by conducting a factual knowledge test (Multiple choice exam) and procedural knowledge test (Objective Structured Clinical Examination). All the questionnaires were presented to a formal expert panel consisting of two established researchers in questionnaire development. Based on the experts' remark, some items were removed from the questionnaire, while some were rephrased. The items for the engagement questionnaire were evaluated using a 5-point Likert type scale (1=Never, 2=Almost Never, 3=Seldom, 4= Occasionally, 5=Frequently, 6=Almost Always, and 7=Always). All other items were evaluated using a 5-point Likert type scale, which ranged from 1 ("strongly disagree") to 5 ("strongly agree"), except for some reversed items (R) which were scored as 1 ("strongly agree") to 5 ("strongly disagree"). A pre-test was conducted prior to the administration of questionnaires to 30 participants of this study. A total number of 30 medical students who were not involved in the study completed the preliminary questionnaire after playing GaMED@TM.

Data Analysis

The data obtained from all sections of the questionnaire were analysed using SPSS 24.0 software package to compute the descriptive statistics (frequencies, percentages, and mean) for the students' demographic

Table 1. Survey constructs, definitions, items and references

Construct	Definitions	Items	References
Perceived Self-efficacy of learning and performance (SE)	A belief in one's capability to organize and execute the courses of action required to produce given attainments.	I was confident using gamified e-learning system to learn ECG.	Bandura (1997, p. 3)
		I got an excellent mark in ECG by learning from gamified e-learning.	
		I feel confident using gamified e-learning contents.	
		I was able to learn ECG by using gamified e-learning.	
Game Characteristics (Points, leaderboard, badge)	Elements used in course design.		Codish and Ravid (2014)
Game Point (GP)		In games, I enjoyed getting more points than my friends.	
		I preferred games that have a score.	
		During competition, I checked my points more often.	
Game badge (GB)		In games, I was willing to put in extra effort in order to gain a trophy	
		I was willing to put in extra effort to get a pretty badge	
		It was important to me to get as many badges as possible in the course.	
Game leader-board (GL)		The decrease in my ranking on the leaderboard made me feel less happy.	
		I always strive to be in a leading position in the game.	
		A leaderboard helped me know my position compared to other players.	
Intrinsic motivation (IM)	"the process where goal-directed activity is instigated and sustained.	Academic Motivation Scale (AMS)	Vallerand et al. (1989)
	The doing of an activity for its inherent satisfaction, not for some separable consequence.	For the intense feelings, I experienced when I play GaMED®™.	
		For the pleasure, I experienced while surpassing myself in GaMED®™.	
		Because I experienced pleasure while I play GaMED®™.	
		For the high feeling that I experienced while playing GaMED®™.	
Learning Engagement (LE)	A positive, fulfilling, and work-related state of mind that is characterized by vigor, dedication, and absorption.	Utrecht Work Engagement Scale for Students (UWES-S)	Schaufeli et al. (2002)
		Time flies quickly when I was playing GaMED®™.	
		I felt happy when I was playing GaMED®™ intensively.	
		I thought about other things during playing GaMED®™.	
		I was easily distracted during playing GaMED®™. (R)	
		I can get carried away by playing GaMED®™.	
Learning climate (LC)		Gamified e-learning was interesting.	Chou and Liu (2005)
		Gamified e-learning climate in GaMED®™ was relaxing.	
		Gamified e-learning climate in GaMED®™ was enjoyable.	
		Gamified e-learning climate in GaMED®™ was boring (R).	
Learning Satisfaction (LS)	*Academic satisfaction questionnaire (ASQ)*	If I had an opportunity to play GaMED®™ in the future, I would gladly do so.	Gunawardena and Zittle (1997)
		I was satisfied with all the features of GaMED®™.	
		I was stimulated to do additional readings or research on topics learned in GaMED®™	
		Gamified learning was a useful learning experience.	

and academic profiles. The differences and associations between various variables were statistically analyzed using the t-test (univariate analysis). Harman's single factor test was used to investigate common method variance among the factors (Podsakoff & Organ, 1986). In terms of construct validity, exploratory factor analysis (EFA) was conducted to explore the underlying relationships among the items to finalize the minimum required constructs that should be included in the study. Communalities indicate the amount of variance in each variable that is accounted for by the common factors. If the communality were very low, it means that the variable does not fit the construct well. As suggested by Tabachnik and Fidell (2007), 0.30 was used as the cut-off score to suppress the survey items that held low communalities in the pilot test. Six items were excluded from the scale along with the factor extraction due to respectively low communalities. Eight factors with total of 30 items were revealed from Principal component analysis (PCA) as the extraction method, which is a widely used method for factor extraction in EFA (table 2). There was no single factor with the majority of covariance in both the dependent and independent variables. Factor loading of each item and total variances indicated a good construct validity. Based on the measurement of the scale's reliability (using the value of Cronbach's alpha), all the questionnaires were reliable. Structural equation modeling (SEM) was used to examine the multivariate causal relationships between the observed and latent variables and test the hypotheses between the predictors in this research model (Hoyle, 1995). The main advantage of using SEM is that it can give an estimate of the measurement and structural model. In addition, SEM integrates factor analysis, principal components analysis, discriminant analysis, path analysis, and multiple regression analysis from first-generation techniques as a comprehensive statistical approach. To test the model of this research, SmartPLS 3.2.7 software was used to carry out the partial least squares' analysis of the proposed measurement model and structural model (Richter et al., 2015). The maximum likelihood method was adopted to estimate the model's parameters.

RESULTS

A total number of 142 students from gamified learning completed the gamified learning survey questionnaire, of which 140 responses were valid. Majority of the participants were female (64%) while the average age of the respondents was 21 years (SD=1.23). Among them, 27% were Year 1 & 2 medical students, followed by Year 3 medical students (33%), Year 4 medical students (15%) and Year 5 medical students (25%). The majority of participants were of Chinese ethnicity (28%) followed by Malays (22%), Indian (18%) and other ethnicities (13%).

Structural Equation Modeling (SEM) Data Analysis

Structural Equation Modeling (SEM) was used to predict the impact of gamified learning on learning achievement. The two-step approach, measurement model and structural model, was used to confirm the reliability and validity of the items before measuring the structural relationship between constructs.

Measurement Model

The measurement model was examined via the evaluation of reliability, convergent, and discriminant validity of the construct measures. The factor structure values are summarized in Table 2. The internal consistency properties of the respective latent variables are calculated using Cronbach's Alpha. The Cronbach's alpha values ranged from 0.777 to 0.915, thus exceeding the minimum threshold of 0.70 as suggested by Peterson (1994). Similarly, confirmatory factor analysis (CFA) was performed to measure the convergent validity of the study which is meant to examine whether each variable measured its intended factor of interest (Bagozzi et al., 1991). CR which was found to be higher than 0.7 to indicate the adequate internal consistency (Hair et al., 2011). The standardized loading items were considered significant as the cut-off value was set at 0.50 (Hair et al., 2010). The average variances extracted (AVE) of latent constructs in the study showed good convergent validity, which ranged from 0.826 to 0.936. The CR values exceeded the recommended threshold value of 0.50 (Hair et al., 2010), which meant more than half of the variances involved in the items were accounted for their hypothesized constructs. Besides, the discriminant validity was examined for confirmation that each factor was distinct or uncorrelated. The heterotrait-monotrait (HTMT) ratio of correlations approach was used to examine the discriminant validity (Henseler et al., 2015). According to HTMT criterion by Kline (2011), it must be <0.85. HTMT inference using bootstrapping technique (Henseler et al., 2015) was used and 90% bootstrap confidence interval included the value of -1 <HTMT<1 (liberal criterion). Table 3 shows the HTMT analysis of the study which reveals a good discriminant validity.

Model Testing Criteria

Many indices can be used to evaluate the fit of a model; however, no single index can serve as the only standard for judging the quality of a model. Thus, this study adopted the following indices recommended by Hoyle (1995), as the criteria for this model's evaluation (Table 4). The closer the observed data is to the theoretical model, the better the fit of the model, and the easier it is to satisfy the thresholds of the aforementioned indices. The model fit result showed the model is fit enough to analyze the study.

Evaluation of Structural Model

Figure 1 shows the causal relationship between the constructs and the standardized path coefficients (R^2).The result of the t-test showed that game point had a significant positive effect on motivation ($\beta = 0.184$, $P < 0.05$) and engagement ($\beta = 0.126$, $P < 0.05$); game badge had a significant positive effect on motivation ($b = 0.322$, $P < 0.001$) and engagement ($\beta = 0.306$, $P < 0.001$); game leaderboard had a significant positive effect on motivation ($\beta = 0.388$, $P < 0.001$) and engagement ($b = 0.339$, $P < 0.001$). Thus, H1to H6 were supported and accepted. The t-test result also showed that intrinsic motivation had a significant positive effect on learning satisfaction ($\beta = 0.391$, $P < 0.001$) and learning engagement ($\beta = 0.367$, $P < 0.001$) of learners had a significant positive effect on learning achievement. Thus, H7 and H10 were supported and accepted.

In addition, the t-test showed that learning satisfaction had a significant positive effect on learning achievement ($\beta = 0.231$, $P < 0.05$). Therefore, H 12 was supported and accepted. However, the learning climate didn't have a significant positive effect on the learning engagement ($\beta = 0.033$, $P = 0.326$) and motivation ($\beta = 0.005$, $P = 0.470$) of users. Additionally, Learners' self-efficacy didn't show a significant positive effect on satisfaction (($\beta = 0.117$, $P = 0.111$) and hence, rejected the hypothesis. Thus, H8 and H9 were rejected. The explained variances include learning engagement ($R^2 = 0.334$), intrinsic motivation ($R^2 = 0.426$), learning satisfaction ($R^2 = 0.172$) and learning achievement ($R^2 = 0.249$). The paths that affect the learning achievement have an explained variance of 0.50.

GB, GL, GP, IM, LA, LC, LE, LS, SE denote game badge, game leaderboard, game point, intrinsic motivation, learning achievement, learning climate, learners' engagement, learning satisfaction, and self-efficacy respectively.

Table 2. Reliability, construct, and convergent validity of the reflective items in the measurement model.

Latent variables	Items	M	SD	Factor loadings	Cronbach's alpha	Composite reliability[a]	AVE[b]
Game Point (GP)					**0.766**	**0.865**	**0.682**
	GP_1	3.76	1.17	0.883			
	GP_2	3.81	0.98	0.821			
	GP_3	3.88	0.91	0.771			
Game Badge (GB)					**0.777**	**0.889**	**0.684**
	GB_1	3.92	0.76	0.854			
	GB_2	3.80	0.85	0.858			
	GB_3	3.84	0.91	0.767			
Game Leaderboard (GL)					**0.814**	**0.826**	**0.727**
	GL_1	4.29	0.81	0.84			
	GL_2	4.14	0.80	0.864			
	GL_3	4.02	0.89	0.854			
Learning Climate (LC)					**0.904**	**0.867**	**0.629**
	LC_1	4.36	0.75	0.824			
	LC_2	4.35	0.72	0.721			
	LC_3	3.99	0.88	0.571			
	LC4	4.47	0.77	0.996			
Self-Efficacy (SE)					**0.853**	**0.896**	**0.683**
	SE_1	4.33	0.68	0.817			
	SE_2	4.17	0.73	0.897			
	SE_3	4.06	0.78	0.759			
	SE_4	4.23	0.68	0.827			
Learners' Engagement (LE)					**0.915**	**0.936**	**0.745**
	LE_1	4.51	1.36	0.883			
	LE_2	4.55	1.36	0.866			
	LE_3	4.08	1.26	0.866			
	LE_4	4.06	1.29	0.876			
	LE_5	3.96	1.10	0.824			
Intrinsic Motivation (IM)					**0.900**	**0.930**	**0.770**
	IM_1	3.54	1.15	0.846			
	IM_2	3.83	0.87	0.86			
	IM_3	3.81	0.96	0.929			
	IM_4	3.66	1.25	0.874			
Learning Satisfaction (LS)					**0.899**	**0.929**	**0.765**
	LA_1	3.72	1.26	0.844			
	LA_2	4.26	0.92	0.892			
	LA_3	4.13	0.99	0.882			
	LA_4	4.22	0.91	0.880			

M-mean; SD-standard deviation

Note: [a] Composite reliability = (square of the summation of the factor loadings) / [(square of the summation of the factor loadings) + (square of the summation of the error variances)]

[b]Average Variance Extracted = (summation of squared factor loadings) / (summation of squared factor loadings) (summation of error variance)

Table 3. Discriminant validity (HTMT results)

	GB	GL	GP	IM	LA	LC	LE	LS
GB								
GL	0.301							
GP	0.2	0.437						
IM	0.373	0.618	0.585					
LA	0.301	0.46	0.322	0.526				
LC	0.135	0.098	0.107	0.094	0.018			
LE	0.276	0.542	0.535	0.708	0.464	0.093		
LS	0.296	0.375	0.256	0.419	0.364	0.141	0.376	
SE	0.243	0.102	0.097	0.113	0.243	0.089	0.188	0.142

GB= game badge, GL= game leaderboard, GP= game point, IM= intrinsic motivation, LA= learning achievement, LC= learning climate, LE= learners' engagement, LS= learning satisfaction. SE= self-efficacy.

Hypotheses Testing and Path Analysis

Table 5 shows the direct, impact of each construct. The learning achievement and satisfaction are the outcome variables used to determine whether students benefit from gamified learning. It shows that the determinant with the strongest direct impact on learning satisfaction is intrinsic motivation ($b = 0.391$), followed by game leader-board on intrinsic motivation ($b = 0.388$). This result shows that the more motivated, the stronger the learning satisfaction in the future. In terms of the total effect of the learning achievement, learning engagement has the strongest effect, followed by learning satisfaction and then motivation.

DISCUSSION

The objective of this study was to evaluate the impact of online gamified learning on learning performance among the different academic years of undergraduate medical students. GaMED$^{@TM}$ ECG learning activities were centered on ECG interpretation skills, which is a major course in the medical education

Table 4. Goodness-of-fit Indices for the sample (N=140).

Model fit measure	Recommended value	Model value
SRMT	<0.08	0.073
NFI	>0.90	0.904
RMS theta	<0.14	0.138
dG	<95% bootstrap quantile	1.722
dULS	<95% bootstrap quantile	2.667

SRMR: standardized root mean square residual; NFI: Normed fit index ; RMS theta: root mean square residual covariance: dG & dULS: Exact model fit by bootstrapping.

Figure 1. Structural model.

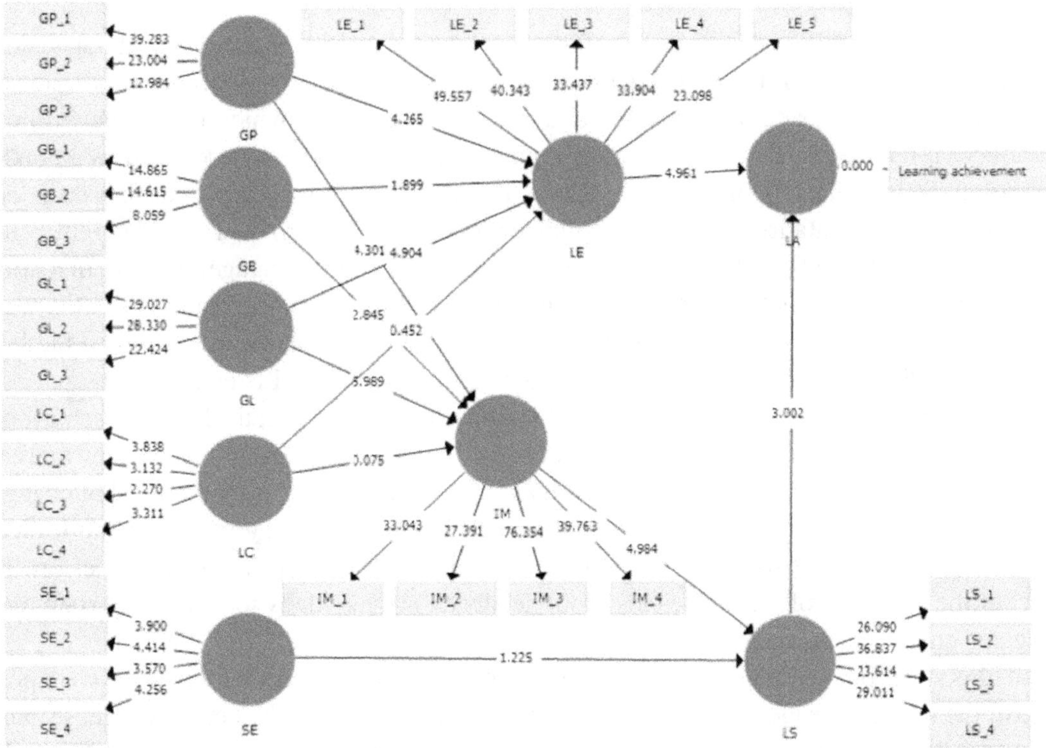

Table 5. Testing the hypotheses

Hypotheses	Relationship	Estimate	Std. Deviation	t-value (one-tailed)	p-value	Decision	5%CI	95%CI	VIF	f^2
H1	GB -> IM	0.184	0.065	2.845	0.002	**Accepted**	0.078	0.294	**1.065**	**0.056**
H2	GB -> LE	0.126	0.067	1.899	0.029	**Accepted**	0.032	0.242	**1.065**	**0.022**
H3	GL -> IM	0.388	0.065	5.989	0.000	**Accepted**	0.285	0.495	**1.174**	**0.223**
H4	GL -> LE	0.339	0.069	4.904	0.000	**Accepted**	0.222	0.446	**1.174**	**0.147**
H5	GP -> IM	0.322	0.075	4.301	0.000	**Accepted**	0.198	0.443	**1.164**	**0.155**
H6	GP -> LE	0.306	0.072	4.265	0.000	**Accepted**	0.18	0.42	**1.164**	**0.121**
H7	IM -> LS	0.391	0.078	4.984	0.000	**Accepted**	0.263	0.522	**1.004**	**0.184**
H8	LC -> IM	0.005	0.062	0.075	0.470	**Rejected**	-0.082	0.122	**1.028**	**0**
H9	LC -> LE	0.033	0.072	0.452	0.326	**Rejected**	-0.086	0.154	**1.028**	**0.002**
H10	LE -> LA	0.367	0.074	4.961	0.000	**Accepted**	0.242	0.483	**1.146**	**0.156**
H11	LS -> LA	0.231	0.077	3.002	0.001	**Accepted**	0.108	0.364	**1.146**	**0.062**
H12	SE -> LS	0.117	0.096	1.225	0.111	**Rejected**	-0.087	0.272	**1.004**	**0.017**

H= hypothesis, GB= game badge, GL= game leaderboard, GP= game point, IM= intrinsic motivation, LA= learning achievement, LC= learning climate, LE= learners' engagement, LS= learning satisfaction, SE= self-efficacy, CI= confidence interval, VIF= variance inflation factor, p value < 0.05 is statistically significant.

program. The gamification elements used in this study include points, leader-boards and achievement badges.

As hypothesized, gamified learning was found to have a positive impact on students' learning achievement and satisfaction through engagement and motivation. The result of this study showed that game elements (point and badge) increase motivation and engagement which in turn have significant positive effect on learning. This finding can be explained by similar theory proposed by Poondej and Lerdpornkulrat (2016) who documented the positive impact of autonomy which enhances deep learning via motivational goal-orientation approach. A study conducted by Ribeiro et al. (2018) highlighted that possession of game elements motivate self-regulation which enhances engagement, participation and learning experience by stimulating active learning theory. Furthermore, the findings in this study are in consonance with other existing literature on the positive effects of game attributes on the learning (Geelan et al., 2015; Gressick & Langston, 2017; Kuo & Chuang, 2016; Lister 2015).

Another possible explanation of how gamified learning activity stimulates learning achievement is rooted from game dynamic (leaderboard) which has positive impact on learners' motivation and engagement. The findings in this study indicate that GaMED@™ activities generate a high level of engagement and intrinsic motivation in medical students contributed by dynamic progression in the leaderboard which provides formative feedback about the level of competence, intrinsic motivative effort. Hence, the impact of the provision of formative close-loop feedback is most likely to be an important mediator between game enhanced engagement and motivation of students.

Overall, this study proves that the use of achievement badges, points and leaderboards were powerful indicators of the learner's academic accomplishment for completion of assisgned tasks. These game elements served as learner goals that stimulated participants to be dedicated to pursuing and accomplishing them. The participants saw the achievement badges as rewards for their hard work. Moreover, studies conducted to investigate the impact of gamification have documented that those virtual achievement may be used to improve the learner's engagement and intrinsic motivation (Ribeiro et al., 2018; Hakulinen & Auvinen, 2014). According to Hamari (2015), the effect of the point system, leader-board and achievement badges on the level of engagement of learners can be explained using the social comparison theory. This theory states that learners tend to compare their achievements with others and participate in the learning activities that their peers participate in. Other theories that explain the impact of leader-boards and badges on intrinsic motivation include Alderfer's ERG theory, Maslow's hierarchy of needs, and McClelland's need theory of motivation (McClarty et al., 2012). This, in turn, all game elements in this study indirectly increase the perceived learning satisfaction of students via enhanced learning motivation. Also, learning satisfaction is considered as an effective indicator of the academic performance of a student.

The t-test result showed that intrinsic motivation had a significant effect on learners' satisfaction ($\beta = 0.391$, $P < 0.001$) while the engagement of learners ($\beta = 0.367$, $P < 0.001$) had a significant positive effect on learning achievement. This result is in consonance with the study conducted by Sailer, Hense, Mayr & Mandl (2017), which documented that the intrinsic motivation triggered by game characteristics resulted in an increase in the perceived satisfaction of learners. The result of this study is also in accordance with the study conducted by Lister (2015), which documented that the active engagement of learners resulted in an increase in academic performance. In addition, this result is in agreement with existing literature on the effect of intrinsic motivation and engagement on the perceived satisfaction and academic achievement of learners (Dichev & Dicheva, 2017; Papp, 2017).

Also, learning satisfaction is considered as an effective indicator of the academic performance of a student. Werbach (2014) also stated that the gaming environment plays a crucial role in the perceived satisfaction of learners. This study also showed that the satisfaction of learning had a significant positive effect on learning achievement ($\beta = 0.231$, $P < 0.05$). This finding is in consonance with the study conducted by Sailer, Hense, Mayr and Mandl (2017), which documented that the perceived satisfaction of learners positively influences the level of competence of learners. The result of this study is also in accordance with existing literature on the effect of learning satisfaction on learning achievement (Peng et al., 2012). The result of this study may be due to the level of interactivity in the online environment. These strong emotions evoke the perceived satisfaction of learners with the gaming environment (Liaw & Huang, 2013).

However, the learning climate did not have a significant positive effect on learners' engagement ($\beta = 0.033$, $P = 0.326$) and the motivation ($\beta = 0.005$, $P = 0.470$) of users. The result of this study is not in agreement with the study conducted by Lerdpornkulrat et al., (2018) which documented that the student perception of learning climate positively influences learning engagement and motivation which contributes to intention to study. A study conducted by Noe et al. (2010) also documented that an active learning climate stimulates individual exploration which enhances the level of motivation and engagement in learning. However, to date, there's no study on impact of gamification on climate of learning. Thus, it is mysterious to understand why learning climate didn't support motivation and engagement in gamified learning. We suppose the fostering of perceived competitive climate or complex interactivity can sometimes demotivate students which can have negative impact on learning experience.

In addition, learners' self-efficacy did not show a significant positive effect on the perceived satisfaction of learners ($\beta = 0.117$, $P=0.111$) in our study. This finding is in agreement with the study conducted by Ortiz-Rojas et al. (2017), which documented that gamification has no significant impact on self-efficacy. However, this finding is not in agreement with most studies (Banfield & Wilkerson, 2014; Polo-Peña et al., 2020; Richter et al., 2021) that showed gamification has positive impact on self-efficacy and motivation. As per Bandura et al. (1997), social relatedness positively relates to self-efficacy of learners. As such, we suppose the result in this study may be due to the inability of the game elements to foster social relatedness amongst students.

Overall, this chapter provides an evaluation study of the impact of gamification on learning performance among undergraduate medical students at a local university. With the statistical evidence, the game characteristics (such as points, badges, and leader-boards) had shown a positive effect on education via students' intrinsic motivation and learning engagement. Remarkably, climate of learning environments and self-efficacy were not found to be essential factors in influencing outcome in gamified learning.

RECOMMENDATIONS

Based on the promising findings generated in this study, further studies should be conducted on the development of a sustainable gamified learning environment for the entire course over a more extended time-frame (from 5 weeks to 14 weeks) to get a more reliable result. Other recommendations for future research studies include the empirical evaluation of other factors that affect learning outcomes and effectiveness of gamified learning.

LIMITATIONS

The first limitation of the study is the small sample size which can affect the power of the results. The second limitation of the study is the generalization of this study's findings across other academic fields due to the fact that this study was restricted to a local university in Malaysia and focused on gamified ECG learning among undergraduate medical students, thus, the findings in this study cannot be generalized to the entire population. The third limitation is the potential gender bias. In this simple randomised study, women were more likely to participate than men (64% vs. 36%). This result has been discussed in several works (Curtin et al. 2000; Moore & Tarnai, 2002; Singer et al., 2000). Another major limitation is the short experimental timeframe (2 weeks) that can arise big concerns on the reliability of the results. Study period was short due to the limited students' available time to participate in the study period. Due to the relatively shorter timeframe compared with other studies (Baydas & Cicek, 2019; Cheong et al., 2013; Pakinee & Puritat, 2021), changes in how students exhibit their learning behaviours over time (long-term effect of gamified learning) could not be detected from this analysis. The last limitation is the novelty effect. Since gamified learning is relatively new, the level of enthusiasm of researchers may skew data.

CONCLUSION

The result of this study showed that game characteristics positively influence the learning engagement and intrinsic motivation of learners which increases learning experience and achievement. However, the learning climate and self-efficacy did not influence motivation and perceived satisfaction of users respectively. It is noteworthy that learning motivation had the strongest influence on satisfaction while engagement had the strongest effect on learning achievement in gamification. In essence, the findings generated in this study indicate that students' performance and learning achievement can be positively influenced by game elements through motivation and engagement. Furthermore, these game elements can be used as a teaching and learning approach to enhance learning outcomes. However, educators must consider using appropriate game attributes in creating positive and interactive learning environment during the development of a suitable gamified learning platform.

REFERENCES

Akl, E. A., Pretorius, R. W., Sackett, K., Erdley, W. S., Bhoopathi, P. S., Alfarah, Z., & Schünemann, H. J. (2010). The effect of educational games on medical students' learning outcomes: A systematic review: BEME Guide No 14. *Medical Teacher*, *32*(1), 16–27. doi:10.3109/01421590903473969 PMID:20095770

Akl, E. A., Sackett, K., Pretorius, R., Erdley, S., Bhoopathi, P. S., Mustafa, R., & Schunemann, H. J. (2013). Educational games for health professionals. *Cochrane Database of Systematic Reviews*, (1), CD006411. doi:10.1002/14651858.CD006411.pub2 PMID:23440807

Annetta, L. A., Minogue, J., Holmes, S. Y., & Cheng, M.-T. T. (2009). Investigating the impact of video games on high school students' engagement and learning about genetics. *Computers & Education*, *53*(1), 74–85. doi:10.1016/j.compedu.2008.12.020

Armstrong, M. B., & Landers, R. N. (2014). Reactions to Gamified Training. Poster Presented at the *Old Dominion University 4th Annual Graduate Research Achievement Day*, Norfolk, VA. 10.13140/2.1.2264.3848

Bagozzi, R. P., Yi, Y., & Phillips, L. W. (1991). Assessing construct validity in organizational research. *Administrative Science Quarterly*, 421–458. doi:10.2307/2393203

Bakker, A. B., Sanz Vergel, A. I., & Kuntze, J. (2015). Student engagement and performance: A weekly diary study on the role of openness. *Motivation and Emotion*, *39*(1), 49–62. doi:10.100711031-014-9422-5

Bandura, A. (1997). *Self-efficacy: The exercise of control.* Macmillan. doi:10.1891/0889-8391.13.2.158

Banfield, J., & Wilkerson, B. (2014). Increasing student intrinsic motivation and self-efficacy through gamification pedagogy. *Contemporary Issues in Education Research*, *7*(4), 291–298. doi:10.19030/cier.v7i4.8843

Bateman, J., Allen, M., Samani, D., Kidd, J., & Davies, D. (2013). Virtual patient design: Exploring what works and why. A grounded theory study. *Medical Education*, *47*(6), 595–606. doi:10.1111/medu.12151 PMID:23662877

Baydas, O., & Cicek, M. (2019). The examination of the gamification process in undergraduate education: A scale development study. *Technology, Pedagogy and Education*, *28*(3), 269–285. doi:10.1080/1475939X.2019.1580609

Bicen, H., & Kocakoyun, S. (2018). Perceptions of Students for Gamification Approach: Kahoot as a Case Study. *International Journal of Emerging Technologies in Learning*, *13*(02), 72–93. doi:10.3991/ijet.v13i02.7467

Buckley, P., & Doyle, E. (2017). Individualising gamification: An investigation of the impact of learning styles and personality traits on the efficacy of gamification using a prediction market. *Computers & Education*, *106*, 43–55. doi:10.1016/j.compedu.2016.11.009

Çakıroğlu, Ü., Başıbüyük, B., Güler, M., Atabay, M., & Memiş, B. Y. (2017). Gamifying an ICT course: Influences on engagement and academic performance. *Computers in Human Behavior*, *69*, 98–107. doi:10.1016/j.chb.2016.12.018

Campillo-Ferrer, J. M., Miralles-Martínez, P., & Sánchez-Ibáñez, R. (2020). Gamification in higher education: Impact on student motivation and the acquisition of social and civic key competencies. *Sustainability*, *12*(12), 4822. doi:10.3390u12124822

Carini, R. M., Kuh, G. D., & Klein, S. P. (2006). Student engagement and student learning: Testing the linkages. *Research in Higher Education*, *47*(1), 1–32. doi:10.100711162-005-8150-9

Chang, C.-C., Lin, C.-Y., Chen, Y.-C., & Chin, Y.-C. (2009). Predicting information-seeking intention in academic digital libraries. *The Electronic Library*, *27*(3), 448–460. doi:10.1108/02640470910966899

Cheong, C., Cheong, F., & Filippou, J. (2013). Quick Quiz: A Gamified Approach for Enhancing Learning. *PACIS 2013 Proceedings*, 1–14.

Chou, S.-W., & Liu, C.-H. (2005). Learning effectiveness in a Web-based virtual learning environment: A learner control perspective. *Journal of Computer Assisted Learning*, *21*(1), 65–76. doi:10.1111/j.1365-2729.2005.00114.x

Chou, Y. (2015). *Actionable gamification: Beyond points, badges, and leaderboards*. Octalysis Group.

Codish, D., & Ravid, G. (2014). Academic Course Gamification: The Art of Perceived Playfulness. *Interdisciplinary Journal of E-Learning and Learning Objects*, *10*, 131–151. doi:10.28945/2066

Compeau, D., Gravill, J., Haggerty, N., & Kelley, H. (2006). Computer Self-Efficacy: A Review. Human-Computer Interaction in Management Information Systems: Foundations, 225-261.

Courteille, O., Bergin, R., Courteille, O., Bergin, R., Stockeld, D., Ponzer, S., & Fors, U. (2008). The use of a virtual patient case in an OSCE-based exam–a pilot study. *Medical Teacher*, *30*(3), e66–e76. doi:10.1080/01421590801910216 PMID:18484444

Curtin, R., Presser, S., & Singer, E. (2000). The effects of response rate changes on the index of consumer sentiment. *Public Opinion Quarterly*, *64*, 413–428. doi:10.1086/318638 PMID:11171024

Dichev, C., & Dicheva, D. (2017). Gamifying education: what is known, what is believed and what remains uncertain: a critical review. *International Journal of Educational Technology in Higher Education*, *14*. doi:10.1186/s41239-017-0042-5

Ding, L., Er, E., & Orey, M. (2018). An exploratory study of student engagement in gamified online discussions. *Computers & Education*, *120*, 213–226. doi:10.1016/j.compedu.2018.02.007

Freeman, S., Eddy, S. L., McDonough, M., Smith, M. K., Okoroafor, N., Jordt, H., & Wenderoth, M. P. (2014). Active learning increases student performance in science, engineering, and mathematics. *Proceedings of the National Academy of Sciences of the United States of America*, *111*(23), 8410–8415. doi:10.1073/pnas.1319030111 PMID:24821756

Geelan, B., de Salas, K., Lewis, I., King, C., Edwards, D., & O'Mara, A. (2015). Improving learning experiences through gamification: A case study. *Australian Educational Computing, 30*(1).

Gibson, D., Ostashewski, N., Flintoff, K., Grant, S., & Knight, E. (2015). Digital badges in education. *Education and Information Technologies*, *20*(2), 403–410. doi:10.100710639-013-9291-7

Gressick, J., & Langston, J. B. (2017). The Guilded Classroom: Using Gamification to Engage and Motivate Undergraduates. *The Journal of Scholarship of Teaching and Learning*, *17*(3), 109. doi:10.14434/v17i3.22119

Gunawardena, C. N., & Zittle, F. J. (1997). Social presence as a predictor of satisfaction within a computer-mediated conferencing environment. *American Journal of Distance Education*, *11*(3), 8–26. doi:10.1080/08923649709526970

Hair, J. F., Black, W. C., Babin, B. J., & Anderson, R. E. (2010). *Multivariate Data Analysis* (7th ed.). Pearson.

Hair, J. F., Ringle, C. M., & Sarstedt, M. (2011). PLS-SEM: Indeed a silver bullet. *Journal of Marketing Theory and Practice*, *19*(2), 139–152. doi:10.2753/MTP1069-6679190202

Hakulinen, L., & Auvinen, T. (2014). The effect of gamification on students with different achievement goal orientations. *Proceedings - 2014 International Conference on Teaching and Learning in Computing and Engineering, LATICE 2014*, 9–16. 10.1109/LaTiCE.2014.10

Hamari, J. (2015). *Gamification - Motivations & Effects*. Academic Press.

Hanus, M. D., & Fox, J. (2015). Assessing the effects of gamification in the classroom: A longitudinal study on intrinsic motivation, social comparison, satisfaction, effort, and academic performance. *Computers & Education*, *80*(October), 152–161. doi:10.1016/j.compedu.2014.08.019

Hattie, J., Biggs, J., & Purdie, N. (1996). Effects of Learning Skills Interventions on Student Learning: A Meta-Analysis. *Review of Educational Research*, *66*(2), 99–136. doi:10.3102/00346543066002099

Heng, K. (2014). The Relationships between Student Engagement and the Academic Achievement of First-Year University Students in Cambodia. *The Asia-Pacific Education Researcher*, *23*(2), 179–189. doi:10.100740299-013-0095-8

Henseler, J., Ringle, C. M., & Sarstedt, M. (2015). A new criterion for assessing discriminant validity in variance-based structural equation modeling. *Journal of the Academy of Marketing Science*, *43*(1), 115–135. doi:10.100711747-014-0403-8

Hoyle, R. H. (1995). Structural equation modeling: Concepts, issues, and applications. *Sage (Atlanta, Ga.)*.

Huang, B., & Hew, K. F. (2018). Implementing a theory-driven gamification model in higher education flipped courses: Effects on out-of-class activity completion and quality of artifacts. *Computers & Education*, *125*, 254–272. doi:10.1016/j.compedu.2018.06.018

Huang, W. H. Y., & Soman, D. (2013). *A practitioner's guide to gamification of education. Research reports series, behavioural economics in action*. Academic Press.

Johnson, R. D., & Marakas, G. M. (2000). Research Report: The Role of Behavioral Modeling in Computer Skills Acquisition: Toward Refinement of the Model. *Information Systems Research*, *11*(4), 402–417. doi:10.1287/isre.11.4.402.11869

Jurgelaitis, M., Čeponienė, L., Čeponis, J., & Drungilas, V. (2019). Implementing gamification in a university-level UML modeling course: A case study. *Computer Applications in Engineering Education*, *27*(2), 332–343. doi:10.1002/cae.22077

Kapp, K. M. (2012). *The gamification of learning and instruction: game-based methods and strategies for training and education*. John Wiley & Sons.

Khaleel, F. L., Sahari Ashaari, N., Tengku Wook, T. S. M., & Ismail, A. (2016). Gamification Elements for Learning Applications. *International Journal on Advanced Science, Engineering and Information Technology*, *6*(6), 868–874. doi:10.18517/ijaseit.6.6.1379

Kline, R. B. (2011). *Principles and practice of structural equation modeling (3. Baskı)*. Guilford.

Kuo, M.-S., & Chuang, T.-Y. (2016). How gamification motivates visits and engagement for online academic dissemination – An empirical study. *Computers in Human Behavior*, *55*, 16–27. doi:10.1016/J.CHB.2015.08.025

Landers, R. N. (2014). Developing a Theory of Gamified Learning: Linking Serious Games and Gamification of Learning. *Simulation & Gaming*, *45*(6), 752–768. doi:10.1177/1046878114563660

Landers, R. N., & Landers, A. K. (2014). An Empirical Test of the Theory of Gamified Learning. *Simulation & Gaming*, *45*(6), 769–785. doi:10.1177/1046878114563662

Lerdpornkulrat, T., Koul, R., & Poondej, C. (2018). Relationship between perceptions of classroom climate and institutional goal structures and student motivation, engagement and intention to persist in college. *Journal of Further and Higher Education*, *42*(1), 102–115. doi:10.1080/0309877X.2016.1206855

Liaw, S. S., & Huang, H. M. (2013). Perceived satisfaction, perceived usefulness and interactive learning environments as predictors to self-regulation in e-learning environments. *Computers & Education*, *60*(1), 14–24. doi:10.1016/j.compedu.2012.07.015

Lister, M. (2015). Gamification: The effect on student motivation and performance at the post-secondary level. *Issues and Trends in Educational Technology*, *3*(2). Advance online publication. doi:10.2458/azu_itet_v3i2_Lister

Looyestyn, J., Kernot, J., Boshoff, K., Ryan, J., Edney, S., & Maher, C. (2017). Does gamification increase engagement with online programs? A systematic review. *PLoS One*, *12*(3), e0173403. doi:10.1371/journal.pone.0173403 PMID:28362821

McClarty, K. L., Orr, A., Frey, P. M., Dolan, R. P., Vassileva, V., & McVay, A. (2012). A Literature Review of Gaming in Education. *Gaming in Education*, 1–36.

McCoy, L., Lewis, J. H., & Dalton, D. (2016). Gamification and Multimedia for Medical Education: A Landscape Review. *The Journal of the American Osteopathic Association*, *116*(1), 22. doi:10.7556/jaoa.2016.003 PMID:26745561

Moore, D. L., & Tarnai, J. (2002). Evaluating nonresponse error in mail surveys. In R. M. Groves, D. A. Dillman, J. L. Eltinge, & R. J. A. Little (Eds.), *Survey Nonresponse* (pp. 197–211). John Wiley & Sons.

Noe, R. A., Tews, M. J., & McConnell Dachner, A. (2010). Learner engagement: A new perspective for enhancing our understanding of learner motivation and workplace learning. *The Academy of Management Annals*, *4*(1), 279–315. doi:10.5465/19416520.2010.493286

Ohn, K. M., Yusof, S., Urban, D., & Arifin, Z. (2018). ID NO. UMS001 TOPIC: Gamified Online Learning Design: GOLD for score in medical education. *University Carnival on e-Learning (IUCEL)*, 274.

Ohn, M. H., & Ohn, K. M. (2020). An evaluation study on gamified online learning experiences and its acceptance among medical students. *Tzu-Chi Medical Journal*, *32*(2), 211. PMID:32269957

Ohn, M. H., Ohn, K. M., Souza, U. D., Yusof, S., & Ariffin, Z. (2019). Effectiveness of innovative gamified learning among undergraduate medical students. *Journal of Physics: Conference Series*, *1358*(1), 012060.

Ortiz-Rojas, M., Chiluiza, K., & Valcke, M. (2017). Gamification in Computer Programming: Effects on Learning, Engagement, Self-Efficacy and Intrinsic Motivation. *The 11th European Conference on Game-Based Learning ECGBL 2017*, 507–514. 10.1109/EDUCON.2017.7943073

Özdener, N. (2018). Gamification for enhancing Web 2.0 based educational activities: The case of pre-service grade school teachers using educational Wiki pages. *Telematics and Informatics*, *35*(3), 564–578. doi:10.1016/j.tele.2017.04.003

Paas, F., Tuovinen, J. E., van Merriënboer, J. J. G., & Aubteen Darabi, A. (2005). A motivational perspective on the relation between mental effort and performance: Optimizing learner involvement in instruction. *Educational Technology Research and Development*, *53*(3), 25–34. doi:10.1007/BF02504795

Pakinee, A., & Puritat, K. (2021). Designing a gamified e-learning environment for teaching undergraduate ERP course based on big five personality traits. *Education and Information Technologies*, *26*(4), 4049–4067. doi:10.100710639-021-10456-9 PMID:33613080

Pappas, C. (2017). What are the most effective uses of gamification in learning? *How Gamification Reshapes Learning*.

Patrício, R., Moreira, A. C., & Zurlo, F. (2018). Gamification approaches to the early stage of innovation. *Creativity and Innovation Management*, *27*(4), 499–511. doi:10.1111/caim.12284

Patrício, R., Moreira, A. C., & Zurlo, F. (2021). Enhancing design thinking approaches to innovation through gamification. *European Journal of Innovation Management*, *24*(5), 1569–1594. doi:10.1108/ejim-06-2020-0239

Peng, W., Lin, J.-H., Pfeiffer, K. A., & Winn, B. (2012). Need Satisfaction Supportive Game Features as Motivational Determinants: An Experimental Study of a Self-Determination Theory Guided Exergame. *Media Psychology*, *15*(2), 175–196. doi:10.1080/15213269.2012.673850

Peterson, R. A. (1994). A meta-analysis of Cronbach's coefficient alpha. *The Journal of Consumer Research*, *21*(2), 381–391. doi:10.1086/209405

Pettit, R. K., McCoy, L., Kinney, M., & Schwartz, F. N. (2014). A multimedia audience response game show for medical education. *Medical Science Educator*, *24*(2), 181–187. doi:10.100740670-014-0038-x

Podsakoff, P. M., & Organ, D. W. (1986). Self-reports in organizational research: Problems and prospects. *Journal of Management*, *12*(4), 531–544. doi:10.1177/014920638601200408

Polo-Peña, A. I., Frías-Jamilena, D. M., & Fernández-Ruano, M. L. (2020). Influence of gamification on perceived self-efficacy: Gender and age moderator effect. *International Journal of Sports Marketing & Sponsorship*. Advance online publication. doi:10.1108/IJSMS-02-2020-0020

Poondej, C., & Lerdpornkulrat, T. (2016). Relationship between motivational goal orientations, perceptions of general education classroom learning environment, and deep approaches to learning. *Kasetsart Journal of Social Sciences*, *37*(2), 100–103. doi:10.1016/J.KJSS.2015.01.001

Rajani, N. B., Mastellos, N., & Filippidis, F. T. (2021). Impact of gamification on the self-efficacy and motivation to quit of smokers: Observational study of two gamified smoking cessation mobile apps. *JMIR Serious Games*, *9*(2), e27290. PMID:33904824

Ribeiro, L., Leal da Silva, T., & Quadrado Mussi, A. (2018). Gamification: A methodology to motivate engagement and participation in a higher education environment. *International Journal of Education and Research*, *6*(4), 249–264.

Richter, N. F., Cepeda, G., Roldán, J. L., & Ringle, C. M. (2015). European management research using partial least squares structural equation modeling (PLS-SEM). *European Management Journal, 33*(1), 1–3. doi:10.2196/27290

Sailer, M., Hense, J. U., Mayr, S. K., & Mandl, H. (2017). How gamification motivates: An experimental study of the effects of specific game design elements on psychological need satisfaction. *Computers in Human Behavior, 69*, 371–380. doi:10.1016/J.CHB.2016.12.033

Schaufeli, W. B., Martínez, I. M., Pinto, A. M., Salanova, M., & Barker, A. B. (2002). Burnout and engagement in university students a cross-national study. *Journal of Cross-Cultural Psychology, 33*(5), 464–481. doi:10.1177/0022022102033005003

Shin, N., Sutherland, L. M., Norris, C. A., & Soloway, E. (2012). Effects of game technology on elementary student learning in mathematics. *British Journal of Educational Technology, 43*(4), 540–560. doi:10.1111/j.1467-8535.2011.01197.x

Simões, J., Redondo, R. D., & Vilas, A. F. (2013). A social gamification framework for a K-6 learning platform. *Computers in Human Behavior, 29*(2), 345–353. doi:10.1016/j.chb.2012.06.007

Singer, E., van Hoewyk, J., & Maher, M. P. (2000). Experiments with incentives in telephone surveys. *Public Opinion Quarterly, 64*, 171–188. doi:10.1086/317761 PMID:10984332

Sousa-Vieira, M. E., Ferreira-Pires, O., López-Ardao, J. C., & Fernández-Veiga, M. (2021). *Effectiveness of Gamification in Undergraduate Education*. doi:10.5220/0010495603760385

Sun, P.-C. C., Tsai, R. J., Finger, G., Chen, Y.-Y. Y., & Yeh, D. (2008). What drives a successful e-Learning? An empirical investigation of the critical factors influencing learner satisfaction. *Computers & Education, 50*(4), 1183–1202. doi:10.1016/j.compedu.2006.11.007

Tabachnik, B. G., & Fidell, L. S. (2007). *Using multivariate statistics* (5th ed.). Allyn and Bacon.

Tay, L. (2010). Employers: Look to gaming to motivate staff. *IT News for Australian Business.*

Toda, A. M., do Carmo, R. M., da Silva, A. P., Bittencourt, I. I., & Isotani, S. (2019). An approach for planning and deploying gamification concepts with social networks within educational contexts. *International Journal of Information Management, 46*, 294–303. doi:10.1016/j.ijinfomgt.2018.10.001

Vallerand, R. J., Blais, M. R., Brière, N. M., & Pelletier, L. G. (1989). Construction et validation de l'échelle de motivation en éducation (EME). *Canadian Journal of Behavioural Science/Revue Canadienne Des Sciences Du Comportement, 21*(3), 323.

Wang, M.-T., & Eccles, J. S. (2013). School context, achievement motivation, and academic engagement: A longitudinal study of school engagement using a multidimensional perspective. *Learning and Instruction, 28*, 12–23. doi:10.1016/J.LEARNINSTRUC.2013.04.002

Werbach, K. (2014). (Re) defining gamification: A process approach. In *International conference on persuasive technology* (pp. 266–272). Springer. 10.1007/978-3-319-07127-5_23

Whitton, N., & Moseley, A. (2014). Deconstructing Engagement. *Simulation & Gaming, 45*(4–5), 433–449. doi:10.1177/1046878114554755

Wilson, K. A., Bedwell, W. L., Lazzara, E., Salas, E., Burke, S. C., Estock, J. L., Orvis, K. L., & Conkey, C. (2009). Relationships between game attributes and learning outcomes: Review and research proposals. *Simulation & Gaming*, *40*(2), 217–266. doi:10.1177/1046878108321866

Yi, M. Y., & Davis, F. D. (2003). Developing and Validating an Observational Learning Model of Computer Software Training and Skill Acquisition. *Information Systems Research*, *14*(2), 146–169. doi:10.1287/isre.14.2.146.16016

Zhao, C.-M., & Kuh, G. D. (2004). Adding Value: Learning Communities and Student Engagement. *Research in Higher Education*, *45*(2), 115–138. doi:10.1023/B:RIHE.0000015692.88534.de

Zichermann, G., & Cunningham, C. (2011). *Gamification by design: Implementing game mechanics in web and mobile apps*. O'Reilly Media, Inc.

Chapter 6
The Efficacy of Gamification for the Involvement of Students in Distance Education

Fernando S. C. Pimentel
https://orcid.org/0000-0002-9180-8691
Federal University of Alagoas, Brazil

Daniel A. M. de Barros
https://orcid.org/0000-0002-1788-3474
Federal University of Alagoas, Brazil

Janaina M. da Silva
https://orcid.org/0000-0001-7491-2254
Federal University of Alagoas, Brazil

Emerson M. P. da Silva
Federal University of Alagoas, Brazil

Margarida M. Marques
https://orcid.org/0000-0002-4325-9122
Research Centre on Didactics and Technology in the Education of Trainers (CIDTFF), Department of Education and Psychology, University of Aveiro, Portugal

ABSTRACT

This chapter presents quantitative research that analyzes gamification's effectiveness in a distance learning mathematics undergraduate course. First, the growth of the culture of digital games and the development of gamification from a methodological perspective were discussed. Then, the fundamentals regarding gamification in distance education are presented. Methodologically, the research followed the research steps done by Rahman, Ahmad, and Hashim with some adaptations are indicated in this chapter. The data collection instrument used for this investigation consisted of a questionnaire for 37 students. The research data suggest that gamification promoted students' engagement with learning. It is concluded that the categories presented in the study indicate that students perceive gamification as an alternative to create more dynamic classes and promote learning.

INTRODUCTION

In the contemporary educational scenario, students' lack of interest, motivation and engagement are identified both face-to-face and Distance Learning (DL) contexts. Student motivation and engagement

DOI: 10.4018/978-1-6684-4287-6.ch006

during learning processes is a relevant problematic to study, since the more the student is involved and motivated to learn, the more likely it is to occur (Rahman et al., 2018). In this sense, institutions have been seeking to take advantage of techniques and tools to engage students and, thus, to enable more effective teaching and learning processes (Rahman et al., 2018). In addition, the digital culture pervasiveness has been prompting researchers and teachers to develop methods that integrate digital technologies, such as digital games, with teaching and learning processes (Gee, 2003; Zichermann & Cunningham, 2011; Prensky, 2012).

Regarding DL, it is seen as an educational modality in which the pedagogical mediation processes take place through digital technologies, where teachers and students may be in diverse geographic environments and time zones (Moore & Kearsley, 2007). In addition, the pedagogical processes that occur in DL are different from those that occur in face-to-face environments, thus requiring adequate planning, focused on this modality's specific needs.

In the last few years, DL has been moving into the spotlight and expanding through the occupation of spaces that face-to-face educational processes are unable to fill in. For example, it allows students to be more active in the teaching and learning processes through the development of their autonomy while building their own knowledge (Moore & Kearsley, 2007). The demand for methods that increase students' motivation and engagement in the construction of knowledge becomes urgent, which brings us back to methodologies that involve digital games' elements, such as gamification.

In the student motivation and engagement perspective, a relevant aspect of gamification is the narrative, with the ability to promote playful scenarios that can favor the construction of knowledge. What is sought is that students become involved in a universe in which learning becomes less tiring than in methods focused on content exposure, for example (Domínguez et al., 2013). Another issue to highlight is the game balance, which requires, for instance, finding the balance between the player's skills and the challenges that are presented to him. This balance provides a more intense immersive experience, in which the player remains in a state of flux of constant challenge, between the borders of boredom and anxiety, according to the Flow theory (Csikszentmihalyi, 2008). Consequently, the balance of the game promotes motivation in the player to advance in what is proposed, helping him/her in the improvement or acquisition of skills, as well as in the construction of knowledge (Whitson & Consoli, 2009). In this sense, developing gamification in educational environments, aiming to promote student involvement in teaching and learning processes, has been a fertile field for research with promising results for teachers and students (Swacha, 2021).

It is in the above presented perspective that gamification fits as a method that uses the elements of games in non-game environments to promote engagement and motivation among those involved (Kapp, 2012). Going deeper into the educational dimension, it is worth mentioning that gamification not only intents to motivate and engage students, but it also aims at learning processes based on the interaction between those involved, the technologies and the context in which they are inserted (Pimentel, 2018). In this way, teaching and learning processes may integrate game elements to promote student success (Al-Azawi et al., 2016).

When successful gamification techniques are used, it is possible to transform simple tasks into pleasurable learning processes for students, because it can minimize unpleasant emotions characteristic in traditional educational formats. For example, in gamification one can learn from failures, which are typical and naturally accepted in game contexts, without facing embarrassment situations (Huang & Soman, 2013).

Game elements incorporated in teaching and learning may use automatic elements or social elements. The first one includes points, achievement badges, levels or simply time restrictions, allowing the student to compete autonomously. The second, on the other hand, inserts students into shared communities where achievements and progresses are public and preferably regularly updated, concurring to a sense of increased participation and motivation to learn (Huang & Soman, 2013).

Considering the above, student motivation and engagement in DL contexts still require further research (Rahman et al., 2018). In this line, this chapter presents a quantitative survey study (Ponto, 2015) of the effectiveness of a gamification approach in the involvement of students in DL, from the perspective of Brazilian higher education students. For this, a theoretical context of gamification is presented, including its bases in digital games and the perspective of increasing students' motivation and engagement for the construction of knowledge, based on scientific literature. In addition, an in-depth look at gamification in education is made, especially regarding gamification in distance education contexts.

The data collection instrument used for this investigation consisted of a survey questionnaire, with its development in the form of a self-report, as the respondent himself must complete it. The questionnaire is aimed at students in 'Degree in Mathematics' course, at the blind review (blind review), in the context of the Open University of Brazil (OUB). In this data gathering instrument, the variables of perceived utility, ease of use, attitude towards gamification, skill engagement, and interaction engagement were considered, as observed in the study developed by Rahman and colleagues (2018).

The analysis of the data collected indicates that the students of this distance learning course perceive positively the use of gamification in the teaching and learning processes.

Despite this result, it is necessary to develop more empirical research on the students' perception of the effectiveness of gamification in other courses, also considering the contents of the disciplines. In this sense, the chapter is relevant for the scientific community, as it will present a quantitative investigation of the effectiveness of gamification in DL, with data showing that gamification has promoted greater student engagement.

GAMIFICATION IN EDUCATION

Technological growth in recent years favored the increasing number of digital games fans, being these present in the lives of much of the population. The Survey Game Brazil 2021 (Sioux Group & Go Gamers, 2021) shows that about 72% of Brazilians play digital games. This expression has a much greater meaning than the number itself, as digital games are pointed as already being part of the culture (Huizinga, 2014) and they reach a diverse audience, from different genders and social classes.

According to the yearbook of the Asociación Española de Videojuegos (AEVI, 2019), digital games appear as the main audiovisual and cultural choice in Spain, with a revenue of 1,479 million euros for the digital games industry in 2019. Data shows players' profile, being 58% men and 42% women. Overall, these players devote 6.7 hours per week to play (AEVI, 2019). This high acceptance of games and digital games happened for several reasons, such as the variety of game genres available or the increasingly realistic sound and visual effects in each new game generation.

The game experience is more than just fun. The game is a significant experience for the full development of the subject, as it allows him/her to develop skills, such as the ones focused on social aspects, creativity, and imagination (Lázaro, 2019). In this sense, Huizinga (2014) states that the game can be defined as a voluntary activity, with established rules, where the environment indices a series of emotions and feelings in the players.

The literature mentions that digital Game-Based Learning (DGBL) is more meaningful and fun, when compared to traditional methods (Van Eck, 2015). One of the factors that contribute to this is the fact that students are embedded within the digital culture and are already using games at various times of their daily lives (Prensky, 2012). Therefore, from the theory (DGBL) and how game culture researchers analyze the development of new relationships between games and learning, it is argued that the rise of game culture has given rise to a trend, which aims to provide people with the same feeling, motivation and engagement caused by games in any environment, digital or analogue. According to Kapp (2012), gamification is characterized by the application of game design elements in an environment unrelated to the game, to promote interaction, motivation and audience engagement through problem solving.

Game design elements can be used in different environments, such as within educational environments, enhancing learning (Busarello, 2016). For Van Eck (2015) gamification is one of the DGBL variations. In addition to Kapp's (2012) concept, Pimentel (2018, p. 78) proposed that "[...] gamification is the process of using game mechanics, style and thinking, in a non-game context, as a medium to engage and motivate people, aiming at learning through interactions among people, technologies and the environment", where the concept of technology comprises its critical view of the human-technology relationship.

The design elements found in games, and which are used in gamification, act directly on the motivation of individuals. This motivation can be classified as an intrinsic or extrinsic. According to Bussarello (2016), intrinsic motivation causes a greater engagement in the individual, as it is associated with emotions and meanings, and can be much more lasting. On the other hand, extrinsic motivation is also important, as factors such as external rewards (e.g., score attribution associated with performance) also promote significant engagement in individuals. Pimentel (2018) indicates that the main goal of gamification in the educational field is associated with the engagement and motivation of individuals through their interaction with other people, with the world around them, and with technologies (whether analog or digital) for the development of learning experiences. Thus, it is understood that the perceptions placed in relation to the game have allowed the use of its elements in teaching-learning processes. This reasoning is also explained because gamification allows for a more flexible application, whether in online or offline environments (Sanmugam, Abdullah et. al., 2016), and it is not necessary for gamification to occur exclusively with the integration of digital technologies.

With the adoption of gamification in education it is expected to be able to engage and involve students in learning. This is because it is understood that there is a relationship between the student's involvement in a set of activities and positive results regarding the individual's development, which includes satisfaction, persistence, performance, and social involvement. Therefore, one of the biggest challenges in the context of education is to think about how to make students remain motivated for the time necessary to learn (Eltegani & Butgereit, 2015). All this adds to the claim that gamification has the potential to motivate and involve students in teaching-learning processes and to contribute to student's active role.

Engagement has to do with some improvements acquired in the teaching-learning process, such as cognitive development, student satisfaction, better grades, and persistence. In this way, it can be achieved through well-defined goals and assuring students stay on task. In gamification planning, initially student interest and engagement with the course should be encouraged; then active engagement with the learning materials and finally appropriate assessment with feedback that allows for an understanding of what has been learned (Eltegani & Butgereit, 2015).

In the educational field, it is possible to observe that gamification influences as a learning tool and provokes collaborative behavior, as students prefer to learn in a playful way. However, to be successful in using gamification, one must be active and willing to deal with any issues that may arise, and offer feedback where necessary (Lazarus, 2019). In gamification, collaboration may provide teamwork by allowing students to master a range of problems and challenges that they otherwise would not be able to overcome on their own. A gamification proposal that advocates individual activities may cause certain actions to result in feelings of competence (Sailer, 2020).

GAMIFICATION IN DISTANCE EDUCATION

Distance Education (DE) has gained relevant space in the contemporary social context. One of the reasons is the strong presence of digital technologies in our daily lives, serving as instruments for solving a wide variety of problems. Such technologies allow an acceleration of events in society. Moreover, thinking of education only from a face-to-face perspective, with fixed study hours and physical displacement of teachers and students, becomes a counterpoint to a scenario where mobility and ubiquity provided by digital technologies. These technologies can allow greater interaction between people in different times and spaces, increasing productivity in the execution of tasks. Thus, DE is an educational modality in which pedagogical mediation takes place with the support of digital technologies, providing communication between teachers and students that may be separated in time and space (Moore & Kearsley, 2007), in an adaptation to current social demands.

Another point to be highlighted is that DE has occupied spaces that face-to-face education cannot reach, in addition to allowing students to take a more active role in the teaching and learning processes through the development of their autonomy (Moore & Kearsley, 2007). Many DE students choose this teaching mode due to the possibility of being able to reconcile their personal and professional schedules with study (Gillett-Swan, 2017; Kortemeyer, 2016). However, the autonomy and organization levels required are constant challenges for students in this modality, which is evident in the high dropout rates compared to face-to-face teaching (Vogel et al., 2018).

According to Bitterncourt and Mercado (2014), the dropout rate is directly related to the institution that offers the course. In this sense, it is necessary that the institution develops experiences that promote student engagement with the course, minimize dissatisfaction with tutors and teachers and encourage didactic-pedagogical development. These strategies aim to overcome possible limitations and problems with the support technology. Another strategy is the improvement of face-to-face meetings, as moments of configuration of hybrid and multimodal spaces of coexistence. Therefore, when planning a discipline or a course in the DE modality, special attention is needed to aspects such as student motivation and engagement (Rahman et al., 2018). In other words, it is essential to look for methods that promote these aspects, so that the student does not drop out of the course and build their knowledge in a pleasurable way. This assumption leads us to consider the gamification perspective, as it involves the constituent elements of digital games, being a common language for contemporary students.

In general, institutions that offer DE courses use learning management platforms known as Virtual Learning Environments (VLE), such as Moodle. Such platforms are designed to provide the various DE actors (teachers, tutors, students, administrators) a system that makes it possible to create personalized learning environments, becoming the means where students develop their activities, building knowledge with their colleagues and teachers in the diverse collaborative tools available, such as forums, wikis, chats, and blogs. These collaborative tools are designed as spaces for interaction and knowledge exchange. But, as previously mentioned, DE students spend much of their study time in a solitary way, exercising their autonomy in learning, supported by study contents proposed by the teacher, which can in some cases generate discouragement (Hartnett, 2019). The motivation of the DE student is identified as a success factor for this modality (Hartnett, 2016; 2019).

To plan a course or discipline in DE, it is relevant to know the profile of the students who will participate, in order to understand what can or cannot be implemented to achieve the aimed educational objectives, without losing sight of the motivation issue. In general, DE students tend to be heterogeneous in terms of goals and preferences for learning methods, and each one may employ different cognitive and metacognitive strategies to learn (Koper, 2015). Thus, planning is carried out considering interests, preferences, learning needs and previous experiences of students, aiming to build a favorable learning environment, based on strategies or methods that motivate them while they learn (Hartnett, 2016; 2019). Understanding that most contemporary students have digital wisdom (Prensky, 2012) and that they have a daily habit of playing digital games (Sioux Group & Go Gamers, 2021; AEVI, 2019) may support the strategic option of selecting gamification to promote the needed motivation for student involvement in the learning process, especially regarding the DE modality.

Motivated by the growing number of researches on gamification in other areas, interest in gamification and in its use has also increased in the area of education (Lee & Doh, 2012). According to Kapp (2012), gamification has the potential to influence, engage and motivate people, which can respond to the growing interest in research on this topic. However, studies that present an overview of the gamification strategies investigated in the context of higher education and teacher education are still elementary. This instigates new research to deepen the theme, as well as studies that confront this reality with the theoretical proposition of Connectivism (Downes, 2005; 2007; Siemens, 2010; 2012). This theory defends the assumption that learning consists of the ability to build, remain and circulate in networks of connection through digital technologies, with the aim of developing the ability to reflect, decide and share information.

For Braga and Obregon (2015), gamification strategies are the way to insert the elements of digital games in the context of learning, transforming the contents so that they can be made available in an online environment. For Deterding (2011), a gamification strategy is based on three main aspects, namely, meaning, domain and autonomy, which combines gamification with DE, as it requires students with a more autonomous profile.

Gamification and its applications in the educational field have been the target of a series of production and research initiatives on apps, software and theories on the process of using game design in educational activities. Schlemmer (2015, 2016) points a set of favorable implications for teaching and learning. For Pimentel (2018), gamification in education must go beyond the fun elements, without ceasing to use such elements, promoting more and more interactive learning experiences, since gamification works from the perspective of building experiences that can motivate students to study.

When well planned, gamification can be a method capable of motivating and engaging students in their activities while immersed in a narrative that playfully involves them in the learning process (Huang & Soman, 2013; Al-Azawi et al., 2016; Rahman et al., 2018). However, it is necessary to support this idea with real data on the effectiveness of gamification in DE. In this sense, some studies have already shown positive aspects regarding the implementation of gamification in DE, as can be seen in Alabbasi (2017), Kaufmann (2018) and Oliveira e Silva (2020).

According to Alabbasi (2017), students have a positive perception regarding gamification in DE, as they believe that the incorporation of game elements generates feelings of belonging and reduced loneliness, increases connectivity, decreases boredom, anxiety and stress in the learning process. However, the author points limitations this study, namely regarding the small sample size and the short period of gamification use, making it difficult to understand students' perception in long-term use. Another highlighted limitation is that among the game elements, only game mechanics were used in this particular study.

Studies by Kaufmann (2018) indicate that gamification helps students to overcome the complexities of academic challenges, based on their engagement in the learning process. In addition, it points out that the isolation and little feedback, between teacher and student, can be compensated through a process of continuous student reward, and that the student's creativity work in a gamified environment can lead to academic success and satisfaction with their course, faculty and the academic program in general. According to the study of Oliveira and Silva (2020), students are able to identify that gamification promotes the academic achievement; however, they claim that the aspects of scoring, medals and confidentiality should be improved.

A study of particular relevance for the present research is one conducted by Rahman et al. (2018). In face of the discussions on the extent to which gamification can promote student engagement, the authors carried out an investigation to analyze the effectiveness of gamification to improve student engagement. The investigation was carried out within a discipline of Database Design of the Information and Communication Technology Department at Polytechnic Muadzam Shah Pahang, Malaysia. Fifty students participated in this research. In the first phase of the study, the students participated in gamified classes, and in the second phase a questionnaire was applied. The questionnaire assessed the acceptance of gamification and its effects on students and student involvement during classes. This questionnaire was based on the Technology Acceptance Model (TAM); thus, the result of this adaptation was the creation of the Gamification Acceptance Model (GAM).

Rahman et al. (2018) used analysis categories that proposed in the Gamification Acceptance Model (GAM):

1. Perceived Usefulness Items (PU): degree to which students believe gamification will increase their learning performance;
2. Perceived Ease of Use Items (PEOU): degree to which students expect gamification to be user-friendly;
3. Attitude (A): students' attitude towards gamification;
4. Skill Engagement (SKE): student's engagement in skills practice, which includes general learning strategies;
5. Interaction Engagement (IE): involvement in participation/interaction in the class.

As Figure 1 shows, PU category is influenced by the PEOU, and both affect A. The latter can influence engagement in relation to skill development - Skill Engagement (SKE) -, and participation/interaction in class - Interaction Engagement (IE).

In analyzing and discussing the data, Rahman et al. (2018) indicate that gamification technology used in the educational environment should be easy to use and be appealing to students to the point of increasing engagement in activities. This involvement, or engagement, can be defined as the positive and enduring work-related mental state characterized by vigor, dedication and immersion. This concept is directly related to the assumptions of the self-determination theory of Deci & Ryan (2004), widely used in the context of employee management.

Figure 1. Gamification acceptance model (GAM) (adapted from Rahman et al., 2018)

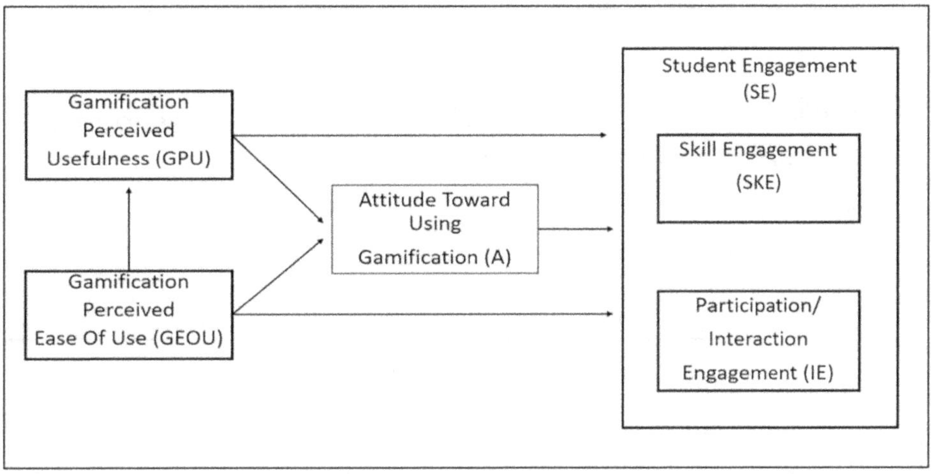

The self-determination theory (SDT), proposed by Ryan & Deci (2000) can be understood as a macro-theory, because it focuses on the influence of the satisfaction of basic psychological needs on the motivation and well-being of the individual. The authors argue that these needs are at the basis of motivation and personality integration.

In the context of gamification, flow theory (Csikszentmihalyi, 2008), which is conceptualized as a mental state of immersion in an activity, with a sense of intensified focus, total involvement and enjoyment in the process of the activity, may be associated with SDT theory to understand how motivation and engagement promote satisfactory learning outcomes.

METHODOLOGY

This research theoretical foundation was based on studies on the relationship of metacognition and DE courses, allowing the planning and development of this study, involving students from the curricular unit 'Information and Communication Technology for Distance Learning'. In this research, metacognition refers to any cognitive knowledge or process related to the evaluation, monitoring and adjustment of cognition (Flavell, 1979).

All participants are students of the "Degree in Mathematics", at the Federal University of Alagoas (Ufal), in the context of the distance learning courses offered by this institution and are part of the Open University of Brazil (OUB) network.

The research was carried out in the set of activities developed by the Virtual Communities Research Group – Ufal, and followed all ethical requirements, including the determinations of the Brazilian General Data Protection Law. Participants had their identities preserved, being able to participate in the study or leave it at any time.

OUB offers bachelor's, degree, specialization and master's courses in Brazil since 2006. At the Ufal, OUB started in 2007 and continues its activities, mainly in teacher training courses (Pimentel & Mercado, 2019).

Figure 2. Operational framework

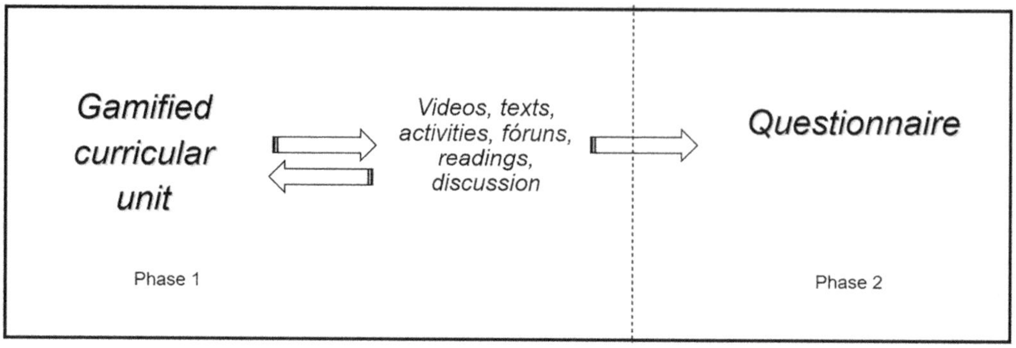

The research model adopted in this quantitative survey study (Ponto, 2015) is an adaptation of the study carried out by Rahman, et al (2018), comprising two phases: (1) realization of the gamified discipline; (2) application of the questionnaire (Figure 2).

In phase 1, the curricular unit was carried out, using dynamics, mechanics and components of digital games, transforming the methodology of the curricular unit. It has a workload of 60 hours and was developed over a two months period. Most students in this study used the computer to access the curricular units' virtual learning environment, set in a gamified way, using the institution's Moodle. Texts, videos, discussion forums, readings, discussion in virtual classes and other individual or pair activities were used. Table 1 shows some of the procedures of how the elements of games were inserted in the development of gamification.

The curricular unit is offered in the 1st semester of the 'Degree in Mathematics' course. Its objectives are as follows: 1) To train teachers to use technologies in the school environment, as a tool in exploring the possibilities of ICT in relation to the construction of knowledge, developing skills for using technologies critically; 2) To analyze school incorporation of resources sustained by new technologies; 3) To select available technological materials taking into consideration educational criteria, and use them both critically and didactically; 4) To introduce ICT in the teaching-learning processes, with themes of interest for students' specialty and from practical models.

The curricular unit adopted a gamified methodology, with practical activities using Internet resources. The narrative used elements from the Star Wars saga. The course is designed in 8 phases, all named after the titles of the Star Wars films. The titles of the phases were chosen by relating the theme to the phase's content and the proposed activities. Work was carried out in pairs and in individual work with reference texts/activities for discussion. Analyses of experiences and studies involving the use of digital technologies in education were carried out. Finally, the students were required to produce a lesson plan.

Phase 2 included the questionnaire application, after phase 1 conclusion. It is a self-administered tool, where the respondent must fill it out, and addresses questions related to the following categories: Perceived Usefulness Items (PU); Perceived Ease of Use Items (PEOU); Attitude (A); Skill Engagement (SKE) and Interaction Engagement (IE). It was developed and validated by Rahman, et al (2018).

The questionnaire was made available online, through Google Forms (https://forms.gle/rHEw4p9uv-vX2wMAT8), and contained two parts. The first part comprises three demographic questions and the second part contains 18 questions distributed to the categories presented in Table 2. Questions 4 to 21

Table 1. Elements and procedures of gamification

Dynamics	Progression	Students had to complete the activities of a certain phase (stage) to be able to access another phase. Students could complete the activities until they reached the required score.
	Narrative	The narrative was built from the Star Wars films. Each of the stages was inspired by one of the films, such as Rogue One, Star Wars: the rise of skywalker, The last Jedi, The Force Awakens, Return of the Jedi, The Empire Strikes Back, Revenge of the Sith, Attack of the clones…
Mechanics	Challenges	The course activities were designed as challenges that the student had to complete in order to reach the score that would allow them to advance to the next level. The time factor was also thought of as a challenge, as the students had a certain amount of time to complete each activity.
	Cooperation	Some challenges were designed to be carried out in pairs, others in groups. In the individual challenges, students could communicate, exchanging ideas, information, content or strategies for the development of the challenges, collaborating with each other.
	Feedbacks	The feedbacks were done by the subject teacher through a discussion forum, or using the chat available in the learning environment. A tutor also provided feedback on the activities, indicating what the students had accomplished and whether the learning objectives had been met.
Components	Points	Each challenge had a point scale that depended on how long the activity was completed or how well the rules were followed. The students were aware of what score they could achieve, because in each challenge it was presented how many points could be achieved.
	Levels	The course was divided into 8 phases. Each stage corresponded to a level. The course did not follow an obligatory linearity, as it was possible for students to be in different levels during the same week of activities
	Ranking	At the end of each phase the teacher made the students' ranking available.
	Avatar	At the beginning of the course the students had to create their avatar (a graphical representation of the user, the user's character or persona) that expressed their identity in the Star Wars saga. The avatar should be in the student's profile in the learning environment.

were prepared with a 5-point Likert scale (1 - strongly disagree, 2 - disagree, 3 - neutral, 4 - agree and 5 - strongly agree).

Collected data were analyzed with Jamovi 1.8.2, R 4.1.0 and RStudio Desktop, systematizing the data and allowing the analysis by the research team. The Cronbach´s alpha of the categories is presented in Table 2. This result considers that the instrument is highly reliable (Cohen, Manion & Morrison, 2018), even considering that in PEOU and in IE we have results above 0.9. Such a result may indicate that some of the items are redundant, but in this research, we preferred not to change the original questionnaire due to validity issues.

The gamification effectiveness in student engagement was measured through the applied questionnaire as the questions were answered. Questionnaires were made available, but validated answers corresponded to students who attended the curricular unit, and later all answers were turned into graphs and the numbers are presented in percentages.

For the analysis of the categories, we used the formula for the sum of the items, given that the procedure proposed by Likert does not analyze the individual questions or items, but rather their sum (BOONE JR.; BOONE, 2012).

Table 2. Questionnaire analysis categories, corresponding questions and computed Cronbach's Alpha

Analysis category	Questions	Cronbach's Alpha
Perceived Usefulness Items (PU)	4, 5, 6, 7	0.888
Perceived Ease of Use Items (PEOU)	8, 9, 10, 11	0.916
Attitude (A)	12, 13, 14	0.883
Skill Engagement (SKE)	15, 16, 17	0.856
Interaction Engagement (IE)	18, 19, 20, 21	0.902

Example of the formula used:
=ROUND.UP((SUM(F2;H2;J2;X2;)/4);0)

DATA ANALYSIS AND DISCUSSION

Demographic Analysis

The questionnaire obtained 37 answers (N=37), but 8 answers were invalidated (N2= 8), as they were repeated or from students who did not attend the course. Thus, 29 responses were validated (N3=29). As the total number of students who completed the course was 55 students (16 from the Maceió hub, 14 from the Palmeira hub, 11 from the Penedo hub, 3 from the Delmiro hub and 11 from the Camaragibe hub), N3 corresponds to 52.72% of total students.

In the first part of the questionnaire, participating students answered three questions that allow a demographic overview (polo city, gender and age). Of the 29 student respondents, 15 are male and 16 female. This occurrence is not common in exact sciences courses in Brazil, when the majority are male students. This data raises the hypothesis that this result has its origin in the fact that it is a degree course that is more sought after by women than by men. This hypothesis may or may not be confirmed by other studies.

Figure 3 shows data regarding participants' age. Data was collected in a five options scale, starting from 18 years old. The most frequent age-range was 18 to 22 (10 respondents), as can be expected in a 1st semester class. However, this particular cohort of respondents includes students from all age-ranges, revealing an heterogenous group.

Category Analysis

In Table 3, with the descriptives of the categories, it is observed that the mean of the responses is higher for the categories attitude (4.21), usefulness (4.17) and interaction engagement (4.14). The significance level for these data was $p<.001$. This result indicates that the proposed gamified course met its objectives in terms of promoting student engagement and learning, but it also shows that other activities can be proposed for a higher result in the "ease of use" and "skill engagement" categories.

Figure 4 presents a synthesis of the analysis of all questions, related to the five categories (PU; PEOU; A; SKE and IE). The results reveal a tendency for the participants to confirm the effectiveness

Figure 3. Graph presenting participants' age

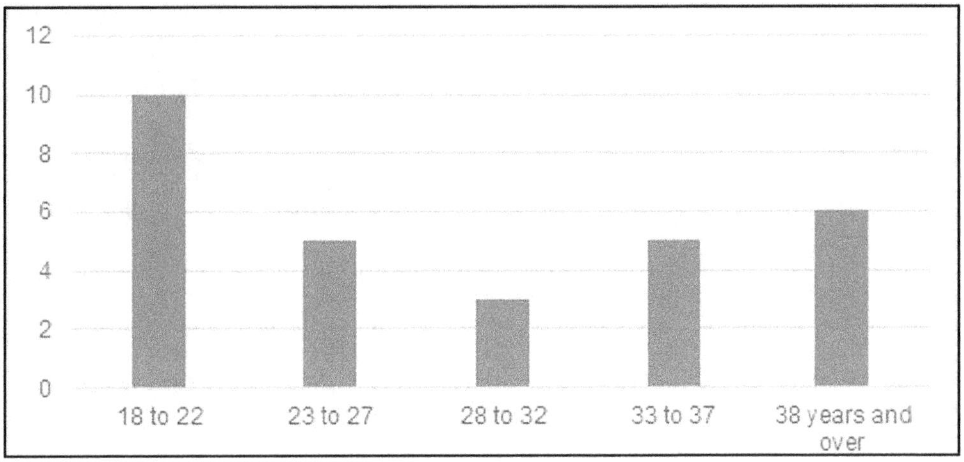

of gamification in promoting their involvement in the curricular unit, as the option 'totally disagree' was not selected. These results are in line with the study developed by Rahman, et al (2018).

Follows a more detailed analysis of the results, considering each category.

Perceived Usefulness (PU)

Most respondents (82.8%) agree with the usefulness of the gamification approach conducted in this study. Moreover, Figure 5 highlights that 41.4% of respondents agreed with the usefulness of the gamification and another 41.4% strongly agreed. This shows that the majority of students agreed that using gamification in the classroom can benefit their learning experience.

In this perspective, the graph in Figure 5 corroborates the findings for the PU category of the study carried out by Rahman et al (2018), which indicates that all students who participated in the research agreed that gamification is useful and that its use within the educational context can benefit teaching and learning processes. This perception of usefulness in relation to gamification is positively related to the educational experience of students. From this perspective, it is necessary that students involved in the gamification process understand that they can learn from the material or strategy being applied, thus generating satisfaction and/or meaning in relation to their learning (Bussarello, 2016).

Thus, acknowledging that gamification is useful for student learning, its use in the educational field emerges as a possibility to develop situations that enhance learning, specifically in the DE context.

Table 3. Descriptive categories

	Ease of Use	Attitude	Usefulness	Skill Engagement	Interaction Engagement	
N	29	29	29	29	29	
Mean	3.97	4.21	4.17	3.97	4.14	
Standard deviation	0.778	0.902	0.889	0.944	0.833	

Figure 4. Graph presenting the analysis of all questions related to the five categories

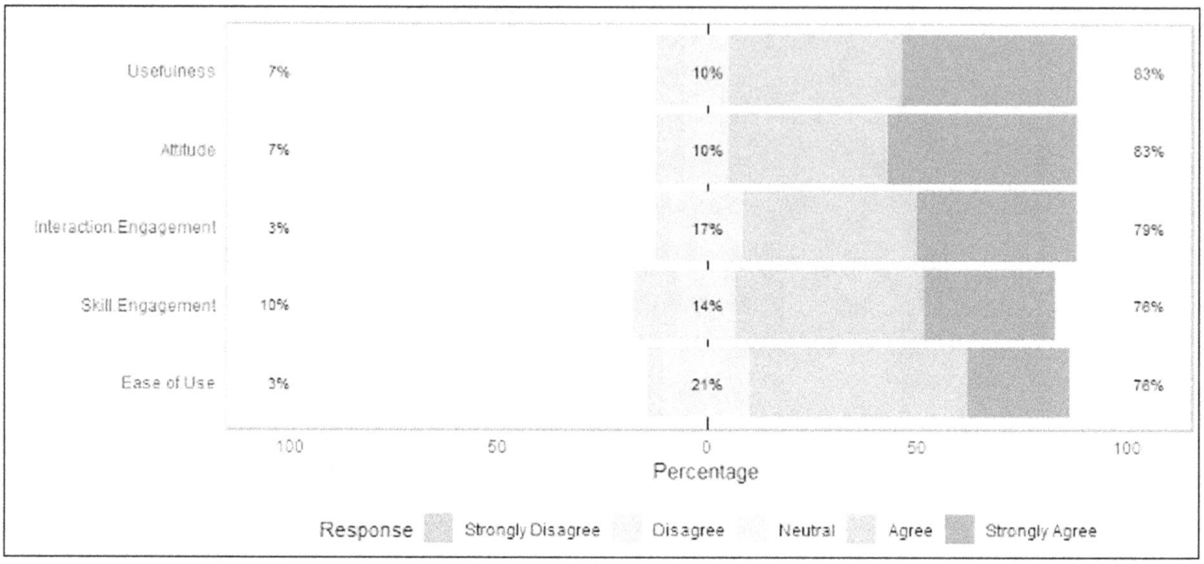

Perceived Ease of Use (PEOU)

Figure 6 reveals that most respondents agree or strongly agree with the easiness of use of the gamification used in this study (a total of 75.8%, from summing up 51.7 and 24.1). This result is particularly significative as the gamified curricular unit occurred in the first semester of the course, and it is assumed that most students never had a previous DE experience, as reported in class by the students themselves.

Figure 5. Graph presenting the frequency regarding Perceived Usefulness (PU)

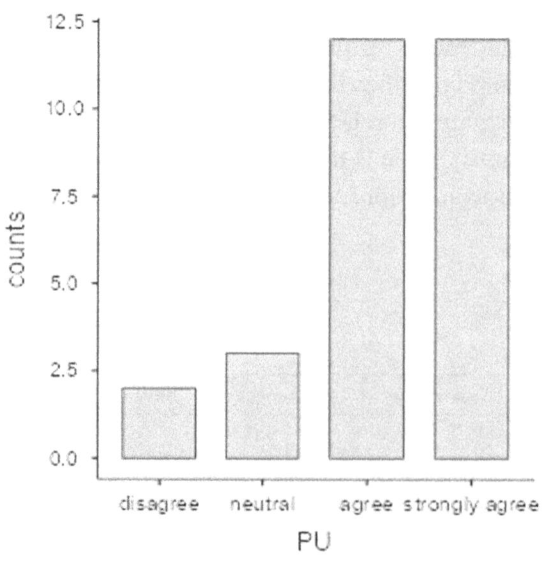

Figure 6. Graph presenting the frequency regarding Ease of Use (PEOU)

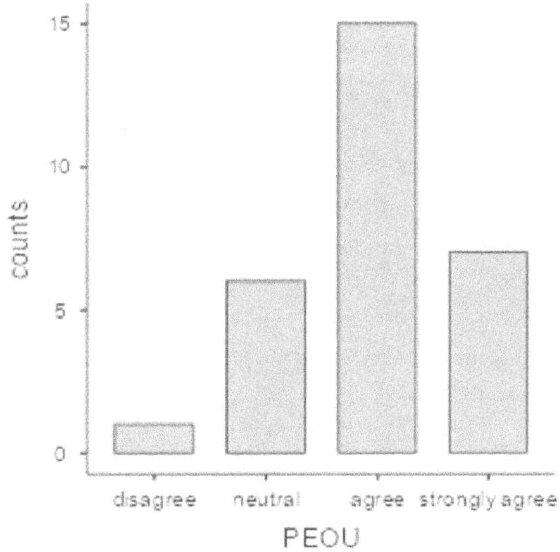

Still, in these particular conditions, it is observed that the gamification approach was easy to use. Nevertheless, it is also possible to observe that the frequency of respondents that selected the neutrality option is relevant, with 20.7%, and that the greater frequency of responses (51.7%) falls in the 'I agree option'. Hence, more can be done to increase the gamification PEOU for students. It would be opportune to carry out the same study at another moment of the course, when the students are no longer those who are having their first formative experience. As well as at the end of the course, which occurs after 4 years (on average).

By identifying that gamification is an easy enough methodology to be used, students become more willing to accept and use gamification during learning processes (Rahman et al., 2018). In this perspective, the application of gamification in DE environments becomes viable and more likely to be accepted by students in this modality, as shown by the results above. In general, the interface of the gamified environment proved to be clear and objective, without requiring new skills development and facilitating student interaction with online gamification.

In the context of DE, the virtual learning environment is the most favorable place for meaningful learning to take place, in which take place a large part of the pedagogical processes, communication between students and tutors, and student participation in forums (Pimentel, 2013). This perception regarding the ease of use of the gamified environment (in this study Moodle was used) points to benefits in relation to the student's interaction with the virtual learning environment.

Attitude (A)

Figure 7 shows the analysis of the respondents' attitude towards the use of gamification. The frequency of responses to the options 'agree' (37.9%) and 'strongly agree' (44.8%) shows the general positive attitude of respondents towards the use of gamification in educational context. This positive attitude may be related to the didactic change in which the teacher was not in a perspective of content transmission.

Figure 7. Graph presenting the frequency regarding Attitude (A)

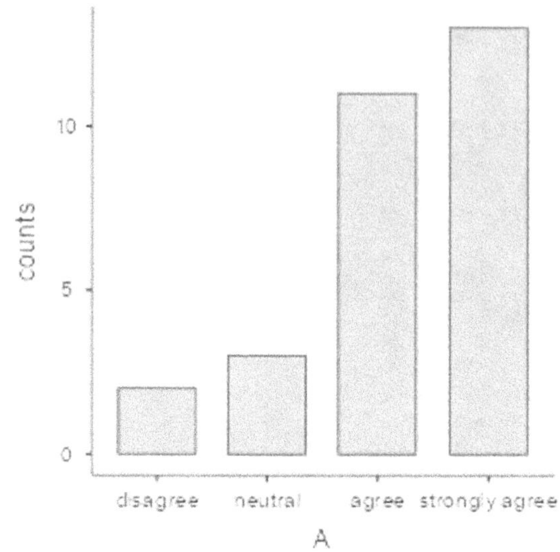

It cannot be stated, based on these results, that it is for sure. It could be related, but this aspect was not investigated in this study.

Skill Engagement (SKE)

The curricular unit was designed with the aim of effectively promote students' engagement with their own learning. In this sense, autonomy and organization skills were needed for good academic performance. Figure 8 shows the frequency analysis of skill engagement category. For instance, respondents generally agreed (44.8%) or strongly agreed (31.0%) with the statement that claimed that gamification elements used in the curricular unit promoted engagement with leaning. According to the students' responses, the gamification system encouraged them to take good notes in virtual classroom, to pay more attention to the instructions given under the curricular unit, its contents and activities, and to remember to study regularly.

Interaction Engagement (IE)

The curricular unit was planned from the assumption that the more interaction with gamification is promoted, the more likely it is to achieve learning (Pimentel, 2018). The last category analyzed concerns the effective engagement of students with learning, that is, their engagement in interaction. Figure 9 shows the frequency analysis of the respondents' interaction engagement category. Once more, the 'agree' (41.4%) and 'strongly agree' (37.9%) options were the most selected, indicating that the curricular unit promoted interaction actions among students and between students and the teacher.

In this set of questions, students were asked whether the online gamification system contributes to the perception that they can have fun while studying, whether it has contributed to actively participating in discussions in the forums, and whether it contributes to helping other students. It was also asked if the online gamification system helps to ask questions when they do not understand the teacher. The

Figure 8. Graph presenting the frequency regarding Skill Engagement (SE)

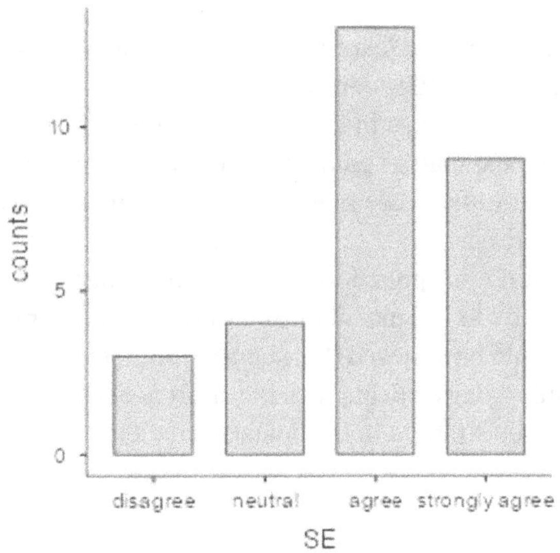

high incidence of 'agree' and 'strongly agree' answers show that, in the students' view, gamification is a way to promote interaction engagement.

STUDY LIMITS

The first limitation of this investigation is related to the number of participants (N=29), although the results are similar to those of Rahman et al., (2018). The same experiment can be implemented with

Figure 9. Graph presenting the frequency regarding Interaction Engagement (IE)

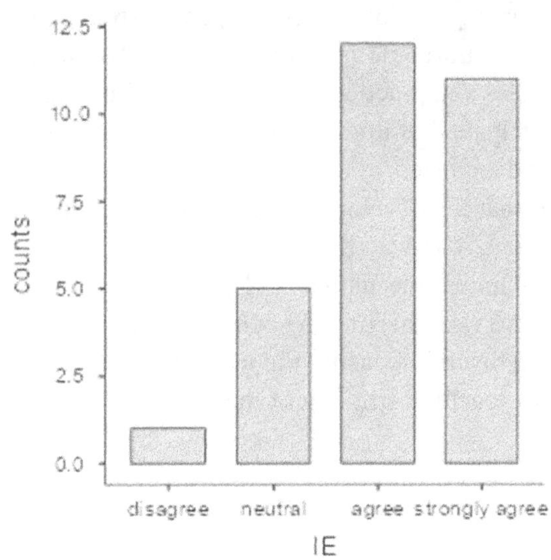

other classes, involving more students, verifying how gamification promotes student engagement aimed at learning.

The Covid-19 pandemic has hampered learning, as social distance prevents students from physically attending educational institutions. In OUB courses, including Mathematics, in addition to online moments, students have face-to-face moments in central cities. However, since the pandemic, these meetings cannot be held. We understand that, as gamification in DE courses are still recent in the Brazilian context, the impossibility of face-to-face meetings may have impaired the effectiveness of gamification. Further study can test this hypothesis.

Considering that gamification was applied to an initial curricular unit of the course, many students had no knowledge of how to study in DE modality, and they were not familiar with the virtual learning environment. This limitation could be removed if the course promoted an introductory environment unit, or a workshop, aiming at familiarizing students with the skills needed to study at a distance and with the use of the digital technologies set explored in the course's curricular units.

FINAL CONSIDERATIONS

This survey study found that gamification promoted student engagement with learning. As in the study by Rahman et al (2018), this investigation also revealed that the student engagement construct can be used as an indicator to measure student acceptance of gamification.

The five categories used in the study reveal that students perceive that gamification is a way to create more dynamic classes and to promote learning. The Perceived Usefulness (PU) and Attitude (A) categories had approximate scores and reveal the students' relationship with these categories. The results of the Perceived Ease of Use (PEOU) category demonstrate that technology familiarity strategies can be promoted, aiming at greater student achievement. Finally, the Skill Engagement (SKE) and Interaction Engagement (IE) categories demonstrated that gamification is a way to promote engagement and interaction. The more dynamic the curricular unit is, namely with activities that allow effective student participation, the more engagement with learning and the more interaction. There was even a satisfactory reception from the students, as they did not just have to watch videos or read texts. These strategies are necessary and meaningful for learning but focusing on exposure strategies does not allow for interaction.

As a methodological strategy, gamification served the curricular unit planning and objectives. It also promoted engagement, playfulness and practical activities, enabling participants to deepen the content. There was a change in the participants' attitude, with a greater commitment to their own learning, noticeable in the data collected and analyzed.

In sum, it can be concluded that the development of a gamified curricular unit can promote student involvement, focusing on learning. The way the discipline was planned, with a narrative close to the students' experiences, with dynamics, mechanics and game components, promoted engagement and interaction, allowing students who were starting the course to learn in a playful way. This way of elaborating and promoting a gamified discipline, using the institution's own Moodle, as well as other digital platforms, may be proposed as a teaching strategy of the blind review, blind review.

ACKNOWLEDGMENT

The authors kindly thank the voluntary participation of university students in this study, who contributed to advance knowledge in this field. The authors also thank the anonymous reviewers for critically reading the initial manuscript and suggesting substantial improvement. The work of Margarida M. Marques is funded by Portuguese funds, through University of Aveiro, in the scope of the framework contract foreseen in the numbers 4, 5 and 6 of the article 23, of the Decree-Law 57/2016, of August 29, changed by Law 57/2017, of July 19.

REFERENCES

Al-Azawi, R., Al-Faliti, F., & Al-Blushi, M. (2016). Educational Gamification Vs. Game Based Learning: Comparative Study. *International Journal of Innovation, Management and Technology*, (September), 131–136. doi:10.18178/ijimt.2016.7.4.659

Alabbasi, D. (2017). Exploring graduate students' perspectives towards using gamification techniques in online learning. *Turkish Online Journal of Distance Education*, *18*(3), 180–196. doi:10.17718/tojde.328951

Associassíon Española de Videojuegos - AEVI. (2019). *The Video Game Industry in Spain: Yearbook 2019* [La Industria del Videojuego En España: anuario 2019]. http://www.aevi.org.es/web/wp-content/uploads/2020/04/AEVI-ANUARIO-2019.pdf

Boone, H. N. Jr, & Boone, D. A. (2012, April). Analyzing Likert Data. *Journal of Extension*, *50*(2).

Bussarello, R. I. (2016). *Gamification*. Pimenta Cultural.

Csikszentmihalyi, M. (2008). *Flow: the psychology of optimal experience*. Harper & Row.

de Oliveira, A. M., & Silva, S. (2020). A boss in higher education: Enunciative look at gamification in the teaching of textual genres [Um chefão no ensino superior: olhar enunciativo sobre a gamificação no ensino de gêneros textuais]. *Revista Docência do Ensino Superior*, *10*, 1–20. doi:10.35699/2237-5864.2020.14942

Deci, E. L., & Ryan, R. M. (2004). *Handbook of self-determination research*. University Rochester Press.

Domínguez, A., Saenz-de-Navarrete, J., De-Marcos, L., Fernández-Sanz, L., Pagés, C., & Martínez-Herráiz, J. J. (2013). Gamifying learning experiences: Practical implications and outcomes. *Computers & Education*, *63*, 380–392. doi:10.1016/j.compedu.2012.12.020

Downes, S. (2005). *An introduction to connective knowledge*. https://www.downes.ca/post/33034

Downes, S. (2007). *What connectivism is*. https://www.downes.ca/post/38653

Eltegani, N., & Butgereit, L. (2015). Attributes of students engagement in fundamental programming learning. In *2015 International Conference on Computing, Control, Networking, Electronics and Embedded Systems Engineering* (pp. 101-106). IEEE. 10.1109/ICCNEEE.2015.7381438

Flavell, J. H. (1979). *Metacognition and Cognitive Monitoring. American Psychological Association.*

Gee, J. P. (2003). What video games have to teach us about learning and literacy. *Computers in Entertainment, 1*(1), 20–20. doi:10.1145/950566.950595

Gillett-Swan, J. (2017). The challenges of online learning: Supporting and engaging the isolated learner. *Journal of Learning Design, 10*(1), 20–30. doi:10.5204/jld.v9i3.293

Hartnett, M. (2016). The importance of motivation in online learning. In M. Hartnett (Ed.), *Motivation in online education* (pp. 5–32). Springer. doi:10.1007/978-981-10-0700-2_2

Hartnett, M. (2019). Motivation in distance education. In M. G. Moore & W. C. Diehl (Eds.), *Handbook of Distance Education* (4th ed., pp. 145–157). Routledge.

Huang, W. H. Y., & Soman, D. (2013). *A Practitioner's Guide to Gamification of eEducation. Rotman School of Management.* University of Toronto.

Huizinga, J. H. L. (2014). *Homo Ludens: the game as an element of culture* [Homo Ludens: o jogo como elemento da cultura]. Perspectiva. doi:10.4324/9781315824161

Kapp, K. M. (2012). *The gamification of learning and instruction: game-based methods and strategies for training and education.* John Wiley & Sons.

Kaufmann, D. A. (2018). Reflection: Benefits of Gamification in Online Higher Education. *Journal of Institutional Research, 7*(1), 125–132. doi:10.9743/JIR.2018.12

Koper, R. (2015). How do students want to learn in online distance education? Profiling student preferences. *The International Review of Research in Open and Distributed Learning, 16*(1), 307–329. doi:10.19173/irrodl.v16i1.2000

Kortemeyer, G. (2016). Work habits of students in traditional and online sections of an introductory physics course: A case study. *Journal of Science Education and Technology, 25*(5), 697–703. doi:10.100710956-016-9624-6

Lázaro, I. G. (2019). Escape Room as a proposal for gamification in education [Escape Room como propuesta de gamificación en educación]. *Revista Educativa Hekademos*, (27), 71–79.

Lee, H., & Doh, Y. Y. (2012, August). A study on the relationship between educational achievement and emotional engagement in a gameful interface for video lecture systems. In *International Symposium on Ubiquitous Virtual Reality* (pp. 34-37). IEEE. 10.1109/ISUVR.2012.21

Lee, H., & Doh, Y. Y. (2012, August). A study on the relationship between educational achievement and emotional engagement in a gameful interface for video lecture systems. In *2012 International Symposium on Ubiquitous Virtual Reality* (pp. 34-37). IEEE. 10.1109/ISUVR.2012.21

Moore, M., & Kearsley, G. (2007). *Distance education: an integrated vision* [Educação a distância: uma visão integrada]. Thomson Learning.

Pimentel, F. S. C. (2013). *Online Interaction: A challenge of mentoring* [Interação On-line: um desafio da tutoria]. Edufal.

Pimentel, F. S. C. (2018). Gamification in education, coining a concept [Gamificação na educação, cunhando um conceito]. In E. Fofonca, G. S. Brito, M. Estevam, & N. P. V. Camas (Eds.), *Metodologias pedagógicas inovadoras: contextos da educação básica e da educação superior* (pp. 76–87). Editora IFPR.

Pimentel, F. S. C., & Mercado, L. P. L. (2019). The policy of expansion of higher education through the UAB in Alagoas [A política de expansão do ensino superior por meio da UAB em Alagoas]. *EDUCAÇÃO, 7*(3), 127–138. doi:10.17564/2316-3828.2019v7n3p127-138

Ponto, J. (2015). Understanding and Evaluating Survey Research. *Journal of the Advanced Practitioner in Oncology, 6*(2), 168.

Prensky, M. (2012). Learning based on digital games [Aprendizagem baseada em jogos digitais]. São Paulo: SENAC.

Rahman, R. A., Ahmad, S., & Hashim, U. R. (2018). The effectiveness of gamification technique for higher education students engagement in polytechnic Muadzam Shah Pahang, Malaysia. *International Journal of Educational Technology in Higher Education, 15*(1), 1–16. doi:10.118641239-018-0123-0

Ryan, R. M., & Deci, E. L. (2000). Self-determination theory and the facilitation of intrinsic motivation, social development, and well-being. *The American Psychologist, 55*(1), 68–78. doi:10.1037/0003-066X.55.1.68 PMID:11392867

Sailer, M., & Homner, L. (2020). *The gamification of learning: A meta-analysis.* https://link.springer.com/article/10.1007/s10648-019-09498-w

Sanmugam, M., Zaid, N. M., Abdullah, Z., Aris, B., Mohamed, H., & van der Meijden, H. (2016). The impacts of infusing game elements and gamification in learning. In *2016 IEEE 8th international conference on engineering education (ICEED)* (pp. 131-136). IEEE. 10.1109/ICEED.2016.7856058

Schlemmer, E. (2015). *Gamificação em contexto de hibridismo e multimodalidade na educação corporativa* (Vol. 5). Revista FGV Online.

Schlemmer, E. (2016) Hybridism, Multimodality and Nomadism: co-determination and coexistence for an Education in the context of ubiquity [Hibridismo, Multimodalidade e Nomadismo: codeterminação e coexistência para uma Educação em contexto de ubiquidade]. In Educação a distância, qualidade e convergências: sujeitos, conhecimentos, práticas e tecnologias. São Carlos: EdUFSCar.

Siemens, G. (2010). *Knowing knowledge* [Conociendo el conocimiento]. Ediciones Nodos Ele. https://archive.org/details/2010ConociendoElConocimiento

Siemens, G. (2012). Connectivism: a theory of learning for the digital age [Conectivismo: uma teoria da aprendizagem para a era digital]. In *Conectados no ciberespaço. Paulinas.*

Simpson, O. (2003). *Student retention in online, open, and distance learning*. Psychology Press. doi:10.4324/9780203416563

Sioux Group & Go Gamers (2021). *Game Brasil 2021 Search* [Pesquisa Game Brasil 2021]. https://www.pesquisagamebrasil.com.br/pt/ebooks/

Swacha, J. (2021). State of research on gamification in education: A bibliometric survey. *Education Sciences*, *11*(2), 1–15. doi:10.3390/educsci11020069

Van Eck, R. (2015). Digital game-based learning: Still restless, after all these years. *EDUCAUSE Review*, *50*(6), 13.

Vogel, C., Hochberg, J., Hackstein, S., Bockshecker, A., Bastiaens, T. J., & Baumöl, U. (2018). Dropout in distance education and how to prevent it. In *Proceedings of EdMedia: World Conference on Educational Media and Technology* (pp. 1788-1799). Association for the Advancement of Computing in Education (AACE).

Whitson, C., & Consoli, J. (2009). Flow Theory and Student Engagement. *Journal of Cross-Disciplinary Perspective In Education*, *2*(1), 40–49.

Zichermann, G., & Cunningham, C. (2011). *Gamification by design: Implementing game mecha-nics in web and mobile apps*. O'Reilly Media.

ADDITIONAL READING

Huang, W. H. Y., & Soman, D. (2013). Gamification of education. *Report Series: Behavioural Economics in Action, 29*.

Kapp, K. M. (2012). *The gamification of learning and instruction: game-based methods and strategies for training and education*. John Wiley & Sons.

Kapp, K. M. (2013). *The gamification of learning and instruction fieldbook: Ideas into practice*. John Wiley & Sons.

Kingsley, T. L., & Grabner-Hagen, M. M. (2015). Gamificação. *Journal of Adolescent & Adult Literacy*, *59*(1), 51–61. doi:10.1002/jaal.426

Patricio, R., Moreira, A., Zurlo, F., & Melazzini, M. (2020). Co-creation of new solutions through gamification: A collaborative innovation practice. *Creativity and Innovation Management*, *29*(1), 146–160. doi:10.1111/caim.12356

Patrício, R., Moreira, A. C., & Zurlo, F. (2018). Gamification approaches to the early stage of innovation. *Creativity and Innovation Management*, *27*(4), 499–511. doi:10.1111/caim.12284

Pimentel, F. S. C., Nunes, A. K. F., & Sales, V. B. D. (2020). Teacher training in digital culture through gamification. *Educar em Revista*, 36.

Werbach, K., & Hunter, D. (2012). *For the win: How game thinking can revolutionize your business.* Wharton Digital Press.

Werbach, K., & Hunter, D. (2015). *The gamification toolkit: Dynamics, mechanics, and components for the win*. Wharton School Press.

Zahedi, L., Batten, J., Ross, M., Potvin, G., Damas, S., Clarke, P., & Davis, D. (2021). Gamification in education: A mixed-methods study of gender on computer science students' academic performance and identity development. *Journal of Computing in Higher Education*, *33*(2), 1–34. doi:10.100712528-021-09271-5

KEY TERMS AND DEFINITIONS

Distance Learning: Educational modality in which the pedagogical mediation processes take place through digital technologies, where teachers and students may be in diverse geographic environments and time zones.

Efficacy: Is what perfectly fulfills a certain task or function, reaching the proposed objective. Effectiveness is directly linked to the result.

Flow Theory: Mental state in which a person doing some activity is fully immersed in a feeling of heightened focus, total involvement, and enjoyment in the process of the activity. In essence, flow is characterized by complete immersion in what one is doing and a resulting transformation in one's sense of time.

Gamification: Defines the use of techniques common to games in non-game situations. A feature that normally appears in games is adapted for a different context, usually to motivate or make a task more enjoyable.

Gamification in Education: Gamification in education is the process of using the mechanics, style, and thinking of games, in a non-gaming context, as a possibility to engage and motivate people, aiming at learning through interaction among people, with technologies, and with the environment.

Interaction: Reciprocal influence between one thing and another, between one person and another: the interaction of theory and practice. In distance education interaction is pointed out as a necessary action for the development of learning.

Likert Scale: A survey scale that represents a set of response options (numeric or verbal) covering a range of opinions on a topic. It is used in a closed-ended question, when respondents have pre-populated response options.

Chapter 7
The Game Pentade:
A Design Model Proposal for Games for Education

Lazaro Raposo
Cereal Games, Portugal

Helia Guerra
https://orcid.org/0000-0002-4130-417X
University of Azores, Portugal

Carla Morais
https://orcid.org/0000-0002-2136-0019
University of Porto, Portugal

Antonio Coelho
https://orcid.org/0000-0001-7949-2877
University of Porto, Portugal

ABSTRACT

The use of digital games as support tools for education has proven to be effective. To explore their potential, it is crucial to design them carefully. This chapter considers the design of games for education, where players cultivate their knowledge and practice their skills by multiplying numerous hindrances during gaming. Educational elements are integrated into the gameplay, which players acquire while playing. The game's effectiveness depends on the players' ability to form a cheerful and encouraging environment to continue playing while increasing their interest in gameplay and improving academic performance. Following a design-first development approach, an innovative proposal for this design is presented, adding a new dimension to the game's tetrad: learning dynamics. Benefiting from years of professional practice, this game pentad design framework fulfills the learning and user experience requirements while overcoming the design limitations of more conventional approaches not based on an educational purpose.

DOI: 10.4018/978-1-6684-4287-6.ch007

INTRODUCTION

The use of digital games as support tools for Education has proven to be effective (de Freitas, 2018). To explore the potential of this form of active learning - active review sessions (using games and simulations) and role-playing have a high position on the spectrum of active learning activities arranged by complexity and classroom time commitment (CEI, n.d.), it is important to separate the games regarding their purpose. The games' purpose can be educational, when the game aims to teach certain contents or develop certain skills, such as "Where in The World is Carmen Sandiego" by Brøderbund in 1985, or "Vasco da Gama: A Grande Viagem" by Grupo Forum in 1998. But the game's purpose can also be entertainment, despite having features that allow it to be used in an educational context, such as "Age of Empires II" by Ensemble Studios in 1999, or "Portugal 1111" by Ciberbit in 2004 (Zagalo, 2013; Perrotta *et al.*, 2013).

This chapter is concerned with the design of digital games for educational purposes since its inception. According to the classification proposed by the Taxonomy of Serious Games (Sawyer & Smith, 2008), it corresponds to Games for Education. Games for Education is a category of a much wider specter that is Serious Games, which are games that have a purpose beyond just entertainment. It can be applied to, besides the aforementioned education, health (escape from Diab by Archimage Inc. in 2006), marketing (Magnum Pleasure Hunt by Lowe Brindfors in 2011), exercise by Nintendo wiiFit in 2007, recruitment by US Army in 2002, arts by Samorost Amanita Design in 2005), news (Darfur is Dying by interFUEL LLC in 2006) among many other subjects.

As mentioned, Serious Games can be entertaining tools, such as games for Education, where players cultivate their knowledge and practice their skills by rewarding numerous hindrances during gaming. Educational elements can be integrated into the gameplay, which the players will acquire during the gaming process. Effective serious games attempt to form a cheerful mood to encourage players to continue the play, leading to increased interest in gameplay and better academic performances (Zhonggen, 2019; Nazry & Romano et.al., 2017).

In this chapter we present a new proposal for a game design framework that allow us to successfully obtain pieces of educational software, in the form of games, that can fit the mentioned characteristics. But, first, we briefly describe the background needed to understand the proposed design model. The main section devoted to the model description, describes, and discusses the core activities for the game design process. Moreover, it complements the model description presenting two case studies of Game for Education design that followed the proposed model. Next section summarizes, in a roadmap format, the core activities for beginning the game design process and how they may be integrated into a single design process. We conclude with future research challenges.

BACKGROUND

Before discussing a new model for the game design process, it is important to analyze and discuss other well-known educational game design framework proposals. So, a literature review for Game Design Frameworks towards educational purposes is needed.

In general, the goal of design is to solve problems, and game design is no exception (Schell, 2008). Game design corresponds to the entire process of finding solutions, structuring ideas, and conceptualizing the entire game. It is "designing" first the game before starting to allocate resources on its development (Bethke, 2003).

The design phase of educational games allows us to develop the initial idea for the game, through the design and analysis of solutions, all this before investing in its construction. It forces us to define the game's objectives, to characterize the target audience and the knowledge and skills we intend to promote. It also contributes to clearly identifying the game's objective and its restrictions, essential for realizing its pedagogical potential and minimizing development risks. We focus on game-based learning and not in gamification in the learning process (Apostol et. al., 2013). Although, gamification can be a good approach to influence behavior (Bunchball, 2010) and also a good approach for co-creation (Patrício et. al., 2020) and for creativity and innovation (Patrício et. al., 2018; Patrício et. al., 2020).

Jesse Schell (Shell, 2008) considers that a complete game design will have to encompass four elements: Mechanics, Story, Technology and Aesthetics. Together, these elements form what is called the "Elemental Tetrad of the game". Mechanics refer to how the game's objectives are achieved (*e.g.*, jumping, running, pushing objects). We can consider that the Mechanics of a game, in a way, define the game genre (*e.g.*, sport, action, strategy). Technology refers to the platforms for which the game will be developed (*e.g.*, programming language, rendering engines, hardware).

The Technology element can affect the design of a game. Therefore, decisions regarding the technology to adopt must be made at the beginning of the game design process. The Story is the element of the game responsible for its narrative thread. The main and secondary objectives of the game, as well as protagonists and antagonists, are foreseen in the Story. The Aesthetics element is related to artistic factors, such as the graphic aspect or music, constituting the element responsible for creating a virtual environment where the game's action takes place, and should be appropriate to the game concept, and to its target audience (Schell, 2008).

Regarding educational purposes, we have the eMDAx framework (Paz, 2019), which is an extension of the MDA framework (Hunicke et.al., 2004). The MDA stands for Mechanics, Dynamics, and Aesthetics (see Figure 1). While Mechanics and Aesthetics have the same meaning as those from Jesse Schell's Game Tetrad, Dynamics refers to the way the player experiences and decides to interact with the game world through the game mechanics. For example, Counter-Strike: Global Offensive (CS:GO), developed by Valve Corporation in 2012, is a FPS (First Person Shooter) game where the main objective is to eliminate the opposing team. We can notice the mechanics of life, mouse click fire, weapon damage and areas of the body where the damage dealt is different. One strategy a player can have is to aim at the opponent's controlled character's head to deal more damage, thus eliminating him more efficiently. This way of playing is not mandatory, and there is no guarantee that doing it will bring a victory, but it is up to the players to analyze the situation and the mechanics presented and choose to use this strategy or not (Paz, 2019).

The eMDAx framework (Paz, 2019) means Educational, Mechanics, Dynamics, Aesthetics and Experience. It is a more educational oriented framework. When adding a fourth element - Educational - to the MDA framework, the author creates a new dimension to include the educational content related directly and exclusively to the Mechanics and Dynamics elements. The Experience in this model refers to the post-game "luggage" the player carries after playing. The eMDAx framework is depicted in Figure 2.

Figure 1. The MDA model (Hunicke et.al., 2004)

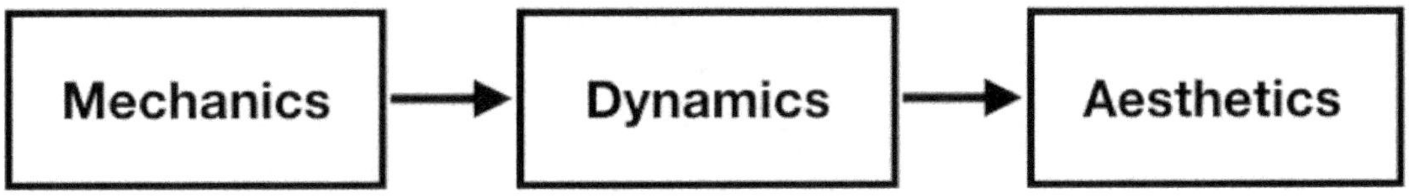

Figure 2. The eMDAx framework structure (Paz, 2019)

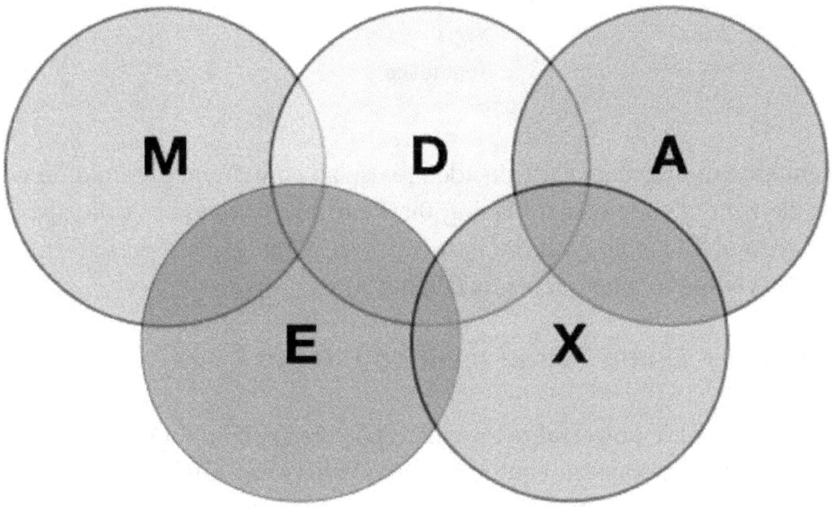

THE GAME PENTAD FRAMEWORK

In this section, we present a design model that aims to provide true gaming experiences, while maintaining its educational purposes. We work directly from Jesse Schell's Game Tetrad (Schell, 2008), because we consider it a solid framework to design entertainment games. That said, it makes sense to adopt it as the ground basis for an educational game design approach.

As an innovative/original aspect, we add a new element to the game's tetrad, thus obtaining the Game Pentad. We call this fifth element "Learning Dynamics".

The main difference between the Game Pentad and the eMDAx framework is how they relate Dynamics with the other elements. Game Pentad relates Dynamics to all elements, while eMDAx only relates Dynamics with Mechanics. It is important here to highlight the difference between game dynamics and game mechanics (Grünberg, 2014). Moreover, the term Dynamics has a slightly different meaning in both models. In order to differentiate the term in both models, instead, we use in Game Pentad Learning Dynamics.

In the context of the Game Pentad, Learning Dynamics will focus on the educational content covered in the game, and in its "dynamic" relationship with the game's mechanics, game's story, game's aesthetics and even the game's technology. For our framework, we adopt the term Narrative instead of Story.

Figure 3. The new Game Pentad framework structure (adapted from (Schell, 2008))

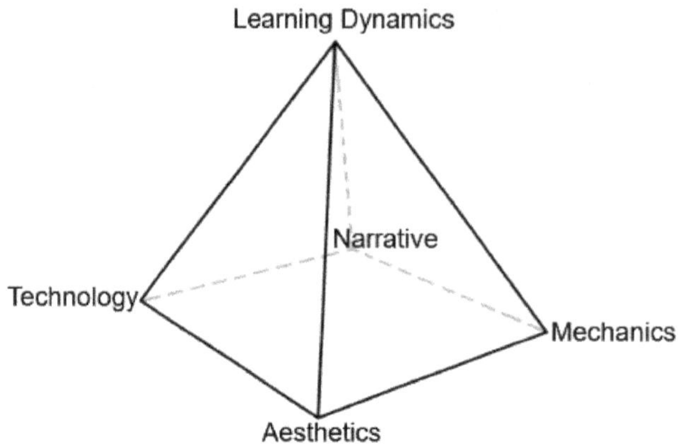

For the representation of this model, we decided to use an equilateral pyramid, in which each vertex corresponds to an element of the Pentad, placing the Learning Dynamics at the apex and Mechanics, Aesthetics, Narrative, and Technology at the base vertices. Side edges represent the relation between the Learning dynamics with the other elements (Figure 3).

Learning Dynamics + Game Tetrad = Game Pentad

It is well-known that games are powerful tools where players spend a lot of time and energy trying to win. Thus, it is important to ensure an equitable balance between all elements of the Game Pentad. Striking a balance among narrative, mechanics, aesthetics, and learning objectives is a critical issue for every educational game design process.

To explain in detail, Learning Dynamics in design, it is important to separate the theme of the game from the Game Dynamics. It is considered that the theme is broad in scope and, therefore, too broad to be covered in a single game. Learning dynamics should focus on the specific subjects which the game will provide. For example, we can have a game whose theme is Biology, while Learning Dynamics will focus on identifying, analyzing, and communicating specific topics in Biology, such as taxonomy, or human body.

The importance for the existence of Learning Dynamics in the Game Pentad is to highlight the process of how to identify, select and work on more specific subjects within the proposed theme, and to relate them in an organic and dynamic way with the other elements.

The relationship between Learning Dynamics and the other elements is explained in detail as follows:

1. **Mechanics:** The game core Mechanics should be designed to support the Learning Dynamics. As said before, Mechanics comprise a whole set of actions necessary for the player to reach his goal. These actions correspond to pre-conceived rules authored by the game creator, to try to determine how the player's experience and interactions will be (Adams & Dormans, 2012). Since a game can be defined as a system of rules that limit and specify its whole (Tekinbas & Zimmerman, 2003), relating or integrating these rules to support a specific Learning Dynamics, aiming at the learning objectives, is essential to allow the player to learn directly through the act of playing.

2. **Aesthetics:** It is very important to consider Aesthetics right from the beginning of the game design process, so that the game art is best fitted to the target audience. Aesthetics encompasses the representation of the "game world", and it should not appear detached from the rest of the experience. The graphical user interface of the game represents a simulation of spaces and objects interacting with the player's senses and influences her/his actions, unlike cinema, for example, where such interaction does not exist (Grodal, 2003). This visual representation of what is perceived by the player should not be seen apart as it contributes to the combined game experience. It is important to consider that the sound representation is also an aesthetic extension of the game, and as the visual part, it must be designed to represent the learning topics in an effective and immersive way to the player, maintaining a connection to the game's theme so as not to break the imaginary created by the player. For example, a game about marine biology should have an aesthetics element consistent with the sea, while a game about astronomy should already allow an aesthetic approach to the idea, we have of what science fiction is.
3. **Narrative:** Narrative is one of the most important dimensions of the game pentad, regarding a series of more sensitive topics related with social stereotypes, such as gender equality or social prejudice, among others. Educational software can be seen as a healthier and family-oriented solution, which leads to minorize attention to potential negative effects, such as those mentioned above. Thus, they can be ignored as possible sources of negative influence on children (Sheldon, 2004). Due to the content of the Narrative, which is the dimension responsible for the story and the characters, this, in the context of the game pentad, turns out to be the contact point to work on issues related with stereotypes, such as gender equality, cultural representation and social prejudice, but without compromise learning dynamics. Narrative also allows anchoring the game's plot around the learning plan, as well as segmenting the game's chapters/episodes according to the organization designed for the Learning Dynamics.
4. **Technology:** The purpose and context of using the game for playing determines the choice of technologies to adopt, both for development and distribution platforms. The game provides an experience that takes place in a certain space and time (Atwood-Blaine & Huffman, 2017; Giannakos *et al*, 2014). To respect this principle, when a game is designed with the purpose of being educational, its design is conditioned by the respective usage context. For example, a game with Augmented Reality might be perfect for communicating in a Science Center, while a game developed for mobile devices might be the best solution to extend its use in learning periods after classes (Raposo, 2012). Therefore, the adoption of technology always presents a series of constraints and restrictions, due to the impact it has on all other game elements.

In the next sections we exemplify the framework application in practice, concerning two selected games from a company, Cereal Games, that has been developing games for education under this game pentad framework, since 2014.

Example of Application: Bike a Planet

"Bike a planet" is a game for education developed by Cereal Games for the Santana Astronomical Observatory - Azores (OASA) useful to exemplify the application of the proposed model.

OASA is one of the centers that integrate the network of Science Centers in the Azores (OASA, n.d.). This network is a structure created by the Government of the Azores that brings together various spaces for scientific dissemination. OASA aims to promote scientific culture in Astronomy and knowledge of the Universe, through interactive activities open to the society, in particular the educational community and the public and private schools in the Azores.

A fundamental requirement of OASA for this project was to provide entertainment experiences for their visitors, while maintaining the educational contents (Raposo & Garcia, 2016). OASA has its activities organized by modules and dispersed throughout the physical space of the observatory. Each module provides an experience on a specific theme, whose duration should respect a predefined time interval.

The experience to be provided by "Bike a planet" should be in a separate module of OASA and entail physical activity.

This led to basically two main decisions.

- Physical activity was achieved with the installation of sensors and actuators on a Static bike. Hence, the concept "Bike a planet" was born - Riding on a planet!
- Since Astronomy is a very vast scientific field, the game experience was designed around the dynamics of rotation, orbit periods, and gravitational differences of the planets.

This specific choice of learning dynamics was crucial to develop a focused experience and, therefore, richer, and more efficient. Since it was intended to be a game experience of 7 minutes on average, we selected only a few Learning dynamics. Otherwise, it would limit the adoption of game mechanics.

The vertices of the game's Pentad cannot appear isolated. These dynamics were selected to keep the aspirations of having an educational game that also promotes physical activity. This activity results in the form of "Pedal", which is the main game mechanics.

The game experience is adapted to the planet of the Solar System that the player selects. The way the player pedals until it completes the orbital period movement is dependent on its orbital movement around the sun. Depending on the planet selected, a motor drove the gears to simulate these differences. When pedaling 687 times to complete the translation of Mars, for example, the player can have a comparison term with planet Earth that "costs" 365 cycles to complete the orbital period. This experience allows the player to learn directly from the mechanics and not through memorizing "spit" facts through a quiz!

Of course, pedaling a planet is something unrealistic. But games are usually fanciful. However, when giving to the player fantasy, immersion, challenge, catharsis, we are providing a magic circle (Huizinga, 2007) where the player can learn in an escapist context, that is, out of reality.

For instance, since the outer planets require an extraordinary effort to complete, a "warp speed" mechanic was developed, inspired by the tv series StarTrek. Warp Speed allows that each pedaling counts for several weeks instead of one single day, as long as the players achieve a specific velocity and maintain it above that threshold. The amount of physical effort required to keep above the threshold was carefully balanced to reward tenacious players.

This mechanic allows the player to finish the game with planets like Neptune, for example, which have an orbital period of 60182 days. We present, in Table 1 a short summary of the elements of the Game Pentad, resulting from the initial design stage of Bike a Planet.

To better understand the Game Pentad, we provide below a different example of an educational game.

Table 1. Short summary of the Game Pentad for Bike a Planet

Learning Dynamics	Orbital Periods, Planet names and relative dimensions, gravitical forces
Mechanics	Warp Speed, Pedal
Aesthetics	3D planets and asteroids with non -realistic textures (cartoonish), Sci-Fi UI
Technology	Static bike equipped with sensors, Arduino, computer
Narrative	Context provided by OASA monitors with the finishing goal, Planets as protagonists associated with difficulty levels.

Example of Application: Geo-GO: A Geographical Adventure

Geo-GO - a geographical adventure, is an educational game that was designed to be used on mobile devices as a complementary tool for teaching Geography to students of the 7th grade year aged 12-13 years (Raposo *etal.*, 2012).

Learning Dynamics were previously discussed and selected with a sample of Geography teachers. The selection of learning dynamics includes Climates, Flora and Fauna, Latitudes and Longitudes, and Time Zones, corresponding to the subjects where students experience more difficulties (Raposo, 2012).

Thus, for the design of this game, Mechanics were designed and adapted from the games with the purpose of entertaining due to their familiarity for the target audience. In this way, it is intended to present the player with a distinct experience from what is recommended by school manuals. For example, we have the "Sudoclima" mechanic which, as the name means, is an adaptation of the "Sudoku" game, so that the player can understand the differences between different climates. Another example is the "disc system", which has mechanics based on code padlocks, in which the player needs to rotate the disks to get the correct combinations.

As for the Narrative element, the story depicts a humorous adventure, whose protagonists try to prevent the "harmless" villain from changing the climate of Earth. It has a certain non-sense humor and a narrative style specific for the age group and inspired by tv series, such as "Phineas and Ferb" by Disney Television Animation in 2007. For the protagonists of the game, the option is given for the player to choose between a female or male character, also leaving the name at the player's choice. This option allows that there is no gender inequality imposed by the game design.

We present, in Table 2 a short summary of the elements of the Game Pentad, resulting from the initial design stage of Geo-Go - a geographical adventure.

Table 2. Short summary of the Game Pentad for "Geo-GO- a geographical adventure"

Learning Dynamics	Climates, Flora and Fauna, Latitudes and Longitudes, Time zones, relative and absolute location, political geography
Mechanics	Sudoclima, Tile Puzzles, Disc System, ClimaBowling, Point and click
Aesthetics	Cartoon graphics, UI colors change according to continents
Technology	Mobile devices, internet connection for sharing scores and results
Narrative	Character selection with gender options, game levels structured by continents

Table 3. Issues and questions for supporting the Game Pentad design

Learning Dynamics	1. What are the learning objectives? 2. Which learning content is essential to reach these objectives? 3. Which content should we focus on? Is this content balanced for a good learning experience?
Mechanics	1. How to apply the given learning dynamics to specific mechanics? 2. Does the intended mechanics blend with the learning dynamics? 3. Are the mechanics intuitive to provide understanding? 4. Does the mechanics combined with the learning dynamics provide challenge?
Aesthetics	1. What is the target audience of our game? 2. Should it be in 2D or 3D? 3. If 2D, what do we expect from the Look & Feel? 4. If 3D, what do we expect from the Look & Feel?
Narrative	1. Does the story add to the experience? 2. Do we provide gender equality? 3. How can we use the story structure to organize our game? 4. How can we use the story plot to support the learning dynamics? 5. Are we somehow not providing good examples through the story?
Technology	1. Where will this game be available? Distribution platforms? 2. What's the context for it? Classroom? Museum? Home? 3. Does it require an internet connection? 4. Which Engine will we use for this development? The Engine must guarantee the previous requirements.

SOLUTIONS AND RECOMMENDATIONS

This section presents an overview of the game design process following the model proposed in the previous section complemented with practical application examples. It highlights the key issues for the design of games for education, strongly influenced by practice.

According to Jesse Schell, "The game begins with an idea." (Schell, 2008). This sentence is true for entertainment games, yet, while not entirely wrong for Educational Games, it is more accurate to say that "the (educational) game begins with a problem".

In an educational context, most games are designed because there is a necessity to provide additional tools for learning, more immersive experiences, or to create new materials about a given subject.

This is usually the kick start for the creation of an Educational Game because this need already gives us the context and provides us with the theme/ subject. After that, there is several issues about the several elements of the Game Pentad that must be solved/answered back and forward, to find a good balance for a good gaming learning experience.

When starting to design the game, it is important to question ourselves about some of the goals we need to achieve and if our ideas are going towards it. For that, and based on previous development experience, we suggest some questions that can be placed not only to the development team, but also to educators, trainers, and pedagogical leaders. Table 3 provides the main aspects we propose to consider during an educational game design process under the Game Pentad.

FUTURE RESEARCH DIRECTIONS

The proposed Game Pentad is a framework to design games for education that results from the best practices over 7 years in a company specialized in game design and development. Several games for education were developed under this framework having different learning proposes and learning environments. A mindset of this framework has been empirically evaluated over this time, contributing to its consolidation.

It is intended to extend this research project in some directions to validate, evaluate, test, and improve the framework. Moreover, it is also considered in the short term to prepare documentation explaining how to start design projects in a nutshell, providing tips and templates for novices.

Some further studies include:

1. Evaluate the framework externally with samples of game developers from other companies, researchers, and undergraduate students from courses of game development. Since this model has only been used at Cereal Games, it can benefit from input from other developers with other experiences. These developers can bring a fresh perspective and validation of the model.
2. Evaluate the framework externally with samples of researchers, and undergraduate students from courses of game development. Promote workshops with the selected participants can be useful to obtain results during practice, besides preparing questionnaires and interviews.
3. Extend the framework to explicitly consider several actors during the design, such as representatives of the product owner, teachers and students, besides game's developers specific roles of designers, participating in the design process in a collaborative manner as a multidisciplinary team.
4. Extend the framework to be more flexible, having specific processes for different teaching/learning approaches.
5. Compare the framework with other design frameworks for educational games, starting by identifying the key indicators for such a design process. An experimental approach with control groups can be useful to consider in the comparative study.
6. Structure existing educational games, preferably familiar ones, with the Game Pentad. This process would be a kind of reverse design, in which taking a successful and popular educational game, we can disassemble it under this model, analyzing the elements of the base of the pyramid and realizing its effective correlation with the apex, that is, the Learning dynamics.

CONCLUSION

Games for Education are Serious Games that can be entertaining tools where players cultivate their knowledge and practice their skills by rewarding numerous hindrances during gaming. These requirements can be more easily achieved when the game has an educational purpose, and its design is based on this purpose, from the start of the project. In this chapter, it is presented a new proposal for a game design framework concerning game development for educational purposes since their inception. The framework allows to successfully design pieces of educational software, in the form of games, to achieve the learning and user experience requirements and overcoming design limitations of entertainment games approaches not based on an educational purpose. The framework named Game Pentad is depicted by a square pyramid, where the base is composed by the elemental game's tetrad of Mechanics, Narrative,

Aesthetics, and Technology, and the apex is reserved to a new element representing the Learning Dynamics dimension and related with the base's four elements.

The Game Pentad framework results from the best practices over seven years in a company specialized in game development, in solving specific educational problems, having different learning proposes and learning environments. A mindset of this Framework has been empirically evaluated over this time, contributing to its consolidation with the potential to be extended in several directions to validate, evaluate, test, and improve. Moreover, it is also considered in the short term to prepare documentation explaining how to start design projects in a nutshell, providing tips and templates for novices.

We believe that this new design approach can contribute to being more effective in exploring the potential of a form of active learning driven by playing digital games. Such games are designed for educational purposes but integrate engagement elements provided by digital games designed for entertainment purposes.

REFERENCES

Adams, E., & Dormans, J. (2012). *Game mechanics: advanced game design*. New Riders.

Apostol, S., Zaharescu, L., & Alexe, I. (2013). Gamification of learning and educational games. In *Proceedings of the 9th. International Scientific Conference eLearning and Software for Education* (pp. 67-72). Academic Press.

Atwood-Blaine, D., & Huffman, D. (2017). Mobile gaming and student interactions in a science center: The future of gaming in science education. *International Journal of Science and Mathematics Education, 15*(1), 45–65. doi:10.100710763-017-9801-y

Bethke, E. (2003). *Game development and production*. Wordware Publishing, Inc.

Bunchball, Inc. (2010). *Gamification 101: An introduction to the use of game dynamics to influence behavior*. Bunchball. Available at: http://jndglobal.com/wp-content/uploads/2011/05/gamification1011.pdf

Center for Educational Innovation – CEI. (n.d.). *University of Minnesota*. https://cei.umn.edu/active-learning

de Freitas, S. (2018). Are games effective learning tools? A review of educational games. *Journal of Educational Technology & Society, 21*(2), 74–84.

Giannakos, M. N., Jones, D., Crompton, H., & Chrisochoides, N. (2014, June). Designing Playful Games and Applications to Support Science Centers Learning Activities. In *International Conference on Universal Access in Human-Computer Interaction* (pp. 561-570). Springer. 10.1007/978-3-319-07440-5_51

Grodal, T. (2003). Stories for Eye, Ear, and Muscles: Video Games, Media, and Embodied Experiences. In M. Wolff & B. Perron (Eds.), *The Video Game Theory Reader* (pp. 129–156). Routledge.

Grünberg, T. K. (2014). *What's the difference between game mechanics and game dynamics?* Available at: http://www.quora.com/Whats-the-difference-between-game-mechanics-and-game-dynamics

Huizinga, J. (2007). *Homo ludens: the game as an element of culture* [Homo ludens: o jogo como elemento da cultura]. Perspectiva.

Hunicke, R., LeBlanc, M., & Zubek, R. (2004, July). MDA: A formal approach to game design and game research. In *Proceedings of the AAAI Workshop on Challenges in Game AI* (*Vol. 4*, No. 1, p. 1722). Academic Press.

Juan, A. A., Loch, B., Daradoumis, T., & Ventura, S. (2017). Games and simulation in higher education. *International Journal of Educational Technology in Higher Education*, *14*(1), 1–3. doi:10.118641239-017-0075-9

Nazry, N. N. M., & Romano, D. M. (2017). Mood and learning in navigation-based serious games. *Computers in Human Behavior*, *73*, 596–604. doi:10.1016/j.chb.2017.03.040

Patricio, R., Moreira, A., Zurlo, F., & Melazzini, M. (2020). Co-creation of new solutions through gamification: A collaborative innovation practice. *Creativity and Innovation Management*, *29*(1), 146–160. doi:10.1111/caim.12356

Patrício, R., Moreira, A. C., & Zurlo, F. (2018). Gamification approaches to the early stage of innovation. *Creativity and Innovation Management*, *27*(4), 499–511. doi:10.1111/caim.12284

Patrício, R., Moreira, A. C., & Zurlo, F. (2021). Enhancing design thinking approaches to innovation through gamification. *European Journal of Innovation Management*, *24*(5), 1569–1594. doi:10.1108/EJIM-06-2020-0239

Paz, I. (2019). *eMDAx Tool Proposed game design framework for educational games* [Ferramenta eMDAx Proposta de framework de game design para jogos educacionais] [Master Thesis]. Universidade da Beira Interior, Portugal.

Perrotta, C., Featherstone, G., Aston, H., & Houghton, E. (2013). *Game-based learning: Latest evidence and future directions*. NFER.

Raposo, L. (2012). *Design of educational game design document and development of a prototype educational game for mobile devices* [Conceção do educational game design document e desenvolvimento de um protótipo de jogo educativo para dispositivos móveis] [Master Thesis]. Faculdade de Engenharia da Universidade do Porto. Portugal.

Raposo, L., & Garcia, P. (2016). *Bike a Planet: Educating through a healthy video game* [Bike a Planet: Educando através de um videojogo saudável] [Poster communication]. 4º Congresso de Comunicação de Ciência, SciCom PT 2016, Lisboa, Portugal.

Raposo, L., Morais, C., & Paiva, J. (2012). "GEO-GO" – a geographical adventure in the form of educational game: description of the project and its development ["GEO-GO" – uma aventura geográfica sob a forma de jogo educativo: descrição do projeto e seu desenvolvimento]. In *Proceedings of Encontro sobre Jogos e Mobile Learning*. Universidade de Coimbra.

Santana Astronomical Observatory of Azores - OASA. (n.d.). http://oasa.centrosciencia.azores.gov.pt

Sawyer, B., & Smith, P. (2008). *Serious games taxonomy*. Serious Games Initiative.

Schell, J. (2008). *The Art of Game Design: A Book of Lenses*. Morgan Kaufmann Publishers. doi:10.1201/9780080919171

Sheldon, J. P. (2004). Gender stereotypes in educational software for young children. *Sex Roles*, *51*(7), 433–444. doi:10.1023/B:SERS.0000049232.90715.d9

Tekinbas, K. S., & Zimmerman, E. (2003). *Rules of play: Game design fundamentals*. MIT press.

Zagalo, N. (2013). *Video games in Portugal: History, Technology and Art* [Videojogos em Portugal: História, Tecnologia e Arte]. FCA Editora.

Zhonggen, Y. (2019). A meta-analysis of use of serious games in education over a decade. *International Journal of Computer Games Technology*. doi:10.1155/2019/4797032

Chapter 8
The Rise of Educational Escape Rooms:
Designing Games as Formative Tasks

José Carlos Piñero Charlo
https://orcid.org/0000-0001-7583-4729
University of Cadiz, Spain

ABSTRACT

Nowadays, the rise of escape rooms as a worldwide extended leisure activity is a reality. Such success has been achieved briefly and has motivated its use as a formative tool at various academic levels. Some authors have reported successful use of educational escape rooms in multiple topics (nursery, pharmacy, psychology, telecommunications, and STEM courses, among others). Furthermore, evidence of a learning process during educational escape room experiences has been published in the last years. Educational escape rooms are nowadays considered a valid, innovative formative methodology. This chapter aims to provide background, information, case reports, and guidelines for using educational escape in various curricular disciplines.

BACKGROUND: GAME-BASED LEARNING

Gamification becomes an object of interest for education researchers since it rose to popularity in the early 2010s. This interest is mainly based on the idea of gamification as "the ideal process for creating engaging learning environments" (Kapp, 2012). Furthermore, game-based mechanics implicitly points out its key virtue (the ability to build engagement and motivation) "using game-based mechanics, aesthetics and game thinking to engage people, motivate action, promote learning, and solve problems" (Kapp, 2012). Such game mechanics can be articulated by means of computer-supported games, board games, videogames, and many others. In this regard games, used as a tool for an educational or formative process, have some characteristics (Chamoso et al., 2004) that leads to a learning process centered on exploiting the features of this resource:

DOI: 10.4018/978-1-6684-4287-6.ch008

Figure 1.

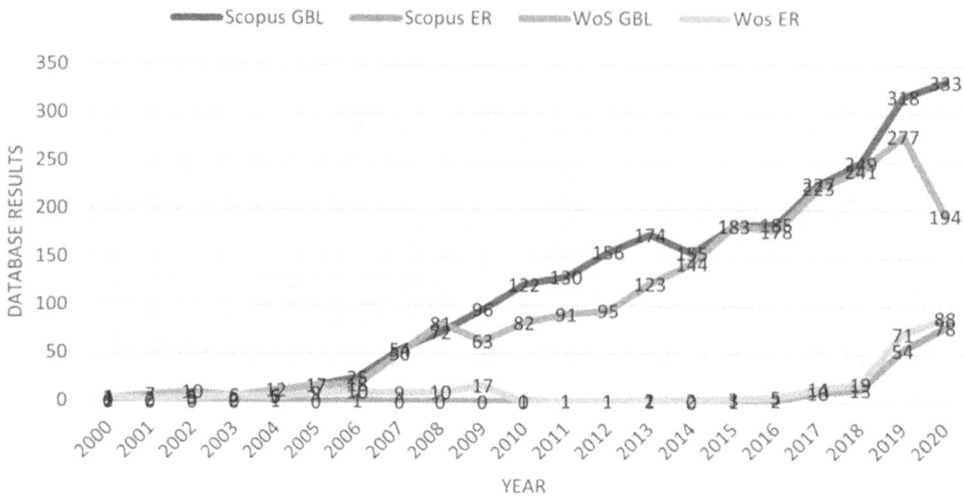

- **Being a leisure activity:** Games have a social and emotional impact due to its psychological and emotional factors (in terms of joy, stress, and motivation).
- **Freedom of action:** The limited spatial and temporal extension of games allows players to instantly appreciate the value of their work, being publicly recognized.
- **Being a universal activity:** gaming is a universal phenomenon (animals and humans play games in which they test and get to know their bodies and the surrounding world) that is practiced just for the sake of playing; without knowing anything about the game's features or effects.

Consequently, applying games to education converts education in a universal activity, because games are a natural activity (we all know how to play). In this regard, (Vygotsky, 1978) described games as a mechanism for providing opportunities to children to experience scenarios which they are not yet able to live through in real life. When it comes to the effects of playing, prominent psychologists and educational researchers such as (Montessori, 1916) and (Piaget, 1945) have acknowledged the value of playing for the development of children through the last century (Murray, 2018).

Thus, the importance of games for one's development has led to the inclusion of game-based settings for learning purposes (S. Kim et al., 2018) both in lower and upper secondary as well as in higher education. From the research interest point of view, the literature indicates that game-based learning has received increasing attention some researchers even consider educational games being one of the biggest interest attractors of the last decade in the educational context (Swacha, 2021). Indeed, a growing research interest is evidenced when searching in the most prominent databases (Scopus and Web of Science), as can be observed in Figure 1.

So, game-like activities can be designed for a primary purpose other than pure entertainment. A "serious game" is, indeed, a game designed following these intentions. Serious games are applied "outside the context of entertainment, where the narration progresses as a sequence of patterns impressive in quality ... and is part of a thoughtful progress" (Lugmayr et al., 2017). The concept shares aspects with simulation generally, including flight simulation and medical simulation, but explicitly emphasizes the added peda-

Table 1. Four Polya phases, connected to the comprehension of a problem/game.

Polya Phase	Comprehension of the Problem	Comprehension of the Game
Understanding the problem	• What is the problem asking for? • Identifying problem data	• Which requirements do we have to fit? • Identifying possible actions
Devising a plan	• Comparing to similar problems • Making guesswork	• Comparing to similar games • Making strategies
Carrying out the plan	• Guesswork assessment • Execution of the plan	• Strategy assessment • Gaming
Looking back	• Strategy generalization: is it worth in any problem? • Modeling the strategy for "certain types of problems"	• Strategy generalization: is it worth it in any condition? • Modeling the strategy for "certain types of games"

gogical value of fun and competition. Serious games can be classified in two broad categories (Djaouti et al., 2011), depending on the game structure: process-oriented games and outcome-oriented games.

Gamification, on the other hand, consist in the application of game-like elements (like badges, leaderboards, and point systems) to non-game activities, normally with intention to increase engagement and effectiveness. It can also be defined as a set of activities and processes to solve problems by using or applying the characteristics of game elements. Taking this into account, Game-Based Learning (GBL) can be defined as a process where game characteristics and principles are embedded within learning activities (intending to promote student engagement and motivation to learn). At this point, one could consider that a GBL approach can be an outcome-focused serious game, designing the game to train people in essential skills or competencies.

Game-Based Learning as a Problem-Based Learning Approach

Games and team-play may awake relational aspects, favoring imagination and divergent thinking because of the socialization and group discussions linked to independent work (which may ease the exploration of a diversity of solutions by sharing ideas). Such elements are connected to the formative potential of games, conceived as a problem-based methodology. Indeed, stages in problem solving and gaming are equivalent (Edo et al., 2008), as detailed in Table 1 -where Polya phases (Polya, 1945) are connected with the comprehension of a problem/game (Carmona & Cardeñoso, 2019)-.

The use of specific game's dynamics to strength motivation and to stimulate individuals to achieve previously determined goals is known as "gamification". Even when "gamification" admits other definitions on the literature (Bunchball, 2010; Llorens Largo et al., 2015), all these definitions share a common aim: increasing the interest of a part of the population over a determined subject. Finally, gamification has been studied in the literature; to fulfil the goal of "transforming work into games", some specific properties have to be respected (Oprescu et al., 2014). In the context of learning/teaching processes, the interest of applying educational gamification is related to its capability to mobilize specific competences and knowledges. However, most educational games are designed not to learn, but to apply previously acquired knowledge. In this regard, some studies (Obando Zapata & Muñera Córdoba, 2003) invite one to subtend the acquisition of the knowledge (more specifically, mathematic knowledge) taking a "situation-problem" as a starting point (so that a scenery and a context is specifically built for a problem-based approach).

Learning in Educational Escape Rooms Games

In agreement with the available literature, an escape room (ER) can be defined as live-action team-based game where players discover clues, solve puzzles, and accomplish tasks in one or more rooms in order to accomplish a specific goal (usually escaping from the room) in a limited amount of time (Nicholson, 2018). In addition to its leisure capability, ERs have gained research and educational interest due to potential applications for mobilizing abilities such as team building (Warmelink et al., 2017), leadership (Wu et al., 2018), creative thinking (Williams, 2018), and communication (Pan et al., 2017). So, is not surprising that some educational institutions have started to integrate this resource in educational programs, using escape rooms with formative scopes. In this regard, some educators have gone a step forward in creating educational escape rooms which can be defined as "escape rooms whose resolution requires the mobilization of curricular knowledge".

The rise of escape rooms as a worldwide extended leisure activity is nowadays a reality. Such a success has been achieved in a brief period and has motivated its use as a formative tool at various academic levels. Some authors have reported a successful use of educational escape rooms in a wide variety of topics (nursery, pharmacy, psychology, telecommunications and STEM courses among others). Furthermore, during the last years, evidence of a learning process during educational escape room experiences have been published. Educational Escape Rooms are nowadays considered a valid, innovative formative methodology. This chapter aims to provide background, information, references to case-reports and guidelines for the use of educational escape on a variety of curricular disciplines. Playing/designing EERs as formative tasks will be widely discussed below, here we provide a brief introduction to both approaches.

Playing an Educational Escape Room as a Formative Task

Educational Escape Rooms (EERs) constitutes an attractive formative opportunity since students/players have a chance to manipulate physical models in an autonomous way while sharing the experience with their peers. This possibility becomes more important at early formative stages, due to the cognitive development stage in which the players might be (Huitt & Hummel, 2003). Particularly, children at the concrete operational stages (aged between 7 and 11, middle childhood and preadolescence) may benefit from the chance of solving problems that apply to actual (concrete) objects or events, rather than working with abstract concepts or hypothetical tasks -in this regard, evidence of learning processes have already been reported in literature (Piñero Charlo, 2020)-. However, EERs might be also useful at higher educational stages because of the opportunity to have a "controlled environment" in which a real/academic situation can be reproduced.

Designing an Educational Escape Room as a Formative Task

On the other hand, EERs can constitute a way to develop a teacher-centered design (it is, a courseware management system that supports instructors' needs for course and curricular administration, management, and development). So, the design and implementation of EER can be posed as a formative task to be developed by student teachers -future teachers-. Here, student teachers would have to consider a variety of didactic parameters such as the sequencing of problems and clues, the timing, didactic supports, manipulative tools, evaluation method, etc. These student-designed EERs can be also implemented in schools (attending to a collaborative, service-learning approach) that might have a positive impact if correctly designed (Piñero Charlo et al., 2021).

ISSUES AND CONTROVERSIES

The growing interest in GBL is not exempt of controversy. In this regard, some authors states that "Many educationally interesting games exist, yet evidence for their impact on student achievement is slim" (Young et al., 2012). One of the most prominent arguments provided is that although the games themselves may be able to spur scientific thoughts, critical thinking, and knowledge construction, players often must be prompted to become metacognitively aware that they are using the scientific method and discussing scientific strategies that are rooted in the physical world before they become capable of utilizing those skills outside of the game. It is: educational games should be implemented only in concert with good teaching. The transfer of science information from isolated in-game activities requires metacognitive scaffolding by a skilled educator who can encourage student reflection, provide students with thought questions that force them to reference the specific curricular science skills, and bridge content from the game into their real lives (B. Kim et al., 2009).

More specifically, concerning to "Escape Room" games, most of the authors do not provide evidence of a learning process during educational escape room (EER) experiences. Indeed, state of the art in educational escape rooms (Piñero, 2019) highlights the lack of empirical evidence supporting the positive impact of educational escape rooms and game-based learning in general (de Freitas, 2013; Wouters et al., 2009). In this regard, EER-related literature lacks on transcriptions of learning experiences, didactic analysis of the learning process and analysis of the didactic suitability of the EER. The lack of weight of evidence in some Game Based Learning (GBL) published papers opens the discussion of the real performance not only of GBL-EER approaches, but also of other GBL-serious games approaches (Connolly et al., 2012).

As can be seen, according to the database consulted, there are no significative manuscripts prior to 2017 (as illustrated in Fig.1) that seriously reports on the success rate by using educational escape rooms -that is, the percentage of students who solve the room before it is time is up-. In several cases, the most recent literature discusses this point and difference in cases in which some groups of students manage to escape from the room (Hermanns et al., 2018) and in cases in which all groups of students manage to escape (Monaghan & Nicholson, 2017). However, this discussion is not extensive to most of the articles referenced in this book chapter, even though this type of data is essential to assess the difficulty of the activity and modulate it in future iterations.

THE DESIGN OF EDUCATIONAL ESCAPE ROOMS

As can be appreciated in Fig.1, escape-room-based games have arisen in the last decade. Nowadays, some educational institutions have started to integrate this resource in educational programs, using escape rooms with formative scopes. To do so, educational escape rooms have been created. Educational Escape Rooms are defined as "escape rooms whose resolution requires the mobilization of curricular knowledge". However, due to the novelty of the "educational escape room" concept, there is a real paucity of research reporting and examining the potential educational use of escape rooms, as well as the application of non-educational escape rooms in educational settings. In this section, EER design criteria, theoretical background and common alternatives will be discussed.

Fitting the Experience: The Flow State

The design of Escape Room-games with educational purposes must consider the abilities, knowledges, difficulties… and other theoretical or practical skills that are part of the participant background. Each educational escape room shall fit to the students so that the game remains challenging but approachable. In this regard, one of the most commons challenges highlighted in literature is to fit the difficulty level of the activities composing the experience -in fact, this is not easy even in conventional and commercial escape rooms (Nicholson, 2015)-. This is even more complex in the case of educational purposes, where the fit must take into account nor only the "mechanic" difficulty of the activity, but also the difficulty to dominate the conceptual tools, materials and models; which should be specific of each knowledge domain (tools and models provided should not be the same for a "chemistry-based" EER or a "medicine-based" one).

In educational escape rooms, the complexity of the activities plays a crucial role in the success of the experience as too many simple puzzles will quickly bore students, while a too high difficulty level can lead to frustration or anxiety. This equilibrium is known as "flow state" and is illustrated in Figure 2 -adapted from (Vittersø & Csikszentmihalyi, 2000)-. The flow state can be defined as a mental state of operation in which a person, performing an activity, is fully immersed in a feeling of energized focus, full involvement, and enjoyment in the process of the activity. This theory suggests keeping the player in a state of total immersion so that they are never in a state in which the challenges posed are neither excessive nor simple. However, other approaches suggest that the chain of problems in the room must be of increasing difficulty (Nicholson, 2016b). This approach considers that getting stuck in the first puzzle can be very discouraging for the participants. However, if the bottleneck is in one of the last puzzles, the feeling of frustration is not the same (since it has been preceded by a large dose of adrenaline when solving all the previous problems.

Csikszentmihalyi's theory states that mental states that results in stress or depression should be avoided. In this regard, the possibility of designing a "flow channel" -see Fig.2- with the strategic goal of increasing the task performance as well as an augmented cognition has been discussed (Csikszentmihalyi, 1990).

Stablishing Design Criteria: Structuring an EER

Some educational escape rooms design guidelines are available in literature (Nicholson, 2016b; Walsh, 2017), lacking—in some cases—scientific references supporting such guidelines. Literature has plenty of approaches that are not escape rooms in the strict mean (Hermanns et al., 2018; Ma et al., 2018): players are accompanied by the teacher (Diago Nebot & Ventura-Campos, 2017), or the escape room experience is reduced to "opening a box" (Veldkamp et al., 2020) during a conventional lecture (indeed, in some of these approaches, players does not have to escape from any room). Educational escape rooms are yet in an emergent situation, so there is still some misinformation and confusion. This situation sets the point to establish specific criteria for defining "what an educational escape room is". To the author's knowledge, there is no "educational escape room design criteria" published in relevant media (it is, in well indexed journals or book chapters). So, the design criteria here presented have been developed by the author and have been demonstrated to provide reliable results (Piñero Charlo, 2020):

Figure 2.

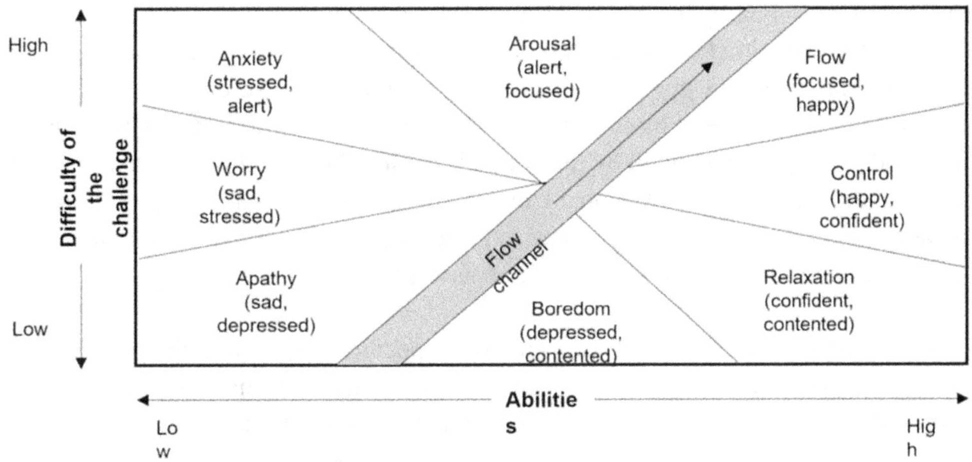

- **Dynamism:** This criterion is connected to the problems, activities and enigmas, which should be solved in a brief time. A good EER should be composed by many "little problems" rather than a single big problem.
- **Performance:** To achieve the previously described "flow state", the EER must fit to the knowledge the student/players. Specific difficulties, detected during the conventional course, should be addressed during the game; creating a framework where peer-to-peer discussions help to overcome such difficulties. This information should be used to group students in a specific manner.
- **Manipulation:** Escape room-based experiences constitutes an opportunity to manipulate tools and models that might ease the understanding of some curricular concepts. Other games might use cards, images, texts… or other forms that might be useful to manage the escape room setup. However, to the author's consideration, as escape rooms are "physical games"; the physical, manipulative and experimental dimension should not be neglected if a proper simulation want to be delivered to the student.
- **Communication:** In the case of an educational escape room, obtaining the final code should not be the end of the activity; once finished with the escape experience, students/players should be interviewed in order to discuss and to think about the problems solved (which should be connected to the story). This is due to the excitation of the players: the emotional dimension must be reduced to avoid diluting the formative scope.
- **Isolation:** Isolation of the players is fundamental not only to promote autonomous work, but also to promote cooperative work. In the context of education, the game master becomes a "game teacher"; which may provide orientation, reformulate sentences, highlight clues, or even remind the players the position of a forgiven object. His role is to grant an optimum experience, both emotionally and formatively. Moreover, communication among players and the "game teacher" in real educational escape rooms is quite limited (normally, to audio–radio communication). In this regard, difficulty of the challenges and resources provided to the players plays a key role to deal with this limitation.
- **Continuity:** Educational escape rooms should be meaningfully connected to the concepts and knowledges that are being taught on the conventional course at the moment of the implementa-

tion. Furthermore, an EER might be useful to introduce new concepts, being later discussed in the conventional course. Finally, narrative, scenery, and storytelling are useful not only to create an immersive experience (Nicholson, 2016a) but to fit to an integrated curriculum approach.
- **Curriculum:** Enigmas and problems of an EER should mobilize curricular concepts. For example, in the particular case of mathematics (field of specialty of the author), they should fit to the standards and principles described by the NTCM (National Council of Teachers of Mathematics) for each educational stage (The National Council of Teachers of Mathematics, 2000).
- **Assessment:** Finally, as in any educational experience, an EER constitutes an activity where the development of certain competences should be assessed.

In case any (or various) of these principles are not respected in an EER experience, authors should consider that they are not designing a conventional "escape room experience" or maybe such experience is nor "educational" enough (and so cannot be labeled as Educational Escape Room).

Furthermore, the way in that an EER conducts the narrative, connects the clues, and provides the tools can ease or make more difficult the research and, thus, the learning and the mathematization process. So, different perspectives can be used to schedule and design an EER. The choice will depend on the expertise of the students, the complexity of the curricular concepts mobilized, the available resources and many other factors. Literature highlights three main categories (Piñero, 2019) depending on how the problems that composes the whole activity are connected among them:

- **Linear escape rooms:** in this distribution, problems are following a linear sequence and have to be resolved following a strict order.
- **Non-linear escape rooms:** which offers a higher number of clues and puzzles that can be resolved in any sequence (so players can decide how, when and who is going to solve each problem).
- **Distributed escape rooms:** this is a singular design where players are "isolated" among them (each player is in a different room). Distributed escape rooms can also be linear or non-linear, but the fact of isolating each player makes them different enough to have their own category.

Escape Room-like Alternatives

The above-mentioned design criteria may help to a proper use of the specific strengths of EERs as a collaborative environment where a simulation can be developed (so that curricular knowledge and professional tools or models are mobilized). An example of the specific strength of a conventional EER is presented in Fig.3a, where a group of students are autonomously exploring the use of specific tools for measuring weights (Piñero Charlo, 2020). However, there are some GBL approaches that becomes an alternative to "normative" EERs. While these alternatives are inspired (or adapted) from normative EERs, there are some criteria that are not respected so that some of the specific EER's strengths are not appearing. Among them virtual escape rooms, escape boxes and augmented reality-based EER becomes the most spread.

Virtual Escape Rooms

Virtual escape rooms are online-based setups where players can connect to the experience by using internet (from home or from the classroom itself). In this setup, there is no opportunity to manipulate physical

Figure 3.

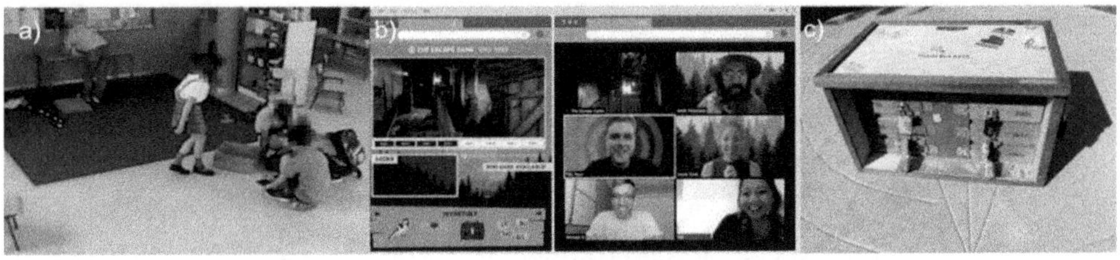

tools… so the simulation loose reality. Furthermore, players are not "isolated", so they have no real need to "escape" from anything. The only real need comes from the fact that they wish to win the game. This setup can be also adapted to fit curricular knowledge but miss a point of reality and simulation that has to be considered. An image to illustrate this setup can be consulted in Fig.3b (*Remote Adventures*, 2021).

Escape Boxes

A common alternative to escape rooms (that can also be adapted to educational purposes) is the "escape box" approach. In this setup, there is no room to escape for. Rather, players are committed to open a box which may have a similar structure to a conventional Escape Room. Here, there is no isolation of the players; but there is margin to allocate tools in the box (so that some manipulation and physical experimentation can be achieved). An image to illustrate this approach can be consulted in Fig.3c (*Dorno Escape Boxes*, 2021).

Augmented Reality in Escape Rooms

This is a blended form of Escape Rooms that combines the game mechanics of a physical and conventional ER with the use of Augmented Reality (AR) technology. The mixed approach is used to conduct real-physical environment (which can deliver a good simulation experience) with enriched information that cannot be physically provided due to limitations (Tzima et al., 2021).

PLAYING AN EDUCATIONAL ESCAPE ROOM AS A FORMATIVE TASK

While meaningful literature (it is, well recognized in prestigious databases, journals and books) in educational escape rooms is still under development -see Fig.1-, some researchers have already reported successful implementation of EER experiences in a variety of fields:

- Surgery (Adams et al., 2018; Brown et al., 2019).
- Medicine (Kinio et al., 2018; Wu et al., 2018).
- Pharmacy (Cain, 2018; Clauson et al., 2019; Gordon et al., 2019).
- Physiotherapy (Jiménez et al., 2017).
- Chemistry (Peleg et al., 2019; Vergne et al., 2019).
- Computer networks (Borrego et al., 2017)

Table 2. Example (simplified) of a puzzle description in an EER

Task number	Diagram	Narrative	Support
Task 1: Use marbles in the balance to weight objects. **Formative goal:** Use real tools to weight objects.		Provide the narrative goal, the mission to be accomplished and the implications for the whole story.	**Solution:** 7 – 5 – 9 **Padlock:** Padlock #3 (black, numeric/3) **Resources:** Balance, marbles, book… **Guidelines:** Weight three objects. **Time:** 15 minutes **Clues:** • 5 min: redistribute objects • 9 min: weight a single object • 12 min: wait for the equilibrium
Task 2: Brief description of the puzzle **Formative goal:** Brief description of the goals.	Diagram of the puzzle	Mission 2	Solution: Padlock: Resources: Guidelines: Time: Clues:

- Cryptography (Ho, 2018).
- Mathematics (Diago Nebot & Ventura-Campos, 2017; Piñero Charlo, 2020).
- Programming (López-Pernas et al., 2019).

On the other hand, there are other EER initiatives aimed at pre-university students with the aim of motivating informal learning on topics such as earthquake preparedness (Novak et al., 2019), criminology (Ferreiro-González et al., 2019), or radiology (Jambhekar et al., 2019). It is evident that the nature of the puzzles that make up the room will depend on the area of knowledge dealt with, although there are generic resources that appear repeatedly in the use of educational escape rooms (that is, the same resource is used to work on different concepts).

Getting Started in EERs

The designer of an educational game-based experience might be interested in Escape Rooms for a variety of educational purposes such as developing teamworking, strengthening prioritization (learners have to decide what to expend their time focusing on), creativity, skill practice, engagement and others. However, the most common intention is to promote higher levels of learning. It is, rather than teaching basic facts and figures to students, an EER approach tends to require them to apply knowledge in different situations than those in which they will have been initially learnt.

To reach proper formative standards, the designer shall follow the design guidelines of a conventional lecture (van de Walle et al., 2013); thus, considering the schedule, tools, tasks, questions… and many other parameters. However, all these facts are now in coordination with a specific narrative and under a GBL-PBL perspective. So, this section will briefly present all dimensions that should be considered for a proper learning environment based on an EER.

A Proposed Template

In our experience, a good EER starts with the consideration of the narrative, scenery and tasks involved. We name these three pillars "the environment", so that a diagram could be useful to provide a sequence of the ideas, narrative steps, formative scopes, etc. In our experiences, we use two main tools to clarify the design:

- **Map and overview:** Even when this might seem something trivial, a map would help to visualize the spatial distribution of the tasks. This would also help to determine the position of the camera (live videorecording is highly recommended), the expected sequence and similar considerations. The overview of the activity should state: the learning objectives, the key constraints, the outline of the narrative, a brief discussion of the puzzle organization and a brief draw outlining the puzzle organization.
- **Detailed puzzle description**: That should present a brief description of the puzzle (accompanied with images and diagrams), the solution of the puzzle, the locks used on the puzzle, the guidelines that will be provided, the clues that can be provided and the connection with the narrative.

Table 2 presents the simplified puzzle description used in one of our EER (Piñero Charlo, 2020); a map and an overview of the whole experience can be consulted in the referred study.

Resources that Might be Considered

Resources and manipulative tools play a key role in EERs, due to the possibility of helping students to learn by allowing them to move from concrete experiences to abstract reasoning (Heddens, 1986; Ross & Kurtz, 1993). Indeed, the use of manipulatives helps students hone their mathematical thinking skills:

Manipulatives can be important tools in helping students to think and reason in more meaningful ways. By giving students concrete ways to compare and operate on quantities, such manipulatives as pattern blocks, tiles, and cubes can contribute to the development of well-grounded, interconnected understandings of mathematical ideas. (Stein & Bovalino, 2001)

In this regard, to gain a deep understanding of mathematical ideas, students need to be able to integrate and connect a variety of concepts in many ways. (Clements, 2000) calls this type of understanding "Integrated-Concrete" knowledge. The effective use of manipulatives can help students connect ideas and integrate their knowledge so that they gain a deep understanding of mathematical concepts.

In addition to specific knowledge-related manipulatives and models (that will depend on the specific knowledge and ideas to be developed in the EER), there are some common manipulatives that are used in EERs. Among these common manipulatives one can enumerate -of course- common, directional and word padlocks or cryptex (a cylinder that can be opened with the right combination), among others -see Fig.4a-. In addition, the following resources could be considered in an EER:

Figure 4.

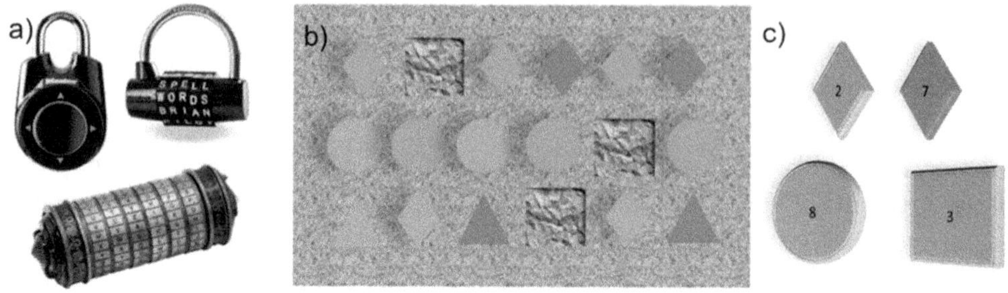

- **Hearing/sound:** sound can be used to either reveal clues or to be the puzzle (showing heartbeat patterns for medicine students or music-related material for musicians). This could be done by a soundtrack, noise signaling of something hidden (for example, a sound that is set off when you are near an object), or a lock being triggered by the players tapping a rhythm.
- **Light:** a common resource to use in escape rooms is invisible ink, combined with a UV light that reveals the hidden message. It could also be more subtle though, such as spot lighting (or colored lighting) that highlight clues.
- **Logic puzzles:** a good starting point for players that are first experiencing a EER experience is a logic puzzle, which consist in a set of clues that combine logically to give the solution of a question. This type is often seen in books of logic puzzles solved by filling in a grid to work out the missing pieces of information. Adapt this in an EER so that subject knowledge must also be deployed to solve the logic puzzles. An example of logic puzzle, using geometric figures and colors, is presented in figure 4b-c (note that the figures can be replaced by, for example, chemical elements).
- **Maths:** Often part of other puzzles, the designer can set simple math puzzles that need to be solved when the numbers have been revealed in some way (this is also a convenient wat of reinforcing basic math skills as part of another lesson).
- **Mazes:** Move an item along a maze to trigger an action. It could be physically moving something through a physical maze that triggers an electronic lock (or frees an item) or using the directions to open a directional lock. The mace could even represent steps in a process in an EER to check (or reinforce) knowledge of that process.
- **Matchmaker:** A type oz puzzle where pairing up items from two lists, reveals the answer. Letters or numbers between these lists reveal the answer when the items are linked correctly.
- **Assembly:** Physically putting together objects to from something new. At its simplest, it could be a jigsaw, or add a cog or handle to a mechanism to make it work. It's often less obvious than this though, and a proper example for EERs is to put a sheet of acetate with highlighted areas, or cards with sections cut out, to reveal a hidden message.

FURTHER CONSIDERATIONS ABOUT REAL IMPLEMENTATIONS

In addition to the above-mentioned design criteria, real implementations require additional routines to be considered:

- Presentation of the norms and rules of the game and discussion of such norms by asking questions as: what does the game consist of? What I understand… is coincident with what you have understood? how do you start playing? How will we organize the cooperation in the room?
- Show a brief simulation of the experience in which teacher helps to clarify doubts.
- Deliver a "questionnaire" after the experience, including questions such as: "explain what the game consisted of (connecting and discussing the narrative), what would you change in the way you play in a second attempt? Was it easy to win? This questionnaire can take the form of an interview right after the experience.
- Make a connection with the concepts that are being taught in conventional lectures: is this familiar to you? Did we discuss something similar?
- Collect data (video, audio transcriptions) to deliver evidence of learning to the educational community. This is a matter of interest for educational researchers, which would like to know strengths and limitations of educational escape rooms.

In our experience, some players use take a while to engage with the escape room (not knowing exactly what to do, touch or consider relevant on the room). The situation drastically improves when players become familiar with the tool, but these considerations have demonstrated to be useful for those that are first living an educational escape room experience.

Currently there are already some documents that describe the parameters to design educational escape rooms (Walsh, 2017). However, these studies lack the necessary scientific basis that, even today, is insufficient. Therefore, we believe that the main research point to which present and future efforts should be directed in the medium and short term should be the critical collection of evidence of learning in educational escape rooms, as a previous step to the validation of this tool and its alleged institutionalization.

Finally, it has been observed that considerations prior to the selection of student groups are not established (in fact, the criteria with which the groups are formed in the provided literature, are not indicated). We believe that it is positive to indicate the criteria for group composition: heterogeneous, homogeneous, etc... to clarify the results presented in future studies.

DESIGNING AN EDUCATIONAL ESCAPE ROOM AS A FORMATIVE TASK

The previous section presented some indicators and guidelines to consider, so that students on an EER achieve the formative scopes while clarifying the process through the narrative and the EER adventure itself. One can realize on the difficulty of designing a proper educational escape room. Indeed, the design and development of an EER has shown to mobilize professional skills and knowledge of mathematics' student teachers (Piñero Charlo et al., 2021).

Progressive Learning

Didactic trajectory is defined as "a hypothetical path through which primary school students can progress in their learning of a specific mathematical topic" (Clements & Sarama, 2014). While this construct is applied to mathematic education, it can be extended to other knowledge disciplines. Learning trajectories are a construct that can help student teachers (it is, future teachers) to learn to design teaching proposals that consider a progression in the understanding of mathematical topics in elementary school students. If we consider middle school children (aged between 6 and 12) This progression takes place in three stages:

- **Concrete stage:** A mathematical concept is introduced with manipulatives; students explore the concept using the manipulatives in purposeful activity.
- **Representational stage:** A mathematical concept is represented using pictures of some sort to stand for the concrete objects (the manipulatives) of the previous stage; students demonstrate how they can both visualize and communicate the concept at a pictorial level.
- **Abstract stage:** Mathematical symbols (numerals, operation signs, etc.) are used to express the concept in symbolic language; students demonstrate their understanding of the mathematical concept using the language of mathematics.

The reader can directly connect these stages with the way an EER works (driving through these three stages). In this regard, teachers play a crucial role in helping students use manipulatives successfully, so that they move through the three stages of learning and arrive at a deep understanding of mathematical concepts (as well as other knowledge disciplines). Furthermore, an EER can be an appropriate tool to develop this progressive learning.

Skills Mobilized

Designing an EER is a challenge from many points of view: organization, evaluation, tools to be used, scheduling, and a wide etcetera. Indeed, we have already demonstrated that these challenges mirrors that of the design of a conventional lecture (Piñero Charlo et al., 2021), concluding that student teachers can be committed to design and implement EERs as a part of their formative tasks; thus, developing some key professional competencies in the process.

As future teachers, the aim of the designed tasks should establish a problem-based-learning approach by applying gamification strategies; using the EER to foster cooperation, motivation and exploration; thus becoming an optimum tool for working mathematic-related content. So, student-teachers could be invited to design educational escape rooms, covering curricular aspects. A co-design strategy with a service-learning perspective allows fitting the escape room design to the real needs of schoolchild, also stimulating the implication of the participant students in the process.

This task (designing an EER) should be evaluated as a conventional task so that key didactic-professional knowledge is assessed. In doing so, we have detected specific skills and key competencies mobilized by the students during the development process, such as: (i) Meeting the curriculum. (ii) Understanding the basic principles and fundamental laws of the experimental, social, and exact sciences. (iii) Developing and evaluating appropriate teaching resources able to promote the acquisition of basic skills in students. (iv) Developing problem-solving skills. (v) Establishing connections among subjects and developing a problem-solving perspective strongly related to real problems.

We've successfully proposed the design and implementation of EER, so that trainee teachers were committed to do the whole task (designing, implementing, documenting, etcetera). We found that the professional competencies mobilized were: (i) Meet and promote interaction processes, cooperation strategies and team-working. (ii) Promote educational and scientific values (for an active and democratic citizenship), fostering the democratic education of citizens and the practice of critical social thinking. (iii) Identify, report, and collaborate in the treatment of learning difficulties by identifying and planning

Figure 5.

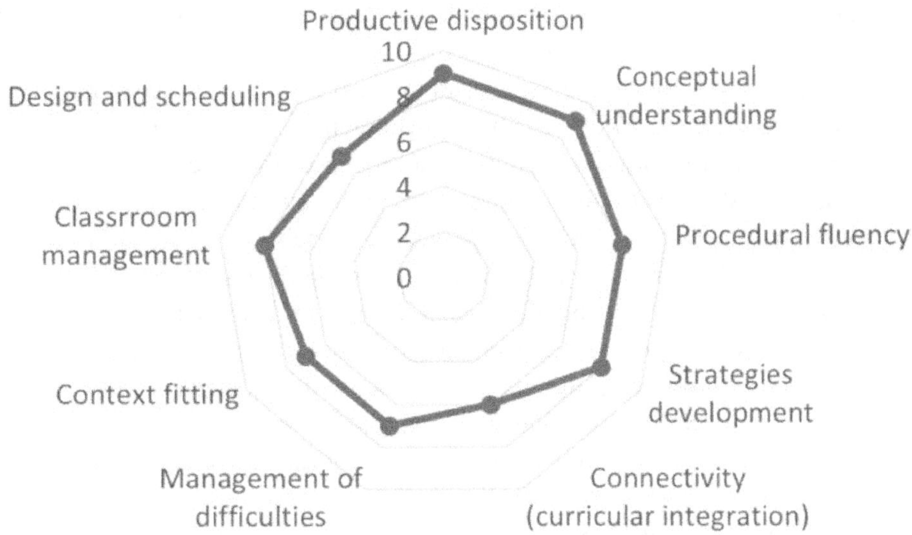

the resolution of educational situations that affect students with different abilities and different learning rates. (iv) Evaluate curriculum content and teaching resources and its influence in the promotion of basic skills in students. (v) Communicative and interactional skills.

Finally, we provide a "skill radar" plot with the main didactic-professionals skills that a trainee teacher should develop. This chart can be adapted to specific formative programs.

CONCLUSIONS AND FUTURE PROSPECT

Educational Escape Rooms have been reported to be a useful formative tool, both for students -experimenting the EER game- and as a formative task for trainee teachers. This chapter has provided wide literature, evidencing successful uses of EER in a variety of disciplines. We've also provided some templates that could be of interest for some teachers/researchers that would like to initiate in the use of Educational Escape Rooms.

Finally, we could conclude that the use of Educational Escape Rooms still has a wide margin for improvement; while it is also a matter of growing interest from the educational research point of view (as evidenced in Figure 1). The author would like to highlight the key importance of delivering learning evidence to the community; it is: publishing EER implementations with a proper analysis and discussion that shows the lights and shadows of this methodology -that is still in its very first stage of use-.

SUGGESTED USES FOR EDUCATIONAL ESCAPE ROOMS

To close this chapter, the author would like to clarify and summarize the most extended uses of Educational Escape Rooms:

- **As starting point:** While the interest of applying educational gamification is related to its capability to mobilize specific competences and knowledge, most educational games are designed not to learn, but to apply previously acquired knowledge. In this regard, some studies (Obando Zapata & Muñera Córdoba, 2003) invite one to subtend the acquisition of the knowledge (more specifically, mathematic knowledge) taking a "situation-problem" as a starting point (so that a scenery and a context is specifically built for a problem-based approach). The use of EERs to introduce a topic could lead to the students to "ask themselves the right questions"; thus, becoming a curiosity generator, creator of needs and an idoneous knowledge sustainer.
- **To create a context:** A mathematician would not communicate results "as obtained". Rather he will reorganize them, giving it the most general form and endowing knowledge with a communicable, decontextualized, depersonalized, and timeless structure. Instead, a teacher first performs an inverse work to the scientific one through a recontextualization and re-personalization of knowledge (looking for situations that give meaning to the knowledge to be taught). In this regard, designing EERs constitutes an opportunity to create a situation where knowledge becomes recontextualized.
- **As evaluation method:** An EER might imply the use of specific tools and models, whose mastering might be a matter of interest for the teacher (or for the purposes of the related course). In this regard, primary school children could be invited to use measuring tools like rulers, compass, balances, etcetera, while university students might use other specific tools. Furthermore, the information provided during peer-to-peer discussions can be a valuable source of data for an evaluator (and can also be an opportunity to identify errors and difficulties).
- **Designing as a formative task:** The design of an educational escape room unravels and fosters most of the didactic-professional skills that a trainee teacher shall develop during its formation. It is also an innovative way to deliver curricular tasks to future teachers.

REFERENCES

Adams, V., Burger, S., Crawford, K., & Setter, R. (2018). Can You Escape? Creating an Escape Room to Facilitate Active Learning. *Journal for Nurses in Professional Development*, *34*(2), E1–E5. doi:10.1097/NND.0000000000000433 PMID:29481471

Borrego, C., Fernández, C., Blanes, I., & Robles, S. (2017). Room escape at class: Escape games activities to facilitate the motivation and learning in computer science. *Journal of Technology and Science Education*, *7*(2), 162. doi:10.3926/jotse.247

Brown, N., Darby, W., Practitioner, N., Nurse, C., Coronel, H., & Practitioner, N. (2019). An Escape Room as a Simulation Teaching Strategy. *Clinical Simulation in Nursing*, *30*, 1–6. doi:10.1016/j.ecns.2019.02.002

Bunchball. (2010). *Gamification 101: An Introduction to the Use of Game*. doi:10.1016/j.compedu.2012.12.020

Cain, J. (2018). Exploratory implementation of a blended format escape room in a large enrollment pharmacy management class. *Currents in Pharmacy Teaching & Learning*, *11*(1), 44–50. doi:10.1016/j.cptl.2018.09.010 PMID:30527875

Carmona, E., & Cardeñoso, J. M. (2019). Situations based on board games to attend to the elaboration of school mathematical knowledge [Situaciones basadas en juegos de mesa para atender la elaboración del conocimiento matematico escolar]. *Épsilon, 101*, 7–30.

Chamoso, J. M., Durán, J., García, J., Martínez, J., & Rodríguez-Sánchez, M. (2004). Analysis and experimentation of games as instruments to teach mathematics [Análisis y experimentación de juegos como instrumentos para enseñar matemáticas]. *Suma, 47*, 47–58. http://revistasuma.es/IMG/pdf/47/047-058.pdf

Clauson, A., Hahn, L., Frame, T., Hagan, A., Bynum, L. A., Thompson, M. E., & Kiningham, K. (2019). An innovative escape room activity to assess student readiness for advanced pharmacy practice experiences (APPEs). *Currents in Pharmacy Teaching & Learning, 11*(7), 723–728. doi:10.1016/j.cptl.2019.03.011 PMID:31227096

Clements, D. H. (2000). 'Concrete' Manipulatives, Concrete Ideas. *Contemporary Issues in Early Childhood, 1*(1), 45–60. doi:10.2304/ciec.2000.1.1.7

Clements, D. H., & Sarama, J. (2014). *Learning and teaching early math: The learning trajectories approach*. Routledge. doi:10.4324/9780203520574

Connolly, T. M., Boyle, E. A., MacArthur, E., Hainey, T., & Boyle, J. M. (2012). A systematic literature review of empirical evidence on computer games and serious games. *Computers & Education, 59*(2), 661–686. doi:10.1016/j.compedu.2012.03.004

Csikszentmihalyi, M. (1990). *Flow: The Psychology of Optimal Experience*. Herper Perennial.

de Freitas, S. (2013). *Learning in immersive worlds: A review of game-based learning*. https://www.jisc.ac.uk/media/documents/programmes/elearninginnovation/gamingreport_v3.pdfhttp://curve.coventry.ac.uk/open

Diago Nebot, P. D., & Ventura-Campos, N. (2017). Escape Room: Educational gamification for learning mathematics [Escape Room: gamificación educativa para el aprendizaje de las matemáticas]. *Suma, 85*, 33–40.

Djaouti, D., Alvarez, J., & Jessel, J.-P. (2011). Classifying serious games: The G/P/S model. In Handbook of Research on Improving Learning and Motivation through Educational Games: Multidisciplinary Approaches. IGI Global. doi:10.4018/978-1-60960-495-0.ch006

Dorno escape boxes. (2021). https://www.oio-7.top/products.aspx?cid=42&cname=escape+box

Edo, M., Baeza, M., Deulofeu, J., & Badillo, E. (2008). Study of the parallelism between the phases of solving a game and the phases of solving a problem [Estudio del paralelismo entre las fases de resolución de un juego y las fases de resolución de un problema]. *Union- Revista Iberoamericana de Educación Matemática, 14*, 61–75.

Ferreiro-González, M., Amores-Arrocha, A., Espada-Bellido, E., Aliano-Gonzalez, M. J., Vázquez-Espinosa, M., González-De-Peredo, A., Sancho-Galán, P., Álvarez-Saura, J. Á., Barbero, G. F., & Cejudo-Bastante, C. (2019). Escape ClassRoom: Can You Solve a Crime Using the Analytical Process? *Journal of Chemical Education, 96*(2), 267–273. doi:10.1021/acs.jchemed.8b00601

Gordon, S. K., Trovinger, S., & Delellis, T. (2019). Escape from the usual : Development and implementation of an ‘ escape room ’ activity to assess team dynamics. *Currents in Pharmacy Teaching & Learning*, *11*(8), 818–824. doi:10.1016/j.cptl.2019.04.013 PMID:31227197

Heddens, J. W. (1986). Bridging the gap between the concrete and the abstract. *The Arithmetic Teacher*, *33*(6), 14–17. doi:10.5951/AT.33.6.0014

Hermanns, M., Deal, B., Campbell, A. M., Hillhouse, S., Opella, J. B., Faigle, C., & Campbell, R. H. IV. (2018). Using an “Escape Room” toolbox approach to enhance pharmacology education. *Journal of Nursing Education and Practice*, *8*(4), 89. doi:10.5430/jnep.v8n4p89

Ho, A. M. (2018). Unlocking Ideas: Using Escape Room Puzzles in a Cryptography Classroom. *PRIMUS (Terre Haute, Ind.)*, *28*(0), 1–13. doi:10.1080/10511970.2018.1453568

Huitt, W., & Hummel, J. (2003). Piagets Theory of Cognitive Development. In *Educational Psychology Interactive: cognitive development*. Valdosta State University. https://www.google.com/url?sa=t&rct=j&q=&esrc=s&source=web&cd=&cad=rja&uact=8&ved=2ahUKEwjijvjfpuLxAhWSHRQKHVJSBHcQgAMoAHoECAIQAg&url=http%3A%2F%2Fscholar.google.es%2Fscholar_url%3Furl%3Dhttps%3A%2F%2Fintranet.newriver.edu%2Fimages%2Fstories%2Flibrary%2Fstennett_psychology_articles%2FPiagets%252520Theory%252520of%252520Cognitive%252520Development.pdf%26hl%3Des%26sa%3DX%26ei%3DsrXuYJrZONzSsQLa-bb4DA%26scisig%3DAAGBfm1v3pK0vg0T8d5QUl1dSac91MMN_g%26nossl%3D1%26oi%3Dscholarr&usg=AOvVaw1_dbqUkiMk_8j2wv5gZCBG

Jambhekar, K., Pahls, R. P., & Deloney, L. A. (2019). Benefits of an Escape Room as a Novel Educational Activity for Radiology Residents. *Academic Radiology*, 1–8. doi:10.1016/j.acra.2019.04.021 PMID:31160173

Jiménez, C., Lafuente, R., Ortiz, M., Bruton, L., & Luna, V. M. (2017). Room Escape: Proposal of Gamification in the Degree of Physiotherapy [Room Escape: Propuesta de Gamificación en el Grado de Fisioterapia]. *Proc. Congreso Nacional De Innovación Educativa Y De Docencia En Red*, 537–551.

Kapp, K. M. (2012). *The gamification of learning and instruction: game-based methods and strategies for training and education*. Pfeiffer.

Kim, B., Park, H., & Baek, Y. (2009). Not just fun, but serious strategies: Using meta-cognitive strategies in game-based learning. *Computers & Education*, *52*(4), 800–810. Advance online publication. doi:10.1016/j.compedu.2008.12.004

Kim, S., Song, K., Lockee, B., & Burton, J. (2018). What is Gamification in Learning and Education? In Gamification in Learning and Education. Advances in Game-Based Learning (pp. 25–38). doi:10.1007/978-3-319-47283-6_4

Kinio, A. E., Dufresne, L., Brandys, T., & Jetty, P. (2018). Break out of the Classroom : The Use of Escape Rooms as an Alternative Teaching Strategy in Surgical Education. *Journal of Surgical Education*, *76*(1), 134–139. doi:10.1016/j.jsurg.2018.06.030 PMID:30126728

Llorens Largo, F., Gallego-Durán, F. J., Villagrá-Arnedo, C.-J., Compañ, P., Satorre Cuerda, R., & Molina-Carmona, R. (2015). Lessons learned by gamifying when it was not yet called gamification [Lecciones aprendidas gamificando cuando aún no se llamaba gamificación]. *La Sociedad Del Aprendizaje. Actas Del III Congreso Internacional Sobre Aprendizaje, Innovación y Competitividad. CINAIC 2015*, 214–219.

López-Pernas, S., Gordillo, A., Barra, E., & Quemada, J. (2019). Examining the Use of an Educational Escape Room for Teaching Programming in a Higher Education Setting. *IEEE Access: Practical Innovations, Open Solutions*, *7*, 31723–31737. doi:10.1109/ACCESS.2019.2902976

Lugmayr, A., Sutinen, E., Suhonen, J., Sedano, C. I., Hlavacs, H., & Montero, C. S. (2017). Serious storytelling – a first definition and review. *Multimedia Tools and Applications*, *76*(14), 15707–15733. Advance online publication. doi:10.100711042-016-3865-5

Ma, J.-P., Chuang, M.-H., & Lin, R. (2018). An innovated design of ER box by STEAM. In P.-L. P. Rau (Ed.), *Cross-Cultural Design: Applications in Cultural Heritage, Creativity and Social Development* (Vol. 2, pp. 70–79). Springer. doi:10.1007/978-3-319-92252-2_6

Monaghan, S. R., & Nicholson, S. (2017). Bringing Escape Room Concepts to Pathophysiology Case Studies. *HAPS Educator*, *21*(2), 49–65. doi:10.21692/haps.2017.015

Montessori, M. (1916). *The Montessori Method*. Schocken Books.

Murray, J. (2018). The play's the thing. In International Journal of Early Years Education (Vol. 26, Issue 4). doi:10.1080/09669760.2018.1527278

Nicholson, S. (2015). *Peeking Behind the Locked Door: A Survey of Escape Room Facilities*. https://scottnicholson.com/pubs/erfacwhite.pdf

Nicholson, S. (2016a). Ask Why: Creating a Better Player Experience through Environmental Storytelling and Consistency in Escape Room Design. *Meaningful Play 2016*, 1–17. https://scottnicholson.com/pubs/askwhy.pdf

Nicholson, S. (2016b). The State of Escape: Escape Room Design and Facilities. *Meaningful Play 2016*, 20. https://scottnicholson.com/pubs/stateofescape.pdf

Nicholson, S. (2018). Creating engaging escape rooms for the classroom. *Childhood Education*, *94*(1), 44–49. doi:10.1080/00094056.2018.1420363

Novak, J., Lozos, J. C., & Spear, S. E. (2019). Development of an Interactive Escape Room Intervention to Educate College Students about Earthquake Preparedness. *Natural Hazards Review*, *20*(1), 06018001. doi:10.1061/(ASCE)NH.1527-6996.0000322

Obando Zapata, G., & Muñera Córdoba, J. J. (2003). Problem situations as a strategy for mathematical conceptualization [Las situaciones problema como estrategia para la conceptualización matemática]. *Revista Educación y Pedagogía*, *15*(35), 183–199.

Oprescu, F., Jones, C., & Katsikitis, M. (2014). I PLAY AT WORK-ten principles for transforming work processes through gamification. *Frontiers in Psychology*, *5*(JAN), 1–5. doi:10.3389/fpsyg.2014.00014 PMID:24523704

Pan, R., Lo, H., & Neustaedter, C. (2017). Collaboration, Awareness, and Communication in Real-Life Escape Rooms. *Proceedings of the 2017 Conference on Designing Interactive Systems - DIS '17*, 1353–1364. 10.1145/3064663.3064767

Peleg, R., Yayon, M., Katchevich, D., Moria-shipony, M., & Blonder, R. (2019). *A Lab-Based Chemical Escape Room: Educational, Mobile, and Fun!* doi:10.1021/acs.jchemed.8b00406

Piaget, J. (1945). *Play, Dreams, and Imitation in Childhood*. Norton.

Piñero, J. C. (2019). Análisis sistemático del uso de salas de escape educativas: estado del arte y perspectivas de futuro. *Espacios, 40*(44), 9. http://www.revistaespacios.com/a19v40n44/19404409.html

Piñero Charlo, J. C. (2020). Educational Escape Rooms as a Tool for Horizontal Mathematization: Learning Process Evidence. *Education in Science*, *10*(9), 213. doi:10.3390/educsci10090213

Piñero Charlo, J. C., Ortega García, P., & Román García, S. (2021). Formative Potential of the Development and Assessment of an Educational Escape Room Designed to Integrate. *Education in Science*, *11*(3), 131. doi:10.3390/educsci11030131

Polya, G. (1945). *How To Solve It*. Academic Press.

Remote Adventures. (2021). https://theescapegame.com/blog/remote-adventures-our-answer-to-friendly-family-competition-over-the-holidays/

Ross, R., & Kurtz, R. (1993). Making Manipulatives Work: A Strategy for Success. *The Arithmetic Teacher*, *40*(5), 254–257. doi:10.5951/AT.40.5.0254

Stein, M. K., & Bovalino, J. W. (2001). Manipulatives: One Piece of the Puzzle. *Mathematics Teaching in the Middle School*, *6*(6), 356–359. doi:10.5951/MTMS.6.6.0356

Swacha, J. (2021). State of Research on Gamification in Education: A Bibliometric Survey. *Education Sciences, 11*, 69.

The National Council of Teachers of Mathematics. (Ed.). (2000). *Principles and Standards for School Mathematics*. https://www.nctm.org/Standards-and-Positions/Principles-and-Standards/Principles,-Standards,-and-Expectations/

Tzima, S., Styliaras, G., & Bassounas, A. (2021). Revealing hidden local cultural heritage through a serious escape game in outdoor settings. *Information (Switzerland)*, *12*(1), 1–17. doi:10.3390/info12010010

van de Walle, J. A., Karp, K. S., Williams, B., & Jennifer, M. (2013). Elementary and Middle School Mathematics: Teaching Developmentally (8th ed.). Pearson.

Veldkamp, A., Daemen, J., Teekens, S., Koelewijn, S., Knippels, M. C. P. J., & van Joolingen, W. R. (2020). Escape boxes: Bringing escape room experience into the classroom. *British Journal of Educational Technology*, *51*(4), 1220–1239. doi:10.1111/bjet.12935

Vergne, M. J., Simmons, J. D., & Bowen, R. S. (2019). Escape the Lab: An Interactive Escape-Room Game as a Laboratory Experiment. *Journal of Chemical Education*, *96*(5), 985–991. doi:10.1021/acs.jchemed.8b01023

Vittersø, J., & Csikszentmihalyi, M. (2000). Finding Flow. The Psychology of Engagement with Everyday Life. *Journal of Happiness Studies*, *1*(1), 121–123. Advance online publication. doi:10.1023/A:1010032312178

Vygotsky, L. (1978). *Mind in Society*. Harvard University Press.

Walsh, A. (2017). *Making Escape Rooms for Educational Purposes: A Workbook*. Academic Press.

Warmelink, H., Mayer, I., Weber, J., Heijligers, B., Haggis, M., Peters, E., & Louwerse, M. (2017). AMELIO: Evaluating the Team-building Potential of a Mixed Reality Escape Room Game. *Extended Abstracts Publication of the Annual Symposium on Computer-Human Interaction in Play - CHI PLAY '17 Extended Abstracts*. 10.1145/3130859.3131436

Williams, P. (2018). Using escape room-like puzzles to teach undergraduate students effective and efficient group process skills. *ISEC 2018 - Proceedings of the 8th IEEE Integrated STEM Education Conference*, 254–257. 10.1109/ISECon.2018.8340495

Wouters, P., van der Spek, E. D., & van Oostendorp, H. (2009). Current Practices in Serious Game Research. In L. Boyle, M. Stansfield, & T. Connolly (Eds.), *Games-Based Learning Advancements for Multi-Sensory Human Computer Interfaces* (pp. 232–250). doi:10.4018/978-1-60566-360-9.ch014

Wu, C., Wagenschutz, H., & Hein, J. (2018). Promoting leadership and teamwork development through Escape Rooms. *Medical Education*, *52*(5), 561–562. doi:10.1111/medu.13557 PMID:29508433

Young, M. F., Slota, S., Cutter, A. B., Jalette, G., Mullin, G., Lai, B., Simeoni, Z., Tran, M., & Yukhymenko, M. (2012). Our Princess Is in Another Castle: A Review of Trends in Serious Gaming for Education. *Review of Educational Research*, *82*(1), 61–89. doi:10.3102/0034654312436980

Chapter 9
Converting Course Material to Educational Escape Room Formats

Robert Ross
La Trobe University, Australia

Richard Hall
La Trobe University, Australia

Sarah Lynne Ross
Escape Room Education, Australia

ABSTRACT

Game-based learning and gamification concepts are growing as educators look to engage, motivate, and create memorable learning experiences for their students. In this chapter, the authors provide a primer to bring teachers and academics up to date on developing educational escape rooms for their classrooms. Hence, this chapter gives an overview of what education escape rooms are, how they can be run, narratives, the pedagogical purpose of the escape room, and how puzzles can be generated. The chapter provides categories of puzzle types with examples and concludes with a STEM-based escape room activity targeted toward secondary school students.

INTRODUCTION

Humans have enjoyed playing games for thousands of years. Early records suggest that ancient forms of backgammon (Game of Ur) and checkers have their origins around 3000BC (Masukawa, 2016; Pietroszek et al., 2021). Although traditional 'recreational games may have some educational benefit (e.g., teaching counting, sequences, teamwork), games and game principles can also be purposefully employed as a pedagogical teaching practice.

DOI: 10.4018/978-1-6684-4287-6.ch009

Active learning is a broad concept which has significantly leveraged gamification and GBL. Active learning, in contrast to passive learning, requires learners to actively participate in the classroom as part of their learning experience – in contrast to passively receiving information (Bonwell & Eison, 1991; Coorey, 2016). Although active learning approaches are varied (e.g., problem-based learning, peer learning, clickers, GBL) it has demonstrated positive effects on student understanding, engagement, and collaboration (De Caprariis et al., 2001; Prince, 2004).

Pedagogy encompassing games and game-concepts broadly includes several distinct implementations including gamification, game-based learning (GBL) and serious games (Becker, 2021). Gamification involves integrating game-based elements into education (e.g., points, badges, or leaderboards). Serious games are games which are not just for recreation but may also seek to change a behaviour or an attitude of players. Finally, GBL use games specifically designed with educational learning goals in mind (Kapp, 2012).

Gamification and GBL approaches have been used in many different educational contexts to engage, motivate, and enhance learning. More recently educational escape rooms have risen to prominence as a new wave of GBL which has been embraced across many different disciplines (Lathwesen & Belova, 2021; Veldkamp et al., 2020a).

The objective of this chapter is to provide readers with the fundamentals of what educational escape rooms, how they can be run and how they can be created. The chapter is organised as follows: the background section provides a background to the origins of recreational and educational escape rooms whilst highlighting the breadth of topics that educational escape rooms have been adapted for. The solutions and recommendations section discusses different escape room implementations, puzzle design, evaluation, and storyline design. Following this an example of a complete educational escape room with student study data is provided. Finally future research directions around escape room design and use are provided along with a conclusion.

BACKGROUND

Educational escape rooms, as described in this chapter have their roots in table-top forms of recreational escape rooms. The history of recreational escape rooms is relatively recent. In 2007, the first in-person recreational escape room began and quickly spread around the world (Nicholson, 2015). Currently there are tens of thousands of recreational escape rooms spread across over 50 different countries (Ferguson, 2019). These in-person games were preceded by adventure-based computer games of a similar genre like Crimson Room and Myst (Bartlett & Anderson, 2019)

The basic premise of recreational escape rooms is that a group of participants need to solve puzzles to unlock a series of solutions and escape from a room within a specified time interval (Wiemker et al., 2015). Each room has a narrative storyline which the participants work within. Common storylines include prison breaks, horror, detective, and virus outbreaks. Although they are referred to as an 'escape room', many contain several adjoining rooms each with puzzles and locks to unlock. Studies indicate the recreational escape room clientele are an approximately equal mix of males and females and have been used as corporate team bonding, date nights and as a fun activity among friends (Nicholson, 2015).

More recently the escape room game genre has expanded to table-top games including both board-game varieties (e.g., EXiT, Unlock! Escape Room the Game) and computer-based online games (e.g. The

Experiment, Escape F1rst). Although these table-top variants don't rely on being locked in a physical room, they include the teamwork, puzzle solving, narrative and time-pressure of traditional escape rooms.

Even more recently, educational escape rooms have risen to prominence as an engaging form of team-based learning (Clarke et al., 2016; Veldkamp et al., 2020a). In contrast to recreational escape rooms, which are primarily designed for enjoyment and experience, educational escape rooms are designed with specific learning objectives in mind. In contrast to traditional (passive) learning approaches (where students merely listen to a teacher), educational escape rooms are a form of active learning where participants actively discuss, problem solve, reason, collaborate and synthesise knowledge (Bonwell & Eison, 1991). Importantly, active learning approaches have been shown to be beneficial for learning (Prince, 2004).

Educational escape rooms have quickly grown in number and scope. For primary and secondary students, Breakout-Edu has been a platform that has proven popular with thousands of teachers designed games. These have been helpfully shared and aligned with learning standards (O'Brien & Pitera, 2019). Within the health domain there are recent examples of nursing, dentistry, and toxicology (Adams et al., 2018; Boysen-Osborn et al., 2018; Zaug et al., 2021). Recent examples within science disciplines include chemistry, physics, and molecular biology (Peleg et al., 2019; Ross & Bell, 2019; Vörös & Sárközi, 2017). Classically, problem-solving based disciplines within Engineering have a natural match for escape room puzzles including digital electronics, telecommunications and more widely in student recruitment (Ross & Bennett, 2020).

MAIN FOCUS OF THE CHAPTER

The focus of this chapter is to act as a primer to bring teachers and academics up to date with how to develop educational escape rooms for their classroom. Hence, this work will give an overview of how educational escape rooms can be run, the pedagogical purpose of the escape room and how puzzles can be generated.

SOLUTIONS AND RECOMMENDATIONS

This section starts by outlining the different formats that educational escape room concept that can be used in. Following this there is a description with examples of different puzzle types which can be used to highlight how puzzles can be created. Escape rooms are more than just a series of puzzles, so following this the concept of narratives is discussed to give concept and coherence to the GBL environment. The following section provides keys to evaluating educational escape rooms as not all GBL experiences or puzzles are created equal. To complete this section, the full puzzles and narrative for an educational escape room are provided. Data from participant testing is presented to measure effectiveness of the educational escape room.

Educational Escape Room Formats

Educational escape rooms have been implemented across classrooms in several different styles. These largely fall into four main categories:

- Physical rooms with physical puzzles that are solved in-person by teams of participants. There are several different examples of these styles of escape rooms which closely mimic the recreational escape rooms (Novak et al., 2019). Although this form of escape room is the most immersive of all (the participants are in a real room environment) it scales poorly for larger class groups of learners. Let us consider some of the drawbacks in using physical escape rooms for education. Firstly, there is significant cost in setting up purpose-built rooms for a learning activity. Secondly, only a small number of participants can complete the activity simultaneously. Thirdly, there is a significant time to reset the room after each game. Fourthly, a booking system to schedule games is required. Finally, a game master (the teacher/lecturer) is required to be present to observe all the games (López-Pernas et al., 2021).
- Online escape room games where participants work using a webpage and may communicate with other students online or within the same classroom. Although there are recent examples of online escape room development platforms (López-Pernas et al., 2021) many online escape rooms repurpose existing platforms such as Google Forms (Cain, 2019). The online educational escape-room environment benefits from scalability, ease of setup, COVID safeness and low cost (López-Pernas et al., 2021). Some drawbacks to the online model include decreased group interaction, greater abstraction from the real world, potential internet connectivity issues, limitations on the puzzles that can be used (e.g., they can't be folded) and finally the pushback against doing everything "on a screen".
- Lockbox escape rooms (e.g., Breakout-EDU) are where students need to solve a series of puzzles which unlock combination locks to unlock a box. In contrast to breaking out of a room, the lock-box approach has participants solving puzzles to break into a locked box, typically by unlocking a series of combination locks as solutions to each of the puzzles (O'Brien & Pitera, 2019; Veldkamp et al., 2020b). This approach is more hands-on and is less abstracted compared to the online variants and provides possibility for tangible prizes (locked within the box). Compared to the physical rooms, the lock-box approach is much lower cost, and many groups can simultaneously participate (using multiple lockboxes) all within the one room. Some drawbacks of the lock-box approach are that timing is still required, reconfigurability, although possible, can be time consuming, and clue delivery is still heavily dependent on teaching staff.
- Electronic decoder boxes where participants solve paper-based or physical puzzles and then validate their answers by typing them into an electronic decoder box as shown in Figure 1 (Ross, 2019). The decoder box method provides a hands-on, less abstracted approach compared with the online approaches. Similar to the lock-box approach, the decoder box allows many groups to complete the activity all within the one space at relatively low cost. The electronic decoder box has significant advantages over the lock-box approach including: a built-in timer, automated clue delivery, penalties for incorrect guesses and data analytics to measure learner performance.

In contrast to the traditional physical room approach, the online, lock-box and decoder box approaches can be viewed as table-top educational escape room activities which, aside from being much cheaper, allow many groups to complete the same activity within the same physical space. Given these particular advantages around scalability, this chapter focusses on the table-top approaches. For these table-top escape rooms there are different ways that puzzles can be presented to users, which will in-part reflect the type of escape room game being played. The four predominate approaches are:

Figure 1. Decoder box for puzzle validation (Ross & Hall, 2021).

- **Paper based:** The simplest and most cost-effective approach is to print puzzles and distribute these to the teams. Printed puzzles can be distributed in sealed envelopes (to prevent participants going onto the next puzzle before completing earlier ones). These are disposable and can be directly written on which can be helpful in the problem-solving process.
- **Online:** For the online escape rooms the most natural way of presenting the puzzles is online (e.g. shown on a webpage). This approach allows puzzles to be easily altered, allows for multimedia, but does make it harder for teams of students to 'draw on the puzzles' and means that puzzles requiring folding or overlaying of different parts will not be available.
- **Paper-based technology mediated:** Puzzles may combine aspects of augmented reality or virtual reality. Examples would include QR codes which provide additional information or fiducial markers which provide augmented reality overlays when viewed with a participants phone or tablet.
- **Physical objects:** Some physical objects may be used (which fit the tabletop format) to provide a less abstracted and more hands-on experience.

Figure 2. Mathematical puzzles requires antenna gain to be ordered based on free space path loss

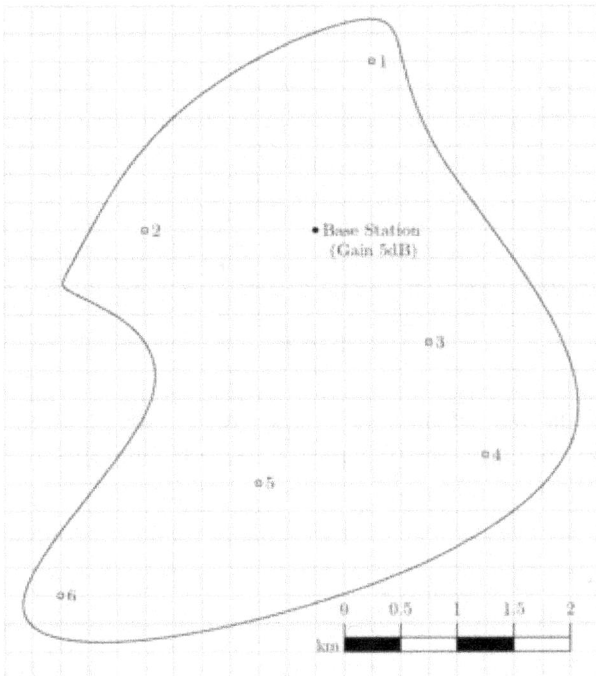

Sensor	Transmitter Antenna Gain (dB)	Frequency (MHz)
1	1	915
2	2	915
3	3	915
4	3	433
5	3	433

Educational Escape Room Puzzle Types

Having discussed the different escape room implementations (how the game is played) this section will provide examples of different ways puzzles can be constructed to contain learning elements. These puzzles will be primarily targeted towards table-top escape rooms (i.e. not the full physical room) as they are lower cost, more scalable and better suited to the classroom environment. Many of the locking/validation approaches require a numerical answer (e.g. a combination lock) so some of the puzzle answers in the following section will specifically result in numerical answers. The different puzzle types include:

- **Mathematical reasoning:** Many puzzles within STEM fields require some mathematical reasoning or computation to determine a result. Many different mathematical computations are possible including computation of chemical concentrations, computations of forces in physics, computation of variables within geometry or conversions between different number bases for digital mathematics (Ross & Bell, 2019; Ross & Bennett, 2020). In these circumstances, the unlocking code may be the direct result of the mathematical computation (rounded to a known number of significant figures). Figure 2 shows an example of one element of a puzzle using mathematical reasoning to compute in order the free-space path loss of various radio transmitters for a telecommunications engineering subject (Ross & de Souza-Daw, 2021).

- **Unscrambling:** Words, collections of words or even individual letters may be scrambled to hide their intended meaning (e.g. a famous historical quote). Each of the groups of words can be as-

Table 1. Puzzle requiring reordering within a sentence

faith in Jesus Christ, so we also have believed	1
in Christ Jesus, in order to be justified	8
yet we know that a person is not	5
by faith in Christ and not	2
justified by works of the law but through	7
by works of the law, because	4
no one will be justified.	6
by works of the law	3

signed a number and the correct order of the words will generate a number which is the solution. The example shown below is taken from the book of Galatians (Chapter 2, verse 16) and the correct numerical solution would be 57182436. Another approach which may take unscrambling a step further would be to perform a frequency analysis – count how many times the unscrambled words are found in a block of text.

- **Cipher:** Many different ciphers or encoding means (e.g. morse code, pigpen, phone, Caesar, Braille) are commonly used within escape rooms. These could be used to hide clues, add fun or form the point of the whole activity (e.g. a communications engineering task involving decoding serial bitstrings). Three examples are shown below in Figures 3-5 which respectively encode: 'TWO', 'TUCKER' and 'ULTRASOUND'.

- **Physical reasoning:** Some physical phenomena (which is generally well known) may form the basis of puzzles (e.g. water flow, direction that each gear turns in a drivetrain). The example puzzle provided (Figure 6) requires students to work out the direction each of the gears are turning (clockwise or counter clockwise) and use the key extractor to deduce a code based on this. For this set of gears the code would be 5.

- **Logical deduction**: Some puzzles may involve some logical deduction to successfully remove some options and order the remaining options. The example shown in Figure 7 is a variant of the popular 'open this lock' viral puzzle. Students need to work out the correct 3 digit sequence of numbers and the correct order by using the clues. The correct answer for this puzzle is 183.

- **Physical objects:** Although table-top escape rooms will not be as elaborate as the full physical room implementation, there may be some elements where physical objects can be provided to solve the puzzle (e.g. multi-meter, laser-cut gears, UV torch). Figure 8 shows two electrical circuits enclosed by acrylic. The circuit on the left has some of the inputs connected to different outputs and participants need to use a multimeter to determine the connectivity. The circuit on the

Figure 3. Serial BitString which spells out the word TWO

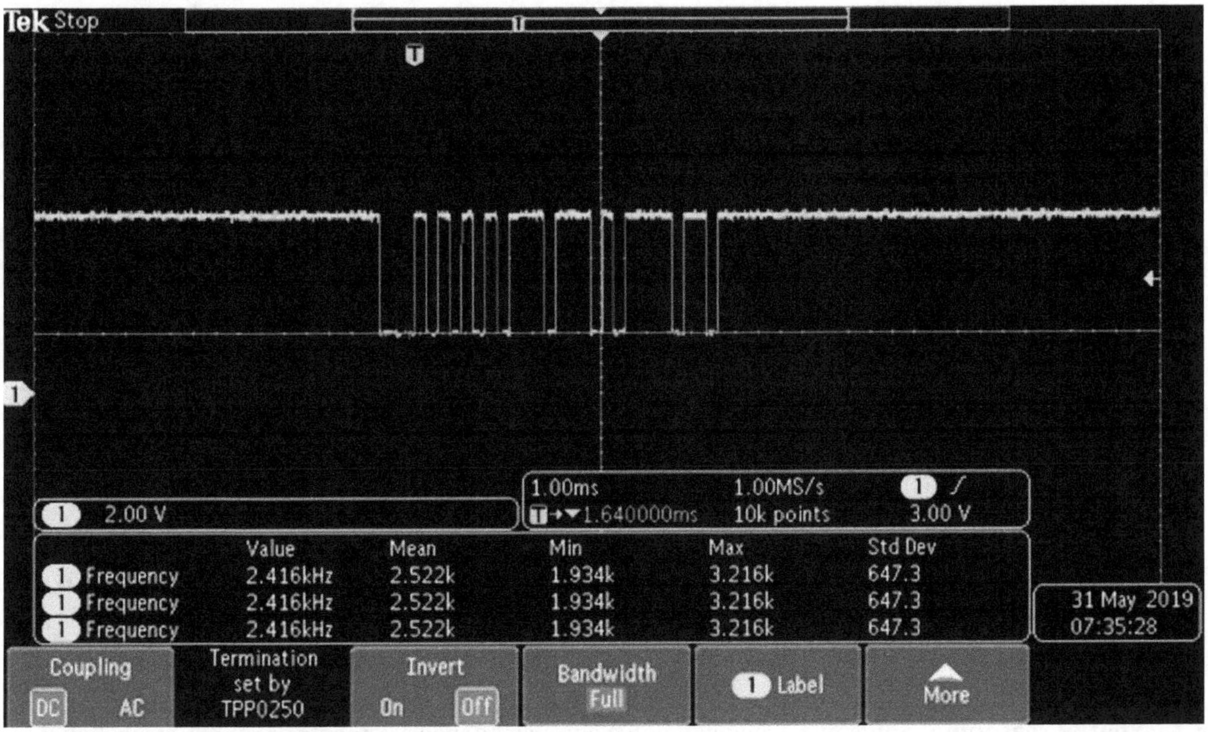

right has different analog voltages produced at each pin (1-5) which participants measure with a multi-meter.

Figure 4. Pigpen cipher which spells out the word 'TUCKER'

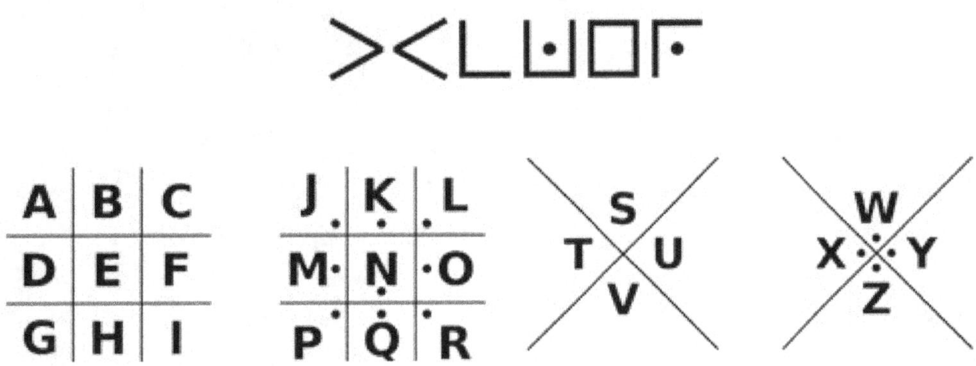

- **Hidden within text**: Early recreational escape rooms often encoded solutions or clues directly as anomalies or elements within the text (e.g. errors, capitalization, changing colour, anagrams). Figure 9 shows a slab of text with 5 missing characters which spell out the word "NINE". Figure

Figure 5. T9 phone keypad cipher which spells out 'ULTRASOUND'

10 shows two sections of C-Code with errors on lines 5 (left - missing a semi-colon) and 6 (right – misspelling checkSum).

- **Spatial reasoning:** Some puzzles may involve comparing measurements or other physical quantities between objects (e.g. distance measurements or angles for a geography based puzzle). The puzzle shown in Figure 11 requires participants to measure the distance from scrambled place

Figure 6. Gear-train puzzle

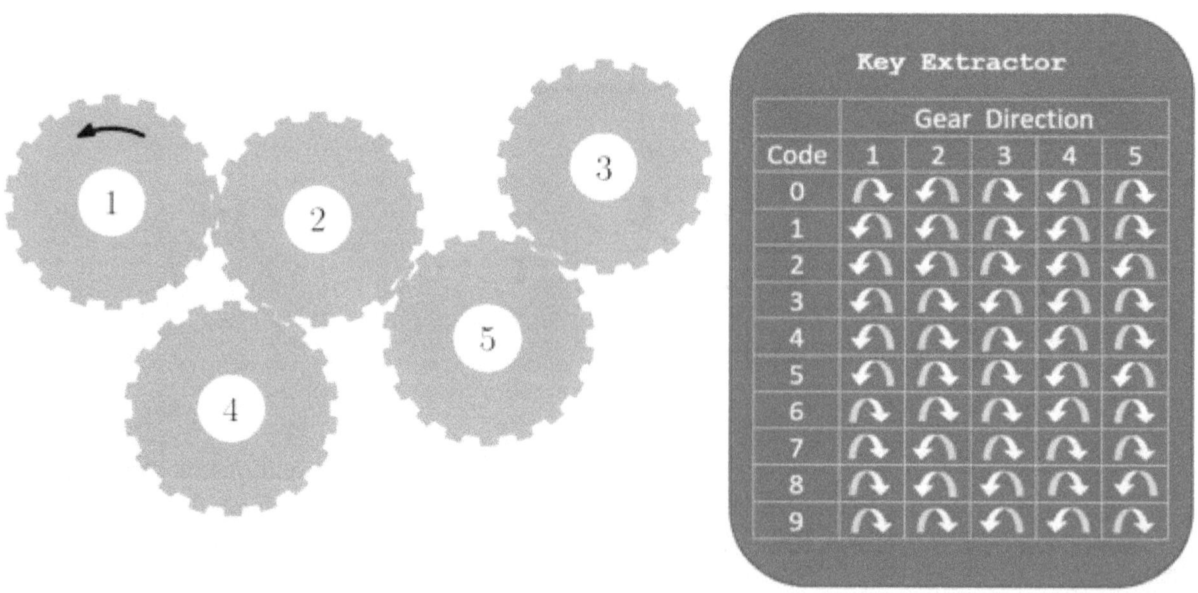

Figure 7. Logical deduction puzzle

529	All numbers are wrong
415	One number is right but in the wrong place
563	One number is right and in the correct place
351	Two digits are right but are in the wrong place
984	One number is right and in the correct place

names (MELBOURNE -> DARWIN is the first) and round the number to the nearest 1000km to get the solution.

- **Paper manipulation:** Some puzzles may comprise paper that needs to be folded, manipulated, overlayed or joined together. (e.g. several pieces overlayed may form a number). The Caesar cipher puzzle example provided in example puzzle 3 is of this type as it requires two pieces of paper which need to be overlayed and adjusted with respect to each other. Another example is a scytale

Figure 8. Electrical circuits puzzle to be solved using a multimeter

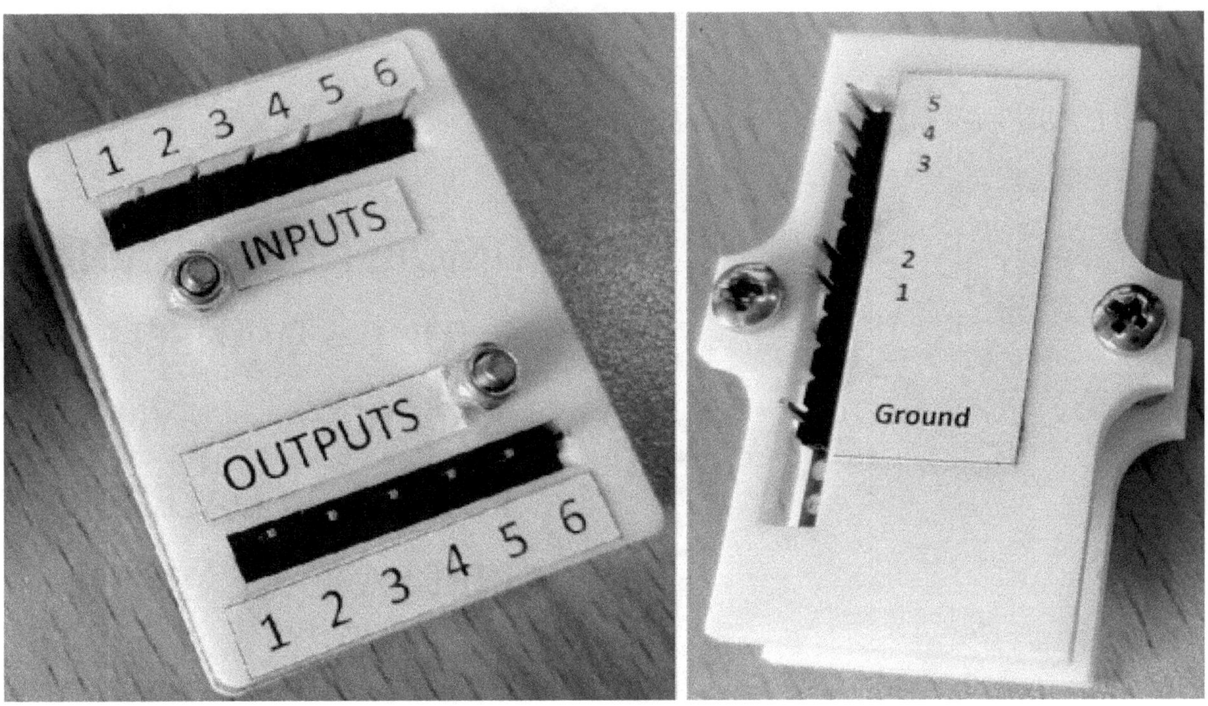

transposition cipher which is decoded by rolling up the strip of letters with the correct diameter as shown in Figure 12.

Figure 9. Missing letters in the text spell out NINE

Whe Mary when to the market the only th ng that she could see was a little fluffy lamb. The lamb followed her home and became her best frie d. She fed the lamb grass flavoured ice-cr am.

Figure 10. Puzzle requiring errors in code to be identified

```
int a = 1;
int b = 2;
int c = 3;
while(a < 1000){
    a += 2
}
a = 0;
c = b - a;
```

```
int checkSum = 0;
int b = 119;

for (int i = 0; i < 255; i++){
    b = checkSum + i;
    checksum ^= i;
}
b++;
```

Figure 11. Place names need to be unscrambled and distances measured

RUMOBENLE -> RIWNAD

RUUUL-> WANSELECT

MORBOE -> DEYNYS

TOBRAH -> DALEIEAD

SIRBBEAN -> BACRENAR

Figure 12. Scytale cipher decoded by wrapping strips with the correct diameter

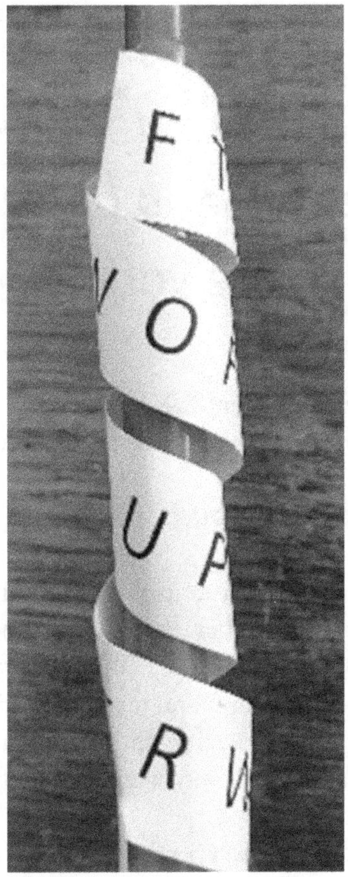

- **Obfuscation:** There are many other common ways of obfuscating text to make it more difficult to read and derive the meaning. Common techniques include: mirror writing, letters in reverse, jumbling text within words (typoglycemia), writing in accents, using phonetics and inverting characters. Figure 13 has the first line in mirror writing, the second upsidedown, the third has characters reversed while the fourth has a German accent. These puzzles were generated using the helpful puzzle generator website dCode (https://www.dcode.fr/en).

- **Technology mediated:** Augmented reality or virtual reality could be used to display puzzles or puzzle elements. When a tablet or handset is pointed at an image or a fiducial marker it may display new information in the form of a video, 3D, photo or audio overlay.
- **Hybrids:** Many puzzles may contain elements of more than one of the different puzzle types (e.g. they may involve augmented reality and require some mathematical reasoning as well).

Many puzzles contain multiple common sub-puzzles (a similar puzzle to be completed multiple times) which have a similar way to unlock all of them. However each needs to be solved and put in order. Doing the same style of puzzle multiple times helps solidify the decoding process and encourages teamwork.

Figure 13. Obfuscated text describing different countries around the world

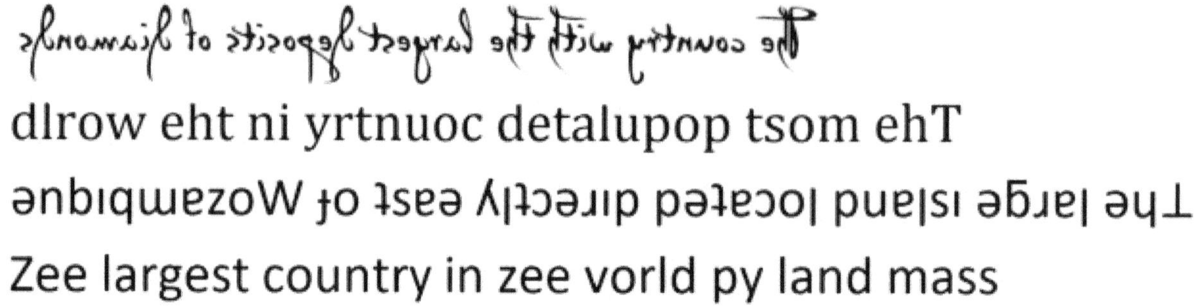

Hence, both the solution of each puzzle element is as well as the order of these solutions is required. Typically, some simple ordering scheme (e.g. the order is printed on the back of the puzzles) can be used.

Narratives for Educational Escape Rooms

One distinctive thing about educational escape rooms is the narrative or storyline that accompanies the activity. These storylines, similar to those found in recreation escape rooms, give a premise and urgency for why the group needs to escape (Clarke et al., 2017). The storyline can be presented in many different ways (e.g. written, video, AR, VR, actors) and tends to work well if it is progressively revealed throughout the activity – rather than simply starting and finishing bookends. One way to do this is to integrate puzzles directly into the storyline in a way which can both provide clues but also connect the puzzles together.

A good storyline should include some tension (i.e. a reason that an escape is required), a clear link to the puzzles and have some descriptor as to why there is some urgency involved (hence the time limit). Some sample storylines could include:

- Being stuck in a cave, in catacombs, in a tomb or a dungeon and needing to escape before the oxygen is depleted.
- Defusing a bomb planted by a criminal mastermind with specific knowledge of the field that you are meant to be studying.
- Solving a mystery and catching a criminal by a process of deductive reasoning.
- Escaping from jail after being wrongly accused so that you can catch the real culprit.
- Escaping from a pirates treasure lair before the pirates return and you are caught.
- A top secret spy mission to uncover nefarious plans and escape before being discovered and blowing the mission.
- Repairing the time machine before the invading zombies or dinosaurs attack.

Evaluating Educational Escape Rooms

Educators may employ educational escape rooms for different purposes. Hence, there are different ways that educational escape rooms can be run and evaluated depending on the desired purpose of the activity. Unlike traditional tests or exams, if marks are assigned to educational escape rooms they tend to be lower (e.g. 5%) and open-book activities are common (Ross & de Souza-Daw, 2021). The open-book nature of the escape rooms places greater emphasis on applying knowledge in problem solving domains rather than simply memorising knowledge. Likewise, educational escape rooms may have several different purposes including: introducing a new topic, improving learner engagement, revisiting topics already covered, applying theory to a solution domain or even as part of a corporate training module (Clarke et al., 2017).

Educational escape rooms have been evaluated on multiple levels. Before they are deployed within the classroom it is considered good practice to test them with Alpha and Beta testers. Alpha testers tend to be content experts and ensure that the puzzles are correct, have educational value and can provide expert feedback required to identify issues in clarity (e.g. the puzzles too cryptic). Whereas, Beta testers are real users (e.g. students) in a real environment that can ensure the puzzles present sufficient (but not excessive) difficulty and can provide a measure of domain knowledge for the target group (Mohd & Shahbodin, 2015).

Besides simply evaluating the playability of the educational escape room game there are other things that can also be studied for different cohorts of learners. Researchers have called for more systematic approaches and evidence to evaluate the educational usefulness of educational escape rooms (Lathwesen & Belova, 2021). These metrics, which are educationally important, include measures such as effectiveness, learner engagement, teamwork and depth of learning. Some of the currently used evaluation approaches include:

- **Participant Surveys:** Participants complete a survey with relevant questions directly after the activity. The survey may contain questions on perceived enjoyment, difficulty, learning, teamwork, engagement and questions that relate to flow (e.g. did you loose track of your surroundings during the activity). Such surveys are common and universally point to high levels of learner engagement and enjoyment of educational escape rooms (Ross & Bennett, 2020). Some surveys have included a self-assessment on perceived learning which can be difficult for learners to accurately assess (Moore & Campbell, 2021; Ross & Hall, 2021).
- **Teacher Observation:** Teacher observation can be a useful qualitative tool in evaluating escape room effectiveness. These observations may be particularly useful if teachers know their students well and observe changes in behaviour, attentiveness or concentration associated with the activity. Generally, these observations have noted high levels of active participation and higher levels of motivation compared to many traditional pedagogies (López-Pernas et al., 2019; Veldkamp et al., 2020a).
- **Pre/Post Testing:** In terms of learning effectiveness, pre-testing (to see what learners knew before the activity) coupled with post-testing (to see what they have learned) is a useful mechanism for testing the activity. Results between pre and post testing shows improvement which validate the educational escape room approach (Eukel et al., 2017; López-Pernas et al., 2019)
- **Data Analytics:** Analysing data gathered within the activity can be another measure to evaluate educational escape rooms. This data may include time taken to solve each puzzle (as a measure of comparative difficulty) and number of wrong guesses - as a measure of complexity (Ross & Hall, 2021). Between different groups these metrics may vary significantly depending on teamwork, knowledge coming into the activity and prior problem-solving experience.

Studies have pointed high levels of student engagement as a result of educational engagement for educational escape room activities (López-Pernas et al., 2019; O'Brien & Pitera, 2019; Ross & Bell,

2019; Ross & Bennett, 2020). Many participants reported that they strongly enjoyed the various activities and would like to see more of them within the classroom. One aspect that the educational escape rooms highlight is that of teamwork. Many team-based projects cause some level of disdain for students (particularly when non-active team-members are in their group). In contrast, the escape room activities are relatively short in duration but encompass an intense teamwork exercise where application of knowledge and problem solving are used together.

The escapED framework is a useful design framework which allows for escape room puzzles, environments, and interactions to be analysed holistically (Clarke et al., 2016). The escapED framework focusses first on Participants and delineates on topics of: User Type, Time, Difficulty, Mode, and Scale. Clearly, some users will come with different backgrounds and problem-solving abilities and so a master's student should be able to perform faster and at a higher level than a high school students.

The second escapeED field focusses on Objectives, in other words, what are we trying to do from a learning point of view. These Objectives are further broken down into categories of: Learning, Solo/Multidisciplinary, Soft Skills and Problem Solving. Although these educational escape rooms are often content focussed, helpful soft skills around teamwork, communication and delegation are often helpfully practiced by participants. The escape room may be designed so that these soft skills may be central to the learning objectives or simply to accompany the core content within the activity.

The third escapeED field is on the Theme of the escape room. Encompassed within the Theme are categories of: Escape Mode, Mystery Mode, Narrative Design and Standalone/Nested. This Theme category is a major element in creating a cohesive structure and reason for the escape room beyond solving some isolated questions (making it fun – unlike an exam). Several standard escape modes are popular including lockboxes, padlocks around rooms, online environments, and decoder boxes. There are different ways the narrative and mystery can be woven into the escape room activity including text-based representations, virtual reality, augmented reality or through use of non-playing characters.

The next category revolves around the Puzzles. Within the Puzzles category the prominent elements are Design, Reflex Learning Objectives, Instruction/Manuals, Clues/Hints. As puzzles are key to the escape room experience, they should go beyond simply copying and pasting a question out of a past exam. Designers need to consider how students are prepared for the activity if the puzzles teaching anything and how students can keep progressing when they have gotten stuck.

The fifth category encompasses Equipment, as every variety of escape room requires some mediated form of technology that goes simply beyond pen and paper (e.g., locks, lockboxes, decoder boxes, PC). Important considerations within Equipment include Location/Space, Physical Props, Technical Props and Actors. Each of these elements can help either facilitate the activity (e.g., locks to validate solutions) or can help reinforce the underlying theme of the escape room.

The final escapED category is around Evaluation, which is important for improving the escape room and ensuring that it meets the fundamental objectives. Key elements within Evaluation include Testing, Reflection, Evaluate Learning Objectives, Adjust and Reset. As these evaluation parameters suggest, designers rarely get the educational escape room perfect the first time and several feedback cycles may be required to improve the escape room before release.

STEM Educational Escape Room Sample

This section gives the readers a sample educational escape room to show the complete package-including puzzles with an accompanying storyline. This escape room is aimed towards middle-secondary school level with a focus on STEM and logical reasoning skills. Normally 30 minutes is allocated to solve this escape room, with most groups finishing within 20 minutes.

Introduction

CRASH! That was the noise of the enormous stone door crashing down behind you, sealing you in. For years you have been searching for the legendary Aztec cave of gold and your research and travels have finally led you here – only to be trapped in the cave having triggered the trip wire for the door. In the corner you see an enormous egg-timer with what looks like about 25 minutes remaining. Who knows what will happen when the time is up – maybe the cave will be flooded or maybe it will cave in! "How do we get out of this one?" you ask your compatriots.

The legends allude to some sort of a vague puzzle cave – claiming only the master puzzler is worthy of the gold. One of your merry crew suggests you press on to look for some puzzles.

Open Envelope 1 and solve the first puzzle. Enter the code into the decoder box. Don't open the next puzzle until the current puzzle is solved.

Puzzle 1

You approach the first puzzle which looks a bit like a confused kids playground – a whole bunch of see-saws with the axle in all different spots. Each see-saw has a weight on one end. At the edge of the cavern a pile of weights have been dumped. An inscription on the wall reads "Bring balance to the world – alas to the one who tips the scales over"

Puzzle 2

Well done! You have achieved balance and caused a new passageway to be opened. In this passage you see a series of clay buckets with connecting channels and the inscription "The key bucket will be the first to fill". You have almost run out of water so you can't just tip your own water supply in to test it out. Time to use your mind!

Puzzle 3

Congratulations, you are puzzling your way through tremendously. Another passageway has been opened up to you. Surely that gold (and a path to escape) is almost within reach. What's this inscribed on the wall? A series of SEVEN sets of letters and some weird wheels. Maybe the wheels somehow allow you to swap one letter for another to decode the word. Solve the last puzzle and escape to your freedom and golden riches.

Narrative Conclusion

Upon solving the last puzzle, a hidden passage opens up to your left. As you peer through you see piles of glittering gold and an arrow with the word EXIT marked beneath it.

Congratulations! It seems your team are the master puzzlers worthy of escape and that long sort after AZTEC gold. You take a deep breath of relief and step into the treasure room.

Figure 14. Balance Beams for Puzzle 1

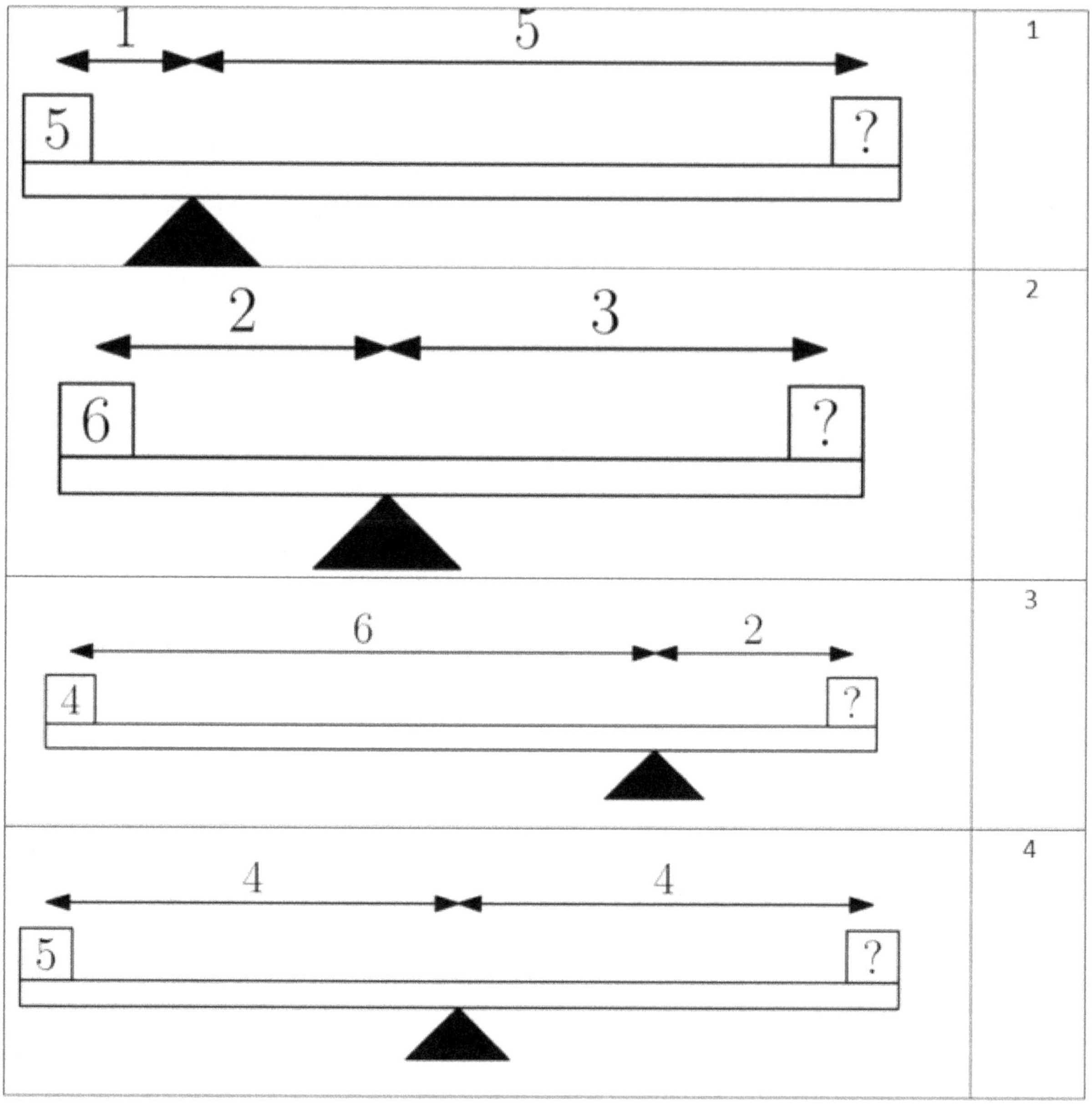

Solutions to sample escape room:

Puzzle 1: Solution – 14125

This first puzzle uses the basic physics concept of a balance beam in equilibrium. A clue of $M_1D_1 = M_2D_2$ is often provided which means that the further a mass is away from the fulcrum the smaller it can be to maintain equilibrium.

Figure 15. Water path puzzle for puzzle 2

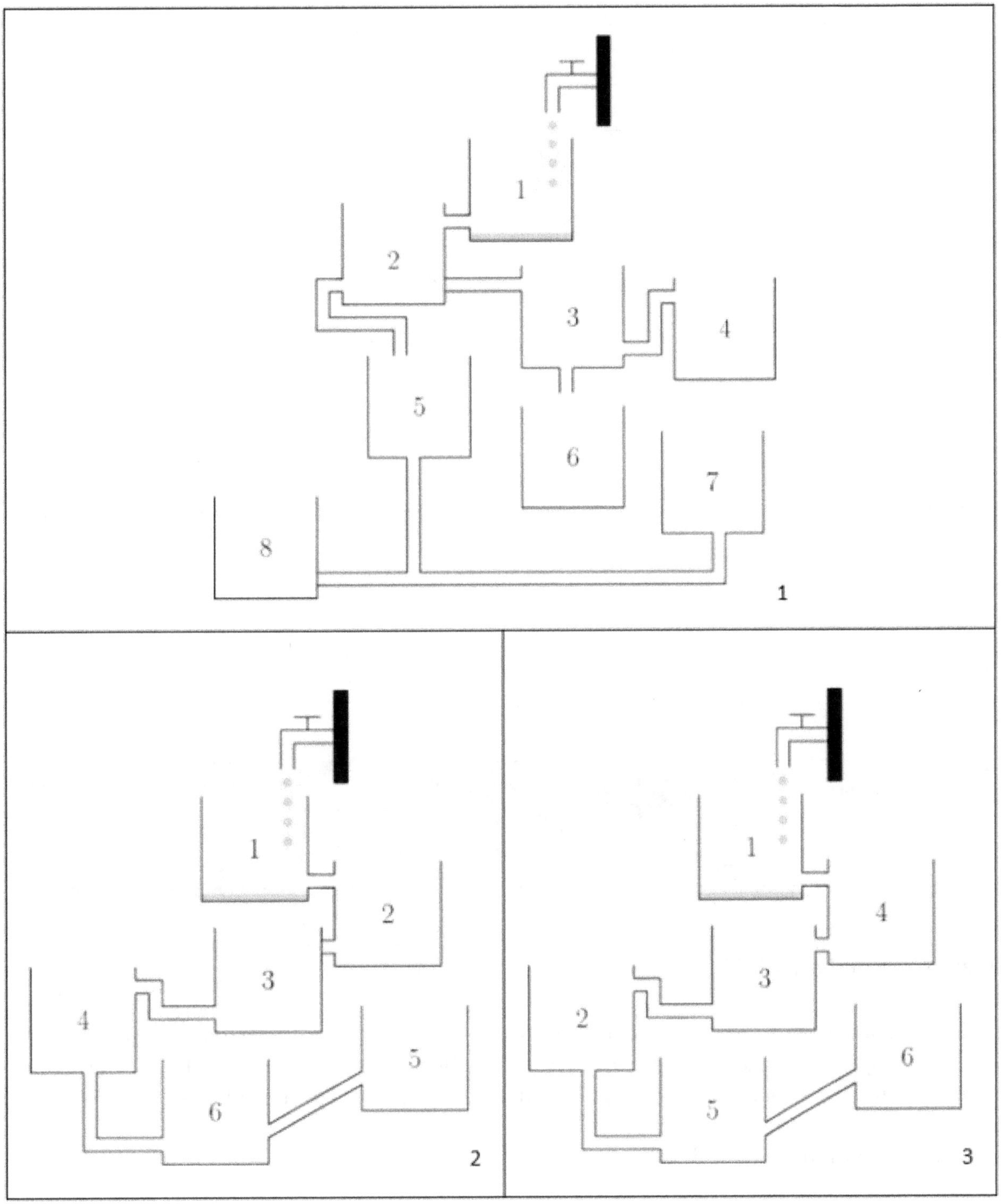

Figure 16. Puzzle 3 containing cipher text

NBCLNYYH	1
IHY	2
NBLYY	3
NBLYY	4
NQI	5
YCABN	6
ONE	7

Puzzle 2: Solution – 725

The keys to solving this puzzle is to recognise that water will find its lowest level (due to gravity) and that some of the pipes are blocked off and hence no water can flow into some of the cups. Interestingly, many players initially don't notice the blocked pipes and attempt to proceed as if no blockages were present.

Puzzle 3: Solution – 13133281

This puzzle uses the classic Caesar replacement cipher to spell out the solutions. The two number wheels are provided to participants and they need to work out the orientation of the wheels with respect to each other to solve the puzzle. There are several ways to solve this puzzle including checking all possible

Figure 17. Caesar cipher wheels for decoding cipher text

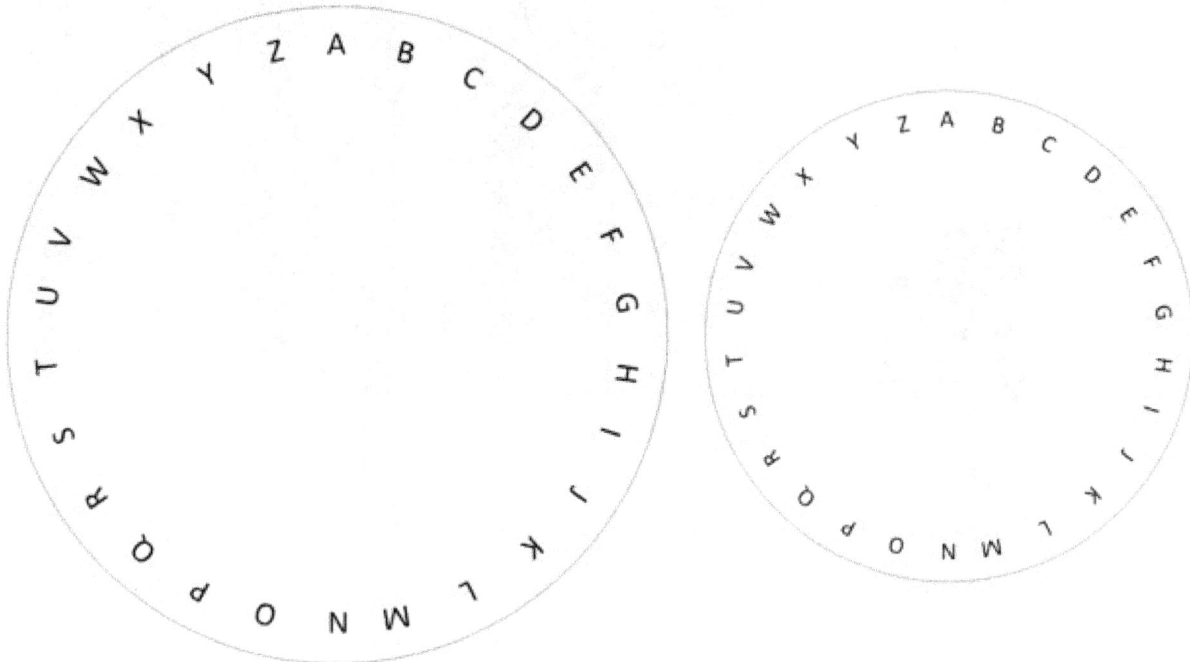

three-letter numbers (ONE, TWO, SIX) or recognising that the only number with a double letter is THREE and so Y=E.

Evaluation of STEM Educational Escape Room

The STEM educational escape room described in the previous section has been successfully run with approximately 400 secondary school students aged 12-16. This escape room was designed with a primary aim of engaging potential future engineering students as a school outreach activity. Hence, the time provided for the activity is shorter (30 minutes) than what may be traditionally used in a classroom to provide opportunity for a discussion about courses and career pathways.

Group sizes of 2-4 attempted the activity with a success rate of 98%. Post-activity Likert surveys were conducted with a subset of 160 of the participants who attended the university open day as reported in (Ross & Bennett, 2020). Considering the purpose of the activity was to engage potential future students, the survey questions were used to student motivation (questions 1 and 4), gauge possible measures of flow (questions 2 and 3) and finally the perceived difficulty of the puzzles.

Survey Questions:

1. I wanted to complete the escape room activity?
2. I became unaware of my surroundings while doing the escape room activity?
3. I felt absorbed in the escape room activity?
4. If I had to vote, I would be in favour of using escape room learning in the classroom?
5. I found the activity difficult?

Figure 18. Survey results from STEM Escape room (Ross & Bennett, 2020)

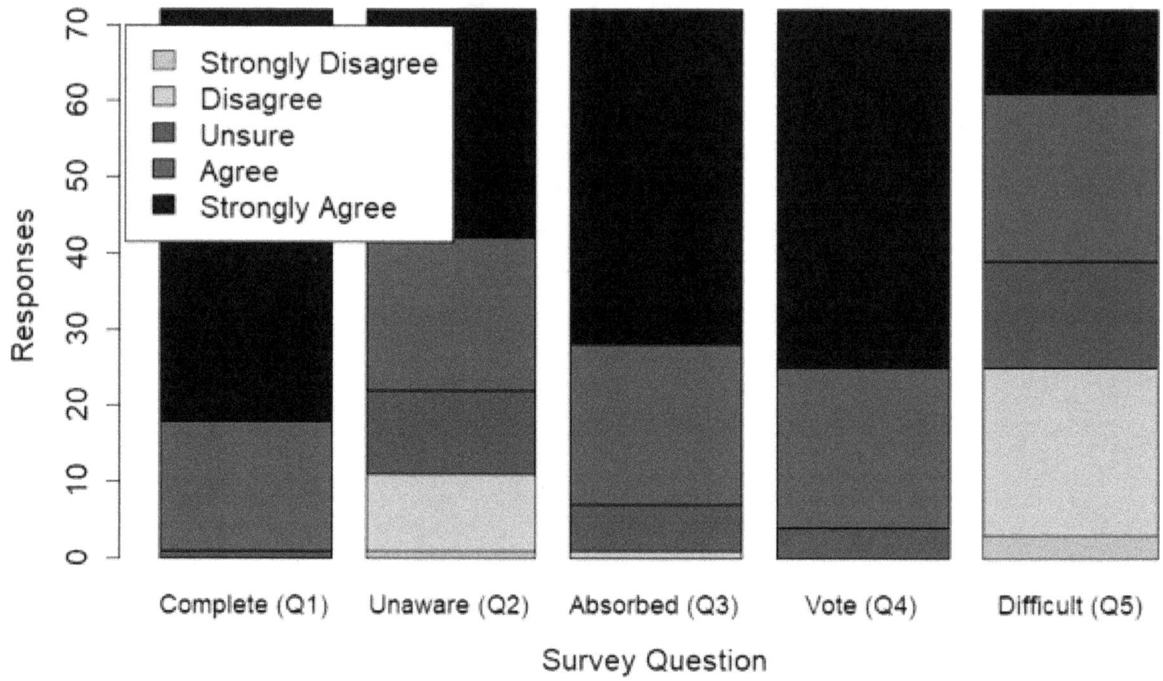

Figure 14 summarises the responses received from students. The responses to questions 1 and 4 suggest that the student motivation for an activity like this is high and that they would like to have more similar activities for learning within the classroom.

Survey responses to questions 2 and 3 suggest that many students experienced some measure of flow as they became un-aware of the environment external to the game as they focussed on collaboratively solving problems. Given that this was conducted as an open-day activity, this flow is even more encouraging as many distractions, people, and external constraints (timetabled seminars) are present.

Finally, the question with the largest variance in responses related to the difficulty of the activity. We suspect this is in part relates to the age of participants (some of the concepts will be easier for upper-secondary school compared to lower secondary school).

FUTURE RESEARCH DIRECTIONS

Educational escape rooms are an area which has significant scope for further research considering puzzle development, playability and assessing the educational outcomes for learners.

In relation to puzzle development, there is scope in studying different classes of puzzles and how educators and learners approach the puzzle development process. There is also potential in evaluating puzzles with A/B testing to optimise the use of puzzles within the learning environment.

In relation to playability, there is significant potential in studying the learning environment and user interfaces. In particular understanding user perceptions for different classes of escape rooms (e.g. online/full-scale/tabletop). Time intervals are typically aligned with normal class period lengths (e.g. 1 hour) although possible optimisation around time limits (e.g. shorter escape rooms for younger students) may yield more suitable learning environments. Measuring effectiveness of different storyline/narratives on learner performance and different ways these narratives can be mediated (e.g. text, videos, augmented reality, virtual reality) would also be useful.

Finally, there is significant scope in measuring escape room effectiveness using control groups where confounding factors as minimised. The improvements in engagement are well represented in the literature, but the quantification of learning or improvements in teamwork are less well documented.

CONCLUSION

Educational escape rooms present an exciting active learning frontier of learning pedagogy. Not only are the activities engaging and fun but they also encourage teamwork and problem solving to create a memorable learning experience. Given the interest innovative educators have invested in educational escape rooms, we expect to see these growing and reaching more classrooms into the future. We also see wides scope beyond school/university environments including possibilities of escape rooms for corporate training and interactive museum exhibits.

ACKNOWLEDGMENT

This research was funded by a grant from the Telematics Trust.

REFERENCES

Adams, V., Burger, S., Crawford, K., & Setter, R. (2018). Can you escape? Creating an escape room to facilitate active learning. *Journal for Nurses in Professional Development*, *34*(2), E1–E5. doi:10.1097/NND.0000000000000433 PMID:29481471

Bartlett, K. A., & Anderson, J. L. (2019). Gaming to learn: Bringing escape rooms to the classroom. In *Handbook of Research on Innovative Digital Practices to Engage Learners* (pp. 1–27). IGI Global. doi:10.4018/978-1-5225-9438-3.ch001

Becker, K. (2021). What's the difference between gamification, serious games, educational games, and game-based learning. *Acad. Lett, 209*.

Bonwell, C. C., & Eison, J. A. (1991). Active Learning: Creating Excitement in the Classroom. 1991 ASHE-ERIC Higher Education Reports. ERIC Clearinghouse on Higher Education, The George Washington University.

Boysen-Osborn, M., Paradise, S., & Suchard, J. (2018). The toxiscape hunt: An escape room-scavenger hunt for toxicology education. *Journal of Education and Teaching in Emergency Medicine*, *3*(1), 9–19. doi:10.5070/M531037616

Cain, J. (2019). Exploratory implementation of a blended format escape room in a large enrollment pharmacy management class. *Currents in Pharmacy Teaching & Learning*, *11*(1), 44–50. doi:10.1016/j.cptl.2018.09.010 PMID:30527875

Clarke, S., Arnab, S., Morini, L., Wood, O., Green, K., Masters, A., & Bourazeri, A. (2016, October). EscapED: A framework for creating live-action, interactive games for higher/further education learning and soft skills development. In *Proceedings of the 10th European conference on Games Based Learning, ECGBL* (pp. 968-672). Academic Press.

Clarke, S., Peel, D. J., Arnab, S., Morini, L., Keegan, H., & Wood, O. (2017). escapED: A framework for creating educational escape rooms and Interactive Games For Higher/Further Education. *International Journal of Serious Games*, *4*(3), 73–86. doi:10.17083/ijsg.v4i3.180

Coorey, J. (2016). Active learning methods and technology: Strategies for design education. *International Journal of Art & Design Education*, *35*(3), 337–347. doi:10.1111/jade.12112

De Caprariis, P., Barman, C., & Magee, P. (2001). Monitoring the benefits of active learning exercises in introductory survey courses in science: An attempt to improve the education of prospective public school teachers. *The Journal of Scholarship of Teaching and Learning*, *1*(2), 13.

Eukel, H. N., Frenzel, J. E., & Cernusca, D. (2017). Educational gaming for pharmacy students–design and evaluation of a diabetes-themed escape room. *American Journal of Pharmaceutical Education*, *81*(7), 6265. doi:10.5688/ajpe8176265 PMID:29109566

Ferguson, K. (2019). *International Escape Room Markets analysis*. The Logic Escapes Me. https://thelogicescapesme.com/news/international-escape-room-markets-analysis

Kapp, K. M. (2012). *The gamification of learning and instruction: game-based methods and strategies for training and education*. John Wiley & Sons.

Lathwesen, C., & Belova, N. (2021). Escape Rooms in STEM Teaching and Learning—Prospective Field or Declining Trend? A Literature Review. *Education Sciences*, *11*(6), 308. doi:10.3390/educsci11060308

López-Pernas, S., Gordillo, A., Barra, E., & Quemada, J. (2019). Examining the use of an educational escape room for teaching programming in a higher education setting. *IEEE Access: Practical Innovations, Open Solutions*, *7*, 31723–31737. doi:10.1109/ACCESS.2019.2902976

López-Pernas, S., Gordillo, A., Barra, E., & Quemada, J. (2021). Escapp: A Web platform for conducting educational escape rooms. *IEEE Access: Practical Innovations, Open Solutions*, *9*, 38062–38077. doi:10.1109/ACCESS.2021.3063711

Masukawa, K. (2016). The Origins of Board Games and Ancient Game Boards. In Simulation and Gaming in the Network Society (pp. 3-11). Springer. doi:10.1007/978-981-10-0575-6_1

Mohd, C. K. N. C. K., & Shahbodin, F. (2015). Personalized learning environment: Alpha testing, Beta Testing & user acceptance test. *Procedia: Social and Behavioral Sciences*, *195*, 837–843. doi:10.1016/j.sbspro.2015.06.319

Moore, L., & Campbell, N. (2021). Effectiveness of an escape room for undergraduate interprofessional learning: A mixed methods single group pre-post evaluation. *BMC Medical Education*, *21*(1), 1–8. doi:10.118612909-021-02666-z PMID:33879150

Nicholson, S. (2015). *Peeking behind the locked door: A survey of escape room facilities*. Academic Press.

Novak, J., Lozos, J. C., & Spear, S. E. (2019). Development of an interactive escape room intervention to educate college students about earthquake preparedness. *Natural Hazards Review*, *20*(1), 06018001. doi:10.1061/(ASCE)NH.1527-6996.0000322

O'Brien, K., & Pitera, J. (2019). Gamifying instruction and engaging students with Breakout EDU. *Journal of Educational Technology Systems*, *48*(2), 192–212. doi:10.1177/0047239519877165

Peleg, R., Yayon, M., Katchevich, D., Moria-Shipony, M., & Blonder, R. (2019). A lab-based chemical escape room: Educational, mobile, and fun! *Journal of Chemical Education*, *96*(5), 955–960. doi:10.1021/acs.jchemed.8b00406

Pietroszek, K., Agraraharja, Z., & Eckhardt, C. (2021, March). The Royal Game of Ur: Virtual Reality Prototype of the Board Game Played in Ancient Mesopotamia. In *2021 IEEE Conference on Virtual Reality and 3D User Interfaces Abstracts and Workshops (VRW)* (pp. 647-648). IEEE.

Prince, M. (2004). Does active learning work? A review of the research. *Journal of Engineering Education*, *93*(3), 223–231. doi:10.1002/j.2168-9830.2004.tb00809.x

Ross, R. (2019). Design of an open-source decoder for educational escape rooms. *IEEE Access: Practical Innovations, Open Solutions*, *7*, 145777–145783. doi:10.1109/ACCESS.2019.2945289

Ross, R., & Bell, C. (2019, August). Turning the classroom into an escape room with decoder hardware to increase student engagement. In *2019 IEEE Conference on Games (CoG)* (pp. 1-4). IEEE. 10.1109/CIG.2019.8848020

Ross, R., & Bennett, S. (2020). Increasing Engagement with Engineering Escape Rooms. *IEEE Transactions on Games*, *14*(2), 161–169. doi:10.1109/TG.2020.3025003

Ross, R., & de Souza-Daw, A. (2021, June). Educational Escape Rooms as an Active Learning Tool for Teaching Telecommunications Engineering. In Telecom (Vol. 2, No. 2, pp. 155-166). Multidisciplinary Digital Publishing Institute. doi:10.3390/telecom2020010

Ross, R., & Hall, R. (2021). Towards Teaching Digital Electronics Using Escape Rooms. *Advances in Engineering Education*, *9*(2), 1–19.

Veldkamp, A., Daemen, J., Teekens, S., Koelewijn, S., Knippels, M. C. P., & van Joolingen, W. R. (2020b). Escape boxes: Bringing escape room experience into the classroom. *British Journal of Educational Technology*, *51*(4), 1220–1239. doi:10.1111/bjet.12935

Veldkamp, A., van de Grint, L., Knippels, M. C., & van Joolingen, W. (2020a). Escape education: A systematic review on escape rooms in education. *Educational Research Review*, *31*, 100364. doi:10.1016/j.edurev.2020.100364

Vörös, A. I. V., & Sárközi, Z. (2017, December). Physics escape room as an educational tool. In AIP Conference Proceedings (Vol. 1916, No. 1, p. 050002). AIP Publishing LLC.

Wiemker, M., Elumir, E., & Clare, A. (2015). Escape room games. *Game Based Learning*, *55*, 55–75.

Zaug, P., Gros, C. I., Wagner, D., Pilavyan, E., Meyer, F., Offner, D., & Strub, M. (2021). Development of an innovative educational escape game to promote teamwork in dentistry. *European Journal of Dental Education*, *26*(1), 116–122. doi:10.1111/eje.12678 PMID:33561894

Chapter 10
Escape Rooms and Breakouts:
Novel Educational Strategies

Janio Jadán-Guerrero
Universidad Tecnológica Indoamérica, Ecuador

Marcos Chacón-Castro
Universidad de Investigación y Desarrollo, Colombia

Luis Aimacaña-Espinosa
https://orcid.org/0000-0003-1707-6557
Universidad Tecnológica Indoamérica, Ecuador

ABSTRACT

The escape rooms and breakouts are immersive games in which the participants are locked in a room and must solve a series of puzzles to escape. In virtuality, these games have also aroused interest in the educational field as a learning tool to transform students from passive spectators to active participants. Immersive learning allows students to learn about a topic while practicing teamwork and communication. This chapter aims to explain how these tools work and describe the implementation process using digital educational resources available on the web. Some examples developed by the authors are mentioned, and the evaluation results concerning the students' motivation, satisfaction, and participation in a virtual environment are presented.

INTRODUCTION

Nowadays, the gamification in the educational context is generating a greater impact on educational actors due to the motivation and diversity of environments that are generated at the time of transferring the games mechanics to school environment, which can be applied in an individual or group way.

A micro gamification model is the Escape Rooms and the Breakouts, both have similarities in learning-teaching development. The Escape Room is defined as an escape room where one or a group of students solve enigmas in a certain time to be able to leave (Garcia, 2019). On the other hand, a Breakout is an

DOI: 10.4018/978-1-6684-4287-6.ch010

immersive game derived from Escape Rooms, with the difference that in a breakout you don't have to leave a room where a group is locked up; here the objective is to open a box closed with different types of padlocks. To get the codes that open them it is necessary to solve problems, questionnaires and riddles. A short narrative transforms the participants into secret agents, scientists, adventurers, or any character we imagine Negre (2017).

Matínez and Chivite (2020) affirm: "under the Castilian name of Escape Games, two terms are associated in English: Escape Room and Breakout. Both terms refer to a set of gamification tools where a group of students, normally grouped into teams, compete to solve a series of challenges in order to get out of a specific space in a given time "(p.38). The use of this type of playful strategies in the classroom is can be adapted to any curricular content and allows students to develop various skills, which are mentioned below:

1. collaboration and teamwork,
2. critical thinking development and problem-solving skills,
3. improvement of communicative competence,
4. strengthening continuous and constant work
5. deductive thinking construction,
6. under pressure work,
7. learning protagonist and
8. increase motivation

For Palomo (2019), these educational micro gamification tools allow students' participation motivation and improvement when acquiring their knowledge. Where the student becomes the protagonist of their own learning. Through participation, collective thinking is prioritized in order to meet the challenges posed. Each of the participants must demonstrate and share their knowledge or skills to solve the riddles and thus generate cooperative learning.

Escape Rooms and Breakouts can be applied to different academic areas such as: Mathematics, Physical Education, Chemistry, English, among others. As examples, experiences carried out in different subjects are cited, such as: Analysis of an Educational Escape Room in Primary Education Mathematics Class carried out by (García, Solano and Sánchez, 2020). The designing and participating experience in an educational Escape Room in Physical Education and Technology carried out by (López and Ortega, 2018). Study carried out for chemistry subject on: Escape room in ESO 3rd year for a meaningful chemistry learning (Reñe, 2020) and the Design of an Educational Escape Room as a gamified and motivating tool for learning English in Primary by (O'Brien and Yebra, 2019).

They can also be applied to different educational levels such as primary, secondary and university. At the initial level, the research "Educativa Escape Room" is cited as a motivating and innovative resource in early childhood education, carried out by (Poza, 2018). At the secondary level, the study carried out by Morales (2020) on the implementation of Escape Rooms for the fourth year of Secondary Education in the subject of Physics and Chemistry. Finally, the study carried out at the Faculty of Pharmacy of the University of Seville, on a multidisciplinary Escape Room as an educational tool carried out by (Gutiérrez et al., 2019).

Indeed, the gamified spaces use provide an experience that enhances the teaching-learning process between the contents and competences for students, which favor the construction of knowledge, skills development and problem solving, obtaining immediate feedback and cooperative learning. Communication through the game makes players be more tolerant with the opinion of others because they are playing. In the game there is no risk, there are opinions and playing the rules are clear. Playing the divergent opinions are not a reason for conflict, on the contrary, they are complementary and enriching (Moreno, 2019).

GAME THINKING

Game Thinking or project design inspired by games, is the art and science of engaging people on a complex, innovative, and uncertain business environments. This approach combines game design, systems thinking, Agile/Lean UX and design thinking to help people build deeply engaging experiences and accelerate the learning (Parapanos & Michopoulou, 2021).

Game thinking and Design thinking have many aspects in common, both focuses on costumer empathy and rapid prototyping. Game thinking crystallizes aspects of game design and Design thinking is conceptually appropriate to support innovative, complex, and uncertain business environments (Patrício et al., 2021).

There are some other concepts related to employment of the game or its characteristics to motivate and create an environment conducive to learning: Gamification, Game-Based Learning, Serious Games and Exergames. There are also other concepts that follow the principles of gamification known as Scape Rooms and Breakouts described below.

GAMIFICATION

Gamification consists of the use of elements games (e.g. Storytelling, rules, challenges, and badges) designed in the game in non-game scenarios to promote motivation, collaborative work, enjoyment, and engagement, particularly when performing a challenging and complicated task or when achieving a goal. (Deterding et al., 2011).

Gamification works as a motivational didactic strategy in the teaching-learning process to provoke specific behaviors in the student within an environment that is attractive to them, that generates a commitment to the activity in which they participate and that supports the achievement of positive experiences to achieve meaningful learning

GAME-BASED LEARNING

Game-Based Learning (GBL) consists of the use of games as vehicles and support tools for learning, assimilating, or evaluating knowledge. It is an innovative methodology that offers both students and teachers a different and practical educational experience that can be applied to a subject or topic or integrate several subjects.

Serious Games

Serious games are learning tools, based on virtual reality, whose main objective is learning. Serious games can be considered to simulations, such as video games, flight simulators, military or police training simulators, medicine simulators, among others. Participants will be able to face individual or collective challenges, putting into practice all their knowledge and skills. In conclusion the application of serious games is effective, innovative and safe way of learning, especially in the commercial or industrial field (Urquidi & Tamarit, 2015).

Exergames

Exergames stimulates the mobility of the whole body by using interactive environments with immersive experiences that simulate different sensations of presence. The Exergames become the physical activity technological approach that supplies users' needs evidenced in exercise, stimulating through of play and competition of the physical activity. The use and interpretation of gestures allow great applicability in different scenarios (such as in rehabilitation). Emerging technologies used by consoles such as PlayStation Move ® by Sony ®, Xbox Kinect ® by Microsoft ®, or Wii ® by Nintendo ®, offer data entry through gestures without surfaces contact. The constant use of interactive systems can make a therapy, a rehabilitation process or physical exercise in general more pleasant and motivating. In older adults, analyzing the use and user experience proposed by video games with different systems, positive results have been demonstrated in therapies by combining elements of physical exercise with entertainment, and this population tends to improve different behavioral attitudes, staying physically active and with positive and funny perception towards videogames. Additionally, increases in energy expenditure, muscle mass and motivational level have been shown in children with cerebral palsy undergoing active video game therapy (Giraldo and et.al, 2013).

Escape Rooms

Escape Room has its origin in Japan by Takao Kato, in 2008 where the first adventure game was made that consisted of solving different enigmas through groups participation. As of 2013, this game has moved to other continents such as: Europe and Australia. Today the Escape Rooms trend has been very welcomed by many people. Worldwide there are approximately 6,500 companies that offer ER games. In the educational context, it is an activity considered as a game system within the educational perimeter, in which different methodologies are used such as game-based learning or gamification (Zarco, Machancoses & Fernández, 2019, p.25).

The Escape Room is a game of fun and collaboration in which it is proposed to a group of students who are locked in a room from which they will have to leave using their knowledge and creativity in a certain time (García, 2019). To carry out this activity they will have to solve challenges, open locks, discover clues or enigmas (Ayuso, 2019).

Escape Rooms are gamification activities, where different learning opportunities are created for students, where they become the protagonist of their own learning to demonstrate their skills or knowledge of their educational work. This type of strategy can be used physically and digitally, is currently being used by many teachers in different subjects and has a high pedagogical value when it is related to the curricular content. This strategy encourages cooperation, logical thinking, problem solving and the assimilation of content in a simpler way (Diago and Ventura, 2017, p. 35).

Breakouts

Negre (2017) states that Breakout is an immersive game coming from the Escape Rooms. A breakout is a playful activity (game) where the participant has to open a closed box with different types of locks, and it is not necessary to leave a room in which a group is locked. To get the codes that open them it is necessary to solve problems, questionnaires and riddles.

A breakout is called the 'lock game' is a very versatile educational strategy, adaptable to any content or age, its design can be developed in a real way (physical world) or in a simulated way (virtual world). Its application improves the students' motivation, promotes creativity development of and facilitates the contents understanding.

Benefits of Escape Rooms and Breakouts

The benefits that Escape Rooms and Breakouts provide in the educational context are many, including offering a playful and active learning, generating teamwork by solving the challenges, managing time, applying content or skills, improving transversal skills and strengthen intrinsic motivation (Sempere, 2020). Figure 1 shows the main benefits.

For Sánchez (2018), the use of Escape Rooms and Breakouts generate in participants the development of the 4 C's: creativity, collaboration, communication, and critical thinking. Promotes active learning, increases tolerance to frustration and strengthens motivation due to the attractive and playful environment that is generated.

Escape Rooms and Breakouts promote active learning in which students work together against the clock to solve contextualized problems like those they will encounter in their future professional practice. Each student becomes the protagonist of his own learning, manages the correct use of time, enhances cognitive development, social skills development, affective development, educational development, and psychomotor development. Finally, these strategies develop skills related to the competencies of learning to learn, improving deductive thinking and problem-solving ability.

In formal education, depending on the educational goals, Escape Rooms and Breakouts can get adapted to any curricular. The content embedded in the curriculum of a course is intended to foster student knowledge and develop skills related to a specific area. Educators start their design process with defining educational goals, which guide choices on the puzzle path, the role of technology and the teacher's role during the gameplay (Veldkamp et al., 2020).

Escape Rooms and Breakouts employ mechanisms associated with both intrinsic and extrinsic motivation with brief activities that produce a high level of involvement in those who participate in solving cases or problems, while developing teamwork, communication, and other general skills (Calvo et al., 2018).

Finally, Escape Rooms and Breakouts increase tolerance for frustration. They Generate the need to try again, in situations that may fail. Teachers try to create authentic environments with meaningful activities and room for failure. Educational developers aim for a high success rate; success gives students positive learning experiences, and solving all puzzles will help to achieve all learning goals (Veldkamp et al., 2020).

Figure 1. Escape Room and Breakout Benefits

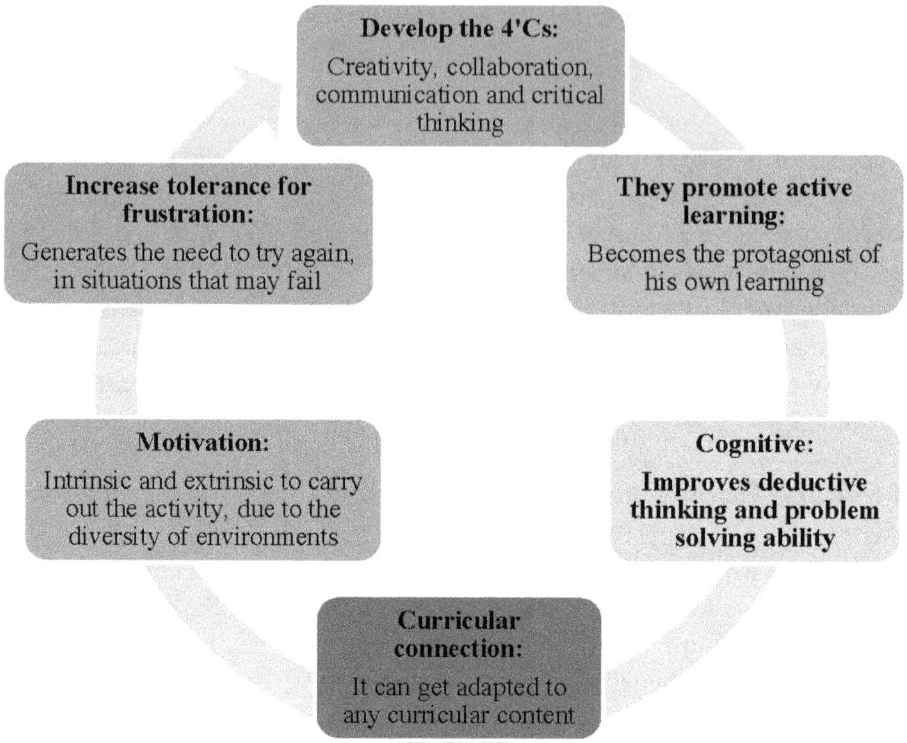

Differences Between Escape Rooms and Breakouts

Escapes Rooms and breakouts are very similar strategies, however, the main difference is that in Breakout, students must open a closed box with different types of locks according to the codes they obtain from different problems or enigmas, while in Escape Room the student must escape from the confinement room by solving the challenges posed.

The design of Escape Rooms or Breakouts will greatly influence how students learn, so it is necessary to consider the decoration, music, light, enigmas. This will make learning meaningful for them.

How to Design a Didactic Strategy using Escape Room and Breakouts?

During the research process, the Escape Rooms and Breakouts have been approached as microgamification scenarios for the creation of educational activities.

The Escape Rooms is a micro gamification strategy where the student escapes from the traditional classroom (Aimacaña, Chacon & Jadan, 2021) that requires prior planning to establish the mechanics, dynamics, and components of the virtual or physical environment. Within the review of the state of the art of gamified scenarios, experiences have been systematized that theoretically deepen the leading role of students, collaborative work, pedagogical practice, increased motivation, and active participation by students (Brusi & Cornella, 2020; Veldkamp et al., 2020).

The design of Escape Rooms allows learning in a fun, practical and dynamic way to increase the motivation of students in learning moments, which lead to problem solving, the use of technology, collaborative work, logical reasoning (Chacón, Aimacana, & Jadan, 2021).

Indeed, there are multiple reasons for the creation of an educational Escape Rooms and Breakouts from the incorporation of real and immersive experiences where the main protagonist is the student and the teachers become a guide of the process, being an action-participatory research. For this reason, it is essential to follow a path that allows the process to be more learning and meaningful for students and teaching practice by selecting the model of Kemmis and McTaggart (1998), cited by Latorre (2005) that addresses the cyclical process that they are carried out in a spiral way in the following phases: observation, planning, action, and reflection. The strategic axis that encompasses action and reflection, the organizational one that is made up of the planning and observation phases. According to Latorre (2005), each of the moments requires "a retrospective look and a prospective intention that together form a self-reflective spiral of knowledge and action" (p. 35). Next, Figure 2 shows the process carried out in this study from this theoretical approach, so that permanent reflection makes the construction of knowledge visible and pedagogical practice is enriched.

In the first cycle considered by the authors as the exploration phase, it is considered the key moment for the researcher teacher to know clearly from his students their tastes, hobbies, or activities that they are passionate about, in particular games, video games or virtual environments, such as mentioned by Chacón, Aimacaña & Jadán (2021). Therefore, it is necessary to carry out an instrument based on the laker test to know the skills and students' competencies, allowing the design to be closer to the characteristics of the group of students. (Brusi & Cornella, 2020) states:

With what objective do we propose the activity? Will it be a motivating proposal to introduce a topic? Do we use it as a didactic resource to inspect into content that has already been developed in the classroom? Will it provide the opportunity to develop practices that complement the theoretical treatment of some concepts? Do we reserve it as an evaluation activity? Do we present it as a multidisciplinary initiative in which establish interactions with other subjects? (p. 76)

Therefore, it is necessary to consider the exploration stage as one of the basic tasks to make a reflection of the key elements for the beginning of this investigative process.

In the next ***planning phase***, considering the data taken from the previous stage, an exposition of the problem is made, likewise, the problematizing question and the research objective that define the path of the research work are identified. According to Corral, Corral, & Franco (2016) cited Chacón (2021), the diagnosis and exploration of the initial situation is required to organize, group, and relate the data, based on the objectives of the research, in order to proceed to its analysis and interpretation (p.38). Also, it has been selected to incorporate one or more ways of learning: visual learning, auditory learning, tactile learning, kinesthetic, the learning environment and identifying their previous knowledge.

For the next ***action phase***, it implies that the researcher teacher makes a review of the activities, tasks and proposes a game scheme. According to Murillo (2011): "Deliberate and controlled action is projected as a careful and reflective change in practice" (p.21). During this process, the design and implementation of the educational Escape Room or Breakout is carried out as immersive experiences in a game mode that is the natural process, motivating for students (Guerrero & Ramon, 2018).

In the next ***observation phase***, the teacher has two fundamental roles. The first role is a constant observer of the student's team or individual work process, collecting information through instruments such

Figure 2. Research moments according to Kemmis and McTaggar (1998)
Source: Chacón (2021)

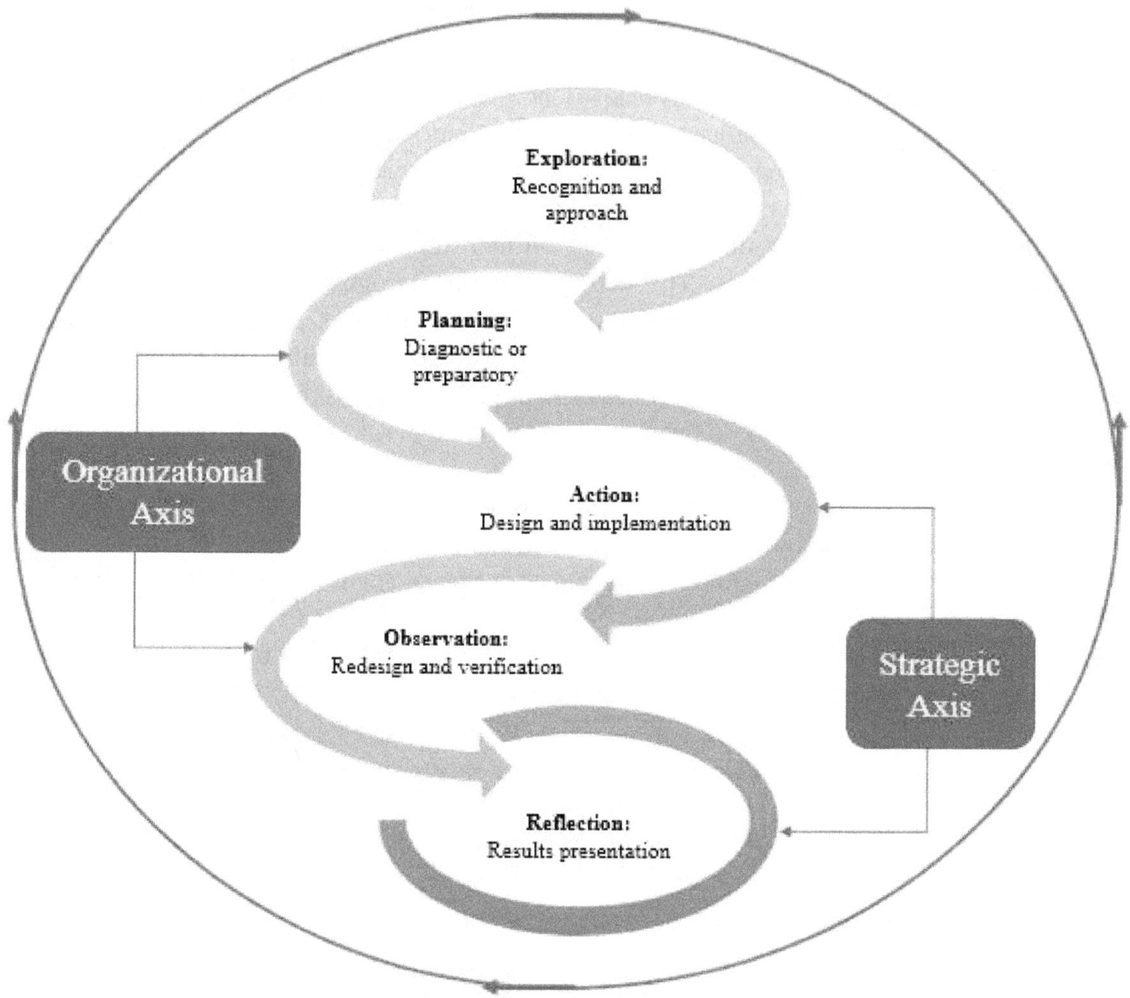

as pedagogical diaries, videotapes, interactive tasks, and dialogue between academic peers; its second function lies on being a guide to the teaching-learning process, that is, having a prior preparation for what may happen in the face of the proposed tasks, the research teacher being a mediator of the process and promoting the active participation of students. According to Bernal and others (2010) "Observation involves the collection and analysis of data related to some aspect of professional practice. We observe the action in order to reflect on what we have discovered and apply it to our professional action" (p. 18). Finally, the ***reflection phase*** is subject to the previous one since it is the moment of constant reflection on the part of the research teacher. Therefore, at this moment in the cycle, the information is organized in an orderly and rigorous way to present and evaluate it according to the categories of analysis that are oriented to the question and the objective of the research. In this regard, Murillo (2011) states that:

We understand reflection as the set of tasks aimed at extracting relevant meanings, evidences or proofs in relation to the effects or consequences of the action plan. The task of analyzing and interpreting gives meaning to creativity, in this sense it is a unique and creative process, where the artistic component has an important weight (p. 23).

That is why the researcher must carry out certain tasks in the analysis process such as: reducing the information, gathering the information, validating and interpreting the information, in order to clearly describe the data, categorize it and explain theoretically the investigation.

As mentioned above, for the design of an Escape Rooms or Breakouts it is necessary to consider the following points to develop it: virtual or physical scenario, it is important when planning immersive moments; participants, knowing and identifying the ages, tastes, and the approach designed for the students will allow to establish the levels of difficulty and rules when proposing the tasks; The narrative is one of the most powerful dynamics of gamification since it defines the beginning, the development, and the end of the activities proposed by the research teacher, for example:

- Escape from somewhere (prison, bank ...)
- Solve a crime
- Investigate a mystery
- Military mission
- Defuse a bomb
- Commit a robbery
- Help find a cure
- Save the world from an alien attack
- Save the world from an asteroid
- Ancient Egypt, among others; challenges or missions, it is time to propose riddles, enigmas and puzzles among others; virtual or physical environments, it is necessary to manage the programming of the game or video game using effect, sound, music, lighting so that the experience is immersive; The didactic sequence allows proposing a series of sequential activities using Flow theory, in order to maintain the interest and motivation of the students.

According to Díaz (2013) states:

The meaning of the opening activities is varied at first, it allows to open the learning climate, if the teacher manages to ask them to work with a real problem, or to open a discussion in small groups about a question that starts with questions significant for students, they reacted by bringing to their thoughts several information that they already possess, either because of their previous school education or because of their daily experience (p. 6).

Using clues, these curious facts allow students to feel like playing as they approach the Game Master level, in such a way that in communication letters or codes are deciphered to solve challenges. Finally, the rules are presented to the players to know the clear, precise conditions before starting any activity.

The respective designs for the creation of the Educational Escape Rooms or Breakouts are shown in Figure 3.

Each of the interactive activities generated from the different applications have an educational escape room or breakout mechanics, with the purpose of promoting teamwork, increasing motivation, examin-

Figure 3. Escape Room and Breakout Edu Typology.

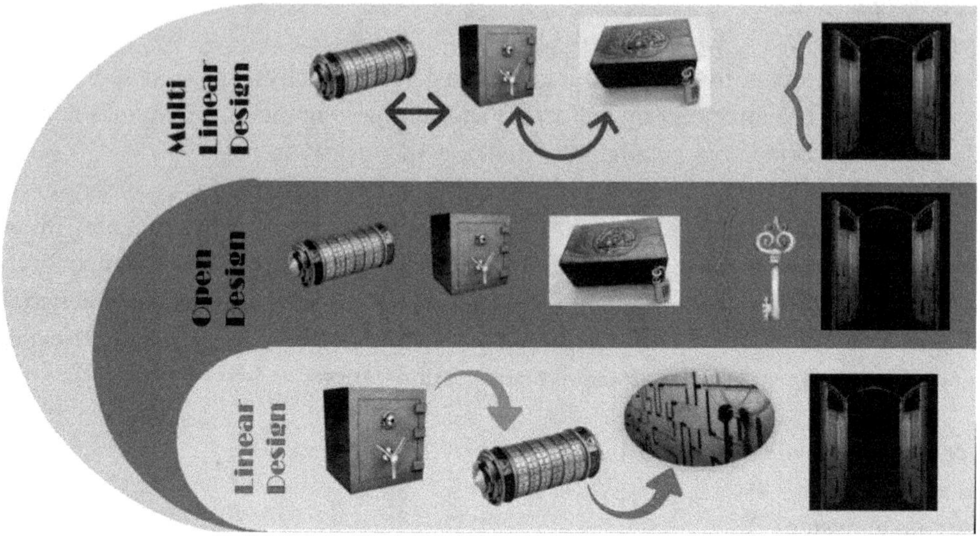

ing, observing, solving problems, calculating, arguing and enhancing the skills development. Next, the typology of the Escape Rooms and Breakouts will be explained in detail:

- **Linear design:** the missions or challenges posed are carried out sequentially, which allows obtaining the key, code or elements that will allow to advance in each of the stages, where physical skills, argumentation and critical and constructive dialogue are put to test, through values such as: respect, responsibility, tolerance and constant collaboration. From the authors' point of view, it is important to include clues, sublevels that motivate students to review the topics proposed by the teacher, as shown in Figure 4.

In figure 4, a linear design is evidenced for the creation of challenges in the different areas of knowledge, having an alternative route in case of presenting difficulties to carry it out.

- **Open design:** in this mode the user can start in a scenario, where they can find missions or challenges in any order, with the purpose of finding the keys, codes or elements to leave the place or proposed scenario to exit in the stipulated time.
- **Multi-linear design:** the user will have the combined experience of linear and open design; these challenges can be elaborated sequentially or alternative routes.

Technological Tools for Designing Escape Rooms or Breakouts

There are numerous technological tools and web pages for creating Escape Rooms or Breakouts. The design can start from a simple initial idea, then create elements (codebooks, clips, QR codes, box, locks, keys, cards, etc) for later integration. Some of them are described below.

Figure 4. Escape Rooms formulation, taken and adapted from: Chacón, Aimacaña & Jadán (2021)

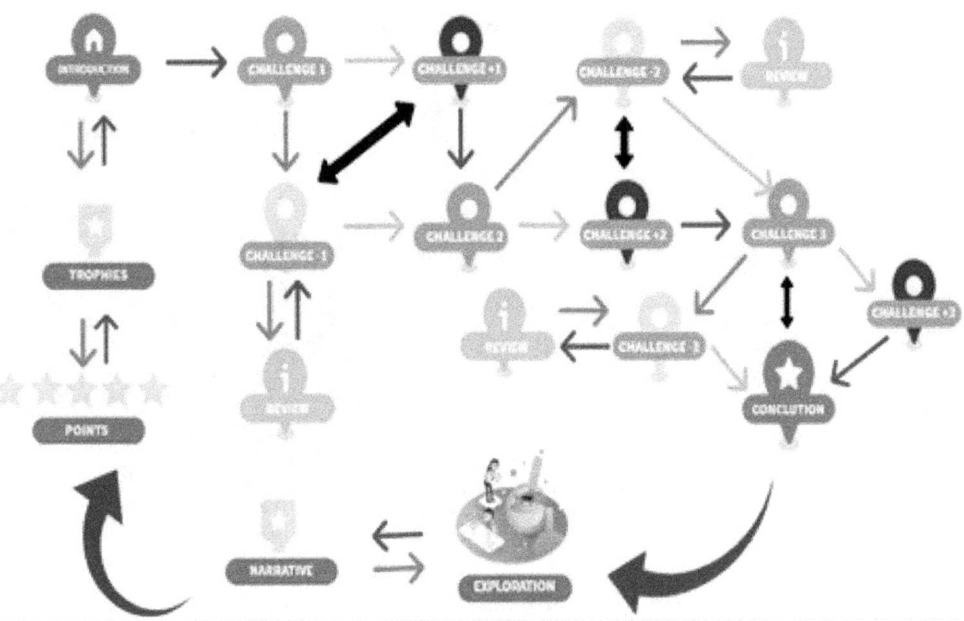

Genially is an application that combines the user immersion, the creation of transcendent knowledge to pass flat content into interactive, which makes students have infinite possibilities to explore stories, characters, narrative, aesthetics and consolidating a fun learning space, dynamic and handy (Figure 5).

Students have the option to interact through windows, labels, texts, documents and activities integration. With Genially it is possible to create countless presentations, games (escape room or edu breakout), interactive images, infographics, gamification, interactive books, among others.

Genially's superpowers such as interactivity allow the exploration of information in an enriching way for the learning process, these activities come to life making the class dynamic, fun and practical. The animation of the elements promotes visual effects that generate active participation on the part of the students. Monitoring allows you to measure and analyze the performance of your genially, reviewing the changes made to the presentation in real time. Finally, the integration potentiates the use of all the content that is hosted on the web, allowing the inclusion of games, documents, links, additional applications and incorporating active learning methodologies such as gamification, flipped classroom, among others.

These Genially's superpowers make it possible for teachers to create their educational materials in virtual or face-to-face classroom. For example, the creation of a Breakout edu titled: "Math Roblox" designed in Genially using the narrative from the popular Roblox video game, where the student will put into practice his knowledge of logical reasoning, problem solving and spatial thinking.

In this Breakoutedu four challenges are proposed, with the purpose of strengthening the logical reasoning of the students to find the codes to open the proposed locks and strongboxs. Each team put their knowledge of: arithmetic operations, sequences, patterns and spatial thinking into practice.

Figure 5. Interactive content creation

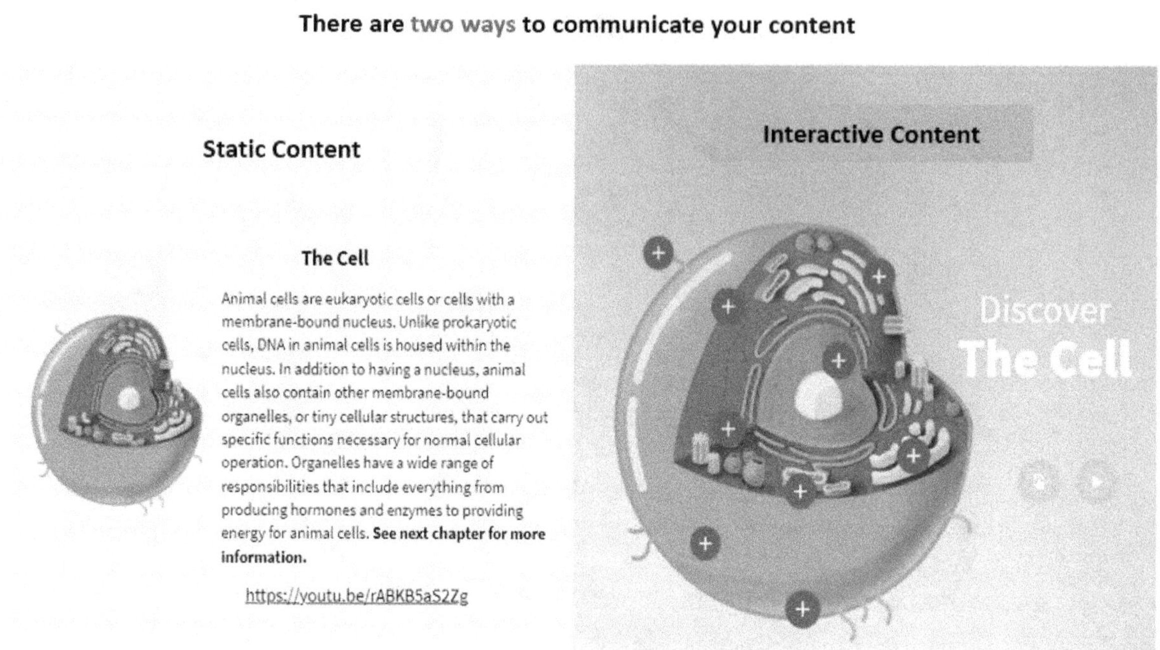

Figure 6. Superpowers for cool people

Figure 7. Breakout Edu Math Roblox

Figure 8. Locks and codes

Figure 9. Math Lab Each of these activities provides the student with excitement, enjoyment and teamwork in the stipulated time.

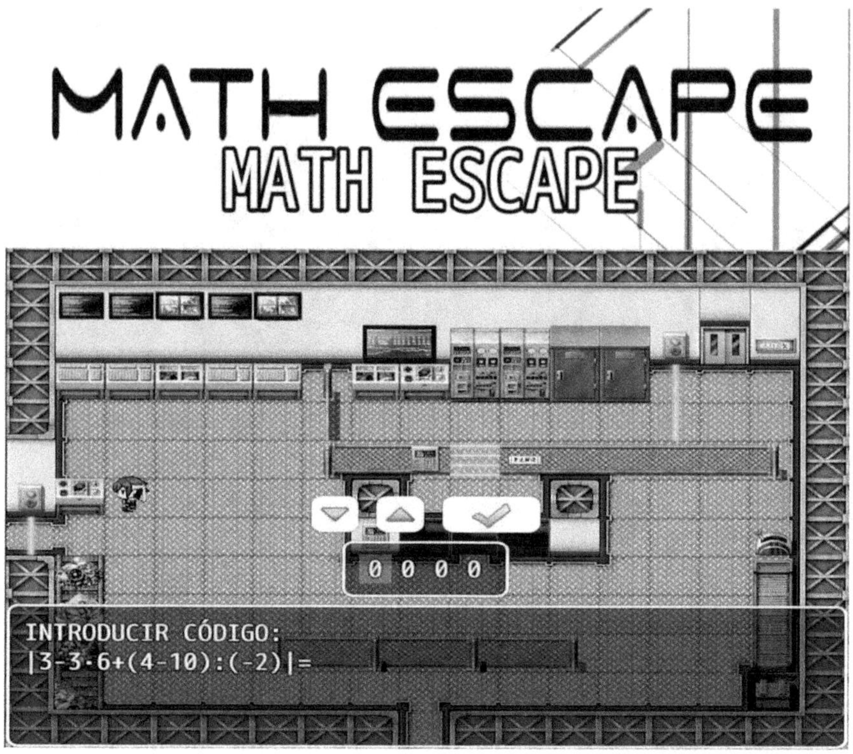

RPG Maker

RPG Maker is a free premium platform that allows it to create 2D simulated Role playing Game style videogames providing the user with an immersive environment of adventure, action and emotion, this can be found at the following link: https://rpgplayground.com/. Below is a game created by LudoMath with the purpose of strengthening the development of arithmetic operations.

Google Sites

Google sites is a tool that allows it to create websites easily and for free. It is an application that allows it to link a variety of information, videos, presentations, files. It is a free service from Google that is currently applied in the educational context for the design of immersive games such as Escape Rooms and Breakouts. An example of an online escape room designed with the Google sites tool is shown in Figure 10.

Class Craft

Class Craft is a digital platform that aims to create a playful environment to develop dynamic classes and increase the intrinsic motivation of students. One of the most immediate advantages obtained by

Figure 10. Example of a Escape Room designed with Google sites, from https://www.bespokeclassroom.com/blog/2019/10/4/how-to-build-a-digital-escape-room-using-google-forms

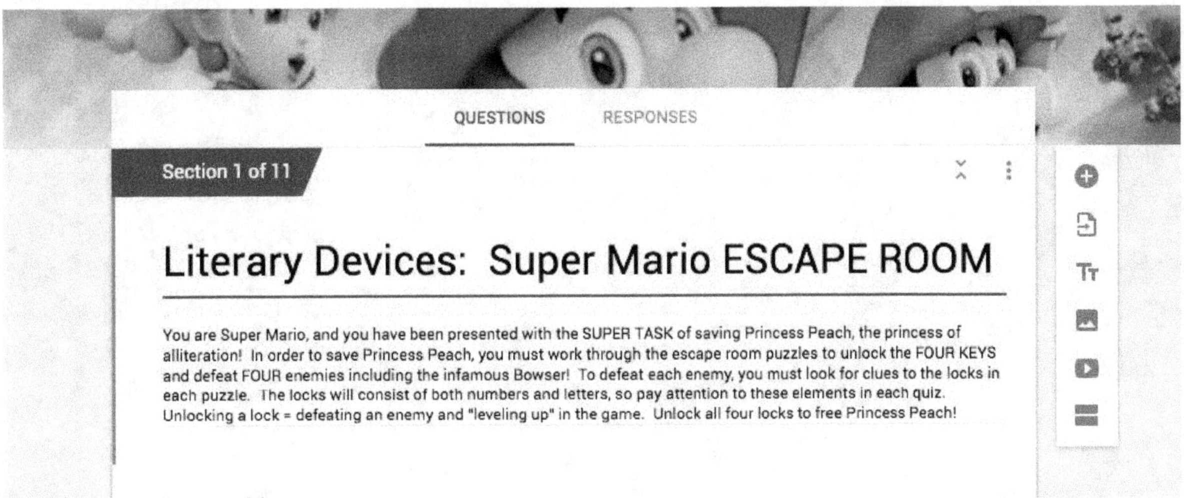

using this platform in the classroom is the visible and immediate increase in the motivation of students towards classes, in addition to extraordinarily favoring their self-regulation.

In the classroom it becomes a stage in which, in a completely virtual way, the students play at being Warriors, Magicians and Healers. As classes progress, they acquire more powers and faculties (experience) gained from their performance in the classroom (participation, delivery of assignments, completion of work, etc.). Also, as they develop favorable attitudes for the classroom, they will have more experience and gold coins, which increases their level in the game and enables them to have more faculties within the classroom. Although it is more oriented to the field of gamification, elements of Escape Rooms and Breakouts can be incorporated. Figure 11 shows the main interface of Class Craft.

Examples of an Escape Room

An example developed by the authors is the Escape Room "Hogwarts Castle Mystery" for teaching Chemistry. The Escape Room was designed on the Genially platform, using the narrative related to Master Snape's Laboratory to brew potions. Figure 12 shows the main interface.

Six activities were created for related to mass, volume, molarity and normality. The estimated time to overcome the challenges and solve the problems was sixty minutes. The figure 13 shows the challenge on the mass / mass percentage, where students had to prepare 400 grams of 5% herbal vitalizing potion. In this activity students had to find the amount of solute and solvent that is required for said solution.

Once the challenges are finished, the participant registers the requested code to open the main potions's classroom door of and escape from Master Snape. See figure 14.

Figure 11. Escape Room designed with Google sites

Figure 12. Master Snape's Potions Classroom

Figure 13. Potions classroom challenges

Figure 14. Final Challenge

CONCLUSION

Escape Rooms and Breakouts are an innovative and attractive learning strategy that generates emotion, motivation and critical thinking, due to the fact that the student participates in the learning process by putting their knowledge or skills into practice by solving the problems. and promote their creativity and imagination. The use of Escape Rooms and Breakouts constitute an educational strategy where the contents can be adapted according to the interests and needs of the students, due to the variety of activities, resources and materials that can be included in their design that can be in a physical or digital environment.

The implementation of the Escape Room and Breakouts are a didactic strategy that favors learning in a fun, practical and dynamic way, with the purpose of increasing the interest and participation of the students. Each one of the virtual or face-to-face scenarios consists of escaping from a closed space in a stipulated time, through different challenges, enigmas and games that promote teamwork, being a meaningful experience for the student.

REFERENCES

Ayuso Tapia, G. (2019). *Creation of an Educational Escape Room for Compulsory Secondary Education* [Creación de un Escape Room Educativo para Educación Secundaria Obligatoria]. Universidad de Valladolid, Escuela de Ingeniería Informática de Valladolid. https://uvadoc.uva.es/handle/10324/38983

Calvo, S., Lafuente, R., Jiménez, J., Bruton, L., Pérez, S., & López-Royo, M. (2018). Room escape a transversal gamification strategy for Physiotherapy students, Edulearn 18. *10th International Conference on Education and New Learning Technology*, 4149-4154.

Deterding, S., Dixon, D., Khaled, R., & Nacke, L. (2011). From game design elements to gamefulness:defining "Gamification". *Proceedings of the 15th International Academic MindTrek Conference on Envisioning Future Media Environments - MindTrek '11*, 9-11. 10.1145/2181037.2181040

Diago Nebot, P., & Ventura Campos, N. (2017). Escape Room: educational gamification for learning mathematics [Escape Room: gamificación educativa para el aprendizaje de las matemáticas]. *Suma: Revista sobre Enseñanza y Aprendizaje de las Matemáticas, 85*, 33-40.

García Lázaro, I. (2019). Escape Room as a proposal for gamification in education [Escape Room como propuesta de gamificación en educación]. *Revista Educativa Hekademos*, *27*(XII), 71–79.

García Tudela, P., Solano Fernández, I., & Sánchez Vera, M. (2020). Analysis of an educational escape room in elementary school mathematics class [Análisis de una escape room educativa en clase de matemáticas de educación primaria]. *Journal for Research in Mathematics Education*, *9*(3), 273–297.

Giraldo, J., Muñoz, J., & Villada, J. (2013). Exergames: A technological tool for physical activity [Exergames: una herramienta tecnológica para la actividad física]. *Revista Medica de Risaralda*, *19*(2), 126–130. doi:10.22517/25395203.8527

Gutiérrez Praena, D., Rios Reina, R., Ruiz, R., Talero, E., Callejón, R., Callejón, R., & Sanchez Hidalgo, M. (2019). *The use of an escape room as a teaching resource in the Faculty of Pharmacy* [El uso de una escape room como recurso docente en la Facultad de Farmacia]. https://riunet.upv.es/handle/10251/128803#

López Secanell, I., & Ortega Torres, E. (2020). *Educational Escape Room: Conception of future secondary education teachers in the specialty of physical education and technology on the experience of designing and participating in an educational escape room* [Escape Room Educativa: Concepción de los futuros maestros de educación secundaria en especialidad de educación física y tecnología sobre la experiencia de diseñar y participar en una escape room educativa]. DIDACTICAE, Universitat de Barcelona. https://revistes.ub.edu/index.php/didacticae/article/view/22648/pdf doi:10.1344/did.2020.8.176-192

Martínez Felipe, M., & Chivite Pérez, D. (2020). Escape games in education. [Juegos de escape en educación.] Padres y maestros. *Journal of Parents and Teachers*, *383*(383), 37–42. doi:10.14422/pym.i383.y2020.006

Morales Moreno, N. (2020). *Teaching-learning of Physics and Chemistry Through Play: Didactic Proposal based on an Escape-Room* [Enseñanza-aprendizaje de la Física y la Química Mediante el Juego: Propuesta Didáctica basada en un Escape-Room]. Universidad de Granada. https://digibug.ugr.es/bitstream/handle/10481/62767/TFM%20Noelia%20Morales%20Moreno.pdf?sequence=1&isAllowed=y

Moreno Fuentes, E. (2019). Breakoutedu as a key tool for gamification in the initial training of teachers [El Breakoutedu como herramienta clave para la gamificación en la formación inicial de maestros/as]. *Revista electrónica de Tecnología Educativa, 67*, 66–79. https://www.edutec.es/revista/index.php/edutec-e/article/view/1247/665

Negre, C. (2017). *"BreakoutEdu", microgamification and meaningful learning* [«BreakoutEdu», microgamificación y aprendizaje significativo]. https://www.educaweb.com/noticia/2017/07/26/breakout-edumicrogamificacion-aprendizaje-significativo-15068

O'Brien, N. B., & Yebra, J. M. (2019). *Design of an Educational Escape Room as a Gamifying and Motivating Tool for learning English in Primary* [Diseño de una Escape Room Educativa como Herramienta Gamificadora y Motivadora para el Aprendizaje del Inglés en Primaria]. Universidad de Zaragoza, Facultad de Ciencias Humanas y de la Educación. https://core.ac.uk/download/pdf/290000125.pdf

Palomo Blázquez, A. (2019). *Escape room in the classroom: Learning through challenge* [Escape room en el aula: Aprender a través del desafío]. Revista Digital Docente.

Parapanos, D., & Michopoulou, E. (2021). Gamification, Game Mechanics, Game Thinking and Players' Profile and Life Cycle. In X. Feifei & D. Buhalis (Eds.), *Gamification for Tourism* (pp. 13–34). Channel View Publications. doi:10.21832/9781845418236-004

Patrício, R., Moreira, A. C., & Zurlo, F. (2021). Enhancing design thinking approaches to innovation through gamification. *European Journal of Innovation Management, 24*(5), 1569–1594. doi:10.1108/EJIM-06-2020-0239

Poza García, M. (2018). *Educational escape room as a motivating and innovative resource in early childhood education* [Escape room educativa como recurso motivador e innovador en educación infantil]. Universidad de Valladolid. Facultad de Educación de Soria. https://uvadoc.uva.es/handle/10324/34270

Reñe Bru, M. (2020). *Escape room in 3rd year of ESO for meaningful learning of chemistry* [Sala de escape en 3° de ESO para el aprendizaje significativo de la química]. Re-UNIR. https://reunir.unir.net/handle/123456789/10572

Sánchez Lamas, A. (2018). *Educational Escape Rooms: practical example and guide for its design* [Escape Rooms educativas: ejemplo práctico y guía para su diseño]. Universitat Oberta de Catalunya.

Sempere Pla, S. (2020). Gamification project based on the escape room applied to a bilingual classroom of primary education with CLIL approach [Proyecto de gamificación basado en el escape room aplicado a un aula bilingüe de educación primaria con enfoque AICLE]. *Tecnología. Ciência & Educação (Bauru), 16*, 5–40.

Urquidi, A., & Tamarit, C. (2015). Serious games as a facilitating instrument of learning: Empirical evidence [Juegos serios como instrumento facilitador del aprendizaje: evidencia empírica]. *Opción, 31*(3), 1201–1220.

Veldkamp, A., Grint, L., Knippels, M., & Joolingen, W. (2020). Escape education: A systematic review on escape rooms in education. *Educational Research Review, 31*, 100364. doi:10.1016/j.edurev.2020.100364

Zarco Claudio, N., Machancoses, M., & Fernández Piqueras, R. (2019). The effectiveness of the Escape Room as a strategy for motivation, cohesion and learning mathematics in sixth grade [La eficacia de la Escape Room como estrategia de motivación, cohesión y aprendizaje de matemáticas en sexto de educación primaria]. *Edetania, 56*, 23–42.

Chapter 11
Development of Computer Games by Students

Chulpan Minnegalieva
https://orcid.org/0000-0003-4648-1623
Institute of Computational Mathematics and Information Technologies, Kazan Federal University, Russia

ABSTRACT

People have a different attitude towards computer games – from their complete rejection to delight. However, representatives of different professions agree that computer games can and should be used with benefit. This chapter describes practical tasks related to developing computer games in students' education. Tasks of that type are offered to students studying information technology. Game development uses modern platforms that provide ample opportunities. Students develop 3D models, write scripts, and research interaction principles between different applications. Such tasks will help protect the younger generation from misuse of computer games, improve programming and modeling skills, and develop spatial thinking and creativity.

INTRODUCTION

People of different ages view computer games in different ways. According to the surveys, children and teenagers play more often. If a child plays rarely, this usually does not bother parents and members of the older generation. But if a player spends a lot of time playing games, this negatively affects his studies and work. The development of the games by the students themselves will help to protect them from game addiction.

BACKGROUND

Gamification today covers more and more areas of public life and is being explored by various experts. For example, O. Pedreira and colleagues examined the application of gamification in software development

DOI: 10.4018/978-1-6684-4287-6.ch011

(Pedreira et al., 2020). J. Wozniak analyzes the problems of gamification in reward systems (Wozniak, 2020). Experts note that gamified approaches create a space for inspiration (Patricio et al., 2018). Also, R. Patricio et al. believe that gamification enhances co-creation by providing a structured peer-to-peer approach that ensures close interaction between different participants (Patricio et al., 2020). When using gamification approaches in teaching, teachers note that student engagement increases in all categories: from junior school children to adults. Fun (interest) had a significant and positive indirect effect on perceived learning through young students' attitudes towards coding (Tizsa and Markopoulos, 2021). By thoroughly utilizing gamification, teachers could direct their classroom activity towards success in raising engagement and achievement (Stott and Neustaedter, 2013). Sergi Villagrasa and his colleagues found that students who study 3D using gamification techniques perform better (Villagrasa et al., 2014). Gamification applications are effective in developing positive student behavior. Students and parents had positive views of the gamification applications (Hursen and Bas, 2019). Of course, gamification is not only beneficial. Toda A.M. and colleagues identified four negative effects: Indifference, Loss of performance, Undesired behavior, and Declining effects (Toda et al., 2017).

When introducing gamification in education, teachers use approaches typical for games, including computer games. Game techniques and mechanisms can be implemented in the learning process by activities aimed at achieving specific educational goals, increasing student motivation, and involving students in a friendly competitive environment (Kiryakova et al., 2014). Game training has deep historical roots. Games have been used in schools long before the advent of computers. Carers especially effectively utilize this method for preschoolers and primary school teachers. A game teaches, develops, educates, and socializes. A computer game can be viewed as a development of an ordinary game. Of course, there is a fundamental difference – in a computer game, a child communicates with virtual talkers or rivals. Or communication can be with friends but through the network. Even when children participating in an online game are in the same room, they rarely speak directly to each other.

But a computer game has other advantages – it has more opportunities for modeling the environment and developing an interesting dynamic algorithm. For example, Maskeliūnas et al. (2020) authors describe a serious interactive game for teaching JavaScript programming. The game encourages interactivity and pursues deeper learning of programming concepts. Educational computer games have a positive impact as a pedagogic tool on the educational process. At the same time, experts note that games with highly integrated educational content perform better than those games with loosely integrated content (Mostafa and Faragallah, 2019).

Currently, teachers are paying attention to the development of games by the students. Developing own game helps the all-around development of students (Minnegalieva et al., 2020). By designing and developing educational game projects, students learn how to use computers to solve mathematical problems, apply tasks, and make informed decisions using digital resources (Soboleva et al., 2021). Therefore, teachers began to use game development teaching for children and students in their practice. For example, in Chen (2021), the authors describe the Cardboard game development tool, which allows students to learn game production and design incrementally from beginners to experienced learners. This chapter will provide examples of assignments that were offered to undergraduate students. School students interested in information technology can also perform such tasks.

DEVELOPMENT OF COMPUTER GAMES

A group of developers creates a modern computer game; this process requires vast labor and financial inputs. A school child or a student can do the development of a simple game; platforms facilitating this process are widely used now. There are many step-by-step instructions and tutorials on the Internet, using which young people understand the game development process independently. In teaching information technologies to students, it is helpful to offer them tasks related to game development.

Benefits of Computer Games Development by Students

Considering the benefits of developing computer games by students, there are three main aspects. The game development process is interesting for the students (increasing interest in learning and developing creative thinking). Using modern platforms for game development allows you to develop modeling and spatial thinking skills (development of modeling skills). A complex game, even when using modern platforms, requires writing program code; accordingly, programming skills are developed (development of programming skills).

Increasing Interest in Learning and Development of Creative Thinking

According to research results, it is worth noting a high interest of teachers and students in creating and using educational computer games (Dobroskok et al., 2020). At a younger age, students do not yet know that the game is based on a program written by someone. As learners grow older, they realize this is some simple or complex algorithm. Keen on computer science and programming, schoolchildren come to realize this fact earlier. Accordingly, when a student begins to develop a game himself, he stops treating computer games as magic and starts understanding the essence of this process. Some of the students even feel disappointed; they see that there is no wizard. Students will learn that the game is based on a program written by someone and that this program can be appropriately configured. Students who develop games themselves are less likely to become overly addicted to the game.

Young people are usually more creative than older people. They have outside-the-box thinking; they treat all tasks creatively, not according to templates. Therefore, the development of games allows you to channel their energy in a helpful direction. Of course, there are many tutorials on the Internet. They demonstrate the process of developing a particular game. Teachers also give examples during the class. Students often offer interesting scenarios. But at the moment, it is quite difficult since the number of different games is vast, and it is not so easy to come up with an original scenario. So, another positive aspect of independent game development is the development of students' creative thinking.

Students may be offered tasks related to developing educational/ training games. Teachers know that students are usually good at explaining incomprehensible educational content to each other. When a student understands a specific algorithm or, for example, how he solves a task, he demonstrates this to his friends or classmates in an accessible and understandable manner. When students get an assignment to develop an educational computer game, they usually make up a good algorithm to explain the educational material. They try to make it easy to understand the topic. For example, a student-developed a game to solidify the road rules. In this game, the character cannot cross the road in the wrong place; he must go to a traffic light or pedestrian crossing. This is implemented in Unity by adding colliders and setting constraints. It would seem a very simple approach, but it allows you to remember the rule for a pedestrian well.

Development of Modeling Skills

Augmented Reality and Virtual Reality technologies are currently being used in teaching (Falah et al., 2021). The combination of Augmented Reality (AR) technology with educational content aims to create new ideas that can improve the effectiveness and attractiveness of learning. One of the features of AR technology is that it has three dimensions (3D) for virtual objects (Mina et al., 2021).

The Unity platform provides the ability to develop augmented reality objects. Special tools allow you to create and use an application on AR devices. Students can be offered tasks related to creating small training programs with augmented reality objects. In this case, the augmented reality objects' work skills and programming competencies are developed. This assignment also appears to be interesting for students. For example, you can create a small training game by "animating" learning objects when you hover your camera over them.

It is known that some of the students experience problems when solving problems in stereometry. They do not represent objects in space well and do not know how to work with spatial objects. While developing 3D computer games, the student can consider each object, each spatial model from different points of view, from different angles. This develops spatial thinking. Also, when working with modern game development platforms, you can add "physics," that is, the movement of an object will correspond to the laws of gravity, mechanics, and interaction of bodies. For example, the Unity platform has a Rigidbody component that connects physical behavior for objects and controls an object's position through physics simulation. Adding a Rigidbody component to an object puts its movement under the control of the Unity physics engine. An object with a Rigidbody will be subject to gravity and react to collisions with other objects. In Unity, you can adjust the parameters of gravity, drag, and friction and study the behavior of physical bodies. Thus, you can consolidate the knowledge of the main sections of physics. For example, you can adjust various parameters for gravity and show the falling of bodies on the surfaces of different planets. You can change friction coefficients and show objects' movement on different surfaces. The development of games allows you to consolidate your skills and abilities in geometry and physics.

Development of Programming Skills

Game development is software development. Game projects require uncommon developers' technical and creative skills compared to non-game projects (Carranza et al., 2021). The game is based on some algorithm or program. Often, when teaching programming, students are presented with standard, monotonous study assignments. When developing games, students learn the basics of programming through interesting examples. In this case, they want to get the result faster; they can see the constructed game scene after completing the task. Unity supports the object-oriented programming language C#. Teachers use Unity game development to improve their programming skills. Students can develop complex game scenes using scripts in this language. For example, a student has developed a program showing the operation of a quadcopter. He showed the influence of different parameters on flight change. In this case, scripts were written in C#, and with their help, the training game was compiled.

SAMPLES OF PRACTICAL TASKS FOR STUDENTS

This part of the work provides examples of tasks successfully used to teach students (field "Information systems and technologies"). In completing the assignments, students were motivated, demonstrated creativity, and developed modeling and programming skills. Tasks were allocated to groups: Review of existing games, Study applications for game development, Modeling in Unity, Development of computer games in Unity, Modeling in 3ds Max, Scripting in 3ds Max, and Game development in Blender.

Review of Existing Games

Task Example

To begin with, you can suggest reviewing existing games. For example, to analyze any computer game, pay attention to the following points: the number of players and the way they interact; visual presentation (two-dimensional, three-dimensional); platform, multiplatform; genre (adventure, strategy, action, simulator, puzzle, educational, etc.); theme (fantasy, historical, etc.); the environment where the game takes place; a positive effect on the player, whether the game helps in the development of memory, thinking, attention, reaction, etc .; negative impact on the player – what undesirable consequences are possible; the popularity of the game; advantages and disadvantages. In this case, the student can analyze a familiar for him game.

Students' Answers

The most significant interest in this analysis is the students' assessment of the positive and negative impact on the player. Game development companies usually post Detailed descriptions of games on the Internet for advertising purposes, and anyone can get acquainted with them. Table 1 shows the students' positive and negative aspects in analyzing different games (without specifying the game's name).

Study Applications for Game Development

There are different applications for game development. Game engines help developers create video games and avoid duplication of code and efforts, like frameworks for traditional software systems (Politowski et al., 2021). Unity is used to develop games, models, and simulators (Kim et al., 2021).

Task Example

This assignment is offered to students to study game development applications. For instance, one considers Unity, a real-time interactive content development platform. The company provides an opportunity for students to explore the platform for free. Unity is a system of several components: an editor, the ability to publish to multiple platforms, a resource and plugin store, and a community. There is an Asset Store. Assets (property) – in this case, files of content (sounds, scripts, images, videos)

1. Develop a teaching model demonstrating the dropping of bodies from a certain height on different planets. To do this, you can use 3D Object ® Sphere, adjust the parameters, and specify the

Table 1. The result of student games analysis

Positive impact on the player	Risks of negative impact
It trains your analytical mind.	Not marked
The game has a good storyline, excellent graphics, and a good sense of humor, which generally has a beneficial effect on the psychological state of a person.	The risk of computer addiction.
Development of strategic thinking, reaction, and the ability to make the right decision quickly.	The person loses track of time; the game begins to "drag out," taking away all the person's free time.
Memory, the ability to plan and carry out the intended plan, develops.	The state of nervousness and fear increases and excitement appears. Deterioration of vision, development of hypodynamia.
Acquaintance with the culture of fantasy.	The risk of computer addiction.
Spatial thinking develops when you have to think constantly, as it is difficult to understand the game's intricacies immediately. Studying the world of animals, plants, planets, and other things plays an educational function.	The game is very addictive due to the wide variety of systems, planets, and landscapes, negatively affecting a person's real life. The player becomes emotionally impoverished, leaving emotions in virtual reality. It also affects health.
It helps in the development of reaction, puzzles contribute to the development of thinking and attention, thanks to this game you will learn a lot about the history of those times, and the graphics make it possible to see the real historical monuments of Venice and other cities of Italy during the Renaissance. Urban architecture, famous historical figures and events, and features of people's households of that time all can be easily studied in an accessible form simply by playing.	The risk of computer addiction.
This game, like any strategy, teaches you to plan actions, place bets on some events that may occur, and be prepared for them. In addition, team play is one of the most important features of this game. To win your team, you must contact other members to plan further actions. If you play five with friends against another random five people who do not know each other, the chance of winning the match is significantly increased, even if you are newbies. Since there may be foreigners on your team in the match, there is a good opportunity to improve your English. Accordingly, such qualities as attention, thinking, and reaction are developed.	The risk of computer addiction.
Original puzzle concept; the gameplay attracts with the difficulty of passing a particular level; the game can be safely recommended to people of all ages; during the game, you need to use logical thinking; the game is not deprived of a sense of humor.	Not marked
The game develops strategic thinking while looking for the best team strategy to defeat others or to survive among the zombies. It also helps to develop hand movements' eye, sight, and accuracy.	The genre of this game is war, which negatively affects mental health; a person sees what is happening in the war, but at the same time sees that the game starts anew every time, which gives a kind of illusion of immortality.
Affects emotions – allows you to feel joy, sadness, admiration, regret, etc., depending on the emotional spectrum of the player; responsibility for their decisions is clearly shown; a simulator in which you can play various options and outcomes (you can create a family, buy and rent housing, the player does not receive money for completing tasks, for this, he is hired to work, where the level of payments depends on skills and abilities).	The player may draw wrong conclusions, not those the author laid down. That is, in the game, you can be an evil person and bear almost no consequences for this; excessive involvement in the game that generates dependent behavior is possible.
Develops tactical and strategic thinking, as well as knowledge of history.	Not marked
Develops thinking, ingenuity, and quickness.	Increased aggressiveness and lack of control over the time spent in the game.
Planning, resource management, and logistics. Players learn to manage limited resources and make decisions about the best use, just like in real life. The creators claim that the game has inspired many users to pursue urban planning and architecture careers. The game is very good at helping to develop a design look. Some aspiring designers use the game to fill their portfolios or practice.	The game has a very high emotional response since the character is the player himself or the dream to be like the character. Therefore, the player perceives any disappointment or joy of the character as his failure or victory. In my opinion, not all people can cope with emotions; for someone, loss in the game will be too destructive to return to the real world; this is the negative quality of all games for people who do not want to live a real life. I know from my own experience that this game can take up a considerable amount of real-time since, during the game, you don't even notice that 10-12 hours have passed, or even more; you completely forget about food and sleep.
It greatly affects a person's reaction since he must react to the enemy's attack at the right moment. Also, a person gains experience in team play. Usually, the players' roles are distributed in the team: some attack from the flank, others go around, and someone remains at the base. Intra-game communication develops, as it is necessary to maintain communication within the team. And there is also the opportunity to make new friends worldwide.	A person may show signs of aggression, as he may be dissatisfied with another person's game (for example, due to cheating – gaining an advantage by fraudulent means) or because of a loss. There are often situations when a verbal confrontation begins between players. A person does not notice the passage of time and stays up in the game for a long time while forgetting to do important things (and even eat). This can happen due to the passion for the gameplay or the desire to escape from their problems into virtual reality (addictive behavior). In this case, a sedentary lifestyle is bad for your health.
Develops reaction, attentiveness, thinking, and teamwork skills.	There is a lot of eye strain and stress from losing.
The game helps develop a good reaction and allows you to improve your memory by keeping route maps in mind. You can learn to understand cars and their characteristics when pumping your vehicle.	As with any other game, this is an uncontrolled pastime behind it.
Develops attentiveness and motor skills; instills a love for sports; teaches to compete with rivals.	Family and friends disregard; the deterioration of performance.
The game helps to learn the tricky strategy and combat skills; it allows to sort out such science as economics using artificial examples; and will teach you extraordinary thinking in a particular situation and lightning-fast reaction. To benefit his team, a player needs constant monitoring and analysis of the situation. It is solidarity and tactics that are the key to victory.	Rage and intolerance during the game are becoming quite common. In a short period, you need to perform 2-3, and sometimes more tasks at the same time. The weak psyche of a teenager may not withstand the constant tension during a play session. But the victory depends on each of the five players. Another negative impact on the player is that a person loses track of time, and the game begins to catch the player, taking away all the free time and private life of a person.
During the game, children gain programming, engineering, architecture, and mathematics skills.	Fatigue and irritation after extended periods of play.

Collider. Next, add the RigidBody component, and adjust the Gravity, Drag, and Angular Drag values. To complete the task, you must repeat the knowledge of physics and astronomy. In this case, it is the teaching model that is obtained. It will show the approximate difference in bodies dropping. Computer algebra systems can be used for precise experiments.

2. Develop a training model demonstrating planets' movement around the sun. In this case, 3D Object ® Sphere is also applied. On the surface of the spheres depicting different planets, impose different Materials, change the color, Tiling, and Offset. To complete the assignment, the student recalls the trajectories of the planets that move around the Sun. In Unity, you must learn the principles of building animation clips, working with the Animation window and the Animator component. In reality, the trajectories of the planets are quite complex. Depending on the students' training level, the tasks may differ: show the trajectories approximately or in more detail.
3. Using 3D Object ® Terrain, design a landscape containing hills, a lake, trees (a grove and a free-standing tree), grass, and wind effect. Develop different reliefs. Think over and propose a game algorithm for teaching various topics in geography, history, or the basics of life safety.
4. Create two objects. Add a script describing some event that occurs during a collision via a search by name or tag. Use OnCollisionEnter, OnCollisionStay, or OnCollisionExit. Design and implement an algorithm for a teaching model showing the collision of two bodies and an algorithm of the model demonstrating the bounce of a ball from the wall.
5. Create terrain with obstacles. Add a third-person controller, change the Slope Limit and Step Offset parameters, and test the operation. Think over the algorithm of a training lesson on the basics of medical knowledge or the basics of life safety using this controller.

Modeling in Unity

Task Example

Think over the logic and implement a model to demonstrate the attraction of particles to a magnet.

Student's Answer

Sphere, Plane, Main Camera, and Directional Light are used to complete the task. When the model is run, the particles are generated in random places of the site. The magnet moves, and the range of its magnetic field are shown. Material and Rigid Body components are added to all particles and magnets. The tag "part" is added to the particles. Then the particles will be initialized using the GameObject.FindGameObjectWithTag ("part") function. The initial location of the particles is generated randomly. The initial direction of movement of the magnet is set. If a particle enters a magnetic field, it begins to move in the direction of the magnet, with speed inversely proportional to the distance between them. This is done using the OnCollisionEnter () function. If the distance exceeds the radius, the particle stops; this is done using the OnCollisionExit () function.

Development of Computer Games in Unity

Task Example

Think over the educational game's logic and graphical user interface (with or without software implementation). Indicate the course of the game in the form of diagrams, flowcharts, or text descriptions. The game should help in mastering a specific topic of a school subject or university discipline. Think over 3-4 levels of the game and the scoring logic.

Student's Answer 1

Educational game for elementary grades. Game theme: Information Security

- Game progress: To start the game, you must select a character: A girl or boy of 8-10 years old. Next comes a window with tasks (where the difficulty increases with each level). The game starts when you select 1 level.
- Foreword (sample text): Good afternoon, our friend! Today we will get into the World of information technologies together, where we will learn a lot about information security, protecting ourselves and our data, and having fun.

Next, the task begins. You need to go through a maze; you will need to complete tasks and answer questions while going through it. For example, "What is information?", "What is data?" After passing the labyrinth, a sign comes out: "Well done, you got ... points, and you can go to the next level or stay and improve your result."

- Second level: Crossword. When completing a crossword puzzle, task completion time and the number of correct answers are considered. To solve a crossword puzzle, you need to guess the terms related to information security from their descriptions.
- Third level. At this level, information will be given about passwords, what passwords are, and how best to protect yourself. A task to compose a strong password. Points are awarded for strength.
- Fourth level. Video clip with information about anti-virus programs. It is necessary to name at least three antivirus programs. The maximum score will be given if one writes the names of 5 antivirus programs.

Student's Answer 2

The theme of the game is the study of history. The goal is to get out of the estate.

- Description: The game is played in the third or first person. The player is in the room; he has 100 points. One hint – minus 5 points, one direct answer to one task – minus 10 points. If the points end before the end of the game – you have lost 0 points. At the end of the game, the number of points indicates the student's knowledge of the subject.
- Levels to complete: exit from the room, exit from the house, exit from the territory of the estate.

- The first level: find a picture and indicate the name, by whom, and when it was drawn. Find a chest with a key from the door with a code – the year of birth of the person associated with the picture. Upon completing these and similar tasks, the exit of their room opens. For this level, some database is created with data about the paintings.
- Second level: passing the maze, finding any historical thing (scepter, crown, pendant, ring, etc.), identifying the thing's owner, finding a secret door that opens according to the year of birth of the owner of the thing being found. A database of any historical things and their owners is being created from where the data is derived; the maze is present to distract attention from figures and historical facts. The result is leaving the house.
- The third level: to reach the gate, you need to walk only along with the cells in the correct chronology of the reign of the tsars. A lock on the gate with questions concerning these rulers must be answered correctly to open the gate. Upon reaching the gate, the player receives a question regarding any tsar involved in the chronology. This can be a question about the dates of life, reign, the number or names of children, the wars in which he participated, etc. The result is going out of the territory of the estate.

Student's Answer 3

The logic has been thought over, and a game has been implemented to teach the basics of software testing. The "theory" section contains the main definitions, which are displayed in the form of blocks. Definitions are shown in text and graphic format, and some descriptions are animated. It doesn't matter if the user has familiarized himself with the theory in this game or already knows the basics of testing, a section with a test is always available to consolidate the theory. There are twenty questions in the test; ten seconds are given for each question. The presented game is designed in a 2d measurement. The game's plot lies in the fact that the main character, namely the user of our game while solving tasks and receiving the necessary educational information, passes levels that familiarize him with the software testing process. The game has five levels of difficulty. The user opens the first level, and the first thing he sees is a dialog box. The virtual teacher explains the workflow, describes the assignment and gives advice. The tasks follow. For example, select functional requirements among data. Another task is writing a test case for one program's functions. The test case structure is displayed on the screen with empty fields. You must drag blocks with text from the bottom of the screen into these fields. At the next level – the player will need to enter the answers in the empty fields to the question regarding the analysis of boundary values. And at the end, the user must fill in the bug report with the mandatory fields for entering values. The user will always have access to the task data for repeating or working on mistakes after the game-level completion. Also, the user always has access to the "Theory" and "Test" sections.

Modeling in 3ds Max

The Unity development environment provides ample opportunities for creating 3D models. But this platform is primarily intended for creating games. 3D editors have more possibilities specifically for 3D modeling. Therefore, it is a common practice that models are created in 3D editors and then imported into the game development environment.

Autodesk 3ds Max is professional 3D modeling, animation, and rendering software for game creation and design. The application is considered one of the most extensive 3D modeling packages. It contains many plugins and add-ons for a variety of tasks. The program implements tools for animation, and there is a physics calculation mechanism, thanks to which it is possible to achieve realism in modeling hard and soft bodies.

In this case, the practice assignment is not a game development assignment. It involves the development of interactive models that can be applied to individual learning and lectures. These models can also be used in games as separate tasks.

Task Example

Create a model showing a physical phenomenon or process.

Student's Answer 1

A model has been developed that demonstrates the free fall of bodies in various gravitational fields. 4 standard Plane primitives and four standard Sphere primitives, textures for materials are used in model creation. The force of gravity and the falling speed depend on which surface (Plane) the sphere is located. To work with physical objects, Mass FX is used. Spheres are defined as Dynamic Rigid Bodies, Planes as Static Rigid Body. The sphere's direction will be negative on the z-axis and zero on the x and y axes. Materials are applied to the spheres and the Planes, and a Bitmap is added. With the help of this map, ready-made images are superimposed on objects. The animation created using the Mass FX Toolbar is not a standard keyframes animation. To obtain a standard animation, the resulting model must be "baked" (Mass FX ® Simulation ® Bake All Objects).

Student's Answer 2

A model has been developed that demonstrates the attraction of particles to a magnet. Dummy, Box (magnet model), Sphere (particles models), Target Spotlight (lighting), materials are used to create the model. When particles hit the magnetic field area, they begin to move at a certain speed, depending on the distance to the magnet. The code specifies that the script is calculated only once per frame using a variable responsible for ticks. The distance between the magnet and the particle is calculated. The particle's position changes towards the magnet if it is less than a given radius.

Scripting in 3ds Max

MAXScript is a scripting language built into 3ds Max designed to automate routine tasks and create new editing tools and user interfaces. Using this language, you can control and modify objects in a 3D scene, such as geometry, textures, animation, and more. It is possible to develop new software tools for the independent work of students in an interactive mode (Khoroshko et al., 2019).

Task Example

Create a script that allows you to demonstrate various actions on an object in 3D space.

Student's Answer 1

A script has been created to demonstrate how light sources work. Plane and Box objects with the specified parameters are made on the scene. After that, buttons responsible for different light sources become available. The Create Spotlight button creates a directional light that radiates out in a cone shape. The "Create Directional Light" button creates a directional light source in the shape of a cylinder. The Create Omni Light button creates an omnidirectional light source. The "Create Skylight" button creates a light source in the form of a hemisphere, all points of which are sources of light rays. When one of the available light sources is selected, the radio buttons responsible for the position of the light source on the scene, as well as the "High Quality," "Render," and "Delete Light" buttons become available. The High-Quality button enables a high-quality display for the viewport to see how the light works in the scene. The "Render" button is responsible for obtaining the final image. The Delete Light button will remove the current light from the scene (Gabdrakhmanov, 2020).

Student's Answer 2

A script has been developed to demonstrate forward and reverse kinematics using the Bones object as an example. By clicking the "Create Bones" button on the scene, create three bones connected based on the "ancestor/descendant" principle. Further, the radio buttons responsible for activating the forward and inverse kinematics become available. After selecting one, the animation control button and the button returning to the selection of kinematics become available. The Play Animation button allows you to start a looped animation of one of the selected actions, and pressing it again stops the animation (Gabdrakhmanov, 2020).

Snippets of Code:

```
rollout r "Task2" width:178 height:167
(
button btn1 "Create Bones" pos:[46,7] width:86
groupBox grp1 "FK and IK" pos:[13,33] width:152 height:75
radioButtons rdo1 "" pos:[32,58] enabled:false labels:#("Forward Kinematics")
default:0
radioButtons rdo2 "" pos:[32,73] enabled:false labels:#("Inverse Kinematics")
default:0
checkButton ckb1 "Play Animation" pos:[46,113] width:86 enabled:false
button btn2 "FK and IK" pos:[46,139] width:86 enabled:false
on r open do
(
viewCubeOps.goHome()
max select all
max delete
stopAnimation()
sliderTime=0f
```

```
)
on btn1 pressed do
(
global b1=boneSys.createBone [29.716,0,26.993] [2,0,15.512] [0,0,1]
b1.wireColor=(color 255 255 255)
b1.width=4
…
global b2=boneSys.createBone [2,0,15.512] [-25.716,0,26.992] [0,0,1]
…
b3.taper=90
b3.parent=b2
b2.parent=b1
btn1.enabled=false
...
)
on rdo1 changed state do
(
animate on
(
rot1=eulerAngles 0 22.5 0
...
at time 80 rotate b2 rot4
)
rdo2.enabled=false
ckb1.enabled=true
btn2.enabled=true
)
on rdo2 changed state do
(
c=ikSys.ikChain b1 b3 "IKHISolver"
c.transform.controller.dispGoal=false
deselect c
animate on
(
at time 20 move c [13.858,0,5.741]
...
)
rdo1.enabled=false
ckb1.enabled=true
btn2.enabled=true
)
on ckb1 changed state do
(
if state==true then
```

```
(
ckbl.text="Stop Animation"
playAnimation()
)
else
(
ckbl.text="Play Animation"
stopAnimation()
)
)
...
on r close do
(
viewCubeOps.goHome()
max select all
max delete
stopAnimation()
sliderTime=0f
)
)
createDialog r
```

Student's Answer 3

A script has been developed that allows you to demonstrate moving, scaling, and rotating objects. A window is created that contains such interface elements as a button, a frame to restrict interface elements visually, and a radio button. The controller allows you to take any action by clicking on it. The frame groups specific interface elements for a better understanding of their purpose. A radio button is used to select a specific action. By clicking on the "Create Point" button, a point is created on the scene with the display of the X, Y, and Z axes. The "Create Box" button creates a Box object on the scene with the specified parameters. Next, several radio buttons become available, allowing you to activate the transformation prescribed after it with the Box object. Object transformations include moving, rotating, and scaling the object along with the scene's X, Y, and Z axes. After the desired action is selected, the animation control button and the button for activating all available transformations become available. The "Play Animation" button allows you to start a looped animation of the selected action, and pressing the button again stops the animation. If you need to choose another transformation with an object, you can click the corresponding button, "Transform," and then all actions will become available again (Gabdrakhmanov, 2020).

Game Development in Blender

Blender is free and open-source 3D object creation software. It supports the full range of actions with 3D objects – modeling, rigging, animation, rendering, compositing, motion tracking, and video edit-

Table 2. Recommendations for choosing practical tasks

	Increasing interest in learning, development of creative thinking	Development of modeling skills	Development of programming skills
Review of existing games	+		
Study applications for game development	+	+	+
Modeling in Unity	+	+	+
Development of computer games in Unity	+	+	+
Modeling in 3ds Max	+	+	
Scripting in 3ds Max	+	+	+
Game development in Blender	+	+	+

ing. For example, Khan et al. (2019) authors have used the 3D creation software Blender to develop 3D models of various types and to provide complete, user-friendly control to the user. With the Blender Game Engine (BGE), you can create 3D games. Now this engine has been removed from new Blender packages. Still, there is information that the UPBGE (Uchronia Project Blender Game Engine) code will become part of the future official release of Blender. Blender's functionality can be extended with scripts written in Python.

An Example of a Task

Develop a game in Blender. The game is played in the first person. The player flies through obstacles in the form of various 3D objects, which he must not touch. By touching objects, the player loses a life. The player collects points and sets records for the distances covered when moving. Sensors, controllers, and actuators were used as tools. Sensors are the event system that triggers an action when an object collides with another object or when using a joystick. As soon as one or more sensors are triggered, the controller checks if this set of events will lead to an event in the game. Controllers evaluate sensors using simple Boolean conditions such as and, or, and no. When the controller checks a set of sensors, it activates the actuators. Actuators are responsible for a specific action in the game, for example, the end of the game, the movement of an object, the appearance of a new object, etc.

When completing this task, you can put additional requirements, fulfilling which the student will develop modeling skills. As noted above, Blender allows you to perform all stages of modeling with high quality.

SOLUTIONS AND RECOMMENDATIONS

As mentioned above, the development of computer games in students' education has positive aspects. (Soboleva et al., 2021; Chen, 2021). The work considered various tasks for students that increase interest in learning. These tasks can develop modeling and programming skills (Table 2).

The teacher's assistance to the student is important at all stages of collaboration (Galbraith and Winterbottom, 2011; Onrubia and Engel, 2012; Onrubia, 2016). Table 3 shows the actions that are proposed

Table 3. Recommendations for practical tasks implementation

Stages	Teacher	Teacher and student together	Student
Preliminary	Recommends platforms and tools for game development.	The teacher and students provide an overview of the features of the modern game and explore the capabilities of modern game development platforms.	Selects platforms for game development.
Clarification of the assignment	Suggests themes for the game and defines requirements.	They discuss the logic of the game together.	Thinks over the logic of the game. Get acquainted with the requirements for the game.
Completing the assignment	Checks the models' quality and the developed game's correspondence to the task.	Discuss scenes developed by the student.	Performs the task. Demonstrates each level (scene) to the teacher.
Testing	Whenever possible, the teacher involves other students in the group in this process.	Check the game by choosing different levels.	Demonstrates the result. Places the game on the application store, if possible.
Grade	Evaluates the result.	Involve other students in the assessment of the game.	Participates in the evaluation of the work of other students.

to be performed by the teacher and the student at different stages of work with an assignment related to the development of a game

FUTURE RESEARCH DIRECTIONS

As already mentioned, developing a game is a rather laborious process. Working alone or in pairs, a student will not be able to create a big game in 1-to 2 semesters. It is helpful to develop teamwork skills if students work in groups. Perhaps 5-7 or more people. In this case, the distribution of responsibilities is possible. Each student will be responsible for their part of the work – modeling, thinking through the design, writing scripts, debugging the program, etc. It is planned to study the group's game development results in the future.

CONCLUSION

When working with students, researchers ask their opinion on independent game development. Students like such tasks; some students include tasks on game development in the top 5 most interesting tasks during their studies at universities and colleges. Some students choose to study the problems of game development as an assignment for their final qualifying work. They show good results. Game development assignments have been used in teaching over the past years, and it is planned to continue this practice in the future.

ACKNOWLEDGMENT

This paper has been supported by the Kazan Federal University Strategic Academic Leadership Program ("PRIORITY-2030").

REFERENCES

Carranza, D. B., Negrón, A., & Contreras, M. (2021). Videogame development training approach: A virtual reality and open-source perspective. *Journal of Universal Computer Science*, *27*(2), 152–169. doi:10.3897/jucs.65164

Chen, M.-B. (2021). The development of a two-level cardboard game tool. *Zhongguo Gongcheng Xuekan*, *44*(5), 448–454. doi:10.1080/02533839.2021.1919559

Dobroskok, I., Rzhevska, N., Ayyildiz, H., Zaimova, D., & Zheliazkov, G. (2020). Game development software tools in higher educational institutions: Experience of Ukraine, Turkey and Bulgaria. *Technologies and Learning Tools*, *78*(4), 90–104. doi:10.33407/itlt.v78i4.3370

Falah, J., Wedyan, M., Alfalah, S. F. M., Abu-Tarboush, M., Al-Jakheem, A., Al-Faraneh, M., Abuhammad, A., & Charissis, V. (2021). Identifying the characteristics of virtual reality gamification for complex educational topics. *Multimodal Technologies and Interaction*, *5*(9), 53. doi:10.3390/mti5090053

Gabdrakhmanov, R. (2020). *Interactive Computer Graphics Models for Distance Courses* [Unpublished master's thesis]. Kazan Federal University, Kazan, Russian Federation.

Galbraith, J., & Winterbottom, M. (2011). Peer-tutoring: What's in it for the tutor? *Educational Studies*, *37*(3), 321–332. doi:10.1080/03055698.2010.506330

Hursen, C., & Bas, C. (2019). Use of Gamification Applications in Science Education. *International Journal of Emerging Technologies in Learning*, *14*(1), 4–23. doi:10.3991/ijet.v14i01.8894

Khan, S., Channa, S., Ali, S. A., Khan, M. H., Qazi, A.H., & Mengal, K. (2019). 3d Modeling for Wildlife Encyclopedia Using Blender. *3C Tecnologia*, 133-147. doi:10.17993/3ctecno.2019.specialissue3.133-147

Khoroshko, L. L., Ukhov, P. A., & Keyno, P. P. (2019). Development of massive open online courses based on 3d computer graphics and multimedia. *International Journal of Engineering Pedagogy*, *9*(4), 4–15. doi:10.3991/ijep.v9i4.10193

Kim, S. B., Kim, K.-T., Kim, O., Seo, E. Y., & Lee, S. J. (2021). A research tool for biomechanics toward sensory-motor manipulation, Unity 3D. *Journal of Biomechanical Science and Engineering*, *16*(2), 1–7. doi:10.1299/jbse.21-00068

Kiryakova, G., Angelova, N., & Yordanova, L. (2014). *Gamification in Education.* Conference: 9th International Balkan Education and Science Conference, Edirne, Turkey.

Maskeliūnas R., Kulikajevas A., Blažauskas T., Damaševičius R., & Swacha J. (2020). An interactive serious mobile game for supporting the learning of programming in javascript in the context of eco-friendly city management. *Computers*, *9*(4), 1–18. doi:10.3390/computers9040102

Mina, D., Salah, J., & Abdennadher, S. (2021). ARcode: Programming for Youngsters Through AR. *Lecture Notes in Networks and Systems*, *326*, 65–74. doi:10.1007/978-3-030-86618-1_7

Minnegalieva, C. B., Galimyanov, A. F., & Khambelov, A. I. (2020). Development of environmental conservation in digital era. *Procedia Environmental Science, Engineering and Management*, *7*(3), 469–477.

Mostafa, M., & Faragallah, O. S. (2019). Development of Serious Games for Teaching Information Security Courses. *IEEE Access: Practical Innovations, Open Solutions*, *7*, 169293–169305. doi:10.1109/ACCESS.2019.2955639

Onrubia, J. (2016). Learning and teaching in virtual environments: Joint activity, teacher assistance and knowledge construction. *Red-Revista de Educacion a Distancia,* (50).

Onrubia, J., & Engel, A. (2012). The role of teacher assistance on the effects of a macro-script in collaborative writing tasks. *International Journal of Computer-Supported Collaborative Learning*, *7*(1), 161–186. doi:10.100711412-011-9125-9

Patricio, R., Moreira, A., Zurlo, F., & Melazzini, M. (2020). Co-creation of new solutions through gamification: A collaborative innovation practice. *Creativity and Innovation Management*, *29*(1), 146–160. doi:10.1111/caim.12356

Patrício, R., Moreira, A. C., & Zurlo, F. (2018). Gamification approaches to the early stage of innovation. *Creativity and Innovation Management*, *27*(4), 499–511. doi:10.1111/caim.12284

Pedreira, O., García, F., Piattini, M., Cortiñas, A., & Cerdeira-Pena, A. (2020). An architecture for software engineering gamification. *Tsinghua Science and Technology*, *25*(6), 776–797. doi:10.26599/TST.2020.9010004

Politowski, C., Petrillo, F., Montandon, J. E., Valente, M. T., & Guéhéneuc, Y.-G. (2021). Are game engines software frameworks? A three-perspective study. *Journal of Systems and Software*, *171*, 110846. doi:10.1016/j.jss.2020.110846

Soboleva, E. V., Sabirova, E. G., Babieva, N. S., Sergeeva, M. G., & Torkunova, J. V. (2021). Formation of Computational Thinking Skills Using Computer Games in Teaching Mathematics. *Eurasia Journal of Mathematics, Science and Technology Education*, *17*(10), 1–16. doi:10.29333/ejmste/11177

Stott, A., & Neustaedter, C. (2013). Analysis of Gamification in Education. Academic Press.

Tisza, G., & Markopoulos, P. (2021). Understanding the role of fun in learning to code. *International Journal of Child-Computer Interaction*, *28*, 100270. doi:10.1016/j.ijcci.2021.100270

Toda, A. M., Valle, P. H. D., & Isotani, S. (2017). The Dark Side of Gamification: An Overview of Negative Effects of Gamification in Education. In Higher Education for All. From Challenges to Novel Technology-Enhanced Solutions. Springer. doi:10.1007/978-3-319-97934-2_9

Villagrasa, S., Fonseca, D., Redondo, E., & Duran, J. (2014). Teaching case of gamification and visual technologies for education. *Journal of Cases on Information Technology*, *16*(4), 38–57. doi:10.4018/jcit.2014100104

Wozniak, J. (2020). Gamification for sales incentives. *Contemporary Economics*, *14*(2), 144–161. doi:10.5709/ce.1897-9254.337

ADDITIONAL READING

Aktaş, A. Z., & Orçun, E. (2016). A survey of computer game development. *Journal of Defense Modeling and Simulation: Applications, Methodology. Technology*, *13*(2), 239–251.

Andrea, R., Nursobah, & Kopel, M. (2019). Design and Development of "Battle Drone" Computer-Based Trading Card Game (CTCG). *11th International Conference on Multimedia and Network Information Systems (MISSI)*, *833*, 574-585 10.1007/978-3-319-98678-4_57

Patrício, R., Moreira, A. C., & Zurlo, F. (2021). Enhancing design thinking approaches to innovation through gamification. *European Journal of Innovation Management*, *24*(5), 1569–1594. doi:10.1108/EJIM-06-2020-0239

KEY TERMS AND DEFINITIONS

AR (Augmented Reality): The result of introducing any sensory data into the visual field to supplement information and change the perception of the environment.

C#: An object-oriented programming language.

Colliders (Unity Component): Collider components define the shape of a GameObject for physical collisions. An invisible collider must not be the same shape as the GameObject's mesh.

Computer Game Development: The process of developing a computer game.

Educational Computer Game: Software that teaches the user in a game mode.

GameObject (Unity component): GameObjects are the fundamental objects in Unity that represent characters, props, and scenery. They do not accomplish much in themselves, but they act as containers for Components that implement the functionality.

Rigidbody (Unity Component): Rigidbodies enable GameObjects to act under the control of physics. The Rigidbody can receive forces and torque to make objects move realistically. Any GameObject must contain a Rigidbody to be influenced by gravity, act under added pressures via scripting, or interact with other objects through the NVIDIA PhysX physics engine.

Scene (Unity Component): Scenes contain the environments and menus of the game. In each Scene, the programmer place environments, obstacles, and decorations, essentially designing and building the game in pieces.

Unity: A cross-platform computer game development environment.

Chapter 12
Creation of a Distance Communication Channel With Gamification Elements

Alona Yuriivna Yurzhenko
Kherson State Maritime Academy, Ukraine

Julia Yuriivna Bevzenko
Maritime Applied College, Kherson State Maritime Academy, Ukraine

Olena Yuriivna Kononova
Maritime Applied College, Kherson State Maritime Academy, Ukraine

ABSTRACT

The chapter investigates the ways of a distance communication channel with gamification elements created in the electronic educational environment of maritime higher education institutions. The example of the gamified educational electronic environment on LMS Moodle is presented in the chapter. The chapter also gives examples of gamified activities on LMS Moodle to form communicative competency of future maritime professionals. The distance communication channel presented in the chapter contains the use of a social virtual reality platform. The static 360-degree virtual environment with a 2D video stream for English classes was analyzed. According to the received results, the quality and success of training increased. The use of gamification proved useful and helpful in the distance education of future maritime specialists.

INTRODUCTION

In the fight against the outbreak of the COVID-19, countries have replaced face-to-face education with distance education as a defensive tool. The world is looking now at distance technologies in a different way, they have become needed, especially in E-teaching. Teaching, which everyone considered impossible with distance learning only, is now compulsory in this mode. Forced distance learning has become a

DOI: 10.4018/978-1-6684-4287-6.ch012

challenge for all participants in the educational process. It was not easy to organize high-quality training with the use of digital technologies, to inspire and motivate students, to give advice on technical problems. The move to the online space is presenting considerable hardship as teachers struggle to adapt to the rapid move to online modes of delivery in order to keep students engaged in learning (Amriani et al., 2014). Today, one of the main problems of distance education for us is the inability of teachers to create channels of communication with their students. Therefore, the main goal of introducing gamification in an educational context is to increase the involvement of students in the learning process without their own awareness of this fact by modeling the behavior of participants. Unconsciousness plays an important role in this case, because this contributes to the substitution of external motivation for internal. Moreover, due to unconscious involvement, involuntary attention is activated, the activation of which is considered more effective in the learning process. Speaking about the implementation of gamification in distance learning, it should be noted that in this form of education there is little emotional component that connects the teacher and students, as well as students with each other. Therefore, the use of such elements of gamification as levels, awards, winners 'scoreboard, enhances engagement by engaging studying. Another important psychological problem that teachers and students face is the fear of making mistakes. The introduction of gamification changes the way the educational process is organized, this can "help to overcome the fear of mistakes and use mistakes as an important source of acquiring new knowledge. When using gamification (especially meaningful), the edges of the educational process are erased, students abstract from their usual social roles and get used to the role of their characters, using, for example, avatars and acting in accordance with the plot. All this minimizes the fear of making a mistake. In such way teacher and student can communicate. In teaching English, communication is the most important element, because the main task of this discipline is to form the student's communicative competence (the ability to communicate using English). The main task of English for professional purpose is to form professional English-speaking competence (the ability to solve professional problems using English).

BACKGROUND

Education today is becoming an area that is capable of progress through the use of the gamification method thanks to clear parallels between learning and playing. If we play game we pass the levels, then according to the results of the learning we proceed to the next course. Games are based on overcoming obstacles. Learning is based on surrender examination session. Both during the game and during learning we get new knowledge and skills. In both cases, a very significant element is social interaction. Gamification not only uses game elements and game design techniques in non-game contexts (Werbach & Hunter, 2012), but also empowers and engages the learner with motivational skills towards a learning approach and sustaining a relax atmosphere.

Technology also gives the student much access to information and promotes the creation and sharing of knowledge, but it requires teachers to work to find ways of increasing students' motivation and engagement. Thus, a great amount of work has also been devoted to develop new teaching strategies that enhance students' motivation and commitment and maximize their knowledge acquisition. Among different strategies, gamification has attracted the interest of educators, who in the last times have been exploring its potential to improve student learning (Dichev & Dicheva, 2017). Studies about the effectiveness of gamification are promising, with variable to positive results (Caponetto et al., 2014). Although "game" is an ambiguous term and different game formats have been used by researchers and educators

(Hanghøj, 2013), gamification can be defined as the use of game elements in non-entertainment contexts to promote learning. The fact that games have many elements that are naturally appealing for young and adults and have a strong influence in their lifestyle helps to introduce an extra motivation for learning and to improve learning outcomes. The symbiosis between gaming and learning is also evidenced by the progressive development of best practices for courses gamification and game design. Another reason for including game elements in education is that it has been reported that games can provide social links (Waytz & Gray, 2018), promote knowledge seeking (Toh & Kirschner, 2020), develop creativity (Vartanian and Beatty, 2015).

Our course with gamification in MOODLE is designed to progressively introduce new concepts to be mastered. Students must then apply these concepts to increasingly challenging problems and ultimately apply prior knowledge to new situations, improve skills and reduce fear of making decisions. In most of the cases, the gamified activity is well-received by learners, considered effective, educational, and engaging, and in some cases also fun. Our students are the representatives of the new generation Z. They grew up in the century of the technological boom, the development of the Internet and social networks. They are fans of online communication. That is why the gamification of learning can help us to create exciting, educational, and entertaining content and motivate the current generation of students to the realities of the future profession. The introduction of elements of gamification into the learning process increased the interest of students in the course. In order to increase the motivation of students, awards, points, ratings and other game attributes were used. One of the key benefits of gamification is that it makes learning informative, mainly thanks to its interactivity. Role-play and competitive elements add an immersive angle, which, if set up well, can quite simply make learning fun. The creation of a successful situation contributed to the development of students` learning satisfaction.

MAIN FOCUS OF THE ARTICLE

Literature Research

There are a lot of scientists who studied the use of distance technologies in English teaching (Xiao, Hurd, Sherman, Spivakovsky, and others), those who considered the creation of communication channel (Wang, Huang, Kammoun, Chaaban) and others. The creation of communication channel using distance learning was explored by Kearns, Frey, Thach, Murphy. However, the use of the distance communication channel with gamification elements in the electronic information environment for the formation of professional communicative competence of future maritime professionals hasn't been fully investigated. The purpose of our study is to analyze the potential of using distance learning with gamification elements to create communication channel between tutor and student of maritime higher education institution for forming a communicative competence.

Hypotheses and Objectives

The objective of this article is to use gamification as a psychological, didactic and methodological potential in teaching English language, to analyze some tools that allow creating electronic educational resources using gamification elements. Such types of educational work as lectures, readings, audio-visualization and demonstration are passive forms of learning and have low rates of memorization of information.

While discussion, application in practice, cases, teaching others and using in real situations are active forms of learning and will contribute to the development of competencies, including communicative one.

The perception and memorization of information when presenting material with elements of gamification is equated with the assimilation of information applied in practice or even through use in real life, and gives up to 90% of the effectiveness of assimilation of educational material. Moreover, when gamification is used in teaching, the individual's capabilities are activated, and their creative abilities are realized, since the game is characterized by pleasure, improvisation and competitiveness. According to the studies of modern scientists, the introduction of gamification in the educational environment contributes not only to an increase in the level of intrinsic motivation, productivity in the work of students, but also leads to an increase in the percentage of class attendance (Patel & Sakadasariya, 2018, Diahyleva et al., 2020).

Speaking about the introduction of gamification in teaching a foreign language, it should be noted that the non-imitative nature of activity inherent in gamification allows one to develop not only foreign language communication skills, but also professional skills, abilities and gain experience, as well as develop critical thinking, the ability to work together, readiness to cooperation, tolerance. This makes gamification a unique way of organizing educational activities in foreign language classes, in which there is a departure from passive teaching methods, where knowledge is given in a ready-made form, and it becomes possible to implement problem teaching methods, search activities and research projects, organization of self-assessment and group assessment, simulation of the learning process by creating a virtual language space, the creative potential of the personality of the participants in the educational process is activated. In addition, at the present stage of development of language education, special attention should be paid to the development of the self-education system, which requires stimulating the educational and cognitive activity of students in the organization of their independent activity. Gamification provides stimulation of self-education by creating an information and learning environment, which contributes to the independent desire of students for self-development and disclosure of creative abilities, as well as through a strong increase in the level of internal motivation and overall satisfaction with the learning process. In distance and mixed forms of foreign language teaching, various forms of gamification are used: computer games, educational mobile applications, programs and applications with augmented reality elements and with 3D communication using avatars.

METHODOLOGY

The participants of this research are a total of 60 cadets (male) aged 16-17 from Ukrainian maritime education establishment - Maritime Professional College of Kherson State Maritime Academy (KSMA). They are cadets of ship engineering department.

The participants of the research during COVID-19 pandemic had to study English for professional purpose using such distance tool - Learning Management System (LMS) MOODLE with gamification and videoconference facilities. The materials to be used in the mentioned above elements of distance learning are from "While Ashore: coursebook" (Bobrysheva et al., 2021). The stages of the survey were following:

- The course "Maritime English" was created on LMS MOODLE of KSMA. Gamification elements were created (badges, levels, missions, avatars, progress loops/bars, maps etc.). Videoconferencing module (BigBlueButton) was used on LMS MOODLE to conduct the meetings of tutor with students in order to form their professional communicative competence.

- The collection of results and their analysis was done by the tutor.
- To receive proper feedback from students the questionnaires using Google forms were created.
- The collection and analysis of data received in questionnaires was conducted.
- The results of survey were presented in graphical form.

RESULTS

It is important to integrate language learning strategies into oral English learning. For instance, teachers can guide students to develop the good habit of watching English TV programs, English movies or listening to English broadcasts; help students to master some fixed sentence patterns and use them in oral learning and encourage students to try to use English to express their ideas in real life and learning. In the context of the pandemic, the priorities of technologies used to achieve learning outcomes have shifted towards distance education, the main problem of which is to create a two-way communication channel, both in writing and oral forms, with the help of digital technologies. Online learning in its entirety is dependent on technological devices and Internet.

Many scientists were engaged in the study of distance learning, among them is researcher Li who theoretically and practically considered the possibilities of massive open online courses (MOOCs) in classroom teaching of English and wider education field at home and abroad. The use of online courses for English teaching was studied by Voloshynov, Popova, Sherman, Chen, Sonnert, Sadler, Sasselov, Alturkistani, Lam, Foley (Bing, 2017). The use of VR technologies in English teaching was studied by Symonenko, Zaitseva, Osadchyi, Osadcha, Shmeltser and others. Gamification in teaching English for special purpose was studied by Blum-Dimaya, A., Reeve, S. A., Reeve, K. F., David Dodgson (Bobrysheva et al., 2021). The analysis of scientific literature and personal pedagogical experience of authors in higher education institution allows us to highlight the peculiarities of the use of distance learning. While creating distance activities the first and most important is to analyze distance learning and gamification elements used (Table 1).

There is no doubt that the skillful use of distance learning and gamification elements which we've described above can be used to create communication channel necessary for formation of communicative competence of students (Koster, 2004). Analyzing creation of communication channels through forums use the researchers found out that the communication between student and tutor same as student with other students can be achieved here only with the use of texting. Students use their avatars (gamification elements) while working in forums. The communicative competence of future seafarers according to International convention on Standards of Training, Certification and Watch-keeping means use of English in written and oral forms. Thus one more element of written communication skills check is feedback option in Assignment activity which proposes tutor to comment student's work through texting window below the submitted document or to send file of any format (Laster, 2010). Using the last variant of communication tutor has possibility to correct mistakes/underline specific information/comment the work directly in the text. After sending his comments tutor waits for student to reply – this process can be endless (Lazzaro, 2004). The grade (points achievement as gamification element) written by tutor is automatically going to e-gradebook of LMS MOODLE course (McGonigal, 2011).

Table 1. Gamification elements incorporated in the developed system

Name of the element	Description	Examples of use
e-schedule	a unified class schedule system located in Google Sheets, with which you can create the visual presentations needed for your classes, create the handouts. It is s a very powerful real-time collaboration.	With the help of comment option students can ask the questions according to their schedule and receive the answers (Caponetto et al., 2014).
Forum	The Forum allows students and teachers to discuss topics and exchange ideas by posting comments. It is a place where students can interact and get to know each other. Forum activity is a powerful communication tool in MOODLE. There are several forum types to choose from, such as a standard forum where anyone can start a new discussion at any time; a forum where each student can post exactly one discussion; or a question and answer forum where students must first post before being able to view other students' posts.	Tutor can set the subscription to forced mode and continue texting an issue raised previously in VR or video session (Corbett, 2010).
LMS MOODLE Assignment activity	The electronic system LMS MOODLE provides an opportunity to create and send project works through the activity "Assignment", providing individual work of teachers for each student. This includes not only e-mail and file sharing, but also forums, chats, and blogging.	With the help of Feedback option tutor can create and send comments/annotated PDF/Offline grading worksheet/Feedback files back to student (Caponetto et al., 2014).
Messaging drawer in LMS MOODLE	This activity module enables participants to have text-based, real-time discussions, also helps students to prepare for tests where the teacher, or other students, would pose questions, teacher can contact, communicate, give all the necessary recommendations to the participants.	During training, student can write a personal message to the teacher or discuss any questions with colleagues on training (in person or in a group). This can be done using the internal LMS MOODLE messages (Corbett, 2010).
Audio vocabulary in LMS MOODLE	The pages with new words, their transcription, audio file and image or video are connected and presented by Glossary. With the help of the other activity (Book), teacher also can create a presentation of words with audio transcription, pictures and definitions. With the help of this, future ship engineers can correctly pronounce words; understand its meaning on a particular topic of the lesson.	Audio vocabulary lays a certain foundation, thanks to which student can study topics on his own, at any time and at any time to go to the course and listen to the words again. With the help of the audio vocabulary students can learn the correct pronunciation of words, put the English intonation, effectively replenish active and passive vocabulary, develop speaking and writing (Caponetto et al., 2014).
Video room in BigBlueButton Meet	One of the most important elements of distance learning is video conferencing. BigBlueButton is one of the modules on LMS MOODLE for video conferencing and online meetings. BigBlueButton is now helping students to study in quarantine.	With the help of BigBlueButton teacher can check the oral competence of the cadets on a particular topic. Participants answer questions. Teacher can also use the zoom to make notes, use interactive elements to engage participants; conduct online lessons. BigBlueButton has an integrated interactive whiteboard that can be shown to all participants in the video conference. This function is used during lessons, also there is record of a video conference. Then this video can be sent to students who were late for the video meeting or could not attend (Corbett, 2010).
Badges	Badges are awarded based on set criteria and are then displayed on a user's profile. They can also push to a user's Open Badges backpack since MOODLE Badges are compatible with Mozilla Open Badges. A badge can be either a site badge or a course badge. Site badges are awarded for a set of site-wide activities whereas course badges are awarded for interactions within a course.	As a teacher you can add a badge to a course by navigating to *Settings > Course administration > Badges > Add a new badge*. In configuring the badge details you will enter a name and description for the badge as well as select an image for the badge. This image displays when the badge is issued to students. The Issuer details will require you to enter the name of the issuing agent or authority for this badge. You will also need to make decisions regarding the badge expiry by setting if and when the badge expires. You can choose to set the badge to never expire on a given date or expire a set number of days after being issued (Caponetto et al., 2014).
Missions and levels	Mission is basically a task which users need to complete. The levels function as a "gamified" version of learning chapters, which provide that extra fun factor while organizing content progression in a useful manner.	In LMS MOODLE e-course modules are used as missions. Levels are used in LMS MOODLE as module activities connected between each other (restrict option when the access is impossible without previous activity completion). Levels are a fun way for students to see their progress in a game and it gives them something to look forward to as they learn (Corbett, 2010).
Progress bars	The Progress Bar is a time-management tool for students.	It visually shows what activities / resources a student is supposed to interact with in a course. It is colour coded so students can quickly see what they have and have not completed/viewed. The teacher selects which pre-existing activities/resources are to be included in the Progress Bar and when they should be completed/viewed. Ordering can be done by times/deadlines or by the ordering of activities in the course. There is an overview page allowing teachers to see the progress of all students in a class, which is helpful for finding students at risk (Dyagileva et al., 2020).
Loops	Within a lesson activity, the multiple answer option appears to be having issues with displaying feedback and going to the correct page after submission. When a student partially answers a question correctly, the question continues to loop until the user answers it correctly.	It should show the student feedback then go to the end of the lesson as it specified in the jump. It should only stay on that page if set to "This page", but all are set to "End of lesson". This functionality appears to have changed, and as a result a student can not score partial points anymore (previous students in the course scored partial points.)
Avatars	Avatar is used in LMS MOODLE by course participants to immerse themselves into the English educational processю	The use of avatar in the context of learning can make students to feel themselves more safe and relaxed. It can lead to the more active participation and to immersion (Diahyleva et al., 2020).
Rules	A rule is a statement telling students what they should do in order to achieve success or a benefit of some kind.	Teachers can easily create games` rules and customize each game to suit a specific theme or subject. The first step is to create the game rules and define how many points are required to pass each level in the game. The points that students earn for completing lessons, assignments, and more will help them advance through the levels (Popovych et al., 2019).
Points	The marks which course participants earn through learning.	The more points students get – the higher is their positions in leaderboards automatically created on LMS MOODLE via Results blocks (Dyagileva et al., 2020).
Maps	A map is a drawing of a particular area such as a city, a country, or a continent, showing its main features as they would appear if you looked at them from above.	This setting determines whether students' personal locations will show up on this map. This setting determines if an address field will be shown for the extra locations. If the address field is not shown, then locations will only be able to be shown to the city level. Personal locations never have the address field for privacy reasons (Shalar et al., 2019).
Plot	Plot in LMS MOODLE is a strategy or a course of action, carefully planed step by step.	Plot summarising the effects of gamification on engagement and downstream behaviours (Klopfrer et al., 2009). To aid interpretability, the direction of the effects is presented such that positive effects support the hypothesized effect of gamification (i.e. positive effects suggest positive impact of gamification, while negative effects suggest detrimental impact).

In order to develop listening skills tutor of "Maritime English" e-course uses Book module which creates lists of web pages in a book-like format with audio and visual aids. Chapters and subchapters are possible in this module (Mnatsakanyan, 2012). To present new lexical units at the beginning of every lesson tutor creates minimum 7 pages of the Book according to new topic. Every page can contain written and audio formats of new lexical unit, its visual aid, definition, synonym/antonym, example of its use in context etc. (Patel & Sakadasariya, 2018).

Wide range of audio task types also trains students to be ready to pass external independent evaluation exam.

Listening tasks allow to teach students to listen carefully to the sounding speech, to form the ability to anticipate the semantic content of the text and, therefore, to foster a culture of communication in English. Educational value in the formation of skills to understand speech by ear, including that it has a beneficial effect on the development of students' memory, imagination, perception and thinking. During the period of distance learning, the authors also tried to diversify both the exercises and the approach to form the speaking competence of future seafarers.

With the help of activity "Assignment" in MOODLE teacher records audio questions with his/her own voice, and students, in turn, can get ready for passing the competence, and not only.

Many students became interested in this format of training in order to earn additional points. Students download live audio responses into the MOODLE, where, in turn, dialogue and feedback between teacher and student arise.

DISCUSSIONS

Thus, all the distance learning technologies enable students while pandemic COVID-19 to achieve the main goal of Maritime English study at Maritime Professional College of KSMA – to form professional communicative competence of future ship engineers (Polat, 2004). Thus, using video conferencing, students can work in groups (BigBlueButton module). After completing the group`s work, the teacher evaluates it. How is the work of the group evaluated? First, during the work of groups, the teacher monitors the group dynamics and individual activity of educational recipient, so at the end of the work they can already make a conclusion about the learning process (Pidkasisty et al., 1999; Rasheed Hasan, 2020). Second, the usual way to test student`s achievement is to take a sample survey of one of the them from the subgroup (Pope, 2003; Shepel, 2013). The teacher can then meet with the educational recipient in a chat and ask him a few questions, the answers to which require a good command of the material. The success of such group`s work directly depends on the teacher's ability to plan the work of groups and the ability of educational recipients to build their own learning activities, combining individual work with work in pairs and the group as a whole. The goals of such work should be clear and accessible to them. At the same time, educational recipient must understand that this is a joint activity, but each of them has a "special" share in this activity, retains its individuality (Sherman & Chernikova, 2013).

Gamification as the use of game elements and gaming technologies in an out-of-game context is widely heard nowadays. This is an attempt to move towards new tools that motivate and retain members and users. This is the desire to change and adapt to a new way of life, to compete successfully, to be worthy of attention. This is not about "must", but about "want" and "like". It is not about "correctness" but about motivation. Gamification in education focuses on using the basic desires of students in order to become more involved in the process and achieve strong performance and high results. Participants

Figure 1. An educational mini-video (instruction with gamification elements – plot and badges) for 2020 and 2021 years at Maritime Professional College of KSMA ship engineering department (1-year students).

prefer excitement, history, play, which means this is a natural way of acquiring skills. As a matter of interest, in a gamified system, the player reveals his true self, getting into stressful or curious situations. This can be a good recruiting method without relying on previous grades or diplomas. Gamification makes it easy to achieve many educational goals. But education itself is the simplification of difficult life situations. The competencies that participants learn during training are a value, a means of application owned by the participants themselves, and feedback in gamification can be an instant and important step.

Gamification, due to visualization, shows the capabilities, type of thinking, logical abilities of an individual student. Based on this, a professional teacher will be able to accurately determine the student's inclinations for certain activities, direct the further development of his skills in the right direction.

When a player logs into the system and does not know "what to do, how to do it and where", he begins to investigate. The process of passing should be intuitive; this is the best. But, so that at any moment you can be sure that you understand what is happening, you need an instruction, available from any stage, describing the passage in simple language. It can be a stream or an educational mini-video, because just reading the rules is boring for many. As an example rules can be created and placed in a file, including a video file, using the "Instruction" resource (Fig.1), or implemented with the "Forum" tool on LMS MOODLE.

Thus Figure 1 shows educational mini-video on "Sport" topic with some gamification elements of LMS MOODLE – plot and digital badges added by teacher into e-course.

One of the main elements of motivation in all games is the game "currency". For completed tasks, the user receives rewards for each action, for example, bonus points. It is necessary that the points are felt by the player, and he knows exactly what they are given for: speed, accuracy, the number of attempts used, etc. The scores are generated automatically on LMS MOODLE, converted into a gradebook, or the teacher puts scores manually within the course.

Figure 2. Badges for different levels (1-year students).

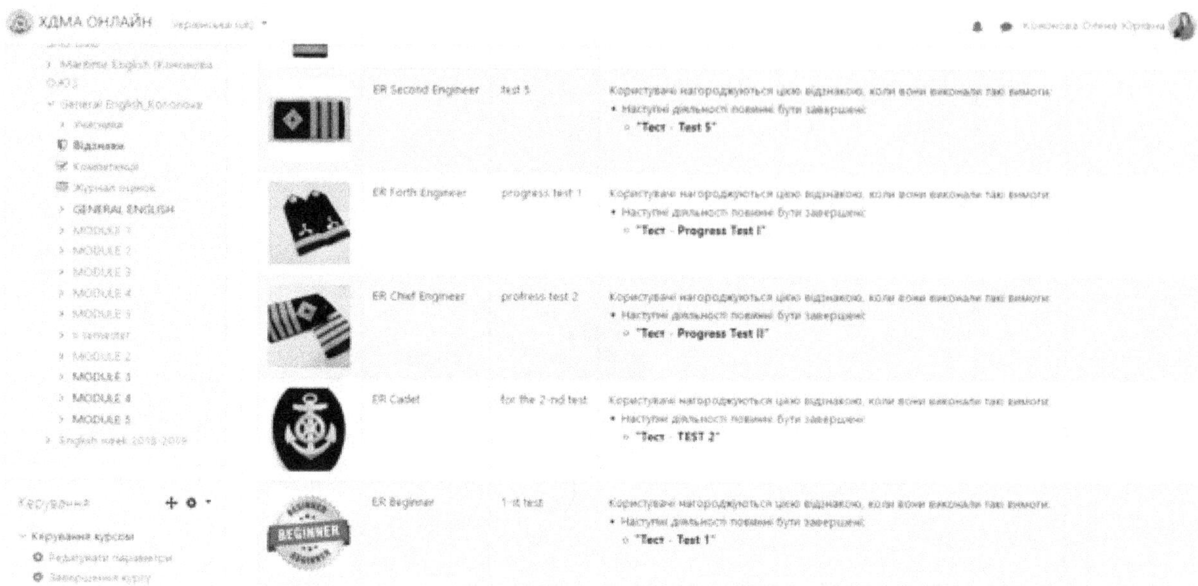

Badges, trophies or statuses that are assigned for a set of actions - mastering a topic, passing the final test, solving a problem on MOODLE are uploaded by the teacher independently. Getting the next thing from the collection yourself brings pleasure and makes you want to continue (Fig. 2). Figure 2 shows digital badges for 1st-year students added into e-course manually by the teacher. Completing tasks of different levels of complicity students receive epaulets of different maritime professional ranks – from engine cadet to the Chief engineer.

At the same time, the ability to compare your result with others is a working way to increase motivation. Competition is modeled during design work through the functionality of streaming and access restriction. You can use the function of the rating system inside assignments and courses (each student can only see his place in the rating).

Students enjoy communicating within a game or course and can help each other understand the material. This feature is very important for design assignments. It is possible to connect chats and forums to assignments and courses. There is a system of individual messages.

The time frame encourages the student to pack up, tune in, sit down and walk through. Plus, the share of excitement starts. In MOODLE one can set a time limit for each task. If you need to complete tasks on specific days or due dates, you can use the calendar. The calendar shows the points of the course, progress and achievements.

All elements of gamification are divided into mini-lessons or separate tasks within larger topics. This is necessary in order to maintain interest, to better assimilate what has been passed. In MOODLE the tools “access restriction” and “delimitation by streams” are used as a tiered passage. Access can be limited by timing or by results (according to the conditions of the assignment). “Delimitation” allows you to direct the passage in the correct sequence or divide information for different groups during the competition.

All these activities, that we use to create a remote communication channel, have elements of gamification and all these make a very positive effect on the studying process as better learning experience:

1. It is not boredom when you undergo while learning, but fun, and at the same time, you get skills.
2. The best learning environment. Gamification helps create a safe environment for skill development, where the cost of error is low. This leads to more active learning due to the lack of fear.
3. Instant feedback. You immediately understand what you are doing right, and where you need to tighten yourself.
4. Encouragement to change behavior. Points, badges and leaderboards make learning fun.
5. Can be used in any field. English, History, Math, programming, negotiation, interviewing - everything can be learned by playing.
6. By increasing the motivation of students, acquisition of skills and abilities can increase significantly.

Increased student engagement allows teacher to gradually increase the difficulty of tasks. This is comparable to a computer game, where the first levels are easy, and the difficulty increases with each subsequent one (Fig. 3). Figure 3 shows map example of e-course where all the modules studied by students are shown with competencies to be achieved, activities needed to be performed, total score and name of Student's book.

It is good that education is moving into online learning. And lest the lack of control diminish the motivation to learn, gamification supports continued interest in learning through the competitive principle.

The analyze of data of success comparing 2019 and 2020 years shows the following results: increase of success and knowledge quality (Smiderle et al., 2020, Symonenko et al., 2019).

The aim of online communication is the same as that of face-to-face communications: bonding; exchanging information; being heard and being understood. When teachers communicate with students, whether in a face-to-face class or an online class, they communicate for the purpose of offering knowledge or having information to gain understanding and develop relationships. This study aims to explore whether online learning has an effect on communication between instructors and students in a negative way, if online learning during Covid-19 pandemic affects students' productivity levels. As well as, to evaluate and suggest ways of improving effective communication between instructors and students in online courses. This study aims to answer the following research questions: (1) Does online learning have a negative impact on communication between instructors and students? (2) How communication between instructors and students in educational Institutions can be improved? (3) What are the problems that students face in online learning and does online learning have a negative effect on students' participation and their productivity level as a whole?

The MOODLE course also used a questionnaire compiled using a Google form, which was used by 60 cadets (male) aged 16-17 from Ukrainian maritime education institution (Maritime Professional College of KSMA - ship engineering department).

They all are using distance learning technologies with gamification elements while studying Maritime English. The goal of the survey was to check whether the communication channel between the student and the tutor is well established. The questions listed were the following: quality of the interaction, relevance of the material studied, reflective thinking, interactivity of e-course, tutor and peer support, interpretation.

The results of questionnaire prove that for those who do have access to the right technology, like LMS MOODLE learning online can be more effective and interesting (Fig. 4).

Our research shows that on average, students retain more material when learning online compared to face-to-face learning. This is mostly due to the students being able to learn faster online; e-learning requires less time to learn than in a traditional classroom setting because students can learn at their own

Figure 3. The beginning of e-course on LMS MOODLE with map and other gamification elements.

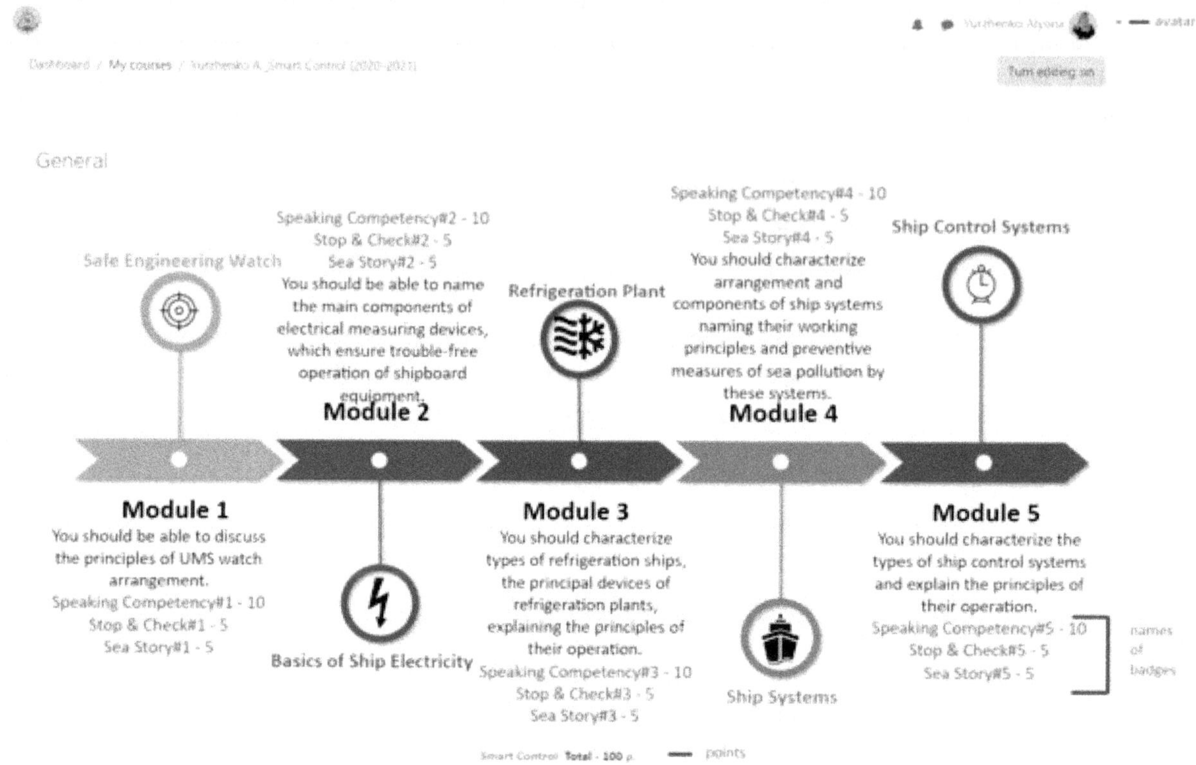

pace, going back and re-reading. Teachers should encourage students to speak and hold the right attitude towards their speaking errors. Besides, teachers play significant roles in helping learners create more opportunities for students to speak English and take a variety of oral practice activities. For students, they should cultivate interest and control their emotional conditions in spoken English learning.

You can see a graphical representation of the results in Figure 4, which shows that the majority of students are satisfied.

Figure 4. The results of Google questionnaire on the quality of interaction with tutor while distance learning of Maritime English.

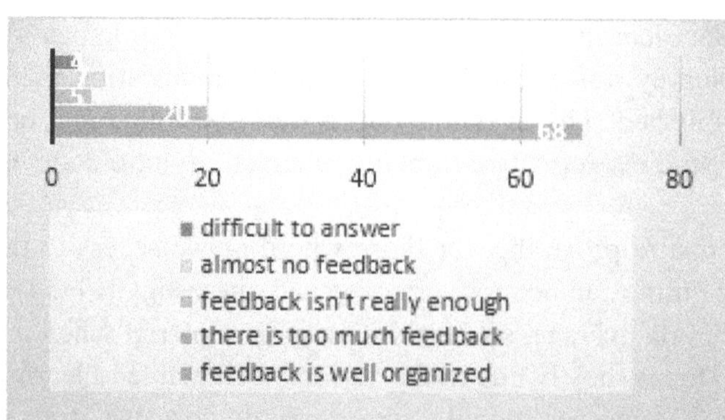

Figure 5. Comparison of statistics for 2020 and 2021 years at Maritime Professional College of KSMA ship engineering department (2-year students).

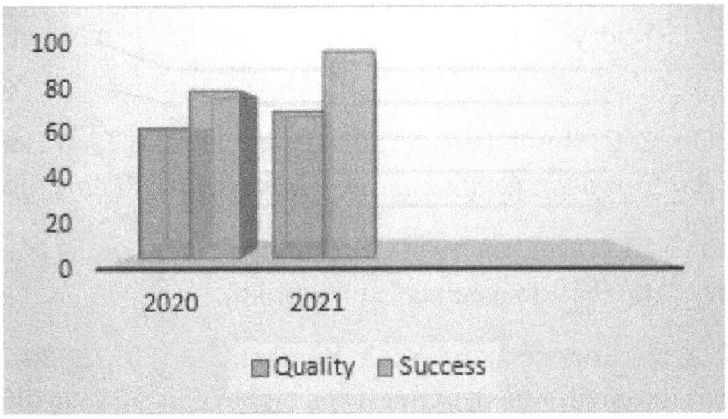

CONCLUSION

Due to the pandemic, the world now looks at distance technologies in a different way, they have become very necessary, and the English language is important for seafarers, because the great amount of technical failures is caused by the inadequate English language skills since and therefore special attention is paid to teaching it, especially during distance education.

The researchers see a solution to this problem in the use of such technology of distance education as LMS MOODLE with gamification elements.

Thus, the psychological potential of introducing gamification elements is used to increase the level of motivation and involvement of students, as well as their satisfaction with the learning process; in better assimilation and systematization of information; in reducing the fear of making mistakes. Due to the implementation of the basic didactic principles by means of gamification elements (instant (corrective) inverse) multimedia-dynamic form of material presentation, etc.) we can talk about the didactic potential of using gamification in teaching foreign languages. The methodological potential of the technology is revealed in the special organization of educational activities in foreign language classes (without changing the content), which allows you to move from passive to active methods, implement problem teaching methods, search activities and research projects, organize self-assessment and group assessment, develop critical thinking, reveal creativity, stimulate students' self-education. A topic for further research can be a comparative analysis of existing models for integrating gamification technologies into the educational process in order to select the most adequate models depending on the audience and course goals.

The perspectives of further research are found in the study of different distance learning trends (e.g. Flipped Classroom, Game-Based Learning, Collaborative Learning) and their implementation in the system of professional training of future maritime professionals to form their communicative competency.

REFERENCES

Amriani, A., Aji, A., Utomo, A. Y., Wahidah, F., & Junus, K. (2014). Gamified E-learning model based on community of inquiry. *2014 IEEE International Conference on Advanced Computer Science and Information Systems*, 474–480. 10.1109/ICACSIS.2014.7065830

Bing, W. (2017). The college English teaching reform based on MOOC (Vol. 10, No. 2). Canadian Center of Science and Education. doi:10.5539/elt.v10n2p19

Bobrysheva, N., Frolova, O., Kudryavtseva, V., & Moroz, O. (2021). *While Ashore: coursebook.* Helvetica PH.

I. Caponetto, J. Earp, M. Ott, & C. Busch (Eds.). (2014). Gamification and Education: a Literature Review. *Proceedings of the 8th European Conference on Games-Based Learning.*

Corbett, S. (2010, September 19). *Learning by playing: Video games in the classroom.* Retrieved from: https://www.nytimes.com/2010/09/19/magazine/19video-t.html

Diahyleva, O. S., Gritsuk, I. V., Kononova, O. Y., & Yurzhenko, A. Y. (2020). Computerized adaptive testing in educational electronic environment of maritime higher education institutions. *CEUR Workshop Proceedings, 2879,* 411-422.

Dichev, C., & Dicheva, D. (2017). Gamifying education: what is known, what is believed and what remains uncertain: a critical review. *International Journal of Educational Technology in Higher Education., 14*(1), 9. Advance online publication. doi:10.118641239-017-0042-5

Dyagileva, O., Goridko, N, Popova, H., Voloshynov, S., & Yurzhenko, A. (2020) *Zabezpechennya staloho rozvytku osvity maybutnikh fakhivtsiv mors'koho transportu za dopomohoyu merezhevoyi vzayemodiyi* [Ensuring sustainable development of education of future maritime transport professionals by means of network interaction]. E3S Web of Conferences.

Figueroa Flores, J. F. (2015). Using gamification to enhance second language learning. *Digital Education Review, 27.* Retrieved from https://revistes.ub.edu/index.php/der/article/download/11912/pdf http://education.mit.edu/papers/MovingLearningGamesForward_EdArcade.pdf /

Hanghøj, T. (2013). Game-based teaching: practices, roles, and pedagogies. In S. de Freitas, M. Ott, M. M. Popescu, & I. Stanescu (Eds.), *New Pedagogical Approaches in Game Enhanced Learning: Curriculum Integration* (pp. 81–101). IGI Global. doi:10.4018/978-1-4666-3950-8.ch005

Klopfer, E., Osterweil, S., & Salen, K. (2009). *Moving learning games forward.* Academic Press.

Koster. (2004). A theory of fun. Paraglyph Press.

Laster, J. (2010). *At Indiana U., A class on game design has students playing to win.* Retrieved from: http://chronicle.com/blogs/wiredcampus/at-indiana-u-a-class-on-game-design-has-students-playing-to-win/21981

Lazzaro, N. (2004). *Why we play games: Four keys to more emotion without story.* Retrieved from: http://www.xeodesign.com/xeodesign_whyweplaygames.pdf /

McGonigal, J. (2011). *Reality Is Broken: Why Games Make Us Better and How They Can Change the World.* Penguin Press.

Mnatsakanyan, O. L. (2012). Organizatsiya kollektivnoy deyatel'nosti shkol'nikov s ispol'zovaniyem servisov sotsial'nykh setey [Organization of collective activities of schoolchildren using social networking services]. *Computer Science Education.*

Patel, J. K., & Sakadasariya, A. (2018). Survey on virtual reality in social network. In *Proceedings of the 2nd International Conference on Inventive Systems and Control*. ICISC.

Pidkasisty, P. I., Friedman, L. M., & Garunov, M.G. (1999). Psikhologo-didakticheskiy spravochnik prepodavatelya vysshey shkoly [Psychological and didactic reference book of a teacher of higher education]. Moscow: Pedagogical Society of Russia.

Polat, E. S. (Ed.). (2004). Teoriya i praktika distantsionnogo obucheniya: Uchebnik. razresheniye [Theory and practice of distance learning: Textbook. allowance]. Center "Academy".

Pope, D. (2003). *Doing school: How we are creating a generation of stressed-out, materialistic, and miseducated students*. Yale University Press.

Popovych, I. S., Blynova, O. Y., Aleksieieva, M. I., Nosov, P. S., Zavatska, N. Y., & Smyrnova, O. O. (2019). Research of the relationship between the social expectations and professional training of lyceum students studying in the field of shipbuilding. *Espacios, 40*(33).

Rasheed Hasan, L. (2020). Is It Possible to Use Facebook instead of MOODLE Learning Management Systems (LMS) to Support the Learning Process? *ACM International Conference Proceeding Series*. 10.1145/3421682.3421695

Selevko, G. K. (2006). Entsiklopediya obrazovatel'nykh tekhnologiy [Encyclopedia of educational technologies] (Vol. 2). Research Institute of School Technologies.

Shalar, O., Huzar, V., Strykalenko, Y., Yuskiv, S., Homenko, V., & Novokshanova, A. (2019). Psycho-pedagogical aspects of interaction between personality traits and physical qualities of the young gymnasts of the variety and circus studio. *Journal of Physical Education and Sport, 19*(6), 2283–2288. doi:10.7752/jpes.2019.s6344

Shepel, E. V. (2013). *Razvitiye poznavatel'noy samostoyatel'nosti studentov-ekonomistov v strukture individual'noy trayektorii professional'noy podgotovki* [Development of the cognitive independence of economics students in the structure of the individual trajectory of vocational training]. Academic Press.

Sherman, M., Chernikova, V. (2013) *Inozemna kompetentnist' yak faktor rozvytku tvorchykh zdibnostey maybutnikh sudnovodiiv* [Foreign language competence as a factor in the development of creative abilities of future navigators]. Kherson State Technical University.

Smiderle, R., Rigo, S. J., Marques, L. B., Peçanha de Miranda Coelho, J. A., & Jaques, P. A. (2020). The impact of gamification on students' learning, engagement and behavior based on their personality traits. *Smart Learn. Environ., 7*(1), 3. doi:10.118640561-019-0098-x

Symonenko, S. V., Zaitseva, N. V., Osadchyi, V. V., Osadcha, K. P., & Shmeltser, E. O. (2019) *Virtual'na real'nist' u navchanni inozemnykh mov u vyshchykh navchal'nykh zakladakh* [Virtual reality in foreign language training at higher educational institutions]. *2nd International Workshop on Augmented Reality in Education.*

Toh, W., & Kirschner, D. (2020). Self-Directed Learning in Video Games, Affordances and Pedagogical Implications for Teaching and Learning. *Computers & Education, 154*, 103912. doi:10.1016/j.compedu.2020.103912

Vartanian, O., & Beatty, E. (2015). Cognitive brain training, video games, and creativity. *Video Games and Creativity, 2015*, 185–198. doi:10.1016/B978-0-12-801462-2.00009-6

Waytz, A., & Gray, K. (2018). Does Online Technology Make Us More or Less Sociable? A Preliminary Review and Call for Research. *Perspectives on Psychological Science, 13*(4), 473–491. doi:10.1177/1745691617746509 PMID:29758166

KEY TERMS AND DEFINITIONS

Augmented Reality: Is an enhanced version of the real physical world that is achieved through the use of digital visual elements, sound, etc. delivered via technology.

BigBlueButton: Is an open source web conferencing solution for e-learning that provides real-time sharing of audio, video, slides, whiteboard, chat and screen.

E-Teaching: Is training of students using various electronic media (e.g., LMS).

Electronic Educational Resources: Are educational resources, represented in digital form.

Gamification: Is the technology with the help of which game mechanics are added into nongame environment.

Gamification Elements: Are the components that make up gamification (badges, leaderboards, maps, avatars, etc.).

Maritime English: Is the English language used by seafarers both at sea and in port and by individuals working in the shipping and shipbuilding industry.

Chapter 13
Games and Gamification in Sustainability Learning:
A Peer-Based Approach for Thai Design Education

Treechada Chotiratanapinun
https://orcid.org/0000-0002-2581-4700
Silpakorn University, Thailand

Suphichaya Suppipat
https://orcid.org/0000-0003-3244-8806
National Taipei University of Technology, Taiwan

ABSTRACT

This chapter explores the intricate socio-political-cultural factors affecting Thai design students' learning and examines the potential of games and gamification in sustainability learning as an unconventional design pedagogical approach in Thai higher education. This chapter's heart is an extensive participatory action research case study from the sustainable design course of two universities in Bangkok. The project allows students to learn from game design to raise awareness of sustainability-related issues and use the games to enhance their sustainability learning through peer interactions. Games and gamification can assist Thai design students in obtaining skills essential to education for sustainable development while reducing power distance and uncertainty avoidance among classroom members. Research findings also reveal the complex relationships between game-based pedagogical practice and cultural characteristics, such as fun-pleasure orientation and interdependence orientation.

INTRODUCTION

The chapter articulates how gamification and socio–politico–cultural factors come into play in sustainable design education in the context of higher education in Thailand. Design education involves practice-based

DOI: 10.4018/978-1-6684-4287-6.ch013

teaching and learning (Tovey, 2015) and generally concerns instruction in design theory and application for products, services, and environments at school levels (Campbell, 2018). Thai design education refers to formal instruction in design, beginning at the higher education level and concentrating on skills-based training, to serve existing industries (Chotiratanapinun, 2018; Suwankarjank & Rugwongwan, 2021). The growing interest in sustainable development recently gained momentum and affected design businesses and curricula (Apisitniran & Theparat, 2018; Thailand Sustainability Expo, 2021). Sustainable development is "development that meets the needs of the present without compromising the ability of future generations to meet their own needs" (World Commission on Environment and Development, 1987). In response to challenges, the sustainable design approach emerged, requiring designers to consider environmental, social, and economic impacts throughout the life cycle of a designed product or service (Ceschin & Gaziulusoy, 2016; Piscicelli et al., 2015). Sustainable design education is essential to current design curricula and considered as a core issue in industrial and product design courses (Lilley & Lofthouse, 2009; Ramirez, 2007; Watkins et al., 2021).

The Sustainable Development Goals (SDGs) were formulated in 2015 by the United Nations General Assembly as a blueprint for achieving a bright and sustainable future for all by 2030 (United Nations Department of Global Communications, 2018). Education for sustainable development (ESD) is considered as a key enabler for the successful achievement of the SDGs (UNESCO, 2020). Specifically, ESD is a learning process for how to make decisions that consider the long-term future of community equity, economy, and ecology. In addition, ESD encourages educational institutions to stimulate learners to reflect on their lifestyle concerning sustainability issues (Laurie et al., 2016; Scott, 2002). The ESD movement in Thailand is in its initial phase, and design educators are the key change agents in integrating ESD into Thai design education (Chotiratanapinun, 2018; Pasupa, 2016). The number of studies on the use of games and gamification in sustainable development is increasing (Guillen et al., 2021). Nevertheless, studies rarely highlight the use of games and gamification in sustainable design education, especially in non-Western contexts.

The chapter provides a contextual background focusing on the factors that influence the learning of Thai design students and identifies the situation of sustainable design education. The chapter also describes the aspects of Thai design education that are resistant to change and subsequently the steps to tackle them. The game design assignments at Chulalongkorn University and Silpakorn University from 2017 to 2020 are brought into focus to justify the emergence of gamification in sustainable design pedagogy in Thailand. The project allowed students to develop their own games based on their sustainability interests. The case study shows that gamification can be taught implicitly to students, who in turn can apply it freely to their design process to develop their games. The findings are discussed in depth. Toward the end of the chapter, the authors urge design educators to assume the role of change agent while using gamification for ESD. Therefore, the chapter aims to contribute directly to the emerging debate on the use of gamification in sustainable design education.

BACKGROUND

This section examines the Thai education culture through two prominent theoretical frames and an analysis of the recent student-led, pro-democracy protest which gives a complete, up-to-date picture of the changes in students' value orientations. It lays out a foundation before moving onto the more context-specific discussion around the use of games and gamification for sustainable design education in Thailand.

Looking at Thailand through Hofstede's Cultural Dimensions Theory

Hofstede's (1997; 2011) cultural dimensions theory is an approach to classify a country's culture and the effects of culture on the values of its members and how these values relate to the behavior of the members. Hofstede identified six dimensions representing differences among national cultures including power distance, individualism/collectivism, masculinity/femininity, uncertainty avoidance, long-term orientation/short-term orientation, and indulgence versus restraint. The chapter is particularly interested in the outstanding levels of power distance, collectivism, and uncertainty avoidance of the Thais and how they impact Thai education.

First, Thai culture exhibits high power distance. As a hierarchical society, individuals' status is typically determined by their general appearance, age, education level, social status, financial status, or family name. Respect for seniority and recognition of who is superior, equal, or inferior to oneself are important. High power distance can affect the education system as a whole, especially teaching and learning patterns, teacher–student interactions, and student participation in classroom activities (Raktham, 2008). Second, as a collectivist society, loyalty to the in-group is paramount, and interaction with peers can be highly desirable in the learning process (Chotiratanapinun, 2018). Third, owing to their high uncertainty avoidance, Thais tend to feel threatened by ambiguous situations and favor strong social norms. Dislike for uncertain situations and tendency to avoid the unknown are major outcomes of the conventional education approach. Thai students are accustomed to teacher-centered pedagogy, revolving around the transmission of a teacher's ideas of right and wrong to students (Gunawan, 2016).

Komin's Nine Clusters of Thai Cultural Values and the Thai Education System

According to Komin's (1990) investigation of empirical studies on the Thai socio-cultural system, the most important cultural characteristics relate to nine value clusters. Table 1 explores the value clusters in connection with Thai education: ego orientation, grateful relationship orientation, smooth interpersonal relationship orientation, flexibility and adjustment orientation, religio-physical orientation, education and competence orientation, interdependence orientation, fun-pleasure orientation, and achievement-task orientation. Examples of practical keywords to put the values into use for pedagogical development are also given.

The foremost value clusters to be particularly examined include interdependence orientation and fun-pleasure orientation. The interdependence orientation, derived from Hofstede's collectivist dimension, sheds a positive light for a shift toward a more participatory style of education. This value cluster can lead to the success of the implementation of peer learning, teamwork, and collaborative design process (Chotiratanapinun, 2018). As the *sanuk* attitude can come into play as a feature of peer learning, the fun-pleasure orientation can be the major factor that drives the interactions among all classroom members. Given that Thais generally dislike discussing critical issues, one significant question arises. How can the attitude of *sanuk*——enjoying oneself and having a good time——that comes with gamification support design students to involve in a serious dialogue on sustainability? Additionally, other Thai cultural values and characteristics remain the stumbling blocks for change and often limit learners from taking on challenging tasks (Gunawan, 2016). The authors decided to conduct the game design project as classroom research to reduce bias from being interdependence-oriented and avoid adopting foreign concepts without careful consideration and adaptation.

Table 1. How Komin's nine clusters of Thai cultural values influence Thai education

Value cluster (Komin, 1990)	**How each value cluster affects the Thai educational system** (Chotiratanapinun, 2018; Lao, 2015; Laopongharn & Sercombe, 2009; Mounier & Tangchuang, 2010)	**Examples of practical keywords for pedagogical development** (Chotiratanapinun, 2018; Shawyun, 2005)
Ego orientation (This cluster leads to characteristics such as face-saving and criticism avoidance.)	Ego orientation underpins the teacher-centered approach and passive learning among students.	Self-advancement
Grateful relationship orientation (This cluster is rooted in the concept of indebted goodness——a psychological bond between one who renders another the needed favors.)	Students are expected to be grateful for their teachers. Sharing ideas or asking questions in the classroom can be interpreted as an act of questioning the teacher's knowledge.	Reciprocal, mutual respect, and relationship building
Smooth interpersonal relationship orientation (This cluster focuses on pleasant interactions and maintenance of surface harmony.)	Students often avoid conflicts of ideas with the teacher.	Suppression of patronage system
Flexibility and adjustment orientation (This cluster correlates with the laxness in principle as Thais are situation-oriented rather than system-oriented.)	Students tend to cut corners or take the easy way out when overwhelmed by challenges.	Being flexible over fixed rules
Religio-physical orientation (This cluster reflects the engagement in spiritual ceremonies of conservative Thais. Although the Buddhist concept of karma principally conveys the law of cause and effect, Thais tend to only think of it as bad karma.)	Believing in bad karma associate with learned helplessness——a condition in which a person feels unable to change their circumstances and characteristics of passive learning.	Considering interconnectedness as a spiritual value
Education and competence orientation (This cluster presents that Thais consider education a means of climbing up the social ladder of having a higher prestige rather than an end value in itself.)	This perception can lead to ethical issues in education such as cheating and plagiarism.	Placing content over forms
Interdependence orientation (This cluster expresses the values of mutual help and the spirit of community collaboration. Thais tend to pick things up easily and superficially from other cultures.)	Thai higher education has adopted multiple Western policies and practices at the surface level without careful consideration and reference to its own context.	Peer learning, team-working, conducting a curriculum intervention to trial new ideas from other cultures
Fun-pleasure orientation (This cluster, characterized by the attitude of *sanuk*——to enjoy oneself and have a good time, is a means to support and maintain the interpersonal value system of the Thai people.)	Thai students tend to avoid engaging in classroom discussions that address critical topics because they are not enjoyable.	Easy going or fun-seeking activities
Achievement-task orientation (This cluster concerns the achievement motivation need. Thais hold low achievement value and consider ambition and hard work as less important than social relationships.)	This value is in direct conflict with the student-centered learning approach.	Incorporating social relationships into learning

Sources: (Chotiratanapinun, 2018; Komin, 1990; Lao, 2015; Laopongharn & Sercombe, 2009; Mounier & Tangchuang, 2010; Shawyun, 2005)

Changes in Students' Attitudes and Lertchoosakul's Analysis of the White Ribbon Movement

A thorough analysis of Thai cultural characteristics of university students was conducted two decades ago, and the findings reflect high values of humbleness, gratefulness to parents and teachers, and loyalty to the monarchy (Ngammuk, 2001). Globalization has become a key external force pushing on the localities and resulting in a diminishing of the sense of nationality and culture. In 2014, the junta government attempted to ascertain that children are socialized to be highly nationalist through the Twelve Thai national core values communication campaign embedded in the school curricula (Draper et al., 2019; Ngammuk, 2016). Liberals had criticized the campaign as a tool of the military to indoctrinate people or "an attempt to drag Thai society into the deep past" (Chaitrong, 2020). Explicitly, the aim of the campaign is chiefly for national securities, especially fostering unity among the Thais rather than for the sake of education development (Nawawi, 2016; Silraungwilai, 2016). In 2016, the junta set out Thailand 4.0, a new economic policy aiming to elevate Thailand to the status of a high-income nation, reduce inequality, and promote environmentally sustainable growth and development (The Economist Intelligence Unit, 2017). Scholars have discussed the challenges to the policy in which learners must be at the center of the educational ecosystem (Wittayasin & Wittayasin, 2017). Buasuwan (2018) suggested that Thai education requires socio-cultural-institutional transformation.

In 2020, Thailand saw an unprecedented, pro-democracy, anti-government movement, which the key protest leaders are university students. Demonstrations erupted in universities, colleges, and high schools across the country. Different groups used social media to coordinate rallies nationwide. Along with raising a three-finger salute which originated in the movie titled The Hunger Games, but now adopted by the Thai protest movement, school students wore white ribbons to stand in solidarity with the protestors (Ratcliffe, 2020; Wongcha-um, 2020). White ribbon becomes a symbol of the broader youth-led protest movement. Lertchoosakul's (2021) analysis of the movement is a recent study on Thai students' view toward the nation's educational system in relation to the political landscape. The findings indicate that the motivations behind the involvement of students in the anti-government protests countrywide include grievances against repressive, authoritative, and unaccountable conservative educational systems as well as the long-established political institutions.

Lertchoosakul categorizes Thai citizens into three different generations in society: the Cold War generation, the In-between generation, and the White Ribbon generation (Voice Online Editorial Division, 2021). The Cold War generation refers to the Baby Boomers. The In-betweens, the children of the Cold War generation and parents to the White Ribbon generation, stand in the middle of the power conflict crisis. Meanwhile, the Cold War generation holds the highest power in society, the White Ribbons, including school students, university students, and young professionals, have insufficient power to contribute to change. Lertchoosakul describes this younger generation in four features. First, as they have grown up in a fast-paced world, they believe that change is inevitable. Second, they question the hierarchical structure of the society. Being young and powerless, they think that the notion of hierarchy is problematic. Third, they regard democracy as the only means for change and hold the nation accountable, and they want to be part of the change. Fourth, they reject misuse of power in problem solving. They have learned from real-life experience that authoritarian power fails to provide sustainable solutions. They also feel that they have been abused by the authoritative educational system. Lertchoosakul urges the In-betweens to empathize with the White Ribbons, come forward, and help effect positive change. In other words, the answer to change lies in the middle generation.

From the students' stance, the Thai educational system fails to provide a foundation for students to tackle present-day challenges in a fast-changing world. "A top–down and unresponsive administrative structure, outdated curricula, and authoritarian teaching methods based on rote memorization and a focus on forcing students to conform to strict rules and hierarchical structures have remained unchanged for a century" (Lertchoosakul, 2021, p. 212). Changing values and attitudes in Thai students seems to signal a need for emancipatory education (Freire, 1970)——a pedagogical process that goes beyond the transmission of knowledge but questions the given structure of socio-politico-cultural relations and explores alternative perspectives. Tackling the power structure in the conservative Thai educational system as a whole is truly challenging. Instead of a quick fix, it is more likely to see a long-term societal adjustment. The chapter later explores how sustainable design education can prepare in responding to the phenomenon, through the synergy between educators, who are the In-betweens, and students who are the White Ribbon generation.

CURRENT SITUATION OF SUSTAINABLE DESIGN EDUCATION IN THAILAND

As sustainability confronts the capitalistic nature of production and consumption, design education must adapt and transform accordingly and be reactive to global challenges (Meyer & Norman, 2020; Watkins et al., 2021). Design educators hold the promise of a sustainable future in the hearts, hands, and minds of the students they instruct (Chotiratanapinun, 2018; Fleming, 2013). This phenomenon will inevitably affect the content and learning approach employed in all design schools.

The author's previous research (Chotiratanapinun, 2018) reveals that there are three characteristics of Thai design education that are resistance to change. The first is the steep hierarchical structure in teaching and learning. The master–apprentice model remains the dominant pedagogical practice. The second is the imbalance among the affective, psychomotor, and cognitive domains of learning in the curriculum. Most design educators hold a conservative view of design, deeply rooted in the making tradition and focusing heavily on hand skills. The third is the rigid, single disciplinary perspective. The lack of an interdisciplinary stance in the curriculum is the consequence of the object-oriented tradition of design. As a result, educators perceive sustainability as a trend and often treat it as an add-on in the curriculum.

To achieve the SDGs, ESD must be an integral part of design education. Skills essential to ESD include envisioning, critical thinking and reflection, systemic thinking, building partnerships, and participation in decision making (Tilbury & Wortman, 2004). The author's previous study (Chotiratanapinun, 2018) proposes the three pedagogical steps to Thai design educators to facilitate the integration of ESD into the curriculum: taking the teacher-as-facilitator role, putting less emphasis on the making and more on the thinking and the caring, and introducing interdisciplinary perspectives to design learning. The shift from the object-oriented view to the system-oriented one provides a systemic framework for solving complex problems. By doing so, students are able to think critically and realize that sustainability is highly relevant to their lives.

Given that universities have a critical role in helping the world achieve SDGs, an increasing number of Thai universities declare that they have adopted the framework. And many have gone as far as holding places in the Times Higher Education Impact Rankings 2021 (Raksaseri, 2020). The rankings are the global performance tables assessing universities against SDGs concerning four broad areas: research, stewardship, outreach, and teaching (Times Higher Education, 2021). However, university executives tend to focus on the top–down approach in management, using an autocratic style of decision making rather than constant learning with and empowering staff and students, to drive organizational change (Chotiratanapinun, 2018). Design educators and students need to be valued and empowered to contribute to the paradigm shift toward sustainability and play an active part in co-creating change.

Further, the fun-pleasure orientation value can be employed to unlock the potential for positive change in sustainability learning among design students, and sustainable design educators need to explore ways to integrate the attitude of *sanuk* with the three steps to tackle resistance to change. As sustainability is perceived as a challenging subject, students prefer the learning sessions to be less academic and more entertaining. Sakunprasert (2018) regards game and gamification as the concepts that "match Thai culture, which is a fun culture. Thai people love activities that they can share and enjoy with their friends." (p. 26). The chapter will explore further how the *sanuk* attitude fits in with the use of games and gamification in Thailand's sustainable design education.

EMERGENCE OF GAMIFICATION AND GAME-BASED LEARNING IN DESIGN EDUCATION AND SUSTAINABLE DESIGN PEDAGOGY

Gamification, which is defined as the use of game design elements in non-game contexts (Deterding et al., 2011), can be implemented under various serious circumstances to promote learning, solve problems, and provide gameful experiences. In the field of design, gamification is used in industries to support design thinking, solution co-creation, idea generation for new product concept development, entry into new markets, and customer engagement (Harwood & Garry, 2015; Patrício et al., 2018, 2021). Gamification is also used in design education (Leonard & Oberprieler, 2018). The gamification of education through the incorporation of game design elements into educational settings is considered as a developing approach for increasing learners' motivation and engagement (Dichev & Dicheva, 2017). Gamification is beneficial to ESD, as it is widely adopted to promote behavioral changes in engagement in pro-environmental behaviors (Du et al., 2020; Morganti et al., 2017; Ouariachi et al., 2020; Ro et al., 2017). By harnessing individuals' abilities and interests, gamification can further advance sustainability communication (Rajanen & Rajanen, 2019).

Game-based learning, that is, the use of games in the process of teaching and learning (Foster et al., 2015), can be a crucial aspect of ESD (Janakiraman et al., 2018). Games provide a learning environment that engages and gives learners a chance to understand the world around them and develop their capabilities (Wortley, 2016). Particularly, board games can be powerful learning tools in ESD (Douglas & Brauer, 2021) and highly effective in illustrating and visualizing the connections between a player's actions and their impact (Fjællingsdal & Klöckner, 2020). Educators at the Autonomous University of the State of Mexico used board games in sustainable design courses (Uribe et al., 2014). Game-based learning proved to be an effective tool for deepening design students' understanding of certain sustainability topics through play, experimentation, interaction, and repetition (Uribe et al., 2017). In Thailand, game design is used as a curriculum intervention to support student-centered, problem-based learning pedagogy (Suppipat et al., 2021).

Game design and gamification strategies have played a significant role in echoing Thai design students' sustainability interests. Themes around social sustainability explored by students largely include social equity and people with disabilities. For example, Chinwattanawongwan, a Product Design bachelor's graduate from Silpakorn University designed a board game to instruct visually impaired children and their peers about the blind guidance blocks, focusing on how to plan walking routes effectively (Dec Graduate Exhibition, 2019). The game also aims to enhance interaction and communication between both the able and visually impaired players. Game themes concerning environmental sustainability are mostly associated with climate change and waste management. For instance, Manoopun's (2020) postgraduate thesis at Thammasat University proposed that gamification can be used as a strategy in Design Management for changing concert attendees' behavior to reduce single-use plastics at electronic dance music festivals.

GAME DESIGN ASSIGNMENTS AT CHULALONGKORN UNIVERSITY AND SILPAKORN UNIVERSITY FROM 2017 TO 2020

At Chulalongkorn University and Silpakorn University, gamification is used in the educational context through the application of some game elements like social interaction, challenge, and goals. Game design is considered a vital tool for strengthening shared values in sustainability. So, the game design project entails two fundamental aspects. One is the opportunity to deepen students' understanding of a subject matter. Another is the ability to empower students to take control of their own learning.

Rationale of the Assignment

The game design project aims to encourage students to realize the critical role of designers related to ecological impacts and social problems. Engagement is an overriding reason for introducing gamification to the classroom. The problem-based learning (PBL) process, which revolves around students learning from the challenge of their interest and choice, is key to this 4-week assignment. The project requires students to work in groups in designing a physical game to raise environmental awareness and developing games for themselves as a specific audience of sustainability learning. By designing and playing games in the classroom, all students and instructors were engaged in a collaborative learning experience. Group tutorials were given throughout the design and development process. In the last session of the project, final prototypes were played and evaluated by all students and instructors. Despite the different contexts, the approach is comparable to the game design project of an introductory ecology course at Cornell University implemented in 2020, in which students were required to develop a novel game based on the ecological topics discussed in class (Heim & Holt, 2021).

METHODOLOGY

The study employs participatory action research (PAR). Its focus lies in enabling everyone's full participation in the research process (Shura et al., 2011). PAR has been increasingly used in educational research to achieve better levels of communication, collaboration, and trust among stakeholders (Lennie & Tacchi, 2013). PAR is particularly suitable for bringing change in the quality of education through its multiple iterative cycles of planning, action, observation, and reflection (Rajbanshi & Chandra Luitel, 2020). The authors' classroom research was conducted extensively in the Sustainable Design course at Chulalongkorn University from 2017 to 2019 and Silpakorn University in 2020. Thus, the study was carried out in four PAR cycles with four different groups of undergraduate Industrial Design and Product Design students. Mixed methods were used, and various types of research data provided depth and richness to understand the entire picture of the circumstance. Since most data are qualitative, the authors predominantly employed thematic analysis——a systematic approach that involves identifying themes of meaning, coding textual data according to themes, and interpreting the results by identifying the overarching patterns of students' experiences.

KEY FINDINGS FROM THE GAME DESIGN OUTPUTS

Table 2 presents the details of the final prototypes of the game design project at Chulalongkorn University and Silpakorn University from 2017–2020. Through the analysis of the game design outputs, along with data from classroom observations, and unstructured interviews during group tutorials, four aspects are explored: a) game content, b) physical game types, c) game mechanics, and d) how to win the games. Figures 1 to 11 are the images of the game design outputs.

Game Content

The students' assignments contain three main themes, including solid waste problems, climate change and carbon footprint issues, and eco-material selection. Solid waste management was the top concern. The students explored waste issues in various directions such as waste separation methods at a household level, waste generation and waste sorting in daily life, waste management at different scales, marine plastic waste problems, recycling of plastic waste, and upcycling of various waste materials. Several teams dealt with context-specific content. For example, one team [Waste Survival/ 2018C] was interested in scavengers, who are stakeholders in the informal sector and play a major role in the waste management process in Thailand. The issues regarding climate change and carbon footprint were presented from a global perspective. For instance, the team interested in carbon credit and carbon trading transformed came up with a strategic planning card game [INTEGRO/ 2017B]. Each player is required to act as a world leader, dealing with the annual carbon emission while attempting to achieve economic growth and mitigate the nation's environmental impact. Concerning eco-materials, the students integrated life-cycle thinking into the game storylines [Susseat/ 2018B and CO-BLOC/ 2020B]. Their games aim to provide material selection guidelines for reducing the negative environmental impact at the early stage of a design process.

Physical Game Types

The selection of physical game type was based on the nature of the data that the students would like to deliver and narrate. The most popular game type is card game. Students translated and visualized their data into text and images on the cards, which can be categorized as information cards, Q&A cards, consequence cards, and event cards. For board games, storytelling plays a central role. Students used graphics and various types of foldable paper boards to illustrate the background and storyline, along with game pieces such as equipment for each player to manage cards in their hands, special tokens, and coins. For tile-based games, the tile technique can leverage the complexity of the game and help increase the physical actions of the players such as flipping, moving, and rearranging game pieces.

Game Mechanics

Most teams chose to combine strategic planning and role-playing to portray the storyline in connection with the skill set applicable to real-world situations. For instance, the game addressing the impacts of global warming, especially severe natural disasters likely to take place on all seven continents, requires each player to take the role of nature photographer traveling for wildlife photography [7Disasters/ 2018A]. Players must work cooperatively and take preventive actions to handle the climate change consequences.

Table 2. Game design assignments at Chulalongkorn University and Silpakorn University from 2017–2020

Year created (Game code)	Game title	Theme	Area of interest	Physical game type	Game mechanics	How to win the game
2017A	Drop N Go	Solid waste problems	Daily waste separation and segregation	Board game	- Dice rolling - Knowledge challenging (Q&A) - Role-playing (Elementary school students)	- Competition. - To accomplish a mission.
2017B	INTEGRO	Climate change and carbon footprint	Greenhouse gas emission, carbon credit, and carbon trading	Card game	- Bidding - Strategic planning - Role-playing (World leaders)	- Competition. - 4 rounds of play. - Time consuming. - Count points to find a winner.
2017C	Save the polar bear!	Climate change and carbon footprint	Climate change, polar ice cap melting, and endangered polar bears	Tile-based game	- Dice rolling - Knowledge challenging (Q&A)	- Competition. - To accomplish a mission.
2018A	7Disasters	Climate change and carbon footprint	Climate change and natural disasters	Board game	- Dice rolling - Strategic planning - Role-playing (Nature and wildlife photographers)	- Collaboration. - To accomplish a mission. - 7 rounds of play. - Time consuming.
2018B	Susseat	Eco-material selection	Life cycle analysis of furniture and eco-indicators of materials	Tile-based game	- Dice rolling- Role-playing (Furniture designers)	- Competition. - To accomplish a mission. - Count points to find a winner.
2018C	Waste Survival	Solid waste problems	Municipal waste separation and waste sorting by an informal sector	Card game	- Knowledge challenging (Q&A) - Strategic planning - Role-playing (Waste pickers)	- Competition. - 15 rounds of play. - Count points to find a winner. - Time consuming.
2019A	Circular Factory	Solid waste problems	Circular economy, plastic waste problems, and plastic recycling	Board game	- Strategic planning - Role-playing (Plastic manufacturers and business owners)	- Competition. - To accomplish a mission. - Count points to find a winner. - Time consuming.
2019B	Magic Village	Solid waste problems	Household waste separation	Card game	- Knowledge challenging (Q&A)	- Competition. - Quick game, getting rid of cards.
2019C	Trash Eater	Solid waste problems	Marine plastic waste, micro plastics, nano plastics, and life below water	Board game	- Fly rodding (To clean up ocean trash) - Strategic planning - Role-playing (Environmental activists and marine conservationists)	- Competition. - To accomplish a mission. - 15 rounds of play. - Requiring speedy actions and decisions. - Count points to find a winner.
2020A	The Campus Waste Challenge	Solid waste problems	Municipal waste separation and waste sorting at a university campus scale	Card game	- Dice rolling - Role-playing (Students and staff in a university)	- Competition. - To accomplish a mission.
2020B	CO-BLOC	Eco-material selection	Green architecture, life cycle analysis of building materials, and natural resource management	Board game	- Strategic planning - Role-playing (University students)	- Competition. - To accomplish a mission.

Figure 1. Drop N Go [2017A]

Figure 2. INTEGRO [2017B]

Figure 3. Save the polar bear! [2017C]

Another example is the game that introduces players to the concept of circular economy [Circular Factory/ 2019A]. Each player is required to act as a plastic manufacturer or a business owner, make use of plastic waste by recycling and remanufacturing for new products, and then sell the recycled items back to customers. Other less popular game mechanics are unique in their ways. Q&A cards are used as an environmental trivia quiz to challenge players' sustainability knowledge. Dice rolling and other game pieces involving physical actions such as bidding, fly rodding, and wheel rotating are used to escalate the levels of fun and excitement.

How to Win the Games

For most games designed by students, players must compete against each other to win. Competition is based on the accumulation of points, the ability to exchange points for prizes, or the minimum time spent on completing the task. Competition motivates individual players, leading to higher engagement levels. Only one team created a game to stimulate collaboration, using the "everyone wins, or no one does" concept. All players are required to accomplish a mission by the synergy among themselves. This concept implies that environmental preservation is everyone's responsibility.

A limit of rounds is a distinguishing factor adding to the mechanics of winning the game in relation to the game storyline. The carbon credit trading game [INTEGRO/ 2017B] is designed to be played in

Figure 4. 7Disasters [2018A]

four rounds following four quarters of one fiscal year. The player with the highest score at the end of the fourth round wins the game. The game about natural disasters [7Disasters/ 2018A] consists of seven rounds referenced from the seven continents of the world. The game portraying the role of a waste picker [Waste Survival/ 2018C] recaps the amount of money each player earned after fifteen rounds. It is based on the life of a scavenger who sells recyclable waste every fifteen days to make a living. The number of rounds also determines the play duration. A long play may not be able to attract the players to stay focused unless it can offer a high level of joy.

KEY RESULTS FROM THE STUDENTS' POST-SUBMISSION REFLECTIVE NOTES

At the end of each game testing session, all participants were requested to complete an online evaluation questionnaire and write their reflections about the games on the condition of anonymity. Through thematic analysis, the following insights were derived from four aspects of the game design project: game content, game system, design elements in the game, and game engagement. This section clarifies these aspects in relation to students' learning experiences.

Figure 5. Susseat [2018B]

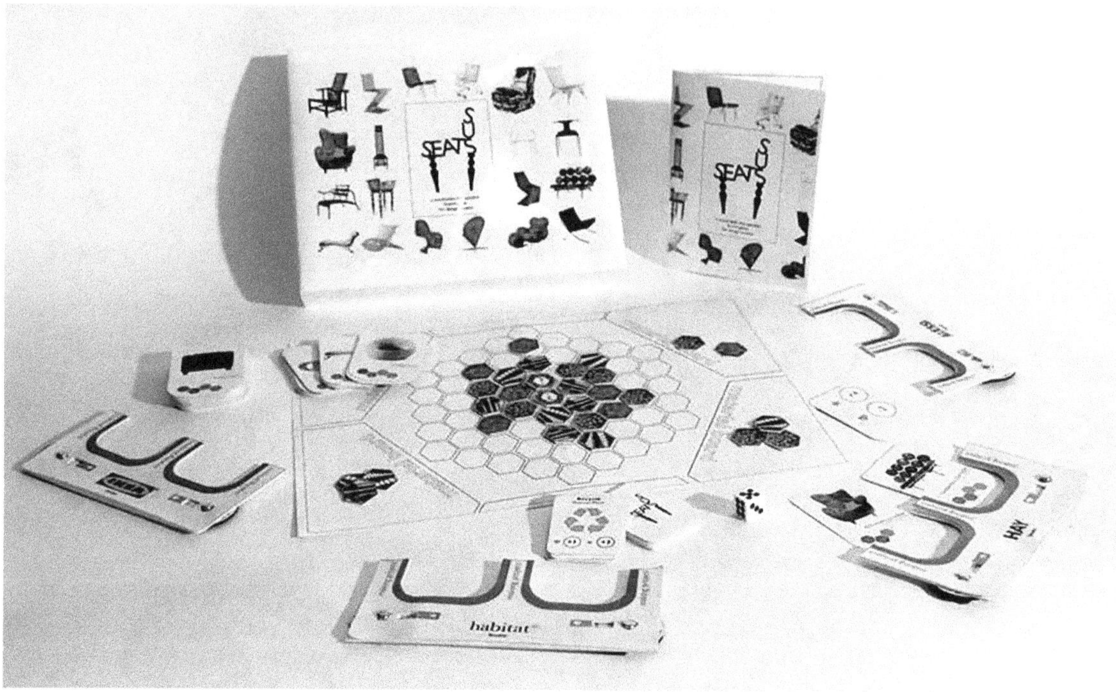

Figure 6. Waste Survival [2018C]

Figure 7. Circular Factory [2019A]

Link between Game Content and Students' Area of Interest

The students asserted that powerful game content should be relevant to current issues or existing problems and provide fundamental information to assist players in adopting behavioral change toward sustainability in their real lives. Accordingly, students proposed the topics and themes of their games from their personal experiences, individual unsolved problems, and information gained from the media. More than half of the students initiated their first ideas from waste problems that they had encountered themselves, such as solid waste separation, municipal waste management, single-use plastic waste, and marine plastic waste. They continued to observe particular issues such as the amount and types of waste generated among elementary school students in a day and the differentiation of the colors of the local trash bins and the designated types of waste; problems regarding waste sorting in a university campus; and a day in a life of a scavenger who picks, sorts, and sells recyclable waste to earn a living. High interest in waste management issues among students reflects an urgent need for information and a skill set relevant to problem-solving.

Storytelling is key to engagement. Role-playing assists in the understanding of the players' positions in the game. The students used viral images from the media in the visual presentation of the game content. Striking pictures include polar bears starving in the Arctic [Save the polar bear!/ 2017C], the deadliest natural disasters and extreme weather conditions from around the globe [7Disasters/ 2018A], the microplastics found in the ocean, a sea turtle with a plastic straw stuck in its nose, and a pilot whale found dead with hundreds of plastic bags in its stomach in Thailand [Trash Eater/ 2019C]. Role-playing can motivate and engage students to act and play their part as someone else with a sense of involvement in environmental protection.

Figure 8. Magic Village [2019B]

From Systems thinking to Game System Design

Instructors and game creators need to determine the optimization of the game system for sustainable design education. The simplicity of games can facilitate the students to comprehend the overall game system easily and quickly. The complexity of games can contribute to challenges and interests. Time is also a pivotal factor. Design for a specific time duration can affect the dynamic of the game and the level of physical and emotional engagements between players and game elements. Players can concentrate on a game for a certain period, ideally 30–60 minutes. The clarity of instructions and the game rules can facilitate the game flow and define the role of game players. To work out the game flow, indicating clear instructions and preparing adequate time for prototype testing are profoundly important. Students found that creating a game system involves the interconnection between various game elements and different stages of the development process. In this way, the project enhanced systems thinking skills in students.

Students demonstrated their ability to think in systems by applying various game mechanics and playing techniques. Supporting systemic interactions between the player and the game, many teams chose to visualize a large amount of data about environmental issues onto Q&A, consequence, and event cards. All teams working on strategic planning games selected role-playing as an integral part of their game mechanics, highlighting the cause-effect relations between human behavior and their impacts on the environment. Students inspired by the plastic waste problem did not limit themselves only to waste separation but extended to incorporate the concept of circular economy as the highlight of their game

Figure 9. Trash Eater [2019C]

[Circular Factory/ 2019A]. The team tackling the consequences of global warming specifically represented the idea that no one on earth is safe from the accelerating effects of climate change [7Disasters/ 2018A]. Their game poses a question about how we make decisions as today's practices may become tomorrow's problems. However, the evaluation questionnaire findings report that the level of complexity in a strategic planning game may reduce the level of satisfaction and willingness to learn among design students. Only a certain level of complexity can challenge and encourage them to learn more.

Design Elements in a Game as Reflection of the Design Competencies of Learners

Working on the elements in a game can enhance the design competencies of learners in many ways. Design elements are created according to the designated game type to communicate the game content, support the game mechanics, and assist in the game flow. They represent the aesthetics, ergonomics, and usability of the game and direct game attraction. Each team's aesthetic preference in styling is what makes their game stand out. For example, one group chose to deal with the familiarity of styles of contemporary furniture [Susseat/ 2018B]. Using furniture design exemplars produced by celebrated designers, the game

Figure 10. The Campus Waste Challenge [2020A]

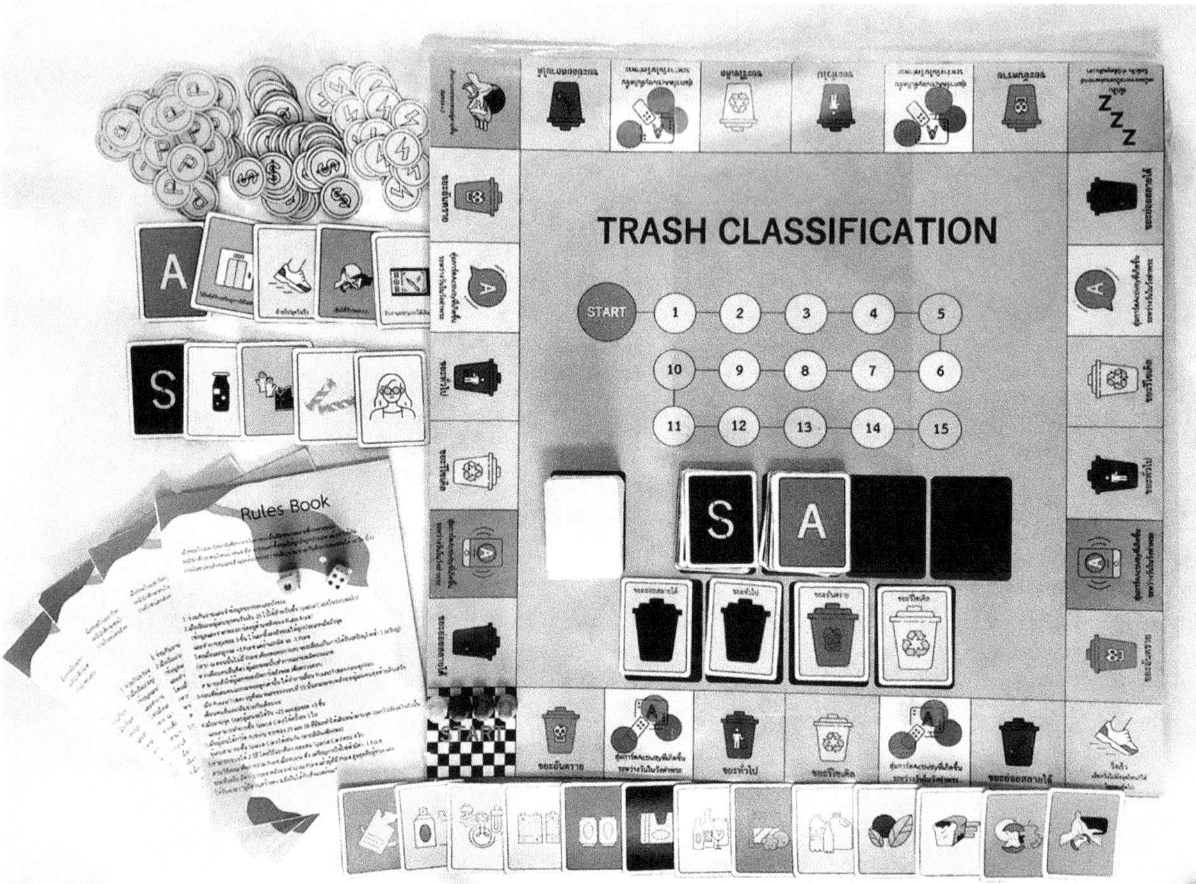

opens up the discussion on features such as form, function, color combination, material selection, and production technique, in relation to the environmental impact throughout the entire product life cycle. Students even carefully developed appropriate art direction to support storytelling and the role-playing nature of their games. Two teams attempted to communicate serious waste problems in a light-hearted manner through a fantasy representation of garbage [Magic Village/ 2019B] and a watercolor-painted illustration of sea creatures [Trash Eater/ 2019C].

The notion of usability aids in communication and delivering a more promising gameplay experience. The students dealt with visualization of semantic data, development of symbols and metaphors, and readability of the texts used. For instance, multiple groups [Drop N Go/ 2017A, INTEGRO/ 2017B, 7Disasters/ 2018A, and Waste Survival/ 2018C] decided to differentiate functions of the cards by color-coding, applying dissimilar colors on the backsides to communicate various issues on waste separation and climate change mitigation. The usability of the game pieces directly affects the physical movement of the players. The students considered the ergonomic quality of the game pieces, especially the visibility and sizing of the tokens. The game in reference to an environmental activist and a marine conservationist [Trash Eater/ 2019C] comes with properly sized fishing rod tools for players to collect trash in the ocean conveniently.

Figure 11. CO-BLOC [2020B]

Lastly, the design outputs speak for the students' prototype-making ability. Throughout the game design and development process, students experienced hands-on learning with a problem-solving mindset. By testing their prototype, each team can establish a trial of their game system and flow, while simultaneously spotting the weaknesses of game elements and interface design.

Game Engagement in Support of Peer Learning

Game engagement is considered an approach to interactions between players and game elements. The verbal interactions among players enhance the negotiation and communication skills of the students. The process of game testing and playing facilitates the dialogue among classmates as well as the dialogue between the students and the instructors. Physical actions and emotional expressions can break the ice, improve the learning-teaching environment, and bring students and instructors closer to one another. The physical reactions include snatching, rotating, and moving tokens, flipping cards, bidding, teasing other players, and challenging each other by asking questions. The games involving physical actions can assist in developing sustainability-related skills. For example, the actions of mixing and matching colors and objects are used for a game about waste sorting and waste separation techniques, cultivating and understanding of waste management in everyday life. However, excessive actions required in a game can confuse players and divert the main objective and the message of the game that the creator intends to deliver. In a nutshell, to support the students' satisfaction, interactions with other players, physical actions, and emotional expressions during playing games are necessary for a higher level of game engagement.

KEY INSIGHTS FROM POST-PROJECT FOCUS GROUP DISCUSSION

Using game elements in the classroom can have a lasting impact on the students' lifelong development, but insufficient high-quality evidence cannot support the long-term benefits of gamification in an educational context (Dichev & Dicheva, 2017). Hence, the focus group discussion with seven students from Silpakorn University was conducted sixteen months after the course ended to apprehend the thoughts and ideas occurring and developing over a long period through their critical reflections on the project. Doing so affords the students sufficient time to let key takeaways from the experience sink in. The dialogue encompasses four interlinked aspects: the *sanuk* attitude, peer learning, the learner–teacher relationship, and the students' view on sustainability.

Link Between the Sanuk Attitude and Peer Learning

The students' experiences were intricately conformed to the *sanuk* attitude. Students were engaged in the non-linear process of game design, involving designing, testing, and playing the games. As they learned through the user-centered design process, game testing was voted the least pleasant part because they had to deal with the failure of expectation, boredom from repetitiveness, and extensive time consumption. It was even more problematic for students who were unfamiliar with games and did not play games as a hobby. Moreover, the time constraints associated with other ongoing coursework assignments in the semester affected both the fun in the process and the overall quality of the design outputs. Owing to the strong making tradition deeply embedded in the curriculum, students would enjoy the sense of achievement that comes with success in completing the fully functional prototypes. The combination of the sense of achievement along with the *sanuk* attitude can create a more positive feeling toward the project.

Peer learning accelerates the *sanuk* attitude in students. Constructive interaction and freedom of expression brought fun to the learning process. The challenges, positive results of strategic play, visual elements, and surprise elements in the game lead to increasing fun. Observing how their peers enjoy the game they designed is also a kind of pleasure. In the students' opinion, a typical Thai classroom is rarely associated with games, and laughing out loud while studying may be considered impolite and disrespectful to the instructor. Little bits and pieces of fun began to appear only when the instructor amicably adjusted the power relations in the classroom.

Power Relations in Classroom Interaction: Peer Relationship

All participants proclaimed that working with teammates during the game design stage offered them an opportunity to see the good in others. Peers brought different expertise and skills contributing to their collective success. Collaborative learning was essential to improve their communication skills by listening to different opinions from team members, compromising, and negotiating. Designing a game as a team enabled students to practice inclusivity and respect for others' viewpoints. Students who did not play games as a hobby had thought that they were inferior team members. Other members insisted that questions and feedback from the non-gamer peers are valuable to the design process because they brought a fresh eye. One non-gamer student asserted that she became more open-minded as the project continued.

All participants informed that they got to know more about their peers during game testing and playing. Three students who consider themselves reserved stated that the project was a powerful ice-breaker, allowing them to converse with and learn from unfamiliar classmates. Some others were impressed by how their peers handled role-playing, making unexpected decisions, and exploring the game rules to determine ways of using them to maximum advantage. One student who was a game moderator elaborated specifically on developing designerly observation skills for user experience research. For designers, observation is a cognitive tool that appears as a fundamental stage in the design process. During game testing, he carefully moderated the event and monitored whether gaps and bugs existed in the game. The experience granted him a better understanding of the target audience of sustainability communication.

Power Relations in Classroom Interaction: Learner–teacher Relationship

In the students' view, the teacher-as-facilitator role is a striking factor contributing to the effectiveness of ESD through the game design project. The students appreciated when the instructor took a backseat instead of taking over and leading the lesson. Learning by playing games helps students learn from failure in a safe environment and free themselves from fear of being judged in the classroom. All participants indicated that they had nothing to lose because they knew they were playing games. They felt that they could simply be themselves and became more comfortable with trying something new. The background knowledge of and previous experience with the instructor are influential for the trust-building process. Using gamification as pedagogy may be effective only when the students have positive familiarity with the instructor. All participants asserted that they would feel awkward and skeptical if they were asked to be active in the activity facilitated by an instructor who had always used the traditional teacher-centered approach.

The classroom layout is a contributory factor to the learner–teacher relationship. In their opinion, the sitting-in-circle ritual represented the democratic approach to learning, provided a positive vibe of inclusivity, and created a sense of trust among the group. When sitting together in a circle, the students tended to be more mindful of the task at hand and felt that the instructor became more attentive and considerate of all members.

Using Game as a Critical Lens for Looking into the Reality

Inevitably, the game design project can bring the political dimension into the ESD practice by emphasizing power relations among various stakeholders. All participants thought of their games as a critical lens to examine the actual world they live in. The games they designed and played with peers, one about waste management [The Campus Waste Challenge/ 2020A] and another about natural resource management [CO-BLOC/ 2020B], are crucial to visualize inequality, the root cause of many structural problems in Thai society and a threat to the nation's sustainable development. For them, in the game world, the rules depend on the authority of the designers as rule setters. In reality, as of their experience, the rule setters may benefit the most from the rules they set. Players who exploit bugs in the games mirror the people who legitimize legal loopholes for their advantages in reality.

All participants highlighted the game about resource management and material selection for green architecture [CO-BLOC/ 2020B], critiquing crony capitalism, which leads to air pollution, water contamination, soil degradation, deforestation, and biodiversity destruction. As players must deal with the circumstance of limited resources, the game accents social classes, the gaps between the rich and the poor, survival instinct, and use of power. Role-playing underlines how players use their abilities for competition. The different individual abilities of players symbolize the power each player holds. Toward the end of the game, if everyone loses, it conceptualizes an overall systems breakdown, that is, the interconnected collapse of the systems that support life on this planet.

Considering that the games are complex systems, the game design project fostered students to become systems thinkers, engaging complex problems from multiple perspectives and viewing them holistically. All participants agreed that tackling sustainability challenges requires purposeful individual and collective endeavors, and they are committed to doing their bit because they believe that individual action is essential to achieve systemic change.

SOLUTIONS AND RECOMMENDATIONS

The study shows that applying games and gamification in a sustainable design course can be an innovative student-centered learning approach. The socio-politico-cultural factors play an instrumental role throughout the pedagogical practice in shaping sustainability literacy and encouraging a shift in attitudes toward sustainability in Thai design students. The authors wish to discuss the solutions and recommendations through the reflections from the educator's stance.

Uniting the Hierarchical Repositioning of the Instructor with the *Sanuk* Attitude

The study unveils that the game design project can assist Thai design students in not only capturing the multifaceted aspects of sustainability but also critiquing the hierarchical nature of conventional learning. To enhance the *sanuk* attitude among students, the traditional power relations need reconsideration and strategic reversal. The hierarchical repositioning of the instructor tends to be a challenge for Thai educators rather than students. To promote the changing role of designers in students for their sustainable future, the role of design instructors must become responsive to the dynamic landscape of education. From the authors' impression on the game design project, the experience offers an idea that while industrial or product designers can take the role of instructional designers, instructors can become learners as well.

The authors recommend Thai, and even non-Thai, design educators teaching sustainability-related courses to attempt reviving their attitude of *sanuk* by engaging in gamification or game-based learning with their students. In this way, the role of an educator can be shifted naturally to embrace the voices of the learners in addressing their perspectives and needs of sustainability.

Fostering Change Agents while Holding the Small-is-Beautiful Mindset

The potential of higher education as a change agent in accelerating society's transition toward sustainability has long been acknowledged by international scholars (Stephens et al., 2008). Undeniably, cultivating in students the ability to become change agents requires instructors to take on the role themselves, helping an organization or part of an organization transform how it operates. However, to be an impactful change agent within the Thai educational system is challenging to achieve. Landers et al. (2018) stated that gamification design succeeds based on its effect on individuals, not organizations. From the authors' view, although the individual-level effects cannot directly influence the organization as a distinct entity, this phenomenon represents the bottom-up process of change, which educators can make in their work boundaries.

Many students continued the journey with their games after the course ended. For instance, a group of Chulalongkorn University students went on to test their waste separation game with teachers and students at the institution's Demonstration School for further development. Another example is a team from Silpakorn University who reappropriated their game for a design contest. After spending three months collecting data regarding sustainable energy and developing the new design, the team won first runner-up by creating a board game that allows players to co-create an ideal smart city through balanced resource allocation and energy management.

The authors recommend embracing the small-is-beautiful concept and localizing gamification as a kind of appropriate technology in ESD. It is the little things that count. Change occurs a little bit at a time, and collectively, small actions can change the big picture.

FUTURE RESEARCH DIRECTION

The authors are keen to further explore how the findings of this chapter can be adapted or scaled to other relevant areas or contexts. Collaboratively working on physical game designs may be unsuitable to the current situation of the COVID-19 pandemic. Owing to the high uncertainty avoidance culture of Thais, the authors are interested in seeking ways to proceed with the project on an interactive online learning platform without causing students stress. As industrial and product design curricula in Thailand continue to place strong emphasis on object making, learning additional digital skills can be an overloaded learning situation for students. Thus, the question of how to reposition the game design project to serve students' needs, complement the ESD goals, and suit the current complex circumstances remains.

CONCLUSION

The chapter provides insightful implications on how to integrate gamification and game-based learning in Thailand's sustainable design education. The present political crisis fosters critical thinking and gives rise to significant changes in Thai students' values and attitudes toward social issues and environmental problems. The study verifies that the White Ribbon generation is becoming increasingly aware of sustainability as they stand in the conflicts that are rooted in inequalities. Evidently, more than ever, now is the best time for Thais to learn sustainability. The Thai design education has already paved the way for ESD. As media and scholars argue that Thai schools and universities are a breeding ground for authoritarianism, tackling the dilemma is an urgent task for design educators who are advocates of sustainability at least within the scope of their academic responsibilities. The authors propose that sustainable design pedagogy can be enriched by incorporating the Thai cultural values of the fun-pleasure orientation and the interdependence orientation. The high levels of power distance and uncertainty avoidance in Thai design students, which are stumbling blocks to student-centered learning, can be reduced through gamification. According to the case study, although the core of the project is sustainability communication, the payoff exceeded the expected learning outcomes in many ways. Remarkably, this project can advance the students' ability to visualize interconnectedness. Through game design, students realized that the complex environmental problems that all lives on earth are currently facing are indeed a consequence of the way human beings have organized themselves socially, economically, and politically.

The findings clarify that the game design project contributed to all five key skills of ESD. Systems thinking is the most apparent. The connections between a player's actions and their impact were illustrated during the gameplay, as students learned that the collective impact of human behaviors is contributing to the current global sustainability challenges. Peer learning, combined with the attitude of *sanuk*, contributes to building partnerships and individual participation in decision making. The games are evidence of how students envision their sustainable futures. The reflective notes and the dialogue from the focus group discussion actually speak for the students' critical thinking and reflection abilities. The improvement of the learner–teacher relationships is another important aspect for consideration. Educators need to create an atmosphere conducive to learning along with learning tools that are compatible with the emerging trends and interests of students. The project required the authors, the instructors of the course, to assume the role of open-minded listener, advisor, and reflective practitioner throughout the game design and development process. Allowing the students to propose their self-initiated topics and themes from the start can diversify a broad range of knowledge in the course. By implementing gamification in the classroom, the authors also experienced pleasure in the challenges and excitement to explore new areas of knowledge offered through the games designed by students. Gaining the findings from the multiple PAR cycles, the authors can recognize students' actual needs in their sustainable design learning. Finally, the process of cultivating in students the ability to become change agents continues.

ACKNOWLEDGMENT

The authors express their gratitude to students from Chulalongkorn University and Silpakorn University who participated in the study. The authors also extend their thanks to Kevalin Saksiamkul for her kind assistance in manuscript preparation. Further, the authors are grateful for the financial support for copy editing provided by the Institute of Environmental Engineering and Management, National Taipei University of Technology.

REFERENCES

Apisitniran, L., & Theparat, C. (2018, October 15). Creating the virtuous circle. *The Bangkok Post*. https://www.bangkokpost.com/business/1558130/creating-the-virtuous-circle

Bakhanova, E., Raffe, W. L., Voinov, A., & Marin, J. G. (2019, December 1-6). *Gamification of participatory modeling in the context of sustainable development: Existing and new solutions* [Conference presentation abstract]. 23rd International Congress on Modelling and Simulation, Canberra, Australia. https://opus.lib.uts.edu.au/bitstream/10453/137302/1/bakhanova-3.pdf

Buasuwan, P. (2018). Rethinking Thai higher education for Thailand 4.0. *Asian Education and Development Studies*, *7*(2), 157–173. doi:10.1108/AEDS-07-2017-0072

Campbell, J. (2018). *Sociology & Education*. Scientific e-Resources.

Ceschin, F., & Gaziulusoy, I. (2016). Evolution of design for sustainability: From product design to design for system innovations and transitions. *Design Studies*, *47*, 118–163. doi:10.1016/j.destud.2016.09.002

Chaitrong, W. (2020, August 3). Clash of old and new values: Is Thailand heading for a big change? *The Nation Thailand*. https://www.nationthailand.com/perspective/30392327

Chotiratanapinun, T. (2018). *Transformative learning for a shift towards sustainability in Thailand's design education* [Doctoral thesis, Goldsmiths, University of London]. http://research.gold.ac.uk/id/eprint/23309

Dec Graduate Exhibition. (2019, May 10). *Board game design for instructing visually-impaired children and peers about Braille blocks*. Facebook. https://www.facebook.com/1090561811128660/photos/a.1111302605721247/1111304399054401/?comment_id=1112929428891898

Deterding, S., Dixon, D., Khaled, R., & Nacke, L. (2011). From game design elements to gamefulness: Defining "gamification." *Proceedings of the 15th International Academic MindTrek Conference: Envisioning Future Media Environments, MindTrek 2011*, 9–15. 10.1145/2181037.2181040

Dichev, C., & Dicheva, D. (2017). Gamifying education: what is known, what is believed and what remains uncertain: a critical review. *International Journal of Educational Technology in Higher Education*, *14*(1), 9. Advance online publication. doi:10.118641239-017-0042-5

Douglas, B. D., & Brauer, M. (2021). Gamification to prevent climate change: A review of games and apps for sustainability. *Current Opinion in Psychology*, *42*, 89–94. Advance online publication. doi:10.1016/j.copsyc.2021.04.008 PMID:34052619

Draper, J., Sobieszczyk, T., Crumpton, C. D., Lefferts, H. L., & Chachavalpongpun, P. (2019). Racial "Othering" in Thailand: Quantitative Evidence, Causes, and Consequences. *Nationalism & Ethnic Politics*, *25*(3), 251–272. doi:10.1080/13537113.2019.1639425

Du, H. S., Ke, X., & Wagner, C. (2020). Inducing individuals to engage in a gamified platform for environmental conservation. *Industrial Management & Data Systems*, *120*(4), 692–713. doi:10.1108/IMDS-09-2019-0517

Fjællingsdal, K. S., & Klöckner, C. A. (2020). Green Across the Board: Board Games as Tools for Dialogue and Simplified Environmental Communication. *Simulation & Gaming*, *51*(5), 632–652. Advance online publication. doi:10.1177/1046878120925133

Fleming, R. (2013). *Design Education for a Sustainable Future*. Routledge. doi:10.4324/9780203584071

Foster, A. N., Shah, M., & Duvall, M. (2015). Game Network Analysis. In M. Niess & H. Gillow-Wiles (Eds.), *Handbook of Research on Teacher Education in the Digital Age* (pp. 380–411). IGI Global. doi:10.4018/978-1-4666-8403-4.ch015

Freire, P. (1970). *Pedagogy of the oppressed*. Seabury Press.

Guillen, G., Hamari, J., & Quist, J. (2021, January 5). Gamification of Sustainable Consumption: a systematic literature review. *Proceedings of the 54th Hawaii International Conference on System Sciences*. 10.24251/HICSS.2021.163

Gunawan, J. (2016). Understanding culture in higher education in Thailand. In Education for Health: Change in Learning and Practice (Vol. 29, Issue 2, pp. 160–161). Network: Towards Unity for Health. doi:10.4103/1357-6283.188783

Harwood, T., & Garry, T. (2015). An investigation into gamification as a customer engagement experience environment. *Journal of Services Marketing*, *29*(6–7), 533–546. Advance online publication. doi:10.1108/JSM-01-2015-0045

Heim, A. B., & Holt, E. A. (2021). From Bored Games to Board Games: Student-Driven Game Design in the Virtual Classroom. *Journal of Microbiology & Biology Education*, *22*(1), ev22i1.2323. Advance online publication. doi:10.1128/jmbe.v22i1.2323 PMID:33884075

Hofstede, G. (1997). *Cultures and Organizations: Software of the Mind*. McGraw-Hill.

Hofstede, G. (2011). Dimensionalizing Cultures: The Hofstede Model in Context. *Online Readings in Psychology and Culture*, *2*(1). Advance online publication. doi:10.9707/2307-0919.1014

Janakiraman, S., Watson, S. L., & Watson, W. R. (2018). Using Game-based Learning to Facilitate Attitude Change for Environmental Sustainability. *Journal of Education for Sustainable Development*, *12*(2), 176–185. doi:10.1177/0973408218783286

Komin, S. (1990). Culture and Work-Related Values in Thai Organizations. *International Journal of Psychology*, *25*(3–6), 681–704. doi:10.1080/00207599008247921

Lao, R. (2015). *A Critical Study of Thailand's Higher Education Reforms: The culture of borrowing*. Routledge.

Laopongharn, W., & Sercombe, P. (2009). What relevance does intercultural communication have to language education in thailand? In ARECLS (Vol. 6, pp. 59–83). Academic Press.

Laurie, R., Nonoyama-Tarumi, Y., Mckeown, R., & Hopkins, C. (2016). Contributions of Education for Sustainable Development (ESD) to Quality Education: A Synthesis of Research. *Journal of Education for Sustainable Development*, *10*(2), 226–242. doi:10.1177/0973408216661442

Lennie, J., & Tacchi, J. A. (2013). *Evaluating Communication for Development: A framework for social change*. Routledge. doi:10.4324/9780203078495

Leonard, S., & Oberprieler, K. (2018). Gamifying design education. *Conference Proceedings of the Academy for Design Innovation Management*, *1*(1). 10.33114/adim.2017.79

Lertchoosakul, K. (2021). The white ribbon movement: High school students in the 2020 Thai youth protests. *Critical Asian Studies*, *53*(2), 206–218. doi:10.1080/14672715.2021.1883452

Lilley, D., & Lofthouse, V. (2009). Sustainable design education – considering design for behavioural change. *Engineering Education*, *4*(1), 29–41. doi:10.11120/ened.2009.04010029

Manoopun, M. (2020). *A design strategy for changing attendee behavior to reduce single-use plastics at EDM festivals in Thailand.* Academic Press.

Meyer, M. W., & Norman, D. (2020). Changing Design Education for the 21st Century. *She Ji, 6*(1), 13–49. Advance online publication. doi:10.1016/j.sheji.2019.12.002

Morganti, L., Pallavicini, F., Cadel, E., Candelieri, A., Archetti, F., & Mantovani, F. (2017). Gaming for Earth: Serious games and gamification to engage consumers in pro-environmental behaviours for energy efficiency. In Energy Research and Social Science (Vol. 29, pp. 95–102). Elsevier Ltd. doi:10.1016/j.erss.2017.05.001

Mounier, A., & Tangchuang, P. (2010). *Education and Knowledge in Thailand: The Quality Controversy.* Silkworm Books.

Nawawi, R. (2016). *The formation of the value of Thai society in the context of national security.* National Defence College of Thailand.

Ngammuk, P. (2001). *An analysis of Thai cultural characteristics of students in higher education institutions under the Ministry of University Affairs* [Doctoral thesis]. Chulalongkorn University.

Ngammuk, P. (2016). A Comparison of the Twelve Core Values of Thai people defined by the Head of the National Council for Peace and Order (NCPO) found in Thai private and public university students. *Hawaii International Conference on Education.*

Ouariachi, T., Li, C. Y., & Elving, W. J. L. (2020). Gamification approaches for education and engagement on pro-environmental behaviors: Searching for best practices. *Sustainability, 12*(11), 4565. Advance online publication. doi:10.3390u12114565

Pasupa, S. (2016). *Sustainable Development in Thailand Supported by Industrial Design Education* [Doctoral thesis, Loughborough University]. https://repository.lboro.ac.uk/articles/thesis/Sustainable_development_in_Thailand_supported_by_industrial_design_education/9355721

Patrício, R., Moreira, A. C., & Zurlo, F. (2018). Gamification approaches to the early stage of innovation. *Creativity and Innovation Management, 27*(4), 499–511. doi:10.1111/caim.12284

Patrício, R., Moreira, A. C., & Zurlo, F. (2021). Enhancing design thinking approaches to innovation through gamification. *European Journal of Innovation Management, 24*(5), 1569–1594. doi:10.1108/EJIM-06-2020-0239

Piscicelli, L., Cooper, T., & Fisher, T. (2015). The role of values in collaborative consumption: Insights from a product-service system for lending and borrowing in the UK. *Journal of Cleaner Production, 97*, 21–29. doi:10.1016/j.jclepro.2014.07.032

Rajanen, D., & Rajanen, M. (2019). Climate change gamification: A literature review. In J. Koivisto & J. Hamari (Eds.), *GamiFIN Conference 2019* (pp. 253–264). GamiFIN Conference. http://ceur-ws.org/Vol-2359/

Rajbanshi, R., & Chandra Luitel, B. (2020). Transformative Learning: An Approach to Understand Participatory Action Research. *Transformations, 6*(1). https://nsuworks.nova.edu/transformations

Raksaseri, K. (2020, April 25). 19 Thai unis list on "THE Impact" ranks. *Bangkok Post*. https://www.bangkokpost.com/thailand/general/1906975/19-thai-unis-list-on-the-impact-ranks

Raktham, C. (2008). *Cultures and Learner Behaviours: A Qualitative Investigation of a Thai Classroom*. Academic Press.

Ramirez, M. (2007). *Sustainability integration in industrial design education: A world wide survey Sustainability integration in industrial design education: a worldwide survey*. www.ulsf.org

Ratcliffe, R. (2020, December 24). "We want a true democracy": students lead Thailand's protest movement. *The Guardian*. https://www.theguardian.com/world/2020/aug/24/we-want-a-true-democracy-students-lead-thailands-protest-movement

Ro, M., Brauer, M., Kuntz, K., Shukla, R., & Bensch, I. (2017). Making Cool Choices for sustainability: Testing the effectiveness of a game-based approach to promoting pro-environmental behaviors. *Journal of Environmental Psychology*, *53*, 20–30. doi:10.1016/j.jenvp.2017.06.007

Sakunprasert, T. (2018). *The application of gamification in Thai organization*. Academic Press.

Scott, W. (2002). *Education and Sustainable Development: challenges, responsibilities, and frames of mind*. The Trumpeter. https://trumpeter.athabascau.ca/index.php/trumpet/article/view/123/134

Shawyun, T. (2005). *Values of Thai Undergraduate and Graduate Students: A Case Study of Assumption University*. doi:10.13140/RG.2.2.30591.71848

Shura, R., Siders, R. A., & Dannefer, D. (2011). Culture Change in Long-term Care: Participatory Action Research and the Role of the Resident. *The Gerontologist*, *51*(2), 212–225. Advance online publication. doi:10.1093/geront/gnq099 PMID:21163911

Silraungwilai, U. (2016). The Twelve Thai National Core Values : The Intersection Between Thai Identities and Thai Cultural Competences. *APHEIT Journal*, *22*(1), 134–140.

Suppipat, S., Hu, A. H., & Chotiratanapinun, T. (2021). Gamifying Sustainable Design to Enhance Environmental Consciousness of Industrial Design Students. In Y. Kishita, M. Matsumoto, M. Inoue, & S. Fukushige (Eds.), EcoDesign and Sustainability II (pp. 291–310). Springer. doi:10.1007/978-981-15-6775-9_19

Suwankarjank, V., & Rugwongwan, Y. (2021). Design Thinking Model in Design Education for Thai Product Design Student. *Review of International Geographical Education Online*, *11*(3). Advance online publication. doi:10.33403/rigeo.800453

Thailand Sustainability Expo. (2021). *Thailand Sustainability Expo 2021*. https://tsx2021.thailandsustainabilityexpo.com/index.php

The Economist Intelligence Unit. (2017, November 16). Thailand 4.0: in sight but not in reach. *The Economist*. http://www.eiu.com/industry/article/786131662/thailand-40-in-sight-but-not-in-reach/2017-11-16

Tilbury, D., & Wortman, D. (2004). *Engaging People in Sustainability*. Commission on Education and Communication, IUCN. https://www.researchgate.net/publication/255964013

Times Higher Education. (2021). *Impact Rankings 2021*. Times Higher Education. www.timeshighereducation.com/impactrankings

Tovey, M. (2015). *Design Pedagogy: Developments in Art and Design Education* (M. Tovey, Ed.). Gower Applied Research.

UNESCO. (2020). *Education for sustainable development: A roadmap*. https://unesdoc.unesco.org/ark:/48223/pf0000374802

United Nations Department of Global Communications. (2018, April 21). *The 17 Goals - Sustainable Development Goals*. United Nations. https://sdgs.un.org/goals

Uribe, R. V., Alicia, S., & Cobos, U. (2014). *Board Games as Tool for Teaching Basic Sustainability Concepts to Design Students*. The European Conference on Sustainability, Energy and the Environment 2014.

Uribe, R. V., Santamaría Ortega, A., Alicia, S., & Cobos, U. (2017). *Sustainability Should Be Fun. Designing Boardgames to Teach Sustainability*. The Asian Conference on Sustainability, Energy & the Environment 2017.

Voice Online Editorial Division. (2021, April 15). วิจัย ‘คนรุ่นใหม่’ ทำความเข้าใจม็อบเพดานสูง – คำตอบการเปลี่ยนแปลงอยู่ที่รุ่นกลาง! [Research ‘the new generation’ to understand the high ceiling mob – the answer to the change lies in the middle generation!]. *Voice Online*. https://www.voicetv.co.th/read/nW0ygLK3U?fbclid=IwAR07HcQjqbB2UZTH0yLilcf-in0sK3CyxliHZiLAxJvb6wy9eae1GF71lI4

Watkins, M., Casamayor, J. L., Ramirez, M., Moreno, M., Faludi, J., & Pigosso, D. C. A. (2021). Sustainable Product Design Education: Current Practice. *She Ji: The Journal of Design, Economics, and Innovation*, *7*(4), 611–637. doi:10.1016/j.sheji.2021.11.003

Wittayasin, S., & Wittayasin, S. (2017). Education Challenges to Thailand 4.0. *Int. J. Integr. Educ. Dev*, *2*(2), 29–35.

Wongcha-um, P. (2020, August 18). Thai school “Hunger Games” salute protests spread. *Reuters*. https://www.reuters.com/article/us-thailand-protests-idUSKCN25E1AT

World Commission on Environment and Development. (1987). *Our Common Future*. Oxford University Press.

Wortley, D. J. (2016). The Education Game Using Gamification in the Classroom. *ThaiSim Journal: Learning Development*, *1*(1), 18–24.

KEY TERMS AND DEFINITIONS

Education for Sustainable Development (ESD): Education that encourages changes in knowledge, skills, values, and attitudes to enable a more sustainable and just society for all.

Industrial Design: A discipline and professional practice that involves the design of products, services, and systems through a strategic problem-solving process.

Participatory Action Research (PAR): A research approach in which stakeholders are involved in the entire process as co-researchers and knowledge collectively generated in the process is used for the development of strategies for social change.

Pedagogy: The approach to teaching, focusing on how the process influences and is influenced by the social, political, and psychological development of learners.

Product Design: A discipline and professional practice that involves the innovation process of tangible products.

Sustainability: An interdisciplinary subject which pertains to all living systems on earth. It spans from environmental studies to social sciences and requires efforts and expertise from a variety of backgrounds.

Sustainable Development: A principle for meeting human development goals while concurrently sustaining the ability of ecological systems to provide the natural resources and ecosystem services on which the economy and society depend.

Thai Design Education: The formal teaching of design theory and application, beginning at the higher education level, wherein students are predominantly offered practical, skill-based training.

Thailand: A country formerly known as Siam, located in Southeast Asia, and with a constitutional monarchy. Throughout its modern history, the form of government has ranged from military dictatorship to electoral democracy.

Chapter 14
Gamification 101:
An Exploration of a Gamified Instructional Approach

David R. Hill
University of Michigan, Dearborn, USA

Stein Brunvand
University of Michigan, Dearborn, USA

ABSTRACT

Higher education is currently experiencing a period of self-examination as tuition costs soar, academic relevance is being challenged, and institutions experience stagnant enrollment. This changing collegial landscape has prompted higher education faculty and administration to reexamine many of their current practices. One area that some faculty have begun to explore is their pedagogical approach to instruction. Having realized that the lecture format is no longer sufficient for delivering engaging education, faculty have started to embrace alternative pedagogies such as games or game elements to enhance assignments and increase student engagement. This chapter will explore gamification implementation as an alternative pedagogical method and examine various elements of a gamified class structure at the university level. Other key features discussed in this exploration include the design and evaluation of course assignments, the use of locks on assignments, and the relevance of competition within gamified courses.

INTRODUCTION

Higher education is currently experiencing copious amounts of scrutiny regarding tuition costs, universal accessibility, and relevance (Chamorro-Premuzic & Frankiewicz, 2019; Ivancheva, 2020; Moore & Morton, 2017). These critiques have prompted higher education administrators and faculty to reexamine many of their current practices to lessen and, in some instances, alleviate such criticisms. As university administrators focus on solutions for the systemic issues associated with higher education, faculty have started to address some of the public's concerns in a more micro way. More specifically, many faculty have begun to reexamine their pedagogical approach to instruction precipitated by decreased student

DOI: 10.4018/978-1-6684-4287-6.ch014

engagement and overall satisfaction with course content and mode of instruction (Aiken et al., 2016; Brint & Cantwell, 2014; Kumar & Khurana, 2012). The impetus of this reexamination is a result of realizing that the lecture format is no longer sufficient for capturing student interests within a classroom setting. As a result, more and more faculty have started to investigate alternative pedagogies and one such pedagogical method is gamification of learning which uses commonly implemented game design elements in non-game settings to enhance assignments and increase student engagement by providing assignment choice and self-directed learning pathways (Deterding et al., 2011; Sampayo-Vargas, et al., 2013; Simões et al., 2013).

Often mistaken for gamification, educational games have been a part of the k-12 classroom routine for years, but they have been typically used for the exclusive purpose of teaching a specific academic skill such as grammar (Tuan & Doan, 2010; Yolageldili & Arikan, 2011) or problem-solving. This isolated and limited application of games resulted in them being used as a tool to supplement class instruction or assess content knowledge rather than being a pedagogy. However, due to the popularity of video game playing by student aged individuals over the last several decades, a new trend emerged. A select group of educators began recognizing the power and allure of video game playing on many young adult learners and started to explore ways of incorporating gamified or gamification elements commonly used in video games into their classroom instruction and course design (Dominguez et al., 2013). What started in the K-12 classroom as educational games has evolved into gamification of learning and has transitioned to university-level courses (Hill & Brunvand, 2017) across a variety of academic disciplines.

Gamification is not exclusive to the field of education, as evidenced by other professions that have embraced gamified elements by embedding them into their work culture. For example, over the last decade, gamification has made its way into various facets of both corporate and private industries at an increasing rate (Humari, 2017). This growth can be attributed to the many positive effects of gamification, which include user motivation, productivity, and the development of valued technology skills (Brunvand & Hill, 2018; Hamari, Koivisto, & Sarsa., 2014). By adopting a gamified approach to teaching, select higher education faculty across the country are redesigning their courses. Some are even conducting research studies that examine the effects of gamification. Results indicate gamification does have a positive impact on assignment choice and student engagement (Bencsik, Mezeiova, and Samu, 2021; Goksun & Gursoy, 2019; Tsay, Kofinas, & Luo, 2018). This empirical evidence provides faculty with novel options on how courses can be taught and designed through gamification.

The overall focus of this chapter is to highlight the many facets of implementing a gamified approach to instruction in the post-secondary educational setting. The primary target audience for this chapter is higher education personnel (e.g., faculty, administrators) and software developers working on innovative gamified learning management systems (LMS). Additionally, this chapter will explore gamification implementation as an alternative pedagogical method to the traditional lecture format and examine various elements of a gamified class structure at the university level. Other key features discussed in this exploration include the design and evaluation of course assignments, the use of locks on assignments, and the relevance of competition within gamified courses. Lastly, limitations and implications for practice are also addressed and future research areas are suggested.

BACKGROUND

Recently, Bencsik, Mezeiova, and Samu (2021) examined the impact of gamification on motivation and preferred classroom tasks. More specifically, the authors designed a gamified curriculum for a group of 260 graduate students pursuing economics degrees and collected data through student surveys. The authors reported that gamification did have a positive effect on the majority of students surveyed when asked to compare the gamified class to traditional courses (non-gamified). More specifically, 86% of the participants indicated they liked having the opportunity to be more creative with assignments, and 76% of students believed the gamification made the assignments easier to understand the curriculum. Overall, the majority of students surveyed have a positive view of gamification, but the authors did note that gamification does not automatically lead to increased activity by all students. Especially students who are initially skeptical of gamification and do not fully immerse themselves and utilize the various gamified features.

Similarly, Goksun and Gursoy (2019) investigated the relationship between student success and engagement by focusing on the effects of gamification used as a formative assessment tool to academic achievement and student engagement by conducting a mixed-methods study that included 71 pre-service teachers enrolled in an educational assessment course. In addition to academic achievement and student engagement, the authors also examined the professional and personal views of the participants on gamification applications. Results indicated that academic achievement did improve when gamified assessments were implemented, and the majority of participants viewed the gamified element as positive and a tool that they would use in the future.

A third study involved a group of researchers (Tsay, Kofinas, & Luo, 2018) who collected data on 136 undergraduate business majors over two academic terms to see how a gamified course structure impacted student performance. Data from the cohort were compared with a control group of students who chose not to participate in a gamified version of the same course. Results indicated that students who participated in the gamified version performed significantly higher than the control group. Also, the authors reported that behavioral engagement was positively connected to course performance.

The previous paragraph highlighted a sample of the recent studies that have been conducted that focus on the effects of gamification on higher education courses and more specifically, student engagement and assignment choice. It is worth noting that the classes featured in each study are from different academic disciplines and are not exclusive to one content area. This facet further supports the flexibility of how gamifying a course is not contingent upon a specific topic or format.

MAIN FOCUS OF THE CHAPTER

As with any instructional approach, gamification has an impact on the pedagogy employed in the classroom. To better understand that impact, this chapter will explore the relationship between pedagogy and the gamified class structure utilizing an LMS. Some key elements that will be discussed in this exploration include the design and evaluation of course assignments, the use of locks on assignments, and the role of competition within gamified courses.

Use of Locks

Locks are often used in a gamified course to require students to demonstrate foundational knowledge before they are able to advance to more complicated assignments. In a video game, players generally have to complete certain tasks before they can unlock different powers, levels, tools, and features within the game. Locks can help players develop a cycle of expertise (Bereiter & Scardamalia, 1993) by giving them the chance to repeat a series of tasks until they have developed a sufficient knowledge base and skill set. Gee (2003) includes this intentional repetition of foundational skills as a core principle of good game design. In essence, a good game requires players to repeat specific skills until they are proficient because those skills will be necessary throughout the remaining levels of the game. This notion of actively building a foundation of understanding harkens back to Dewey's (1916) notion that true learning is built around the discovery of knowledge rather than just passive instruction.

Locks can be used in a similar way in a gamified course to help students construct the knowledge they will need to be successful as the content becomes more complex. Blocking direct access to challenging assignments can strategically scaffold students so they are working within their personal zones of proximal development (Vygotsky, 1978) rather than risking them jumping into assignments and content that would be overwhelming. Providing regular feedback can be one way to support students as they develop foundational knowledge in a gamified setting (Khaleel et al., 2016). In addition, locks can also be an effective way to guide students towards certain choices that you want them to make. For instance, if you have core assignments that you prefer all students complete you can always require those assignments rather than making it a choice. Most video games have required elements that must be completed in order for players to advance through the game. While you might be able to exercise choice in the sequence those required elements are completed, you generally don't have the choice to just skip over them and still expect to advance to the next level of the game. Therefore, having required assignments in a gamified course is not contradictory to the core philosophy of gamification.

Another option would be to make core assignments an "unlock" for a variety of other assignments. This would create a situation where students would essentially be forced to complete the core assignments in order to unlock and get access to the other assignments they want to choose so they can advance through the different levels of your grading system. In this arrangement, students could choose not to complete the core assignments, but this also means they would be choosing not to access and complete a range of other assignments, which will have a detrimental impact on their progress in the course. One example of this can be found in an educational technology class taught by one of the authors. The goal of this class is to introduce preservice teachers to a wide range of technologies, and associated pedagogies for integrating those technologies, that they can use to teach across the curriculum. A core assignment in this class is the creation of a technology enhanced learning activity. This assignment is a lock for several other larger point assignments in the course, so students must complete it and earn a minimum grade of 80% in order to get access to those other assignments. Students are able to revise and resubmit the learning activity assignment so that they have multiple opportunities to achieve the 80% threshold and thereby unlock the remaining assignments.

Obviously, the use of locks can quickly infringe on student choice and autonomy with regard to selecting assignments for completion. It may seem like a "false" sense of choice when students have to pick their way through locked assignments in order to get to the activities they really prefer to complete. However, this is not unlike most video games where player choice is constrained by a variety of parameters. You can't simply jump from level 1 to level 14 just because you *choose* to do so. There is a sequence to the game and that sequence is embedded in the design of the game so that the entire experience has coherence and doesn't result in complete frustration. Likewise, assignments and other tasks created in a gamified course can be expected to have a strategic sequence that supports students through the pathway they choose while also providing logical boundaries for those different pathways. The challenge for the instructor is in designing a range of assessments that are different enough that students perceive them as discrete options but also similar enough that they can be used to assess understanding of an identified concept or set of skills.

Competition

Competition is a core element of video games. Players compete against the game itself and the different characters present in the game that are designed to slow their progress. In multiplayer games, there is competition between other players, which can sometimes result in teams of players competing against each other. Competition can be present in gamified settings as well and is particularly common when gamification is used in the service industry (Korn & Schmidt, 2015). One of the more common ways competition is utilized in a gamified setting is in the exercise and fitness sector where apps are used to see who runs the farthest, pedals the longest, and lifts the most. Results of different workouts can be made public, so everyone sees how they rank against other "competitors" and set individual goals for improvement. Gamified courses can incorporate competition as well through the use of leaderboards, which make visible the accomplishments of each student (Eleftheria et al., 2013). Proponents of Competition-based Learning argue that when a competitive element is introduced in the classroom, student learning is independent of the actual score received or how someone ranks against their classmates (Burguillo, 2010). In other words, even if a student doesn't "win" the competition they are still able to learn from the experience. It is also important to note that while competition can increase motivation and attention to a task, it can also add an additional cognitive load to the learner as they work to simultaneously complete an assigned set of tasks and monitor the progress of the classmates they are competing against (Nebel, Schneider & Ray, 2016). Seeing where they stack up against their peers may be motivating for some students, but it could also have a detrimental effect on others who may be embarrassed or experience performance anxiety, so deciding to make a leaderboard public should be determined on a course-by-course basis.

One option that could provide a workable compromise would be to allow students to be identified by an alias or nickname on the leaderboard. This would provide them with a level of anonymity while still showing each student how they stack up against their peers. Being able to hide behind an alias could relieve some of the pressure students feel when their performance in the class is made public. It is also important to remember what the leaderboard represents. A leaderboard shows the cumulative point total for each student, or player in a game. It doesn't provide a detailed breakdown of how the student performed on each individual assignment nor does it reveal any information about what assignments the student has even completed. A leaderboard is also dynamic as students constantly have the opportunity to complete additional assignments and revise previous ones in an attempt to earn more points and improve their position or ranking on the board. This is one of the benefits of the additive grading approach used in gamified courses that has students start with zero points and then work towards the grade, or level, they hope to achieve. With additive grading, students have far more control over their progress since they can pick and choose as many, or as few, assignments to complete in order to move through the grading levels of your class. Being able to see a class leaderboard is one way to help them track their progress and compare that to the progress of their peers.

Another way to incorporate competition into a gamified course is by creating challenges, sometimes referred to as quests or boss battles, where teams of students compete against each other on course related tasks. These challenges can be designed in a variety of ways. For instance, a challenge could be structured where there is one clear winner who earns more points than the other teams or participants. One of the more common examples of this is when students are asked to build an actual structure (i.e., tallest building, strongest bridge) out of specific materials in order to learn more about the strength of those different materials. In a competition such as this all groups would be given the same amount of time, materials, and parameters to build their structure. When structuring a competition this way it is important to consider what a team has to do in order to finish first. Is it simply a matter of completing the task before everyone else or will their work be evaluated some other way? In some cases where there is a "first place" option peer review could be used to help determine the top team. For instance, if the assignment is a design challenge where each group is tasked with developing a solution to a common problem, the class could be asked to vote on the best design or solution. Another option is to create a situation where each team can earn equal points for successfully completing a challenge. Students might be more inclined to collaborate across groups when they know that each team can be considered victorious. Again, decisions about how and when to include competitive elements into a gamified course will vary based on the preferences of the instructor and the discipline/topic of the course.

Considering how the design of assignments, the use of locks, and the role of competition might factor into the design of a gamified course is definitely important. But these aren't the only factors that need deliberation when implementing gamification. The following section explores a variety of other implications for practice with regards to teaching a gamified course.

SOLUTIONS AND RECOMMENDATIONS

Limitations

Gamification provides instructors with a level of flexibility when it comes to creating unique and engaging assignments. Students also benefit from a gamified class structure because students work at their own pace and are empowered by being able to choose which tasks to complete (Banfield & Wilkerson, 2014). However, there are also limitations to a gamified class that need consideration before deciding to gamify a particular course. Three general limitations associated with gamification are addressed in this chapter. These limitations include the following: a) the accessibility of reliable technology for all users; b) delivery model (face-to-face instruction, fully online, and hybrid; and c) course equality (fairness to the student who may prefer a more traditional class but is required to enroll in a gamified course). These specific limitations have been carefully selected due to their sizable impact on decision-making when one is contemplating a gamified approach for a class.

Accessibility

Any gamified class at the university level will require the use of an LMS to assist the instructor in organizing the course content. The LMS serves as the assignment hub, provides students with any rules and directions associated with specific assignments, and provides users with scoring rubrics as well as results. The LMS is an integral piece of the gamified classroom because it is the focal point of the class

- think of it as a more interactive and virtual syllabus but with vastly more capabilities and functions. However, the LMS can only be accessed through a personal computing device connected to the internet. So, what this means is that any student who does not have a computer, smartphone, or tablet and internet access may not be able to participate fully in a gamified class if the class is offered exclusively online.

At the beginning of 2020, the world encountered a pandemic that significantly impacted and altered every person's life. None more so than people's everyday routines and restrictions on physical human contact and socialization. Furthermore, businesses shut down, travel ceased, and schools (both K-12 and post-secondary) made the immediate shift to fully online instruction. This move to fully online teaching was far from smooth but manageable for the fortunate individuals who had a reliable and accessible internet connection and equipment. Others were less fortunate, particularly those who were from rural communities or lower socioeconomic families. More specifically, families living in rural areas lacked a reliable internet network to access, and families from lower socioeconomic backgrounds simply could not afford broadband internet. Other groups also experienced similar obstacles to online learning, and the result for these less fortunate was a loss of academic instruction for most of the school year/semester. Without empirical evidence, it is difficult to pinpoint what single factor contributed to the loss of instructional time, but an argument can be made that technology access, or lack of, was instrumental in how successful online education was delivered and received by students.

In addition to accessible technology, having access to reliable technology is equally important. For example, newer and more efficient technology has steadily replaced many of the traditional learning tools commonly used in education. Moreover, paper products such as physical copies of textbooks are quickly being replaced with digital versions that are cheaper and can be accessed on multiple personal computing devices. Additionally, course-related assessments can now be designed and administered via computer learning management systems, thus eliminating the need for excess paper copies of assignments.

All of this newer technology has enhanced classroom instruction in various ways. For example, increasing accessibility for multiple users, reducing material costs, and expanding functionality, but one significant barrier to this technology renaissance is the ability for all students to access it. Furthermore, the user must be able to afford a personal computing device in addition to having internet access or this significant barrier will continue to impede online learning. In this day and age, some type of personal computing device is needed in order to access course documents and engage in some digital-based assignments within a typical instructional setting and this is especially true of a gamified course.

Delivery Model

Gamification can be used for a variety of academic classes and because there is a degree of assignment autonomy involved, the class structure is not limited to one type of format. Currently, there are three types of class designs available at the university level: face-to-face, online, and hybrid. How gamification impacts all three will be examined in greater detail. Also, the importance of knowing what options are available when considering using a gamified approach cannot be understated because each type of class can present challenges. This is especially relevant when designing assignments and creating grading scales because both must be explained clearly, time-sensitive, and motivational. The first type of class to be discussed is face-to-face instruction.

This delivery model consists of students physically attending a class on campus and by far has been the most offered form of class. This is further evidenced by the fact that for decades the traditional collegiate class has looked very similar regardless of the institution (Stark, 2003). For example, a typical course would meet once or twice a week and primarily consist of an instructor standing in front of a classroom full of students delivering a lecture. Sometimes the instructor would use a projector or chalkboard to physically write content or draw graphs that supplemented the lecture content, but that was the extent of classroom technology use because the professor was the focal point. Then new technology started to emerge circa the late 1980s and early 1990s in the form of PowerPoint software and alternative writing surfaces like the dry erase board to expand the capabilities of disseminating course content and increase student interactions with the presented material. Newer, more sophisticated technology soon followed, such as LMS interfaces, laptop computers, tablets, and smartphones.

Face-to-face classes provide many advantages to hosting a gamified course because students have in-person access to the instructor on a weekly basis. Having that in-person contact with the instructor is helpful when there are technical issues with the LMS, confusion about specific assignments, and the need to clarify rules that are part of the gamified class. Instructors also benefit from the in-class format because they can explicitly explain the gamified elements multiple times, physically guide students through the features on the LMS, and monitor students' performance and provide corrective feedback immediately when students are confused or incorrectly completing the various assignments.

Advancement in technology-enabled universities to offer online instruction as a novel alternative to the traditional face-to-face class and to this day, online classes are still an option at most universities. Interestingly, this shift to online learning can be traced back to 1989 when the first online classes were offered at the University of Phoenix (The University of Phoenix, n. d.). The benefits of online learning are many such as online learning allows students to attend classes regardless of where they live and provides an asynchronous class schedule that enables students to have much more flexibility with their schoolwork. Even with the infusion of new technologies, the majority of higher education institutions still offer just a conservative number of online courses as face-to-face instruction continues to be the default model. However, after being forced to move all classes to online this past year due to the pandemic, more universities may decide to offer future classes remotely.

So, how does gamification align with an online class structure? From a technical standpoint, it aligns well with gamification. As stated previously, any gamified class will use an LMS which is naturally accessed through a computer device and internet. Additionally, the majority of assignments are designed so that students can choose which ones to complete, and many do not have concrete deadlines. This limitation on assignment deadlines aligns with an asynchronous class schedule. However, instructors must be cognizant of how students typically engage in online courses, more specifically, how students organize their time and the completion of assignments. Without regular check-ins by the instructor, students may be at risk of falling behind and possibly missing opportunities to complete time-sensitive tasks.

The third type of class offering is a hybrid model that combines both online and face-to-face instruction. This method of instruction may be the optimal design for faculty and students alike because it provides each group with maximum flexibility and support. There is also an assumption that if a student has enrolled in a hybrid class, they are well aware of the requirements like having internet access and a personal computer, so access to the course material should be barrier-free. From an instructor's standpoint, a hybrid class does not pose any substantial restrictions to implementing a gamified class. The only significant concern with gamifying a hybrid class is that some students may procrastinate on completing assignments when there are minimal face-to-face interactions with other students and the instructor.

Course Equality

As discussed previously in this chapter, one of the major tenets of class gamification is "choice," more specifically, the ability for students to make choices about the assignments to complete and learning pathways to take. But what about the students who do not want to participate in a gamified class and prefer the traditional class model? As the instructor, this must be taken into consideration when designing a gamified course because not all students want to participate in one. A solution is that multiple sections of the same course be offered so that students have options if the faculty member's department is small and cannot provide multiple sections, then another plan must be available. That is not to say that one must abandon the gamified approach, but a difficult decision will have to be made and questions answered. More specifically, can a gamified course accommodate students who prefer the traditional mode of instruction, or are they simply out of luck and forced to suffer through the current gamified course? There are no correct or straightforward answers to these questions but one way to lessen the stress on students who prefer a more traditional approach to instruction (i.e., face-to-face) is to provide them with extensive explanations of what a gamified class entails before they enroll and during the first week of class. Another suggestion is to provide the students with the requisite resources to be successful, and that includes resources such as laptops, universal internet access, and detailed written instructions.

FUTURE RESEARCH DIRECTIONS

While the gamification of learning has grown in popularity over the past several years, some significant holes remain in the body of research surrounding this pedagogical strategy. For instance, student choice is a primary tenet of gamified learning so it would be helpful to learn more about how students make decisions when faced with choices about what assignments to complete and the pathway they chart through a particular class. This line of research could also provide key insights on how to structure a gamified class such that students feel like they have a genuine choice rather than feeling like they are being guided towards an obvious set of options.

Another area of research that needs deeper exploration is the impact gamification has on student learning and academic achievement. Much of the existing research sheds light on the impact of gamification on student engagement and motivation, which is useful, but since engagement doesn't automatically lead to learning it would be useful to learn more about how, and even if, gamification can be used to positively impact learning. Research of this nature could also create a better understanding of the transferability of gamification across different content areas. Understanding if and how a gamified approach impacts learning would allow educators to make more informed decisions about the structure of their classes and the implementation of this pedagogical strategy.

This chapter has focused exclusively on the use of gamification in higher education, but it would be interesting to learn more about the use of gamified instruction with younger students as well. Considering the amount of responsibility placed on a student in a gamified course, it is often assumed that older and more mature students would do better in this type of learning environment. However, it is entirely possible that younger students would excel in a situation where they were given more choice over what assignments they completed and the path they took towards mastery of different content. Research that explored the applicability of gamified teaching across different age ranges could help teachers at all levels better understand whether or not this instructional approach was suitable for them or not.

CONCLUSION

As gamification grows in popularity, it is useful to take a look into the pedagogy behind this instructional approach. It is also helpful to explore the limitations of this teaching style and the implications it presents for practice and, most importantly, the impact it can have on the learner. University faculty have options when it comes to delivering classroom instruction. Long gone are the days of a professor standing in front of a classroom full of students lecturing for an hour. Students want to be academically engaged in a meaningful way as well as having a certain level of autonomy when it comes to course assignments. That is why some higher education faculty have started to explore the use of gamification as an alternative pedagogy to the traditional lecture approach.

In addition to providing students with more control over their learning, gamification provides the instructor with unique tools and strategies to enhance the course material. Not only can a gamified approach allow students choice in assignments, it also makes it possible to strategically embed competition within a class and utilize non-traditional assessments. Each of these components requires students to take a more involved approach to their learning because the traditional course rules do not apply. One such example is that assignments in a gamified class are not necessarily sequential so students can skip certain assignments until they are ready to complete them. Class leaderboards can also be used to stimulate friendly competition across individual students or small groups. Gamification can also allow the instructor to create assessments that are unique and separate from the traditional formal assessments so commonly used. When combined and utilized, these elements create a class that is truly original and engaging. Once the blueprint of the gamified class has been designed, the next decision is to select the course structure.

Faculty can opt for the traditional face-to-face class, teach fully online or use a hybrid model. All three models are viable options, and each come with their own benefits and limitations. Regardless of what type of class structure is chosen, instruction must be relevant and engaging to all students. Instructors must decide which model best fits with the type of gamification they intend to use and also consider the type of students who will be enrolling. Specifically, not all students may be receptive to a gamified class so their needs and preferences must be considered. However, there are no limitations when it comes to gender, academic classification (i.e., undergraduate/graduate), or academic major so gamification is not limited to a select few. Since the academic area is not constrained in a gamified course, instructors need to contemplate other factors that may impact their desire to use a gamified approach. These factors include the size of the academic institution and more specifically, the resources available to the faculty. For example, does the institution have the capabilities to offer multiple sections of one particular course? Does the institution offer technology assistance to students who may not have access to computers or the internet off-campus? These are both important considerations when contemplating a gamified approach to instruction.

Research results have shown that gamification does lead to greater student engagement and overall satisfaction (Bencsik, et al., 2021; Goksun & Gursoy, 2019; Kofinas & Luo, 2018) but there are other areas that still need to be examined. Especially in the areas of assignment preference and learning outcomes. When it comes to assignment preferences, there is a need to understand why a student chooses a particular assignment from an array of options. Is it because the student perceives the assignment as easy or is it because the assignment aligns with the student's learning preferences? The same goes for learning outcomes because in a gamified class, many of the assignments can be attempted multiple times so a completed assignment does not automatically mean the student has mastered the content. This is particularly true when non-traditional forms of assessment are being used.

The purpose of this chapter is to provide the reader with a more in-depth examination of gamified teaching and provide higher education faculty and administrators a useful resource for more effective ways to connect with their students. In addition to higher education personnel, others who may benefit from this chapter are software developers and curriculum specialists looking to expand their products to include post-secondary instruction. One concluding thought for the reader is that gamification is just one option that is available to faculty. Hopefully, this chapter has provided enough information on gamification to show that it is a viable alternative pedagogy for instructors who are interested in engaging their students in an unconventional way to increase productivity and interest. Gamification implies fun but just because a course is entertaining does not lessen the course rigor. It simply reimagines it.

REFERENCES

Aiken, K. D., Heinze, T. C., Meuter, M. L., & Chapman, K. J. (2016). Innovation through collaborative course development: Theory and practice. *Marketing Education Review*, *26*(1), 57–62. doi:10.1080/10528008.2015.1091679

Banfield, J., & Wilkerson, B. (2014). Increasing student intrinsic motivation and self-efficacy through gamification pedagogy. *Contemporary Issues in Education Research*, *7*(4), 291–298. doi:10.19030/cier.v7i4.8843

Bencsik, A., Mezeiova, A., & Samu, B. O. (2021). Gamification in Higher Education (Case Study on a Management Subject). *International Journal of Learning, Teaching and Educational Research, 20*(5).

Bereiter, C., & Scardamalia, M. (1993). *Surpassing Ourselves: An Inquiry into the Nature and Implications of Expertise*. Open Court.

Brint, S., & Cantwell, A. M. (2014). Conceptualizing, Measuring, and Analyzing the Characteristics of Academically Disengaged Students: Results From UCUES 2010. *Journal of College Student Development*, *55*(8), 808–823. doi:10.1353/csd.2014.0080

Burguillo, J. C. (2010). Using game theory and Competition-based Learning to stimulate student motivation and performance. *Computers & Education*, *55*(2), 566–575. doi:10.1016/j.compedu.2010.02.018

Chamorro-Premuzic, T., & Frankiewicz, B. (2019). Does higher education still prepare people for jobs. *Harvard Business Review*, 7.

Deterding, S., Dixon, D., Khaled, R., & Nacke, L. 2011. From game design elements to gamefulness: Defining “Gamification.” *Proceedings of the 2011 Annual Conference Extended Abstracts on Human Factors in Computing Systems - CHI EA ’11*, 2425.

Dewey, J. (1916). *Democracy and Education*. The Free Press.

Domínguez, A., Saenz-de-Navarrete, J., De-Marcos, L., Fernández-Sanz, L., Pagés, C., & Martínez-Herráiz, J. J. (2013). Gamifying learning experiences: Practical implications and outcomes. *Computers & Education*, *63*, 380–392. doi:10.1016/j.compedu.2012.12.020

Eleftheria, C. A., Charikleia, P., Iason, C. G., Athanasios, T., & Dimitrios, T. (2013). An innovative augmented reality educational platform using Gamification to enhance lifelong learning and cultural education. *IISA 2013 - 4th International Conference on Information, Intelligence, Systems and Applications*. 10.1109/IISA.2013.6623724

Gee, J. P. (2003). What video games have to teach us about learning and literacy. *Computers in Entertainment*, *1*(1), 20. doi:10.1145/950566.950595

Gee, J. P. (2005). Learning by Design: Good Video Games as Learning Machines. *E-Learning and Digital Media*, *2*(1), 5–16. doi:10.2304/elea.2005.2.1.5

Göksün, D. O., & Gürsoy, G. (2019). Comparing success and engagement in gamified learning experiences via Kahoot and Quizizz. *Computers & Education*, *135*, 15–29. doi:10.1016/j.compedu.2019.02.015

Hamari, J., Koivisto, J., & Sarsa, H. (2014). Does gamification work?--a literature review of empirical studies on gamification. In *2014 47th Hawaii international conference on system sciences* (pp. 3025-3034). IEEE.

Hill, D. R., & Brunvand, S. (2017). Gaming the system: Helping students level-up their learning. *International Journal on Teaching and Learning in Higher Education*, *30*(1), 70–79.

Hill, D. R., & Brunvand, S. (2018). Gamification. In *The K-12 Educational Technology Handbook*. https://edtechbooks.org/k12handbook/gamification

Ivancheva, M. (2020). Unbundling: A new gendered frontier of exclusion and exploitation in the neoliberal university. *Journal of New Materialist Research*, *1*, 80–109. doi:10.1344/jnmr.v1i1.29204

Khaleel, F. L., Siti, T., Tengku, M., Sahari Ashaari, N., & Ismail, A. (2016). The Architecture of Dynamic Gamification Elements Based Learning Content. *Journal of Convergence Information Technology*, *11*(June), 164–177. https://www.researchgate.net/publication/304639660

Korn, O., & Schmidt, A. (2015). Gamification of Business Processes: Re-designing Work in Production and Service Industry. *Procedia Manufacturing*, *3*, 3424–3431. Advance online publication. doi:10.1016/j.promfg.2015.07.616

Kumar, B., & Khurana, P. (2012). 2012 Gamification in education – learn computer programming with fun International. *Journal of Computers and Distributed Systems*, *2*(1), 46–53.

Moore, T., & Morton, J. (2017). The myth of job readiness? Written communication, employability, and the 'skills gap' in higher education. *Studies in Higher Education*, *42*(3), 591–609. doi:10.1080/03075079.2015.1067602

Nebel, S., Schneider, S., & Rey, G. D. (2016). From duels to classroom competition: Social competition and learning in educational videogames within different group sizes. *Computers in Human Behavior*, *55*, 384–398. doi:10.1016/j.chb.2015.09.035

Sampayo-Vargas, S., Cope, C. J., He, Z., & Byrne, G. J. (2013). The effectiveness of adaptive difficulty adjustments on students' motivation and learning in an educational computer game. *Computers & Education*, *69*, 452–462. doi:10.1016/j.compedu.2013.07.004

Simões, J., Redondo, R. D., & Vilas, A. F. (2012). A social gamification framework for a K-6 learning platform. *Computers in Human Behavior*, *29*(2), 345–353. doi:10.1016/j.chb.2012.06.007

Stark, M. (2003, September 1). Derek Bok: Business lessons for education leaders. *Harvard Business School Working Knowledge*. Retrieved from http://hbswk.hbs.edu/ archive /3646.html

Tsay, C. H. H., Kofinas, A., & Luo, J. (2018). Enhancing student learning experience with technology-mediated gamification: An empirical study. *Computers & Education*, *121*, 1–17. doi:10.1016/j.compedu.2018.01.009

Tuan, L., & Doan, N. (2010). Teaching English Grammar through Games. *Studies in Literature & Language*, *1*(7), 61–75. cscanada.net/index.php/sll/article/ download/j.sll.1923156320100107.006/1463

Vygotsky, L. S. (1978). *Mind and Society: The Development of Higher Mental Processes*. Harvard University Press.

ADDITIONAL READING

Anderson, C. G., Campbell, K., & Steinkuehler, C. (2019). *Building persistence through failure*. doi:10.1145/3337722.3337741

Bedwell, W. L., Pavlas, D., Heyne, K., Lazzara, E. H., & Salas, E. (2012). Toward a Taxonomy Linking Game Attributes to Learning. *Simulation & Gaming*, *43*(6), 729–760. doi:10.1177/1046878112439444

Biggs, J. (1999). What the student does: Teaching for enhanced learning. *Higher Education Research & Development*, *18*(1), 57–75. doi:10.1080/0729436990180105

Deci, E., Vallerand, R., Pelletier, L., & Ryan, R. (1991). Motivation and Education: The Self-Determination Perspective. *Educational Psychologist*, *26*(3), 325–346. doi:10.120715326985ep2603&4_6

Duckworth, A. L., Peterson, C., Matthews, M. D., & Kelly, D. R. (2007). Grit: Perseverance and passion for long-term goals. *Journal of Personality and Social Psychology*, *92*(6), 1087–1101. doi:10.1037/0022-3514.92.6.1087 PMID:17547490

Dweck, C. (2016). What having a "growth mindset" actually means. *Harvard Business Review*, *13*(2), 2–5.

Gagne, M., & Deci, E. L. (2005). Self-Determination Theory and Work Motivation. *Journal of Organizational Behavior*, *26*(4), 331–362. doi:10.1002/job.322

Hamari, J. (2017). Do badges increase user activity? A field experiment on the effects of gamification. *Computers in Human Behavior*, *71*, 469–478. doi:10.1016/j.chb.2015.03.036

Morschheuser, B., Werder, K., Hamari, J., & Abe, J. (2017). How to gamify? A method for designing gamification. *Proceedings of the Annual Hawaii International Conference on System Sciences*, 1298–1307. 10.24251/HICSS.2017.155

Park, D., Tsukayama, E., Yu, A., & Duckworth, A. L. (2020). The development of grit and growth mindset during adolescence. *Journal of Experimental Child Psychology*, *198*, 104889. doi:10.1016/j.jecp.2020.104889 PMID:32629233

Thibodeaux, T., Harapnuik, D., & Cummings, C. (2019). Student Perceptions of the Influence of Choice, Ownership, and Voice in Learning and the Learning Environment. *International Journal on Teaching and Learning in Higher Education*, *31*(1), 50–62.

KEY TERMS AND DEFINITIONS

Accessibility: Capable of being reached.

Assessment: A belief that one's own culture is superior to other cultures.

Assignment Choice: The belief that family is central to wellbeing and that family members and family issues take precedence over other aspects of life.

Higher Education: Education beyond the secondary level provided by a college or university.

Learning: The activity or process of gaining knowledge or skill by studying or being taught something in a structured educational environment.

Pedagogy: The art, science, or profession of teaching.

Student Motivation: The act or process of giving someone participating in a instructional setting a reason for doing something academically.

Technology: Any device, software, or equipment that helps people learn, communicate, or function better.

Chapter 15
Gamification in the Space Sector:
How Gamification Activities Can Foster the Passion and Interest for STEM-Related Studies

Annalisa Galeone
https://orcid.org/0000-0003-0031-3077
Catholic University of the Sacred Heart, Italy

ABSTRACT

Firstly, the authors introduce the concept of gamification design applied to various contexts. Then, they discuss how the gamification approach is used within the space sector to develop online and offline resources to foster passion and interest in STEM-related subjects. Indeed, a decreasing number of students nowadays decide to take up STEM-related studies and careers. Therefore, following an edutainment logic, it is essential to design more gamification activities to increase students' motivation and engagement with STEM topics. Given this, they consider the cases of the videogames Kerbal Space Program (KSP) and MinecraftEdu, the ESA Kids website, Mission X, CanSat Competition, Moon Camp, Climate Detectives, Astro-Pi Challenge, and the ESERO Project. They also carry out a netnographic study on some social media pages. Moreover, they discuss how gamification activities may promote the company's corporate brand for NASA and the European Space Agency (ESA). Finally, they focus on the digital divide, which might limit the gamification methodology in approaching disadvantaged socio-economic countries.

INTRODUCTION

Tell me and I forget, teach me and I may remember, involve me and I learn. - Benjamin Franklin

Gamification is defined as "the use of game elements and game-design techniques in non-game contexts" (Deterding et al., 2011, p. 1) to encourage users' motivation, enjoyment, and engagement in perform-

DOI: 10.4018/978-1-6684-4287-6.ch015

ing a challenging task with the aim to achieve a specific goal (Patrício, Moreira, & Zurlo, 2018). On a business level, gamification can be applied to many different business functions including Marketing and Sales, Human Resources and Customer Service, with different impacts inside and outside the firm's boundaries (Patrício, Moreira, & Zurlo, 2018).

The aim of this book chapter is to describe how the gamification approach has been applied within the space sector with the goal to promote the study and passion for STEM (Science, Technology, Engineering and Mathematics) subjects. Therefore, beyond the mere illustration of specific cases, we will explain the advantages of using online and offline gamification activities as an educational source in primary, middle and secondary schools along within universities.

In the following paragraphs, we will go through the literature review about gamification, and cover more in detail the gamification activities carried out by the European Space Agency (ESA) and NASA (2021) to foster the passion and interest for STEM-related studies and careers. For example, we will discuss the case of the videogames Kerbal Space Program (KSP) (2021) and MinecraftEdu (2022), the ESA Kids (2021) website, Mission X (2021), CanSat (2021) competition, Moon Camp (2022), Climate Detectives (2022), Astro-Pi Challenge (2022), and the ESERO (2021) project (see table 1).

Primary and secondary data were collected thanks to the documentary reading carried out on several sources (see reference list at the end of the book chapter); a netnogrpahic study was carried out on Reddit (2022a; 2022b) and Quora (2022); the information was provided thanks to a traineeship within ESA Education Office in 2015 and my current job as contractor at ESTEC, the European Space Agency (ESA)'s technical heart in the Netherlands. Indeed, I carried out a participant observation study, working as an insider at ESA Education Office with the responsible people who are in charge still nowadays of managing the ESA Kids website, Mission X, the CanSat competition, Moon Camp, Climate Detectives, Astro-Pi Challenge, and the ESERO project (ESA Teach with Space Conference, 2021).

Furthermore, we will also consider how the gamification activities may have a positive influence on the corporate brand in terms of brand loyalty, brand awareness and brand love. Therefore, a netnographic analysis was carried out on Paxi's Facebook (2022) and Twitter (2022) pages to study the comments and reactions of the followers.

Finally, in the last part of the chapter, when discussing about future research directions, we will consider the topic of the digital divide which may become a limit in designing online gamification activities in developing countries.

LITERATURE REVIEW

Gamification is an essential tool for edutainment activities which aim to educate while having fun (Aksakal, 2015). Indeed, *edutainment* is a derived word which states the marriage of education with entertainment (Colace et al., 2006). Hence, gamification and edutainment are two concepts tightly linked together. On one hand, the edutainment formula has been employed to produce educational computer games over the years (Aksakal, 2015). On the other hand, gamification has been employed in the field of education as an edutainment activity within several contexts: physical education (Parra-González, 2021); engineering courses (Díaz-Ramírez, 2020); statistics education (Legaki, 2020); language learning, e.g., the educational app Duolingo (2021) counts 300 million active users (Legaki, 2020); and high school classes to teach algebra concepts (Faghihi, 2014). Specifically, the gamification method aims to "foster human motivation and performance in regard to a given activity" (Sailer et al., 2017).

Table 1. The cases analyzed throughout the book chapter

Case	Type	Developer	Target group	Benefits
Kerbal Space Program (KSP)	Videogame	Developed by Squad (2021) and published by Private Division (2021)	Space lovers: junior players (from 11 to 17 years-old) and adult players (from 18 years-old on).	-Realism of the videogame -Learn basic concepts on orbital mechanics, physics, math, and spacecraft design -User-friendly interface -Fun and engaging videogame
MinecraftEdu	Videogame	TeacherGaming (2021)	Primary and secondary school level	-User-friendly interface -Fun and engaging videogame -Learn concepts related to science, history & culture, math, art & design, digital citizenship, climate & sustainability, etc. -Suitable to all learning levels
ESA Kids	Website	Education Office - European Space Agency (ESA)	Kinder garden and primary school children from 4 years-old on	-User-friendly interface -Fun online and offline activities -Learn concepts about math, physics, biology, astronomy, etc. -Paxi, the mascot for a storytelling experience
Mission X	Challenge	Education Office - European Space Agency (ESA)	Students from 8 to 12 years-old	-Fun online and offline activities -Identify yourself with an astronaut -Learn how to keep fit and eat healthy -Promote group bonding and team building
CanSat competition	Competition	Education Office - European Space Agency (ESA)	Secondary school level	-Educational and fun offline activities -Learn the principles to build a small satellite -Promote group bonding and team building
Moon Camp	Challenge	Education Office - European Space Agency (ESA)	Primary and secondary school level	-Educational and fun offline activities -Promote group bonding and team building -Learn the principles to live on the Moon and 3D design a human shelter
Climate Detectives	Challenge	Education Office - European Space Agency (ESA)	Primary and secondary school level	-Learn to analyse Earth Observation data, identify a climate-related issue, and propose positive actions to monitor or mitigate the problem -Educational offline activities -Promote group bonding and team building
Astro-Pi Challenge	Challenge	Education Office - European Space Agency (ESA)	Upper primary/lower secondary school level	-Learn to design a scientific experiment, write the computer code to run it and have it operated on the International Space Station (ISS) -Educational online and offline activities -Promote group bonding and team building
ESERO project	Programme	Education Office - European Space Agency (ESA) and National Space Agencies or National Space Offices (depending on the country involved)	Primary and secondary school level	-User-friendly interface -Engaging online and offline activities -Learn concepts about math, physics, biology, astronomy, etc. -Present at national level in each country

Gamification applies different learning elements, such as game designs and structures (Attali & Arieli-Attali, 2015). This methodology is based on the increased capability of players to learn and retain information when they have fun while learning (Molina et al., 2017).

There are three main gamification categories: immersion-based gamification, social-based gamification, and achievement/challenge-based gamification (Xi & Hamari, 2020; Koivisto & Hamari, 2019). The immersion-based game design attempts primarily to engulf the player into a story and interpret a roleplay, e.g., using an avatar in a videogame like it happens with the aliens in Kerbal Space Program (KSP) (2021) and Paxi (2021) on the ESA Kids (2021) website. The social-based game design is focused on several forms of competition and/or collaboration: thanks to the teams and online communities, the player develops a sense of belonging to a group. Finally, the achievement/challenge-based game design is focused on overcoming challenges, progressing and earning rewards through points, leaderboards, levels and badges; experiencing a winning state which leads to social prestige as it happens to players of the Kerbal Space Program (KSP) (2021). According to the self-determination theory, these elements are considered as achievement-related features and immediate performance indicators leading to intrinsic motivation for players. Moreover, they also maximize the players' knowledge acquisition (Xi & Hamari, 2020; Koivisto & Hamari, 2019).

In particular, there are two types of motivation: extrinsic motivation which is derived from a goal, purpose, or reward; intrinsic motivation which is experienced by inherently enjoying the task itself. So, when designing gamification activities, it would be more effective to attract people into an experience with extrinsic rewards, and then ensure a long-term engagement moving toward more intrinsic motivators (Chou, 2016). Rewards are the most popular type of dynamic. By rewarding someone who has achieved a goal, their motivation and engagement will be boosted, thus, they will repeat their actions to make progress into a better condition. The other popular dynamic is role-playing. With role-playing, people can play as a character while following a scenario, exploring the world related to the game, choose activities to be completed in order to get rewards (Kusuma et al., 2018). For example, players can act as the aliens Kerbals in the videogame Kerbal Space Program (KSP) (2021) or the alien Paxi (2021) on the ESA Kids (2021) website.

Therefore, gamification is an interactive learning method, much more interesting compared to listening to lectures in class. This learning method, challenges the person in many ways: it gives the players reasons to keep trying and finishing a level or mission, which makes them motivated to keep learning at the same time; it makes the players curious because they must explore and discover the virtual world, they are playing in; the competition among players increases when they are assigned points (i.e., leaderboard) which prompts them to do always better in the videogame; players experience management-simulation by building their own spacecraft and completing their missions using the game resources (Kusuma et al., 2018); real-world forecasting problems (Legaki, 2020) when they apply their knowledge, skills and resources to evaluate, for instance, the flight risks before making their spacecraft fly as it happens in Kerbal Space Program (KSP) (2021). When the players overcome the challenges, they feel satisfaction and reach a sense of achievement and mastery. For example, in the videogame Kerbal Space Program (KSP) (2021), there are obstacles that players must overcome using their own characters, the Kerbals, while gathering objects to complete tasks, acquire knowledge and skills along the missions with the aim to make their spacecraft fly. Indeed, giving feedback to players for their actions makes them realise what is wrong and correct, thus, changing the course of their strategy to perform better in the future (Kusuma et al., 2018).

GAMIFICATION TO PROMOTE STEM SUBJECTS IN THE SPACE SECTOR

As Agency we have the duty to educate citizens and communicate with them. Kerbal Space Program is a perfect channel for doing both. This is important to us, because today's young players have the potential to become the engineers or astronauts of tomorrow. - Emmet Fletcher, Head of the ESA Branding and Partnerships Office, Wired, 2021

In education, gamification is used to increase the engagement and motivate students to learn. Specifically, gamification activities in the space industry have the aim to promote the study of STEM (Science, Technology, Engineering and Mathematics) subjects for primary and secondary school students. Indeed, gamification is increasingly employed in learning environments as a tool to enhance student motivation and consequent learning outcomes (Legaki et al., 2020). In fact, the gamification concept and its operationalisation in non-gaming contexts has become a growing practice in several contexts (Xi and Hamari, 2020). Therefore, gamification represents one of the greatest tendencies of the last decade, given the interest shown by organisations, which are seeking to increase the involvement and motivation of their audiences (Kotler, Kartajaya, and Setiawan, 2017; Shen et al., 2020). Indeed, gamification has shown to foster a high incrementation in the motivation, development of cooperative work, and problem-solving skills (López-Quintero, Pontes-Pedrajas, and Varo-Martínez, 2019).

Furthermore, gamification has been found to be positively associated with brand loyalty (Xi and Hamari, 2020), brand attitude (Yang, Asaad, and Dwivedi, 2017), brand awareness (Lucassen and Jansen, 2014), brand engagement (Berger, Schlager, Sprott, and Herrmann, 2017), brand involvement (Nobre and Ferreira, 2017) and brand love (Hsu and Chen, 2018). Indeed, as we will see more in detail in the following paragraph, the collaboration between NASA (2021), the European Space Agency (ESA) (2021) and the videogame company Squad (2021) positively affected the relationship between the players and their corporate brands. In fact, these two space agencies allowed Squad (2021) to insert in the videogame Kerbal Space Program (KSP) (2021) references to their space missions, spacecrafts, launch vehicles and corporate brands. All above-listed elements concur to develop a passionate attachment to the brands with the support of their loyal players.

The Case of the Videogames, Kerbal Space Program (KSP), and MinecraftEdu

Kerbal Space Program has already been an inspiration for an entire generation of future engineers and scientists - Daniel Neuenschwander, ESA's Director of Space Transportation, ESA, 2020

Kerbal Space Program (KSP) (2021) is a space flight simulation videogame developed by the Mexican multimedia company Squad (2021) and published by the American company Private Division (2021). The videogame was released in April 2015, and the sequel, Kerbal Space Program (KSP) 2, is expected to be launched in 2022. The game features a realistic orbital physics engine, allowing for various real-life orbital maneuvers such as Hohmann transfer orbit (i.e., an elliptical orbit used to transfer between two circular orbits of different radii around a central body in the same plane) and orbital rendezvous (i.e., a set of orbital maneuvers during which two spacecrafts, one of which is often a space station, arrive at the same orbit and approach to a very close distance).

In Kerbal Space Program (KSP) (2021) the players take charge of the space program for aliens known as the Kerbals. The player has access to a set of several parts to assemble fully functional spacecrafts that fly based on realistic aerodynamic and orbital physics. The Kerbal crew is launched into space with the aim to explore moons and planets in the Kerbol Solar System, constructing bases and space stations to expand the reach of the expedition.

Kerbal Space Program (KSP) (2021) features three gameplay modes: Science Mode, Career Mode and Sanbox. In Science Mode, the players can perform space experiments to unlock new technology and advance the knowledge of Kerbalkind. In Career Mode, the goal is to oversee every aspect of the space program, including construction, strategy, and funding. Finally, in Sandbox, the players use their skills and the technology in the game to build any spacecraft they can think of.

People and agencies in the space sector have taken an interest in the game, including NASA (2021), the European Space Agency (ESA) (2021), and the Rocket Lab (2021) (Wired, 2021).

The game takes inspiration from NASA (2021)'s space mission OSIRIS-REx (2021) (i.e., Origins, Spectral Interpretation, Resource Identification, Security, Regolith Explorer). The OSIRIS-REx (2021) spacecraft was launched in 2016 and traveled to the asteroid Bennu. It reached the asteroid in 2018 and it is now bringing a small sample back to Earth for study. OSIRIS-REx (2021) will reach Earth in 2023. Therefore, in the game, the players are challenged to use the virtual tools and supplies to construct their own OSIRIS-REx (2021) spacecraft with the aim to collect an asteroid sample and return it safely to Kerbin (NASA, 2016).

Thanks to the collaboration with the European Space Agency (2021), a new update, Shared Horizons (ESA, 2020), was released on 1st July 2020. Players are now able to build and launch European rockets. The game now features all stages, engines and systems of Ariane 5, Europe's launch vehicle that has been in operation since 1996 and has launched many ground-breaking science missions. The players can build a perfect Ariane 5 replica or create a hybrid by combining multiple rocket parts. Once their rocket is launched, players can navigate two new scenarios based on some of Europe's well-known science missions – the BepiColombo (2021) Mercury explorer and the Rosetta (2021) comet chaser (ESA, 2020).

The first new scenario is based on BepiColombo (2021), an ongoing joint mission between ESA (2021) and the Japan Aerospace Exploration Agency (JAXA, 2021), launched on an Ariane 5 rocket in 2018 and currently travelling to Mercury. Players attempt to reach orbit and land on Moho, the equivalent of Mercury in the Kerbal universe, while performing various scientific tasks from the actual ESA/JAXA mission such as mapping the celestial body's surface and magnetosphere.

The second scenario is based on Rosetta (2021), ESA'S iconic mission to Comet 67P/Churyumov-Gerasimenko. Launched in 2004, also on an Ariane 5 rocket, Rosetta (2021) travelled through the Solar System for ten years before reaching a two-lobed comet, dropping the Philae lander on its surface, and studying the comet for over two years. The mission gathered large amounts of data as the comet swung around the Sun, helping scientists to learn more about the role comets have in the evolution of the Solar System.

Kerbal Space Program (2021) also features some Rocket Lab (2021)'s launch vehicles such as Electron and Neutron (Peter Beck, 2021).

We carried out a netnographic analysis on Reddit (2022a; 2022b) and Quora (2022) to read about the experience of several teachers and players. In general, teachers agree that the Kerbal Space Program (KSP) (2021) is ideal to be used to introduce students to the basic concepts of the orbital mechanics. For example, a college math and physics teacher has been hosting every year a "Physics of rocketry" summer workshop for incoming first-year students and/or visiting high school students, using Kerbal Space Program (KSP) (2021) to teach the basics of orbits and orbital maneuvering. First, he has some preliminary discussion about the physics of why orbit works (i.e., gravitational force, centripetal force, equating the formulas) and explains the meaning of certain concepts (i.e., prograde, retrograde, radial, normal, pitch) using a toy X-Wing as a visual aid. Then he gathers the students in small groups in a computer lab to load up a saved KSP game with a small rocket already in orbit. The students try pointing the rocket in a certain direction, turn on engines, switch to map view so they can see how the orbital trajectory is changing, draw before/after sketches of their orbit, and repeat this experiment for each of the six directions. Once they get a general feel for what each maneuver does, they are asked to try changing their trajectory to get to the satellite Mun. After they have tried that for a while, the students load another saved KSP game with the same rocket plus launch vehicle on the launchpad and try to get to orbit. Once they figure that out, they are told to try putting it all together and go from Kerbin to Mun and back (Reddit, 2022a).

Someone else from the Civial Air Patrol (2022) used the Kerbal Space Program (KSP) (2021) to teach to middle schoolers how to get into space, getting to orbit, rendevous/docking, landing on the Moon, and spaceplanes (Reddit, 2022b). He formatted the sessions into a 20-minute presentation describing the basics of space flight and the characteristics of the corresponding NASA (2021) mission. Then the students split into groups of 5 to build a ship based on the instructions received and the lists of relevant parts. Sometimes the different groups get to compete to make the best design, sometimes they are asked to work together (i.e., one group has to design a probe whereas one group has to design the manned docking ship). Once finished, a student is asked to pilot the ship, and the rest of the group is told to debrief about flaws and strengths in the design (Reddit, 2022b).

In addition, some professors have used Kerbal Space Program (KSP) (2021) in aerospace engineering courses to introduce their students to orbital mechanics and assigning extra-credit questions on the exam (Reddit, 2022a; Quora, 2022). Whereas, someone working in a science museum also used the Kerbal Space Program (KSP) (2021) to host workshops about orbital mechanics for the children and their parents visiting the museum (Reddit, 2022a).

In view of the above-mentioned, we can state that Kerbal Space Program (KSP) (2021) has a strong educational element allowing players to gain a deeper understanding of orbital mechanics, rocket science and more in general of space exploration. Hence, the players are in control of their own learning and understanding of science, while keeping things appealing, interesting and fun. This makes Kerbal Space Program (KSP) (2021) a fantastic scientific teaching resource for teachers and research providers who are always looking to teach science in a fun and accessible way. Indeed, a fun leisure activity can help to pick up on tough subjects such as rocket science and orbital mechanics more naturally and easily.

Therefore, Kerbal Space Program (KSP) (2021) is used in many middle schools, secondary education institutions, and universities around the world through the partnership with the start-up TeacherGaming (2021) to help teachers to educate their students in science. The videogame was used to teach higher education physics in lessons revolving around circular motion and it has been used by students giving school presentations about astronomy (Kerbal Space Academy, 2021). Also, thanks to the virtual fieldtrips published on the website Kerbal Space Academy (2021), viewers can learn about space missions, space exploration technologies, and interact with astronauts, rocket scientists, and other guests.

Furthermore, according to the netnographic analysis carried out on Reddit (2022a; 2022b) and Quora (2022), several players affirmed that they started developing a deeper interest in NASA (2021) after playing with Kerbal Space Program (KSP) (2021) and started dreaming of becoming an aerospace engineer. Indeed, the mentions to NASA (2021)'s missions, its logo in the videogame, NASA (2021)'s spaceship components, and the realism of the videogame, helped players to develop a deeper bond with the brand NASA (2021). Therefore, all of the above-mentioned contributes to increase brand awareness

(Lucassen & Jansen, 2014), brand engagement (Berger et al., 2017) and brand loyalty (Xi & Hamari, 2020) with NASA (2021).

The start-up TeacherGaming (2021) also launched the Minecraft Education Edition (MinecraftEdu) which has been acquired by Microsoft (2022). MinecraftEdu (2022a) is a game-based learning platform that promotes creativity, collaboration and problem-solving in an immersive digital environment. Its aim is to bridge the gap between learning at school and learning with games (TechCrunch, 2018). Among the different worlds you can build in the videogame, you can also select space-themed activities. For example, to celebrate the 20th anniversary of the International Space Station (ISS) in space, MinecraftEdu (2022a) in 2020 partnered with NASA (2021). Therefore, the players had the possibility to design a new module for the space station and describe what hypothetical scientific experiments could be carried out (MinecraftEdu, 2022b). In another challenge, to celebrate the launch in 2020 of the Mars rover Perseverance, MinecraftEdu gave the players the possibility to build a Mars rover (MinecraftEdu, 2022c).

In addition, teachers can join the Minecraft Teacher Academy to take free courses and become a Minecraft-certified teacher with the aim to learn how to use MinecraftEdu (2022a) to teach in class. The teacher needs to progress in three different levels (i.e., Beginner, Intermediate, Advanced) to earn the Minecraft-certified Teacher badge (MinecraftEdu, 2022d).

An interesting study has been conducted with six primary schools in Australia to understand the impact of MinecraftEdu (2022a) in the math classroom (MinecraftEdu, 2022e; Digital Media Research Centre, 2020a; 2022b). In 2019, MinecraftEdu (2022a) partnered with the Queensland University of Technology's Digital Media Research Centre (2020a) in Australia to understand the impact that MinecraftEdu (2022a) can have for younger students as they learn mathematics. Researchers were eager to examine the ways that engagement was built thanks to the videogame's environment. To make sure the activities were aligned to the Australian curriculum and accompanied by accessible support materials, the team chose the *Algebra Architecture* and *Area and Volume* lessons. The *Algebra Architecture* lesson explores math models to learn about arithmetic patterns, and students use this knowledge to build architectural designs. *Area and Volume* encourages learners to create and solve problems involving spatial mathematics. The videogame was used by the teachers to illustrate concepts like scale, addition, multiplication, area, volume, and perimeter. After a three-month study, students showed remarkable progress in both their understanding of math and their confidence around the subject (Digital Media Research Centre, 2020a; 2022b). Indeed, according to the educators who used this videogame with their students, MinecraftEdu (2022a) is a creative way to synthesize understanding of maths concepts, engage all learners, and to provide open-ended activities to cater to all learning levels, making it possible to scaffold for students who need more support. The students affirmed that they would have liked to use MinecraftEdu (2022a) again for math learning because they felt their understanding of math concepts had grown after using the videogame and it made learning maths fun. In addition, the students felt very comfortable in the digital environment and their overall experience was reported to be overwhelmingly positive (Digital Media Research Centre, 2020a; 2022b).

Gamification Activities Carried out by the European Space Agency (ESA)

Hi! My name is Paxi. I'm an explorer from another planet. I've parked my spaceship in orbit and parachuted down to Earth to meet you. My home planet orbits a star not too far from your Sun, so you could say we are neighbours. - Paxi, the alien and mascot of the ESA Kids website, ESA Kids, 2021

"The importance of sustaining students' motivation has been a longstanding challenge to education" (Dichev & Dicheva, 2017). Therefore, there has been a growing interest in gamification since 2013 which has grown rapidly thereafter (Subhash & Cudney, 2018). In the education context, gamification refers to the introduction of game design elements and gameful experiences in the design of learning processes (ibid). This is an active-learning approach (García-Peñalvo et al., 2019) with the aim to motivate and engage students in their learning process by incorporating game design principles, hoping that emotions such as fun, derived from games, can put the players in a "receptive frame of mind for learning" (Demkah & Bhargava, 2019). The benefits derived from the gamification approach include an improvement in the academic performance, more engagement and motivation, and better attitude (ibid).

Nowadays a decreasing number of young people decide to take up STEM-related studies and careers (ESERO, 2021). Consequently, one of the goals of the European Space Agency (ESA) is to make a difference and reverse this negative trend through an education program which targets European students starting from an early age. In particular, ESA is addressing primary and secondary education in Europe through the activities of the ESA Education Office (2021).

Gamification can be developed, utilising various technological resources or didactic resources (Parra-González et al., 2021). The range of gamification possibilities is broad and has various application forms (White Shellenbarger, 2018). The ESA Education Office (2021) has launched the ESA Kids (2021) website, a portal which targets primary school children from 3 to 12-years old. This is an e-learning portal dedicated to the alien Paxi (2021) with many didactic resources, mostly presented with a gamification approach. Paxi (2021) is the website's mascot. He is a friendly green and red alien who introduces children to fun and educational activities related to space and STEM subjects. The ESA Kids (2021) website is divided into the following sections: Learn, News, Things to do, Multimedia, Teachers, Games, Language and Search. The website is available in five different European languages, and you can switch from a language to another one through the "Language" section.

In the "Learn", "Things to do" and "Multimedia" sections, students can read or watch videos about several space-related topics and learn about the Solar System, the Universe, the Moon, the Sun, Earth, Mars, the stars, gravity, and much more. Whereas in the "News" sections, children can keep up to date by reading the most recent news about the space missions.

In the "Teachers" section, schoolteachers can download learning materials to teach geography, mathematics, science, art and design, literacy, social studies, and biology. For example, students can learn about "Astrofarmer", the conditions for plant growth on Earth and in space; "Astrofood", the edible plants in space; how to build a bionic hand; how to extract water on the Moon; and the history of the Universe. Teachers can also apply for the ESA Teachers' Workshop or join the e-technology lab. The Teachers' Workshop features keynote lectures from top-level space experts and visits at the European Space Research and Technology Centre (ESTEC) in the Netherlands. Over the course of a four-day programme, participants engage in practical training sessions that demonstrate how to use space in the classroom as an inspirational context. The e-technology lab workshop uses a range of educational technology tools (i.e., LEGO education, Raspberry Pi and Arduino) within the space context to enable teachers to engage and inspire their students in STEM subjects.

In the section called "Games", primary school students have the possibility to choose among seven different games to play with: Space Cleanup, Solar System Explorer, Colour with Paxi, Catch the craft, Milky Way Match, Spacecraft Assemble, and Space Memory Game. Children can play with these games on their laptop and/or mobile by downloading the mobile app available on the website. Thanks to the use of these gamification activities, children learn about STEM or space-related topics (i.e., the Sun, the Universe, the Moon, Mars, Earth, the Solar System) while having fun always accompanied by Paxi (2021), the explorer from another planet (ESA Kids, 2021). One of the aims of the ESA Education Office (2021) is to make gamification part of the formal education setting. Indeed, the philosophy of ESA Kids (2021) is to learn while having fun.

The ESA Kids (2021) team is active on the social media through Paxi's Facebook (2022) and Twitter (2022) pages. Therefore, a netnographic analysis was carried out on Paxi's Facebook (2022) and Twitter (2022) pages. According to the results, thanks to the ESA Kids (2021) website and Paxi (2021), children develop a brand interest (Nobre & Ferreira, 2017) and love (Hsu & Chen, 2018) with the European Space Agency (ESA) since an early age and even beyond European borders. Indeed, many primary, middle, and secondary school students from all over the world follow with great interest Paxi's adventures posted on his social media pages. Paxi's Facebook (2022) page counts 11,000 followers and Paxi's Twitter (2022) page counts 5,670 followers. Indeed, a mascot-themed social media page helps to create a nice storytelling, and a fun and engaging way to present space-related information to the children. Hence, children learn in a creative way while having fun (Sciamarelli, 2015). Several children send their drawings to Paxi's competitions demonstrating passion and love for space since an early age. The entries to the drawing competitions come from all over the world: Europe (i.e., Germany, Italy, France, Luxembourg, the Netherlands, Spain, Portugal), Turkey, Brazil, India, and the United Emirates, to mention some of them. In addition, many teachers use the ESA Kids (2021) website to find inspiring hands-on activities to be carried out in class with their students. Also, the Teachers' Workshop organised every year in Autumn and Spring in ESTEC (i.e., the European Space Agency's (ESA) technical heart), helps to create a deeper bond with the primary and secondary school teachers who come from all over Europe to gather for the workshop in the Netherlands.

The ESA Kids (2021) website is part of the activities of the European Space Education Resource Office (ESERO) project (ibid). The ESERO (2021) project helps to stimulate young people's awareness of Europe's space programme and of its importance for modern society and economy. The most effective form of space-based education must be the one that supports the specific educational needs of the various Member States, all having different educational systems, different school curricula and languages. To that end, the ESEROs are distributed across Member States, and staffed by local experts who work in partnership with their national education authorities and networks. Currently, ESA has established eighteen ESERO (2021) national offices in its Member States: Austria, Belgium, Czech Republic, Denmark, Estonia, France, Germany, Ireland, Italy, Luxembourg, Finland, Netherlands, Norway, Poland, Portugal, Romania, Spain, and the UK.

ESERO (2021) uses space related themes and the fascination felt by young people for space to enhance school pupils' literacy and competence in STEM-related subjects; it highlights the associated applications from space and raises awareness of the large range of career prospects in the space domain. Hence, ESERO (2021) disseminates space-related STEM classroom resources with this aim. By using the space context to make the teaching and learning of STEM subjects more attractive and accessible, students feel more comfortable and familiar with sciences in general. The ESERO (2021) activities help bring STEM subjects within the pupils reach, demolishing the misconception that science is only for geniuses. According to the ESERO (2021) project, the ESA Kids (2021) website is very popular among primary school children. It can be a valid complementary support for primary school teachers looking into innovative ways to engage their young students with gamification space-related topics. These resources provide students with content in a motivating way and encourage them to actively build their own learning. This leads to meaningful learning that is better remembered by students (Ayén, 2017).

The gamification approach is not restricted to digital tools such as software for computers and smartphones (Patrício et al., 2020). It can be developed for other educational resources which will be used offline. Indeed, each ESERO (2021) member state has its own website translated in the national language and with several learning resources divided per age range. For example, on ESERO UK (2021), 14 year-old students, learn how to design and build their own paper rockets and launch them. They learn what it takes for a rocket to be stable, and they can calculate the rocket's trajectory and velocity. Students learn about the velocity required to leave Earth in a rocket and uncover why the Moon has the potential to be a stepping-stone for further space exploration. Lastly, they calculate the acceleration of their rocket at launch and put this into a context of the g-force experienced by astronauts during launch (ESERO UKb, 2021). This is just one of the many learning resources and activities available on ESERO UK (ESERO UKc, 2021).

The ESEROs also encourage and promote the participation to European competitions organised by the European Space Agency (ESA) (2021): the CanSat (2021) competition, Mission X (2021), Moon Camp (2022), Climate Detectives (2022), and Astro-Pi Challenge (2022).

The CanSat (2021) competition provides secondary school students with the opportunity to have practical experience working on a small-scale space project. A CanSat is a simulation of a real satellite, integrated within the volume and shape of a soft drink can. The challenge for the students is to fit all major subsystems found in a satellite, such as power, sensors, and a communication system, into this minimal volume (ESERO UKd, 2021). The CanSat competition can be considered as a social-based gamification activity which focuses on forms of collaboration in teams; and it is also based on the achievement/challenge-based game design, focused on overcoming challenges, progressing and earning rewards until students succeed to fly their CanSat experiencing a winning state.

Mission X (2021) is an international educational challenge that focuses on health, science, fitness, and nutrition and encourages pupils to train like an astronaut. Mission X (2021) is designed for students 8-12 years-old, but open to all ages. The challenge is open worldwide and it is supported by a set of physical and educational hands-on classroom activities, developed by space scientists and fitness professionals working with real astronauts. Therefore, teams of students complete Mission X activities to earn points. Every submitted activity helps the Mission X (2021)'s mascots, Luna and Leo, to walk closer to the Moon until they reach it. Each year, the "Walk To The Moon Challenge" runs from January to May (ESERO UKe, 2021). Mission X (2021) presents the characteristics of an immersion-based game design since the students identify themselves (Kusuma et al., 2018) with the mascots Luna and Leo who aim for the Moon. It also has the characteristics of a social-based game design since students are encouraged to form teams and collaborate to complete the challenge (Xi & Hamari, 2020; Koivisto & Hamari, 2019). Finally, Mission X (2021) has also an achievement/challenge-based game design focused on overcoming challenges, progressing, and earning rewards until they reach the Moon with Luna and Leo (Xi & Hamari, 2020; Koivisto & Hamari, 2019).

Moon Camp (2022) is a challenge organised in collaboration with Airbus Foundation (2022). Primary and secondary school students learn what it takes to live on the Moon and 3D design a human shelter on its surface.

Climate Detectives (2022) is an ESA school project for students between 8 and 15 years old. Students are challenged to 'make a difference' in understanding and protecting Earth's climate. They will identify a climate problem by observing their local environment and be tasked to investigate it. They will use available Earth Observation data or take measurements on the ground. Based on their investigation, teams will propose a way to help monitor or reduce the problem. At the end, all participating teams will share their research findings on the Climate Detectives (2022) website. At key phases of the project, scientists, and experts in the field of Earth Observation and climate will support the teams.

Finally, Astro-Pi Challenge (2022) is a challenge for upper primary/lower secondary school students. They are asked to design a scientific experiment, write the computer code to run it and have it operated on the International Space Station (ISS). Within the Astro-Pi Challenge (2022), students can choose between *Mission Zero* which targets primary school pupils and only takes one hour to be completed, and *Mission Space Lab* which targets secondary school students and takes six months to conduct the experiment. This challenge is organised in collaboration with the Raspberry Pi Foundation (2022).

SOLUTIONS AND RECOMMENDATIONS

The importance of sustaining students' motivation has always been a challenge within the education field (Dichev & Dicheva, 2017). Therefore, there has been a growing interest in gamification since 2013 which has grown rapidly thereafter (Subhash & Cudney, 2018). This is an active-learning approach (García-Peñalvo et al., 2019) with the aim to motivate and engage students in their learning process by incorporating game design principles, hoping that emotions such as fun, derived from games, can put the players in a "receptive frame of mind for learning" (Demkah & Bhargava, 2019).

Specifically, the gamification approach has several advantages in terms of hedonic outcomes (i.e., engagement, enjoyment, and fun), utilitarian benefits (i.e., academic performance, increased productivity, creative problem-solving, sense of usefulness), and social benefits (i.e., recognition, social influence, and self-esteem) (Patrício, Moreira, & Zurlo, 2018).

Consequently, given the advantages of this approach, it would be advisable to design and implement even more online and offline gamification activities to promote the interest and study of STEM-related subjects. Therefore, we would need to invest more in companies or start-ups like TeacherGaming (2021) which launched the Minecraft Education Edition (MinecraftEdu, 2022a) with the aim to bridge the gap between learning at school and learning with games (TechCrunch, 2018). Indeed, Microsoft (2022) spotted this business opportunity and has acquired MinecraftEdu (2022a) launching the Minecraft Teacher Academy (MinecraftEdu, 2022d) to teach teachers how to use MinecraftEdu (2022a) in classroom with their students (TechCrunch, 2018). Research shows that the primary school children who have been using MinecraftEdu (2022a) to learn math concepts, have shown a positive response in terms of knowledge increase, self-confidence and felt very comfortable in learning in a digital environment (Digital Media Research Centre, 2020a; 2022b). Therefore, the students experienced extrinsic motivation which was derived from achieving a goal or reward while progressing in the videogame; and intrinsic motivation which was experienced by inherently enjoying the task of learning math while having fun in playing MinecraftEdu (2022). So, when designing gamification activities, it would be more effective to attract players into an experience with extrinsic rewards, and then ensure a long-term engagement moving toward more intrinsic motivators (Chou, 2016).

Moreover, it is extremely important to find new ways to encourage students to apply for STEM-related careers, for example within the space sector. We advise to design also offline gamification activities otherwise students from developing countries run the risk to be cut out since their internet connection is not always ensured. For example, the internet penetration in Nigeria stands at 42%, implying that more than half of the population is not connected to the Internet (International Telecommunication Union, 2019). Luckily, the gamification methodology is not restricted to digital tools such as software for computers and smartphones (Patrício et al., 2020). It can be employed to develop educational resources which will be used offline as shown with the educational materials available on the ESERO (2021) and ESA Kids (2021) websites, and the Mission X (2021), CanSat (2021) competition, and Moon Camp (2022), organised by the European Space Agency (ESA) (2021).

In addition, gamification may play an essential role in promoting a company's corporate brand since it has been found that it is positively associated with brand loyalty (Xi & Hamari, 2020), brand attitude (Yang, Asaad, & Dwivedi, 2017), brand awareness (Lucassen & Jansen, 2014), brand engagement (Berger at al., 2017), brand involvement (Nobre & Ferreira, 2017) and brand love (Hsu & Chen, 2018). Indeed, as shown from the results of our netnographic study on Reddit (2022) and Quora (2022), the collaboration between NASA (2021), the European Space Agency (ESA) (2021) and the videogame companies Squad (2021) and TeacherGaming (2021) positively affected the relationship between the players and their corporate brands. In fact, the two space agencies allowed the videogame companies to insert references to their space missions, spacecrafts, launch vehicles and corporate brands. All above-listed elements concurred to develop a passionate attachment to these brands with the support of their loyal gamers.

According to the results of the netnographic analysis on Paxi's (2022) Facebook and Twitter (2022) pages, children developed a deep brand engagement (Berger et al., 2017), brand involvement (Nobre & Ferreira, 2017) and brand love (Hsu & Chen, 2018) with ESA because they enjoy performing the educational activities accompanied by Paxi, the alien mascot of the ESA Kids (2021) website. Children from all over the world follow Paxi on his social media pages and demonstrate their affection and engagement by sending their drawings to join drawing competitions. Paxi (2021) helps to develop a fun and engaging storytelling experience for the children who bond with the character. Indeed, the benefits of project-based teaching with mascots are numerous: creativity is essential for learning, and with mascot-inspired projects it is developed and not forced (Sciamarelli, 2015); thematically organised materials are easier to remember and learn (Singer, 1990). Therefore, we suggest developing online and offline gamification activities with a mascot to guide the learners because teaching children with mascot-inspired projects is teaching children through play. Children learn better through play, being curious, exploring things and sharing them with others (Sciamarelli, 2015).

FUTURE RESEARCH DIRECTIONS

Nowadays a decreasing number of young students decide to take up STEM-related studies and careers (ESERO, 2021). Consequently, one of the aims of the European Space Agency (2021) and other international organisations is to make a difference and reverse this negative trend. This is done thanks to various means which include online, and offline educational resources designed according to a gamification logic to address primary and secondary students. Indeed, gamification can be developed, utilising various technological or didactic resources (Parra-González et al., 2021). The range of gamification possibilities is broad and has various application forms (White Shellenbarger, 2018). Furthermore, following the results of our netnographic study on Paxi's (2022) Facebook and Twitter (2022) pages, we suggest focusing on developing mascot-based educational materials because there are several advantages: children engage, have fun, and learn while playing and identifying themselves with the mascot (Sciamarelli, 2015).

At the same time, future research needs to consider the digital divide when designing gamification activities in the education field. The digital divide is defined as "a division between people who have access and use of digital media, and those who do not" (Van Dijk, 2020, p. 1). There are three main gap impact areas: economic (i.e., absence of technology), usability (i.e., difficulty in using the technology), and empowerment (i.e., not being able to realise the technology potential for self-empowerment) (Gandolfi, Ferdig, & Kratcoski, 2021).

Nowadays, Information Communication Technologies (ICT) usage is considered as a basic utility that is comparable to electricity, water, and gas (Walton et al., 2013). In 2019, about 53.6% of the world's population (i.e., 4.1 billion people) were reported to be using the Internet (International Telecommunication Union, 2020). People from most developing countries have gained access to digital technology through lower mobile prices (Naik et al., 2012) as well as reduced costs of infrastructure, equipment, and internet accessibility through smartphones (Donner, 2015). This has contributed to partially bridge the digital divide in several countries.

However, the digital divide increased in several countries during the COVID19 pandemic. Hence, it became even more timely and important to tackle this gap and foster digital inclusion. Many governments instituted a shutdown of their economies which led to the closure of traditional school services. About 1.6 billion learners in 190 countries across the world were affected by the pandemic, with 94% of the world's school population impacted by school closures (United Nations, 2020). In response to this education emergency, each country instituted measures to cushion the effect of the school closures by implementing various learning interventions using technological platforms, internet-based tools, and traditional media. However, many students around the world, especially those living in disadvantaged socioeconomic backgrounds, could not attend their online classes due to a lack of ICT tools (ex. no laptop, no tablet, no internet connection, etc.). For example, this was the case of many Nigerian students. Indeed, according to the International Telecommunication Union (2019), internet penetration in Nigeria stands at 42%, implying that more than half of the population is not connected to the Internet. Children from poorer socioeconomic backgrounds tend to have limited access to internet connectivity, computers, mobile phones, functional ICT skills and active parental support (Azubuike et al., 2021). The inequity in access to ICT-based learning has the adverse effect of further intensifying the existing disparities in learning outcomes along socioeconomic and geographic (i.e., urban-rural) areas (United Nations, 2020). For example, Chair and De Lannoy (2018)'s study of Nigeria, Tanzania and Rwanda showed that young people especially in rural areas, were deprived of internet resources due to low-level of education, low income and lack of digital skills. On the other hand, also in more developed countries such as the United States, the learning technologies disparity was exacerbated during the pandemic. In fact, low-income students and families were particularly disadvantaged in accessing hardware and software technologies to support teaching and learning (Gandolfi, Ferdig, & Kratcoski, 2021).

Consequently, future research on gamification design needs to take into consideration also the digital divide gap which still needs to be filled in. This gap needs to be addressed in future research since it can be an opportunity to innovate and reduce the socioeconomic disparities. Hence, it would be advisable to invest in the gamification design of both online and offline resource materials to mitigate the digital divide.

Finally, although this is not the focus of this book chapter, it is important to remind that on a business level, gamification can be applied as well to different business functions including Marketing and Sales, Human Resources and Customer Service, with different impacts inside and outside the firm's boundaries (Patrício, Moreira, & Zurlo, 2018). Subsequently, it would be advisable to invest more in the future on the design of gamification activities at several corporate levels.

CONCLUSION

In this book chapter, we focused on how the gamification approach may have the important role to promote the passion, interest, and study of STEM-related subjects within the space sector. Indeed, gamification is an essential tool for edutainment activities which aim to educate while having fun (Aksakal, 2015). Unfortunately, nowadays a decreasing number of young students decide to take up STEM-related studies and careers (ESERO, 2021). Consequently, one of the goals of the European Space Agency (2021) and other international organisations is to make a difference and reverse this negative trend. This is done thanks to various means which include online, and offline educational resources designed according to a gamification logic to address primary and secondary students. In truth, gamification can be developed, utilising various technological resources or didactic resources (Parra-González et al., 2021). The range of gamification possibilities is broad and has various application forms (White Shellenbarger, 2018).

Therefore, we focused on the videogames Kerbal Space Program (KSP) (2021) and MinecraftEdu (2022a), the ESERO (2021) project, Mission X (2021), CanSat (2021) competition, Moon Camp (2022), Climate Detectives (2022), Astro Pi Challenge (2022), and the ESA Kids (2021) website. All these means contribute to increase engagement and motivation in the students and players to achieve their goals. Indeed, research shows that gamification has several advantages in terms of hedonic outcomes (i.e., engagement, enjoyment, and fun), utilitarian benefits (i.e., academic performance, increased productivity, creative problem-solving, sense of usefulness), and social benefits (i.e., recognition, social influence, and self-esteem) (Patrício, Moreira, & Zurlo, 2018).

Moreover, gamification is an important asset for corporate brands since it may influence brand loyalty (Xi & Hamari, 2020), brand attitude (Yang, Asaad, & Dwivedi, 2017), brand awareness (Lucassen & Jansen, 2014), brand engagement (Berger, Schlager, Sprott, & Herrmann, 2017), brand involvement (Nobre & Ferreira, 2017) and brand love (Hsu & Chen, 2018). Consequently, the collaboration between NASA (2021), the European Space Agency (ESA) (2021) and the videogame companies Squad (2021) and TeacherGaming (2022) positively affected the relationship between the players and their corporate brands. In fact, the two space agencies allowed these companies to insert references to their space missions in the videogames (e.g., in Kerbal Space Program (KSP) (2021) they inserted references to Rosetta (2021), Bepicolombo (2021), OSIRIS-REx (2021), spacecrafts, launch vehicles such as Ariane 5, and corporate brands). In addition, according to the netnographic analysis carried out on Reddit (2022a; 2022b) and Quora (2022), several players affirmed that they started developing a deeper interest in NASA (2021) after playing with Kerbal Space Program (KSP) (2021) and started dreaming of becoming an aerospace engineer. Indeed, the mentions to NASA (2021)'s missions, its logo in the videogame, NASA (2021)'s spaceship components, and the realism of the videogame, helped players to develop a deeper bond with the brand NASA (2021). All above-listed elements concur to develop a passionate attachment to these space brands with the support of their loyal fans.

According to the results of the netnographic analysis on Paxi's (2022) Facebook and Twitter (2022) pages, children developed a deep brand engagement (Berger et al., 2017), brand involvement (Nobre & Ferreira, 2017) and brand love (Hsu & Chen, 2018) with ESA because they enjoy performing the educational activities accompanied by Paxi, the alien mascot of the ESA Kids (2021) website. Indeed, the benefits of project-based teaching with mascots are numerous: children learn while playing and having fun in a creative way (Sciamarelli, 2015).

Finally, future research within the gamification field, should bear in mind the existence of the digital divide which might represent an obstacle for online-based gamification activities. Therefore, it would be useful to work on developing offline gamification resources to mitigate the gap between advanced economic countries and disadvantaged socioeconomic countries.

ACKNOWLEDGMENT

This research received no specific grant from any funding agency in the public, commercial, or not-for-profit sectors.

A lot of the information provided in this book chapter derives from the traineeship period in 2015 at ESA Education Office, and from further information collected more recently thanks to my current job as Change and Adoption Officer for ATG Europe B.V. at ESTEC, the European Space Agency (ESA)'s technical heart in the Netherlands. I thank the ESA Education Office for the traineeship opportunity in 2015 which helped me to write this book chapter focusing on the ESA Kids website, Mission X, the CanSat competition, Moon Camp, Climate Detectives, Astro-Pi Challenge, and the ESERO project.

REFERENCES

Airbus Foundation. (2022). *Homepage.* Available at https://www.airbus.com/en/sustainability/airbus-foundation

Aksakal, N. (2015). Theoretical View to The Approach of The Edutainment. *Procedia: Social and Behavioral Sciences, 186*, 1232–1239. doi:10.1016/j.sbspro.2015.04.081

Astro-Pi Challenge. (2022). *Homepage.* Available at https://astro-pi.org/

Attali, Y., & Arieli-Attali, M. (2015). Gamification in assessment: Do points affect test performance? *Computers & Education, 83*(4), 57–63. doi:10.1016/j.compedu.2014.12.012

Ayén, F. (2017). ¿Qué es la gamificación y el ABJ? Iber: Didáctica de las ciencias sociales. *Geografía e Historia, 1*(86), 7–15.

Azubuike, O. B., Adegboye, O., & Quadri, H. (2021). Who gets to learn in a pandemic? Exploring the digital divide in remote learning during the COVID-19 pandemic in Nigeria. *International Journal of Educational Research Open, 2*(2), 1–10. doi:10.1016/j.ijedro.2020.100022 PMID:35059664

Bepicolombo. (2021). *Bepicolombo overview.* Available at https://www.esa.int/Science_Exploration/Space_Science/BepiColombo_overview2

Berger, A., Schlager, T., Sprott, D. E., & Herrmann, A. (2017). Gamified interactions: Whether, when, and how games facilitate self–brand connections. *Journal of the Academy of Marketing Science, 81*(2), 1–22.

CanSat. (2021). *Homepage.* Available at https://www.esa.int/Education/CanSat

Chair, C., & De Lannoy, A. (2018). *Youth, deprivation and the internet in Africa.* Https://researchictafrica.net/after-access-survey-papers/2018/After_Access:_youth_and_digital_inequality_in_Africa.pdf

Chou, Y.-K. (2016). Actionable gamification: Beyond points, badges, and leaderboards. Octalysis Media.

Civil Air Patrol. (2022). https://www.gocivilairpatrol.com/

Climate Detectives. (2022). https://climatedetectives.esa.int/

Colace, F., De Santo, M., & Pietrosanto, A. (2006). Work in Progress: Bayesian Networks for Edutainment. *36th ASEE/IEEE Frontiers in Education Conference*.

Demkah, M., & Bhargava, D. (2019). Gamification in education: a cognitive psychology approach to cooperative and fun learning. *Proceedings - 2019 Amity International Conference on Artificial Intelligence*. 10.1109/AICAI.2019.8701264

Deterding, S., Dixon, D., Khaled, R., & Nacke, L. (2011). From game design elements to gamefulness: defining gamification. *Proceedings of the 15th International Academic MindTrek Conference: Envisioning Future Media Environments*. 10.1145/2181037.2181040

Díaz-Ramírez, J. (2020). Gamification in engineering education – An empirical assessment on learning and game performance. *Heliyon*, *6*(9), 1–10. doi:10.1016/j.heliyon.2020.e04972 PMID:32995639

Dichev, C., & Dicheva, D. (2017). Gamifying education: what is known, what is believed and what remains uncertain: a critical review. *International Journal of Educational Technology in Higher Education*, *14*(9), 1–36. doi:10.118641239-017-0042-5

Digital Media Research Centre. (2020a). *M:EE – Minecraft for Educational Impact*. Available at https://research.qut.edu.au/dmrc/projects/mee-minecraft-for-educational-impact/

Digital Media Research Centre. (2020b). *Project Publication - Minecraft: Education Edition for Educational Impact*. Available at https://research.qut.edu.au/dmrc/wp-content/uploads/sites/5/2019/10/MEE-Research.pdf

Duolinguo. (2021). https://www.duolingo.com/

ESA. (2020). *Kerbal includes Ariane 5 and real ESA missions for gamers*. Available at https://www.esa.int/About_Us/Partnerships/Kerbal_includes_Ariane_5_and_real_ESA_missions_for_gamers

ESA Education Office. (2021). *Education*. Available at https://www.esa.int/Education

ESA Kids. (2021). https://www.esa.int/kids/en/learn

ESA Teach with Space Conference. (2021). https://educationforms.esa.int/booklet.pdf

ESERO. (2021). *European Space Education Resource Office*. Available at https://www.esa.int/Education/Teachers_Corner/European_Space_Education_Resource_Office

ESERO UK. (2021). https://www.stem.org.uk/esero

ESERO UKb. (2021). *Quality assured 3...2...1...lift off! - Building your own paper rock*. Available at https://www.stem.org.uk/resources/elibrary/resource/460411/321lift-building-your-own-paper-rocket

ESERO UKc. (2021). *Resources*. Available at https://www.stem.org.uk/esero/resources

ESERO UKd. (2021). *Cansat*. Available at https://www.stem.org.uk/esero/cansat

ESERO UKe. (2021). *Mission X*. Available at https://www.stem.org.uk/missionx

European Space Agency. (2021). https://www.esa.int/

Faghihi, U., Brautigam, A., Jorgenson, K., Martin, D., Brown, A., Measures, E., & Maldonando-Bouchard, S. (2014). How Gamification Applies for Educational Purpose Specially with College Algebra. *Procedia Computer Science*, *41*, 182–187. doi:10.1016/j.procs.2014.11.102

Gandolfi, E., Ferdig, R. E., & Kratcoski, A. (2021). A new educational normal an intersectionality-led exploration of education, learning technologies, and diversity during COVID-19. *Technology in Society*, *66*(8), 1–8. doi:10.1016/j.techsoc.2021.101637

García-Peñalvo, F. J., Alarcón, H., & Dominguez, A. (2019). Active learning experiences in engineering education. *International Journal of Engineering Education*, *35*(1), 305–309.

Hsu, C. L., & Chen, M. C. (2018). How gamification marketing activities motivate desirable consumer behaviors: Focusing on the role of brand love. *Computers in Human Behavior*, *88*(11), 121–133. doi:10.1016/j.chb.2018.06.037

International Telecommunication Union (ITU). (2019). *Measuring digital development: Facts and figures 2019*. https://www.itu.int/en/ITU-D/Statistics/Documents/facts/FactsFigures2019.pdf

JAXA. (2021). https://global.jaxa.jp/.

Kerbal Space Program (KSP). (2021). https://www.kerbalspaceprogram.com/

Koivisto, J., & Hamari, J. (2019). The rise of motivational information systems: A review of gamification research. *International Journal of Information Management*, *45*(4), 191–210. doi:10.1016/j.ijinfomgt.2018.10.013

Kotler, P., Hermanwan, K., & Iwan, S. (2016). *Marketing 4.0: Moving from traditional to digital*. John Wiley & Sons Inc.

Kusuma, G. P., Wigati, E. K., Utomo, Y., & Suryapranata, L. K. P. (2018). Analysis of Gamification Models in Education Using MDA Framework. *Procedia Computer Science*, *135*, 385–392. doi:10.1016/j.procs.2018.08.187

Legaki, N. Z., Xi, N., Hamari, J., Karpouzis, K., & Assimakopoulos, V. (2020). The effect of challenge-based gamification on learning: An experiment in the context of statistics education. *International Journal of Human-Computer Studies*, *144*(12), 1–14. doi:10.1016/j.ijhcs.2020.102496 PMID:32565668

López-Quintero, J. L., Pontes-Pedrajas, A., & Varo-Martínez, M. (2019). Las TIC en la enseñanza científico-tecnica hispanoamericana: Una revisión bibliográfica. *Digitital Education Review*, *35*(6), 229–243. doi:10.1344/der.2019.35.229-243

Lucassen, G., & Jansen, S. (2014). Gamification in consumer marketing-future or fallacy? *Procedia: Social and Behavioral Sciences*, *148*, 194–202. doi:10.1016/j.sbspro.2014.07.034

Microsoft. (2022). https://www.microsoft.com/it-it

MinecraftEdu. (2022a). https://education.minecraft.net/en-us/homepage

MinecraftEdu. (2022b). *International Space Station*. Available at https://education.minecraft.net/en-us/challenges/a-visit-to-the-international-space-station

MinecraftEdu. (2022c). *Build a Mars rover*. Available at https://education.minecraft.net/en-us/challenges/build-a-mars-rover

MinecraftEdu. (2022d). *Minecraft Teacher Academy*. available at https://education.minecraft.net/en-us/resources/get-trained

MinecraftEdu. (2022e). *New study: understanding the impact of Minecraft in the math classroom*. Available at https://education.minecraft.net/en-us/blog/new-study-understanding-the-impact-of-minecraft-in-the-math-classroom

MissionX. (2021). https://www.esa.int/Science_Exploration/Human_and_Robotic_Exploration/Education/Mission_X_-_Train_like_an_astronaut

Molina, J. J., Ortiz, A., & Agreda, M. (2017). Analisis de la integracion de procesos gamificados en Educacion Primaria. In Innovacion docente y uso de las TIC en eduacion. Universidad de Malaga (UMA).

Moon Camp. (2022). https://mooncampchallenge.org/

NASA. (2016). *Gamers Tackle Virtual Asteroid Sampling Mission*. Available at https://www.nasa.gov/feature/goddard/2016/gamers-tackle-virtual-asteroid-sampling-mission

NASA. (2021). https://www.nasa.gov/

Nobre, H., & Ferreira, A. (2017). Gamification as a platform for brand co-creation experiences. *Journal of Brand Management*, *24*(4), 349–361. doi:10.105741262-017-0055-3

OSIRIS-REx. (2021). https://www.nasa.gov/osiris-rex

Parra-González, E., López-Belmonte, J., Segura-Robles, A., & Moreno-Guerrero, A.-J. (2021). Gamification and flipped learning and their influence on aspects related to the teaching-learning process. *Heliyon*, *7*(2), 1–10. doi:10.1016/j.heliyon.2021.e06254 PMID:33659757

Patrício, R., Moreira, A., Zurlo, F., & Melazzini, M. (2020). Co-creation of new solutions through gamification: A collaborative innovation practice. *Creativity and Innovation Management*, *29*(1), 146–160. doi:10.1111/caim.12356

Patrício, R., Moreira, A. C., & Zurlo, F. (2018). Gamification approaches to the early stage of innovation. *Creativity and Innovation Management*, *27*(4), 499–511. doi:10.1111/caim.12284

Paxi. (2021). *About Paxi*. Available at https://www.esa.int/kids/en/about_Paxi/Paxi

Paxi Facebook. (2022). https://www.facebook.com/PaxiESAKids

Paxi Twitter. (2022). https://twitter.com/Paxi_ESAKids

Peter Beck. (2021). *Rocket Lab CEO Peter Beck & Kerbal Space Program*. Available at https://www.youtube.com/watch?v=FWKLiJu7EtA

Private Division. (2021). https://www.privatedivision.com/

Quora. (2022). https://www.quora.com/Why-should-Kerbal-Space-Program-be-played-in-schools

Raspberry Pi Foundation. (2022). https://www.raspberrypi.org/

Reddit. (2022a). https://www.reddit.com/r/KerbalSpaceProgram/comments/ac7dyi/do_schools_use_ksp_to_teach_students/

Reddit. (2022b). https://www.reddit.com/r/KerbalAcademy/comments/k6p9qx/kerbaledu_2/

Rocket Lab. (2021). https://www.rocketlabusa.com/

Rosetta. (2021). https://www.esa.int/Enabling_Support/Operations/Rosetta

Sailer, M., Hense, J. U., Mayr, S. K., & Mandl, H. (2017). How gamification motivates: An experimental study of the effects of specific game design elements on psychological need satisfaction. *Computers in Human Behavior*, *69*(4), 371–380. doi:10.1016/j.chb.2016.12.033

Sciamarelli, M. (2015). *11 – Teaching children with mascot-inspired projects*. Available at https://www.teachingenglish.org.uk/sites/teacheng/files/pub_F004_ELT_Creativity_FINAL_v2%20WEB.pdf#page=108

Shen, Y. S., Choi, H. C., Joppe, M., & Yi, S. (2020). What motivates visitors to participate in a gamified trip? A player typology using Q methodology. *Tourism Management*, *78*(6), 1–14. doi:10.1016/j.tourman.2019.104074

Singer, M. (1990). *Psychology of language: An introduction to sentence and discourse processing*. Lawrence Erlbaum.

Squad. (2021). https://squad.com.mx/

Subhash, S., & Cudney, E. A. (2018). Gamified learning in higher education: A systematic review of the literature. *Computers in Human Behavior*, *87*(10), 192–206. doi:10.1016/j.chb.2018.05.028

TeachCrunch. (2018). *TeacherGaming, a startup from MinecraftEdu team, raises $1.6M to put games into the classroom*. Available at https://techcrunch.com/2018/01/24/teachergaming/?guccounter=1&guce_referrer=aHR0cHM6Ly93d3cuZ29vZ2xlLmNvbS8&guce_referrer_sig=AQAAAJuibv_w-QUMmS72W-ktDoG9dgmmOdYBwhxgM5o7gyajidgZ7YsY3ESOfYyzR6c2RlcR5Cj1uSAPuCwx-lyxHRLF-uMXDpOFxjiKtw980eNOJQWa0gP5wAT1K81FG3bkK9x7zE0qv7_8TplZ8iF9bo52Th9AIt-Ny4J1pd01v4unBU

TeacherGaming. (2021). https://teachergaming.com/

United Nations. (2020). *Policy Brief: Education during COVID-19 and beyond*. https://www.un.org/development/desa/dspd/wp-content/uploads/sites/22/2020/ 08/sg_policy_brief_covid-19_and_education_august_2020.pdf

Van Dijk, J. (2020). *Digital Divide*. Polity Press.

Wired. (2021). *Kerbal Space Program: dieci anni di voli spaziali insegnati da un videogioco*. Available at https://www-wired-it.cdn.ampproject.org/c/s/www.wired.it/amp/308408/gadget/videogiochi/2021/06/24/kerbal-space-program-anniversario/

Xi, N., & Hamari, J. (2019). Does gamification satisfy needs? a study on the relationship between gamification features and intrinsic need satisfaction. *International Journal of Information Management*, *46*, 210–221. doi:10.1016/j.ijinfomgt.2018.12.002

Xi, N., & Hamari, J. (2020). Does gamification affect brand engagement and equity? A study in online brand communities. *Journal of Business Research*, *109*(3), 449–460. doi:10.1016/j.jbusres.2019.11.058

Yang, Y., Asaad, Y., & Dwivedi, Y. (2017). Examining the impact of gamification on intention of engagement and brand attitude in the marketing context. *Computers in Human Behavior*, *73*, 459–469. doi:10.1016/j.chb.2017.03.066

ADDITIONAL READING

Anikina, O. V., & Yakimenko, E. V. (2015). Edutainment as a Modern Technology of Education. *Procedia: Social and Behavioral Sciences*, *166*(1), 475–479. doi:10.1016/j.sbspro.2014.12.558

Asquer, A. (2013). Not Just Videogames: Gamification and its Potential Application to Public Services. In *Digital Public Administration and E-Government in Developing Nations: Policy and Practice* (pp. 146–165). IGI Global Publisher. doi:10.4018/978-1-4666-3691-0.ch008

Cristoforetti, S. (2020). *Diary of an Apprentice Astronaut*. Penguin.

Koivisto, J., & Hamari, J. (2014). Demographic differences in perceived benefits from gamification. *Computers in Human Behavior*, *35*(6), 179–188. doi:10.1016/j.chb.2014.03.007

Patrício, R., Moreira, A. C., & Zurlo, F. (2021). Enhancing design thinking approaches to innovation through gamification. *European Journal of Innovation Management*, *24*(5), 1569–1594. doi:10.1108/EJIM-06-2020-0239

Peak, T. (2020). *Limitless: The Autobiography: The bestselling story of Britain's inspirational astronaut*. Century.

KEY TERMS AND DEFINITIONS

CanSat: It is a simulation of a real satellite, integrated within the volume and shape of a soft drink can. The challenge for students is to fit all major subsystems found in a satellite, such as power, sensors, and a communication system, into this minimal volume. This challenge is organised by the European Space Agency (ESA).

Corporate Brand: It encompasses the name, design, symbol, or any other feature that identifies a company as distinct from other companies. It describes an organisation as a whole and aims to create a consistent corporate image.

Digital Divide: A division between people who have access and use digital media (e.g., the Internet, mobile, PC, etc.) and those who do not. Typically, this gap is more prominent in developing countries where the socioeconomic living conditions are worse.

Edutainment: It is a derived word which states the marriage of education with entertainment. The aim is to design educational activities which teach and entertain at the same time.

ESA Kids: It is ESA website targets primary school children from 3 to 10-years old. This e-learning portal is dedicated to the alien Paxi and it has many didactic resources, mostly presented with a gamification approach.

ESERO: This ESA project helps to foster interest and passion for STEM-related studies and to stimulate young people's awareness of Europe's space programme. The ESEROs are distributed across Member States and staffed by local experts who work in partnership with their national education authorities and networks. Currently, ESA has established eighteen ESERO national offices.

European Space Agency (ESA): It is an intergovernmental organisation of 22 Member States dedicated to the exploration of space. It was established in 1975 and headquartered in Paris, France.

Kerbal Space Program (KSP): It is a space flight simulation videogame developed by the Mexican multimedia company Squad and published by the American company Private Division. The players take charge of the space program for aliens known as the Kerbals. The game features a realistic orbital physics engine, allowing for various real-life orbital maneuvers.

Mission X: It is an international educational challenge, designed for students age 8-12, that focuses on health, science, fitness, and nutrition and encourages pupils to train like an astronaut. Teams of students complete Mission X activities to earn points and help the mascots, Luna and Leo, to virtually walk closer to the Moon until they reach it.

NASA: It is the acronym of National Aeronautics and Space Administration. It is an independent agency of the U.S. federal government responsible for the civilian space program, as well as aeronautics and space research.

Space Sector: It refers to the economic activities related to manufacturing components that go into Earth's orbit or beyond, delivering them to those regions, and related services. This sector encompasses intergovernmental organisations, private companies, and several other actors who contribute to deliver the final product or service.

Chapter 16
Interdisciplinary Communication:
Paving the Way for Gamification in Entrepreneurship Education – A Case Study From a Medium-Sized UK University

Alicia Danielsson
University of Bolton, UK

Denis Hyams-Ssekasi
https://orcid.org/0000-0002-5022-1210
University of Bolton, UK

ABSTRACT

This chapter presents a collaborative autoethnography study whereby two academics at a medium-sized UK university explore their experiences of teaching entrepreneurship in different business and law school departments to combine expertise and resources to develop interdisciplinary gamification solutions. The combined experiential reflections have contributed to the generation of ideas that will prompt future interdisciplinary content to be created to bridge together fields such as business, social, legal, and technical studies. The chapter concludes that critical factors limiting developments in interdisciplinary entrepreneurship games include a lack of focus on entrepreneurial skills in departments within HEIs other than business schools and a lack of cross-departmental communication and collaboration. Although all the required expertise and resources are present within the university, a genuinely holistic approach can only be developed if innovative teaching tools combine multidisciplinary content from all faculties.

INTRODUCTION

The Covid-19 pandemic intensified and, in some cases, created many dynamics within higher education teaching. This chapter was prompted by two enhanced dynamics, namely, the sudden leap forward

DOI: 10.4018/978-1-6684-4287-6.ch016

in the use of remote technology and the reduction of communication between academics, most notably between academics of different departments, due to the move to working from home and online teaching practices during times of lockdown and the social distancing measures in place which reduced social interaction to a minimum (Koren & Pető, 2020; Rashid & Yadav, 2020). As cross-departmental communication begins to re-emerge, it is important to communicate individual experiences and reflect on these collectively to restore inter-institutional synergies. As such, this chapter is the result of a collaborative effort to bring together the autoethnographic experiences of entrepreneurship teaching in order to develop strategies in the future that will ensure interdisciplinary needs of industry will be met moving forward: The concluding result of this study has been to develop cross-departmental, multidisciplinary entrepreneurship simulation games as a holistic and practical approach to entrepreneurship education.

In relation to the material scope of the proposed project on which the research of the chapter is based, the foundation of the project is found in the contemporary challenges to design an entrepreneurship education framework that is effective in driving enterprising skills and fostering entrepreneurship post graduating. Like any other taught disciplines in higher education institutions (HEIs), entrepreneurship education has become an essential element of the curriculum, a preparation for future careers and priority for the government. In recent times, higher education institutions have been grappling with the problem of engaging learners in their acquisition of new knowledge and relevant skills. Facilitated activities where students visit new ventures, indulge in business plan competitions, elevator pitch contests, start-ups competitions that are judged by 'dragons', placements and internships, and business consultancies through working with businesses under supervision have been adopted (Vanevenhoven & Drago, 2015).

Wilson (2011) identifies that most successful courses in developing professional skills include activities such as simulations and games, interactive teamwork, and group activities. Mason and Rennie (2006) the use of innovative methods such as gamification and virtual reality do improve the teaching quality and effectiveness. In relation to the issue of gamification, it needs to be noted that the type of game genres which are considered to be serious games is debated within the literature, with little consensus. For instance, Annetta (2010) distinguishes between serious games, simulations, serious educational games, and virtual worlds. Here, serious games on the one hand, are described as digital games which have been designed to educate players by teaching and training specific skills. Serious educational games (SEGs), on the other hand, require an additional layer of academic content. Simulations are described as a form of SEGs, yet without the element of scorekeeping. However, in contrast Hays (2005) claims that simulations which contain certain features, for instance certain challenges or competitions would also fall under the umbrella-term of games, while simulation games which have the purpose of instructing and supporting learning outcomes and aims would most likely be categorized as serious games. Virtual worlds, while still related to the category, are more likely to describe a related tool for gamification, namely a form of virtual three-dimensional environment in which players interact (Almeida & Simoes, 2019). For this chapter, it is important to note, that all the above categories are viewed as forms of gamification, as they all contain some of the key interactive components, regardless of the sub-categories the described tools could be placed.

Within the contemporary higher education sector, learners are constantly exposed to technology and as such they are more adept with technological skills (Ahmad, 2019; Chernikova, et al. 2020). Yet, the utilization of the above forms of gamification remain underutilized and the available serious educational simulation games appear to be missing the necessary complexity to merge the practical illusion with the realities of entrepreneurship in practice (Schofield, 2021).

In particular, this collaborative autoethnography project brings together the experiences of two academics from a medium sized UK university, who separately engaged in forms of gamification to teach entrepreneurship, yet from entirely different subject perspectives – business and law. As such, the nature of this research has been explorative, to uncover potential areas of collaboration. The two guiding research questions were set as the following:

1. What individual successes and development needs were experienced in relation to the use of gamification elements in the two separate accounts of entrepreneurship education?
2. What implications does our collaborative reflection have for the future of entrepreneurship education and gamification within our higher education institution?

Unlike more traditional scientific research methods, this chapter will begin by laying out the research methodology before delving into the review of key literature on the subject matter. This is not uncommon in the humanities, especially within the sphere of qualitative research methods. In particular, as will be demonstrated in the next section, collaborative autoethnography brings together an array of different accounts of issues, which also include different core literature. As such, to ensure readers are guided logically through the key elements of the study, the conscious decision is made to lead with the methodology, which consitutes the fundamental compontent that holds the individual elements of the project together. Thus, the following section will lay out the selected research methods employed for the purpose of answering the set research questions, with the aim of exploring ways to enhance entrepreneurship education by embedding gamification and simulation within higher education teaching.

METHODOLOGY

The foundation upon which this study was built can be found in Schön's reflection-in-action framework. This framework, which is almost four decades old, is still a leading model to effectively uncover what teachers across faculties encounter, think, and do in their teaching practices. In this framework, Schön, (1983) assumes that faculty members reflect on their teaching practice by carrying out continuous conversations with their lived experiences and their own practice. Reflection-in-action showcases the way teaching professionals undertake actions which then generate effects, which then in turn are used as feedback for professional repetition, reframing or modification of teaching approaches. This process continues in a continuous cycle of revision and the development of new pedagogical approaches.

This particular study has been built on Schön's reflective-in-action framework by adopting three key reflective stages: Firstly, the "descriptive reflection" whereby the individual accounts of a situation are described, thereby identifying key problems; Secondly, "comparative reflection" whereby the two accounts of lived experiences are combined via a process of collaborative reflection, and thirdly, with "critical reflection" which involved thinking about likely solutions or arrangements (Jay & Johnson, 2002, pp. 77–79).

Accordingly, this study has opted to follow the qualitative research method of collaborative autoethnography (CAE), which is a subcategory of autoethnography, whereby more than one researcher uses their autobiographical experiential data to further the understanding on a phenomenon (Chang et al., 2012). Thus, autobiographical as well as other sociocultural data are collated, analyzed and interpreted in a similar process as found in ethnographic research for the purpose of advancing understanding

(Chang, 2016; Lapadat, 2017; Ngunjiri et al., 2010; Polczyk, 2012). Chang et al. (2012) explain more specifically that within "collaborative autoethnography, each participant contributes to the collective work his/her distinct independent voice. At the same time, the combination of multiple voices to interrogate a social phenomenon creates a unique synergy and harmony that autoethnographers cannot attain in isolation (p. 24)."

While the popularity of all forms of autoethnography is increasing within academic scholarship, it is still a controversial choice of research method. As such, its more radical criticisms include comments, such as those made by Delamont (2009), which describe autoethnography as "an intellectual cul de sac" (p. 51), or "an abrogation of the honorable trade of the scholar" (p. 61). When researching autoethnography as a research tool, we came across the work by Gregersen (2019), which we found to be one of the most in-depth analyses of the method we had seen so far. We were surprised to find that in her experience, the starkest criticisms of autoethnography emanated from ethnographers. This is particularly surprising, as ethnography as a method, has historically been criticized for similar reasons as autoethnography, such as the difficulties to eliminate bias and the lack of generalizability of the research (Ali & Yusof, 2011; Duff, 2006; Herriott & Firestone, 1983). However, what we believe to be more significant is the fact that a key limitation of ethnography as a research method is that it relies on the sincerity of the research subjects and the correct interpretation of the researcher, even when the data will not showcase the full picture (Fine, 1993). In contrast, in autoethnography, the researcher and the research subject form the same person, which means that the researcher has access to the full set of experiential data, even when this processing of these cannot be objective.

This brings me to the limitations of this part of the study, which are an absence of generalizability and objectivity. Generalizability requires research findings to be applicable in wider contexts. The emphasis on this requirement stems historically from the quantitative research approaches, often found within positivism. However, in relation to qualitative research, the need for generalizability is often strongly debated. Yet, supporters of qualitative methods often highlight that despite the lack of generalizability, there are certain "redeeming qualities" (Myers, 2000, p. 1), which justify its absence. In particular, the idiographic nature or qualitative research (Thomae, 1999) whereby interpretivism prioritizes gaining understanding of circumstances and behaviors rather than the wider ability to predict and generalize cause and effect (Macionis & Gerber, 2010) render the positivist understanding of generalizability immaterial.

In line with the selected autoethnographic method, this part of the study seeks to create and disseminate a close-up, ground-levelled perspective on a specific experience (Adams et al., 2015), and, thus, embraces subjectivity in the typical autoethnographic fashion. As such, our observations and experiences will, and should, influence the research process.

Our reflections of student feedback, both verbal or written in forms of completed internal module evaluation forms, as well as and wider cross-departmental communications on the subject were included, which were further collaboratively reflected on during systematic, critical friend discussions. The sections of the study have been aligned with the stages of Schön's reflection-in-action framework. As such, Part I and Part II correspond with the "descriptive reflection" stage of the framework. Hereafter, Part III forms the "comparative reflection" stage and finally, the recommendations and solutions section corresponds with the "critical reflection" of Schön's framework.

THE BUSINESS SCHOOL PERSPECTIVE

Exploring the Current Literature on Simulations and Serious Games as Interdisciplinary Models of Teaching Entrepreneurship within Business Schools

Entrepreneurship Education as a Non-exhaustive Educational and Economic Priority

The past few years have seen a drastic change in the way entrepreneurship is perceived. In particular, policy-makers are increasingly looking towards entrepreneurship as an opportunity to generate economic growth, in particular, with the goal of establishing innovative and inclusive entrepreneurial ecosystems (Visvizi, et. al., 2018; Roundy et. al., 2018). This shift in focus has also transferred into educational settings. Here, entrepreneurship education is increasingly focused on the acquisition of skills and knowledge that will enable learners to grasp business opportunities. Thus, the teaching of entrepreneurship in higher education institutions seeks to stimulate and instigate graduates into successful entrepreneurship aiming at graduates starting their own businesses following graduation (Bakar, 2015). Hence, entrepreneurship is viewed as new business ventures as a means for economic growth (Holcombe, 1998; Sergi et al., 2019).

From the outset, there is an abundance of literature on the subject matter of entrepreneurship. The term entrepreneurship is not all that new, it was used for the first time in 1732 when Richard Cantillon, an Irish economist was referring to individuals with "a willingness to carry out forms of arbitrage involving the financial risk of a new venture" (Minniti & Lévesque, 2008, p. 603). The term is derived from the French word entreprendre, which translates into English to mean to undertake or start something. Generally, entrepreneurship is known as the process of developing a business plan and transforming this plan into an opportunity with a view to making a profit. It involves searching as well as exploiting new and old opportunities. It is by no means risk free, as it requires key aspects of business: creativity, innovation, enthusiasm, planning, developing, as well managing a business with significant initiatives and risks. It is believed that entrepreneurship fosters innovation and sustainable business growth (Diaz Garcia et al. 2015) and economic growth (Grivokostopoulou, 2019; Gurol & Astan, 2006; Wong et al., 2005).

Busenitz, et al. (2003) argue that the driving force behind a contemporary economy is entrepreneurship. It plays an important role in the economic output as well as overall employment. Zaman (2013) adds that entrepreneurship is the foundation to the growth of an economy and a contributory factor to the development and stability of an economy in every developed country.

Entrepreneurship has been considered a more strategic and important means of reverting the cyclic economic downturns as well as the driver for development and creation of business. Advocates for entrepreneurship believe that it can be learnt or acquired through experience, but the majority can be taught (Martin & Iucu, 2019; Nabi et al, 2018). It is argued that most HEIs do not teach clear approaches to entrepreneurship and instead "focus more on lengthy risk and return calculations" (Bhatia & Levina, 2020). Designing an effective entrepreneurship education framework is not straightforward. However, innovation methods have been introduced to ensure there is a good grasp of entrepreneurship in practice. Matlay and Carey (2006) argue that entrepreneurship education has grown too fast in most developed countries. Bhatia and Levina (2020) acknowledge that business schools still have a place for entrepreneurship as a formal education discipline. In their study, they noted that in some business schools, steps have been made to develop internal institutional philosophies in entrepreneurship education. In some instances, the emphasis has been on real-life experiences, inculcating in the students that entrepreneurship skills can only be advanced through experience, experiential learning and in others teaching entrepreneurship in the same way as any other subjects are taught.

The rise of the Covid-19 pandemic has changed the face of the economy, and this has forced different economic approaches within the labor market, and resulted in many people considering the importance of entrepreneurship. According to Entrepreneur Education (2015), being self- employed allows people to create jobs that lead to growth in the economy. Zaman (2013) explains that with the uncertainty of the labor market it will not be a bad idea for people to own their own businesses, with individuals who are aspiring to become entrepreneurs likely being propelled and stimulated by entrepreneurship education.

The European Commission points out that the "primary purpose of entrepreneurship education [at higher education level] is to develop entrepreneurial mindsets and capacities" (European Commission, 2008, p. 11). It also suggests that HEIs should include entrepreneurship as a subject within its programs.

Notably, there is a wide recognition and acknowledgement of the role of education in promoting more entrepreneurial behaviors and attitudes (European Commission, 2008). Across the board, there is still a general belief that entrepreneurship education is vital in HEIs. Souitaris, Zerbinati, & Al-Laham (2007) suggest that, to introduce entrepreneurship education programs, initiators must take into consideration "conventional wisdom" which incorporates the widely accepted ideas, opinions or beliefs as true.

Traditionally, the teaching of entrepreneurship is premised on stirring self-employment and the capacity to act in entrepreneurial ways in solving challenges in order to address issues of unemployment. Inspiring entrepreneurial ways in solving problems is important in the current pandemic era. There is a need to generate new and innovative entrepreneurial ways to resuscitate economies. The need for entrepreneurial minds is crucial and demands a redefining of the current curriculums. A well-designed entrepreneurship curriculum should be able to create business opportunities, widen horizons and bring about innovation. In essence, the entrepreneurial skills should mirror the curriculum. such as innovativeness, creativity and risk-taking tendencies, alertness exploiting opportunities, self-confidence and networking skills (Schumpeter, 1926; Kirzner, 1979; Denslow and Giunipero, 2003; Peters, 2005; and Platt, 2004). The ingenuity of the graduates should demonstrate the superiority, robustness and pragmatic the program is. However, this calls into question whether entrepreneur education is able to produce entrepreneurs in practice.

The attitude towards entrepreneurship is generally influenced by educational attainments. According to Srirejeki and Faturokhman (2020), the ideas of Linan (2004) on the types of Entrepreneurship education still stand today. Accoringly, there are four different types of entrepreneurship education programs. The first, "Entrepreneurial Awareness Education", intends to develop know-how about entrepreneurship and have an influence on perspective that may impact intentions. The second type is represented as "Education for Start-Up". These programs are designed for people who normally already have an entrepreneurial idea and need to figure out practical questions about becoming self-employed. The third type, which we can refer to as "Education for Entrepreneurial Dynamism", targets people who are already entrepreneurs and want to encourage dynamic attitudes after the start-up phase. The last type, "Continuing Education for Entrepreneurs" depicts life-long learning programs and targets experienced entrepreneurs. (Linan, 2004). Together with the different types of entrepreneurship education, there are four analysis paths of entrepreneurship education research (Bechard & Gregoire, 2005). The first analysis path focuses on the impact of entrepreneurship programs on the individual and society. The second analysis path is geared towards the structure of entrepreneurship programs, for example, social Innovation to build the capacity of system entrepreneurs around innovation, system change, and resilience; learn new ways of thinking about old problems and figuring out how to put theoretical ideas into practice. The third path analyses the content and its delivery in entrepreneurship programs, and the fourth path focuses on the needs of individual participants in entrepreneurship programs (Bechard & Gregoire, 2005).

In his study, Jamieson (1984) divides the entrepreneurial education in three categories: education for, about and in enterprise. Hoppe et al. (2017) argue that the concept of for/in/through/about leads to highly different pedagogical approaches for entrepreneurship education depending on their purpose. They further argue that the inclusion of the notion of "in" offers new opportunities to enhance complementary student learning in higher education. Herrmann et al. (2008) point out the need to move from teaching students [learning "about"] to something more hands on that is experiential learning which is [learning "for "] to provide students a better understanding of what is happening in the real world. However, there is a need to have a teaching method that is strategic and has a long and positive impact on the students' developmental knowledge of entrepreneurship.

Entrepreneurship education is perceived to be more attractive and, thus, better suited to result in new businesses or start-ups (Fayolle et al., 2006). Efforts have been made by HEIs to provide a wide range of entrepreneurship education (Kuratko, 2005). Such initiatives give ample opportunities for students to assess whether they wish to pursue an entrepreneurial career or not. It is still unclear as to whether entrepreneurship education prepares students to become entrepreneurs (Graevenitz, Harhoff and Web, 2010). They further state that "depending on what they learn students may adjust their entrepreneurial intentions upwards or downwards" (p. 5). Nevertheless, the effects of entrepreneurship education are noted (Fiet, 2001), influences individual knowledge and skills (Graevenitz, Harhoff and Web, 2010), influences entrepreneurial insights and intents (McMullan et. al 2002). Particular entrepreneurship programs or courses offered by HEIs encourage some students to start their own businesses, (Gerba, 2012), "to engage in entrepreneurial activity in an experimental setting" (Graevenitz, Harhoff and Web, 2010, p. 6). They add that the experience gained can be emulated in the classroom e.g., in start-up simulations (p. 6).

Teaching Methods in Entrepreneurship Education: The Ideal Setting for Gamification Simulations

Entrepreneurship as an academic discipline entail conveying skills and knowledge in areas such as capturing business plans and translating these into tangible products and/or services, as well as the marketing thereof. As such, fundamental components within the curriculum of Entrepreneurship education involve the teaching of skills such as risk-taking, showing initiative and innovativeness (Iscenco & Li, 2014; Hassan et. al., 2021). Moreover, other interdisciplinary areas of knowledge need to be conveyed, such as financial management, accounting, credit management, taxation and business projection are crucial for future entrepreneurs (Winarno & Wijijayanti, 2018). Hence, the development of an awareness of these aspects of entrepreneurship should be taught and trained as a core component of entrepreneurship education, from as early stages as possible. According to Bahador & Haider (2017) this should already be taking place in early years education and should be continuously reinforced within higher education courses. Similarly, to the trends in most higher education disciplines, teaching and learning in entrepreneurship in higher education settings are continuously evolving with the aim of making teaching methods more effective to achieve future success in Entrepreneurship amongst graduates (Mason, 2011; Kelley and Johnston, 2012). Yet, studies still reveal that students struggle with the application of their entrepreneurial skills and theoretical knowledge in practical settings when faced with the challenge of making important business decisions (Rosli et. al., 2019). There are already numerous studies suggesting that gamification within teaching approaches approach can enhance the interest of learners as well as their motivation, critical thinking ability and perseverance (see for example: Fratto, 2011; Kiili, 2007). Other studies also suggest that gamification is more effective for improving social and collaborative skills, especially when the gamification elements require students to work together in the completion of tasks within the games (Kiili, 2007; Nitkin, 2012; Wan Tahir, 2018). According to Apostol et. al (2013), reasons for this include enhanced engagement and with that interest for the subject matter, as well as the promotion of learner motivation and enhanced cognitive growth, including factual knowledge, practical application ability and increased critical problem-solving skills. With increasing development in the technological areas, most studies focus on the digital development of computer games (Hamari, et al., 2016, Rapp et. al., 2016), however, this move overshadows some of the more fundamental academic questions, including the core design elements and academic components necessary to achieve the correct disciplinary balance. This can at times result in the misconception of gamification referring to digital forms of games. However, studies focusing, for instance, on board games, have revealed that the social interactions alongside the learning games that were undertaking in face-to-face settings, such as verbal discussions, resulted in an additional layer of learning, most notably in developing understanding for the reasons behind answers and choices taken (Rosli et. al., 2019).

As is also the case in other areas of education, entrepreneurship education aims to improve the quality of its content and methods. The use of simulations or games in the business world is well developed and companies are benefitting from such methods. Houtari & Hamari (2012) argue that gamification is widely used in learning, customer engagement and employee performance. Games are utilized not only to reinforce knowledge, but also as a means of explaining concepts which would be rather impossible to expound using merely verbal tools such as ordinary spoken words (Caponetto et al., 2014). Antonaci et al. (2015) claim that gamification, due to the view that they engage, motivates and rewards the target audience to learn new skills or change behaviors via active involvement (Isabelle, 2020; Iscenco & Li, 2014). In their study, Agogué, Levillain and Hooge (2015) explore the serious games as a collaborative tool that has been used since the 1960s to support learning processes. They further explore the impact of gamification and how it can be used to improve learning.

Educators use methods such as simulations to encourage and achieve learning. Mayer et al. (2014) point out the importance of simulations in learning and argue that simulations come in different forms, such role plays (technical and no-technical) computer simulations, written case studies, and board games. In particular, simulations and serious games are attributed to effectively assist in the development of self-efficacy. The literature links this with the ideal of Social Cognitive Theory, which purports that a crucial part of knowledge acquisition takes place via social interactions, the observing of others and experiences (Bandure, 1989). Simulations and serious games create environments in which this kind of learning can take place within educational settings (Klimmt & Hartmann, 2006), as the mastery of the games and simulations promote self-efficacy, which then transfers into real-life behaviours (Peng, 2008). Whilst this is an ideal goal for entrepreneurship education, knowing the theoretical benefits and being able to affectively transfer this knowledge into the classroom setting is another matter. As such, the following will examine the experience of entrepreneurship education within a sample higher education business school setting.

A Case for Multidisciplinary Entrepreneurship Education Simulations from the Perspective of Business Schools – An Autoethnographic Case Study

Setting the Context

I have been teaching Business Management in higher education for at least 20 years, of which 6 years have been spent delivering Enterprise and Entrepreneurship modules at the medium sized UK university within which this study is placed. I have taught, co-taught and acted as a module leader across many related business management modules. The entrepreneurship module was introduced in the business school of this university six years ago. The main objective was to develop entrepreneurship mind-sets and capacities in students, whilst also encouraging them to start their own businesses after the completion of their courses. It is important to note that this module is currently only available to students on particular undergraduate business programs within the Business School.

The aim of this module is to enable students to develop the knowledge and understanding of entrepreneurship and small business development. More emphasis is placed upon an appreciation of enterprise resource requirements, skills and competencies as a medium to develop employability and innovation. Fundamentally, students are expected to analyses the processes involved in generating ideas, developing, producing and marketing new goods and services in new and mature industries. The module is designed in such a manner that students should develop a growing interest in enterprise and entrepreneurship as a means of addressing a range of social and economic problems.

The content of the module, despite the intended practical implications, is mostly theoretical and fails to offer a holistic understanding of what it actually means to start a business. The module is delivered over 15 weeks, with 3 hours of scheduled class participation time. In essence, an hour of this is dedicated to traditional class input (lecture) whilst two hours are spent on business related practical activities. During the weekly hour-long lecture, the theoretical perspective of entrepreneurship is emphasized – making the student a passive listener. The two-hour activities each week are utilized to expose students to business expert guest speakers, who are mostly business managers. Topics covered by these managers include finance, information communication systems (ICT) and marketing. The value of these two hours a week is thought to be that these practitioners share their own experiences with the students rather than merely the theoretical concepts, thereby bringing the industry realities closer to the students. In view of this, the guest speakers talk about how they initiated their companies from scratch and became successful. The 8 guest speakers who support the students are recruited before the beginning of the semester and are all well-recognized within their areas. Apart from these 8 guest lectures, two of the weekly practical sessions are dedicated to practical activities, including mentoring sessions from a further 4 external mentors who offer support on matters such as running live projects, which focusses on starting enterprises and exploiting business opportunities. These sessions and activities are set and facilitated by the module lecturer.

Experience of Embedding Practical Entrepreneurship Elements within the Teaching of the Entrepreneurship module within the Business School

From my experience of delivering this module, I noted that students' main reasons for undertaking the module were mostly merely for the completion of their degrees, as the module is compulsory rather than optional. This is in itself counterproductive, as one would hope that students would attend the classes with the drive to start a business. In its current format, the completion of the module is viewed more as a box-ticking exercise than a quest to achieve knowledge and skills. The time given for this module was not enough for the students to develop the necessary skills nor to be enticed to become entrepreneurs. What makes this module different from other business modules is that students get involved in live projects and trade fairs. Essentially, the experience of running a business starts 3 weeks after the start of module and runs for a minimum of 11 weeks, with the trade fair taking place in the final week of the module. Over the course of these 11 weeks, students are placed into a group of 5 students, who were allocated to the individual groups randomly. The intention behind the random allocation is to encourage the realization that within employment, employees also do not choose who they will be working or sharing offices with. In these 11 weeks, students also benefit from mentorships which are provided for by the previously mentioned external business mentors. Each group is given £20 as a start-up investment from which they are tasked to make a profit. The groups are also encouraged to be resourceful and venture out into other practices, such as seeking out other business opportunities with a view to generating more funds. The group members are expected to run the project like a business, which means that they are required to have an organizational structure (with each individual playing a role that would add value to the project). It is my role to ensure that a trade fair is organized and students are encouraged to take an active part. At the trade fair, each group displays its products and explains how they have generated an income. The group that displayed their products well, traded and generated the most income is considered the winner.

Although teaching the entrepreneurship module has been a rewarding experience in which I was able to provide students with a space to consider the potential of running a business as a possible future career, I have also found that the limited experiential learning embedded within the module, is not achieving the sought objectives, namely to appreciate the implementation of theory into practice, which is an often-ignored aspect of business and management modules. I have also realized that to develop entrepreneurial attitude and skills, requires a number of learning phases. Students need longer programs with more time to reflect on their experiences. I am not suggesting that some students are not drawn towards entrepreneurship in their future career choices following entrepreneurship education, yet hands on experience are still not playing a sufficient role in teaching. If the mindset was embedded throughout the module, the dissipation of the beliefs and an increasing awareness of entrepreneurship as a career would be enhanced. Having said all this, it needs to be reiterated that none of the students I have taught over the past 6 years have come back to me and said that they started their business and it was running well. In a way, one can argue that there is a dichotomy of what students study in the business schools and what they do after completing their courses. They know about what is taught especially in entrepreneurship module but they don't pursue the self-employment opportunities. It is also clear that other disciplines taught in the business are not linked to entrepreneurship. No holistic approach as far as teaching business management courses are concerned. A shift towards a multidisciplinary course seems to be more realistic and a way forward. In light of this, the next section of this study will entail the situation within the law school of the same institution. As indicated at the beginning of this chapter, the key issue in paving the way towards increased multidisciplinary modes of teaching entrepreneurship education is a lack of multidisciplinary collaboration between subject areas in higher education institutions. The purpose is to expose the needs and experiences of other departments while tacking similar skills development needs with the aim to enhance communication, collaboration and multidisciplinary cooperation in future educational settings.

THE LAW SCHOOL PERSPECTIVE

Questioning the Current Literature on Simulations and Serious Games as Interdisciplinary Models of Teaching within Law Schools

Across jurisdictions, a persistent fundamental requirement sought for quality assurance purposes from regulatory bodies within the legal sectors is that professional training must be closely connected to both the theoretical knowledge of the law as well as its practical application and the skills to be able to do this as a professional. As examples, references to this can both be found in the available communications released by the American Bar Association (ABA) (2013) and the English Solicitors Regulation Authority (SRA) (2020). Further, the ABA (2014) has previously explained that when examining the existing training provided to students targeting future professional employment, it becomes evident that the majority of law schools are still not offering sufficient practical training courses. As such, calls are becoming louder for law schools to enhance their practical components of educational provisions to add to the practical experience students gain. In particular, the areas of preparation for advocacy and independent legal practice are highlighted. Similarly, the newly introduced Solicitors Qualifying Examination in England and Wales has sought implement an increased focus on the practical skills training of future solicitors. In particular, the embedding of targeted skills training and the newly implemented SQE 2 exam which assesses legal practical skills as a prerequisite to professional qualification (Solicitors Regulation Authority, 2021).

In light of the changes to the education and practice environment in which the amount of information is continuously expanding, while maintaining the fundamental traditional theoretical content of the law, it is vital to branch out into new innovative teaching methods within higher education to ensure learning takes place as effectively as possible (Alexander, 1999; Justice et al., 2007; Mykhailyshyn, 2018; Tokareva, 2019). As such, the increasingly utilized practice-oriented teaching methods within law schools are intended to immerse law students into realistic future professional conduct as early as possible (SRA, 2020).

Jacob (2015) is representative of a growing number of scholars (see also Kuhn 2009; Petkov et al., 2020; Steegh, 2005) who advocate the importance of multidisciplinary approaches within universities to meet the needs of future legal professionals. In basic terms, interdisciplinarity refers to educational approaches which concentrate on at least two, if not more, subjects (Kozakiewicz, 2008). As such, the aim is to "enhance the ability to work in teams and collaborate among representatives of different professions, thereby enhancing practical training within the subject" (Weinberg & Harding, 2004). According to Newell (2007) interdisciplinarity is understood to be the solution to the contemporary issue of increasing complexity, as it encourages comprehensive understanding.

Over the past three decades, the academic focus has increasingly been placed on developments and implementation methods for multidisciplinary approaches and possible interactive teaching techniques for the purpose of improving the teaching within professional disciplines (Anft, 2017; Barton, 2021; Faria & Dickinson, 1994; Nancarrow et al., 2013; Pometun, 2007; Tavares, 2017; Wiratraman, 2019). Yet, particularly in the subject matter of law, one finds that not only are interdisciplinary models insufficiently addressed, but the approaches to interactive teaching methods remain focused on the traditional employment sector with little diversification, ultimately leading to a lack of flexibility in terms of employment potential for law graduates (see for example: Joy, 2017; Lytvyn et al. 2017; Petkov et al., 2020).

The objective of this part of the study, is to challenge and showcase the missing potential for law schools to tap into interdisciplinary education options within the Entrepreneurial sphere, by collaborating with business schools and other subject departments to enhance interdisciplinary content and training and ultimately better the future working prospects for their graduates across institutions.

The need to Diversify Targeted Labor Sectors of Law Graduates within Higher Education's Employability Skills Training

Similarly to the situation found the world over, the higher education sector in the United Kingdom (UK) is driven by a need to develop and enhance new methods of teaching which corresponds with the demands of the economic and social dimensions of society, while simultaneously providing graduates with the necessary competitive advantages to succeed in the labor market (Durazzi, 2019; Jacob et al., 2019; Tholen & Brown, 2017; Pham, 2021; Pitan, 2017). This also coincides with increasing demands by employers that graduates possess diverse, interdisciplinary skillsets, as well as skills that allow for easy adaptation into various sectors, such as the ability to solve complex problems, or creativity (Jacobson & Wilensky, 2006; Sarfraz et al. 2018; Suarta et al., 2017; Suleman, 2018). As such, the contradiction of expectations for graduates, whereby they need to be specialists on the one hand, and generalists on the other, poses significant challenges on higher education providers (Bridgstock et al., 2019; Edge, et al., 2019; Gannaway & Sheppard, 2019; Healy et al., 2021).

Within law schools, this contradiction is more pronounced than in many other disciplines. On the one hand, the traditional subject area of law remains renowned for its traditional disciplinary shackles of imposed requirements by professional bodies without which the programs cannot achieve professional accreditation (Solicitors Regulation Authority, 2014). However, on the other hand, the increased pressures from the wider higher education sector also demands high rates of graduate employment following the completion of the programs (Tran, 2016). From the outside, these two requirements do not seem contradictory per se. However, when also taking into consideration the difficulties of entering the traditional accredited legal professions, another picture emerges.

When reviewing the data released by the Higher Education Statistics Agency (HESA) from the past 4 years (HESA, 2021), the picture emerges that in the UK alone, Higher Education institutions release between 20,000 and 30.000 new law graduates into the job market each year, while research undertaken by High Fliers Research Limited reveals that the number of annual legal sector vacancies, also increasing, remain below 1000 (High Fliers, 2021). Accordingly, the ratio of law graduates to legal sector vacancies lies approximately around 30 graduates to each employment opportunity within the traditional legal sector. Moreover, the available graduate outcome data indicates that law programs account for the lowest rates of graduate employment within non-scientific disciplines throughout the United Kingdom with less than half of law graduates securing employment in any industry over the same period (Law Monthly, 2019). The consequence of this situation is that many law graduates find themselves requiring retraining towards alternative careers in order to find their place within the labor market.

Research carried out by MMA Digital found that some of the leading alternative sectors that law graduates seek employment within include professional services, such as Human Resources, Sales or Marketing. However, less than 30% of law graduates tend to successfully secure employment within these sectors compared to approximately half of graduates from other disciplines.

Due to the restricted focus of law schools towards graduate employment within the traditional legal sector and the corresponding targeting of labor sectors within the curriculum of law schools, entrepreneurship as a potential career goal is not prioritized within most law schools. As seen in the previous section, even research into entrepreneurial skills within law schools and the teaching thereof merely sees the purpose of this as a beneficial skill for dealing with clients or other legal practice related roles. However, the as is seen across many other disciplines, entrepreneurship has been contributing to growing labor markets, higher graduate employment, including within professional industries, and ultimately assists governments in the development of innovative and entrepreneurial economies (Bell, 2016; OECD, 2014).

Considering the lack of interdisciplinary training overall within law schools more generally as well as the annual graduate outcome data (HESA, 2021), it is evident that entrepreneurship is a potential area of future employment for law graduates, which is far from being exhausted.

The Need to Rethink the Functions of Law Schools and Legal Education

As explained earlier in this chapter, the university training provided within law schools remains strongly focused on traditional forms of employment within the legal sector. As such, the key objective continues to prioritize training students to think and behave like solicitors or barristers (Abonyi et al. 2020; Biviano, 2017; Menkel-Meadow, 2019; Natt Gantt, 2012). Although there have been changes to the way this operates across the globe, such as a growing focus on the effects of globalization of the sector, whereby international law and the ability to navigate across cultures and jurisdictions (Galloway, 2017; Goodwin, 2021; Maxeiner, 2008), there appears to be a strong current against branching out across disciplines and sectors. Without evidence to substantiate this claim, it is nonetheless presumed from the experience's details later within this chapter, that a reason preventing the branching out into other disciplines, in part, can be based on the lack of academic collaboration across subject areas. As such, the insufficient interdisciplinary exchange of knowledge and experiences in academia is holding back the vital intertwining of disciplinary training. Considering the developments found within many industries, whereby a more symbiotic environment has developed across subject matters due to the natural collaboration and merging of disciplines in practice, a logical consequence can arguably be a growing divide between academic subject matter education and the realities of employment in practice. Ultimately, this means that any attempts within higher education teaching to enhance employability with more practically focused teaching methods would remain ineffective without the inter- and multidisciplinary adjustments to reflect industry realities.

Hoffman (2012) pinpoints a key issue in the fact that there exists a long-standing inter-subject war within scholars involved in legal training pertaining to the understanding of the purpose of law schools. As such, one side believes that law schools are meant to train students in the theory of the law, while the other side prioritizes the training of skills required for legal practice.

However, even if employment within sectors other than the traditional legal ones is disregarded as a focus, the contemporary lawyer requires more than the skills of legal practice and analysis in order to work collaboratively with professionals outside the scope of the legal sector (Hyams, 2012). As such, the demands of an increasingly competitive legal employment sector as well as the growing complexity and multifacetedness of the global economy mean that neither legal theory, nor legal practice skills are insufficient to prepare law graduates for the multilayered employment realities lying ahead.

Evans and Gable (2016) address this issue while concluding that a key missing link is the need to train law students to be entrepreneurial. They argue that the inclusion of entrepreneurial skills would combine both the theoretical as well as the experiential elements. This is also thought to bridge the philosophical divide between law school academics, while simultaneously empowering law students to not only navigate between theory and practice, but also develop an understanding of the experiences of their clients. While Evans and Gable's innovative concept of Legal Entrepreneurship education is not disputed, this chapter's proposal takes the ideas a step further. While recognizing that legal entrepreneurship education is vital for the training of contemporary lawyers, this study is based on the acceptance of the reality that many law school graduates do not in fact enter the traditional legal professions. Thus, this chapter proposes embedding a more multidisciplinary focused entrepreneurship education within law schools' curricula to increase employability of law graduates overall, not merely those who decide to pursue a career in the traditional legal professions.

A Case for Multidisciplinary Entrepreneurship Education Simulations from the Perspective of Law Schools – An Autoethnographic Case Study

Setting the Context

It was August 2018 and I was about to enter into my second year of higher education teaching in law. In my first year as a lecturer, I had co-taught on a number of modules, which I was well-versed in, yet not an expert. I had also been the module leader and primary teacher on a few other modules, which I can confidently state I am an expert in. However, I had now been given the module International Business Law to teach on my own, without any prior experience of teaching the subject. This, of course, did not mean that I did not know the legal theoretical content of the subject, but the key issue, when teaching international business law, is the fact that the subject itself does not exist in the same way other standalone law subjects do. One needs to understand that international business law is more of an umbrella-term that covers any areas of law which are applicable in the context of international business. As such the content of such a module, when narrowed down to the 45 allocated teaching hours is at risk of either only covering certain niche areas of the matter, such as international trade law, or be unrealistically broad, making it almost impossible to cover everything in 45 teaching hours. At the same time, the nature of the subject matter itself, considering the increasing acceptance within legal academia that globalization has a disproportionate impact on law graduates and the way they are taught (see Kuntz, 1946; Henderson, 2013), meant that the module in many cases may be one of the most significant for the future employment of my students.

When preparing the module, I thus, not only needed to prepare the content of the module and make a conscious selection of areas of law that would offer a realistic representation of the demands of international business, but I also needed to consider the teaching methods and types of exposures I would provide the students to achieve independent life-long learning and the necessary flexibility and adaptability to navigate the multilayered industry context they may one day be faced with in their work. During my research I found academic commentary which highlighted the need to expose students to the practicalities of globalization, which also included law students (Silver, 2013; Cassidy, 2012; Lutz, 2012).

At the time of the preparation of the module, I did know appreciate what an impact my teaching would have on the development of entrepreneurial skills, which I will lay out in the next section.

Experience of Embedding Entrepreneurship Simulations within the Teaching of International Business Law

For the sake of sincerity and academic rigor, I must confess that the research into an approach to teaching the international business law module took up so much time, that my options ended up being more limited than I would have liked. Accordingly, I had spent more time trying to figure out how to teach the module and what key components to include, that there was not much time left for the writing up of the actual content. As such, the decision to embed a simulation into the module was only in-part derived from the desire to train students in the necessary skills for future success in the areas of law and international business, but also in-part based on now even more limited time to create teaching materials. In hindsight, however, this time-pressure was the force I needed to move away from the traditional teacher-centric lecturing styles I was accustomed to.

For the purpose of the simulation, I started to explore the different kinds of simulations used in education, which brought me to my first hurdle. The quantity of information surrounding simulations and teaching online is extensive, however, I could not find a format that suited me needs. The key issue was a lack of multidisciplined approaches. There were academic papers, and more general websites that provided guidance for the embedding of simulations in many disciplines. I found that the disciplines most represented which suited my needs were found in the field of business studies, however, logically, these did not involve the key legal problems I needed to embed. Instead, the focus was on simulations relating to marketing, strategic management, product design or business processes (see for example: Abdullah et al., 2013; Löffler, 2020; Uhleman et al., 2020; Vos & Brennan, 2010). Although, I felt that many of these aspects would be beneficial to be included, the lack of interdisciplinary components also meant that the matters were overly specialized for law students to navigate without studying the underpinning matter. In contrast, the law related simulations, as indicated in the previous sections of this chapter, focused solely on the simulation of traditional legal environments, such as moot courts, simulated negotiations, client interviews or other legal practice activities.

I found myself drawn towards total enterprise simulations (Washbush & Gosen, 2001; Lohman at al. 2019; Goi, 2019). One of the key definitions of total enterprise simulations was already provided more than three decades ago by Key and Biggs (1990):

A total enterprise game is one which includes decisions in most of the main functions of business: marketing, production, finance, and personnel. Such games require integration of the various functional areas. In addition, total enterprise games incorporate environmental factors, such as general economic conditions and interest rates as important components of the learning experience (p. 49).

However, as a law academic, I was inhibited by my own lack of business and management expertise. As such, although totality simulations would have been my ideal preference, I did not have the knowledge to design a simulation that could replicate entire business operations and I certainly would not have the depth of knowledge to break down the complex subject matter into comprehendible sections to ensure student learning. Thus, I carefully approached aspects of functional and concept simulations, whereby I placed the concentration on particular areas of international business, which were focused on potential legal problems.

The first lecture was then used to set the scene. The students were introduced to the simulation, whereby they were tasked to set up their own fictitious business. The only requirement for the business was that the operation had to involve an international component. What the component consisted of what left to the students to decide. The tools they were given included some instructional videos on how to develop business ideas, a business plan template, a PC to work on and an online platform where they could upload any files or comments, which I was able to access in order to monitor their progress. In terms of setting up the business, students, thus, had to take their business idea and place this into a real-life format, including deciding on the jurisdiction for the establishment and the type of business formation and set-up. Depending on the selections made, other requirements would emerge, such potential governing documents. Following the initial setting-up of the businesses, students had to present their initial ideas to the rest of the class, who then temporarily slipped into the roles of potential investors.

Here again, my lack of business expertise prevented me from delving deeper into the financial specifics of the investments and any other financial simulations, which I would have ideally liked to implement. Instead, the simulation was limited to an assessment of the feasibility of the proposed business under the scrutiny of a panel of peers.

Over the next 13 weeks, the fictitious businesses were taken on a simulated journey through the legal world of international business law. Here, new legal challenges were encountered each week which required solving, whereby the students were required to undertake legal research into the problem and find solutions that would apply to their specific businesses. The challenges covered various issues, including the following:

- Business ethics, including environmental and human rights issues
- International trade
- Business within various regional systems, such as the EU and China
- Export and Import Problems
- Hiring Agents and Distributors
- International Commercial Dispute Resolution
- Foreign Direct Investments
- International E-Commerce
- Intellectual Property Law
- Competition Law

At the end of each session, the students would showcase their individual solutions to the simulated legal problems they had been given with certain points being discussed within the class.

Some of the predicted benefits of the simulation included that it encouraged students to learn not only the content of the law, but also how to independently navigate the international legal realm. This meant that I would not have to cover every aspect of international business law within the module, but could instead trust that post graduating, the students would have gained the necessary skills to find any relevant law in the context of international business if so required. Another predicted consequence, which exceeded my initial expectations was the impact the sharing of the individual findings would have. The fictitious businesses the students developed over the course were wide ranging, and included both services and products, with barely any sector overlaps. In one instance, two students had developed a similar business and undertook a fictitious merger, which further enriched the overall experience. The diversity of represented international businesses also meant that the solutions to the weekly legal dilemmas were unique and, thus, resulted in the class being exposed to wider legal issues than initially intended.

The most valuable insight into the experience of teaching this simulation for me as an educator, was the passion showcased by the students. Students developed a personal attachment to their businesses and were driven to see the businesses through any challenges that came their way. The level of motivation within the class to learn the subject matter was unlike any experience I had had in my previous teaching.

Students reported that "[the module] helped with the application of law, and understanding the connection between theory and practice" and that "[t]he practical simulation fit [their] learning style perfectly."

One student explained in the module feedback that it "opened [their] eyes to maybe working in a startup or running my own business in the future. I loved the entrepreneurial aspect." Several students expressed similar notions, with some students thinking seriously about making their fictitious businesses a reality. Although the long-term data on the student outcomes will remain a few years away, the reactions already showcase a shift in the future perspectives of the students and their long-term career aspirations. One student already embarked on an MBA programme following the completion of the masters course following the positive experience of the module.

Although the intention of the simulation was to train students in legal research and the ability to independently navigate the subject matter of international business law, an unintended consequence was the development of entrepreneurial skills and ambitions within the cohort of students. Ideally, this consequence could be built upon and expanded, however, my expertise to achieve this without interdisciplinary input is limited.

BRINGING THE TWO EXPERIENCES TOGETHER: MICRO AND MACRO FINDINGS AND REFLECTIONS

According to Durate (2007), within the process of autoethnographic research into teaching practices, the focus progresses from the personal sphere (micro-context) towards the institutional domain (macro-context) when seeking to link micro and macro contexts (p. 1).

The following will present the findings from the combined separate experiences of the two authors of this paper, which will be reported in an aggregated format. These findings have been derived from the two separate personal experiences as higher education teachers in two separate departments, the law school and the business school of a small to medium sized higher education institution in the Northwest of England.

The findings were derived on the basis of Schön's (1983) model of practitioners developing and improving their teaching practice through the reflection in, on and for action. As such, when the two cross-disciplinary experiences are linked in reflection, they provide the foundation for a multi- and interdisciplinary collaborative model for entrepreneurship simulations that draws on the cross-departmental expertise of higher educational institutions to provide graduates with the tools needed to excel in an increasingly multilayered and complex world of employment.

Looking back to the beginning of this chapter, one recalls the initial research questions, which guided the study:

1. What successful strategies and development needs were revealed in our separate experiences with elements of gamification in entrepreneurship education?
2. What implications does our collaborative reflection have for the future of entrepreneurship education and gamification within our higher education institution?

When reviewing, comparing and contrasting our experiences, a metaphor that repeatedly emerged was that of a jigsaw puzzle. As such, the study was embarked upon in the hope to learn from the experiences of colleagues within other disciplines who undertake teaching in related areas. What we found was that many of the successful strategies employed in one department formed a potential missing piece that could fill experienced gaps in the other and vice versa. For instance, the experiences within the business school had revealed a lack of practical motivation amongst students to encourage future business start-ups. When reflecting on this need in light of the success experienced in this area within the law school, it was deduced that the active participation in the simulation, and the ownership taken by the students in developing their own individual fictitious businesses could potentially solve this issue. It also confirmed the assumption that the business school approach to entrepreneurship education was not interactive enough to stimulate the experiential learning. The experiences from the law school simulation lacked in-depth knowledge of business processes and financial considerations, which are vital for any entrepreneurial endeavors. As such, it was seen that graduates who wished to pursue entrepreneurship in their futures decided to embark on further study to fill the missing gaps. As such, the required expertise to close this gap was already being utilized in a module within another department, namely the business school.

The study also confirmed many of the findings from the literature review. Most notably it has been confirmed within the experiences, that simulations are a useful teaching tool to encourage practical and immersive learning. The case studies also demonstrated the common lack of interdisciplinary teaching of entrepreneurship within HEIs and how total enterprise simulations cannot realistically be created within multidisciplinary input.

SOLUTIONS AND RECOMMENDATIONS

Following the findings and reflections, the key learning we have taken from combining our teaching experiences of entrepreneurship across departments has been that as academics and subject experts of our individual subjects we tend to see ourselves as isolated islands of knowledge, tasked with passing on our experiences and knowledge to the next generation of workers. However, this understanding of our roles as separate isolated knowledge entities does not mirror the realities of the various industries, we are seeking to prepare our students for. As such, each academic is only a small part of a piece of a jigsaw puzzle, and each department or school is one of these pieces, which when placed together should mirror society as it will be found by students once they graduate. In our cases, we realized that for the purpose of entrepreneurship education, our practices in business and law each had a number of needs and offers which corresponded to the needs and offers from the other school. Figuratively, it seemed just like each of our experiences showcased how the teaching practices could be merged into a wider jigsaw puzzle. This prompted us to reach out to more of our academic colleagues in other schools and departments to assess what other needs and offers pertaining to entrepreneurship education existed within the university. In hindsight our findings may appear obvious, however, this was also possible to be established via cross-departmental and multidisciplinary communication.

For the purpose of showcasing our wider findings in this area, a table has been created, showcasing some of the relevant exposed cross-departmental input and output potential, which have been derived from the findings of this study as well as communications with academics from other departments following the findings.

Table 1. Potential inputs and outputs for future cross-departmental collaboration on accessible entrepreneurship simulation games in the sample HEI

School/ Department	Interdisciplinary input needs	Entrepreneurship Education Utility Output Potential
Business School	• Interactive Engagement Tools • Interdisciplinary expertise (law, politics, technology, design, innovation etc.) • Social/Psychological models and understanding of human behaviors • Technology and related support facilities	• Expertise of business processes and related subject matters (i.e., marketing, product design, strategic management, accountancy and finance) • Experience of entrepreneurship education • Knowledge of business and entrepreneurship methodologies • Network of entrepreneurs and business management experts
Law School	• Expertise of business processes and related subject matters (i.e., marketing, product design, strategic management, accountancy and finance) • Interdisciplinary expertise (business, politics, technology, design, innovation, teaching and learning approaches etc.) • Social/Psychological models and understanding of human behaviors • Technology and related support facilities	• Experience of engaging enterprise simulation • Expertise in the laws relating to Entrepreneurship and business operations • Experience in developing problem scenarios • Experience and knowledge of relevant communication skills and how to teach these (i.e., negotiations, discussions, interviews, presentations)
Findings derived from communications with academics from other departments on the basis of the initial findings from this study		
Psychology School	• Expertise of business processes and related subject matters (i.e., marketing, product design, strategic management, accountancy and finance) • Interdisciplinary expertise (law, politics, technology, design, innovation etc.) • Technology and related support facilities	• Experience in simulation games • Trialed models of online gamification • Expertise in Social/Psychological models and understanding of human behaviors • Interactive Engagement Tools
Education School	• Expertise of business processes and related subject matters (i.e., marketing, product design, strategic management, accountancy and finance) • Interdisciplinary expertise (law, politics, technology, design, innovation etc.) • Technology and related support facilities • Interactive Engagement Tools	• Expertise in teaching and learning approaches • Experience in innovative teaching methods • Network of Teaching and Learning Experts
Creative Arts Schools	• Expertise of business processes and related subject matters (i.e., marketing, product design, strategic management, accountancy and finance) • Interdisciplinary expertise (business, law, politics, technology, design, innovation, teaching and learning approaches etc.) • Social/Psychological models and understanding of human behaviors • Technology and related support facilities	• Expertise in innovation and design • Experience in encouraging students to take creative risks • Ability to design aesthetic virtual simulation tools/ environments • Network of creative human capital • Higher success rates of enterprising graduates • Interactive Engagement Tools
Information Technology Related Schools	• Expertise of business processes and related subject matters (i.e., marketing, product design, strategic management, accountancy and finance) • Interdisciplinary expertise (business, law, politics, design, innovation, teaching and learning approaches etc.) • Social/Psychological models and understanding of human behaviors	• Higher success rates of enterprising graduates • Technical and technological knowhow • Experience of an expertise in creating virtual games and learning spaces • Access to specialist IT equipment and the knowledge/ ability to use it • Expertise in gaming models and theories

A closer look at the potential inputs and outputs from various HEI departments enhances the puzzle metaphor used earlier in this chapter. In this sense, it becomes clear that collaborative efforts to create an institution wide entrepreneurship simulation game are viable without external input, as all the required expertise and facilities are already present within the organization. However, there are two major requirements for this kind of endeavor to be realized: Firstly, entrepreneurship must be considered a standalone skill rather than a sub-category of business studies. Secondly, separate schools within HEIs need to enhance cross-departmental communication and experience exchange.

FUTURE RESEARCH DIRECTIONS

There are clear indications that the experiences in teaching entrepreneurship will continue to move towards more innovative and practical methods, such as simulations. However, what this study has revealed in the untapped potential of cross-disciplinary collaboration to enhance the authenticity of gamification, such as realistic simulation games, by adding interdisciplinary layers. The complexities found within the world of work, particularly commercial sectors, will require significant academic attention in the future to enable HEIs to prepare students for the realities post-graduation. The interdisciplinarity of gamification across HEIs, thus, cannot solely apply to methods or content, but needs to be holistic and embed multidisciplinary layers in all aspects. It is the intention of this project to have inspired academics to reach out to colleagues in other departments to work towards implementing these findings in practice.

CONCLUSION

This study utilized collaborative autoethnography to bring together the experiences of two academics from different schools within a medium sized HEI to improve the use of gamification for entrepreneurship education. The idea is to design a novel form of entrepreneurship education, which uses games as a way to practically train entrepreneurship skills in a more realistic, multidimensional and multidisciplinary fashion. The contributors seek to highlight the wide-ranging contextual dimensions required of entrepreneurship in practice and embed this into education and training tools. The chapter covers a broad variety of pedagogical settings, objectives and tools within entrepreneurship education, whilst offering a plurality of disciplinary, cultural and departmental perspectives, which address a range of contemporary issues and substantial developments in the area.

Despite the importance and interests in games, most of the games developed concentrate on single specialist subjects and are often not fit for educational purposes that seek to prepare graduates for successful employability within entrepreneurship in practice. This chapter highlights to conceptual and practical steps taken within a study which explores the theoretical perspectives of multidisciplinary entrepreneurship education from a learner's perspective. It acknowledges the dilemmas HEIs experience whilst supporting learners in their entrepreneurship education. The innate desire of learners to have accessible games to develop more practical skills in the classroom is vital in achieving engaging learning environments and processes (the simulation game). The use of games enables learners to sustain entrepreneurship knowledge, skills and competencies (Antonaci et, al 2015), increases learners' interests (Ruiz-Alba et al, 2019), motivates learners and as a result enhances the employability of students and graduate outcomes results (Huotari & Hamari, 2012).

The findings of this study pave the way for the development of future accessible solutions for all learners, regardless of socio-economic background or discipline to enhance entrepreneurship post-graduation. Using the experiential learning as a means to generate ideas and stimulate interests, interdisciplinary content has been created, bridging together fields such as business, social, legal and technical studies.

In conclusion, the collaborative reflections of the individual teaching experiences have revealed that the key factors that are currently holding developments back in the area of interdisciplinary gamification solutions to entrepreneurship education include a lack of focus on entrepreneurial skills in departments within HEIs other than business schools, and a lack of cross-departmental communication and collaboration. The required multidisciplinary and holistic approach to develop innovative teaching tools must engage students via the interconnectedness of innovation, economic considerations, laws and legal environments, technical know-how and creativity in a clear, concise and comprehensible style that will be understood regardless of the subject-specific area of expertise.

REFERENCES

Abdullah, N. L., Hanafiah, M. H., & Hashim, N. A. (2013). Developing Creative Teaching Module: Business Simulation in Teaching Strategic Management. *International Education Studies*, *6*(6), 95–107. doi:10.5539/ies.v6n6p95

Abonyi, A. U., Okafor, M. G., & Okongwu, J. (2020). Law, specialization, teaching and practice. *Chukwuemeka Odumegwu Ojukwu University Law Journal, 5*(1).

Adams, T. E., Jones, S. L. H., & Ellis, C. (2015). *Autoethnography*. Series in Understanding Statistics.

Agogué, M., Levillain, K., & Hooge, S. (2015). Gamification of creativity: Exploring the usefulness of serious games for ideation. *Creativity and Innovation Management*, *24*(3), 415–429. doi:10.1111/caim.12138

Ahmad, T. (2019). *Scenario based approach to re-imagining future of higher education which prepares students for the future of work*. Higher Education, Skills and Work-Based Learning. doi:10.1108/HESWBL-12-2018-0136

Alexander, S. (1999). An evaluation of innovative projects involving communication and information technology in higher education. *Higher Education Research & Development*, *18*(2), 173–183. doi:10.1080/0729436990180202

Alexandre-Leclair, L. (2014). Diversity as a motive for entrepreneurship? The case of gender, culture and ethnicity. *Journal of Innovation Economics & Management*, *2*(14), 157–175. doi:10.3917/jie.014.0157

Ali, A. M., & Yusof, H. (2011). Quality in qualitative studies: The case of validity, reliability and generalizability. *Issues in Social and Environmental Accounting*, *5*(1), 25–64. doi:10.22164/isea.v5i1.59

Anft, M. (2017). Breaking professional schools out of their silos. *The Chronicle of Higher Education*, (April), 30.

Antonaci, A., Dagnino, F. M., Ott, M., Bellotti, F., Berta, R., De Gloria, A., Lavagnino, E., Romero, M., Usart, M., & Mayer, I. (2015). A gamified collaborative course in entrepreneurship: Focus on objectives and tools. *Computers in Human Behavior*, *51*, 1276–1283. doi:10.1016/j.chb.2014.11.082

Bahador, K. M. K., & Haider, A. (2017). Incorporating information technology competencies in accounting curriculum: A case study in Malaysian higher education institutions. *Journal of Engineering and Applied Sciences (Asian Research Publishing Network)*, *12*(21), 5508–5513.

Bakar, R., Islam, M. D. A., & Lee, J. (2015). Entrepreneurship education: Experiences in selected countries. *International Education Studies*, *8*(1), 88–99.

Barton, A. M. (2021). Teaching Lawyers to Think Like Leaders: The Next Big Shift in Legal Education. *Baylor Law Review*, *73*, 115.

Béchard, J. P., & Grégoire, D. (2005). Entrepreneurship education research revisited: The case of higher education. *Academy of Management Learning & Education*, *4*(1), 22–43. doi:10.5465/amle.2005.16132536

Bell, R. (2016). Unpacking the link between entrepreneurialism and employability: An assessment of the relationship between entrepreneurial attitudes and likelihood of graduate employment in a professional field. *Education + Training*, *58*(1), 2–17. doi:10.1108/ET-09-2014-0115

Bhatia, A. K., & Levina, N. (2021) Can Entrepreneurship be taught in a classroom, Business Education. *Harvard Business Review*. https://hbr.org/am/2020/08/can-entrepreneurship-be-taught-in-a-classroom

Biviano, T. (2017). Practical Lawyering: Intervention in Law School Curriculum Requirements to Prepare New Lawyers for Ethically Competent Practice. *The Georgetown Journal of Legal Ethics*, *30*, 619.

Bridgstock, R., Grant-Iramu, M., Bilsland, C., Tofa, M., Lloyd, K., & Jackson, D. (2019). Going beyond "getting a job": Graduates' narratives and lived experiences of employability and their career development. In Education for Employability (Volume 2) (pp. 89-104). Brill Sense.

Busenitz, L. W., West, G. P. III, Shepherd, D., Nelson, T., Chandler, G. N., & Zacharakis, A. (2003). Entrepreneurship research in emergence: Past trends and future directions. *Journal of Management*, *29*(3), 285–308. doi:10.1016/S0149-2063(03)00013-8

Caponetto, I., Earp, J., & Ott, M. (2014, October). Gamification and education: A literature review. In *European Conference on Games Based Learning* (*Vol. 1*, p. 50). Academic Conferences International Limited.

Caruso, J. V. (2019, March). Using Business Simulations to Prepare Students to Think Critically, Make Better Decisions, and Solve Business Problems. In *Developments in Business Simulation and Experiential Learning: Proceedings of the Annual ABSEL conference* (*Vol. 46*). Academic Press.

Chang, H. (2016). Autoethnography. In *Autoethnography as method* (pp. 43–58). Routledge. doi:10.4324/9781315433370

Chang, H., Ngunjiri, F., & Hernandez, K. A. C. (2016). *Collaborative autoethnography* (Vol. 8). Routledge. doi:10.4324/9781315432137

Chernikova, O., Heitzmann, N., Stadler, M., Holzberger, D., Seidel, T., & Fischer, F. (2020). Simulation-based learning in higher education: A meta-analysis. *Review of Educational Research, 90*(4), 499–541. doi:10.3102/0034654320933544

Clouse, V. G. (1990). A controlled experiment relating entrepreneurial education to students' start-up decisions. *Journal of Small Business Management, 28*(2), 45.

Crecente-Romero, F., Giménez-Baldazo, M., & Rivera-Galicia, L. F. (2016). Subjective perception of entrepreneurship. Differences among countries. *Journal of Business Research, 69*(11), 5158–5162. doi:10.1016/j.jbusres.2016.04.097

Daly, S. P. (2001). Student-operated Internet businesses: True experiential learning in entrepreneurship and retail management. *Journal of Marketing Education, 23*(3), 204–215. doi:10.1177/0273475301233006

Delamont, S. (2009). The only honest thing: Autoethnography, reflexivity and small crises in fieldwork. *Ethnography and Education, 4*(1), 51–63. doi:10.1080/17457820802703507

Denslow, D. L., & Giunipero, L. C. (2003). *Improving purchasing success through entrepreneurial behaviour*. Paper presented at the ISM's 88th Annual International Supply Management Conference.

Díaz-García, C., Sáez-Martínez, F., & Jiménez-Moreno, J. (2015). Assessing the impact of the "Entrepreneurs" education programme on participants' entrepreneurial intentions. *International Journal of Educational Technology in Higher Education, 12*(3), 17–31.

Duff, P. A. (2006). Beyond generalizability. *Inference and generalizability in applied linguistics: Multiple perspectives, 12*, 65.

Durazzi, N. (2019). The political economy of high skills: Higher education in knowledge-based labour markets. *Journal of European Public Policy, 26*(12), 1799–1817. doi:10.1080/13501763.2018.1551415

Edge, N., Fitzgerald, E., & Willcoxson, L. (2019). Addressing Key Concerns in Graduate Employability: Changing Our Expectations of Universities. In Education for Employability (Volume 2) (pp. 51-64). Brill Sense.

Enterprise, D. G. (2008). *Entrepreneurship in higher education, especially within non-business studies. Final report of the expert group*. European Commission.

Eurydice Network. (2012). *Education Information Network in Europe*. https://eacea.ec.europa.eu/national-policies/eurydice/about_en

Fayolle, A., Gailly, B., & Lassas-Clerc, N. (2006). Assessing the impact of entrepreneurship education programmes: A new methodology. *Journal of European Industrial Training, 30*(9), 701–720. doi:10.1108/03090590610715022

Fiet, J. O. (2001). The theoretical side of teaching entrepreneurship. *Journal of Business Venturing, 16*(1), 1–24. doi:10.1016/S0883-9026(99)00041-5

Fine, G. A. (1993). Ten lies of ethnography: Moral dilemmas of field research. *Journal of Contemporary Ethnography, 22*(3), 267–294. doi:10.1177/089124193022003001

Galloway, K. (2017). Getting back to our roots: global law schools in local context. In *Legal Education In The Global Context* (pp. 17–30). Routledge. doi:10.4324/9781315563244-2

Gannaway, D., & Sheppard, K. (2019). Pursuing Employability through Generalist and Specialist Degree Programs: Australian Perspectives. In Education for Employability (Volume 2) (pp. 155-166). Brill Sense.

Genson, G. L. (1992). Teaching entrepreneurship through the classics. *Journal of Applied Business Research*, *8*(4), 135–140. doi:10.19030/jabr.v8i4.6135

Gibb, A. (2011). Concepts into practice: meeting the challenge of development of entrepreneurship educators around an innovative paradigm: The case of the International Entrepreneurship Educators' Programme (IEEP). *International Journal of Entrepreneurial Behaviour & Research*, *17*(2), 146–165. doi:10.1108/13552551111114914

Goi, C. L. (2019). The use of business simulation games in teaching and learning. *Journal of Education for Business*, *94*(5), 342–349. doi:10.1080/08832323.2018.1536028

Goodwin, A. L. (2021). Teaching standards, globalisation, and conceptions of teacher professionalism. *European Journal of Teacher Education*, *44*(1), 5–19. doi:10.1080/02619768.2020.1833855

Graevenitz G.v., Harhoff, D., & Weber, R. (2010) The effects of entrepreneurship education. *Journal of Economic Behaviour and Organisation, 76*(1), 1-39.

Gregersen, E. (2019). *The lived experience of a university law clinic supervisor: an autoethnographic inquiry*. University of Northumbria at Newcastle.

Grivokostopoulou, F., Kovas, K., & Perikos, I. (2019). Examining the impact of a gamified entrepreneurship education framework in higher education. *Sustainability*, *11*(20), 5623. doi:10.3390u11205623

Gürol, Y., & Atsan, N. (2006). Entrepreneurial characteristics amongst university students: Some insights for entrepreneurship education and training in Turkey. *Education + Training*, *48*(1), 25–38. doi:10.1108/00400910610645716

Haines, G. H. Jr. (1988). The ombudsman: Teaching entrepreneurship. *Interfaces*, *18*(5), 23–30. doi:10.1287/inte.18.5.23

Hamari, J., Shernoff, D. J., Rowe, E., Coller, B., Asbell-Clarke, J., & Edwards, T. (2016). Challenging games help students learn: An empirical study on engagement, flow and immersion in game-based learning. *Computers in Human Behavior*, *54*, 170–179. doi:10.1016/j.chb.2015.07.045

Hassan, M. A., Habiba, U., Majeed, F., & Shoaib, M. (2021). Adaptive gamification in e-learning based on students' learning styles. *Interactive Learning Environments*, *29*(4), 545–565. doi:10.1080/10494820.2019.1588745

Healy, M., Brown, J. L., & Ho, C. (2021). Graduate employability as a professional proto-jurisdiction in higher education. *Higher Education*, 1–18.

Herriott, R. E., & Firestone, W. A. (1983). Multisite qualitative policy research: Optimizing description and generalizability. *Educational Researcher*, *12*(2), 14–19. doi:10.3102/0013189X012002014

Herrmann, K., Hannon, P., Cox, J., Ternouth, P., & Crowley, T. (2008). *Developing entrepreneurial graduates: putting entrepreneurship at the centre of higher education.* NESTA.

HESA. (2021). *Graduates in work | HESA.* Retrieved 5 August 2021, from https://www.hesa.ac.uk/data-and-analysis/graduates/activities/work

High Fliers. (2021). *High Fliers.* Retrieved 8 August 2021, from https://www.highfliers.co.uk/

Hindle, K. (2002). A grounded theory for teaching entrepreneurship using simulation games. *Simulation & Gaming, 33*(2), 236–241. doi:10.1177/1046878102332012

Holcombe, R. G. (1998). Entrepreneurship and economic growth. *Quarterly Journal of Austrian Economics, 1*(2), 45–62. doi:10.100712113-998-1008-1

Hoppe, M., Westerberg, M., & Leffler, E. (2017). Educational approaches to entrepreneurship in higher education: A view from the Swedish horizon. *Education + Training, 59*(7/8), 751–767. doi:10.1108/ET-12-2016-0177

Huotari, K., & Hamari, J. (2012, October). Defining gamification: a service marketing perspective. In *Proceeding of the 16th international academic MindTrek conference* (pp. 17-22). 10.1145/2393132.2393137

Iscenco, A., & Li, J. (2014). *The game with impact: Gamification in environmental education and entrepreneurship. Moldovan Environmental Governance Academy.* MEGA.

Jacob, M., Kühhirt, M., & Rodrigues, M. (2019). Labour market returns to graduates' international experience: Exploring cross-country variation in Europe. *European Sociological Review, 35*(4), 491–505. doi:10.1093/esr/jcz022

Jamieson, I. (1984). Education for enterprise. In *CRAC* (Vol. 19). Ballinger.

Jay, J. K., & Johnson, K. L. (2002). Capturing complexity: A typology of reflective practice for teacher education. *Teaching and Teacher Education, 18*(1), 73–85. doi:10.1016/S0742-051X(01)00051-8

Joy, P. A. (2017). The uneasy history of experiential education in US law schools. *Dickinson Law Review, 122*, 551.

Justice, C., Rice, J., Warry, W., Inglis, S., Miller, S., & Sammon, S. (2007). Inquiry in higher education: Reflections and directions on course design and teaching methods. *Innovative Higher Education, 31*(4), 201–214. doi:10.100710755-006-9021-9

Kelley, T. M., & Johnston, E. (2012). Discovering the appropriate role of serious games in the design of open governance platforms. *Public Administration Quarterly*, 504–554.

Kelmar, J. H. (1992). Business plans for teaching entrepreneurial behaviour. *Education + Training, 34*(1). Advance online publication. doi:10.1108/00400919210007511

Kiili, K. (2007). Foundation for problem-based gaming. *British Journal of Educational Technology, 38*(3), 394–404. doi:10.1111/j.1467-8535.2007.00704.x

Kirzner, I. (1979). *Perception, opportunity, and profit: studies in the theory of entrepreneurship. University of Chicago Press.*

Koren, M., & Pető, R. (2020). Business disruptions from social distancing. *PLoS One, 15*(9), e0239113. doi:10.1371/journal.pone.0239113 PMID:32946463

Kuhn, R. (2009). Information literacy for law students: An approach to meeting the challenges of professional training and practice. *Innovation, 38*(1). Advance online publication. doi:10.4314/innovation.v38i1.46973

Kuratko, D. F. (2005). The emergence of entrepreneurship education: Development, trends, and challenges. *Entrepreneurship Theory and Practice, 29*(5), 577–597. doi:10.1111/j.1540-6520.2005.00099.x

Lapadat, J. C. (2017). Ethics in autoethnography and collaborative autoethnography. *Qualitative Inquiry, 23*(8), 589–603. doi:10.1177/1077800417704462

Liñán, F. (2004). Intention-based models of entrepreneurship education. *Piccolla Impresa/Small Business, 3*(1), 11-35.

Löffler, A., Prifti, L., Levkovskyi, B., Utesch, M., & Krcmar, H. (2018, April). Simulation games for the digital transformation of business processes: Development and application of two prototypes from the automotive and online retail sector. In *2018 IEEE Global Engineering Education Conference (EDUCON)* (pp. 1475-1483). IEEE. 10.1109/EDUCON.2018.8363407

Low, M., Venkataraman, S., & Srivatsan, V. (1994). Developing an entrepreneurship game for teaching and research. *Simulation & Gaming, 25*(3), 383–401. doi:10.1177/1046878194253006

Lytvyn, A., Lytvyn, V., Rudenko, L., Pelekh, Y., Didenko, O., Muszkieta, R., & Żukow, W. (2020). Informatization of technical vocational schools: Theoretical foundations and practical approaches. *Education and Information Technologies, 25*(1), 583–609. doi:10.100710639-019-09966-4

Martin, C., & Iucu, R. B. (2014). Teaching entrepreneurship to educational sciences students. *Procedia: Social and Behavioral Sciences, 116*, 4397–4400. doi:10.1016/j.sbspro.2014.01.954

Mason, C. (2011). Entrepreneurship education and research: Emerging trends and concerns. *Journal of Global Entrepreneurship, 1*(1), 13–25.

Mason, R., & Rennie, F. (2006). *Elearning: The key concepts*. Routledge. doi:10.4324/9780203099483

Matlay, H., & Carey, C. (2006, October). Entrepreneurship education in the UK: a critical perspective. *ISBE Conference, Cardiff, November.*

McMullan, W., Chrisman, J. J., & Vesper, K. H. (2002). Lessons from successful innovations in entrepreneurial support programming. *Innovation and entrepreneurship in Western Canada: From family businesses to multinationals*, 207-223.

Menkel-Meadow, C. (2019). Thinking or Acting Like A Lawyer? What We Don't Know About Legal Education and are Afraid to Ask. In *The State of Legal Education Research: Then and Now and Tomorrow*. TaylorFrancis/Routledge.

Meyer, M., Libaers, D., Thijs, B., Grant, K., Glänzel, W., & Debackere, K. (2014). Origin and emergence of entrepreneurship as a research field. *Scientometrics, 98*(1), 473–485.

Minniti, M., & Lévesque, M. (2008). *Recent developments in the economics of entrepreneurship*. Academic Press.

Myers, M. (2000). Qualitative research and the generalizability question: Standing firm with Proteus. *Qualitative Report*, *4*(3), 9. doi:10.46743/2160-3715/2000.2925

Mykhailyshyn, H., Kondur, O., & Serman, L. (2018). Innovation of education and educational innovations in conditions of modern higher education institution. *Journal of Vasyl Stefanyk Precarpathian National University*, *5*(1), 9–16. doi:10.15330/jpnu.5.1.9-16

Nabi, G., Holden, R., & Walmsley, A. (2010). Entrepreneurial intentions among students: Towards a re-focused research agenda. *Journal of Small Business and Enterprise Development*, *17*(4), 537–551. doi:10.1108/14626001011088714

Nabi, G., Walmsley, A., Liñán, F., Akhtar, I., & Neame, C. (2018). Does entrepreneurship education in the first year of higher education develop entrepreneurial intentions? The role of learning and inspiration. *Studies in Higher Education*, *43*(3), 452–467. doi:10.1080/03075079.2016.1177716

Naudé, W. (2010). Entrepreneurship, developing countries, and development economics: New approaches and insights. *Small Business Economics*, *34*(1), 1–12. doi:10.100711187-009-9198-2

Newell, W. H. (2007). *13 Decision Making in Interdisciplinary Studies*. Academic Press.

Ngunjiri, F. W., Hernandez, K. A. C., & Chang, H. (2010). Living autoethnography: Connecting life and research. *Journal of Research Practice*, *6*(1), E1–E1.

Oosterbeek, H., Van Praag, M., & Ijsselstein, A. (2010). The impact of entrepreneurship education on entrepreneurship skills and motivation. *European Economic Review*, *54*(3), 442–454. doi:10.1016/j.euroecorev.2009.08.002

Penaluna, K., Penaluna, A., & Jones, C. (2012). The context of enterprise education: Insights into current practices. *Industry and Higher Education*, *26*(3), 163–175. doi:10.5367/ihe.2012.0098

Peters, M. A. (2005). The new prudentialism in education: Actuarial rationality and the entrepreneurial self. *Educational Theory*, *55*(2), 123–137. doi:10.1111/j.0013-2004.2005.00002.x

Petkov, S., & Savishchenko, M., V., Semenyshyna-Fihol, B., A. Poda, T., & M. Chaika, I. (2020). Application of Mock-Court as an Interdisciplinary Model for Consolidation of Professional Training of Law Students. *Journal Of Education And E-Learning Research*, *7*(2), 122–129. doi:10.20448/journal.509.2020.72.122.129

Pham, T. (2021). Communication competencies and international graduates' employability outcomes: Strategies to navigate the host labour market. *Journal of International Migration and Integration*, 1–17.

Pitan, O. S. (2017). *Graduate employees' generic skills and training needs*. Higher Education, Skills and Work-Based Learning. doi:10.1108/HESWBL-04-2017-0026

Platt, L. (2004). Accepting Risk-Daring Greatness. *Vital Speeches of the Day*, *70*(17), 541.

Polczyk, P. (2012). *Autoethnography as an accessible method of research*. Academic Press.

Porter, L. W. (1994). The relation of entrepreneurship education to business education. *Simulation & Gaming, 25*(3), 416–419. doi:10.1177/1046878194253008

Quality Assurance Agency for Higher Education. (2012). *Enterprise and entrepreneurship education: guidance for UK higher education providers*. QAA.

Rapp, A., Cena, F., Hopfgartner, F., Hamari, J., & Linehan, C. (2016, October). Fictional game elements: Critical perspectives on gamification design. In *Proceedings of the 2016 Annual Symposium on Computer-Human Interaction in Play Companion Extended Abstracts* (pp. 373-377). 10.1145/2968120.2968125

Rashid, S., & Yadav, S. S. (2020). Impact of Covid-19 pandemic on higher education and research. *Indian Journal of Human Development, 14*(2), 340–343. doi:10.1177/0973703020946700

Robertson, M., & Collins, A. (2003). The video role model as an enterprise teaching aid. *Education + Training, 45*(6), 331–340. doi:10.1108/00400910310495987

Robertson, M., Collins, A., Medeira, N., & Slater, J. (2003). Barriers to Start-Ups and Their Effect on Aspirant Entrepreneurs. *Education and Training, 45*(6), 308-316. Available: www.lmu.ac.uk/business-start-up

Rosli, K., Khairudin, N., & Saat, R. M. (2019). Gamification in entrepreneurship and accounting education. *Academy of Entrepreneurship Journal, 25*(3), 1–6.

Roundy, P. T., Bradshaw, M., & Brockman, B. K. (2018). The emergence of entrepreneurial ecosystems: A complex adaptive systems approach. *Journal of Business Research, 86*, 1–10. doi:10.1016/j.jbusres.2018.01.032

Sarfraz, I., Rajendran, D., Hewege, C., & Mohan, M. D. (2018). An exploration of global employability skills: A systematic research review. *International Journal of Work Organisation and Emotion, 9*(1), 63–88. doi:10.1504/IJWOE.2018.091339

Schofield, M. (2021). Gamification Tools to Facilitate Student Learning Engagement in Higher Education: A Burden or Blessing? In Fostering Communication and Learning With Underutilized Technologies in Higher Education (pp. 21-35). IGI Global. doi:10.4018/978-1-7998-4846-2.ch002

Schön, D. A. (1983). *The reflective practitioner: How professionals think in action*. Basic Books.

Schumpeter, J. A. (1926). *Theorie der wirtschaftlichen Entwicklung* (2nd ed.). Duncker & Humboldt.

Sergi, B. S., Popkova, E. G., Bogoviz, A. V., & Ragulina, J. V. (2019). Entrepreneurship and Economic Growth: The Experience of Developed and Developing Countries. In Entrepreneurship and Development in the 21st Century (Lab for Entrepreneurship and Development). Emerald Publishing Limited. doi:10.1108/978-1-78973-233-720191002

Sexton, D. L., & Upton, N. B. (1987). Evaluation of an innovative approach to teaching entrepreneurship. *Journal of Small Business Management, 25*(1), 35.

Solicitors Regulation Authority. (2014). *Academic Stage Handbook*. Solicitors Regulation Authority.

Solicitors Regulation Authority. (2021). *SQE2 assessment specification | SQE | Solicitors Regulation Authority*. SQEWebsite. Retrieved 5 August 2021, from https://sqe.sra.org.uk/exam-arrangements/assessment-information/sqe2-assessment-specification

Souitaris, V., Zerbinati, S., & Al-Laham, A. (2007). Do entrepreneurship programmes raise entrepreneurial intention of science and engineering students? The effect of learning, inspiration and resources. *Journal of Business Venturing*, *22*(4), 566–591. doi:10.1016/j.jbusvent.2006.05.002

Spiegel, M., & Marxt, C. (2011). Defining Technology Entrepreneurship. *2011 IEEE International Conference on Industrial Engineering and Engineering Management*, 1623-1627. 10.1109/IEEM.2011.6118191

Srirejeki, K., & Faturokhman, A. (2020). An Experimental Study on the Effectiveness of Entrepreneurship Education. *Economy Transdisciplinarity Cognition, 23*(1).

Steegh, N. (2005). Using Externships to Introduce Family Law Students to New Professional Roles. *Family Court Review*, *43*(1), 137–148. doi:10.1111/j.1744-1617.2005.00013.x

Stewart, J., & Knowles, V. (2003). Mentoring in undergraduate business management programmes. *Journal of European Industrial Training*, *27*(2/3/4), 147–159. doi:10.1108/03090590310468967

Styhre, A. (2020). Governing Innovation-Led Economies: The Role of Business Creation and Creativity. In Indie Video Game Development Work (pp. 37-77). Palgrave Macmillan.

Suarta, I. M., Suwintana, I. K., Sudhana, I. F. P., & Hariyanti, N. K. D. (2017). Employability skills required by the 21st-century workplace: A literature review of labour market demand. *Advances in Social Science, Education and Humanities Research*, *102*(58), 337–342. doi:10.2991/ictvt-17.2017.58

Suleman, F. (2018). The employability skills of higher education graduates: Insights into conceptual frameworks and methodological options. *Higher Education*, *76*(2), 263–278. doi:10.100710734-017-0207-0

Tavares, B. L. (2017). Changing the construct: Promoting cross-cultural conversations in the law school classroom. *Journal of Legal Education*, *67*(1), 211–241.

Tholen, G., & Brown, P. (2017). *Higher education and the myths of graduate employability*. Academic Press.

Thomae, H. (1999). The nomothetic-idiographic issue: Some roots and recent trends. *International Journal of Group Tensions*, *28*(1), 187–215. doi:10.1023/A:1021891506378

Tokareva, E. A., Smirnova, Y. V., & Orchakova, L. G. (2019). Innovation and communication technologies: Analysis of the effectiveness of their use and implementation in higher education. *Education and Information Technologies*, *24*(5), 3219–3234. doi:10.100710639-019-09922-2

Tran, T. T. (2016). Enhancing graduate employability and the need for universityenterprise collaboration. *Journal of Teaching and Learning for Graduate Employability*, *7*(1), 58–71. doi:10.21153/jtlge2016vol7no1art598

Uhlemann, J., Costa, R., & Charpentier, J. C. (2020). Product design and engineering—Past, present, future trends in teaching, research and practices: Academic and industry points of view. *Current Opinion in Chemical Engineering*, *27*, 10–21. doi:10.1016/j.coche.2019.10.003

Ulijn, J. M., Duill, M. O., & Robertson, S. A. (2004). Teaching business plan negotiation: Fostering entrepreneurship among business and engineering students. *Business Communication Quarterly*, *67*(1), 41–57. doi:10.1177/1080569903262040

Vanevenhoven, J., & Drago, W. A. (2015). The structure and scope of entrepreneurship programs in higher education around the world. In *Entrepreneurial Learning* (pp. 117–133). Routledge. doi:10.4324/9781315857817-6

Visvizi, A., Lytras, M. D., Damiani, E., & Mathkour, H. (2018). Policy making for smart cities: Innovation and social inclusive economic growth for sustainability. *Journal of Science and Technology Policy Management*.

Vos, L., & Brennan, R. (2010). Marketing simulation games: Student and lecturer perspectives. *Marketing Intelligence & Planning*, *28*(7), 882–897. doi:10.1108/02634501011086472

Wan Tahir, W. M. M., Mohd Noor, I. H., Daud, D., & Hussin, A. H. (2018). Towards interactive learning style in accounting: The game approach. *Academic Journal of Business and Social Sciences*, *2*, 1–8.

Washbush, J., & Gosen, J. (2001). An exploration of game-derived learning in total enterprise simulations. *Simulation & Gaming*, *32*(3), 281–296. doi:10.1177/104687810103200301

Wilson, R. D. (2011). *External validation of an instructional design model for high fidelity simulation: model application in a hospital setting*. Arizona State University.

Winarno, A., & Wijijayanti, T. (2018). Does Entrepreneurial Literacy Correlate to the Small-Medium Enterprises Performance in Batu East Java? *Academy of Entrepreneurship Journal*, *24*(1), 1–13.

Wiratraman, H. P. (2019). The Challenges of Teaching Comparative Law and Socio-Legal Studies at Indonesia's Law Schools. *Asian Journal of Comparative Law*, *14*(S1), S229–S244. doi:10.1017/asjcl.2019.15

Wong, P. K., Ho, Y. P., & Autio, E. (2005). Entrepreneurship, innovation and economic growth: Evidence from GEM data. *Small Business Economics*, *24*(3), 335–350. doi:10.100711187-005-2000-1

Zaman, M. (2013). Entrepreneurial characteristics among university students: Implications for entrepreneurship education and training in Pakistan. *African Journal of Business Management*, *7*(39), 4053–4058.

ADDITIONAL READING

Bagheri, A., Alinezhad, A., & Sajadi, S. M. (2020). Entrepreneurship Education and Gamification: An Analysis of Students' Learning Outcomes. In *The Entrepreneurial Behaviour: Unveiling the cognitive and emotional aspect of entrepreneurship*. Emerald Publishing Limited. doi:10.1108/978-1-78973-507-920201005

Breuer, H., Gudiksen, S., Abril, C., & Lehmann, C. (2019). Gamification and Games as Facilitation Methods for Innovation and Entrepreneurship. In *ISPIM Conference Proceedings* (pp. 1-21). The International Society for Professional Innovation Management (ISPIM).

Chorney, A. I. (2012). Taking the game out of gamification. *Dalhousie Journal of Interdisciplinary Management, 8*(1).

Golipour, R., Gholamreza, J., Mirzaei, M. A., & Rosh, T. (2011). The impact of organizational trust on innovativeness at the Tehran oil refinery company. *African Journal of Business Management, 5*(7), 2660–2667.

Hernández, M. I. O., Lezama, R. M., & Gómez, S. M. (2021, April). Work-in-Progress: The Road to Learning, Using Gamification. In *2021 IEEE Global Engineering Education Conference (EDUCON)* (pp. 1393-1397). IEEE. 10.1109/EDUCON46332.2021.9453892

Hindle, K. (2002). A grounded theory for teaching entrepreneurship using simulation games. *Simulation & Gaming, 33*(2), 236–241. doi:10.1177/1046878102332012

Kessel, R. (2019). Pracademic collaboration: Hacking into the future of legal education. *Alternative Law Journal, 44*(1), 73–75. doi:10.1177/1037969X18814980

Klofsten, M. (2000). Training entrepreneurship at universities: A Swedish case. *Journal of European Industrial Training, 24*(6), 337–344. doi:10.1108/03090590010373325

Kuratko, D. F. (2005). The emergence of entrepreneurship education: Development, trends and challenges. *Entrepreneurship Theory and Practice, 29*(5), 577–597. doi:10.1111/j.1540-6520.2005.00099.x

Leitch, C. M., & Harrison, R. T. (1999). A process model for entrepreneurship education and development. *International Journal of Entrepreneurial Behaviour & Research, 5*(3), 83–109. doi:10.1108/13552559910284065

Menzies, T. (2004). Are universities playing a role in nurturing and developing high-technology entrepreneurs? The administrators' perspective. *International Journal of Entrepreneurship and Innovation, 5*(3), 149–157. doi:10.5367/0000000041513385

Pilar, L., Moulis, P., Pitrová, J., Bouda, P., Gresham, G., Balcarová, T., & Rojík, S. (2019). Education and Business as a key topics at the Instagram posts in the area of Gamification. *Journal on Efficiency and Responsibility in Education and Science, 12*(1), 26–33. doi:10.7160/eriesj.2019.120103

Robertson, M., & Collins, A. (2003b). The video role model as an enterprise teaching aid. *Education + Training, 45*(6), 331–340. doi:10.1108/00400910310495987

KEY TERMS AND DEFINITIONS

Autoethnography: A research method involving self-reflection that aims at drawing on one's own lived experience to impart knowledge, whereby the researcher is also the research subject.

Business Studies: The academic subject discipline which involves the study of economics and management, in particular as an educational topic.

Collaborative Autoethnography: A multivocal research approach whereby two or more researchers work collaboratively to share their personal stories and reflect on and interpret the pooled autoethnographic data.

Higher Education Teaching: The teaching that takes place at university or third level education after someone leaves school and usually refers to both undergraduate and postgraduate studies.

Law: The subject discipline and profession which is concerned with customs, rules, and practices of conduct within a community, which are considered binding within said community, and the enforcement of the totality of the rules by authorized authorities.

Multidisciplinary Education: The teaching and learning of a topic from the perspectives of more than one discipline.

Serious Games: Games which are considered "serious", which can include both physical as well as digital games, of which the purpose is to educate and train rather than merely to entertain.

Simulations: A model or representative example of something that reflects the real-life dynamics in a simplified, yet realistic manner.

Chapter 17
Science Fair Project in the Teacher Training Process:
Its Emotional Response and Implications

Miriam Andrea Hernández-Barco
https://orcid.org/0000-0002-3196-0421
University of Extremadura, Spain

Jesús Sánchez-Martín
University of Extremadura, Spain

Isaac Corbacho-Cuello
https://orcid.org/0000-0003-1768-8270
University of Extremadura, Spain

Florentina Cañada-Cañada
University of Extremadura, Spain

ABSTRACT

In this chapter, the authors describe a Star Wars scientific gamification experience, presented as a gymkhana with seven different activities to be carried out in the classroom. This proposal was designed to be done with prospective primary teachers during their science training studies. The prospective teachers have to observe, explore, experiment, and describe the different physical and chemical phenomena involved. The emotional response of prospective teachers was studied to describe their affective dimension after this "science fair." Such gamification promotes high rates of positive emotions (such as surprise or curiosity) and very low rates of negative emotions (such as boredom or rejection). The affective domain should be considered during teacher training, which is possible with this kind of experience.

DOI: 10.4018/978-1-6684-4287-6.ch017

INTRODUCTION

Despite the need to have scientifically literate citizens, students are increasingly turning away from studying science subjects (Vázquez & Manassero, 2008). The current context of permanent change requires a versatile and resolute population capable of adapting to the uncertain times ahead. A solid basic scientific education helps to have a critical vision of the world and to make appropriate decisions. Educational institutions, especially universities, are responsible for providing the population with a foundation which then will facilitate and promote lifelong learning.

Higher education should not only serve to offer theoretical knowledge about various types of content but also to train students in how to behave when faced with different situations, to be able to reflect and make reasoned decisions. The functions of university education are not limited to professionalism and research, but also apply to an education adapted to the profile of the students themselves. However, despite the immense responsibility there should be towards the scientific education of the population, over the last few years there has been a noticeable abuse of the positivist orientation in science teaching. Science teaching has traditionally been done in a very different way to how science is actually carried out. This leads to numerous misconceptions among primary and secondary students about scientific concepts, as well as undesirable attitudes towards science (Vázquez & Manassero, 2007). A methodological change is required in order to eradicate these misconceptions and to enhance the affective dimension of students towards science. Gamification strategies has emerged as resource to improve the teaching and learning process.

The proposal that we shall be describing offers as a didactic resource a hybrid method of gamification together with inquiry. It was designed to enhance the affective dimension of prospective teachers. It consists of seven different activities to promote the students' engagement while learning in the context of a gamified subject set in "Star Wars". Throughout the course, students can earn different badges and cards that will help them pass the exam and improve other cognitive and emotional skills. Inquiry fosters active learning and empowers students in their learning process. This type of method improves the student's autonomy and other soft skills (such as critical thinking, collaborative work, or creativity). Students become the protagonists of the teaching and learning process, and teachers only guide and help them through the activities the students themselves organize autonomously.

The main objective of the present research study was to analyse the emotional dimension of a sample of prospective teachers after implementing a gamified inquiry activity called "science fair", set in "Star Wars" movies. The objective of the authors with this experience was to awaken positive emotions (such as joy, surprise, fun, or enthusiasm) towards science in a prospective teachers sample by making a change in the methodological approach that was aimed at enhancing emotional responses. In the literature, there is evidence for the transmission of emotions by teachers – in particular, the emotions experienced by the teacher are those they then transmit to their pupils (Frenzel et al., 2009, 2018; Olson et al., 2019; Poon et al., 2019). "Hard science" content should be worked on during primary education teacher training through methods that actively engage the students in order to foster their positive emotions and to ensure that the future transmission of content is done correctly without damaging their own pupils' emotional dimension, with a special emphasis on gender differences (Frenzel et al., 2007; Steegh et al., 2019).

THEORETICAL BACKGROUND

Consideration of the Affective Domain during Science Lessons

Traditionally, science teaching has been carried out following an academic approach centred on the teacher and based on the teacher transmitting the content using the textbook. The pupil's role was limited to assimilating the information and memorizing the content – a method far removed from what it really means to do science. One result of such poor didactics over the years has been that the science taught in school has not led to the pupils' general scientific literacy, and has given them a wrong idea of what science and the scientific method really are (Vázquez & Manassero, 2007).

Consideration of the pupil's affective domain and its impact on education is quite recent (Izquierdo, 2007). Previously, the affective and cognitive domains, and emotions and learning, were subjects of separate research. Today it is known that they form an inseparable duality: there is no learning without interaction with the affective domain (Mora, 2017). However, this dissociation between the emotional and the epistemological dimensions of science learning has in many cases led to the generation of bad experiences during the school stage (Gargallo & Bargalló, 2011; Tomas et al., 2016). Many pupils feel a true emotional rejection towards scientific subjects, which then conditions their decisions concerning higher education, causing many of them to choose to move away from scientific and technological subjects (Mellado et al., 2014).

The lack of a citizenry with an appropriate level of scientific literacy leads to what is being seen recently with the anti-vaccine, flat-Earther, or climate change denial movements. To be able to fight against this type of thought current, it is necessary for pupils during their basic education to learn science without feeling rejection. It is also necessary for the teachers to have scientific knowledge on the one hand, and the skills and competencies that will allow them to teach science in an exciting way that generates positive emotions in their pupils on the other. Emotions influence knowledge, but knowledge also influences emotions. Acting consciously springs from the affective domain. In the literature about affectivity from Hume (1711-1776) to Plutchik (1927-2006), there is the underlying idea that intelligence is at the service of emotions (Marina, 2004). With regard to the importance that can be attributed to emotions in learning, it is known that they can help or hinder the fixation of concepts in memory – episodes associated with an emotion are easier to remember and last longer in memory (Mora, 2012).

The inclusion of the affective domain and emotions in research about the didactics of experimental sciences has meant a change of direction which has led to reorganizing objectives and addressing the development of new skills that are needed in today's societies. This new approach places the pupils at the centre of the teaching and learning processes, promoting in each of them their own personal constructions, and also taking into consideration their prior knowledge (Anđelković et al., 2018).

There are numerous taxonomies, definitions, and classifications of emotions. For this research, the authors considered the definition given by Bisquerra (2003) which takes emotions to be reactions of different intensity depending on the information received from the environment, the subjective assessment of it that each individual makes, and how it affects their well-being. The emotions chosen for the study were an adaptation of those used in previous research about academic emotions (Dávila-Acedo, 2018) which came from the classification into positive and negative emotions proposed by Fernández-Abascal et al. (2001). They are listed in Table 1.

Joy, confidence, fun, enthusiasm, satisfaction, surprise, and tranquillity have been included in the list of positive emotions. These emotions are those that ensure well-being, and are felt when a goal is

Table 1. Positive and negative emotions used in this research.

Positive emotions	Negative emotions
Joy	Boredom
Confidence	Frustration
Enthusiasm	Nervousness
Fun	Rejection
Satisfaction	Worry
Surprise	
Tranquillity	

attained, or personally some improvement can be seen. In some classifications, surprise forms part of the neutral or ambiguous emotions since it can be both positive and negative (Bisquerra, 2003). However, earlier studies that collected qualitative information noted that in most cases, in indicating the emotion surprise, the students made allusions to positive causes (Dávila-Acedo et al., 2016). In the present research therefore, it has been included in the category of positive emotions. These emotions are not essential for survival, but are focused on increasing happiness (Bisquerra, 2019). Boredom, frustration, nervousness, worry, and rejection have been included in the list of negative emotions. The fact of classifying emotions as positive and negative has no connotation of good or bad. Negative emotions are identified as causing unpleasant feelings to the individual who experiences them, but they have their role in people's lives. Indeed, and contrary to the case with positive emotions, negative emotions do have a fundamental role for survival (Bisquerra, 2009, 2019; Pekrun & Stephens, 2010). These taxonomies, despite being applied in the area of didactics, emerged from research in psychology. Recently, new classifications have been incorporated into research about science teaching that go beyond such valency, and respond to the degree of activation an emotion generates in pupils (Agen & Ezquerra, 2021), thereby overcoming the classic positive or negative dichotomy, and suggesting that one needs to go further, differentiating in terms of the effect that the emotion has on learners. In the classroom, emotions can reach high levels of activation (positive emotions such as surprise and curiosity, or negative such as frustration and uncertainty) or low levels (positive emotions such as satisfaction and tranquillity, or negative such as sadness and boredom). In this way, it is easier to interpret the effect that different affective environments have on learning. In the following subsection, we shall look more deeply into the relevance of considering the affective domain in teacher training.

Affective Domain in Teacher Training

Teachers and their forms of behaviour have a real impact on their pupils and their pupils' academic achievements (Eccles, 2009). It is therefore fundamental, and indeed a requisite, for primary education teachers to feel interest and enthusiasm towards science in order to be able to transmit it, but there have been studies reflecting the concern about deficiencies in the scientific training of teachers (Oliva & Acevedo, 2005). Research in the area of the Didactics of Experimental Sciences suggests that prospective teachers in general feel negative emotions towards science and do not feel prepared to teach it (Dávila-Acedo et al., 2015; Pipitone et al., 2019). Prospective teachers also consider science particularly hard to learn and they do not perceive science learning as being something motivating – a result of their own bad emotional experiences generated by the transmissive teaching model (Gargallo & Bargalló, 2011).

If, as noted by Bisquerra & Pérez (2007), pupils learn academic knowledge better when they have emotional competencies, it is essential to train, through intervention programs that include both the cognitive and the affective, emotionally competent teachers who know how to diagnose and self-regulate emotions (Mellado et al., 2014). Improving scientific competence also means first improving the emotions of prospective teachers.

A teacher must feel prepared to teach the subject. It is impossible for them to be able to teach something they do not know (Mellado et al., 2014). This is why they must master the subject in order to feel effective, improve their self-confidence, and successfully transmit the content. Prospective primary teachers must have a solid scientific training. This will help them feel more confident and improve their perception of self-efficacy, both of which have a direct impact on their classroom practice: teachers who show more confidence in their abilities in these subjects are readier to take risks in their methods and carry out more complex tasks than those who have low expectations from their knowledge (Brígido et al., 2012). Furthermore, students who are confident in their abilities in a specific domain are more likely to regulate their behaviour by adopting more effective learning strategies (Wu et al., 2019).

The focus is therefore on training the teachers: if they do not teach science well, they do not convey enthusiasm for science and mathematics, it is because they themselves do not feel that enthusiasm. That prospective teachers value and perceive the usefulness of scientific knowledge is key for them during the development of their future professional work to ignite their pupils' emotions and effectively transmit scientific knowledge.

The last decades have been marked by rapid changes and periods of transformation and renewal of education policies in European countries, materialized in the Bologna plan and the European Higher Education Area (EHEA). These contexts of globalization have required higher education (including teacher training, of course) to adjust to these new systems and today's societies, transforming university teaching and learning processes (Murga-Menoyo, 2015).

Present currents in didactics propose a change in the educational paradigm to one in which the pupil is the protagonist of the teaching and learning process (Andrews & Higson, 2008; Gerstein & Friedman, 2016). This change of direction to a pupil-centred approach is based on constructivist theories. Higher education must therefore foster the development of skills of communication, adaptation, creativity, emotional intelligence, critical thinking, and empathy (also termed soft skills) at the same time as providing students with knowledge and competencies (Rieckmann, 2018). But lectures alone are incapable of responding to these demands. A multitude of active methods are now being used as support to attain scientific literacy among the population. At the same time as working on the curricular content, they are allowing for the development of other dimensions and abilities, including the students' affective domain (Sanchez-Martin et al., 2018; Zamora-Polo et al., 2019). With this paradigm shift in science education research, the present study was designed to explore the students' emotional dimension after the implementation of a gamified inquiry activity termed "science fair" in which the learner is the protagonist of their own process of learning, while the teacher guides the path that process takes.

Gamification and Other Active Methods for Emotional Enhancement

The role of universities is not only to train professionals. Our new societies need competent citizens who can adapt to the future environment and contexts that they will have to face. The structure of the curriculum, however, facilitates neither critical, innovative, creative learning nor the development of personal skills (such as responsibility, teamwork, or empathy). Therefore, to promote the integral learning of higher education students, there have arisen such teaching methods as problem-based learning and game-based learning (Gallego-Durán et al., 2019; Sánchez-Martín et al., 2017), service-learning (Hernández-Barco et al., 2019), inquiry (Pedaste et al., 2015), or gamification (Robson et al., 2015; Gallego-Durán et al., 2019; Sánchez-Martín et al., 2020).

Gamification is a method that consists of including aspects of play (mechanical and dynamic) into educational contexts (for example, competitions, badges, role-play, avatars, rankings, levels, …) with the objective of motivating the learner and letting them live rewarding and transformative learning experiences by turning the class into a true playful context with a didactic objective (Brezovszky et al., 2019; Sánchez-Martín et al., 2017).

The use of games as a classroom method has experienced exponential growth over the last decade. It of course has full inclusion as a learning strategy when speaking about pre-primary education (learning without playing at those stages is inconceivable). In primary education however, it loses value as a didactic tool even though Vigotsky or Piaget advocated play as having great educational potential and that it facilitates learning. Instead, play is considered to be a tool exclusively for fun and is replaced by methodological practices based on effort (Cornellà, Estebanell & Brusi, 2020). Game-playing was born with the human and has evolved with the human as a free activity but with rules voluntarily accepted by the player (Legerén & Rada, 2014). The use of games in the classroom has provided the educational community with the opportunity to carry out a multidisciplinary approach in real environments and improve the classroom experiences of teacher education students through typical elements and techniques taken from games (Yllana-Prieto, Jeong & González-Gómez, 2021).

There is evidence that the implementation of different active methods for science teaching generates emotional experiences that have an impact on increasing pupils' motivation and meaningful learning (Sanchez-Martin et al., 2018). The pupils' emotional involvement is necessary for them to have correct learning, so that the teacher likewise has to be involved and excited when transmitting this knowledge (Mellado et al., 2014). These methods are based on the idea that pupils learn better when they apply their knowledge directly to real life situations. For the prospective teacher, the teaching promoted is that which connects with other content of the curriculum and allows it to be applied in other potentially useful contexts, in addition to developing other types of specific and cross-cutting competencies of the profession (Sánchez-Martín et al., 2020). These techniques are also used to improve pupils' motivation and are good strategies with which to improve their social relationships and self-confidence (Pérez, 2011).

Gamification is considered a powerful way to improve education through its application in a non-game environment but engaging people in important task with the same intrinsic motivation than in games (Gallego-Durán et al., 2019). An appropriate design should focus the learners on their objectives by allowing them to try different routes and alternatives freely and easily, even fail and not suffer penalty.

The "science fair" to be described in this book chapter is a gamified inquiry activity. The inquiry method consists of activities in which students develop knowledge and understand the scientific ideas of the natural world. It comprises an entire intentional process of diagnosing problems, critiquing experiments and distinguishing alternatives, planning the investigation, searching for information, building models, debating with peers, and constructing coherent arguments (Fernández-Marchesi, 2018).

Numerous skills can be worked on through scientific inquiry. Starting from the pupils' prior ideas, their conceptual, procedural, and attitudinal development can be fostered through reflection (Retana-Alvarado et al., 2018). With the use of inquiry activities, it is possible to work not only on scientific content through experimentation itself, but also on soft skills, thus promoting the acquisition of curricular content and achieving learning objectives.

Inquiry-based learning begins with the posing of questions, problems, or scenarios instead of just presenting and stating facts, or considering that learning is a straightforward unobstructed path (Frank & Stanszus, 2019). Pupils who participate in inquiry activities identify and investigate issues to actively develop their knowledge and provide solutions to specific challenges. This is a process planned and guided by their teachers whose role is one of facilitating the process. The pupils are the protagonists. It is they who autonomously experiment with procedures, formulate hypotheses, record data, draw conclusions, etc. (Solís-Espallargas et al., 2015).

Cognitive and emotional processes are linked. Gamification adopt psychological perspectives based on how emotions influencing learning process, based on engaging and enjoyable experiences for players (Mullins & Sabherwal, 2020). In the following section, we shall describe the activity that was carried out in this research study.

THE STUDY

The sample selection was non-random convenience sampling. In total, data were collected from 47 students in the 4th year of the Bachelor's degree in Primary Education at the University of Extremadura.

To achieve the initial objectives proposed in the research, a questionnaire was designed in which the students had to indicate whether or not, after they had carried out a practical inquiry activity, they felt the emotions suggested to them in a list which consisted of 7 positive and 5 negative emotions, and to explain why.

Analyses

After the elaboration of the questionnaire and the selection of the sample, the questionnaire was handed out to the students of the different groups in paper format. The data were collected, processed, and transferred to digital support to then be analysed through the webQDA qualitative analysis program. Excel and JASP were used for the quantitative treatment of the data.

Results

The Science Fair

The gamification activity, a science fair, was carried out in a science laboratory. Only common, basic materials such as those described below were required. The duration of the science fair was 80 minutes. In the laboratory, there were seven recreational science experiments: every ten minutes a bell rang to signal that it was time to move on to the next stall. Once the teacher had prepared and equipped the laboratory to simulate a fair, it was necessary to explain to the students that they were in a science fair which they would have to explore for themselves, knowing that the activities involved are ones that they as teachers could implement with their future pupils. The students were divided into groups of two or three. At each stall there was a card with explanations about what they had to do. The students spontaneously moved towards the fair stalls they wanted, and discussed the activity with their classmates. All the students had

Figure 1. Cover page of a document offered to students in the context of the gamified subject. The sentence contains "Laws of force". Source: The authors.

to experience all the stalls. The gamification experience includes ranking and badges in the context of the film "Star Wars" (Figure 1).

Points can be earned in a step-by-step way, and they can be bought and sold during the course and at the end. The gamification experience allowed prospective teachers to ask for help to teachers or other classmates and they also can transfer their own points to other students (Figure 2). After submitting the report, students entered a ranking where they could win cards (coffee, bribery or safe-conducts) that give them privileges in the exam (or a breakfast in the café): they can use the calculator, they are allowed to use formulas, they can eliminate a question from the exam…

Figure 2. Cards used in the game. Source: The authors.

Before the students entered the laboratory, eight working places had to be prepared and equipped with the following elements:

1. **Weightless water.** Material: a glass bottle filled with water and marked with a grid. Procedure: when the bottle is turned upside down quickly, the water does not fall out. However, when it is turned slowly it does. Physics concepts: atmospheric pressure, liquid behaviour.
2. **Climber fluid.** Material: a candle, artificial colouring (methylene blue), a copper coin, a Petri dish, a volumetric flask. Procedure: put the coin in the Petri dish, place the candle on the top of the coin, light the candle, pour water into the Petri dish and add artificial colouring, cover the candle with the flask. Physics concepts: atmospheric pressure.
3. **Giant soap bubbles.** Material: a large container, bubble wands in different shapes and sizes. Procedure: blow bubbles in the air. Physics concepts: surface tension.
4. **Colour changes.** Material: round-bottomed flask, droppers, phenolphthalein, caustic soda, Congo red, hydrochloric acid. Procedure: fill the flask half full of water, add four drops of phenolphthalein, observe its colour. Add, drop by drop, caustic soda until the colour changes. Add four drops of Congo red. Add hydrochloric acid drop by drop until the colour begins to change. Observe the changes and explain what happens. Physics concepts: chemical reactions.
5. **Non-Newtonian fluid.** Material: Cornflour, water, and a bowl. Procedure: stir cornflour into water in the bowl. Slowly dip your hand into the bowl of cornflour mix. Softly pull it out. Try to hit the mixture violently with your clenched fist. What happens? Physics concepts: non-Newtonian fluid.
6. **Elephant's toothpaste.** Material: hydrogen peroxide (25 mL), 50 mL flask, detergent, potassium iodide, a spatula. Procedure: add the hydrogen peroxide to the flask (be careful, it is abrasive), add detergent and with the spatula a small amount of potassium iodide. Wait for the reaction. Physics content: exothermic and endothermic reactions.
7. **Secret message.** Material: filter paper, cotton swabs, sodium bicarbonate solution, cooker. Procedure: write a secret message using a cotton swab and the sodium bicarbonate solution. Then, put it on the cooker and wait. Physics concepts: chemical reactions.

At each of the stalls, the students had to complete a card where they included the following information from each of the experiments: (i) how it works, (ii) what happens, (iii) what modifications could be included, and (iv) what the explanation of the phenomenon is. Although the research does not seek to compare with traditional methods, prospective teachers express they prefer learning through inquiry gamification to traditional lectures. This gamification experience offers the knowledge content such a way that players will discover while playing and discovering.

The Emotional Responses

With regard to the questionnaires about emotions, the results showed that, after carrying out a gamified inquiry activity (the science fair), the prospective teachers indicated around 90% positive emotions and less than 10% negative emotions (Figure 3).

Table 2 shows the percentages of positive and negative emotions indicated by the prospective teachers. These data were obtained by adding up the total number of emotions reported by prospective teachers and calculating the total percentage of prospective teachers who selected to feel the emotions shown.

These students have been previously informed about the emotions and the meaning of each one, so they know what we mean by each emotion shown to them.

Figure 3. Box and violin plot representing the percentages of positive and negative emotions reported by the prospective teachers after conducting the science fair. The horizontal line inside each box represents the median, the lower and upper limits correspond to the 25th and 75th percentiles, and the lower and upper endings of the vertical lines to the 5th and 95th percentiles. The violin curve represents the density of points. Source: The authors.

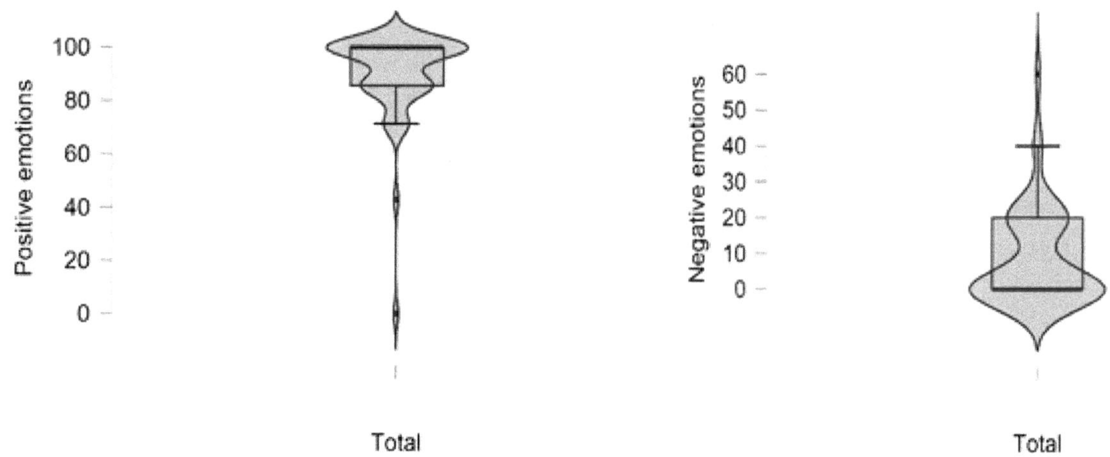

Table 2. Percentages of positive and negative emotions reported by the prospective teachers towards the science fair.

Positive emotions	*Percentage*	*Negative emotions*	*Percentage*
Joy	80.85	*Boredom*	0
Curiosity	100	*Frustration*	14.89
Fun	97.87	*Nervousness*	17.02
Enthusiasm	85.11	*Worry*	10.64
Satisfaction	95.74	*Rejection*	2.13
Surprise	100		
Tranquility	80.85		

After the science fair had finished, all the participants expressed surprise and curiosity. Some of the reasons the students mentioned to justify these emotions were, for example, curiosity and interest generated by participating in a science fair, and surprise when doing unknown experiments and seeing the final result. In general, they felt joy, fun, and curiosity in handling laboratory equipment and in experiencing something new and unusual that they had never done before. Other causes of positive emotions were (i) learning science through practical activities, (ii) working in groups, and (iii) seeing how their own learning evolved.

Regarding negative emotions, none of the prospective teachers indicated boredom, and only 2.13% indicated rejection. The most indicated were frustration, nervousness, and worry. Nevertheless, despite being negative emotions, these are activators (Agen & Ezquerra, 2021), which means that they generate within the individuals feelings that motivate them to act. They are therefore desirable emotions during science learning. The reasons the students mentioned when feeling frustration referred to the initial ignorance that they had, which prevented them from carrying out some of the experiments. However, this motivated them to keep trying until they successfully completed the activity. Nervousness was generated because of anticipation, and by wanting to know quickly what was happening and how the experiments of the science fair were coming out.

Thus, the percentage of positive emotions indicated was greater than that of negative emotions. The science fair, which was implemented in a gamified way as an inquiry activity, generated positive emotions in the prospective teachers, and these were related to the experience itself. Despite working on scientific content related to Physics and Chemistry, experimentation and working in the laboratory aroused interest and put the prospective teachers in a favourable emotional predisposition towards these types of experiments, increasing their motivation towards learning.

DISCUSSION

The existence of scientifically and emotionally competent teaching staff is necessary to improve schools' educational quality and the emotional experiences of their pupils. Both prospective and in-service teachers need to be aware of their own emotions, have high self-efficacy in science teaching, and take responsibility for the effects their classroom activity may generate, especially in those areas such as Physics and Chemistry which generate negative emotions (Dávila-Acedo, 2017). Authors encourage for this ends the inclusion of some topics close to the real life of students, such as TV series or movies. In this case, gamification take place in the context of "Star Wars", with a system of badges and point, where students can easily see their score in real time on a daily basis.

Sierra and Fernández-Sánchez (2019) carried out a gamification experience with undergraduate students who also manifest to feel fun, joya and pleasure, only a few of participants manifested to feel frustration. Students who participated in this research reported some benefits they found within the teaching and learning process, based on the motivation to achieve de goals. We agree with their results, prospective teachers also point to working in a group, companionship and collaboration as causes of positive emotions.

Continuing with what Crujeiras & Jiménez (2015) put forward, the teaching method must be inspired by the scientific process itself, and should promote inquiry-based, pupil-centred learning, with a practical scientific component. Education professionals need to generate positive emotions towards science teaching since they have an enormous responsibility in creating emotional skills in their students, through both the example of direct contact and the use of emotional intelligence in science classes, thus helping to create an emotionally healthy institutional environment. The development of positive attitudes in their students, through the promotion of favourable feelings and emotions, will facilitate a change in beliefs and expectations about the subject, and encourage those students' approach to science (Dávila-Acedo et al., 2021).

That prospective primary school teachers know their emotions is the first step towards being able to act and make the pertinent modifications to their attitudes through reflection and awakening them to the importance of their performance in the classroom as teachers. Future teachers must take responsibility and recognize their social involvement in human and scientific development. The repercussions of the generation of scientific vocations mean that they must take risks and implement didactic strategies designed to promote positive experiences for pupils in the primary school science classroom (Gargallo & Bargalló, 2011).

The interest of the present study was to be able to turn the negative emotions initially presented by prospective primary teachers (Hernández-Barco et al., 2021a) into positive emotions, thus promoting meaningful learning through the implementation of active methods. These methods have already demonstrated their emotional benefits in science teaching in both secondary education (Dávila et al., 2016) and higher education (Hernández-Barco et al., 2021b). Other studies too on teacher training have obtained emotional improvements after the implementation of active methods (Jeong et al., 2016, Sierra & Fernández-Sánchez, 2019).

Sanchez-Martin et al. (2018) analysed the emotional responses of a sample of prospective teachers towards different methods of teaching science (oral presentation, oral presentation plus audiovisual support, guided inquiry, gamification, and hands-on activities). They observed significant differences in the responses to the different methods, with hands-on activities and gamification being those preferred by the prospective teachers to learn science and those which generated most activating emotions. Through gamification, it is possible to develop and show prospective teachers skills and tools that they will be able to use in their future teaching practice in science subjects (Brezovszky et al., 2019). Gallego-Durán et al. (2019) offer some resources for gamification based on game design, such as characters, stories and aesthetics, and suggest that students can be given the freedom to create their own characters. Preferred approaches for educational environments are working in teams, sharing challenges and achieving common goals. Gamification also brings emotional benefits for undergraduate students (Sierra & Fernández-Sánchez, 2019).

Carrying out practical activities with prospective teachers not only improves their emotional dimension, but also their cognitive dimension in its aspects of the acquisition of knowledge and the development of such scientific skills as the manipulation of tools. This makes learning more motivating (Dávila-Acedo et al., 2021) and generates greater tranquillity and well-being for the prospective teachers (Retana-Alvarado et al., 2018).

In this case, the experience at the "science fair" can be defined as a "hands-on" activity (Sanchez-Martin et al., 2017) in the context of a gamified course, focused on learning by doing, to generate significant learning with a strong influence on the prospective teachers' affective domain. However, it is necessary and important for the emotion to be contextualized within the teaching and learning processes. Feeling just fun (or some other positive emotion) because of having a good time in class with classmates but with no relation to the task at hand may lead the pupil to be distracted instead of immersed in the activity (Pekrun, 2014). On many occasions during gamification, students consider negative or adverse emotions to actually be positive since they stimulate their reflection on different topics and favour their social behaviour (Mekler et al., 2016).

The results of this study concur with those of Solís-Espallargas et al. (2015) who concluded that their prospective primary teachers who worked using the inquiry method highlighted as positive aspects of the method that they were responsible for the inquiry process itself, and that they were working with procedures that help them to develop reasoning criteria. Frank & Stanszus (2019) noted that there is a key factor in the inquiry method – the role of the teaching staff. The students who work using this method stress that the teachers decisively influence the perception of and participation in the activity.

Working using this method leads to changes in prospective teachers that cause them to reflect on their science teaching methods, modifying their initial transmissive approach towards a new one focused on posing questions that involve their pupils. These findings were reported in studies carried out by Martínez-Chico et al. (2015), which also showed a conceptual evolution together with the development of inquiry skills and abilities (such as the explanation of hypotheses, the search for evidence, or posing questions).

Pipitone et al. (2019) observed the emotional and attitudinal change occurring when prospective primary teachers were taking the Didactics of Science subject. They found as causes for the observed improvement: (i) the method, i.e., teaching classes where the pupil takes on a large part of the leading role, showing the connection of science with daily life, etc., (ii) affective aspects, such as the bond that is created between the instructors of the subject and the prospective teachers; and (iii) their enhanced self-efficacy.

The results reported in this book chapter are coherent with those of Marcos-Merino et al. (2020) who analysed the emotional effect of the implementation of a practical activity based on inquiry in science teaching. They found that, after carrying out the practice, their prospective teachers stated that they felt all the positive emotions analysed (joy, confidence, satisfaction, enthusiasm, and fun) with greater intensity, and a decrease in negative emotions (boredom and uncertainty). The inquiry method can also serve to modify other personal components, such as improving the perception of self-efficacy, finding the science class to be greater fun, or reducing anxiety (van Aalderen-Smeets et al., 2012). Gómez-Carrasco et al. (2019) also explored the positive effect on the motivation and perception of learning of students when gamification is carried out.

Emotions influence pupils' learning outcomes (Carmona-Halty et al., 2019) since they help to direct attention, which is a requisite for learning (Phelps, 2006). The classroom and the teaching and learning processes are therefore charged with affectivity (Garritz, 2010). However, the study of emotions and the need for the existence of a good classroom environment for an advantageous, motivating, and interesting educational process has been insufficiently studied (Garritz, 2009). As Mullins and Sabherwal (2020) concludes, gamified experiences should be pleasant however the experience involves both positive and negative emotions (like watching a film or playing a game), emotions are an uncharted territory in gamification. It is therefore necessary to continue investigating into the emotional effects of the implementation of gamification in the classroom.

FUTURE RESEARCH DIRECTIONS AND CONCLUSIONS

This study has described transcendental implications in primary education teacher training: it provides evidence of how important it is to contemplate the affective dimension during teacher training to improve the students' emotions and attitudes towards science. It is interesting for them that during their academic training they participate in this type of experience which generates positive emotions and other characteristics, such as curiosity, surprise, or a spirit for inquiry, that are equally necessary to foster scientific attitudes.

The implementation of gamification as a method to teach science in higher education has shown itself to be an emotionally effective resource due to its capacity to generate positive emotions and to reduce negative emotions. Contemplating the emotional dimension of students is key to the successful completion of their studies. Teacher training must offer experiences that generate changes in the affective domain, igniting activating emotions, and in which the students themselves understand that it is possible to teach and learn science using other methodological strategies – strategies in which the pupils are involved, confront their own difficulties, see their weaknesses, and modify their attitudes towards science.

With this activity, prospective teachers familiarize themselves with the main Physics and Chemistry concepts of the commonest activities in primary education – density, volume, pressure, chemical reactions, acids and bases – while enjoying themselves and experiencing positive emotions during their science learning. This gamified experience in the context of a "science fair" led to the improvement of the prospective teachers' affective dimension. They claimed that they felt curiosity, surprise, and fun. None of them noted the emotion of boredom during the science fair.

An instructor's methodological approach has a considerable influence on their students' affective component. Getting students involved in the subject and adding dynamics to the theoretical content is necessary to facilitate a good classroom environment that encourages meaningful learning and an improvement in the prospective teachers' confidence. This study has shown how conducting a "science fair", following an inquiry-oriented gamification method, can serve to foster prospective teachers' positive emotions and reduce their negative emotions towards science learning. Alternative approaches were proposed to overcome some of the challenges that arise in teacher training. They were based on implementing active methods far removed from the traditional teaching model, in order to generate positive emotional experiences and meaningful learning, integrating affective and cognitive aspects, and promoting autonomous and collaborative learning. In addition to meeting the requirements of the curriculum of the degree course, in this way the prospective teachers become familiar with such methodological alternatives as gamification and inquiry. This is of particular interest in the degree in Primary Education due to the repercussions it will have for their future work in teaching.

ACKNOWLEDGMENT

This research was supported by the Research Project PID2020-115214RB-I00/AEI/10.13039/501100011033, the Government of Extremadura [Grant GR21047 and the Proyect IB18004], and the Ministry of Science, Innovation and Universities [BES-2017-081566].

REFERENCES

Agen, F., & Ezquerra, Á. (2021). Analysis of emotions in the work of inquiry: "The Black Box" [Análisis de las emociones en el trabajo de indagación: "La Caja Negra"]. *Investigación en la Escuela*, *3*, 125–138. doi:10.12795/IE.2021.i103.09

Anđelković, S., Dedjanski, V., & Pejic, B. (2018). Pedagogical benefits of fieldwork of the students at the Faculty of Geography in the light of the Bologna Process. *Journal of Geography in Higher Education*, *42*(1), 110–125. doi:10.1080/03098265.2017.1379058

Andrews, J., & Higson, H. (2008). Graduate Employability, 'Soft Skills' Versus 'Hard' Business Knowledge: A European Study. *Higher Education in Europe*, *33*(4), 411–422. doi:10.1080/03797720802522627

Bisquerra, R. (2003). Emotional education and basic life skills [Educación emocional y competencias básicas para la vida]. *Revista de Investigación Educacional*, *21*(1), 7–43.

Bisquerra, R. (2009). *Psychopedagogy of emotions* [Psicopedagogía de las emociones]. Editorial Síntesis.

Bisquerra, R. (2019). Universe of emotions: A didactic material for emotional education [Universo de emociones: un material didáctico para la educación emocional]. *Cuadernos de Pedagogía, 499*, 105–111.

Bisquerra, R., & Pérez, N. (2007). Socio-emotional competences [Las competencias socioemocionales]. *Educacion XXI, 10*, 61–82.

Brezovszky, B., McMullen, J., Veermans, K., Hannula-Sormunen, M. M., Rodríguez-Aflecht, G., Pongsakdi, N., Laakkonen, E., & Lehtinen, E. (2019). Effects of a mathematics game-based learning environment on primary school students' adaptive number knowledge. *Computers & Education, 128*, 63–74. doi:10.1016/j.compedu.2018.09.011

Brígido, M., Borrachero, A. B., Bermejo, M. L., & Mellado, V. (2012). Prospective primary teachers' self-efficacy and emotions in science teaching. *European Journal of Teacher Education, 1*, 1–18.

Carmona-Halty, M., Salanova, M., Llorens, S., & Schaufeli, W. B. (2019). Linking positive emotions and academic performance: The mediated role of academic psychological capital and academic engagement. *Current Psychology (New Brunswick, N.J.)*, 1–10.

Cornellà, P., Estebanell, M., & Brusi, D. (2020). Gamification and game-based learning. General considerations and some examples for the Teaching of Geology [Gamificación y aprendizaje basado en juegos. Consideraciones generales y algunos ejemplos para la Enseñanza de la Geología]. *Enseñanza de las Ciencias de la Tierra, 28*(1), 5–19.

Crujeiras, B. P., & Jiménez, M. P. (2015). Challenges posed by open research activities in the laboratory: Articulation of theoretical and practical knowledge in scientific practices [Desafíos planteados por las actividades abiertas de indagación en el laboratorio: articulación de conocimientos teóricos y prácticos en las prácticas científicas]. *Enseñanza de las Ciencias, 33*(1), 63–84.

Dávila-Acedo, M. A. (2017). Emotions and their causes in the learning of Physics and Chemistry, in the students of Secondary Education [Las emociones y sus causas en el aprendizaje de Física y Química, en el alumnado de Educación Secundaria]. *Revista Eureka Sobre Enseñanza y Divulgación de las Ciencias, 14*(3), 570–586.

Dávila-Acedo, M. A. (2018). *Emotions in the learning of physics and chemistry in secondary school students. An emotional intervention program* [Las emociones en el aprendizaje de física y química en el alumnado de educación secundaria. Un programa de intervención emocional]. Universidad de Extremadura.

Dávila-Acedo, M. A., Borrachero, A. B., Cañada-Cañada, F., Martínez-Borreguero, G., & Sánchez-Martín, J. (2015). Evolution of the emotions experienced by students of the degree of teacher in primary education, in didactics of the subject and energy [Evolución de las emociones que experimentan los estudiantes del grado de maestro en educación primaria, en didáctica de la materia y la energía]. *Revista Eureka Sobre Enseñanza y Divulgación de Las Ciencias, 12*(3), 550–564.

Dávila-Acedo, M. A., Cañada-Cañada, F., Sánchez, J., & Mellado, V. (2016). Emotions in learning physics and chemistry in secondary education [Las emociones en el aprendizaje de física y química en educación secundaria]. *Causas relacionadas con el estudiante. Educación en la Química, 27*(3), 217–225.

Dávila-Acedo, M. A., Cañada-Cañada, F., Sánchez, J., & Mellado, V. (2016). Emotions in learning physics and chemistry in secondary education [Las emociones en el aprendizaje de física y química en educación secundaria]. *Causas relacionadas con el estudiante. Educación en la Química, 27*(3), 217–225.

Dávila-Acedo, M. A., Cañada-Cañada, F., Sánchez-Martín, J., Airado-Rodríguez, D., & Mellado, V. (2021). Emotional performance on physics and chemistry learning: The case of Spanish K-9 and K-10 students. *International Journal of Science Education, 43*(6), 1–21. doi:10.1080/09500693.2021.1889069

Eccles, J. (2009). Who am I and what am I going to do with my life? Personal and collective identities as motivators of action. *Educational Psychologist, 44*(2), 78–89. doi:10.1080/00461520902832368

Fernández-Abascal, E., Martín, M., & Domínguez, J. (2001). *Psychological processes* [Procesos psicológicos]. Pirámide.

Fernández-Marchesi, N. (2018). Practical laboratory activities and inquiry in the classroom [Actividades prácticas de laboratorio e indagación en el aula]. *TED: Tecné. Episteme y Didáxis, 44*, 203–218.

Frank, P., & Stanszus, L. S. (2019). Transforming consumer behavior: Introducing self-inquiry-based and self-experience-based learning for building personal competencies for sustainable consumption. *Sustainability, 11*(2550), 1–19. doi:10.3390u11092550

Frenzel, A. C., Becker-Kurz, B., Pekrun, R., Goetz, T., & Lüdtke, O. (2018). Emotion transmission in the classroom revisited: A reciprocal effects model of teacher and student enjoyment. *Journal of Educational Psychology, 110*(5), 628–639. doi:10.1037/edu0000228

Frenzel, A. C., Goetz, T., Lüdtke, O., Pekrun, R., & Sutton, R. E. (2009). Emotional transmission in the classroom: Exploring the relationship between teacher and student enjoyment. *Journal of Educational Psychology, 101*(3), 705–716. doi:10.1037/a0014695

Frenzel, A. C., Pekrun, R., & Goetz, T. (2007). Girls and mathematics – A "hopeless" issue? A control-value approach to gender differences in emotions towards mathematics. *European Journal of Psychology of Education, 22*(4), 497–514. doi:10.1007/BF03173468

Gallego-Durán, F. J., Villagrá-Arnedo, C. J., Satorre-Cuerda, R., Compañ-Rosique, P., Molina-Carmona, R., & Llorens-Largo, F. (2019). A Guide for Game-Design-Based Gamification. *Informatics (MDPI), 6*(4), 49. doi:10.3390/informatics6040049

Gargallo, J. B., & Bargalló, C. M. (2011). What experiences do future teachers have about science classes? Implications for their formation [¿Qué experiencias manifiestan los futuros maestros sobre las clases de ciencias? Implicaciones para su formación]. *Review of Education, 354*, 447–472.

Garritz, A. (2009). Affectivity in the teaching of science [La afectividad en la enseñanza de la ciencia]. *Educación en la Química, 20*, 212–219.

Garritz, A. (2010). The teaching of science in a society with uncertainty and accelerated change [La enseñanza de la ciencia en una sociedad con incertidumbre y cambios acelerados]. *Enseñanza de las Ciencias, 28*(3), 315–326. doi:10.5565/rev/ec/v28n3.4

Gerstein, M., & Friedman, H. (2016). Rethinking higher education: Focusing on skills and competencies. *Psychosociological Issues in Human Resource Management, 4*(2), 104–121. doi:10.22381/PIHRM4220165

Gómez-Carrasco, C. J., Monteagudo-Fernández, J., Moreno-Vera, J.-R., & Sainz-Gómez, M. (2019). Effects of a gamification and flipped-classroom program for teachers in training on motivation and learning perception. *Education Sciences*, *9*(299), 1–15. doi:10.3390/educsci9040299

Hernández-Barco, M., Cañada-Cañada, F., Corbacho-Cuello, I., & Sánchez-Martín, J. (2021a). An Exploratory Study Interrelating Emotion, Self-Efficacy and Multiple Intelligence of Prospective Science Teachers. *Frontiers in Education*, *6*(March), 1–12. doi:10.3389/feduc.2021.604791

Hernández-Barco, M., Sánchez-Martín, J., Blanco-Salas, J., & Ruiz-Téllez, T. (2019). Teaching Down to Earth. Service-Learning methodology for science education and sustainability at University level. A practical approach. *Sustainability*, *12*(542), 1–23.

Hernández-Barco, M., Sánchez-Martín, J., Corbacho-cuello, I., & Cañada-Cañada, F. (2021b). Emotional Performance of a Low-Cost Eco-Friendly Project Based Learning Methodology for Science Education: An Approach in Prospective Teachers. *Sustainability*, *13*(3385), 1–19. doi:10.3390u13063385

Izquierdo, M. (2007). Teaching science, a new science [Enseñar ciencias, una nueva ciencia]. *Enseñanza de las Ciencias Sociales*, *6*, 125–138.

Jeong, J. S., González-Gómez, D., & Cañada-Cañada, F. (2016). Students' perceptions and emotions toward learning in a flipped general science classroom. *Journal of Science Education and Technology*, *25*(5), 747–758. doi:10.100710956-016-9630-8

Legerén, B., & Rada, F. (2014). *The rules of the game* [Las reglas del juego]. Avanca Cinema.

Marcos-Merino, J. M., Esteban Gallego, R., Ochoa De Alda, J. A. G., & Mellado, V. (2020). Effect of practical teaching on the emotions of teachers in training towards Biology: Analysis of the influence of gender [Efecto de la enseñanza práctica en las emociones de los maestros en formación hacia la Biología: análisis de la influencia del género]. *Revista Internacional de Pesquisa em Didática Das Ciências e Matemática*, *1*, 1–22.

Marina, J. A. (2004). *Failed intelligence. Theory and practice of stupidity* [La inteligencia fracasada. Teoría y práctica de la estupidez]. Editorial Anagrama S.A.

Martínez-Chico, M., Liso, M. R. J., & Lucio-Villegas, R. L. G. (2015). Effect of a training program to teach science by inquiry based on models, on the didactic conceptions of future teachers [Efecto de un programa formativo para enseñar ciencias por indagación basada en modelos, en las concepciones didácticas de los futuros maestros]. *Revista Eureka Sobre Enseñanza y Divulgación de las Ciencias*, *12*(1), 149–166.

Mekler, E. D., Birk, M. V., Rank, S., Iacovides, I., & Steinemann, S. T. (2016). Designing for emotional complexity in games: The interplay of positive and negative affect. *CHI PLAY 2016 - Proceedings of the Annual Symposium on Computer-Human Interaction in Play Companion*, 367–371.

Mellado, V., Borrachero, B., Melo, L. V., Dávila-Acedo, M. A., Cañada, F., Conde, M. C., Costillo, E., Cubero, J., Esteban, R., Martínez, G., Ruiz, C., Sánchez, J., Garritz, A., Mellado, L., Vázquez-Bernal, B., Jimenez-Pérez, R., & Bermejo, M. L. (2014). Emotions in science teaching [Las emociones en la enseñanza de las ciencias]. *Enseñanza de las Ciencias*, *32*(3), 11–36.

Mora, F. (2012). What are emotions? [¿Qué son las emociones?]. In R. Bisquerra (Ed.), *Cómo educar las emociones? La inteligencia emocional en la infancia y la adolescencia* (pp. 14–24). FAROS.

Mora, F. (2017). *Neuroeducation: you can only learn what you love* [Neuroeducación: sólo se puede aprender aquello que se ama]. Alianza Editorial.

Mullins, J. K., & Sabherwal, R. (2020). Gamification: A cognitive-emotional view. *Journal of Business Research, 106*, 304–314. doi:10.1016/j.jbusres.2018.09.023

Murga-Menoyo, M. Á. (2015). Competences for sustainable development: The capacities, attitudes and target values of education within the framework of the post-2015 Global Agenda [Competencias para el desarrollo sostenible: las capacidades, actitudes y valores meta de la educación en el marco de la Agenda global post-2015]. *Foro de Educación, 13*, 55–83. doi:10.14516/fde.2015.013.019.004

Oliva, J. M. O., & Acevedo, J. A. D. (2005). Science teaching in primary and secondary today. Some proposals for the future [La enseñanza de las ciencias en primaria y secundaria hoy. Algunas propuestas de futuro]. *Revista Eureka Sobre Enseñanza y Divulgación de las Ciencias, 2*(2), 241–250.

Olson, R. E., McKenzie, J., Mills, K. A., Patulny, R., Bellocchi, A., & Caristo, F. (2019). Gendered emotion management and teacher outcomes in secondary school teaching: A review. *Teaching and Teacher Education, 80*, 128–144. doi:10.1016/j.tate.2019.01.010

Pedaste, M., Mäeots, M., Siiman, L. A., de Jong, T., van Riesen, S. A. N., Kamp, E. T., Manoli, C. C., Zacharia, Z. C., & Tsourlidaki, E. (2015). Phases of inquiry-based learning: Definitions and the inquiry cycle. *Educational Research Review, 14*, 47–61. doi:10.1016/j.edurev.2015.02.003

Pekrun, R. (2014). Emotions and Learning. In UNESCO (Ed.), Emotions and Learning (pp. 6–30). Gonnet Imprimeur.

Pekrun, R., & Stephens, E. J. (2010). Achievement Emotions: A Control-Value Approach. *Social and Personality Psychology Compass, 4*(4), 238–255. doi:10.1111/j.1751-9004.2010.00259.x

Pérez, M. C. (2011). Board games in early childhood education [Los juegos de mesa en la educación infantil]. *Pedagogía Magna, 11*, 354–359.

Phelps, E. A. (2006). Emotion and Cognition: Insights from Studies of the Human Amygdala. *Annual Review of Psychology, 57*(1), 27–53. doi:10.1146/annurev.psych.56.091103.070234 PMID:16318588

Pipitone, C., Guitart, J., Agudelo, C., & García, À. (2019). Favoring the positive emotional change towards the sciences in the initial training of teachers [Favoreciendo el cambio emocional positivo hacia las ciencias en la formación inicial del profesorado]. *Ápice. Revista de Educación Científica, 3*(1), 41–54.

Poon, C. Y. S., Hui, V. K. Y., Yuen, G. W. C., Kwong, V. W. Y., & Chan, C. S. (2019). A well-slept teacher is a better teacher: A multi-respondent experience-sampling study on sleep, stress, and emotional transmission in the classroom. *PsyCh Journal, 8*(3), 280–292. doi:10.1002/pchj.282 PMID:30983162

Retana-Alvarado, D. A., De las Heras-Pérez, M. Á., Vázquez-Bernal, B., & Jiménez-Pérez, R. (2018). The change in the emotions of teachers in initial training towards the classroom climate in an intervention based on school research [El cambio en las emociones de maestros en formación inicial hacia el clima de aula en una intervención basada en investigación escolar]. *Revista Eureka Sobre Enseñanza y Divulgación de las Ciencias*, *15*(2), 2602.

Rieckmann, M. (2018). Learning to transform the world: key competencies. In Issues and trends in Education for Sustainable Development in Issues and trends in education for sustainable development (1st ed., pp. 39–59). United Nations Educational, Scientific and Cultural Organization.

Robson, K., Plangger, K., Kietzmann, J. H., McCarthy, I., & Pitt, L. (2015). Is it all a game? Understanding the principles of gamification. *Business Horizons*, *58*(4), 411–420. doi:10.1016/j.bushor.2015.03.006

Sanchez-Martín, J., Cañada-Cañada, F., & Dávila-Acedo, A. (2018). Emotional responses to innovative science teaching methods: Acquiring emotional data in a general science teacher education class. *Journal of Technology and Science Education JOTSE*, *8*(4), 346–359. doi:10.3926/jotse.408

Sánchez-Martín, J., Cañada-Cañada, F., & Dávila-Acedo, M. A. (2017). Just a game? Gamifying a general science class at university: Collaborative and competitive work implications. *Thinking Skills and Creativity*, *26*, 51–59. doi:10.1016/j.tsc.2017.05.003

Sánchez-Martín, J., Corrales-Serrano, M., Luque-Sendra, A., & Zamora-Polo, F. (2020). Exit for success. Gamifying science and technology for university students using escape-room. A preliminary approach. *Heliyon*, *6*(7), e04340. doi:10.1016/j.heliyon.2020.e04340 PMID:32671257

Sierra, M. C., & Fernández-Sánchez, M. R. (2019). Gamifying the university classroom. Analysis of an Escape Room experience in higher education [Gamificando el aula universitaria. Análisis de una experiencia de Escape Room en educación superior]. *Revista de Estudios y Experiencias en Educación*, *18*(36), 105–115.

Solís-Espallargas, C., Colomar, I. E., & García, A. R. (2015). A research-based learning experience with Black Boxes in initial teacher training [Una experiencia de aprendizaje por investigación con Cajas negras en formación inicial de maestros]. *Revista Eureka*, *12*(1), 167–177.

Steegh, A. M., Höffler, T. N., Keller, M. M., & Parchmann, I. (2019). Gender differences in mathematics and science competitions: A systematic review. *Journal of Research in Science Teaching*, *56*(10), 1431–1460. doi:10.1002/tea.21580

Tomas, L., Rigano, D., & Ritchie, S. M. (2016). Students' regulation of their emotions in a science classroom. *Journal of Research in Science Teaching*, *53*(2), 234–260. doi:10.1002/tea.21304

van Aalderen-Smeets, S. I., van der Molen, J. H., & Asma, L. J. F. (2012). Primary teachers' attitudes toward science: A new theoretical framework. *Science Education*, *96*(1), 158–182. doi:10.1002ce.20467

Vázquez, A., & Manassero, M. A. (2007). In defense of attitudes and emotions in scientific education (II): Empirical evidence derived from research [En defensa de las actitudes y emociones en la educación científica (II): evidencias empíricas derivadas de la investigación]. *Revista Eureka Sobre Enseñanza y Divulgación de las Ciencias*, *4*(3), 417–441.

Vázquez, A., & Manassero, M. A. (2008). The decline in students' attitudes towards science: A disturbing indicator for science education [El declive de las actitudes hacia la ciencia de los estudiantes: un indicador inquietante para la educación científica]. *Revista Eureka Sobre Enseñanza y Divulgación de las Ciencias*, *8*(3), 274–292.

Wu, Y.-J., Kiefer, S. M., & Chen, Y.-H. (2019). Relationships between learning strategies and self-efficacy: A cross-cultural comparison between Taiwan and the United States using latent class analysis. *International Journal of School & Educational Psychology*, 1–13.

Yllana-Prieto, F., Jeong, J. S., & González-Gómez, D. (2021). An online-based edu-escape room: A comparison study of a multidimensional domain of psts with flipped sustainability-stem contents. *Sustainability*, *13*(3), 1–18. doi:10.3390u13031032 PMID:34676112

Zamora-Polo, F., Sánchez-Cortés, M. M., Reyes-Rodríguez, A. M., & Sanz-Calcedo, J. G. (2019). Developing project managers' transversal competences using building information modeling. *Applied Sciences (Basel, Switzerland)*, *9*(4006), 1–17. doi:10.3390/app9194006

ADDITIONAL READING

Allen, K., Kern, M. L., Vella-Brodrick, D., Hattie, J., & Waters, L. (2018). What Schools Need to Know About Fostering School Belonging: A Meta-analysis. *Educational Psychology Review*, *30*(1), 1–34. doi:10.100710648-016-9389-8

Davidson, S. G., Jaber, L. Z., & Southerland, S. A. (2020). Emotions in the doing of science: Exploring epistemic affect in elementary teachers' science research experiences. *Science Education*, *104*(6), 1008–1040. doi:10.1002ce.21596

De Castella, K., Goldin, P., Jazaieri, H., Ziv, M., Dweck, C. S., & Gross, J. J. (2013). Beliefs about emotion: Links to emotion regulation, well-being, and psychological distress. *Basic and Applied Social Psychology*, *35*(6), 497–505. doi:10.1080/01973533.2013.840632

Goetz, T., Sticca, F., Pekrun, R., Murayama, K., & Elliot, A. J. (2016). Intraindividual relations between achievement goals and discrete achievement emotions: An experience sampling approach. *Learning and Instruction*, *41*, 115–125. doi:10.1016/j.learninstruc.2015.10.007

Mellado, V. (2003). Cambio didáctico del profesorado de ciencias experimentales y filosofía de la ciencia. *Enseñanza de las Ciencias*, *21*(3), 343–358. doi:10.5565/rev/ensciencias.3913

Mullins, J. K., & Sabherwal, R. (2020). Gamification: A cognitive-emotional view. *Journal of Business Research*, *106*(8), 304–314. doi:10.1016/j.jbusres.2018.09.023

Posner, J., Russell, J. A., & Peterson, B. S. (2015). The circumplex model of affect: An integrative approach to affective neuroscience, cognitive development, and psychopathology. *Development and Psychopathology*, *17*, 715–734. PMID:16262989

Rosiña, E., Bermejo, M. L., del Barco, M., Cañada, F., & Sanchez-Martin, J. (2020). Multiple Intelligences analysis and emotional implications in STEM education for students up to K-12. In R. Zheng (Ed.), Examining Multiple Intelligences and Digital Technologies for Enhanced Learning Opportunities (pp. 261–280). University of Utah.

von Scheve, C. (2012). Emotion regulation and emotion work: Two sides of the same coin? *Frontiers in Psychology*, *3*(496), 1–10. doi:10.3389/fpsyg.2012.00496 PMID:23181041

Wolf, T., Weiger, W. H., & Hammerschmidt, M. (2020). Experiences that matter? The motivational experiences and business outcomes of gamified services. *Journal of Business Research*, *106*, 353–364. doi:10.1016/j.jbusres.2018.12.058

KEY TERMS AND DEFINITIONS

Emotions: These are psycho-biological reactions that people experience with different intensity depending on the information and the perceptions they receive from the environment and after a subjective assessment that each person makes, and which directly affects their personal well-being.

European Higher Education Area: Educational organization (founded in 1999) in the European Union with the aim of harmonizing the different European educational systems, constituting a flexible and common university system that facilitates the recognition of degrees and mobility throughout the European community.

Gamification: Didactic method that includes aspects of play (mechanical and dynamic), and that is aimed at improving students' motivation to achieve learning objectives.

Inquiry: Didactic method that comprises an intentional process directed by the teacher and based on the diagnosis of problems, research, debate, and construction of arguments following the scientific method, in order for the student independently to provide solutions to specific challenges.

Scientific Literacy: Knowledge that the general population has about scientific procedures, methods, and ideas, which facilitates their being able to get involved, reflect, and make decisions related to scientific fields.

Self-Efficacy: The teacher's perception of their own abilities to carry out a task or activity. It is closely related to self-concept, emotions, and knowledge of the subject.

Soft Skills: Skills other than cognitive skills that have to do with the students' social, personal, and emotional dimension, for example, the ability to speak in public, collaborative work, positive attitude, or responsibility.

Chapter 18
The Use of an Educational Digital Game in Higher Education:
Design and Application to Increase the Motivation in Calculus Learning

Vinicius Lunkes Cezar
https://orcid.org/0000-0002-8888-7018
Federal University of Health Sciences of Porto Alegre, Brazil

Patrick Vicente Garcia
https://orcid.org/0000-0002-4865-8624
Pontifical Catholic University of Rio Grande do Sul, Brazil

Viviane Rodrigues Botelho
Federal University of Health Sciences of Porto Alegre, Brazil

Evandro Manara Miletto
https://orcid.org/0000-0001-7888-9047
Federal Institute of Rio Grande do Sul, Porto Alegre, Brazil

ABSTRACT

Grabbing students' attention is becoming more challenging in the digital age, distance education, and increasing low literacy. This complex educational phenomenon needs to be mitigated to prevent negative social and economic consequences. This work presents the use of gamification in higher education to engage and motivate students in Calculus, a course that traditionally presents high failure and dropout rates. The main goal is to report an experience developing an RPG-style educational digital game to be used and tested in part of the course during one semester. The project applied concepts of gamification, educational digital games, digital game-based learning, and the theory of meaningful learning as a theoretical basis for the formulation of the game. The results showed positive acceptance of this approach by the students and an increase of interest in proceeding with using the game for learning purposes. According to the results, 73% of students declared the game contributes to the learning process, and 82% showed interest in using the game for the whole semester.

DOI: 10.4018/978-1-6684-4287-6.ch018

INTRODUCTION

Historically, Calculus has high dropout rates and failure. According to Barufi (1999), the subject presented a 66% failure rate between 1990 and 1995 at the Institute of Physics of University of São Paulo (USP). This same subject at the Institute of Geosciences between 1990 and 1993 reached an alarming 72% non-approved rate at USP. A survey conducted by the Mathematical Association of America (MAA), concluded that students considered Calculus learning ineffective, lacking aspiration, with an excessive amount of content and at a very fast pace. In addition, the lack of connection between the teacher and the students was identified (Bressoud et al., 2012). Another problem, reported by Mendes and Giostri (2008) is that the student arrives in higher education with inadequate math knowledge and without motivation to maintain a regular study.

According to Kessler et al. (2011), many Calculus students have gaps in fundamental mathematics knowledge, however these concepts are essential for calculus understanding. The Meaningful Learning Theory proposed by Ausubel et al. (1968) says that this basic knowledge of mathematics is called "subsumers for meaningful learning". The reinforcement of contents through lectures (the traditional pre-calculus courses) has sometimes proved to be ineffective, since the difficulties of students in this area and the learning style are very diverse.

Nowadays, most students in higher education belong to a group called digital natives, composed of people born in the 1980s or later and grew up surrounded by technology. Digital natives have access to information very easily and quickly. They are not usually motivated by traditional instruction. Instead, they prefer inductive reasoning with fast interactions. Therefore, to keep the interest of digital natives, the education needs to fit these student profiles and use the technological resources to improve the teaching and learning process (Prensky, 2010). Obviously, the conventional teaching process is essential. However, in some cases, the massive and purely conceptual expository lectures demotivate students (Bezerra, 2016). In that regard, gamification arises as an alternative to deal with this gap since it could make learning more interesting and engaging (Surendeleg et al., 2014).

Gamification is defined as the application of game techniques and game-oriented thinking in non-game contexts. It emerges in applications of marketing, training s, productivity, finance, health, sustainability, as well as news and entertainment media (Deterding et al., 2011). However, over the years, the phenomenon of gamification is spreading also through the educational area (Fardo, 2013). Several studies report the success of gamification in education. Silva et al. (2016) focused on the problem of programming learning, which usually presents a high rate of evasion. The authors developed a model based on student engagement with gamification techniques and applied it in three classes containing 24 students. The results showed that the students became more engaged, and the teachers stated that the model helped in the learning process. An exploratory case study was conducted by Machajewski (2017), containing dense descriptions of students in the subject of Introduction to Computing at Grand Valley State University. 1184 comments from students enrolled in a gamified version of the discipline were qualitatively analyzed and pointed to the success of the purpose.

The research by (Rincon-Flores et al., 2020) analyzed the use of gamification in Calculus through telepresence and holographic projection. All thirty-four students who participated stated that the gamified strategy made the classes more motivating. This was reflected in grade improvement of the second evaluation period. The literature review by Manzano-León (2021) analyzed articles published between 2016 and 2020 that implemented gamification in the education context formal. Fourteen works were selected for analysis from 750. The results support that educational gamification has a potential impact on student academic performance, commitment and motivation.

The gamification based on digital games is becoming increasingly popular due to the technological profile of digital natives. According to Wijman (2021), the gaming market generated $177.8 billion in 2020, an increase of 23.1% compared to 2019. This was the biggest market growth since Newzoo began tracking revenues in 2012. The related blocking measures to COVID-19 generated huge interest in games across all regions and platforms. The trend is that the gaming market will continue to grow in the coming years, surpassing US$ 200 billion by the end of 2023. For this potential, as Prensky (2010) argues, learning based on digital games is in accordance with the needs and learning styles of digital natives, motivating students in their studies and being able to be adjusted to all subjects.

The educational digital games are part of the reformulation that mathematics has undergone, not in the sense of reducing the rigor or exclusion of content, but in the way it is seen and addressed by students and teachers. That said, games emerge as an auxiliary tool to meet the new educational guidelines arising from this process of change (Rafael, 2017).

Based on this, the present chapter presents a case study about the development and application of a game using educational and game industry concepts. In the next section, the theoretical framework is explained. Afterwards, the development of the educational digital game called The Fellowship of the Calculus is discussed. Finally, the case study, results, and conclusions are presented.

THEORETICAL BACKGROUND

In this section, the main concepts applied to the conception of the proposed digital game are presented.

Meaningful Learning

Meaningful Learning is the process through which new information, new knowledge or concept is related in a non-arbitrary and substantive way to the student's cognitive structure (Ausubel et al. 1980). This definition presents what the authors consider one of the most important factors for learning to occur, the relationship between the new concept and the student's cognitive structure, according to Ausubel et al. (1980) "If we had to reduce all educational psychology to a single principle, we would say that the singular factor influencing learning is what the learner already knows, find that out and base your teachings on that." (p. 137).

Two conditions are necessary for meaningful learning to occur:

1. The materials must be potentially significant, that is, there must be a relationship with the learner's cognitive structure.
2. The student needs to be willing to meaningful learning and not simply memorize, arbitrarily and literally, thus generating mechanical learning.

In mechanical learning new information has little or no connection with the relevant concepts in the student's cognitive structure, even so, Ausubel does not consider that there is a dichotomy between meaningful and mechanical learning, as shown in Figure 1:

Figure 1. Relationship between mechanical and meaningful learning (Adapted from Moreira, 2012)

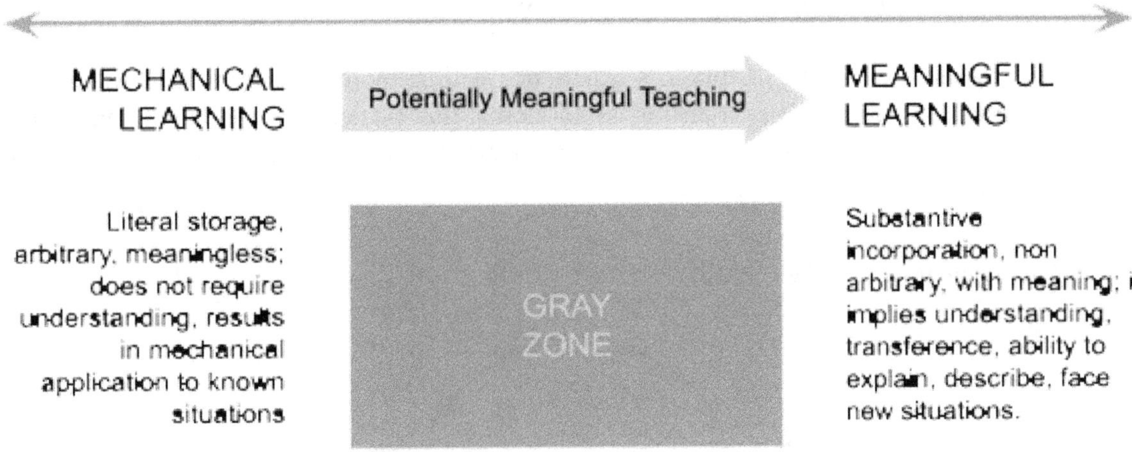

Thus, the individual acquires information in an area of knowledge that is completely new to him, so that, with his development, he acquires subsumers that allow the occurrence of significant learning However, this process is not natural and depends on the previously mentioned conditions of the student's predisposition, potentially significant material and subsumers.

The specific knowledge that the student already has in their cognitive structure are called subsumers. Through them, new knowledge can have meaning, if it has a relationship with the existing subsumer. This occurs through specifically relevant prior knowledge and the interaction with them of new knowledge. Subsumers have a degree of cognitive stability, that is, their meanings can be more or less elaborated. However, even the subsumer that will serve as an anchor idea for a new knowledge is modified, acquiring new meaning, this due to the process being interactive (Moreira, 2012).

The concepts of Meaningful Learning Theory can be applied to improve calculus learning. Barbosa (2004) shows that the traditional methodologies with ready-made assessments working only on memorization and a lot of abstraction make learning difficult.

Gamification

It can be considered that the word gamification is correlated with gamification's expression. Therefore, the meaning and usage are the same for all of them. This term first appeared in 2003, being coined by the computer programmer and inventor Nick Pelling. It began to be strengthened from 2010, generating reports and statistics on the subject (Alves, 2015). According to Zichermann and Cunningham (2011), people are motivated by gamification to master a certain subject, for entertainment and socializing purposes.

According to Alves (2015), three characteristics of gamification are able to motivate people:

- **Challenges:** the learner needs to meet meaningful goals at different levels, but the outcome is uncertain with constant feedback on their performance.
- **Fantasy:** using an environment that is not present in the student's real experience favors cognitive and emotional aspects with the use of fantasy in learning environments.

- **Curiosity:** the well-built environment provokes the learner's curiosity, offering knowledge in the right measure, that is, not too complicated or too simple.

By employing these elements, the player's experience will be more pleasurable and will motivate him to perform the desired activities. For this, all tasks that will be performed by the player must be thought of in terms of what you want to achieve. Alves (2015) defined this process as an engagement loop, as shown in Figure 2:

Figure 2. Engagement Loop (Alves, 2015).

One of the most important features of a game is the quick feedback. It is essential to keep the player more motivated and, thus, make even the mistake something normal within the engagement loop. Immediate feedback contributes to greater engagement when applied also to virtual awards, such as game points, for example, not only for completing a task or activity, but also for the quality of contributions (Patrício et al., 2018).

Digital Education Games

Digital games have playful activities formed by actions and decisions limited by a set of rules controlled by a computer program (Schuytema, 2008). These games are a subset of fun and play that may or may not lead to learning. There are formal and structured ways that put into practice the full power of fun and games in the learning process (Prensky, 2010). Games are educational when they act as motivators of the learning process (Tarouco et al., 2004). Thus, when a digital game is applied in the teaching and learning process in education, it can be considered an Educational Digital Game.

According to Prensky (2012), the success of learning in a digital game depends on the variables of involvement and learning. Commercial digital games usually only work on the issue of involvement to attract more players to buy the game. On the other hand, if only learning is aimed at without involvement, the student will probably not be motivated to use the tool. The great challenge is to equalize the two variables so that learning based on the digital game takes place.

The Digital games can be classified into 8 categories that usually overlap, as shown in the Table 1:

In the context of this research, the educational digital game is classified and has the characteristics of an RPG, so it is important to address this type of digital game more deeply in the next sections.

Table 1. Educational digital game classification (Adapted from Prensky, 2012)

Category	Characteristic
Action	When the player needs to shoot falling things or enemies, car races and chases.
Adventure	Where unknown worlds are explored, objects are picked up, and problems solved.
Sports	Most are action games where the player controls his character within a sport. There are sports with less action that the game is more statistical.
Strategy	Generally, the player is responsible for evolving an army or a civilization to progress and in most cases defeat their opponents.
Fight	Two or more characters fight a battle until one side is defeated.
Puzzle Game	The plot is simply a pretext for problems to be solved.
RPG (Role Playing Game)	They often feature characters known as dwarfs, hobbits, humans, orcs, elves, wizards, etc., who interact with medieval images involving quest tasks to save someone or something.
Simulation	The player pilots air, land or water machines, usually military. Worlds are built and companies are run that are very connected to reality.

THE RPG GAME

The game in RPG format is very effective in the educational field for researchers and educators who can use its broad simulation and fantasy features to aid teaching and learning (Wu et al., 2016). This type of game is difficult and complex to be developed, but if applied to instruction purposes, it can motivate and offer an engaging environment for students (Tarouco et al., 2004). The RPG games can be digital or not, but the game components remain the same, changing only the game master, as shown in Table 2:

Table 2. RPG components. (Adapted from Dormans, 2006; Frias, 2009).

Component	Description
Fictional universe	Parameters of a fictitious reality in an equally fictitious time, such as a medieval or futuristic past, are established.
Adventure	The journey can be short, medium or long duration, collectively or individually.
Trauma	Where adventure's essence is hidden as well as the conflicts, problem-situations, enemies, and obstacles to overcome.
Narrative	It connects the characters to share an imaginary reality in a defined and controlled space of time by the game.
Master	A specific player guides players through the game, defining the rules, composing, and presenting the plot and challenges to the players. In the case of the digital game, this role is within the story defined for the game.
Characters	They are players with skills and defects that are improved and associated with other attributes throughout the adventure's course.
Non-player character (NPC)	These are digital game-controlled characters that players can interact with but cannot engage in combat.

Computer-based RPGs adopt a simple model presenting an improved aesthetic, making the playing more enjoyable. This is so different from the real world, where you have to work hard to find out what are the rules of the game, and players work even harder to achieve them, without being sure if they are doing the right thing (Schell, 2008).

According to Schell (2008), some characteristics to have a good educational digital game in RPG format need to be considered are:

- Avoid offering only one problem or challenge at a time. It is much more common to give two or more parallel challenges at the same time, so the player is less likely to get frustrated quickly (Schell, 2008).
- Screen data must be changed when the player enters combat mode, presenting statistics, menus and information about the battle and the player (Schell, 2008).
- The villain (main enemy) is usually included in educational simulations and can challenge heroes in areas where the simulation seeks to develop specific skills (Mattar, 2010).
- In the use of an RPG players need to determine the actions of their heroes based on the game situation, from the rules that should result in success or failure (Wu et al., 2016).
- NPCs should be primarily concerned with helping players in the various missions presented by the game (Machado et al., 2017).

The Game Design

This chapter aims to present details of the proposed game development. The premises to ensure students' learning and engagement are: (i) create a digital game with an interface like commercial games, and (ii) always keep the relation between the game context and the theoretical content of Calculus. The development guide followed the three main gamification elements described by Kapp (2012):

1. **Mechanics:** are usually the elements used in many games such as levels or phases, badges, ranking, score, and time control. They are important tasks in the gamification process. However, they are not enough to transform a boring experience into something engaging.
2. **Aesthetics:** gamification experience needs to be pleasant, and it is strongly related with game aesthetics. The graphic quality, art pieces, sound effects, and soundtrack are examples of important features to be worked on.
3. **Thoughts:** Probably the most important of gamification, thoughts are the ideas that compose the game history. The thoughts define the experiences carried out by the students that lead to the learning that is desired with gamification. Aspect as contexts, goals, and fantasy need to be designed to ensure a motivating experience. Besides, since the game has an educational purpose, it is necessary to ensure that players' competition will not overlap the cooperative relation between the students.

The game is in RPG format, where players assume the role of a character in simulated scenarios, following a defined story (Cover, 2014). Pedagogically, the RPG games help to improve several skills such as social inclusion, attention, concentration, creativity, and socialization (Frias, 2009; Pessini et al., 2015).

For the design of a successful digital game the investment in the game contextualization and in the development of graphical interfaces are crucial, in as much as it attracts players attention and, due to this, the development is usually carried out in several phases. Mattar (2010) and Schuytema (2008) suggest the following development phases for educational digital games: pre-production with the survey of requirements for the design and concept of the game; production with implementation and coding; and post-production by applying the tests.

To define the main elements that are part of the game, the Game Design Document (GDD) proposed by Schuytema (2008) was adapted. The GDD supports the team during the process of developing a digital game (Aleem et al., 2016; Pedersen, 2003). Table 3 and 4 show the GDD for game development:

Table 3. The Fellowship of the Calculus' GDD

1. Essential overview	
Title	The Fellowship of the Calculus
Gender	educational
Category	RPG
Platform	Windows
Resume	An RPG game where students will choose between 5 heroes named with inspiring mathematician names, following an established script where the discipline content is inserted into the story.
Fundamental aspects	The game has a 3D scenario with limits that prevent the player from leaving, through scenario and story elements to indicate the path to be followed.
Differentials of the game	The educational digital game uses heroes inserted in a medieval fantasy story to build paths, stages, objectives, tasks, and characters. This approach is very popular among digital natives. These playful activities are important in the teaching and learning process.
2. Game context	
Game history	A new mage has emerged, making several friendships with others of his race. However, over the years he has perfected his magic for evil, becoming an evil wizard as never seen before. The magician acquires powers from calculus content that allow the creation of monsters, called Orcs, to help him. His ultimate goal is to develop the Ring of Calculus to summon the powers of evil and dominate the Land of Calculus. The players' mission is to progress through 4 cities in the game, overcoming midway challenges imposed by Orcs, solving problems and puzzles from the World of Calculus. The player's ultimate goal is to reach the 4th city, Ptolomeya to face the final challenge imposed by the evil wizard and avoid the creation of the Ring of Calculus. In all phases, they will go through activities about the concepts necessary for their journey, which involve mathematical calculations in an attempt to save the Earth of Calculus from evil.
Previous events	There was a time when the Land of Calculus was almost taken over by the powers of evil with the use of a magic ring. However, he was eliminated and destroyed, preventing evil from taking over the Land of Calculus. However, with the destruction of the ring, it is a mistake to think that the secret for the ring to be recreated is eliminated. In reality, there is the possibility of developing the most powerful new Ring of Calculus, from the use of mathematical formulas and the connection with the evil spirits that once tried to dominate the Land of Calculus.
Main players	Johann Carl Friedrich Gauss (Hobbit). Skill: quick attack with your dagger; Baptiste Joseph Fourrier (Dwarf). Skill: agility with your axe; Adrien-Marie Legendre (Elf). Skill: quick with the sword; Amalie Emmy Noether (Human). Skill: strong sword attacks; Évariste Galois (Mage). Skill: Use of magic staff.

The GDD was constantly updated until reaching its final version, characterized as a "living" document. According to Mattar (2010), the GDD must be constantly consulted as the reference document for the game development.

The prototyping process supports the game development mainly at the beginning of the project in the scope definition Schuytema (2008). According to Pressman and Maxim (2016), prototyping helps those involved in understanding what will be built, as it assists in defining and adjusting requirements by presenting versions that allow quick user feedback.

Table 4. The Fellowship of the Calculus' GDD

3. Essential game objects	
Characters	Mage named Kyrus the players' main enemy, Orcs who face players in battles and characters from the hero races who interact with them during the game.
Weapons	Axe, sword, dagger and staff.
Objects	Keys, books, maps, breastplate, helmet and leggings.
4. Conflicts and solutions	
Player action in game	The player interacts with the scene by moving and talking to characters, selecting items, answering content questions, and conducting battles with enemies.
Feedback	At the end of each task, information about the answers given by the players (correct and incorrect) will appear on the feedback message screen. At the end of each phase, the ranking with the badges is displayed.
Progress	All questions related to the calculus content have a time of 10 minutes, as indicated by the subject professor as being enough time to answer the questions with the required calm and attention. This time took into account the available 2 hours of game application, as well as the volume of content covered throughout the regular class week. There is no score difference for whoever responds faster. If the time ends without an answer, the question is considered wrong. The player will be able to advance to the next stage as soon as he finishes the current stage tasks. It is allowed to return at any time to access the prior knowledge.
Scoring system	Getting the question right on the first attempt earns 50 points; on the second attempt, 25 points; and after the third attempt, 5 points.
5. Game Flow	
The game develops in an increasing sequence of 4 stages: 1. Humans' City called Talea. 2. Dwarves' City called Pitaghorum. 3. Elves' City called Arkipedia. 4. Wizards' City called Ptolomeya.	
6. Game variations	
The game is single user without interaction between users, being played individually by each student without exchanging experiences within the game. However, a ranking with badges is generated and shared among all players to convey an idea of competition and allow interaction outside the game.	

First, low-fidelity paper prototyping was used to speed up the development of a low-cost first version of the game's general idea, which was considered very useful at the beginning of the development phase. Afterwards, the initial screen of the high-fidelity prototype was developed, presenting the trajectory to be performed by the player and the numbering of each city. This model features materials with a better finish suitable for carrying out the usability and user experience tests (Rogers et al., 2013). The Figure 3 and Figure 4 show the two prototype screens developed in this work:

The name of the chosen game was "The Fellowship of the Calculus", referring to the book The Fellowship of the Ring by (Tolkien, 2012). The game was developed using the Unity[1] computer program using a free license for students, and with the ability to target games for multiples platforms. The Unity game engine is widely used in the production of commercial games such as Super Mario Run[2], Sonic Forces[3], Pokémon GO[4], Call of Duty[5] and Angry Birds[6].

According to the need to reinforce previous mathematical knowledge, an item called "Tome of Knowledge" was inserted in the game's history. The player could access the item containing the prior mathematical knowledge, subsumers needed to perform the mathematical questions. Access to the file was allowed at any time until the end of the game.

Figure 3. Paper Prototyping.

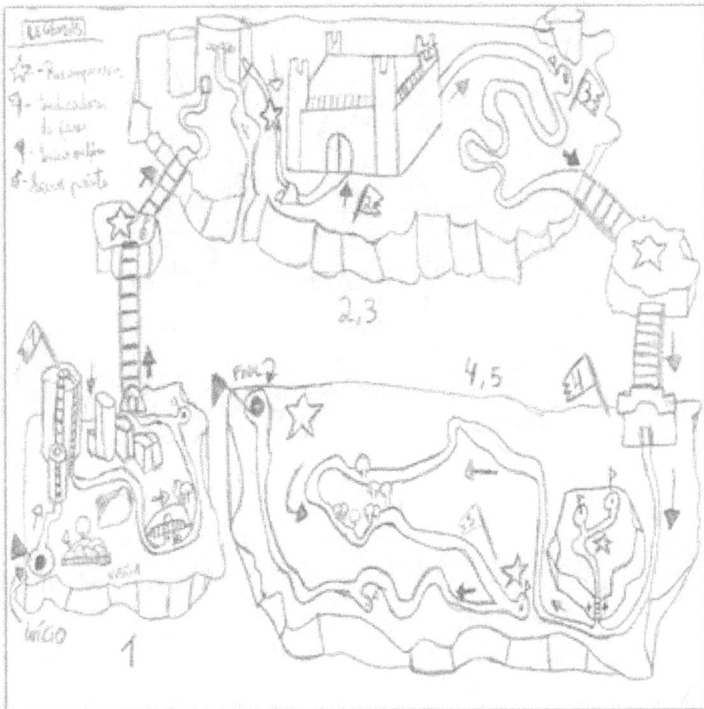

Figure 4. The Fellowship of the Calculus' Map

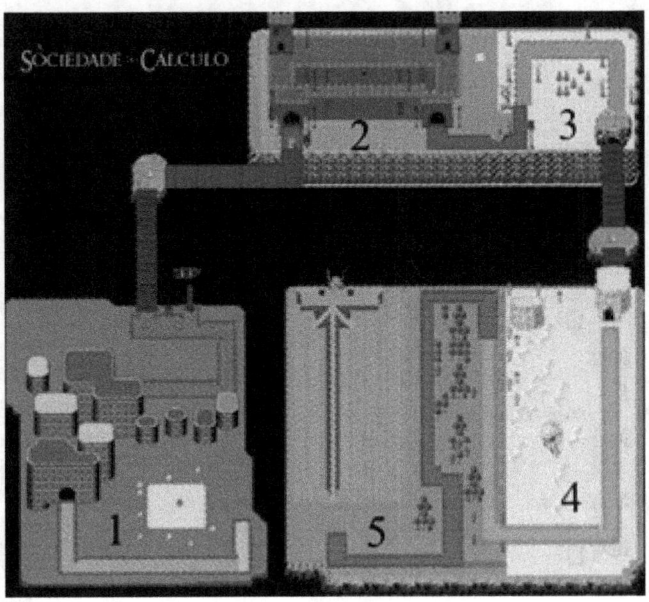

Figure 5. Screenshot of the game "The Fellowship of the Calculus".

Figure 6. Screenshot of a quest in the "The Fellowship of the Calculus"

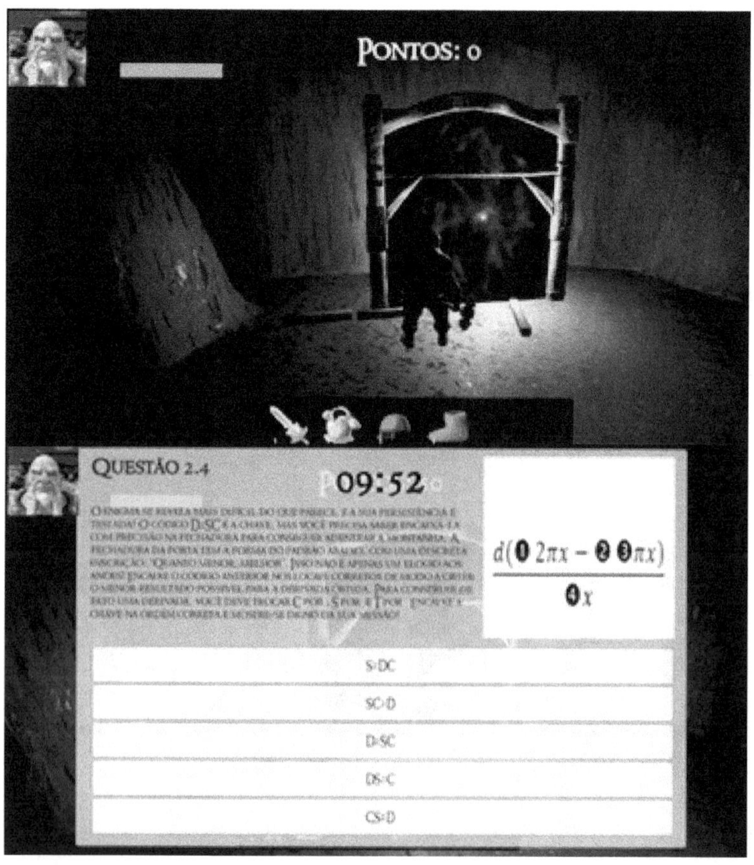

To increase the game immersion of users, the calculus content issues were inserted in the story, challenges, and mysteries involved throughout the player's trajectory. The game includes five phases, each one representing a Calculus content. Figure 5 and Figure 6 illustrate the final version of the game "The Fellowship of the Calculus".

In the post-production phase, extensive testing of the game mechanics was carried out: general functioning and feedback (Sato, 2010). It is noteworthy that this test aimed to assess only the development of the research product, and not the learning process. It was decided to carry out a test with six undergraduate students (Cezar et al., 2019). The students played the game prototype, and the researchers qualitatively analyzed the reported difficulties.

The test of the prototype had positive feedback regarding usability, reliability, and satisfaction issues. From this result, it was possible to see that the game could help teachers in the teaching and learning process of Calculus.

Case Study Description

To evaluate the gamification potential in Calculus learning, the developed game was applied to 20 Calculus students from the Biomedical Informatics undergraduate course of Universidade Federal de Ciências da Saúde de Porto Alegre - UFCSPA (Federal University of Health Sciences of Porto Alegre), who agreed to participate of the study. The confidentiality of information provided by them was guaranteed, as well the right to leave the research at any time. The participants had the following profiles:

- Age: 65% under 20-year-old, 24% aged from 20 to 30 years old and 11% upper 30-year-old.
- Sex: 53% male and 47% female.
- Calculus knowledge: 88% were studying Calculus for the first time, while 12% were repeating the subject.
- Digital games experience: 94% of students enjoy playing digital games.

The test took place at the UFCSPA computer lab along 4 weekly meetings lasting 2 hours each. Students answered one questionnaire per week. The Table 5 shows the application schedule of the game The Fellowship of the Calculus and the participants of each meeting:

Table 5. Meeting's questionnaire and participants

Meeting	Date	Data Collection Instrument	Participants
Week 1	16/10/2019	Weekly questionnaire	20
Week 2	30/10/2019	Weekly questionnaire	20
Week 3	06/11/2019	Weekly questionnaire	18
Week 4	20/11/2019	Weekly questionnaire	17

The questionnaires applied weekly had 10 closed questions with answers on the 5-point Likert scale, elaborated according to Savi (2011). At the end, an open question was available for students, to enter comments on that day's activity.

The objective of the educational game evaluation model proposed by Savi (2011) is to carry out quality assessments through the students' perception about the levels of motivation, user experience and learning promoted by a game. The model has already been applied in some studies demonstrating its applicability in this context of digital games aimed at education. Below are examples of its application:

- El Mochilero: Educational Digital Game for the Development of Intercultural Competence of Spanish Language Learners (Paz et al., 2017).
- Project Detective - A Game for Teaching Earned Value Management (Von Wangenheim et al., 2014).
- SCRUMIA - An educational game for teaching SCRUM in computing courses (Von Wangenheim et al., 2013).

In the first week, the students were notified that there would be a ranking and that the first place would receive a symbolic prize on the last day of the game play. The idea of the ranking encouraged competition, even though there was no score for the subject. This was noticeable in the game application meetings and reported by the Calculus professor, since the students were concerned with the scoring rules and studying to get the questions right.

According to the researchers' perception during the meetings, the connection between the game story and Calculus content favored student's concentration, most students remained involved and motivated to answer the questions since students often consulted their class notes and performed calculations manually. The Figure 7 illustrates the students' participation in the computer lab during the Calculus class:

Figure 7. Calculus Class

Students were participative and provided rich feedback, both at the time of application and in the open question of the weekly questionnaire. Table 6 presents some comments filled in by students in response to the question (Please leave a comment about our activity today. Your participation is very important to us).

Table 6. Student's feedback about week 1.

Feedbacks
"The game contributes a lot to the immersion in the idea that is proposed. It fully meets what is seen in class and I consider it an excellent study/learning tool."
"I found the game to be a very cool learning object, which teaches differently way and reminds us of the lesson content, as well as having a backstory. A lot of things can be improved, but for an early version it's pretty cool, and I really enjoyed playing it."
"Decrease the noise level of the participants as it makes concentration difficult."

From the feedback from Week 1, improvements were worked out for phase 2. The need for silence during the activity was reinforced because the noise made the study difficult for some students. The "WASD" movement system (also known as Was-duh, WSAD or ASDW) was implemented, which works with a set of four keys on the left side of a computer keyboard (Gkikas et al., 2007). The W/S keys make the character move back and forth, and the A/D keys move left and right. Thus, the mouse was left for player actions such as opening chests, talking with the characters, and conducting battles. This change has improved movement issues and combat mechanics, as seen in some Week 2 feedback comments presented in the Table 7:

Table 7. Student's feedback about week 2.

Feedback
"The way of moving the keyboard greatly improved the gameplay. Moving could be faster or slow down scenarios. Indicating the way forward could be made easier. If the indication of the functions (which appears in the upper right field) follows the game design, it would promote a greater immersion."
"I had more fun than the week before, and I feel I did better because I managed to concentrate."
"There could be an option to run, maybe a "double w", because when traveling long distances, walking normally takes a long time. The game design could be a little clearer; it is a bit tricky sometimes to see. The noise in the room is disconcerting, but there is not much to be done as silence is requested, and they do not."

It was noticed that the way of movement increased the fun and increased the motivation for students to play. In the week 3 meeting, the request for silence was reinforced with more emphasis. The option for players running using the keyboard shift and space keys has been implemented. Also, the text size of the user interface has been reduced as much as possible, even though it is an RPG. The lighting of the scenarios was increased based on the feedback received.

These changes resulted in some comments in the week 3 open question, as can be seen in Table 8:

Some students reported their difficulty in solving phase 3 questions. This may have come from the greater complexity of the contents covered this week, as reported by the regent teacher. Last week, the

Table 8. Student's feedback about week 3.

Feedback
"I believe that the new running option has greatly improved the speed of the game, other than that today the instructions were clearer, and consequently it was easier to understand, but the derivation issues towards the end were quite complicated."
"Most of my answers are based on my difficulty with calculus, as this is the first time, I have seen all this content. I like the game. I think for the first time, it is being done well. One of the few things that bothers me is not moving the camera with the mouse, but that is because I am used to it. For the rest, the game is getting better. I think that one day it will be great for the learning of students and other people interested in the subject, or even in the style of the game itself."
"I find it interesting to have questions of varying difficulty. It discourages me a little to play each stage because there are many difficult questions one after the other."

students pointed out that the game in general evolves a lot, addressing many issues raised by them in the previous three weeks. This can be seen in the open question of week 4 that only presented the comments in the Table 9:

Table 9. Student's feedback about week 4.

Feedback
"The game is an effective way as much or even more than making exercise lists, being even more stimulating and rewarding."
"The questions were very calm, and the game design was very good."

The quantity answers to the first closed questions of the questionnaire, prepared according to Savi (2011), addressed aspects of usability, attention, relevance, trust, satisfaction and are summarized in Figure 8.

In general, the game proved to be adequate in terms of its usability, since the percentage of students who checked options 4 and 5 for this item varied between 65% and 75% over the weeks. The number of students who marked option 2 was always less than 12% and option 1 was selected as a response only in week two with 5%. This indicates ease in learning and handling the game in general. In addition, it can be considered that the game has an attractive design that helps to keep the students' attention during the activity in the class, since most marked options 4 and 5 for this item. The results also suggest that the improvements made to the game received through the feedback were evident to some students, especially during weeks 3 and 4, as there were no responses 1 and 2 marked in this time in relation to the design.

Students' percentage who marked options 4 and 5 for the relevance criterion varied between 70% and 80% throughout the weeks. In addition, the students answered options 1 and 2 only in weeks two and three, and in none of the two weeks the percentage for these options exceeded 5%. Most of the students considered the game relevant as an auxiliary tool in their studies.

As for the confidence criterion, the results indicate that, although most students consider the game to be an adequate method, not the majority feel confident about their learning. This is evident, especially in Week 4, where the response percentage at all levels of the scale is similar. In this case, there is the possibility of distrust due to the new way of learning to use gamification in the Calculus context. Other factors may have generated a certain distrust that the students were learning: the activity took place only once a week; the control environment imposed by restricted time to answer the questions; and the fact that the game is a complementary method, which they will not learn without lessons and study.

Figure 8. Results about Usability, Relevance, Trust, and Satisfaction.

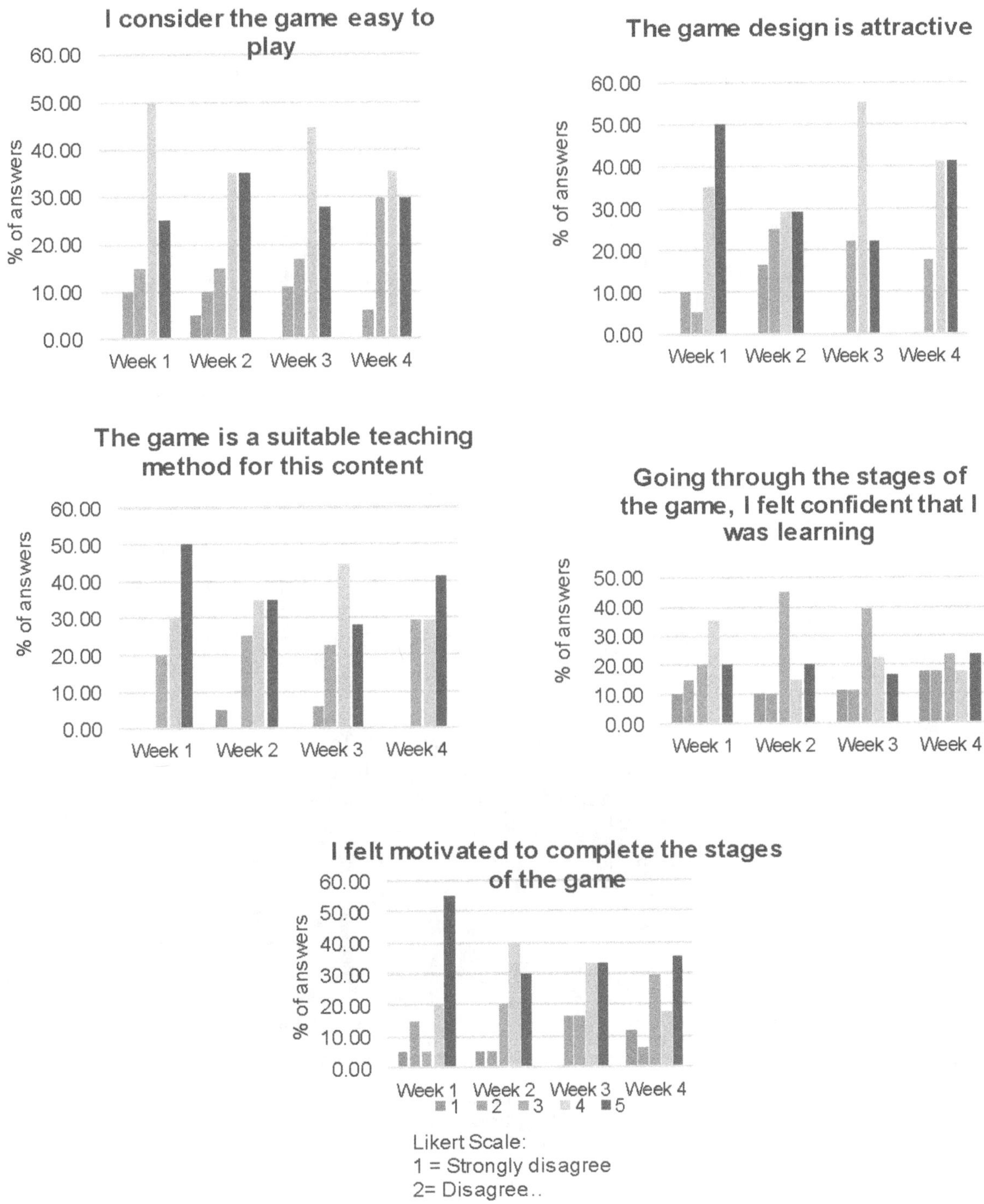

Figure 9. Results about Immersion, Challenge, Fun and Learning

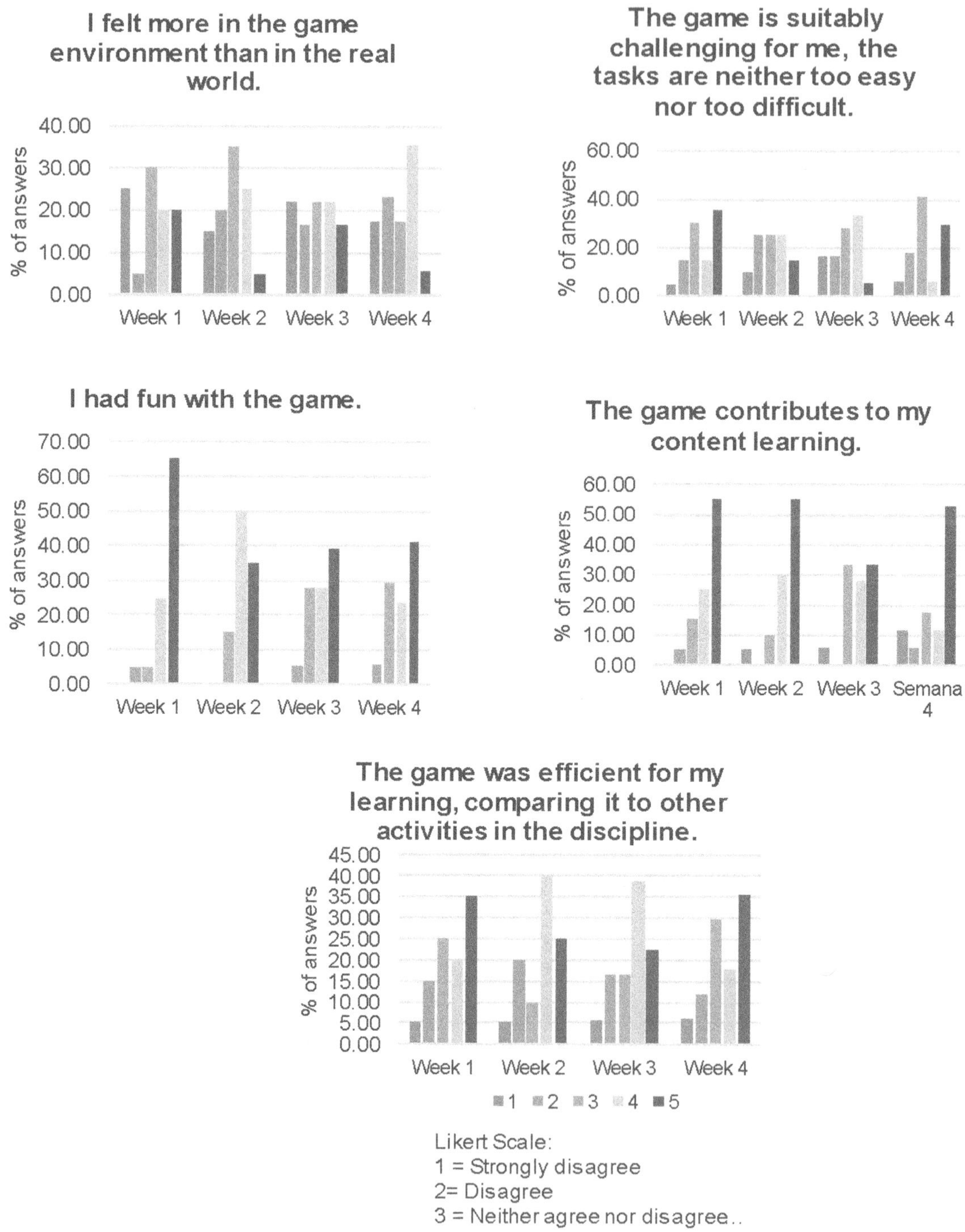

The motivation to complete the steps over the weeks was high, since there was a majority of 4 and 5 responses in the four weeks. However, there was a slight decline in the first three weeks and a little more pronounced in the last (and an increase in the number of responses 3). This may have occurred due to the question's type from week 4. They mostly dealt with problems that required deeper interpretation and, at times, becoming more tiring to solve. Furthermore, there was an evaluation activity a week before the application of the game, which may have contributed to some students' demotivation.

The questions answer that addressed aspects of immersion, challenge, fun, and learning, according to Savi (2011):

The immersion criterion analyzed whether the student felt disconnected from the real world for playing. Over the weeks, the results remained balanced between the five options. This result can be considered satisfactory, because students are used to the features present in multi-user commercial games. Furthermore, the single-user game may have caused a decrease in immersion due to the lack of communication between players within the game.

The question about the challenge criterion showed a steady decline of answers 4 and 5: first week 50%; second week 40%; third week 39%; and fourth week 35%. The mission that the player performed mixed common activities in games with application of the content and, over the four weeks, the task's level of difficulty gradually increased. Thus, it was noticed that some more difficult tasks involving the need to understand the game's history to move forward, as well as the difficulty of the required calculations, might have affected this result over the four weeks. As in the previous question, there was a decline for the fun criterion for answers 4 and 5, which may have been generated for the same reason: first week 90%; second week 85%; third week 67%; and fourth week 65%. However, the percentage remained high for the four weeks. Beyond that, there was no answer 1 in all the fun questionnaires answered. It can be concluded that most students had fun while playing.

The statement that the game contributes to the content's learning obtained the percentage for answers 4 and 5 varying between 85% and 61% in the four weeks. Alternatives 1 and 2 obtained: first week 5%; second week 5%; third week 6%; and fourth week 18%. Most students believed that, from the use of the game as a tool in classes, there was a gain in learning. Finally, the last statement of the game being efficient in learning, compared to other subject activities, obtained a similar percentage over the weeks for alternatives 4 and 5: first week 55%; second week 65%; third week 61%; and fourth week 53%. That said, the game obtained good acceptance from the perspective of learning in the students' view, compared to other activities applied in the subject.

After completing the game's last phase and answering the weekly questionnaire, students answered four more questions regarding their perception of the game's use throughout all phases. The results are shown in the following Figure 10:

For 47% of students, the game helped in solving the exercises proposed in regular classes and 35% of students only studied calculus during the four weeks because of the game. The game increased the study load for 47% of students who answered 4 (partially agree) and 5 (strongly agree), 29% chose answer 3 (neither agree nor disagree) and 24% answered 1 (strongly disagree) and 2 (partially disagree) for the denial of increase in the study. When asked if they would play since the beginning of the semester, 82% of students answered "yes" and only 6% discarded this possibility. These data demonstrate the potential that gamification and the developed digital game generated in the research students. Here, it was seen as a hypothesis that, if applied from the beginning of the semester and with the possibility of access at home (via computer or smartphone), the game could be used as a study tool on a larger scale and improve student performance in Calculus.

Figure 10. Results about the application of the game.

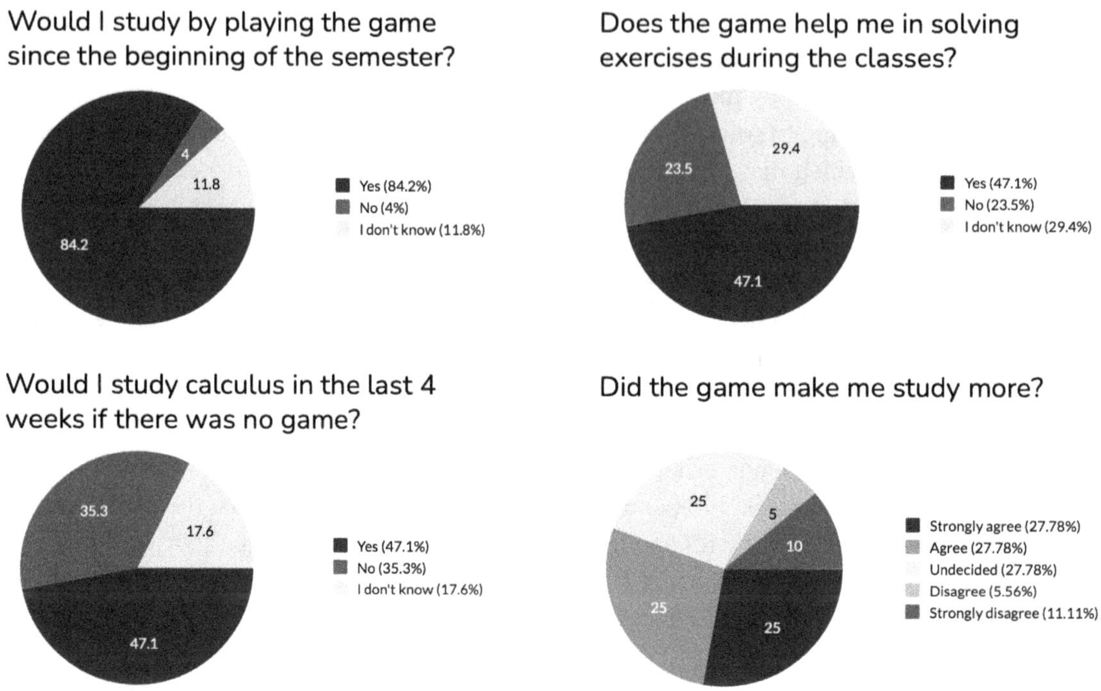

CONCLUSION

The development of innovative solutions that aim to alleviate the problem of high demotivation and the difficulties faced by students in higher education is essential. Mainly in subjects that have high dropout and failure rates. In this sense, the game The Fellowship of the Calculus, presented in this work, evaluated the potential of motivating students through gamification using an educational digital game in RPG format. This research developed a product that helped the student to keep studying regularly through playful activities, and consequently motivating them inside and outside the classroom.

The game development process using standards and concepts from education and the game industry, shown to be crucial to this research. The story as an essential element for gamification is reinforced with the use of an RPG. Furthermore, the Meaningful Learning Theory supported understanding of the subsumers, allowing to define the ideal trajectory for this educational digital game. Following this idea, the mathematical contents were aligned with the story involved in the player's trajectory. This demonstrated that the criterion to achieve real learning based on digital games was carried out, mixing involvement between playful and learning.

After the game design, tests were carried out through four meetings with the Calculus students of the Biomedical Informatics undergraduate course at UFCSPA. In all of them, it was observed that the students played studying, that is, they tried to solve the problems manually, consulted their materials and the Internet to search for information. This is all done in a fun way, despite the content's complexity.

Students, mostly digital natives, found the game's features easy to understand. The design was somewhat impactful, as the game presented a graphical user interface comparable to some commercial games. These students would probably not be motivated if the quality were much lower than what they are used to in their daily lives.

The experiment with the game was carried out in a computer laboratory at UFCPA at a pre-established time, because the current version requires a computer configuration with specific high-performance features. In addition, single-user play has negatively affected immersion and this requirement can be improved. Thus, in order to make it a study tool accessible to everyone, an application for smartphones is being developed to be played online. There is the idea as a future work to apply the game developed in this research to increase the amount of data collected. Thus, it will be possible to make a comparison with data from previous years to verify possible changes in the dropout and failure rate.

Applying gamification using digital games meets the students' profile, according to the data presented in this research. The qualitative feedback from students and professors allows us to conclude that the product of this research has the potential to add value to the teaching and learning process.

REFERENCES

Aleem, S., Capretz, L. F., & Ahmed, F. (2016). Game development software engineering process life cycle: A systematic review. *Journal of Software Engineering Research and Development*, *4*(1), 1–30. doi:10.118640411-016-0032-7

Alves, F. (2015). *Gamification: how to create engaging learning experiences* [Gamification: como criar experiências de aprendizagem engajadoras] (2nd ed.). DVS Editora.

Ausubel, D. P., Novak, J. D., & Hanesian, H. (1968). *Educational psychology: A cognitive view*. Holt McDougal.

Ausubel, D. P., Novak, J. D., & Hanesian, H. (1980). *Educational psychology* [Psicologia educacional]. Interamericana.

B., B. M. (1999). *The construction/negotiation of meanings in the initial university course of Differential and Integral Calculus* [Unpublished Doctoral Thesis]. University of São Paulo, São Paulo, Brazil.

Barbosa, M. A. (2004). *Failure in teaching and learning in the discipline of differential and integral calculus* [O insucesso no ensino e aprendizagem na disciplina de cálculo diferencial e integral] [Doctoral dissertation]. Pontifícia Universidade Católica do Paraná.

Bezerra, N. J. (2016). *The organization of the Teaching of Differential and Integral Calculus from the perspective of the Theory of Step Formation of Galperin's Mental Actions* [Doctoral thesis]. Federal University of Mato Grosso.

Bressoud, D., Carlson, M., Pearson, J. M., & Rasmussen, C. (2012). Preliminary results of the study on characteristics of successful programs in college calculus. *12th International Congress on Mathematics Education*, 8-15.

Cezar, V., Garcia, P., Botelho, V., & Miletto, E. (2019). Towards an RPG game to teach calculus. In *2019 IEEE 19th International Conference on Advanced Learning Technologies (ICALT)* (pp. 116-118). 10.1109/ICALT.2019.00037

Cover, J. G. (2014). *The creation of narrative in tabletop role-playing games*. McFarland.

Deterding, S., Dixon, D., Khaled, R., & Nacke, L. (2011). From game design elements to gamefulness: defining" gamification. *Proceedings of the 15th international academic MindTrek conference: Envisioning future media environments*, 9-15. 10.1145/2181037.2181040

Dormans, J. (2006). On the Role of the Die: A brief ludologic study of pen-and-paper roleplaying games and their rules. *Game Studies, 6*(1). http://gamestudies.org/0601/articles/dormans

Fardo, M. L. (2013). Gamification applied in learning environments [A gamificação aplicada em ambientes de aprendizagem]. *Renote, 11*(1). Advance online publication. doi:10.22456/1679-1916.41629

Frias, E. R. (2009). *Play of representations (RPG) and aspects of autonomous morality* [Jogo das representações (RPG) e aspectos da moral autônoma] [Master dissertation]. University of São Paulo.

Gkikas, K., Nathanael, D., & Marmaras, N. (2007). The evolution of FPS games controllers: How use progressively shaped their present design. *Panhellenic Conference on Informatics (PCI)*, 37–46. http://pci2007.upatras.gr/proceedings/PCI2007_volA/A_037-046_Gkikas.pdf

Kapp, K. M. (2012). *The gamification of learning and instruction: game-based methods and strategies for training and education*. John Wiley & Sons.

Kessler, M. C., de Paula, C. G., & Lemos, R. S. M. (2011). PROMA: In search of answers to successive repetitions in differential calculus [PROMA: Em busca de respostas para as repetências sucessivas no Cálculo Diferencial]. *Proceeding of XXXIX COBENGE - Congresso Brasileiro de Ensino de Engenharia, 29*, 1–10.

Kim, S., Song, K., Lockee, B., & Burton, J. (2018). Gamification cases in education. In Gamification in Learning and Education: Enjoy Learning Like Gaming. (pp. 117–123). Springer International Publishing. doi:10.1007/978-3-319-47283-6_10

Machajewski, S. T. (2017). *Application of Gamification in a College STEM Introductory Course: A Case Study* [Doctoral Thesis, Northcentral University]. ProQuest Dissertations Publishing.

Manzano-León, A., Camacho-Lazarraga, P., Guerrero, M. A., Guerrero-Puerta, L., Aguilar-Parra, J. M., Trigueros, R., & Alias, A. (2021). Between Level Up and Game Over: A Systematic Literature Review of Gamification in Education. *Sustainability, 13*(4), 2247. doi:10.3390u13042247

Mattar, J. (2010). *Games in education: how digital natives learn* [Games em educação: como os nativos digitais aprendem]. Pearson Prentice Hall.

Mendes, K. B., & Giostri, E. (2008). Teaching calculus I and the reality of engineering and technology students [Ensino de cálculo I e a realidade dos alunos de engenharia e tecnologia]. *XXXVI Congresso Brasileiro De Ensino De Engenharia*, 36.

Moreira, M. A., & Mansini, E. A. (2011). *Meaningful Learning: David Ausubel's Theory* [Aprendizagem Significativa: A Teoria de David Ausubel]. Centauro.

Patrício, R., Moreira, A. C., & Zurlo, F. (2018). Gamification approaches to the early stage of innovation. *Creativity and Innovation Management, 27*(4), 499–511. doi:10.1111/caim.12284

Paz, D. P., Franco, M. H., & Bertagnolli, S. d. (2017). Educational digital game for the development of intercultural competence of Spanish-speaking learners [Jogo digital educacional para o desenvolvimento da competência intercultural de aprendizes de língua espanhola]. *Proceedings of SBGames 2017*.

Pedersen, R. E. (2003). *Game design foundations*. Wordware Publishing, Inc.

Pessini, A., Kemczinski, A., & Hounsell, M. d. (2015). An Authoring Tool for the development of Serious RPG Games [Uma Ferramenta de Autoria para o desenvolvimento de Jogos Sérios do Gênero RPG]. *Computer on the Beach 2015*, 71-80.

Prensky, M. (2012). *Digital Game-Based Learning* [Aprendizagem Baseada em Jogos Digitais]. Senac São Paulo.

Prensky, M. R. (2010). *Teaching digital natives: Partnering for real learning*. Corwin Press.

Pressman, R., & Maxim, B. (2016). *Software Engineering* [Engenharia de Software] (8th ed.). McGraw Hill Brasil.

Rafael, R. C. (2017). *Differential and Integral Calculus: a study on strategies to reduce the percentage of non-approval* [Cálculo Diferencial e Integral: um estudo sobre estratégias para redução do percentual de não aprovação] [[Master Dissertation]. Federal University of Juiz de Fora.

Rincon-Flores, E. G., López-Camacho, E., & López, O. O. (2020). Engaging a Calculus Course with Telepresence through Gamification. *2020 IEEE Global Engineering Education Conference (EDUCON)*, 1055-1059. 10.1109/EDUCON45650.2020.9125163

Rogers, Y., Sharp, H., & Preece, J. (2013). *Interaction design: beyond human-computer interaction* [Design de interação: além da interação humano-computador] (3rd ed.). Bookman Editora.

Sato, A. K. (2010). Game design and prototyping: Concepts and applications throughout the design process [Game design e prototipagem: conceitos e aplicações ao longo do processo projetual]. *Proceedings of SBGames, 2010*, 74–84.

Savi, R. (2011). *Evaluation of games aimed at the dissemination of knowledge* [Avaliação de jogos voltados para a disseminação do conhecimento] [Doctoral dissertation]. Federal University of Santa Catarina, Brazil.

Schell, J. (2008). *The Art of Game Design: A book of lenses*. CRC Press. doi:10.1201/9780080919171

Schuytema, P. (2008). *Game Design. A Practical Approach*. Charles River Media.

Silva, T., Melo, J., & Tedesco, P. (2016). A model to promote student engagement in programming learning using gamification [Um Modelo para Promover o Engajamento Estudantil no Aprendizado de Programação Utilizando Gamification]. *Brazilian Journal of Computers in Education*, *26*(3), 120–138. doi:10.5753/rbie.2018.26.03.120

Surendeleg, G., Murwa, V., Yun, H. K., & Kim, Y. S. (2014). The Role of Gamification in Education – A Literature Review. *Contemporary Engineering Sciences*, *7*(29), 1609–1616. doi:10.12988/ces.2014.411217

Tarouco, L. M., Roland, L. C., Fabre, M. C., & Konrath, M. L. (2004). Educational games [Jogos educacionais]. *RENOTE: Revista Novas Tecnologias Na Educação,* 1-7.

Tolkien, J. R. (2012). *The Lord of the Rings: one volume*. Houghton Mifflin Harcourt.

Von Wangenheim, C. G., Rausis, B., Soares, G. M., Savi, R., & Borgatto, A. F. (2015). Project detective – A game for teaching earned value management. *International Journal of Teaching and Case Studies*, *5*(3-4), 216–234.

Von Wangenheim, C. G., Savi, R., & Borgatto, A. F. (2013). SCRUMIA— An educational game for teaching SCRUM in computing courses. *Journal of Systems and Software*, *86*(10), 2675–2687. doi:10.1016/j.jss.2013.05.030

Wijman, T. (2021). *Global Games Market to Generate $175.8 Billion in 2021; Despite a Slight Decline, the Market Is on Track to Surpass $200 Billion in 2023*. Newzoo. https://newzoo.com/insights/articles/global-games-market-to-generate-175-8-billion-in-2021-despite-a-slight-decline-the-market-is-on-track-to-surpass-200-billion-in-2023/

Wu, W. H., Yan, W.-C., Kao, H.-Y., Wang, W.-Y., & Wu, Y.-C. J. (2016). Integration of RPG use and ELC foundation to examine students' learning for practice. *Computers in Human Behavior*, *55*, 1179–1184. doi:10.1016/j.chb.2014.10.023

Zichermann, G., & Cunningham, C. (2011). *Gamification by design: Implementing game mechanics in web and mobile apps*. O'Reilly.

ENDNOTES

1 Unity: https://unity.com/

2 Super Mario Run: https://supermariorun.com/

3 Sonic Forces: https://en.wikipedia.org/wiki/Sonic_Forces

4 Pokémon GO: https://pokemongolive.com/

5 Call of Duty: https://www.callofduty.com

6 Angry Birds: https://www.angrybirds.com/

Chapter 19
The Role of Gameful Elements, Bodily Interactions, and Musical Features in Fostering Engagement and Learning in Musical Serious Games

Marcella Mandanici
https://orcid.org/0000-0003-1863-4178
Brescia Music Conservatory, Italy

ABSTRACT

This contribution explores the connections between gameful elements, bodily interactions, and musical features in the context of three case studies of music learning applications, demonstrating the role of these components in accomplishing the application's task. The critical essential element common to the three case studies is engagement due to gameful elements and other design characteristics such as the choice of music materials and the link between their structural elements and full body/gestural interaction. Assessment and experimental results demonstrate that these characteristics deeply influence users' involvement, memory, and learning.

INTRODUCTION

The great diffusion of electronic devices and ICT technologies have made gamification pervasive in everyday digital life. Gameful elements, video games and game-inspired design seem to be intimately connected to a great deal of computer activities such as work (Oravec, 2015), entertainment (Sharma & Somani, 2019), advertising (Terlutter & Capella, 2013), behavior modeling (Volkswagen, 2009), business management (Lim & Rubasundram, 2018) and education (Nordby et al., 2016). There are probably many reasons to explain this phenomenon, the most obvious of which are the involvement, the fun, the role of challenges and the power of attraction demonstrated by gamification. Previously employed to

DOI: 10.4018/978-1-6684-4287-6.ch019

improve market strategies or for military training, gamification has spread to many sectors of activity, including education. Since the dawn of computer-assisted education, programmers have always sought new ways to grab students' attention leveraging the power of multimedia content through the use of plasma displays, bitmapped graphics and sound (Hofstetter, 1981). Nowadays, gamification seems to respond to the same needs, but reinterpreting the multimedia paradigm in the light of the new possibilities offered by human-computer interaction. However, while the use of gamification brings certain advantages when used inside its original domains, its employment in educational contexts raises some problems, especially in relation to educational strategies and game mechanics. Arnab et al. (2015) define the serious game mechanic as the element that actually realizes effectiveness in the instructional design as it links the gameplay to pedagogical practices. Particularly, just the lack of reflection about the relationships between the gameful elements and the learning process has been addressed by the Game Object Model (GOM) proposed by Amory et al. (1999). In this model the idea of abstract and concrete interfaces is introduced. Abstract interfaces relate to the pedagogical approach, while concrete interfaces represent the actual design elements (gameplay and software). Leveraging the Object-oriented programming paradigm[1], the GOM connects these interfaces to objects organized according to encapsulation, inheritance and polymorphism, concepts which are used to guarantee the interrelationships between the pedagogical and the gamification domain.

In this book chapter the same problem is tackled from the point of view of music serious games based on gameful elements and bodily interaction. The contribution does not focus on the theory but rather on the analysis of the design elements and the critical evaluation of three case studies. The first one is "Harmonic Walk", a large-space interactive space where users' movements are tracked by a camera hanging from the ceiling. Six interactive landmarks trigger six connected musical chords to be played according to the position of the user. This allows to link the movements of the user to the timed harmonic changes implied in a tonal melody, thus creating a dance movement which follows the changes of the musical chords in accompaniment to the melody[2].

A desktop version of "Harmonic Walk" is "Harmonic Touch", a web platform for the study and practice of tonal harmony. The platform leverages interactive maps, graphical representations, score calculation, audio elements, and positive/negative reinforcement to engage students in three experiences related to fundamental aspects of the musical language such as implicit harmony, harmonic rhythm and melody harmonization. Using the platform through their customized accounts allowed teachers to control the activities of their students and prepare targeted assignments for them during the Covid-19 pandemic. Thus teachers could experiment the effects of engagement in the music learning process of elementary school children during the period of school closure[3].

The third case study is "Good or Bad", a two-players game based on full-body interaction. The two players have to rebuild track by track a musical piece by accepting or rejecting music excerpts belonging to two different songs. This happens in a large-scale interactive environment where the landmarks of the gameplay appear as floor projections[4].

To properly organize the analysis of the three case studies, this contribution introduces in the "Background" section an overview of the theories upon which the three case study applications are based. Gamification is the basic element which is directly related to engagement and learning. Acquiring a knowledge of the psychological aspects of embodied cognition is a necessary step for understanding the importance of gestural and bodily interaction in the music learning applications. The definition of gestures necessary to trigger structured music events is essential in the design of such applications, while the theory of conceptual metaphors finds its realization in the interactive maps designed for the three music learning applications. All these features are thoroughly described in "The three case studies" section, where a framework depicting the interrelations among the basic elements employed in the applications' design is presented. The "Results" section deals with the outcomes obtained through the assessment and experimental sessions performed with the three applications presented above, while the "Future research directions" and "Conclusion" sections outline current limitations and perspectives for future work. "

BACKGROUND

The use of games in music education has a long tradition which is solidly rooted in teaching practices. The renowned method Music for children: Orff-Schulwerk American edition (1991) offers tens of suggestions of music games starting from pre-school level. Many of these include movements which aim at teaching basic musical abilities through the involvement of the whole body. A simple example are the numerous ball games present above all in the first volume of the method, where children learn to perform regular rhythmic beats by playing with ball throwing and bouncing. The movement control and the regularities required for these games are the best prerequisites for learning fluency and precision in rhythmic execution. Another meaningful example is represented by the practices related to Dalcroze's eurhythmics (Juntunen & Hyvönen, 2004), where the elements of the musical form are represented through simple choreographic combinations[5]. In these dance-like executions children literally play-act the musical piece, performing in a perceptible way its formal development. These two examples well represent the concept of embodied cognition, which claims that knowledge does not depend only on the acquisition of abstract mental concepts, but that it is mediated by physical experiences related to the body and its movements (Wilson et al., 2019). Embodied cognition - as well as enactive learning which occurs when sensory-motor and affective processes actually engage the mind in the training experience (Gallagher & Lindgren, 2015) - are well known to musicians, who spend a lot of their time practicing an instrument and moulding the best sound quality out of it.

On the other hand, while looking at the same concepts from the digital domain it is worth observing that gestural/full-body interaction and gamification are directly connected in the field of music video games, and particularly of rhythm games. Greatest hits such as Guitar Hero (Arsenault, 2008) and Dance Dance Revolution (Hoysniemi, 2006) well testify the role that physical actions play. In Dance Dance Revolution the user has to occupy a position on a special platform, while in Guitar Hero s/he is urged to press keys on a guitar-shaped controller through a computer screen. The system plays the music and shows colored buttons according to some musical elements (notes, chords, etc.), while the player follows the video by pressing the same buttons depicted on the controller. If on the one hand these systems highlight some interesting aspects of musical performance such as experience sharing, sociability and challenge, on the other hand it should be noted that in this type of interaction the user is called to blindly respond to the input conveyed by the video, without any cognitive or perceptual aspect being called into question. Another field where gamification is widely employed is serious games for rehabilitation (González-González et al., 2019; Rego et al., 2019), and for fitness or physical activity (Biddiss & Irwin, 2010) where it is used to try to cope with the boredom produced by the continuous repetitions of the exercises.

However, gestural interaction and gameful elements employed for music education have a completely different nature. First of all the applications in this domain are not always games but - following the taxonomy proposed by Deterding et al. (2011) - they can simply incorporate some gameful element.

For instance the "Music Paint Machine" (Nijs & Leman, 2014) exploits motion tracking techniques and a pressure mat to draw a colored track derived from the audio recording of a musical performance. The loop established by this audio-visual interaction fosters engagement and enactive learning necessary for the control of the drawing through the sound produced by the instrument. Another form of control happens in the "You're The Conductor" system (Lee et al., 2004), which allows to guide the performance of a virtual orchestra by following the speed and the amplitude of the movements of an infrared light baton that acts as a conductor's wand. Also if designed to respond to use and misuse from very young children, the system seems to be responsive enough to induce movement control, a skill that should not always be taken for granted in children. The last example of a music education application employing full-body interaction is "Resonant Memory" (Camurri et al., 2010). While in the previous examples the movements used in the interaction belong to the traditional performance habits, in the "Resonant Memory" a new concept is introduced, that is the use of space and of an interactive map to guide the interaction. The system employs a camera hanging from the ceiling and oriented perpendicularly to the floor. The images captured by the camera are processed by motion tracking algorithms which produce the Cartesian coordinates of a user moving inside the range of the camera. By partitioning this area, eight peripheral interactive landmarks are created, corresponding each to different sounds. As soon as the child has explored all the landmarks and has carefully listened to the sounds, a central landmark begins to play its spoken story. The tale contains a reference to the sounds and the child has to match the right sound when its reference text occurs. This mechanism activates a spatial memory because the child has to build a mental map of the positions of the sounds for matching them to the story. The gameful element in this case is directly connected to full-body interaction and to the map that the child has to build, remember, and use[6].

THE THREE CASE STUDIES

Starting from the experience of "Resonant Memory" a series of three educational applications for teaching music concepts were designed. Keeping well in mind the relationships among gameful elements, educational purposes and gestural/full-body interaction, a general framework of seven basic elements emerges, as it is represented in the conceptual map depicted in Figure 1.

The elements are interconnected through arrows and are subdivided into three levels. In the first level there are four elements (light gray) which represent the base of the application's design (''Material'', ''Musical feature'', ''Gameful elements'' and ''Gestural/full-body interaction''). At the second level there are two intermediate elements (middle gray). They are ''Engagement'' (the result of the action of the 1st level elements) and ''Levels/user category'', which descends directly from the choice of the music material. At the third level - as a result of the combined effects of the 2nd level elements - there is the final goal of the application, that is ''Learning'' (dark gray).

The music material is the first element in the schema because it is the source of the musical feature, which is the core of the application. To foster the learning process, the choice of the music material must accommodate the characteristics of the user category. It also plays a fundamental role in stimulating engagement because it has a great potential in strengthening a feeling of identity in the users (Campayo–Munoz & Cabedo–Mas, 2017). The musical feature derives from the chosen music material and from its characteristics depend the gameful elements and gestural/full-body interaction. Gameful elements (namely graphics, interactive maps, score calculation, positive/negative reinforcement, social comparison

Figure 1. Conceptual map of the connections among the seven basic elements of the music learning applications analyzed as case studies

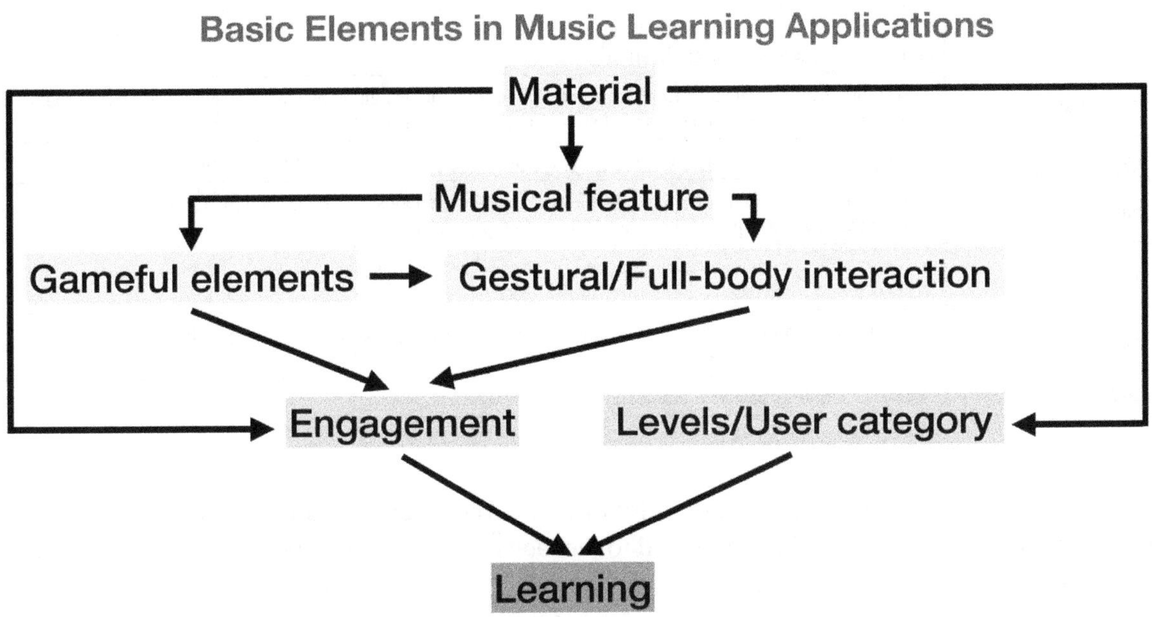

and pressure) are directly connected to the second level element of engagement. But interactive maps are also linked to gestural/full-body interaction, because the user moves according to the spatial organization expressed in the map. The role of bodily interaction and movement in users' engagement while playing games has been investigated by Bianchi-Berthouze et al. (2007). In this study the embodied gaming experience is considered beyond the mere cognitive aspect and includes also affective processes which have been proven to help better results in the game's score and in participants' well being. On the other hand interactive maps are also the graphical representation of the musical feature upon which the application is based. Here another important concept comes into play, that is the theory of conceptual metaphors (Lakoff & Johnson, 2008), which states that a notion in a specific domain can be expressed and understood also through another domain perceptually related to the first. Particularly, image schemas applied to musical concepts have been investigated by Saslaw (1996) who - as an example - emphasizes the kinesthetic commonalities between the dominant-tonic progression and the source-path-goal schema, while also Johnson & Larson (2003) explain the metaphors of music movement as related to the motion of the bodies in space. As the interactive maps employed in the applications are built following these principles, the characteristics of the musical feature inspire also the coordinated movements necessary to interact with the application, and this is the reason for the connection between the musical feature and the interaction element.

Second level elements (engagement and user category) determine the educational effectiveness of the application. Engagement is not only dependent from the use of gameful elements but also from gestural/full-body interaction. Also if the effectiveness of the involvement of the body has not yet been proven (Birchfield & Johnson-Glenberg, 2012), full-body interaction may positively impact the learning process by fostering social participation and amusement (Maes et al., 1997; Malinverni & Burguès, 2015).

Table 1. Grid table for the evaluation of the three case studies

1. Aim	What is required of the user? How s/he understands what is the goal to be achieved?
2. Material	Description of the characteristics of the music materials employed. What is the role of the music material in enticing the user to use the application?
3. Musical feature	Description of the musical feature at the heart of application design. How can this be communicated to the user? Are there educational actions to be undertaken for preparing the users to the game?
4. System	Description of the environment, system architecture, technologies and hardware employed.
5. Interaction	What kind of interaction is required of the user? Is it spontaneous or does it need instructions? What is the relationship between interaction and engagement?
6. Gameful elements	Are there any gameful elements employed in the application's design? What is their role in engaging the users in the task?
7. Usability	Is this application fit for use in school context? How can this application be employed for educational practices?
8. Assessment	What methodology has been employed for the assessment?

The definition of the various levels of difficulty of the activities proposed is still problematic, due to the complex nature of the musical material and to the lack of theoretical work thereupon. However, the Zone of Proximal Development (ZPD) theory from L. S. Vygotskij (Wertsch, 1984) explains well that learning can happen only between the borders of what the child already knows and what s/he can learn with the help of an external agent. Thus the definition of ZPD's for every category of users (pre-school, primary, upper elementary, middle school, high school, experienced, and so on) would represent a useful tool to organize the music material into subsequent levels of difficulty.

Finally, at the third level there is learning that is the desired effect of the whole process. Experiential learning is the proper outcome of the activity in these environments (Gentry, 1990), because also in more structured games what is evaluated is the result of a performance - i.e. of a game experience - and not the knowledge of the musical feature. On the other hand experiential learning can be the starting point for more formal educational activities such as frontal lessons, reflections and assessment.

In order to discuss each element of the framework, the presentation of the three case studies follows the evaluation grid depicted in Table 1.

Harmonic Walk

1. **Aim.** The aim of "Harmonic Walk" is to allow young children to hear musical chords and to accomplish the very complex task of harmonizing a melody in a playful way (Mandanici et al., 2016). A child can enter the "Harmonic Walk" environment and trigger the chords to play the accompaniment while the remainder of the class sings a song or nursery rhyme. Usually tonal harmony is not addressed at all in early music education due to the complexity of the subject and to the amount of theoretical background necessary to understand it. However, "Harmonic Walk" is designed to approach such complexity in a very easy and intuitive way. As in the current implementation no interactive floor projection is provided, the child has to be briefly introduced to the use of the application also through a guided exploration phase.

2. **Material.** The application is designed mainly for children. Thus the material employed can be music excerpts (usually the first phrase) of simple and possibly well known nursery rhymes as well as popular songs. A particular attention should be paid to the harmonic structure of the musical excerpt, which must remain always in the same tonality. Also the speed of the harmonic changes has to accommodate the speed rate of physical interaction. For didactic purposes customized rhymes can be composed by the teacher or by the children, this activity being the best introduction to the use of the application.
3. **Musical feature.** Melody harmonization is based on melody segmentation, which depends on musical meter and on the detection of harmonic changes. The notes of the melody that occur on the main beats are usually the notes which determine the so-called "implicit harmony" (Trainor & Trehub, 1994). As soon as these notes change, also the accompanying chord must be changed accordingly. The detection of the harmonic changes and the recognition of the chord that better fits the melody are the tasks of "Harmonic Walk". Also if these musical features are among the most complex in the tonal language, children are able to perceive them (Schellenberg et al., 2005) and to decide if a chord can fit a melody or not. These perceptual abilities can be trained and reinforced through various physical games both in the "Harmonic Walk" environment or outside it (Mandanici et al., 2019).
4. **System.** As depicted in Figure 2 the "Harmonic Walk" environment is based on a motion tracking system consisting of a camera hanging from the ceiling and of a green carpet which avoids unwanted light reflections and facilitates the detection of the contrast between the pixels of a moving user and the background.

The images captured by the camera are processed by motion tracking algorithms for producing the Cartesian coordinates of a user walking inside the active area. These are used to define six interactive landmarks corresponding to the harmonic space of a major tonality.

Starting from the work of the Swiss mathematician Leonard Euler (1707 - 1783), harmonic spaces have been represented through the *tonnetz* (literally "web of tones") that describes musical chords as the intersections of a grid formed by three interval axes (the 5th, major and minor 3rd). According to the Neo-Riemannian theory (Riemann, 2016) the harmonic space of a major tonality is subdivided into primary chords (major chords built on the I, IV and V degree) and parallel chords (minor chords built on the vi, ii and iii degree). The map depicted in Figure 3 has been employed to allow the user to reach a chord from any position without touching the adjacent ones. However, in the "Harmonic Walk" environment the chords are not labeled by names or by their harmonic degree, but rather by paper crosses attached to the carpet, with only an arrow marking the position of the tonic chord. Thus children can leverage only their perception and memory to remember the position and the sound of the chords and to accomplish the melody harmonization task.

5. **Interaction.** The interaction required in the "Harmonic Walk'' environment is the step necessary to play any adjacent chord in the map of Figure 3, or the short leap used to reach the more distant locations. All in all the interaction looks like a kind of dance where children follow the proceeding of the harmonic changes in time with the melody. This is very similar to the already mentioned play-acting activities typical of Dalcroze's eurhythmics, except that here it is the children who produce the sound of the chord by moving on the position that better fits the melody. After some exploratory activities this results pretty easy for some children as well as rather difficult for some

Figure 2. The setup of "Harmonic Walk" with the camera hanging from the ceiling, the carpet on the floor, two audio monitors and the control station. The white crosses show the interactive landmarks corresponding to the position of the six chords of the harmonic space, the white arrow shows the position of the tonic chord.

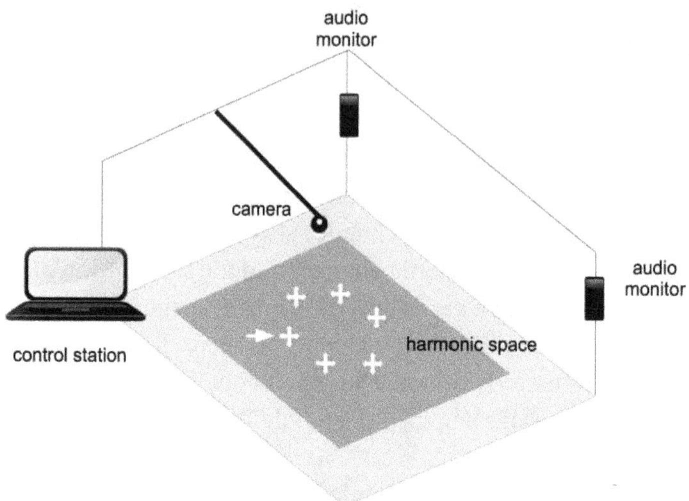

others. During the experiments it emerged that it is not at all obvious that the children know how to coordinate their movements to the melody. In some cases it has also been observed that the disposition of the crosses suggests a circular motion to the child, who thus produces a sequence of chords with scarce musical meaning. For these reasons preparatory activities are highly recommended.

6. **Gameful elements.** The gameful element of "Harmonic Walk'' is the interaction mechanism itself, because the sensation of producing a chord by simply moving a step on one side is engaging and produces fun and curiosity in the children. The challenge of finding the chord that better fits a melody is mediated by motor memory and kinesthetic interaction which are powerful means to foster engagement and learning. Fogtmann et al. (2008) define kinesthetic interaction at the crossroad of interactive technologies, kinesthetic experience and physiology. Kinesthetic experiences involve the body, which is the principal actor in the perception of pleasantness (Rozendaal & Schifferstein, 2010). Probably these are the reasons why the act of producing a sound by bodily interaction is so appealing, gratifying and exciting.
7. **Usability.** "Harmonic Walk'' can be easily used in elementary schools because the system depicted in Figure 2 is not too demanding from the technological point of view. However, it is necessary to control light conditions to avoid system malfunction. "Harmonic Walk'' can be used in many interesting music education activities. The first one can be the exploration of harmonic space. Children can take turns in exploring a chord progression of their choice, remember the related movement pattern and discuss its musical quality. This activity enhances the peculiar properties of the coupling between movement and musical quality, which is very important from the kinaesthetic point of view. Another basic practice is having a child repeatedly perform simple chord progressions (I-V-I or I-IV-I) while another child sings free melodic improvisations echoed by the remainder of the class. These activities, beyond introducing the children to the use of the interactive environment,

Figure 3. The map of the harmonic space used in the "Harmonic Walk" environment with the primary chords in the lower part of the circle and the parallel chords in the upper part.

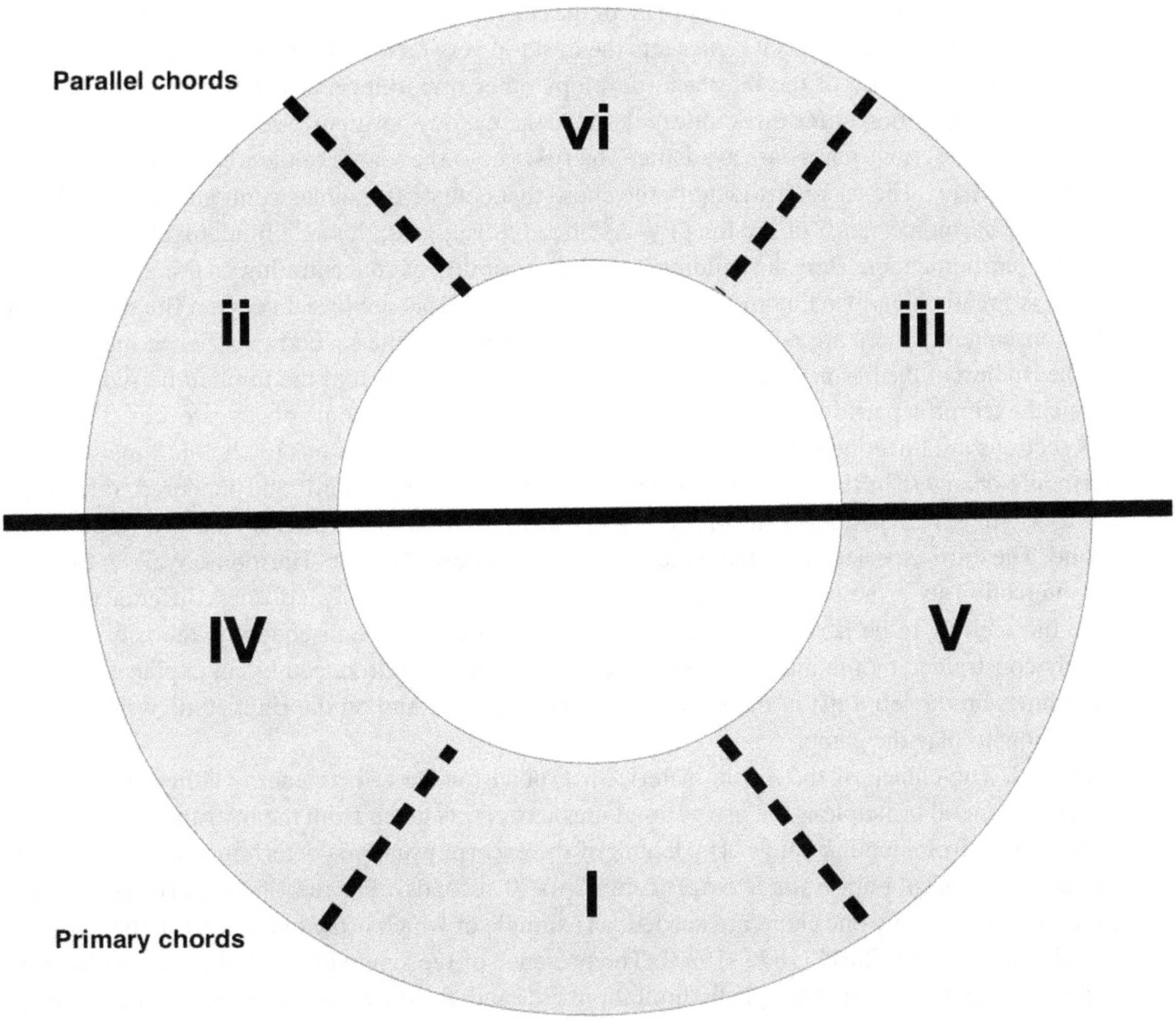

foster musical listening, social participation and suggest the necessary coordination between melody and accompaniment.

8. **Assessment.** Also if it can be used in many other ways, the main function of "Harmonic Walk'' is melody harmonization. This has been tested in December 2014 with 22 high school students aged from 16 to 20 years. After a short presentation of the task and 3 minutes of free exploration of the harmonic space, the students were asked to sing a well known song by an Italian singer together with the test conductor and try to harmonize it. As the possibilities of harmonization are more than one, there is no absolute correct solution. Thus the test conductor considered that the test was successful when the student found a possible harmonization and was able to repeat it without interruptions within the limit of 5 minutes (Mandanici et al., 2016).

Harmonic Touch

1. **Aim.** "Harmonic Touch'' is a web platform for the study and practice of tonal harmony (Mandanici et al., 2019). In some respects it represents the desktop version of "Harmonic Walk '' but, thanks to the major versatility of the interface, develops other important musical features which are a kind of decomposition of the difficulties related to the melody harmonization task. Three different experiences or serious games are available. The first one is the search of the implicit harmony of a musical excerpt[7]. The user must identify the chord that better fits the music among the six belonging to the harmonic space of the tonality. As already discussed, this is a fundamental ability for melody harmonization. Here the children have the possibility of concentrating on this specific task, which is greatly simplified by the fact that the music excerpts are based only on the tonic chord and consequently there are no harmonic changes to detect. In the second experience_the focus is on the rhythm of the harmonic changes rather than on the detection of the implicit harmony[8]. The musical excerpt is partitioned according to the points where harmonic changes occur. The various sections are linked to a series of interactive buttons that the user has to click in time with the harmonic changes. In this case the musical excerpt is correctly rebuilt and rendered; otherwise the user will experience musical delays or superpositions, that the system signals with a crashing sound. The third experience_has the same task as already described for "Harmonic Walk"[9]. Beyond the interaction style, melody harmonization in the "Harmonic Touch" platform is different because here the melody to be harmonized is played by the system and, consequently, the user is more tightly constrained by the music material. Each experience is introduced by an explanatory page that shows on the left a list of the musical excerpts available and on the right some written notes about how to play the game.
2. **Material.** The choice of the music material is crucial for the effectiveness of the three experiences. A general principle is the use of tonal music excerpts taken from the instrumental classical repertoire or from popular songs. The length of the excerpt usually is determined by the duration of the first musical phrase (on average from 20 to 30 seconds). For the first experience musical phrases based on only one chord are needed, an example of which is the famous "Bolero" from the french composer M. Ravel (1875 -1937). The presence of the sung voice is not necessary for this experience, thus there are no stylistic limitations. Instead, for the second experience the presence of a text helps a lot the perception of the exact point where the harmonic changes occur. For this reason the music excerpts eligible for this experience are popular songs chosen from the most various styles (pop, rock, traditional, children songs, etc.). Particularly, the use of songs that are well known by the children or that have even been proposed by them represent a strong stimulus in the use of the game (Campbell, 2010). However it is better to choose songs with clearly perceptible harmonies because sometimes the presence of inversions or subtle harmonic differences can raise doubts about the points where the changes occur, and consequently cause confusion in the user. The melodies to be harmonized in the third experience are subject to greater constraints, due to the limitations imposed by the model of representation of the harmonic space (discussed at point 4 of the present list). The melodies must not have modulations nor must employ harmonies extraneous to the harmonic space composed of the fundamental harmonies and their parallels. For example, the secondary sevenths - very frequent even in many nursery rhymes - are not represented in the current map of the harmonic space.

Figure 4. a) the main page of "Harmonic Touch"; b) the page of experience 1 with the list of available music excerpts and the instructions for the game; c) the map for the detection of the harmonic changes for experience 2; d) the gameplay page for experience 3

3. **Musical feature.** Implicit harmony, harmonic changes and the combination of the two (melody harmonization) are the musical features developed in the three experiences proposed in the "Harmonic Touch" platform. Many supportive educational activities can be carried out to facilitate the understanding of these important concepts, with the employment of keyboards, singing, and games. Some digital tools such as Hookpad[10], Song Maker[11], and Arpeggios[12] offer useful insights of the harmonic relationships and of melody harmonization. Particularly, physical activities as reported in the already cited Mandanici et al. (2019) can counterbalance the use of the web interface. The intertwining of physical activities (i.e. in the classroom) and computer activities (online, at school but also at home) can also be the backbone of a blended learning approach, where the learning spaces (physical and virtual) and times (class and home working) complement each other.
4. **System.** The platform supports three kinds of users: anonymous, teacher and student. Anyone can play the games as an anonymous player but if a user is logged as a teacher s/he can control the accounts of her/his students, select from the database the music to use during the teaching sessions and control the progress of her/his classes. The students can access only the materials chosen by the teacher.

The "Harmonic Touch" platform is organized according to the following framework:

a. Main page (Figure 4a): This is the presentation page, from which it is possible to enter the three experiences through the numbered buttons. The small buttons on the right of the upper bar are:

the blue one for reading some information about the application (explanation, staff, references), the red one for entering the login page.

b. Experience page (Figure 4b): This page is similar for the three experiences and displays on the left the list of available music materials and on the right some instructions for playing the game. Once the music is selected the gameplay page opens.

c. Gameplay page (Figures 4c and 4d): here it is possible to listen to the selected music more than once or/and to explore the harmonic space before starting the game. At the end the user must confirm the session by using a special button.

Also "Harmonic Touch" leverages interactive maps to guide users' interaction. For experiences 1 and 3 the representation of the harmonic space is similar to that used for "Harmonic Walk" (Figure 4b and 4d), while for experience 2 the sequence of the sections with the harmonic changes is represented by a treasure map (Figure 4c). Starting from the image of a ship, a sequence of interactive buttons drives the player to the treasure positioned at the end of the path. However, also if the graphical representation of the harmonic space is similar in experience 1 and 3, there are some differences. In experience 1 the user has to identify the implicit harmony (the tonic) of the music excerpt; thus no indication of the musical chord appears on the interface and the system assigns a random position to the tonic chord at each game. The user has to explore the harmonic space before deciding where the tonic chord is and before confirming the selected choice (Figure 4b). Conversely, in experience 3 the interactive landmarks are labeled with the harmonic degree to facilitate the memory and the recognition of the sound of the various chords.

5. **Interaction.** The interaction on the web platform is operated through mouse clicks on the various interactive landmarks. Except that in experience 1- where the search of the implicit harmony is free from any rhythmic constraint - the mouse movements must be precisely directed and timed according to the music. This kind of interaction requires some amount of control that is not to be taken for granted for all the categories of users (Smith et al., 1999). Particularly, for experience 2 some difficulties in coordinating the movement of the mouse and of the click have been observed in children with even mild disabilities. For them a facilitated interaction set up has been prepared, where the advances along the path are produced only through the spacebar input.
6. **Gameful elements.** The use of gameful elements is pervasive in the "Harmonic Touch" platform.
    a. *Graphics.* All the graphical elements employed in the platform (background image, text fonts, buttons and other illustrative elements such as pointing fingers, arrows, etc.) refer to the communicative style of video games.
    b. *Interactive maps.* The functions of interactive maps have already been discussed in their relationships with the image schemas of the musical features represented. While the interactive map of experience 3 is made playful only in the graphic aspect, the map of experience 1 adds the element of the rotation at random position of the tonic chord, which makes the search for implicit harmony resemble a treasure hunt. The same metaphor is made more explicit in experience 2 which in the present implementation is the only one that is configured as a real game (i.e. with score calculation).
    c. *Audio elements.* A jingle and a crashing sound have been added in experience 2 to signal respectively that the next harmonic change has been reached in time or in advance/delay.
    d. *Score calculation.* In the left part of the gameplay page of experience 2 (Figure 4c) appears a score calculation window, which shows the number of harmonic changes for the selected

song. For each change a maximum score of 100 points is calculated. This score can decrease according to the advance or delay of the clicks on the different interactive points. At the end of the game the total score is displayed.

e. *Positive/negative reinforcement.* Once the user has confirmed the game session, written messages and images announcing the success or the failure of the game are displayed.

f. *Social comparison and pressure.* These elements have been crucial for engaging children in the use of the game experience 2. Experimental sessions evidenced an important element missing in the "Harmonic Touch" platform, that is shared leaderboards and social communication tools such as a blog. As a matter of fact during class and home activities children took screenshots of their victories and shared them across social media external to the platform. This testifies the need of sharing the experience and the role of social pressure in tempting the children to reach a good result.

7. **Usability.** "Harmonic Touch" is a web platform that requires only a computer/tablet and internet connection to be used. For this reason it is the most suitable tool to be used in schools. From the educational point of view the platform allows many activities that can complement and help better achievements in playing the games. In experience 1 the children have to recognize the implicit harmony of a melody. Melodic improvisations performed with voice or keyboard, recorders, Orff instruments, and based only on the notes of a tonic chord can help the perception of the relationships that occur between harmony and melody, such as passing and grace notes. The same experience may be extended developing the melody until it reaches the point where a harmonic change is needed. Reflection about why the tonic chord is no longer fit for accompaniment and what chord is the best solution can introduce game experience 2. Here the melody is correctly rebuilt only if children have a clear idea of when a harmonic change occurs. Finally, discussion about what chord better fits the melody leads the children to play experience 3. A very gradual approach is recommended for this complex game. Songs employing only two chords are the best for practicing at the beginning. Other songs with more and more chords can be introduced little at a time, allowing the children to get more and more confident with the richness of the whole harmonic space. The platform allows children a lot of experimentation; Listening games where different harmonizations can be performed by the teacher, offer the possibility for discussing and evaluating the perceptual qualities of the various chords.
8. **Assessment.** An experimentation of "Harmonic Touch" has been carried out in two elementary schools in February 2021 with 46 children aged between 8 and 11 years. Teachers planned 4 weeks of activities employing experience 2 (detection of the harmonic rhythm) with the aim of trying to understand the relationship between the musical characteristics of a selected group of popular songs and children's performances. This has been done by analyzing the data collected by the web platform that stores all data about the games played, the song chosen by the user, the gestures performed, time and result of the game (Avanzini et al., 2019).

Good or Bad

1. **Aim.** "Good or Bad" is a large-space interactive musical game where two players have to rebuild a music piece track by track (Mandanici et al., 2018). The game has been used in a public space for demonstration and entertainment purposes although it is easily adaptable for education. The activity upon which "Good or Bad" is based is called "active listening", that is how users can interact

with what they listen, changing the audio output through their actions (Volpe & Camurri, 2011). The MIDI[13] tracks of two pieces belonging to the same style are appropriately merged and used to record four audio tracks corresponding to percussion, bass, and two accompanying parts. When the game begins the system randomly selects the first track to be played. Then player 1 selects another track and player 2 has to decide if it belongs to the same piece of the first track or not. If yes the two tracks play together, if not the disturbing track is discarded. The same process is repeated until all the four tracks have been selected and the whole piece recomposed. The game is implemented in a large-scale environment with interactive floor projections and is played in the presence of many bystanders. Thus some information is delivered to the players directly from the projections, some other is obtained by the observation of the other players. If something is missing a game assistant can explain to the participants all relevant information about the gameplay.

2. **Material**. Any kind of musical piece or style can be used for the game. What must be carefully evaluated are the differences between the couple of pieces to be compared during the game. If the two pieces are too different (i.e. they belong to very conflicting tonalities such as G and C#) it is very easy to decide if the tracks are concordant or not. On the contrary, if the pieces belong to the same key or/and are written in the same musical meter the game can be much more difficult. On the other hand it must be observed that the difficulty depends also from the order followed in the track's evaluation. For instance, bass vs. accompaniment if belonging to the same key may have some commonalities that make the evaluation particularly easy; or percussion vs. percussion can be easy to evaluate if written in different musical meters, and so on. Anyway, the difficulty decreases as soon as more and more tracks are selected and then superimposed, because the listening of a contrasting track is more evident against two or more according ones.
3. **Musical feature.** The musical tracks belonging to the same composition have strong horizontal and vertical relationships. Each track displays musical elements which have the same timbre, metrical organization and musical phrasing, whereas each horizontal track shares with the others the same musical tempo, concordant musical accents, and key. These strong connections make listeners perceive the superimposed tracks as a whole musical piece. The identification of these musical features are the core of the game, which – leveraging multitrack recording – offers to the users the unique possibility of listening to music from its very inner structure, i.e. superimposing instrumental parts in various ways.
4. **System.** The motion tracking technologies employed for the "Good or Bad" game are much more complex than those used for "Harmonic Walk". Also if the large-scale interactive environment is conceived in a similar way, here the system is composed by a ceiling-mounted projector, two Kinect v2 sensors[14] and four computers connected through a local network. All the system is controlled by the OpenPTrack software (Munaro et al., 2016), which allows a very robust tracking of more than one user.

As depicted in Figure 5a the game-space is subdivided into two sections, one for each player. Player 1 selects the new track to be evaluated by moving on the interactive landmarks, while player 2 decides if the new track belongs to the same piece of the previously selected ones or not by moving on the "good" or "bad" landmarks. The tracks of the two pieces are numbered 1-4 for the first piece and 5-8 for the second. At the beginning of the game the system produces a random sequence of eight numbers which decide the spatial disposition of the landmarks of player 1. Thus the number of the first track determines which of the two pieces will be rebuilt and which will play the role of the disturbing one. The tracks

Figure 5. Two different phases of the gameplay of the "Good or Bad" game

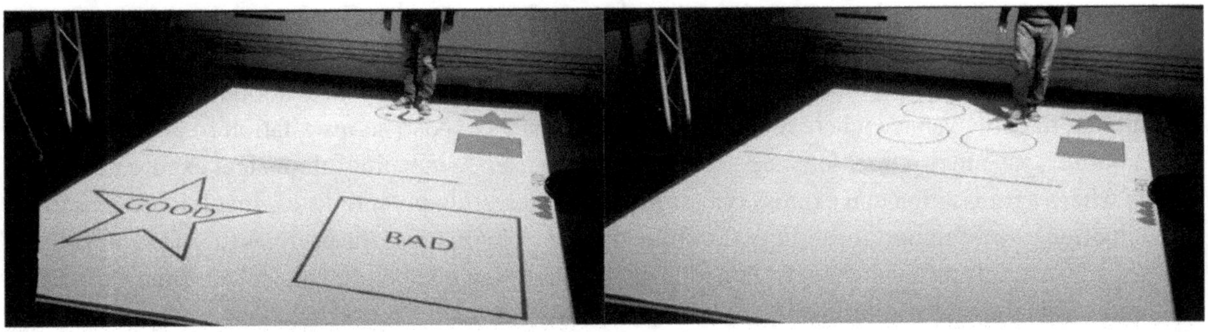

a) b)

of the piece to be rebuilt are represented by a star (good) and the track of the disturbing one by squares (bad), which are colored in green if player 2 has given the right answer or in red if the answer is wrong. Any wrong answer involves the loss of a life.

5. **Interaction.** The interaction required for the "Good or Bad" game can be expressed by the paradigm select --> evaluate--> decide, which is realized through the interaction of the two players. Player 1 selects the track, both evaluate it, and player 2 decides if the track is good or bad. Note that the order of evaluation of the tracks is subject to a double randomization. One depends on the random number sequence produced at the beginning of the game, the other on the choice of player 1, who every time has at least three different options of selection (see Figure 5b).
6. **Gameful elements.** Also in the "Good or Bad" game plenty of gameful elements are employed.
   a. *Graphics.* The graphical elements are the geometric forms used to distinguish among the two pieces and the color code to visualize right and wrong answers. Other elements are text, 3 little hearts to symbolize the lives that the players have at their disposal at the beginning of the game, and two different emoticons (one for the right and the other for the wrong answer).
   b. *Interactive maps.* The two different sections subdivide the game-space showing clearly their different functions. In this case the use of space does not express the peculiarities of the musical feature but rather the functionalities necessary for the gameplay.
   c. *Audio elements.* Two different jingles mark the right and the wrong answer. Victory is accompanied by written text and the performance of the whole song (the four audio tracks plus the sung voice) at a higher volume. Defeat, which happens when all the lives have been lost, is notificated with written text and a repeated ironic sentence.
   d. *Score calculation.* Every time player 2 gives a wrong evaluation a life is lost. When three lives have been consumed, the game finishes with a defeat.
   e. *Positive/negative reinforcement.* These are the text, audio and graphical displays which the system outputs at every evaluation and at the end of the game.
   f. *Social comparison and pressure.* The gameplay of "Good or Bad" happens in public sessions where not only the players directly involved in the interaction but also many other bystanders take part in the game. The social sharing of the gaming experience and co-located users participation in the solution of the game's challenges make the game a transparent, public

process. This may lead to various outcomes such as social facilitation, evaluation apprehension, audience enjoyment and emotional arousal enhancement (De Kort & Ijsselsteijn, 2008).

7. **Usability.** This game has a very complex set up, which makes it much more suitable for an interactive technologies laboratory or public installation rather than for use in schools. However, schools are not the only venues where music education takes place. Also an installation freely available in a public space may attract lots of people and offer to users a meaningful musical experience. Here is where gamification can express one of its more interesting potentialities, involving the users in situations where important abilities are called into play. In this case the user has to listen carefully to the music track and evaluate it from a musical point of view (detecting musical accents, harmonies and musical meter similarities)
8. **Assessment.** The "Good or Bad" game was evaluated during a public event in September 2016. During the working time of the installation (7 hours) the system has been experimented by 150 people with a total of 120 games played. The system recorded all users data such as total number of games, successful games and selected repertoire (Mandanici et al., 2018).

RESULTS

The applications described in the three case studies have been tested in many contexts and with different categories of users. Quantitative and qualitative results of the various experiments are reported here with respect to some meaningful evaluation benchmarks, the first of which is functionality. All three applications disclose to the user some structural functionality of the musical language otherwise not easily accessible especially by non-musicians. Perhaps the major contribution of these experimental prototypes is to demonstrate that also very complex musical concepts can be explored by children and non-expert users through the use of gameful elements. This approach is destined not only to revolutionize music education in the near future but also to change the very role of music in educational contexts (for instance by contributing to develop STEAM[15] programs including music).

Another important benchmark is engagement. From an experiment with an early prototype of "Harmonic Walk" a very positive behavior could be observed from the children. Some of them were fascinated by hearing the sound changing with movement and some others improvised with dance-like movements while entering the environment (Mandanici et al., 2014). A similar behavior has also been documented with adult users in the experiments with the large-scale interactive environment "Harmony Space", an application similar to "Harmonic Walk" (Holland et al., 2009). Engagement has also been highlighted in a more recent experiment with "Harmonic Touch", where teachers could observe that children after playing the games at school tend to repeat the experience at home (64% of the overall number of the games) and even with better results: 6% of games were successful at school versus 16% at home; 50% of games were lost at school versus 37% at home. In this case engagement has the important function of extending considerably the learning time which is no longer limited to class hours also for very young students. As far as the "Good or Bad" game, the system reported that during its public presentation 60% out of 150 users asked to play more than one game and among them about 30% tried all the 3 repertories available. These data suggest that gameful elements linked to gestural and full-body interaction have a great appeal for every category of users.

The last benchmark is performance, that is users ability to accomplish the task required by the three case study applications. "Harmonic Walk '' has been tested in a high school where out of 22 subjects

26% were able to accomplish the melody harmonization task leveraging only on their implicit knowledge of harmonic structure. Of course this result can be much improved with practice and with appropriate educational activities such those described in the "Harmonic Walk" section, point 7. Anyway, it proves the potential of even just the simple use of the application. In the "Harmonic Touch" environment some tests were performed with experience 2 involving elementary school children aged from 8 to 11. One of the aims of the experiment was to discover how a song excerpt could be classified based on its musical characteristics. For this purpose the performances of the six song excerpts employed have been analyzed. The results show that the best performance is obtained by a song with a high level of harmonic complexity but with regular harmonic changes, always corresponding to the main beats and at a speed very near to one second (average chord duration 1.14 s). On the contrary, the worse results were obtained by a song with very slow harmonic changes (average chord duration 4.43 s) and where their distribution did not always match the accents deriving from the musical meter (Avanzini et al., 2021). These kinds of findings are very important for the evaluation of the levels of difficulty of the music material and for the definition of the criteria for planning the educational activities.

Finally, only 34.5% of the 99 complete games played with the "Good or Bad" ended with a defeat, which means that people were able to listen to the various music tracks and to evaluate them in the correct way.

FUTURE RESEARCH DIRECTIONS

Many research questions emerge from the general framework expressed by the design approach depicted in Figure 1, which involves gamification and engagement as primary tools to foster music learning. The development of point 6, Table 1, provides a detailed list of the gameful elements employed in the design of each case study. But, what is exactly their role in producing engagement? Are they really useful to increase learning in the students? This last question represents the key problem for the use of gamification in educational contexts. There is no doubt that learning experiences with gameful applications produce profound mutations both in the relationship between teachers and learners and in the contents that are conveyed. Hence the important point for teachers, designers and policy makers is to understand what exactly these mutations are and if they can really be used to produce a lasting and conscious form of knowledge. And if this is the case, what is the relationship between traditional and these new emerging forms of knowledge? Finally, from the point of view of teachers and students it is important to understand how teaching strategies that use gamified approaches can be embedded in regular class activities, how they can complement school curricula and enrich the musical experience of the students.

CONCLUSION

The use of gamification in music education applications is not an ancillary and optional element, but rather it is intimately intertwined in the design of the applications. This has been demonstrated by the development of the deep interrelationships existing among material, musical features, gameful elements and interaction style. The interplay of these fundamental elements has produced the three case studies which have been presented and evaluated in this contribution. The three applications provide the users with unique musical experiences, foster engagement, and allow a good level of task accomplishment.

Also if the benchmarks considered in the results analysis (functionality, engagement and performance) offer clues for a positive evaluation for the use of these applications in educational contexts, there are still many open questions which require further study. The main of these is if the use of such applications may result in a real increased learning, what kind of knowledge they deliver to the students and how it can be integrated into school curricula. Answers to these important questions should be the core of future research in the field.

This research received no specific grant from any funding agency in the public, commercial, or not-for-profit sectors.

REFERENCES

Amory, A., Naicker, K., Vincent, J., & Adams, C. (1999). The use of computer games as an educational tool: 1. Identification of appropriate game types and game elements. *British Journal of Educational Technology*, *30*(4), 311–322. doi:10.1111/1467-8535.00121

Arnab, S., Lim, T., Carvalho, M. B., Bellotti, F., De Freitas, S., Louchart, S., Suttie, N., Berta, R., & De Gloria, A. (2015). Mapping learning and game mechanics for serious games analysis. *British Journal of Educational Technology*, *46*(2), 391–411. doi:10.1111/bjet.12113

Arsenault, D. (2008). Guitar Hero: "Not like playing guitar at all"? *Loading...*, *2*(2).

Avanzini, F., Baraté, A., Ludovico, L. A., & Mandanici, M. (2019). Metrics for the automatic assessment of music harmony awareness in children. In *Sound & Music Computing Conference* (pp. 372–379). SMC.

Avanzini, F., Baraté, A., Ludovico, L. A., & Mandanici, M. (2021). Songs in Music Education: Design and Early Experimentation of a Web Tool for the Recognition of Harmonic Changes. In *International Conference on Computer Supported Education* (pp. 709-720). SCITEPRESS. 10.5220/0010540407090720

Bianchi-Berthouze, N., Kim, W. W., & Patel, D. (2007, September). Does body movement engage you more in digital game play? and why? In *International conference on affective computing and intelligent interaction* (pp. 102-113). Springer. 10.1007/978-3-540-74889-2_10

Biddiss, E., & Irwin, J. (2010). Active video games to promote physical activity in children and youth: A systematic review. *Archives of Pediatrics & Adolescent Medicine*, *164*(7), 664–672. doi:10.1001/archpediatrics.2010.104 PMID:20603468

Birchfield, D., & Johnson-Glenberg, M. (2012). A next gen interface for embodied learning: SMALLab and the geological layer cake. In Interdisciplinary Advancements in Gaming, Simulations and Virtual Environments: Emerging Trends (pp. 51-60). IGI Global.

Campayo–Munoz, E., & Cabedo–Mas, A. (2017). The role of emotional skills in music education. *British Journal of Music Education*, *34*(3), 243–258. doi:10.1017/S0265051717000067

Campbell, P. S. (2010). *Songs in their heads: Music and its meaning in children's lives*. Oxford University Press.

Camurri, A., Volpe, G., Canazza, S., Canepa, C., Roda, A., Zanolla, S., & Foresti, G. L. (2010). The 'Stanza Logo–Motoria': an interactive environment for learning and communication. In *Proceedings of SMC Conference* (*Vol. 51*, No. 8). Academic Press.

De Kort, Y. A., & Ijsselsteijn, W. A. (2008). People, places, and play: Player experience in a socio-spatial context. *Computers in Entertainment*, *6*(2), 1–11. doi:10.1145/1371216.1371221

Deterding, S., Dixon, D., Khaled, R., & Nacke, L. (2011, September). From game design elements to gamefulness: defining "gamification". In *Proceedings of the 15th international academic MindTrek conference: Envisioning future media environments* (pp. 9-15). 10.1145/2181037.2181040

Fogtmann, M. H., Fritsch, J., & Kortbek, K. J. (2008, December). Kinesthetic interaction: revealing the bodily potential in interaction design. In *Proceedings of the 20th Australasian conference on computer-human interaction: designing for habitus and habitat* (pp. 89-96). 10.1145/1517744.1517770

Gallagher, S., & Lindgren, R. (2015). Enactive Metaphors: Learning Through Full-Body Engagement. *Educational Psychology Review*, *27*(3), 391–404. doi:10.100710648-015-9327-1

Gentry, J. W. (1990). What is experiential learning. *Guide to business gaming and experiential learning*, *9*, 20.

González-González, C. S., Toledo-Delgado, P. A., Muñoz-Cruz, V., & Torres-Carrion, P. V. (2019, September). Serious games for rehabilitation: Gestural interaction in personalized gamified exercises through a recommender system. *Journal of Biomedical Informatics*, *97*, 103266. doi:10.1016/j.jbi.2019.103266 PMID:31408732

Hofstetter, F. T. (1981). *Computer-Based Instruction: Roots*. Origins, Applications, Benefits, Features, Systems, Trends and Issues.

Holland, S., Marshall, P., Bird, J., Dalton, S., Morris, R., Pantidi, N., ... Clark, A. (2009, February). Running up Blueberry Hill: Prototyping whole body interaction in harmony space. In *Proceedings of the 3rd international Conference on Tangible and Embedded interaction* (pp. 93-98). 10.1145/1517664.1517690

Hoysniemi, J. (2006). International survey on the Dance Dance Revolution game. *Computers in Entertainment*, *4*(2), 8. doi:10.1145/1129006.1129019

Johnson, M. L., & Larson, S. (2003). Something in the way she moves"-metaphors of musical motion. *Metaphor and Symbol*, *18*(2), 63–84. doi:10.1207/S15327868MS1802_1

Juntunen, M. L., & Hyvönen, L. (2004). Embodiment in musical knowing: How body movement facilitates learning within Dalcroze Eurhythmics. *British Journal of Music Education*, *21*(2), 199–214. doi:10.1017/S0265051704005686

Lakoff, G., & Johnson, M. (2008). *Metaphors we live by*. University of Chicago press.

Lee, E., Nakra, T. M., & Borchers, J. (2004, June). You're the conductor: a realistic interactive conducting system for children. In *Proceedings of the 2004 conference on New interfaces for musical expression* (pp. 68-73). Academic Press.

Lim, D., & Rubasundram, G. A. (2018). Disruption in teaching & learning: Experiential learning and gamification in practice. *Electronic Journal of Business & Management, 1*, 87–93.

Maes, P., Darrell, T., Blumberg, B., & Pentland, A. (1997). The ALIVE system: Wireless, full-body interaction with autonomous agents. *Multimedia Systems, 5*(2), 105–112. doi:10.1007005300050046

Malinverni, L., & Burguès, N. P. (2015, June). The medium matters: the impact of full-body interaction on the socio-affective aspects of collaboration. In *Proceedings of the 14th International Conference on Interaction Design and Children* (pp. 89-98). 10.1145/2771839.2771849

Mandanici, M., Altieri, F., Pretto, N., Munaro, M., Canazza, S., & Menegatti, E. (2018, November). The "Good or Bad?" Game: Stimulating Listening Skills through Playful Engagement. In *Proceedings of the 4th EAI International Conference on Smart Objects and Technologies for Social Good* (pp. 177-182). 10.1145/3284869.3284917

Mandanici, M., Ludovico, L. A., & Avanzini, F. (2019). A computer-based approach to teach tonal harmony to young students. In *International Conference on Computer Supported Education* (pp. 271-279). SCITEPRESS. 10.5220/0007700402710279

Mandanici, M., Ludovico, L. A., Avanzini, F., & Baraté, A. (2019). Learning tonal harmony through bodily interactions and gamification. In *Music Educators and Researchers of Young Children* (pp. 237–246). Ghent University.

Mandanici, M., Rodà, A., & Canazza, S. (2014, September). The "Harmonic Walk": An interactive educational environment to discover musical chords. ICMC.

Mandanici, M., Rodà, A., & Canazza, S. (2016). The Harmonic Walk: An interactive physical environment to learn tonal melody accompaniment. *Advances in Multimedia.*

Munaro, M., Basso, F., & Menegatti, E. (2016). OpenPTrack: Open source multi-camera calibration and people tracking for RGB-D camera networks. *Robotics and Autonomous Systems, 75*, 525–538. doi:10.1016/j.robot.2015.10.004

Music for children: Orff-Schulwerk. (1991). (American edition). Schott.

Nijs, L., & Leman, M. (2014). Interactive technologies in the instrumental music classroom: A longitudinal study with the Music Paint Machine. *Computers & Education, 73*, 40–59. doi:10.1016/j.compedu.2013.11.008

Nordby, A., Øygardslia, K., Sverdrup, U., & Sverdrup, H. (2016). The art of gamification; teaching sustainability and system thinking by pervasive game development. *Electronic Journal of e-Learning, 14*(3), 152-168.

Oravec, J. A. (2015). Gamification and multigamification in the workplace: Expanding the ludic dimensions of work and challenging the work/play dichotomy. *Cyberpsychology (Brno), 9*(3). Advance online publication. doi:10.5817/CP2015-3-6

Rego, P., Moreira, P. M., & Reis, L. P. (2010). Serious games for rehabilitation: A survey and a classification towards a taxonomy. In *5th Iberian conference on information systems and technologies* (pp. 1-6). IEEE.

Riemann, H. (2016). *Harmony simplified, or the theory of the tonal functions of chords (classic reprint)*. Academic Press.

Rozendaal, M. C., & Schifferstein, H. N. (2010). Pleasantness in bodily experience: A phenomenological inquiry. *International Journal of Design*, *4*(2), 55–63.

Saslaw, J. (1996). Forces, containers, and paths: The role of body-derived image schemas in the conceptualization of music. *Journal of Music Therapy*, *40*(2), 217–243. doi:10.2307/843889

Schellenberg, E. G., Bigand, E., Poulin-Charronnat, B., Garnier, C., & Stevens, C. (2005). Children's implicit knowledge of harmony in Western music. *Developmental Science*, *8*(6), 551–566. doi:10.1111/j.1467-7687.2005.00447.x PMID:16246247

Sharma, S., & Somani, A. (2019). Gamification in Entertainment Industry: Glimpses From Indian Film Industry. In P. Mishra & S. Dham (Eds.), *Application of Gaming in New Media Marketing* (pp. 236–243). IGI Global. doi:10.4018/978-1-5225-6064-7.ch014

Smith, M. W., Sharit, J., & Czaja, S. J. (1999). Aging, motor control, and the performance of computer mouse tasks. *Human Factors*, *41*(3), 389–396. doi:10.1518/001872099779611102 PMID:10665207

Terlutter, R., & Capella, M. L. (2013). The gamification of advertising: Analysis and research directions of in-game advertising, advergames, and advertising in social network games. *Journal of Advertising*, *42*(2-3), 95–112. doi:10.1080/00913367.2013.774610

Trainor, L. J., & Trehub, S. E. (1994). Key membership and implied harmony in Western tonal music: Developmental perspectives. *Perception & Psychophysics*, *56*(2), 125–132. doi:10.3758/BF03213891 PMID:7971113

Volkswagen. (2009). *The Fun Theory*. Retrieved from Thefuntheory.com: http://www.thefuntheory.com/

Volpe, G., & Camurri, A. (2011). A system for embodied social active listening to sound and music content. *Journal on Computing and Cultural Heritage*, *4*(1), 1–23. doi:10.1145/2001416.2001418

Wertsch, J. V. (1984). The zone of proximal development: Some conceptual issues. *New Directions for Child and Adolescent Development*, *1984*(23), 7–18. doi:10.1002/cd.23219842303

Wilson, R. A., Foglia, L., Shapiro, L., & Spaulding, S. (2019). Embodied Cognition. In *The Stanford Encyclopedia of Philosophy*. https://plato.stanford.edu/archives/win2019/entries/embodied-cognition/

ENDNOTES

1. The Object-oriented programming paradigm (OOP) is based on the idea of "objects" (data and code). Data are named "fields", and code or procedures are named "methods".
2. https://youtu.be/c4ru468eqM0
3. http://harmonictouch.lim.di.unimi.it/
4. https://youtu.be/XEliaFxKGeQ
5. https://youtu.be/EQZc58vqMhM

6 https://youtu.be/hd3rbsEaLks
7 http://harmonictouch.lim.di.unimi.it/experience_1_explain.php?s=uun4hrqrmo6se56qprvcqd8697
8 http://harmonictouch.lim.di.unimi.it/experience_2_explain.php?s=uun4hrqrmo6se56qprvcqd8697
9 http://harmonictouch.lim.di.unimi.it/experience_3_explain.php?s=uun4hrqrmo6se56qprvcqd8697
10 https://www.hooktheory.com/hookpad
11 https://musiclab.chromeexperiments.com/Song-Maker/
12 https://musiclab.chromeexperiments.com/Arpeggios/
13 MIDI is the acronym for Musical Instruments Digital Interface, a protocol for the recording, transmission and storing of music performance data.
14 The Kinect sensor allows the tracking of human motion using the data of a RGB camera and a depth map generated by an infrared camera.
15 STEAM is an acronym for Science, Technology, Engineering, Arts and Mathematics and stands for an educational multidisciplinary approach which takes into consideration a specific theme from the point of view of these various disciplines.

Chapter 20
Commercium and Cognitionis Project:
A Gamification Experience in an Undergraduate Course

Alexandre Farbiarz
https://orcid.org/0000-0002-2237-7074
Fluminense Federal University, Brazil

Jackeline L. Farbiarz
Pontifical Catholic University of Rio de Janeiro, Brazil

Guilherme Xavier
Pontifical Catholic University of Rio de Janeiro, Brazil

Cynthia M. Dias
https://orcid.org/0000-0002-4412-0878
Oswaldo Cruz Foundation, Brazil

Lucas L. A. Bastos
Fluminense Federal University, Brazil

Eloisa F. F. S. Gonçalves
Fluminense Federal University, Brazil

ABSTRACT

This chapter presents the Commercium & Cognitionis project, which aligns technology and playfulness, implementing DICTs and gamification as pedagogical tools that value didactic content and engagement, combining competition and collaboration in the search for knowledge to solve the proposed challenges. The proposal is aligned with the insertion of urban youth into a highly imagetic and technological contemporary culture. Adopting active pedagogical methods that exploit skills and abilities in the game allows the combination of systemic and procedural evaluation in the discipline and the evaluation of knowledge construction. To reach the play goal, it was necessary for the student-player to pursue the didactic objectives, as the evaluation of the experience indicates that dedication to the game positively influenced the academic dedication, also stimulating access and meaningful learning on the programmatic contents and guaranteeing autonomy and independence in the educational process.

DOI: 10.4018/978-1-6684-4287-6.ch020

INTRODUCTION

In their first year, students of the Fluminense Federal University (UFF) Journalism undergraduate course, in Brazil, have a mandatory 60-h Visual and Graphic Languages discipline. The authors decided to develop strategies and solutions to the problems identified in the discipline focusing on imparting initial knowledge about basic elements of graphic-visual systems.

The authors started from the UFF Journalism course curriculum, established with a vision that "In recent years, Communication studies have evolved towards understanding the language and theory of media not only as a field of action, but as a place of knowledge" (Universidade Federal Fluminense, 2016, p. 2). It indicates that subjects in the graphic area with an emphasis on Editorial Design, among the seven different areas of emphasis that students have at their disposal, were the core influence on the creation of the Graduate Program in Media and Everyday Life, back in 2013.

Given the clear insertion of urban youth in a contemporary culture that is highly imagetic and technological (Kellner, 2001), the authors' premise seeks to combine technology and teaching practice playfully, developing tools that value didactic content and interaction, helping and stimulating learning. So, the first pedagogical strategy adopted was the insertion of Digital Information and Communication Technologies (DICTs) through smartphones as an interactive tool of a pedagogical nature. The second was the use of gamification as the mainstay of the discipline's pedagogical project. It is important to remark that gamification is the use of game elements in other situations than amusement ones, with a focus on developing the motivation and engagement of participants (Deterding et al., 2011). At the same time, the use of games and playful practices as pedagogical resources can be a way to train people who are both intimate and critical of DICTs (Gee, 2007). This approach can relate to both ways games have content: as a story designed by someone else or the record of its player's decisions, actions, and feedback (Gee, 2015).

Thus, the research that supports this project confirms that the accelerated flow of information (Lipovetsky, 2004) from the media culture (Kellner, 2001) offers information quickly and superficially to young people, sometimes without critical training to deal with them. That is a complex phenomenon and, in this sense, the combination of digital technologies, gamification, and Critical Pedagogy (Giroux, 2016) presents the possibility of rehearsing new forms of interaction between students, educators, and content, promoting the expression of creativity and critical thinking through the use of media. Even immersed in this context of extremes, educators can seek its most favorable face, flee from the mercantile logic and value the processes of interaction between subjects, avoiding the exacerbated individualism characteristic of hypermodernity (Lipovetsky, 2004).

The *Commercium & Cognitionis* project (CetC) seeks to associate technology and teaching practice playfully, developing tools that value didactic content and interaction and help meaningful learning through cooperation. The project, in addition to its application as a discipline, develops experimental field research that investigates how young university students enhance and develop skills necessary for their trajectory in the university environment and everyday life outside the campus, starting from the perspective of the constructing and sustaining discourse in the media as a central element in these processes.

Gamification was a chosen strategy for the CetC project because of its configurative approach to game elements, applied in non-game situations (Deterding et al., 2011; Rivera & Garden, 2020). Zichermann and Cunningham (2011) regard gamification as the use of mechanics, style, and thinking involved in game design techniques to promote the engagement of participants in the solution of a problem, also clarifying that gamifying a process or system will not generate a game *per se*, despite the use of game elements.

According to Patricio, Moreira, Zurlo, and Melazzini (2020), "[...] gamification holds the potential to improve the results of collaborative innovation practices by encouraging the involvement and participation of all key actors in the development of new solutions [...]" (p. 146).

Gamification can be applied to tackle the central issues of collaborative innovation, more specifically its dynamics and messy nature that is a consequence of the challenges of managing multi-actors in knowledge creation. This type of approach can also be used to solve research problems related to actors' alignment and participation in complex collaborative environments, e.g. conflicting parties reaching out for consensus (Patricio, Moreira, Zurlo, & Melazzini, 2020, p. 156).

One of the most characteristic gamification principles is the tripod points, badges, and leaderboards (PBL). According to Werbach and Hunter (2011), points are a way for the player to track their progress; badges are symbolic indications of tasks fully or to be performed; and leaderboards are the comparative way in which players rank their positions in comparison to others, being a fine resource for generating feedback.

These features, so characteristic among a variety of games, resemble the system of grades, distinctions, and classifications in educational tests and exams. The difference lies in what Hunicke et al. (2004) characterize in games, structurally, by the acronym MDA: mechanics, dynamics, and aesthetics. To promote dialogue and collaboration dynamics between different people, there is a need of mediating "objects", or mechanics, starting from something "in common" that enables listening, understanding, collaboration, and collective creation. Therefore, while gamification establishes mechanics that determine the causes and consequences of rules among players' interactions, the interest in the process lies in the dynamics produced and, in greater depth, in the aesthetics experienced.

Gamification involves planning interactions to optimize results, influencing interactors' positive actions and attitudes through game resources, without defining absolute win and defeat conditions. Such experiences include matching metrics that monitor the "game" outcome process and skill development. By promoting such processes among groups, intrinsic motivation can be stimulated from socialization and relatedness (Ryan & Deci, 2000), in which gamification approaches the Connectivism of George Siemens and Stephen Downes (Siemens, 2005). In addition, according to Bíró (2014), gamification, when lining flexible itineraries to meet different learning styles, approaches concepts related to Constructivism.

The report produced for the World Government Summit by Oxford Analytica (World Government Summit, 2016), the literary review by Surendeleg et al. (2014), the meta-analysis by Sailer and Homner (2020), among other studies, have focused on the subtleties of gamification when applied in educational processes. Mechanics, dynamics, and aesthetics in games are diverse, as are the possibilities for effects to be produced by their use in instructional contexts. In this sense, the authors do not seek to adhere to generalizations – either of efficacy or uselessness of gamification as a one-fits-all solution – but to present an experience of applying certain concepts in an undergraduate course.

THE EXPERIMENT

The experiment has been developed in two distinct phases, having been carried out so far with a total of 218 students, with five face-to-face classes in the pre-pandemic period and, more recently, with three remote classes until the current semester, amid the Covid-19 pandemic.

Figure 1. Accessing a video format content
Source: Authors

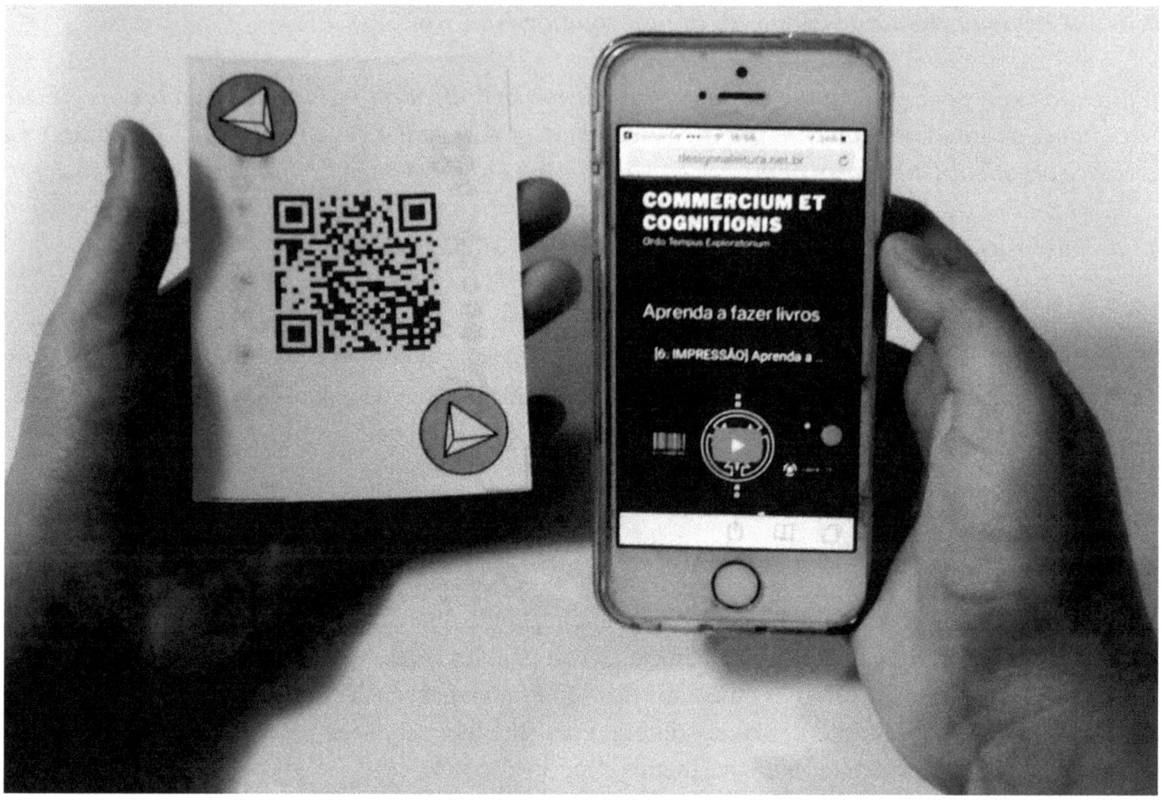

The project seeks, through a system of rules and mechanics aimed at engagement and motivation, to

> *[...] enhance the skills and abilities of students for: 1) collaboration, interaction, and partnership; 2) autonomy in the search for knowledge; 3) responsibility in building the path of knowledge; 4) flexibility to different teaching-learning styles; and 5) diversity of forms of expression. (Farbiarz et al., 2019, p. 234).*

The basic game mechanics, established in the first phase, consist of 540 playing cards divided into nine thematic decks related to the syllabus of the discipline. Each card has a QRCode printed on its back that, through the smartphone camera (Figure 1), allows the student-player to access one of the contents hosted on the discipline's site, whether text, images, or short videos, edited, subtitled and royalty-free.

Each week, the student-players raffled two playing cards of the current theme and received a group mission: to relate their contents with other external ones and make a presentation that met the specific demand of that theme. The student-players were encouraged to exchange the playing cards between them through some mechanics with points rewards, as well as several other ways to encourage collaboration and partnership.

Mattar (2009) states that playful teaching-learning environments provide greater interaction among students and between them and the educators, configuring a form of collaborative and cooperative learning. According to him, "This interaction also develops the critical sense and the ability to work as a team, and often creates the feeling of belonging to a community. [...] All of this, of course, contributes to learning" (Mattar, 2009, p. 116). Pedagogically, it was intended that the articulation between student-players actions and different genres of information, within a common goal, should bring meaning to the accessed content and so, to stimulate research and the construction of new knowledge beyond the game, in line with the goals of autonomy, responsibility, and flexibility.

The missions represent an invitation to the solution of a challenge by competence and skill of the student-player. Because in mission evaluations it is possible to accumulate more points than those needed to meet the requirements of discipline evaluation, the student-player can choose which missions to perform. This mechanics meets the flow theory, essential in the gamified process (Csikszentmihalyi, 2020), by balancing the level of difficulty of the activity with the possibilities of the student-players. As in Education for Liberation (Freire, 2020), in the gamified course, the subject also practices his/her own "process of discovery and construction" (Alves, 2009, p. 141).

Every week, interspersed with the missions, a class, workshop, or activity was realized, seeking to articulate the theory and practice of the syllabus. Finally, at the end of the school semester, the student-players had to produce a final group work, a journalistic publication, either printed or digital. It's possible to see an example of these results in Figure 2. Although with a free editorial line, the articles should be related to the syllabus of the discipline. In this sense, the missions also aim to gradually develop the skills and competencies needed by student-players to carry out this more complex task, since, in addition to the content of the publication, both the graphic design and the creativity reward them points.

The academic results of the project during the face-to-face phase with the students were increasingly encouraging, both for the engagement and for the final works presented. From the responses to the survey form sent at the end of each academic semester (answered by approximately 40% of the students who attended the course in these five semesters), it was concluded that, to achieve the playful objective, the student-player needed to pursue the didactic objective, as its dedication to the game positively influenced its academic dedication. Besides, this behavior provided meaningful learning about the contents, guaranteeing autonomy and independence in the educational process.

Especially, 83.33% of respondents in this phase believed that the contents of the discipline will be important for their academic and professional lives, even being in the first period of the journalism course. But the most relevant answer was that 66.7% of respondents stated that gamification would have contributed to their better understanding of the contents, participation in the discipline, and the development of their autonomy, confirming the initial objectives of the project.

But how to expect the unexpected? How to prepare to experience two years (by now) of remote learning, intensely and completely mediated by digital media and technologies that, until recently, were perceived by many Brazilian educators as fetish objects; somewhat used in classroom practices as a kind of "fireworks" pedagogy (Farbiarz & Farbiarz, 2008) that values the resources at the expense of education?

THE LUDIC SAGA OF THE KINGDOM OF MAGISTERIUM

Undoubtedly, the pragmatism of the situation preceded the theoretical-conceptual concerns: how to transform into a fully digital activity an experience that, even though relied heavily on digital media and technologies, was carried out in person, with mechanics that depended on the interaction between student-players? The pandemic, which imposed total social distancing and the use of digital technologies in the remote teaching format, showed how, as pointed out by Rossini, Amaral, and Santos (2021):

Figure 2. Final work "Nona Arte" magazine
Source: Authors (Produced by Lucas Silva Marciano dos Santos, Lucas Wesley Kelly dos Anjos, Matheus de Abreu Taranto)

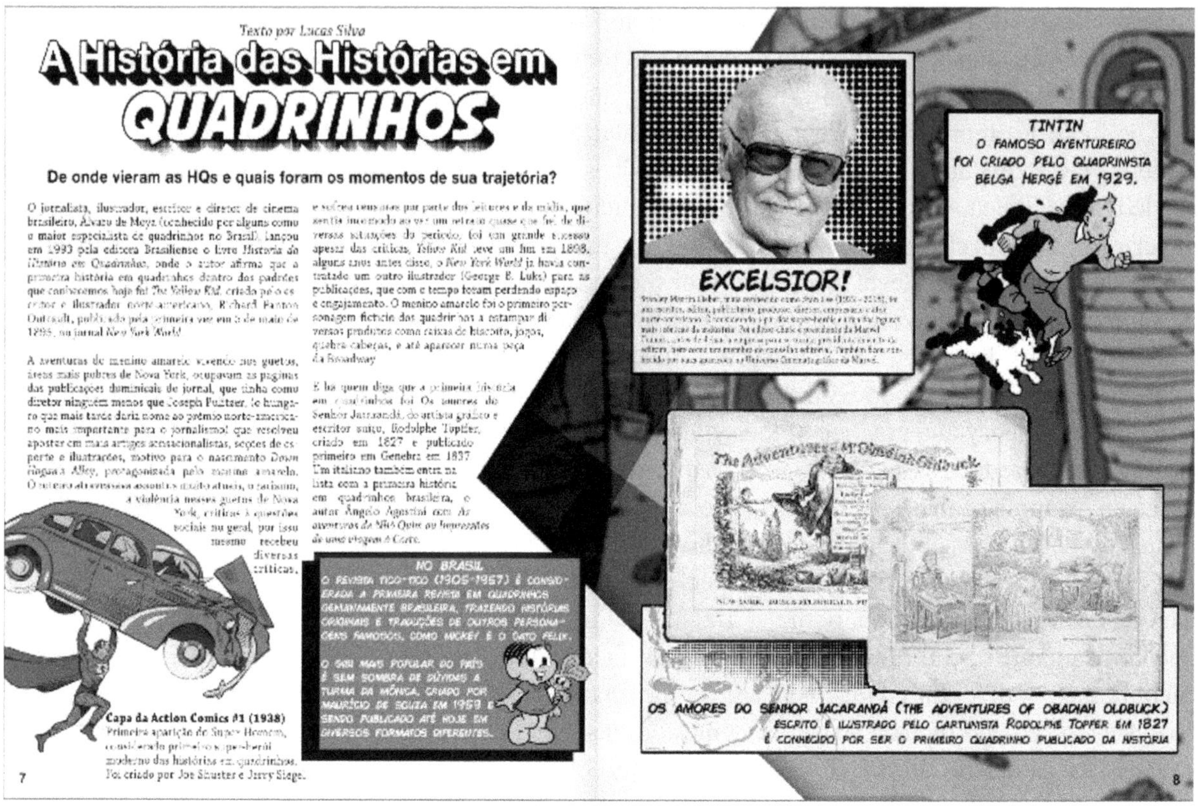

Online education requires its own teaching methodology—one that profoundly changes conventional teaching models that are based on the transmission, memorization, and repetition of information and knowledge. In this scenario, it is necessary to rethink education as an emancipatory human construct that allows subjects to understand themselves as actors and authors in the cyberculture—that is, in contemporary culture mediated by digital networking—which alters modes of communication, production, sociability, and ways of learning and teaching. (p. 286).

With this in mind, as in the development of the first phase of the project, in the second phase, the authors were focused on solving these and other difficulties. The first one was to see the real possibilities of young Brazilian people's access to the same media and technologies that would sustain the gamified course, either because of the concrete difficulties of resources or because of the anxiety imposed by this new form of educational interaction. In this sense, the authors seek again accessible solutions and rely on the notion proposed by Rossini, Amaral, and Santos (2021),

Knowledge is made available in a way that enables the learners to experience and participate in the development of their learning. Learning exchanges can be made with both teacher-students and teacher(s)-teacher(s). These open connections foster teacher and student autonomy and favor the exchange of knowledge because nothing is static and consolidated. Knowledge is (re)constructed and (re)signified for each interaction between the participants. (p. 290).

Despite the synchronous encounters, all syllabus and gamified elements should be available asynchronously too, through low-tech and easily accessible resources. Likewise, there should be space for reflection and discursive media production by students, in compliance with the competencies of responsibility and diversity of forms of expression.

The authors, therefore, perceive the gamified discipline as a hybrid space that articulates practical knowledge to curricular knowledge, breaking the hierarchical form of teaching and learning, aiming at meaningful and contextualized learning, where technology emerges in the communication process, changing spaces and times of learning as shown by Santos and Weber (2013),

Communication technologies give rise, each in its own time, to distinct but not exclusive learning processes. With printed communication technologies, we have teaching-learning processes based on the textbook. With networked digital technologies we have teaching-learning processes that take place through virtual environments [...] This is because no form of communication eliminates the previous ones. What we observe is a change in the social functions of each technology involved in communication processes, giving rise to new social practices, causing changes also in the space-times of learning. (p. 291).

Also according to Santos and Weber (2013), the experience in digital culture provided by networked digital technologies "alters the forms of communication, production, creation, and circulation of information" (p. 300), and in this sense, the ways of teaching and learning in contemporary culture.

The second major issue reverberated around a perception supported by the two and a half years of interaction with the classes and the results of ongoing research: that motivation and engagement could be improved. It was noticeable that the didactic-pedagogical proposal, supported by a systemic evaluation, ended up being perceived by some students as a traditional teaching proposal, summarized as simple preparation of thematic seminars and a final work that would be scored, despite all the game mechanics.

To transform gamified platforms, services, or products into more rewarding experiences, researchers suggest avoiding mechanics that favor social isolation, automatic behaviors conditioned to extrinsic rewards, and competition for points. In their place, they recommend pursuing the design of systems based on cooperation and altruism, through game design patterns that promote friendship and empathy among participants (Cook et al., 2016).

Vasconcellos et al. (in press) point out two main approaches which could broaden the scope and improve engagement in gamified practices: the focus on aesthetic aspects and social ones. Regarding the aesthetic aspects and their impact on the adoption, engagement, and perceived value of the system by users, they propose that these elements reflect feelings such as beauty, enchantment, welcoming, safety, and stimulation, not mere decoration. Concerning the social aspects, they suggest:

[...] game mechanics that give the participant a sense of the social context. Avatar customization, sharing photos and texts, tagging friends and forming more stable groups are just initial recommendations. Ideally, cause-and-effect relationships should be felt socially, in the form of gains shared by a certain group. Gamification that promotes the social would make the rewards obtained in groups proportionately more significant than those obtained individually. Participants would act more organically as a group without the need for instructions to do so.

The competition among groups and cooperation inside them was already a part of the gamified discipline in the first phase. Although, the authors considered that the alternative to reverse the situation of low engagement, although not predominant, and still expand the positive effects of the project, would be connecting all the mechanics, in synchrony with the didactic-pedagogical proposal, in a narrative that would promote the immersion of student-players so considered student-player-characters.

About immersion, Murray (2003) states that:

The experience of being transported to an elaborately simulated place is pleasurable in itself, regardless of the fantasy content. We refer to this experience as immersion. Immersion is a metaphorical term derived from the physical experience of being submerged in water. We seek the same feeling from a psychologically immersive experience that we do from a dip in the ocean or a swimming pool: the feeling of being surrounded by a completely other reality, as different as water is from air, that takes over all of our entire attention, our whole perceptual apparatus. (p. 102).

Immersion is a passive and active process at the same time: it presupposes a new reality acceptance, with its own rules and values, while at the same time it requires a "creative faculty" from those who immerse in the narrative (Murray, 2003, p. 111). This creative activity of consumers of these narratives contributes to their experience with a game, for example, as they not only understand and accept the attributes of the playful world in which they operate but also establish new practices, behaviors, and ways of communicating, among others. Within the context of this project, stimulating this creative profile in the immersion of students-players is essential, as the aim of the authors is to encourage student-players to develop new relationships between the content and their everyday lives, to express themselves in innovative ways, to add new elements to the game narrative itself.

Thus, with Murray (2003), the authors understand that immersion is a simulated experience that can transport through a narrative to another place, which is not the real one. As Murray (2003) teaches, by stating that "[...] a stirring narrative in any medium can be experienced as a virtual reality because our brains are programmed to tune into stories with an intensity that can obliterate the world around us" (p. 101). Of course, the gamified experience is not a digital game and will never achieve its level of immersion, but the use of narrative and involvement of students-players in this narrative pursues some level of immersion, through the role-play developed among the narrative.

Allied to immersion, in the playful proposal of the discipline, there is the issue of agency. According to Murray (2003), "Agency is the gratifying ability to carry out significant actions and see the results of our decisions and choices" (p. 127). When someone clicks on a certain smartphone button looking for a result and sees a task being completed after this action, or when someone answers a question in a quiz and receives positive feedback indicating that he/her received a good score, for example, the subject exercises his/her agency within of these systems. Not because it was simply possible to interact and exercise simple commands, but because those actions built some meaning into that system. From the author's perspective, games, especially electronic ones, are environments in which conditions are offered for players to exercise significant movements and decision-making. In addition to being able to control a character, explore an environment or face an enemy, these actions can contribute to the development of one or more meanings that fit the narrative proposal or expand it. Encouraging this students-players agency is essential for the pedagogical project´s success, as they need to feel that their decisions produce real and significant effects both in the academic sphere, such as reaching a certain grade or not, for example, and in the playful sphere, such as success or failure of the characters involved in the narrative.

Narrative is a powerful element of games, many times used in gamified experiences, for its immersion and interaction properties. Frasca (1999) highlights that because of their narrative elements, games' rules can be open enough to allow the player to determine how he/she wants to participate in the experience. This relative "freedom" gives them the authorship of the actions performed, unlike a traditional narrative where the plot is pre-defined. In this way, he believes that, by presenting believable and identifiable elements, a game can stimulate critical thinking on the part of the player, as an ideal medium to discuss and explore personal and social issues.

According to Salen and Zimmerman (2003), the player interacts with and within a representational universe, a space of possibilities full of narrative dimensions. Compared to the classic structure of a story, many games contain a beginning, development, and conclusion, but this is related to the structure of the game as a system of rules, and events are triggered by playing. At the same time, creating game narratives means playing with fields of culture, as well as conventions in popular culture, literature, entertainment, art, and media in general (Salen & Zimmerman, 2003). No representation is neutral and, in a game, the more relevant they are, the more likely they are to encourage an inviting and engaging experience (Protasio & Dias, 2016).

Salen and Zimmerman (2003) present two ways of understanding how a game system produces narrative: embedded and emergent narrative. The embedded narrative is "[...] pre-generated narrative content that exists prior to a player's interaction with the game. Designed to provide motivation for the events and actions of the game [...]" (Salen & Zimmerman, 2012, p. 383). It is the story that gives meaning and context to the rules, authored by the game creator, which aims to provide the player with meaningful participation through plot elements. A dialogue between characters, a text to be read, music, and even visual representations and interaction mechanics, essentially any element that is immutable and pre-established, contribute to the narrative experience in games and participate in the embedded narrative (Protasio & Dias, 2016). The emergent narrative is composed of the elements that "[...] arise during play from the complex system of the game, often in unexpected ways" (Salen & Zimmerman, 2012, p.383). As such, it is the story created from the player's interactive experience, based on the experience planned by the game designers, but impossible to predict in its entirety, because the events developed are a consequence of the freedom exercised by the player in face of game mechanics and their production of meanings (Protasio & Dias, 2016). The emergent narrative also depends on the context, or on what is happening in the game system at that exact moment (Salen & Zimmerman, 2012). The result of the player's actions and the sequence of events created – planned or not by the creator of the game – generate a narrative in which the player feels authorship. Salen and Zimmerman (2012) believe that the two modes of narrative, when properly worked, coexisting in balance, reach a form of symbiosis and promote a mutually beneficial relationship of communication and collaboration that allows for the creation of unique narrative experiences.

In this sense, the authors elaborated the *Ludic Saga of the Kingdom of Magisterium*, a mystical kingdom situated in indefinite time and space (Figure 3). Student-players-characters enter this fictional universe by embodying one of the six character categories, which represent different communication specialists: Papermakers, Colorists, Typographers, Engravers, Editors, or Printers. The backstory states that the realm is being invaded by an ancient dragon called Silentium, which, with its horde of half-living, destroys all forms of communication and interaction wherever it goes. Each of the specialist classes has a particular role in the narrative, but they are all heroes who, armed with the knowledge of communication, must find the means to combat this great threat.

Figure 3. Coats and Arms from Magisterium Kingdom
Source: Authors

The game mechanics utilized are the same as in the first phase, however, several elements were eliminated, either because of their complexity or because of their inadequacy in the remote format. They gave way to other mechanics more typical of Role-Playing Games (RPG), such as the character's attributes that evolve in achievements through badges and bonuses (Werbach & Hunter, 2012) directly connected to the narrative. According to Hunicke et al. (2004), these features, so characteristic of games, resemble the system of grades, distinctions, and classifications in disciplines or tests. That is, as the student-player-characters carry out the missions and accumulate points, they rise to different Levels of Mystic Wisdom (Figure 4), and when they reach each one of them, they receive a different spell that they can use (Figure 5), under certain conditions, during the adventure.

In addition to these mechanics, weekly, one of the discipline syllabus' contents serves as a narrative motto, which is presented to student-players-characters through a five-minute video narrating the events in Magisterium, the attacks of the Silentium dragon, and the discovery of some knowledge (associated with the programmatic content of the week) that expert heroes should use to combat the threat. At this point, the plot is presented and a mission is indicated to the specialists. In support of each mission, a spell was revealed to them (Figure 6), composed of magical words in a mysterious language inscribed on a mystical artifact, which the student-players-characters must decipher. This spell may help them in resolving the mission, integrating the narrative and academic content.

The student-players-characters also receive two virtual playing cards weekly, covering the same programmatic content. In the remote format, the cards are distributed through personal pages (Figure 7), built for each of them on the discipline's website, and have "Kameas" printed on, the QRCodes that allow smartphone access to the hidden contents hosted on the Magisterium library, the course's website, based on a WordPress blog structure. Individual access to content intends to empower responsibility and autonomy in the search for information, as well as to accommodate different learning styles and rhythms.

For each syllabus topic, different missions are proposed, which are equally valued as they include a brief presentation of research results, either orally, through videos, or other media products, thus stimulating collaboration and diversity of expression forms. Pedagogically, it is intended that the articulation between student-players-characters and different contents with a common goal bring meaning to the accessed material. Besides, it stimulates the research and the construction of new knowledge, in consonance with the autonomy, accountability, and flexibility objectives.

The audiovisual narratives presented to students, game cards, mission spells, and other playful elements seek to encourage players' immersion in the narrative and proposal of the discipline as a whole but always seeking to feed students' creativity and not restrict it. Although the narratives develop the game's initial story and create a setting for each stage, students are free to create meanings, and bring different images or perspectives to the story. The game's villain, the dragon Silentium, is verbally presented in the narrative as a mystical silvery being, but students often use images and videos in which this threat is represented by different colors, in addition to varying sizes and attributes. A similar situation presents itself in other aspects of the game, such as concerning the map of the Kingdom of Magisterium: although certain locations of the fictional nation are mentioned in the game, different groups of students draw their own maps, creating meanings and stories during the course of the game. The absence of an official map for the game does not limit students' immersion but sometimes ends up stimulating their creativity.

At the apex of knowledge construction, at the end of the semester, student-players-characters gather in teams to produce a final assignment, supported by the "library" contents, missions, classes, and any other material, external to the discipline, which they access according to their interest. For the final assignment, student-players-characters have to produce a digital journalistic publication (Figure 8) focused

Figure 4. Sorcerer's mystic level
Source: Authors

Figure 5. Spell that protects the player's group from two bad grades given by other players in the Final Work assessment
Source: Authors

Figure 6. Second spell about colors and inks
Source: Authors

on the Kingdom of Magisterium, which is connected to the overall narrative by representing the collective effort of all the specialists in trying to preserve all the information to the next generations and the nearby kingdoms, in the case the Silentium dragon came again to threaten the dissemination of communication.

Teams create editorial lines and develop articles with a direct or indirect focus on the topics discussed. Therefore, the missions also aim to gradually develop the necessary skills and abilities for student-players-characters to accomplish this more complex task. In addition to the publication content, both graphic design and creativity are scored. The missions developed weekly by students are evaluated based on the competencies aimed at the pedagogical project of the discipline. As the groups demonstrate that they were able to develop the necessary skills at that stage, the result of the audiovisual narrative presented at the end of the mission is also changed. If they've been able to articulate skills satisfactorily in their presentation, the in-game characters solve the week's problem more completely and shrewdly. When the result is not so satisfactory, their playful avatars do not overcome obstacles in the best way, learning from their mistakes in the process. Therefore, their actions within the discipline build academic and playful meanings: they gain or lose points, but they also contribute or not to the characters' success against the enemy.

Figure 7. Personal page at discipline's website
Source: Authors

Based on the gamification processes, all activities are rewarded with points, according to their importance concerning the discipline objectives. The final grade includes the missions and the final assignment, within a systemic and procedural student development assessment through the learning process. The

Figure 8. "Magisterium Diary"
Source: Authors (Produced by Ingrid Madureira Cury, Julia Barbosa de Mattos Ferreira, Samara Inocêncio Barboza)

dynamics of game ranking disclosure and related points obtained are used as a motivation and engagement strategy, as well as control encouraging over their development, both in the game and the course.

Figure 9. Sixth mission report using TikTok
Source: Authors (Produced by Ana Carolina Modesto, Bernardo Pinho, Carolina Maria Gobbeiro)

CONCLUSION

Evaluation of the Experiment

The third semester is still in progress, but the academic results achieved in the first and second semesters of this second phase have been very encouraging. In addition to a noticeable growth in engagement and motivation, given that many student-players even choose to present more missions than academically necessary, the association of syllabus with playful narrative has provided a better relationship between theory and practice, albeit fictional. The production of digital media discourses by students has exacerbated any expectations in this regard, with videos via YouTube, Instagram, and TikTok, like the one exemplified in Figure 9, either reproducing the playful narrative or appropriating journalistic languages, like the one exemplified in Figure 10, in addition to the simultaneous production of websites, blogs, and podcasts. In this way, they experimented with a wide range of multimodal discourse genders.

Lemke (2010) explains that, in addition to new discourses whose construction is made possible and emphasized by new technologies, multimodality is constitutive of any discourse, even if it is apparently formed by a predominant mode, such as verbal language. Linguistic meanings carry non-linguistic meanings, such as choosing typography, and a tone of voice. That is, when a sign materializes, this material

Figure 10. "Magisterium News"
Source: Authors (Produced by Douglas Ribeiro, Beatriz Riscado, Gabriella Gomes)

reality carries meanings beyond just a code: "All semiotics is multimedia semiotics and all literacy is multimedia literacy" (Lemke, 2010, p. 456). Thus, Lemke highlights that the interactions between modes do not add, but a "multiplication" of meanings and these are born from - and feed - social contexts: "Every new system of conventional practices for meaningful communications it is already a new literacy, encompassed by new technologies" (Lemke, 2010, p. 460).

Also, most of the digital publications presented in the final course assignments demonstrated quality, both visual and content-wise. These results indicate the competence development through the missions was central to the student-player's appropriation of Graphic and Visual Language basic concepts, especially considering they are newcomers to a Journalism course, with expectedly little or no skills in the matter.

Considering the experience as a whole, at the end of each of the seven semesters in which the project was applied, 71 student-players responded to an online survey hosted on Google Drive. This consisted, actually, of 11 open and 17 closed questions, about different experiment aspects. About the weekly missions, on average, 84% of the students stated these were necessary for learning, and 74% stated the missions stimulated their research skills. Most relevant, however, was that 89% agreed the missions encouraged the student-players' collaboration.

Collaboration, as it seems, was the most developed skill within the gamified experience, according to 88% of respondents, especially when pointing out that their participation in the game was more collaborative than competitive. Answers also indicate the proposed interactive format was successful as a way to value collaboration above competition between students. In this way, the answers affirmed the alignment of the project with the propositions of Vasconcellos et al. (in press), Cook et al. (2016), discussed above. The authors also detected identities and sociability construction, especially in the accomplishment of weekly group missions (Moita, 2007). Also about the collaborative students´ profile throughout the course, their interactions during the weekly mission presentations can be highlighted. Students interact via chat and microphone in remote classes during the report's screenings, and it is common for them to congratulate themselves on their success, as well as express intimacy and joy through playing with each other and even with the teacher.

The results of the survey at the end of the school semester with the students of the second phase show 96% of them believe that they had success in the subject, and 61% preferred the gamified format to the traditional one. In particular, we went from 66.7% of respondents in the first phase to 78% in the second phase, stating that gamification would have contributed to their better understanding of the contents, ratifying the initial project objectives. Above all, the survey revealed that there was an increase from 83.33% in the first phase to 100% in the second phase of respondents who believed that the contents of the discipline would be important to their academic and professional lives.

According to one of the students, the missions made them create a 'professional' and personal bond with their group, something that would be difficult to occur in remote education. Another important topic pointed out by the student is that they learn the real content and not just memorize it. In this sense, it seems reasonable to assume that the experience achieves a good level of immersion among students based on the gamified proposal with the fictional narrative.

Kapp (2012) believes that gamification systems based solely on the PBL Triad (Points, Badges, and Leaderboards) don't motivate or keep users engaged for a long time, as they are elements associated with extrinsic motivation. In this sense, it's necessary to deepen game strategies and dynamics, providing more meaningful experiences that meet the inherent needs and users' desires, the intrinsic motivation.

One way to develop more effective strategies in a gamified system is the identification of players' profiles, mapping out what motivates them to play, and, from this, establishing dynamics that meet this motivation, providing players with greater engagement. Thus, the authors decided to raise this profile, using Marczewski's (2015) model, based on Bartle's original model (1996), where profiles are classified as to the type of reward they are interested in.

Marczewski's (2015) typology classifies players into six distinct types, seeking to provide gamified system designers with an insight into the users' profiles to indicate the most appropriate gamification techniques. Marczewski's typology describes the following players' types:

- **Achiever:** motivated by mastery, they seek to learn new things and improve themselves, always looking for challenges to overcome;
- **Disruptor:** motivated by change, want to break the rules, acting directly or through other users to force a positive or a negative change in the system;
- **Free Spirit:** motivated by autonomy and self-expression, creating things and exploring the system;
- **Philanthropist:** motivated by a collective purpose, they are selfless and like to assist and provide achievements to other users without any expectation of reward;
- **Player:** motivated by rewards, they do what is necessary to collect them and always seek the best for themselves;
- **Socializer:** motivated by the relationships that the system provides, seeking interaction and social connections with others.

The questionnaire defined by Marczweski (2015), with 24 questions, 4 for each type, was applied. Questions should be answered according to a 5-point Likert scale, where 1 is equivalent to "Totally

Figure 11. The 26 students' profiles.
Source: Authors

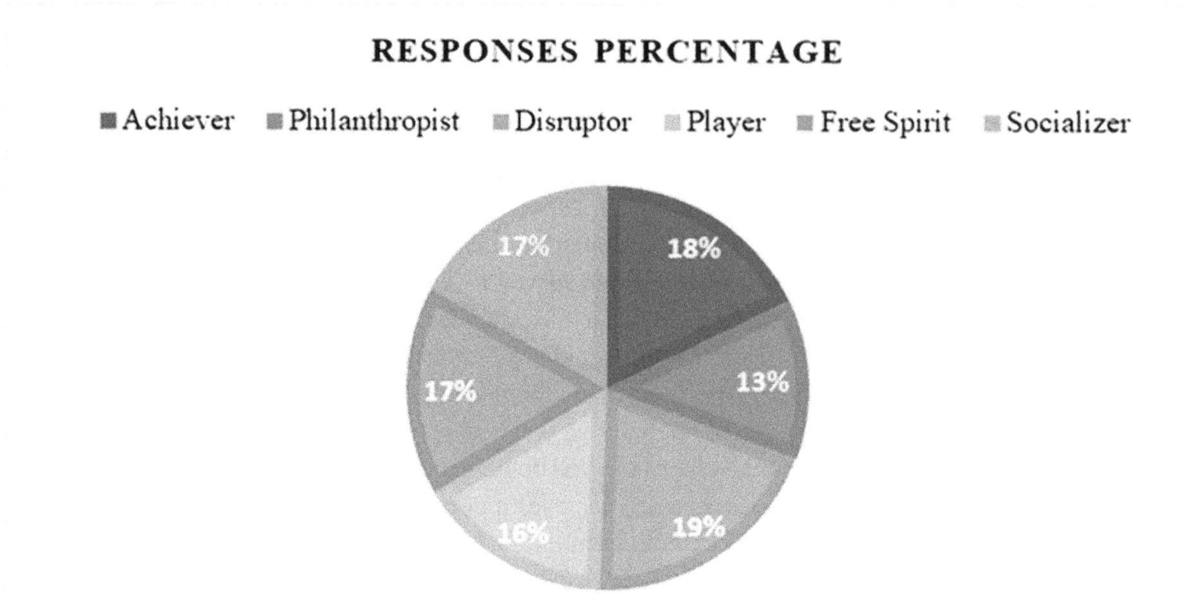

Disagree" and 5 is equivalent to "Totally Agree". As a result, the questionnaire returns the percentage of each type of student-players, defined by its predominant type and secondary types.

The authors sent a Google Form link to the 244 students who attended the course in phases 1 and 2, including the 26 of the recently closed academic semester, and in four days obtained responses from 26 students, which allowed a glimpse at a profile trend, presented at Figure 11:

The graph indicates a good balance between almost all six profiles, with a slightly higher value for the Disruptors type. According to Marczewski, players who identify themselves with this profile seek change, using all possible ways to change the system, or act and find how to take advantage of possible loopholes in it. It is the group that Marczewski cites at the Gamification World Congress (2014) as a group that deserves special attention. If players of this group feel they can help modify the gamified system, they will contribute to the environment, otherwise, they may try to boycott the system.

On the other pole, the profile highlighted with less identification by the students was the Philanthropist, typically altruistic and motivated by the collective purpose. Although this is a relatively not common profile among players, it is curious that the answers to a post factum questionnaire of students who participated in a system with a great focus on collaboration are not perceived in this profile, although they highlighted this competence as one of the ones that most impacted their experience, in the responses to the end-of-course questionnaires over four years of the project.

Based on the results obtained from the survey of the players' types, the authors evaluated the mechanics and strategies adopted in the *Commercium et Cognitionis* (CetC) project, according to some of the Marczewski (2015) recommendations.

The most relevant project's mechanics is undoubtedly the use of challenges that, according to Marczewski, is recommended for almost all six players' types, except precisely the two lowest scores in the survey among students, Player and Philanthropist. The famous PBL Triad (Points, Badges, and Leaderboards), also present among the mechanics of CetC, is not as relevant among the various types, but especially meets Achiever, the second main type among the student's respondents. The content unlocking, present among the game mechanics as *Cognitionis Spell*, which a student-player can receive if he reaches a score on specific competencies in each mission, meets the motivation of the Disruptor type, in addition to the Free Spirit, indicating its relevance to the gamified experience.

Although the achievement system, reproduced weekly in the game associated with Points, Badges, and Leaderboards related mechanics, doesn't meet the main type indicated by the student-players, it meets the following two, Achiever and Free Spirit. Finally, the clear rules system meets the Disruptor type, which is relevant for evaluating the experiment mechanics.

Thus, the authors believe the survey of types according to Marczewski's theory confirms the adequacy of the strategies and mechanics used in the project, ratifying the good path adopted in phases 1 and 2.

Discussion

For Huizinga (2017), playing is a voluntary and liberating act, a temporary escape from real life, transcending the immediate needs of life and giving meaning to this action. This concept, "Magic Circle", later re-discussed by Salen and Zimmerman (2003, 2012), proposes that the game creates a spatiotemporal delimitation around itself and the participants, within "the laws and customs of everyday life lose validity" (Huizinga, 2017, p. 16).

[...] a free activity, consciously taken as "non-serious" and external to normal life, but at the same time capable of absorbing the player intensely and totally. It is an activity disconnected from any material interest, with which no profit can be obtained, practiced within its own spatial and temporal limits, according to a certain order and certain rules. It promotes the formation of social groups that tend to surround themselves with secrecy and emphasize their difference from the rest of the world through disguises or other similar means. (Huizinga, 2017, p. 16).

Based on Wittgenstein's notion of "family resemblance", Raessens (2012) revisits and updates Huizinga's ideas, thinking beyond the notion of "game" as formalized play. Raessens argues that the six elements proposed by Huizinga's definition should be taken as criteria to consider the level of "playfulness" of different activities: 1) freedom and disinterest; 2) separation from everyday life – belonging to symbolic life, "make-believe"; 3) time and space limits and possibility of repetition; 4) fundamental and indisputable rules; 5) creating order in an imperfect world; 6) social engagement. The author thus separates "play" as a broader category, and "game" as formalized play. In his view, play is widely distributed in society, and even participates in a "playful turn" in media studies.

In this way, Raessens amplifies the debate and argues that ambiguities be included in the notion of game. In addition to education, he detects the interpenetration of play and playful elements in other areas, such as political mobilization, the military industry, and writing practices that emerge on the internet, even stating that we live in a "gamification of culture" (Raessens, 2006). Social media, film narrative experiments, and new ways of relating to media sources, including amateur production that resembles professional productions, would be signs of recent changes in the media ecosystem, which have boosted studies on the pervasiveness of the "play" in contemporary culture. If, for Huizinga, the technological development in the 20th century would have destroyed the meaning of playing in modern culture, for Raessens (2012) the Digital Technologies of Information and Communication enabled new ways of playing.

Considering the criteria posited by Raessens, the rules established, associated with the narrative and "make-believe" of the plot, the time and space limits of the discipline, and the social engagement on "creating order" in the imperfect Kingdom of Magisterium promoted an immersive, collaborative and creative context for the students from the first semester of the Journalism course. Thus, the adoption of active and innovative pedagogical methods which explore competencies and skills with game elements made it possible to combine systemic and procedural assessment in the discipline, as well as in knowledge construction, involving the production of media by students in the context of a playful experience. The gamification dynamics combined competition and collaboration in the search for knowledge and solution for proposed challenges. Associating the didactic challenge (in the week-by-week presentations elaboration and final assignment) with the playful challenge (in the points conquest to a personal score) balanced the gradual discipline content acquisition and the rules knowledge that structured the experience. To achieve the ludic objective, the student-players needed to pursue the didactic objective. The project evaluation indicates that dedication to the gamified course positively influenced academic engagement, stimulating access and meaningful learning about the contents, guaranteeing the student-player autonomy and independence in the educational process.

The authors believe they have presented an alternative to traditional learning methods, which consider the multimodal media context in which students are inserted, opening the way for greater interaction between them and their professors, which culminates in engagement and learning (Kapp, 2012). With such strategies, students are kept in a flow zone (Csikszentmihalyi, 2020), while promoting the development of cognitive processes through stimuli so absent in traditional teaching methods but clearly recognized when games are nearby.

The authors consider this project as a possible way to face the challenge of representing information and knowledge, in this socio-historical and technological reality, allowing students to experiment with verbal-visual forms (Brait, 2013) in different formats. Games, and gamified activities in general, allow contact with different realities, the weighing of rules and their negotiation, and the representation of causes and consequences within systems of relationships. Furthermore, they enable players, whether students or not, to develop their character potential in critical ways.

Vision of Future

This project, started in 2017, has been constantly evaluated and reconfigured, either because of the final evaluations of student-players about their experience and the systematic observation of the authors about the activities performed and their immediate results, or by the discussion of these data in the research group the authors integrate. In addition, it is necessary to remember the environmental change that teaching has undergone in recent years.

The first change that the authors intend to implement refers to the format of the game rules manual. Currently, it comprises a Power Point© file (Figure 12) with fifteen slides of information, due to the complexity of mechanics adopted in the game. Since the first phase of the experience, the manual has been redesigned, with concomitant use of verbal and visual language, to achieve a more effective understanding (Mayer & Clark, 2002). However, although with a decreasing rate, there are still student-players who reach the end of the school semester without having fully understood all the rules.

Figure 12. Slide page of the manual about the expert classes
Source: Authors

The first strategy adopted was the fragmentation of the rules' presentation during the academic semester, emphasizing the mechanics pertinent to each stage of the game experienced by the student-players. The second strategy will be to convert the manual from a non-interactive format to an interactive format, through an online app in which student-players can experience dynamically and interactively the game's rules and mechanics. This decision is part of an understanding that a gamified experience that uses interactive digital language needs to have a manual consistent with this same language, agreeing with Ham (2016) and Léste (2021), when they claim that the manual should mimic the game experience as much as possible, providing greater immersion of student-players

I'd like games to get to the point that when I buy one for a newbie they don't feel the need to wait for my teaching to be available before they can play. Better manuals certainly help in that regard, but if we're really going to appeal to a mainstream audience we have to have tutorial experiences that are frictionless and fun. We have that in precious few games now, but there's no reason we couldn't have it in many more. I'd much rather have a good manual than a bad one, but I'd much rather even a mediocre but interactive tutorial over a good manual. (Ham, 2016)

The second adjustment that is needed refers to the environmental change in Higher Education in Brazil. Because of the Covid-19 pandemic, the project was initially carried out in face-to-face format, phase 1, and is currently in phase 2, in remote format. However, the return to face-to-face teaching is approaching, due to the greater control of Coronavirus from the vaccination growth in Brazil. At this time, it is still unclear whether the next academic semester will be in a face-to-face or a hybrid format, but such changes need to be evaluated and implemented for a third phase of the project.

This is a challenge for which the authors haven't defined a clear strategy yet. On the one hand, the success of the project in recent semesters brings the hope that even with changes, the experience can still be successful. However, after two years of remote teaching, with intense use of technologies and digital media in various disciplines of Higher Education in Brazil (Eliezer, Ribeiro & Schutz, 2020), it is reasonable to assume that students do not adapt again to fully face-to-face and conventional teaching, as in the pre-pandemic format.

In this sense, the authors believe that they should maintain as many playful and academic mechanics as possible in the digital format, converting only the necessary to a face-to-face format, together with well-evaluated mechanics in the first and second phases. One of these mechanics refers to the distribution and exchange of playing cards between student-players. In digital format, the playing cards are distributed two by two on student-players' course's web pages, without a draw, which eliminates the luck factor in acquiring more "valuable" and interesting content instead of more casual ones. This variability is still one of the most commented mechanics by former students of the discipline, strengthening the playful aspect and engagement in the game.

Although the authors do not have, at this moment, clarity of some of the strategies to be adopted to adapt the project to changes in scenario and increasingly improve the experience, this quick look at the future allows them a glimpse of what's to come, brings the hope of longevity for the project and the possibility of contributing even more to higher education in Brazil.

REFERENCES

Alves, L. R. G. (2009). *Educação a distância: O estado da arte* [Online distance learning: The state of art]. Pearson Education do Brasil.

Bartle, R. (1996). Hearts, clubs, diamonds, spades: Players who suits MUDs. *Journal of MUD Research, 1*(1), 19.

Bíró, G. I. (2014). Didactics 2.0: A pedagogical analysis of gamification theory from a comparative perspective with a special view to the components of learning. *Procedia: Social and Behavioral Sciences, 141*, 148–151. doi:10.1016/j.sbspro.2014.05.027

Brait, B. (2013). Olhar e ler: Verbo-visualidade em perspectiva dialógica [Looking and reading: verb-visuality in a dialogic perspective]. *Bakhtiniana, 8*(2), 43–66. doi:10.1590/S2176-45732013000200004

Cook, D., Fulton, B., Gonzales, J., Bialoskursky, Y., & Fitch, M. (2016). *Game Design Patterns that Facilitate Strangers Becoming "Friends"* (The Eleventh Annual Game Design Think Tank: Project Horseshoe, 2016). Fat Labs Inc.

Csikszentmihalyi, M. (2020). *Finding Flow: The Psychology of Engagement with Everyday Life*. Basic Books.

Deterding, S., Khaled, R., Nacke, L. E., & Dixon, D. (2011). Gamification: toward a definition. In *Proceedings of Gamification Workshop - Conference on Human Factors in Computing Systems (CHI 2011)*. ACM.

Eliezer, C. R., Ribeiro, E. A., & Schutz, J. A. (2020). *A educação em tempos de pandemia: desafios e possibilidades* [Education in pandemic times: challenges and possibilities]. Dialética.

Farbiarz, A., & Farbiarz, J. L. (2008). A educação a distância online: a dicotomia no ciberespaço [Online distance learning: the dichotomy in cyberspace]. *Anais II Simpósio ABCiber - Associação Brasileira de Pesquisadores em Cibercultura,* 1-15. http://cencib.org/simposioabciber/PDFs/CC/Alexandre%20%20Farbiarz%20e%20Jackeline%20%20Farbiarz.pdf

Farbiarz, A., Xavier, G. A., Dias, C. M., & Farbiarz, J. L. (2019). A gamificação como processo metodológico na formação crítica contemporânea: Uma experiência aliando tecnologia, inovação e ludicidade no Ensino Superior [Gamification as a methodological process in contemporary critical education: an experience combining technology, innovation and playfulness in higher education]. *Logos, 26*, 229–244. https://www.e-publicacoes.uerj.br/index.php/logos/article/view/45676

Freire, P. (2020). *Pedagogia do oprimido* [Pedagogy of the oppressed] (17th ed.). Paz e Terra.

Gee, J. P. (2007). *What video games have to teach us about learning and literacy*. Macmillan.

Gee, J. P. (2015). *Unified discourse analysis: language, reality, virtual worlds, and video games*. Routledge.

Giroux, H. A. (2016). Pedagogia crítica, Paulo Freire e a coragem para ser político [Critical pedagogy, Paulo Freire and the courage to be politician]. *Revista e-Curriculum, 14*(1), 296-306. https://revistas.pucsp.br/index.php/curriculum/article/view/27356

Ham, E. (2016). *Tabletop Game Design for Video Game Designers*. Focal Press.

Huizinga, J. (2017). *Homo Ludens: o jogo como elemento da cultura* [Homo Ludens: the game as a cultural element] (8th ed.). Perspectiva.

Hunicke, R., Leblanc, M., & Zubek, R. (2004). MDA: a formal approach to game design and game research. In *Challenges in Games AI Workshop, Nineteenth National Conference of Artificial Intelligence Proceedings*. AAAI Press.

Kapp, K. M. (2012). *The gamification of learning and instruction: Game-based methods and strategies for training and education*. Pfeiffer.

Kellner, D. (2001). *A cultura da mídia – estudos culturais: Identidade e política entre o moderno e o pós-moderno* [Media culture - cultural studies: Identity and politics between the modern and the post-modern]. EDUSC.

Lemke, J. L. (2010). Letramento metamidiático: Transformando significados e mídias [Metamediatic literacy: transforming meanings and media]. *Trabalhos em Lingüística Aplicada, 49*(2), 455–479. doi:10.1590/S0103-18132010000200009

Léste, J. V. (2021). *The Informational Ergonomics of Tabletop Games' Rulebooks. An analysis on informational hierarchy and organization* (1916169/CA) [Masters Dissertation, Pontifical Catholic University of Rio de Janeiro]. Maxwell database.

Lipovetsky, G. (2004). *Os tempos hipermodernos* [Hypermodern times]. Bacarolla.

Marczewski, A. (2014) User types & player types in gamification. *Proceedings of Gamification World Congress.*

Marczewski, A. (2015). User Types. In A. Marczewski (Ed.), Even Ninja Monkeys Like to Play: gamification, game thinking and motivational design (pp. 65-80). CreateSpace independent Publishing Platform.

Mattar, J. (2009). Interatividade e aprendizagem [Interactivity and learning]. In F. M. Litto & M. Formiga (Eds.), *Educação a distância: o estado da arte* (pp. 112–118). Pearson Prentice Hall.

Mayer, R. E., & Clark, R. C. (2002). *E-Learning and the Science of Instruction: Proven Guidelines for Consumers and Designers of Multimedia Learning*. Pfeiffer.

Moita, F. (2007). *Game on: Jogos eletrônicos na escola e na vida da geração* [Game on: Electronic games at school and in the life of the generation @]. Alínea.

Murray, J. H. (2003). *Hamlet no Holodeck* [Hamlet on the Holodeck]. Itaú Cultural, UNESP.

Patricio, R., Moreira, A., Zurlo, F., & Melazzini, M. (2020). Co-creation of new solutions through gamification: A collaborative innovation practice. *Creativity and Innovation Management, 29*(1), 146–160. doi:10.1111/caim.12356

Protasio, A., & Dias, C. M. (2016). Narrativa nos jogos: uma oportunidade para autoria coletiva na escola [Narrative in games: an opportunity for collective authorship in schools]. In J. L. Farbiarz, A. Farbiarz, & B. J. W. Hemais (Eds.), *Design para uma educação inclusiva* (pp. 117–128). Blucher. Blucher.openaccess.blucher.com.br/article-details/narrativa-dos-jogos-uma-oportunidade-para-autoria-coletiva-na-escola-20195

Raessens, J. F. F. (2006). Playful Identities, or the Ludification of Culture. *Games and Culture, 1*(1), 52–57. doi:10.1177/1555412005281779

Raessens, J. F. F. (2012). *Homo Ludens 2.0: The ludic turn in media theory* (A. G. Fokkema, Trans.). Universiteit Utrecht, Faculteit Geesteswetenschappen.

Rivera, E. S., & Garden, C. L. P. (2021). Gamification for student engagement: A framework. *Journal of Further and Higher Education, 45*(7), 999–1012. doi:10.1080/0309877X.2021.1875201

Rossini, T. S. S., do Amaral, M. M., & Santos, E. (2021). The viralization of online education: Learning beyond the time of the coronavirus. *Prospects, 51*(1-3), 285–297. doi:10.100711125-021-09559-5 PMID:33967347

Ryan, R. M., & Deci, E. L. (2000). Self-determination theory and the facilitation of intrinsic motivation, social development, and well-being. *The American Psychologist, 55*(1), 68–78. doi:10.1037/0003-066X.55.1.68 PMID:11392867

Sailer, M., & Homner, L. (2020). The Gamification of Learning: A Meta-analysis. *Educational Psychology Review, 32*(1), 77–112. doi:10.100710648-019-09498-w

Salen, K., & Zimmerman, E. (2003). This is not a game: play in cultural environments. In *Level Up Conference Proceedings*. DIGRA.

Salen, K., & Zimmerman, E. (2012). *Regras do jogo: Fundamentos do design de jogos* [Rules of play: Game design fundamentals]. Blucher.

Santos, E. O., & Weber, A. (2013). Educação e cibercultura: Aprendizagem ubíqua no currículo da disciplina didática [Education and cyberculture: ubiquitous learning in the didactic subject curriculum]. *Revista Diálogo Educacional, 13*(38), 285–303. doi:10.7213/dialogo.educ.7646

Siemens, G. (2005). Connectivism: A learning theory for the digital age. *International Journal of Instructional Technology & Distance Learning, 2*(1), 3–10. http://www.itdl.org/Journal/Jan_05/article01.htm

Surendeleg, G., Murwa, V., Yun, H. K., & Kim, Y. S. (2014). The role of gamification in education – a literature review. *Contemporary Engineering Sciences, 7*(29), 1609–1616. doi:10.12988/ces.2014.411217

Universidade Federal Fluminense. (2016). *Curso de Jornalismo - Projeto Pedagógico de Curso (PPC): Formulário nº 02 - Princípios Norteadores* [Journalism Course - Pedagogical Course Project (PPC): Form nº 02 - Guiding Principles]. Journalism Course.

Vasconcellos, M., Dias, C. M., Ribeiro, D., & Carvalho, F. G. (in press). Gamificação para o mundo real: Repensando práticas [Gamification for the real world: rethinking practices]. In Educação para Práticas Inovadoras, Lúdicas e Inclusivas: Contribuições para o ensino de graduação. Editora da UFF.

Werbach, K., & Hunter, D. (2012). *For the win: How game thinking can revolutionize your business.* Wharton Digital Press.

World Government Summit. (2016). *Gamification and the future of education.* Oxford Analytica. http://www.oxan.com

Zichermann, G., & Cunningham, C. (2011). *Gamification by Design: Implementing Game Mechanics in Web and Mobile Apps.* O'Reilly.

KEY TERMS AND DEFINITIONS

Critical Media Literacy: Subjects formation to media products critically reading, promoting critical and transformative social awareness.

Digital Information and Communication Technologies: Digital media, that is, technologies based in binary code that allow exchange of information and communication among people.

Embedded Narrative: The narrative developed by game designers, and embedded in the game, in the form of character descriptions, speech and dialogue, texts, music, visual representations, and even mechanics can compose the embedded narrative.

Emergent Narrative: The narrative, sequence of events and their meaning, which emerges from the interaction of players with the game and depends on the possibilities granted by the game system, the choices of players and the game state at each moment.

Gamification: The application of game elements, as systems of engagement, and game design principles to contexts other than games, especially education, marketing, and work environments.

Gender of Discourse: Relatively stable forms of discourse, linked to specific spheres of human communication and social action, realized through multimodal means of meaning production.

Mechanics: In games, the ways of "functioning", that is, the different ways in which objects relate to each other, and which generates dynamics through players' interactions.

Multimodality: A property of messages and media, which states that meaning is always produced via multiple modes of communication and their combinations (written, oral, visual, procedural, gestural, sound).

Suspension of Everyday Life: Elevation of the individual from his alienating routine to a moment of critical distance through art or science.

Chapter 21
Educational Opportunities of Virtual Game-Based Initiatives for Students With Disabilities

Adrián Martín-Gutiérrez
https://orcid.org/0000-0002-9309-9796
University of Valladolid, Spain

Luis Leal-Vega
https://orcid.org/0000-0002-7847-413X
University of Valladolid, Spain

Irene Alcoceba-Herrero
University of Valladolid, Spain

Joaquín Herrera-Medina
University of Valladolid, Spain

Juan Francisco Arenillas-Lara
University of Valladolid, Spain

María Begoña Coco-Martín
University of Valladolid, Spain

ABSTRACT

Digital game-based learning (DGBL) is a novel methodology implemented in many educational virtual settings to improve students´ attention, motivation, and engagement while learning. This chapter aims to provide insight into how game-based methods can enhance students' learning process with sensory, intellectual, and learning disabilities. Specifically, the key of this chapter is to assess the possibilities offered by the introduction of DGBL in educational contexts from a theoretical perspective to understand better the range of opportunities that it can mean for learning and, therefore, for the personal and professional development of people with sensory, intellectual, and learning disabilities.

DOI: 10.4018/978-1-6684-4287-6.ch021

INTRODUCTION

Today, disabled students continue to face certain difficulties in being able to actively participate in higher education or to successfully complete their curricula. In this sense, the development of digital tools is encouraging the introduction of electronic learning (e-learning) in educational environments, which can serve as a transformative agent to facilitate the learning process for all students. Within the educational methodologies compatible with e-learning, digital game-based learning (DGBL) is one of the trends that may have the greatest potential to involve students with different types of disabilities in primary, secondary, and post-secondary education. For this reason, these systems must be adapted to the specific needs of sensory-, intellectual-, and learning-disabled students in order to increase their access and participation in higher education and employment, especially now that the COVID-19 pandemic has led to the widespread use of distance learning.

It has been stated that DGBL can be beneficial for the development of learning skills and formative development of people with sensory, intellectual, and learning disabilities (Zin et al., 2009). In this sense, it has been argued that the introduction of game-based mechanics in the educational context stimulates students' intellectual development, motivates their curiosity for further discovery, and enhances their creativity. In addition, from an emotional point of view, DGBL facilitates the possibility of acquiring confidence and independence, as the games force them to make decisions on their own, also allowing the idea of complying with the rules and requirements established in the game, which is fundamental for the student's development in the context of society.

The objective of this chapter is to assess whether, as a theoretical approach, e-learning systems complemented with a DGBL approach can lead to better learning outcomes or contrasted improvements in skills involved in learning for students with sensory, intellectual, and learning disabilities. In this way, this chapter seeks to emphasize the importance of the possibilities offered by the introduction of DGBL in the field of students with sensory, intellectual, and learning disabilities. The literature review of DGBL applied to the learning process of these types of students hopes to contribute to an increase in these students' access to DGBL, which could increase their opportunities of access to education and future employment. The methodology of literature review and analysis is based on an exploratory search of articles published in the last 20 years, written in English, taking into account PubMed and Google Scholar online databases, and introducing terms related to DGBL initiatives applied to students with sensory, intellectual, and learning disabilities.

BACKGROUND

Traditional games focus solely on entertainment, whereas gamified education serves to achieve objectives and provide values beyond leisure. In this sense, the incorporation of game elements has the potential to enhance the experience of the individuals participating in this educational methodology (Patrício et al., 2018). Currently, DGBL is performed through digital media such as computers or mobile phones in different areas (education, health, business, etc.) to meet the learning demands of a target population by simulating real-world situations and training a wide range of skills while promoting entertainment, motivation, satisfaction, ideation, and so forth (Agogué et al., 2015; Kultima et al., 2008).

The methodological foundations of DGBL applied in educational settings are based on a number of key aspects (Huang et al., 2019). First, the sharing of future goals or objectives allows for the establishment and maintenance of social relationships with others. Next, the concession of merits or rewards provides strong and positive feedback that motivates continuous learning. In addition, the comparison of merits achieved among students increases competitiveness and encourages their involvement in improving their learning outcomes. It is therefore essential that game-based educational interventions provide appropriate feedback to users through positive reinforcement such as notifications, badges, points, and medals to let them know they are on the right track in their academic journey.

DGBL applied to support people with sensory, intellectual, and learning disabilities should comprise three areas: therapy, immersion, and personalization. First, the therapeutic aspect should be included in any design within a DGBL framework, as it has been shown that the application of gamified techniques can contribute to achieving therapeutic goals for students with disabilities by improving impaired skills and increasing motivation and engagement to achieve long-term behavioral change (Malinverni et al., 2017). Second, regarding the immersive aspect, modern technologies such as virtual reality have been shown to stimulate user interactivity and offer greater opportunities for immersion and interaction. Thirdly, personalization is another essential component, as it is necessary to respond to the wide range of needs expressed by different groups of learners, especially those with disabilities. In this sense, as stated by Van Dooren et al. (2019), the ultimate goal of DGBL is to provide an experience that is as realistic and tailored as possible, with which users can identify and be aware of the benefits it can bring them.

Students with sensory disabilities (visual, hearing, or both) face a number of barriers to achieving their academic goals. The main challenges faced by these students are related to factors such as using handheld devices, completing timed tasks, obtaining appropriate feedback, and adopting teamwork mechanisms. In this regard, information and communication technologies have certainly become the most appropriate tool to help this group exercise their right to education, mainly through the development and distribution of adapted educational content (Laabidi et al., 2014). However, another key aspect to ensure good learning outcomes for these students is the introduction of appropriate educational methods that motivate and engage them, as it has been proven that successful learning does not depend exclusively on the use of information and communication technologies, but also on the students' own self-motivation to study (Gillet-Swan, 2017). In this way, it is understood that the introduction of game mechanics can encourage students with sensory disabilities to become more motivated and interact more intensely with electronic educational content, giving them the freedom to fail without fear when learning and providing immediate feedback through the achievement of badges, medals, trophies, or rewards (Lee & Hammer, 2011).

Within intellectual disabilities, one of the most common neurodevelopmental disorders is autism spectrum disorder (ASD), which affects three main areas: communication, social interaction, and impulse control. ASD include various forms depending on its grade of severity, from Asperger's syndrome, as high-functioning ASD, to the so-called Rett syndrome, the most acute type of ASD (Wong & Kasari, 2012). In this sense, Wong & Kasari (2012) affirm that the introduction of individual gamified practices for educational purposes for children with ASD, especially from mild to moderate, can positively influence their learning process as these students often show less interest in joining a shared activity or staying focused on a common goal Accordingly, DGBL can provide reinforcement to motivate these students to remain committed to their learning goals and serve as a valuable tool for teaching them not only educational contents, but also principles on social skills, emotion recognition, and other abilities they find difficult to develop (Hassan et al., 2021).

Dyslexia, one of the most prevalent learning difficulties, can have a negative impact on both self-esteem and academic aspirations of a student. Through the use of DGBL, the severity of this disorder can be reduced by implementing interactive exercises based on reading fluency, phonetical awareness, phonics, vocabulary, and comprehension, increasing the student's desire to continue the learning process and progress in their academic pathway (Vellutino et al., 2004). In other hand, attention deficit hyperactivity disorder (ADHD) is another prevalent learning disability in which students present impulsivity, difficulty concentrating, and difficulty controlling behavior. ADHD is usually diagnosed before the age of 18, which can be a major impediment to the achievement of adequate academic qualifications for those affected, whose numbers have been significantly increasing in the last years (Lis et al., 2016). In this sense, Lis et al. (2016) affirm that DGBL applied to students with ADHD principally aims to make the learning process more engaging and enjoyable.

MAIN FOCUS OF THE CHAPTER

The chapter presents a compilation of real DGBL initiatives applied to students with sensory, intellectual, and learning disabilities. In this sense, DGBL aims to be a tool for students with disabilities, providing a series of opportunities to improve their learning.

Opportunities for Students with Sensory Disabilities

There are several practical examples of how DGBL can contribute to the learning process of students with sensory disabilities (visual, hearing, or both). Authors such as Smith and Abrams (2019) affirm that the main challenges faced by these students in this regard are the use of handheld devices, the completion of timed tasks, the provision of appropriate feedback, and the adoption of multilevel scenarios. These same authors expose how DGBL can contribute to improve this experience for students, highlighting the potential of implementing audio and video tracks in online courses, accompanied by written transcripts compliant with the assistive technology of W3C Web Accessibility Initiative standards that implements alternative audio and text cues in headings, spaces, tables and form fields. Table 1 below lists the analyzed game-based initiatives for students with sensory disabilities.

In the field of mathematics, Ferreira and Cavaco (2014) decided to design a DGBL personal computer learning environment for students with visual disabilities in order to enhance their learning and expand their opportunities to pursue higher education in related areas such as science and engineering. The system sought to motivate and engage students in the learning process as they played, using a captivating story that integrated a reward system with audible "Correct!" feedback each time the student got a particular mathematical question right. Importantly, during the development of the platform, the graphics were adapted to provide accessibility for both low-vision and blind students, as all features were complemented with spatialized 2D-audio throughout the scenes. The final prototype was tested with six ninth-grade students from two different secondary schools (one blind and one visually impaired student had access to the game compared to two visually impaired and two sighted students who did not play). Finally, the analysis of the test results used to evaluate the effectiveness of the intervention before and after one month of use showed that DGBL had a positive impact on students' performance in learning mathematics, interest in lessons, and the student-teacher relationship. In addition, the students enjoyed the adventure and story modes proposed of the game and reported that the audio was sufficient to enjoy the activity.

In other areas such as geometry, DGBL can also be implemented to enhance learning for students with sensory impairments through the design of accessible gamified learning objects (GLOs). In this

Table 1. Analysis of game-based initiatives for students with sensory disabilities

Authors	Name	Participants	Results
Ferreira & Cavaco (2014)	DGBL personal computer learning environment	6 9th-grade students from two Portuguese secondary schools (2 sighted, 3 visually impaired, and 1 blind)	Positive impact on students' performance in mathematics, interest in lessons and the student-teacher relationship.
De Souza Sombrio et al. (2016)	Accessible gamified learning objects	N/A: technical paper	The learning objects bring the possibility for people with disabilities to personalize their learning environment and to promote the knowledge access.
Ferreira et al. (2016)	Development process of a gamified learning object for teaching geometry	N/A: technical paper	Showing great interest in the game like a great tool to make educational activities concerned from accessibility criteria.
Rodríguez et al. (2018)	CPRforBlind	16 volunteer graduate students from the University of Girona (8 sighted, 8 blind)	All participants enjoyed the game, and blind users found it especially easy to play. Nevertheless, the students said that the game needs to be repeated several times.
Ghergulescu et al. (2019)	Atomic Structure Virtual Lab	12 hearing impaired students from an Irish secondary school	There were positive changes in students' motivation, attitude, and affective state. Students found the platform accessible, useful, and easy to use.
Samonte (2020)	Assistive technology, speech recognition, online handwritten character recognition	5 hearing-impaired and speech-impaired 11th- and 12th-grade students from a Philippine secondary school	Hearing and speech disabilities could benefit more from the use of the assessed assistive technologies, improving their performance in basic statistics.
Neto et al. (2020)	Em Busca do Santo Grau	17 volunteers (5 sighted, 4 color blind, 5 visually impaired, and 3 blind).	The adapted version of the game can be a valuable tool for primary and higher education teachers who want to have a digital resource to work with their students in a playful way.

Source: Own elaboration

line, De Souza Sombrio et al. (2016) proposed to relate the concepts of learning objects (LOs) in order to produce educational content accessible to students with visual and hearing disabilities. The objective was to improve the teaching and learning process of calculating the perimeter of triangles presented in an accessible platform, in which the character Elvis led the student's immersion in the flow state together with the accessibility features: audio description, video in sign language, high contrast, font size, subtitles, and other possibilities of exploring accessibility resources. As result, the LOs bring the possibility for people with sensory disabilities to personalize their learning environment and to promote the knowledge access.

Similarly, Ferreira et al. (2016) presented an accessible platform designed for deaf and hard-of-hearing students and an accessible development process of a GLO for teaching geometric content about "Triangles and their characteristics." This GLO, developed by the Graduate Program in Design at the Federal University of Parana, consisted of requirements, conceptual design (concept map and storyboard), and digital modeling. That interface incorporated playful elements in order to present immersive and interactive content, with a practical navigation module for blind and visually impaired students in which information was transmitted with a voice-over. As result, this game had very positive reactions from visually impaired students and their teachers, showing the game was a great tool to make educational activities more accessible.

In a different way, Rodríguez et al. (2018) opted to use a DGBL approach with the aim of teaching the steps of the cardiopulmonary resuscitation (CPR) protocol to students with visual impairment. The proposed game (CPRforBlind) was intended to teach the CPR steps proposed by the European Resuscitation Council through a series of mini-games in which the student had to save the main character using a high-sensitive touch screen as an input method while a recorded voice message described the situation, the challenge, and the actions to be performed to achieve the goal. A pilot study was conducted in which eight sighted and eight blind students from the University of Girona (Spain) answered a questionnaire related to their CPR knowledge before and after playing. Before playing, participants had an average score of 2 on the CPR knowledge questionnaires, but after playing, this average score increased to 9.43 and 10, respectively. In addition, all participants enjoyed the game, and blind users found it especially easy to play. Nevertheless, the students said that the game needs to be repeated several times. In the future, new versions of the game with extra aids are suggested, with the addition of a practice mode for students to feel more confident with the mini-game before achieving the final goal.

With regard to improving the practice of sensory-impaired students in STEM disciplines (science, technology, engineering and mathematics), Ghergulescu et al. (2019) developed a virtual laboratory that allows students with hearing disabilities to perform science experiments remotely whenever they wish as part of the European Horizon 2020 (H2020) project NEWTON. The aim was to place the student at the center of the learning experience by applying innovative pedagogies like self-directed learning-based learning with DGBL and special adaptations such as sign language translation for the target population. The Atomic Structure Laboratory designed was tested in a pilot study that included 12 hearing-impaired students from an Irish secondary school. Specifically, an analysis was conducted before and after a trial session in order to assess the effectiveness of the virtual lab in terms of knowledge achievement, students' motivation in relation to STEM subjects, and creative thinking. At the end of the session, only a small increase in students' learning outcomes was observed. However, there were positive changes in students' motivation, attitude, and affective state in relation to STEM dimensions and creative thinking in terms of originality, fluency, and flexibility, as measured by the Torrance Creative Thinking Test questionnaire. Moreover, most students found the platform accessible, useful, and easy to use.

The introduction of game mechanics to teach applied statistics to students with different forms of disabilities, including hearing, has been also studied by authors such as Samonte (2020), who proposed using a web-based application containing different assistive technologies to teach statistics to disabled students. The system can be opened in laptops, tablets, and smartphones and is able to read 90 characters including numbers, lower and upper case letters, and special characters. Particularly, the system was intended to teach statistics to students with hearing and speech disabilities, through the practical activity of mathematical problems and the use of online handwriting recognition to verify their handwritten answers. The usability results showed that five 11th- and 12th-grade students with hearing and speech disabilities could benefit more from the use of the assessed assistive technologies, suggesting that repeated exposure to these gamified materials may further improve their performance in basic statistics.

Lastly, Neto et al. (2020) developed a version of the educational video game Em Busca do Santo Grau adapted to secondary and post-secondary students with visual disabilities. This game was integrated into the REMAR platform (an open platform in which it is possible to create customized instances of games directly by the teacher) and was based on EduGameAccess, a set of recommendations that integrate some important aspects such as playability, accessibility, and educational considerations for people with visual disabilities. The usability test was carried out with 17 volunteers (five sighted, four color blind, five with low vision, and three totally blind) to identify the main problems related to playability according to the eGameFlow scale (Fu et al., 2009), a validated instrument to measure student's enjoyment of a game. Preliminary results showed that the adapted version of the game can be a valuable tool for primary and higher education teachers who want to have a digital resource to work with their students on different content in a playful way. Despite this, there is still not enough evidence of the learning outcomes that can be achieved with this resource.

Opportunities for Students with Intellectual Disabilities

Children with ASD have difficulties practicing social skills, finding it difficult to understand non-verbal cues and to interact socially with others. Over the years, different game-based initiatives have been proposed to address these problems. According to Alvares et al. (2019), the use of a wide variety of educational games aimed at these students has recently been explored, with promising results in terms of improving their learning outcomes. These findings have led to the widespread design and evaluation of gamified interventions that aim to foster independence and improve learning outcomes for children with ASD. Table 2 below shows the analyzed game-based initiatives for students with ASD.

In the study by Battocchi et al. (2010), involving both children with typical development (70) and children with ASD (16), it was observed that both groups benefited from the presence of rules that shaped the interaction when solving the task of completing a puzzle on an interactive touch screen table. Specifically, the study was conducted with the collaborative puzzle game, which involved two players moving pieces together with their fingertips. After completing the puzzle, users received visual and auditory feedback alerting them if they had made a mistake or congratulating them on successfully completing the puzzle. The results showed how there were more coordinated interactions between players who had to move the puzzle pieces together. In this way, GPC can be a useful tool to foster social interactions and communication skills among children with ASD, having the potential to even improve problem-solving skills and coordination of body movements, which is essential for ASD children with motor difficulties.

On the other hand, Tanaka et al. (2010) developed the Let's Face It! video game, comprising seven interactive computer games targeting specific face impairments associated with ASD, including the recognition of identity across image changes in expression, viewpoint and features, analytic and holistic face processing strategies, and attention to information in the eye region. In addition, the game also integrated a series of rewards and incentives for ASD children, such as a high-score table. For the purposes of the study, a group of 42 children with ASD received 20 hours of training with Let's Face It! compared to a control group that comprised 37 children with ASD who did not play the game. After training, participants experienced some improvement in two of the seven skills tested: eye and mouth recognition. Although the rest of the subtests did not show substantial improvement after the intervention, it could be interesting to continue testing Let's Face It! to train facial identity recognition skills in children with ASD for longer periods of time, as the game is freely available and not very demanding in terms of computational requirements.

Similarly, Whalen et al. (2010) focused on developing the computer skills of students with ASD through another computer-based game, TeachTown. A total of 47 preschool and K-1 students with ASD participated in the trial, which involved 20 minutes per day of TeachTown use and 20 minutes per day of other complementary non-computer activities over a period of three months. At the end of the trial, ASD students showed more improvement overall on language and cognitive outcome measures. ASD

Table 2. Analyzed Game-based initiatives targeting students with intellectual disabilities

Authors	Name	Participants	Results
Battocchi et al. (2010)	Collaborative Puzzle Game	16 children with ASD 70 children with typical development	Can be a useful tool to foster social interactions and communication skills, having the potential to even improve problem-solving skills and coordination of body movements.
Tanaka et al. (2010)	Let's Face It!	42 children with ASD 37 children with ASD (control group)	Participants experienced some improvement in two of the seven skills tested: eye and mouth recognition, but, the rest of the subtests did not show substantial improvement.
Whalen et al. (2010)	TeachTown	47 preschool and K-1 students with ASD	Students showed more improvement overall on language and cognitive outcome measures, and better develop their computer skills.
Ferguson et al. (2013)	Wii Sports	6 children with ASD	The autistic children were observed to improve their physical object control skills and their ability to socially interact competitively or cooperatively with their peers.
Mazurek et al. (2015)	Adaptive Video Games	11 children with ASD	Participants enjoyed challenge with adaptive game technologies because automatically adjust game difficulty for each individual player, fostering competence while minimizing their frustration.
Malinverni et al. (2017)	Pico's Adventure	10 children with ASD	The use of elements and mechanics that were appealing for the children were an essential aspect of the study's success.
Silva-Calpa et al. (2018)	CoASD	7 children with ASD	The game helped to draw the users' attention to perceive and perform the tasks, motivating them to act and collaborate with their peers.
Navan & Khaleghi (2020)	LIFE is GAME	10 children with ASD 10 children with typical development	This game can have a positive effect on the development of their social skills, and identify facial expressions associated with emotional states.
Lee et al. (2020)	PuzzleWalk	9 adults with ASD 9 adults with typical development	This app could contribute to improve various aspects of cognitive and personal development in people with ASD: psychological outcomes such as autonomy, perceived competence, intrinsic enjoyment and motivation.
Bukvic et al. (2014), Greitemeyer & Mügge, (2014), Cadieux & Keenan, (2020)	Minecraft	N/A: technical paper	This game makes it possible for players to explore the entire virtual world by creating their own narrative. Can be a valuable tool to promote active socialization with other people, building interaction skills applicable to the real-world problems faced by children with ASD.

Source: Own elaboration

students who used TeachTown also demonstrated significant progress in the software and those students who used the program for more time demonstrated larger gains within the software and in cognitive outcome measures. In this way, the game enriched typical classroom teaching and was observed that young children with ASD who used the system were able to better develop their computer skills and make progress in their learning.

In a similar way, Ferguson et al. (2013) used a behavioral skills training approach to teach three sportsmanship skills (i.e., complimenting, turn taking, and being a good sport) during video game play (Wii Sports). Specifically, six children with ASD participated in this study, practicing their social skills through whole body movement. The authors decided to use the Nintendo Wii game console, as it has motion-sensing technologies and a pointing device (remote control) as a means of transmitting whole body or arm movement. In this way, students with ASD were able to interact within the video game environment using whole body movement to mimic real-life reactions, such as hitting a virtual tennis ball by moving the arm. As a result, the children were observed to improve their physical object control skills and their ability to socially interact competitively or cooperatively with their peers.

Within this line of research, it is worth mentioning that individuals with ASD increasingly suffer from health problems stemming from physical inactivity as a result of pervasive social deficits and restricted behavior patterns. In the study carried out by Mazurek et al. (2015), a trial was also conducted with adaptive video games that required participants to perform whole-body movements to interact with the game. This pilot study investigated whether playing video games can increase real object control skills in 11 children with ASD, with the results showing how this practice improved not only their psychomotor skills, but also their self-esteem. Specifically, the results indicate that many participants enjoyed challenges with adaptive game technologies because they automatically adjust game difficulty for each individual player based on their in-game performance, fostering competence while minimizing their frustration. The study also exposes that the game features that may enhance player experiences are greater emphasis on visual graphics, story-based elements, game rewards, and achievements. In addition, it has also been proposed that this methodology may be suitable for mixed classrooms of children with typical development and children with ASD.

Malinverni et al. (2017) aimed to promote social initiation in high-functioning children with ASD by playing the video game Pico's Adventure for the Xbox 360 Kinect console. Notably, the game was co-designed with children with ASD and with professionals who work with people with ASD, focusing on creating an interesting narrative and a game system that motivates body movement and social interaction among these students. In Pico's Adventure, children basically had to help the alien Pico complete different missions to fix his spaceship over the course of four sessions in which children practiced skills of cooperation and joint attention to the goal with their peers. Findings from a first exploratory study in which 10 children with ASD were recruited showed the potential of the game to elicit social initiation behaviors. Thus, the researchers argued that Pico's Adventure could be included in school curricula to encourage the development of social skills in children with ASD, concluding that the use of elements and mechanics that were appealing for the children were an essential aspect of the study's success.

Following this line of research, Silva-Calpa et al. (2018) evaluated the effectiveness of the game CoASD (Collaborative Game for people with Autism Spectrum Disorder), consisting of driving a car along a road and parking it inside a garage before the garage door closes on a multi-touch laptop, to promote collaborative work in students with ASD. The intervention involved seven children with ASD, and the results showed that the game helped to draw the users' attention to perceive and perform the tasks, motivating them to act and collaborate with their peers. In this sense, is concluded that collaborative games contribute positively to motivate users with ASD, mainly those with a higher degree of impairment, enabling them to learn about collaboration. However, during the study, some difficulties faced by some participants when dealing with the interface elements provided highlights the great importance of a careful design of all game features.

In another study, Navan and Khaleghi (2020) evaluated the effectiveness of LIFE is GAME, a serious game designed for learning facial emotions based on the interaction between humans and three-dimensional avatars using real-time synthesis and automatic analysis of facial expressions. LIFE is GAME consisted of four different modules (Face Detection, Face Creation, Avatar Creation, and Story Experience). With this structure, various activities were presented to the user to understand emotions, their causes and consequences, and facial expressions tailored to any sense. For the evaluation of the system, 10 children with ASD and 10 typically developing children (control group) performed eight sessions of one hour in which a Child Behavior Checklist (CBCL) was used to measure the effectiveness of the intervention in reducing the behavioral problems of children who participated. The results indicated that the use of DGBL to educate autistic children, especially those with mild to moderate ASD, can have a positive effect on the development of their social skills, as at the end of the test, ASD participants were able to detect and identify facial expressions associated with emotional states taught in the game.

The use of mobile technologies in conjunction with DGBL also presents a great innovative opportunity to enhance the abilities of children with ASD. For example, in the study conducted by Lee et al. (2020), a mobile application centered on the IDEAS (Integrate, Design, Evaluate, and Share) framework and that incorporated a gamified approach was developed for children with ASD: PuzzleWalk mobile application. To test the system, 18 adults with (9) and without (9) ASD participated in a mixed methods study consisting of a cognitive walkthrough, usability testing, and qualitative interviews. The results of the usability testing indicated a satisfactory quality of the system that can be easily applied to both adults with and without ASD. On the other hand, qualitative interviews identified notable issues that address critical insights into the social needs of adults with ASD. Finally, it was concluded that this app could contribute to improve various aspects of cognitive and personal development in people with ASD in real-world settings, based on psychological outcomes such as autonomy, perceived competence, desire to continue, and intrinsic enjoyment and motivation.

Finally, one of the most widespread initiatives in the field of educational DGBL is the use of the video game Minecraft, which employs a block-based construction mechanics in an open world, where users navigate through an avatar viewing the environment in first person, increasing their sense of immersion. According to Bukvic et al. (2014), one of the differences between Minecraft and other DGBL initiatives is that the game is completely free-form, with no specific goals or objectives. This makes it possible for players to explore the entire virtual world by creating their own narrative while adapting the environment to their liking. Furthermore, in today's world, where social and online games are becoming increasingly popular, it has been argued that video games such as Minecraft can be a valuable tool to promote active socialization with other people (Greitemeyer & Mügge, 2014). For these reasons, more recently, some authors such as Cadieux and Keenan (2020) have highlighted the opportunities that Minecraft can have for building interaction skills applicable to the real-world problems faced by children with ASD.

Opportunities for Students with Learning Disabilities

Students With Dyslexia

Dyslexia is considered a prevalent learning condition that affects an individual's ability to read, spell, and comprehend language when reading or writing. According to Vellutino et al. (2004), professionals need to spend between 80 and 100 hours to engage students with dyslexia in class, compared to students without dyslexia, who need between 30 and 60 hours. Often, this amount of instruction does not take place in schools. In this sense, the use of DGBL systems can improve the attention span of these students, as well as allow access to educational resources at any time and place. Table 3 presents the analysis of game-based initiatives for learners with dyslexia.

One of the first authors to explore this line of research was Saputra and Risqi (2015), who developed a learning model for dyslexic children using DGBL as motivational affordance to improve the

Table 3. Analysis of game-based initiatives targeting students with dyslexia

Authors	Name	Participants	Results
Saputra & Risqi (2015)	Lexi Pal	40 children with dyslexia	The participants remained interested throughout the session, had fun while playing, and agreed they would use it again.
Dymora & Niemiec (2019)	Mobile application	12 children with dyslexia	The use of this mobile application improved the text-retention capacity during the dictations performed by school children.
Tulloch & Pammer (2019)	Portable game-like technology	83 children with dyslexia	This portable technology can serve to detect children at greater risk of learning disabilities and to improve the skills affected in the classroom and at home.
Bjekić et al. (2020)	Augmented Reality	N/A: technical paper	Game-based AR systems can lead to saving time in explanations as well as to an increase in students' interest in the lesson, through a three-dimensional environment that engages students with dyslexia.
Jaramillo-Alcázar et al. (2021)	Puzzle Pieces Video Game	N/A: technical paper	This method could contribute to improving the neurocognitive skills of children with dyslexia, taking into account the premise of short task duration to avoid loss of attention and interest.

Source: Own elaboration

psychological outcomes of engagement and enjoyment. The resulting application (Lexi Pal), based on Windows Presentation Foundation technology, was tested in 40 children with dyslexia through two steps, qualitative and quantitative. The results of the usability testing showed that 92.5% of the participants remained interested throughout the application session, 100% had fun while playing, and 96.67% agreed they would use it again.

Similarly, Dymora and Niemiec (2019) designed another mobile application based on the implementation of original algorithms and scenarios of DGBL on mobile devices to improve the effects of therapy for dyslexic children. For the study, 12 school children with dyslexia were asked to take a dictation test before and after accessing the application. As result, the control group that did not have access to the application omitted 24.12% of the text in the first dictation and up to 28.85% in the second, compared to 5.88% and 7.66% in the group that used the application. Thus, it could be said that the use of this mobile application improved the text-retention capacity during the dictations performed by school children.

As recent evidence suggests a link between deficits in visuo-spatial attention and reading ability, Tulloch and Pammer (2019) proposed to determine whether subtle visual deficits in poor readers could be detected in relatively uncontrolled environments using portable game-like technology. For the purpose of the research, the classic visual search and change detection programs were modified to a game format and administered on a portable tablet computer to 83 children with dyslexia. Results were consistent with the visuo-spatial attention deficit hypothesis, indicating that reading ability is related to the visual search task of these people. This is a strong argument for the development of portable visual assessment tools that can be used to detect children at greater risk of learning disabilities. Importantly, the influence of incorporating DGBL into programs designed not only to assess, but also to improve the skills affected by these individuals in the classroom and at home should also be explored.

In a novel way, Bjekić et al. (2020) addressed the implementation of augmented reality (AR) as a supportive tool for the learning of school children with dyslexia. AR is an information and communication technology tool that enables users to see and experience the real world mixed with various virtual objects, without losing the sense of reality. In this context, AR can integrate interactive reading and

DGBL elements to create a suitable environment for learner-centered and experience-based education. Notably, Game-based AR systems can lead to a saving of time in explanations as well as to an increase of student's interest in the lesson, as content is immediately represented in a three-dimensional environment that engages students to a greater extent. All these reasons support the functionality of game-based AR systems as a useful resource to consider in inclusive education.

More recently, Jaramillo-Alcázar et al. (2021) proposed the Puzzle Pieces Video Game to improve the treatment of dyslexia through the collection of data obtained from two puzzles designed to train certain cognitive skills affected by this disorder. The game had a friendly design for intuitive interaction, with colorful backgrounds to attract attention, large print with a font for children, simple words and instructions, and children's background music. Unfortunately, there are no data available on their effectiveness, although it is known that DGBL incorporated into current dyslexia treatment methods could contribute to improving the neurocognitive skills of children with dyslexia. In this sense, the design of video games for this group of people should be based on the premise of short task duration to avoid loss of attention and interest.

Students With ADHD

ADHD is defined as a prevalent neurobehavioral disorder and is commonly diagnosed in a large number of children and adolescents under the age of 18. According to the grade of attention presented by the children, ADHD can be divided into three types: predominantly inattentive ADHD-I (when the person continuously switches activities and has difficulty concentrating on a task), impulsive ADHD-HI predominantly hyperactive (when the person has difficulty sitting still or waiting), and ADHD-C hybrid type (combining the symptoms of the two previous typologies) (Lis et al., 2016).

A characteristic shared by children with ADHD is that they quickly lose interest in activities that they are performing and do not tend to pay attention continuously to complete long tasks, which causes them to require immediate rewards in a short time period. As stated by Bul et al. (2018), gamified initiatives can significantly contribute to engage these students in the learning process. In addition, Fabio and Antonietti (2012) demonstrated that the use of multimedia content such as images, videos, graphics, or hyperlink texts can lead ADHD students to reach achievement levels similar to those of typically developing students. Table 4 shows the analysis of game-based initiatives for students with ADHD.

In a systematic review exploring original studies investigating the efficacy of video game-based interventions or video-game-based assessment tools in children with ADHD, Peñuelas-Calvo et al. (2020) found that assessment tools incorporating gamified elements are effective in discriminating ADHD cases from controls, as well as in discriminating between different ADHD subtypes. Specifically, it is pointed out that the evaluation and performance of therapeutic interventions for children with ADHD through the use of video games can be a complement to traditional health care, serving as an objective measurement tool before specialized medical care is carried out.

Likewise, video-game-based therapeutic interventions are well accepted and generally effective in improving cognition and decreasing ADHD symptoms. Evidence of this was provided by Crepaldi et al. (2020), who presented a computer-based game (Antonyms) in which the user plays a superhero who had to free the planet from enemies, crossing different scenarios. To do so, the user should change their attitude by thinking before performing any action rather than acting on impulse. Results from the evaluation of a preliminary version of the game in eight children with ADHD and 30 children with typical development, matched for age and gender, showed that the ADHD group obtained very similar scores

Table 4. Analysis of game-based initiatives targeting students with ADHD

Authors	Name	Participants	Results
Peñuelas-Calvo et al. (2020)	Game-based assessment for therapeutic interventions	N/A: systematic review	Assessment tools incorporating gamified elements are generally effective in discriminating ADHD cases from controls, and between different ADHD subtypes.
Crepaldi et al. (2020)	Antonyms	8 children with ADHD 30 children with typical development	ADHD group obtained very similar scores to the larger sample of typically developed children, representing a promising methodology to target impulsivity control in children with ADHD.
Ahmad et al. (2020)	Mathefunic	Children with ADHD (N/A: number of participants)	The participants enjoyed the mobile game and agreed that it was able to capture and retain their attention, being satisfied with how easy it was to start, navigate through, and play.

Source: Own elaboration

to the larger sample of typically developed children, concluding that DGBL represents a promising methodology to target impulsivity control in children with ADHD.

On the other hand, DGBL applied to mobile learning can also be seen as a promising tool for ADHD students, given its ease of access at any time and place, thus eliminating the distance-time barrier between teachers and learners (Ally & Prieto-Blázquez, 2014). Following this line of research, Ahmad et al. (2020) designed the Mathefunic mobile game to engage children with ADHD and retain their attention. Participants (children with ADHD) played the mobile game for an average of 20 minutes voluntarily, and then responded to usability testing, which showed they enjoyed the game and agreed that it was able to capture and retain their emotion and increase it motivation. In addition, children were also satisfied with how easy it was to start, navigate through, and play the mobile game.

DISCUSSION

Throughout this chapter, publications have been compiled and analyzed that affirm that the implementation of DGBL initiatives for students with sensory, intellectual, and learning disabilities allows the creation and sharing of information in a structured digital environment, achieving the proposed educational objectives (Patrício et al., 2020). In this way, it can be understood that DGBL can be a powerful method not only to improve results related to the learning process, but also to develop psychological communication and socialization skills in children with these disabilities. In this way, the implementation of DGBL initiatives provides positive reinforcement to motivate these people to stay committed to their learning goals. However, when developing DGBL initiatives, the perceived benefits of video game use (e.g., social connection, stress reduction) as well as the perceived negative effects (e.g., time use, addictive potential) must be taken into account.

For students with sensory disabilities, authors like De Souza Sombrio et al. (2016) affirmed that the introduction of digital LOs offers the possibility for these students to personalize their learning environment and to promote knowledge access, introducing accessibility elements such as audio description, subtitles, or sign language translation. However, authors such as Rodríguez et al. (2018) stated that while blind participants enjoyed the personalized educational game, they had to repeat it several times until they fully understood how it worked. In this sense, DGBL initiatives must continue to improve in terms of accessibility and ease of use.

When developing new game-based interventions for individuals with intellectual disabilities like ASD, it has been shown that learning in a virtual environment minimizes problems related to learning transfer for students with ASD (Politis, 2017). In addition, multi-player or cooperative DGBL may be helpful in promoting social skills for individuals with ASD. A good example of this is the famous video game Minecraft, which makes it possible for players to explore the entire virtual world by creating their own narrative. Authors like Bukvic et al. (2014) and Cadieux and Keenan (2020) affirmed this can be a valuable tool to promote active socialization with other people and build interaction skills applicable to the real-world problem for children with ASD. However, authors like Mazurek et al. (2015) concluded that many individuals experienced negative social interactions through existing online multiplayer formats. Thus, it is important that DGBL developers consider ways of ensuring attractive and useful game communities for individuals with ASD.

In the field of students with learning disabilities like dyslexia, the initiatives with DGBL show that the participants remained interest throughout the session, had fun while playing, and agreed they would use it again (Saputra & Risqi, 2015). In this way, it is observed that the use of DGBL initiatives causes a greater commitment in the learning of this type of students. On the other hand, in the case of students with ADHD, authors such as Crepaldi et al. (2020) concluded that the DGBL implementation represents a promising methodology to target impulsivity control in children with ADHD. Furthermore, assessment tools incorporating gamified elements can be effective in discriminating between different ADHD subtypes (Peñuelas-Calvo et al., 2020). However, it is understood that more empirical evidence is still necessary to demonstrate that its use is appropriate in all types of situations, both learning and diagnostic.

FUTURE RESEARCH DIRECTIONS

This chapter compiles a number of game-based initiatives for students with sensory, intellectual, and learning disabilities. The great interest that exists on the subject is evident, since the number of research found is very high and continues to expand today. Even so, there is still much to be done to explore the influence of DGBL on the learning outcomes of students with sensory, intellectual, and learning disabilities. The benefits of DGBL are related to the possibility for educators to have more options to choose the most appropriate presentation of stimuli or content adapted to the specific needs of students. At the same time, most students with disabilities prefer to learn through educational games rather than books (Zain, 2021). Thus, there is a need for more research on DGBL that can overcome the limitations identified in terms of methods, sample, and short-term versus long-term results.

The possibility of incorporating DGBL as a multidisciplinary skills training method adapted to the special needs of students with sensory, intellectual, and learning disabilities is considered very interesting. In this way, the effectiveness of new online platforms and computer-based video games as modern educational technologies can be explored both in the classroom and at home. For this, new technological equipment is used to adapt DGBL to media such as computers, smartphones, large televisions, or even game consoles, usable anywhere and anytime. In general, all these forms of DGBL can increase motivation, engagement, and satisfaction of learners, whether they are typically developed students or students with sensory disabilities. Furthermore, the use of DGBL can improve behavior, attention, self-control, and communication and social skills.

It has been shown that in the case of ASD students, the introduction of DGBL initiatives helped to draw the users' attention to perceiving and performing the tasks, motivating them to act and collaborate with their peers (Silva-Calpa et al., 2018). In this sense, DGBL can be a useful tool to foster social interactions and communication skills, having the potential to even improve the coordination of body movements (Battocchi et al., 2010). Specifically, according to Tanaka et al. (2010), participants with ASD experienced some improvement in eye and mouth recognition, but the rest of the subtests did not show substantial improvement. In this sense, more research can be carried out to analyze what is the effect of DGBL on the identification of body movements and facial expressions associated with emotional states (Navan & Khaleghi, 2020). Likewise, the development of DGBL in mobile apps represents an opportunity to obtain positive psychological outcomes such as autonomy, perceived competence, intrinsic enjoyment, and motivation, as stated by Lee et al. (2020).

For students with dyslexia, DGBL could contribute to improving their neurocognitive skills, but future studies should take into account the premise of short task duration to avoid loss of attention and interest (Jaramillo-Alcázar et al., 2021). A possible solution to increase interest in the lesson is the introduction of new game-based AR initiatives in a three-dimensional environment that can save time in explanations and engage students with dyslexia (Bjekić et al., 2020). In this sense, virtual three-dimensional scenarios are interesting tools to improve students' immersion capacity in the DGBL initiative, thus achieving more lasting learning.

In the world of today, mobile games, such as the one designed by Ahmad et al. (2020), are also being developed to engage and retain the attention of students with ADHD. New technologies, such as AR, could also contribute to this goal, as they make it possible for educational content to be represented in a real-world environment, engaging students to a greater extent. Therefore, in future lines of research, developers are increasingly interested in the design of educational games for smartphones, since this medium gives students total control over their learning by allowing them to decide when and where to view the content.

Finally, it is worth noting that there are common features of DGBL systems that influence all types of students in a similar way. However, each type of disability has different nuances when designing game-based initiatives. As one of the challenges of e-learning systems is to maintain the engagement of students while learning, DGBL can be a valuable element to incorporate into these systems. One of the aspects that has exponentially increased the importance of these game-based initiatives is the easy availability of the devices needed to play games, as computers, smartphones, large televisions, and game consoles are in almost every home. Future studies should analyze the use of DGBL systems combined with modern technologies, such as augmented reality, virtual reality, extended reality, and mixed reality, which allow for a greater sense of immersion to stimulate to a greater extent the interaction and motivation of participants (Alvares et al., 2019).

CONCLUSION

The implementation of DGBL can be beneficial for both the intellectual and personal development of students with sensory, intellectual, and learning disabilities (Zin et al., 2009). It is important to note that the biggest challenge is often how to motivate and engage students with sensory, intellectual, and learning disabilities (Gillet-Swan, 2017). In this sense, DGBL initiatives have the potential to promote intrinsic motivation of students, as well as their satisfaction, enjoyment, fun, and other desired hedonic aspects (Kultima et al., 2008).

The use of technology can develop DGBL personalized for each student according to their needs and allow access to these educational resources at anytime and anywhere. In this sense, one of the aspects that has exponentially increased the importance of these initiatives is the easy availability of the necessary devices needed to play, such as mobile phones, computers, large televisions, and game consoles (Alabdulakareem & Jamjoom, 2020). The impact of DGBL interventions on psychological outcomes such as motivation, satisfaction, and enjoyment among students with sensory, intellectual, and learning disabilities has been well reported in the literature.

It is important to adapt the digital systems to the recommendations of playability, accessibility, and education for students with visual or hearing disabilities, as Neto et al. (2020) did with the educational game Em Busca do Santo Grau. In this sense, results indicate that there were positive changes in students' motivation, attitude, and affective state, finding the platform accessible, useful, and easy to use (Ghergulescu et al., 2019). For example, students with sensory disabilities have increased their academic performance in subjects like mathematics following the implementation of a game-based learning environment (Ferreira & Cavaco, 2014). In other subjects like statistics, Samonte (2020) affirmed that the use of the assessed assistive technologies can improve the access for students with hearing and speech disabilities.

To improve the learning process of children with ASD, the three areas—therapy, immersion, and personalization—are crucial to provide a realistic and tailored experience in which users can identify and become more aware of the potential benefits that DGBL can bring them (Van Dooren et al., 2019). Game-based initiatives can improve the psychomotor skills of children with ASD, as well as their self-esteem, adjusting game difficulty for each individual player, fostering competence while minimizing their frustration (Mazurek et al., 2015). For example, using the video game Pico's Adventure for the Xbox 360 Kinect console, students with ASD improved their social skills for cooperation and joint attention to a common goal (Malinverni et al., 2017). Moreover, using the Wii Sports video game, children with ASD improved their physical object control skills and their ability to interact socially, competitively, or cooperatively with their peers (Ferguson et al., 2013). Another popular initiative for students with ASD is the use of the Minecraft video game, which makes it possible to explore the entire virtual world by creating their own narrative while build interaction skills to people (Greitemeyer & Mügge, 2014).

In the field of students with learning disabilities, the use of DGBL can especially improve the reading outcomes of children with dyslexia by implementing interactive exercises based on phonological awareness, phonics, reading fluency, vocabulary, and comprehension (Velluntino et al., 2004). In this sense, game-based assessment digital tools can be useful to detect children at greater risk of learning disabilities (Tulloch & Pammer, 2019). On the other hand, to improve the effectiveness of the current treatment methods for dyslexia, Jaramillo-Alcázar et al. (2021) presented the Puzzle Pieces video game, a promising tool whose effectiveness in improving the neurocognitive skills of children with dyslexia has yet to be proven. Furthermore, new trends like the use of this mobile application improved the text retention capacity during the dictations performed by school children (Dymora & Niemiec, 2019).

In students with ADHD, DGBL aims to facilitate the implementation of rules and behaviors, facilitating social relations and feedback with peers and teachers to make the learning process more effective, fun, and enjoyable (Lis et al., 2016). In this sense, according to Alqithami (2021), game-based digital environments serve as a promising tool to improve the attention state of children with ADHD, which can lead to a better focus. In addition, the incorporation of multimedia content and regular or frequent rewards in DGBL systems can significantly increase the attention and concentration of children with ADHD (Antonietti, 2012). Recently, according to the study of Ahmad et al. (2020), the success of mobile games in learning is measured by being able to capture and retain students' attention and students' satisfaction with how easy it was to start, navigate through, and learn while playing.

To conclude, this review of game-based initiatives applied to special education concludes that the use of game elements and dynamics generally increases the motivation, engagement, and enjoyment of students with sensory, intellectual, and learning disabilities. In this context, the use of DGBL systems adapted to the special needs of each group can contribute to start or continue with their learning process in a proactive way, encouraging to improve their educational curriculum and to pursue higher education.

REFERENCES

Agogué, M., Levillain, K., & Hooge, S. (2015). Gamification of creativity: Exploring the usefulness of serious games for ideation. *Creativity and Innovation Management*, *24*(3), 415–429. doi:10.1111/caim.12138

Ahmad, I. S., Ahmad, H. K., Aliyu, S. M., & Ahmad, A. M. (2020). Mathefunic: A mobile based game for engaging children with ADHD. *International Journal on Perceptive and Cognitive Computing*, *6*(2), 60–66. doi:10.31436/ijpcc.v6i2.158

Alabdulakareem, E., & Jamjoom, M. (2020). Computer-assisted learning for improving ADHD individuals' executive functions through gamified interventions: A review. *Entertainment Computing*, *33*, 100341. doi:10.1016/j.entcom.2020.100341

Ally, M., & Prieto-Blázquez, J. (2014). What is the future of mobile learning in education? *International Journal of Educational Technology in Higher Education*, *11*(1), 142–151. doi:10.7238/rusc.v11i1.2033

Alqithami, S. (2021). A serious-gamification blueprint towards a normalized attention. *Brain Informatics*, *8*(1), 1–13. doi:10.118640708-021-00127-3 PMID:33856585

Alvares, G. A., Chen, N. T., Notebaert, L., Granich, J., Mitchell, C., & Whitehouse, A. J. (2019). Brief social attention bias modification for children with autism spectrum disorder. *Autism Research*, *12*(3), 527–535. doi:10.1002/aur.2067 PMID:30632321

Battocchi, A., Pianesi, F., Tomasini, D., Zancanaro, M., Esposito, G., Venuti, P., & Weiss, P. L. (2010). Collaborative puzzle game: A tabletop interactive game for fostering collaboration in children with autism spectrum disorders (ASD). *Journal of Assistive Technologies*, *4*(1), 4–13. doi:10.5042/jat.2010.0040

Bjekić, D., Obradović, S., & Bojović, M. (2020). The challenges for teachers: Augmented reality as educational technology for students with dyslexia. *8th International Scientific Conference Technics and Informatics in Education*, *43*(5), 40-49.

Bukvic, I. I., Cahoon, C., Wyatt, A., Cowden, T., & Dredger, K. (2014). OPERAcraft: Blurring the lines between real and virtual. *2014 ICM/SMC*. https://vtechworks.lib.vt.edu/handle/10919/106442

Bul, K. C., Doove, L. L., Franken, I. H., Oord, S. V. D., Kato, P. M., & Maras, A. (2018). A serious game for children with Attention Deficit Hyperactivity Disorder: Who benefits the most? *PLoS One*, *13*(3), e0193681. doi:10.1371/journal.pone.0193681 PMID:29543891

Cadieux, L., & Keenan, M. (2020). Can social communication skills for children diagnosed with autism spectrum disorder rehearsed inside the video game environment of Minecraft generalize to the real world? *JMIR Serious Games*, *8*(2), e14369. doi:10.2196/14369 PMID:32396129

Crepaldi, M., Colombo, V., Mottura, S., Baldassini, D., Sacco, M., & Antonietti, A. (2020). Antonyms: A computer game to improve inhibitory control of impulsivity in children with attention deficit/hyperactivity disorder (ADHD). *Information (Basel)*, *11*(4), 230. doi:10.3390/info11040230

De Souza Sombrio, G., Schimmelpfeng, L. E., & Ulbricht, V. R. (2016, October). The production of a gamified learning object accessible to people with visual or hearing disabilities for teaching geometry. In *2016 XI Latin American Conference on Learning Objects and Technology (LACLO)* (pp. 1-10). IEEE. 10.1109/LACLO.2016.7751787

Dymora, P., & Niemiec, K. (2019). Gamification as a supportive tool for school children with dyslexia. *Informatics (MDPI)*, *6*(4), 48. doi:10.3390/informatics6040048

Fabio, R. A., & Antonietti, A. (2012). Effects of hypermedia instruction on declarative, conditional and procedural knowledge in ADHD students. *Research in Developmental Disabilities*, *33*(6), 2028–2039. doi:10.1016/j.ridd.2012.04.018 PMID:22750359

Ferguson, B. R., Gillis, J. M., & Sevlever, M. (2013). A brief group intervention using video games to teach sportsmanship skills to children with autism spectrum disorders. *Child & Family Behavior Therapy*, *35*(4), 293–306. doi:10.1080/07317107.2013.846648

Ferreira, F., & Cavaco, S. (2014, October). Mathematics for all: A game-based learning environment for visually impaired students. In *2014 IEEE Frontiers in Education Conference (FIE) Proceedings* (pp. 1-8). IEEE. 10.1109/FIE.2014.7044493

Ferreira, G. P., Andrade, R., Oliveira, S. T., & Ulbricht, V. R. (2016, July). Learning object design for teaching descriptive geometry: A study from the perspective of gamification and accessibility. *International Conference on Universal Access in Human-Computer Interaction* (pp. 38-48). Springer. 10.1007/978-3-319-40238-3_4

Fu, F. L., Su, R. C., & Yu, S. C. (2009). EGameFlow: A scale to measure learners' enjoyment of e-learning games. *Computers & Education*, *52*(1), 101–112. doi:10.1016/j.compedu.2008.07.004

Ghergulescu, I., Moldovan, A. N., Bratu, M., Muntean, C. H., & Muntean, G. M. (2019). A case study in STEM education for learners with special education needs. *Proceedings of the 11th International Conference on Education and New Learning Technologies*, 10152-10157. 10.21125/edulearn.2019.2539

Gillett-Swan, J. (2017). The challenges of online learning: Supporting and engaging the isolated learner. *Journal of Learning Design*, *10*(1), 20–30. doi:10.5204/jld.v9i3.293

Greitemeyer, T., & Mügge, D. O. (2014). Video games do affect social outcomes: A meta-analytic review of the effects of violent and prosocial video game play. *Personality and Social Psychology Bulletin*, *40*(5), 578–589. doi:10.1177/0146167213520459 PMID:24458215

Hassan, A., Pinkwart, N., & Shafi, M. (2021). Serious games to improve social and emotional intelligence in children with autism. *Entertainment Computing*, *38*, 100417. doi:10.1016/j.entcom.2021.100417

Huang, B., Hwang, G. J., Hew, K. F., & Warning, P. (2019). Effects of gamification on students' online interactive patterns and peer-feedback. *Distance Education*, *40*(3), 350–379. doi:10.1080/01587919.2019.1632168

Jaramillo-Alcázar, A., Venegas, E., Criollo-C, S., & Luján-Mora, S. (2021). An approach to accessible serious games for people with dyslexia. *Sustainability*, *13*(5), 2507. doi:10.3390u13052507

Kultima, A., Niemelä, J., Paavilainen, J., & Saarenpää, H. (2008, November). Designing game idea generation games. In *Proceedings of the 2008 conference on future play: Research, play, share* (pp. 137-144). 10.1145/1496984.1497007

Laabidi, M., Jemni, M., Ayed, L. J. B., Brahim, H. B., & Jemaa, A. B. (2014). Learning technologies for people with disabilities. *Journal of King Saud University-Computer and Information Sciences*, *26*(1), 29–45. doi:10.1016/j.jksuci.2013.10.005

Lee, D., Frey, G. C., Min, A., Kim, B., Cothran, D. J., Bellini, S., Han, K., & Shih, P. C. (2020). Usability inquiry of a gamified behavior change app for increasing physical activity and reducing sedentary behavior in adults with and without autism spectrum disorder. *Health Informatics Journal*, *26*(4), 2992–3008. doi:10.1177/1460458220952909 PMID:32951500

Lee, J. J., & Hammer, J. (2011). Gamification in education: What, how, why bother? *Academic Exchange Quarterly*, *15*(2), 146.

Lis, S., Baer, N., Franzen, N., Hagenhoff, M., Gerlach, M., Koppe, G., Sammer, G., Gallhofer, B., & Kirsch, P. (2016). Social interaction behavior in ADHD in adults in a virtual trust game. *Journal of Attention Disorders*, *20*(4), 335–345. doi:10.1177/1087054713482581 PMID:23564736

Malinverni, L., Mora-Guiard, J., Padillo, V., Valero, L., Hervás, A., & Pares, N. (2017). An inclusive design approach for developing video games for children with autism spectrum disorder. *Computers in Human Behavior*, *71*, 535–549. doi:10.1016/j.chb.2016.01.018

Mazurek, M. O., Engelhardt, C. R., & Clark, K. E. (2015). Video games from the perspective of adults with autism spectrum disorder. *Computers in Human Behavior*, *51*, 122–130. doi:10.1016/j.chb.2015.04.062

Navan, A. A., & Khaleghi, A. (2020). Using gamification to improve the education quality of children with autism. *Revista Científica (Maracaibo)*, *1*(37), 90–106. doi:10.14483/23448350.15431

Neto, L. V., Fontoura, P. H. Jr, Bordini, R. A., Otsuka, J. L., & Beder, D. M. (2020). Design and implementation of an educational game considering issues for visually impaired people inclusion. *Smart Learning Environments*, *7*(1), 1–16. doi:10.118640561-019-0103-4

Patrício, R., Moreira, A., Zurlo, F., & Melazzini, M. (2020). Co-creation of new solutions through gamification: A collaborative innovation practice. *Creativity and Innovation Management*, *29*(1), 146–160. doi:10.1111/caim.12356

Patrício, R., Moreira, A. C., & Zurlo, F. (2018). Gamification approaches to the early stage of innovation. *Creativity and Innovation Management*, *27*(4), 499–511. doi:10.1111/caim.12284

Peñuelas-Calvo, I., Jiang-Lin, L. K., Girela-Serrano, B., Delgado-Gomez, D., Navarro-Jimenez, R., Baca-Garcia, E., & Porras-Segovia, A. (2020). Video games for the assessment and treatment of attention-deficit/hyperactivity disorder: A systematic review. *European Child & Adolescent Psychiatry*, 1–16. doi:10.100700787-020-01557-w PMID:32424511

Politis, Y., Robb, N., Yakkundi, A., Dillenburger, K., Herbertson, N., Charlesworth, B., & Goodman, L. (2017). People with disabilities leading the design of serious games and virtual worlds. *International Journal of Serious Games*, *4*(2), 63–73. doi:10.17083/ijsg.v4i2.160

Rodríguez, A., Boada, I., Thió-Henestrosa, S., & Sbert, M. (2018). CPRforblind: A video game to introduce cardiopulmonary resuscitation protocol to blind people. *British Journal of Educational Technology*, *49*(4), 636–645. doi:10.1111/bjet.12627

Samonte, M. J. C. (2020, June). An assistive technology using FSL, speech recognition, gamification and online handwritten character recognition in learning statistics for students with hearing and speech impairment. In *Proceedings of the 2020 The 6th International Conference on Frontiers of Educational Technologies* (pp. 92-97). 10.1145/3404709.3404746

Saputra, M. R. U., & Risqi, M. (2015). Lexipal: Design, implementation and evaluation of gamification on learning application for dyslexia. *International Journal of Computers and Applications*, *131*(7), 37–43. doi:10.5120/ijca2015907416

Silva-Calpa, G. F. M., Raposo, A. B., & Suplino, M. (2018, May). CoASD: A tabletop game to support the collaborative work of users with autism spectrum disorder. In *2018 IEEE 6th International Conference on Serious Games and Applications for Health (SeGAH)* (pp. 1-8). IEEE. 10.1109/SeGAH.2018.8401358

Smith, K., & Abrams, S. S. (2019). Gamification and accessibility. *The International Journal of Information and Learning Technology*, *36*(2), 104–123. doi:10.1108/IJILT-06-2018-0061

Tanaka, J. W., Wolf, J. M., Klaiman, C., Koenig, K., Cockburn, J., Herlihy, L., Brown, C., Stahl, S., Kaiser, M. S., & Schultz, R. T. (2010). Using computerized games to teach face recognition skills to children with autism spectrum disorder: The Let's Face It! program. *Journal of Child Psychology and Psychiatry, and Allied Disciplines*, *51*(8), 944–952. doi:10.1111/j.1469-7610.2010.02258.x PMID:20646129

Tulloch, K., & Pammer, K. (2019). Tablet computer games to measure dorsal stream performance in good and poor readers. *Neuropsychologia*, *130*, 92–99. doi:10.1016/j.neuropsychologia.2018.07.019 PMID:30030193

Van Dooren, M. M., Siriaraya, P., Visch, V., Spijkerman, R., & Bijkerk, L. (2019). Reflections on the design, implementation, and adoption of a gamified eHealth application in youth mental healthcare. *Entertainment Computing*, *31*, 100305. doi:10.1016/j.entcom.2019.100305

Vellutino, F. R., Fletcher, J. M., Snowling, M. J., & Scanlon, D. M. (2004). Specific reading disability (dyslexia): What have we learned in the past four decades? *Journal of Child Psychology and Psychiatry, and Allied Disciplines*, *45*(1), 2–40. doi:10.1046/j.0021-9630.2003.00305.x PMID:14959801

Whalen, C., Moss, D., Ilan, A. B., Vaupel, M., Fielding, P., Macdonald, K., Cernich, S., & Symon, J. (2010). Efficacy of TeachTown: Basics computer-assisted intervention for the intensive comprehensive autism program in Los Angeles unified school district. *Autism*, *14*(3), 179–197. doi:10.1177/1362361310363282 PMID:20484002

Wong, C., & Kasari, C. (2012). Play and joint attention of children with autism in the preschool special education classroom. *Journal of Autism and Developmental Disorders*, *42*(10), 2152–2161. doi:10.100710803-012-1467-2 PMID:22350340

Zain, N. H. M. (2021). Learning through games: An approach for children with autism spectrum disorder during COVID-19 pandemic. *Turkish Journal of Computer and Mathematics Education*, *12*(5), 1820–1829. doi:10.17762/turcomat.v12i5.2196

Zin, N. A. M., Jaafar, A., & Yue, W. S. (2009). Digital game-based learning (DGBL) model and development methodology for teaching history. *WSEAS Transactions on Computers*, *8*(2), 322–333.

ADDITIONAL READING

Chen, C. H., Shih, C. C., & Law, V. (2020). The effects of competition in digital game-based learning (DGBL): A meta-analysis. *Educational Technology Research and Development*, *68*(4), 1855–1873. doi:10.100711423-020-09794-1

Flores-Gallegos, R., Rodríguez-Leis, P., & Fernández, T. (2021). Effects of a virtual reality training program on visual attention and motor performance in children with reading learning disability. *International Journal of Child-Computer Interaction*, *100394*. Advance online publication. doi:10.1016/j.ijcci.2021.100394

Gul, N., Noor, H., & Chaudhary, F. R. (2021). Using Technology to enhance the performance of intellectually disabled students: Mobile game-based Urdu learning. *UMT Education Review*, *4*(1), 42–57. doi:10.32350/uer.41.03

Keller, C., Döring, A. K., & Makarova, E. (2021). The potential of serious games to foster learning among children and adolescents with disabilities: A systematic review. *Digital Culture and Education*, *13*(2), 6-36.

Martinez, L., Gimenes, M., & Lambert, E. (2022). Entertainment video games for academic learning: A systematic review. *Journal of Educational Computing Research*. Advance online publication. doi:10.1177/07356331211053848

Patrício, R., Moreira, A. C., & Zurlo, F. (2021). Enhancing design thinking approaches to innovation through gamification. *European Journal of Innovation Management*, *24*(5), 1569–1594. doi:10.1108/EJIM-06-2020-0239

Tay, J., Goh, Y. M., Safiena, S., & Bound, H. (2022). Designing digital game-based learning for professional upskilling: A systematic literature review. *Computers & Education, 104518*. Advance online publication. doi:10.1016/j.compedu.2022.104518

KEY TERMS AND DEFINITIONS

Attention Deficit Hyperactivity Disorder (ADHD): Is a prevalent learning disability defined as a prevalent neurobehavioral disorder commonly diagnosed in a large number of children and adolescents under the age of 18.

Autism Spectrum Disorder (ASD): Is one of the most common neurodevelopmental disorder that affects three main areas: communication, social interaction, and impulse control.

Digital Game-Based Learning (DGBL): Consists of the introduction of game-based mechanics performed through digital media such as computers or mobile phones in different areas (education, health, business, etc.) to meet the learning demands of a target population by training a wide range of skills while promoting entertainment, motivation, satisfaction, ideation, etc.

Dyslexia: Is considered a prevalent learning condition that affects an individual's ability to read, spell, and comprehend language when reading or writing, having a negative impact on both self-esteem and academic aspirations of the students.

Educational Game Skills: The games force to make decisions on their own, allowing the idea of complying with the rules and requirements with confidence and independence, which is fundamental for the student's development in the real context of society.

Game-Based Education: Game-based mechanics in the educational context that provide appropriate feedback to users through positive reinforcement such as notifications, badges, points, and medals to let them know that they are on the right track in their academic journey.

Sensory Disabilities: Refer to visual, hearing, or both, that face a number of barriers to achieving the academic goals of these students, using handheld devices, completing timed tasks, obtaining appropriate feedback, and adopting teamwork mechanisms.

Chapter 22
Flow, Motivation, Social Interaction, and Design Issues of Serious Games in Education

Nuri Kara
https://orcid.org/0000-0002-0115-383X
Istanbul Bilgi University, Turkey

ABSTRACT

This chapter aims to discuss the flow, motivation, social interaction, and design issues in serious games in education from a theoretical perspective. Serious games in education aim to improve students' skills or provide them with knowledge while entertaining. Flow theory indicates that balancing the difficulty level of a game with players' abilities helps immerse players in serious gameplay. Intrinsic motivation components in serious games contribute to players' achievement of learning goals. Social presence and communication make it easier to understand players' interactions with friends, other players, and the game in serious online games designed for educational purposes. The serious game design process and its challenges help create serious games that meet students' needs and expectations. This chapter analyzes these concepts, their components, and how they interact or influence each other.

INTRODUCTION

"Serious games" are games used for education, management, training, simulation, or health (Susi et al., 2007). Although the "serious game" term was firstly used in the 1970s, this term in a digital framework began to be used with the Serious Gaming Initiative that started in 2002 (De Gloria et al., 2014). Hence, this chapter focuses on serious games played on different platforms using various digital technologies such as computers, consoles, and mobile devices. In recent years, there has been increased scholarly interest in serious games, especially in the field of education (De Gloria et al., 2014; Gómez & Suárez, 2021). Serious games can be considered entertaining educational tools that allow players to develop their knowledge and skills through immersive gaming experiences (Almeida & Simoes, 2019; Zhonggen, 2019). Serious games can contribute to adolescents' educational use of computers (Cilesiz, 2009), as

DOI: 10.4018/978-1-6684-4287-6.ch022

computer games are fun and interactive, creating an enjoyable environment for young learners (Prensky, 2001). Serious games can also improve metacognition skills, as students like to strategize, plan, and organize in digital game environments. As Ritterfeld and Weber (2006) noted, "it seems plausible that video game players benefit from metacognitive strategies in situations in which a challenge cannot be mastered" (p. 403). Existing strategies in digital games can enhance metacognitive skills, which play an important role in educational settings, as they help students recognize others' thoughts. From this point of view, serious games can be beneficial not only in developing students' sense of aesthetics but also in their metacognitive skills.

When creating serious games, developers should consider several features that support effective learning. For example, Lieberman (2006) outlined nine areas of interactive games and learning: "motivation to learn, perception and coordination, thinking and problem solving, knowledge, skills and behaviors, self-regulation and therapy, self-concepts, social relationships, and attitudes and values" (p. 380). Of these concepts, motivation to learn is especially important, as it highlights how serious games encourage effective learning. In serious games, the content, appeal, challenge to reach a goal, emotions and fun, interactivity, engagement, flow, and storyline all these concepts contribute to a player's motivation to learn (Lieberman, 2006). Although entertainment is the primary means of grabbing players' attention in digital games, other components such as flow, interactivity, and challenge engage players in serious games while also supporting educational goals. In other words, because entertainment is not an independent mechanism offered in serious games, entertainment must be supplemented with other effective components to keep players interested.

Zhonggen (2019) listed five main technical components affecting serious game practices in education: realism, backstory and production, artificial intelligence, interaction, and debriefing. According to Zhonggen (2019), realism describes how much the game satisfies students' needs. Backstory and production concern the impacts of the main game generation process. Artificial intelligence concerns the balance between game components and students' responses. Interaction describes various communication types, such as game–student, game–teacher, and student–teacher. Finally, debriefing refers to the reporting and communication process that emerges as a result of gameplay. All these factors can enhance the success of serious game practices in education. Therefore, educators, students, game designers, and other officials should apply these factors to serious game development and use in education. In addition to these factors, there are three main components directly related to serious games: flow, motivation, and social interaction. When reviewing game studies literature, these concepts are less often studied, especially in the context of serious games in education. To address this gap, this study mainly focuses on the theories and practices of flow, motivation, and social interaction within serious games in education.

SERIOUS GAMES FROM THE PERSPECTIVE OF FLOW

Flow is characterized by easiness and effectiveness. Csikszentmihalyi (1990) described flow as "making [the] optimal experience easier to achieve" (p. 72). Flow activities include certain influential features that draw players' attention to the process. These involve various actions such as providing feedback, setting goals, maintaining control, and directing skills (Csikszentmihalyi, 1990). Thus, flow activities evoke players' emotions by identifying certain attractive characteristics. Chen (2007) listed Csikszentmihalyi's observations, describing flow as "a challenging activity requiring skill; a merging of action and awareness; clear goals; direct, immediate feedback; concentration on the task at hand; a sense of control;

a loss of self-consciousness; and an altered sense of time" (p. 31). Thus, creating flow in a particular activity requires a systematic view that considers these eight components. For example, it is difficult to progressively maintain flow in an event or game without providing immediate feedback. Additionally, goals must be set clearly within the game to keep players focused. All eight components help players reach goals by maintaining players' flow.

While flow plays a supportive and positive role in serious game-based learning (Kiili & Lainema, 2008), an in-depth analysis of flow in serious games is still needed (Perttula et al., 2017). Individual gaming experiences emerge while in flow; therefore it is important to investigate the relationships between flow dimensions and their effects on players (Moizer et al., 2019; Perttula et al., 2017). The first dimension of flow is a challenging activity requiring skills. Challenge is a component that must be effectively integrated into serious games to enhance learning outcomes. As Hamari et al. (2016) stated, the degree of "challenge" should correspond to students' expectations, capacities, and needs in serious game-assisted learning environments because it affects academic performance. As noted by Chan et al. (2021), the challenge level could determine the success of serious game-assisted learning. Determining the challenge level in serious games is important when striving to maintain players' flow. Wang et al. (2019) conducted a study aiming to design a digital serious game and test its effectiveness in environmental education. Based on the results, casual players could easily complete the in-game missions and overcome the obstacles in the game because it was challenging enough for them but was not too difficult. However, experienced gamers could not concentrate and achieve flow because the game was too simple (Wang et al., 2019). This finding suggests that there should be a balance between a game's difficulty and players' skills in serious games. Hence, players must be kept within the flow zone to create effective learning and playing experiences. In the context of the flow zone, the complexity of an activity or game should match the player's abilities. As Chen (2007) emphasized, a challenge level that exceeds the player's ability may cause anxiety. In contrast, if the player's skill exceeds the challenge level, the player becomes bored. Thus, the flow zone keeps the players engaged in serious gameplay by balancing the player's skill with the game's difficulty.

The second dimension of flow is a merging of action and awareness. Combining action with awareness enables players to focus on the missions or tasks presented in serious gameplay. Increased awareness contributes to flow while playing an educational serious game. The third dimension of flow is clear goals. In their study, Chan et al. (2021) found that goal clarity significantly impacted learning outcomes. Clear goals allow learners to concentrate on the main tasks during serious gameplay. Hence, instructional goals and game goals should be determined before playing the game. For instance, in a dental game designed to educate people on major dental operations like fillings, filtration, and tooth discoloration, instructional goals could include educating people on major dental operations, increasing strategy and time management skills, or helping patients avoid their fear of dentists. In this case, the game goals could include completing each level to finish the game and earning points by completing operations and decreasing the characters' dentist fear levels.

The fourth dimension of flow is direct, immediate feedback. Buzady (2017) claimed that continuous, context-specific, and adaptive feedback is crucial for an effective learning experience and a fun game atmosphere. In serious games, players should receive prompt and appropriate feedback on their actions so they can complete in-game tasks without getting lost in the game. The fifth dimension of flow is concentration on a task, which means focusing on and becoming immersed in the game. Immersion is a critical concept because it is often emphasized in game and educational studies. According to Oksanen (2013), immersion is the state of being fully present and embedded in an activity. In serious games, immersion not only provides players with a fun gaming experience but can also help achieve effective learning outcomes. As Alexiou et al. (2020) stated, immersion helps provide a suitable learning environment by improving players' in-game experiences. Furthermore, players immersed in the game have better learning outcomes because of their gaming experience and learn the educational content more easily (Wang et al., 2019). Therefore, elements that increase immersion should be prioritized in the design process of serious games (Bachen et al., 2016).

The sixth dimension of flow is a sense of control. Hummel et al. (2021) found that student control of in-game missions and teaching tasks improved their gameplay performance and enjoyment. That is, when players have full control of a serious game, the decisions they make in-game can keep them in a state of flow. In-game decisions may have the greatest potential for helping players follow the pedagogical elements and progress in the game. The seventh dimension of flow is a loss of self-consciousness, defined as the player's decreased ability to perceive the outside world because the player is too immersed in the game. Finally, the eighth dimension of flow is an altered sense of time, which refers to players' inability to understand how time passes while in a state of flow. All these flow dimensions provide important support in improving players' serious gameplay experience and increasing their educational outcomes.

SERIOUS GAMES AND MOTIVATION

Malone's motivation theory is related to intrinsic motivation, which compels people to succeed without punishment or reward. According to Malone and Lepper (1987), intrinsic motivation can be divided into two categories: "individual" motivations such as challenge, curiosity, control, and fantasy and "interpersonal" motivations such as cooperation, competition, and recognition. In serious games, the challenge may be comprised of goals, uncertain results, performance feedback, and self-esteem. These components are important for providing a constant challenge in a serious game. For example, if a serious game does not indicate short- and long-term goals or performance feedback does not meet the player's needs, the game's difficulty will be reduced. Hence, the player may lose his or her motivation to play the game. To overcome this problem, students should be able to choose difficulty levels that suit their competencies and learning needs in serious games (Sipiyaruk et al., 2021).

Curiosity is another important component of individual motivation. According to Malone and Lepper (1987), curiosity consists of two main components: sensory and cognitive. Sensory curiosity deals with the environmental aspects of the game, while cognitive curiosity focuses on the player's knowledge during the game. Sensory curiosity corresponds to design elements in serious games. For example, the interface design should attract students' attention, and the in-game components should be pleasant and suited to the students' tastes to stimulate their sensory curiosity. As evidence, Bui et al. (2020) affirmed that an aesthetically pleasing and clear interface design contributed positively to students' gaming experiences. Cognitive curiosity, on the other hand, corresponds with educational tasks, content, or missions in serious games. Providing students with a wide variety of educational content can appeal to their cognitive curiosity in serious gameplay. In support of this view, Hummel et al. (2021) revealed that a high number of resources in a game both increased students' pleasure and created a more effective learning experience.

Control is another individual motivational component. Contingency, choice, and power are the main aspects of control (Malone & Lepper, 1987). Players must take control of the game by making critical decisions during the game process. Wang et al. (2019) emphasized that learner control is an important factor in students' ability to learn from serious games and be motivated in a fun way. The final component of individual motivation is fantasy. In game environments, players take on different roles in virtual environments as leaders or other characters. Character identification can have a positive effect on interacting with different game characters and learning by experience (Bachen et al., 2016).

Furthermore, interpersonal motivation is a driving force for players to acquire the desired skills, especially in serious multiplayer games. The first component of interpersonal motivation is cooperation. In-game tasks that require input from many individuals emphasize cooperation (Schäfer et al., 2013). Therefore, cooperation should be employed in serious games to increase players' interpersonal motivation. Anyaegbu et al. (2012) conducted a study to test the effectiveness of a serious game designed to improve motivation to learn English in primary school students. The researchers found that the cooperation components of the game created interaction between the players, increasing their motivation and allowing them to learn from each other.

The second component of interpersonal motivation is competition. Competition can motivate different types of players and involves elements such as difficulty, goal fulfillment, and winning the game. Low-skilled students attach more importance to social competitive activities that focus more on entertainment, while highly skilled students attach more importance to competitive activities in which they can demonstrate their performance (Chen, 2014). Hence, the competitive element in serious games should accord with the needs of different players, their pace of play, and their expectations of difficulty level. For example, offering single-player and multiplayer options in serious games is one way to use competition as a motivator.

The final interpersonal motivating factor is recognition. Recognition is associated with the concept of reward in games. According to Westera (2019), rewards in games can be divided into three categories: post-practice rewards, dynamic in-game scores, and affordance-oriented rewards. Post-practice rewards are outputs received after the game ends (Westera, 2019), such as leader board rankings or total game scores. Dynamic in-game scores reflect the player's current achievement status or progress in the game (Westera, 2019), such as updated health points or number of completed missions. Finally, affordance-oriented rewards focus on adaptive incentives that will improve gameplay and create extra gains for the player in the game (Westera, 2019). For example, unlocking a level, gaining prestige points, or reaching an extra level after finding a secret item may enhance players' gameplay experiences. These awards allow players to demonstrate their in-game performances and social presence to other players. Therefore, rewards in serious games are related to recognition as an interpersonal motivator.

Malone's motivation theory can also enhance the entertainment value of serious games. Individual motivations such as challenge, curiosity, fantasy, control, and interpersonal motivations such as cooperation, competition, and recognition (Malone & Lepper, 1987) can create an enjoyable and educational game environment. It is critical to implicitly deliver learning objectives in a particular game setting. The game environment should maintain its fantastic components, and the learning objectives should be integrated into the game's fantasy world. Thus, serious games should include entertaining components that will attract students' attention while also delivering educational content (Sipiyaruk et al., 2021). Moreover, learning objectives should consist of challenges that need to be overcome in the game environment, and game developers should focus on including valid educational goals in these games.

Flow theory and Malone's motivational theory are compatible, as both prioritize players' feelings. Users in a game or other types of play become immersed in the game by following the characteristics of flow and intrinsic motivational components. Most importantly, games or other types of play should offer these options to users. When comparing flow theory and Malone's intrinsic motivation components, the similarities are apparent. For instance, the concepts of challenge, control, goals, and feedback are similar in both theories. Additionally, both theories focus on the player's satisfaction and enjoyment during the play process and strive to make the game environment more fun by using characteristics of the game and players, such as control, feedback, curiosity, strategies, and fantasy.

Although fun is the main component influencing players' preference for specific game environments, the environments' strategies, and characteristics determine how fun a game is. From this perspective, flow and intrinsic motivation cannot be entirely separated. Effectively employing flow characteristics may not be sufficient for keeping players continuously integrated into the game environment. If the player exits the flow zone, leading the player back to the game environment can be difficult. In this circumstance, motivation is crucial because intrinsic motivation is the starting point for players' enjoyment of the game and the sustainability of the game process. According to Csikszentmihalyi (1990), "the motivation to enjoy himself again will push him to get back into the flow channel" (p. 75). Since intrinsic motivation is necessary for users to start the game and progress by completing specific tasks, both theories are equally important. Flow and motivation share attributes such as control, feedback, and challenge, and there is a direct link between flow and motivation since motivation sustains flow during the game process.

SERIOUS GAMES AND ONLINE SOCIAL INTERACTIONS

Massive multiplayer online role-playing games provide an environment where players can interact with other players and use the virtual attributes of these environments (Yee, 2006). The social aspects of these game-based environments can contribute to players' flow experiences. Studies have shown that, in the game environment, players belonging to various groups feel more in the game and spend more time playing these games (Axelsson & Regan, 2002; Cole & Griffiths, 2007). Social interactions can support players to remain in a state of flow. One component of flow is an "altered sense of time," which is facilitated by social interaction. For instance, players can build a community by sharing gameplay-related issues via interactive chat tools. Thus, they can be included in a gaming environment and lose their sense of time. Feedback from other communities or players in the game environment can also support players' continued playing. Moreover, these game environments help players shed their self-consciousness because the features of virtual game environments provide an alternative space where players can express their emotions freely. Similarly, Cole and Griffiths (2007) noted that, in virtual games, players can express themselves by taking on characteristics such as gender, age, and appearance that differ from their real-life traits.

Social presence is part of the gaming experience, especially in multiplayer games (Oksanen, 2013). Game mechanics that support sociability and collaborative play provide players with highly interactive, motivating, and immersive gaming experiences. Therefore, social gaming components that increase motivation and engagement should be integrated into serious games to enrich learning experiences. Several studies have investigated social presence and collaborative play in serious games. For example, Pellas (2017) examined correlations between social presence, cognitive presence, and teaching presence in a multiplayer serious game and found that social presence positively correlates with both teaching presence and cognitive presence. Thus, social presence that focuses on interaction and collaborative play should support both cognitive presence that aims to improve players' in-game learning processes and teaching presence that focuses on delivering in-game learning tasks. As evidence, Sajjadi et al. (2019) studied the effect of a humanized conversational agent on the social presence of players in a serious game and found that the agent with high emotional intensity and strong communication with the player improved players' perceived social presence and offered an effective gaming experience. This finding suggests that non-player characters should engage in dialogue with the player and create emotional effects in collaborative serious games. Furthermore, Jerčić et al. (2018) conducted an experiment to analyze human–robot interaction in a collaborative serious game and found that robot collaborators reflected similar emotions as human collaborators and had a similar effect on players' game performances. Therefore, robot agents can be as successful as humans in creating social interaction with players in collaborative multiplayer serious games. Finally, Oksanen and Hämäläinen (2014) explored collaborative learning and game design pathways in the design and development of serious collaborative games. They found that collaborative serious games tended to prioritize educational theories, and the integration of game design models was limited in the design of collaborative serious games (Oksanen & Hämäläinen, 2014). However, pedagogical elements and game design components should be given equal weight and integrated into the design and development of an effective collaborative serious game.

Social communication is another critical aspect that should be emphasized in online serious games. Players can establish positive relationships with other players or communities in online serious gaming environments designed and developed to suit players' needs and expectations. Players in a gaming environment spend their time not only completing challenges but also interacting with other players and communities. Player–player and game–player interactions allow students to become deeply immersed in the gameplay by increasing the effectiveness and value of serious games (Whitton, 2010). Notably, Axelsson and Regan's (2002) research indicated that people in online groups have significant offline contact with other players. These serious game-based environments give players an opportunity to engage them and develop social skills.

However, the negative impacts of social communities in online serious games should also be considered. Firstly, players can distort their social presence in these game-based environments because players cannot interact face-to-face in the virtual game environment. Thus, they may identify themselves as different characters or people. This situation may negatively affect the psychology and attitudes of adolescents or young players, damaging their personal development. Secondly, players may become addicted to social communities in online gaming environments. Virtual social interaction can negatively affect players' real-time social activities if they spend most of their time participating in online multiplayer games. Lastly, young or adolescent players may be exposed to cyberbullying in online games. Cyberbullying is defined as "an aggressive, intentional act carried out by a group or individual, using electronic forms of contact, repeatedly and over time against a victim who cannot easily defend him or herself" (Smith et al., 2008, p. 376). Bullying is on the rise in online gaming environments, so actionable strategies and evaluations are needed to prevent it (Huang et al., 2019; McInroy & Mishna, 2017). In conclusion, the positive and negative effects of social interaction should be considered when evaluating the effectiveness of online serious games.

DESIGN ISSUES FOR SERIOUS GAMES

Designers aim to create games that are fun and improve players' gaming experiences (Barry 2005). Thus, designers are responsible not only for the technical process of game design but also for creating an enjoyable game environment for players. Gaming has several attributes that reflect the dynamic structure of the design process, which make it difficult to separate its technical and aesthetic aspects. Barry (2005) described the process of computer game design as "an art form that, like most others, requires good technical discipline to be applied successfully and consistently" (p. 102). Therefore, game design cannot focus solely on the artistic or technical process because both are necessary to create effective and enjoyable games for players.

Serious game design in education must incorporate the technical, entertainment, and artistic aspects of casual game design while also integrating educational material (Cowley et al., 2011). Components such as target audience, story, distribution media, price, platform, storytelling, development team, goals and objectives, resources and economies, game genre, layout, pacing, and landmarks must be considered during effective serious game design. Of these components, one must first determine the target audience (Cowley et al., 2011). Considering the target audience in the game design process allows designers to create games that meet audience members' expectations and needs. Regardless of audience members' age or maturity, their thoughts, preferences, styles, and other personal characteristics should determine the game design process.

Participatory design may improve the serious game design and development process. Scaife and Rogers (1999) stated that the "participatory design approach is to respect users more as partners in the design process and, in so doing, explicitly give them a more equal and responsible role" (p. 29). Akilli and Cagiltay (2006) used participatory design as one of the underlying principles of their proposed Fidge instructional design model for creating game-like learning environments. According to Scaife and Rogers (1999), involving users in the game design process is important to determine the effectiveness of the design. Similarly, Akilli and Cagiltay (2006) mentioned the role of players from specific target groups in the pre-analysis and analysis phases. Mature gamers, especially, can offer guidance to designers on how to include learning tasks and motivating game mechanics in the serious game design process. Therefore, designers should seek opinions and suggestions from the target audience in the preliminary analysis and learner analysis stages (Akilli & Cagiltay, 2006). There is no doubt that "children can be brought into the design process and make a contribution" (Scaife & Rogers, 1999, p. 30). To do so, designers or instructional technologists need to find an effective way to obtain insightful views from children. For example, Scaife and Roger (1999) used low-tech techniques to get children to think and imagine and found that low-tech sessions obtained valuable reflections from children. Graphic representation, conversations with children, animated objects, and imagination are low-tech techniques that can be used to gain valuable feedback from children during the design process. Children should play a significant role in the game design process by offering feedback on components of the game environment design process such as storytelling, goals and objectives, and pacing. Getting children's feedback and reactions during the analysis phase of the design process helps the designer and other experts determine how the player progresses through the game.

Developing serious games in education is not the sole responsibility of educational designers or game developers. If serious games are designed only by game designers, educational objectives may be ignored, but if they are designed only by instructors, the motivational aspects of the game, such as entertainment value and pleasure, may be missing (Braad et al., 2016). Instead, these two groups should cooperate while designing and developing serious games for education. A multidisciplinary team must include game designers, software engineers, psychologists, instructional designers, and others (Ávila-Pesántez et al., 2017; Strzalkowski & Symborski, 2017). Together with game artists, game designers and developers handle programming, technical drawing, and game fantasy world development. Meanwhile, instructors and instructional designers help determine in-game learning goals and outcomes and monitor their suitability. Moreover, assessment and evaluation experts perform playtests and usability tests to detect technical and pedagogical deficiencies and errors in the game. As Strzalkowski and Symborski

(2017) emphasized, playtesting contributes greatly to game development by finding in-game bugs and providing suggestions to improve players' learning experiences. In summary, experts on the "serious" side should work cooperatively with experts on the "game" side in the design and development of serious games (Braad et al., 2016).

According to Dimitriadou et al. (2021), educators state that they encounter various difficulties in designing serious games, including administrative, design-related, communicative, and attitudinal challenges. Administrative challenges involve educators using their time and resources to work as game designers in addition to their teaching roles (Dimitriadou et al., 2021). An excessive workload can make it difficult for educators to focus on game design, so educators involved in serious game design must balance their teaching and game design duties. Design challenges are related to the effects of serious game design on the target group (Dimitriadou et al., 2021). That is, while well-designed serious games can increase students' motivation and success, badly designed serious games cannot achieve their objectives. Dividing the work among a multidisciplinary team and ensuring that everyone works harmoniously are examples of communicative challenges (Dimitriadou et al., 2021). Intra-team communication strategies should be determined, and everyone's roles and responsibilities should be clearly arranged to eliminate communication difficulties. Attitudinal challenges include critical perspectives on the inclusion of games in educational settings (Dimitriadou et al., 2021). One way to combat negative attitudes is to present various studies from the literature that support the positive effects of serious games on learning.

Despite the growing popularity of serious games in education, there are very few post-secondary courses focused on serious game design and development, and K-12 students are almost ignored in existing courses (Kapralos, 2021). Examples mostly relate to the implementation of serious games in classroom settings. For instance, Hess and Gunter (2013) compared students' learning experiences and achievements between a serious game-based and non-serious game-based online course. According to the findings, students were more motivated in the online serious game-based lesson than in the non-game-based lesson. One of the interesting results of the study was that while multimedia components such as graphics, interface, sound, and videos in games supported learning, technical and management problems negatively affected learning (Hess & Gunter, 2013). These findings can be an important guide in the design and development of serious games to be used in classroom environments. In another study, Barros et al. (2020) investigated the effect of a serious game about arithmetic operations on students' learning experiences. The results indicated that the serious game had a positive effect on students' learning of arithmetic operations. On the other hand, the music and sound effects of the game were not used by students (Barros et al., 2020). Such preferences of students should be considered in designing serious games for classroom settings.

FUTURE IMPLICATIONS AND RECOMMENDATIONS

The quality of digital worlds has increased with advances in technology (Squire, 2003). Gamers investing their money and countless hours in digital games indicates that the gaming industry has increased in popularity. In addition to the technical capacities of games, the social aspects of games attract players' attention. Shaffer et al. (2005) suggested that digital games can offer new approaches to the future of learning because well-structured digital worlds involve not only facts or specific skills but also players' social practices. These digital worlds can increase players' social community practices. For instance, serious games in health education that support children battling cancer and allow doctors to operate remotely can contribute to social practices by allowing real-time interaction between doctor and player (Shaffer et al., 2005; Wattanasoontorn et al., 2013). Likely, serious games for social community practices will become more popular soon as simulation technology progresses. Technological advancements may also help games transition from computers to mobile technologies. As Wattanasoontorn et al. (2013) stated, mobile devices with Internet access will increase their PC-like features and will become more dominant in the serious gaming industry in the near future. Therefore, more serious games should be designed and developed for mobile devices.

Various factors must be considered in the design of serious games, especially when integrating them into educational settings. The first factor is economic: a sufficient budget should be allocated for serious game designers, developers, and practitioners. The second factor is the inclusion of the target audience in the game design and development process. Child and adult play testers can contribute significantly to the design of serious games by sharing their pedagogical expectations and visual tastes. The final factor is the potential and diversity of the serious game design team. A strong team of educators, game designers, and developers is instrumental in making serious games effective from educational and entertainment perspectives.

Game technologies can offer players more realistic worlds, and players can take responsibility for their playing in a more realistic manner. Shaffer et al. (2005) pointed out that "video games have potential to change the landscape of learning towards a new model of learning through meaningful activity in virtual worlds as preparation for meaningful activity in our postindustrial, technology-rich, real world" (p. 18). Therefore, many studies are needed to investigate students' attitudes towards implementing serious games in education (Martí-Parreño et al., 2018). Not only can serious games offer meaningful educational activities, but players' attitudes can guide the integration of serious games into educational environments. Integrating serious games into educational curricula should be carefully studied and employed (Arnab et al., 2015). Examining affective characteristics such as players' attitudes, empathy, and enjoyment can help researchers understand how to integrate serious games into educational settings by revealing players' flow experiences and motivational states (Alexiou et al., 2020; Zhonggen, 2019). In addition to these affective characteristics, players' interactions with other players, their roles in online gaming communities, and the relationship between game features and their real-life implications should be investigated to better describe players' flow experiences.

REFERENCES

Akilli, G. K., & Cagiltay, K. (2006). An Instructional Design/Development Model for the Creation of Game-like Learning Environments: The FIDGE Model. In M. Pivec (Ed.), *Affective and emotional aspects of human computer interaction: Game-based and innovative learning approaches* (pp. 93–112). IOS Press.

Alexiou, A., Schippers, M. C., Oshri, I., & Angelopoulos, S. (2020). Narrative and aesthetics as antecedents of perceived learning in serious games. *Information Technology & People*, *35*(8), 142–161. Advance online publication. doi:10.1108/ITP-08-2019-0435

Almeida, F., & Simoes, J. (2019). The role of serious games, gamification and Industry 4.0 tools in the Education 4.0 paradigm. *Contemporary Educational Technology*, *10*(2), 120–136. doi:10.30935/cet.554469

Anyaegbu, R., Ting, W., & Li, Y. I. (2012). Serious game motivation in an EFL classroom in Chinese primary school. *The Turkish Online Journal of Educational Technology*, *11*(1), 154–164.

Arnab, S., Lim, T., Carvalho, M. B., Bellotti, F., De Freitas, S., Louchart, S., Suttie, N., Berta, R., & De Gloria, A. (2015). Mapping learning and game mechanics for serious games analysis. *British Journal of Educational Technology*, *46*(2), 391–411. doi:10.1111/bjet.12113

Ávila-Pesántez, D., Rivera, L. A., & Alban, M. S. (2017). Approaches for serious game design: A systematic literature review. *Computers in Education Journal*, *8*(3), 1–11.

Axelsson, A. S., & Regan, T. (2002). *How belonging to an online group affects social behavior – A case study of Asheron's Call* (Technical Report MSR-TR-2002-07). Microsoft Research, Microsoft Corporation.

Bachen, C. M., Hernández-Ramos, P., Raphael, C., & Waldron, A. (2016). How do presence, flow, and character identification affect players' empathy and interest in learning from a serious computer game? *Computers in Human Behavior*, *64*, 77–87. doi:10.1016/j.chb.2016.06.043

Barros, C., Carvalho, A. A., & Salgueiro, A. (2020). The effect of the serious game Tempoly on learning arithmetic polynomial operations. *Education and Information Technologies*, *25*(3), 1497–1509. doi:10.100710639-019-09990-4

Barry, I. (2005). Game design. In S. Rabin (Ed.), *Introduction to Game Development* (pp. 99–160). Charles Rive Media, Inc.

Braad, E., Žavcer, G., & Sandovar, A. (2016). Processes and models for serious game design and development. In R. Dörner, S. Göbel, M. Kickmeier-Rust, M. Masuch, & K. Zweig (Eds.), *Entertainment computing and serious games* (pp. 92–118). Springer. doi:10.1007/978-3-319-46152-6_5

Bui, P., Rodríguez-Aflecht, G., Brezovszky, B., Hannula-Sormunen, M. M., Laato, S., & Lehtinen, E. (2020). Understanding students' game experiences throughout the developmental process of the number navigation game. *Educational Technology Research and Development*, *68*(5), 2395–2421. doi:10.100711423-020-09755-8

Buzady, Z. (2017). Flow, leadership and serious games – A pedagogical perspective. *World Journal of Science. Technology and Sustainable Development*, *14*(2–3), 204–217. doi:10.1108/WJSTSD-05-2016-0035

Chan, K. H. W., Wan, K., & King, V. (2021). Performance over enjoyment? Effect of game-based learning on learning outcome and flow experience. *Frontiers in Education*, *6*, 1–10. doi:10.3389/feduc.2021.660376

Chen, J. (2007). Flow in games (and everything else). *Communications of the ACM*, *50*(4), 31–34. doi:10.1145/1232743.1232769

Chen, Z. H. (2014). Learning preferences and motivation of different ability students for social-competition or self-competition. *Journal of Educational Technology & Society*, *17*(1), 283–293.

Cilesiz, S. (2009). Educational computer use in leisure contexts: A phenomenological study of adolescents' experiences at internet cafes. *American Educational Research Journal*, *46*(1), 232–274. doi:10.3102/0002831208323938

Cole, H., & Griffiths, M. D. (2007). Social interactions in massively multiplayer online role-playing gamers. *Cyberpsychology & Behavior, 10*(4), 575–583. doi:10.1089/cpb.2007.9988 PMID:17711367

Cowley, B., Moutinho, J. L., Bateman, C., & Oliveira, A. (2011). Learning principles and interaction design for 'Green My Place': A massively multiplayer serious game. *Entertainment Computing, 2*(2), 103–113. doi:10.1016/j.entcom.2011.01.001

Csikszentmihalyi, M. (1990). *Flow: The psychology of optimal experience*. Harper Perennial.

De Gloria, A., Bellotti, F., & Berta, R. (2014). Serious games for education and training. *International Journal of Serious Games, 1*(1), 1–15. doi:10.17083/ijsg.v1i1.11

Dimitriadou, A., Djafarova, N., Turetken, O., Verkuyl, M., & Ferworn, A. (2021). Challenges in serious game design and development: Educators' experiences. *Simulation & Gaming, 52*(2), 132–152. doi:10.1177/1046878120944197

Gómez, R. L., & Suárez, A. M. (2020). Gaming to succeed in college: Protocol for a scoping review of quantitative studies on the design and use of serious games for enhancing teaching and learning in higher education. *International Journal of Educational Research Open, 2*(2), 1–7. doi:10.1016/j.ijedro.2020.100021

Hamari, J., Shernoff, D. J., Rowe, E., Coller, B., Asbell-Clarke, J., & Edwards, T. (2016). Challenging games help students learn: An empirical study on engagement, flow and immersion in game-based learning. *Computers in Human Behavior, 54*, 170–179. doi:10.1016/j.chb.2015.07.045

Hess, T., & Gunter, G. (2013). Serious game-based and nongame-based online courses: Learning experiences and outcomes. *British Journal of Educational Technology, 44*(3), 372–385. doi:10.1111/bjet.12024

Huang, C. L., Yang, S. C., & Hsieh, L. S. (2019). The cyberbullying behavior of Taiwanese adolescents in an online gaming environment. *Children and Youth Services Review, 106*, 1–10. doi:10.1016/j.childyouth.2019.104461

Hummel, H. G., Nadolski, R. J., Eshuis, J., Slootmaker, A., & Storm, J. (2021). Serious game in introductory psychology for professional awareness: Optimal learner control and authenticity. *British Journal of Educational Technology, 52*(1), 125–141. doi:10.1111/bjet.12960

Jerčić, P., Wen, W., Hagelbäck, J., & Sundstedt, V. (2018). The effect of emotions and social behavior on performance in a collaborative serious game between humans and autonomous robots. *International Journal of Social Robotics, 10*(1), 115–129. doi:10.100712369-017-0437-4

Kapralos, B. (2021). Learning about serious game design and development at the K-12 level. *International Journal of Information and Learning Technology, 38*(3), 316–327. doi:10.1108/IJILT-01-2021-0003

Kiili, K., & Lainema, T. (2008). Foundation for measuring engagement in educational games. *Journal of Interactive Learning Research, 19*(3), 469–488. doi:10.1016/j.iheduc.2004.12.001

Lieberman, D. A. (2006). What can we learn from playing interactive games? In P. Vorderer & J. Bryant (Eds.), *Playing video games—Motives, responses, and consequences* (pp. 379–397). Lawrence Erlbaum Associates.

Malone, T. W., & Lepper, M. R. (1987). Making learning fun: A taxonomy of intrinsic motivations for learning. In R. Snow & M. J. Farr (Eds.), Aptitude, learning, and instruction volume 3: Conative and affective process analyses (pp. 223–253). Lawrence Erlbaum Associates.

Martí-Parreño, J., Galbis-Córdova, A., & Miquel-Romero, M. J. (2018). Students' attitude towards the use of educational video games to develop competencies. *Computers in Human Behavior*, *81*, 366–377. doi:10.1016/j.chb.2017.12.017

McInroy, L. B., & Mishna, F. (2017). Cyberbullying on online gaming platforms for children and youth. *Child & Adolescent Social Work Journal*, *34*(6), 597–607. doi:10.100710560-017-0498-0

Moizer, J., Lean, J., Dell'Aquila, E., Walsh, P., Keary, A. A., O'Byrne, D., Di Ferdinando, A., Miglino, O., Friedrich, R., Asperges, R., & Sica, L. S. (2019). An approach to evaluating the user experience of serious games. *Computers & Education*, *136*, 141–151. doi:10.1016/j.compedu.2019.04.006

Oksanen, K. (2013). Subjective experience and sociability in a collaborative serious game. *Simulation & Gaming*, *44*(6), 767–793. doi:10.1177/1046878113513079

Oksanen, K., & Hämäläinen, R. (2014). Game mechanics in the design of a collaborative 3D serious game. *Simulation & Gaming*, *45*(2), 255–278. doi:10.1177/1046878114530799

Pellas, N. (2017). An exploration of interrelationships among presence indicators of a community of inquiry in a 3D game-like environment for high school programming courses. *Interactive Learning Environments*, *25*(3), 343–360. doi:10.1080/10494820.2015.1127819

Perttula, A., Kiili, K., Lindstedt, A., & Tuomi, P. (2017). Flow experience in game based learning–a systematic literature review. *International Journal of Serious Games*, *4*(1), 57–72. doi:10.17083/ijsg.v4i1.151

Prensky, M. (2001). Fun, play and games: What makes games engaging. In M. Prensky (Ed.), *Digital game-based learning* (pp. 106–145). McGraw-Hill.

Ritterfeld, U., & Weber, R. (2006). Video games for entertainment and education. In P. Vorderer & J. Bryant (Eds.), *Playing video games. Motives, responses, and consequences* (pp. 399–413). Lawrence Erlbaum Associates.

Sajjadi, P., Hoffmann, L., Cimiano, P., & Kopp, S. (2019). A personality-based emotional model for embodied conversational agents: Effects on perceived social presence and game experience of users. *Entertainment Computing*, *32*, 1–10. doi:10.1016/j.entcom.2019.100313

Scaife, M., & Rogers, Y. (1999). Kids as informants: Telling us what we didn't know or confirming what we knew already. In A. Druin (Ed.), *The design of children's technology* (pp. 29–50). Morgan Kaufmann.

Schäfer, A., Holz, J., Leonhardt, T., Schroeder, U., Brauner, P., & Ziefle, M. (2013). From boring to scoring–a collaborative serious game for learning and practicing mathematical logic for computer science education. *Computer Science Education*, *23*(2), 87–111. doi:10.1080/08993408.2013.778040

Shaffer, D. W., Squire, K. D., Halverson, R., & Gee, J. P. (2005). Video games and the future of learning. *Phi Delta Kappan*, *87*(2), 104–111. doi:10.1177/003172170508700205

Sipiyaruk, K., Hatzipanagos, S., Reynolds, P. A., & Gallagher, J. E. (2021). Serious games and the COVID-19 pandemic in dental education: An integrative review of the literature. *Computers*, *10*(4), 1–15. doi:10.3390/computers10040042

Smith, P. K., Mahdavi, J., Carvalho, M., Fisher, S., Russell, S., & Tippett, N. (2008). Cyberbullying: Its nature and impact in secondary school pupils. *Journal of Child Psychology and Psychiatry, and Allied Disciplines*, *49*(4), 376–385. doi:10.1111/j.1469-7610.2007.01846.x PMID:18363945

Squire, K. (2003). Video games in education. *International Journal of Intelligent Simulations and Gaming*, *2*(1), 49–62.

Strzalkowski, T., & Symborski, C. (2017). Lessons learned about serious game design and development. *Games and Culture*, *12*(3), 292–298. doi:10.1177/1555412016673524

Susi, T., Johannesson, M., & Backlund, P. (2007). *Serious games, an overview* (Technical report HIS-IKI-TR-07-001). University of Skvde.

Wang, C. H., Wu, K. C., & Tsau, S. Y. (2019). Flow learning experience: Applying marketing theory to serious game design. *Journal of Educational Computing Research*, *57*(2), 417–447. doi:10.1177/0735633117752454

Wattanasoontorn, V., Boada, I., García, R., & Sbert, M. (2013). Serious games for health. *Entertainment Computing*, *4*(4), 231–247. doi:10.1016/j.entcom.2013.09.002

Westera, W. (2019). Why and how serious games can become far more effective: Accommodating productive learning experiences, learner motivation and the monitoring of learning gains. *Journal of Educational Technology & Society*, *22*(1), 59–69.

Whitton, N. (2010). *Learning with digital games: A practical guide to engaging students in higher education*. Routledge.

Yee, N. (2006). Motivations for play in online games. *Cyberpsychology & Behavior*, *9*(6), 772–775. doi:10.1089/cpb.2006.9.772 PMID:17201605

Zhonggen, Y. (2019). A meta-analysis of use of serious games in education over a decade. *International Journal of Computer Games Technology*, *5*(1), 1–8. doi:10.1155/2019/4797032

ADDITIONAL READING

Calderón, A., Ruiz, M., & O'Connor, R. V. (2018). A serious game to support the ISO 21500 standard education in the context of software project management. *Computer Standards & Interfaces*, *60*, 80–92. doi:10.1016/j.csi.2018.04.012

Hara, C. Y. N., Goes, F. D. S. N., Camargo, R. A. A., Fonseca, L. M. M., & Aredes, N. D. A. (2021). Design and evaluation of a 3D serious game for communication learning in nursing education. *Nurse Education Today*, *100*, 1–7. doi:10.1016/j.nedt.2021.104846 PMID:33751998

Hart, S., Margheri, A., Paci, F., & Sassone, V. (2020). Riskio: A serious game for cyber security awareness and education. *Computers & Security*, *95*, 1–16. doi:10.1016/j.cose.2020.101827

Hess, T., & Gunter, G. (2013). Serious game-based and nongame-based online courses: Learning experiences and outcomes. *British Journal of Educational Technology*, *44*(3), 372–385. doi:10.1111/bjet.12024

Kliem, A., Wendel, V., Winter, C., Wiemeyer, J., & Göbel, S. (2012). Virtual sports teacher–a serious game in higher education. *International Journal of Computer Science in Sport*, *10*, 100–110.

Lameras, P., Arnab, S., Dunwell, I., Stewart, C., Clarke, S., & Petridis, P. (2017). Essential features of serious games design in higher education: Linking learning attributes to game mechanics. *British Journal of Educational Technology*, *48*(4), 972–994. doi:10.1111/bjet.12467

Rosyid, H. A., Palmerlee, M., & Chen, K. (2018). Deploying learning materials to game content for serious education game development: A case study. *Entertainment Computing*, *26*, 1–9. doi:10.1016/j.entcom.2018.01.001

Tubelo, R. A., Portella, F. F., Gelain, M. A., de Oliveira, M. M. C., de Oliveira, A. E. F., Dahmer, A., & Pinto, M. E. B. (2019). Serious game is an effective learning method for primary health care education of medical students: A randomized controlled trial. *International Journal of Medical Informatics*, *130*, 1–6. doi:10.1016/j.ijmedinf.2019.08.004 PMID:31442848

Vahldick, A., Farah, P. R., Marcelino, M. J., & Mendes, A. J. (2020). A blocks-based serious game to support introductory computer programming in undergraduate education. *Computers in Human Behavior Reports*, *2*, 1–12. doi:10.1016/j.chbr.2020.100037

Whalen, K. A., Berlin, C., Ekberg, J., Barletta, I., & Hammersberg, P. (2018). 'All they do is win': Lessons learned from use of a serious game for Circular Economy education. *Resources, Conservation and Recycling*, *135*, 335–345. doi:10.1016/j.resconrec.2017.06.021

KEY TERMS AND DEFINITIONS

Flow: Flow is the complete immersion of the player into the gameplay.

Intrinsic Motivation: Intrinsic motivation is a desire that comes from within a person without expecting any external reward.

Serious Game Design: Serious game design is the process of creating entertaining digital games that are also educational or skill-enhancing by using design, aesthetic, and technical elements.

Serious Games: Serious games are digital games aiming to improve players' skills or to provide them with knowledge while also being entertaining.

Social Presence: Social presence describes a person's being, along with all of his or her feelings, thoughts, and relationships, in a highly participatory and interactive environment.

Chapter 23
Gamification Framework:
Understanding the Critical Success Factors for Using Gamification as a Pedagogical Tool

Asha S. Kutty
Mar Dionysius College, India

Manu Melwin Joy
CUSAT, India

ABSTRACT

The effectiveness of any teaching-learning process (TLP) can be evaluated based on results obtained after using it. Any learning result relies upon the pedagogical methods adopted to teach learners. The more the technique's suitability, the better will be the results. Game-based learning is where game features and principles are implanted within learning activities. Game-based learning is also an effective learning technique in which games boost student learning. Game-based learning (GBL) brings advancement, experimentation, and disclosure of internal ability in learners. For the educators, it creates original thoughts and ways to deal with the teaching-learning process, allowing instructors to learn new methodologies lined up with research on how students learn. This chapter attempts to sort out the requirement for game-based learning as a creative educating approach. The significant finding of this chapter is a conceptual framework that will enable researchers to identify critical factors for the successful implementation of GBL.

INTRODUCTION

The economy of any nation relies upon significant two angles - Industry and the Education. Industry implies the creation, conveyance and the pay and employment age, which is reflected in GDP and per capita pay. Education implies the information change, the schooling framework, and the way the network is bestowing education. If we take a glimpse at the education area, the taking in initial stages from age

DOI: 10.4018/978-1-6684-4287-6.ch023

4 till the individual has the inclination of learning, for example long lasting learning. The NEP-New Education Policy of India, 2020 which is actualized from this2020, and goes till 2040, calls for changed philosophy to be followed to confer knowledge and education. Because of unexpected circumstance (like COVID 19), most of the educating happens on the web. This is seen from the first degree of school till the PhD courses. A huge number of learners depend on online mode, with various techniques adopted to give knowledge. Over many years, we have utilized a wide range of modes - Chalkboard; OHP-Overhead Projector; PPT slides; notes, videoconferencing, mixed mode and so forth. Every one of these techniques have both advantageous view and limitations. Because of fast changes in economy and the instruction area, more current approaches are required, to arrive at the enormous populace and to have more noteworthy effect on learning outcomes and implementation progress.

Success of learners depend on upon different components - instructional method, approach of educating, educator's information base and so on. Exploration has deplored that "the test of instructing has expanded when encountered with dynamically impassive learners" (Reiners, 2012) found that good old educating system doesn't raise learners' competency to take care of issues freely or to move learning matter to new situations. Educators have recognized a necessity for the variety of teaching procedures that tackle the test of efficient information flow, learner commitment, just as ideal flexibility obviously substance and critical thinking aptitudes. As a possible arrangement, game based learning has accrued increased consideration from the schooling area, just as industry, since it guarantees innovative methods to create skills and increase knowledge (Yee, 2006); (Voogt, 2012); (Scharkow M, 2015). Game-based learning includes planning learning exercises so that game qualities and game standards impact inside the learning exercises themselves. For instance, in an Economics course, learners may compete in a virtual stock-exchanging competition; in a Political Science course, learners may pretend as they participate in simulated activities including a quiz. Games can present objectives, connection, criticism, critical thinking, rivalry, story, and fun learning climate, components that can build student commitment and maintain inspiration. Furthermore, we are seeing more individuals talk about and investigate the possibility of "gamification" — acquainting gaming ideas with generally non-gaming climate. Game and Gamification which are currently broadly utilized in scholastics and work environment, have a few similarities and differences, with regards to practical use.

GAMIFICATION VERSUS GAME-BASED LEARNING

Gamification and game-based learning are similar in that both strategies promote engagement and sustained motivation in learning. However, gamification and game-based learning can also be usefully distinguished. Gamification is the integration of game elements like point systems, leader boards, badges, or other elements related to games into "conventional" learning activities to increase engagement and motivation. For example, an online discussion forum for a Physics course might be gamified via a badge system: students might be awarded a "Ptolemy" badge after they have made 10 postings, a "Galileo" badge after 20 postings, "Kepler" after 30, "Einstein" after 40, and so on. In ideal gamified learning environment, students can see online badges that their peers have earned to create a sense of comradery or competition. Gamification and game-based learning both promote engagement and sustained motivation in learning, but they do not necessarily result in improved learning outcomes. According to Educause's, there are Seven outcomes about Game Based Learning, viz.: 1. Draw students into a course more actively 2. Competition can arouse motivation 3. Hone student abilities while achieving interim goals that makes them feel like they are progressing 4. Reinforce the fact that failure is not a setback nor an outcome but indication that more skill building is needed 5. Through discrete steps, students can see the interrelationship of tactics and strategy 6. Learn about procedure and the value of alternative paths, and 7. Help students become more confident, independent thinkers who are more prepared to take on large projects and carry them through to completion. Toccura Porter, in his article "Games and Activities: Alternative Foundation for Library Instructional Learning," says that there should be consideration of the educational outcomes that need to be fulfilled, whenever a game is incorporated into the classroom. He also states that educational emphasis in 21st century encourages inclusive teaching and learning approaches that are student centred, and that games are an emerging media that play a central role in the development of current generation.

GAME BASED LEARNING: CHALLENGES

Similarly, as with any new instructive methodology, there are various difficulties to utilizing games in the study hall. In the article, "Gaming and Learning: Winning data education cooperation," Spiegelman and Glass talk about potential Barriers to Games Based learning, viz.: 1. Games set aside effort to learn and plan appropriately 2. Squandered endeavours will be the best managerial dread 3. Include materials that range from the modest to the exorbitant 4. Plan endeavours are frequently financed through awards which should be overseen 5. Academic and specialized backings may be essential (extra assets) 6. Issues of access and the computerized partition 7. An assessment is required with respect to whether understudies incline toward this way to deal with educating.

Notwithstanding, it should be noticed that the Spiegelman and Glass express that a ton of game-based learning should be possible with a little venture of assets, and many can be executed with next to no overhead. Also, the advantages of games-based getting the hang of, including expanded commitment and inspiration, more prominent learning, are too convincing to even consider ignoring. Boyhun Kim, in the article "Bridling the Power of Game Dynamics," not all games are fun or worth playing. On the off chance that there is helpless plan, the game won't be fun, and afterward understudies won't play it. The suggestions that the creator makes is to not over gamify. She suggests beginning little and making the game client focused. Educause's in the work on "7 Things You Should Know About Gaming," express that coming up next are a few worries that may emerge out of adopting a games strategy in guidance are as per the following: Games may have instructive allure; however, their overall allure probably won't be general. They are habitually connected with recreation instead of scholarly drive can cause some to feel reluctant. Game elements can be hard to line up with learning goals. As to meet the instructive model, it should meet targets and be entertaining. They should accomplish appropriate arrangement with educational plan. An examination of GBL writing shows the huge positive results in learning and greater commitment of understudies. Games, which centre around learning results, planned logically, executed methodologically, sway adapting emphatically.

REVIEW: OVERVIEW OF STUDIES

As per (Grabinger, 1995), good old educating does not raise understudies' competency to take care of issues autonomously or to move learning substance to new circumstances. Thus, its profoundly prudent to consider a showing philosophy which can assist students with applying hypothetical information in pragmatic/genuine circumstances. Game Based Learning is an imaginative technique which can possibly be a superior academic methodology in educating learning measure. Games animate a few positive feelings in people, for example, feeling consumed, connected with, and achieved (Sailer, 2017). Individuals become more drawn in and gainful during games a lot can possibly inspire people (Garris R. A., 2017); (Gee, 2007).Games are seen as certain enthusiastic encounters from the elements of joy, excitement, and strength ((Poels, 2012). The result of the exploration work accompanies the end that games lead to Challenge, Curiosity, Fun, Fantasy, Interest and Enjoyment ((Admiraal, 2011). Games help in gathering learning destinations like the improvement of sensible thinking, memory, representation, speedy reflexes and critical thinking aptitudes, group building and inspiration abilities; encouraging logical proficiency among residents; to give a thought regarding civic establishments and history, to show geology; and improving specific visual consideration (Morschheuser B. H., 2017); (Steinkuehler, 2008); (Admiraal W. H., 2011); (S, 2016); (Belchior P. M., 2013). GBL writing, analysts proposed commitment as the basic factor which encourage learning. Commitment is characterized as important student association all through the learning climate ((Hamari J. S.-C., 2016); (da Rocha Seixas L. G., 2016). Examination work appreciated why games are so alluring. As indicated by them, it would occur because of a combination of imagination, challenge, and interest, in addition to a degree of commitment portrayed as "stream", where clients don't get unfocussed ((Farlane, 2004). Learning is situated and happens through a cycle of estimating, testing, and gleaming upon the re-enacted world inside the game. This makes the learning cycle additionally captivating (Hamari, 2016); (da Rocha Seixas L. G., 2016). Games can make commitment, and drew in students show more exertion, additionally seeing, more sure feelings, and give more consideration to the learning climate (Fredricks J. A., 2004). Commitment prompts more consideration from the piece of the understudy, and this makes the learning cycle more compelling (Admiraal W. H., 2011). Inborn motivation and the autotelicy of learning are estimated as perhaps the most noteworthy peak of effective training. In games, nonetheless, it is normally seen that gamers who are every now and again occupied with are naturally inspired, just as having the option to start psychological, passionate and social advantage (Cerasoli, 2014). A significant number of the investigations led concur with the way that important learning happens when students connect effectively in learning so that they can choose applicable approaching data, coordinate the chose data into understandable mental models and acclimatize the psychological models with relevant earlier information (Hess, 2013); (Fitz-Walter Z. J.-P., 2017); (Erhel, 2018); (Georgiou, 2018). Studies done in GBL demonstrated that the foreseen value and the foreseen straightforwardness of learning games affected student's overall aim to utilize them than fun or pleasure, though there is by all accounts no connection among delight and intellectual learning pick up (Iten, 2016). GBL writing expressed that effect of stream (operationalized as elevated test and expertise), commitment, and submersion on learning in game-based learning conditions could viably draw in understudies in a learning action (Admiraal W. H., 2011); (Hamari J. S.-C., 2016).Most games permit the player to control the degree of challenge and permits the player to expand abilities, produce stream and consequently inherently inspiring players to improve their aptitudes to address the raised difficulty and re-emerge stream (Huotari, 2017); (Erhel S. &., 2018). Exploration work in GBL have demonstrated the significance of stream and capacity of games to produce stream. The equilibrium of expertise and challenge is the fundamental condition for stream to happen (Eppmann, 2018). Studies have likewise asserted that gamified frameworks can turn into a wellspring of characteristic inspiration on the off chance that they incorporate six components: play, work, decision, data, commitment, and reflection (Yang Y. A., 2017) emphatically.

Learners don't enter a learning climate like 'void vessels' yet carry their own involvement in them; such foundation factors impact their view of and commitment in GBL (Blohm, 2013); (Deterding, 2011). The writing in advanced education and GBL recommends that different factors might be similarly significant, for example, character (Codish, 2014), gamer sort (Hamari J. &., 2014); (Hamari, 2014),and mentalities toward game-based learning and involvement in games (Landers, 2015).The investigations in the field of GBL have considered different results which speak to the viability and adequacy of this method of learning on the student, and famous among them are joint effort (Van der Meii, 2011), basic reasoning (Angeli, 2009); (Galarneau, 2007); (Silva, 2009); (Wang Q. W., 2009)innovative aptitudes.

METHODOLOGY

A systematic review methodology was used to classify how game-based learning systems have been used in education. The authors wanted to identify the most widely documented benefits and components of gamified learning. It is important to identify the contexts in which game-based learning systems prosper/ succeed, and factors for its active implementation. The systematic review methodology suggested by ((Kush, 2011)was conducted. All papers included in the literature review were published after 2007. Systematic review methodology was followed in this study which consists of the following steps. First, we will have to identify objectives of the literature review, then select keywords and databases based on their relevancy to the research area. Search these databases, review title and abstract to eliminate papers for duplication, foreign language, and non-educational application. Then go for a detailed review to eliminate those articles which are not applicable to our context. After this, group the selected reviews based on some common themes and finally report the findings. The systematic review began by assessing each of the A-Z databases pertinent to the research area, with the preliminary search of keywords "Game-based learning" "AND" "Education" in the "All Text" field of the advanced search for each database and restraining the search to include only peer-reviewed journal articles listed in ABDC. The databases used include Taylor & Francis, Web of Science, Proquset, Science Direct, and Scopus. These databases were selected as they widely cover the broad base of application areas of game-based learning. A total of 670 papers were identified in the first search. Grey literature, repetitive search results, and papers which did not contain full text in English were omitted. A detailed review of the title and abstract of the remaining papers was conducted to remove those that did not meet the inclusion criteria for this systematic review. 64 papers remained after this step. Only papers found in the databases through the authors' institutional library were included.

OPPORTUNITY FOR STUDY IN GBL

Games are an omnipresent piece of life in our way of life, and specialists propose they will turn out to be considerably more profoundly implanted in the coming years. Games assist individuals with building up an attitude toward cooperation, critical thinking, correspondence, experimentation, and investigation of characters, all credits that advance achievement in a quickly evolving, data-based culture. Investigation into the psychological and socio-social parts of gaming has detonated in the most recent decade as individuals have understood the potential for game-based learning (Shaffer, 2006).

A few games mean to build content information by letting the players "live" the situation. They may likewise make such an apprenticeship model in which players relate to specialists and take on those parts as they move further into the game. Interest in supposed "genuine games" has appeared to help change perspectives and influence players' activities (TED Talk by Jane McGonigal). Games appear to be especially fruitful in assisting individuals with creating critical thinking and dynamic aptitudes and empowering development. Undoubtedly, gaming prompts individuals to do an enormous measure of exploration and rouses members to invest an uncommon measure of energy on undertaking. Investigating the open door in GBL, the interest emerges in understanding 3 viewpoints, which make GBL besides successful and centred.

1. First, we need to understand the students you want to teach. People have different aptitude and abilities when it comes to learning various subjects. How can we validate GBL on student learning and led to better literacy outcomes?
2. Teachers should ensure that their students are engaging with relevant content as they play. Otherwise, you may risk your students rejecting the games since they do not offer much or any assistance in their academics. How do we validate assessment tools and what are the parameters of assessment, and measurement of educational outcomes?
3. Teachers should make their students accountable for the time they spend playing. Keeping a watchful eye on their progress does not remove the stress-free elements of the game. Instead, you get the opportunity to see how well they are doing. After all, outcomes need to be measurable if you want to continue directing the students to areas they can improve in their academics. The game-based learning is based on three basic points: quality content, relevance, rigour, and simulators. How do we address these issues looking into cultural and scholastic difference among students?

Thus, the present study drives into understanding and addressing issues-game impact-learning outcomes-engagement- scholastics achievements and find better solutions and methodology for further focused approach. A framework and model are developed which will be empirically tested by the author.

While each framework has around it-the positive and negative factors related, there is consistently a way that can be found or find, for more prominent advantage, if that framework is embraced and has better ramifications and result. There is a chance (research work hole) for taking a gander at the GBL. framework, and expand on in making a fresher methodology through Game Based Learning in Education area, with creative and best practice approach. A system and model that address the understudies and personnel (teachers) would be the result of study here. This article centres around taking a gander at independent and dependent including the moderate factors a lot affecting GBL approach and what makes the framework shared benefit results.

The main actors in this GBL are Student-Teacher. The central point is the technology received. The trigger is the substance significance meticulousness of games embraced. Furthermore, the outcome is the paste of the info and the yield, viz: the utilization of games in getting the hang of driving towards meeting the destinations. The model talks about all the players and the technique utilized. While the stream is totally attracted to show the pathway, understudies and instructors structure the principal layer, the learning destinations and stage utilized structure the subsequent layer; the results both in type of subjective and subjective quantifiable structure the third layer; and the last layer is the learning results. The outcomes can be measured again in quality-quantity. The scope of the study in terms of Actors, Objectives, Methodological Approach, and the Results is drawn in the Conceptual Framework.

Figure 1. GBL conceptual framework

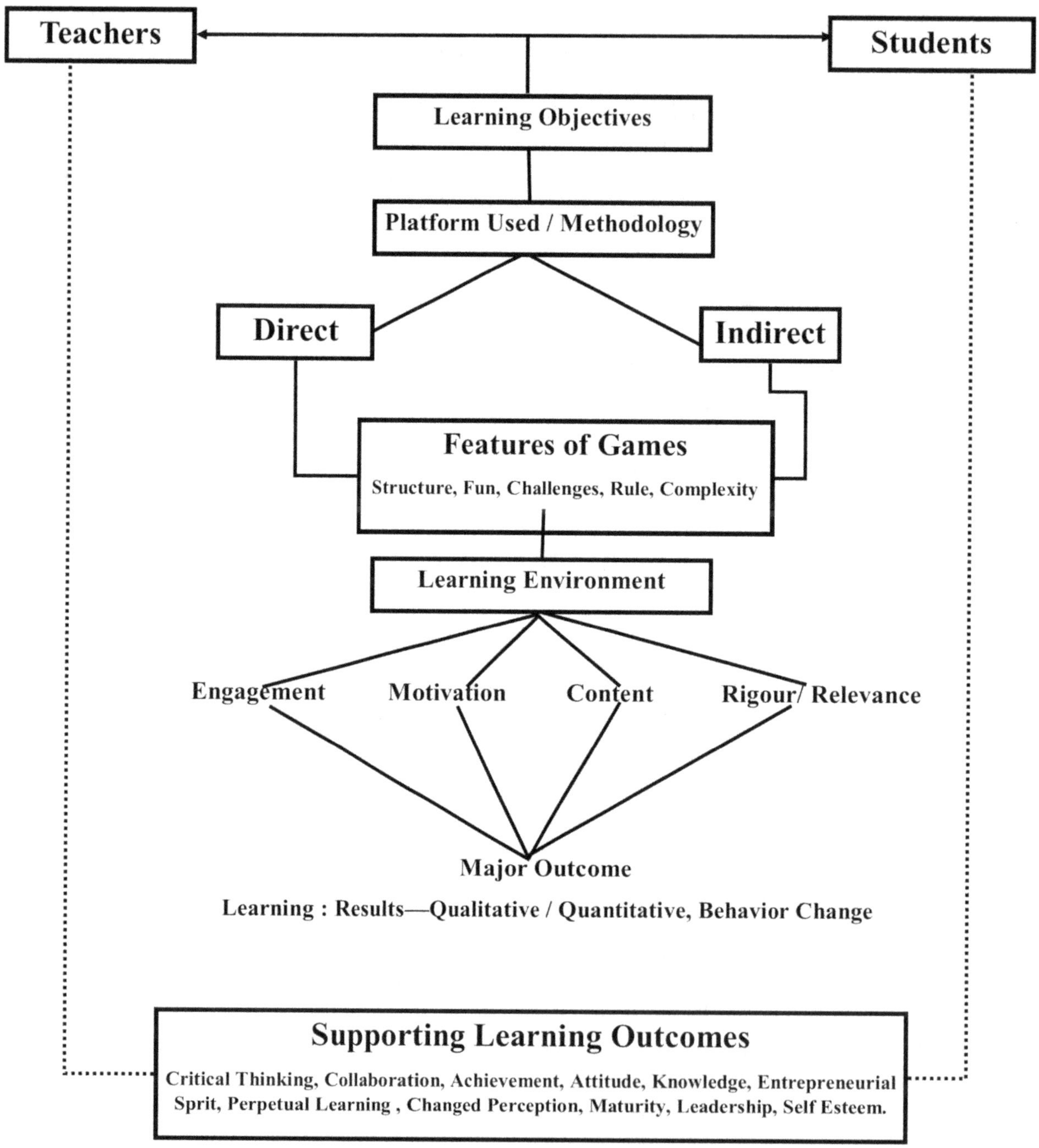

CONCLUSION

We are in a time where information is accessible in bounty. Students can discover information surrounding them. Yet, whatever be the amount and nature of information accessible, understudies think that it's hard to apply their learning, all things considered, circumstance. However, it is a lot of significant for understudies to comprehend the handy relevance if whatever they are learning in schools and universities. Aside from this a large portion of present-day understudies are effectively withdrawn and need inherent inspiration to learn. We should discover an approach to connect with understudies even more likely, propel them characteristically lastly make them equipped for applying information at whatever point and any place required. This article attempts to reveal the capability of games and use of Game Based Learning as an educational intercession to propel and connect with learners more readily.

REFERENCES

Admiraal, W., Huizenga, J., Akkerman, S., & Ten Dam, G. (2011). The concept of flow in collaborative game-based learning. *Computers in Human Behavior*, *27*(3), 1185–1194. doi:10.1016/j.chb.2010.12.013

Angeli, C., Valanides, N., & Christodoulou, A. (2016). Theoretical considerations of technological pedagogical content knowledge. In Handbook of technological pedagogical content knowledge (TPACK) for educators (pp. 11-32). Routledge.

Belchior, P., Marsiske, M., Sisco, S. M., Yam, A., Bavelier, D., Ball, K., & Mann, W. C. (2013). Video game training to improve selective visual attention in older adults. *Computers in Human Behavior*, *29*(4), 1318–1324. doi:10.1016/j.chb.2013.01.034 PMID:24003265

Blohm, I., & Leimeister, J. M. (2013). Gamification. *Wirtschaftsinformatik*, *55*(4), 275–278. doi:10.100711576-013-0368-0

Cerasoli, C. P., Nicklin, J. M., & Ford, M. T. (2014). Intrinsic motivation and extrinsic incentives jointly predict performance: A 40-year meta-analysis. *Psychological Bulletin*, *140*(4), 980–1008. doi:10.1037/a0035661 PMID:24491020

Codish, D., & Ravid, G. (2014). Personality based gamification-Educational gamification for extroverts and introverts. In *Proceedings of the 9th CHAIS Conference for the Study of Innovation and Learning Technologies: Learning in the Technological Era* (Vol. 1, pp. 36-44). Ra'anana: The Open University of Israel.

da Rocha Seixas, L., Gomes, A. S., & de Melo Filho, I. J. (2016). Effectiveness of gamification in the engagement of students. *Computers in Human Behavior*, *58*, 48–63. doi:10.1016/j.chb.2015.11.021

Deterding, S. (2011, May). Situated motivational affordances of game elements: A conceptual model. In Gamification: Using game design elements in non-gaming contexts, a workshop at CHI (Vol. 10, No. 1979742.1979575). Academic Press.

Eppmann, R., Bekk, M., & Klein, K. (2018). Gameful experience in gamification: Construction and validation of a gameful experience scale. *Journal of Interactive Marketing*, *43*, 98–115. doi:10.1016/j.intmar.2018.03.002

Erhel, S., & Jamet, E. (2019). Improving instructions in educational computer games: Exploring the relations between goal specificity, flow experience and learning outcomes. *Computers in Human Behavior*, *91*, 106–114. doi:10.1016/j.chb.2018.09.020

Fitz-Walter, Z., Johnson, D., Wyeth, P., Tjondronegoro, D., & Scott-Parker, B. (2017). Driven to drive? Investigating the effect of gamification on learner driver behavior, perceived motivation and user experience. *Computers in Human Behavior*, *71*, 586–595. doi:10.1016/j.chb.2016.08.050

Fredricks, J. A., Blumenfeld, P. C., & Paris, A. H. (2004). School engagement: Potential of the concept, state of the evidence. *Review of Educational Research*, *74*(1), 59–109. doi:10.3102/00346543074001059

Galarneau, L., & Zibit, M. (2007). Online games for 21st century skills. *Games and simulations in online learning: Research and development frameworks*, 59-88.

Garris, R., Ahlers, R., & Driskell, J. E. (2017). Games, motivation, and learning: A research and practice model. In *Simulation in Aviation Training* (pp. 475–501). Routledge. doi:10.4324/9781315243092-25

Georgiou, Y., & Kyza, E. A. (2018). Relations between student motivation, immersion and learning outcomes in location-based augmented reality settings. *Computers in Human Behavior*, *89*, 173–181. doi:10.1016/j.chb.2018.08.011

Grabinger, R. S., & Dunlap, J. C. (1995). Rich environments for active learning: A definition. *ALT-J*, *3*(2), 5–34. doi:10.3402/rlt.v3i2.9606

Hamari, J., Shernoff, D. J., Rowe, E., Coller, B., Asbell-Clarke, J., & Edwards, T. (2016). Challenging games help students learn: An empirical study on engagement, flow and immersion in game-based learning. *Computers in Human Behavior*, *54*, 170–179. doi:10.1016/j.chb.2015.07.045

Hamari, J., & Tuunanen, J. (2014). *Player types: A meta-synthesis*. Academic Press.

Hess, T., & Gunter, G. (2013). Serious game-based and nongame-based online courses: Learning experiences and outcomes. *British Journal of Educational Technology*, *44*(3), 372–385. doi:10.1111/bjet.12024

Huotari, K., & Hamari, J. (2017). A definition for gamification: Anchoring gamification in the service marketing literature. *Electronic Markets*, *27*(1), 21–31. doi:10.100712525-015-0212-z

Iten, N., & Petko, D. (2016). Learning with serious games: Is fun playing the game a predictor of learning success? *British Journal of Educational Technology*, *47*(1), 151–163. doi:10.1111/bjet.12226

Kirriemuir, J., & McFarlane, A. (2004). *Literature review in games and learning*. Academic Press.

Kush, P., Cudney, E. A., Materla, T., & Antony, J. (2021). Systematic literature review of quality maturity matrix. *Total Quality Management & Business Excellence*, *32*(3-4), 289–297. doi:10.1080/14783363.2018.1552130

Landers, R. N., & Armstrong, M. B. (2017). Enhancing instructional outcomes with gamification: An empirical test of the Technology-Enhanced Training Effectiveness Model. *Computers in Human Behavior*, *71*, 499–507. doi:10.1016/j.chb.2015.07.031

Morschheuser, B., Hamari, J., Koivisto, J., & Maedche, A. (2017). Gamified crowdsourcing: Conceptualization, literature review, and future agenda. *International Journal of Human-Computer Studies*, *106*, 26–43. doi:10.1016/j.ijhcs.2017.04.005

Reiners, T., Wood, L. C., Chang, V., Gütl, C., Herrington, J., Teräs, H., & Gregory, S. (2012). *Operationalising gamification in an educational authentic environment*. Academic Press.

Sailer, M., Hense, J. U., Mayr, S. K., & Mandl, H. (2017). How gamification motivates: An experimental study of the effects of specific game design elements on psychological need satisfaction. *Computers in Human Behavior*, *69*, 371–380. doi:10.1016/j.chb.2016.12.033

Shaffer, D. W., & Gee, J. P. (2006). *How computer games help children learn*. Palgrave Macmillan. doi:10.1057/9780230601994

Silva, E. (2009). Measuring skills for 21st-century learning. *Phi Delta Kappan*, *90*(9), 630–634. doi:10.1177/003172170909000905

Steinkuehler, C., & Duncan, S. (2008). Scientific habits of mind in virtual worlds. *Journal of Science Education and Technology*, *17*(6), 530–543. doi:10.100710956-008-9120-8

VandeWalle, D. (1997). Development and validation of a work domain goal orientation instrument. *Educational and Psychological Measurement*, *57*(6), 995–1015. doi:10.1177/0013164497057006009

Voogt, J., & Roblin, N. P. (2012). A comparative analysis of international frameworks for 21st century competences: Implications for national curriculum policies. *Journal of Curriculum Studies*, *44*(3), 299–321. doi:10.1080/00220272.2012.668938

Wang, Q., Woo, H. L., & Zhao, J. (2009). Investigating critical thinking and knowledge construction in an interactive learning environment. *Interactive Learning Environments*, *17*(1), 95–104. doi:10.1080/10494820701706320

Yang, Y., Asaad, Y., & Dwivedi, Y. (2017). Examining the impact of gamification on intention of engagement and brand attitude in the marketing context. *Computers in Human Behavior*, *73*, 459–469. doi:10.1016/j.chb.2017.03.066

Yee, N. (2006). The demographics, motivations, and derived experiences of users of massively multi-user online graphical environments. *Presence (Cambridge, Mass.)*, *15*(3), 309–329. doi:10.1162/pres.15.3.309

Chapter 24
Gamification to Engage Students:
Integrating the Use of Discord Chat App

Suzanne Brown-McBride
University of Hawaii, Manoa, USA

Peter Leong
https://orcid.org/0000-0003-1549-0893
University of Hawaii, Manoa, USA

ABSTRACT

This chapter describes a case study of the gamification of an educational technology graduate course at the University of Hawaii. The chapter will provide some background literature about chat apps, chat apps in education, and gamification. Next, the chapter will discuss how gamification design elements, framed by the curricula, were implemented in the Discord chat app server using roles, bots, and participation-based experience points. Finally, the chapter will discuss the benefits, challenges, and lessons from incorporating gamification in the Discord server for a graduate online asynchronous course. Recommendations will be provided for instructors who are considering gamifying their college courses.

INTRODUCTION

Originally created to facilitate communication between casual game players online, Discord has become a popular platform for remote groups to connect with 13.5 million active servers per week (About Discord, n.d.). With features similar to chat platforms like Slack and Teams, some educators are already using Discord to host student discussions (Kruglyk et al., 2020; Tom & Joakim, 2017). Less common, however, is the use of Discord's integrations and automations to ease and speed the use of gamification mechanics such as cooperative communication, leveling, experience points, leaderboards, polling and team quests for online learning.

DOI: 10.4018/978-1-6684-4287-6.ch024

This chapter describes a case study of the gamification of an educational technology graduate course using the Discord chat app. The chapter will provide some background about the development of chat apps, a brief literature review of essential concepts related to gamification and a discussion of chat apps in education and gamification. Next, the chapter will discuss how gamification design elements, framed by the curricula, were implemented in Discord chat app server through the use of roles, bots and participation-based experience points. Finally, the chapter will discuss the benefits, challenges and lessons learned of incorporating gamification in Discord server for a graduate online asynchronous course. Recommendations will be provided for instructors who are considering gamifying their college courses.

Gamification is a strategy that resonates with many, but not all students who participate. Discord's integration of gamification with communications components allows for students to benefit from just-in-time communication with their classmates and instructors, even if they choose not to fully participate in the course's gamified elements. For those students who are interested and willing to immerse themselves in the narrative of a course, gamification through Discord can provide a rich and collaborative environment to learn.

BACKGROUND

Why Chat?

Since the inception of the public internet, users have looked for ways to shrink the distance between them to communicate and share ideas (Tarud, 2021). In particular, technologies that facilitate real-time conversation have been a driving force behind digital innovation. Before the launch of the graphical world wide web, early internet enthusiasts used newsgroups, file transfer protocol (FTP), text-based bulletin boards (BBS), Internet Relay Chat (IRC), and Multi-User Dungeons (MUDS) to engage in real-time, or nearly-real time (McCullough, 2018; Oikarinen & Reed, 1993). These platforms were used to host discussions, text-based adventure games, breaking news, and topical repositories of information but were accessible to only the most elite users (McCullough, 2018).

Appealing to a more mainstream audience, CompuServe created the first commercial chat platform CB Simulator in 1980. At the height of its use, CB simulator offered 40 separate chat channels where any subscriber to CompuServe could chat with other subscribers. This feature quickly accounted for 20% of the time that users spent on that platform (Tweney, 2009).

Building on this success, other dial-up service providers began to offer Instant Messaging services that incorporated features like buddy lists where users could chat with a curated list of contacts and friends and voice chat ("Instant Messaging," 2021). The integration of these features into the 'walled garden' of subscription service platforms like America Online helped expand the popular userbase for these services and dramatically increased other kinds of technology investment, like ad revenue (Wu, 2016). While the use of the original bulletin board and IRC technologies have been dropping steadily since the turn of the century, the use of modern chat apps is growing with the top five platforms reaching nearly 5.6 billion active users (Pingdom, 2012; Tankovska, 2021).

Chat apps, like their historical predecessors' bulletin boards, instant messaging, and IRC, are seen by some as superior to asynchronous communication platforms like email because chat apps more closely resemble spontaneous, natural conversation (Wang, 2004). Additionally, chat apps have evolved to become project management and data storage platforms that centralize how people collaborate and track information.

In the workplace, the private sector has used chat and the functionality of real-time file sharing to develop an array of technical tools to help employees collaborate across remote work locations (Herrman, 2019). Platforms like Slack, Google Hangouts, and Microsoft Teams were designed to allow software workgroups to share text, audio, photos in real-time (Cyders & Hilterbran, 2016). Often seen as the modern answer to antiquated technologies like telephone and email, business-style chat apps can serve as catch-alls to manage a team or as one developer put it "having a place to put audio files, random phone numbers, breaking news or even memes from our listeners has made all of our jobs easier" (Herrman, 2019). Especially as the world enters the post-pandemic, chat apps are seen as providing a flexible alternative to face-to-face interactions and live meetings (Miller, 2021).

The gaming community has also seen the potential of real-time chat as a tool to help remotely located gamers communicate while playing online. The most popular chat app for gamers, Discord, was created to be a lightweight, free, and secure alternative to other chat platforms (Lazarides, 2015; Tankovska, 2021). In addition to text and voice chat, Discord also features easy integrations with gamified features such as XP point generation, leaderboards, and spaces for collaboration and team decision making. Discord continues to add features and functionality which has increased its appeal to non-gaming users, including in education (Bailey et al., 2020; Schwartz, 2021).

LITERATURE REVIEW

Gamification

Gamification is the practice of adding game-like elements into instruction such as quests, badges, awards, leveling, leaderboards, non-linear navigation, and timed activities which invite the learners to compete individually or in teams (Deterding et al., 2011; Huang et al., 2020). Gamification is widely used in the private and public sector including retail business, employee training, service marketing and education (Landers, 2014).

While gamification is not solely a digital strategy, as more instruction moves online it has become a popular way to enrich content and engage learners (Looyestyn et al., 2017). Distinct from game-based learning, gamification employs a series of mechanics within the context of instruction instead of simply playing a game that contains educational content (Alsawaier, 2018). Similarly, the gamification of learning is often referred to as 'serious games' in an effort to differentiate the play elements from games that are designed to purely entertain (Susi et al., 2007). Wilson et.al. built on the construct of serious games and went on to argue that it was possible to begin to align instructional objectives with game attributes that positively influence skill and affective outcomes, but that it was difficult to conclusively link any one particular approach with a specific outcome (2009). The connection between gamified strategies and learning outcomes was further refined by Lander's gamified learning theory which argued that instructional content was the fundamental component of successful learning which can be enhanced by gamified approaches (Landers, 2014).

The evidence related to the impact of gamified learning on student outcomes, however, is inconsistent. In a recent meta-analysis of gamification and learning outcomes 30 different interventions were examined and the literature suggests a significant to medium effect size in positive outcomes over non-gamified learning (Bai et al., 2020). Other studies, however, demonstrate that the learner and their educational context can undermine, or even reverse potentially positive outcomes (Rivera & Garden, 2021). It is also unclear if the positive effect is persistent (Dichev & Dicheva, 2017).

While the research is not clear on which particular gamification element is most effective, there is evidence that gamification generally can influence a learner's level of interest and intrinsic motivation (Rivera & Garden, 2021).

Motivation and Engagement

A student's ability to participate and persist in programming is one of the fundamental requirements for academic success. Motivation and engagement are closely aligned, but not dependent, concepts that describe a learners internal process and external factors that shape learner interactions with instruction.

Generally, the use of gamification seems to increase the motivation and engagement of learners (Huang et al., 2020; Sailer & Homner, 2020). In fact, tools like the Pleasure Experience (PLEX) framework can be used to describe and contextualize how gamification can support intrinsic motivation through activities such as discovery, thrill, competition, and captivation (Korhonen et al., 2009).

Self -Determination Theory

Self-Determination Theory (SDT), as originated by Deci and Ryan argues that people are motivated to develop and learn based on three universal needs:

- Autonomy: the learner's ability to feel in control of their own conduct and goals
- Competence: the ability to gain expertise and mastery
- Connection or relatedness: feeling belonging and attachment to others (1985)

While self-determination theory argues that the internal, or intrinsic, desire to gain autonomy, competence and connection drives behavioral change, external (or extrinsic) factors can boost or detract from an individual's motivation to accomplish these goals. There is a fairly significant body of literature that has discussed the connection between gamification and the elements of SDT which correlate to better intrinsic motivation (Alsawaier, 2018; Rivera & Garden, 2021; Shi & Cristea, 2016).

Interaction and Collaboration

Early educational theories such as Bandura's social learning theory and Vygotsky's social development theory highlight the importance of the social aspects of learning. Bandura argues that learners acquire, in part, through the imitation and rehearsal of model behaviors. Desirable behaviors are rewarded and affirmed within the context of culture and learners retain and reproduce those behaviors that they value (Bandura & Walters, 1977). Similarly, Vygotsky's social development theory argues that learners first perceive knowledge as it occurs between people before it is internalized (Tudge & Winterhoff, 1993) . In the digital context, the intensity of interaction between participants on a platform or learners in an online class is often referred to as social presence (Tu, 2000).

Social Presence Theory

Initially constructed as a way to measure physical engagement between people (such as with eye contact or proximity), social presence theory has evolved to include digital interactions.

Online, the degree of social presence can be measured along three dimensions:

1. **Social Context:** participants are oriented to the task at hand, and have relationships with other participants, and they are familiar with relevant social processes such as ways of interacting or making decisions.
2. **Online communications:** participants are familiar with the mores of how others communicate in this particular digital context. For example, participants can effectively communicate ideas using the patois of the medium such as acronyms and memes.
3. **Interactivity:** participants expect to receive feedback in real-time, or near real-time (Tu, 2000).

Collaborative Learning

One way to reinforce learners' motivation and engagement is through collaboration and feedback. The empirical literature on gamification shows an especially strong positive relationship between learner motivation, engagement and performance when the gamification strategies include instant feedback and collaboration (Alsawaier, 2018; Leaning, 2015). Courses that focus gamification strategies on specific course exercises and outcomes or limit choice are less successful than gamification strategies that focus on promoting collaborative learning and intra-student learning, which can be more impactful and have the added benefit of improving course communication (Knutas et al., 2014).

Faculty Engagement and Capacity

Gamification can help instructors, and students, reconcile and connect with their roles as learners and interconnected members of a community by tapping into the ideas and interactions that motivate their best work (Lockee & Song, 2021).

While the concept of gamification is fairly popular among instructors, very few actually adopt gamification strategies in their classrooms (Martí-Parreño et al., 2016; Pernelle et al., 2021). This gap between idea and implementation may be related to resource and technical support constraints that make instructors hesitant to embrace new, technology-assisted approaches like gamification (Dermeval & Bittencourt, 2020). Simply put, instructors are interested in gamification but lack the technical skills and time to integrate this strategy into their coursework.

Chat Apps in Education

While distance learning and the use of technology is not a new concept in the instructional community, the rise of the public internet created new possibilities, and challenges for educators (Reiser, 2001). During the late 1990s and early 2000s, some educators struggled to manage the expansive, unorganized trove of information that could be found online with one instructor despairing that the internet was a "vast and treacherous sea" (Towsend, 2003).

Since that time, the use of online instruction and resources has become a mainstay of modern education with the majority of classrooms in the United States routinely using internet-connected technologies. More recently, chat apps have been used as an adjunct to instruction to help students collaborate on projects and assignments. Within the educational context, there has been a preference for chat applications that more closely resemble the business platform model which includes information and project management features in addition to text, voice, and video communication.

Chat and Motivation

While instruction should remain the core strategy for influencing learner behavior, interactive approaches that promote collaboration and encourage positive behaviors and attitudes can be a helpful compliment (Landers, 2014). Chat apps have been used as an adjunct to both in-person and hybrid instruction to facilitate the competition of projects and group tasks. Instructors who have used chat apps like Teams, Hangouts, Slack, and Discord in the classroom have found that they increase student engagement and promote interaction between students (Cyders & Hilterbran, 2016; Kruglyk et al., 2020).

Chat apps also demonstrate many of the motivational qualities described by self-determination theory:

- **Autonomy:** For younger students, in particular, the use of chat apps is facilitated by their deep familiarity with mobile platforms which makes it easier to quickly respond and interact with the instructor or student-led discussions (Hussain et al., 2018). Furthermore, being able to digitally create, or recreate elements of the user persona are consistent with how Gee constructs autonomy volition online (2005).
- **Competence:** Many students enjoy using chat apps and plan to continue to use the platforms in their personal life (Lacher & Biehl, 2019).
- **Cohesion:** For remote learners, chat apps have also been found to be an important tool for maintaining classroom cohesion. During the Covid-19 pandemic, chat apps helped maintain the conditions for natural interaction between instructors and students, and between students themselves which is an important condition to maintaining motivation in remote contexts (Kruglyk et al., 2020; Wahyuningsih & Baidi, 2021).

Chat for Gamification in Education

While chat apps have increasingly been used in the context of education, it is less common for them to be used as a means to actually gamify instruction itself. More specifically, there are some practice examples of instructors using platforms like Discord to host the audio and note-taking related to educational gaming but do not utilize any of the platform's extensible features that are suited to gamification (Bailey et al., 2020; Kleiber, 2020).

Chat to Promote Teamwork

The ability to successfully design and implement group projects is a critical competency for students to master as they contemplate entering the workforce. Members of a project team must be able to share ideas, store research materials, collaborate on task delegation, and iterate product drafts. Unsurprisingly, chat apps like Slack, and Teams which were designed for the workplace are well-suited to track and manage these kinds of interactions. One class that deployed Slack found that it made communication and idea exchange easier between team members and assisted with the delegation of tasks (Lacher & Biehl, 2019). In another case study, engagement with team members in a chat app was correlated with the successful completion of a group project (Cyders & Hilterbran, 2016). Chat apps are well suited to promote the collaboration and real-time feedback that has been shown to increase learner motivation and engagement (Alsawaier, 2018).

Faculty and Chat Apps

Like students, faculty members have brought their experience with chat apps in their personal lives into their strategies for classroom management. Faculty have also found that students make frequent use of chat apps to ask questions and seek guidance (Cyders & Hilterbran, 2016). However, student satisfaction with using chat apps as a method of connecting with instructors may diminish when class sizes are large, particularly for undergraduates (Hussain et al., 2018).

Additionally, the introduction of a chat app to the classroom can also be time-consuming for instructors as students manage their expectations around instructor access and the learning curve associated with learning a new technology (Lacher & Biehl, 2019; Vladoiu & Constantinescu, 2020). Particularly in the university setting, the heterogeneity of student experiences with technology may highlight differences in comfort with using chat apps.

Filling an Unmet Need

During the Covid-19 pandemic, many universities discovered that their preexisting capacity to host online learning was not sufficient to meet the needs of their students who were transitioning to entirely remote learning (Kruglyk et al., 2020). While traditional discussion forums can provide students with opportunities to interact with one another, they lack the instantaneous, just-in-time features of chat apps which are more appropriate for collaboration and remote work (Vladoiu & Constantinescu, 2020). In particular, there was a need to identify platforms that could host both synchronous and asynchronous content to match the patterns of class offerings (Cyders & Hilterbran, 2016; Kruglyk et al., 2020).

THE CASE STUDY

LTEC 643: Educational Technology in Learning in Informal Learning Environments is a graduate elective course that provides students in the Learning Design and Technology graduate program with an overview of the use of educational technology in informal learning environments. The purpose of this course is to help students gain an understanding of the nature, application, and use of educational technology in museums, cultural institutions, tourist attractions and visitor information centers through readings, lectures, case studies, discussions, digital resources, guest speakers and site visits.

A hero's journey monomyth was used to drive the narrative element of the gamification. This monomyth, which involves a hero who departs on an adventure, and in a pivotal ordeal, triumphs and then returns home transformed, was first introduced in Joseph Campbell's The Hero with a Thousand Faces (1949). At the start of the course, students are introduced to the hero's journey gamification narrative using the following mission description:

"The future isn't what it used to be... The world fell into war in 2077, and mankind has barely survived. As it became clear that mankind would never recover, the world's leading thinkers developed a plan to restore the once great civilization - time travel. A thorough examination of the events leading up to the travesty which befell the planet, identified you and your fellow classmates as having a pivotal role in preventing the catastrophe that ultimately destroyed mankind."

This narrative was designed to act as the critical framework for the instruction which would be supported an amplified by the gamification elements. Centering the course narrative in this manner was designed to amplify and give purpose to the gamification elements which should lead to deeper and more persistent motivation (Dichev & Dicheva, 2017; Landers, 2014).

In order for the class to experience the gamification narrative, the instructor, the teaching assistant and all students created their avatar images and wrote their character storylines. The class was divided up into leagues and each league created their motto or slogan.

Students earn experience points (XPs) by successfully completing their class assignments ("missions"). The XPs students earn will determine their level and rank in the game. There are eight levels beginning with Level 1 "Space Time Cadet" to Level 8 "General Gravity". In addition, students can earn reward points ("Thorium Fuel Cells") which could be exchanged into XPs or used to "purchase" items such as assignment extensions, opportunity to resubmit assignments, etc. in the LTEC 643 Marketplace. To enhance team collaboration and accountability amongst team members, league-based reward points were also awarded to reward positive team behavior (Knutas et al., 2014). A portal website was used to incorporate the course and students' storylines as well as displaying student progress in the game.

Using Discord for Gamification

LTEC 643's Discord server was intended to serve several functions: act as a platform for class communication, facilitate collaborative work and deepen the gamification narrative that framed the entire semester.

Server Preparation and Student Orientation

The initial setup of the server was fairly straightforward - a #general channel was created for whole class discussion, an #announcements channel was designated for one-way communication from the instructor regarding class events, and a #ask-general-gravity channel was created for direct questions to the instructor and teaching assistant. Three team text and voice channels were also created with placeholder names for small collaborative breakouts. Changing the designations for any of these text and voice channels is trivial so the collaborative group names on each channel were updated when teams self-selected the name of their in-game league which reinforced the connection between the server and the gamification narrative.

Like the other business-style chat apps, Discord also has the ability to extend its functionality with integrations. However, Discord's integrations are less focused on traditional productivity offerings and more focused on the needs of online gamers and gaming community managers. Discord's focus on gaming creates some natural opportunities for educators who are looking to gamify instruction.

Discord can use automated 'bots' to perform a variety of tasks such as new-user onboarding, scheduling, content moderation, memes, games, and user role management. For instructors who use Discord, this architectural affordance can extend the platform's capabilities to automate some of the repetitive tasks associated with gamification such as awarding XP and managing roles and ranks. Bots can either be added from a public repository managed by Discord or designed bespoke for specific servers. In the classroom context, custom bots have been developed to track attendance, upload homework, provide links to online exams, and notify students of the grades they have received for their work (Vladoiu & Constantinescu, 2020).

For LTEC 643, several bots were configured to automate portions of the gamification workflow: a member management bot, a scheduling bot, and a polling bot. The member management bot automated some elements of XP generation, managed the class leaderboard, and automated rank promotions. The member management bot could also be set to automate communications such greeting each user when they logged into the server for the first time and reminding them of the channel they could use to reach out to the instructor and teaching assistant. Because the bot was constantly monitoring the Discord, it could reinforce gamification achievements by immediately awarding promotions as users accrued XP points.

The polling bot was used later in the semester when participants were asked to choose their favorite presentation from among both their entire class and their collaborative team. The polling bot set up polls in the main channel for all students to vote, as well as in each collaborative team channel for each team to vote within their group. Also, while the class was largely asynchronous, there were several optional synchronous sessions offered for students to discuss material and ask questions. The scheduling bot was used to confirm dates and participants for each synchronous session.

Using any new technology often requires a learning curve to ensure that all users are able to use the tool to its fullest extent. Discord, in particular, has been found to be a platform that is easy to use and less technically resource-intensive than other platforms (Kleiber, 2020; Kruglyk et al., 2020; Vladoiu & Constantinescu, 2020). Most of the students who joined the LTEC Discord server were first-time users of the platform with some experience using other chat apps like Teams or Slack. In order to ease their entry onto the server, an orientation video was created to help students navigate logging onto the server, and to help describe the general layout and purpose of the channels.

Avatars as a Tool for Gamification

Upon joining the class Discord server, LTEC 652 students in the case study were encouraged to change their user nicknames and login images to reflect their game-based avatar names and to also change their profile photo to their avatar photo. This customization of image and name further reinforced their participation in the underlying game narrative (Jannicke, et al., 2017).

Earning Experience Points (XP)

Earning experience points or "XP" is a classic game mechanic that rewards players for persistence and experience. When used in the classroom, XP points should serve not only as reward for achievement, but also as a reinforcement for positive behaviors (Nah et al., 2013). For educators, it can often be labor-intensive and difficult for instructors to manually maintain a sabermetric-style inventory of XP-worthy activities. Furthermore, there are reward-worthy behaviors that are difficult to quantify in the classroom setting such as collaboration.

Enhancing Collaboration and Real-time Feedback

While most chat platforms are able to host real-time communications, LTEC 643's Discord server was able to help automate some of these tasks and expand the number of activities that could be rewarded with XP points, including collaborative conversations with classmates. Adding chat participation into leaderboard scores created an around-the-clock feedback loop of positive reinforcement which is positively correlated with increased student engagement and motivation (Alsawaier, 2018; Rivera & Garden, 2021). With the bot installed, students were able to gain XPs and rank by participating in class discussions and interacting with each other. Every time a student communicated with other classmates on the Discord server via chat or postings, that student automatically gained XP points. The Discord bot automatically tabulated the scores and those XPs were displayed on the class leaderboard. Ranks on the server were set to trigger at predetermined points intervals and were announced immediately when a student achieved a new rank.

To move up the leaderboard, or to get a higher ranking, students were encouraged to converse and interact within their league, as well as with their other classmates on Discord. Rewarding even passive conversation on the server was designed to positively reinforce the use of Discord as the center of each team's collaborative efforts. For LTEC 643, points earned during league communication on Discord was decisive in the final rounds of rank promotions.

XPs were also manually awarded and added to each student's total on the Discord server when they participated in activities that were not hosted on Discord such as Flipgrid video blogs and submitted assignments. Bonus XPs were also awarded and manually added to the student totals on the Discord server for other types of participation, for example, there were several "Easter egg phrases" scattered inside of the course syllabus. XPs were given to the first two students to identify the "Easter egg phrases'' in the syllabus which immediately increased their rank. Students also earned additional XPs by completing optional quests or missions offered over the duration of the course. Based on the case study reported by Vladoiu and Constantinenscu (2020), it is likely that a customized bot could even more fully automate this practice.

Server Ranks Roles as a Tool for Gamification

Unlike Slack or Teams, Discord natively integrates the notion or roles which, when configured correctly, can more deeply integrate gamification. On a standard Discord server, the owner of the server can set up different classes of members that have different levels of permissions to participate in specific channels, invite other server members, mute, or ban other members. In essence, promoted members have access to additional server permissions and privileges.

In an educational context, roles can allow instructors and teaching assistants to create layers of management (such as to invite members or bots) or create access rules for certain conversations. For example, it is possible to set permissions on a team chat channel to allow only team members and the instructors to join - which might be helpful if teams are competing against one another. Similarly, an instructor could set up an 'announcements' channel that was viewable by all on the server but did not allow comment.

In terms of gamification, roles on Discord can also serve as designations of title or status. It's possible to create roles that are linked to XP achievements so that as XP is earned, higher ranks are achieved. In this case study, the gamification narrative of the class was reinforced by assigning every student an initial rank of "Space-Time Cadet". As students gained XP by collaborating with each other and completing assigned tasks, their rank increased. When a promotion occurred, it was announced server-wide and the rank was noted under the name of the promoted student. While in this instance increased rank did not result in specific additional server permissions when participants were online, their active-status avatars in the Discord server member list were ordered by rank achieved. So not only were rank achievements noted by the instructors, students were reminded of each other's progress every time they logged into the Discord server.

Using a Leaderboard

As students gained ranks on the Discord server based on the XPs earned, their progress was captured by a class leaderboard. The membership management bot on the server tracked each participant's running XP total, including any manual entries that the instructor added on an ad hoc basis. The leaderboard also noted the level each student had achieved. The leaderboard was constantly accessible at a private weblink or when students used the !leaderboard command on Discord.

BENEFITS AND CHALLENGES

Benefits

Discord's ability to reward learner interactions and collaboration set it apart from other chat solutions in terms of gamifying educational content, especially those features that automatically reinforce collaborative interactions and team decision-making.

Discord's extensible, gaming-focused features make it an attractive platform to enhance educational gamification. Its popularity in the gaming community increases the odds that students will be familiar with its basic operation. Discord is also an accessible, lightweight technology that is suited for desktop or mobile platforms which greatly simplifies user onboarding and adoption.

Discord is a stable, easy to use platform for anyone of almost any technical skill level to use, and administer. Because the initial cost for the platform is free, there is a low barrier to entry for educators who are interested in using it as a communication platform, as well as a tool for gamification.

With the use of bots, it is possible to automate and reward learners in real-time for participating in class activities on the server. Bots can help automate some tasks like scheduling, polls, and interaction leaderboards which reduce the burden of some classroom administrative tasks. Discord roles can also be used to create ranks and status rewards that reinforce gamification elements.

Challenges

While Discord is exceptionally easy to use and does not require any payment to establish a server, some of the more sophisticated bots require a fee to fully use their features. Additionally, some of the more complicated automation may require a higher level of technical skill to fully implement. And, even with automations, some manual recordkeeping may still be required to gamify every part of a curriculum.

As a platform, Discord has limited user analytics which might make it difficult to understand how students are using, or not using, different server features. Instructors may need to use other feedback and assessment mechanisms to determine how students are interacting with content and the success of gamification efforts.

LESSONS LEARNED AND RECOMMENDATIONS

About 86% of the participants agree that using Discord for collaborating with their classmates and their team had an impact on their experience. It was observed that the teams that most frequently used the text chat messaging function in Discord to collaborate with their team mates seem most motivated by the course gamification. This concurs with Knutas et al. (2014) that gamification strategies that focus on promoting collaborative learning and intra-student learning can be more impactful and have the added benefit of improving course communication.

In a previous iteration of this gamified course, Google Sheet was used to manually keep track of students' XPs. Implementing bots to automate the process awarding XPs definitely made it easier compared to manually inputting XPs into Google Sheet. Additionally, there are many different ways to creatively use bots or design bots to increase student engagement such as using a bot to automatically award XPs when a particular word appears in the chat messages. To encourage students to help each other by answering questions posted, a bot could be programmed to award XPs whenever the word "star" is associated with a student's name in the chat messages.

This process of implementing gamification for a graduate online asynchronous course using the Discord server provided many insights. One participant's comment seems to sum up the general sentiment for the gamified course:

I really like the idea. I think for me, being pressed for time often, I didn't feel as though I could buy-in to the game aspect as much. But the overall idea is great and I think it can impact people a lot in a positive way.

The use of gamification appears to impact students' motivation differently. It's not for every student. For some learners, it's really motivating, while others "personally did not care for using Discord or competing with classmates to earn points."

The use of the hero's journey monomyth narrative for this gamified course is contingent upon the students' ability and willingness to suspend their disbelief. Mature, adult graduate students seem to find it difficult to be immerse in the narrative as they are simultaneously learning about gamification as part of the course content. One student commented that:

Gamification confuses me more than a traditional classroom system (thinking about rewards and ranks and storylines), but it might be more effective for other students, and it certainly helps to learn the concepts presented in the course.

The findings of this study have several implications for the design of gamified courses. Some recommendations for instructors who are considering gamifying their college courses include:

1. start small with something that they are familiar or comfortable with; teachers need to have a realistic learning target and should ideally begin by using Discord as a chat tool and award points for student participation, then add more gamification elements as they go along;
2. when attempting to gamify a course, the goals of instruction and the objectives should be centrally unchanged. Gamification as a method of instruction is not about fundamentally changing the nature of the course, but rather including mechanisms which promote collaboration and engagement;

3. set very clear game rules for your gamified course; and
4. be actively present in the Discord chat by responding regularly and promptly to questions posed.

CONCLUSION

In conclusion, this chapter presented a case study of how gamification was implemented in Discord chat app server through the use of roles, bots and participation-based experience points. Many educators are interested in gamification but lack the technical skills or time to implement gamification in their courses. The novel use of bots in Discord chat app makes it possible to automate the process of rewarding learners for active participation in class activities on the server as well as to automate tasks like scheduling, polls, and interaction leaderboards which reduces the burden of some gamification administrative tasks. Additionally, Discord roles can be used to create ranks and status rewards that reinforce gamification elements. There are potentially numerous other bots can that be used to support other gamification elements. This case study hopes to encourage educators to consider gamifying their own classes using a chat app server like Discord.

REFERENCES

Alsawaier, R. S. (2018). The effect of gamification on motivation and engagement. *The International Journal of Information and Learning Technology*, *35*(1), 56–79. doi:10.1108/IJILT-02-2017-0009

Bai, S., Hew, K. F., & Huang, B. (2020). Does gamification improve student learning outcome? Evidence from a meta-analysis and synthesis of qualitative data in educational contexts. *Educational Research Review*, *30*, 100322. doi:10.1016/j.edurev.2020.100322

Bailey, K., Bullington, T., & Maclever, L. (2020). *The emergency campaign: Discord, D&D, and distance learning*. Faculty Focus | Higher Ed Teaching & Learning. https://www.facultyfocus.com/articles/online-education/online-course-delivery-and-instruction/the-emergency-campaign-discord-dd-and-distance-learning/

Bandura, A., & Walters, R. (1977). *Soical Learning theory* (Vol. 1). Prentice Hall.

Campbell, J. (1949). *The Hero with a Thousand Faces*. Princeton University Press.

Cyders, T., & Hilterbran, A. (2016). *Classroom integration of the Slack team collaboration tool*. Academic Press.

Dermeval, D., & Bittencourt, I. I. (2020). Co-designing gamified intelligent tutoring systems with teachers. *Revista Brasileira de Informática Na Educação*, *28*, 73–91. doi:10.5753/rbie.2020.28.0.73

Deterding, S., Dixon, D., Khaled, R., & Nacke, L. (2011). From game design elements to gamefulness: Defining "gamification." *Proceedings of the 15th International Academic MindTrek Conference on Envisioning Future Media Environments - MindTrek '11*, 9. 10.1145/2181037.2181040

Dichev, C., & Dicheva, D. (2017). Gamifying education: What is known, what is believed and what remains uncertain: a critical review. *International Journal of Educational Technology in Higher Education, 14*(1), 9. doi:10.118641239-017-0042-5

Gee, J. P. (2005). Learning by Design: Good video games as learning machines. *E-Learning and Digital Media, 2*(1), 12. doi:10.2304/elea.2005.2.1.5

Herrman, J. (2019, June 19). Slack Wants to Replace Email. Is That What We Want? *The New York Times*. https://www.nytimes.com/2019/06/19/style/slack-replace-email-ipo-listing.html

Huang, R., Ritzhaupt, A. D., Sommer, M., Zhu, J., Stephen, A., Valle, N., Hampton, J., & Li, J. (2020). The impact of gamification in educational settings on student learning outcomes: A meta-analysis. *Educational Technology Research and Development, 68*(4), 1875–1901. doi:10.100711423-020-09807-z

Hussain, S., Mills, A., & Sanders, A. K. (2018). Use of Slack in the undergraduate classroom as a means of fostering student/faculty engagement. *Qatar Foundation Annual Research Conference Proceedings*. 10.5339/qfarc.2018.SSAHPP995

Instant messaging. (2021). In *Wikipedia*. https://en.wikipedia.org/w/index.php?title=Instant_messaging&oldid=1031867862

Jannicke, B. H., Anna, B., & Klaus-Dieter, T. (2017). Avatars as motivational factors in simulation games. *The International Scientific Conference eLearning and Software for Education, 1*, 263. 10.12753/2066-026x-17-039

Kleiber, I. (2020). (Video) games in the language classroom. HINT. *Heidelberg Inspirations for Innovative Teaching*, 45-59. doi:10.11588/HINT.2020.1.77690

Knutas, A., Ikonen, J., Nikula, U., & Porras, J. (2014). Increasing collaborative communications in a programming course with gamification: A case study. *Proceedings of the 15th International Conference on Computer Systems and Technologies - CompSysTech '14,* 370–377. 10.1145/2659532.2659620

Korhonen, H., Montola, M., & Arrasvuori, J. (2009). *Understanding playful user experience through digital games. International Conference on Designing Pleasurable Products and Interfaces*, Compiegne, France.

Kruglyk, V., Bukreiev, D., Chornyi, P., Kupchak, E., & Sender, A. (2020). Discord platform as an online learning environment for emergencies. *Ukrainian Journal of Educational Studies and Information Technology, 8*(2), 13–28. doi:10.32919/uesit.2020.02.02

Lacher, L. L., & Biehl, C. (2019). *Investigating team effectiveness using Discord: A case study using a gaming collaboration tool for the CS classroom*. Academic Press.

Landers, R. N. (2014). Developing a Theory of Gamified Learning: Linking Serious Games and Gamification of Learning. *Simulation & Gaming, 45*(6), 752–768. doi:10.1177/1046878114563660

Lazarides, T. (2015, September 14). *Ex-'Fates Forever' developers making "Discord", a voice comm app for multiplayer mobile games.* TouchArcade. https://toucharcade.com/2015/09/14/ex-fates-forever-developers-making-discord-a-voice-comm-app-for-multiplayer-mobile-games/

Leaning, M. (2015). A study of the use of games and gamification to enhance student engagement, experience and achievement on a theory-based course of an undergraduate media degree. *Journal of Media Practice*, *16*(2), 155–170. doi:10.1080/14682753.2015.1041807

Lockee, B., & Song, K. (2021). Three Perspectives to See Students in Gamified Classes. *ISSUU*. https://issuu.com/bainespsa/docs/a76891_isa_journal_issue_24_issuu/s/11678935

Looyestyn, J., Kernot, J., Boshoff, K., Ryan, J., Edney, S., & Maher, C. (2017). Does gamification increase engagement with online programs? A systematic review. *PLoS One*, *12*(3), e0173403. doi:10.1371/journal.pone.0173403 PMID:28362821

Martí-Parreño, J., Seguí-Mas, D., & Seguí-Mas, E. (2016). Teachers' attitude towards and actual use of gamification. *Procedia: Social and Behavioral Sciences*, *228*, 682–688. doi:10.1016/j.sbspro.2016.07.104

McCullough, B. (2018). *How the Internet happened: From Netscape to the iPhone* (1st ed.). Liveright Publishing Corporation.

Miller, C. C. (2021, June 23). Do Chance Meetings at the Office Boost Innovation? There's No Evidence of It. *The New York Times*. https://www.nytimes.com/2021/06/23/upshot/remote-work-innovation-office.html

Mills, S. C. (2006). *Using the internet for active teaching and learning*. Pearson/Merrill/Prentice Hall.

Nah, F. F., Venkata, R. T., Shashank, R., & Pavani, R. (2013). Gamification of Education Using Computer Games. In Human Interface and the Management of Information. Information and Interaction for Learning, Culture, Collaboration and Business. Springer Berlin Heidelberg. doi:10.1007/978-3-642-39226-9_12

Oikarinen, J., & Reed, D. (1993). *"Internet Relay Chat Protocol." Request for Comment:1459*. Network Working Group.

Pernelle, P., Carron, T., Talbot, S., & Wayntal, D. (2021). Fast gamification approach: Increase of the motivation in remote classes. *Proceedings of the 13th International Conference on Computer Supported Education*, 282–287. 10.5220/0010461702820287

Pingdom. (2012). *IRC is dead, long live IRC*. Pingdom.Com. https://www.pingdom.com/blog/irc-is-dead-long-live-irc/

Reiser, R. (2001). A history of instructional design and technology: Part i: A history of instructional media. *Educational Technology Research and Development*, *49*(1), 53–64. doi:10.1007/BF02504506

Rivera, E. S., & Garden, C. L. P. (2021). Gamification for student engagement: A framework. *Journal of Further and Higher Education*, *45*(7), 999–1012. doi:10.1080/0309877X.2021.1875201

Sailer, M., & Homner, L. (2020). The gamification of learning: A meta-analysis. *Educational Psychology Review*, *32*(1), 77–112. doi:10.100710648-019-09498-w

Schwartz, D. (2021). *Using Discord to facilitate student engagement*. https://digitalscholarship.unlv.edu/btp_expo/122

Shi, L., & Cristea, A. I. (2016). Motivational Gamification Strategies Rooted in Self-Determination Theory for Social Adaptive E-Learning. In A. Micarelli, J. Stamper, & K. Panourgia (Eds.), *Intelligent Tutoring Systems* (Vol. 9684, pp. 294–300). Springer International Publishing. doi:10.1007/978-3-319-39583-8_32

Susi, T., Johannesson, M., & Backlund, P. (2007). *Serious Games*. Academic Press.

Tankovska, H. (2021). *Most popular messaging apps*. Statista. https://www.statista.com/statistics/258749/most-popular-global-mobile-messenger-apps/

Tarud, J. (2021, March). *The Evolution of Chat Apps—Koombea Weekly Blogpost*. Koombea. https://www.koombea.com/blog/chat-apps-evolving/

Towsend, R. (2003). *The Internet and the History Classroom: Introduction*. American Historical Association. https://www.historians.org/publications-and-directories/perspectives-on-history/may-2003/the-internet-and-the-history-classroom

Tu, C.-H. (2000). On-line learning migration: From social learning theory to social presence theory in a CMC environment. *Journal of Network and Computer Applications*, *23*(1), 27–37. doi:10.1006/jnca.1999.0099

Tudge, J. R. H., & Winterhoff, P. A. (1993). Vygotsky, Piaget, and Bandura: Perspectives on the Relations between the Social World and Cognitive Development. *Human Development*, *36*(2), 61–81. doi:10.1159/000277297

Tweney, D. (2009). Sept. 24, 1979: First Online Service for Consumers Debuts. *Wired*. https://www.wired.com/2009/09/0924compuserve-launches/

Vladoiu, M., & Constantinescu, Z. (2020). Learning during Covid-19 pandemic: Online education community, based on discord. *2020 19th RoEduNet Conference: Networking in Education and Research (RoEduNet),* 1–6. 10.1109/RoEduNet51892.2020.9324863

Wahyuningsih, E., & Baidi, B. (2021). Scrutinizing the potential use of Discord application as a digital platform amidst emergency remote learning. *Journal of Educational Management and Instruction*, *1*(1), 9–18. doi:10.22515/jemin.v1i1.3448

Wang, W. (2004). *Steal this file sharing book: What they won't tell you about file sharing*. No Starch Press.

Wilson, K. A., Bedwell, W. L., Lazzara, E. H., Salas, E., Burke, C. S., Estock, J. L., Orvis, K. L., & Conkey, C. (2009). Relationships Between Game Attributes and Learning Outcomes: Review and Research Proposals. *Simulation & Gaming*, *40*(2), 217–266. doi:10.1177/1046878108321866

Wu, T. (2016). *The attention merchants: The epic scramble to get inside our heads* (1st ed.). Alfred A. Knopf.

KEY TERMS AND DEFINITIONS

Bot: A software application that can perform automated, often repetitive, user tasks on internet-connected platforms.

Chat App: Digital application or platform that facilitates synchronous and asynchronous communication between individuals and groups using text, digital files, images, or voice.

Collaborative Features: Affordances offered by digital platforms designed to promote the exchange of information among teams.

Experience Points (XP): A unit of measurement for a scaled reward or bonus system in games, usually based on duration or intensity of interaction.

Gamification: The addition of strategic, competitive, or ranked interactions to facilitate engagement in educational content.

Leader Board: A ranked display of teams or individuals within teams, specifically in the context of a competitive event.

Remote Learning: Instruction conducted with the learner and instructor in separate locations, usually outside of a traditional classroom. It can be offered synchronously, asynchronously or as a hybrid of the two.

Chapter 25
Gamified Learning in Higher Education:
An Instructional Design Method to Improve Engagement

Claire Louise Palmer Garden
https://orcid.org/0000-0001-7961-2170
Edinburgh Napier University, UK

Errol Scott Rivera
https://orcid.org/0000-0002-2818-0205
Cardiff University, UK

ABSTRACT

Gamification and design thinking can be considered part of instructional design (ID) in the higher education (HE) context. Each of these fields has much to learn from the others. For example, although there is a lack of an agreed method to gamify learning, there are established models for ID. Furthermore, ID and gamified learning share limitations, notably a lack of reflection and empathy/systems approach in the processes used, that can be remedied by borrowing from design thinking. In the context of HE, it is appropriate to frame that empathy as student engagement to draw on the literature base. A gamification method is presented that incorporates reflection and student engagement to remedy these limitations. Although conceived to improve student engagement with formative assessment in UK HE, the process may be widely applied to other settings to support user engagement and enhance relevant outcomes (e.g., satisfaction) in different global locations.

INTRODUCTION

In this chapter, we will compare Instructional Design (ID), Design Thinking and Gamification in order to place them into the context of each other. We explore notions proposed by others that gamification

DOI: 10.4018/978-1-6684-4287-6.ch025

is an extension to ID and Design Thinking (Broer, 2015; Hung, 2018; Patrício et al., 2020), and that gamification is in fact what educators have been doing for a long time (Broer, 2015; Rieber, 1996). We will briefly examine limitations of these theories in the context of education, paying particular regard to the Higher Education (HE) setting, before presenting our own gamification method as a solution.

The gamification method proposed, although conceived as a means to improve student engagement with formative assessment in the UK Higher Education (HE) context, can be more widely applied to support user engagement to enhance academic or social outcomes (e.g. satisfaction) in other global locations (Rivera & Garden, 2021). Furthermore, gamification and ID/ Design Thinking have broad applicability to many other settings, for example training and business (e.g. see Landers & Armstrong, 2017; Patrício et al., 2018; Robson et al., 2016). This chapter will draw on many fields such as systemic design (Nelson, 2019), organisational psychology (Landers et al., 2015), student engagement (Kahu, 2013), ID (Vovides & Lemus, 2019), design thinking (Gibbons, 2003) and gamification (Nacke & Deterding, 2017), and will necessarily adopt an interdisciplinary approach.

BACKGROUND

Given the context of the discussion of gamification and ID/ Design Thinking that follow, a brief introduction to learning in the HE context is required. According to UNESCO, the HE sector can be defined as "All universities, colleges of technology and other institutions providing formal tertiary education programmes (i.e. ISCED levels 5, 6, 7, or 8).." (*Higher Education Sector (for R&D Data) | UNESCO UIS*, n.d.)." The sector plays an important role in the global economy, e.g. UK HE generated an estimated 1.2% of British GDP 2017 (*The Economic Impact of Universities in 2014–15*, n.d.).

The degree programmes provided by HE are taught by subject matter experts, akin to instructors in the training field. The teaching approach of these programmes has evolved from traditional didactic strategies to incorporate a number of learning theories that have emerged over the past half century. These, together with ID models, guide curriculum design in HE institutions to support students to achieve learning outcomes (Khalil & Elkhider, 2016). There are three main theories that define learning differently. These are: Behaviourism (learning as acquisition of new behaviour), Cognitivism (leaning as organisation of knowledge) and Constructivism (learning as searching for meaning; see Table 1). In reality, educators adopt a blend of these in their practice, dependant on their own training and experience. Behaviourism is the most traditional, didactic approach, and can be viewed as somewhat exploitative. Cultural sensitivity is required when considering the appropriateness of an approach (Raina, 2011). Learning outcomes, or what is achieved through the learning process, are usually organised across the five domains of knowledge: psychomotor, cognition and metacognition, and affect and self (Gagné, 1972; Krathwohl, 2002). Achievement of these outcomes is assessed differently according to which learning theory is adopted, and we can see a trend from behavioural (exams) through cognitive (essays, reports and projects) to constructivist (ungrading and peer review) approaches as the field of education develops. Those engaged in instructional design must therefore choose appropriate strategies that support learning as they define it to achieve intended learning outcomes in the relevant domain(s) of knowledge. In other words, the components of the system used in teaching: the environment and activities (including the method and assessment approach), must all be oriented in the same direction to achieve the learning outcomes. This theory is called constructive alignment (Biggs, 1996) and its implementation is the basis of the field of ID (Reigeluth, 1987).

Table 1. Summary of traditional learning theories

	Behaviourism	Cognitivism	Constructivism
Primary Target Domain of Knowledge	Psychomotor	Cognition and meta-cognition	Cognitive/Affective
Definition of Learning	Acquisition of new behaviour	Organisation of knowledge	Search for meaning
Focus of Instruction	Skills and competency based	Mapping and reflection based	Reflective practice
Example Instruction Method	Passive traditional lectures and demonstrations	Active problem solving	Active collaborative authentic cases
Assessment Approach	Criterion-based exams	Essays, reports and projects	Ungrading and peer review

Source:(Khalil & Elkhider, 2016)

Instructional Design Theory and Practice

ID models were developed in the 1970s to support systematic planning, design and development of instruction to facilitate learning, and various models continue to persist (Branch & Dousay, 2015; Stefaniak & Xu, 2020). The ID approach is most prevalent in Turkey and the USA where individuals formally trained in ID undertake this work, explaining the predominance of this context in the literature (Stefaniak & Xu, 2020). However, in much of the rest of the world, subject matter experts, instructors, undertake this work with limited training, adopting a similar, albeit less formal or systematic, approach. The Analysis, Design, Development, Implementation, Evaluation (ADDIE, Table 2) model is the most common and traditional ID model, and shares characteristics with other approaches (Stefaniak & Xu, 2020). Using this model, instructional designers first analyse the goals of instruction (the learning outcomes) before designing, developing and implementing a curriculum and teaching and learning strategy to meet these needs. The final stage involves evaluating the effectiveness of the approach and may use Kirkpatrick's four level evaluation model as a guide, taking into account user Reaction, Learning, Performance, Organizational Impact (Kirkpatrick & Kirkpatrick, 2009). However, this evaluation can be difficult to achieve across all levels and many practitioners focus instead on collecting and analysing feedback data concerning the learner experience and attainment to guide revision of their materials/ approach (Khalil & Elkhider, 2016; Kirkpatrick & Kirkpatrick, 2009; Reio et al., 2017).

The traditional ID approach is limited by this reliance on generic models and processes which can limit designer creativity (Stefaniak & Xu, 2020). Furthermore, the learning theories on which ID is based (Table 1.) are limited in that they ignore the individual, environmental and social context of the learner, and the affect this might have on their learning and thus the effectiveness of a teaching strategy. This causes strategies to fail and is seen as learner disengagement/ lack of motivation, dissatisfaction and/ or failure to achieve assessed learning outcomes (Trowler, 2010). Part of the solution to these issues lies in refining both the learning theories and ID approaches to better incorporate the learner experience and their context. For example, Adult Learning Theory (Merriam, 2008), Cognitive Load Theory (Sweller, 2011) and Multimedia Theory (Mayer, 2002) extend the learning theories described above, and the incorporation of design thinking (Stefaniak, 2019) and systems thinking (Wolfson et al., 2014) can improve the ID approach, to better consider some aspects of the learner's individual context or the system in which they operate. However, context is not formally incorporated into traditional ID models and remains a large limitation.

Design Thinking is an approach to solving 'wicked problems' that cannot be definitively described, in contrast to the 'tame problems' dealt with by science. This approach involves empathy, abductive reasoning, framing and progressive refinement in order to define the problem and come up with a solution (Table 2). The empathy component focusses the solution on the user and has parallels in education with student-centred approaches to teaching, learning and assessment (Banter et al., 2019), and in collaborative approaches to innovation (Patricio et al., 2021). Furthermore, in this context we can also view empathy as student engagement and instructor experience. Student engagement literature (Kahu, 2013) can help to make sense of this component where we define student engagement as a variable, context-dependent psychological state experienced whilst learning. Abductive reasoning relies on an understanding of the desired outcome when all other aspects of the problem are unclear (thus making them 'wicked'), whilst framing is a means to articulate an approach to the problem, helping to set the problem (Hung, 2018). In HE, these outcomes are usually defined as learning outcomes which are selected according to the relevant domains of knowledge (Krathwohl, 2002). Taken together, a more interdisciplinary and reflective approach to ID, incorporating elements of Design Thinking and relevant engagement literature may help better inform the implementation of these theories and methods.

Gamification Theory and Practice

Gamification has been called upon in recent times as a solution to some of the ID limitations in training and education, especially lack of learner motivation (often conflated with engagement), and has largely evolved separately from the field of ID (Dichev & Dicheva, 2017; Rivera & Garden, 2021). However, gamification can in some ways be considered to be an extension of Design Thinking (Hung, 2018; Patrício et al., 2020) and an extension or re-packaging of well -known principles of teaching and learning e.g. badges, autonomy, relatedness and competence (Broer, 2015; Landers et al., 2015; Wiggins, 2016). Because of this, arguably it is the *process* of gamification that is more meaningful and powerful for educators than the outcome, lending focus, purpose and structure to instructional design (Broer, 2015; Hung, 2018; Patrício et al., 2021).

In the context of teaching and learning, gamification sits at one end of a spectrum with serious games at the other, and game-based learning in the middle (Fig. 1). These differ in the extent to which the approach resembles a game: serious games are games used for the purposes of education, and thus contain all the components of a game. In contrast, gamification only uses one or more game components, and not enough to fully resemble a game (Deterding et al., 2011). It is very important to disambiguate these terms, so that the evidence base may be properly interpreted and applied (Broer, 2015; Hung, 2017). Indeed, the field is currently awash with seemingly contradictory and difficult to interpret findings because of this, and the many different definitions of gamification currently in use (e.g. see Broer 2015). Here we adopt the Gamified Learning definition of Landers: 'the use of game attributes to facilitate learning and related outcomes' (Landers, 2014), with game attributes categorised into action language, conflict/challenge, control, environment, game fiction, human interaction, immersion and rules/ goals (Wilson et al., 2009).

Gamified learning is thought to work by modifying the recipient's behaviour and attitude, such as interest, time and effort, to support the achievement of intended outcomes (Landers, 2014). It is important to gamify effective instructional material because gamification does not enhance learning by itself, gamification plus the instructional material/ strategy does this (Landers, 2014). There is no agreed method to gamify learning, which we attempt to remedy here. There are descriptions of *what* to do, but not *how*

Figure 1. Gamified learning lies at one end of a spectrum with serious games at the other and game-based learning in the middle. Serious games gave the highest resemblance to games, being fully fledged games, and gamified learning has the least.

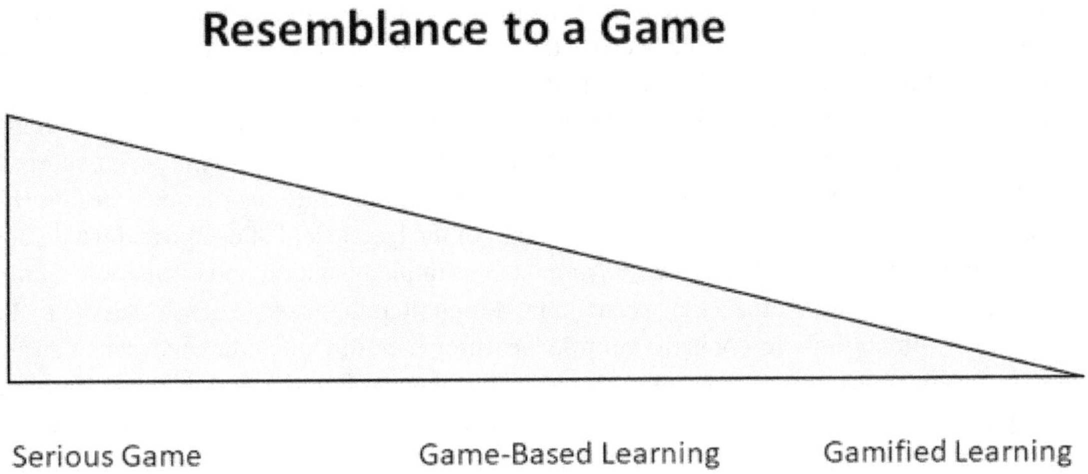

to do it. The gamifier = designer *may* exert choice over which aspect of the recipient's psychological state to modify, and they *will* select one or more game attributes to modify it through gamification to achieve an outcome albeit inadvertently in some cases. Outcomes may include satisfaction, spend or in the context of gamified learning, learning outcomes (Rivera & Garden, 2021; Wilson et al., 2009). The meaning of the gamified experience is conveyed through feedback not just on actions, but also on decisions and guiding values (Kim & Werbach, 2016; Tobon et al., 2020; Werbach, 2014). For meaningful gamified learning, this has been framed as a requirement to build in opportunities for play, exposition, choice, information, engagement and reflection to support the user to find links between their experience with the real world (Nicholson, 2015). In other forms of gamification such as commerce, gamification adds feedback to what is an otherwise inherently transactional situation. In the case of learning, the responsibility of feedback to convey meaning is paramount (Kim & Werbach, 2016; Landers, 2014).

It is possible to find aspects of design thinking and ID that are shared with gamification (Table 2). For example, the initial stage of for all three processes is an attempt to understand and articulate the problem, and there are different ways to carry this out. In traditional ID, this is the Analysis phase, where instructional goals are refined and articulated as learning outcomes. This step might incorporate abductive reasoning and framing if Design Thinking is used to get to grips with a difficult problem (Stefaniak, 2019). There is no set way to do this for gamified learning, but reflection is a common first step that practitioners take when considering their learning and teaching strategy – indeed, reflective practice has been an important part of practice in HE for at least the past decade (Clegg et al., 2010). Empathy is found in Design Thinking and some gamification approaches (Rivera & Garden, 2021) and is incorporated from the beginning of the process as a way of acknowledging and sometimes including users and their context into the design process. Although this is missing from the traditional ADDIE approach, it is possible to consider the 'system' as part of the Analysis process at the beginning (Stefaniak & Xu, 2020). This is taken one step further as engagement in our and approach to gamification (Rivera & Garden, 2021). This is particularly important if gamification is to be meaningful to the user, especially if gamification is being deployed as an intervention to improve user engagement, one facet of which is motivation (Kahu, 2013). This engagement aspect missing from traditional ID and has been articulated as a need for a systems approach (Stefaniak & Xu, 2020). This remains a substantial limitation to the ID approach which would benefit from incorporating the empathy/ engagement aspects of DT and gamification. Finally, ID and DT incorporate evaluation/ refinement into their design process, but this is missing from gamification (Table 2). This may be because the iterative nature of games design is often brought over into gamification processes, but is not explicitly articulated. Nevertheless, the field of gamification would benefit from formally adopting systematic evaluation into the process in order to strengthen the evidence base (Hung, 2018). Taken together, one may consider gamification to be an approach to design, and gamified learning in particular to be one possible approach to instructional design (Hung, 2018). Therefore, the field of gamification is actually part of the larger field of design and would benefit from incorporating aspects of that field into its approach to implementation and evaluation. Similarly, gamified learning would benefit from the instructional design literature base (e.g. see (Ali et al., 2021).

There are many limitations present in the gamified learning literature, including the lack of an agreed methodology for implementation as discussed above. This may explain the limited adoption of gamified learning outside the fields of computing and game design to date (Hung, 2017). Furthermore, most evidence focuses on the use of leader boards, points and badges in Learning Management Systems, probably because they are the most familiar to practitioners and relatively easy to implement (Dicheva et al., 2015; Nicholson, 2015). This is problematic because this narrow viewpoint leaves the majority of available game attributes without an evidence base, and there is in fact no technology requirement for gamification (Broer, 2015; Nicholson, 2015; Wilson et al., 2009). Indeed according to Broer, gamification is "likely to transcend the choice of medium" (Broer, 2015), a statement agreed with by others (Hung, 2017; Rivera & Garden, 2021). The re-use of concepts already present in education e.g. stars and badges, and the focus on autonomy, competence and relatedness in gamification can also make its application in this context more difficult to study (Broer, 2015; Nicholson, 2015).

A further major criticism of the way gamification has been applied and evaluated to date lies in the (perhaps unintended) focus on behavioural elements, and concomitant failure to address cognitive and affective aspects of the user experience, something we and others are attempting to rectify (Ali et al., 2021; Rivera & Garden, 2021). When extended to learners, this means there tends to be a focus on what students DO to achieve learning outcomes, ignoring what students think, and especially, feel. This is manifested as a focus on the selection of game attributes that target user behaviour such as leader boards, the effects of which are measured as behavioural outcomes such as time on task and number of posts on LMS in evaluations of gamified learning (Landers & Landers, 2014). This behavioural approach can also be clearly seen in Lander's Theory of Gamified Learning (Landers, 2014) and Nicholson's RECIPE for meaningful gamification (Nicholson, 2015). Likewise, Kahu's work illustrates the ways in which student engagement, and therefore learning, might be endangered by a similar narrowing of account, wherein student engagement is viewed largely in terms of the behavioural (psychomotor) domain of experience (Kahu, 2013). As a further complication, in ID the learning outcomes which guide the design process are often confined to the *cognitive* domain of learning where the student's thinking occurs, with little thought to the emotionality or physicality of experience in learning (A.J. Harrow, 1972; Krathwohl, 2002; Morshead, 1965). This *also* potentially ignores who they are, and how they act and feel. This is problematic if we agree with the notion that learning and engagement have cognitive, affective *and* behavioural dimensions (Kahu, 2013; Kraiger et al., 1993; Krathwohl, 2002). By focussing on just one of these, we neglect much of what is beneficial to the student/ user in the gamified experience and render the intervention less effective.

Student behaviour doesn't always lead to a change in grades (Song and McNary 2011), perhaps because of the failure of constructive alignment between the learning strategy (often behavioural as in gamified learning), learning outcomes situated in other domains of learning (often cognitive), and assessment (often behavioural) which reinforces a reward-dependent approach that erodes intrinsic motivation (Biggs, 1996; Nicholson, 2015). This is especially important because many practitioners turn to gamification as an intervention to support improved motivation or engagement. This is also why others search for 'meaningful gamification' (Hung, 2017; Nicholson, 2015) and why we put forward the theoretical basis to our Gamification for Student Engagement Framework (Rivera & Garden, 2021). This limitation also leaves practitioners open to criticism around the ethics of manipulating behaviour through gamification e.g discussions around exploitationware Hung (2017). It is this surface approach to gamification, coupled with a confusing and contradictory evidence base and the presentation of some established ideas as new that has led to cynicism in the education field (Attali & Arieli-Attali, 2015; Broer, 2015). However, like many other approaches to teaching and learning, gamification is not intrinsically good or bad, the outcome depends on how it is applied (Hung, 2017). Some limitations of gamified learning are also shared with traditional instructional design. These include over-simplification of the problem/ solution (e.g. gamification over simplifies game design and ID oversimplifies the design process), selective focus on behavioural outcomes, and lack of user input and consideration of context (depending on the model used). Engagement research is a useful means of addressing the final limitation and underpins our Gamification for Student Engagement framework (Rivera & Garden, 2021).

A Gamification Method to Improve Student Engagement

We present a process that uses a modified ADDIE ID approach that focuses on the Analysis stage in order to address the lack of empathy/ design thinking limitation of ID. In addition, the process explains *how* to carry out gamification rather than listing *what* steps to take in order to address this gamification limitation. Here, an instructor is supported, through facilitated reflection by an instructional designer, to gamify instructional material to improve student engagement using the Gamification for Student Engagement Framework (Rivera & Garden, 2021). The method is an attempt to enable instructors/ instructional designers to select how learning outcomes (as defined by Bloom: (Krathwohl, 2002) will be achieved through supporting an engagement state (as defined by (Kahu, 2013) they choose to influence through gamification (as defined by (Landers, 2014) through the application of appropriate game attributes (as defined by (Wilson et al., 2009). That choice is not achieved via learning analytics or student satisfaction surveys, but through reflection of expertise and empathy that can be underpinned by research in gamification and engagement to provide the substance for reasoned and accountable decisions in learning design (see Table 1 Rivera & Garden, 2021, Fig. 2). This method includes many of Hung's recommendations for instructional designers interested in gamification (2017): it is student-focused, starts small with one or two game elements, does not rely on learning analytics but is considerate of scalability, revision and reiteration.

We use an example where gamification aims to improve student engagement with formative assessment, to improve attainment of the associated learning outcome. The Analysis phase begins by examining whether or not there is constructive alignment of the assessment and the learning outcome, because misalignment between intentions and teaching strategies/ material can result in student disengagement and failure, and gamification cannot fix broken instructional material (Biggs, 1996; Landers, 2014; Reigeluth, 1987). Once the learning outcome is better defined in the context of the assessment, it is expanded

*Table 2. A comparison of Traditional Instructional Design, Design Thinking and Gamification approaches to facilitating learning. Note that it is possible to incorporate Design Thinking and Gamification into Instructional Design to move on from the traditional approach– these should not be seen as separate entities. *A list of models is available here: (Branch & Dousay, 2015).*

	Traditional Instructional Design	Design Thinking	Traditional Gamification
Focus	Medium	Problem	Problem
Process	Analysis, Design, Development, Implementation, Evaluation*.	Abductive Reasoning, Framing, Empathy, Progressive Refinement.	Ill-defined.
Approach to Understanding and Articulating Problem	Analysis of instructional goals.	Abductive Reasoning, Framing, Empathy.	Not well defined. Can be incorporated as Engagement (Rivera & Garden, 2021).
Role of Context	May be present in analysis of the system in the first phase, and the evaluation phase.	'Baked in' via empathy.	Not well defined. Can be incorporated as Student Engagement (Rivera & Garden, 2021) or choice, exposition and engagement (Nicholson, 2015) if these approaches are taken.
Predominant Mode of Evaluation/ Measurement	Reaction, Learning, Performance, Organizational Impact .	Not well defined, includes qualitative analysis of experience.	Behaviour change e.g. time on task.
Predominant Learning Theory	Dependant on instructor approach.	Unclear, likely to be constructivist.	Behaviourism.

to incorporate all the domains of learning in order to identify which is most problematic and optimise the opportunity for student engagement. The next stage is rooted in what the socio-cultural approach to student engagement identifies as a danger to student learning, wherein qualities and skills which are advantageous to a student success can be taken for granted and assumed to be inherent, becoming unwritten rules or expectations which underpin how a learning institution interacts with students, otherwise known as the institution's 'habitus' (Thomas, 2010). A habitus which succumbs to these assumptions can create methods of teaching which are exclusionary to students who may not posses these qualities or skills, but are otherwise capable of achieving the learning outcomes. In the gamification process presented, the instructor reflects on their assumptions through experience in conjunction with their learning outcomes to identify which psychological domain of engagement could be improved through gamification targeted towards an antecedent of engagement. These antecedents are factors that exist within and outside the student and influence the student's engagement states at any given moment. They can be found more proximally within the student, which are themselves influenced by more distal antecedents such as their socioeconomic background, family support, and culture (Kahu, 2013). The number and types of antecedents to engagement, and their interactions are numerous and intricate, however we focus on the proximal antecedents within the student, their skills, motivation, self-efficacy, and identity. The final part of this stage involves identifying the appropriate intervention by linking this engagement antecedent to the desired state of engagement through an analysis of the relevant pedagogic literature.

Figure 2. The gamification for engagement method involves instructor reflection and constructive alignment throughout the process. First, learning outcomes across the three domains of learning for the instructional material (curriculum/ assessment) to be gamified are clarified. Then a problematic learning outcome is identified in one domain of learning that is aligned to state of engagement to be targeted through gamification. The instructor identifies a personal quality that supports their success in the field and selects a specific antecedent and state of engagement to target that fits best. The link between the antecedent and engagement state is sought using academic literature before an appropriate game attribute is selected that would support this process, which is then implemented into the instructional material.

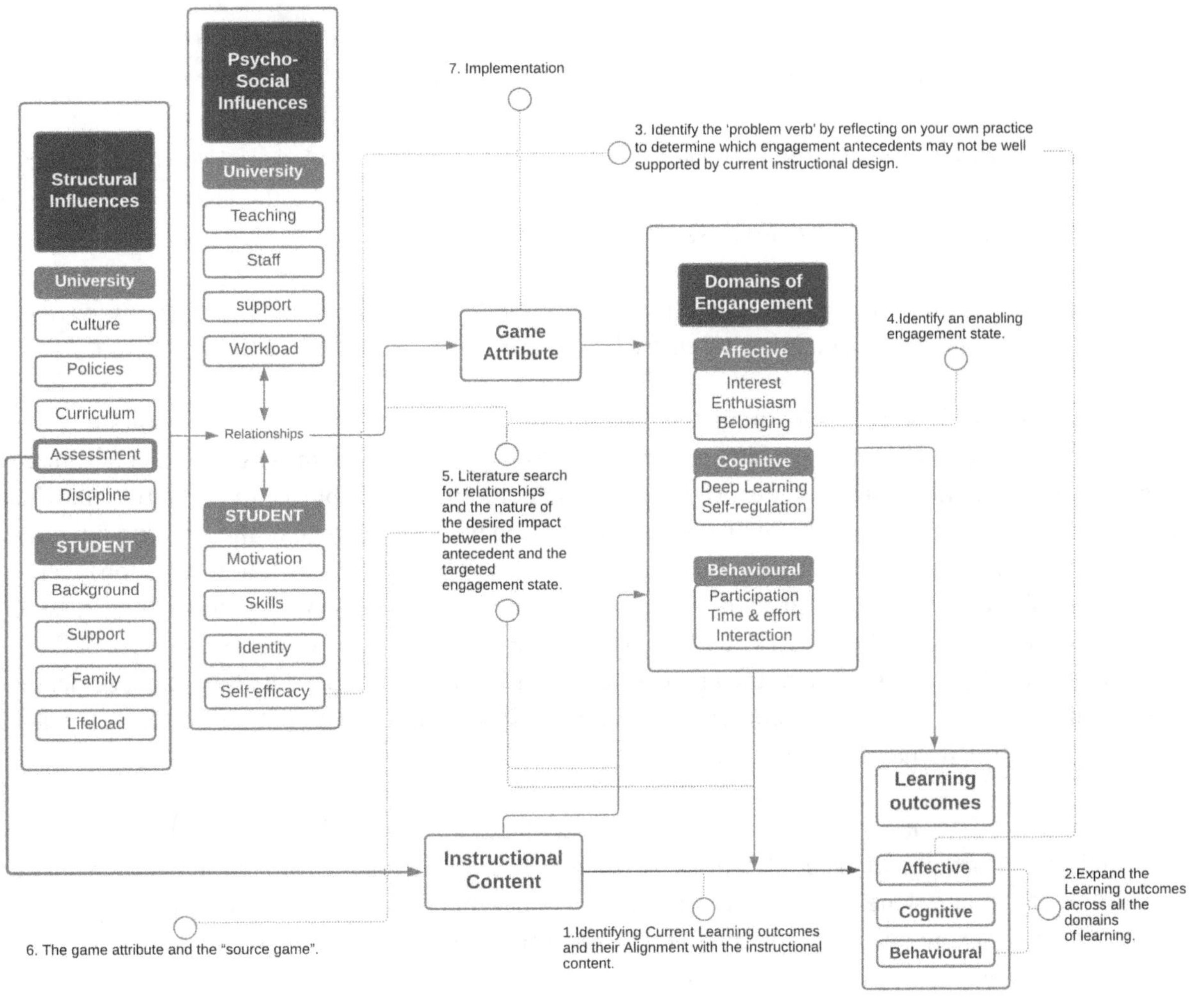

In the Design and Development stage, the instructor identifies which game attribute influences player engagement in much the same way that the intervention (described in the pedagogic literature in the previous stage) impacts the student (Table 1, Rivera & Garden, 2021). At this point, it is important to remember that while there are only 19 game attributes, their uses are very variable, and they are often implemented in various ways and in conjunction with other game attributes.

How to Gamify Learning in Seven Steps, an Example

Analysis

1. **Identify Learning Outcomes and their Alignment with Assessment:** The example used here is the gamification of a formative assessment (a multiple-choice quiz) for a first-year undergraduate course in cell biology, where the learning outcome for the course, and thus the formative assessment, is written as follows:

Understand the structure of animal cells and identify its composite parts.

This part of the process considers how the verb in the learning outcome (understand, a cognitive learning outcome, Table 3) is aligned to the design of the assessment by re-writing the learning outcome to describe the intended result of formative assessment:

By the end of this formative assessment, the student will be able to identify the correct response to questions about the fundamental principles of cell biology.

In taking a closer look at this learning outcome, it can be seen that 'identify' is an accurate way to describe what happens during the formative assessment, but applies more to the cognitive act of remembering than understanding, stated in the original learning outcome (See Table 3). In a situation like this, we begin to question whether the formative assessment could be better aligned to the learning outcome. Perhaps a redesign of the formative assessment is required. Alternatively, we may start to question whether a multiple choice quiz is actually an act of association (a verb in the category of understanding), rather than simply identifying or choosing. That questioning is key to this art of the process.

No matter what position is taken, the process benefits from this reflection. At this stage, semantics are everything, as this more accurate learning outcome will serve as the foundation for the next stage, integrating the other domains of learning.

2. **Expand the Learning Outcome:** Consideration of all domains of learning is necessary when gamifying instructional material such as a formative assessment for engagement (Rivera & Garden, 2021). This is best done by re-writing learning outcomes that includes verbs from all three domains of Bloom's Taxonomy of Learning: affective, cognitive and psychomotor (Krathwohl, 2002), and contextualising them within the formative assessment.

To begin with, most courses do not incorporate learning outcomes that acknowledge the affective or psychomotor domains. In the case of the example, we must focus on the verb of 'understanding' in the learning outcome and consider the ways in which the formative assessment tests that understanding and look for verbs in the other domains of learning with similar complexity. 'Understand' refers to a lower complexity level of the cognitive domain of learning in Bloom's revised taxonomy of learning (Anderson et al., 2001; Krathwohl, 2002), thus a lower complexity verb from the affective domain would likely be appropriate (Morshead, 1965). However, if the lowest complexity 'remember' is more appropriate (Table 3.), the most basic levels of complexity in the affective and psychomotor domains should also be

Table 3. Typically, learning outcomes are written exclusively using verbs from the cognitive domain of learning as found in Bloom's Revised Taxonomy, describing the cognitive aspect of learning (Krathwohl, 2002). The outcomes increase in complexity from left to right, the ones used in the example are highlighted.

Cognitive Domain: Categories of Learning Outcomes Aspects of learning dealing with knowledge, how it is obtained, recalled, processed, and manipulated.									
Remember		**Understand**		**Apply**	**Analyse**	**Evaluate**		**Create**	
Retrieval of knowledge		Constructing meaning from knowledge		Procedural use of knowledge	Networked knowledge to extrapolate/ interpolate	Utilisation of knowledge as criteria		Reorganising/repurposing of knowledge	
Arrange Cite Choose Count Define Describe Duplicate Identify Label	List Locate Match Outline Recall Recite Record Review State	Abstract Associate Categorize Clarify Classify Conclude Contrast Exemplify Extrapolate	Generalize Illustrate Interpret Map Predict Represent Summarize Translate	Apply Carry out Demonstrate Determine Develop Employ Execute Implement Operate Show Sketch Solve Use	Analyse Attribute Deconstruct Differentiate Discriminate Distinguish Focus Organize Outline Parse Select Structure	Argue Assess Check Conclude Coordinate Criticize Critique Detect	Judge Justify Monitor Prioritize Rank Rate Recommend Test	Assemble Build Combine Compose Construct Create Design	Draft Formulate Generate Hypothesize Integrate Plan Produce

selected (Tables 4 &5). The verbs in those domains are chosen according to which is more representative of what the student does in the yet-gamified formative assessment. It is helpful to write formative assessment tailored learning outcome in the present tense:

In this formative assessment, the student identifies (cognitive) the correct response to questions about the fundamental principles of cell biology by asking (affective) fundamental questions about biology, replicating (psychomotor = behavioural) the command of cell biology the instructor showed in week 1.

In the above example, the instructor has concluded that while the learning outcome for the *course* is written using a cognitive verb from the category of understanding, the *formative assessment* is in fact asking the student to display learning that is more appropriately categorised as remembering (highlighted in Table 3). They have decided that this is appropriate for where the formative assessment falls in the semester. They have also chosen to use verbs from all three domains of learning in a single learning outcome that describes what the formative assessment currently asks the students to do (highlighted in Tables 4 &5).

3. **Identify the Problem Learning Outcome and Learning/ Engagement Domain:** Once the learning outcome is envisioned across all three domains of learning, it becomes easier to identify which domain is proving problematic for student engagement and subsequently, achievement. This stage employs empathy, where the instructor considers their experiences with students and reflects on the design and effectiveness of their formative assessment. This is done by contrasting observed student experience to the instructor's experience in the discipline, i.e., what strengths

Table 4. Verbs used in the articulation of learning outcomes in the affective domain of learning (Morshead, 1965). The outcomes increase in complexity from left to right, the ones used in the example are highlighted.

Affective Domain: Categories of Learning Outcomes This domain concerns the aspects of learning that deal with emotions as expressions of value and attitudes.									
Receiving		**Responding**		**Valuing**		**Organization**		**Characterization**	
Openness to new experiences		Interaction with new experiences		Attaching worth to new experiences		Integration into an existing value system		New attitudes/beliefs through internalisation	
Ask Choose Describe Follow Give Hold	Identify Locate Name Select Reply Use	Answer Assist Compile Conform Discuss Greet Label Perform	Practice Present Read Recite Report Select Tell Write	Complete Demonstrate Differentiate Explain Follow Form Initiate	Join Justify Propose Read Share Study Work	Adhere Alter Arrange Combine Compare Complete Defend Formulate	Generalize Identify Integrate Order Organize Prepare Relate Synthesize	Act Discriminate Display Influence Listen Modify Perform Practice	Propose Qualify Question Revise Serve Solve Verify Use

does the instructor have (but students may not) that makes inhabiting that learning outcome verb easier for the instructor? This stage is an attempt to enable the instructor to identify their role in creating an assumptive habitus in the design of a specific learning experience, such as a formative assessment. After having expanded their aligned learning outcomes to all three domains of learning, the instructor may now step back from the material to reflect on their own experiences as a student and a practitioner. Here, they may begin a simple list of personal characteristics, strengths, or attitudes that helped them master the material. This gives the instructor the chance to consider how the formative assessment may have been designed amidst their own blind spots, assumptions, or narrow expectations for what a successful student must be capable of during or even prior to the formative assessment. Likewise, the instructor may also remember challenges they may have experienced as a student, subsequently, overcome, and have since forgotten about. The goal here is for the instructor to articulate their own personal strengths which have contributed to their success in their discipline, and articulate them as clearly as possible. Instructors who have used this method have been encouraged to sum up each quality in a single word where possible, and prioritise clarity where not. Every item on the list should be clear enough for the instructor to remember exactly what

Table 5. Verbs used in the articulation of learning outcomes in the psychomotor (behavioural) domain of learning (Armstrong, 1970; Harrow, 1972). The outcomes increase in complexity from left to right, the ones used in the example are highlighted.

Psychomotor Domain Levels: Categories of Learning Outcomes This domain concerns the aspects of learning that deal with physical experiences and skills.									
Imitation		**Manipulation**		**Precision**		**Articulation**		**Naturalization**	
Copying via observation		Reproduction via instruction		independent adroit execution		Consistent execution of networked skills		Automatic high level execution	
Adhere Copy Follow	Repeat Replicate	Build Execute Implement	Perform Recreate	Calibrate Complete Control	Demonstrate Perfect Show	Adapt Combine Construct Coordinate	Develop Formulate Master Modify	Design Invent Manage	Project Specify

was meant when they were written down. This kind of specific and positive reflection/ articulation can be an uncomfortable and even embarrassing experience because it is experiential. At this stage, it is important for an instructor to be aware of that type of reticence and dissuade themselves of it, as it can lead to creating a list of personal strengths that is generalised or otherwise hedged. Modesty is also counterproductive because while each item on that list is one of the instructor's strengths, each one is also a potentially crucial challenge to one or even all of their students.

Completed lists of strengths may range from three items to fifteen, taking between five and twenty minutes to complete, and often require a colleague to provide a sounding board. Once complete, it can then be looked at as a list of challenges, wherein the instructor should take further time to reflect on whether students have expressed or displayed difficulty with any of the items on the list. This should be done primarily within the context of the activity that is being gamified using experiences of previous students who had difficulty with it. This reflection can be supported by referencing records available to the instructor such as student feedback, class representative meetings, or marks and achievement statistics. However, in nearly every case since this method was first tested, a instructor's own experiences with their students has allowed them to quickly and confidently identify the personal strength or quality they have which historically has proven most challenging to students' success with the assignment in question.

For the example used thus far, the instructor made a list of their own traits and qualities that would aid them in their discipline, particularly where this formative assessment and its subject matter is concerned:

1. Good memory
2. Diligent
3. Excited to prove myself
4. Disciplined
5. Comfortable admitting when I don't know something
6. Optimistic
7. Like working with others

The instructor looked over this list while thinking about their past students and found themselves thinking of students who displayed lots of enthusiasm for the material but performed poorly on this formative assessment. They even thought of students with whom they often 'butted heads'. This reflection was enough for the instructor to hone in on item 5: *'being comfortable admitting when I don't know something.'*

This is where the 'problem learning outcome' is identified, i.e. where the instructor begins to understand which domain of learning is more directly suffering from students' current level of engagement. If one of the learning outcomes is synonymous with the most problematic challenge, or if one of them has a more immediate and logical causal relationship with that challenge, then it is most likely the 'problem learning outcome'. In our example, the instructor in has written three separate learning outcomes:

- **Cognitive:** <u>Identify</u> the correct response to questions about the fundamental principles of cell biology
- **Affective:** <u>Ask</u> fundamental questions about biology.
- **Psychomotor (Behavioural):** <u>Replicate</u> the command of cell biology the instructor showed in week 1.

After reflecting on their own strengths, the instructor concluded that a personal characteristic of their own is also something they typically observed in promising students, that being:

Quality 5: 'being comfortable admitting when I don't know something.'

In this case, the instructor considers which verb (underlined) would be rendered most difficult if they were not comfortable admitting when they didn't know something. After discussing the matter with a colleague, it quickly becomes obvious that asking a question is in and of itself an admission that you *'don't know something.'* From this, the instructor concludes that 'asking' is the 'problem verb', and thus 'affective' is the problem domain.

However, it is not always that straightforward. For example, imagine that same instructor elected to use all three domains in a single learning outcome, which was also less ambitious and more descriptive in its articulation, such as:

In this formative assessment, the student adheres (psychomotor) to the fundamental principles of cell biology by identifying (cognitive) the correct response to questions after choosing (affective) from a bank of similar but incorrect responses.

In this situation, the quality still remains the guiding influence, however the instructor cannot see a clear relationship between it and any of the verbs used in this version of the learning outcome. In which case, rather than the specific verbs used, the quality/challenge can be compared to other verbs within the same category, or the category itself (see Tables 3-5). Here, the instructor observes that being 'comfortable admitting what I don't know something' is conceptually very similar the category of affective verbs known as 'receiving', described as 'an openness to new situations' (see Table 4). Thus, the instructor has established the 'choosing' as the problem verb, and subsequently the affective domain remains the most problematic of the three domains of learning.

NB: Currently, it is advised that this means of identifying the 'problem learning outcome/domain' only be used when a clear relationship cannot be established between the quality and learning outcomes as written, as instructors have had better success gamifying when they remain rooted in the learning outcomes that have been aligned to the activity in question.

4. **Identify an Enabling Engagement State:** Like the domains of learning, student engagement is divided among the affective, cognitive, and psychomotor (behavioural) domains (Kahu, 2013). However, where learning outcomes are characterised by verbs, Kahu describes student engagement using states of being. In *Framing Student Engagement in Higher Education (2013),* Kahu provides a non-exhaustive but critical list of states of engagement within each domain.

This stage of gamification is about identifying the 'target' student engagement state, and making an important choice about how the instructor will impact that student engagement using gamification. It should be emphasised that this is more a matter of choice for the instructor. Unlike the previous stages of gamification, this stage requires the instructor to make a proposition about the most useful state of engagement they wish to impact, and by what means. To do this, there are crucial assumptions we make about Kahu's framework that must be accepted:

Table 6. Domains of engagement, and the states within those domains, as described by Ella Kahu (Kahu, 2013).

Student Engagement		
Affect	Cognition	Behaviour
Enthusiasm Interest Belonging	Deep Learning Self Regulation	Time and Effort Interaction Participation

- **Assumption 1:** states of engagement are dynamic, i.e. there is no ideal level at which these states must exist for learning to be possible. E.g. A particular level of enthusiasm may be appropriate for one activity, and that same level of enthusiasm in the same student could be insufficient for a different one.
- **Assumption 2:** to learn within a domain the student must be appropriately engaged in that domain. For example, if the instructor has concluded that the affective learning outcome has proven challenging for their students, it reasonable to assume that the affective domain of engagement is likely not sufficient for the student to achieve the desired learning outcome. In implementing this method, choosing which affective state of engagement to augment has proven to be the most subjective activity. Instructors have been served well by interrogating both their own quality and the description of engagement states that Kahu employs, looking for overlaps.
- **Assumption 3:** to change engagement, one must first know what influences it. In much the same way that learning is a consequence of engagement, states of engagement are themselves a result of what Kahu refers to as antecedents to engagement (Kahu, 2013).

In the example case, the instructor must focus on augmenting an affective state of engagement (as per assumption 2). The instructor examines Quality 5: 'being comfortable admitting when I don't know something' and finds synergy in between their own use of the word 'comfort' and Kahu's concept of 'belonging' in the affective domain of engagement (Finn, 1993; Kahu, 2013). This reflection feels compatible with student informal feedback that their discipline can feel elitist. The instructor reflects on which antecedent of the four antecedents to engagement: skills, motivation, self-efficacy, and identity (as they exist within the student) can be intervened upon to create the state of belonging they wish to engender in students. They may look for the antecedent they believe will result in an optimal state of belonging, or one they believe is more directly responsible for the students' current state of belonging. After reflection, discussion with colleagues, and even students, the instructor proposes that being comfortable with admitting what they don't know has allowed them to avoid feeling like they don't belong, because it allowed them feel secure in the way they perceived current skill level even if they knew it wasn't yet up to the task. Thus, the instructor chooses to continue targeting the engagement state of belonging, and elects to impact that state via the antecedent of students' self-efficacy, which is most allied to belonging in this context.

NB: At this point, after articulating this relationship between their personal quality (comfort), a specific antecedent (self-efficacy), a specific state of engagement (belonging), and a specific learning outcome (ask) in a specific domain (affective), the power of this method will begin to assert itself. Previous instructors have described this as an "ah-ha moment", many of their experiences with struggling students (and their course feedback) quickly make sense in a way they had not before. Every instructor who completed this process took comfort in their newfound ability to articulate something they previously could not always perceive, or claimed to have experienced a kind of professional catharsis. If an instructor has completed this stage and is not confident in their conclusion, they are advised to work backwards from this point, reviewing their progress for the point at which their conclusions began to feel arbitrary or forced, perhaps in discussion with a colleague.

5. **Explain the Relationship between the Engagement State and the Antecedent to Define the Desired Intervention:** This stage builds on the propositions made by the instructor in the previous stage with more substantial and objective considerations. To do this, the instructor must identify pedagogic literature that describes the relationship between the target state of engagement (e.g. belonging) and the antecedent they've proposed to be most crucial (e.g. self-efficacy). The goal here is for the instructor to be able to conceptualise the relationship between the antecedent and the state of engagement, and how an intervention might impact that relationship. Instructors have done this with a simple search through peer reviewed pedagogy research and scholarship, using their chosen antecedent and engagement states as search terms. Continuing with our example, the instructor finds pedagogic literature after searching for research that links belonging to self-efficacy. They also include additional search terms that ensure the findings of the research are compatible with the learning theories underpinning their own teaching practice, e.g. constructivism.

This stage challenges the instructor/ designer to understand and analyse the literature well enough to be able to succinctly narrate the relationship between the antecedent and the state of engagement. The literature that instructors used varied in how succinctly they described the nature of those relationships, what impacted those relationships, and the nature of that impact. Often, instructors found literature with clear implications, e.g. a peer reviewed article entitled "Student Motivation and Self-Regulation" which has both an antecedent and a state of engagement in the title, and concluded that students with low motivation showed higher self-regulation with they collaborated with a partner and a clear reason as to why. Other, less well-defined articles may have similar value, but use different language, so support and discussion with colleagues can be vital for this stage as well as a firm grasp of the decisions, terms, propositions, and rationale the instructor has established thus far.

Here, our example instructor identifies an influential article that describes how a specific concept intervenes in the relationship between their chosen engagement antecedent and their chosen engagement state, and writes out a succinct encapsulation of the article:

Discussions (intervention) of the subject material between students helps students' confidence (self-efficacy) by allowing them to see that they are not the only ones (belonging, affective engagement) who have been unsure about the material, making them feel more comfortable with asking questions of the teacher in class (learning outcome, affective).

It is this narration of the relationship and how it may be intervened upon which forms the basis for the choice of game attribute to be employed, and how it must be employed to achieve the effect. This intervention is the ultimate objective for gamification.

Design and Development

6. **Identify an Appropriate Game Attribute and the Source Game:** In this stage the instructor identifies the game attribute to be used to gamify their learning, and describe what it will need to accomplish. At this point, it is important to remember that while there are only 19 game attributes, their uses are incredibly variable, and they are often implemented in various ways and in conjunction with other game attributes. The goal is to find a game that utilises a game attribute to create engagement in a player in much the same way that the intervention (described in the pedagogic literature in the previous stage) impacts the student. The challenge for the lecturer to is be able to conceptually translate the intervention identified in stage 5 with one of the game attributes described by Wilson and Bedwell (Bedwell et al., 2012; Wilson et al., 2009).

In our example the instructor reads descriptions of game attributes (Wilson et al., 2009) and selects the game attribute of 'interpersonal interaction' as the most similar to the description of discussion found in the literature used in stage 5. The instructor does not play games frequently, and is unsure about whether they can identify relevant examples to exemplify how this game attribute may be implemented. However, in this case, simple games such as pub-quizzes employ many of the concepts described by the relationship/intervention in stage 5: employing a group dynamic, picking a team, choosing team name, thematic questions, competition, and time limitations, and a question master. Moreover, interpersonal interaction is employed to a similar effect, i.e., people in groups, where self-efficacy is key, and interaction requires individuals acknowledging that they may not know a key piece of information, facilitating the engagement state of belonging. The instructor suggests that the formative assessment can be restructured to ensure students have similar discussions during the quiz, while trying to meet all of the original learning outcomes of the formative assessment, as well as the newly expanded learning outcomes written to reflect the affective and behavioural domains of learning.

Implementation and Evaluation

7. **Incorporate the Game Attribute into the Instructional Material: Gamification:** The end-goal for the previous step is the identification of a game attribute to use and a specific game to serve as a model for its implementation. Rather than recreate the game itself, (which would be game-based learning, and not gamification) the instructor simply extracts the game attribute used in the game and implements it within the part of the instructional material most associated with the 'problem-learning outcome'. The multiple-choice quiz formative assessment is restructured (or gamified) to incorporate the 'interpersonal interaction' attribute to ensure students have discussions during the quiz (as described in step 5 above), while trying to meet all of the original learning outcomes of the formative assessment (step 1), as well as the newly expanded learning outcomes written to reflect the affective and behavioural domains of learning (step 3).

In our example, the final gamified formative assessment is now a quiz that is taken by teams instead of individual students. Each question is generated by a team of students given a limited amount of time to discuss what they do and don't know and formulate a question that the other teams must answer. This ensures students ask questions as well as answering them, all through discussion which is implemented in a co-operative, competitive atmosphere that makes it easier for students to feel welcome within the discipline, despite any knowledge gaps they may possess in the subject matter. This makes them feel less self-conscious about actions that reveal what they don't know, including actions necessary for learning more, such as asking questions or asking for help.

Lastly, the instructor can now evaluate the learning outcomes based on the accuracy of students' answers and the quality of the questions they formulate. This is the beginning of the evaluation step, which is also informed by other forms of student feedback, e.g. course survey.

LIMITATIONS

The goals of this method, and the Gamification for Student Experience Framework that underpins it are to highlight that context is important, and to provide a gamification method as a way through which this context can influence the design of learning (Rivera & Garden, 2021). However there are some limitations present in our method that remain:

1. The method focuses most on the Analysis step of the ADDIE process, and does not adequately describe how the gamified material may be evaluated or modified, the final ADDIE step. However, the learning outcomes are clearly articulated as part of the process, and achievement of these may be measured. Furthermore, student feedback mechanisms are commonplace in HE and may easily be incorporated (e.g. see Jessop et al., 2013; Shah et al., 2017, Figure 3)
2. This method of gamification is not designed in partnership with students and so therefore some assumptions about the student experience may have carried over, impacting on its effectiveness. However, incorporation of user feedback during and after the process would remedy this to some extent.
3. Although this method is reflective in approach and incorporates engagement theory, the resulting gamified learning experience does not necessarily include aspects of design that others have put forward as being necessary for it to be meaningful (e.g. play, Nicholson, 2015). However, it is necessary to simplify the process, at least while the evidence base is being built, and not all these aspects need to be present for the experience to be meaningful (Hung, 2017). Therefore, it is likely that the game attributes selected as part of this process are compatible with meaningfulness because of the purposeful incorporation of engagement theory.
4. It is likely that not every gamification strategy will benefit all learners, therefore an element of choice should be incorporated (Hung, 2017; Nicholson, 2015), a concept borrowed from Universal Design for Learning (Rose & Meyer, 2009). Repeating the gamification process one or more times would result in different gamified versions of the instructional material that could conceivably offer choice.

Game Attributes were applied to instructional material (curriculum/ assessment) to improve learning outcomes according to our Gamification for Student Engagement framework (Rivera & Garden, 2021). However, 'curriculum' and 'assessment' are just two possible antecedents of engagement that may be amenable to gamification and there are many other aspects of a student's individual and socioeconomic context that are not addressed here. Therefore, gamification of instructional material using this framework is not a panacea that fixes all elements of student engagement. Rather, it is the part that as instructors, we can influence. Furthermore, there are consequences of engagement other than learning outcomes, e.g.

Figure 3. The gamification method outlined in this chapter can be mapped to the ADDIE approach to instructional design to further situate it into this body of work. The first step in the method involves instructor reflection (the Analysis step, akin to Empathy in Design Thinking) to take into account their context and experiences in order to identify a problematic learning outcome and engagement state, and constructively align them. In the Design and Development steps a relevant game attribute is identified that should theoretically facilitate engagement, and an example or source game is found that demonstrates how the game attribute might usefully be applied to the curriculum in the Implementation stage. The Evaluation stage is not explicit in the method shown but would logically include investigations into whether the gamified approach improved desired learning outcomes and student experience of engagement.

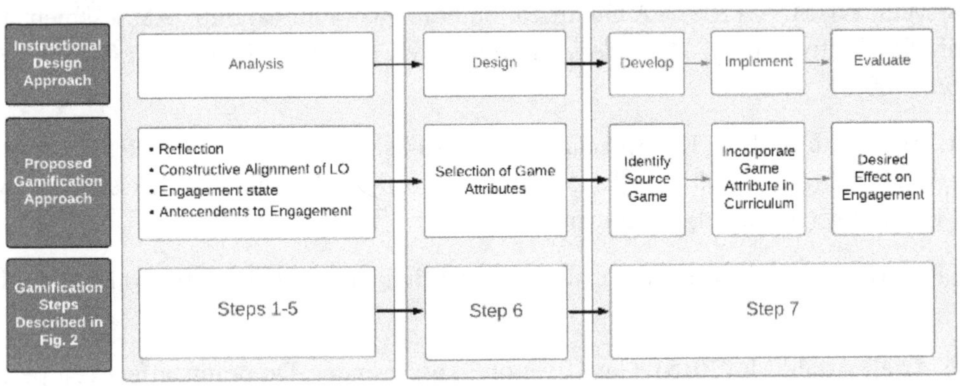

satisfaction and a sense of community that may be affected by gamification. Therefore, the potential to gamify other aspects of the student experience to support other outcomes is tantalizing.

CONCLUSION

We have shown that gamification is one approach to instructional design that, in order to be successful, must contain elements of engagement, something that Design Thinking and meaningful gamification have in common. The method of gamification for student engagement detailed here was built on the principle that current best practice must be reflected upon and that instructional design, student engagement, and gamification must be reconcilable if each is treated as an opportunity to provide checks and balances to the other. Building on Hung's contemplation of meaningful gamification (2017), this method demonstrates that the quality of meaning a student derives from a gamified learning experience is dependent on the quality of reflection pursued by the instructor in the gamification process itself. During the development and testing of the gamification example presented here, the instructor's reflections led them to consider the intricate influence of personal values and physical actions (the context) on their instructional design and articulate these as facets of affective and psychomotor/behavioural domains of learning. More generally, instructors found that reflecting on the context of their practice led to great insight into the students' learning experience.

Moving beyond the application of gamification onto learning, the incorporation of engagement literature into ID/ Design Thinking and Gamification theories has the potential to revolutionize practice through clearly articulated relationships between designer input and user experience that impact on outcomes.

This approach may be more widely applied to support user engagement to enhance other outcomes (e.g. satisfaction). Furthermore, gamification and ID/ Design Thinking have broad applicability to many other settings, (e.g. see Landers & Armstrong, 2017; Robson et al., 2016), therefore this approach may be applied to disciplines outside learning and education to broaden the evidence base for gamification, something that is necessary for the progress of the field (Hung 2017).

REFERENCES

Ali, A. Z., & Mahdavi, M. A. (2021). A Gamification Framework for Cognitive Assessment and Cognitive Training: Qualitative Study. *JMIR Serious Games, 9*(2). Https://Games.Jmir.Org/2021/2/E21900 doi:10.2196/21900

Anderson, L. W., Krathwohl, D. R., Airasain, P. W., Cruikshank, K. A., Mayer, R. E., Pintrich, P. R., Raths, J., & Wittrock, M. C. (2001). A Taxonomy for Learning, Teaching, and Assessing: A Revision of Bloom's Taxonomy (Abridged). Longman.

Armstrong, R. J. (Ed.). (1970). Developing and Writing Behavioral Objectives. Educational Innovaters Press.

Attali, Y., & Arieli-Attali, M. (2015). Gamification in assessment: Do points affect test performance? *Computers & Education*, *83*, 57–63. doi:10.1016/j.compedu.2014.12.012

Bedwell, W. L., Pavlas, D., Heyne, K., Lazzara, E. H., & Salas, E. (2012). Toward a taxonomy linking game attributes to learning: An empirical study. *Simulation & Gaming*, *43*(6), 729–760. doi:10.1177/1046878112439444

Biggs, J. (1996). Enhancing teaching through constructive alignment. *Higher Education, 32*(3), 347–364. doi:10.1007/BF00138871

Branch, R. M., & Dousay, T. A. (2015a). Survey of instructional design models. In D. R. Walling (Ed.), *Survey of Instructional Design Models* (5th ed.). Association for Educational Communications and Technology.

Broer, J. (2015). Is this new? Family Resemblances in Gamification in Education. *Bulletin of the Technical Committee on Learning Technology*, *17*(4), 14–17.

Clegg, S., Tan, J., & Saeidi, S. (2010). *Reflecting or Acting? Reflective Practice and Continuing Professional Development in Higher Education.* doi:10.1080/14623940220129924

Dichev, C., & Dicheva, D. (2017). Gamifying education: what is known, what is believed and what remains uncertain: a critical review. In International Journal of Educational Technology in Higher Education (Vol. 14, Issue 9, pp. 1–36). doi:10.118641239-017-0042-5

Dicheva, D., Dichev, C., Agre, G., & Angelova, G. (2015). Gamification in Education: A Systematic Mapping Study. *Journal of Educational Technology & Society*, *18*(3), 75–88. doi:10.1109/EDUCON.2014.6826129

Gagné, R. M. (1972). Domains of learning. *Interchange, 3*(1), 1–8. doi:10.1007/BF02145939

Harrow, A. J. (1972). *Taxonomy of the psychomotor domain : A guide for developing behavioral objectives*. David McKay.

Higher education sector (for R&D data) | UNESCO UIS. (n.d.). Retrieved July 30, 2021, from http://uis.unesco.org/en/glossary-term/higher-education-sector-rd-data

Hung, A. C. Y. (2017). A Critique and Defense of Gamification. *Journal of Interactive Online Learning*, *15*(1).

Hung, A. C. Y. (2018). Gamification as Design Thinking. *International Journal on Teaching and Learning in Higher Education*, *30*(3), 549–559.

Kahu, E. R. (2013). Framing Student Engagement in Higher Education. *Studies in Higher Education*, *38*(5), 758–773. doi:10.1080/03075079.2011.598505

Khalil, M. K., & Elkhider, I. A. (2016). Best Practices Applying learning theories and instructional design models for effective instruction Khalil MK, Elkhider IA. Applying learning theories and instruc-tional design models for effective instruction. *Advances in Physiology Education*, *40*(2), 147–156. doi:10.1152/advan.00138.2015 PMID:27068989

Kirkpatrick, D. L., & Kirkpatrick, J. D. (2009). Evaluating: part of a ten-step process. In *Evaluating training programs*. Berrett-Koehler Publishers Inc.

Kraiger, K., Ford, J. K., & Salas, E. (1993). Application of cognitive, skill-based, and affective theories of learning outcomes to new methods of training evaluation. *The Journal of Applied Psychology*, *78*(2), 311–328. doi:10.1037/0021-9010.78.2.311

Krathwohl, D. R. (2002). A Revision of Bloom's Taxonomy: An Overview. *Theory into Practice*, *41*(4), 212–218. doi:10.120715430421tip4104_2

Landers, R. N. (2014). Developing a Theory of Gamified Learning: Linking Serious Games and Gamification of Learning. *Simulation & Gaming*, *45*(6), 752–768. doi:10.1177/1046878114563660

Landers, R. N., Bauer, K. N., Callan, R. C., & Armstrong, M. B. (2015). Psychological Theory and the Gamifcation of Learning. In Gamification in Education and Business. doi:10.1007/978-3-319-10208-5_9

Landers, R. N., & Landers, A. K. (2014). An Empirical Test of the Theory of Gamified Learning: The Effect of Leaderboards on Time-on-Task and Academic Performance. *Simulation & Gaming*, *45*(6), 769–785. doi:10.1177/1046878114563662

Mayer, R. E. (2002). Multimedia learning. *Psychology of Learning and Motivation - Advances in Research and Theory, 41*, 85–139. doi:10.1016/S0079-7421(02)80005-6

Merriam, S. B. (2008). Adult learning theory for the twenty-first century. *New Directions for Adult and Continuing Education*, *2008*(119), 93–98. doi:10.1002/ace.309

Morshead, R. W. (1965). Taxonomy of Educational Objectives Handbook II: Affective Domain. *Studies in Philosophy and Education, 4*(1), 164–170. doi:10.1007/BF00373956

Nicholson, S. (2015). A RECIPE for Meaningful Gamification. *Gamification in Education and Business*, 1–20. doi:10.1007/978-3-319-10208-5_1

Patricio, R., Moreira, A., Zurlo, F., & Melazzini, M. (2020). Co-creation of new solutions through gamification: A collaborative innovation practice. *Creativity and Innovation Management*, *29*(1), 146–160. doi:10.1111/caim.12356

Patrício, R., Moreira, A. C., & Zurlo, F. (2018). Gamification approaches to the early stage of innovation. *Creativity and Innovation Management*, *27*(4), 499–511. doi:10.1111/caim.12284

Patrício, R., Moreira, A. C., & Zurlo, F. (2021). Enhancing design thinking approaches to innovation through gamification. *European Journal of Innovation Management*, *24*(5), 1569–1594. doi:10.1108/EJIM-06-2020-0239

Raina, V. (2011). *Between behaviourism and constructivism*. doi:10.1080/09502386.2011.534578

Reigeluth, C. M. (1987). *Instructional theories in action : Lessons illustrating selected theories and models*. Academic Press.

Reio, T. G., Rocco, T. S., Smith, D. H., & Chang, E. (2017). A Critique of Kirkpatrick's Evaluation Model. *New Horizons in Adult Education and Human Resource Development*, *29*(2), 35–53. doi:10.1002/nha3.20178

Rivera, E. S., & Garden, C. L. P. (2021). Gamification for student engagement: A framework. *Journal of Further and Higher Education*, *45*(7), 999–1012. Advance online publication. doi:10.1080/0309877X.2021.1875201

Stefaniak, J. (2019). The Utility of Design Thinking to Promote Systemic Instructional Design Practices in the Workplace. *TechTrends*, *64*(2), 202–210. doi:10.100711528-019-00453-8

Stefaniak, J., & Xu, M. (2020). An Examination of the Systemic Reach of Instructional Design Models: A Systematic Review. *TechTrends*, *64*(5), 710–719. doi:10.100711528-020-00539-8

Sweller, J. (2011). Cognitive Load Theory. *Psychology of Learning and Motivation - Advances in Research and Theory*, *55*, 37–76. doi:10.1016/B978-0-12-387691-1.00002-8

The economic impact of universities in 2014–15. (n.d.). Retrieved July 30, 2021, from https://www.universitiesuk.ac.uk/economic-impact

Trowler, V. (2010). Student Engagement Literature Review. The Higher Education Academy. doi:10.1037/0022-0663.85.4.571

Wiggins, B. E. (2016). An overview and study on the use of games, simulations, and gamification in higher education. *International Journal of Game-Based Learning*, *6*(1), 18–29. doi:10.4018/IJGBL.2016010102

Wilson, K. A., Bedwell, W. L., Lazzara, E. H., Salas, E., Burke, C. S., Estock, J. L., Orvis, K. L., & Conkey, C. (2009). Relationships Between Game Attributes and Learning Outcomes. *Simulation & Gaming*, *40*(2), 217–266. doi:10.1177/1046878108321866

Wolfson, A. J., Rowland, S. L., Lawrie, G. A., & Wright, A. H. (2014). Student conceptions about energy transformations: Progression from general chemistry to biochemistry. *Chemistry Education Research and Practice*, *15*(2), 168–183. doi:10.1039/C3RP00132F

ADDITIONAL READING

Alsawaier, R. S. (2018). The effect of gamification on motivation and engagement. *International Journal of Information and Learning Technology*, *35*(1), 56–79. doi:10.1108/IJILT-02-2017-0009

Biggs, J., Medland, E., & Vardi, I. (2003). Aligning teaching and assessing to course objectives. *Assessment & Evaluation in Higher Education*, *38*(5), 1–16. doi:10.1080/02602938.2012.670197

Black, P., & Wiliam, D. (2009). *Developing the theory of formative assessment*. doi:10.1007/s11092-008-9068-5

Deterding, S., Sicart, M., Nacke, L., O'Hara, K., & Dixon, D. (2011). Gamification. using game-design elements in non-gaming contexts. *Proceedings of the 2011 Annual Conference Extended Abstracts on Human Factors in Computing Systems - CHI EA '11*. 10.1145/1979742.1979575

McDonald, J. K., & Yanchar, S. C. (2020). Towards a view of originary theory in instructional design. *Educational Technology Research and Development*, *68*(2), 633–651. doi:10.100711423-019-09734-8

Mora, A., Riera, D., González, C., & Arnedo-Moreno, J. (2017). Gamification: A systematic review of design frameworks. *Journal of Computing in Higher Education*, *29*(3), 516–548. doi:10.100712528-017-9150-4

Nicol, D. J. (2009). Assessment for learner self-regulation: Enhancing achievement in the first years using learning technologies. *Assessment & Evaluation in Higher Education*, *34*(3), 335–352. doi:10.1080/02602930802255139

Werbach, K. (2014). *(Re) Defining Gamification : A Process Approach*. Persuasive Technology. doi:10.1007/978-3-319-07127-5_23

Whitton, N., & Moseley, A. (2014). Deconstructing Engagement: Rethinking Involvement in Learning. *Simulation & Gaming*, *45*(4–5), 266–275. doi:10.1177/1046878114554755

Yorke, M. (2003). Formative assessment in higher education: Moves towards theory and the enhancement of pedagogic practice. *Higher Education*, *45*(4), 477–501. doi:10.1023/A:1023967026413

KEY TERMS AND DEFINITIONS

Affective Domain: The psychological category related to feeling or affect.

Behavioural Domain: The psychological category related to doing, or behaviour. Analogous to the psychomotor domain.

Cognitive Domain: The psychological category related to thinking, or cognition.

Constructive Alignment: Orientation of system components used in teaching: the environment and activities (including the method and assessment approach), in the same direction in order to achieve the learning outcomes.

Game Attribute: Distinct game design features used in gamification.

Gamified Learning: The use of game attributes to facilitate learning and related outcomes.

Higher Education: All universities, colleges of technology and other institutions providing formal tertiary education programmes.

Instructional Design: Design of instructional material, taking into account constructive alignment.

Learning Outcome: What is achieved through the learning process, organised across five domains of knowledge: psychomotor, cognition, metacognition, affect, self.

Student Engagement: The variable, context-dependent psychological state students experience while learning.

Chapter 26
Scrumming:
Gamifying a Dashboard for Undergraduate Student Motivation

Adriana Peña Pérez Negrón
https://orcid.org/0000-0001-6823-2367
CUCEI, Universidad de Guadalajara, Mexico

Jose Luis David Bonilla Carranza
https://orcid.org/0000-0002-8690-4865
CUCEI, Universidad de Guadalajara, Mexico

Mirna Muñoz
https://orcid.org/0000-0001-8537-2695
Centro de Investigación en Matemáticas, A.C., Mexico

Sonia Osorio Angel
https://orcid.org/0000-0003-4540-4191
CUCEI, Universidad de Guadalajara, Mexico

ABSTRACT

Software project management is a multitask process that involves planning, organizing, monitoring, and controlling. And Scrum is an agile project management method based on self-organized teams; that is, the team members, although guided by a product owner and the Scrum master, evaluate the project's tasks and decide who will take care of them and the schedule. However, in academia, the Scrum method might not work as expected in a professional environment because of the commitment of the team members. Also, it seems more proper for the students to be motivated to take care of more diverse tasks, not just those they are comfortable with. By gamifying the Scrum dashboard for their final subject project, the motivation to take varied and challenging activities is expected. A study was conducted where the main results indicate that the teams under a gamified project in the academy context, have a greater tendency to complete the project.

DOI: 10.4018/978-1-6684-4287-6.ch026

INTRODUCTION

Project management involves planning, organizing, monitoring, and controlling all aspects of a project with an agreed schedule, budget and performance criteria, the so-called "iron triangle". Yet, project management is also in charge of integration, scope, human resource, communication, risk, and procedure management (Radujković & Sjekavica, 2017). Besides, Project management is a multitask process, often dealing with more than one project at the same time; this, in turn, requires several IT tools to support handling, monitoring, and communicating in time with everyone involved in such projects (Horváth, 2019).

For software development, currently, the most known project management approaches are the traditional and the agile ones. The traditional approach seems to represent a better solution for projects with well-defined requirements, while agile approaches better suit when requirements are not well defined, and the software release is expected to be continuous with complete functionality (Andrei et al., 2019). Because of the changing market and software requirement conditions, agile approaches are gaining popularity; furthermore, the agile project management approach has been adopted beyond IT (Ćirić & Gračanin, 2017). Among the most widely used agile methods, Scrum is located at the top (Madampe, 2017).

The Scrum method is grounded on a self-organized team that manages planning and responsibilities division; therefore, the project manager tasks are somehow assumed by the team. Here the team members estimate the development effort, and they also establish who will be in charge of each activity.

The emerging use of the agile methods created a gap between academia and the industry (Fitsilis & Lekatos, 2017; Pérez-Castillo, et al., 2018), which according to Kropp and Meir (2013) should be covered not only theoretically, but practically applied, and integrated into other courses (e.g., programming, algorithms, or data structure) and not only in Software Engineering courses, a practice that has been proved to be appropriate (Fitsilis & Lekatos, 2017).

Several approaches have been proposed for teaching project management as part of Software Engineering, including traditional approaches, real life projects, simulations and gamification (Metrôlho, Ribeiro, & Passão, 2020). Rush & Connolly (2020) proposed a teaching framework for integrating Scrum in an IT project management course. For its adaptation in the classroom they presented a scheme of pre-semester activities and adapting the class schedule for Scrum activities. Their approach is Scrum based but to teach traditional project management content in undergraduate students. According to the authors, the approach supports developing also confidence and social skills needed in project management. For training in Scrum, Schäfer (2017) proposed using a game-based approach for different background students (i.e. computer science and electronic engineering bachelor degrees). They used Minecraft 3D blocks open world where players build landscapes and buildings, and asked the students to construct a project using Scrum for its management. As a result, they consider this approach as helping different background students together, a motivational factor. Steghöfer, et al. (2017), proposed a workshop to use Scrum for building a logo city, as a strategy to observe the students during the process of learning team work and project management. They found it proper to rise the students' confidence in applying Scrum practices and that the workshop format introduces the students to the importance of communication in project management. De Souza et all, (2017) presented SCRUMI as a serious game to teach Scrum, based on questions and answers regarding the concepts of the Scrum framework. They found that most of the students felt motivated seeking to achieve the proposed challenges.

Finally, Scrum principles have been applied to foster team work skills, for example, Vogelzang, Admiraal & Van Driel (2020) used the framework for secondary chemistry lessons, as a results teachers agreed that the clear structure contributes to the learning environment. And Carvalho et al. (2018) used

Scrum in the fourth year of the Industrial Engineering and Management degree program for Project Based Learning (PBL), their results show that Scrum in complex PBL learning environments provide an effective support for the students to self-manage their projects.

In our case, the goal is not to teach Scrum but to use it as a means to manage a real-life software development project. In the Scrum method, students should be allowed to select the tasks to be in charge of, however, this might not be as straightforward as when it comes to a professional team committed to the project's success. As a solution, we argue that by including gamification, the students' incentive to challenge themselves for tasks that might require a greater effort could be reinforced, promoting also diversity in the selection.

Gamification aims to engage and intrinsically motivate people by applying game elements in a non-gaming context since games present cognitive, emotional, and social benefits. This premise comes from the assumption that gamification can satisfy the intrinsic needs of the users and consequently leading to activities relevant to the gamification target (Patrício, et al., 2018; Xi & Hamari, 2019; Patrício, et al., 2020).

This chapter presents a proposal for including gamification in the dashboards that agile software development management use, in order to motivate undergraduate students to challenge themselves to accomplish tasks that might require a greater effort.

BACKGROUND

In this section are presented key concepts for the proposal related to both main topics, gamification and the Agile methods.

Games are fun to play. They present a control structured arrangement that can be avoided giving a sense of freedom. While playing, we create a pretended reality in which rules are agreed, and to which we are committed, generating the so-called "magic circle". And then, when the game ends, we take with us the game memories and experiences (Adams, 2014; Von Ehren, 2020).

Gamification is the integration of game elements in activities that are not games. Gamification represents a practice that can change behavior because of its motivational aspect by reinforcement and emotions. Positive and negative reinforcement encourage or discourage behavioral repetition, same as satisfying outcomes lead people to repeat certain behaviors (Robson et al. 2015).

Nowadays, students are digital natives. Modern paradigms in education boost the use of technology to promote active learning, where gamification has become a trend with proven benefits (Kiryakova, Angelova, & Yordanova, 2014), teaching programming and programming practices are not an exception.

Gamification in Computer Programs

In Software Engineering, gamification has been applied in software development to help in the achievement of activities related to motivate and improve communication skills, having an increasing trend since 2010 (Knutas, et al., 2014; Galeano-Ospino, Machuca-Villegas, & Gasca-Hurtado, 2020; Gasca-Hurtado, et al. 2021). Then, it has been broadly implemented in education, as well as in marketing, finance, human resources, environment, government, and mobile applications with different objectives (Muñoz, et al., 2019). The most famous example of gamification in a software application is the speed camera lottery of the fun theory initiative carried out by Volkswagen at the end of 2010 in Stockholm, by financially rewarding drivers according to their proper behavior, this initiative resulted in drivers better respecting speed limits (Volkswagen, 2010).

Regarding teamwork, one of the important works was the presented by Latulipe et al., (2015) where the established objective was the formation of a team. They obtained the same results on team with and without the application of the gamification elements, but, through the use of the gamification elements, authors highlighted that the students created more friends during the course.

Another study is the presented by Jurado et al., (2015), which objectives focuses on improving the social interaction of team members to share their knowledge. Their conclusions showed good results from the application of the gamification elements, because not only was the knowledge sharing improved, but also three key aspects for teamwork were strengthened (participation, collaboration, and the contribution).

Agile Methods

Agile methods are known for bringing software product conception to its delivery, which means to reduce the time to produce software products associated with heavyweight or plan-based methods (Bourque & Fairley, 2014). The most popular agile methods, according to the survey of CollabNet VersionOne enterprise in their 13th Annual State of Agile Report are Scrum, Scrum-XP hybrid, Scrumban, Kanban, iterative development, Lean Startup, and XP (Digital.ai. 2021).

The agile methods promote a project management process reinforcing teamwork, organization, and self-responsibility, that promotes a quick delivery of quality software with a business approach aligned to the customer needs and the organizational goals (SINTECO, 2009).

The agile project management life cycle starts with the stakeholders determining the features to be developed. Those requirements are broken into smaller pieces of work, the user stories, which are prioritized and stored in a backlog. The software is developed in iterative cycles where phases are connected, and each phase represents the feedback to the others (Molhanec, 2007).

In education, agile methods have inspired several approaches. Agile seems to be effective specially in active and project-based learning is applied, allowing students to work in a targeted and effective way (Salza, Musmarra, & Ferrucci, 2019). In Krehbiel, et al (2017) study, they found that Agile adaptation to higher education increases students' engagement, encourage them to be responsible of their learning, enhances the collaboration quality, producing higher quality deliverables.

Scrum Method

Scrum is a framework developed to address complex adaptive problems to produce delivering products with the highest possible value, providing an empirical process control (Schwaber, Sutherland & Beedle, 2017). According to Bourque & Fairley (2014), Scrum is the agile method with more friendly management.

The Scrum team is a set of associated roles, events, artifacts, and rules that have a specific purpose for its success and usage. Then, it has three main components: roles, events, and artifacts (Hayat, et al., 2019), next briefly explained:

- **Roles:** Scrum has three roles, the Product Owner, who mainly handles setting the project goals, and is the only person responsible to manage the product backlog; the Scrum Master, who guides and coach the team to perform theory, practices, rules, and values, the Scrum Master also removes the impediments that the development team faces to achieve its progress; and the Development team, a self-organized team that handles the task assignment, the daily detail management, and the progress, quality, and control of the product (Schwaber, Sutherland & Beedle, 2017)

- **Events:** Scrum is organized in time-boxed events, such as the sprint (a 1-4 weeks' period), that should perform a sprint planning meeting, in which is planed the sprint, and set its goal. During the sprint, the tasks are taken from the product backlog and executed, which are part of the project artifacts. In this approach, the team members select from the backlog the tasks they commit to execute. The daily Scrum meeting is a 15-minute meeting performed every day carried to help the development team to inspect the work process. At the end of the sprint, a sprint review meeting should be held to inspect achievements and to adapt the product backlog (if needed). And a Sprint Retrospective meeting is also carried out to provide the opportunity to improve the development team based on self-inspection (Deemer et al., 2010; Schwaber, Sutherland & Beedle, 2017).
- **Artifacts:** The Scrum products are product backlog, sprint backlog, increment, the definition of "done", and burn down chart, all of them defined to represent the work and evaluate it, providing transparency as well as the identification of opportunities and adaptations when needed (Schwaber, Sutherland & Beedle, 2017).

The rules of Scrum keep together roles, events, and artifacts, so the rules govern the relationships and interaction among the three main components (Schwaber, Sutherland & Beedle, 2013).

Besides, to monitor sprint's progress, the development team should focus on the remaining work in the Sprint's backlog, by keeping track of its progress in the Daily Scrum meeting to manage it (Schwaber, Sutherland & Beedle, 2013), for this task Kanban boards are a useful tool to support Scrum.

Kanban is a Japanese term that refers to a sign, poster, or billboard that is translated as a visual board (Agile alliance, 2018). It is an agile tool for agile project management designed to help the development team to have a better visualization of its job, limit its work in progress, and maximize its workflows (Rehkopf M, 2021).

A Kanban board is mainly composed of columns, for the development team to see in a visual way, the different processing states of each product backlog item, and a set of cards or tickets representing a unit of value, which generally is associated with a user story (Rehkopf M, 2021). Also, each column of the board is associated with a work in progress, and the work in process limit (WIP limit), which purpose is not allowing the implementation of sequential tasks (Rehkopf M, 2021, Agile alliance, 2018). Due to the increasing use of Scrum boards by development teams, Kanban boards underwent a digital transformation, an example of the most used are Trello and Jira software (Rehkopf M, 2021).

In this context, some students have been performing in the educational file to teach Kanban using boards as main tools, among other, we selected three studies as example: (1) the university of Aalto teaches Kanban and lean thinking in a software project management course using a collaborative Kanban board game. This study analyzes a quantitative data from 57 learning diaries. The results show that students' perception was that they had learned substantially from the game. Besides, students evaluated the game very positively. But the learning goals were only partially reached (Heikkilä, Paasivaara, & Lassenius, 2016); (2) a prototype of a computer-aided task board with information technology BSc students was used to track their project work and project management to detect any changes in board status, with real-time update online. The advantages of the proposed blended solution were: an in-depth understanding of the students regarding the product development phase, students using physical Kanban boards did a better work than the students raining only in a theorical way or using only common virtual task boards without having physical interaction (Bacea, Ciupe, & Meza, 2017); and (3) an experience report of the use of Trello with a software supported version of Kanban board to support agile and lean learning for in-service teachers undertaking professional development. Their results of analyzing several hundred teachers showed that Trello provides an excellent tool for this type of learning environment (Parsons, 2018).

SCRUM METHOD GAMIFICATION

Game Elements Implementation

As mentioned, agile teams are in charge of their own schedule by monitoring and measuring project progress, where the visualization and dissemination measurement results are often based on information radiators; based on this metaphor, a visible dashboard seems a perfect tool to highlight all major indicators of the software development process (Meding, 2017). In this context, dashboards support a wide-ranging view of what is happening on a project, with dynamic parts of what is getting done, what needs to be done, and what is finished, allowing the development team to have better visibility of their remained work, so they can take extra actions when needed. This chapter provides a dashboard where gamified elements were inserted to increase the motivation of students to carry out their final project.

Based on a systematic literature review, Muñoz et al. (2018) established the most used game elements used for gamification in software development teams next briefly described:

- **Leaderboards**, a rank of players as a competitive indicator to determine who performs best. They tend to motivate the players to constructive participation or as a demotivate factor if they are at the lowest places (Sailer et al., 2017).
- **Points systems**, a basic element to reward the successful accomplishment of a goal that provides continuous and immediate feedback; they represent a status (Werbach & Hunter, 2015).
- **Badges,** a visual representation of achievements, earned or collected (Werbach & Hunter, 2015). They symbolize social influence, while lead to select certain routes and challenges (Sailer et al., 2017).
- **Levels,** which represent challenges increasing difficulty according to the game progress. Usually, a higher level is unlocked as a reward (Gnauk, Dannecker & Hahmann, 2012).
- **Progress bars,** informs about progress related to the final goal of the game. Usually, a bar or a numeral percent displays the degree of total goals to motivate the player to continue (Xu, 2011).
- **Rewards,** the main motivators of the gamified system, they have specific characteristics such as type (points or virtual money), trigger (the accomplishment of certain actions that trigger the reward), and usage (Darejeh & Salim, 2016).
- **Scores,** which measure the player performance, represent the number of points, goals and achievements in the game (Darejeh & Salim, 2016).
- **Challenges,** similar to goals, but players have to face some kind of pressure to complete the task such as time limit (Darejeh & Salim, 2016).
- **Achievements,** an activity or task completed, they can be obtained for one activity or for a small group of them, contrary to badges that require a set of activities. From a group of achievements, the gamer can get a badge (Darejeh & Salim, 2016).

- **(Immediate) Feedback,** to provide information identifying how to perform an activity. A common use is to give information when the system asks a question or to perform a specific task (Darejeh & Salim, 2016).
- **Storyline,** a scenario or theme, typically for a role playing to interact with the others (Darejeh & Salim, 2016).

Among them, the most used gamification elements in software engineering teamwork are the interplay of badges, points, and leaderboards, recognized as highly effective (Muñoz et al. 2018). Therefore, they were selected for gamifying the dashboard as follows:

Points

Points systems are useful to have visibility of the user's progress or success; they support comparing users' or gamers' performance. The points were implemented in the dashboard as next described:

- The participant that takes care of a task receives the same points as the effort evaluation assigned to that task. If the task is not completed or if it has not the required quality, then instead of earning points, the participant loses the task effort value.
- Participants can achieve the task in collaboration, in this case, the points are divided based on the number of people that participated e.g. for 2 people, each one receives the 60% of the effort value; 3 persons, get 35% of the effort value; 4 persons get 30% of the effort value; and for 5 persons, they receive 25% of the task effort value. We believe that this will encourage collaboration, but not enough to work all the time with others or to perform low-value tasks in collaboration.
- At the end of the project, diversification of tasks is rewarded with extra points. Every task was classified according to the software development cycle, see Figure 1. The types are A (planning, requirements definition, and design), B (implementation), C (launch, deployment, and maintenance), D (testing), and the E category was included because the students need to document the code. Besides, the task diversity is rewarded at the end of the project as follows:
    - The participant with three different categories gets 20% extra points
    - Participants with four different categories get 35% extra points
    - Participants with five different categories get 50% extra points

Badges

Badges are useful to represent the success or achievement of the user's goals, so it helps to motivate an individual to achieve his/her goals. Therefore, it should be meaningful for the user. Then, the proposed badges implemented in the Kanban dashboard are associated with software development best practices (SBP) and behavior best practices (BBP). Table 1 shows the badges implemented in the Kanban dashboard, their purpose, and how the students obtain them.

Figure 1. Task project categorization

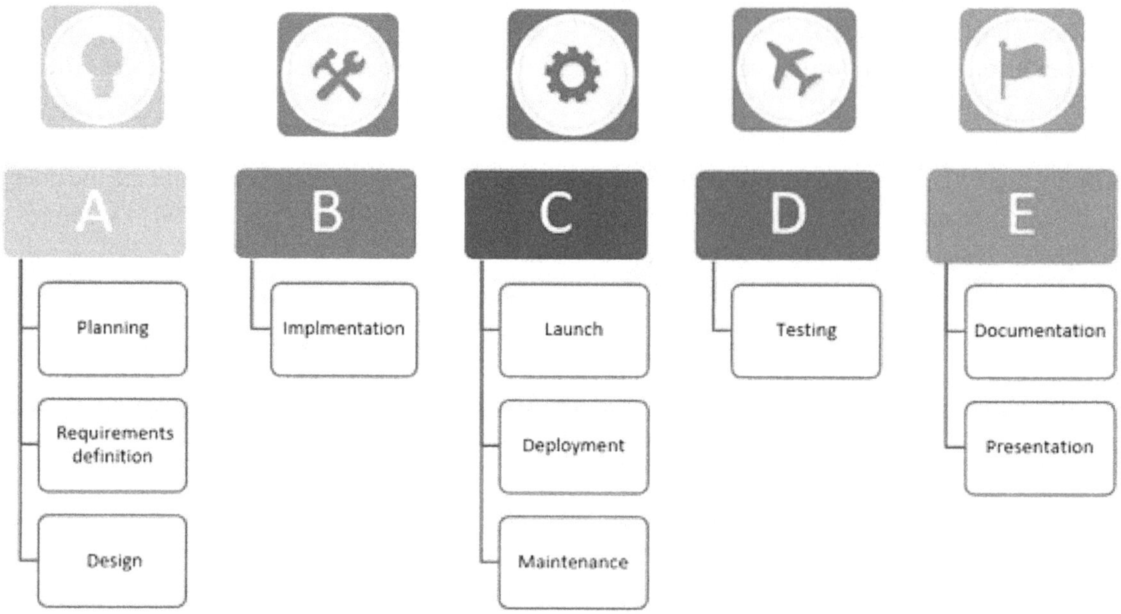

Leaderboards

Leaderboards are useful to show the user's progress or success and to compare it with other users' progress. Then, two leaderboards were implemented, one for each team, the leader team board, and one for all the teams, the leader projects board. In the team leaderboard are displayed the team members with their points, their earned badges, and also the tasks classification they achieved in the Sprint. The participant with more points, the leader, has the benefit of first choosing tasks in the next Sprint.

The other leaderboard presents the punctuation by team or project. In this leaderboard the leader is selected by the number of team members participating in the Sprint, the uncompleted task, and the number of tasks accomplished. In case of a tie, the categories of the tasks performed are taken into account, and the participants' effort points are considered as the last criteria.

The gamification elements, selected present intrinsic need satisfaction as proposed by Robson et al. (2015), of 1) autonomy, predicted by immersion-related gamification features, in this case by the badges of the developer/player; 2) competence, predicted by achievement-related gamification features, covered by the points account, and 3) relatedness, predicted by social-related gamification elements, like the leaderboard. The implementation is next presented.

By gamifying the project, it is expected that the students feel motivated to finish the project or at least to complete a major part of it. Also, it was observed that some students tend to avoid certain tasks (e.g. documentation or programming) leaving that to their teammates. Then, it is also expected that through the points system by task categories, the participants try to do a higher diversity of tasks. Finally, the badges are intended to promote best practices in software development as well as beneficial individual behavior for the team as a whole.

Table 1. Badges for coding and behavior good practices.

Badges	Name	Type SBP/BBP	Purpose	Obtained when
	Speed (time to make the task)	SBP	Obtain the highest number of tasks completed in the shortest amount of time	After each Sprint, the time of each task is counted, and an average time is calculated. The team member with more tasks and less average time wins the badge.
	Quality (errors)	SBP	Generate fewer code errors	After each Sprint, in the Sprint Review meeting, all team members analyze the tasks that do not need to be reworked, based on that they vote to propose who wins this badge.
	Clean code (easy to understand)	SBP	Use good coding practices	After each Sprint, in the Sprint Review meeting, all team members vote which of them wins this badge according to their code reviews.
	Code correct documentation	SBP	Generate the habitus for documenting the code in an adequate way	After each sprint, the project repository is reviewed, so that this badge is assigned to the one with the most number of comments.
	Greater number of tasks in the Sprint	SBP	Encourage them to perform more tasks during the sprint.	After each Sprint, the total number of tasks per team member is counted, and the one with the most completed tasks wins the badge.
	Peers support (sharing knowledge)	BBP	Resolve doubts for the team members	After the Sprint, in the Sprint retrospective meeting, all team members vote which team member resolved more doubts to win this badge.
	Learning willingness	BBP	Look for new solutions	After the Sprint, in the Sprint retrospective meeting, all team members vote which team member proposed new solutions applying new knowledge.

METHODS

In order to understand the impact of the gamification, we define a method based on the empirical research method: controlled experiments. The controlled experiment method will allow us to have control over a variable and having a set of participants carrying out a set of tasks (Wohlin, Höst, & Henningsson 2003). Therefore, the variable to control is the gamified dashboard, or as we call it Scrumming, and the tasks to carry out are the project and the participants are the students who were involved in the project.

Controlled experiment context: a set of students should execute a final project of the Internet programming subject, which is part of the undergraduate program of Computer Science Engineering and Informatics Engineering. It is important to mention two reason for selecting this context: 1) due to the COVID-19 pandemic, this regularly face-to-face course was online; 2) the final project is part of the grade of the course; it represents 30% of the grade. This means that even if the students do not complete

Table 2. Sprint Leaderboard

Team ranking	Team member	Team member ranking	Points	Accomplished task category	Number of tasks accomplished
Leaderboard 2nd Sprint					
2nd place	TM1-1	1st place	11	A,B	2
	TM1-2	3rd place	4	A	1
	TM1-3	2nd place	8	A,B	2

the final project, it does not represent a negative impact or a threat to them, because they can approve the course. Also, they receive a grade for the project according to their progress.

Controlled experiment set goals: The project had to be developed in teams, which could select the type of Website development, as far as they follow the next project requirements:

- It has to solve any type of social problem.
- The solution has to involve the use of the Internet of Things (IoT).
- The project has to present the front and back end.
- It also has to be responsive.
- The project has to be developed applying the tools learned in the course (i.e. HTML, CSS, JavaScript, Angular, Phaser, Laravel, and Nodemcu).
- Each project has to be unique, which means, it should be different from those presented by other teams.
- Projects with more than the indicated modules and tools will get extra points.

Controlled experiment execution: Twenty-two students, 20 males, and 2 females, enrolled in the subject were randomly assigned in triplets to get a total of eight teams. None of the students had previous experience on gamification in their regular classes or in the Scrum framework. Four teams followed a gamified dashboard for the project development and four teams followed a traditional Trello dashboard for the project development. It is important to highlight that the eight teams used the Scrum method to develop their project.

The instructions for all the teams were to use Trello™ tool for project management. Trello™ is a collaboration tool that organizes the project into boards. Trello draws on the Kanban principles of workflow through boards, lists, and cards. Then, the project tasks were listed and evaluated by all teams. The gamified project dashboard received the rules as explained in the section "Scrum method gamification".

The final project took 4 Sprints, each one with a one-week duration. At the end of the Sprint, the professor presented the leaderboard of each team as the example in Table 2, which shows the dashboard for the second Sprint including ranking, point, tasks categories, and the number of tasks accomplished.

The analysis of the results is showed in next section.

Table 3. Results of Scrumming vs traditional dashboard results

Team number	Type of team	Unfinished Tasks	Not assigned tasks	Completed tasks	Total of not completed tasks	Total of project tasks	Percentage of not completed tasks
1	non-gamified Scrum dashboard	10	5	4	15	19	78%
2	Scrumming	0	0	14	0	14	0%
3	non-gamified Scrum dashboard	4	0	13	4	17	23%
4	Scrumming	0	1	26	1	27	3%
5	non-gamified Scrum dashboard	1	2	11	3	14	21%
6	Scrumming	0	8	14	8	22	36%
7	non-gamified Scrum dashboard	6	5	0	11	11	100%
8	Scrumming	0	0	15	0	15	0%

RESULTS

Teams with Gamified Dashboard versus Non-gamified Dashboard

This section analyzes the performance of teams using Scrumming versus teams using a traditional Trello dashboard. Table 3 shows the result focusing on the unfinished tasks, not assigned tasks, and completed tasks.

The results for element were:

- **Unfinished task:** analyzing data of column three, the results showed that all teams using Scrumming (team 2, 4,6, and 8) have no unfinished tasks, but the teams using non-gamified Scrum dashboard have from 1 to 10 unfinished tasks.
- **Not assigned task:** analyzing data of column four, two teams using Scrumming (team 4 and 6) have 1 and 8 not assigned tasks respectively, besides, the team having 8 not assigned tasks (team 6) is the team that partially completed the project. Related to the teams using non-gamified Scrum dashboard teams (team 1 and team 2) having less not assigned tasks 0 and 1 respectively are the teams that partially completed the project.
- **Completed tasks:** analyzing data of column five, teams using Scrumming have more completed tasks than teams using non-gamified Scrum dashboard. Besides, teams 1 and 7 that do not complete the project have 5 and 9 completed tasks.
- **Total of not completed tasks:** this result is obtained by adding data of columns three (unfinished tasks) and four (not assigned tasks) to get the total of tasks not completed by teams. As column five shows, teams using Scrumming keep 1 and 8 not assigned tasks. However, teams using a non-gamified Scrum dashboard have increased the number of not completed tasks.
- **Completed projects:** this result is obtained by analyzing data of columns six (total of not completed tasks) and seven (total of project tasks) to get the percentage of not completed tasks that

will help us to identify teams that finish the project. The results showed greater participation in the four gamified teams, three of them finished the project and one was partially completed. In contrast, in the non-gamified teams, three projects were partially finished and the other three were not completed at all.

In summary, teams using Scrumming got better results. Moreover, the grades of the gamified teams assigned by the teacher of the subject in a 100 scale were 90, 95, and 90 for teams 2, 4, and 8 respectively that finished the project, and 35 for the team 6 that did not finish it. And the grades for teams using the non-gamified Scrum dashboard were 55, for teams 3 and 5 that partially finished projects, 25 for team 1 that did not finish the project, and 0 for team 7 that did not do the project.

This is consistent with the expected gamified motivation to complete the project, and its quality.

Gamified Dashboard Teams

This section provides the results of teams using the gamified dashboard named Scrumming focused on the project achievement and their members' motivation.

a) Project Achievement

The complete results are provided in Table 4, with the four Sprints' leaderboards containing team ranking, team member ID, Sprint ranking, points, task category, and a total of tasks.

As can be observed in Table 4 teams that completed the project 2, 4 and 8 were placed in the first three places ranking throughout the Sprints (see column 1), having more team members' participation (columns 2 and 3). Column 3 is related to points assigned based on the user story completed, as the column shows teams have an increase in the tasks performed in the last two sprints increasing the obtained story points. Column four is related to the task category, as it is observed in the first Sprints team members carried out tasks related to only one category A (planning, requirement definition, and design) or B (implementation). However, in the last two Sprints, most of the team members carried out at least two categories being the most common implementation B(implementation) and C (launch, deployment, and maintenance). Finally, in column five, it is observed an increase in the tasks performed by team members in the last two Sprints. Related to team 6 that did not finish the project, in the third Sprint only one of the team members made his/her task, and in the fourth Sprint, none of them made any task at all.

None of the students did the five categories. Accomplished categories are presented in Table 5. As mentioned only gamified teams finished the project, therefore it was not possible to compare the diversity of task with non-gamified teams. It can also be observed that it was not possible to take care of three different types of tasks during a Sprint, and therefore the points' reward should be adapted to the software development cycle.

b) Team Members' Motivation

Related to the team motivation, this analysis was focused on the badges earned by team members, which allow us to analyze the tendency to win badges. It is important to mention that each badge was earned according to the software development best practices (SBP) and behavior best practices (BBP) used by the team members. The rules to win a badge are provided in Table 1 column 5 *How to get it?* The complete results of earned badges are presented in Table 6.

Table 4. The follow-up for each Sprint by teams.

Team ranking	Team member	Team member Sprint ranking	Points	Task category	Total of tasks
Leaderboard Sprint 1					
2ND	TM2-1	1ST	3	A	2
	TM2-2	3RD	2	B	1
	TM2-3	2ND	1	A	1
3RD	TM4-1	1ST	3	A	3
	TM4-2	2ND	2	A	2
	TM4-3	2ND	2	A	2
1ST	TM6-1	2ND	4	A	2
	TM6-2	1ST	7	A,B	5
	TM6-3	2ND	4	A	2
4TH	TM8-1	1ST	5	A	3
	TM8-2	-	0	-	0
	TM8-3	-	0	-	0
Leaderboard Sprint 2					
2ND	TM2-1	1ST	6	A	2
	TM2-2	2ND	3	A	1
	TM2-3	2ND	3	A	1
1ST	TM4-1	3RD	3	B	1
	TM4-2	1ST	6	B	2
	TM4-3	2ND	4	B	2
3RD	TM6-1	3RD	0		
	TM6-2	2ND	8	A	3
	TM6-3	1ST	13	A	3
4TH	TM8-1		-5		
	TM8-2		-8		
	TM8-3		-2		
Leaderboard Sprint 3					
1ST	TM2-1	2ND	4	B	1
	TM2-2	1ST	11	B,C	3
	TM2-3	1ST	11	B,C	3
2ND	TM4-1	1ST	13	B,C	1
	TM4-2	1ST	13	B,C	1
	TM4-3	1ST	13	B,C	1
4TH	TM6-1	3RD	0		
	TM6-2	1ST	10	B,C	2
	TM6-3	3RD	0		
3RD	TM8-1	3RD	-1	B	2
	TM8-2	1ST	11	B,C	3
	TM8-3	2ND	2	A	2
Leaderboard Sprint 4					
2ND	TM2-1	1ST	22.5	C, D	5
	TM2-2	2ND	10.5	C, E	4
	TM2-3	3RD	11.5	B, C	3
1ST	TM4-1	3RD	20	B, D	6
	TM4-2	2ND	22	B, E	6
	TM4-3	1ST	27	B, C	9
4TH	TM6-1		0		
	TM6-2		0		
	TM6-3		0		
3RD	TM8-1	3RD	5	C, D	1
	TM8-2	1ST	10	B, E	3
	TM8-3	2ND	7	C	2

Table 5. Diversity of task accomplished by team member

Team member	Type of task accomplished
TM2-1	A, B, C, D
TM2-2	A, B, C, E
TM2-3	A, B, C
TM4-1	A, B, C, D
TM4-2	A, B, C, E
TM4-3	A, B, C
TM6-1	A
TM6-2	A, B, C
TM6-3	A, B
TM8-1	A, B, C, D
TM8-2	B, C, E
TM8-3	A, C

Table 6. The follow-up for each Sprint by teams.

Team member	1ST Sprint	2ND Sprint	3RD Sprint	4TH Sprint
TM2-1				
TM2-2				
TM2-3				
TM4-1				
TM4-2				
TM4-3				
TM6-1				
TM6-2				
TM6-3				
TM8-1				
TM8-2				
TM8-3				

The results according to Table 6 regarding the earned badges by team members are next described:

- Team 2. TM2-1 got three badges throughout all sprints, in Sprints 1,2 and 3 got the speed badge that means the member performed faster the assigned tasks, and in the last Sprint got the greater number of tasks that means he/she completed more tasks to finish the project. TM2-2 were the team members who made more tasks for the Sprint but he/she was worried about learning more things, documenting his/her code, and providing a clean code. Finally, the TM2-3 got the support badges that meant he/she was worried about other team members.
- Team 4. TM4-1 got more badges related to code correct documentation that means he/she was worried about correctly documenting the code. TM4.2 got more badges related to peer support that means he/she helps to solve problems for other team members and got a speed badge that means he/she works faster than the other members. Finally, TM4.3 got more quality and learning badges that means he/she created the best code and learned new technologies.
- Team 6. TM6-1 was the only one who won the code correct documentation, which means he/she was worried about documenting his/her code in the right way. TM6.2 got a greater number of tasks in the Sprint that means the team member who worked more than the others. TM6.3 got the peer support and speed badge that means work faster and help his/her team members. However, these badges were won in the first three sprints. However, in the four sprints, they do not work.
- Team 8. TM8-1 got more code correct documentation and clean code and quality badges mean he/she was worried about documenting in an adequate way his/her code and there to keep it understandable for the other team members.TM8-2 got a greater number of tasks and speed badges that means he/she works more efficiently. Finally, the TM8-3 got more learning willingness and peer support badges that mean he/she helps his/her team members to resolve problems.

According to the results, in the first Sprint, the team members are motivated to implement more software development best practices (SBP) in order to achieve the Sprint's goal because they are starting to work as a team. However, during the rest of the sprints team members implement both software development best practices (SBP) and behavior best practices (BBP) because they are following the Scrum rules and at least one of them is worried about being collaborative with other team members to achieve the Sprint's target. Finally, in the fourth Sprint, most of the team members were worried about delivering a complete product, which is the reason why they were focused on software development best practices (SBP) and these results are in concordance with the results provided in Table 4.

FUTURE RESEARCH DIRECTIONS

According to the results of the implementation of Scrumming, four research directions are identified as follows:

1. increasing the sample to implement Scrumming dashboard; we are aware that one of the main limitations of this study is the sample size used for experimentation.
2. performing an analysis focused on contrasting the motivation of performing diverse tasks versus the tendency to only win the badges;

3. analyzing the completed Scrum method events and artifacts to identify which of them can be gamified; and,
4. creating an application that automatically assigns badges at both levels the team members level and the team level.

CONCLUSION

Nowadays we can see two features in the software domain industry: 1) software should be done by team due to its complexity and 2) software development teams are preferring the use of agile methods in an effort to reduce the time in which the software product is delivered, however if an agile method is not implemented in an adequate way it could present negative effects on projects. Therefore, two topics addressed in this article might have an important impact on software development projects. On the one hand, there is a real and increasing tendency of the use of agile methods, especially Scrum, for small and medium enterprises in an effort to reduce the time to deliver their software product. On the other hand, the implementation of gamification elements keeps the motivation of team members and increases their participation in the software development activities. This fact highlights the need to provide the software tools that make their usage easy not only in the industry domain but in the academic domain where the future engineers are being trained.

Based on the above mentioned, this article provides a proposal to gamified a Trello Kanban dashboard named Scrumming, which has been proved using a controlled group of 4 teams from a total of 8 teams getting good results. In the context of our sample, we can conclude that the use of Scrumming motivated the students to follow the best practices in the execution of Scrum, it had a very important positive impact a positive impact in the project conclusion. The results of this experiment showed the next improvements: (1) technical improvements such as an increase in the speed to perform project tasks, and an increase in the number of tasks of the number of tasks done, an increase in the implementation of code correct documentation and an increase in clean code; (2) soft skills improvements such as in the support provided to other team members to help solving problems, increase in the learning willingness and a more efficiently work.

However, we are aware that the sample of the controlled groups participating in the experiment is a limitation of this research, and that authors need to broaden the sample as mentioned in future research directions.

REFERENCES

Adams, E. (2014). *Fundamentals of game design*. Pearson Education.

Agile alliance. (2018). *Agile glossary*. https://www.agilealliance.org/agile101/agile-glossary/

Andrei, B. A., Casu-Pop, A. C., Gheorghe, S. C., & Boiangiu, C. A. (2019). A study on using waterfall and agile methods in software project management. *Journal Of Information Systems & Operations Management*, *13*(1), 125–135.

Bacea, I. M., Ciupe, A., & Meza, S. N. (2017, July). Interactive Kanban—Blending digital and physical resources for collaborative project based learning. In *2017 IEEE 17th International Conference on Advanced Learning Technologies (ICALT)* (pp. 210-211). IEEE. 10.1109/ICALT.2017.68

Bourque, P., & Fairley, R. (2014) *Guide to the Software Engineering Body of Knowledge* (SWEBOK Version 3). IEEE Computer Society. www.swebok.org

Carvalho, J. D., Fernandes, S., Lima, R. M., & Mesquita, D. (2018). *Making PBL teams more effective with Scrum.* University of Minho. http://hdl.handle.net/1822/66529

Chou, Y. K. (2015). *Actionable Gamification Beyond Points, Badges, and Leaderboards.* Octalysis Media.

Ćirić, D., & Gračanin, D. (2017). Agile project management beyond software industry. In *proceedings of the XV international scientific conference on industrial systems* (pp. 332–337). Novi Sad: Faculty of Technical Sciences.

Darejeh, A., & Salim, S. S. (2016). Gamification solutions to enhance software user engagement—A systematic review. *International Journal of Human-Computer Interaction, 32*(8), 613–642. doi:10.1080/10447318.2016.1183330

De Souza, A. D., Seabra, R. D., Ribeiro, J. M., & Rodrigues, L. E. D. S. (2017, May). SCRUMI: a board serious virtual game for teaching the SCRUM framework. In *2017 IEEE/ACM 39th International Conference on Software Engineering Companion (ICSE-C)* (pp. 319-321). IEEE. 10.1109/ICSE-C.2017.124

Digital.ai. (2021). *15th State of Agile Report.* https://stateofagile.com/#ufh-i-661275008-15th-state-of-agile-report/7027494

Fitsilis, P., & Lekatos, A. (2017, September). Teaching software project management using agile paradigm. In *Proceedings of the 21st Pan-Hellenic Conference on Informatics* (pp. 1–6). 10.1145/3139367.3139413

Galeano-Ospino, S., Machuca-Villegas, L., & Gasca-Hurtado, G. P. (2020, October). Knowledge transfer in software development teams using gamification: A systematic literature review. In *International Conference on Software Process Improvement* (pp. 115–130). Springer.

Gasca-Hurtado, G. P., Gómez-Álvarez, M. C., Muñoz, M., & Mejía, J. (2021, September). Gamification Principles to Decrease SPI Change Resistance. In *European Conference on Software Process Improvement* (pp. 241-256). Springer. 10.1007/978-3-030-85521-5_16

Gnauk, B., Dannecker, L., & Hahmann, M. (2012, March). Leveraging gamification in demand dispatch systems. In *Proceedings of the 2012 Joint EDBT/ICDT workshops* (pp. 103–110). 10.1145/2320765.2320799

Heikkilä, V. T., Paasivaara, M., & Lassenius, C. (2016, May). Teaching university students Kanban with a collaborative board game. In *Proceedings of the 38th international conference on software engineering companion* (pp. 471-480) 10.1145/2889160.2889201

Horváth, I. (2019). MaxWhere 3D capabilities contributing to the enhanced efficiency of the Trello 2D management software. *Acta Polytechnica Hungarica, 16*(6), 55–71. doi:10.12700/APH.16.6.2019.6.5

Jurado, J. L., Fernandez, A., & Collazos, C. A. (2015, October). Applying gamification in the context of knowledge management. In *Proceedings of the 15th International Conference on Knowledge Technologies and Data-driven Business* (pp. 1–4). 10.1145/2809563.2809606

Kiryakova, G., Angelova, N., & Yordanova, L. (2014, October). Gamification in education. In *Proceedings of 9th International Balkan Education and Science Conference.*

Knutas, A., Ikonen, J., Nikula, U., & Porras, J. (2014, June). Increasing collaborative communications in a programming course with gamification: a case study. In *Proceedings of the 15th International Conference on Computer Systems and Technologies* (pp. 370–377). 10.1145/2659532.2659620

Krehbiel, T. C., Salzarulo, P. A., Cosmah, M. L., Forren, J., Gannod, G., Havelka, D., Hulshult, A. R., & Merhout, J. (2017). Agile Manifesto for Teaching and Learning. *The Journal of Effective Teaching*, *17*(2), 90–111. https://uncw.edu/jet/articles/vol17_2/krehbiel.html

Kropp, M., & Meier, A. (2013, May). Teaching agile software development at university level: Values, management, and craftsmanship. In *2013 26th International Conference on Software Engineering Education and Training (CSEE&T)* (pp. 179–188). IEEE. 10.26041/fhnw-626

Latulipe, C., Long, N. B., & Seminario, C. E. (2015). Structuring Flipped Classes with Lightweight Teams and Gamification. *Proceedings of the 46th ACM Technical Symposium on Computer Science Education*, 392–397. 10.1145/2676723.2677240

Madampe, M. A. K. G. (2017). Successful adoption of agile project management in software development industry. *International Journal of Computer Science and Information Technology Research*, *5*(4), 2327.

Metrôlho, J. C., Ribeiro, F. R., & Passão, P. (2020). Teaching Agile Software Engineering Practices Using Scrum and a Low-Code Development Platform–A Case Study. *ICSEA*, *2020*, 160–165.

Muñoz, M., Peña Pérez Negrón, A., & Hernández, L. (2020). Gamification in Virtual reality Environments for the integration of Highly Effective Teams. In *Virtual Reality Designs* (pp. 151–175). CRC Press. doi:10.1201/9781003019589-7

Owens, D., & Shekhar, G. (2018). Using SCRUM principles to transform the classroom. *AMCIS 2018 Proceedings*, 85. https://aisel.aisnet.org/amcis2018/TREOsPDS/Presentations/85

Parsons, D., Thorn, R., Inkila, M., & MacCallum, K. (2018, December). Using Trello to support agile and lean learning with Scrum and Kanban in teacher professional development. In *2018 IEEE International Conference on Teaching, Assessment, and Learning for Engineering (TALE)* (pp. 720-724). IEEE. 10.1109/TALE.2018.8615399

Patricio, R., Moreira, A., Zurlo, F., & Melazzini, M. (2020). Co-creation of new solutions through gamification: A collaborative innovation practice. *Creativity and Innovation Management*, *29*(1), 146–160. doi:10.1111/caim.12356

Patrício, R., Moreira, A. C., & Zurlo, F. (2018). Gamification approaches to the early stage of innovation. *Creativity and Innovation Management*, *27*(4), 499–511. doi:10.1111/caim.12284

Pérez-Castillo, R., Caballero, I., & Rodríguez, M. (2018, April). Improving the experience of teaching Scrum. In *2018 IEEE Global Engineering Education Conference (EDUCON)* (pp. 1598–1605). IEEE. 10.1109/EDUCON.2018.8363426

Philbin, S. P. (2017). Investigating the scope for agile project management to be adopted by higher education institutions. In *Software Project Management for Distributed Computing* (pp. 345–366). Springer. doi:10.1007/978-3-319-54325-3_14

Radujković, M., & Sjekavica, M. (2017). Project management success factors. *Procedia Engineering, 196*, 607–615. doi:10.1016/j.proeng.2017.08.048

Rehkopf, M. (2021). *¿Qué es un tablero Kanban?* Atlassian. https://www.atlassian.com/es/agile/kanban/boards

Robson, K., Plangger, K., Kietzmann, J. H., McCarthy, I., & Pitt, L. (2015). Is it all a game? Understanding the principles of gamification. *Business Horizons, 58*(4), 411–420. doi:10.1016/j.bushor.2015.03.006

Rush, D. E., & Connolly, A. J. (2020). An agile framework for teaching with scrum in the IT project management classroom. *Journal of Information Systems Education, 31*(3), 196–207. https://aisel.aisnet.org/jise/vol31/iss3/4

Sailer, M., Hense, J. U., Mayr, S. K., & Mandl, H. (2017). How gamification motivates: An experimental study of the effects of specific game design elements on psychological need satisfaction. *Computers in Human Behavior, 69*, 371–380. doi:10.1016/j.chb.2016.12.033

Salza, P., Musmarra, P., & Ferrucci, F. (2019). *Agile methodologies in education: A review. Agile and lean concepts for teaching and learning*. Springer. doi:10.1007/978-981-13-2751-3_2

Schäfer, U. (2017, April). Training scrum with gamification: Lessons learned after two teaching periods. In *2017 IEEE Global Engineering Education Conference (EDUCON)* (pp. 754–761). IEEE. 10.1109/EDUCON.2017.7942932

Schwaber, K., Sutherland, J., & Beedle, M. (2013). *The definitive guide to Scrum: The rules of the game*. Scrum.org. http://www.scrumguides.org/docs/scrumguide/v1/Scrum-guide-us.pdf

Steghöfer, J. P., Burden, H., Alahyari, H., & Haneberg, D. (2017). No silver brick: Opportunities and limitations of teaching Scrum with Lego workshops. *Journal of Systems and Software, 131*, 230–247. doi:10.1016/j.jss.2017.06.019

Vogelzang, J., Admiraal, W. F., & Van Driel, J. H. (2020). A teacher perspective on Scrum methodology in secondary chemistry education. *Chemistry Education Research and Practice, 21*(1), 237–249. doi:10.1039/C9RP00111E

Volkswagen. (2010). *The Speed Camera Lottery*. http://www.thefuntheory.com/speed-camera-lottery-0

Von Ehren, S. (2020, June 11). Why do people love games? *The New York Times*. https://www.nytimes.com/2020/06/11/style/why-people-love-games.html

Wohlin, C., Höst, M., & Henningsson, K. (2003). Empirical research methods in software engineering. In *Empirical methods and studies in software engineering* (pp. 7–23). Springer. doi:10.1007/978-3-540-45143-3_2

Xi, N., & Hamari, J. (2019). Does gamification satisfy needs? A study on the relationship between gamification features and intrinsic need satisfaction. *International Journal of Information Management*, *46*, 210–221. doi:10.1016/j.ijinfomgt.2018.12.002

Xu, Y., & Hi, H. (2011). *Literature review on web application gamification and analytics* (CSDL Technical Report 11-05). University of Hawaii.

KEY TERMS AND DEFINITIONS

Agile Methods: Were created as a solution to reduce the time to produce software products from their conception to their delivery.

Agile Project Management: Set of activities to be performed in a project covering its planification, monitoring and control and its closure by applying agile principles such as reinforcing teamwork, organization, and self-responsibility.

Behavior Best Practices: Are practices related to soft skills such as tobe able to work in teams and to share knowledge among others.

Digital Dashboards: Agile tool that allows Scrum teams to have a better visibility of their work throughout the software development project.

Gamification: Is the use of game elements to boost the motivation and participation of people in a non-game environment.

Project Management: Set of activities to be performed in all projects covering its planification, monitoring and control and its closure to achieve that project can be achieved within the time and budget expected.

Scrum Method: The most popular agile method, that provides a framework focused on an empirical process control highlighting the social engineering to produce delivering products with the highest possible value.

Chapter 27

Understanding the Challenges of Game-Based Training:

Recommendations for Moving Research Forward in Game-Based Learning

Diana R. Sanchez
https://orcid.org/0000-0003-4937-9114
San Francisco State University, USA

Clifton A. Lee
San Francisco State University, USA

ABSTRACT

Substantial resources have been put towards game-based learning and the use of games in multidisciplinary research and practice. Despite this growing popularity, a definitive link has yet to be established between games and learning outcomes such as improved motor skills or recall of information. The problems researchers face are a series of challenges that prevent researchers from conducting research on game-based learning in a consistent and standardized way. Through reviewing and aggregating the literature, the authors describe five challenges currently facing the area of game-based learning and offer recommendations as to what future research could do to resolve these challenges moving forward. The primary purpose of this chapter is to provide a steppingstone in the game-based learning literature to help move the field away from conflicting research findings and toward a clearer understanding of game-based learning as an educational solution across disciplines.

INTRODUCTION

Across disciplines, games have grown in popularity as an innovative medium through which people can learn knowledge and develop skills. This rise in *serious games*, or games that are made for the purpose of education rather than entertainment (Boyle et al., 2011) has included many positive intentions to

DOI: 10.4018/978-1-6684-4287-6.ch027

maintain the ludic elements in games that are associated with immersion and fun. Researchers have been interested in this interplay between fun and the practical outcomes of learning that exist in serious games. This has been pervasive across industries, such as education (Begg et al., 2005), military (Hays, 2005), medicine (Sabri et al., 2010), and pro-environmental behavior, (Kotsopoulos et al., 2019), making game-based learning a multidisciplinary topic. For the purposes of this chapter, we will focus on game-based learning within the organizational training context and extend our recommendations to the broader field of game-based learning across multiple disciplines.

Organizations invest in employee training as is evidenced by a recent report showing that the $17.7 million which companies spent on training in 2019 increased to $22 million in 2020 (Training Industry Report, 2020). This increase suggests that more organizations are recognizing the importance of organizational learning which ensures employees have the knowledge, skills, and abilities needed to complete their work. One training method that has garnered increasing attention is the use of games for training. Although games have been used in organizational settings for decades (Biggs, 1987; Cohen & Rhenman, 1961; Gredler, 1996; Keys & Wolfe, 1990), game-based learning has grown in popularity both in research and in practice over the last 10 years (Brom et al. 2011; DeSmet et al., 2014; Loganathan et al, 2019). Games are a particularly attractive option for training employees because games are often perceived positively and can improve the attention and motivation of the people completing the training. (Coller & Shernoff, 2009; Kalz et al., 2015; Papastergiou, 2009; Prensky, 2001a)

Organizations have recognized the potential benefits of using game-based approaches in their training programs. This has been demonstrated through their continued number of resources put towards the design and implementation of games (both commercially available games as well as games developed by the organization) for training purposes (Akilli & Cagiltay, 2006: Huang et al., 2015; Kalz et al., 2015; Prensky 2001a). For example, one research study compared a paper-and-pencil training manual to a computer game designed to train workers on complex manufacturing tasks. Researchers found that participants who learned using the computer game scored significantly higher on the knowledge assessment and reported feeling more confident and engaged with the training material (Li et al., 2017). This demonstrates that games can improve learning and positively impact the learner's feelings toward the training. These positive feelings toward game-based training can benefit organizations who may need to train less interesting but legally required topics (e.g., sexual harassment training). Games might provide an opportunity to improve engagement with the training while ensuring organizations meet training program requirements.

This practice of using game-based approaches has been speculated as a temporary fad (Calleja & Callus, 2010), with some stating that game elements may act more as *seductive details* to the learner which distract attention away from relevant content (Fisch, 2005). However, in contrast to this, others have demonstrated value and predict continued growth in the sustained use of game-based practices within organizations (Prensky, 2001b; Rutten et al., 2012; Senderek et al., 2015). Given the rapid growth and popularity of this practice of using games for organizational learning, (Akilli & Cagiltay, 2006; Huang et al., 2015) it is warranted to review and discuss the potential challenges that may be faced as the application of game-based learning progresses. The purpose of this chapter is twofold, first to review existing literature on game-based learning to identify potential challenges that researchers across disciplines have faced and may continue to face in applying game-based learning to their respective fields and second to propose recommendations for continued research and application of game-based learning.

While research on game-based learning has grown, there has been conflicting evidence on the benefits of games for organizational outcomes such as learning (Akl et al., 2013; Breuer & Bente, 2010; Harris,

Figure 1.

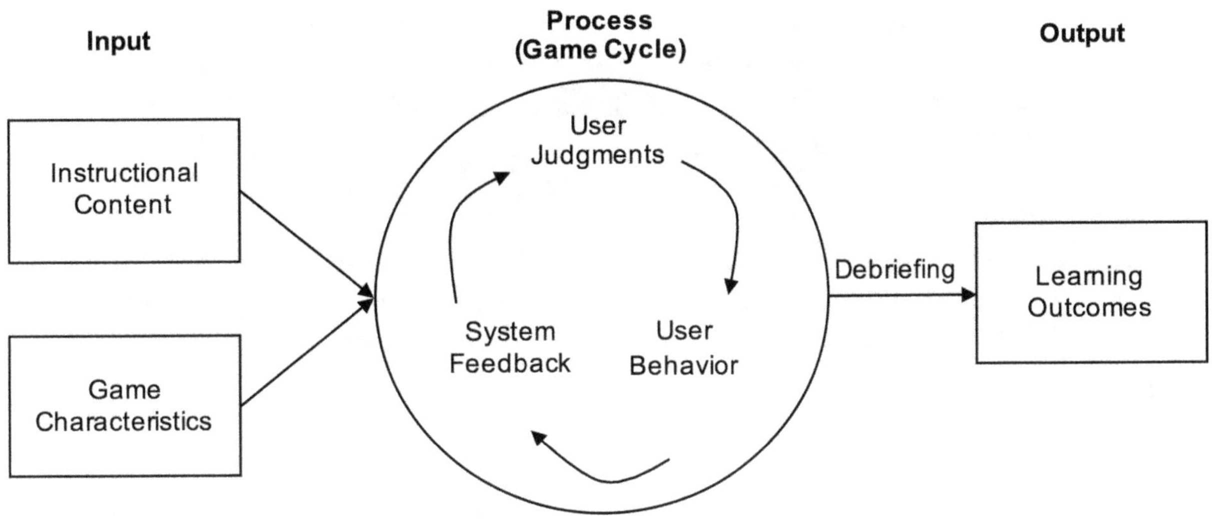

2008). This is a concern because continued disagreement may prevent new developments in game-based learning. To address this problem, we reviewed research on game-based learning and summarized various challenges facing the field. A brief summary of these challenges are: (1) the blurred distinctions between games and similar training media, (2) a growing need to identify game characteristics for specific game-based interventions, (3) the lack of evidence for the mechanisms through which game-based learning is experienced, (4) continued ambiguity in the measurement of different training outcomes, and (5) the need to draw accurate implications from research-based findings. We will discuss relevant research for each challenge in turn, followed by a recommendation for further consideration.

THEORETICAL BACKGROUND: A FRAMEWORK FOR GAME-BASED LEARNING

Current research on game-based learning often applies the methodological framework proposed by Garris et al. (2002), see Figure 1. This model produced a game-specific version of the *Input-Process-Output (IPO)* model introduced by McGrath (1984) to study how people interact within teams. Understanding this model is relevant for the current study as it is the framework through which we will present our challenges identified in the research literature. The IPO model features a progression of three steps in which specific inputs lead to processes, which produce outputs. In Garris et al.'s version of the model, the input step consists of instructional content (e.g., skills being taught) and game characteristics (e.g., degree of fantasy in the game design). Several studies have produced taxonomies of game characteristics to help define and distinguish these features and to provide standardized language for the field of game-based learning (e.g., Bedwell et al., 2012; Connolly et al., 2012; O'Neil et al., 2005). The process step has been given different names in the research literature including game cycle, game play, and user experience. In the presented model, this step includes user judgment (e.g., interest), user behaviors (e.g., decisions made) and system feedback (e.g., changes produced by the user's actions). Garris et

Figure 2.

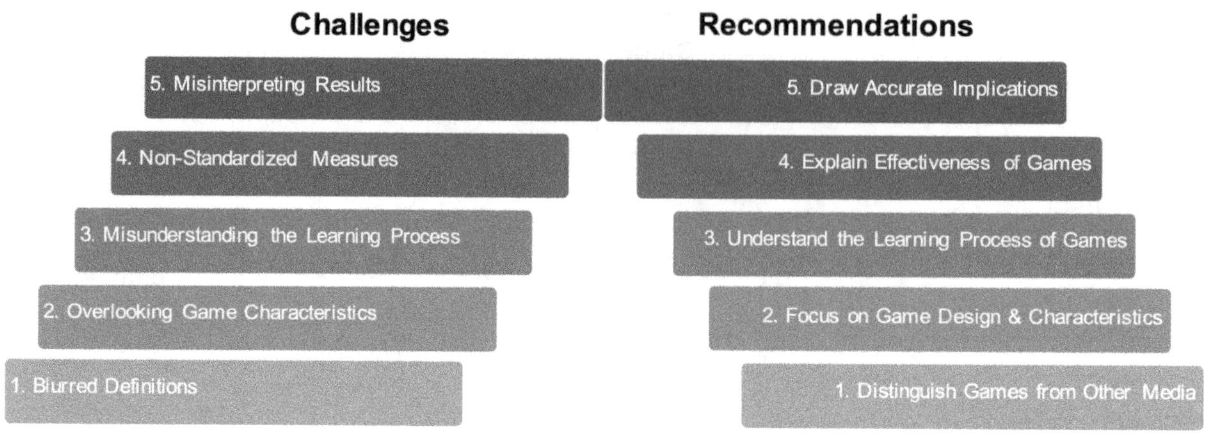

al. (2002) referred to the process step as the key component of the model, believing it could lead to a judgment-behavior-feedback loop (Sanchez & Langer, 2020), motivating users to continually return to the game and re-engage with the activities. The final output step consists of skill-based learning (e.g., motor or technical skills), cognitive-based learning (e.g., declarative knowledge), and affective learning (e.g., attitudes). This model has been particularly important to the gaming research literature because it provided researchers with a framework to build additional evidence for understanding the progression of game-based learning from the first step of design through the final step of evaluation (e.g., Connolly et al., 2012; Ke, 2008; O'Neil et al., 2005; Wilson et al., 2009).

Current Challenges of Game-Based Learning

Several researchers have produced research studies that have applied this model to understand how game characteristics influence training outcomes (e.g., Connolly et al., 2012; Grossman et al., 2014; Hoffman & Nadelson, 2010; Iacovides et al., 2014; Pratt & Hahn, 2015). This has led to a prolific generation of game-based learning research across industries (e.g., Faria et al., 2009; Gee, 2005; Hsu, 1989; Jabbar & Felicia, 2015; Li & Tsai, 2013) with the previously mentioned consequence of also increasing the contradictory results regarding the effectiveness of game-based learning. To better understand these contradictions, we reviewed the literature on game-based learning and present a summary of current challenges to research that may be propagating the concerns and controversies in this field. We will organize the structure of these challenges based on this model from Garris and colleagues, first focusing on challenges related to game components, next challenges addressing game inputs, followed by challenges related to the processes of game-based learning, and finishing with challenges on the outputs of games. We further present recommendations for each of these challenges that will help drive the research and application of game-based learning forward, see Figure 2.

Challenge 1: Blurred Definitions of Games and Game-Based Training

A contributor to the difficulty in establishing a definitive link between games and learning outcomes is in defining the broad concept of a game and establishing what is and is not a game. Over the last several decades there has been an increase of research literature highlighting the ongoing struggle to identify a standardized definition of a game (Aarseth & Grabarcyzk, 2018; Arjoranta, 2014; Emelianenko, 2011; Laas, 2017; Salen et al., 2004; Schell, 2008; Stenros, 2017; Waern, 2012; Zyda, 2005). Many of the papers that approach this topic of generating a definition for a game have stated that using a universal definition of a game would be a benefit because it would help unite the myriad of disciplines that are conducting research on games. (Arjoranta, 2019; Stenros, 2015). Researchers have taken different approaches to developing a definition for a game, some focusing on the philosophical aspects of a game (Laas, 2017; Nguyen, 2017), while others produced definitions based on specific behaviors that players engage in while playing a game (Aarseth & Grabarcyzk, 2018; Purkiss & Khaliq, 2015). Some research has focused on understanding play and how to integrate this concept into the understanding of a game (Amory & Seagram, 2003; Eichberg, 2018; Groh, 2012). This amassed literature is hallmarked by a large variation of how games are defined and understood. Depending on the criteria one uses to identify a game, different aspects of the games become more pronounced than others. In Table 1 we provide a sample of definitions derived from the research on how games have been explained and defined across industries.

A growing position in the effort to identify a universal definition of a game is that games can take different forms and can adapt to many needs, meaning researchers share the perspective that the definition of a game must remain flexible to the current need or application of the game (Aarseth, 2014; Arjoranta, 2014; Emelianenko, 2011; Feige, 2012; Laas, 2017). This position establishes that no universal definition of a game is needed or can be created (Wittgenstein, 2009) because games take on different and distinct forms according to the context in which they are used. Although many definitions of a game may share some similarities, their differences are what make them unique and meaningful given their specific purpose. Without a standard definition of a game, there is still a need to distinguish between games and other similar types of learning interventions (e.g., gamification, simulations).

In a learning context, the format that is used to deliver the content is often referred to as *training media* or *learning media*. For example, in traditional educational institutions, *classroom instruction* is the most common learning medium (National Center for Education Statistics, n.d.), whereas in workplace settings the most common training medium is *computer-based training* (Sugrue & Rivera, 2005). Distinguishing between learning media allows for the benefits and drawbacks to be researched and understood. However, distinguishing games from other similar media can be uniquely challenging. For example, one paper reported a dental simulation as a game although it lacked the common characteristics of a game such as presenting constraints and challenges beyond practicing a skill (Amer et al., 2011). For most definitions, this learning media would be best described as a simulation. In another example, in the videogame *Zero Hour* individuals take on the role and practice the skills of an Emergency Medical Service responder (Virtual Heroes, 2007). Although this game matches common definitions of a simulation, such as taking on a role and applying skills in a replication of real-life, it also includes primary components attributed to a game such as increasing levels of difficulty, playing with an avatar, and active decision making in an interactive virtual world (Bedwell et al., 2012; Garris et al., 2002). Given the number of shared characteristics and similarities between games and other similar media, it is clear why it is difficult to define and distinguish game-based learning.

Previous researchers have addressed this need to provide clear distinctions between different forms of training media (Clark, 2001; Greenblat, 1981; Hays, 2005). Some researchers have presented guidelines intended to help define different training mediums and identify the distinctions between them (e.g., Crookall & Thorngate, 2009; Fletcher & Tobias, 2006; Gredler, 1996; Wilson et al., 2009), see Table 2. Some have used specific terminology such as pure and mixed media to help with these distinctions

Table 1. A summary of definitions used for games and similar constructs across research fields

Construct	Definition	Original Source	Cited by
Play	A voluntary activity that is intrinsically motivating, involves some level of activity (often physical) and may possess make-believe qualities.*	Amory & Seagram, 2003	- -
Play	Actions not consciously performed for the sake of any result beyond themselves.**	Dewey, 1910	40
Play	Involves challenge against uncertain outcomes...the attainment of the goals of the activity are uncertain.*	Driskell & Dwyer, 1984	- -
Play	Describes free-form, expressive, improvisational behaviors and meanings.*	Groh, 2012	- -
Play	To engage in activity directed toward bringing about a specific state of affairs, using only means permitted by specific rules, where the means permitted by the rules are more limited in scope than they would be in the absence of the rules, and where the sole reason for accepting such limitation is to make possible such activity.*	Suits, 1967	22
Play	To attempt to achieve a specific state of affairs [prelusory goal], using only means permitted by the rules [lusory means], where the rules prohibit use of more efficient in favor of less efficient means [constitutive rules], and where the rules are accepted just because they make possible such activity [lusory attitude].*	Suits, 1978	41, 43, 50, 52, 57, 60, 61, 66
Game	Games are facilitators that structure player behavior, and whose main purpose is enjoyment.*	Aarseth, 2007	61
Game	An activity among two or more independent decision-makers seeking to achieve their objectives in some limiting context.*	Abt, 1970	33, 36, 43, 57, 60, 61, 65
Game	A type of play activity, conducted in the context of a pretended reality, in which the participants try to achieve at least one arbitrary, nontrivial goal by acting in accordance with rules.*	Adams, 2012	43
Game	An exercise of voluntary control systems in which there is an opposition between forces, confined by a procedure and rules in order to produce a disequilibrial outcome.**	Avedon & Sutton-Smith, 1971	1, 36, 43, 52, 57, 60, 61
Game	An ongoing series of complementary ulterior transactions progressing to a well-defined, predictable outcome.**	Berne, 1964	36
Game	An activity with rules. It is a form of play often but not always involving conflict, either with other players, with the game system itself, or with randomness/fate/luck. Most games have goals, but not all (for example, The Sims and SimCity). Most games have defined start and end points, but not all (for example, World of Warcraft and Dungeons & Dragons). Most games involve decision making on the part of the players, but not all (for example, Candy Land and Chutes and Ladders). A video game is a game (as defined above) that uses a digital video screen of some kind, in some way.**	Brathwaite & Schreiber, 2008	52
Game	Is free (voluntary), separate (taking place within its own space and time), uncertain (without a pre-defined outcome), unproductive (not creating any value outside of the activity), governed by rules and based on make-believe.*	Caillois, 1961	57, 60, 42, 63
Game	Games are created through the act of gameplay, which is contingent on player acts.**	Consalvo, 2009	52
Game	Is a form of art in which participants, termed players, make decisions in order to manage resources through game tokens in the pursuit of a goal.*	Costikyan, 1994	18, 43, 60, 61
Game	An interactive structure of endogenous meaning that requires players to struggle toward a goal.*	Costikyan, 2002	60, 61
Game	Is a closed formal system that subjectively represents a subset of reality... A game creates a subjective and deliberately simplified representation of emotional reality. A game is not an objectively accurate representation of reality; objective accuracy is only necessary to the extent required to support the player's fantasy. The player's fantasy is the key agent in making the game psychologically real.*	Crawford, 1997	60, 41, 43
Game	Is a system that has: (1) Representation: [a] game is a closed formal system that subjectively represents a subset of reality. By "closed" I mean that the game is complete and self-sufficient as a structure. ...By formal I mean only that the game has explicit rules. ...(2) Interaction: ... to let [the audience] generate causes and observe effects. Thus, the highest and most complete form of representation is interactive representation. Games provide this interactive element, and it is a crucial factor in their appeal (3) Conflict: 'Conflict arises naturally from the interaction in a game. The player is actively pursuing some goal. Obstacles prevent him from easily achieving this goal. ... Conflict is an intrinsic element of all games (4) Safety: ...a game is an artifice for providing the psychological experiences of conflict and danger while excluding their physical realizations. In short, a game is a safe way to experience reality. More accurately, the results of a game are always less harsh than the situations the game models.**	Crookall et al., 1987	61
Game	Contests in which both players and opponents operate under rules to gain a specified objective.*	Cruickshank & Telfer, 1980	19
Game	A set of activities involving one or more players. It has goals, constraints, payoffs, and consequence. A game is rule-guided and artificial in some respects. Finally, a game involves some aspect of competition, even if that competition is with oneself.*	Dempsey et al., 2002	34, 61
Game	First, [a game] must involve overt competition of some sort, either directly between individuals or teams (as for example in bridge or soccer) or between individuals or teams who are each competing against the 'game system' (as, for example, in golf). Second, the exercise must have rules, i.e the players must operate under a set of arbitrary constraints specific to a particular game.*	Ellington et al., 1982	61
Game	A universal form of recreation generally including any activity engaged in for diversion or amusement and often establishing a situation that involves a contest or rivalry.*	Encyclopedia Britannica, 2003	59
Game	A game is a form of play where players agree on a system of rules that assigns social status to their quantified performance.*	Frasca, 2007	61
Game	An activity carried out by cooperating or competing decision-makers who want to achieve their objectives following a set of rules.**	Gibbs, 1974	7, 27, 28
Game	A contest among players operating under a set of rules in order to win or to obtain a payoff.*	Gibbs, 1988	- -
Game	Are world-building activities.**	Goffman, 1961	60
Game	Consist of rules that describe allowable player moves, game constraints and privileges (such as ways of earning extra turns), and penalties for illegal (nonpermissable) actions. Further, the rules may be imaginative in that they need not relate to real-world events.*	Gredler, 1996	51
Game	Competitive contests characterized by discrete plays or moves by the players. The objective is to win by any strategy permitted by the rules.*	Gredler, 1996	- -
Game	Competitive exercises in which the objective is to win and players must apply subject matter or other relevant knowledge in an effort to advance in the exercise and win.*	Gredler, 1996	- -
Game	An artificially constructed, competitive activity with a specific goal, a set of rules and constraints that is located in a specific context.*	Hays, 2005	31
Game	An activity, in which participants follow prescribed rules that differ from those of real life as striving to attain a challenging goal.**	Heinich et al., 2002	3

continued on following page

Table 1. Continued

Construct	Definition	Original Source	Cited by
Game	A contest of physical or mental skills and strengths, requiring the participant(s) to follow a specific set of rules in order to attain a goal.**	Hogle, 1996	38
Game	Interactions among groups of players (decision makers) placed in a prescribed setting and constrained by a set of rules and procedures.*	Hsu, 1989	21
Game	An activity which proceeds within certain limits of time and space, in a visible order, according to rules freely accepted and outside the sphere of necessity or material utility.**	Huizinga, 1938	39, 40, 57, 60
Game	(1) games are based on rules; (2) they have variable outcomes that are quantifiable; (3) different outcomes in a game are assigned different values, both positive and negative; (4) effort must be invested to affect the outcome; (5) the outcome is important to the player; and (6) optionally, games can have real-life consequences.**	Juul, 2003	13, 23, 32, 43, 56, 57 60, 61
Game	A form of recreation constituted by a set of rules that specify an object to be attained and the permissible means of attaining it.*	Kelley, 1988	61
Game	A game is any contest or effort (play) among adversaries or teammates (players) operating under constraints (rules and resources) for an objective (winning, victory, prestige, status, or pay-off). The exercise, or activity, should involve overt competition, or cooperation between the individuals or teams, who are competing against each other, or together (while jointly conquering circumstances) fighting the odds.*	Klabbers, 2006	61
Game	An activity guided and described by some set of rules most especially for the purpose of entertainment or competition.*	Loganathan et al., 2019	- -
Game	Games in the most extensive sense of the word are all sorts of activities which are not "real work" for livelihood or common physiological functions—e.g. connected with digestion and sexual life. Games are performed from mere desire. But as activities connected with the exceptions mentioned above also may arise from desire, it is difficult to draw a definite borderline.**	Maigaard, 1951	60, 61
Game	A semibounded and socially legitimate domain of contrived contingency that generates interpretable outcomes.*	Malaby, 2007	14, 60, 61
Game	A game is a form of play with goals and structure.*	Maroney, 2001	61, 65
Game	Games are the things that (are intended to) produce autotelic and aesthetic (sensitivity-requiring) actions.*	Matsunaga, 2014	61
Game	A tool formed between game, player and contextual context.**	Mäyrä (2008)	57
Game	Powerful tools that can provide solutions to requirements or desires of individuals.**	McGonigal, 2011	57
Game	Are popular art, collective, social reactions to the main drive or action of any culture. Games, like institutions, are extensions of social man and the body politic, as technologies are extensions of the animal organism. Both games and technologies are counter-irritants or ways of adjusting to the stress that occur in any social group. As extensions of the popular response to the workday stress, games become faithful models of culture.*	McLuhan, 1964	57, 61
Game	Voluntary activi[ties], obviously separate from real life, creating an imaginary world that may or may not have any relation to real life and that absorbs the player's full attention. Games are played out within a specific time and place, are played according to established rules, and create social groups out of their players.**	Michael & Chen, 2006	19
Game	[A system in which] each participant is striving for his greatest advantage in situations where the outcome depends not only on his actions alone, nor solely on those of nature, but also on those of other participant.**	Morgenstern, 1968	36
Game	A game has four characteristics: prohibitive rules, goals (such as the most important ones, the winning conditions), opposition (antagonism provided by the game rules), and representation, or a falseness that is contrary to the real.*	Myers, 2009	60
Game	Game is an activity defined by a set of rules, like baseball, sonnet, symphony, diplomacy... game is defined activity with rules and a playing field and participants. It is possible to engage in games like baseball or the composing of fugues as play; it is also possible to experience them as lı¯la(divine play),or as drudgery, as bids for social prestige, or even as revenge.*	Nachmanovitch, 1990	61
Game	Games are algorithmic entertainment.*	Newman & Simons, 2004	61
Game	A game is the formalization of free play via the introduction of rules.*	Newman & Simons, 2004	61
Game	A formal game has a twofold structure based on ends and means: Ends. It is a contest to achieve an objective. [....] Only one of the contenders, be they individuals or teams, can achieve it, since achieving it ends the game. To achieve that objective is to win. Hence a formal game, by definition, has a winner; and winning is the 'end' of the game in both senses of the word, as termination and as object. Means. It has an agreed set of equipment and of procedural 'rules' by which the equipment is manipulated to produce a winning situation. 'Every game has its rules', says Huizinga in Homo Ludens. But we may go further, and say 'Every game is its rules', for they are what define it.*	Parlett, 1999	60, 61, 66
Game	Organized play.**	Prensky, 2001	3
Game	Closed activities that have a beginning and an end with a winner who defines the end of the game. Games require cooperation with other members and competition against another team or players.**	Rixon, 1981	7
Game	An abstract object (either a sequence or a goal) which is designed to have no instrumental value; the realization or pursuit of which is intended to be of absorbing interest to participants or spectators.*	Rowe, 1992	- -
Game	A system in which players engage in an artificial conflict, defined by rules, that results in a quantifiable outcome.*	Salen & Zimmerman, 2003	1, 12, 20, 43, 45, 52, 57, 60, 61, 65
Game	A voluntary activity with: (1) Rules: Games are rule-based, (2) Variable and quantifiable outcome: Games have variable, quantifiable (not necessarily ordered) outcomes, (3) Players assigning values to the outcomes: The different potential outcomes of the game are assigned different values by each player (that is, each player defines its own goals), (4) Player effort: The player invests effort in order to influence the outcome to one he prefers (that is, games are challenging), and (5) Negotiable consequences: The same game [artifact] can be played with different real-life consequences.*	Santos, 2008	- -
Game	A problem-solving activity, approached with a playful attitude.*	Schell, 2008	43, 46
Game	An activity in which people agree to abide by a set of conditions (not necessarily rules) in order to create a desired state or end.**	Shirts, 1975	6
Game	An institutional model of a game situation.*	Ståhl, 1983	60
Game	Is a fun based, voluntary, internally motivated, free choiced and free to leave activity.**	Suttom-Smith, 1997	57

continued on following page

Table 1. Continued

Construct	Definition	Original Source	Cited by
Game	A setting in which participants make choices, implement those choices, and receive consequences of those choices in an effort to achieve given objectives. Explicit rules govern the choices and resources available to the participants, the actions and interactions of the participants, the relationships between a participant's choices and consequences, the consequences of one participant's choices for other participants, and the conditions under which the given objectives are achieved.*	VanSickle, 1978	25, 64
Game	A game is a (designed or emerging) system of rules, goals and opposition, which has as its primary purpose to allow people to engage with it for paratelic reasons, while agreeing that the actions performed are re-signified.*	Waern, 2012	61
Game	A physical or mental contest, played according to specific rules, with the goal of amusing or rewarding the participants.*	Zyda, 2005	- -
Gaming	Any overt instructional or learning format that involves competition and is rule-guided.**	Dempsey et al., 1996b	3
Gaming	Characterizes rule-based playing with determined goals.*	Groh, 2012	- -
Gamification	The use of game design elements, characteristic for games, in non-game contexts.**	Deterding et al., 2011	58, 67
Gamification	The addition of elements commonly associated with games (e.g. game mechanics) to an educational or training program in order to make the learning process more engaging.*	Landers & Callan, 2011	- -
Gamification	The use of game-like mechanisms applied to traditional teaching to increase motivation or engagement (e.g., leader boards, points, badges).*	McClarty et al., 2012	- -
Gamification	The transfer of typical elements and processes of games into a non-game work based context with the aim of raising motivations and changing attitudes of the users.*	Senderek et al., 2015	- -
Workplace Gamification	The adaptation and application of game design principles and game interaction elements to workplace processes and behaviours.**	Oprescu et al., 2014	67
Gamification Quotient	The gamification level of an app…will receive its value, depending on the gamification design elements included in the app.*	Kotsopoulos et al., 2016	- -
Computer Game	A game that is carried out with the help of a computer program.*	Smed & Hakonen, 2003	- -
Computer Game	Defined as such by the author, or inferred by the reader because the activity has goals, is interactive, and is rewarding (gives feedback).*	Vogel et al., 2006	15
Computer Game	Being interactive, based on a set of agreed rules and constraints, and directed toward a clear goal that is often set by a challenge.**	Wouters et al., 2013	15
Computer Game	Interactive, digital games that support learning and/or skill acquisition.*	Shute, 2011	- -
Video Game	A mode of interaction between a player, a machine with an electronic visual display, and possibly other players, that is mediated by a meaningful fictional context, and sustained by an emotional attachment between the player and the outcomes of her actions within this fictional context.**	Bergonse, 2017	5
Video Game	Consist of rule-governed play to obtain specified goals.*	Driskell & Dwyer, 1984	19
Video Game	A videogame can be a puzzle-game, a toy-game, or any kind of game that can be handled by an audiovisual apparatus.*	Esposito, 2005	5
Video Game	Players always face a challenge and have a specific goal, for the accomplishment of which they must struggle with some kind of opposition. Additionally, videogames provide not only the means (i.e., the toys) and the rules to play, but also an interactive gaming environment, as opposed to many other games, and, additionally, the gaming environment is always virtual.*	Fabricatore, 2000	47
Video Game	Simple or complex, 2-dimensional and 3-dimensional games played on game platforms or computers.*	Harris, 2008	- -
Video Game	Videogames are artifacts that evaluate performance.*	Karhulahti, 2015	- -
Video Game	Electronic games that involve interaction with a user interface to generate visual feedback on a video device.*	Levitan, 2010	48
Video Game	An artefact in a digital visual medium, is intended primarily as an object of entertainment, and is intended to provide such entertainment through the employment of one or both of the following modes of engagement: rule-bound gameplay or interactive fiction.*	Tavinor, 2009	37, 61
Video Game	A mental contest, played with a computer according to certain rules for amusement, recreation, or winning a stake.*	Zyda, 2005	17
Micro-Games	Relatively simple computer games that do not require special skills to play and that challenge players with clearly defined goals reachable within minutes or tens of minutes of game-play.*	Brom et al., 2011	- -
Well-Played Game	Something that provides us with a common goal, the achievement of which has no bearing on anything outside the game.*	DeKoven, 1978	60
Casual Game	One that is easy to learn, simple to play and offers quick rewards with forgiving gameplay, which all turns into a fun experience.*	Kultima, 2018	- -
Pervasive Games	Imply some sort of reality expansion of the game.*	Bång et al., 2009	- -
Pervasive Learning Game	A game that has one or more salient features that expand the contractual magic circle of play socially, spatially or temporally.*	Montola, 2005	35
Digital Game	A digital experience in which the participants (a) strive to achieve a set of fictive goals within the constraints of a set of rules that are enforced by the software, (b) receive feedback toward the completion of these goals (e.g., score, progress, advancement, win condition, narrative resolution), and (c) are intended to find some recreational value.*	Clark et al., 2016	- -
Digital Gaming	A complex but intuitive system comprising interactive technologies, media, and simulation technology, often with a story/plot. However, their interactivity is designed to be intuitive as well as stimulating the natural creativity and capabilities of the user.*	Kosmadoudi et al., 2013	- -
Digital Game-Based Learning	Learning from instructional games delivered via computer-based media.*	Adcock, 2008	- -
Digital Game-Based Learning	Any learning on a computer or online.**	Prensky, 2007	11, 17
Technology-Based Learning	Learning via electronic technology, including Internet, intranets, satellite broadcasts, audio and video conferencing, bulletin boards, chat rooms, webcasts, and CD-ROM.*	Koller et al., 2008	- -

continued on following page

Table 1. Continued

Construct	Definition	Original Source	Cited by
Game-Like Learning Environments	Authentic or simulated places, where learning is fostered and supported especially by seamless integration of motivating game elements.*	Akilli & Cagiltay, 2006	- -
Game-Based Learning	An approach using games designed for learning, usually for younger learners raised on interactive technology.*	Blunt, 2000	- -
Game-Based Learning	A subset of [entertainment education] including the use of any type of games (e.g. board games, card games, sports or digital games) for learning/educational purposes.*	Breuer & Bente, 2010	- -
Game-Based Learning	Engages players in learning activities, usually by means of educational video or serious games.*	Burguillo, 2010	- -
Game-Based Learning	A learning method, which contributes to the employees' work based competence development by exploiting the motivation of game mechanism in a virtual, interactive frame. Thus the active learning processes and not the entertainment related aspects are in the focus. The learning content is integrated into the game fostering the active, self-controlled, constructive, explorative and situated learning... game-based learning focusses on the learning processes during the playful application.*	Senderek et al., 2015	- -
Educational Game	An instructional method requiring the learner to participate in a competitive activity with preset rules.**	Fitzgerald, 1997	4
Educational Game Design	A broad subject that groups very different approaches and methodologies...that can be broadly categorized into three groups: (1) Multimedia approaches tightly linked to content presentation; (2) those that repurpose pre-existing games for education; (3) a middle category of specially designed games that seeks a balance between fun and educational content.*	Moreno-Ger et al., 2008	- -
Edutainment Games	Games within the serious games family which are mainly developed for use in K-12 education, have a focus on the conveyance of curricular textbook knowledge and rather pursue additive combinations of entertainment and education in a motivator or reinforcement paradigm.*	Breuer & Bente, 2010	- -
Serious Game	Have an explicit and carefully thought-out educational purpose and are not intended to be played primarily for amusement.**	Abt, 1970	2, 11, 16, 17, 24
Serious Game	Computer application, which aims to combine aspects of both serious as, but not limited to, teaching, learning, communication, or further information with entertainment from the spring game. Such an association has intended to depart from mere entertainment.**	Alvarez, 2007	49
Serious Game	May be defined as utilities video games, productive in other words, whose design aims to bring about a transformation in their recipients in line an improvement of skills (training), the adaptation to the environment (treatment of phobias), understanding of a phenomenon (education) or greater adherence to the message (promotion, advertising, ideological video games), also known as Political games.**	Amato, 2007	49
Serious Game	A computer game that engages the user, and contributes to the achievement of a defined purpose other than pure entertainment.*	Backlund et al., 2007	- -
Serious Game	All games that engage the user and simultaneously contribute to the achievement of a certain objective other than just entertainment, whether the user is aware of that fact or not.*	Bourbia et al., 2014	- -
Serious Game	Games which are intentionally designed for the purpose of learning, skill acquisition and training.*	Boyle, 2011	- -
Serious Game	Designed to promote active participation and interaction as the center of the experience, instead of pure entertainment.*	Burguillo, 2010	- -
Serious Game	Use the characteristics [of games] to provide learners with an authentic learning experience where the entertainment and learning are seamlessly integrated.*	Charsky, 2010	- -
Serious Game	Fully produced games whose main purpose is something other than entertainment.*	Collmus, 2016	- -
Serious Game	Video games whose main purpose is not entertainment but rather teaching and learning.*	Cowan, 2010	55
Serious Game	An explicit and carefully thoughtout educational purpose and are not intended to be played primarily for amusement.*	de Wit-Zuurendonk & Oei, 2011	- -
Serious Game	Games designed with a purpose beyond that of recreation or entertainment. Serious games encompass games designed to educate, train, incite activism, inform, persuade, express, recruit or indoctrinate.*	Dickey, 2011	- -
Serious Game	A fusion of entertainment and instruction, with a careful balance required between engaging gameplay and educational or behavioural goals.*	Dunwell et al., 2014	- -
Serious Game	Games whose primary goal is other than mere entertainment.*	Galaup, 2015	- -
Serious Game	Full-fledged games for non-entertainment purpose.*	Groh, 2012	- -
Serious Game	Games and simulations designed to support formal educational and training objectives and outcomes.*	Harris, 2008	- -
Serious Game	An interactive computer application, with or without a significant hardware component, that (i) has a challenging goal, (ii) is fun to play and/or engaging, (iii) incorporates some concept of scoring, and (iv) imparts to the user a skill, knowledge, or attitude that can be applied to the real world.*	Kapralos, 2012	- -
Serious Game	Encourage active and critical learning through game environments where users enjoy the process of pursuing challenging tasks, achieving goals by making decisions, formulating strategies, construct knowledge, try different alternatives and succeed or fail without worrying about the consequences in real life.*	Kosmadoudi, 2013	- -
Serious Game	Games with purpose beyond just providing entertainment; examples include, but are not limited to, games for learning, games for health, and games for policy and social change.*	Levitan, 2010	- -
Serious Game	Digital games, simulations, virtual environments and mixed reality/media that provide opportunities to engage in activities through responsive narrative/story, gameplay or encounters to inform, influence, for well-being, and/or experience to convey meaning. The quality or success of serious games is characterized by the degree to which purpose has been fulfilled. Serious games are identified along a continuum from games for purpose at one end, through to experiential environments with minimal or no gaming characteristics for experience at the other end.*	Marsh, 2011	29
Serious Game	A game in which education (in its various forms) is the primary goal, rather than entertainment.**	Michael & Chen, 2006	17
Serious Game	Games primarily focused on education rather than entertainment.*	Miller et al., 2011	9
Serious Game	Digital games whose purpose exceeds pure entertainment.*	Reckien & Eisenack, 2013	- -
Serious Game	Digital games whose primary goal goes beyond entertainment to education, outreach or training.*	Stokes, 2005	33, 62

continued on following page

Table 1. Continued

Construct	Definition	Original Source	Cited by
Serious Game	Games for purposes other than mere entertainment.*	Susi et al., 2007	26
Serious Game	A mental contest, played with a computer in accordance with specific rules, that uses entertainment to further government or corporate training, education, health, public policy, and strategic communication objectives.*	Zyda, 2005	33
Serious Digital Game	A type of computer-delivered intervention considered to be both educational and fun.*	DeSmet et al., 2014	- -
Simulation	Products that result when one creates the appearance or effect of something else.*	Cruickshank & Telfer, 1980	- -
Simulation	A program that contains a model of a system (natural or artificial; e.g., equipment) or a process.*	de Jong & van Joolingen, 1998	54
Simulation	A dynamic set of relationships among several variables that (1) change over time and (2) reflect authentic causal processes (i.e., the relationships must be verifiable).*	Gredler, 1996	51
Simulation	Participants take on either (1) demanding, responsible roles such as concerned citizens, business managers, interplanetary explorers, or physicians, or (2) professional tasks such as exploring the causes of water pollution or operating a complex equipment system.*	Gredler, 1996	- -
Simulation	A carefully controlled representation of reality.*	Ochoa, 1969	- -
Simulation	A working representation of reality...maybe an abstracted, simplified, or accelerated model of process.**	Saunders, 1987	25, 30, 53, 64
Simulation	Anything which simulates or models reality.**	Shirts, 1975	6
Simulation Game	A mixed feature of a game-competition, co-operation, participants and rules. Clearly these games take place on a simulated environment.*	Chwif & Barretto, 2003	- -
Simulation Game	Has elements like score, performance rating, conflict, and payoff, and simulates a real world situation for decision-making or alternative evaluation.*	Deshpande & Huang, 2011	- -
Simulation Game	A real in person environment...with all the complexities of the technical and social interactions usually found there. This...maximizes the fidelity of the learning environment so that it more completely represents the real world, combining elements of both games and simulations.*	Landers & Callan, 2011	- -
Simulation Game	Contains characteristics of both a simulation and a game. It is an activity in which participants interact within an artificially produced environment which recreates some aspect of social reality.**	Maidment & Bronstein, 1973	8
Simulation Game	Combines the features of a game (competition, cooperation, rules, participants, roles) with those of a simulation (incorporation of critical features of reality). A game is a simulation game if its rules refer to an empirical model of reality.**	Ruohomaki, 1995	30
Simulation Game	Instruction delivered via personal computer that immerses trainees in a decision-making exercise in an artificial environment in order to learn the consequences of their decisions.*	Sitzmann, 2011	15
Simulation Game	Its rules refer to an empirical model of reality, such as a political process or an economic system.*	VanSickle, 1978	- -
Gaming Simulation	Similar to game-based learning, except simulations target skill attainment.*	Blunt, 2000	- -
Gaming Simulation	A sequential decision-making exercise, with the basic function of providing an artificial but realistic environment that enables players to experience the consequences of their decisions through immediate response. Its objective is to enhance a comprehensive understanding of complex systems and to communicate and develop knowledge and skills.*	Siemer & Angelides, 1995	64
Computer Simulation Game	Any software application that provides access to a model of a theoretical or physical system.**	Thomas et al., 1998	44
Interactive Simulation Activity	Must interact with the user by offering the options to choose or define parameters of the simulation then observe the newly created sequence rather than simply selecting a prerecorded simulation.*	Vogel et al., 2006	15
Epistemic Game	Games that immerse students in real-world professional activities to get them to understand, create, and innovate within those contexts.*	Levitan, 2010	- -
Business Game	A game with a business environment that can lead to one or both of the following results: the training of players in business skills (hard and/or soft) or the evaluation of players' performances (quantitatively and/or qualitatively).*	Greco et al., 2013	- -
Management Game	Used to create experiential environments within which learning and behavioral changes can occur and in which managerial behavior can be observed.*	Keys & Wolfe, 1990	- -
General Management Game	Designed to give people experience in making decisions at a top executive level and in which decisions from one functional area interact with those made in other areas of the firm.**	Cohen & Rhenman, 1961	10

*Quote from original source. **Quote from cited by source.

Note. Cited by sources are coded as: 1 = Aarseth & Grabarczyk, 2018, 2 = Ahmed & Sutton, 2017, 3 = Akilli & Cagiltay, 2006, 4 = Akl et al., 2013, 5 = Arjoranta, 2019, 6 = Aronson et al., 1977, 7 = Bakhsh, 2016, 8 = Bates, 1982, 9 = Bhagat et al., 2016, 10 = Biggs, 1987, 11 = Breuer & Bente, 2010, 12 = Calleja & Callus, 2009, 13 = Calleja & Callus, 2010, 14 = Calleja & Callus, 2011, 15 = Clark et al., 2016, 16 = Coller & Scott, 2009, 17 = Corrigan, 2015, 18 = Costikyan, 2005, 19 = DeRouin-Jessen, 2008, 20 = Djaouti et al., 2008, 21 = Feinstein et al., 2002, 22 = Forcier, 2013, 23 = Forcier, 2014, 24 = Gale, 2011, 25 = Galvao et al., 2000, 26 = García-Mundo et al., 2017, 27 = Gibbs, 1981, 28 = Gilgeous & D'Cruz 1996, 29 = Girard et al., 2013, 30 = Greco et al., 2013, 31 = Hays, 2005, 32 = Högberg, 2019, 33 = Huang et al., 2015, 34 = Huizenga et al., 2009, 35 = Kalz et al., 2015, 36 = Karhulahti, 2013, 37 = Karhulahti, 2015, 38 = Ke, 2009, 39 = Kickmeier-Rust, 2009, 40 = Korteling, 2011, 41 = Laas, 2017, 42 = Landers et al., 2018, 43 = Maranhao et al., 2016, 44 = McCarty, 2001, 45 = McClarty et al., 2012, 46 = Mildner et al., 2015, 47 = Mitchell & Savill-Smith, 2004, 48 = Moshirnia, 2008, 49 = Mouaheb et al., 2012, 50 = Nguyen, 2019, 51 = O'Neil et al., 2005, 52 = Purkiss & Khaliq, 2015, 53 = Ruohomaki, 1995, 54 = Rutten et al., 2012, 55 = Sabri et al., 2010, 56 = Santos, 2008, 57 = Sezgin & Yüzer, 2017, 58 = Simões et al., 2013, 59 = Smed & Hakonen, 2003, 60 = Stenros, 2015, 61 = Stenros, 2017, 62 = Thompson et al., 2010, 63 = Vesa et al., 2016, 64 = Vogel et al., 2006, 65 = Waern, 2012, 66 = Zagal et al., 2019, 67 = Kotsopoulos et al., 2016.

Table 2. A comparison of characteristics in games versus simulations (adapted from Gredler, 1996)

	Games	Simulations	
		Experiential	Symbolic
Setting			
Transportation to another world or environment.	X	X	X
Purpose			
Competition or winning.	X		
Fulfilling a professional role.		X	
Executing a professional task.			X
Event Sequence			
Most often linear.	X		
Typically, nonlinear with branching.		X	X
Mechanisms			
Sets of rules are applied.	X		
Dynamic, authentic relationships between variables.		X	X
Evolving Scenarios			
Execute responsibilities in evolving scenarios.		X	
Databased / Process Interaction			
Interact to explain, predict or correct misconceptions.			X

(Hays, 2005; Leemkuil et al., 2000; Percival & Ellington, 1980), see Figure 3. Despite the effort to help draw these distinctions, other researchers have still used terms like game and simulation interchangeably (Amer et al., 2011; Greenblat & Duke, 1981; Rieber, 1996; Thomas et al., 1997). This can create challenges for researchers when attempting to interpret the aggregated results of game-based learning studies as is done in a meta-analysis or a review. If a researcher cannot accurately parse apart the results of a game-based learning tool from another form of media, their findings will likely lead to inconclusive or erroneous interpretations due to contaminated data. Clear distinctions are imperative for preventing these issues of misattribution or contamination (Clark, 2001; Kobes et al., 2010).

Recommendation 1: Distinguishing Games from Other Training Media

The first challenge in game-based learning research is that poor distinctions have been made between games and other forms of training media. By grouping games with other training media, we misattribute results and may reach inaccurate conclusions. To address this challenge, it is recommended that researchers clearly define and distinguish games from other similar forms of training media using commonly established definitions that fit the context for how the game is being used (e.g., Gredler, 1996; Hays, 2005). This includes distinguishing a game-based learning intervention from other similar forms of training media such as simulations and computer-based learning (Gredler, 1996). We further propose that a broad set of criteria be consistently applied to clearly establish when using a *serious game* (i.e., training that exists within a game context; Zyda, 2005), gamification (i.e., game elements added to a non-game context; Senderek et al., 2015) in learning, or a learning simulation.

Figure 3.

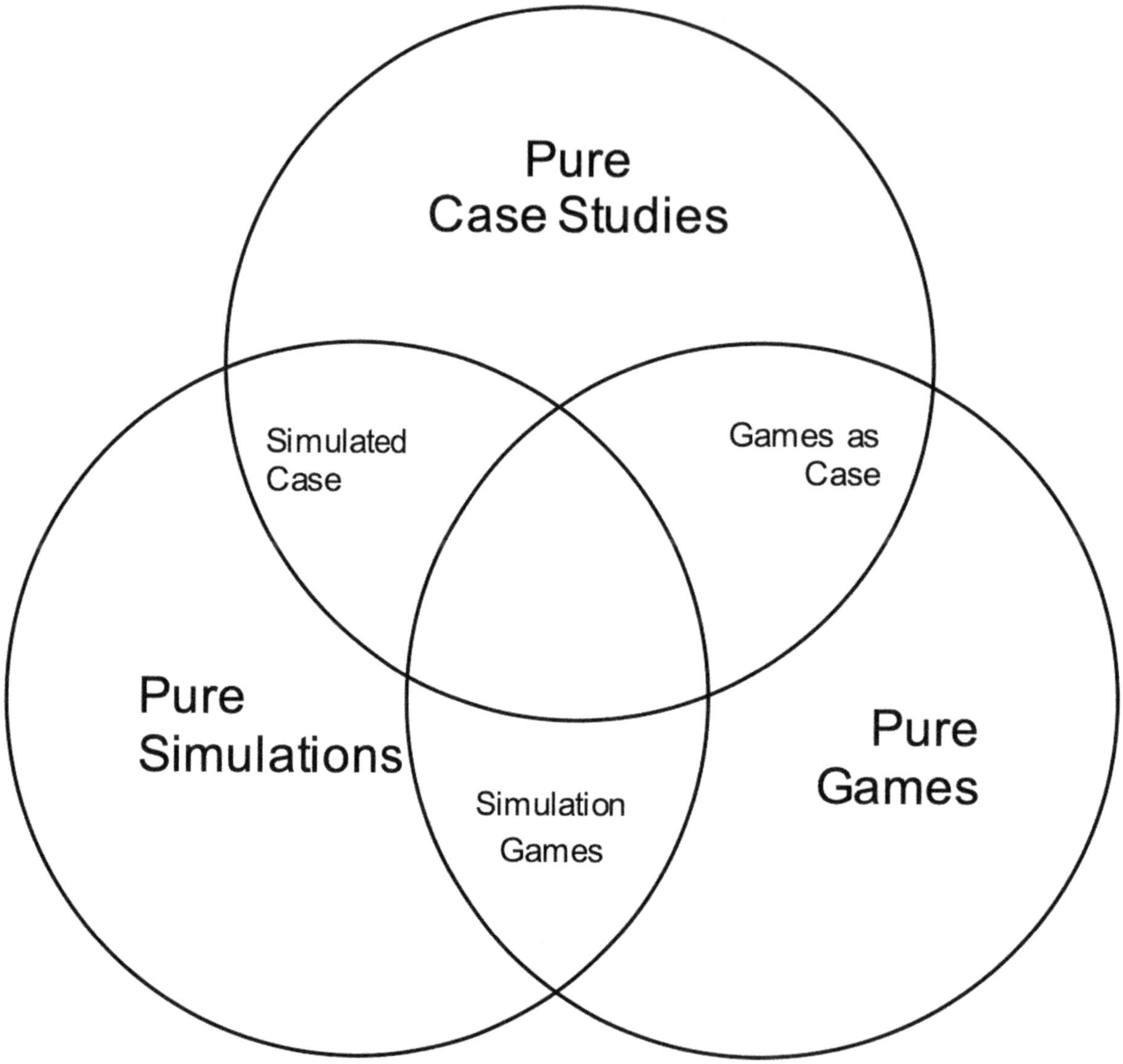

Understanding Gamification and Game-Based Learning.

It is important for researchers to realize the similarities and differences between game-based learning and gamification. Gamification is the integration of game elements into non-game contexts (Landers et al., 2017). These game elements can include things such as points, achievements, and badges (Patrício et al., 2018). Designers of training programs use gamification in order to increase learner interest in the programs. Previous research suggests that increasing learner interest through gamification can positively affect learning outcomes, such as the increased retention of learning material (Landers, 2014). The purposes of gamification draw many parallels with the purposes of game-based learning. They are similar in that both game-based learning and gamification involve the manipulation of game elements in order

Figure 4.

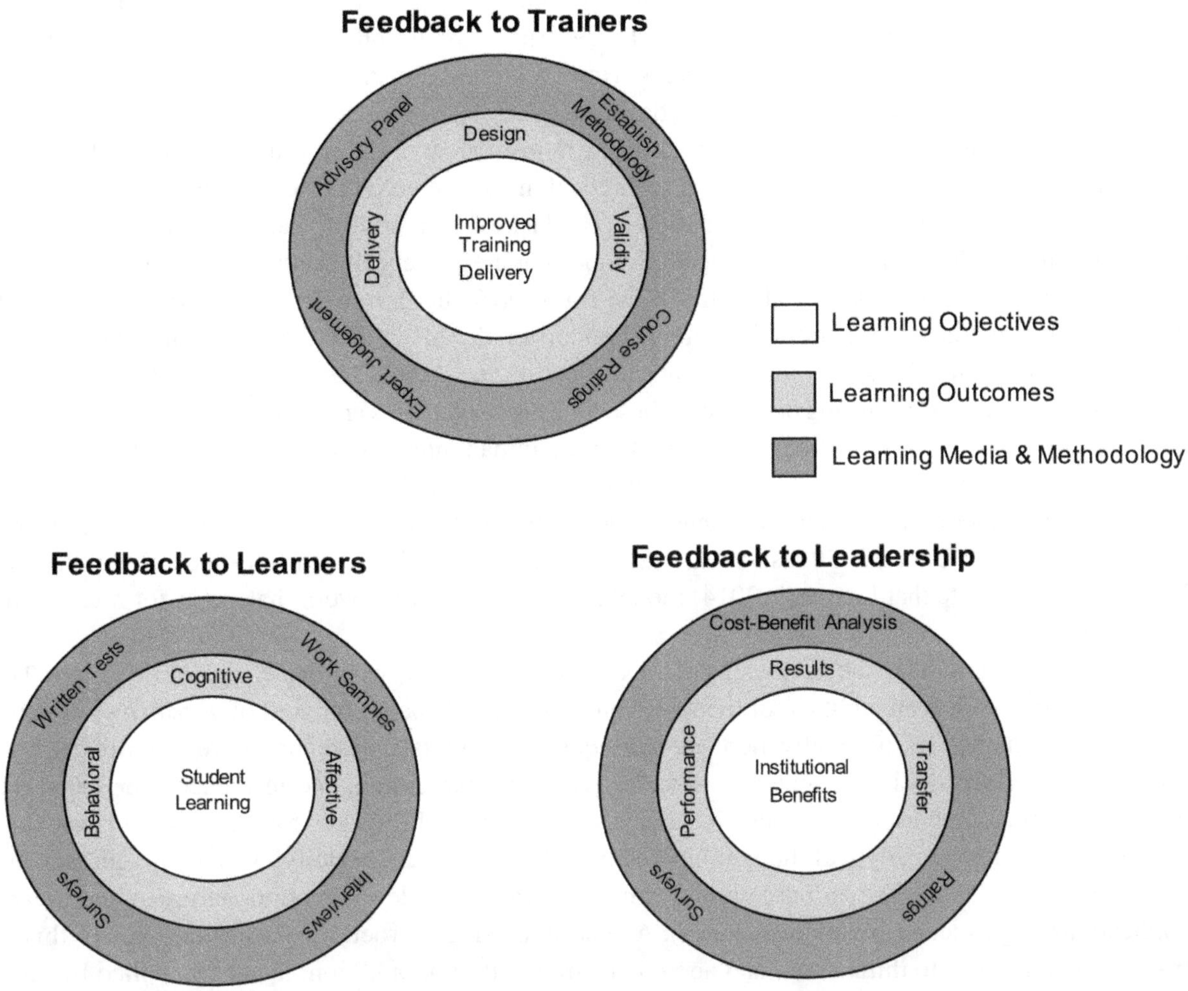

to affect learner behaviors and attitudes. They differ in that game-based learning involves the actual usage of a game, (often a serious game) to deliver educational content. The critical difference here is the game context itself; primarily, gamification does not occur in an actual game. Attitudes and behaviors influence learning by acting as the process through which instructional design and learning outcomes are related to one another. Additionally, attitudes and behaviors directly affect the relationship between game elements and learning outcomes.

Gamification can be used in a wide variety of contexts. As mentioned before, gamification can be used to increase learner interest in a training context, thereby resulting in a positive enhancement of learning outcomes from that training context. However, gamification has also been used in contexts such as creativity and innovation (Patrício et al., 2018), exercise (Blohm & Leimeister, 2013), and the service industry (Huotari & Hamari, 2017). Within the topics of creativity and innovation in particular, research suggests that gamification of the creative process can help groups overcome initial barriers to collaboration (Patrício et al., 2018). Specifically, these barriers include important organizational topics such as hierarchical ambiguity, disunity on group goals, and group accountability (Patrício et al., 2020).

In addition, recent research has suggested that the surmounting of these initial barriers is due in part to group members feeling heightened senses of engagement and coordination due to the gamification of the creative process (Patrício et al., 2021). These results among others highlight the progress that gamification research has made in recent years. However, there are still many aspects of gamification that research has not managed to examine in detail just yet.

For example, the growth of interest in gamification research in the past decade has made it very important for researchers to start developing theoretical models to help isolate and explain why specific facets of gamification result in certain outcomes. The lack of a theoretical framework that researchers can unify and conduct studies on gamification under has negatively impacted the generalizability of gamification research (Landers et al., 2014). One framework that has arisen in gamification research has been Landers' theory of gamified learning (Landers et al., 2014). The theory of gamified learning proposes that there are nine game elements that gamification researchers and practitioners can manipulate that are likely to improve learning outcomes. These nine game elements are action language, assessment, conflict/challenge, control, environment, game fiction, human interaction, immersion, and rules/goals. These nine game elements have their basis in previous literature by Bedwell et al., (2012) and Wilson et al., (2009). This theory has seen use in contexts such as research into goal orientation and self-efficacy, (Garcia-Marquez & Bauer, 2020) as well as classroom learning and assessment (Sanchez et al., 2019). It is important to note that Landers' (2014) model is not the only framework that exists for researching gamification.

Some researchers have taken to using the Octalysis framework when studying gamification. The Octalysis framework is an eight factor model (in an octagonal shape) composed of *core drives* of game design that influence learner motivation and subsequent behaviors. These core drives are divided into four *right brain drives*: (i.e., associated with creativity, self-expression, and influence over social dynamics) meaning, empowerment, social influence, and unpredictability, and four *left brain drives*: (i.e., associated with logic, analytical thought, and ownership) avoidance, scarcity, ownership, and accomplishment (Chou, 2015). The purpose of this framework was to enable applications across industries and applications (e.g., social networks structures). A benefit to using a structured framework such as this, is that it can guide how to think about and approach gamification. In addition, it can be applied by other gamification researchers. For example, this framework has been used in contexts such as the education of traditional Ubuntu oral traditions (Oliveira & Cruz, 2018), and the learning of computer languages (Christopher & Waworuntu, 2021). Having a framework like this allows researchers and practitioners across disciplines to have meaningful conversations about gamification while using the same terminology and discussing the same core components.

We can compare the Octalysis framework with the Garris et al. (2001) IPO model and the Theory of Gamified Learning proposed by Landers (2014). We see that each of them follow the same primary steps of inputs (e.g., game elements), processes (e.g., core drives, learner reactions), and outputs (e.g., effectiveness). In this way each framework shares structural similarities and draws similar conclusions. This overlap between gamification and game-based learning models reinforces a statement made by Landers (2017), who stated that serious games and gamification both have a basis in using game elements to affect learning but only really differ when it comes to how those game elements are applied.

Thus, there is value in utilizing frameworks to help guide and inform research, particularly with topics that span multiple disciplines and industries. These standardized forms enable researchers and practitioners to use shared terminology, forms, and processes that improve the quality and usability of their research and products. A great benefit to this process is testing and providing evidence for the framework and the relationships it proposes. If we apply this train of thought to our three aforementioned models, the Input-Process-Output model, the Theory of Gamified Learning, and the Octalysis framework, then we can see that both the IPO model and the Theory of Gamified Learning have wide bodies of literature supporting the constructs that make up their respective theories. In addition, there have been many studies over the years testing the relationships that they propose and highlighting where future research could seek to expand upon past or present findings. This testable and verifiable research evidence is what makes models like the IPO model and the Theory of Gamified Learning so valuable to research and application. Future research into gamification models like the Octalysis framework should seek to tie together the concepts and constructs presented in the framework with previous research evidence supporting the use of those concepts in research. This will help to establish a body of work that can clearly guide and inform future research using the Octalysis framework.

Challenge 2: Overlooking the Importance of Game Characteristics

The majority of studies in the game-based learning literature are media comparisons (i.e., comparing the effectiveness of one training medium to another; Clark, 1983; 1985; 2001; Mayer, 2011). The field has continued to produce studies about comparing media instead of studying specific aspects of the features within a medium that have an association with training outcomes. These studies have continued despite researchers such as Clark reporting for decades that media comparisons are misguided and produce little progress in learning research (Clark, 1983; 1985; 1994; 2001). The theoretical justification for making comparisons by game characteristics rather than by a broad category of games as a learning medium, is consistent with Garris et al.'s (2002) approach that game characteristics impact the in-game processes that lead to learning outcomes. This is comparable to points made by Clark (1994) that training media are proxy measures for other characteristics and mechanisms within the training that are associated with learning outcomes. This challenge in game-based learning research is that studies do not provide detailed descriptions of game characteristics and do not study the impact of specific attributes on training outcomes. This lack of using a central framework of game characteristics contributes to the unfortunate practice of aggregating evidence of game effectiveness to a broad category of games rather than specifying the specific characteristics of the game that may have contributed to improved learning. In other words, researchers are treating all games as members of a single category even when the games have different features and attributes that likely impact learning outcomes.

There is a need to use research-based frameworks to identify and describe specific game characteristics. Several researchers have supported this claim by stating that different games influence training outcomes in different ways based on specific design characteristics of the game (Bedwell et al., 2012; Garris et al., 2002; Wilson et al., 2009). For example, the amount of control (i.e., multiple possible actions throughout the game) an individual has within the environment of the game is related to their level of motivation and desire to return to the game (Driskell & Dwyer, 1984; Habgood, 2005; Habgood et al., 2005; Lepper, 1985). Previous researchers have provided frameworks and taxonomies that can be used to distinguish different game characteristics (Bedwell et al., 2012; Wilson et al., 2009). Some of these frameworks have focused on different elements such as the structure of the game versus the player's experience in the game (Calvillo-Gámez et al., 2015; Ermi & Mäyrä, 2005; Hassenzahl, 2018; Preece et al., 2002). Despite the different approaches these frameworks have taken to define game characteristics, their key importance is that they identify characteristics that can be used to distinguish different features of a game. Despite the availability of these frameworks to identify game characteristics and the previous connections that have been drawn between game characteristics and training outcomes, little empirical research has examined the impact of game characteristics (Bedwell et al., 2012; Wilson et al., 2009). This includes a lack of empirical evidence isolating and manipulating game characteristics and a lack of information describing game characteristics in enough detail so that game characteristics can be inferred when not explicitly identified. Rather than making these distinctions between games based on their characteristics using the available taxonomies, researchers often group games together, disregarding distinctions in game characteristics. Aggregating games with different characteristics (e.g., in meta-analyses or qualitative reviews) likely leads to misleading or inconclusive evidence on the effectiveness of game-based learning.

Recommendation 2: Focusing on the Impact of Game Design and Game Characteristics

It is important that future research shifts away from media comparisons and towards closer examinations of game characteristics. Thus, to address this challenge, we recommend that game characteristics be clearly defined in the game-based learning research using common taxonomies or frameworks (e.g., Bedwell et al., 2012) and that more attention be given to exploring the relationships between specific game characteristics and training outcomes. Part of this recommendation is to highlight the need to design games so that unique game characteristics match intended outcomes similar to the approach used in the Decision-Based Evaluation (DBE) model (Kraiger, 2002), see Figure 4. The DBE model proposes that the intended objective of the training (i.e., revising the training, impacting learners, institutional benefits) aligns with how the training is designed and evaluated. Like this, game developers need to design game-based learning to match the intended outcomes, paying specific attention to designing game characteristics that facilitate that outcome. Research driven design will help ensure that the game adds beneficial characteristics which support learning, while reducing unnecessary cognitive load (Kalyuga & Plass, 2009).

Challenge 3: Misunderstanding the Black Box of the Learning Process

Learning is a complex process that has been studied for decades (Jarvis et al., 2003). Although research has uncovered many valuable theories and findings that have helped to make sense of the way humans learn, there is still much that is unknown about the experience of learning and how to facilitate this process (Dochy et al., 2003). Previous researchers have referred to the learning process as a *black box* (Fischer, 2009; Long, 1980; Opdal, 2019). where specific information on the mechanisms and processes through which learning occurs has many elements that are not entirely understood. Tying research together from multiple disciplines such as education, psychology, and neuroscience, helps to reveal more about the convoluted connections in the process of learning and each takes a different approach in terms of understanding the physiological, psychological, or cognitive processes that occur during learning. As a result, there is still much to uncover and understand about the learning process.

When looking at the learning process specifically using game-based learning, we are presented with a challenge that research does not entirely understand the different mechanisms that occur and promote learning in this context. There is a need to understand the learning processes of game-based training and to test complex relationships such as mediating relationships with games and training outcomes. Recent research (Kraiger & Ford, 2020) has established that the learning processes or the mechanisms that learners experience are directly related to training outcomes such as learning or reactions to the training. This has resulted in a weak empirical understanding of how games impact learning beyond theoretical arguments. Some researchers have argued that behavioral and attitudinal variables exist that mediate the relationship between game characteristics and training outcomes (Landers, 2014; Landers & Landers, 2014), yet there is little research that has examined these possible indirect effects. These gaps have led some researchers to continue to also label game-based training processes as a *black box* (Arnab et al., 2015; Perrotta et al., 2013), while other researchers have merely posited that there are mechanisms that occur during the training experience without testing what they are and how effective they are.

One common assumption is the claim that game-based learning occurs because games are motivating, engaging, and immersive for learners (e.g., Coller & Shernoff, 2009; Papastergiou, 2009; Prensky, 2001), and that these features of the game experience in turn improve learning. However, there is a lack of evidence to support these assertions (de Freitas & Jarvis, 2007). These assertions also call into question how games are actually responsible for improving learning. Not knowing the processes through which game characteristics impact training outcomes has been identified as an important gap that prevents clear implications and precludes the generation of sound recommendations for practitioners on the value and use of game-based learning solutions (Landers, 2014). More research on the mechanisms that mediate the relationship between game-based learning and training outcomes is necessary.

Recommendation 3: Understanding the Processes through which Games Improve Learning

In the game-based learning context, research needs to isolate and study key processes that games may help facilitate in learning such as attention, immersion, engagement, and motivation. Where current research falls short is in the ability to explain how and why these mechanisms are important to the learning process in game-based learning. Knowing this might allow us to better understand the implications of using game-based learning solutions, such as understanding if a game is engaging and the association this engagement might have with different learning outcomes such as declarative knowledge and affective states. Thus, the third challenge in game-based learning research is the need to identify and test complex mechanisms through which learning occurs in game-based training. To address this challenge, it is recommended that potential mechanisms are identified as potential mediators and empirically testing these specific variables to establish their relationships with different training outcomes. It is important that future research shifts towards closer examinations of the learning processes that occur during gameplay to understand the in-game processes that can lead to learning outcomes.

Challenge 4: Unclear Definitions and Non-Standardized Measures for Learning Outcomes

Measuring *training outcomes (i.e., learning outcomes)* is one of the most important aspects of training as it establishes whether the training has met its goals and objectives (Kraiger, 2002; Kraiger et al., 1993). There are well-established research guidelines for defining and measuring training outcomes (e.g., Kirkpatrick & Kirkpatrick, 2006; Kraiger, 2002; Kraiger et al., 1993; Phillips & Phillips, 2016; Sackett & Mullen, 1993). Aligning training objectives with the most appropriate training outcome is a critical guideline for determining the effectiveness of the training (e.g., de Freitas & Jarvis, 2007). Establishing effective training evaluation provides input to ensure training improves over future iterations (Brown & Gerhardt, 2002; Kraiger, 2002). Despite the importance of understanding learning outcomes there is ambiguity and large variations in how training outcomes are defined and measured.

To better understand this issue, we first look at the different ways learning can be measured. Measures of learning assess the extent to which learners demonstrate that they have acquired the knowledge and/or skills specified in the training objectives (Kraiger, 2002). Learning may be measured either objectively or subjectively. Objective learning is the process of assessing knowledge or skills acquired or developed in training using evaluative methods independent from human judgment (Beach, 1980). Subjective measures of learning refer to self or other assessments of trainee learning (Sitzmann et al., 2010). When the person who is evaluating the learning is also the learner (e.g., perceived learning measures), these include judgments of learning, which are defined as the level of confidence an individual has regarding his or her own knowledge or development in a specific skill set or within a certain domain of knowledge. These measures are valuable when the goals of the training are to understand an individual's perceptions of his or her own learning and are particularly useful in the research fields of memory and human cognition (Koriat, 1997; Koriat et al., 2002; Rhodes & Tauber, 2011). Within game-based training, they can be useful during training as they may guide decisions trainees make about whether to repeat content or move on within the game.

Despite research guidance on how to evaluate learning, there are still large variations in the clarity and consistency of how training outcomes are defined and measured within the context of game-based learning (as discussed by Clark, 2007). There is a need to consistently define and differentiate training outcomes from one another (e.g., objective learning, subjective learning). Hays (2005) stated that deciding to use a game-based learning tool required a leap of faith, because the evidence for games as effective teaching tools was lacking but there was evidence that games are engaging and create positive reactions. A more recent study on this same topic suggests that instead of looking at individual game elements, research needs to look at the interplay of different game elements in order to tie games to desired outcomes (Imlig-Iten & Petko, 2018). This is consistent with other researchers who have identified that games impact training outcomes differently (e.g., Shute, Ventura, & Ke, 2015). It further highlights the importance of measuring training outcomes consistently and accurately using validated methods (Clark, 2001).

Recommendation 4: Distinguishing Types of Learning to Explain the Effectiveness of Games

Currently there is wide variation in how training outcomes are defined and measured, ranging from using validated scales to a single-item indicator. Given that measuring training outcomes is the primary way to determine the effectiveness of the game as a learning intervention, it is critical that more attention is paid to this aspect of game-based learning. Thus, the fourth challenge in game-based training research is the ambiguous definition of training outcomes that poorly define or fail to report a clear explanation of how a study was measured. To address this challenge, it is recommended that future research provide clear descriptions on the definitions and measures used for training outcomes. This includes ensuring there are clear distinctions between subjective based measures (e.g., satisfaction with training, perceived learning) and actual behavioral measures (e.g., a knowledge assessment given post-training). It is imperative that future programs using game-based interventions measure training outcomes consistently and accurately and when possible that these programs use validated measurement methods (Clark, 2001). A

Figure 5.

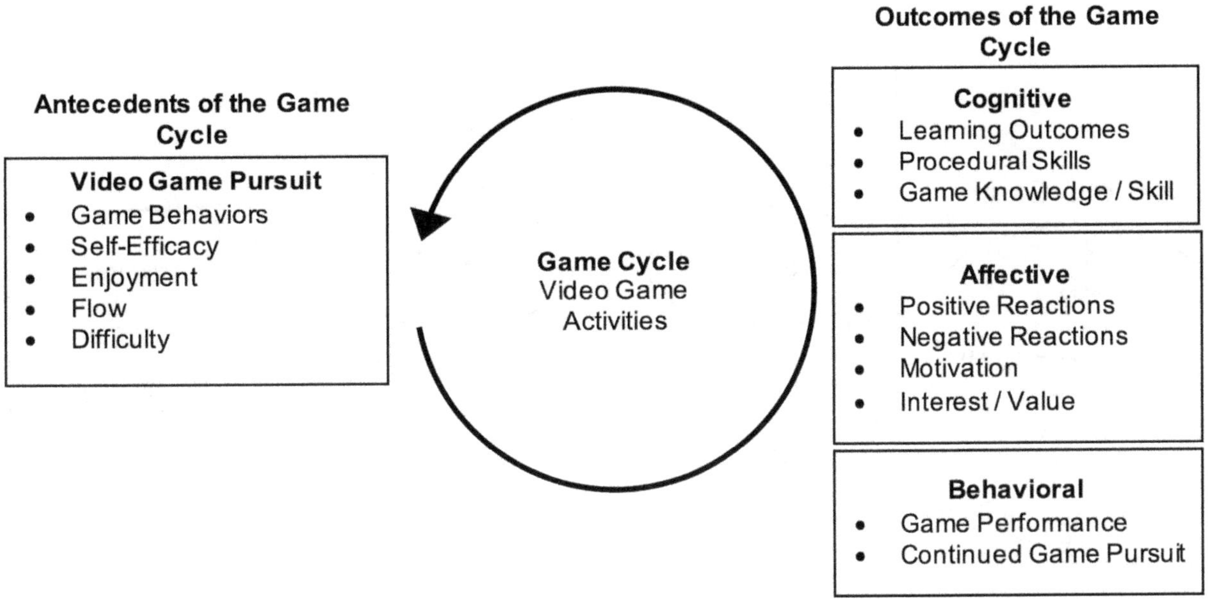

standard framework we recommend is from Kraiger (2002) where learning outcomes are organized into categories of cognitive learning outcomes (e.g., declarative knowledge, procedural knowledge, strategic knowledge), behavioral outcomes (e.g., mental skill demonstration such as problem solving, physical skill demonstration such as operating machinery), attitudinal outcomes (e.g., how motivated one feels after the training), and reactions from the training (e.g., satisfaction with the experience, the ease of the training, the perceived value of the training).

Challenge 5: Misinterpreting and Overstating Research Results for Game-Based Learning

The ambiguity in measuring training outcomes becomes problematic when we measure one learning outcome and then draw inferences about another outcome from that same measure. For example, affective reactions can be useful for measuring whether trainees like the course, whether they will complete it, or whether they will recommend it. However, affective reactions cannot indicate whether an individual learned the intended content or can perform a new skill. There is clear research evidence that one type of training outcome measure (e.g., satisfaction with the training) cannot act as a proxy measure for other outcome measures (e.g., learning declarative knowledge on the topic). Thus, it is unreasonable to assume that subjective measures of learning can accurately represent an objective level of learning (Alliger et al., 1997; Chen, 2005; Clark, 2001; Hays, 2005; Hinds, 1975; Leung, 2006; O'Neil et al., 2005; Sitzmann et al., 2010). This is supported by previous research that has shown that subjective assessments are not highly correlated with actual performance (Murphy, 2008). It is misleading when researchers claim to have measured learning and imply objective learning, but only use measures of subjective learning or affective reactions towards the training. Erroneous measures of learning can lead to false conclusions

Figure 6.

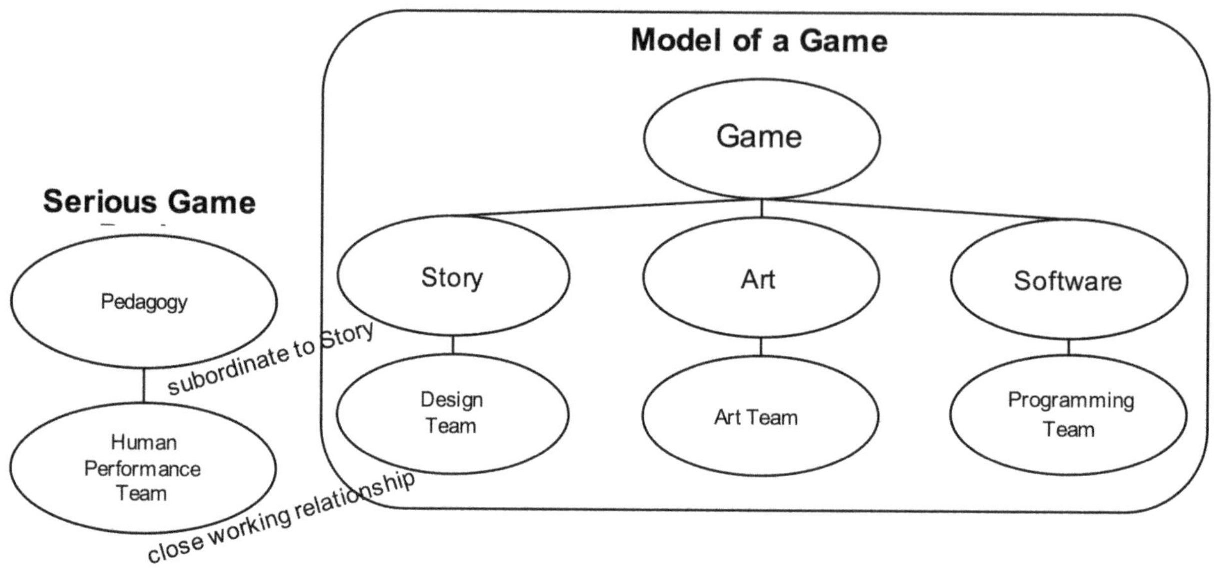

about the effectiveness of a training intervention, which may be contributing to the conflicting results regarding the conditions under which games are viable training options.

In game-based training, common training outcomes which are measured include affective reactions and learning measures, with the latter consisting of both objective and subjective forms. Affective reactions measure the individual's response to the training, including their feelings and liking of the format and materials (Tan et al., 2003). Subjective measures of learning are valuable when applied in the correct context (Alliger et al., 1997; Kraiger, 2002; Leung, 2006). Although each of these results has value in helping to understand game-based learning, confounding them with one another can be misleading to other researchers and practitioners seeking to design and implement their own game-based interventions. This imprecision in assessing learning outcomes has led to inaccurate implications, misconstrued results, and overstated research findings across the literature.

Recommendation 5: Drawing Accurate Implications from Research Findings

The fifth challenge in game-based learning research is a lack of precision in differentiating training outcomes, which at times leads to inaccurate implications, misconstrued results, and overstated research findings. To address this challenge, we recommend that future research draw implications based solely on the training outcomes that were measured. It will benefit future research and practice of game-based learning, to avoid misrepresenting findings, such as measuring one learning outcome (e.g., affective reactions), then drawing inferences about another outcome (e.g., procedural knowledge). This would provide much value to researchers moving forward, since there is a need to draw accurate implications from game-based learning studies that do not overstate or misrepresent the research findings. The concern is that when objective measures of learning are used interchangeably with subjective learning or affective reactions in the research literature that research-based findings are overstated or misrepresented and provide inaccurate direction for practitioners and designers on how to design and implement effective game-based learning interventions. Asking whether a player believes they have learned something or whether they enjoyed the game-based learning experience has been used to make claims that the training was an effective learning tool (e.g., Burguillo, 2010; Johnson, 2010; Levitan, 2010; Loon et al., 2015; Vahed, 2008). In one study, researchers claimed that computer-based learning led to *increased performance* when only self-report survey responses were gathered from participants to make these claims (Burguillo, 2010). Similarly, another study claimed that student learning improved following a game-based simulation, but the only outcome measures were student responses to survey and interview questions along with self-ratings of their own learning on the different learning modules (Loon et al., 2015). It is not uncommon for researchers to use language that implies that learning was achieved in a training in which only subjective, self-report measures were gathered. There are in fact an alarming number of examples in the research literature across industries that demonstrate inaccurate or overstated claims using subjective measures of evaluation (e.g., Aabakken et al., 2000; Chang et al., 2003; Jeong & Bozkurt, 2014; Navarro et al., 2004). This is important because previous research has acknowledged the low correlation between perceptions of learning and actual learning (Makransky & Petersen, 2019). If this overrepresentation continues, practitioners and game designers will continue to receive mixed information on the effective design and development of game-based learning interventions.

DISCUSSION

Our review of the research literature revealed current challenges in how research is being conducted (e.g., vague explanations of game design features that may impact learning outcomes). These challenges may be addressed by changing the focus of the research question to understand the context in which games are effective for learning, and by increasing the scientific rigor of studies in the field. Previous researchers have highlighted the need for quality game-based research, stating that game developers need better guidance on how to design a game in a manner that will facilitate learning outcomes (Adams et al., 2012; O'Neil & Perez, 2008). For example, recent research has suggested that games should be designed to fit the preferences of the players. This involves molding games to address player needs such as self-actualization, self-regulation, and rewards and incentives. By designing games this way, player motivation to complete the game would increase and facilitate the achievement of the aforementioned learning outcomes (Kotsopoulos et al., 2020). Other researchers have called for studies to examine the variables that lead to effective game-based learning (Wong et al., 2007). Some researchers have stated that there is a need for specific studies that isolate game elements to determine their effects (Adams, 2013). However, researchers have been calling for these studies since the mid-1980's (e.g., Lepper, 1985), leading some researchers to criticize the lack of progress that has been made in the field over the last several decades (Butler et al., 2014). Given the amount of time and money invested in producing games for learning, it is apparent that a resolution to this contradictory research is needed.

Developing quality game-based research is further important due to practices in how games are being applied. Some organizations have begun to use games for high stakes purposes such as a step in a multi-hurdle selection process (Amad, 2015; Morgan, 2013). This is concerning in some contexts with inconclusive evidence to justify the use of games for this purpose (i.e., no known published studies validating games as an effective selection assessment method for predicting job performance). Although there seems to be considerable potential in this application for game-based tools, research must catch up with the applications of games to provide evidence on the usefulness of games as high-stakes selection tools. The negative consequences of applying games without sufficient research backing were evident in the outcome of the lawsuit with Lumosity. Certain parties sued Lumosity for making broad reaching claims regarding the cognitive benefits of their *brain training* games (Federal Trade Commission, 2016; Span, 2016). Lumosity settled this case, with substantial financial penalty and changes to their business processes. These negative consequences are also apparent when we consider the rising misuse of gamification and gamification techniques. Landers (2019) highlights a malevolent trend in which vendors of training programs have begun to add game elements to existing training programs or systems without any reason to do so. This trend, known as *rhetorical gamification*, has muddled public perception of gamification and has actually caused harm to the reputation of the gamification field due to the brazen and oftentimes wrong claims that vendors of products with rhetorical gamification make (Landers, 2019)Based on these deleterious outcomes, it is important for researchers and practitioners to be vigilant about the rigor of game research and the recommendations that are made in applying research results. Overstating claims on the benefits of game-based learning can have critical consequences for organizations and institutions. The research to justify the use of games for these means is far from conclusive. It is apparent that organizations need to be cautious when applying games for purposes other than what there is clear and rigorous scientific evidence to support. Below are recommendations we would make for continued research and practice in the area of game-based learning that we believe would benefit the sustained growth and understanding of this topic.

Building a Relationship between Research and Practice

One next step for the future of game-based learning is for researchers to build partnerships with those using game-based learning in practical settings. Studying the actual applications of game-based learning solutions would contribute to an invaluable body of empirical studies. Understandably, concerns about sharing proprietary information or programs may limit a practitioner's ability or willingness to share their products for scientific exploration. However, it would benefit both practitioners and researchers to generate evidence on the effectiveness of game-based learning using the actual games used in organizations and institutions. At present, many researchers use games that are readily available (e.g., commercial games, entertainment-based games) as proxy measures for the training games used in practice. Not only does the use of these games lack face validity for real world application, but the skills the participants are developing (e.g., communication and knowledge sharing) are secondary skills and not the primary focus of the game design. Future studies could address this concern by studying games currently being used within applied settings. This would allow more clear connections to be made between the research and the application of the results.

Understanding the Role of Videogame Experience

Another consideration for future research is the impact of game experience. Previous research has suggested that previous experience with games can confound the results of a research study that uses video games as part of an intervention. Specifically, individuals with more game experience may learn better in game environments for reasons other than the game characteristic which is being studied (Landers & Armstrong, 2017). The benefits of game experience could include preference for the instructional tool, greater enjoyment with the gameplay, or more familiarity with game controls. Despite the prevalence of measuring game experience as a control measure, there is little explanation in the literature as to whether this measure has an impact and the extent of that impact.

Developing and using a valid measure of video game experience would enable additional research to explore the implications that videogame experience has for training outcomes. Exploring the link between experience and performance is not new for psychologists. In the 70's and 80's, researchers explored the link between job experience and job performance. Researchers believed there was a link between experience and performance and frequently measured work experience as a control measure. However, a series of meta-analyses demonstrated that there was a small relationship, but that the definition and measure of experience was inconsistent and had a large impact on how the results should be interpreted (Quiñones et al., 1995). This is not to imply that videogame experience does not have an impact on game-based training. On the contrary, we believe there are strong theoretical arguments for why researchers should be measuring and controlling for videogame experience in game-based training. However, it is clear there needs to be a consistent method for measuring game experience and researchers need to understand and account for the impact that videogame experience has on game-based training outcomes.

Recent research has acknowledged the difficulty in developing a consistent method for measuring game experience. When trying to measure game experience directly, researchers can run into challenges of measuring game experience in a way that is both comprehensive yet still applicable to a wide variety of contexts. One study circumvents these challenges by conceptualizing game experience as part of the game cycle (Sanchez & Langer, 2020). The game cycle includes the processes of pursuing games, investing time in games, and producing game-related outcomes, see Figure 5. These game-related outcomes include cognitive changes, (learning outcomes, procedural skills, game knowledge, and skill), affective changes, (positive/negative reactions, motivation, and interest), and behavioral changes, (game performance and continued game pursuit). Thus, the authors of this study proposed that the more a person engages in the game cycle, the more game experience that person is said to have. By conceptualizing game experience in this way, the authors were able to develop a way of measuring game experience across various applications and contexts. Future research should seek to further explore the relationships between game experience and other individual characteristics.

Drawing a Link to Meaningful Outcomes

Future research should establish a clear link between game-based learning and relevant outcomes (e.g., job performance for workplace training, academic success for educational learning). Prior research has demonstrated a positive correlation between declarative knowledge and *transfer of training* (i.e., the application of learned content outside of the classroom and into an applied setting or context), but not as clearly between affective reactions and transfer of training (Blume et al., 2010). There is some theoretical support to imply that positive affective states experienced in the training (e.g., motivation) may benefit the acquisition of declarative knowledge, which may increase the likelihood that transfer of training will occur (Cheng & Hampson, 2008). However, there are many factors that affect transfer, such as support and opportunity to practice (Cheng & Hampson, 2008). Considering the number of factors that can influence these outcomes, it is important to gather direct transfer measures rather than relying on the relationship between transfer of training and other available measures.

THEORETICAL AND PRACTICAL IMPLICATIONS

The recommendations we provide in our manuscript can act as a primary guide for future research in game-based learning and gamified learning interventions. These five key takeaways can help inform critical considerations and steps that will help ensure rigorous research that can be generalized to other game-based learning studies. In addition, the literature and information we have accumulated here can be also useful for practitioners who are implementing game-based learning solutions in their field (e.g., at work, in an education institution). The frameworks and models we have presented here can be used as a guide for those who are designing and implementing their own game-based solution. They can further use these research-based results to make decisions on their own game design, to help ensure the games will lead to the intended learning outcomes.

Utilizing Advancements in Virtual Reality

The advent of new developments in gaming has been accompanied by research exploring the different ways in which these technologies can be applied in real-world settings. For example, researchers have shared optimistic views on the potential applications of virtual reality (VR) and have stressed that further research be done to take advantage of these applications. (Okada et al., 2019; Pedroli et al., 2016; Rogers et al., 2017) One recent study examined the usage of virtual reality games (VRGs) as a novel way to assess spatial reasoning compared to traditional methods of testing spatial reasoning (Weiner & Sanchez, 2020). Generally, their results suggest that VR games have meaningful similarities to traditional measures of spatial reasoning. Research like this highlights one of the many forms that gaming can take and the need for more researchers across disciplines to investigate and contribute to the literature. Future research will rely on strong relationships between the application of the game and how the game is designed. Other researchers have accounted for the importance of this integration between goal and design. There is a need for game design models to actively incorporate purpose. In one example from Zyda (2005) the game design model was adapted to include the purpose of the game which included a learning component. Their revised model demonstrates the need to identify the application of the game early in the design process, see Figure 6.

In conclusion, there are several current challenges in the research literature that are impacting the progress and understanding of game-based learning and how effective these applications are across disciplines. However, based on our recommendations, we believe that using intentional design with standardized methodology will help generate dependable research findings to inform future frameworks of game-based learning. This will help ensure continued effectiveness of game-based learning solutions.

REFERENCES

Aabakken, L., Adamsen, S., & Kruse, A. (2000). Performance of a colonoscopy simulator: Experience from a hands-on endoscopy course. *Endoscopy*, *32*(11), 911–913. doi:10.1055-2000-8092 PMID:11085483

Aarseth, E. (2014). I fought the law: Transgressive play and the implied player. In N. Segal & D. Koleva (Eds.), *From literature to cultural literacy* (pp. 180–188). Palgrave Macmillan. doi:10.1057/9781137429704_13

Aarseth, E., & Grabarczyk, P. (2018, July 25-28). *An ontological meta-model for game research* [Conference presentation]. DiGRA Conference, Turin, Italy. http://www.digra.org/digra-2018-the-game-is-the-message-cfp/

Adams, D. M. (2013). *Exploring the effect of video game playing on static and dynamic spatial cognition skills* (Unpublished doctoral dissertation). University of California.

Adams, D. M., Mayer, R. E., MacNamara, A., Koenig, A., & Wainess, R. (2012). Narrative games for learning: Testing the discovery and narrative hypotheses. *Journal of Educational Psychology*, *104*(1), 235–249. doi:10.1037/a0025595

Akilli, G. K., & Cagiltay, K. (2006). An instructional design/development model for the creation of game-like learning environments: The FIDGE model. In M. Pivec (Ed.), *Affective and emotional aspects of human-computer interaction: Game-based and innovative learning approaches* (pp. 93–112). IOS Press. http://citeseerx.ist.psu.edu/viewdoc/download?doi=10.1.1.465.6601&rep=rep1&type=pdf#page=108

Akl, E. A., Kairouz, V. F., Sackett, K. M., Erdley, W. S., Mustafa, R. A., Fiander, M., Gabriel, C., & Schünemann, H. (2013). Educational games for health professionals. *Cochrane Database of Systematic Reviews*, *3*(3), 1–47. doi:10.1002/14651858.CD006411.pub3 PMID:23440807

Alliger, G. M., Tannenbaum, S. I., Bennett, W., Traver, H., & Shotland, A. (1997). A meta-analysis of the relations among training criteria. *Personnel Psychology*, *50*(2), 341–358. doi:10.1111/j.1744-6570.1997.tb00911.x

Amad, A. (2015, September 24). *The advantages of Wasabi Waiter Apps in hiring*. The Science Times. Retrieved from https://www.sciencetimes.com/articles/7384/20150924/advantages-wasabi-waiter-apps-hiring.htm

Amer, R. S., Denehy, G. E., Cobb, D. S., Dawson, D. V., Cunningham-Ford, M. A., & Bergeron, C. (2011). Development and evaluation of an interactive dental video game to teach dentin bonding. *Journal of Dental Education*, *75*(6), 823–831. doi:10.1002/j.0022-0337.2011.75.6.tb05111.x PMID:21642529

Amory, A., & Seagram, R. (2003). Educational game models: Conceptualization and evaluation. *South African Journal of Higher Education*, *17*(2), 206–217. https://eric.ed.gov/?id=EJ832934

Anderson, P. H., & Lawton, L. (2009). Business Simulations and Cognitive Learning: Developments, Desires, and Future Directions. *Simulation & Gaming*, *40*(2), 193–216. doi:10.1177/1046878108321624

Arjoranta, J. (2014). Game definitions: A Wittgensteinian approach. *International Journal of Computer Game Research*, *14*(1), 1–13. http://gamestudies.org/1401/articles/arjoranta

Arjoranta, J. (2019). How to define games and why we need to. *Computer Games Journal*, *8*(3-4), 109–120. doi:10.100740869-019-00080-6

Arnab, S., Lim, T., Carvalho, M. B., Bellotti, F., Freitas, S., Louchart, S., Suttie, N., Berta, R., & De Gloria, A. (2015). Mapping learning and game mechanics for serious games analysis. *British Journal of Educational Technology*, *46*(2), 391–411. doi:10.1111/bjet.12113

Bauer, K. N., Brusso, R. C., & Orvis, K. A. (2012). Using adaptive difficulty to optimize videogame-based training performance: The moderating role of personality. *Military Psychology*, *24*(2), 148–165. doi:10.1080/08995605.2012.672908

Beach, D. (1980). *Personnel: The management of people at work*. Macmillan.

Bedwell, W. L., Pavlas, D., Heyne, K., Lazzara, E. H., & Salas, E. (2012). Toward a taxonomy linking game attributes to learning an empirical study. *Simulation & Gaming*, *43*(6), 729–760. doi:10.1177/1046878112439444

Begg, M., Dewhurst, D., & Macleod, H. (2005). Game-informed learning: Applying computer game processes to higher education. *Innovate: Journal of Online Education, 1*(6), 1-7. https://www.learntechlib.org/p/107268/

Biggs, W. D. (1987). Functional business games. *Simulation & Gaming*, *18*(2), 242–267. doi:10.1177/104687818701800206

Blohm, I., & Leimeister, J. M. (2013). Gamification. *Business & Information Systems Engineering*, *5*(4), 275–278. doi:10.100712599-013-0273-5

Blume, B. D., Ford, J. K., Baldwin, T. T., & Huang, J. L. (2010). Transfer of training: A meta-analytic review. *Journal of Management*, *36*(4), 1065–1105. doi:10.1177/0149206309352880

Boyle, E., Connolly, T. M., & Hainey, T. (2011). The role of psychology in understanding the impact of computer games. *Entertainment Computing*, *2*(2), 69–74. doi:10.1016/j.entcom.2010.12.002

Breuer, J. S., & Bente, G. (2010). Why so serious? On the relation of serious games and learning. *Journal for Computer Game Culture*, *4*(1), 7–24. doi:10.7557/23.6111

Brom, C., Preuss, M., & Klement, D. (2011). Are educational computer micro-games engaging and effective for knowledge acquisition at high-schools? A quasi-experimental study. *Computers & Education*, *57*(3), 1971–1988. doi:10.1016/j.compedu.2011.04.007

Brown, K. G., & Gerhardt, M. W. (2002). Formative evaluation: An integrative practice model and case study. *Personnel Psychology*, *55*(4), 951–983. doi:10.1111/j.1744-6570.2002.tb00137.x

Burguillo, J. C. (2010). Using game theory and competition-based learning to stimulate student motivation and performance. *Computers & Education*, *55*(2), 566–575. doi:10.1016/j.compedu.2010.02.018

Butler, Y. G., Someya, Y., & Fukuhara, E. (2014). Online games for young learners' foreign language learning. *ELT Journal*, *68*(3), 265–275. doi:10.1093/elt/ccu008

Calleja, G., & Callus, I. (2011). Game studies. In B. Clarke & M. Rossini (Eds.), *Routledge companion to literature and science* (pp. 323–334). Routledge. doi:10.4324/9780203848739.ch28

Calvillo-Gámez, E. H., Cairns, P., & Cox, A. L. (2015). Assessing the core elements of the gaming experience. In R. Berhnhaupt (Ed.), *Evaluating user experience in games* (pp. 47–71). doi:10.1007/978-3-319-15985-0_3

Capatina, A., Bleoju, G., Rancati, E., & Hoareau, E. (2018). Tracking precursors of learning analytics over serious game team performance ranking. *Behaviour & Information Technology*, *37*(10/11), 1008–1020. doi:10.1080/0144929X.2018.1474949

Chang, J., Lee, M., Ng, K. L., & Moon, K. L. (2003). Business simulation games: The Hong Kong experience. *Simulation & Gaming*, *34*(3), 367–376. doi:10.1177/1046878103255877

Chen, H. H. (2005). *A formative evaluation of the training effectiveness of a computer game* [Unpublished doctoral dissertation, University of Southern California]. https://www.proquest.com/openview/5126be19de8d9deae152bf5514fcf2bb/1?pq-origsite=gscholar&cbl=18750&diss=y

Cheng, E. W., & Hampson, I. (2008). Transfer of training: A review and new insights. *International Journal of Management Reviews*, *10*(4), 327–341. doi:10.1111/j.1468-2370.2007.00230.x

Chou, Y.-K. (2015). *Actionable gamification: Beyond points, badges, and leaderboards*. Octalysis Media.

Christopher, L., & Waworuntu, A. (2021). Java programming language learning application based on Octalysis gamification framework. *International Journal of New Media Technology*, *8*(1), 65–69. doi:10.31937/ijnmt.v8i1.2049

Clark, R. E. (1983). Reconsidering research on learning from media. *Review of Educational Research*, *53*(4), 445–459. doi:10.3102/00346543053004445

Clark, R. E. (1985). Confounding in educational computing research. *Journal of Educational Computing Research*, *1*(2), 137–148. doi:10.2190/HC3L-G6YD-BAK9-EQB5

Clark, R. E. (1994). Media will never influence learning. *Educational Technology Research and Development*, *42*(2), 21–29. doi:10.1007/BF02299088

Clark, R. E. (2001). *Learning from media: Arguments, analysis, and evidence*. Information Age. https://psycnet.apa.org/record/2012-18168-000

Clark, R. E. (2007). Learning from serious games? Arguments, evidence, and research suggestions. *Educational Technology*, *47*(3), 56–59. https://www.jstor.org/stable/44429512

Cohen, K. J., & Rhenman, E. (1961). The role of management games in education and research. *Management Science*, *7*(2), 101–194. doi:10.1287/mnsc.7.2.131

Coller, B. D., & Shernoff, D. J. (2009). Video game-based education in mechanical engineering: A look at student engagement. *International Journal of Engineering Education*, *25*(2), 308–317. https://www.ijee.ie/contents/c250209.html

Connolly, T. M., Boyle, E. A., MacArthur, E., Hainey, T., & Boyle, J. M. (2012). A systematic literature review of empirical evidence on computer games and serious games. *Computers & Education*, *59*(2), 661–686. doi:10.1016/j.compedu.2012.03.004

Crookall, D., & Thorngate, W. (2009). Acting, knowing, learning, simulating, gaming. *Simulation & Gaming*, *40*(1), 8–26. doi:10.1177/1046878108330364 de Freitas, S., & Jarvis, S. (2007). Serious games engaging training solutions: A research and development project for supporting training needs. *British Journal of Educational Technology, 38*(3), 523–525. doi:10.1111/j.1467-8535.2007.00716.x

DeSmet, A., Van Ryckeghem, D., Compernolle, S., Baranowski, T., Thompson, D., Crombez, G., Poels, K., Van Lippevelde, W., Bastiaensen, S., Van Cleemput, K., Vandebosch, H., & De Bourdeaudhuij, I. (2014). A meta-analysis of serious digital games for healthy lifestyle promotion. *Preventive Medicine, 69*, 95–107. doi:10.1016/j.ypmed.2014.08.026 PMID:25172024

Dillenberger, D., & Sandowski, P. (2012). *Subjective learning: Second version* (Report No. 12-007). Penn Institute for Economic Research. https://papers.ssrn.com/sol3/papers.cfm?abstract_id=2017595

Dochy, F., Segers, M., Van den Bossche, P., & Gijbels, D. (2003). Effects of problem-based learning: A meta-analysis. *Learning and Instruction, 13*(5), 533–568. doi:10.1016/S0959-4752(02)00025-7

Driskell, J. E., & Dwyer, J. D. (1984). Microcomputer videogame-based training. *Educational Technology, 24*(2), 11–16. https://www.jstor.org/stable/44427307

Eichberg, H. (2018). *Play in Philosophy and Social Thought*. Routledge. https://www.routledge.com/Play-in-Philosophy-and-Social-Thought/Eichberg-Larsen/p/book/9780367519759

Emelianenko, A. Y. (2010). Проблематичность однозначного определения феномена игры [The difficulty of a clear definition of "game"]. *RUDN Journal of Philosophy, 4*, 77-81. https://journals.rudn.ru/philosophy/article/viewFile/11684/11114

Ermi, L., & Mäyrä, F. (2005, June 16-20). *Fundamental components of the gameplay experience: Analysing immersion* [Paper presentation]. DiGRA 2005: Changing Views – Worlds in Play, Vancouver, Canada. http://www.digra.org/digital-library/publications/fundamental-components-of-the-gameplay-experience-analysing-immersion/

Faria, A. J., Hutchinson, D., Wellington, W. J., & Gold, S. (2009). Developments in business gaming a review of the past 40 years. *Simulation & Gaming, 40*(4), 464–487. doi:10.1177/1046878108327585

Federal Trade Commission. (2016). *Lumosity to pay $2 million to settle FTC deceptive advertising charges for its "brain training" program: Company claimed program would sharpen performance in everyday life and protect against cognitive decline*. https://www.ftc.gov/news-events/press-releases/2016/01/lumosity-pay-2-million-settle-ftc-deceptive-advertising-charges

Feige, D. M. (2012). Computer games as works of art. In J. Fromme & A. Unger (Eds.), *Computer games and new media cultures: A handbook of digital game studies* (pp. 93–106). Springer. doi:10.1007/978-94-007-2777-9_6

Fisch, S. M. (2005). Making educational computer games "educational". In M. Eisenberg & A. Eisenberg (Eds.), *IDC '05: Proceedings of the 2005 conference on interaction design and children* (pp. 56–61). Association for Computing Machinery. doi:10.1145/1109540.1109548

Fischer, K. W. (2009). Mind, brain, and education: Building a scientific groundwork for learning and teaching. *Mind, Brain and Education: the Official Journal of the International Mind, Brain, and Education Society, 3*(1), 3–16. doi:10.1111/j.1751-228X.2008.01048.x

Fletcher, J. D., & Tobias, S. (2006). Using computer games and simulations for instruction: A research review. *Proceedings of the Society for Applied Learning Technology Meeting*, 1–34. https://www.researchgate.net/publication/228511464_Using_computer_games_and_simulations_for_instruction_A_research_review

Garris, R., Ahlers, R., & Driskell, J. E. (2002). Games, motivation, and learning: A research and practice model. *Simulation & Gaming*, *33*(4), 441–467. doi:10.1177/1046878102238607

Gee, J. P. (2005). Learning by design: Good video games as learning machines. *E-Learning and Digital Media*, *2*(1), 5–16. doi:10.2304/elea.2005.2.1.5

Granger, B. P. (2008) *Moderating effect of training content complexity on the relationship between training media and training outcomes* [Master's thesis]. University of South Florida Libraries. https://digitalcommons.usf.edu/etd/1989/

Gredler, M. E. (1996). Educational games and simulations: A technology in search of a (research) paradigm. In D. H. Jonassen (Ed.), *Handbook of research on educational communications and technology* (pp. 521–540). Macmillan. http://citeseerx.ist.psu.edu/viewdoc/download?doi=10.1.1.115.9904&rep=rep1&type=pdf

Greenblat, C. S. (1973). Teaching with simulation games: A review of claims and evidence. *Teaching Sociology*, *1*(1), 62–83. doi:10.2307/1317334

Greenblat, C. S., & Duke, R. D. (1981). *Principles and practices of gaming-simulation*. Sage. https://catalog.princeton.edu/catalog/309032

Groh, F. (2012). Gamification: State of the art definition and utilization. In N. Asaj, B. Konings, M. Poguntke, F. Schaub, & B. Wiedersheim (Eds.), *Proceedings of the 4th seminar on research trends in media informatics* (pp. 39–46). Institute of Media Informatics. https://d-nb.info/1020022604/34#page=39

Grossman, R., Heyne, K., & Salas, E. (2014). Game and simulation-based approaches to training. In K. Kraiger, J. Passmore, N. R. dos Santos, & S. Malvezzi (Eds.), *Handbook of the psychology of training, development, and performance improvement* (pp. 205–224). Wiley Blackwell. doi:10.1002/9781118736982.ch12

Habgood, M. P. J. (2005). *Zombie division: Intrinsic integration in digital learning games* [Unpublished manuscript]. The Learning Sciences Research Institute, The University of Nottingham. https://www.researchgate.net/publication/242288013_Zombie_Division_Intrinsic_Integration_in_Digital_Learning_Games

Habgood, M. P. J., Ainsworth, S. E., & Benford, S. (2005). Endogenous fantasy and learning in digital games. *Simulation & Gaming*, *36*(4), 483–498. doi:10.1177/1046878105282276

Harris, D. (2008). *A comparative study of the effect of collaborative problem-solving in a Massively Multiplayer Online Game (MMOG) on individual achievement* (Publication No. 3317694) [Doctoral dissertation, University of San Francisco]. USF Digital Repository. https://repository.usfca.edu/cgi/viewcontent.cgi?referer=https://www.google.com/&httpsredir=1&article=1259&context=diss

Hassenzahl, M. (2018). The thing and I (Summer of '17 remix). In M. Blythe & A. Monk (Eds.), *Funology 2: From usability to enjoyment* (pp. 17–31). Springer. doi:10.1007/978-3-319-68213-6_2

Hays, R. T. (2005). *The effectiveness of instructional games: A literature review and discussion.* Naval Air Warfare Center Training Systems Division. https://apps.dtic.mil/sti/citations/ADA441935

Hinds, A. P. (1975). Separating the sirloin from the salami. *Training and Development Journal, 29*(3), 42–44. https://eric.ed.gov/?id=EJ113779

Hoffman, B., & Nadelson, L. (2010). Motivational engagement and video gaming: A mixed methods study. *Educational Technology Research and Development, 58*(3), 245–270. doi:10.100711423-009-9134-9

Hsu, E. (1989). Role-event gaming simulation in management education: A conceptual framework and review. *Simulation & Gaming, 20*(4), 409–438. doi:10.1177/104687818902000402

Huang, Y., Liu, R., Zhai, S., Ma, X., Zhou, M., & Deng, Q. (2015). A knowledge-intensive serious game for education of traditional chinese medicine: A pilot study. *International Journal of Hybrid Information Technology, 8*(3), 111–120. doi:10.14257/ijhit.2015.8.3.11

Huotari, K., & Hamari, J. (2017). A definition for gamification: Anchoring gamification in the service marketing literature. *Electronic Markets, 27*(1), 21–31. doi:10.100712525-015-0212-z

Iacovides, I., McAndrew, P., Scanlon, E., & Aczel, J. (2014). The gaming involvement and informal learning framework. *Simulation & Gaming, 45*(4-5), 611–626. doi:10.1177/1046878114554191

Imlig-Iten, N., & Petko, D. (2018). Comparing serious games and educational simulations: Effects on enjoyment, deep thinking, interest and cognitive learning gains. *Simulation & Gaming, 49*(4), 401–422. doi:10.1177/1046878118779088

Jabbar, A. I. A., & Felicia, P. (2015). Gameplay engagement and learning in game-based learning: A systematic review. *Review of Educational Research, 85*(4), 740–779. doi:10.3102/0034654315577210

Jarvis, P., Holford, J., & Griffin, C. (2003). *The theory & practice of learning*. Routledge. doi:10.4324/9780203465653

Jeong, K. Y., & Bozkurt, I. (2014). Evaluating a project management simulation training exercise. *Simulation & Gaming, 45*(2), 183–203. doi:10.1177/1046878113518481

Johnson, W. L. (2010). Serious use of a serious game for language learning. *International Journal of Artificial Intelligence in Education, 20*(2), 175–195. doi:10.3233/JAI-2010-0006

Kalyuga, S., & Plass, J. L. (2009). Evaluating and managing cognitive load in games. In R. Ferdig (Ed.), *Handbook of research on effective electronic gaming in education* (pp. 719–737). IGI Global. doi:10.4018/978-1-59904-808-6.ch041

Kalz, M., Börner, D., Ternier, S., & Specht, M. (2015). Mindergie: A pervasive learning game for pro-environmental behaviour at the workplace. In L. H. Wong, M. Milrad, & M. Specht (Eds.), *Seamless learning in the age of mobile connectivity* (pp. 397–417). Springer. doi:10.1007/978-981-287-113-8_20

Ke, F. (2008). A case study of computer gaming for math: Engaged learning from gameplay? *Computers & Education, 51*(4), 1609–1620. doi:10.1016/j.compedu.2008.03.003

Keys, B., & Wolfe, J. (1990). The role of management games and simulations in education and research. *Journal of Management, 16*(2), 307–336. doi:10.1177/014920639001600205

Khaliq, I., & Purkiss, B. (2015). *A study of interaction in idle games & perceptions on the definition of a game. In 2015 IEEE Games Entertainment Media Conference*. IEEE. doi:10.1109/GEM.2015.7377233

Kirkpatrick, D. L., & Kirkpatrick, J. D. (2006). *Evaluating training programs: The four levels*. Berrett-Koehler. https://www.bkconnection.com/books/title/evaluating-training-programs

Kobes, M., Helsloot, I., de Vries, B., & Post, J. (2010). Exit choice, (pre-)movement time and (pre-) evacuation behaviour in hotel fire evacuation – Behavioural analysis and validation of the use of serious gaming in experimental research. *Procedia Engineering, 3*, 37–51. doi:10.1016/j.proeng.2010.07.006

Koriat, A. (1997). Monitoring one's own knowledge during study: A cue-utilization approach to judgments of learning. *Journal of Experimental Psychology, 126*(4), 349–370. doi:10.1037/0096-3445.126.4.349

Koriat, A., Sheffer, L., & Ma'ayan, H. (2002). Comparing objective and subjective learning curves: Judgments of learning exhibit increased underconfidence with practice. *Journal of Experimental Psychology, 131*(2), 147–162. doi:10.1037/0096-3445.131.2.147 PMID:12049237

Kotsopoulos, D., Bardaki, C., Papaioannou, T. G., Lounis, S., Stamoulis, G. D., & Pramatari, K. (2019). Designing a serious game to motivate energy savings in a museum: Opportunities & challenges. In A. Liapis, G. Yannakakis, M. Gentile, & M. Ninaus (Eds.), Lecture Notes in Computer Science: Vol. 11899. *Games and Learning Alliance* (pp. 572–584). Springer. doi:10.1007/978-3-030-34350-7_55

Kotsopoulos, D., Bardaki, C., Papaioannou, T. G., Pramatari, K., & Stamoulis, G. D. (2020). User-centered gamification: The case of IoT-enabled energy conservation at work. *International Journal of E-Services and Mobile Applications, 12*(2), 15–39. doi:10.4018/IJESMA.2020040102

Kotsopoulos, D., Bardaki, C., & Pramatari, K. (2016). Gamification, geolocation and sensors for employee motivation towards energy conservation at the workplace. *MCIS 2016 Proceedings*. https://aisel.aisnet.org/mcis2016/39

Kraiger, K. (2002). Decision-based evaluation. In K. Kraiger (Ed.), *Creating, implementing, and managing effective training and development: State-of-the-art lessons for practice* (pp. 331–375). Jossey-Bass. https://www.researchgate.net/publication/281601028_Decision-based_evaluation

Kraiger, K., & Ford, J. K. (2020). The science of workplace instruction: Learning and development applied to work. *Annual Review of Organizational Psychology and Organizational Behavior, 8*(1), 45–72. doi:10.1146/annurev-orgpsych-012420-060109

Kraiger, K., Ford, J. K., & Salas, E. (1993). Application of cognitive, skill-based, and affective theories of learning outcomes to new methods of training evaluation. *The Journal of Applied Psychology, 78*(2), 311–328. doi:10.1037/0021-9010.78.2.311

Laas, O. (2017). On game definitions. *Journal of the Philosophy of Sport, 44*(1), 81–94. doi:10.1080/00948705.2016.1255556

Landers, R. N. (2014). Developing a theory of gamified learning linking serious games and gamification of learning. *Simulation & Gaming, 45*(6), 752–768. doi:10.1177/1046878114563660

Landers, R. N. (2019). Gamification misunderstood: How badly executed and rhetorical gamification obscures its transformative potential. *Journal of Management Inquiry*, *28*(2), 137–140. doi:10.1177/1056492618790913

Landers, R. N., & Armstrong, M. B. (2017). Enhancing instructional outcomes with gamification: An empirical test of the Technology-Enhanced Training Effectiveness Model. *Computers in Human Behavior*, *71*, 499–507. doi:10.1016/j.chb.2015.07.031

Landers, R. N., Armstrong, M. B., & Collmus, A. B. (2017). How to use game elements to enhance learning: Applications of the theory of gamified learning. In M. Ma & A. Oikonomou (Eds.), Serious games and edutainment applications. Springer. doi:10.1007/978-3-319-51645-5_21

Landers, R. N., & Landers, A. K. (2014). An empirical test of the theory of gamified learning: The effect of leaderboards on time-on-task and academic performance. *Simulation & Gaming*, *45*(6), 769–785. doi:10.1177/1046878114563662

Leemkuil, H., de Jong, T., & Ootes, S. (2000). *Review of educational use of games and simulations* (No. IST-1999-130). KITS Consortium. https://www.researchgate.net/publication/250740593_Review_of_educational_use_of_games_and_simulations

Lepper, M. R. (1985). Microcomputers in education: Motivational and social issues. *The American Psychologist*, *40*(1), 1–18. doi:10.1037/0003-066X.40.1.1

Leung, A. (2006). A conceptual model of information technology training leading to better outcomes. *International Journal of Business and Information*, *1*(1), 74–95. doi:10.6702/IJBI.2006.1.1.4

Levitan, E. P. (2010). *Higher education administrators' perceptions of the use of simulation games for adult learners* (Publication No. 3406153) [Doctoral dissertation, Argosy University]. ProQuest Dissertation Publishing. http://search.proquest.com/docview/275851740

Li, K., Hall, M., Bermell-Garcia, P., Alcock, J., Tiwari, A., & González-Franco, M. (2017). Measuring the learning effectiveness of serious gaming for training of complex manufacturing tasks. *Simulation & Gaming*, *48*(6), 770–790. doi:10.1177/1046878117739929

Li, M. C., & Tsai, C. C. (2013). Game-based learning in science education: A review of relevant research. *Journal of Science Education and Technology*, *22*(6), 877–898. doi:10.100710956-013-9436-x

Loganathan, P., Talib, C. A., Thoe, N. K., Aliyu, F., & Zawadski, R. (2019). Implementing technology infused gamification in science classroom: A systematic review and suggestions for future research. *Learning Science and Mathematics Journal, 14*, 60-73. http://recsam.edu.my/sub_lsmjournal/images/docs/2019/2019_5_PL_6073_Final.pdf

Long, M. H. (1980). Inside the "black box": Methodological issues in classroom research on language learning. *Language Learning*, *30*(1), 1–42. doi:10.1111/j.1467-1770.1980.tb00149.x

Loon, M., Evans, J., & Kerridge, C. (2015). Learning with a strategic management simulation game: A case study. *International Journal of Management Education*, *13*(3), 227–236. doi:10.1016/j.ijme.2015.06.002

Makransky, G., & Petersen, G. B. (2019). Investigating the process of learning with desktop virtual reality: A structural equation modeling approach. *Computers & Education*, *134*, 15–30. doi:10.1016/j.compedu.2019.02.002

Mayer, R. E. (2011). Multimedia learning and games. In S. Tobias & J. D. Fletcher (Eds.), *Computer games and instruction* (pp. 281–305). Information Age Publishing. https://psycnet.apa.org/reMultimedia learning and games.cord/2011-11269-010

McGrath, J. E. (1984). *Groups: Interaction and performance*. Prentice-Hall. http://users.ece.utexas.edu/~perry/education/382v-s08/papers/mcgrath84.pdf

Michael, D., & Chen, S. (2006). *Serious games: Games that educate, train, and inform*. Thomson Course Technology.

Morgan, J. (2013, December 17). *Want to work here? Play this game first!* Forbes. https://www.forbes.com/sites/jacobmorgan/2013/12/17/want-to-work-here-play-this-game-first/#73827d254249

Murphy, K. R. (2008). Explaining the weak relationship between job performance and ratings of job performance. *Industrial and Organizational Psychology: Perspectives on Science and Practice*, *1*(2), 148–160. doi:10.1111/j.1754-9434.2008.00030.x

National Center for Education Statistics. (n.d.). *Fast facts: Back to school statistics*. https://nces.ed.gov/fastfacts/display.asp?id=372

Navarro, E. O., Baker, A., & Van der Hoek, A. (2004, January 18-21). *Teaching software engineering using simulation games* [Paper presentation]. International Conference on Simulation in Education, San Diego, CA. http://isr.uci.edu/content/teaching-software-engineering-using-simulation-games

Nguyen, C. T. (2017). Philosophy of games. *Philosophy Compass*, *12*(8), e12426. doi:10.1111/phc3.12426

O'Neil, H. F., & Perez, R. S. (2008). *Computer games and team and individual learning*. Elsevier. https://www.semanticscholar.org/paper/Computer-Games-and-Team-and-Individual-Learning-O'Neil-Perez/e7cda4b404d149e70c6675c6ed01efbbff29a54b

O'Neil, H. F., Wainess, R., & Baker, E. L. (2005). Classification of learning outcomes: Evidence from the games literature. *Curriculum Journal*, *16*(4), 455–474. doi:10.1080/09585170500384529

Okada, A., Rocha, A. K. L. T., Fuchter, S. K., Zucchi, S., & Wortley, D. (2019). Formative assessment of inquiry skills for responsible research and innovation using 3D virtual reality glasses and face recognition. In S. Draaijer, D. Joosten-ten Brinke, & E. Ras, (Eds.), *Technology Enhanced Assessment Conference: Revised selected papers* (pp. 91– 101). Springer. 10.1007/978-3-030-25264-9_7

Oliveira, S., & Cruz, M. (2018). The gamification Octalysis framework within the primary English teaching process: The quest for a transformative classroom. *Revista Lusófona de Educação*, *41*(41), 63–82. doi:10.24140/issn.1645-7250.rle41.04

Opdal, P. A. (2020). Inside the black box: On the concepts "teaching" and "learning" and the connections between them. *Scandinavian Journal of Educational Research*, *64*(3), 457–470. doi:10.1080/00313831.2019.1577752

Oprescu, F., Jones, C., & Katsikitis, M. (2014). I play at work-ten principles for transforming work processes through gamification. *Frontiers in Psychology*, *5*(Jan), 1–5. doi:10.3389/fpsyg.2014.00014 PMID:24523704

Papastergiou, M. (2009). Digital game-based learning in high school computer science education: Impact on educational effectiveness and student motivation. *Computers & Education*, *52*(1), 1–12. doi:10.1016/j.compedu.2008.06.004

Patrício, R., Moreira, A. C., & Zurlo, F. (2018). Gamification approaches to the early stage of innovation. *Creativity and Innovation Management*, *27*(4), 499–511. doi:10.1111/caim.12284

Patrício, R., Moreira, A. C., & Zurlo, F. (2021). Enhancing design thinking approaches to innovation through gamification. *European Journal of Innovation Management*, *24*(5), 1569–1594. doi:10.1108/EJIM-06-2020-0239

Patrício, R., Moreira, A. C., Zurlo, F., & Melazzini, M. (2020). Co-creation of new solutions through gamification: A collaborative innovation practice. *Creativity and Innovation Management*, *29*(1), 146–160. doi:10.1111/caim.12356

Pedroli, E., Pallavinci, F., Serino, S., Cipresso, P., Chicchi Giglioli, A., & Riva, G. (2016). The use of virtual reality tools for the assessment of executive functions and unilateral spatial neglect. In F. Hu, J. Lu, & T. Zhang (Eds.), *Virtual reality enhanced robotic systems for disability rehabilitation, edition* (pp. 115–140). Advances in medical technologies and clinical practice. IGI Global. doi:10.4018/978-1-4666-9740-9.ch007

Percival, F., & Ellington, H. I. (1980). The place of case studies in the simulation/gaming field. In P. Race & D. Brook (Eds.), *Perspectives on academic gaming & simulation 5: Simulation and Gaming for the 1980s*. Kogan Pages.

Perrotta, C., Featherstone, G., Aston, H., & Houghton, E. (2013). *Game-based learning: Latest evidence and future directions*. NFER. https://www.nfer.ac.uk/publications/game01/game01.pdf

Phillips, J. J., & Phillips, P. P. (2016). *Handbook of training evaluation and measurement methods*. Routledge. doi:10.4324/9781315757230

Pratt, M. A., & Hahn, S. (2015). Effects of simulation on student satisfaction with a capstone course. *Journal of Hospitality & Tourism Education*, *27*(1), 39–46. doi:10.1080/10963758.2015.998911

Preece, J., Rogers, Y., & Sharp, H. (2002). *Interaction design: Beyond human computer interaction*. John Wiley & Sons. https://www.wiley.com/en-us/Interaction+Design%3A+Beyond+Human+Computer+Interaction%2C+4th+Edition-p-9781119088790

Prensky, M. (2001a). True believers: Digital game-based learning in the military. In M. Prensky (Ed.), *Digital game-based learning*. McGraw-Hill.

Prensky, M. (2001b). Fun, play and games: What makes games engaging. In M. Prensky (Ed.), *Digital game-based learning*. McGraw-Hill.

Quiñones, M. A., Ford, J. K., & Teachout, M. S. (1995). The relationship between work experience and job performance: A conceptual and meta-analytic review. *Personnel Psychology*, *48*(4), 887–910. doi:10.1111/j.1744-6570.1995.tb01785.x

Rhodes, M. G., & Tauber, S. K. (2011). The influence of delaying judgments of learning on metacognitive accuracy: A meta-analytic review. *Psychological Bulletin*, *137*(1), 131–148. doi:10.1037/a0021705 PMID:21219059

Rieber, L. P. (1996). Seriously considering play: Designing interactive learning environments based on the blending of microworlds, simulations, and games. *Educational Technology Research and Development*, *44*(2), 43–58. doi:10.1007/BF02300540

Rogers, C. B., El-Mounaryi, H., Wasfy, T., & Satterwhite, J. (2017). *Assessment of STEM e-learning in an immersive virtual reality (VR) environment* [Paper presentation]. 2016 ASEE Annual conference & exposition, New Orleans, LA, United States. 10.18260/p.26336

Rosen, E. F., & Petty, L. C. (1992). Computer-aided instruction in a physiological psychology course. *Behavior Research Methods, Instruments, & Computers*, *24*(2), 169–171. doi:10.3758/BF03203492

Rutten, N., van Joolingen, W. R., & van der Veen, J. T. (2012). The learning effects of computer simulations in science education. *Computers & Education*, *58*(1), 136–153. doi:10.1016/j.compedu.2011.07.017

Sabri, H., Cowan, B., Kapralos, B., Porte, M., Backstein, D., & Dubrowskie, A. (2010). Serious games for knee replacement surgery procedure education and training. *Procedia: Social and Behavioral Sciences*, *2*(2), 3483–3488. doi:10.1016/j.sbspro.2010.03.539

Sackett, P. R., & Mullen, E. J. (1993). Beyond formal experimental design: Towards an expanded view of the training evaluation process. *Personnel Psychology*, *46*(3), 613–627. doi:10.1111/j.1744-6570.1993.tb00887.x

Salas, E., Tannenbaum, S. I., Kraiger, K., & Smith-Jentsch, K. A. (2012). The science of training and development in organizations: What matters in practice. *Psychological Science in the Public Interest*, *13*(2), 74–101. doi:10.1177/1529100612436661 PMID:26173283

Salen, K., Tekinbaş, K. S., & Zimmerman, E. (2004). *Rules of play: Game design fundamentals*. MIT Press. https://mitpress.mit.edu/books/rules-play

Sanchez, D. R., & Langer, M. (2020). Video game pursuit (VGPu) scale development: Designing and validating a scale with implications for game-based learning and assessment. *Simulation & Gaming*, *51*(1), 55–86. doi:10.1177/1046878119882710

Sanchez, D. R., Langer, M., & Kaur, R. (2019). Gamification in the classroom: Examining the impact of gamified quizzes on student learning. *Computers & Education*, *144*, 103666. doi:10.1016/j.compedu.2019.103666

Savage, D. D., & Bales, R. (2017). Video games in job interviews: Using algorithms to minimize discrimination and unconscious bias. *ABA Journal of Labor & Employment Law*, *32*(2), 211–228. https://heinonline.org/HOL/LandingPage?handle=hein.journals/lablaw32&div=18&id=&page=

Schell, J. (2008). *The art of game design: A book of lenses*. CRC Press. https://www.schellgames.com/art-of-game-design/

Senderek, R., Brenken, B., & Stich, V. (2015). The implementation of game based learning as part of the corporate competence development. In A. Pester, V. Alexandrov, J. J Noguez, & L. J. Neri (Eds.), *Proceedings of the 2015 international conference on interactive collaborative and blended learning* (pp. 44-51). IEEE. 10.1109/ICBL.2015.7387632

Shute, V. J., Ventura, M., & Ke, F. (2015). The power of play: The effects of Portal 2 and Lumosity on cognitive and noncognitive skills. *Computers & Education*, *80*, 58–67. doi:10.1016/j.compedu.2014.08.013

Sitzmann, T., Ely, K., Brown, K. G., & Bauer, K. N. (2010). Self-assessment of knowledge: A cognitive learning or affective measure? *Academy of Management Learning & Education*, *9*(2), 169–191. doi:10.5465/amle.9.2.zqr169

Span, P. (2016, January 19). After the F.T.C.'s failing grade for Lumosity. *The New York Times*. https://www.nytimes.com/2016/01/19/health/ftcs-lumosity-penalty-doesnt-end-brain-training-debate.html?_r=0

Stenros, J. (2015). *Playfulness, play, and games: A constructionist ludology approach* [Doctoral dissertation]. Tampere University Press. https://trepo.tuni.fi/handle/10024/96986

Stenros, J. (2017). The game definition game: A review. *Games and Culture*, *12*(6), 499–520. doi:10.1177/1555412016655679

Sugrue, B., & Rivera, R. J. (2005). *State of the industry: ASTD's annual review of trends in workplace learning and performance*. ASTD. https://www.td.org/research-reports/2005-state-of-the-industry-report

Tan, J. A., Hall, R. J., & Boyce, C. (2003). The role of employee reactions in predicting training effectiveness. *Human Resource Development Quarterly*, *14*(4), 397–411. doi:10.1002/hrdq.1076

Thomas, R., Cahill, J., & Santilli, L. (1997). Using an interactive computer game to increase skill and self-efficacy regarding safer sex. *Health Education & Behavior*, *24*(1), 71–86. doi:10.1177/109019819702400108 PMID:9112099

Tobias, S., & Fletcher, J. D. (2011). *Computer games and instruction*. Information Age. https://eric.ed.gov/?id=ED529495

Training Industry Report. (2020, November/December). *Training Magazine, 57*(5), 22-37. https://pubs.royle.com/publication/?m=20617&i=678873&p=24

Vahed, A. (2008, October). *The tooth morphology board game: An innovative strategy in tutoring dental technology learners in combating rote learning* [Conference Paper]. European Conference on Games-Based Learning, Barcelona, Spain. https://www.researchgate.net/publication/268925737_The_Tooth_Morphology_Board_Game_An_Innovative_Strategy_in_Tutoring_Dental_Technology_Learners_in_Combating_Rote_Learning

Virtual Heroes. (2007). *Zero Hour: America's Medic*. www.virtualheroes.biz/VHFree/Content/ReferenceMaterials/RefMaterialZeroHour.zip

Waern, A. (2012, June). Framing games. *Proceedings of DiGRA Nordic 2012 Conference: Local and Global – Games in Culture and Society, 10,* 1-14. http://www.digra.org/wp-content/uploads/digital-library/12168.20295.pdf

Weiner, E. J., & Sanchez, D. R. (2020). Cognitive ability in virtual reality: Validity evidence for VR game-based assessments. *International Journal of Selection and Assessment*, *28*(3), 215–235. doi:10.1111/ijsa.12295

Wilson, K. A., Bedwell, W. L., Lazzara, E. H., Salas, E., Burke, C. S., Estock, J. L., Orvis, K. L., & Conkey, C. (2009). Relationships between game attributes and learning outcomes: Review and research proposals. *Simulation & Gaming*, *40*(2), 217–266. doi:10.1177/1046878108321866

Wong, W. L., Shen, C., Nocera, L., Carriazo, E., Tang, F., Bugga, S., Narayanan, H., Wang, H., & Ritterfeld, U. (2007). Serious video game effectiveness. In R. Bernhaupt, & M. Tscheligi (Eds.), *Proceedings of the international conference on advances in computer entertainment technology* (pp. 49-55). Association for Computing Machinery. 10.1145/1255047.1255057

Zwikael, O., & Gonen, A. (2007). Project execution game: Training towards managing unexpected events. *Journal of European Industrial Training*, *31*(6), 495–512. doi:10.1108/03090590710772668

Zyda, M. (2005). From visual simulation to virtual reality to games. *IEEE Computer*, *38*(9), 25–32. doi:10.1109/MC.2005.297

KEY TERMS AND DEFINITIONS

Affective Learning: Learning related to changes in learner disposition and emotion. Examples of concepts learned through affective learning include attitudinal changes and motivational changes (Kraiger et al., 1993).

Cognitive-Based Learning: Learning related to the acquisition of knowledge and the relationships among concepts. Examples of concepts learned through cognitive-based learning include verbal knowledge, knowledge organization, and cognitive strategies (Kraiger et al., 1993).

Game-Based Learning: The achievement of learning objectives using games as a way to deliver educational content (Burguillo, 2010).

Input-Process-Output: A framework developed by McGrath (1984) to illustrate how systems develop as a result of inputs leading to processes which in turn lead to outcomes.

Objective Measures of Learning: The methods used to capture learner development throughout a training program using evaluations that are based on verifiable evidence (Anderson & Lawton, 2008).

Seductive Details: Attention-grabbing material that is presented with educational content with the intent that learners' interest in the attention-grabbing material will result in the educational content appearing more memorable. Research has suggested that this does not work and that seductive details tend to be remembered separately from the educational content that they are paired with (Fisch, 2005).

Serious Games: Games played for educational reasons rather than entertainment (Michael & Chen, 2006).

Skill-Based Learning: Learning related to development of technical or motor skills. Examples of concepts learned through skill-based learning include the abilities to compile, proceduralize, and compose different motor or technical skills as well as the ability to refine skills to the point of automaticity (Kraiger et al., 1993).

Subjective Measures of Learning: The methods used to capture the feelings, perceptions, and impressions of the learner regarding the educational material (Dillenberger & Sandowski, 2012).

Training Media: The vehicle through which educational material is delivered. Examples of training media include classroom instruction or learning management systems (Granger, 2008).

Training/Learning Outcomes: Changes in the knowledge or behavior of a learner as a result of instruction or training (Salas et al., 2012).

Chapter 28
Solving a Crime in the Geology Lab:
A Gamification Lesson Plan to Get Familiar With Common Rocks and Minerals

Isaac Corbacho-Cuello
https://orcid.org/0000-0003-1768-8270
University of Extremadura, Spain

Rodrigo González-García
University of Extremadura, Spain

Miriam Andrea Hernández-Barco
https://orcid.org/0000-0002-3196-0421
University of Extremadura, Spain

ABSTRACT

This work shows an innovative and manipulative activity to learn about rocks and minerals using gamification and problem-based learning. This proposal was designed to be carried out with primary school prospective teachers during their training studies but can also be applied in either primary or secondary education levels. Students role-play aspirants who intend to enroll in a fictitious scientific police school. The admission test to that school consists of a practical case, where light has to be thrown on a death case. They need to determine if it could be a self-poisoning or murder case, deciphering some hints and using their basic geology knowledge and skills to show that they deserve a place in that school. This activity takes advantage of the popular TV dramas based on forensics to engage and motivate the students to work in the lab with minerals and rocks that the students could otherwise not have well received.

DOI: 10.4018/978-1-6684-4287-6.ch028

INTRODUCTION

Traditionally, science teaching has relied mainly on a positivist approach, where interpretation of all natural phenomena is achieved through theories and laws, and where the only role of students is to "know" the information (Ruiz, 2007; Vázquez & Manassero, 2007; Torres, 2010). Thus, science teaching has been done in a very different way from what "doing science" means (Vázquez & Manassero, 2007). This academist approach excludes the students' affective domain from the learning process (Mellado, 2014), since encouraging scientific attitudes, and creating a positive class atmosphere has been traditionally considered non-scientific. And one of the sciences where this problem is a great issue is Geology.

When compared to Biology, Geology is undoubtedly less appreciated by students, at all education levels (Betzner & Makerk, 2014; Sherman-Morris & McNeal, 2016). Usually, students link this discipline with boring content, harsh, and difficult, where learning by memorizing is almost the only option (Calonge, 2013; Orion, 2019). Commonly, students do not relate Geology content with their daily life, where Geology has an essential role and importance in our environment and activity. A solid basic scientific training will help students to face the world with a critical eye, and to make appropriate decisions.

On the other hand, since Geology is one of the Natural Sciences, it is indispensable to develop practical lessons to enhance its understanding and knowledge. This could be done through field trips and/or laboratory practices. However, when teachers are not specialized in Geology, this task can be very challenging. Furthermore, as stated before, students do not show a positive attitude towards Geology, which makes it more difficult (Zamalloa & Sanz, 2020). That is why teachers should implement active, motivating, and innovative methodologies, such as gamification.

With the aim of overcoming all the aforementioned difficulties and challenges, a Geology-based gamified lesson plan is proposed in this work. Through this proposal, which shares some characteristics with role-play and escape rooms, students can get familiar with the characteristics, composition and properties of several common rocks and minerals, in an active and motivating way.

BACKGROUND

Geology Low Status among Sciences

In Primary and Secondary education levels, overall interest in Geology (or Earth Sciences in general) is usually low and focused on those topics that students think may have a closer relationship to their daily life like earthquakes, climate change or seas (Hemmer et al., 2007). Generally, students underestimate other aspects related to Geology that have even more impact on their daily life, because they do not receive as much attention as they should during their education: air and water for living beings, soils for food production, energy sources (coal, oil), and materials for building all human constructions and most tools and gadgets used nowadays (Orion, 2019).

The real importance and relevance of Geology in human beings' lives is not properly reflected in society, which leads to a low status in learning plans and studies worldwide, due to a "*vicious cycle of unawareness*" (Betzener & Marek, 2014; Orion, 2017). Traditionally, Earth Sciences education has undergone improper practices, building misconceptions and misapprehensions about the relevance of Earth Science and the importance of Earth Science education. According to Orion (2019):

these attitudes perpetuate the narrow perspectives of reductionist policy makers in education, including politicians, scientists, and educators, with the result that there has been no appreciable change in the profile of Earth Science in schools, or in the way that it is taught.

Different analyses have shown that not only students may have a low opinion on Geology, but also science teachers (Betzener & Marek, 2014), since many times the educational value of Geology is perceived lower than that on Chemistry, Physics, or Biology. And this is a key point since teachers should influence students' interest in Geology. Interest can be encouraged by selecting appropriate topics which can be linked to students' everyday lives, connecting with their reality, to highlight the importance for society, and significance of those subjects.

Active Methodologies to Teach Geology to Prospective Teachers

During the last decades, many fast changes, and renovation/transformation phases, have taken place in education policies among European countries, leading to the European Higher Education Area (EHEA) and Bologna Process implementation. These globalization contexts have required Higher Education to evolve and adjust to new paradigms, transforming the teaching and learning process at university level (Murga-Menoyo, 2015). Bologna Process induced roles reversal in university classrooms, so nowadays students are the keystone of the educative process, being the teacher a guide in that process, through using different didactic methodologies.

Higher education is crucial to reach the goal of modifying attitudes towards Geology learning, especially during teacher training programs. Affective domain research works have shown that when a teacher is enthusiastic while teaching a subject, that enthusiasm is transferred to students, arousing positive emotions in them like enjoyment (Frenzel et al., 2009). Therefore, it is necessary to improve the affective domain towards Geology when training prospective teachers, and for this reason, some changes in sciences didactics are required.

Universities not only should train professionals, but also competent citizens able to adapt to future contexts and environments, and to face current and future problems. However, curricula structures usually do not allow critical, innovative, and creative learning; neither do personal skills such as responsibility, teamwork or empathy. Thus, to promote comprehensive learning in higher education students, several methods have been developed, with many examples available: Project Based Learning (Hernández-Barco et al., 2021), Gamification (Sánchez-Martín et al., 2020) or Flipped Classroom (Jeong et al., 2016).

Although escape rooms (or breakout edu) have their own identity, usually they are included among gamification approaches. In escape rooms, commonly, a group of people has to decipher several enigmas, puzzles, mysteries and riddles, in a limited time, to "escape from a room" or "open a locked box", for example. Usually, in learning environments, these approaches are carried out during a single session.

Many studies have shown that affective domain improves after joining those methodologies in higher education students (Lázaro, 2019; Sánchez-Martín et al., 2020; Sierra & Fernández-Sánchez, 2019; Yllana-Prieto et al., 2021). There are also evidence showing that using escape rooms in Geology teaching generates activating positive emotions, as enjoyment or curiosity, and also a cognitive conflict that allows students to realize which are their own conceptual limitations, leading them to an increase in Geology learning interest (Cañada-Cañada et al., 2021).

In this work, an innovative and different way of teaching Geology to prospective Primary School teachers is presented, based on gamified strategies, which set them (students) as the principal actors of the teaching/learning processes. This increases their motivation and creates an activation state that promotes active learning and empowerment during their learning process.

Forensics Geology and Gamification in Geology Teaching

As it has been highlighted before, when teaching sciences, it could be useful to simulate situations where knowledge and practice in different experimental sciences can be applied. Addressing scientific issues that could affect students' daily lives can be motivating and increase student participation (Casanoves et al., 2017). These approaches contribute to accomplishing science, technology, and society (STS) goals like increasing scientific literacy, highlighting the importance of science in everyday life, and helping to make responsible decisions about how to address different issues and challenges.

Simulating specifically criminal situations is one way to make science more accessible, motivating, and attractive to students and teachers. Geology is not an exception, so *Forensic Geology* can be used as a strategy, taking advantage of different successful TV shows like *Crime Scene Investigation* or *Silent Witness* (Pirrie, 2009; Murray, 2019). Although the portrayal of geology/geologists in these TV dramas may not resemble reality accurately (as it happens with all other scientific roles portrayed), definitely it has helped to raise awareness of Geology importance in actual Forensics. Forensic Geology works on the identification and analysis of geologic materials (sediments, soils, rocks and minerals) involved in a crime, or at a crime scene, using geological techniques. Examples of Forensic Geology contributions are widely available: Murray (2004), Bowen et al. (2005), Pirrie (2009), Ruffel (2010), Donnelly (2010), Ruffel et al. (2013), Di Magio et al. (2017), and Murray (2019).

In this context, Forensic Geology can be a powerful tool for Geology teaching, although so far it has not been exploited properly, with very few published examples (Pirrie et al., 2013; Carrillo et al., 2018). Pirrie et al. (2013) during the International School Science Fair (ISSF) 2013, which took place at Camborne Science and International Academy (Cornwall, United Kingdom), participated in a workshop on forensic geology. There, participant students could practice the recovery and analysis of geological trace evidence in a Forensic Geology-simulated context. In Carrillo et al. (2018) proposal, students develop their skills in map orientation using a compass, which leads them to find laboratories and sand/sediments samples, involved in a murder case.

GAMIFICATION LESSON PLAN

Proposal

In this work a didactic proposal is presented, based on solving a crime analyzing different hints and information, and using basic geologic techniques. This proposal was developed originally to be used in an undergraduate course for prospective Primary School teachers, although it can be easily adapted to Primary or Secondary education levels. Since 2017, around 400 students have passed through this experience, becoming one of the most appreciated and valued activities among students. The proposal is a Problem-Based Learning and Gamification combination, where students need to solve a problem, with common gamification elements (according to Toda et al., 2019) such as: acknowledgement (badges, achievements), points (scores), time pressure (countdown timer), progression, imposed choice, competition, cooperation, and novelty.

Benefits

As aforementioned, this gamified proposal has several benefits and advantages, i.e.:

1. **Motivation:** Students get involved and engaged with the activity once they know how the activity is going to be developed. The popularity of crime scene-related TV dramas, and the potential enjoyment that students feel, are key points to tie them up. What they think is going to be just another boring activity about minerals and rocks becomes a desirable activity.
2. **Autonomy and Reasoning:** Most work has to be done in an autonomous way, and students will need to practice their reasoning skills to solve the case. Activity is very challenging, and this can boost their minds.
3. **Active learning:** In this activity, students become actively involved in their learning process, since they are not just passively listening. They will need to analyze samples, search, and read information, and discuss options with their partners. Thus, the three learning domains (knowledge, skills, and attitudes) are developed.
4. **Student's learning self-control:** Before joining the activity, students have been instructed, in several lessons, about general Geology contents, as it is required in their training studies to become Primary School teachers. They learn about the planet Earth's structure, composition, and dynamics. But also, about formation and characteristics of rocks and minerals. But it is not until they face the problem to solve (the *case*), that they realize how much they need some basic knowledge and tools on Geology. With this activity, students detect which knowledge and/or skills have been properly acquired, and if any of them needs to be further developed.
5. **Information for the teacher:** This gamified activity provides the teacher with valuable information about the learning progress of the students, if they have acquired the required knowledge and skills, if additional emphasis has to be done on some concepts or processes, etc.
6. **Creativity and imagination**: Since the proposal is a gamified role-play, where they need to solve a crime analyzing hints and evidence, to eventually solve the case, some doses of creativity and imagination are required.
7. **Social skills:** Students work in pairs, so it is necessary to discuss and argue to reach an agreement about the possible case solution. Investigation is a collaborative work between the two partners. But, on the other hand, students are discouraged from sharing their findings and ideas with the other pairs, so a healthy dose of competitiveness is developed. Competitiveness has an encouraging effect on students *to perform better* than others.
8. **Digital literacy:** Most of the information required to solve the case set out in the activity can be obtained from the hints, evidence, and tools the students have. But an investigation about heavy metals, poisoning symptoms, etc. has to be done, and the only access to extra information is their cell phones. Reliable and trustworthy information sites will be needed, so they will have to work on their digital literacy skills.
9. **Scientific literacy:** Finally, through this practical experience students will broaden and consolidate their scientific literacy, working on different scientific issues (geology, chemical composition, toxicity, etc.), and also on science-technology-society relationships.

Previous Knowledge

As previously stated, this proposal was developed originally to be used in an undergraduate course of prospective Primary School teachers, although it can be easily adapted to Primary or Secondary education levels. Activity usually takes place during the 6th semester, in the context of a Biology and Geology Teaching subject. Before joining the activity, students have undertaken lessons covering basic knowledge about Earth (origin, structure, and dynamics), minerals (characteristics, properties, formation, usefulness), and rocks (formation, types, characteristics, usefulness). Most of those basic concepts, such as Mohs scale of mineral hardness, or the streak of a mineral, are addressed in a theoretical way during the lessons, so a hands-on activity to explore them is an excellent complement to consolidate learning.

Activity Overview

In our proposal, students become *aspirants* to join a fictitious *Scientific Police School*, which access test is a practical skills exam where they are asked to solve a crime using basic Geology knowledge and techniques. A working place is set up for developing the proposal, so students (*aspirants*) have different tools and resources and are allowed to search on Internet for further information, when needed. Before starting, the teacher introduces the case, telling them that a murder has taken place, and that through preliminary analysis and interrogation some information has been obtained. They are told about the victim's work and relationships with workmates, different observations that colleagues made, and what hypotheses are being considered, so far. In the following sections, all details are provided.

Materials Needed

One of the main advantages of this proposal is that no expensive or technical resources or materials are needed. The key material is a common scholar rocks and minerals collection, where adequate samples should be represented, which is available at almost every school science lab. It may include: aragonite, baryte, basalt, biotite, calcite, cinnabar, conglomerate, flint, fluorite, galena, granite, gypsum, halite, hematite, lava, magnetite, marble, pumice, pyrite, quartz, quartzite, sandstone, slate, sulphur, sylvite, and talc. In this proposal, only 6 minerals and 6 rocks are needed, but the number of samples can be up- or downscaled depending on the students' level and available time. As it will be described below, the selection of minerals has to be done according to the desired outcome of the activity.

In addition to this, some tools and props are required for proper plot and atmosphere setting. Before students enter the laboratory, a working place for each pair has to be prepared and equipped with the following elements: a basic rocks and minerals identification guide, a magnifier lens, a steel nail, a magnet, a copper coin, and a piece of unglazed porcelain (Figure 1). Besides, they are provided with a results sheet, which would be the *Final Report*. The purpose of each element is:

- **Basic rocks and minerals identification guide:** A simple identification guide can be used. Usually, school minerals and rocks collections bring an identification guide. In our proposal, this guide was customized by adding some simulated police anagrams on its cover, to emulate an *official police identification guide*. Guide should include essential information such as color, streak, hardness, relative weight, brightness, composition, habit, etc.

Figure 1. Materials in participants' workbench

- **Magnifier lens:** to take a closer look at the structure of the sample, to determine, for example, if it is composed of smaller fragments.
- **Steel nail and copper coin:** students need to determine, approximately, the hardness of the samples, in order to identify them. If the sample can be scratched using a fingernail, its hardness (on Mohs scale) should be below 2.5. When a fingernail cannot scratch the sample, but a copper coin can do so, the hardness is between 2.5 and 3.5. If the copper coin is not hard enough to scratch the sample, then a steel nail can be used. If it scratches the sample, the harness should be between 3.5 and 6.5, otherwise it should be higher than 6.5.
- **Magnet:** to detect magnetic properties in samples.
- **Piece of unglazed porcelain:** to perform a streak test, a method used to determine the color of a mineral in powdered form. There is no need to use professional (and expensive) streak plates, so a piece of a broken common porcelain coffee mug can be used.
- **Final Report sheet:** In this report, *aspirants* (students) should record their findings and, finally, their opinion about the death hypothesis, based on their findings (Figure 2).

Before starting the activity, the teacher has to prepare an *evidence bench*, where the selected minerals and rocks should be placed into zip bags (*evidence bags*), and conveniently labelled as *Evidence #1*, *Evidence #2*, etc. (Figure 3). The selection may include six rocks and six minerals, carefully selected depending on the desired denouement of the case/activity. Some of the possible solutions for the mystery could be:

Figure 2. Example of a Final Report Sheet

SCIENTIFIC POLICE SCHOOL SELECTION PROCESS

Group [ ] Date [ ]

Team			
Members	1:	2:	
EVIDENCES IDENTIFICATION			
Minerals		*Rocks*	
Evidence #1		Evidence #7	
Evidence #2		Evidence #8	
Evidence #3		Evidence #9	
Evidence #4		Evidence #10	
Evidence #5		Evidence #11	
Evidence #6		Evidence #12	
CONCLUSIONS			

- **Option 1, Mercury self-poisoning:** Among the evidence rocks and minerals the teacher can include cinnabar. This mineral is potentially toxic due to its mercury content, so an accidental self-poisoning could solve the mystery.
- **Option 2, Lead self-poisoning:** In this case, galena can be included among the evidence rocks and minerals the teacher prepares before the activity. Galena could be toxic because of its lead content, being another case of accidental self-poisoning.
- **Option 3, Arsenic, antimony, thallium, or chromium self-poisoning:** If arsenopyrite, stibnite, lorandite, or chromite are available, arsenic, antimony, thallium or chromium self-poisoning, respectively, could be an option.
- **Option 4, No self-poisoning:** No potentially toxic rocks or minerals are included in the evidence set. Therefore, accidental self-poisoning is not an option, and a murderer is needed.

Depending on the minerals and rocks available, the teacher can consider other options, being the aforementioned options some examples.

Figure 3. Evidence bench

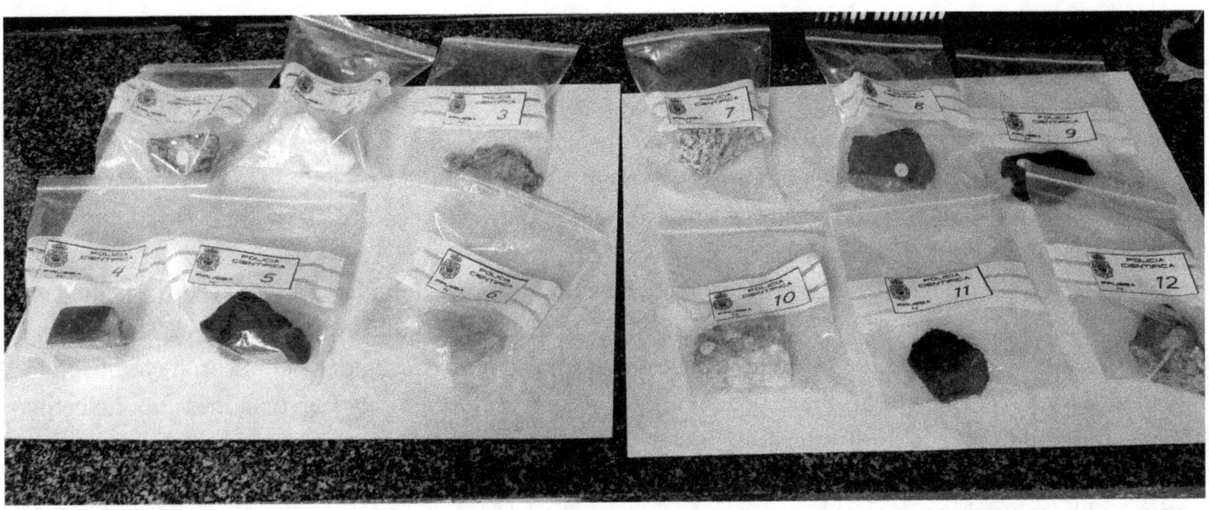

To support the case, it is necessary to adapt the case plot depending on the desired solution previously chosen. For instance, in case the teacher considers the option of mercury self-poisoning, the observed symptoms of the victim, told to the students during the *case explanation*, should match that poisoning: burning in the stomach and throat, bloody diarrhea and vomiting, numbness or pain in certain parts of the skin, uncontrollable shaking or tremor, inability to walk well, blindness and double vision, memory problems and/or seizures (Medline, 2021a). For lead self-poisoning, some of the symptoms could be: abdominal pain and cramping, aggressive behavior, anemia, constipation, difficulty sleeping, headaches, hearing loss, irritability, low appetite and energy, and/or reduced sensations (Medline, 2021b). When using arsenic, self-poisoning symptoms may include: drowsiness, headaches, confusion, severe diarrhea, metallic taste in the mouth and garlicky breath, excess saliva, problems swallowing, blood in the urine, cramping muscles, hair loss, stomach cramps, convulsions, excessive sweating, vomiting, and/or diarrhea

(Biggers & Paddock, 2018). Vomiting, watery diarrhea, collapse, irregular respiration, and hypothermia can be used as antimony poisoning symptoms (Risk Assessment Information System, 1997). For thallium, symptoms may include: severe stomach pain, nausea, vomiting, diarrhea, painful and rapidly progressing peripheral neuropathy (numbness, tingling and pain, especially on the soles and palms), and/or sudden hair loss that progresses to widespread alopecia (Ngan, 2013). Finally, in case chromium is selected, intense gastrointestinal irritation or ulceration and corrosion, epigastric pain, nausea, vomiting, diarrhea, vertigo, fever, muscle cramps, hemorrhagic diathesis, toxic nephritis, renal failure, intravascular hemolysis, circulatory collapse, liver damage, and/or acute multisystem organ failure can be listed as symptoms (Agency for Toxic Substances and Disease Registry, 2008).

It is necessary to state that there is no risk for students in this activity, since the limited handling and exposure time to minerals containing heavy metals makes it totally safe.

Needless to say, that if this activity is carried out with different groups of students, it is necessary to change the case solution between groups; otherwise, they may comment on the solution to their classmates, spoiling the activity.

Running the Activity

After all necessary equipment has been properly set up, students can join the activity. They should be grouped, preferably, in pairs. Usually, the activity requires approximately three hours to be completed, but duration can be easily reduced, if desired (e.g., selecting fewer samples to identify). First of all, students are told by the *instructor* (teacher) that, from then on, they become *Scientific Police School aspirants,* who are about to participate in an *access test*, and only the best candidates will be admitted. The access test consists of *solving* a murder case, where they will need to show their reasoning skills and Geology knowledge.

Obviously, the case plot described below can be customized, and/or adapted, to fit the students' level and interests. With the aid of a visual presentation, the teacher should present the case. The different diapositives shown could include fictious police anagrams, to help to create the appropriate atmosphere. The instructor tells the aspirants that a dead body was found in the Geology Lab two days ago. Investigation has found that the victim was a geologist who used to work there, identified as Professor [fictitious name]. All workmates were conveniently interrogated, and some information has been gathered: (a) the victim had been working several months on some samples of rocks and minerals (all samples have been placed in evidence bags, labeled as Evidence #1, Evidence #2, etc.); (b) some of the victim's workmates described striking symptoms on him [now the teacher should provide symptoms according to the desired solution of the case, as explained before]; (c) preliminary forensics report has indicated that the cause of the death seems to be poisoning, maybe heavy metal poisoning, and that no signs of violence or fighting have been found; (d) workmates revealed that there was an open enmity between the victim and a close collaborator, Dr. [fictitious name]; (e) that collaborator, the main suspect, has no alibi, and stated that the victim might have dead because of accidental poisoning.

After the case explanation, *aspirants* are told that they are going to have one hour to analyze all the evidence in order to identify them, to assess if those samples could be the cause of an accidental self-poisoning, or otherwise a murder is required. A countdown timer is then started. They are asked to work in pairs, collaboratively. But, since their *access to the police school* is at stake, information should not flow between pairs; otherwise, *competitors* may benefit from it. To identify each sample in the evidence bags, students need to use the *Police Rocks and Minerals Identification Guide*, and they need to find out: approximate hardness (using a copper nail, copper coin, and steel nail), strake (with unglazed porcelain), relative weight, magnetic properties, etc. They are allowed to search the internet for additional information, if needed. If the sample is identified, a search for its chemical composition has to be made, to search for heavy metals. Samples without heavy metals, or other potentially toxic compounds, should be discarded as the cause of self-poisoning. All the information about identification has to be recorded in the Final Report. During the analysis, the teacher can be around supervising how the students perform the different tests and solving problems or questions.

When the count-down timer ends, the aspirants are told that they do not have any more time for samples analysis, and all evidence is moved away. Now they have around 15 minutes to fill in the Conclusions section of the Final Report. This is the time to sum up all the information that they collected, and decide if, according to that, the self-poisoning hypothesis could be feasible, or otherwise, should be rejected. Finally, all the filled-in reports are gathered up by the teacher/instructor.

Then, the instructor can comment on the results on the Reports, analyzing each of the samples/evidence, and the answers of the students/aspirants. Finally, identification and results discussion should be done all together, giving the students the opportunity to defend and explain their findings. To end up, with all the samples correctly identified, the correct hypothesis is revealed. Those students capable of solving the case are awarded badges and *are allowed to proceed to the next test.* Students unable to solve the case *are rejected and will not join the Scientific Police School.*

SOLUTIONS AND RECOMMENDATIONS

There is no doubt that when learning sciences it is essential to include practical experiences, where teachers usually pretend to achieve different objectives: motivation, experiential knowledge, close environment knowledge, better understanding of concepts and theories, skills development (observation, problem-solving, etc.) (Carrillo, 1996). Geology teaching studies have been traditionally underdeveloped when compared to other sciences like Biology, Chemistry, or Physics. A brief search for research papers on this topic reveals that there is still a long way to go on this subject. As stated before, Geology commonly has a low relative weight along Primary and Secondary education levels (Lacreu, 2014; Araujo & Toledo, 2014; Casas et al., 2016). In addition to this, it is also true that often Geology teaching is done by teachers from other fields of knowledge. This leads to a situation where Geology-related learning materials are less abundant, less diverse, and more conventional. This makes teaching and learning Geology a challenge not only for the students, but also for the teachers. Therefore, an extra effort has to be done to redirect this situation. And here this is the point where games and gamification can be valuable tools.

Although gaming is still considered mainly as an enjoyment activity, there are many other environments where games can be applied, i.e. in education processes. In the last years, games interest has been increasing: the number of hours spent using video games is constantly increasing, but also board games are recovering their prominence (Corenllà et al., 2020). Even escape rooms, which were created with a non-learning purpose, have gained increasing importance in educative environments, since skills like teamwork, lateral thinking, communication, and working under pressure can be enhanced (Sánchez-Martín et al., 2020). Escape room methodologies can also be useful to increase group cohesion, to help learning immersion, and to set up alternative evaluation methods (Lázaro, 2019).

Since Vigotsky (1978) and Piaget (1999) defended the high educational value of games, many studies have shown that gaming plays a key role in students' learning and development. However, most schools only use games to fill in time gaps, ignoring the real potential (Garaigordobil, 1992; Corenllà et al., 2020). In kindergarten education it is widely accepted that games are an essential part of the learning process, but when moving to Primary Education, games are not considered "serious work" anymore. Games, thus, are related to enjoyment, joy, and fun, but not to yield, effort or productivity (Trujillo, 2017). Nevertheless, things can be different if the game/gamification are carefully selected, because it can help students to engage in the learning activity, increasing their attention, and leading them to memorize, take efforts and learn. Games can help to develop concentration and arouse curiosity, which ultimately, leads to learning. Playing games is a complete activity which encompasses all knowledge areas: physical, psychic (thinking, express), affective (feelings), and social (Marín et al., 2015). It is necessary to develop a favorable attitude in students to reach meaningful learning. Students are the main subjects of their own learning process, so it can be useful to consider their previous knowledge and experiences to promote meaningful learning. It is crucial to connect with their interests, with the things that motivate them, that belong to their world, where games usually are a relevant activity (Coll, 1998).

It has been shown that escape rooms have emotional effects on higher education level students, since they feel enjoyment, happiness, pleasure, stress, anxiety, and even frustration (Sierra & Fernández-Sánchez, 2019). In a similar way, participants who joined the activity described in this work consider that our proposal is motivating and amusing, highlighting teamwork and practical application of theoretical concepts, as two key aspects. Another highly valued aspect is the healthy competition atmosphere created in the classroom. Accordingly, escape rooms may be an indispensable tool in prospective teachers training, since they lead to meaningful learning through a motivating activity (Lázaro, 2019).

Geology, like all other Earth Sciences, has slightly benefited from gamified approaches at different education levels. It is possible to find pioneer approaches based on card games (Muñoz, 1994), word puzzles (Ruiz, 1992), role-playing games (Alda, 1997), and board games (Andaluz, 1994; Castillo, 1994; Gil, 1996) (Cornellà et al., 2020). Later, many teachers have occasionally used gamification in practical lessons, but usually englobed in a more traditional teaching strategy. But gamification and Geology have been linked not only in academic environments, but also in non-formal environments, i.e. scientific fairs, summer camps, museums, etc. In these environments, gamified proposals usually were developed based on adapted board games, traditional games, or gymkhanas. In addition to this, in the last twenty years, digital technologies have widened possibilities through developing video games, websites, and apps related to Earth Sciences content. Even problem-based learning approaches can be designed as gamified experiences, like the proposal described in this and previous work (Carrillo et al., 2018).

Teachers should feel properly trained to teach sciences in general, and Geology in particular; otherwise it will not be possible to generate a desired change in science didactics. Those teachers that trust their capabilities are more prone to enroll in innovative methodologies, far beyond textbooks and traditional lessons (Borrachero et al., 2013), developing better attitudes to science in their students. Therefore, it is important that prospective teachers undergo different active learning methodologies, as the proposal we describe in this work, resulting in a richer professional practice.

But gamification is much more complex than just playing a game. Teachers need to select carefully the desired objectives to reach, so then proper planification and design can be done. This might be hard work; therefore some resistance can be expected from gamification unexperienced teachers. Thus, more research and outreach activities should be done.

FUTURE RESEARCH DIRECTIONS

When teaching Geology, gamification does not need to be a lab- or classroom-only activity. Field trips and open air activities are also perfect settlements for this methodology. Currently, there are different studies being carried out to explore the potential benefits of applying gamification in museums, itineraries, permanent or temporal expositions, and many more environments (Cornellà et al., 2020). Possibilities increase even more if technologies like augmented reality and/or geolocalization are implemented into the gamified activity.

Gamification studies in learning environments allow to analyze gamification benefits in students motivation. Reviewing different works in this direction (Ortiz-Colón et al., 2017), it can be observed that motivation in gamified activities leads to an increase in students compromise and learning. And also the huge influence that gamification has on cognitive development, emotions, and socializing processes developed along the activity.

A systematic review about gamified science experiences research papers (Kalogiannakis et al., 2021), published between 2012 and 2020, revealed that 66% of them used mixed-method approaches, 29% used a quantitative approach, and only 4% used a qualitative approach. This work also revealed that most of the data collection was done using questionnaires, interviews and observation forms. Another two relevant findings where: (1) most of the studies were carried out in secondary and higher education, being primary education studies much less numerous; (2) the most popular topics were related to Biology, followed by Chemistry and Physics, with Geology being underrepresented.

It is also true that gamification learning studies have produced mixed results over the years, raising doubts and controversies over their potential; therefore, further research has to be undertaken to analyze the effects of gamification in learning science (Kalogiannakis et al., 2021).

Back to our proposal, a longitudinal study of several years is being carried out to analyze the effects on the participating students. In our study, different aspects like motivation, science interest, Geology interest, emotions, and self-efficacy are measured before and after joining the activity. Preliminary results are promising, and publication of the results will add light on gamification effects on Geology teaching/learning.

CONCLUSION

As previously discussed throughout the chapter, there are many reasons that make gamification a powerful resource in teaching environments. Not long ago, gamification approaches were restricted and limited to lower education levels; however, currently gamification has spread to all ages in formal and non-formal learning contexts. Although Geology teaching has joined gamification, there is still a long way to go. Gamification experiences increase motivation levels and engagement among students, but also among teachers. The proposal presented in this chapter can help to develop a connection between students and Geology, bringing it to their close reality and connecting it with their interests. Gamification will be an essential tool in the forthcoming years to develop innovative learning plans.

ACKNOWLEDGMENT

This research was supported by the Research Project PID2020-115214RB-I00/AEI/10.13039/501100011033, the Government of Extremadura [Grant GR21047 and the Proyect IB18004], and the Ministry of Science, Innovation and Universities [BES-2017-081566].

REFERENCES

Agency for Toxic Substances and Disease Registry. (2008). *Chromium Toxicity. Clinical Assessment - History, Signs and Symptoms.* https://www.atsdr.cdc.gov/csem/chromium/signs_and_symptoms.html

Alda, F. L. (1997). Tratamiento de residuos: Un juego de simulación. *Enseñanza de las Ciencias de la Tierra*, *5*(1), 49–53.

Andaluz, N. (1994). Necesitamos ayuda; ¡sálvanos!: Un juego para enseñar y aprender geología. *Enseñanza de las Ciencias de la Tierra*, *2*(1), 278–280.

Araujo, E. P. R., & Toledo, M. C. M. (2014). Ciências da Terra em cursos que habilitam ao magistério de Ciências Naturais para o ensino fundamental. *Terræ Didatica*, *10*(3), 319–330. doi:10.20396/td.v10i3.8637347

Betzner, J. P., & Marek, E. A. (2014). Teacher and Student Perceptions of Earth Science and Its Educational Value in Secondary Schools. *Creative Education*, *5*(11), 1019–1031. doi:10.4236/ce.2014.511116

Borrachero, A., Brígido, M., Costillo, E., Bermejo, M. L., & Mellado, V. (2013). Relationship between self-efficacy beliefs and emotions of future teachers of Physics in secondary education. *Asia-Pacific Forum on Science Learning and Teaching*, *14*(2), 1–11.

Bowen, G. J., Wassenaar, L. I., & Hobson, K. A. (2005). Global application of stable hydrogen and oxygen isotopes to wildlife forensics. *Oecologia*, *143*(3), 337–348. doi:10.100700442-004-1813-y PMID:15726429

Calonge, A. (2013). Current state of the Geology Teaching, particulary the cristalography, mineralogy and petrology contents. *Seminarios SEM*, *10*, 22–35.

Cañada-Cañada, F., Hernández-Barco, M. A., Sánchez-Martín, J., & Corbacho-Cuello, I. (2021). Estudo comparativo das diferentes estratégias de aprendizagem baseada em jogos: Rendimento emocional dos professores em formação durante a aprendizagem das ciências. *Revista Internacional de Pesquisa em Didática das Ciências e Matemática*, *2*, 1–25.

Carrillo, L. (1996). Los problemas prácticos en Geología: Problemas, posibilidades y propuestas. *Enseñanza de las Ciencias de la Tierra*, *4*(2), 120–123.

Carrillo, L., Luzón, M. A., Mayayo, M. J., Soria, A. R., Yuste, A., & Gil, A. (2018). Resolviendo un asesinato: Una experiencia con la Geología Forense como estrategia de enseñanza-aprendizaje en la Educación Secundaria. *Enseñanza de las Ciencias de la Tierra*, *26*(2), 163–175.

Casanoves, M., Salvadó, Z., González, A., Valls, C., & Novo, M. T. (2017). Learning genetics through a scientific inquiry game. *Journal of Biological Education*, *51*(2), 99–106. doi:10.1080/00219266.2016.1177569

Casas, N., Maguregi, G., Zamalloa, T., Echevarría, I., Fernández, M., & Sanz, J. (2016). Las salidas de campo y la Geología. El perfil académico y la actitud del profesorado de la ESO en la CAPV. *Enseñanza de las Ciencias de la Tierra*, *24*(2), 213–220.

Castillo, E. (1994). El Rocopoly, un recurso didáctico para la enseñanza de la petrología. *Enseñanza de las Ciencias de la Tierra*, *2*(1), 280–281.

Coll, C. (1998). Significado y sentido en el aprendizaje escolar. Reflexiones en torno al concepto de aprendizaje significativo. *Infancia y Aprendizaje*, *11*(41), 131–142. doi:10.1080/02103702.1988.10822196

Cornellà, P., Estebanell, M., & Brusi, D. (2020). Gamificación y aprendizaje basado en juegos. Consideraciones generales y algunos ejemplos para la Enseñanza de la Geología. *Enseñanza de las Ciencias de la Tierra*, *28*(1), 5–19.

Di Maggio, R., Donnelly, L., Al Naimi, K., Barone, P., Salvador, F., Dawson, L., Dixon, R., Fitzpatrick, R., Gradusova, O., Nesterina, E., Peleneva, M., Ushacova, O., Molina, C. M., Pirrie, D., Ruffell, A., McKinley, J., Sagripanti, G., Villalba, D., Schneck, B., & Forbes, S. (2017). Global developments in forensic geology. *Episodes*, *40*(2), 120–131. doi:10.18814/epiiugs/2017/v40i2/017014

Donnelly, L. J. (2010). *The role of geoforensics in policing and law enforcement*. Emergency Global Barclay Media Limited.

Frenzel, A. C., Goetz, T., Lüdtke, O., Pekrun, R., & Sutton, R. E. (2009). Emotional transmission in the classroom: Exploring the relationship between teacher and student enjoyment. *Journal of Educational Psychology*, *101*(3), 705–716. doi:10.1037/a0014695

Garaigordobil, M. (1992). *Juego cooperativo y socialización en el aula*. Seco Olea.

Gil, S. (1996). Los juegos didácticos en la asignatura Paleontología. Un eslabón en el proceso de aprendizaje de los estudiantes. *Enseñanza de las Ciencias de la Tierra*, *4*(3), 224–226.

Hemmer, I., Bayrhuber, H., Häußler, P., Hemmer, M., Hlawatsch, S., Hoffmann, L., & Raffelsiefer, M. (2007). Students' interest in geoscience topics, contexts and methods. *Geographie und ihre Didaktik. Journal of Geography Education*, *4*, 185–197.

Hernández-Barco, M., Sánchez-Martín, J., Corbacho-Cuello, I., & Cañada-Cañada, F. (2021). Emotional Performance of a Low-Cost Eco-Friendly Project Based Learning Methodology for Science Education : An Approach in Prospective Teachers. *Sustainability*, *13*(3385), 1–19. doi:10.3390u13063385

Jeong, J. S., González-Gómez, D., & Cañada-Cañada, F. (2016). Students' perceptions and emotions toward learning in a flipped general science classroom. *Journal of Science Education and Technology*, *25*(5), 747–758. doi:10.100710956-016-9630-8

Lacreu, H. L. (2014). Aciertos, distorsiones y falacias en la enseñanza de las ciencias naturales de la educación secundaria obligatoria de Argentina. *Terræ Didatica*, *10*(3), 217–226. doi:10.20396/td.v10i3.8637323

Lázaro, I. (2019). Escape Room como propuesta de gamificación en educación. *Revista Educativa Hekademos*, *27*(12), 71–79.

Marín, V., López, M., & Berea, G. (2015). Can gamification be introduced within primary classes? *Digital Education Review*, *27*, 55–68.

MedlinePlus, United States National Library of Medicine. (2021a). *Lead poisoning*. https://medlineplus.gov/ency/article/002473.htm

MedlinePlus, United States National Library of Medicine. (2021b). *Mercury poisoning*. https://medlineplus.gov/ency/article/002476.htm

Mellado, V., Borrachero, B., Melo, L. V., Dávila-Acedo, M. A., Cañada, F., Conde, M. C., Costillo, E., Cubero, J., Esteban, R., Martínez, G., Ruiz, C., Sánchez, J., Garritz, A., Mellado, L., Vázquez-Bernal, B., Jimenez-Pérez, R., & Bermejo, M. L. (2014). Las emociones en la enseñanza de las ciencias. *Enseñanza de las Ciencias*, *32*(3), 11–36. doi:10.5565/rev/ensciencias.1478

Muñoz, J. (1994). Ludolitos. *Enseñanza de las Ciencias de la Tierra*, *2*(1), 282–284.

Murga-Menoyo, M. Á. (2015). Competencias para el desarrollo sostenible: Las capacidades, actitudes y valores meta de la educación en el marco de la Agenda global post-2015. *Foro de Educación*, *13*(19), 55–83. doi:10.14516/fde.2015.013.019.004

Murray, L. (2019). Solving crimes with geology. *Engineering & Technology*, *14*(5), 54–57. doi:10.1049/et.2019.0506

Murray, R. C. (2004). *Evidence from the Earth: Forensic Geology and Criminal Investigation*. Mountain Press Publishing.

Ngan, V. (2013). *Thallium poisoning*. https://dermnetnz.org/topics/thallium-poisoning/

Orion, N. (2017). The relevance of earth science for informed citizenship: Its potential and fulfillment. In L. Leite, L. Dourado, A. Afonso, & S. Morgado (Eds.), *Contextualizing Teaching to Improving Learning: The Case of Science and Geograph* (pp. 41–56). Nova Science Publishers.

Orion, N. (2019). The future challenge of Earth science education research. *Disciplinary and Interdisciplinary Science Education Research*, *1*(3), 1–8. doi:10.118643031-019-0003-z

Ortiz-Colón, M. A., Jordán, J., & Agredal, M. (2018). Gamification in education: An overview on the state of the art. *Educação e Pesquisa*, *44*, 1–17.

Paddock, M., & Biggers, A. (2018). *What is arsenic poisoning?* https://www.medicalnewstoday.com/articles/241860

Piaget, J. (1999). *Play, dreams and imitation in child-hood*. Psychology Press.

Pirrie, D. (2009). Forensic geology in serious crime investigation. *Geology Today*, *25*(5), 188–192. doi:10.1111/j.1365-2451.2009.00729.x

Pirrie, D., Donnelly, L., Rollinson, G. K., Butcher, A. R., Dawson, L. A., & Pirrie, H. A. (2013). Forensic geology at the International School Science Fair 2013. *Geology Today*, *29*(6), 222–228. doi:10.1111/gto.12028

Ruffel, A. (2010). Forensic pedology, forensic geology, forensic geoscience, geoforensics and soil forensics. *Forensic Science International*, *202*(1-3), 9–12. doi:10.1016/j.forsciint.2010.03.044 PMID:20430544

Ruffel, A., Pirrie, D., & Power, M. R. (2013). Issues and opportunities in urban forensic geology. *Geological Society of London, Special Publications*, *384*(1), 147–161. doi:10.1144/SP384.19

Ruiz, F. J. (2007). Modelos didácticos para la enseñanza de las ciencias naturales. *Revista Latinoamericana de Estudios Educativos*, *3*, 41–60.

Ruiz, L. (1992). Pasatiempos y Geología: posibilidades didácticas. In Actas de VII Simposio sobre Enseñanza de la Geología (pp. 313-351). Instituto de Ciencias de la Educación, Universidade de Santiago de Compostela.

Sánchez-Martín, J., Corrales-Serrano, M., Luque-Sendra, A., & Zamora-Polo, F. (2020). Exit for success. Gamifying science and technology for university students using escape-room. A preliminary approach. *Heliyon*, *6*(7), e04340. doi:10.1016/j.heliyon.2020.e04340 PMID:32671257

Sanmugam, M., Abdullah, Z., Mohamed, H., Aris, B., Zaid, N. M., & Suhadi, S. M. (2016). The Affiliation between Student Achievement and Elements of Gamification in Learning Science. In *Proceedings of the 2016 4th International Conference on Information and Communication Technology* (pp. 1-4). 10.1109/ICoICT.2016.7571962

Sherman-Morris, K., & McNeal, K. S. (2016). Understanding Perceptions of the Geosciences Among Minority and Nonminority Undergraduate Students. *Journal of Geoscience Education*, *64*(2), 147–156. doi:10.5408/15-112.1

Sierra, M. C., & Fernández-Sánchez, M. R. (2019). Gamificando el aula universitaria. Análisis de una experiencia de Escape Room en educación superior. *Revista de Estudios y Experiencias en Educación*, *18*(36), 105–115. doi:10.21703/rexe.20191836sierra15

The Risk Assessment Information System. (1997). *Formal Toxicity Summary for Antimony*. https://rais.ornl.gov/tox/profiles/antimony.html

Toda, A. M., Klock, A. C. T., Oliveira, W., Palomino, P. T., Rodrigues, L. R., Shi, L., Bittencourt, I., Gasparini, I., Isotani, S., & Cristea, A. I. (2019). Analysing gamification elements in educational environments using an existing Gamification taxonomy. *Smart Learning Environments*, *6*(16), 1–14. doi:10.118640561-019-0106-1

Torres, M. (2010). La enseñanza tradicional de las ciencias versus las nuevas tendencias educativas. *Revista Electrónica Educare*, *14*(1), 131–142. doi:10.15359/ree.14-1.11

Trujillo, F. (2017). Del juego a la gamificación. Mitos y leyendas de las TIC. *Aula de innovación educativa, 267*, 38-40.

Vázquez, A., & Manassero, M. A. (2007). En defensa de las actitudes y emociones en la educación científica (II): Evidencias empíricas derivadas de la investigación. *Revista Eureka Sobre Enseñanza y Divulgación de las Ciencias*, *4*(3), 417–441. doi:10.25267/Rev_Eureka_ensen_divulg_cienc.2007.v4.i3.03

Vygotsky, L. S. (1978). *Mind in society: The development of higher psychological processes*. Harvard University Press.

Yllana-Prieto, F., Jeong, J. S., & González-Gómez, D. (2021). An Online-Based Edu-Escape Room: A Comparison Study of a Multidimensional Domain of PSTs with Flipped Sustainability-STEM Contents. *Sustainability*, *13*(3), 1–18. doi:10.3390u13031032 PMID:34676112

ADDITIONAL READING

Dichev, C., & Dicheva, D. (2017). Gamifying education: what is known, what is believed and what remains uncertain: a critical review. *International Journal of Educational Technology in Higher Education*, *14*(9), 1–36. doi:10.118641239-017-0042-5

Morris, B. J., Croker, S., Zimmerman, C., Gill, D., & Romig, C. (2013). Gaming science: The "Gamification" of scientific thinking. *Frontiers in Psychology*, *4*, 607. doi:10.3389/fpsyg.2013.00607 PMID:24058354

Pirrie, D., & Ruffell, A. (2012). Forensic Geology and Soils. In N. Marquez Grant & J. Roberts (Eds.), *Forensic Ecology Handbook* (pp. 183–201). John Wiley & Sons. doi:10.1002/9781118374016.ch12

Roca, N., & Garcia-Valles, M. (2020). Trainee Teacher Experience in Geoscience Education: Can We Do Better? *Geoheritage*, *12*(4), 92. doi:10.100712371-020-00518-8

Ruffell, A., & McKinley, J. (2008). *Geoforensics*. Wiley Blackwell. doi:10.1002/9780470758854

Samways, G. (2020). *Gamification of Geosciences - A way to get a new generation engaged?* https://www.linkedin.com/pulse/gamification-geosciences-way-get-new-generation-engaged-samways

Westrin, P., Berthet, T., Brajkovič, R., Pirard, E., Murphy, M., Bellucci, L., Käär, K., Herrera, J., & Kavanagh, R. (2020). Can we teach children geology using one of the world's most popular video games? *European Geologist*, *50*, 83–86.

Zamalloa, T., & Sanz, J. (2020). Attitudes of secondary school students towards geology in Spain. *Research in Science & Technological Education*, 1–24. Advance online publication. doi:10.1080/02635143.2020.1845641

KEY TERMS AND DEFINITIONS

Earth Sciences: Group of sciences related to the planet Earth (lithosphere, atmosphere, hydrosphere, and biosphere). Earth sciences use tools from geology, physics, chemistry, geography, biology, and mathematics.

Forensic Geology: Analysis of crime evidence where minerals, rocks, soils, sediments, and other materials Earth materials are involved, in order to solve a crime.

Gamification: Application of game elements and game dynamics and mechanics in a non-game context.

Geology: Science that focuses on rocks and minerals, which compose the Earth, and the different processes affecting them along time.

Heavy Metal: Metals with relatively high densities, atomic weights, or atomic numbers.

Role-Play: Changing of one's behavior to assume a role.

Toxic Heavy Metal: Any heavy metal potentially toxic, especially in environmental contexts. The main toxic heavy metals are cadmium, mercury, and lead, but also arsenic, manganese, chromium, cobalt, nickel, copper, zinc, silver, antimony, and thallium.

Chapter 29
Entrepreneurial Competences Development Through Game Strategies:
A Case Study of a Card Game Focused on Social Transformation With Health Students

Adriana Justin Cerveira Kampff
https://orcid.org/0000-0003-1581-1693
Pontifical Catholic University of Rio Grande do Sul, Brazil

Ana Cecília B. Nunes
https://orcid.org/0000-0002-4018-2676
Pontifical Catholic University of Rio Grande do Sul, Brazil

Naira Maria Lobraico Libermann
https://orcid.org/0000-0002-6647-0385
Pontifical Catholic University of Rio Grande do Sul, Brazil

Gabriela Birnfeld Kurtz
Pontifical Catholic University of Rio Grande do Sul, Brazil

Débora Conforto
Pontifical Catholic University of Rio Grande do Sul, Brazil

ABSTRACT

Game strategies have been used in educational contexts to enhance engagement. This research discusses a higher education experience using an online tailor-made card game to develop entrepreneurial competencies within health students on an online course. The project counted 892 participants from 12 different health majors and is analyzed to address the following research question: How can playful strategies assist in developing students' entrepreneurial competencies in higher education, especially those focused on a social change goal? The research is qualitative exploratory based on a case study with a non-probabilistic sampling. The findings indicate the implemented strategies greatly enhanced the student engagement and co-responsibility in their learning processes, along with the expansion of interaction and experimentation.

DOI: 10.4018/978-1-6684-4287-6.ch029

INTRODUCTION

One of the biggest challenges in education is to keep the students engaged, i.e. to come up with activities that will keep them motivated and focused. Activities around engagement actions need to consider the relevance of the content and the motivational nature of the intended learning approach, which is mostly about active learning. The literature suggests that it is better for students to take part, rather than just listening. As Bonwell and Eison (1991, p. 5) state: "when they are actively involved, students have to engage in such higher-order thinking tasks as analysis, synthesis, and evaluation". In this sense, active learning is "instructional activities involving students in doing things and thinking about what they are doing" (Bonwell & Eison, 1991, p. 5).

The difficulties in becoming a qualified teacher are complex, therefore their training needs to encourage them to develop those skills that will enable undergraduates and graduates to have a suitable profile of skills for their profession. Ramos (2002) points out that job skills are those that allow the job-seeker to meet the new demands of the productive sectors, in some way, formalizing the methods of managing and teaching the competencies of professionals, so that they are prepared for what is currently required.

The changes in the complex and dynamic world of work, combined with changes in the profile of students, who have new expectations and desires, also indicates the need to change the techniques and methods used in the classrooms. The use of Information and Communication Technology (ICT), especially Digital Technology (DT), can help share knowledge. Mattar (2010) points out that games are closely connected with the way the new generation learns, and could be a way to improve engagement.

Based on this context, this chapter addresses the following research question: how can gamification help to develop students' entrepreneurial skills in Higher Education, especially those focused on achieving social change? The gamification approaches described here were used on a higher education course called Integrated Work in Healthcare. It was provided as an online series to 12 different undergraduates, majoring in healthcare-related subjects. It focused on discussing the interdisciplinary role of healthcare workers, and reached over 892 students who took part between the autumn term in 2020 and the same term in 2021 in Brazil. The issues around using game-like elements in a non-game context is examined based on this case study (Yin, 2003), using an exploratory qualitative non-probabilistic approach. The objective is to discuss gamification as a way to encourage student engagement based on this example from higher education.

ENCOURAGING THE DEVELOPMENT OF DIGITAL COMPETENCES IN HIGHER EDUCATION

The modern world is marked by significant changes in the way we live and relate to the world, linked to globalization and digitalization. In this situation, higher education needs to reinvent itself. It needs to train workers who have broad skills, especially intercultural skills that enable them to understand the diversity of cultures and ideas, and, therefore, means that they are ready to work together as part of multi-cultural, disciplinary, and professional groups. They also need entrepreneurial competences, so that they can identify innovative solutions to the problems that come up and so they pay attention to the social impact, and digital competencies, to enable them to use technology and resources to communicate and access information, create content and learn throughout life.

Table 1. DIGCOMP 2.0 – The digital competence framework for citizens

Areas	Key components of digital competence
Information and data literacy	To articulate information needs, to locate and retrieve digital data, information and content. To judge the relevance of the source and its content. To store, manage, and organize digital data, information, and content.
Communication and collaboration	To interact, communicate and collaborate through digital technology while being aware of cultural and generational diversity. To participate in society through public and private digital services and participatory citizenship. To manage one's digital identity and reputation.
Digital content creation	To create and edit digital content. To improve and integrate information and content into an existing body of knowledge while understanding how copyright and licenses are to be applied. To know how to give understandable instructions to a computer system.
Safety and security	To protect devices, content, personal data, and privacy in digital environments. To protect physical and psychological health, and to be aware of the different digital technology for social well-being and social inclusion. To be aware of the environmental impact of digital technology and its use.
Problem-solving	To identify needs and problems, and to resolve conceptual problems and problem situations in digital environments. To use digital tools to innovate processes and products. To keep up to date with the digital evolution.

Source: The Digital Competence Framework 2.0 (Vuorikari et al., 2016)

When it comes to developing digital competences in students in higher education, we should focus on using technology and resources to find information and reference material for study and research; being able to communicate fluidly using digital tools and social media, with faculty members, colleagues, and everyone else; being able to use the learning platforms from educational institutions; being able to use collaborative resources; and being able to create research and share their ideas. Information is essential. This includes that information that they need for their profession and, in particular, what they need to know to be a citizen. Table 1 acts as a reference, grouping the digital competences in the digital competence framework for citizens established by the European Commission.

To develop these skills, it is important to provide learning situations that can develop them. One area that can help among others, therefore, is online training in Higher Education. The Integrated Work in Healthcare course, for example, examines the subject from the perspective of different professions, as this is believed to be a fundamental part of professional training and it includes students who are majoring in different healthcare subjects. Team working and choosing the right resources are fundamental to resolving complex problems. In the specific case described in this article, competences develop through the interaction between students and professors on an online learning platform, using the game ColabAção, which is described later.

Developing Entrepreneurial Competences in Higher Education

Entrepreneurial skills are known to be important in furthering innovation in universities. This idea is supported by the fact that students and graduates create companies and possess the business skills and attitude that comes from graduating with a range of entrepreneurial skills, regardless of their area of training. This approach is based on having a broad concept of entrepreneurship, together with a practical education and the development of social skills. As highlighted by the Entrepreneurship Survey at Brazilian Universities (Endeavor & Sebrae, 2016), "the University needs to empower and inspire entrepreneurship, big dreams, and innovation in students in order to encourage economic and social development in the community".

In addition to this, experts on the subject have acknowledged that the next generation of jobs will not be based on professions, but on problem-solving skills and the ability to overcome challenges. We will no longer think about jobs, but about the skills to perform a job, many of which may not even exist today. This is achieved by training students for situations rather than professions. The success factors for a higher-level program will no longer necessarily be equivalent to a specific and restricted profession. This approach to education focuses on multi-disciplinary careers and job opportunities.

The main objective of most business education is to develop a level of entrepreneurial skills. Entrepreneurial skills are defined here as the knowledge, skills, and attitudes that affect the will and ability to act as an entrepreneur and create value.

The European Commission (2016) states that Education for Entrepreneurship is based on transforming ideas into entrepreneurial actions; it is a fundamental competence throughout life, as learners become active in society. Therefore, it is important to learn all subjects and receive all types of educational training.

EntreComp – The Entrepreneurship Competence Framework (Bacigalupo et al., 2016) defines entrepreneurship as a crosscutting competence that applies to all spheres of life: from fostering personal development to actively participating in society and when (re)entering the labor market as a worker or as self-employed, or at the beginning of new ventures (cultural, social, or commercial). It is based on a broad definition of entrepreneurship that is about creating cultural, social, or economic value. Therefore, it encompasses different types of entrepreneurship, including intrapreneurship and social entrepreneurship.

We can see that the objective of Entrepreneurship Education as defined by the European Commission Framework (Bacigalupo et al., 2016) is broad. Entrepreneurship as a competence is seen as the ability of an individual to put ideas into practice. It includes creativity, innovation, and risk-taking, as well as the ability to plan and manage projects to achieve these goals. In this context, it is essential to develop entrepreneurial skills as part of the curriculum in higher education, so that students can use these skills over the course of their lives and can act as agents for social transformation. These skills also need to be developed in a crosscutting format. Entrepreneurship is a competency that refers not only to acquiring particular attitudes, skills and knowledge but this competency is also about giving the individual the ability to take action to put ideas into practice. Entrepreneurship in education can therefore help to equip an individual and enable them to be able to do so. It is, therefore, a crosscutting competence for economic and social situations. It helps to develop proactive citizens able to turn ideas into real projects. However, it can sometimes be challenging to ensure students are engaged when developing these competencies. In this article, we suggest the use of gamification to do so, based on the following theoretical approach.

Gamification to Improve Engagement and Learning in Higher Education

Johan Huizinga, a Dutch historian, is believed to be the first researcher to treat games as a cultural element. In his inaugural work, "Homo Ludens", published in 1938, Huizinga (1971) explains that games have an important function, which goes beyond the physiological or a psychological reflex. For him, "every game means something" (Huizinga, 1971, p. 5). He discounts the idea that the reasons people play are just biological, in other words, they are something animalistic and they are an activity designed to discharge excess energy or as practice for the serious activities of adult life. Huizinga emphasizes that entertainment and play are symbolic and human activities. In trying to determine the essence of games, he emphasizes that they have a social function, and they are a cultural element that is based on manipulating images, in an "imaginary" situation. Therefore, in the opinion of Huizinga (1971), a game only exists as a function of the subjects who take part in it. His inaugural thesis was extremely important for the development of game studies, both analog and digital, because, for the first time, they were accepted as part of the social system, in other words they mean something and are uniquely human.

As games studies have developed, especially with the arrival of electronic games, some other features have been added to describe, "what makes a game a game". Salen and Zimmerman, for example, defined a game (in general) as "a system in which the players engage in an artificial conflict, defined by rules, which implies a quantifiable result" (2012, p. 95). In relation to electronic games, Salen and Zimmerman (2012) believe that the physical medium of the game is important, but technology should not be treated as an end, but as part of a larger system.

Educational games play a very important role in innovation in teaching. There are clear advantages over the traditional transmissive model of education at all levels (Savi & Ulbricht, 2008). According to Prieto et al. (2005), educational software – which includes electronic games – needs to have defined teaching objectives and must be part of the teaching context, where the method is to guide the student through interaction, motivation, and discovery, to make it easier for them to learn the content.

However, there are some challenges when it comes to electronic games and education. One important issue is the fact that they need to meet the teaching requirements, which often makes the game uninteresting or unenjoyable (Fortuna, 2000). Therefore, they need to find the right balance between fun and education. As well as being different for the student, they are also different for the teacher. According to Gebran (2009), when using this technique, the professor becomes a mediator, rather than a transmitter. This way, they work together with the students. Another issue can be the generational conflict or lack of familiarity with technology. It is important to help the teacher by providing additional resources, such as manuals, tutorials, and an evaluation framework (Mattar, 2010).

Many studies have investigated the impact of gamification in Higher Education. Vlachopoulos and Makri (2017, p. 25) highlighted that:

games and simulations are educational interventions, which create a supportive environment in which students can acquire knowledge across different subjects and courses. Students have the opportunity to better understand theoretical concepts, provided that games are used as a supplement to traditional lecture-based courses.

Alves (2015) also showed that gamified activities could engage different audiences of different ages, in educational settings, both in person and using online instructional activities. Similarly, Cunha (2008) supports this by saying that in order to be innovative in education, it is essential to change the system and look at things differently. In line with these perspectives, the teaching and learning processes in higher education need to be reexamined. In looking at the implementation of the gamified activities discussed in this article, we choose to use the structural gamification model (Filatro & Cavalcanti, 2018). This model is linked to a behavioral approach to learning. It is designed as a self-regulated teaching process that can reinforce behavior in order to achieve the main goal set by the teacher. This type of gamification can encourage students to be more actively involved by providing feedback and rewards during the process. Further details on how it was implemented, and its benefits can be found in the discussion section.

THE RESEARCH QUESTION AND METHODS

This research examines an example from Higher Education of developing entrepreneurial competences through game-based learning, involving 892 Healthcare student at the Pontifical Catholic University of Rio Grande do Sul (PUCRS) in Southern Brazil. Game-based learning is defined as "the intentional use of electronic or non-electronic games or simulations to achieve one or more specific learning objectives" (Wiggins, 2016, p. 19). Therefore, this paper addresses the following research question: how can gamification help to develop entrepreneurial competences in students in Higher Education, especially those focused on social change objectives?

To answer this, the paper has adopted an action research approach, as defined by Rowley (2014, p. 2):

Action research is a research approach typically applied in an organizational, educational, or community setting whose central characteristic is that the outcomes of the research process are twofold, an action (e.g. a completed project or organizational change) and new knowledge or theory. Action research can be viewed as the ultimate case study approach due to its systematic framework for gathering data and insights into an organization or a community and its processes and behavior.

It is based on a case study (Yin, 2003), using an exploratory qualitative method and a non-probabilistic survey sample for convenience. To provide a broader explanation of the case studied here: a survey of students was conducted, which received 47 responses in total. The questionnaire consisted of 12 questions with open and closed questions (which used a Likert scale). The survey was divided into two sections: the first about usability (how east to play and understand the instructions) and the second related to the learning points and the experience. The written responses were analyzed qualitatively to produce emergent themes. The Survey's results were accompanied by a descriptive report on the online course and the game, with feedback from the professors directly involved in this specific online class and in supporting the game.

DISCUSSION

Creating and Developing Digital Solutions for the Engagement of Faculty Members and Students at PUCRS on the Integrated Work in Healthcare Course

Designing an interdisciplinary activity, that is methodologically based on gamification, is an opportunity to provide a solution to one of the greatest current issues for training, something that has become more important as a result of the Covid-19 pandemic: how to deliver significant teaching plans that encourage student engagement. Engagement is affected by the relevance of the content and the way the proposed learning approach is able to motivate the student.

The gamification models described in this document were provided online for the University course Integrated Work in Healthcare. Its curricular basis was on the importance of the multidisciplinary aspect of the work of healthcare workers. The context of this course is the collaborative teaching of physicians, nurses, psychologists, and other healthcare professions, so that the students are prepared to work as a team in professional healthcare.

The proposal to use game elements in a non-game context, in this strongly multidisciplinary situation designed by the Integrated Work in Healthcare course, shows how gamification can be used as an effective way to improve student engagement and to implement learning processes based on self-control and cooperation.

Self-controlled learning highlights the importance of an active method, as the student has control of their training. The Integrated Work in Healthcare course implements this principle by creating a gamified teaching activity and establishes a set of rules to encourage the healthcare student to take an active part. This academic course aims to establish an educational situation that embodies the words of Freire (2003, p. 47), when he stated that "teaching is not transferring knowledge but creating the conditions for it to be produced or created".

The Integrated Work in Healthcare course is structured into four learning units. These are conceptual, interdependent, and complementary blocks that establish a training path, which is supported and monitored by professors and students, who are able to beat challenges to win medals and online certificates (Figure 1). Each learning unit lasts 4 weeks and they consist of gamified activities and opportunities to apply the concepts, enabling the students to consider what they have learned, based on scenarios that simulate real situations that healthcare workers may find themselves in. The curricular and methodological design of the course is explained by the professor who designed the digital content, as well as the person responsible for the pedagogical mediation:

The Integrated Work in Healthcare course contains crosscutting content for majors in the area of healthcare, which addresses the health-disease process, public health policies, the Brazilian universal health system and interprofessional work in healthcare. The course supports the integration and development of interprofessional work at PUCRS. As it is an online course, the use of innovative pedagogical practices to encourage interactivity, active participation, and the responsibility of students are all essential for the success of the course and to achieve the expected learning results [Teacher and Nurse, AB].

Figure 1. The curriculum design of the Integrated Work in Healthcare course: four interdependent and complementary learning units
Source: The authors (2021)

In order to provide the opportunity for meaningful learning, it is essential that each student is made partly responsible for their learning. Therefore, it is essential to make the learning expectations of the professors clear. Each module of the course has a learning trail (Figure 2) at the beginning, that shows the investigation to be done, identifies the elements that will enable the student to expand their cognitive repertoire and, therefore, how well they will perform in the gamified activity: the opportunity to apply

Figure 2. Learning Trail to the second learning module: The Concept of Expanded Healthcare
Source: The authors (2021)

the concept and work as a team.

The first learning unit has an investigative focus on health concepts and processes. In this conceptual block, historical and interpretative aspects related to the health-disease process are examined, in order to highlight the introduction of the concept of expanded healthcare and to analyze the impact of social determinants on its implementation. The proposed gamified activity consists of a set of everyday social and cultural situations to be analyzed and the social determinants of health identified. Therefore, while it allows the student to look at the concept of expanded healthcare systematically, it also enables the students to practice their argumentation skills in multidisciplinary groups, in order to resolve a case study. The student receives online medals and a first certificate by successfully completing the gamified activities, during which the student takes on the role of Junior scenario analyst I ANVISA I National Health Surveillance Agency (Figure 3).

The students can check and look up their rewards of badges and medals in the participant profile area and in the grade report, both available on the Moodle platform (Figure 4).

The focus of study for the second and third learning units is the development of the concept of healthcare and its relationship with the historical implementation of public policies in this area. It explains the nature of the main systems that healthcare workers operate under, from public policies to the

Figure 3. Challenges and rewards for the first learning unit, "Health: concepts and processes"
Source: The authors (2021)

Figure 4. Image of the badges on the Moodle Platform
Source: The authors, 2021.

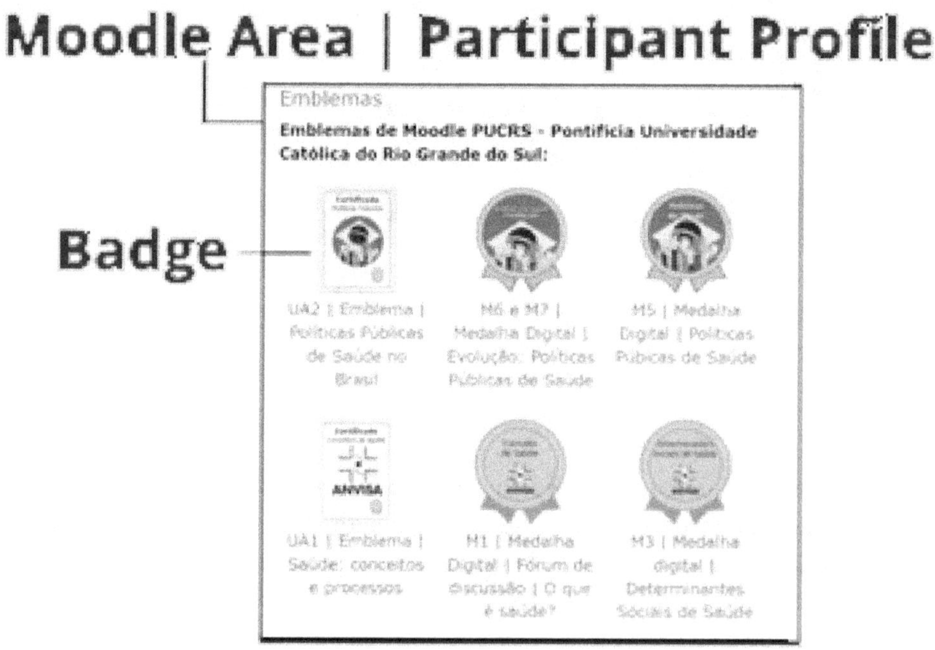

implementation of the Unified Healthcare System, so that students can understand and know how to respond to the current needs of the Brazilian people. The student learns and apples the fundamentals to ensuring care to others is practiced to a high quality, is comprehensive, and longitudinal, by working with multidisciplinary teams (Figure 4).

Having covered the circumstances under which future healthcare workers operate, the last learning unit aims to achieve one of the objectives of the World Health Organization (WHO), Interprofessional Education. The complexity of the individual and collective needs of the Brazilian people highlights the importance of professional health training that takes into account the development of entrepreneurial skills and appreciates interprofessional performance.

Developing entrepreneurial competence becomes part of the training process in the Integrated Work in Healthcare course, which, without doubt, adds to the graduate's profile, making it more suitable for the current demands in healthcare work.

Interprofessional education aims to produce professionals with the ability to undertake, identify problems, and propose solutions, to transform ideas into opportunities to enhance the access of the Brazilian people to social benefits. To include this, the development of personal, collective skills needs to be aligned to the complexity of current issues in the area of healthcare. It is also essential to encourage professionals to develop their interpersonal and intrapersonal skills, by inviting them to overcome complex problems in an innovative, creative, and interdisciplinary way.

This challenge for training is covered by making entrepreneurial competences the focus of study in the last learning module of the Integrated Work in Healthcare course. The training path uses multimodal digital content to develop a specific set of skills that are a fundamental part of multidisciplinary working. The approach uses quiz-format games (Figure 5), for appropriating knowledge up to the application of the concepts, to challenge students to try new and different perspectives on the profile of a healthcare worker.

Figure 5. Game Screen: Entrepreneurial Competences
Source: The authors (2021)

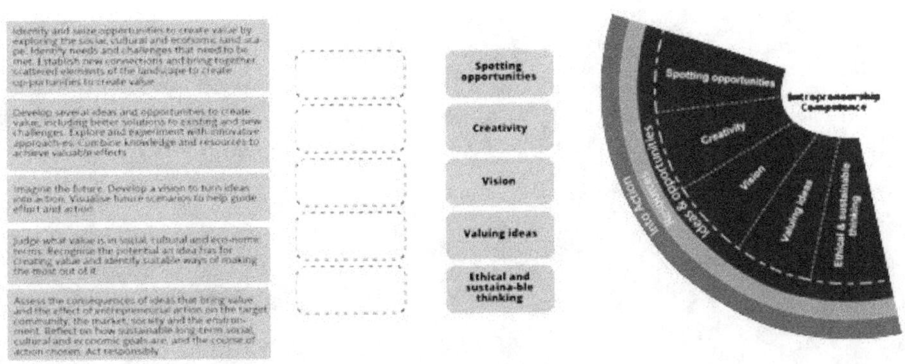

The concluding activity of the Integrated Work in Healthcare course challenges students to suggest an intervention, which is mainly based on the organizing element of a collaborative game – ColabAção. The name is a combination of the words 'collaboration' and 'action'. This gamified teaching resource, conceptualized by IDEAR – The Interdisciplinary Lab for Entrepreneurship and Innovation at PUCRS and Sopro Digital Content, and programmed by a multidisciplinary team from the Online Undergrad and Graduation sector, was customized to help make suggestions for humanitarian action in response to the challenges posed by the COVID-19 pandemic.

The Card Game ColabAção: Development, Teaching strategies, and Entrepreneurial Competences

The multidisciplinary content of the Integrated Work in Healthcare course is more substantial because it can rely on experts from IDEAR – The Interdisciplinary Lab for Entrepreneurship and Innovation at PUCRS and the Online Graduation Coordination Department, to help to develop behavioral skills and create an entrepreneurial attitude, thereby achieve a teaching objective in line with interprofessional education. This concluding activity is going to be described in parallel with the discussion of the premises for including gamification and its potential to be used as an active and meaningful learning strategy. This course establishes a situation where doctors, nurses, psychologists, and other healthcare workers can be taught collaboratively, consisting of training the students to work as a team in different professional fields.

Figure 6 shows the learning path where each interprofessional team is asked to create a Humanitarian Proposal, but the criteria for creating it is organized by the interface to the game. The gamified strategy helps to introduce teams to real situations in which healthcare professionals work. It puts them in situations that are different from those they usually face in practice scenarios.

Figure 6. Learning Trail for creating a Humanitarian Proposal for the COVID-19 pandemic
Source: The authors (2021)

Gamification is an educational approach that consists of bringing the game elements listed by Fardo (2013) to the teaching-learning process – objectives, clear rules, immediate feedback, rewards, intrinsic motivation, the inclusion of errors as part of the process, fun, narrative, levels, abstraction from reality, competition, conflict, cooperation, willingness to take part, etc. – which can all be combined in different ways. The gamified method designed for the Integrated Work in Healthcare course was based on four important elements: willingness to take part, rules, objectives, and feedback.

Willingness points to the need to accept the rules, to understand the objectives, and appreciate the feedback received. The element that encourages volunteering is cooperation: realizing the importance of cooperation between the students making up the interprofessional groups, composed of future professionals in different areas of healthcare: doctors, dentists, nurses, psychologists, nutritionists, physiotherapists, physical education instructors, pharmacists and biologists. The criteria for the composition of the teams was: a maximum number of four members and representatives of at least two different courses in the areas of healthcare. The first activity was to map the profile of the students in each team (which were formed randomly), recording the skills they had and how these could help with creating a humanitarian proposal. Cards are created to record each member and to be shared later within the interprofessional group (Figure 7), as it was important to understand what each team-member could contribute towards the humanitarian proposal.

Figure 7. Charts to map the profile of the members of each interprofessional team
Source: The authors (2021)

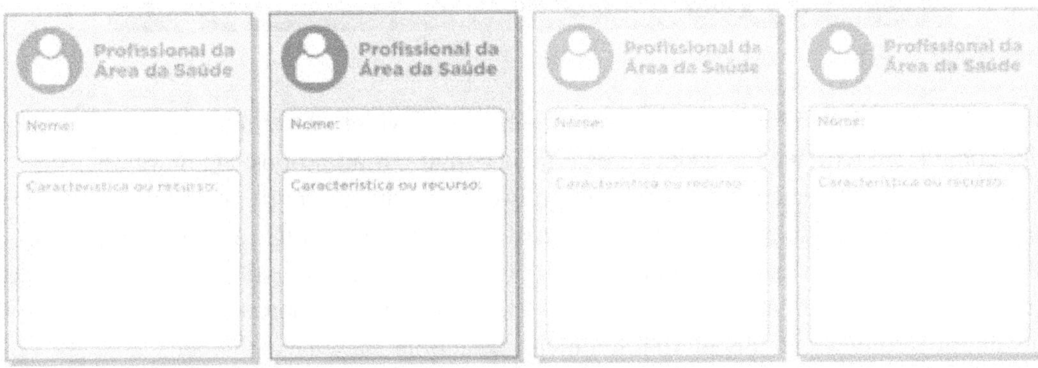

Once the learning path was revealed and the potential of each member mapped, the next action was to find out the objective of the gamified activity. Choosing the objective was the step to identify what the team's next actions in the gamified activity would be.

ColabAção is a card game structured into five categories – Objectives, Team, Partnerships, Time, Resources – representing the central elements of the processes for designing social interventions. The card game is designed to be played among teams (cooperative mode), to develop people's Entrepreneurial Competence. The professor's role is to act as a mediator and a mentor to guide the students and actively help them from start to finish. The activity took place over two weeks.

The objective in a gamified activity is what encourages the participant in the student activity to complete the challenge. As Fardo (2013) mentions, if the game's goals are not clearly defined it can cause confusion and is likely to lead to failure. More complex objectives should be subdivided into smaller objectives to help them to complete the greater objective. There is no time limit in the game, as it maps the scenario in order to propose an innovative solution for healthcare, taking a strategic look at the Covid-19 situation. The ColabAção game starts by asking the team to draw the objective to be covered by the humanitarian proposal. The team of professors – physician, nurse, and social worker – established 15 objectives, based on demands relating to COVID-19, including checking prevention strategies, suggesting activities for health teams dealing with socially vulnerable people and those with various disabilities,

Figure 8. Screen showing the first action in the ColabAção game: selecting an objective to be achieved as part of the humanitarian proposal
Source: The authors (2021)

for example. A card is drawn for the game with the objective, which determines the activities that each interprofessional team will need to take to create their humanitarian proposal (Figure 8).

Once the objective is selected, the system randomly chooses three important elements needed to build the proposal from the following decks: Team, Partnerships, and Time (Figure 9). In the Team Deck, the system draws a card that decides the number of people that the interprofessional group will have available to implement the humanitarian proposal. This element is very important because it tells the team how many employees they can rely on to implement the actions they have planned.

Figure 9. Screen showing the decks
Source: The authors (2021)

From the Partnerships deck, the system selects a card indicating the partners available to help the team implement the proposal. The partners will be supporters of the proposal, and could be the government, a company, a university, an NGO, a Volunteer Group, a Board of Health, or a Health Clinic. This choice is important to the team, as it should give the additional options through partnerships.

From the Time deck the system will select the time that the interprofessional group has to implement their humanitarian proposal. This element is very important as it allows the team to plan the time available to carry out their activities, as well as possible.

The next part of the game is for the interprofessional team to choose the resources they have for implementing their humanitarian proposal. The interprofessional group are allowed to choose two cards from the Resource deck, freely chosen by the team rather than automatically selected by the system. This is a key point in deciding whether the humanitarian proposal is feasible. The interprofessional group must carefully analyze the chosen objective and the other elements – the team, their partnerships, and the time available, and this should tell them which two resources they to ensure they can collaborate effectively and to enable the proposal to be implemented. Each interprofessional team can choose from the following options: kitchen equipment; agricultural equipment; prototyping equipment; construction materials; medical equipment; artistic resources and dissemination media (Figure 10).

Figure 10. Collaboration: Resource Deck screen
Source: The authors (2021)

As they interact with each stage of the ColabAção game, a scenario is steadily built up, which encourages the students to explore the subject and design the scenario themselves. Each objective selected by the interprofessional teams creates a set of challenges that will stimulate the students' cognitive repertoire, which will have improved after completing the 15 learning paths, and it will create a scenario in which they can work together. It is important to note that whatever professions are represented in the teams, the cards drawn are always the same.

The gamified activity of ColabAção encourages students to see the features of each objective that is drawn and to achieve it, all members of each team to examine the information and make decisions. The final screen for the game is an image with a summary of all the cards selected or chosen by the team (Figure 11). The teams then continue, using this summary, and come up with solutions to meet the objective, taking into account the staff available, the partnerships, the time available, and the resources. The result should be a project to address the issues, which they present to the whole class at the end of the assignment.

Figure 11. Collaboration: final screen
Source: The authors (2021)

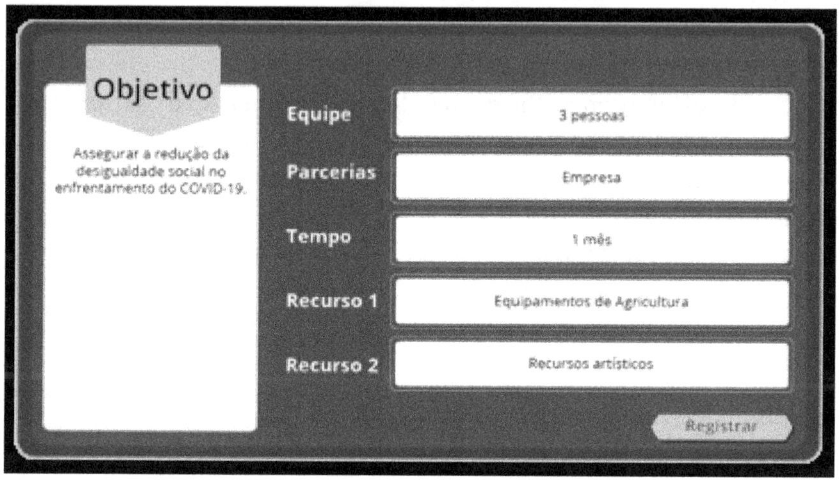

The ColabAção game, as mentioned by Silva et al. (2019), is an example of an entertaining gamified activity, but it is not just intended to be enjoyable with no other end, but also because it is thought-provoking, has tension, enables students to see a simulated world or situation, or the world in a different way. Approaching a problem in a fun way does not often consider the objectives nor does not it tend to establish a more precise methodological approach, which gamification does. The professor of the Integrated Work in Healthcare course who acted as a mediator and monitored the learning process explained the importance of gamification:

Gamification takes place at various points during the course, but it has contributed most significantly to the way the final module was constructed, which very effectively puts students in an interprofessional experience in dealing with a challenge of building a proposal for humanitarian aid to help with Covid-19. To create their proposal, the groups are supported by the ColabAção game, which was developed by the IDEAR – The Interdisciplinary Lab for Entrepreneurship and Innovation at PUCRS and Sopro Digital Content. IDEAR Lab is designed to encourage entrepreneurship among the students, professors, and the academic community and allow them to experience it. Gamification enables students to interact with the game, and use it to identify the objective; partnerships, time, and resources that they will need to carry out the proposal. In addition, the game encourages students to develop entrepreneurial and collaborative skills, which complements the objectives for the course. [Professor and Nurse, AB].

DISCUSSION: GAMIFICATION AND TEACHING IMPLICATIONS

The implementation of gamified activities needs to be carefully planned to ensure that they have a successful impact on the students' learning. Two models of gamification need to be considered in education, as mentioned by Filatro and Cavalcanti (2018): structural gamification and content gamification.

The Integrated Work in Healthcare course was organized around the use of the structural model of gamification, where game elements are used to help motivate and engage students in the learning process. The learning trails (Figures 2 and 6) graphically represent the path that the student needs to follow to meet the challenge in each activity. Other elements of the game, such as different levels of difficulty for the activities and rewards, the achievement of medals and certificates (Figures 3 and 4), were also included in each module.

A third important element in the gamification of the course is the feedback on gamified activities, which enables quick responses and helps to keep the students interested. One of the aspects that most enhances the learning process is undoubtedly the immediate response to students completing activities, as this helps to identify weak points as well as opportunities to go over and review objectives that have not been achieved. On this aspect, as mentioned in a previous study (Patrício et al., 2021, p. 14): "gamification seems to increase participation since everyone is more stimulated and has the same opportunity to contribute to the final idea (…)". Although the study mentioned related to a corporate setting, it would also seem to be true in an academic/classroom environment.

The structural model of gamification is aligned to a behavioral approach to learning. Behavior is reinforced by a self-controlled learning process, which helps students to achieve the objectives set by the teacher. This type of gamification encourages student to actively participate, gives them feedback and rewards, as long as the student meets the learning expectations.

Assessment is the aspect of the pedagogical process that is clearly most affected by the structural model of gamification. By explaining a formative approach to the assessment process, traditional feedback in terms of tests and grades is replaced by scores and rewards from gamified activities. From this point of view, there is more opportunity for the student to be successful and the student comes into contact with different fields of knowledge.

The final course activity, led by the ColabAção game, illustrates the content gamification model, as it uses game elements to enable students to acquire knowledge and apply the concepts. This kind of gamification is related to the theory of self-determination. The game acts as a device to motivate the student to undertake challenges, making use of the internal resources and each student's self-controlled learning. When creating a humanitarian proposal based on the criteria provided by the ColabAção game, students from each interprofessional team have the opportunity to demonstrate their ability to put their practical skills and theoretical knowledge, acquired from the Integrated Work in Healthcare course, into practice to resolve challenges, consisting of problematic situations to be faced by healthcare workers in the future in relation to interprofessional team working.

Structural or content gamification enables different designs to be created, either in – person or online within an educational context. The students' learning experience can clearly be improved, by enabling: (1) students to be more engaged and co-responsible for their learning process; (2) more interaction and experimentation; (3) the students to take charge of their own learning; (4) a formative assessment process: rapid and appropriate feedback and a more opportunities for success; (5) more personalized monitoring, with effective ways to track each student's learning development and to ensure mistakes are treated and accepted as part of the learning process, to be analyzed and thought about.

DISCUSSION: THE OPINIONS OF STUDENTS AND PROFESSORS ON THE CARD GAME

Learning System Management (LSM) platforms provide features that enable gamified activities to be created. These are technical resources that, as well as encouraging more students engagement, make it possible to create self-controlled learning processes by combining the three phases suggested by Boruchovitch and Gomes (2019) – establishing goals; proposing measures for the self-control of performance, and opportunities for self-assessment.

As well as being aimed at better student engagement, ColabAção also focused on encouraging a learning process that was based on self-controlled learning and cooperation. Self-controlled learning demonstrates the importance of using an active method since it puts the student in charge and makes them equally responsible for education. Automatic feedback was used as part of the learning process, where the student was asked about the activity and asked them to think about it as part of a self-assessment (automatic feedback control). This feedback also helps them to appreciate what they have done and encourages them to continue with the work

The Integrated Work in Healthcare course puts this principle into practice by creating a gamified teaching activity, that establishes a strategy to improve the active performance of a healthcare worker in training. The learning path designed for this course demonstrates the principle in education of the idea "learn how to learn", by presenting a set of challenges for students to apply their knowledge to, by establishing objectives, rules, and providing online medals and certificates. Gamification therefore shows how it can use conceptual systematization, but also be an important formative element in enabling the effective tracking of the teaching activities for each student.

Adding the development of entrepreneurial competences to the training process, clearly enhance the profile of graduates, it helps to align them with the current performance needs for healthcare workers. IDEAR's collaboration illustrates how the interdisciplinary performance is improved by the Laboratory team. The proposal for the gamified activity was modeled on "The European Entrepreneurship Competence" (EntreComp) framework, which enabled the students to understand the matrix for entrepreneurial competence, based on three levels of proficiency: basic, intermediate, and advanced.

The degree of student engagement could be seen from the quality of the proposals, which is illustrated by the comments of the mediator, when analyzing one of the humanitarian projects: "I am delighted, I may be overly appreciative, but the team responded very well to the challenge presented by the ColabAção game". This supports the findings of Patrício et al. (2020, p. 11), which highlighted the higher quality of solutions produced in gamified workshops: "the gamified approach makes intangible thoughts more tangible and clearer by delivering a self-explanatory report on the proposed solution". The system's strategy of drawing cards was designed to push the student, and encourage them to take a broader investigative perspective, beyond their own scope. The healthcare worker operates in a diverse and complex environment and, therefore, it is important to know how to deal with what you do not know. The comments from the students demonstrate this view on not being able to choose, as an opportunity to look at something new: "It was the draws that provided the surprises when creating the proposal"; "Creativity to create something different"; "We had to use our creativity to complete the drawn task".

In addition, it is important to highlight the following results, from among the students' survey responses: 48.9% of the students stated that the ColabAção game had helped them to develop entrepreneurial skills and to understand how to design projects as part of the course. In terms of usage, the students stated that the game provided: interactivity, innovation in the teaching method, dynamism, surprising challenges and proposals, and ease of use.

According to the students' feedback, what they learned from the game was the importance of collaboration and cooperation, knowing how to use entrepreneurship in their daily lives, how to include knowledge from other professions, the different forms and options for entrepreneurship, how to be sympathetic in the current state of the world. Patrício et al. (2021) also mentioned that group communication could be improved, because gamified activities attended to create friendly and open environments that encourage team members to converse. This was also true of the ColabAção example in the view of the students.

We can answer our research question, based on the responses by the students, as this provides evidence that the game and gamification helped to develop entrepreneurial skills as part of the course.

Finally, one of the professors mediating the course decided to include it in another course, "Advisory, Consulting and Supervision", part of the Social Work program, as a result of the level of engagement by the students, as demonstrated by the quality of the proposals produced. The game was customized for this new course, to meet its new objectives, which relate to the work of four international humanitarian aid organizations: Doctors Without Borders (MSF), the Red Cross, the United Nations High Commissioner for Refugees (UNHCR), and the International Organization for Migration (IOM).

EPILOGUE AND LESSONS LEARNED

Education is the means, par excellence, to develop autonomy and awareness in people, by expanding their horizons and reviewing and recreating their arguments. Teaching processes need to encourage interaction to overcome a single subject perspective. The ColabAção game and the other gamified activities mentioned treat entrepreneurship as knowledge and a competence, they encourage a multidisciplinary approach and curriculum, and they show the value of gamification as a methodological strategy. In this way, they confirm the importance encouraging more connections between students, professors, communities, and of increasingly using innovation in society and training students to act as effective agents for social transformation. It is also important to note that the game is already being used in another subject, on the Social Work course (appropriately adapted to this field), and the results are to be documented.

The active methodology is an educational concept, which as the name says encourages students to participate in learning through dynamics centered on their interests and according to their situation and motives. Nowadays, learning needs to consider the students' concerns and needs, so that, there is meaning for their personal development with each new piece of content and each new competency.

According to Coutinho (2011), adults build knowledge, based on interpersonal and social networks. In other words, they learn based on relational context. Gamification encourages students to explore and discover, and encourages them to re-examine information, theories, and interpersonal relationships.

The educational institutions need to adopt a new approach if they are going to be able to teach entrepreneurship in university classrooms. First of all, they will need to focus on creative and innovative teaching methods, rather than theoretical, monotonous, and unproductive classes. The ColabAção game is an example of such a method.

ACKNOWLEDGMENT

This work was supported by the Pontifical Catholic University of Rio Grande do Sul (PUCRS).

REFERENCES

Alves, F. (2015). *Gamification: Como criar experiências de aprendizagem engajadoras* [Gamification: How to create engaging learning experiences]. DVS Editora.

Bacigalupo, M., Kampylis, P., Punie, Y., & Van den Brande, G. (2016). *EntreComp: The entrepreneurship competence framework*. Publication Office of the European Union. https://publications.jrc.ec.europa.eu/repository/handle/JRC101581

Bonwell, C. C., & Eison, J. A. (1991). *Active Learning: Creating Excitement in the Classroom*. ERIC Publications.

Boruchovitch, E., & Gomes, M. A. M. (2019). *Aprendizagem autorregulada: Como promovê-la no contexto educativo?* [Self-regulated learning: How to promote it in the educational context?]. Editora Vozes.

Coutinho, C. P., & Lisbôa, E. S. (2011). Sociedade da informação, do conhecimento e da aprendizagem: Desafios para educação no século XXI [Information, knowledge and learning society: Challenges for education in the 21st century]. *Review of Education, 18*(1), 5–22.

Cunha, M. I. D. (2008). Inovações pedagógicas: O desafio da reconfiguração de saberes na docência universitária [Pedagogical innovations: The challenge of reconfiguration of knowledge in university teaching]. *Cadernos de Pedagogia Universitária, 6*, 1–41.

Endeavor & Sebrae. (2017). *Empreendedorismo nas Universidades Brasileiras 2016*. https://www.sebrae.com.br/Sebrae/Portal%20Sebrae/Anexos/Relatorio%20Endeavor%20impressao.pdf

Fardo, M. L. (2013). A gamificação aplicada em ambientes de aprendizagem [Gamification applied in learning environments]. *RENOTE, 11*(1), 1–9. doi:10.22456/1679-1916.41629

Filatro, A., & Cavalcanti, C. C. (2018). *Metodologias inov-ativas na educação presencial, a distância e corporativa* [Innov-ative methodologies in face-to-face, distance and corporate education]. Saraiva Educação SA.

Fortuna, T. R. (2000). Sala de aula é lugar de brincar? [Is the classroom a place to play?]. In M. L. Xavier & M. I. Dalla Zen (Eds.), *Planejamento em destaque: Análises menos convencionais* [Planning in the spotlight: Less conventional analytics] (pp. 147–164). Mediação.

Freire, P. (2003). *Pedagogia da autonomia: Saberes necessários à prática educativa* [Pedagogy of autonomy: Knowledge necessary for educational practice]. Paz e Terra.

Gebran, M. P. (2009). *Tecnologias educacionais* [Educational technologies]. IESDE Brasil S.A.

Huizinga, J. (1971). *Homo ludens: o jogo como elemento da cultura* [Homo ludens: The game as an element of culture]. Editora da Universidade de S. Paulo & Editora Perspectiva.

Mattar, J. (2010). *Games em educação: Como os nativos digitais aprendem* [Games in Education: How digital natives learn]. Pearson Prentice Hall.

Patricio, R., Moreira, A., Zurlo, F., & Melazzini, M. (2020). Co-creation of new solutions through gamification: A collaborative innovation practice. *Creativity and Innovation Management, 29*(1), 146–160. doi:10.1111/caim.12356

Patrício, R., Moreira, A. C., & Zurlo, F. (2021). Enhancing design thinking approaches to innovation through gamification. *European Journal of Innovation Management, 24*(5), 1569–1594. doi:10.1108/EJIM-06-2020-0239

Prieto, L. M., Trevisan, M. D. C. B., Danesi, M. I., & Falkembach, G. A. M. (2005). Uso das tecnologias digitais em atividades didáticas nas séries iniciais [Use of digital technologies in didactic activities in the initial grades]. *Renote: revista novas tecnologias na educação, 3*(1), 1-11.

Ramos, M. N. (2002). A educação profissional pela pedagogia das competências e a superfície dos documentos oficiais [Professional education through the pedagogy of competences and the surface of official documents]. *Educação & Sociedade, 23*(80), 401–422. doi:10.1590/S0101-73302002008000020

Rowley, J. (2014). Data analysis. In D. Coghlan & M. Brydon-Miller (Eds.), *The SAGE encyclopedia of action research* (pp. 239–242). Sage.

Salen, K., & Zimmerman, E. (2012). *Regras do jogo: Fundamentos do design de jogos* [Game Rules: Game design fundamentals]. Blucher.

Savi, R., & Ulbricht, V. R. (2008). Jogos digitais educacionais: Benefícios e desafios. *Renote: revista novas tecnologias na educação, 6*(2), 1-10.

Silva, J. B. D., Sales, G. L., & Castro, J. B. D. (2019). Gamificação como estratégia de aprendizagem ativa no ensino de Física [Gamification as an active learning strategy in the Physics education]. *Revista Brasileira de Ensino de Física, 41*(4), 1–9. doi:10.1590/1806-9126-rbef-2018-0309

Vlachopoulos, D., & Makri, A. (2017). The effect of games and simulations on higher education: A systematic literature review. *International Journal of Educational Technology in Higher Education, 14*(1), 1–33. doi:10.118641239-017-0062-1

Vuorikari, R., Punie, Y., Carretero Gomez, S., & Van Den Brande, G. (2016). *DigComp 2.0: The Digital Competence Framework for Citizens. Update Phase 1: the Conceptual Reference Model.* Publications Office of the European Union. https://publications.jrc.ec.europa.eu/repository/handle/JRC101254

Wiggins, B. E. (2016). An overview and study on the use of games, simulations, and gamification in higher education. *International Journal of Game-Based Learning, 6*(1), 18–29. doi:10.4018/IJGBL.2016010102

Yin, R. K. (2003). *Estudo de Caso: Planejamento e métodos* [Case Study: Planning and methods]. Bookman Editora.

Chapter 30
Fostering Motivation to Learn Through Gamification:
Understanding the Impact of Different Kinds of Rewards on Learner Motivation

Giada Marinensi
https://orcid.org/0000-0002-0588-2554
Link Campus University, Italy

Brunella Botte
Link Campus University, Italy

ABSTRACT

The implementation of gamification in educational contexts has experienced steady growth over the last few years. This may be due to many factors, including that teachers are increasingly familiar with video games and their students and are more willing to experiment with different game-inspired learning approaches in the classroom. However, designing an effective gamified system is a challenging task. Therefore, this paper aims to provide teachers with more guidance in the gamification design process, especially concerning the difficult task of planning a motivating reward system. To do so, the authors conducted a qualitative study of the gamified learning app Duolingo. The study focused on understanding how users respond to the different kinds of rewards the app provides and how rewards affect their motivation to learn by fulfilling their need for competence, relatedness, and autonomy in the framework of self-determination theory.

INTRODUCTION

Gamified learning, defined as the implementation of gamification techniques in educational contexts (Armstrong & Landers, 2017; Landers, 2015), has been widely employed in recent years and has also been the focus of significant research activity aimed at analysing its effectiveness (Sailer & Homner, 2020a). However, despite the number of studies already carried out, the effect of gamification on cogni-

DOI: 10.4018/978-1-6684-4287-6.ch030

tive, motivational, and behavioural learning outcomes is still to be determined (Sailer & Homner, 2020a). This is due to many factors, including the fact that gamification has been applied to a large variety of disciplines and at different educational levels, and also to the fact that gamified learning has been implemented in many different forms, ranging from the simple use during a lesson of playful students' response systems (such as Kahoot!), to very complex gamified systems that redefine the entire students' experience (such as Classcraft).

Even if a definite answer to the question about the effectiveness of gamified learning cannot be provided yet, several literature reviews have been carried out, highlighting at least the general tendency of research findings on this topic (Bertalero et al., 2018; Dichev & Dicheva, 2017; Hamari et al., 2014; Manzano-León et al., 2021; Sailer & Homner, 2020b). According to these reviews, the most common positive effects of gamification, observed at all the educational levels, are related to students' academic achievement, engagement, and motivation. Moreover, gamification seems to be generally well-received by students, given its ability to make them feel empowered while progressing through their learning path and to add an overall level of fun and enjoyment to the learning process.

The appeal of gamification for the new generation of students is consistent with the fact that, as digital natives, they are very familiar with the video games language and very used to having them as part of their everyday life (Glover, 2013). Moreover, they show an overall positive attitude toward the concept of learning from this medium (Prensky, 2003).

Teachers as well are more and more likely to be as familiar with video games as their students already are, since "an entire generation of adults grew up on computers and smartphones. Even for those who didn't, video games are a natural part of their lives and their children's lives" (Entertainment Software Association, 2020). According to data about gamers and games, in the last couple of decades, the gamer profile has radically changed. Nowadays, the average age of gamers is between 35 and 44 years in the U.S. (Entertainment Software Association, 2020) and 31 in Europe (ISFE, 2020). Gamers are almost equally distributed between males and females since in the U.S., across all gamers, 41% are female and 59% are male (Entertainment Software Association, 2020), while in Europe, 45% are female and 55% are male (ISFE, 2020).

These shifts in the gamer profile, combined with the growing pervasiveness of games in our everyday life (Walz & Deterding, 2014), are among the factors that paved the way for the increased adoption of gamification in education we are witnessing and can lead to the assumption that the number of teachers willing to adopt a gamified learning strategy in their courses will increase in the near future.

However, designing an effective gamified system is not an easy task (Chia et al., 2017), and it requires a deep knowledge of how games succeeded in engaging and motivating us.

Among the many different elements to be considered when it comes to designing an effective gamified system for learning, choosing the right kind of rewards and planning the right reward schedule certainly are crucial tasks, with the potential of affecting the effectiveness of the entire system since rewards have a fundamental role in supporting motivation (Deci et al., 1999; Houlfort et al., 2002; Ryan & Deci, 1987). It has to be observed that little research has been carried out so far on the specific topic of how rewards affect users' motivation in the context of gamified learning applications, with the results that teachers attempting to implement a gamified strategy in their course still lack the needed guidance on how to design an effective reward system.

Building on the relevant literature available on how rewards work on games (Deci et al., 1999; Hallford & Hallford, 2001; C. Phillips et al., 2013, 2018; R. S. Phillips et al., 2014; Ryan & Deci, 1987) and on recent studies exploring the rewards system of gamified applications (Botte et al., 2020; Lewis et al.,

2016; Rapp, 2017; Sailer et al., 2017), this study aims at further exploring how rewards can affect players' motivation by fulfilling their need for competence, relatedness, and autonomy, in the framework of the Self-Determination Theory (SDT).

The rest of this chapter is structured as follows. The *Theoretical Framework* section presents a literature review about gamified learning and about the motivational impact of rewards. Then, the gap in the literature is highlighted, and the main research questions are formulated. In the section *The gamified language learning app Duolingo*, we describe the gamified learning app Duolingo, which is used as an example in this analysis. The *Methodological approach* section presents the method and the tools adopted in the research process and provides a description of the participants involved. The main findings of the study are commented in the *Results and discussion section*, and a set of design suggestions on how to build an effective reward system for the specific context of gamified learning will be formulated in the *Conclusions* section.

THEORETICAL FRAMEWORK

The Application of Gamification in Education

The general definition of gamification as "the use of game design elements in non-game contexts" (Deterding, 2011) has been expanded by Lenders (2015) to better capture the essence of gamified learning. According to Lenders, when applied to educational contexts, gamification can be defined as the use of game elements to affect learning-related behaviours and attitudes, with the final aim to foster the formation of positive learning habits. The adoption of positive learning habits should, in turn, lead learners to the achievement of better learning outcomes and academic performance.

A recent meta-analysis carried out by Sailer and Homer (2020), in which they examined a final sample of 38 publications reporting 40 experiments, provided evidence that gamification benefits learning and the results of their study were in line with the theory of gamified learning (Landers, 2015) and self-determination theory (Deci & Ryan, 2002).

Among the most reported benefits of gamified learning, there are the following: better cognitive learning outcomes, higher level of motivation to learn, higher levels of engagement in the learning process (Patrício et al., 2018, 2021).

An empirical study carried out by Freitas et al. (2017) and comparing the results of a total of 150 first-year management students, divided into two equal-sized groups, highlighted that the students taking the gamified version of the course achieved a statistically higher mean score and pass percentage. Similarly, De-Marcos et al. (2017), applying a social gamification approach to an undergraduate course and comparing the students' results with a control group, observed that the gamified group outperformed the control group on practical assignments.

Moreover, on Freitas et al. (2017) students involved in the gamified version of the course showed also higher participation and class attendance than the non-gamified group. Another example is provided by the study of Beemer et al. (2019), which focused on the application of gamification to physical education and highlighted that 55% of the students involved in the study performed a minimum of 20 minutes of daily exercise and only 15% did not regularly participate, with statically significant differences in comparison to the traditional group.

Even though several studies, like those just mentioned, reported beneficial effects of gamification implementations in educational contexts, there are also many studies reporting mixed results and undesirable effects (Buckley & Doyle, 2017; Homer et al., 2018). It is also well documented that gamification can negatively impact intrinsic motivation due to the "overjustification effect" (Cameron et al., 2001; Deci et al., 1999; C. Phillips et al., 2018; Ryan & Deci, 2000). This happens in particular when the appeal of extrinsic rewards catches too much of learners attention, finally becoming for them the main reason to accomplish the foreseen task. This way, the gamification achieves the exact opposite of its initial intent, causing over time an impoverishment of users' initial intrinsic motivation to engage with the system (Marczewski, 2018; Werbach & Hunter, 2012).

In order to design an effective gamified learning initiative and prevent its potential counterproductive effects, it seems evident how important it is to explore deeply the aspects related to the motivational impact of rewards and to the users' individual responses to the rewards offered in a gamified educational system.

The Motivational Impact of Rewards

Since Skinner introduced the concept of reinforcement in his studies about Operant Conditioning (Ferster & Skinner, 1957; Skinner, 1953), the study of the power of rewards as motivators evolved significantly.

Being considered one of the most motivating activities, games have been largely studied in order to understand in which elements, or combinations of elements, such power lies. Scholars focused their attention on the reward system, defining, as a result, taxonomies aiming at knowing rewards at a deeper level.

Hallford & Hallford (2001) made an attempt to categorize rewards in the most inclusive way. Their taxonomy is derived from the study of role-playing games but it has been proposed as suitable also for other games' genres (Salen Tekinbas & Zimmerman, 2003). In their study, four rewards' categories were identified, according to their role in the game: rewards of access, rewards of facility, rewards of sustenance and rewards of glory (Hallford & Hallford, 2001).

Phillips et al. (2013) built upon that taxonomy, extending the four categories of rewards to other game genres. As a result of the study conducted by Phillips et al., the previous taxonomy was expanded and slightly modified, leading to a new categorization including: rewards of access, rewards of facility, rewards of glory, rewards of sustenance, rewards of praise and sensory feedback (C. Phillips et al., 2013).

In 2011 a different approach to categorization was adopted by (Wang & Sun, 2011), which listed the most common types of rewards individually, without grouping them according to their common features. Even if this approach results to be very punctual in summarizing the rewards usually included in games, it lacks inclusivity and requires constant updates, to include new rewards.

In 2017, Rapp attempted the classification of World of Warcraft rewards, through an ethnographic study, based on the value players assigned to rewards and on the effect such rewards had on the gaming experience (Rapp, 2017). Rapp identified three main rewards categories: enabling rewards, exchanging rewards and flexible rewards. In his work, Rapp also highlighted how gamification research rarely confronts itself with game research (Rapp, 2017). Therefore, in this study, as a starting point, we decided to apply the taxonomy proposed by Phillips et al. (C. Phillips et al., 2015) to a gamified application for learning languages.

Multiple studies also investigated the impact of rewards on players' motivation. Most of these studies applied quantitative methods to data collection and analysis (Danner & Lonky, 1981; Deci et al., 1999; Mekler et al., 2017; Sailer et al., 2017), so to find correlations between rewards and Self Determination

Theory basic needs' satisfaction (Danner & Lonky, 1981; Mekler et al., 2017; C. Phillips et al., 2018; Sailer et al., 2017) but also in relation to other motivation theories (Richter et al., 2015).

Also, research about reward's impact on users' motivation, consider specific game elements, usually the most used ones (namely points, badges, leaderboard and few others) more than categories of rewards (Mekler et al., 2017; Sailer et al., 2017).

All this considered, for the purpose of this exploratory study a qualitative approach was chosen, so to examine in depth users' feelings and perceptions derived from the usage of a gamified application. We also contextualized this study in the framework of the SDT, one of the theories mostly considered in game and gamification studies (Dicheva et al., 2018; Seaborn & Fels, 2015).

The Gap in the Research and the Research Questions

As anticipated, it is not usual to find studies exploring the impact of the reward system in a gamified application from a qualitative perspective. This exploratory research aims at answering the following research questions:

- **RQ1:** In what way do the different kinds of rewards offered in a gamified app affect learners' perception of their level of satisfaction of the three basic needs of SDT?
- **RQ2:** Are all the three basic needs of the SDT perceived as satisfied? Is there a predominance of one need perceived as most satisfied compared to the others?
- **RQ4:** Are there other factors in a gamified application that, to some extent, impact on the overall satisfaction of the three basic needs?

To answer these questions, the author analysed Duolingo, one of the most famous gamified applications for learning foreign languages.

THE GAMIFIED LANGUAGE LEARNING APP DUOLINGO

In this study, we decided to examine the reward system included in Duolingo (https://www.duolingo.com/), one of the most popular gamified learning apps. Duolingo, in fact, counts over 500 million registered users, of which 42 million are active at least once a month, and offers a total of 95 courses in 38 languages (https://www.businessofapps.com/data/duolingo-statistics/).

What contributes to distinguishing Duolingo among the various available applications for learning a foreign language is the gamification of the user experience. Duolingo, in fact, makes use of several game elements in its design, including a complex reward system designed to keep users motivated as much, and as long, as possible.

Duolingo contents are organised into Units, each Unit has a variable number of Lessons. Each Lesson is composed of exercises and can be completed from level 1 to a variable top level. The completion of each Lesson awards a predefined amount of Experience Points (XP). Each Lesson includes a variable amount of exercises and has a progress bar that increases and changes colour as the user solves the exercises. The last exercise of the Lesson is more difficult than the others. When the Lesson is concluded, the user receives a recap of the XP earned. The user also receives Daily Streak Points that reward consistency in the use of the application.

For the purposes of this study, all the rewards present in Duolingo were surveyed and were subsequently associated with the categories identified by Phillips (C. Phillips et al., 2015), as we will see further on.

The analysis of the Duolingo mobile application led to the list of rewards summarised in Table 1.

It has to be noted that, depending on the language studied, rewards can vary, along with interface elements; therefore, it is necessary to specify that the languages studied for the purpose of this research were: English, Japanese, German, Klingon.

METHODOLOGICAL APPROACH

In order to answer the research questions of this exploratory study, it was decided to adopt a qualitative approach, based on a diary study.

This method has been adopted on different occasions, by scholars investigating the perception of the individual user experience in different fields. Among others (Czerwinski et al., 2004; Grinter & Eldridge, 2003; Sohn et al., 2008), Rapp adopted the same method to study in which way the gamified elements foster the user's engagement and participation (Rapp, 2015).

In the specific case of gamification design, it has been assessed that the "one size fits all" approach doesn't guarantee the efficacy of gamified solutions (Harviainen, 2014; Monterrat et al., 2017). This awareness leads to the need for more data and insights about users' subjective experiences with gamified systems; the diary study method allows access to single users' thoughts and perceptions which are pivotal for a more qualitative analysis of the gamified experience efficacy, both from the HCI and learning experience point of view.

Traditionally, the efficacy of a gamified system, and therefore of the HCI experience is evaluated through the collection and analysis of qualitative data. In recent times, also in the HCI field arises the need for a deeper understanding of the individual experience (Adams et al., 2008) and, consequently, for the adoption of qualitative methods for such studies (Rode et al., 2012).

Despite the sample size involved in the diary study being smaller than the quantitative one, precious insights on the user experience can be gathered and examined (Fossey et al., 2002; Marshall, 1996).

Diary studies, similarly to the Experience Sampling Method (Csikszentmihalyi, 2014), give users the chance to record their thoughts and feelings almost while they occur. In their diary, users have to take notes about what happens during the use of the application, highlighting relevant events and the feelings related to them. They also have the chance to reflect more thoroughly about the experience, writing down the overall subjective perception of the experience (Church & Smyth, 2009). In the specific case of the present study, the focus is on the learning experience and on the efficacy of the reward system implemented in the Duolingo application.

Adopting the diary study method has several advantages. For example, it is possible to have access to users' thoughts and reflections on an ongoing basis, and in circumstances where the researcher's presence would not be possible. Thanks to the regular annotations, it is also possible to be aware of any changes in user behaviour and perceptions over time (Iida et al., 2012). These are all information fundamental to understanding the effectiveness of a gamified system, and in particular, of the reward system, through time.

Right after completion of the usage period, and of the diary compiling, users were asked to fill in a questionnaire consisting of four sections: section one including demographic information, section two including questions regarding their gaming habits, if any, section three including questions to assess the

Table 1. List of Duolingo rewards and description

Type of rewards	Description
Gems	Represent a sort of in-game currency and can be spent to buy items in the Duolingo shop. They are awarded: • In chests; • When completing a Unit;
XP Points	Through XP it is possible to progress in the leaderboard (league) and to unlock chests. Are awarded: • At the end of each lesson • In chests As a special feature, at the end of each chapter, XP points are doubled for 15 minutes.
Unit progression	The user progresses from one Unit to the next each time all the lessons included in the Unit are completed at least at level 1.
Chests	Chests include surprise rewards, usually Gems, XP or power-ups, in variable amounts. They can be: • Awarded after completing a daily goal • Free, gifted each hour.
Feedback messages	Users receive feedback messages every time a task is completed.
Animations	• Awarded after correctly answering questions in a row • Awarded after completing an exercise • Awarded after completing a lesson.
Audio feedback	Are awarded after each interaction, whether it is right or wrong.
Progression bar on top of the screen	The bar progresses every time a task is accomplished in the system.
Daily streak point	Are awarded to support consistency in the system: for every day of use in continuity a streak point is awarded.
Power-ups	Have the role to give competitive advantages in Duolingo. Can be: Awarded after completing a lesson Bought in the store spending gems Found in chests.
Badge	Are awarded for completing a challenge.
Motivational messages	Are visualised during the lessons, when exercises are completed.
Motivational messages referred to other players	Are visualised when a friend achieves something in the app.
Crowns	Indicate the level reached in single lessons of a learning unit. Are awarded for completing a lesson in a Unit.
Hearts	Are awarded for watching a video ad.
Owl outfits	Can be bought in the store, spending Gems.
Changing colour of the progress bar while progressing in the quizzes	The colour changes every time the user completes 5 exercises.
Unlocking Duolingo Plus freely for 3 days	Is awarded after using Duolingo for 7 days in a row.
Leaderboard	Are unlocked after the fourth lesson.

satisfaction of the three basic needs (Autonomy, Relatedness and Competence) as theorized by the Self-

Table 2. The sample

Participant Code	Age	Gender	Work	Gaming frequency	Favoured kind of games	Experience with Gamification
P1	22	M	Stud.	Very High	Digital and Analog	Yes
P2	24	M	Unemp.	High	Digital	Yes
P3	42	F	Emp.	Very High	Digital	No
P4	25	F	Emp.	Medium	Digital	Yes

Determination Theory (SDT) (Ryan & Deci, 2000), and section four, including questions dedicated to gathering information on their perception of the rewards received during the usage of Duolingo.

In section three, the three basic needs satisfaction is assessed through the Basic Psychological Need Satisfaction Scale (Deci et al., 2001; Ilardi et al., 1993; Kasser et al., 1992), while section four includes questions to investigate the needs' satisfaction generated by the rewards foreseen in Duolingo, through the Activity-Feeling States (AFS) Scale (Reeve & Sickenius, 1994).

Finally, in the light of both diaries and questionnaire results, a focus group was conducted, in order to deepen our understanding of participants' individual responses to the Duolingo reward system.

As for the reward categorization, we were interested not only in better understanding the users' perception of single rewards, but also to try to generalise the results to a whole group of rewards. Therefore, we proceeded to allocate Duolingo rewards in the proper categories foreseen by the Phillips et al. taxonomy, built in its turn on the Halford and Halford one (Hallford & Hallford, 2001; C. Phillips et al., 2013). To proceed in this classification, a group of five experts in the field of gamification design were involved, and invited to use the Duolingo application for one week. After the usage period, they participated in a focus group, aiming at sorting and classifying the Duolingo rewards, according to the Phillips categories.

The Participants

This exploratory study was conducted on a sample of four users, two male and two female, ranging in age between 22 to 42. One of them was a student, two were employed and 1 was unemployed. In the questionnaire they had to fill in before the focus group, they were asked about their gaming habits and two of them reported playing every day, while the others reported playing less frequently but still on a regular basis. Three of the participants mostly played digital games, while one of them enjoyed playing both digital and analogue games.

Regarding their level of familiarity with gamification, all participants were familiar with the concept of gamification and showed a positive attitude towards it, although only three of them had used one or more gamified apps prior to their participation in this research.

Sample size (4) was considered adequate for this study, in consideration of its qualitative nature and its exploratory purpose (Dworkin, 2012; Malterud et al., 2016).

The participants' effort using Duolingo during the one-week research period was on a voluntary basis and they were not compensated for either the diary study or the one-hour focus group.

Table 3. Interview guide

Section of the Focus Group	Questions
Warm-up questions	Which language did you choose to learn and what was your level of knowledge of the language you chose? Why did you choose to try to learn that very language? Have you previously used other gamified applications? If yes, which applications were they, how long did you use them for, and how was your overall user experience?
Transition questions	What were your expectations of the Duolingo app? What did you expect to achieve by using it? Do you feel that your expectations were met or not? Have notifications been an effective trigger in prompting you to use the app?
Key questions	Your motivation to use Duolingo does not seem to have remained constant throughout the week. What was the impact of the rewards you received on your general level of motivation to learn? Did the rewards received somehow balance out/make repetitive tasks less boring, increasing the enjoyment of the experience? Have you ever used power-ups or spent gems to buy power-ups? Would you have appreciated having more opportunities to spend gems?
Additional questions	Do you plan to continue using the app now that your participation in this research has ended? Does anyone have something further to add?

The Procedure

The gamified app chosen for this study was Duolingo not only because it is a very popular app but also because, while many other gamified apps mostly relies on points, badges and leaderboards as the building blocks of their reward system, Duolingo implements a very rich and diverse system of rewards, as shown in Table 1, offering to us the chance to analyse users' responses and preferences in relation to a wider range of rewards and reward mechanisms and schedules.

Participants were instructed to download the app on their smartphone and use it, in its free version, regularly over a period of seven consecutive days. They were let free to decide the language they like to learn, and the time to spend each day to learn it.

Each day, participants were also asked to fill in an electronic diary, shared with them as GoogleDoc, to report their feeling and thoughts about their experience with the app, with a particular focus on emotional response generated by the rewards received.

Once the research time frame was over, participants were invited to fill in a digital questionnaire to gather some more data about their characteristics, and then participated in a focus group to discuss their overall experience. Using the diaries and the questionnaires as prompts, to build an interview guide covering all the aspects relevant for the research (see Table 3).

Two researchers were present during the focus group, one acting as a moderator and the other as an assistant moderator. The session lasted approximately 90 minutes, was audio recorded, transcribed verbatim and then analysed through qualitative content analysis (Hsieh & Shannon, 2005; Krippendorff, 2018; Weber, 1990).

In parallel, the group of five experts used the gamified application as well, with the goal of understanding the role of rewards in the system, and then being able to place them in the appropriate categories of the Phillips taxonomy. During the focus group,

The rewards, summarized in Table 1, have been distributed as shown in Table 4.

Table 4. Rewards' distribution in taxonomy categories

Taxonomy categories	Original definition	Duolingo rewards
Rewards of access	Grant the player admission to otherwise inaccessible environments, environmental objects, or game modes (including narrative cutscenes).	• Chapter progression • Unlocking Duolingo Plus freely for 3 days after using Duolingo for seven days in a row • Crown
Rewards of facility	Increase the effectiveness of the player within the game state.	• Daily streak points
Rewards of sustenance	Mitigate burden, such that a negative play state (such as losing all health or running out of ammunition) is less probable.	• Power ups awarded after completing a lesson • Hearts (lives) awarded for watching a video ad
Rewards of Glory	Are considered to be videogame rewards that do not impact moment to moment gameplay, and that are quantifiable in either the game or meta-game through points, achievements, badges and definitive victory conditions, such as winning the game. However, Rewards of Glory do not extend to non-quantifiable feedback such as praise from an in-game character or visual feedback at the end of a level.	• XP Points • Badge awarded for completing a challenge • Leaderboard
Rewards of Praise	Communicate (verbally or textually) a form of praise or flattery via game systems to the player.	• Feedback messages • Motivational messages • Motivational messages referred to other players
Sensory feedback	Provide the user with overt aesthetic or tactile feedback that is designed to promote positive affect in the player.	• Animations after correctly answering 5/10 questions in a row • Animations after completing an exercise • Audio feedbacks • Progression bar on top of the screen • Animation after completing a lesson • Changing colour of the progress bar while progressing in the quizzes
Rewards of Currency	Can be spent or exchanged in the gamified application.	Gems
Rewards of self-expression	Enable the player to express him/herself in the game, and to express his/her own. individuality/creativity	Owl outfits

During the focus group with experts, devoted to a reflection on the nature of the rewards included in Duolingo, it emerged that two of the rewards included in Duolingo were not classifiable in the existing categories.

Therefore, two more categories were added, one called rewards of currency, in which to include those rewards that can be exchanged or used in the system to purchase other items, and one called Rewards of self-expression, that allow the user to express their own individuality/creativity.

RESULTS AND DISCUSSION

Before starting to discuss participants' perception of the rewards received in Duolingo, it is interesting to notice that often, during their experience with Duolingo, participants' reported doubts about the reward system.

"Having started my lesson today it [the app] gave me a daily 'streak', but about half an hour later it disappeared. I didn't understand if I did something wrong." P1-Day1

Even though the lack of clarity about the reward system didn't prevent the participants to keep using the app and to enjoy the rewards received, it seems to diminish their sense of agency and negatively affect their need for competence. They, in fact, started questioning themselves for not being able to understand why they received a specific reward or what was its meaning.

"I'm starting to understand the reward system better, although I still don't know what I did to deserve the double XP bonus for 10 minutes. Perhaps I missed it, I don't know if it's indicated. I'd like to figure it out so I can take advantage of it later." P3-Day2

"It is still unclear to me how I get the bonuses, sometimes it seems a bit random, but I don't think it is. The fact that I don't really understand the system according to which some rewards are given makes me lose enthusiasm a bit. But I'm still at the stage where I'm getting the hang of it, so maybe it's my fault." P3-Day3

The analysis of diaries, questionnaires and focus group's transcriptions brought to the surface a set of mixed feelings about the reward system included in Duolingo. In Table 5 are synthesized the main impressions about the impact of each reward on the three basic needs.

As can be observed in Table 5, not all rewards were considered by users having a perceived impact one at least one of the three basic needs (ref. Table 1). Most of the rewards are perceived as having an impact on the need for competence. In regard to that, the level progression is considered a source of satisfaction and motivation. Rewards that grant access to new levels/content are perceived as a clear indicator of one's progress.

"[I felt] happiness especially in passing the first stage of learning, and satisfaction in getting both the crown and (as a consequence) the ability to have access to the second level of the language" P1-Day5.

Table 6 summarizes the distribution over the taxonomy categories of the rewards considered as impactful by users.

In spite of the fact that the majority of the rewards is considered as having an impact on at least one of the three basic needs, the overall feeling about the reward system is not positive.

Even if the first moments using the application were engaging and interesting for all the users, boredom set in quite quickly.

The initial enthusiasm starts to wane as the exercises offered are always the same and it doesn't feel like we are really going on anymore. After the first 10 minutes I started making distracting mistakes as I couldn't wait for the game session to end. P4-Day3.

Table 5. Rewards' subjective perceived impact on the three basic needs

	Autonomy	Competence	Relatedness
P1	• Gems • Free chests	• Chapter progression • Progression bar • Animation after lesson • Badge • Motivational messages • Crowns	• Leaderboard
P2	• Gems • Chapter progression • Owl outfits	• XP points • Chapter progression • Progression bar • Motivational messages	• XP points • Leaderboards • Motivational messages referred to other players
P3	• Chapter progression	• Chapter progression • Animations (all) • Power ups	• Leaderboard
P4	• Gems • Crowns • Owl outfits	• Chapter progression • Progression bar • Crowns • Owl outfits • Leaderboard	• Leaderboards • Motivational messages referred to other players

Table 6. Distribution of resources according to the taxonomy

Taxonomy categories	Autonomy	Competence	Relatedness
Rewards of access	Chapter progression Crowns	Chapter progression Crowns	-
Rewards of facility	-	-	-
Rewards of sustenance	-	Power ups	-
Rewards of Glory	-	XP Points Badge awarded for completing a challenge Leaderboard	XP Points Leaderboard
Rewards of Praise	-	Motivational messages	Motivational messages
Sensory feedback	-	Animations after correctly answering 5/10 questions in a row Animations after completing an exercise Progression bar on top of the screen Animation after completing a lesson	-
Rewards of Currency	Gems		-
Rewards of self-expression	Owl outfits	Owl outfits	-

In general, all rewards are perceived as without purpose, or with very limited purpose, therefore, felt as demotivating.

I like getting rewards but it's starting to feel a bit 'purposeless', perhaps because I'm still not clear on what the xp is for. Aside from the gems that are needed in duolingo to receive aesthetic stuff (very limited) and be able to avoid ruining the app's usage streak, the accumulation of rewards seems a bit of an end in itself. P3-Day4.

On the other hand, the learning purpose of the application is appreciated by users, independently from the reward system.

I feel satisfied, entertained, and motivated since through the experience I learned a basic grammar rule that I had long ignored. P4-Day1.

What surfaced in the investigation is that one external factor seems to have had a relevant impact on the overall perception of the reward system, namely the lack of clarity and transparency of the reward system, as previously reported.

The satisfaction grows as the usefulness of the rewards becomes clearer.

I received xp that put me on the bronze leaderboard that opened up for me yesterday. So now I understand what the xp's are for and they make a little more sense. It still remains unclear what advantage I have to moving up in that leaderboard (other than the personal satisfaction of my ranking). P3-Day6.

CONCLUSION

What emerged in this qualitative exploratory study is that the need perceived as the most satisfied, compared to the others, is the need for competence. The majority of the rewards considered relevant for users contributes to give the sense of progression and improvement, while only in few cases the sense of autonomy and relatedness are fostered.

Unfortunately, the lack of variety and progression in the reward system itself, seems to quickly lead users to boredom. It seems also that gamification failed at its primary objective: contribute to making boring tasks less boring and more game-like.

This is exploratory study intended to examine, from a qualitative point of view, the users' experience in a gamified system, to have a better understanding of users' perceptions and thoughts when learning with the support of a reward system.

Further studies can be conducted with a broader sample of users, to verify if the feelings and perceptions of this small sample are confirmed.

REFERENCES

Adams, A., Lunt, P., & Cairns, P. (2008). A qualitative approach to HCI research. In P. Cairns & A. Cox (Eds.), Research Methods for Human-Computer Interaction (pp. 138–157). Cambridge University Press. doi:10.1017/CBO9780511814570.008

Armstrong, M. B., & Landers, R. N. (2017). An Evaluation of Gamified Training: Using Narrative to Improve Reactions and Learning. *Simulation & Gaming*, *48*(4), 513–538. doi:10.1177/1046878117703749

Beemer, L. R., Ajibewa, T. A., Dellavecchia, G., & Hasson, R. E. (2019). A pilot intervention using gamification to enhance student participation in classroom activity breaks. *International Journal of Environmental Research and Public Health*, *16*(21), 1–11. doi:10.3390/ijerph16214082 PMID:31652885

Bertalero, G., Addebito, P., Bancario, C. C., & Cliente, C. A. L. (2018). *Gamified learning in higher education: A systematic review of the literature*. Academic Press.

Botte, B., Bakkes, S., & Veltkamp, R. (2020). Motivation in Gamification: Constructing a Correlation Between Gamification Achievements and Self-determination Theory. *Lecture Notes in Computer Science*, *12517*, 157–166. doi:10.1007/978-3-030-63464-3_15

Buckley, P., & Doyle, E. (2017). Individualising gamification: An investigation of the impact of learning styles and personality traits on the efficacy of gamification using a prediction market. *Computers & Education*, *106*, 43–55. doi:10.1016/j.compedu.2016.11.009

Cameron, J., Banko, K. M., & Pierce, W. D. (2001). Pervasive Negative Effects of Rewards on Intrinsic Motivation: The Myth Continues. *The Behavior Analyst*, *24*(1), 1–44. doi:10.1007/BF03392017 PMID:22478353

Chia, A., Hung, Y., Zarco, E., Yang, M., Dembicki, D., & Kase, M. (2017). Gamification in the wild: Faculty perspectives on gamifying learning in higher education. *Issues and Trends in Educational Technology*, *5*(2), 4–22.

Church, K., & Smyth, B. (2009). Understanding the intent behind mobile information needs. *Proceedings of the 14th International Conference on Intelligent User Interfaces*, 247–256. 10.1145/1502650.1502686

Csikszentmihalyi, M. (2014). *Flow and the Foundations of Positive Psychology*. Springer. doi:10.1007/978-94-017-9088-8

Czerwinski, M., Horvitz, E., & Wilhite, S. (2004). A diary study of task switching and interruptions. *Proceedings of the SIGCHI Conference on Human Factors in Computing Systems*, 175–182. 10.1145/985692.985715

Danner, F. W., & Lonky, E. (1981). A Cognitive-Developmental Approach to the Effects of Rewards on Intrinsic Motivation. *Child Development*, *52*(3), 1043–1052. doi:10.2307/1129110

De-Marcos, L., García-Cabot, A., & García-López, E. (2017). Towards the Social Gamification of e-Learning: A Practical Experiment. *International Journal of Engineering Education*, *1*, 1–14. https://portal.uah.es/portal/page/portal/epd2_profesores/prof23288/publicaciones/0PaperSocialGamificationv5.4_IJEE_preprint.pdf

Deci, E. L., & Ryan, R. M. (2002). Overview of self-determination theory: An organismic dialectical perspective. In E. L. Deci & R. M. Ryan (Eds.), *Handbook of self-determination research* (pp. 3–33). University Rochester Press.

Deci, E. L., Ryan, R. M., Gagné, M., Leone, D. R., Usunov, J., & Kornazheva, B. P. (2001). Need satisfaction, motivation, and well-being in the work organizations of a former eastern bloc country: A cross-cultural study of self-determination. *Personality and Social Psychology Bulletin, 27*(8), 930–942. doi:10.1177/0146167201278002

Deci, E. L., Ryan, R. M., & Koestner, R. (1999). A meta-analytic review of experiments examining the effects of extrinsic rewards on intrinsic motivation. *Psychological Bulletin, 125*(6), 627–668. doi:10.1037/0033-2909.125.6.627 PMID:10589297

Deterding, S. (2011). Situated motivational affordances of game elements: A conceptual model. *CHI Gamification Workshop 2011*, 3–6.

Dichev, C., & Dicheva, D. (2017). Gamifying education: what is known, what is believed and what remains uncertain: a critical review. International Journal of Educational Technology in Higher Education, 14(1). doi:10.118641239-017-0042-5

Dicheva, D., Irwin, K., & Dichev, C. (2018). OneUp: Supporting Practical and Experimental Gamification of Learning. *International Journal of Serious Games, 5*(3), 5–21. doi:10.17083/ijsg.v5i3.236

Dworkin, S. L. (2012). Sample size policy for qualitative studies using in-depth interviews. [). Springer.]. *Archives of Sexual Behavior, 41*(6), 1319–1320. doi:10.100710508-012-0016-6 PMID:22968493

Entertainment Software Association. (2020). 2020 Essential Facts About the Video Game Industry. *Cision*, 1–2. https://www.prnewswire.com/news-releases/new-survey-2020-essential-facts-about-the-video-game-industry-301093972.html

Ferster, C. B., & Skinner, B. F. (1957). *Schedules of reinforcement*. Prentice-Hall, Inc. doi:10.1037/10627-000

Fossey, E., Harvey, C., McDermott, F., & Davidson, L. (2002). Understanding and evaluating qualitative research. *The Australian and New Zealand Journal of Psychiatry, 36*(6), 717–732. doi:10.1046/j.1440-1614.2002.01100.x PMID:12406114

Freitas, S. A. A., Lacerda, A. R. T., Calado, P. M. R. O., Lima, T. S., & Canedo, E. D. (2017). Gamification in education: A methodology to identify student's profile. *Proceedings - Frontiers in Education Conference,* 1–8. 10.1109/FIE.2017.8190499

Glover, I. (2013). Play as you learn : Gamification as a technique for motivating learners. *Proceedings of World Conference on Educational Multimedia, Hypermedia and Telemcommunications, 1*, 1999–2008.

Grinter, R., & Eldridge, M. (2003). Wan2tlk? Everyday text messaging. *Proceedings of the SIGCHI Conference on Human Factors in Computing Systems*, 441–448. 10.1145/642611.642688

Hallford, N., & Hallford, J. (2001a). *Swords and circuitry: A designer's guide to computer role-playing games*. Premier Press.

Hamari, J., Koivisto, J., & Sarsa, H. (2014). Does gamification work? - A literature review of empirical studies on gamification. *Proceedings of the Annual Hawaii International Conference on System Sciences*, 3025–3034. 10.1109/HICSS.2014.377

Harviainen, J. T. (2014). Critical Challenges to Gamifying Education. *Proceedings of the Game On Conference*.

Homer, R., Hew, K. F., & Tan, C. Y. (2018). Comparing digital badges-and-points with classroom token systems: Effects on elementary school ESL students' classroom behavior and English learning. *Journal of Educational Technology & Society*, *21*(1), 137–151.

Houlfort, N., Koestner, R., Joussemet, M., Nantel-Vivier, A., & Lekes, N. (2002). The impact of performance-contingent rewards on perceived autonomy and competence. *Motivation and Emotion*, *29*(4), 279–295. doi:10.1023/A:1022819120237

Hsieh, H. F., & Shannon, S. E. (2005). Three approaches to qualitative content analysis. *Qualitative Health Research*, *15*(9), 1277–1288. doi:10.1177/1049732305276687 PMID:16204405

Iida, M., Shrout, P. E., Laurenceau, J.-P., & Bolger, N. (2012). Using diary methods in psychological research. In *APA handbook of research methods in psychology* (Vol. 1). American Psychological Association.

Ilardi, B. C., Leone, D., Kasser, T., & Ryan, R. M. (1993). Employee and supervisor ratings of motivation: Main effects and discrepancies associated with job satisfaction and adjustment in a factory setting 1. *Journal of Applied Social Psychology*, *23*(21), 1789–1805. doi:10.1111/j.1559-1816.1993.tb01066.x

ISFE. (2020). *Europe Video Game Industry Key Facts 2020*. https://www.isfe.eu/wp-content/uploads/2020/08/ISFE-final-1.pdf

Kasser, T., Davey, J., & Ryan, R. M. (1992). Motivation and employee-supervisor discrepancies in a psychiatric vocational rehabilitation setting. *Rehabilitation Psychology*, *37*(3), 175–188. doi:10.1037/h0079104

Krippendorff, K. (2018). *Content analysis: An introduction to its methodology*. Sage publications.

Landers, R. N. (2015). Developing a Theory of Gamified Learning: Linking Serious Games and Gamification of Learning. *Simulation & Gaming*, *45*(6), 752–768. doi:10.1177/1046878114563660

Lewis, Z. H., Swartz, M. C., & Lyons, E. J. (2016). What's the point?: A review of reward systems implemented in gamification interventions. *Games for Health Journal*, *5*(2), 93–99. doi:10.1089/g4h.2015.0078 PMID:26812253

Malterud, K., Siersma, V. D., & Guassora, A. D. (2016). Sample size in qualitative interview studies: Guided by information power. *Qualitative Health Research*, *26*(13), 1753–1760. doi:10.1177/1049732315617444 PMID:26613970

Manzano-León, A., Camacho-Lazarraga, P., Guerrero, M. A., Guerrero-Puerta, L., Aguilar-Parra, J. M., Trigueros, R., & Alias, A. (2021). Between level up and game over: A systematic literature review of gamification in education. *Sustainability (Switzerland)*, *13*(4), 1–14. doi:10.3390u13042247

Marczewski, A. (2018). Even Ninja Monkeys Like to Play: Unicorn Edition. Gamified UK.

Marshall, M. N. (1996). Sampling for qualitative research. *Family Practice*, *13*(6), 522–526. doi:10.1093/fampra/13.6.522 PMID:9023528

Mekler, E. D., Brühlmann, F., Tuch, A. N., & Opwis, K. (2017). Towards understanding the effects of individual gamification elements on intrinsic motivation and performance. *Computers in Human Behavior*, *71*, 525–534. doi:10.1016/j.chb.2015.08.048

Monterrat, B., Lavoué, É., & George, S. (2017). Adaptation of gaming features for motivating learners. *Simulation & Gaming*, *48*(5), 625–656. doi:10.1177/1046878117712632

Patrício, R., Moreira, A. C., & Zurlo, F. (2018). Gamification approaches to the early stage of innovation. *Creativity and Innovation Management*, *27*(4), 499–511. doi:10.1111/caim.12284

Patrício, R., Moreira, A. C., & Zurlo, F. (2021). Enhancing design thinking approaches to innovation through gamification. *European Journal of Innovation Management*, *4*(27), 499–511. doi:10.1108/EJIM-06-2020-0239

Phillips, C., Johnson, D., Klarkowski, M., White, M., & Hides, L. (2018). The impact of rewards and trait reward responsiveness on player motivation. *CHI PLAY 2018 - Proceedings of the 2018 Annual Symposium on Computer-Human Interaction in Play*. 10.1145/3242671.3242713

Phillips, C., Johnson, D., & Wyeth, P. (2013). Videogame reward types. *ACM International Conference Proceeding Series*, 103–106. 10.1145/2583008.2583025

Phillips, C., Johnson, D., Wyeth, P., Hides, L., & Klarkowski, M. (2015). Redefining videogame reward types. *OzCHI 2015: Being Human - Conference Proceedings*, 83–91. 10.1145/2838739.2838782

Phillips, R. S., Horstman, T., Vye, N., & Bransford, J. (2014). Engagement and Games for Learning: Expanding Definitions and Methodologies. *Simulation & Gaming*, *45*(4-5), 548–568. doi:10.1177/1046878114553576

Prensky, M. (2003). *Don't Bother Me Mom: I'm learning. How computer and video games are preparing your kids for 21st Century success and how you can help*. Paragon House.

Rapp, A. (2015). A qualitative investigation of gamification: Motivational factors in online gamified services and applications. *International Journal of Technology and Human Interaction*, *11*(1), 67–82. doi:10.4018/ijthi.2015010105

Rapp, A. (2017). From Games to Gamification: A Classification of Rewards in World of Warcraft for the Design of Gamified Systems. *Simulation & Gaming*, *48*(3), 381–401. doi:10.1177/1046878117697147

Reeve, J., & Sickenius, B. (1994). Development and validation of a brief measure of the three psychological needs underlying intrinsic motivation: The AFS scales. *Educational and Psychological Measurement*, *54*(2), 506–515. doi:10.1177/0013164494054002025

Richter, G., Raban, D. R., & Rafaeli, S. (2015). Studying gamification: The effect of rewards and incentives on motivation. In Gamification in Education and Business (pp. 21–46). doi:10.1007/978-3-319-10208-5_2

Rode, J., Blythe, M., & Nardi, B. (2012). Qualitative research in HCI. In CHI'12 Extended Abstracts on Human Factors in Computing Systems (pp. 2803–2806). doi:10.1145/2212776.2212725

Ryan, R. M., & Deci, E. L. (1987). The support of autonomy and the control of behavior. *Journal of Personnel Psychology*, *53*(6), 1024–1037. doi:10.1037/0022-3514.53.6.1024 PMID:3320334

Ryan, R. M., & Deci, E. L. (2000). Intrinsic and Extrinsic Motivations: Classic Definitions and New Directions. *Contemporary Educational Psychology*, *25*(1), 54–67. doi:10.1006/ceps.1999.1020 PMID:10620381

Sailer, M., Hense, J. U., Mayr, S. K., & Mandl, H. (2017). How gamification motivates: An experimental study of the effects of specific game design elements on psychological need satisfaction. *Computers in Human Behavior*, *69*, 371–380. doi:10.1016/j.chb.2016.12.033

Sailer, M., & Homner, L. (2020). The Gamification of Learning: A Meta-analysis. *Educational Psychology Review*, *32*(1), 77–112. doi:10.100710648-019-09498-w

Salen Tekinbas, K., & Zimmerman, E. (2003). *Rules of play: Game design fundamentals*. MIT Press.

Seaborn, K., & Fels, D. I. (2015). Gamification in theory and action: A survey. *International Journal of Human-Computer Studies*, *74*, 14–31. doi:10.1016/j.ijhcs.2014.09.006

Skinner, B. F. (1953). *Science and human behavior*. Macmillan.

Sohn, T., Li, K. A., Griswold, W. G., & Hollan, J. D. (2008). A diary study of mobile information needs. *Proceedings of the Sigchi Conference on Human Factors in Computing Systems*, 433–442. 10.1145/1357054.1357125

Walz, S. P., & Deterding, S. (2014). An Introduction to the Gameful World. In S. P. Walz & S. Deterding (Eds.), *The gameful world. Approaches, issues, applications* (pp. 1–13). The MIT Press.

Wang, H., & Sun, C.-T. (2011). Game reward systems: Gaming experiences and social meanings. *DiGRA Conference, 114*.

Weber, R. P. (1990). Basic content analysis (2nd ed.). Sage Publications. doi:10.4135/9781412983488

Werbach, K., & Hunter, D. (2012). *For the win: How game thinking can revolutionize your business*. Wharton Digital Press.

Chapter 31
Gamifying the Refugee Classroom:
Challenges and Potential

Katerina Bizota
Hellenic Open University, Greece

Katerina Makri
Hellenic Open University, Greece

ABSTRACT

This research presents the design, implementation, and evaluation of a theory-driven educational scenario for students with a refugee background based on gamification to support learning Greek as a second language. The scenario was implemented in an educational priority zone (ZEP) classroom of a Greek primary school with eight refugee students aged 9 to 11 with a diverse linguistic background. The gamified educational platform Classcraft was used, transforming the lesson into a fantasy map-based world with heroes and quests. The findings indicate that the game elements significantly impacted engagements were competition and collaboration and some immersion-related features like storytelling, which increased autonomy. The language goal of the scenario was attained by the majority of students displaying that gamification can promote language development if adjusted to students' language level. From the findings, two demotivating factors were detected that should be taken under consideration for future studies.

INTRODUCTION

In Greece, the Covid-19 pandemic has created a game-changing shift in refugee education by bringing into the spotlight ICT teaching models and modernization of Second Language Acquisition (SLA). If we take into account the fact that refugee students are accompanied by a powerful asset, which is the eagerness to explore and learn new things, games are the perfect experience to "learn by doing", filled with intrinsic motivation and engagement. Given that, gamification is one of those practices that look towards this direction.

DOI: 10.4018/978-1-6684-4287-6.ch031

Gamification in education, as a novel field of study, received a great deal of attention during the last decade by encouraging instructional designers to incorporate game elements into learning practices to generate active, experiential and ludic learning to stimulate learners and raise competence (Stott &Neustaedter, 2013). However, the educational gamification field is still in early stages with many unexamined aspects (Koivisto & Hamari, 2019).Zooming into literature, what remains under-exploited are the effects of gamification in refugee education, thus the field calls for well-designed and theory-driven educational scenarios, tailored to the needs of the refugee population (Bock, Haque & McMahon, 2020).

This chapter explores the potential of gamification for one of the most neglected populations in educational technology and gamification literature, namely the refugee young generation. This endeavor will attempt to fill the existing gap by investigating how gamification can be applied in a reception classroom through Classcraft, a digital platform offering a wide range of gamification mechanics. Specifically, the research aimed at designing and implementing a gamified scenario to examine if gamification can promote refugee students' engagement in learning Greek as a Second Language (GSL).

BACKGROUND

Defining the Concept of Gamification in Education

The concept of gamification is not entirely new in the educational arena and has been applied in several educational contexts during the last decade, yet a large amount of information is still unknown (Metwally, Nacke, Chang, Wang & Yousef, 2021).

As a starting point, the definition that dominates the literature pertains to Deterding, Dixon, Khaled and Nacke (2011a), who defined gamification as "*the use of game design elements in non-game contexts*" (p. 2). On its part, Werbach (2014) refined this conceptualization as "*the process of making activities more game-like*" (p. 6). In 2015, the conceptualization has finally moved towards learning by Landers, inaugurating gamification of learning. In his theory of gamified learning, gamification is interpreted as "*the use of game attributes, including action language, assessment, conflict/challenge, control, environment, game fiction, human interaction, immersion, and rules/goals to facilitate learning and related outcomes" (p. 6)*. In other words, gamification in education is a mechanism that conflates game elements and game-like experiences into the learning process with the ultimate goal to change learner's contextual behavior.

With that in mind, an increasing number of educational implementations made their appearancewith positive results on motivation, engagement, performance and interaction (Antonaci, Klemke, & Specht, 2019; Zainuddin, Chu, Shujahat, & Perera, 2020), but outpaced the understanding of gamification and its method (Dichev & Dicheva, 2017; Landers, Bauer, Callan, & Armstrong, 2015).

GameDesign Elements: Beyond PBL

Gamification approaches game designthrough an innovative lens (Patrício, Moreira & Zurlo, 2018, 2021). Werbach and Hunter (2012) pointed out that an engaging game is based on a player's desires. If the objective of gamification is to create a "game-like experience" for players, then the selection of the appropriate elements is of great importance in a game design. Many researchers tried to disclose those elements, without, however reaching consensus, concluding that the one-size-fits-all model is not the answer.

Werbach and Hunter (2012) proposed a three-staged game element's pyramid to illustrate the subset of elements in a bottom-up approach. On its basis, we encounter the Game Components such as achievements, points, levels, quests, teams and avatars that can be used as educational resources to personalize learning. Then, Mechanics follow, which are the processes that can facilitate learning and generate students' engagement (e.g. challenges, chances, competition, cooperation, feedback, rewards). On the higher level tier Dynamics appear, which include more abstract but valuable elements that create a communication rationale like constraints, emotions, narrative, progression, and relationships.

A pertinent question in relevant research is which specific elements have a strong motivational effect on learners. According to a literature review conducted by Hamari, Koivisto and Sarsa (2014), Points, Badges and Leaderboards (The PBL Triad, henceforth referred to as "PBL") are the most commonly used game elements in various learning settings that can affect performance level, engagement and motivation as well as social comparison.However, these game design elements do not address learners as social beings, but rather as rankings (Hamari, Koivisto, & Sarsa, 2014). In this regard, Sailer and colleagues (2017) reviewed the effects of several game design elements suggesting that avatars, guilds and storyline successfully affect experiences of social relatedness. Moreover, Alomari, Al-Samarraie and Yousef (2019) conducted a systematic literature review to examine the role of gamification elements and techniques in promoting students' learning. The majority of studiesareoriented towards PBL, while "other techniques" like avatar-based systems arementioned less frequently. On this neglected category, one can find narrative and storytelling, which are elements with a highly immersive power but still are underrated (Palomino, Toda, Oliveira, Rodrigues, Cristea & Isotani, 2019). Narrative is the element that permeates a purpose of meaning towards a defined goal through its plot, which is supported by storytelling, placing the player into a continuous interaction with the context. That continuous interaction captivates the learner to keep on engaging with the activity for the sake of the ending story (Xi &Hamari, 2019). To elaborate, the study of Xi and Hamari (2019) demonstrated that immersion-related features, like narrative and storytelling, are related to high autonomy levels, as the plot can include an array of choices to be made dependent on learner's personality.

Overall, a "*vital aspect of gamification design is the context of application*" (Antonaci, Klemke& Specht, 2019, p. 21), thus game elements should favor the target audience they address. To achieve that, researchers should deviate from PBL path and welcome other features of game design (Rapp, 2017). Given that, the definition of a theoretical framework that supports the design of specialized game elements, is of great importance (Hamari, Koivisto, &Sarsa, 2014).

Gamification Theories for Education: Building a Framework

The need to establish a theoretical framework on gamification to solidify the game design elements that truly impact learning, led to the birth of a series of theories that traverse the psychological and social domains of users.

The most-frequently used psychological theory in gamification studies is Deci and Ryan's (2008) Self-Determination Theory (SDT), which combines both ends of the motivational spectrum (extrinsic and intrinsic). In SDT, motivation is a gradual process starting from the stage of amotivation, where there is an absence of intentional regulation and control, and through progressive extrinsic sources, the individual approaches intrinsic motivation, attaining to the pure form of motivation, self-determination.

To experience that inherent satisfaction, three intrinsic needs should coexist: Autonomy, Competence, and Relatedness. In a gamification system, students do not engage with learning just for the awards, but for the sense of volition over their environment, the gradual satisfaction of skill mastery and the social connectedness within the gamified community. Nacke and Deterding (2017) examined studies on the PBL through a SDT lens, suggesting that PBL can serve as immediate feedback, providing a gradual sense of internalized competence for the students. In addition, Cruz, Hanus and Fox (2017), revealed that a key tenet of SDT is the way a player ascribes meaning to his/her experiences either intrinsically or extrinsically to boost his/her self-worth. Besides, SDT is not only focused on individual differences, but on how social factors facilitate a sense of volition. Antonaci, Klemke, Kreijns and Specht (2018) developed a ground-breaking theoretical matrix for gamification in a MOOC course, by valorizing the social and individual aspect to scout which game elements can enhance engagement. To this end, the concept of Social Presence theory is of special interest.

Social Presence describes how the sense of community and interdependence can generate a group identity that can impact self-growth and engagement in a blended or computer-mediatedenvironment. It mainly refers to the way individuals establish their "state of being" in a virtual or a traditional way to create interpersonal transactions and social connections (Jusoff& Khodabandelou, 2009). When strong interpersonal relationships are formed in a virtual space, they tend to significantly influence the exchange of information, thereby reinforcing the power of persuasion. In turn, strong social connections can generate feelings of belonging,as long as the members of the group rely on each other to make decisions and take action. Thus, Social Presence relies on group size as a predictor of an effective mediated-communicationas well as the use of an appropriate collaborative "space" to negotiate meaning (Roberts, Lowry & Sweeney, 2006). Small groups are preferable in these cases. Several studies on Social Presence support that face to face interactions can be enhanced through collaborative software like a shared, well-designed interface (Roberts, Lowry & Sweeney, 2006).

Overall, psychological approaches hold the reins in gamification, but theories targeted at education are limited and lack empirical research and practice. The educational realm, nowadays, has been transformed into a multicultural social system with a strong sense of community. Perhaps, what is missing in a gamification conceptual framework is not another theory that describes motivation and behavior patterns, but theories that invest on social capital to fill the missing element of motivational theories, which is social connectedness. Therefore, it is important, when applying gamification in education, to include game elements that can intensify motivation in a *social* way.

Challenges with Gamification

Implementing gamification in education is not an easy task, as there area number of challenges that need to be addressed and negative effects that may emerge if the baseline of the design is flimsy. Toda, Valle and Isotani (2018) identified four negative effects that may transpire when gamification is applied to educational settings. Those are: indifference, loss of performance, undesired effects and declining effects.

Indifference

Indifference may occur when the selected gamification elements may not exert any impact on motivation, engagement or performance, thus no significant difference is perceived between traditional approach and a gamified one. The particular negative effect is noticed, when performance is measured. Several studies pointed out that the performance level of experiment groups did not exert any difference from control groups taught through conventional learning (Papadakis & Kalogiannakis, 2017).

Loss of Performance

Loss of performance is detected when a student's performance is hindered or decreased by the gamification process due to demotivating factors like unclear rules, unfamiliarity with gamification strategies, penalties and difficult tasks. For instance, students' performance may decrease if their name did not appear on a leaderboard (Piteira, Costa, and Aparicio, 2017).

Undesired Behavior

Gamification may exert reversed outcomes such as dissatisfaction, boredom, frustration and demotivation due to fears of failure, insufficient guidance and facilitation or unclear goals. One interesting finding came from Özdener (2018) who reported that the lack of the instructor to gauge the capabilities of the students resulted in students demotivation.

Declining Effects

According to empirical evidence (AlMarshedi,Wills, Wanick & Ranchhod, 2014) a gradual loss of motivation and engagement may occur due to long-term use of the gamified system as students lose their interest in it.Consequently, when designing a gamification system in an educational setting without considering student profiles, instructional objectives and applied theories there is a high chance of a negative effect to occur. If we consider that quite recently the educational use of gamification has been tested rigorously by scholars of the field it is reasonable to extrapolate that the pitfalls of gamification have not been assessed to a great extent. Moreover, the "game master" of gamification in learning is the educator, who needs full support and guidance to design an effective gamified system. Thus, the field calls for well-designed and theory-driven educational gamified initiatives that address the class dynamics to avoid the dark side of gamification.

Refugee Education and Games: Navigating in Uncharted Waters

Zooming into literature, what has remained uncharted is how gamification can be applied in SLA and, more importantly, in refugee education. Although there is a great body of research that focuses on the application of Gamification in education and its effect on students' motivation and engagement, the number of studies conducted on students with a refugee background is limited, almost nonexistent, and mainly oriented in integration purposes through apps or serious games. UNHCR (2020) reported that the number of the forcibly displaced people continues to riseand puts pressure on education to keep the enrolment numbers high by providing equitable and quality education for all beyond reach. Moreover, if we reflect on the global reality and the Coronavirus case, then there is a grave threat of a 'pandemic of inequality' to erupt, as an entire generation has had its education disrupted, and the hard-won increases in school enrolment could be reversed and put the goal of inclusive education in danger. Now more than ever is the need to adopt novel teaching approaches.

According to recent studies on SLA, a refugee has to navigate through different linguistic and cultural worlds by learning the language of the host country to integrate smoothly into a new social context (Mogli& Papadopoulou, 2018). That navigation according to Abujarour, Krasnova and Hoffmeier (2018) is dependent on their capacity to create social connections and thus,nurture a sense of social connectedness that fosters a sense of well-being and stress-reduction. Taking this under consideration, the incorporation of digital games in SLA is able to promote their integration in the classroom and in society. From the work of Lifanova and colleagues (2016), the integration of refugees and migrants is hindered by two major impediments: language barrier and a lack of contacts to local people. However, the main hindrance for integration arises in communication. Learning a language from scratch is not an easy process, but rather full of failure, stressful situations and pressure to become understood and convey meaning. As a result of such frustration, certain learners can become demotivated to continue learning the language and face issues of self-confidence that impedes their progress (Holmes, 2018). To avoid the above negative feelings, we should engage students in a learning process that is fun, intriguing, self-regulated and stress-free.

In a recent study, Castaño-Muñoz, Colucci and Smidt (2018) supported that the adoption of Free Digital Learning (FDL) for inclusion of migrants and refugees in education, is a new area of study and there is little research that assesses its potential and challenges. To fill the existing gap, they conducted a systematic review analysis on studies that provided a design framework for digital learning targeted at this population to find out which teaching approaches best serve their needs. The findings showed that the refugee students prefer:a) guided and personalized approaches that consider cultural/context sensitivities and b) blended learning environments in order to feel connected with their learning environment and build a higher sense of community. On the other hand, if we bear in mind that social connectedness is of paramount importance for refugees (AbuJarour, Krasnova& Hoffmeier, 2018), the use of Information and Communication Technology (ICT) can open new opportunities for pathways to integration and language learning through gamification.

Based on the above reasoning, a number of applications with gamification features have been developed to facilitate the integration of newcomers in the host country and guide them on their first steps. The mobile application, Moin, created by Ngan, Lifanova, Jarke and Broer (2016), is an informal learning and communication application enriched with gamification features aiming at mingling migrant youths with local people in Bremen through participating in an array of social events to create situations of indirect language practice. The incorporated gamification elements include progress bars and leaderboards that are used to keep the young people motivated to continue using the app.However, even if the above application is an original paradigm of how gamification can facilitate integration, it was difficult to map out empirical studies targeted at the refugee populationin formal education and blended learning environments.

The researchers' concluding argument is that gamification in refugee education is a social need. Refugees should stay connected with the globalized reality, now more than ever. Inclusive practices and digital applications can transform their lives and wire them with the rest of the community. While the research on gamification in education has made a leap, there are scarce initiatives addressing this population and their unique needs. Nevertheless, formal schooling is still the gray area of the field with limited research on its premise.

Gamification with Classcraft

Classcraft is characterized as a promising gamification tool in education that raises motivation and participation in a ludic way, but empirical researchis still limited (Sanchez, Young, &Jouneau-Sion, 2017). Classcraft is an online platform based on digital-storytelling that gamifies the learning process by adding elements from RPGs, such as avatars, classes, guilds, talent trees, points, rewards and boss fights, blending the fantasy world with school reality. The platform offers a free of charge basic account, acting as an open source for the educational community. The above characteristics make Classcraft the best possible way to organize and transform your classroom into a game-like system that stimulates students to achieve their learning goals; but that is just the surface of what actually Classcraft can offer.

The supreme feature of this platform is the management system it encapsulates. In this system, the teacher can manage the classroom through variegated and personalized settings like setting up the rules and providingstudents with codes to control theiraccount. Besides, the platform includes a reward/penalty system that can be adjusted by the teacher to meet the needs and behavior patterns of the students, setting the rules for the embedded reality, to encourage desired behavior. The reward system is based on several kinds of points. Specifically, students can earn Experience Points (XP), which allow them to level up and unlock powers, and on the other hand, lose Health Points (HP) if they exhibit an inappropriate behavior.

Moving on to another feature, Classcraft gives students the autonomy to regulate their learning and acquire new roles and identities. Students acquire fantastic characters as avatars like Mages, Guardians, or Healers based on RPG archetypes (tank, support, and damage dealers) with a special skill tree according to their role. Each class has a set of powers that are either beneficial to the individual or the team.

Lastly, Classcraft allows educators to gamify a lesson or an entireteaching course by transforming assignments into fiery quests and personalized learning adventures with new paths to unlock according to the skills or personality of the learner. The educator can create an assignment to any subject area according to his/her expectations in the form of a quest that will be shown in a map. The following step is to set the objectives of the quest, six in total as it is the limit in a free account. The game offers an array of digital elements to add to the classroom tasks, like points and rewards, ludicizing real-life interactions as they occur (Sanchez, Young &Jouneau-Sion, 2016).

Classcraft recently attracted the attention of the research community focusing on its potential for behavior change. For instance, Membrive and Armie (2020) implemented Classcraft in a university course on English as a second language and demonstrated that the platform increased involvement in learning and collaborative practices. Lastly, Rivera-Trigueros and Sánchez-Pérez(2020) employed Classcraft inEnglish as a Foreign Language (EFL)secondaryclassroom and illustrated the beneficial nature of Classcraft in fostering student's motivation.

SOLUTIONS AND RECOMMENDATIONS

Research Proposal: the Gamified Scenario on Classcraft

Looking for ways to leverage this super-diverse environment and investigate the game design elements that can enhance the learning experience of refugee students, the researchers designed a theory-driven educational scenario for students with a refugee background in Classcraft,on the basis of gamification. The added value of using the platform was that it encouraged blended learning practices. The lesson was delivered through computer-mediated technologies, but accomplished via face-to-face teamwork and action. The novelty of the research proposal lies in the researchers' attempt to contribute to the empirical research on gamification as a meaningful teaching practice for refugee education, as well as to trace out its benefits and challenges.

In this context, the following research questions were posed:

1. Which game design elements affect the engagement of refugee students with an activity according to their gaming preferences?
2. Which game design elements of the gamified lesson affected engagement and language permormance of refugee students?

To answer the research questions the researchers set a theory hypothesis to comprehend which game elements compilation best fits refugee students.The researchers' assumption is that a strong sense of community and interdependence among students can increase engagement.Thus, the hypothesis is that the game design elements should be oriented to the social factor of learning as students with a refugee background yearn for social connectedness to negotiate meaning around them. Antonaci's model of action (2019) stimulated the researchers to combine social and psychological theories to increase engagement and achieve an efficient learning outcome. Consequently, the design has drawn elements from Social Presence to establish a sense of community through group cohesion in a blended learning environment, and SDT to activate their intrinsic motivation and develop autonomy to trigger self-learning.

One of the challenges with research on student engagement is the large variation in the measurement of this construct (Fredricks & McColsky, 2012). In this study, engagement is perceived in both behavioural and emotional terms, as defined in the work of Fredricks, Blumenfeld & Paris (2004): a) students attend and are involved, demostrating the absence of disruptive or negative behaviour and b) students experience affective reactions such as interest, enjoyment or a sense of belonging. For both behavioural and emotional engagement, we used observation. Observation was selected as a data collection process due to the researcher's and teachers' familiarity with the children. Under these circumstances, engagement can only be characterized as "perceived", as it wasn't systematically measured, nor triangulated with different data collection tools.

The Educational Scenario: The Voyage of Sinbad and the Fruit Thief

The scenario was developed for the needs of teaching GSL. The first step was to set the goals and the rationale of the gamified scenario to meet the linguistic needs of the target group.The goals were defined along with the teacher.The blueprint of the scenario was based on Fragkaki's (2008) well-structured educational scenario framework.

The didactic goal of the scenario was to formulate properly the singular and the plural of nouns in Greek. The students were grouped according to their personality traits and dynamics. They read the multimodal texts and worksheets were distributedfollowing the story. Tasks became more complex as they advanced on the quests, ranging from communicative to gap filling and scavenger hunt.

Objectives

- Didactic goals:

    - Recall fruit vocabulary
    - Identify singular nouns by the article
    - Construct plural of feminine and neutral nouns
- Social goals:
    - Collaborate with each other to complete the tasks
    - Take decisions all together by negotiating meaning
    - Become autonomous learners

The rationale was based on Vygotsky's sociocultural theory. Under the influence of Vygotsky' viewpoint, learning was produced through scaffolding alongside more skilled peers in a culturally empowering manner, while the incorporated game elements promote teamwork and autonomous learning. Thus, the scenario was articulated around collaborative tasks with a didactic outcome framed with game elements and mechanics to augment engagement and achieve self-regulated learning.

After setting the goals and rationale, an engaging plot framed them. The story was written in both Greek and English by the researchers on Classcraft. The storyline was generatedfollowing Toda's (2019) four points to create an engaging and escalating plot:

- Introduce an extraordinary event
- Invent one protagonist and one antagonist
- Create a conflict
- Escalate the plot

The voyage of Sinbad served as the background story incarnating the famous tale of Arabic folklore, whereas the storyline was taking place in Africa. The researchers wanted to evoke intimacy with the task as the majority of the students were familiar with Arabic folklore, and Africawas the place of birth of one of the students. The tale unfolds in six tasks that students have to get though to find the treasure (Table 1 and Figures 1, 2 and 3).

Figure 1. The Map on Classcraft with the objectives.

Figure 2. The presented story is based on the voyage of Sinbad. Students are asked to read the story and "greet" the hero.

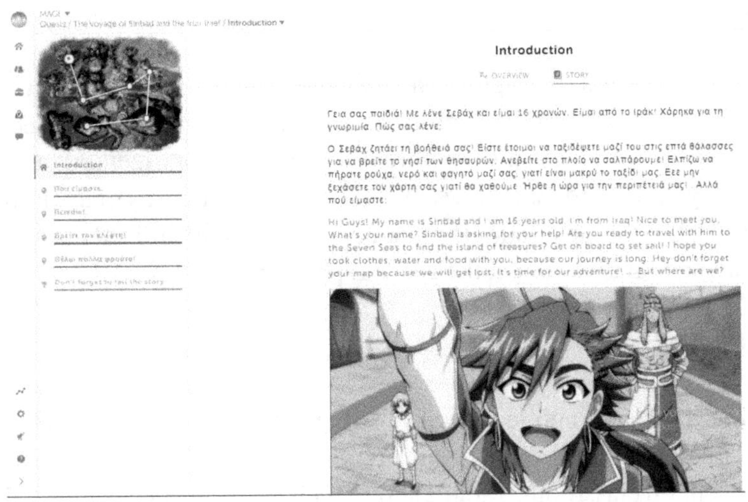

Figure 3. The second task on Classcraft asks students to involve into a treasure hunt.

Table 1. Orchestration of the scenario in Classcraft

Tasks	Experience points	Description
1. Meet Sinbad	0 exp	Introductory quest
2. Where are we?	30 exp	Fill in the word
3. I am hungry	35 exp	Focus on form
4. Find the thief	50 exp	Problem-solving
5. I want more fruit	60 exp	Focus on form
Bonus. Boss Fight	100 exp	Assessment
6. Don't forget to tell the story	100 exp	Sharing personal experience and Artifact

METHODOLOGY

Research Design

The research design adopts a qualitative approach as an interpretive practice to answer the research questions efficiently and open new ways of conducting research for and with the refugee youth. Considering that the research is made with refugee students through a participatory method, a qualitative methodology provides a multi-way boulevard that allows the researchers to draw as much information as possible from the participants in a flexible and dialogic manner avoiding standardized questionnaires, which may confine their expression and narrow down their rich repertoire.

Context and Participants

The research was carried out at a public school in Athens, Greece.It involved eight (8) students from different cultural and linguistic backgrounds, four (4) males and four (4) females between 9 and 11 years old, who attended a reception classroom. Table 2 shows their demographic features. They were classified as A1 learners, according to the Common European Framework of Reference for Languages (CEFR). Education in L1 was interrupted or limitedaffecting L2 writing skills.

Regarding their overall behavior, there was a tendency to avoid homework or keep chatting inconsistently during classroom disrupting the process. School attendance was marked with a fluctuating dropout rate. Some students were away for a long time without informing the school and after quarantine the school faced more casualties.

Table 2. Participants' demographics

Participants	Gender	Age	Nationality	Language(s)	Residency	Prior schooling
P1	Female	9	Congo	English, Portuguese, French	2 years	None
P2	Female	11	Afghanistan	Farsi, Dari, English	3 years (1 in a camp)	One year
P3	Male	11	Afghanistan	Arabic, Farsi, Dari, English	3 years	One year
P4	Male	11	Afghanistan	Farsi, Dari, English	3 years	One year
P5	Female	10	Afghanistan	Farsi, English	3 years	One year
P6	Male	11	Afghanistan	Farsi, Dari, English	2 years	Two years
P7	Female	10	Afghanistan	Turkish Farsi, Dari	2 years	One year
P8	Male	10	Afghanistan	Arabic, Turkish, Farsi, Dari, English	1 year	One year

Data Collection Tools

The researchers carried out five (5) unstructured interviews with the students to draw information on students' demographics, gaming preferences and needs, and gauge their language proficiency. Our base line was the teachers' and researchers' familiarity with the children before the intervention, which ensured a) their trust for them to willingly participate in the tasks and b) teachers' knowledge of children's language levels. The researcher also piloted the reward system before the intervention, by observing a "normal" language lesson and pinpointing students' needs. The data collected from this pilot were combined with interview data to reach the final gamified task design. Systematic observations were employed to record student's behavior, assess team's organization and collaboration as well as detect the engagement level throughout the process. The observations were transcribed into a research diary that gave birth to field notes. To achieve a holistic observation of the process the two ZEP teachers were assigned to keep track of the groups as it was impossible for the teacher-researcher to observe both teams at once. The language performance was assessed by the answers provided on the tasks. For the evaluation of the overall experience, focus group discussions (FGDs) were formulated to document how learners experienced the phenomenon of gamification and identify the factors that affected that experience. FGDs aimed to investigate a) the usability of the platform b) the impressions from the gamified lesson c) the motivation created through the use of the platform d) collaborative learning and e) lesson enhancement through future suggestions.

Process and Phases of the Educational Scenario

The implementation actualized in four phases. This process took place over a week, allot two hours per day consistent with the school curriculum and no deviations were made from the school timeline.Table 3 displays the four phases and a brief description for each one.

It should be noted that the reward/penalty system on Classcraft was adjusted together with the teacher of the classroomunder collaborative innovation practices in order to classify the capabilities the behaviors that need to be addressed(Patricio, Moreira, Zurlo & Melazzini, 2020).The lesson was organized in two groups of four: Team 1 and Team 2 for the record. Team dynamics compromised by heterogeneous groups taking under consideration language levels mixing lower with higher students.

Table 3. The process of the educational scenario

Procedure of the scenario	Allocated time	Title	Description
First Phase	2 hours	Familiarize with Classcraft	Introduction to Classcraft and avatar creation
Second Phase	2 hours	Testing Day of the award/ penalty system	Familiarize students with the rewarding system by distributing points in a "real time" lesson and observe students' reaction towards the gamification system
Third Phase	1 hour and a half	Implementation of the gamified scenario	Implementation of the scenario.The teacher-researcher as game master providing hints and facilitating the smooth functioning of the game.
Fourth Phase	30 min	FGDs	A 15 minutes discussion about their experience with the gamified lesson

Data Analysis

A thematic analysis wasopted for the analysis data. The qualitative data consisted of five (5) interviews, fifteen (15) assignments, observation field notes, and FDGs field notes. Initial coding was produced inductively based on the set of data.Initial coding was produced inductively. All data sources were transcribed and analyzed separately to generate the initial coding. Through coding, the patterns of each data set were identified and grouped together into themes. From data analysis five themes were generated illustrated in Table 4.

Excerpts from interviews generatedthree codes: Relationships, Teams, Avatars and Resourceacquisition. Table 5 below displays the excerpts that apply to each code. Game design elements were based on this codes.The observationnotes generated three themes. Undesired participants' behavior was also identified and grouped in as Demotivators. An overlap was observed between the codes Teams, Competition and Collaboration.

Table 4. Themes and codes extracted from data analysis

<table>
<tr><th>Research resources</th><th>Themes</th><th>Codes</th></tr>
<tr><td>Interviews</td><td>Game design Elements</td><td>Relationships, Teams, Avatars and Resourceacquisition</td></tr>
<tr><td rowspan="3">Observation on student's performance on task</td><td>Effective game elements for engagement</td><td rowspan="3">Narrative,
Competition and Collaboration
Collaboration
Autonomy
Task difficulty
Groups' cohesiveness</td></tr>
<tr><td>Effective game elements for language development</td></tr>
<tr><td>Demotivators</td></tr>
<tr><td>Focus Group Discussions</td><td>Positive andnegative experiences</td><td>Usability
Teams
Satisfaction</td></tr>
</table>

FINDINGS

Interviews: Relationships, Teams, Avatars and Resource Acquisition

The students were asked why they play video games. Table 5 below shows the three codes that extracted from their utterance.Most of the participants seek for communication with a friend while playing a game in order to have fun and share mutual understanding.Moreover, all the participants claimed that before playing a game they set up their own party and community, mainly, with family members. These responses depict the high social connection refugees share with their group and their desire to share common culture and language so as to collaborate and have fun. The participants pointed out indirectly the factors that retain players in a specific group, namely interdependence and a sense of community. Social Presence Theory examines both features.

While communication and teamwork were the codes that dominated the interviews, one participant gave emphasis to another gaming element, the RPG feature. In particular, she pinpointed that avatar creation and character customization catch her attention. Classcraft incorporates all the above features, teams and avatars.

Table 5. Findings extracted from students' utterances

Codes	Utterance
Relationships	"there are people, you can laugh, write something". "Yes I have many friends…" "if I want to play with a friend I call her to get into (the game) and then play together""I have many friends… but I have one that I know her very well… she is from Congo"
Teams	"you play with company… "you can call other kids to play together". "We have a clan" "I play every day with my brother…"
RPG features: Avatars and Resource Acquisition	"we can choose boy or a girl… buy clothes" "you can be very beautiful, have money and clothes…and also magic"

Effective Game Elements for Engagement

The teacher-researcher observed that the students engaged progressively in every part of the scenario. Also, they worked and strived together to accomplish the quests, a behaviour considered as pointing towards a positive and collaborative learning environment, where students focused on learning.In particular, competition contributed significantly in expanding engagement in the project as the students were committed to finish the quest. For instance, Team 1 behavior changed dramatically and got more serious when faced a penalty and lost points falling behind Team 2 on the second task (Figure 4). That incident did not demotivate or affect team's dynamic, on the contrary, the team members took account of his actions and demonstrated resilience and teamwork to move on (taken from field notes). Moreover, observations suggested that two members of the team, a boy and a girl, collaborated perfectly performing in a state of flow leading the whole group. In essence, it was observed that teamwork increased participation as students mutually depended on others. Students, also, engaged through the narration. The rich multimedia of the scenario like gifs, video and images appear to have engrossed their attention and fuelled their participation. Indicative of this interpretation is the instance of one member of Team 2 beinginspired by the narration and decided to participate in the last task and write about their journey, narrating the story in her own way.

Figure 4. One student from Team 1 faced a penalty because he did not follow the rules and used an extra hint resulting in HP loss.

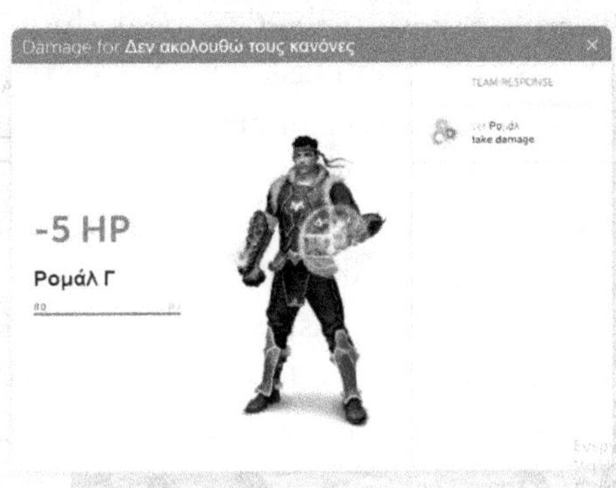

Language Performance

Language performance has been verified from student's performance in the tasks. The students completed four tasks in total with a good score (Figure 6, Task 4 is not included to focus mainly on language form). The final results emerged from Task 5, in which the new knowledge had to be constructed and applied. Data analysis showed that the majority of students grasped the rule, since the percentage of correct answers was quite high (81%, see figure 5).

Collaboration was the key to success for every task. The students supported their team members so as to proceed and accomplish the language goals collectively enhancing language development indirectly. This finding indicated that an extrinsic motivator nurtured an intrinsic one, which developed a sense of community, as the learners seemed to draw satisfaction from this interpersonal space that created, becoming interdependent. That interpersonal space was waxed by the autonomy given to the students. Specifically, it was observed that the students felt confident to complete the task as they relied on their teammates to have their back.

Figure 5. Student's performance on Task 5.

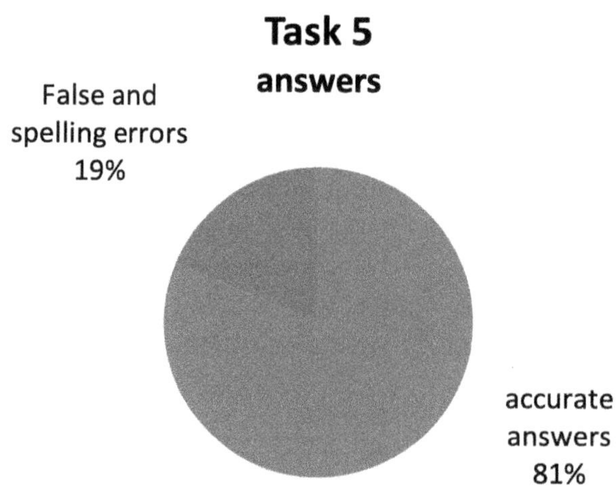

However, language performance did not exert the desired performance in two cases. Participant 4 did not complete the task correctly, his answers in task 5 were all wrong. Participant 4 was assigned as the lower skilled student by the teacher and the less interested in learning Greek. Secondly, a fluctuating performance was exhibited by Participant 8, who was classified as a skilled language learner. His answers in the task even if they were correct grammatically they were inconsistent as he confused a word with another and omitted letters, completing the task in a rush.

Moving on to the bonus quest, which indirectly assessed their gained knowledge, both teams answered all the questions correctly even the student with the lower performance. It is indicated that studentsare performing better orally and generalized the grammar rule quite easily.

Figure 6. The overall performance of students.

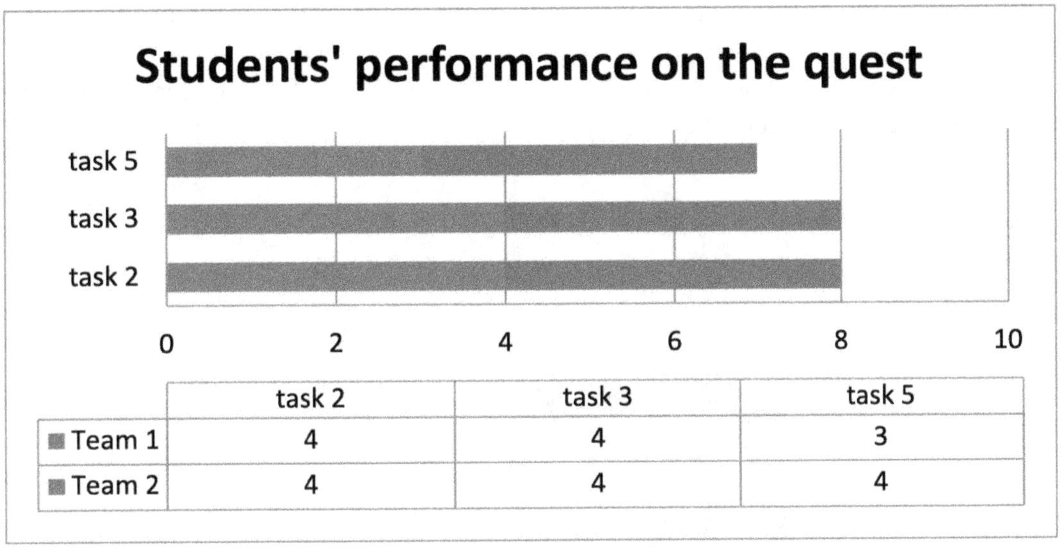

Demotivating Factors

The gamified lesson exerted reversed outcomes such as frustration and demotivation due to wrong choices of the researchers to gauge correctly team's dynamic. Participant 4 resigned and demotivated resulting in a re-arrangement of teams. Without group cohesiveness learners can lose the motivation to keep up with the group. Thus, group's cohesiveness has an impact on the social presence of a learner.

Secondly, task difficulty demotivated some students. Only Team 2 ventured writing about their experience. The purpose of the ending quest was to test the dedication of the students in following the narrative till the end. The two parts of the task were complimentary and it was up to the student which path to choose the easy one or the difficult one as there was no coercion from the part of the teacher-researcher.

Overall Evaluation from FGDs

Regarding the usability of the platform, both teams reported that while it was easy to navigate, they got disappointed from the technological equipment. The non-support of the lesson by the ICT is attributed to the fact that the school was not fully-equipped with the required technological infrastructure.

In relation to the question about the impact of gamification elements on engagement with the learning process, the majority of respondents felt that the gaming elements enhanced their learning experience. All participants admitted that the way learning was delivered through the platform, animated their interest and instigated them to participate in the lesson. Two students commented that they had fun even if they had to write, while one girl stated she wanted to play more and complete more quests. As regards the game elements that motivated and impelled them to continue, Team 1 highlighted that they wanted to win and perform well, while Team 2 emphasized on the character creation, the narrative and the joy of playing. Generally, the competition that existed between the teams escalated within a reasonable framework and was a strong motivator for participation.

Turning to collaboration between the groups, the majority of the students answered that it was satisfactory and empowering. Another point of referencewas the penalty. The members of Team 1 were not discouraged by the boy who "cheated" as they were all accountable; on the contrary, they wanted to heal him praising the Healer of the team (Figure 7). Overall, they agreed that they prefer working in groups with their friends supporting each other.

Figure 7. Team 1 decided to heal the "wounded" member and proceed all together.

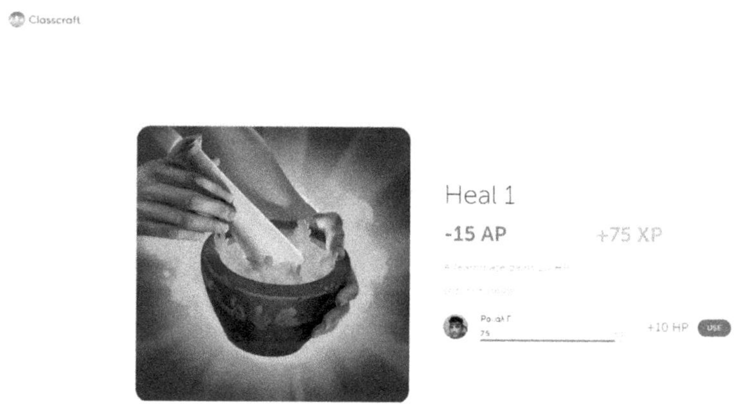

In terms of complexity of the educational content, both teams agreed that the gamified lesson helped them understand the grammatical phenomenon. They stressed that the lesson resembled a game, but knowledge was acquired at the same moment. It is worth mentioning the utterance of a boy from Team 1, who argued that he does not want to play but learn. That depicts exactly their urge to learn and that gamification practice, if structured rigorously, can turn the lesson into a game in a stealth way. Moreover, several students emphasized that they wanted toestablish Classcraft in classroom to get points and watch videos. They stated that the content was quite clear, without any particular difficulty in comprehension.

DISCUSSION

Which Game Design Elements affect the Engagement of Refugee Students with an Activity According to their Gaming Preferences?

From the beginning of the research, it was clear to the researchers that the only way to design an effective gamified scenario for language learning was to delve into students' micro and macro world and understand their needs as a preliminary step. The needs analysis was associated with the game elements of video games as a measure of fun and devotion to a task. From the students' profile we extracted the following game elements that meet the needs of the students for an engaging and entertaining experience: Relationships, Teams, Avatars and Resource acquisition.

Participants articulated the desire to communicate with friends in order to establish their presence in a shared online activity. Relationship is closely related to SDT through the intrinsic need of Relatedness. Conditions supporting individuals' need for affectionate relationships and a sense of belonging are argued to foster higher forms of engagement in an activity (Deci & Ryan, 2000). In the case of refugees, that engagement correlates with higher forms of social inclusion and positive attitudes towards the second language (Abujarour, Kresanova& Hoffmeier, 2018; Mogli&Papadopoulou, 2019). Therefore, gamification in refugee education has the potential to promote social connectedness and strong relationships via rich computer-mediated communication media that fuel their need for relatedness and frequent social interactions.

With respect to Teams, according to the participants, teamwork acted as the ultimate motivator for playing a video game. The students stated that they form "groups" and "clans" with their friends and family members. Refugee students seek to create a powerful game community with their peers for the thrill of winning and entertainment. Turning to Tseng, Huang and Teng (2015), that sense of community can positively impact retention in the game and establish a student's Social Presence. Moreover, teamwork is fueled by competition and cooperation, which are prominent game mechanics that affect motivation, engagement and learning outcomes (Kapp, 2012). Therefore, it could be argued that refugee students prefer defined small groups. That finding has its roots in the pursuit of a common identity as students seek to create affective ties among them (Rapp, 2017).

Moving on, one participant mentioned RPG features like Avatars and Resources acquisition like gold and clothes referred to "fantastic" characteristics which engrossed the participant and produced stronger feelings of autonomy (Xi &Hamari, 2019). That "addiction" derives from their need to inhabit a character they have in their mind and reconstruct their desired identity in order to escape from the confines of the real world (Susaeta,Jimenez, Nussbaum, Gajardo, Andreu & Villalta, 2010).

The Hybrid Model

The above arguments led the researchers to revise the initial theory hypothesis and create a hybrid model with SDT and Social Presence. Thetheory hypothesis was that social theories best fit the refugee population as social connectedness can generate a group identity that impacts self-growth and engagement. That hypothesis proved correct, but not sufficient as autonomy, a prominent feature of Self-Determination Theory (SDT),affected significantly language competence. Reversely, even if SDT has a social component, namely Relatedness, that alone is not enough to support the needs of the refugee minor group as it is targeted mainly on individual goals without considering the sociocultural community scale. By valorising, the social aspect through Social Presence, the focus is on the creation of a strong sense of community. Mainly, the researchers argue that in a gamification design for refugee education social and psychological aspects should be treated together as equal parts.Therefore, we support that Social Presence combined with SDT can create a strong gamification framework for refugee students based on their needs.

Which Game Design Elements of the Gamified Lesson affected Engagement and Language Performance of Refugee Students?

The scope of the second question was to identify which game elements of the gamified scenario significantly affected engagement and language performance. Data analysis showed that the game design elements incorporated in Classcraft had a great impact on students' perceived engagement leading to a satisfactory language perfomance.

Regarding language performance, the results were positive, however the short-term of the research could not consolidate the learning outcome. The tasks got more challenging progressively and performance dropped slightly. The mean score on Quest 5 was 81% showing that the majority of participants grasped the grammatical rule and applied it correctly. That score included spelling errors displaying a minimum number of errors as the students supported each other and revised the answers. The skilled peers took the role of the teacher guiding the learning process. Consequently, the findings demonstrated that the power of gamification lies in collaboration and autonomy which are the two factors that significantly affected SLA verifying related studies on achievement (Xi &Hamari, 2019). It is apparent that collaboration can counterbalance the lack of linguistic skills conforming to Vygotsky's theory and zones of proximal development (ZPD). This result implies that refugee learners are motivated to expand their skills when they experience a feeling of interdependence.

In terms of engagement, competition-collaboration and storyline were the elements that demonstrated a significant difference among others. To begin with, data analysis showed that competition and collaboration were the main game design elements that highly immersed the students into the gamified activity aligning to the preliminary needs analysis and student's initial preferences. The point-based system in the form of reward and penalty produced positive and fair competition among the teams affecting students' satisfaction and enjoyment. It should be clarified that the point system in Classcraft is based on behavioral learning outcomes and a team based-approach avoiding rankings that display their performance in hierarchy. The gamification system of Classcraft affected the medium of the competitive-collaborative model. This finding is in line with empirical research that supports the positive effect of the competitive-collaborative gamification strategy on engagement (Sailer & Homner, 2020).

The second game element that affected engagement was the storyline. The script was created from scratch by the researchers with the inner motive to link students' culture with the real time setting transporting them to familiar lands. By contextualizing the tasks and the characters the task gained meaning beyond mere points (Kapp, 2012). Through the storyline, students expressed self-gratification by unlocking new parts of the story. Considering the findings from the observation, it could be inferred that students captivated by the storyline, but the parts of the story that immersed them more were the media-riched narratives, especially, the music video. The same results are illustrated in other studies, emphasizing the absorbing power of storyline and narrative (Shi & Shih, 2015). Nevertheless, only Team 2 stayed dedicated to the storyline and completed all the parts, whereas Team 1 picked up only one part of the last task under their free will. Even if it is an isolated example it demonstrates that the storyline can provide a level of autonomy to the learners (Xi &Hamari, 2019). Overall it could be argued that the game elements that conquered the interest of students in the gamification process were in line with the game elements students defined in their interviews as prominent features in playing video games. It is worth mentioning that the findings illuminate game elements that go beyond PBL rein portraying the pure intrinsic needs of students with a refugee background.

In a final analysis, the dark side of gamification was verified as several demotivating factors, controllable though, made their appearance and affected the performance level of the students. A distinctive example of undesired behavior was the student that exerted detrimental outcomes like dissatisfaction, boredom and demotivation due to wrong team organization by the researchers and the teacher. Another undesired effect emerged as a by-product of task difficulty. Challenges exert positive learning outcomes when balanced to learners' skills, conversely, can demotivate students to progress and dampen their confidence (Shi & Shih, 2015). Hence, instructors should adjust the skill-level of the gamification process in the educational setting and provide more freedom of choice as refugee students are heterogeneous concerning prior knowledge, cultural background and language levels.Recommendations about how to make a gamification system work with learners with a refugee background are presented below:

1. **Identify student's subjective needs:**Perform needs analysis thoroughly. Pay considerable attention to their social-related aspects.
2. **Identify student's ZPD:** Be aware of their competence level and adjust learning to their skills.
3. **Define the pedagogical objectives** clearly and make sure they correspond to the learners' linguistic level
4. **Increase freedom of choice**when designing a gamification educational model: Extend answer choices to control the degree of learning difficulty and challenge.
5. **Organize**the lesson in small groups to promote group cohesiveness.

CONCLUSION

The aim of this research was to design and implement an educational scenario for teaching the Second Language to students with a refugee background by utilizing gamification elements. In this context, the researchers designed step by step the educational scenario in Classcraft taking under consideration the experiences and preferences of the students and teacher's guidelines. Moreover, an emphasis was given on which gamification theories were compatible with refugee students' needs as there was no research towards this direction. The researchers decided to go with a social theory as a guide concluding that a combination of theories is the most effective way to develop a gamification model for illustrating the refugee group's capabilities and possibilities.The results (a) highlighted the importance of collaborative game elements, (b) recommended the combination of Social Presence and SDT as the ultimate combo for designing gamification scenarios for refugee students and (c) determined that gamification in education demands exceptional facilitation to avoid demotivating factors.

As a starting point, the interviewspersonalized the educational scenario highlighting the importance of needs analysis in gamification. Classcraft came up as the best idea to actualize that endeavor due to the social and costumized features it entails serving both as a classroom management tool as well as a "tabula rasa" for the educational scenario. Regarding the second question, engagement was approached through team reflections and observations, whereas language performance was analyzed throughout student'sscore on the gamified tasks. Data analysis showed that the game design elements incorporated in Classcraft, such as avatars, teams and narrative, had a great impact on students' perceived engagement leading to a satisfactory language performance. The overall experience of students with gamification was considered positive and satisfied their learning needsas the FGDs demonstated. Basically, the study achieved to amplify in an easy and costless way a reception classroom and transform it into an open space that arouses fantasy and attains language goals at the same time. That is very important for learners with a refugee background as their inner motive is to compensate for the lost time and reach their age group learning standards. Gamification is not playing; gamification is the optimal strategy for transferring knowledge in the 21st century.

Traversing into 21st century skills, collaboration is the wheel of gamification in refugee education as the findings indicated. Competition is considered a strong motivator, but only in combination with collaboration aided students to reach their level of potential development through guidance and assistance. Thus, it is argued that collaborative learning combined with gamification practices like challenges and points, on the premise of SDT and Social Presence, provides a fruitful ground for refugee students to advance linguistically and maintain the social bonds with their community. The same collaborative spirit adheres to the teachers, also, as through the action research had the opportunity to participate and observe the possibilities Classcraft can bring on to their classroom.

Ultimately, the results demonstrated that refugee students, like any other kid, are spending their free time playing video games on their mobile devices with their family members and friends. The study highlights the need to stop portraying them as vulnerable, but as a dynamic population that can shape the digital narratives of the future world. Boostingthis dynamic community with gamification is probably the key to language acquisition and smoother integration to the new reality.

FUTURE RESEARCH DIRECTIONS

As an ending note, some suggestions will be presented for further investigation as they sprouted from the research. Firstly, due to the fact that the field of gamification is a new area of study, it requires rigorous long-term empirical research. For this reason, the presented gamified proposal should be tested for a longer period of time to gauge the growth of engagement. In the long-term, motivation can also be measured as the time restriction of the current research prevented the researchers to attain that objective effectively and engagement was considered easier to be observed. Therefore, it would be interesting for future studies to use Classcraft for a respectful period of time to test the motivation patterns of refugee students learning a second language. Moreover, the motivation patterns could be linked to learners' personality types as the ones introduced in Marczewski's User's Types Hexad (2015) and built upon field research on refugee students. Lastly, it is rather plausible to investigate more the social and psychological theories regarding the refugees. The current study supported the combination of SDT and Social Presence, but at a very basic level. Probably, a grounded theory is needed to solidify the research and discover which social theories could be of added value for refugees.

Regarding the participants, the sample was rather small but effective to establish social presence. For future studies, a control group is required; otherwise the results could not be compared to traditional practices. Also, to verify the language performance of students, one solution could be to employ authentic assessment or peer and self- evaluations. Moreover, the refugee minor group is a considerably heterogeneous group; consequently, the game element opted for the specific design may not affect the majority. Lastly, to avoid negative effects it would be plausible to assign groups in an optimal and thoughtful way based on common interests and relationships. For instance, a Google Forms survey could be created for students to share their interests and then form group dynamics.

REFERENCES

AbuJarour, S., Krasnova, H., & Hoffmeier, F. (2018). *ICT as an enabler: Understanding the role of online communication in the social inclusion of Syrian refugees in Germany*. Academic Press.

AlMarshedi, A., Wills, G. B., Wanick, V., & Ranchhod, A. (2014, November). Towards a sustainable gamification impact. In *International Conference on Information Society (i-Society 2014)* (pp. 195-200). 10.1109/i-Society.2014.7009041

Alomari, I., Al-Samarraie, H., & Yousef, R. (2019). The role of gamification techniques in promoting student learning: A review and synthesis. *Journal of Information Technology Education, 18*(08), 2019. doi:10.28945/4417

Antonaci, A., Klemke, R., Kreijns, K., & Specht, M. (2018). Get Gamification of MOOC right! *International Journal of Serious Games, 5*(3), 61–78. doi:10.17083/ijsg.v5i3.255

Antonaci, A., Klemke, R., & Specht, M. (2019, September). The effects of gamification in online learning environments: A systematic literature review. *Informatics (MDPI), 6*(3), 32. doi:10.3390/informatics6030032

Arce, N. H., & Valdivia, A. C. (2020). Adapting competitiveness and gamification to a digital platform for foreign language learning. *International Journal of Emerging Technologies in Learning, 15*(20), 194–209. doi:10.3991/ijet.v15i20.16135

Bock, J. G., Haque, Z., & McMahon, K. A. (2020). Displaced and dismayed: How ICTs are helping refugees and migrants, and how we can do better. *Information Technology for Development, 26*(4), 670–691. doi:10.1080/02681102.2020.1727827

Castaño-Muñoz, J., Colucci, E., & Smidt, H. (2018). Free digital learning for inclusion of migrants and refugees in Europe: A qualitative analysis of three types of learning purposes. *International Review of Research in Open and Distributed Learning, 19*(2). Advance online publication. doi:10.19173/irrodl.v19i2.3382

Cruz, C., Hanus, M. D., & Fox, J. (2017). The need to achieve: Players' perceptions and uses of extrinsic meta-game reward systems for video game consoles. *Computers in Human Behavior, 71*, 516–524. doi:10.1016/j.chb.2015.08.017

Deci, E. L., & Ryan, R. M. (2008). Self-determination theory: A macrotheory of human motivation, development, and health. *Canadian Psychology, 49*(3), 182–185. doi:10.1037/a0012801

Deterding, S., Dixon, D., Khaled, R., & Nacke, L. (2011). From Game Design Elements to Gamefulness: Defining "Gamification". In A. Lugmayr, H. Franssila, C. Safran, & I. Hammouda (Eds.), *Proceedings of the 15th International Academic MindTrek Conference: Envisioning Future Media Environments* (pp. 9–15). ACM. https://dl.acm.org/citation.cfm?id=2181037.2181040 doi:10.1145/2181037.2181040

Dichev, C., & Dicheva, D. (2017). Gamifying education: What is known, what is believed and what remains uncertain: A critical review. *International Journal of Educational Technology in Higher Education, 14*(9), 9. Advance online publication. doi:10.118641239-017-0042-5

Fredricks, J. A., Blumenfeld, P. C., & Paris, A. (2004). School engagement: Potential of the concept: State of the evidence. *Review of Educational Research, 74*(1), 59–119. doi:10.3102/00346543074001059

Fredricks, J. A., & McColskey, W. (2012). The Measurement of Student Engagement: A Comparative Analysis of Various Methodsand Student Self-report Instruments. In Handbook of Research on Student Engagement. doi:10.1007/978-1-4614-2018-7_37

Hamari, J., Koivisto, J., & Sarsa, H. (2014). Does Gamification Work? – A Literature Review of Empirical Studies on Gamification. *Proceedings of the 47th Hawaii International Conference on System Sciences*. 10.1109/HICSS.2014.377

Holmes, J. (2018). Building confidence in foreign language communication through 'Skilled Use of Interaction Strategies'. *Sciences de l'Homme et Société / Education*. https://dumas.ccsd.cnrs.fr/dumas-01942635

Jusoff, K., & Khodabandelou, R. (2009). Preliminary study on the role of social presence in blended learning environment in higher education. *International Education Studies*, *2*(4), 79–83. doi:10.5539/ies.v2n4p79

Landers, R. N. (2014). Developing a theory of gamified learning: Linking serious games and gamification of learning. *Simulation & Gaming*, *45*(6), 752–768. doi:10.1177/1046878114563660

Landers, R. N., Bauer, K. N., Callan, R. C., & Armstrong, M. B. (2015). Psychological Theory and the Gamification of Learning. In T. Reiners & L. Wood (Eds.), *Gamification in Education and Business* (pp. 165–186). Springer International Publishing. doi:10.1007/978-3-319-10208-5_9

Lifanova, A., Ngan, H. Y., Okunewitsch, A., Rahman, S., Guzmán, S., Desai, N., . . . Karayel, M. (2016, July). New locals: Overcoming integration barriers with mobile informal and gamified learning. In *Proceedings of the International Conference on Information Communication Technologies in Education (ICICTE)* (pp. 7-9). Academic Press.

Membrive, V., & Armie, M. (2020). *Beyond gamification: Classcraft as an engagement tool in the teaching of english as a second language*. http://end-educationconference.org/wp-content/uploads/2020/06/2020end016.pdf

Metwally, A. H. S., Nacke, L. E., Chang, M., Wang, Y., & Yousef, A. M. F. (2021). Revealing the hotspots of educational gamification: An umbrella review. *International Journal of Educational Research*, *109*, 101832. doi:10.1016/j.ijer.2021.101832

Mogli, M., & Papadopoulou, M. (2018). "If I stay here, I will learn the language": Reflections from a case study of Afghan refugees learning Greek as a Second Language. *Research Papers in Language Teaching & Learning, 9*(1).

Nacke, L. E., & Deterding, C. S. (2017). The maturing of gamification research. *Computers in Human Behaviour*, 450-454.

Ngan, H. Y., Lifanova, A., Jarke, J., & Broer, J. (2016, September). Refugees welcome: Supporting informal language learning and integration with a gamified mobile application. In *European Conference on Technology Enhanced Learning* (pp. 521-524). 10.1007/978-3-319-45153-4_54

Nowell, L. S., Norris, J. M., White, D. E., & Moules, N. J. (2017). Thematic analysis: Striving to meet the trustworthiness criteria. *International Journal of Qualitative Methods*, *16*(1). doi:10.1177/1609406917733847

Özdener, N. (2018). Gamification for enhancing Web 2.0 based educational activities: The case of pre-service grade school teachers using educational Wiki pages. *Telematics and Informatics*, *35*(3), 564–578. doi:10.1016/j.tele.2017.04.003

Palomino, P., Toda, A., Oliveira, W., Rodrigues, L., Cristea, A., & Isotani, S. (2019, November). Exploring content game elements to support gamification design in educational systems: narrative and storytelling. In *Brazilian Symposium on Computers in Education (Simpósio Brasileiro de Informática na Educação-SBIE)* (Vol. 30, No. 1, p. 773). 10.5753/cbie.sbie.2019.773

Patricio, R., Moreira, A., Zurlo, F., & Melazzini, M. (2020). Co-creation of new solutions through gamification: A collaborative innovation practice. *Creativity and Innovation Management*, *29*(1), 146–160. doi:10.1111/caim.12356

Patrício, R., Moreira, A. C., & Zurlo, F. (2018). Gamification approaches to the early stage of innovation. *Creativity and Innovation Management*, *27*(4), 499–511. doi:10.1111/caim.12284

Patrício, R., Moreira, A. C., & Zurlo, F. (2021). Enhancing design thinking approaches to innovation through gamification. *European Journal of Innovation Management*, *24*(5), 1569–1594. doi:10.1108/EJIM-06-2020-0239

Piteira, M., Costa, C. J., & Aparicio, M. (2017). A conceptual framework to implement gamification on online courses of computer programming learning: implementation. In *10th International Conference of Education, Research and Innovation (ICERI2017)* (pp. 7022-7031). 10.21125/iceri.2017.1865

Rapp, A. (2017). Designing interactive systems through a game lens: An ethnographic approach. *Computers in Human Behavior*, *71*, 455–468. doi:10.1016/j.chb.2015.02.048

Rivera-Trigueros, I., & Sánchez-Pérez, M. D. M. (2020). Conquering the iron throne: Using classcraft to foster students'motivation in the efl classroom. *Teaching English with Technology*, *20*(4), 3–22.

Roberts, T. L., Lowry, P. B., & Sweeney, P. D. (2006). An evaluation of the impact of social presence through group size and the use of collaborative software on group member"voice" in face-to-face and computer-mediated task groups. *IEEE Transactions on Professional Communication*, *49*(1), 28–43. doi:10.1109/TPC.2006.870460

Ryan, R. M., & Deci, E. L. (2000). Intrinsic and extrinsic motivations: Classic definitions and new directions. *Contemporary Educational Psychology*, *25*(1), 54–67. doi:10.1006/ceps.1999.1020 PMID:10620381

Sailer, M., Hense, J. U., Mayr, S. K., & Mandl, H. (2017). How gamification motivates: An experimental study of the effects of specific game design elements on psychological need satisfaction. *Computers in Human Behavior*, *69*, 371–380. doi:10.1016/j.chb.2016.12.033

Sailer, M., & Homner, L. (2020). The Gamification of Learning: A Meta-analysis. *Educational Psychology Review*, *32*(1), 77–112. doi:10.100710648-019-09498-w

Sanchez, E., Young, S., & Jouneau-Sion, C. (2017). Classcraft: From gamification to ludicization of classroom management. *Education and Information Technologies*, *22*(2), 497–513. doi:10.100710639-016-9489-6

Shi, Y. R., & Shih, J. L. (2015). Game factors and game-based learning design model. *International Journal of Computer Games Technology*, *2015*, 1–11. doi:10.1155/2015/549684

Stott, A., & Neustaedter, C. (2013). Analysis of gamification in education. Academic Press.

Susaeta, H., Jimenez, F., Nussbaum, M., Gajardo, I., Andreu, J. J., & Villalta, M. (2010). From MMORPG to a classroom multiplayer presential role playing game. *Journal of Educational Technology & Society, 13*(3), 257–269.

Toda, A. M., Valle, P. H., & Isotani, S. (2017, March). The dark side of gamification: An overview of negative effects of gamification in education. In Researcher links workshop: higher education for all (pp. 143-156). Academic Press.

UNHCR. (2020, September 3). *Coming together for Refugee Education*. https://www.unhcr.org/media-page-coming-together-for-refugee-education.html

Werbach, K. (2014, May). (Re) defining gamification: A process approach. In *International conference on persuasive technology* (pp. 266-272). Springer. 10.1007/978-3-319-07127-5_23

Werbach, K., & Hunter, D. (2012). *For the win: How game thinking can revolutionize your business*. Wharton Digital Press.

Xi, N., & Hamari, J. (2019). Does gamification satisfy needs? A study on the relationship between gamification features and intrinsic need satisfaction. *International Journal of Information Management, 46*, 210–221. doi:10.1016/j.ijinfomgt.2018.12.002

Zainuddin, Z., Chu, S. K. W., Shujahat, M., & Perera, C. J. (2020). The impact of gamification on learning and instruction: A systematic review of empirical evidence. *Educational Research Review, 30*, 1–23. doi:10.1016/j.edurev.2020.100326

ADDITIONAL READING

Garone, P., & Nesteriuk, S. (2019, July). Gamification and learning: A comparative study of design frameworks. In *International Conference on Human-Computer Interaction* (pp. 473-487). Springer. 10.1007/978-3-030-22219-2_35

Kusuma, G. P., Wigati, E. K., Utomo, Y., & Suryapranata, L. K. P. (2018). Analysis of gamification models in education using MDA framework. *Procedia Computer Science, 135*, 385–392. doi:10.1016/j.procs.2018.08.187

Mogli, M., & Papadopoulou, M. (2018). "If I stay here, I will learn the language": Reflections from a case study of Afghan refugees learning Greek as a Second Language. *Research Papers in Language Teaching & Learning, 9*(1).

Nordby, A., Øygardslia, K., Sverdrup, U., & Sverdrup, H. (2016). The art of gamification; Teaching sustainability and system thinking by pervasive game development. *Electronic Journal of E-Learning, 14*(3), 152–168.

Oliveira, S., & Cruz, M. (2018). The gamification octalysis framework within the primary english teaching process: The quest for a transformative classroom. *Revista Lusófona de Educação, 41*(41), 63–82. doi:10.24140/issn.1645-7250.rle41.04

KEY TERMS AND DEFINITIONS

Educational Scenario:The flow of a series of educational activities: usually including the use of digital technology for added pedagogical value.

Game Design: The process of utilizing specific elements and aesthetics for the purpose of creating a game.

Game Elements: In gamification contexts, game elements refer to specific rewards assigned to users after achieving a certain challenge or quest. The aim is to increase level, engagement and motivation.

Hybrid Model: In the context of this research, the term refers to the combination of Self Determination (SDT) and Social Presence theories, to synthesize individual and social elements in order to support the needs of the refugee students' group.

Quest: A concept coming from games and commonly used in gamification research and practice. A quest is a set of challenges that once overcome, result in a defined reward.

SLA: Second Language Aquisition, a term commonly used in the fields of Language Studies and Language Education.

Social Theories: In the context of gamification, the term refers to theories that focus on the social aspect of gamification, aiming at enhancing the feelings of relatedness and connectedness among users.

Chapter 32
Increasing Engagement Through Explicit and Implicit Gamification in Higher Education

Simon Grey
University of Hull, UK

Neil A. Gordon
University of Hull, UK

ABSTRACT

Engagement is essential in higher education but can be problematic to achieve. Successful games are, at their core, designed to be engaging experiences. In attempts to increase engagement in learning, there has been an increase in playful learning, game-based learning, and gamification as educators attempt to encourage engagement by explicitly harnessing the engaging attributes of games. Additionally, other attempts to increase engagement in education have implicitly resulted in the incorporation of game-like attributes. This chapter provides specific definitions of these terms and acknowledges that such attempts to increase engagement often offer an additional layer of extrinsic motivators. The authors propose that this can lead to unexpected and undesirable effects if extrinsic motivators are not well aligned to the desired behavior. This chapter presents a taxonomy of engagement strategies regarding their implicit and explicit game attributes and their implicit and explicit teaching attributes.

INTRODUCTION

This chapter will consider the role of games, game-based learning, and gamification in higher education. It will discuss how encouraging student engagement is of increasing importance in higher education, and the power of successful games to engage players is something that is highly sought after in higher education. This has led to the introduction of games for teaching and the adoption of game related

DOI: 10.4018/978-1-6684-4287-6.ch032

teaching strategies. This adoption of game-based approaches is an area of ongoing research, in terms of the appropriateness, effectiveness and applicability of games and game-based strategies to teaching. The authors will present definitions of the related but distinct terms "game", "game-based learning" and "gamification" and will consider the underlying psychological factors that motivate players to play.

The issue of engagement for higher education is a significant one, with retention and attainment seen as key challenges for the sector globally. The chapter demonstrates how the concepts of intrinsic and extrinsic motivation drive engagement with both with games and with teaching, and proposes that engagement with both games and learning are driven by these same types of motivations. This blurs the line further between what can be considered gamification, and leads to the proposal of the concept of explicit and implicit gamification.

To illustrate this concept a visualisation of the relationship between game and game like artefacts associated with learning, charted in a conceptual space based on their membership of explicit or implicit gamification. To further bolster these ideas, a taxonomy of mechanics and attributes that frequently manifest in gamification is proposed. Finally, an example of the relative alignment of game-like mechanics with desired outcomes or goals is presented – highlighting the need for careful consideration when attempting to incentivize specific behaviour.

BACKGROUND

In this section, the authors briefly outline the importance of student engagement in higher education, and the desire to draw inspiration from games including a description of perspectives from games design on the potential of games as general learning and teaching artefacts, and the role that all games take learning. Next, some definitions of important relevant terms games, game-based learning and gamification are offered. Following this, some theories of motivation of engagement are outlined with explicit links to learning and to games where appropriate – highlighting some of the potential pitfalls that could arise when trying to influence specific behaviour.

Engagement in Higher Education

Student engagement in Higher (also called Tertiary) Education is of vital importance both to the success of education providers, and for the students that make use of them. The growth of Higher Education across the world (Choudaha & Van Rest, 2018) has seen increased staff-student rations and pressures on resources, as institutions adapt to manage larger classes. This growth has also created more varied student qualification profiles and a more varied student cohorts, leading to issues of engagement and support and the need for differentiated teaching, a new challenge for H.E.. Changes in student finance – such as the move in many countries to tuition fees – mean that many students try to balance work alongside their studies, whilst others have to balance family and caring commitments. These changes have an impact on student engagement and attainment. In the UK, Woodfield (2014) considered many of these issues, and how they correspond to different attainment and success outcomes in different disciplines, and later work has considered how to model and approach these diverse populations (Quaye et al, 2019). Work by the authors of this chapter (Gordon & Grey, 2018) considered approaches to measuring engagement, as well as different approaches to increase motivation, as considered below. The political pressure to increase participation in Higher Education in many countries is also altering the nature of students, and in many cases seems to have a negative impact on the level of engagement of these reluctant students.

Motivation for Games and Gamification

In this section, a brief description of games as engaging artefacts is presented. The authors will present perspectives of games designers who argue that learning is a direct outcome of play, and that games are at their core teaching artefacts that promote a lusory attitude. The authors will also discuss challenges such as the view that play is seen as childish, and game players (Gamers) are wasting time.

Play and games are often seen as trivial ventures; however, through his work on the function of play in culture Huizinga (1971) highlights that play is a fundamental part of human culture, with an important role to play. Interestingly, Huizinga points out that the origin of the word 'school' "Meaning originally 'leisure' it has now acquired precisely the opposite sense of systemic work and training" (1971, p.148).

Game designer Chris Crawford claims that "the fundamental motivation for all game playing it to learn" (2011, p.13) claiming that the purpose of games was to learn about the game domain, solve the problems and beat the challenges it presents by developing the required skills to do so. Koster goes further to make the claim that "Fun is just another word for learning" and that games are ultimately teachers (2010, p.46) and further emphasises the link between good games as engaging experiences, and games as teaching artefacts with the definition of a good game as "one that teaches everything it has to offer before the player stops playing." (2010, p.46).

The role of play and games in learning is well established, yet also holds some amount of stigma. As we grow older, there seems to be a drive to distance ourselves from childish things. Adults who play video games adopted the term "gamer", rather than "player" in an effort to add legitimacy to their hobby that they dedicate so much time to. Furthermore, when chastising another for inappropriate behaviour one might ask them "What are you playing at?" yet when we embark of a learning journey, or a journey of discovery we might say that we are "playing around with an idea". This stigma may present barriers to learner engaging in learning through the medium of games.

Definition of Games, Game-Based Learning, Serious Games, Gamification and Playful Learning

In this section, the authors make formal distinctions between games, game-based learning, serious games, gamification and playful learning, and will suggest definitions based upon literature of each. This will set a foundation and context for the idea of explicit and implicit gamification.

Games

Many attempts have been made to define games, and once a definition for games is agreed upon, defining games-based learning comes more easily. Schell presents a detailed, comprehensive and evolving description of definitions for games, highlighting their benefits and shortcomings finally settling upon "a game is a problem-solving activity, approached with a playful attitude" (2008, p.47) Other attempts to define games seem less nuanced, and so more elegant. Esteemed games designer Sid Meier describes games as a "series of interesting decisions." (Alexander, 2012, "GDC 2012" section), however this could be interpreted more like advice to design a game, and without more clarity many things that are not games would be consider as games.

McGonigal presents more pragmatic approach, defining games as anything that has four defining traits; a goal, rules, a feedback system and voluntary participation (2012, p.21). Some important distinctions to make are the necessity for a playful approach, which could manifest itself through voluntary participation. The existence of rules and a goal distinguish games from toys. Finally, a feedback system allows players to assess the consequences of their actions in a game and the efficacy with which they are progressing towards their goal. Under this definition, it is argued that engagement with an institution of higher education could also be considered a game for many students, as they incorporate all four of the elements McGonigal presents. Firstly, goals manifest themselves in the form of marks for modules or units contributing to an overall qualification. Secondly, rules are provided in terms of academic conduct and the requirements of a particular learning activity. Thirdly, feedback should be provided for formative and summative work. Finally, by its nature Higher Education is normally considered a voluntary level of education, though that is under pressure, as it has now become a gateway to an increasing array of careers, and with a variety of incentives or penalties to encourage students to enter Higher Education.

McGonigal claims that video games are not an easy option; citing philosopher Bernard Suits eloquent description of playing a game as "*the voluntary attempt to overcome unnecessary obstacles*" (2012, p.22). Not all games are good games though, and there is active research into what makes a good game as opposed to a bad one. As such, it seems appropriate that the people who design higher education may learn something from this work into the design of good games that engage players.

Game-based Learning

Learning is a core aspect of game playing experience, and this is not lost on game designers. Game designer Chris Crawford points out "... the fundamental motivation for all game-play is to learn" (2011, p.13). Similarly, Koster makes the bold claim "...games are, in the end. Teachers. Fun is just another word for learning." (2010, p.46), and uses the example of tic-tac-toe to demonstrate that once a game system is fully understood they become boring, and the player's desire to engage is diminished. Huizinga (1938) describes how animals play according to a set of rules. The purpose being to learn how to fight, as well as establishing a dominance hierarchy in a relatively low risk environment.

Game-based learning is any learning that is acquired through engaging with a game that was not created with the specific primary goal of creating a teaching artefact. Learning can manifest itself in many ways. Learning could be embedded within the mechanics of the game, and players could learn about patterns of movement, tactics, and strategy. Alternatively, learning could primarily be included within the narrative of the game and the game world itself. Kurt Squire describes the accurate historical, cultural and geographical knowledge he acquired inadvertently through playing Sid Meier's perpetual simulation game "Pirates!" (2011). More recently, the modern action-adventure game franchise "Assassin's Creed" includes over 20 games. In each game, the protagonist uses a device that unlock "genetic memories" of their ancestors to re-enact events during a significant time and place in history. The publishers of the Assassin's Creed franchise take great pride in create accurate depictions of the times and places their protagonist visits, and for Assassin's Creed: Odyssey even enabled players to explore the virtual environment whilst removing any risk mechanics usually found in games in a game mode called "Discovery Tour".

"Discovery Tour is a dedicated game that lets visitors freely roam Ancient Greece and Ancient Egypt to learn more about their history and daily life. Students, teachers, non-gamers, and dedicated players can discover these eras at their own pace, or embark on guided tours curated by historians and experts." (Discovery Tour by Ubisoft: Teacher learning resources I Ubisoft (UK), n.d. "Discovery Tour" section)

For this sort of incidental learning it is important that games remain authentic to their source material, to prevent the spread of misconceptions. One artefact of that is the popular YouTube channel Gamology (n.d.) which regularly publishes "Experts Reacts" videos in which an expert in a particular field provides commentary on the accuracy of the depiction of their field in video games.

Other games that have been credited with this "implicit" domain-based learning effect include titles such as Civilisation (http://www.civilization.com), Transport Tycoon (http://www.transporttycoon.com) and Sim City (http://www.simcity.com/en_US). These are typically games in which success requires strategic planning and systemic thinking. Whilst these are examples of games that can teach something about the domain in which they are set, it seems that they were created as commercial ventures, and were not specifically created with learning in mind. Rather they happened upon the potential of games to teach something almost as a by-product of playing.

These are examples of game based learning. Other games have been created specifically with the aim of providing opportunities of learning, or with the aim of creating lasting behavioural change. Perhaps the most famous example in terms of its reputation and success is "Where in the world is Carmen Sandiego" which was released in 1983 (http://www.carmensandiego.com). Unfortunately, commercial genre of games labelled "edutainment" seems to be more associated with poorly designed, poorly executed games (Goldstein, 2014). It is proposed that this is largely due to a combination of poor game design, poor understanding of learning and teaching, and a lack of funding in comparison to mainstream games. That does not mean that there is not a place for game based learning, but many games make the mistake of taking a good game and trying to retrofit some learning activity. For edutainment to be successful the primary goal, the learning outcomes must be central to the design.

When designing games specifically to be used in teaching, Grey et al. (2017) propose that it is important to closely align game mechanics with the desired learning goals, otherwise there is a risk of emergent behaviour resulting in misleading models of understanding due to the mode of delivery. Abbot (2018) however advocates for adapting existing games. Whilst this may result in all the learning goals being embedded in the narrative which could potentially be removed there is definitely merit in delivering learning games with tried and tested engaging mechanics that provide a lower barrier to entry for players already familiar with games.

Serious Games

A generally more successful application of games for learning is the field of serious games (Burden and Slater 2008). Serious games are games that are made for a specific "serious" purpose. Often serious games take the form of training simulations. Serious games are widely used in the military, where funding is less of an issue. As well as games for training, military simulation games are also created for propaganda purposes (Chacksfield, 2009). The relative success of serious games often seems proportional to the quality of game, which is in turn linked to the available budget.

Similarly to Grey et al. (2017), Supriana et al. (2017) also highlight the need for learning and teaching strategies to be closely aligned to game mechanics, thus avoiding the phenomenon of "chocolate covered broccoli" – which describes serious games in which the learning material is not well aligned or integrated with the game mechanics. Lopez et al. (2021) acknowledge that trainees should approach serious games with an accepting and open mind, highlighting the stigma that games are play-things. Analysis of trainees attitudes towards using lego as a management training tool revealed that trainees perception of the usefulness of serious games was key to acceptance.

The Games for Change movement is also worthy of a mention. Games for change (http://www.gamesforchange.org) is a global organisation founded in 2004 with the primary goal of facilitating "the creation and distribution of social impact games that serve as critical tools in humanitarian and educational efforts". This represents a recent, significant and active body in this field of research.

Gamification

Gamification is a term that describes the use of game based mechanics in nongame contexts. Gamification is by no means a new thing, as any sort of reward system such as giving badges for achievement (as with the boy scouts) points based loyalty scheme can be considered a form of gamification (growthengineering, 2021). Often gamification is reliant upon a layer of intrinsic motivators.

This section will briefly consider what a game is, the impact of play on learning, and the distinction between gamification and game based learning. Next, compelling video games will be considered with reference to the motivational theory covered previously in order to identifying some key concepts of motivational theory that are applied to motivate players to play games. Finally, we will consider how these concepts can be applied to learning and teaching in order to motivate engagement. Key concepts include flow, fast feedback, continual and cumulative feedback, the importance of choice and the idea of tasks having low risk and fun failure.

Zichermann and Cunningham define gamification as *"The process of game-thinking and game mechanics to engage users and solve problems"* (2011, p.xiv). Deterding et al provide a systematic dissection of gamification beginning with the proposed definition that gamification is *"the use of game design elements in non-game contexts"* (2011, p.10). Later Kapp combines elements of a variety of definitions to arrive at the definition *"Gamification is using game-based mechanics, aesthetics and game thinking to engage people, motivate action, promote learning, and solve problems."* (2012, p.10). Werbach and Hunter also offer the definition of gamification as *"The use of game elements and game design techniques in non-game contexts"* (2012, p.26)

Stereotypically gamification is sometimes summarized as giving feedback for engagement through points, badges and leader boards. It is argued that points, badges and leader boards represent little more than another layer of extrinsic motivators (described later) (Zichermann and Cunningham. 2011; Werbach and Hunger, 2012) which can lead to undesirable outcomes. Werbach and Hunter caution that designers should not *"mindlessly attach extrinsic motivators to activities that can be motivated using intrinsic regulators."* (2012, p.62). It is proposed that if implemented appropriately badges in particular can offer the opportunity to reflect on progress to date by providing sustained competence feedback as it is proposed that carefully selected set of badges would give a visually satisfying representation of the cumulative accomplishments to date. Such use needs careful planning, to ensure that the implementation does indeed meet the needs of the learners (Xi & Hamari, 2019).

Playful Learning

Playful learning include games, game-based learning, serious games and any other playful approach that is applied to learning and teaching. Playful learning encompasses all these things and refers to an approach to learning and teaching that adopts a lusory attitude. This more inclusive term removes the tendency to worry about distracting definitions, that can become unhelpful and exclusive. Adopting a lusory attitude can alleviate some of the stigma associated with extrinsic motivation, that can have unintended negative consequences such as narrowing focus, diminishing intrinsic motivation and increasing fear of failure. This can be especially true if extrinsic motivation is not well aligned with the desired learning behaviours. Playful learning could be framed as any practice which rejects the potential negative consequences of systems driven by metrics in favour of embracing low risk experimentation in safe spaces, encourages a process of failure and reflection, and allows participants to be immersed in learning (Whitton, 2018). It is natural to learn through play and playing with ideas, and lowering the social barriers to allow for free play is conducive to this type of learning.

As demonstrated by Lopez et al (2021) order to engage with learning in a playful way participants require an open mind, which could be termed a lusory attitude. This presents a conflict between playfulness, which is sometimes seen as a frivolous activity for children, and the importance of the task in hand. The term "Serious Games" that could be considered to be an oxymoron emphasises this point – games are to some people a playful pursuit for children; they are not "serious". This distinction is also highlighted by Whitton and Langam (2018) who note that many academics consider more playful approaches to learning to be *"inappropriate and frivolous, undermining the academic nature of higher study"* (Whitton and Langam, 2018, p.1002) whilst also finding that students are receptive to efforts to make learning more fun.

Acceptance of games in adulthood is embodied in the concept of the "magic circle" (Nørgård et al, 2016) which can be described as a virtual barrier that must be crossed by players in order to engage with the rules, mechanics and narrative associated with play. Accepting the metaphor of the magic circle and result in greater intrinsic motivation, promoting exploration, reflective risk taking and participation (Nørgård et al, 2017). Parallels can be drawn between the idea of entering the magic circle as a state of acceptance and developing an open mindset (Dweck, 2017). In both cases participants are required to cultivate a specific mental state in which they can be playful, suspend disbelief, encourage risk taking and deliberate experimentation and recognise embrace failure as opportunities that are necessary for learning and growth.

Summary

In this section the terms games, game-based learning, serious games, gamification and playful learning have been introduced. Table 1 presents a summary of key differences between the various terms with respect to their use, their intended use and the degree to which the artifact is a game. These terms are not exclusive. For example, a Serious Game uses an explicit game to deliver an engaging learning experience to its players, and so is encompassed within game-based learning. However in some cases players learn from a game (often through engaging with an accurate narrative) when the intended use for the game was to entertain rather than to be a teaching tool.

Table 1. Summary of the key differences between games, game-based learning, gamification, serious games and playful learning

	Uses a game	Intended use	Actual use
Games	Yes	Engagement in entertainment	Engagement in entertainment
Game-Based Learning	Yes	Engaging entertainment	Learning
Gamification	No	Engagement	Engagement
Serious Games	Yes	Engaging learning	Learning
Playful Learning	Maybe	Learning	Learning

The next section will bridge the gap between motivation of engagement and learning and teaching.

Games and Gamification in Learning and Teaching

In this section, the authors will consider the role of games and gamification in learning and teaching. This includes considering examples of the explicit use of games and gamification in learning and teaching, both computer- mediated and non-technology based ones. Examples here include games for entertainment such as Sid Meier's Pirates and the Assassins Creed franchise, serious games typically used for training such as RescueSim (De Gloria, 2014) and extra-curricular activities that are games, for example Game Jams that are often competitive and sometimes incentivized by prizes. These examples of explicit gamification illustrate the application of actual games in teaching. In this section, will also the authors also highlight game like elements employed in teaching generally that are not typically considered under the banner of games – labelling these implicit gamification. This is consistent with other commentators and authors (Chou, 2013).

Gamification has been making an impact in business for several years (Johnson et al, 2013), but it has only recently been adopted in education. It is perhaps unsurprising that game designer turned lecturer Lee Sheldon redesigned his entire academic course as a game, using his experience as a game designer to fix flaws in the academic system resulting in his "multiplayer classroom" (2011). By using this method within institutional constraints Sheldon was able to increase engagement and improve marks by presenting his course as a game, with rules, goal and feedback, and perhaps most importantly by introducing a playful environment. Sheldon also presents a number of recent case studies playing with similar concepts.

Games and gamification are emerging technologies that are expected to have a significant impact on higher education in the near future as more educators recognize that "games simulate productivity and creative inquiry among learners" (Johnson et al, 2013, p.20). Gordon et al present data from a study that included "natural" game based mechanics such as multiple attempts, low risk, adaptive difficult to match skills and immediate feedback (2013). All of these are qualities that have been borrowed from games and games design. However, in some case these would be considered implicit gamification rather than explicit gamification. For example, natural game mechanics are considered implicit gamification, whereas extrinsic motivators for engagement, such as points, badges or marks for completing work is considered explicit gamification.

Dichev and Dicheeva (2017) present a comprehensive review of gamification in education with a focus on empirical evidence of attainment of learning outcomes. The outcome of this review is inconclusive, with still more study being required. One interesting conclusion however is that *"the practice of gamifying learning has outpaced researchers' understanding of its mechanisms and methods"* (Dichev and Dicheeca, 2017, p.25) which alludes to some of the risks of gamified learning experiences, and the need to align game mechanics with desired behaviours and learning outcomes.

Kusuma et al present an analysis of gamification models in education (2018) drawing inspiration from the MDA model for game design (Hunicke et al, 2004), which places emphasis on the separation between the game mechanics as created by the designer, and the aesthetic experience of the player. Kusuma et al identify a wide variety of mechanics that have been adopted through the gamification of education, but do not evaluate their potential to result in effective learning, of the separation between designing learning mechanics and the learning experience – which is a key feature of the MDA model. Ignoring this aspect can lead to game mechanics that are misaligned with learning outcomes.

Advances in the area of learning analytics can also contribute to the reach of gamification, allowing more ways to monitor engagement and provide fast feedback. It was also predicted that learning analytics would reach the mainstream by 2016 (Johnson et al, 2013) which has proven to be largely accurate. In this context, learning analytics can be considered big data applied to education. Learning analytics is concerned with understanding and making decisions based upon data collected in educational domains. That data could be used to drive systems such as personalized or flexible learning facilities (Gordon 2014). Learning analytics can also be used to measure the impact of such systems.

It is proposed that there is an explicit link between gamification and learning analytics. If the desire for engagement is such that the effort into setting up a gamified solution can be justified it follows that there is a desire to understand how well the gamified solution worked, how engaged its users are and why they were engaged. The scalable technologies often used to implement such systems facilitate the collection of vast amounts of data on user interactions. Therefore, we have a large amount of data, and a desire to derive some understanding from the data. Analytics provides the bridge in between.

Underlying Motivation for Engagement

In all case games, gamification and game-based learning are strongly linked with motivating engagement. For games in their purest form, the primary goal of games is for the player to engage with the game. Even then though, as Crawford and Koster highlight (Crawford, 2011; Koster, 2010), games are about learning about the game itself. When there is no more to learn about the game motivation to engage in play is diminished. In a systematic meta-review of theoretical foundations of gamification, serious games and game-based learning Krath et al identified 118 motivational theories (2021). Gamification is increasingly being used as one of the strategies and tools available in Higher Education (Aguiar-Castillo et al, 2020), however often gamification, game-based learning and other playful approaches to learning have a tendency to focus on motivation through the provision of extrinsic measures of performance that mirror the increasingly metric driven systems found throughout institutions of higher education (Nørgård et al, 2016). This section considers three of the most popular theories in experiential learning theory, self-determination theory and the concept of flow, and their application to games, and to learning and teaching outside of games, both of which play significant roles in what makes games so compelling to players.

Experiential Learning Theory

Experiential learning embraces the idea that knowledge is learned through experience. It includes concepts of building, testing and reflecting upon increasingly abstract mental models. Experiential learning uses experiences, reflection, reactions, feelings and actions to consciously acquire knowledge (Valkanos and Fragoulis 2007).

Figure 1. Kolb's learning cycle (adapted from Kolb, 2014)

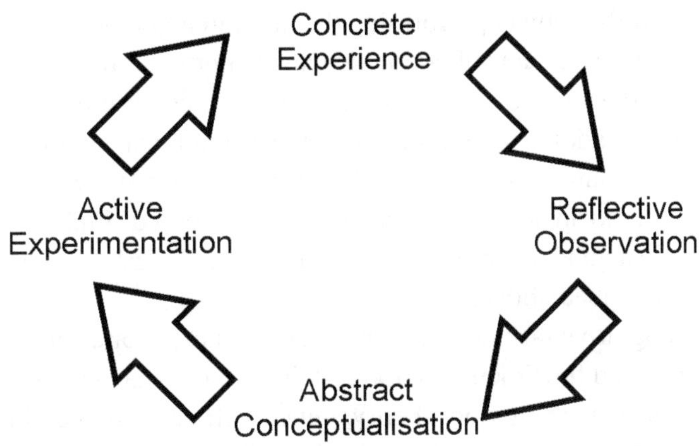

Perhaps the most prevalent theory of experiential learning is Kolb's learning cycle, shown in Figure 1. Kolb clarified that experiential learning requires a participant to immerse themselves fully and openly, without bias, in the experience (2014). The learners' observations must be reflected on from a variety of perspectives, in order to devise logically sound theories, which allow them to make decisions and solve problems. It is worth noting the importance of the role of feedback in experiential learning gained through testing and reflecting, in order to build better mental models of understanding.

Self-Determination Theory

Self Determination Theory is a theory of motivation in which participants of a task are motivated by the task itself. It includes the motivation to fulfil three needs; the need for competence in the task, the need for autonomy and the need for relatedness (Ryan 1982; Ryan and Deci 2000; Ryan, Rigby et al. 2006; Rigby and Ryan 2011). Competence (or mastery (Pink 2011)) refers to the feeling that participants are good (or at least improving their skills) for a particular task. Autonomy refers to the feeling that participants are in control of their actions, and that they are a result of meaningful choices that the participants themselves have made. Relatedness (or purpose (Pink 2011)) refers to the need for participants to be socially connected to others, and that individual participants are personally important to those people.

These three needs can be categorized as intrinsic motivators, which are inseparable from the task at hand, as opposed to extrinsic motivators, such as points, badges, money or marks. Facilitating intrinsic motivation is of particular importance in education. Ryan and Deci state that "intrinsic motivation results in high-quality learning and creativity" (Ryan and Deci 2000, p.55)

At this point, it is important to make a distinction between extrinsic and intrinsic motivators, as these are key to understanding Self-Determination theory. Extrinsic motivators are motivators that are separate to the desired behaviour being motivated, whereas intrinsic motivation comes from the behaviour itself. As such intrinsic motivators are typically highly dependent on the specific task involved but include feelings of satisfaction having achieved a challenging task, or progress towards mastery. Common extrinsic motivators are often less abstract because they are separated from the task. Common extrinsic motivation include financial incentives or other rewards for work, such as marks. Motivators can also be negative sticks, as opposed to carrots, such as fines, or in academia penalties for failing to attend teaching activities.

Extrinsic motivators work well for mundane tasks; however, for cognitive tasks they can have a negative effect, particularly if the subject performing the task already holds some intrinsic motivation in that task. Pink lists seven negative effects of adding extrinsic motivator to a task, claiming that extrinsic motivators can crowd out good behaviour, diminish performance, reduce creativity, encourage short-term thinking and cheating, become addictive, and possible worst of all, can suppress intrinsic motivation.

Pink (Pink 2011); Kohn (Kohn) and Werbach (Werbach and Hunter 2012) cite numerous studies in which the negative effects of extrinsic motivators have been recorded. Pink expands that for mundane tasks extrinsic motivators are a good technique, but for any cognitive task, extrinsic motivators can result in the detrimental effects described above.

Instead, it is better for cognitive tasks if there are intrinsic motivators. These motivators come from the task itself, and from the need fulfilment that the task itself can offer. The theory of intrinsic motivation is best embodied by Self Determination Theory, which will be explained in the following section.

In describing a "Motivational Continuum", Werbach and Hunter (2012, p.67) note that there is not a black and white divide between intrinsic and extrinsic motivators. Werbach gives the example of online role-playing games, which can be played alone or as part of a guild. He notes that certain mundane tasks such as collecting items will be performed as part of a group that would not be performed alone.

"The users need for relatedness dramatically changes the perceived nature of the motivation" (Werbach and Hunter, 2012, p.67)

Cognitive Evaluation Theory (CET) is also worthy of consideration, and is considered a sub-theory for Self Determination Theory (Ryan and Deci 2000). CET places an emphasis on the need for autonomy alongside competence feedback, hypothesising that competence feedback will have no positive affect intrinsic motivation unless it is accompanied by a feeling of autonomy.

Malone et al identified that a focus in educational research on cognitive learning processes have left a comparative void in the area of motivating learning and creating motivating learning environments (Malone 1981; Malone and Lepper 1987). In an effort to fill this perceived void, Malone et al attempted to create conditions for learning that rejected extrinsic motivators and embrace intrinsic motivators through engaging with fantasy, challenge and curiosity.

Flow

Another important motivational theory is that for Flow. Flow is the work of psychologist Mihaly Csikszentmihalyi who described his studies into the concept of happiness as the psychology of optimal experience (Csikszentmihalyi, 1990). The concept of flow describes a state of complete engagement, when a person faces a challenge is well matched to their skill that pushes them towards the limits of their ability. In the world of sports, this concept is often described as being "in the zone". That concept is illustrated in the figure below.

Figure 2. Visualisation of flow state with respect to challenge and skill

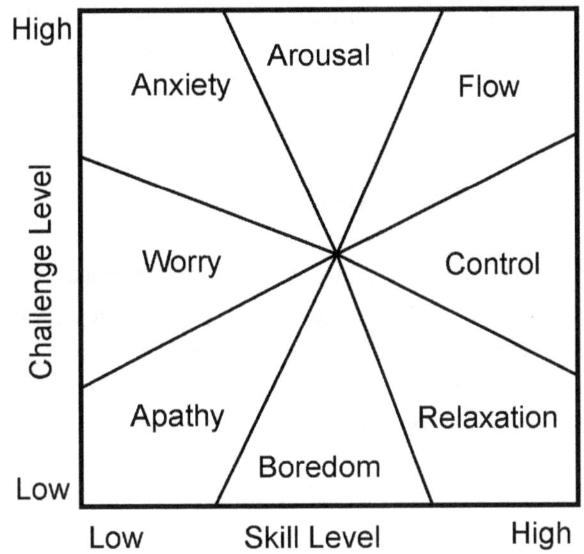

Figure 2 Visualisation of Flow with respect to challenge and skill charts relative challenge against skill level for a person carrying out some task, highlighting their emotions as their skill level changes with respect to the level of challenge they are facing. Consider the individual at the centre of the diagram, and the challenge level and skill level plotted relative to the individual. If the challenge of a task is less that the skill level, the individual is apathetic, bored or relaxed. If the level of skill required by a challenge is greater than the individual's skill level then the individual becomes anxious, aroused, or in the flow state.

Flow is a valuable concept in games. In an effort to create better games, some game designers have latched on to this concept. Although it is unclear whether he was talking specifically about flow, it is claimed that Nintendo's legendary game designer Shigeru Miyamoto described directing players into a flow state in a rare interview (Desert Hat, 2009), describing how it is important to keep the player in a flow channel, enabling them to improve their skills, and to feel mastery. Games designer and founder of ThatGameCompany, Jenova Chen, based his doctoral thesis on the concept of flow in games, and since has made several successful games based around the concept of flow (2007). These examples of game designers in pursuit of the flow state are indicative of the importance of the concept. In particular, Miyamoto's description of the need to follow failure with the opportunity for the player to regain control and further improve their skills has parallels with both self-determination theory (through feelings of competence) (Ryan and Deci 2000; Ryan, Rigby et al. 2006; Rigby and Ryan 2011) and flexible personalized learning (Gordon 2013). Csikszentmihalyi states that in order to achieve flow "goals are usually clear and feedback immediate" (Csikszentmihalyi 1990, p.54). Feedback is a vital and recurring concept in both games as well as learning and teaching, which is reflected within Kolb's learning cycle (2014).

In summary, the role of good games is to engage players through designed experiences. Gamification is the use of game mechanics in non-game contexts to engage people towards a desired goal. People are motivated to engage through the provision of extrinsic and intrinsic motivators and require timely feedback to aid understanding and reflect upon their success moving towards a goal. This is achieved by adding a layer of extrinsic motivators; however, without care extrinsic motivators can have undesirable effects. In the next section, the authors attempt to raise awareness of these risks, by introducing the idea that any extrinsic motivation can be framed as gamification, either explicitly or implicitly. The authors also consider the potential relative alignment of extrinsic motivators with desired goals, theorizing that the negative effect of extrinsic motivation is diminished when the extrinsic motivators are well aligned with the desired goals.

SOLUTIONS AND RECOMMENDATIONS

In the previous sections, the authors have presented the case for increased engagement in higher education, and highlighted the power of games to engage. Some prominent underlying motivational theories of engagement have been considered, and the risks involved in careless implementation of engagement techniques using extrinsic motivators have been highlighted. In this section, the authors will attempt to encourage consideration of this phenomenon when deploying techniques designed to promote engagement.

Taxonomy of Implicit and Explicit Gamification

As highlighted previously gamification manifests itself as a layer of extrinsic motivators to invoke a desired behaviour, and so any extrinsic motivation to engage can be considered gamification. It is important that extrinsic motivators are well aligned with desired behaviours, which in the case of learning and teaching typically refers to acquiring new knowledge or skills. In this section, the authors give examples to support the idea of implicit and explicit gamification. Any additional extrinsic motivators can be considered gamification. The institutional structures that are used to assess and monitor learning, providing feedback and marks, attaining credits and qualifications can be considered to be implicit gamification. Providing achievements, badges or points would be considered explicit gamification.

Figure 3. Game-likeness versus motivation. Examples of how some approaches fit into the space of motivation and gamification

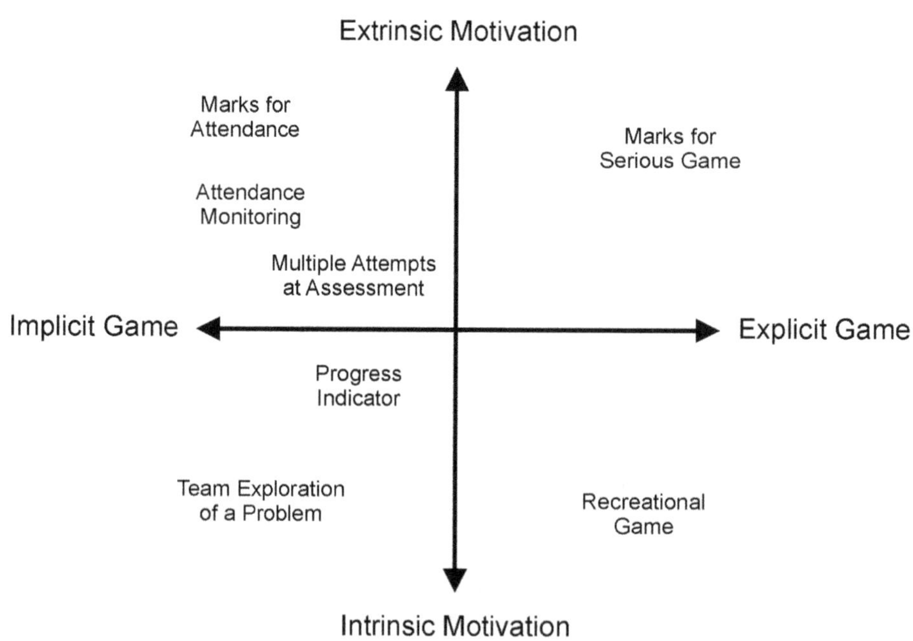

Figure 3 Game-likeness versus motivation shows how some common techniques used in higher education can be consider at implicitly or explicitly to be game-like. These techniques can also be analysed in terms of how far they provide varying levels of extrinsic or intrinsic motivation to engage with a specific task. In the case of higher education, the goal is that students learn about topics and acquire new skills. Awarding marks for work – indeed assessment in general - is considered an extrinsic motivator. Awarding marks for engaging with a serious game specifically designed to deliver the desired knowledge and skills is explicitly a game. Awarding marks for attending a lecture is implicitly game-like, because there are rules, a feedback system and a goal. Playing a recreational game that immerses the player in a world is explicitly a game, but is intrinsically motivated because the goal is to work through the game rather than to acquire skills and knowledge concerning the narrative of the game, for example.

List of Attributes Leading to Gamification

In this section the authors provide a list of game mechanics that can be applied in education, such as points, badges, leader boards, multiple attempts, fast feedback, teaching in narrative etc. (Gordon et al), particularly those that can be enabled through technology. These mechanics are presented in Table 2, and are structured as a taxonomy to show how motivation (intrinsic or extrinsic) and gamification (implicit or explicit) complement one another. Whilst these relate to the issue of engagement – the intention here being to engage students – we have not attempted here to assess how effectively they actually engage students.

Table 2. Taxonomy of gamification techniques

Technique/mechanic	Description	Implicit or Explicit	Intrinsic or Extrinsic
Attendance/access monitoring with rewards or penalties.	Checking presence at a session or accessing an online resource, with marks or other rewards for attendance and/or penalties for non-attendance.	Implicit: a reward mechanism for attempting	Extrinsic
Progress monitoring through learning resources or levels	Graphical or other indicator of progress through a session/module	Implicit	Intrinsic
Multiple attempts	Multiple attempts at an assessment activity	Implicit. Corresponds to multiple lives in a game.	
Low risk attempts/submission	Can have a go without fearing the consequence	Implicit	Extrinsic
Personalised experience	Randomisation or other approach to give a unique experience	Implicit	Intrinsic
Adaptive difficulty	Utilising knowledge or dependency structure to adapt activity to learner's performance	Implicit	Intrinsic
Immediate Feedback	To enable students to understand their current performance, and to try again	Implicit	Intrinsic
Serious Game	A game designed to teach some topic or awareness of issues	Explicit	Intrinsic
High scores and Leader boards	Enables students to understand their relative performance, and what is possible	Implicit	Intrinsic

Examples of Alignment of Extrinsic Motivation with Desired Goals

It is proposed that one method to avoid the negative effects of extrinsic motivation described by Pink (2011) is to ensure that extrinsic motivators are closely aligned with the desired goals. This is similar to the approach proposed by Grey et al. (2017) when designing game-based learning by closely aligning game mechanics with desired behaviour. In the diagram below, techniques used to prompt engagement are speculatively plotted against how well they could potentially be aligned with desired goals. This is speculative because in each case there are many factors involved. For example, awarded marks for the completion of assessment should assess that a student have achieved the learning outcomes and acquired the skills required to complete the assessment, but that is dependent on the quality of the particular assessment. Similarly, penalizing students or for failing to attend at a scheduled teaching activity may not be well aligned with the goal of acquiring skills and knowledge because it is likely that some students would engage with the attendance monitoring system without engaging with the teaching activity itself.

Figure 4. Goal alignment versus motivation. Examples of how some approaches fit into the space of motivation and goal alignment

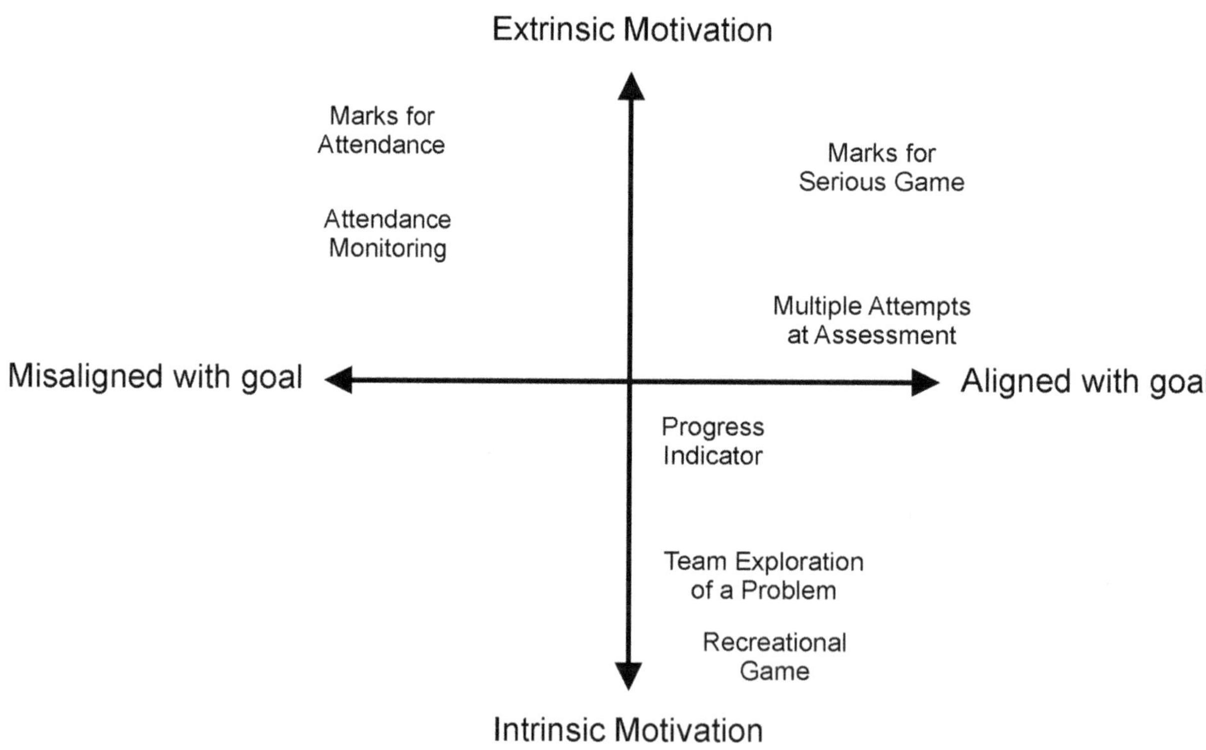

Figure 4 Goal alignment versus motivation speculatively shows how some motivation techniques fall along a spectrum of alignment with the intended goal. Features to note here are that marks and assessment of the acquisition of skills and knowledge are notionally separate from the goal of acquiring skills and knowledge. Thus, it seems that there will always be approaches in the top right quadrant. Anything concerning marks, an extrinsic motivator, would appear in the top half of the diagram.

Similarly, the bottom left quadrant is empty because it is hard to conceive of an approach that is intrinsically motivated by the desired goal, but misaligned with that same goal. This quadrant will always remain empty.

Extrinsic motivators such as monitoring and awarding penalties or benefits for attendance alone are not well aligned with the desired goal, because it is very easy for students to attend and activity without actively engaging in the learning and teaching. This top left quadrant should be avoided.

The ideal space to occupy is the bottom right quadrant. In the example of learning and acquiring skills this can be regarded as learning for the love of learning. It should be noted that in this case the recreational game would be one that is accurate and immerses the player in the desired learning material, otherwise it is not well aligned with the goal – or rather is well-aligned with a different goal. This could then be considered procrastination.

Pragmatically in higher education, it is likely that most initiatives to promote engagement will occupy the top half of the diagram. It is hoped that by presenting techniques designed to promote engagement in this way can raise awareness of the risks of extrinsic motivators, and encourage the use of techniques that move towards the right side of the diagram, and away from the top left quadrant.

FUTURE RESEARCH DIRECTIONS

Three are two things that digital games do particularly well that could be used in higher education. Both are related to flow. The first is the provision of challenges that are closely matched to the current skill of the students. The second is providing immediate feedback on performance. With increasing class sizes, this is becoming more and more challenging, and the two factors together present a particularly difficult problem. Providing a challenge closely matched to skill is synonymous with personalized learning. Providing fast feedback is feasible with very small student numbers, but rapidly becomes a question of automation. Automation makes personalized learning more difficult. Whilst both are theoretically achievable with appropriate resources, it is becoming increasingly challenging to achieve this whilst also avoiding slipping to the top-left quadrant of the diagram in Figure 4.

CONCLUSION

In conclusion, the authors have discussed the distinction between games, game-based learning and gamification, and have examined the underlying theories of motivation that drive engagement both in games and in learning. It has been demonstrated that extrinsic motivators for engagement are not without their risks, and these should be carefully considered. Care should be taken when implementing any initiative to promote engagement, to ensure that the necessary extrinsic motivators are well aligned with the desired goals and intended behaviour.

To demonstrate this the authors have identified some frequently used techniques to promote engagement in learning and plotted the degree that they motivate using intrinsic or extrinsic motivation against the degree that such initiatives are likely to be aligned with the intended learning goals.

The authors have identified some of the approaches to learning that gamification can enable, and have shown how gamification can be applied implicitly or explicitly. How far these approaches can provide intrinsic or extrinsic motivation to engage learners has also been explored. The question of how far these are successful in engaging students, and how far they are successful in enabling actual learning, is something for further investigation. However, empirical evidence and experience of the authors has shown that these approaches do work well for some students, and have value as part of the portfolio of teaching methods. The need for appropriate challenges and fast feedback has also been touched upon, and again, experience has shown that challenges can enable students to engage with their studies, and can encourage students to push themselves further and thus improve their attainment. Improved engagement has the potential to improve student attainment, thereby improving their grades and potential career destinations. These particular measures are typically used in university rankings, and thus this can improve institutional esteem too, though that is very much a by-product and not an aim of the approach.

REFERENCES

Abbott, D. (2018, December). Modding tabletop games for education. In *International Conference on Games and Learning Alliance* (pp. 318-329). Springer.

Aguiar-Castillo, L., Hernández-López, L., De Saá-Pérez, P., & Pérez-Jiménez, R. (2020). Gamification as a motivation strategy for higher education students in tourism face-to-face learning. *Journal of Hospitality, Leisure, Sport and Tourism Education, 27*, 100267. doi:10.1016/j.jhlste.2020.100267

Alexander, L. (2012). *GDC 2012: Sid Meier on how to see games as sets of interesting decisions.* Gamasutra. https://www.gamasutra.com/view/news/164869/GDC_2012_Sid_Meier_on_how_to_see_games_as_sets_of_interesting_decisions.php

Chacksfield, M. (2009). US army spends $32.8 million on propaganda videogame. *TechRadar.* https://www.techradar.com/news/gaming/us-army-spends-32-8-million-on-propaganda-videogame-657121

Chen, J. (2007). Flow in games (and everything else). *Communications of the ACM, 50*(4), 31–34. doi:10.1145/1232743.1232769

Chou, Y. (2013). *Explicit vs Implicit Gamification: How to Define Gamified Design.* https://www.gamification.co/2013/04/09/explicit-vs-implicit-gamification/

Choudaha, R., & Van Rest, E. (2018). *Envisioning Pathways to 2030: Megatrends Shaping the Future of Global Higher Education and International Student Mobility.* ERIC.

Crawford, C. (2011). *The Art of Computer Game Design.* McGraw Hill Osborne Media.

Csikszentmihalyi, M. (1990). *Flow: The psychology of optimal experience.* Harper & Row.

De Gloria, A., Bellotti, F., & Berta, R. (2014). Serious Games for education and training. *International Journal of Serious Games, 1*(1). Advance online publication. doi:10.17083/ijsg.v1i1.11

Desert Hat. (2009). *Game Design the Miyamoto Way: Flow and Difficulty.* https://deserthat.wordpress.com/2009/11/26/game-design-the-miyamoto-way-flow-and-difficulty/

Deterding, S., Dixon, D., Khaled, R., & Nacke, L. (2011, September). From game design elements to gamefulness: defining "gamification". In *Proceedings of the 15th international academic MindTrek conference: Envisioning future media environments* (pp. 9-15). 10.1145/2181037.2181040

Dichev, C., & Dicheva, D. (2017). Gamifying education: What is known, what is believed and what remains uncertain: a critical review. *International Journal of Educational Technology in Higher Education, 14*(1), 1–36. doi:10.118641239-017-0042-5

Discovery Tour by Ubisoft. (n.d.). *Teacher learning resources*. Ubisoft (UK). https://www.ubisoft.com/en-gb/game/assassins-creed/discovery-tour

Dweck, C. (2017). Mindset-updated edition: Changing the way you think to fulfil your potential. Hachette UK.

Gamology. (n.d.). *Home* [YouTube Channel]. YouTube. Retrieved August 4, 2021, from https://www.youtube.com/c/Gamology

Goldstein, K. (2014). Why did edutainment become a bad word. *Computers in Entertainment*.

Gordon, N. (2014). Flexible pedagogies: Technology-enhanced learning. The Higher Education Academy, 1-24.

Gordon, N., Brayshaw, M., & Grey, S. (2013). Maximising gain for minimal pain: Utilising natural game mechanics. *Innovation in Teaching and Learning in Information and Computer Sciences, 12*(1), 27–38. doi:10.11120/ital.2013.00004

Gordon, N. A., & Grey, S. (2018). Approaches to measuring attendance and engagement. *New Directions in the Teaching of Physical Sciences*, (13).

Grey, S., Grey, D., Gordon, N., & Purdy, J. (2017). Using formal game design methods to embed learning outcomes into game mechanics and avoid emergent behaviour. *International Journal of Game-Based Learning, 7*(3), 63–73. doi:10.4018/IJGBL.2017070106

GrowthEngineering. (2019, August 29). *The history of gamification: From the beginning to right now.* https://www.growthengineering.co.uk/history-of-gamification/

Huizinga, J. (1938). *Homo ludens: A study of the play-element in culture.* Beacon Press.

Hunicke, R., LeBlanc, M., & Zubek, R. (2004). MDA: A formal approach to game design and game research. In *Proceedings of the AAAI Workshop on Challenges in Game AI* (*Vol. 4*, No. 1, p. 1722). Academic Press.

Johnson, L., Adams Becker, S., Cummins, M., Estrada, V., Freeman, A., & Hall, C. (2013). *NMC Horizon report: higher education edition. Report.* The New Media Consortium.

Kapp, K. M. (2012). *The gamification of learning and instruction: game-based methods and strategies for training and education*. John Wiley & Sons.

Kolb, D. A. (2014). *Experiential learning: Experience as the source of learning and development.* FT Press.

Koster, R. (2010). *A theory of fun for game design.* Paraglyph Press.

Krath, J., Schürmann, L., & von Korflesch, H. F. (2021). Revealing the theoretical basis of gamification: A systematic review and analysis of theory in research on gamification, serious games and game-based learning. *Computers in Human Behavior, 125*, 106963. doi:10.1016/j.chb.2021.106963

Kusuma, G. P., Wigati, E. K., Utomo, Y., & Suryapranata, L. K. P. (2018). Analysis of gamification models in education using MDA framework. *Procedia Computer Science, 135*, 385–392. doi:10.1016/j.procs.2018.08.187

López, F. R., Arias-Oliva, M., Pelegrín-Borondo, J., & Marín-Vinuesa, L. M. (2021). Serious games in management education: An acceptance analysis. *International Journal of Management Education, 19*(3), 100517. doi:10.1016/j.ijme.2021.100517

Malone, T. W. (1981). Toward a theory of intrinsically motivating instruction. *Cognitive Science, 5*(4), 333–369. doi:10.120715516709cog0504_2

Malone, T. W., & Lepper, M. R. (1987). Making learning fun: A taxonomy of intrinsic motivations for learning. *Aptitude, learning and Instruction III: Cognitive and affective process analysis.*

McGonigal, J. (2011). *Reality is broken: Why games make us better and how they can change the world.* Penguin.

Nørgård, R. T., Toft-Nielsen, C., & Whitton, N. (2017). Playful learning in higher education: Developing a signature pedagogy. *International Journal of Play, 6*(3), 272–282. doi:10.1080/21594937.2017.1382997

Nørgård, R. T., Whitton, N. J., & Toft-Nielsen, C. (2016). *Playful teaching between freedom and control: exploring the magic circle in higher education.* https://www.srhe.ac.uk/conference2016/abstracts/0175.pdf

Pink, D. H. (2011). *Drive: The surprising truth about what motivates us.* Penguin.

Quaye, S. J., Harper, S. R., & Pendakur, S. L. (Eds.). (2019). *Student engagement in higher education: Theoretical perspectives and practical approaches for diverse populations.* Routledge. doi:10.4324/9780429400698

Rigby, S., & Ryan, R. M. (2011). *Glued to games: How video games draw us in and hold us spellbound.* Praeger.

Ryan, R. M. (1982). Control and information in the intrapersonal sphere: An extension of cognitive evaluation theory. *Journal of Personality and Social Psychology, 43*(3), 450–461. doi:10.1037/0022-3514.43.3.450

Ryan, R. M., & Deci, E. L. (2000). Intrinsic and extrinsic motivations: Classic definitions and new directions. *Contemporary Educational Psychology, 25*(1), 54–67. doi:10.1006/ceps.1999.1020 PMID:10620381

Ryan, R. M., Rigby, C. S., & Przybylski, A. (2006). The motivational pull of video games: A self-determination theory approach. *Motivation and Emotion, 30*(4), 344–360. doi:10.100711031-006-9051-8

Schell, J. (2008). *The Art of Game Design: A book of lenses.* CRC Press. doi:10.1201/9780080919171

Sheldon, L. (2020). *The Multiplayer Classroom: Designing coursework as a game.* CRC Press. doi:10.1201/9780429285035

Squire, K. (2011). *Video Games and Learning: Teaching and participatory culture in the digital age*. Teachers College Press.

Supriana, I., Agustin, R. D., Bakar, M. A., & Zin, N. A. M. (2017). Serious games for effective learning. In *2017 6th International Conference on Electrical Engineering and Informatics (ICEEI)* (pp. 1-6). IEEE. 10.1109/ICEEI.2017.8312466

Valkanos, E., & Fragoulis, I. (2007). Experiential learning–its place in in-house education and training. *Development and Learning in Organizations*, *21*(5), 21–23. doi:10.1108/14777280710779454

van Berlo, Z. M., van Reijmersdal, E. A., & Eisend, M. (2021). The gamification of branded content: A meta-analysis of advergame effects. *Journal of Advertising*, *50*(2), 179–196. doi:10.1080/00913367.2020.1858462

Werbach, K., & Hunter, D. (2012). *For the win: How game thinking can revolutionize your business*. Wharton Digital Press.

Whitton, N. (2018). Playful learning: Tools, techniques, and tactics. *Research in Learning Technology*, 26.

Whitton, N., & Langan, M. (2018). Fun and games in higher education: An analysis of UK student perspectives. *Teaching in Higher Education*.

Woodfield, R. (2014). Undergraduate retention and attainment across the disciplines. *Higher Education Academy*, *27*, 1–77.

Xi, N., & Hamari, J. (2019). Does gamification satisfy needs? A study on the relationship between gamification features and intrinsic need satisfaction. *International Journal of Information Management*, *46*, 210–221. doi:10.1016/j.ijinfomgt.2018.12.002

Zichermann, G., & Cunningham, C. (2011). *Gamification by design: Implementing game mechanics in web and mobile apps*. O'Reilly Media, Inc.

KEY TERMS AND DEFINITIONS

Aligned Extrinsic Motivation: Extrinsic motivation that is well aligned with the desired goal.

Explicit Gamification: Extrinsic motivation created in an explicit attempt to gamify a task.

Extrinsic Motivation: Motivation to complete a task that is external to the task.

Game-Based Learning: Learning through playing a game.

Gamification: Promotion of engagement through the application of game mechanics to non-game contexts.

Implicit Gamification: Extrinsic motivation created without an explicit attempt to gamify a task.

Intrinsic Motivation: Motivation to complete a task that originates from the task itself.

Misaligned Extrinsic Motivation: Extrinsic motivation that is not well aligned with the desired goal.

Playful Learning: An inclusive term for taking a lusory approach to learning and teaching.

Serious Games: Games created for a specific purpose of learning and teaching, often in the form or training simulators.

Chapter 33
Merging Tangibles and Gamification to Teach Algorithmic Thinking to KG Children With "Gamirithmic"

Samaa Mohammed Shohieb
Mansoura University, Egypt

Ceymi Doenyas
Yıldız Technical University, Turkey

Waleed Mohamed Al-Adrousy
Mansoura University, Egypt

ABSTRACT

This chapter presents the design, implementation, and evaluation of a new technique to improve children's algorithmic thinking skills that enable solving problems following clearly defined steps. Gamirithmic teaches children to codify ideas by coming up with solutions to problems in systematic and structured ways via its step-by-step procedure with the increasing complexity of commands in each step. The errors of kindergarten children (3-6 years of age) decreased with each trial, but the time taken did not, suggesting that children took time to process the more complicated commands and come up with algorithmic strategies to solve them, yet made fewer errors even though the steps got more complex, as they got used to engaging this type of thinking. Older children made fewer errors and took less time to complete the new tasks. Gamirithmic teaches technology-related concepts using a technology-independent medium that is less likely to induce behavioral problems associated with screen-based methods.

INTRODUCTION

Algorithmic thinking refers to abstracting and modelling a problem and specifying a sequence of in-

DOI: 10.4018/978-1-6684-4287-6.ch033

structions to solve the problem, and since it is placed at the heart of computational thinking, it is recommended to be taught starting from primary school (Bonani et al., 2018). Simple algorithms are designed for children based on repetition, conditional logic, and sequencing to solve fun problems; like puzzles. Algorithmic thinking allows children to conceptualize solutions by breaking down problems using discrete steps in a procedure. As with every skill, children can improve their algorithmic thinking through completing creative projects to which they can apply their skills and with daily practice. Children can build up their algorithmic thinking skills by completing fun coding activities (Futschek & Moschitz, 2011). Since algorithmic thinking is considered to underlie success in science, technology, engineering, and mathematics (STEM) field as well as financial and integrated systems, a strategic realignment of school curricula to include instilling this type of thinking to students has been recommended (Hurlburt, 2018).

Algorithmic thinking, besides the inherent value it holds for problem-solving abilities, has also recently been shown to relate with executive functions, which are top-down and effortfully engaged mental processes that enable mentally playing with ideas, meeting novel challenges, and staying focused. It is believed higher-order executive functions such as reasoning, problem-solving, and planning are built from the core executive functions of inhibitory control, working memory, and cognitive flexibility (Diamond, 2013). However, it was not until recently that how the algorithmic thinking component of problem-solving relates to executive functions was investigated. A recent study has found moderate to strong correlations between computational thinking and executive functions in children, leading the authors to suggest computational thinking activities as an engaging and motivating method to help students improve their executive functions (Robertson et al., 2020). Similarly, another recent study with IT-Engineer students aged between 19-22 years found a positive correlation between executive functions and algorithmic problem solving (Kovari, 2020). Therefore, teaching algorithmic thinking to children starting from an early age emerges as a valuable teaching aim due to the ubiquitousness of it in real life and its relationship with executive functions, which are important for psychological, cognitive, and social development; future academic and life success; and mental and physical health (Diamond, 2013). In programming, functions are created to solve specific repeatable tasks by combining multiple instructions into one line of code, which contains the many steps that would be needed to accomplish that task. Similarly, humans need to mentally solve certain tasks to successfully function in daily life and this cognitive practice of coming up with the appropriate steps to reach a solution resembles writing a code to accomplish a certain task.

Though game-based e-learning can teach engineering and science concepts more effectively than conventional script-based instruction (Boeker et al., 2013), many researchers showed that tangible tools are much more efficient and easier to engage students in exploring introductory programming concepts than equivalent virtual programming environments (Druin, 1999; Frei et al., 2000; Futschek & Moschitz, 2011; Stanton, 2001; Mikhak et al., 1999). Certain toolkits specified for teaching algorithmic thinking and coding concepts exist, yet, they have their limitations. The available tangible toolkits such as LEGO Boost Robotics Creative Toolbox (2019), Fisher-Price Think & Learn Code-A-Pillar (2019), Primo Toys Cubetto (2019), Kibo (2019), Ozobot (2019), Dash & Dot (2019), Sphero SPRK Edition (2019), Puzzlets (Labs, 2019), Kano Computer (2019), Code Monkey Island (2019), Microduino's Cookie (2019), Sullivan et al. (2015), and Jewelbots (2019) are intended for children over 6 years of age and are too expensive for people in developing countries. Moreover, they are too bulky to be deployed in classroom environments. These problems have been repeatedly reported (ANON, 2019; Spin Master - Meccano Meccano, 2019; STEM for Girls, 2019).

In terms of learning, the fundamental difference between game-based learning and gamification is the active learning experience within a game framework that has explicit learning objectives and measurable outcomes (Patrício et al. 2018; 2021 & Patrício et al. 2020). This is what game-based learning is (Shaffer et al. 2005; Torres et al. 2008); learning takes place within the context of a virtual game, necessitates significant student participation, and provides insightful feedback on student progress. On the other hand, gamification is adding game elements or mechanisms to an experience to make it more engaging or enjoyable. The learning content is usually kept separate from the game components. Leaderboards, badges, timed activities, incentives, and points can all be used in gamified classes and activities to engage students.

This chapter presents a creative, low-cost, and easy-to-deploy gamified technique of teaching algorithmic thinking to kindergarten children aged between 3-6 years. The new methodology contains the execution of a set of commands that allow children to solve a problem. It aims to enable children to learn and utilize edutainment-based techniques to fulfil the previously set objectives and to codify their ideas by finding a solution to a problem in systematic and structured ways. This new technique is hereby called "Gamirithmic'' (Gamification + Algorithmic). It is designed to teach algorithmic thinking to children using Gamification techniques with tangibles, which is "an exploitation of game design elements and game mechanics in non-game scenarios" (Shohieb, 2019) to result in maximum edutainment processes for children. The overall design process included Human-Computer Interaction (HCI), Computer Science (CS), and teaching researchers (the authors), and kindergarten teachers. The evaluation of Gamirithmic was performed after obtaining ethical approval from the faculty of computers and information, Mansoura University in Egypt, getting the oral approval of the children and written consents of the children's parents to record the children's behaviour in the tests to use for research purposes. The evaluation of the system took place over 15 weeks in a local school and we recorded the children's reactions, development, and parents' answers to a final informal survey.

BACKGROUND

Technical and Physical Educational Tangibles for Children

Pedagogy has emphasized that tangible interactive objects and physical representations benefit young students (Druin, 1999; Frei et al., 2000; Mikhak et al., 1999; Stanton, 2001). Tangibles are physical objects (manipulatives) that can be perceived by touch and can be grasped and manipulated in various ways. Tangibles in teaching coding can be either technical (robotics-based) or physical (board games). This section reviews tangibles in teaching coding principles to children aged between 3 and 7 years.

Technical Tangibles in Learning Coding Principles

This section overviews different attempts made to teach programming with robotics rather than desktop computers. In this context, robotics may or may not include screens in that the robot can be programmed and directed via an application on a tablet or mobile device or it can be directed via pressing buttons or putting tangible objects on a screenless control board. On the other hand, board games don't need any screens; children need only to think and handle everything manually.

McNerne (2004) presented an early design for a platform to create Microworlds, a tangible programming bricks system for children to explore scientific and computation thinking. Wang et al. (2016) built TanProRobot 2.0 that consists of three parts: robot car, tangible several manipulatives, and programming blocks. Children arrange the programming blocks to program the robotic car to simulate certain actions. Also, manipulatives enable children to interact with the car. TanProRobot has helped children get a general understanding of event handling concepts. Goyal et al. (2016) presented Code Bits, a paper-based toolkit for tangible computational thinking that is scalable, portable, and inexpensive. Code Bits was integrated with the Code Bits android app that runs the code based on the augmented reality technique. Anzoátegui et al. (2017) created the Cubetto robot that enables the child to learn to solve problems with a screenless programming and coding technique.

Mariappan et al. (2016) proposed C-Block that aims to enable infants to explore STEM education and provide tangible methods of performing programming for them. They presented the design and implementation of C-Block sets and described the system to extract the information from the instruction blocks. They concluded that C-Block would be a great advance to enhance the implementation of robotics for education processes.

Chawla et al. (2013) proposed Dr. Wagon, a tangible programming toy with a wagon-shaped robot and a series of programming blocks that include "if" statements, loops ("repeat"), and basic functions ("move"). These blocks could be attached in many ways to control the moving behavior of the wagon. They showed the efficiency of Dr. Wagon by presenting the cognitive, usability, and technical details of the project. Gordon et al. (2015) proposed a social robot toolkit that provides common mechanisms along three dimensions: (i) reusable vinyl stickers enabling tangible programming, (ii) social robots that interact directly with children, and (iii) programming exercises and tasks centered on social interaction are three ways to make coding more real. Strawhacker and Bers (2015) used the "Creative Hybrid Environment"; CHERP for robotic programming. That technique integrated a programming language and LEGO WeDo robotics construction kit. They recorded the qualitative observational data from the classrooms. They concluded that using tangible programming kits with children is an efficient technique to teach computational thinking for children. Sullivan et al. (2015) described the development of KIBO, done by Tufts University and funded by the National Science Foundation, as a newly created robotics kit for children aged 4-7 in which children can program up to 80 steps in one sequence and it has LED lights on the top that show the direction of each step.

Screenless Physical Tangibles (Board Games) in Learning Coding Principles

There are some board games designed to teach coding concepts for children. These games are called screenless coding (coding without screens). Though both robots and board games are tangible methods to teach coding principles, robots may or may not have an application to guide them whereas board games do not need any screens to be used. These games such as CodeMaster (2019) in which the player uses the specified Action Tokens to create a program that will lead the player's avatar to collect all the Crystals on the map and land at the Portal. In Race to the Treasure ("Race to the Treasure Co-operative Game", 2019), the player builds a path with his/her team and collects three keys on a race to beat ogre to the treasure. In this game everyone plays together; no one is left out. With Robot Turtles (Shapiro, 2019) is implemented with the Logo programming language and is designed for children aged 4 and over, 2-5 players can learn main programming concepts in an easy and fun way (Sobodić et al., 2018).

MAIN FOCUS OF THE CHAPTER

Issues

Many Arab children don't have access to affordable coding games because the games are too costly. These same reasons also apply to individuals in other developing countries. Furthermore, existing coding games are too bulky to be used in educational settings (ANON, 2019; Spin Master - Meccano Meccano, 2019; STEM for Girls, 2019). In screen-based coding games, the player can only experience the world via the senses of sight and hearing. Additionally, such games are only accessible in English. This chapter presents a new design that enables using three senses—touch, vision, hearing—to teach coding principles to children and accommodates Arab children whose first language is not English.

SOLUTIONS AND RECOMMENDATIONS

A pilot survey was conducted to determine if a need existed for this new technique. In the survey, parents were asked to compare screen-based (applications, online games, etc.) and screenless (tangible games) methods for teaching their children by reporting if they observed the listed outcome more when a screen-based or screenless method was used. Out of 36 parents, the majority said that their child experienced the following problems more when using screen-based educational methods/games compared to screenless ones: sleep problems/deprivation/disruption; vision problems; health problems such as eye strain, text thumb, phone neck; decreased social interaction/loss of social skills; aggressive behavior; disinterest in other aspects of life; inability to focus on a task long enough to complete it (easily bored/distracted); inability to be patient; language problems (less speaking, inaccurate grammar/words, problems in holding a conversation); constantly preoccupied, distracted, not paying attention to real-life conversations and events; and decreased creative thinking (drawing, crafting, playing with dough, reading tangible books) (see Table 1). Except for 3 parents who declared not allowing their child to use screens or not being able to determine daily screen time, the rest of the parents reported their child to use screens between 1-7 hours per day.

Therefore, given the negative behavioral consequences of screen-based methods and the already present screen time in children's lives outside of education, a screenless technique was developed to teach algorithmic thinking and coding concepts to children. This work presents a complete research design, implementation, and evaluation of Gamirithmic, a creative merging of tangible objects with the gamification technique to teach algorithmic thinking and coding concepts to kindergarten children. This technique was tested with a sample of kindergarten children aged 3 to 6.

Design

At the beginning of the design process, learning of coding principles was broken down into three general phases. Phase 1 includes learning how to codify a problem solution into a sequence of steps. Phase 2 includes how to think of iterations and loops to reduce the number of steps. Phase 3 concentrates on how to use conditional thinking, building, calling simple functions, and optimizing the available solutions.

In this game, the child is expected to mentally come up with the steps needed to solve the given task, build a stepwise method, and call the necessary steps as needed along the way of solving the task of

Table 1. Parents' comparison of outcomes they observed in their children upon using screen-based and screenless methods/games on a questionnaire created by the authors.

Outcome	Screen-based method	Screenless method
Sleep problems/sleep deprivation/sleep disruption	32	1
Vision problems	33	
Health problems (eye strain, "digital/text thumb", "phone neck")	32	
Decreased social interaction/loss of social skills	31	
Aggressive behavior	32	1
Disinterest in other aspects of life	31	
Inability to focus on a task long enough to complete it (easily bored/ distracted)	24	4
Inability to be patient	16	8
Language problems (less speaking, inaccurate grammar/words, problems in holding a conversation)	14	0
Constantly preoccupied, distracted, not paying attention to real-life conversations and events	33	0
Decreased creative thinking (drawing, crafting, playing with dough, reading tangible books)	31	0

each level. Table 2 shows each phase and the corresponding coding principles included. The following subsections explain in more detail how the three phases of coding were designed and matched with algorithmic thinking, 'design for kids' rules, and gamification technique. Subsequently, a complete design for each phase's levels/sublevels is included.

Translating Algorithmic Thinking Steps into Design Issues

Algorithmic thinking steps have been identified as clear learning outcomes and each step has been matched with predefined phases in Table 2. The full details of algorithmic thinking steps and corresponding design issues for each phase are described in Table 3. Table 3 presents the algorithmic thinking steps that are the desired outcomes of each phase and how these outcomes can be translated into a design issue that can be solved and thus incorporated into the game being designed. Design issues refer to rules for designing systems, games, or any other entity that needs to be followed according to HCI science.

Table 2. Each phase and the corresponding coding principles included

Phase #	Coding Principles
Phase 1	Codifying a problem solution into a sequence of steps.
Phase 2	Using iterations and loops.
Phase 3	Conditions, building simple functions, and calling them.

Table 3. Translating Algorithmic Thinking Steps and Learning Outcomes into a Design Issue

Phase #	Algorithmic Thinking Step as a learning outcome	Translating the Required Step into a Design Issue
Phase 1	1.1 Identify inputs and outputs.	Having the child determine a path that begins from the start point and reaches the specified goal in each phase/ level, and do so by avoiding obstacles
	1.2 Identify, select, and employ an algorithmic strategy to attempt to solve a problem.	Analysis by the player of the given board game to achieve his/her goal and thinking about the goal achievement steps
	1.3 Test potential solutions on several datasets.	Having the child practice and gain experience in solving the other levels and sublevels
Phase 2	Identify repetition/ repeatable steps.	Using the symbolic representation of commands integrated with tangible numbers (1 to 9) to clarify iteration and loops in phase 2 and phase 3
Phase 3	3.1 Identify success and failure conditions.	Designing a board game (Figure 3) that can be flexibly adapted with different places for the goal and obstacles 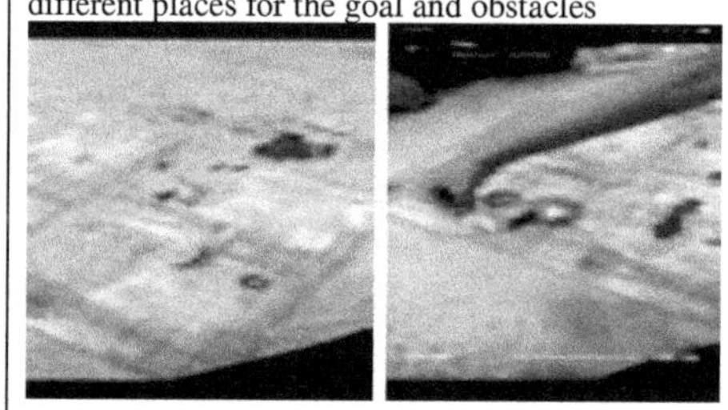
	3.2 Identify problems that lend themselves to an algorithmic solution and reframe problems in ways that clarify what the algorithm needs to do, i.e., using functions, and solution optimization	Generalize children's experience to form a sequence of systematic and logical steps to solve a given problem (the other levels and sublevels) Merging the frequently used steps as a function that can be used later by only calling that function. Applying solution optimization by choosing the best route with the smallest number of steps.

Applying "Design for Kids' Rules" in the Proposed Design

Design for kids resembles those for adults in terms of consistency and affordance, which refers to the user's understanding of the properties of a design or what it can be used for, emerging from the user-device interaction (Still & Dark, 2013). However, as children differ from adults in many ways, this greatly affects designing for them (Said, 2004; Steine & Moher, 1992). "Designing for kids" is a major field in HCI (Gelman, 2014) and there are many principles that should be set as rules while designing for children (Berkovitz, 1994; Druin et al., 2001; Frei et al., 2000; Hanna et al., 1999; Johnson et al., 1999; Said, 2004; Steine & Moher, 1992; Wyeth, & Purchase, 2003). Table 4 describes each principle with the corresponding real design issue to fulfill this principle. Table 4 introduces some terms, such as badges that refer to awards received for completing the given step, and performance graphs (see Figure 1) that visually depict the performance of the participant. During the sessions, feedback is instantly given to children after each step by researchers and teachers to help them learn. After a completed sub-level, the child is given a star on the performance graph. After completing a set of levels, a child is rewarded with a badge (from a set of predefined badges) on his/her performance board. After completing half of each phase, the child is presented with a physical reward. Authors relied on Abrams & Walsh (2014) to choose the correct scheduling of these rewards. Moreover, authors selected the physical rewards to

Table 4. Applying "Design for Kids' Rules" in the Proposed Design

Rule #	"Design for Kids" Rule	Applying in the Real Design
1.	Visual elements (avoid using text) (Druin et al., 2001; Hanna et al., 1999; Steiner & Moher, 1992)	All designed objects are visually based and have no text For example, using arrows, characters, colors, toys made from play dough, and tangible level board
2.	Children are impatient (need immediate feedback) (Said, 2004; Steiner & Moher, 1992)	Every action has immediate feedback from the instructor
3.	Children cannot yet understand abstract concepts (Johnson et al., 1999; Said, 2004; Steiner & Moher, 1992)	The use of abstract concepts, such as feelings, is avoided. Instead, practical and physical objects were utilized.
4.	Appropriately sized objects (Berkovitz, 1994; Frei, Su, Mikhak, and Ishii, 2000).	All objects are designed with sizes suitable for potentially weak muscles of children 
5.	Children like tangible interfaces (Druin, 1999; Mikhak, 1999; Resnick et al. 1998; Stanto, 2001)	Different raw materials were used to stimulate the child's senses (ie; colorful with different texture clerk for handicrafts, tangible numbers, small animals and trees as obstacles and playdough and small rounded moving eyes for the avatar that will be used in the adventure, or other words, in solving the problem)  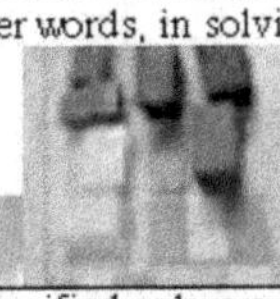
6.	Encouragement of discovery (Wyeth & Purchase, 2003)	Type of materials and using unified colors and themes facilitate discovery process (as described in the previous point)
7.	Using Storytelling and characters (Stanton, 2001)	Each child creates his/her preferred character playdough and small rounded moving eyes for the avatar that will be used in the adventure (with teachers' assistance to use it)
8.	Keep the Environment Child Friendly and Safe (Steiner & Moher, 1992)	All the materials used are safe for children i.e., non-toxic, soft, and flexible materials
9.	Effective use of color and graphics to facilitate learning process (keeping in mind the faster rate of development of children compared to adults) (Druin, 1999; Said, 2004)	Each instruction has unique colors in all levels 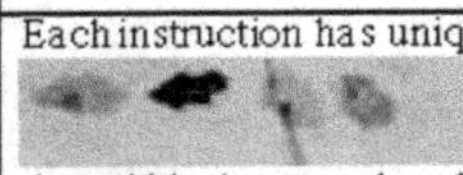 -board blocks are colored in unique colors in all levels  -Badges and performance graph has a unified look; Figures 1 and 2
10.	Supportive reward (e.g., receiving motivational phrases such as good work, go on, excellent, or stickers on their progress board); Children act emotionally, not rationally (Hanna et al., 1999)	The whole design is based on the gamification technique; as described in Table 5 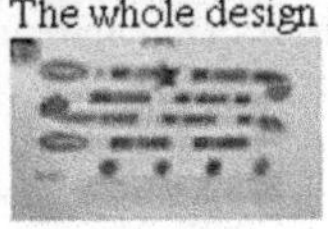
11.	Instructions should be easy to remember and comprehend (Pausch, Vogtle, & Conway, 1992)	The environment and objects used in the teaching process have almost no specified instructions and when there are, they are simple (e.g., each instruction has a unique color and is easy to remember) 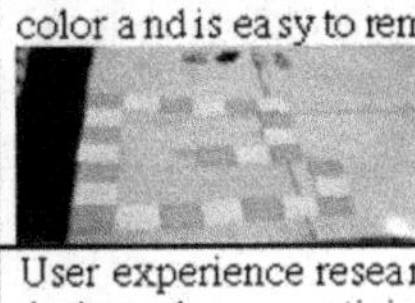
12.	Design Co-designing with Children (Have Patience and Learn to Step Back and Observe) (Sonia & Carl, 2005; Hanna et al., 1999).	User experience research using participatory design methods. In every step of the design phase, participants were asked to solve some levels and redesign some artifacts. This experience was used to confirm the age-appropriateness of each level and artifact. 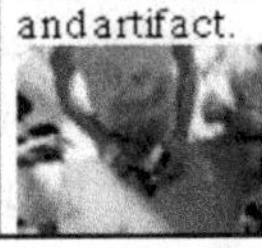

Table 5. Applying "Gamification Technique" in the Proposed Design

Game mechanic #	Game Mechanic Name	Explanation	Applying in the Real Design
1.	Leveling Up (Walz & Deterding, 2015)	Levels are a tool to assist a learner in understanding when he has reached an accomplishment or a milestone. Levels can be an opportunity to provide areas for improvement and meaningful feedback.	Using phases, levels, and sublevels; as described in Table 6.
2.	Challenges (Hopfgartner et al., 2015)	Challenge is a powerful game mechanic to motivate children to act, especially if they believe they are working to achieve something bigger than themselves, something great and something awe-inspiring.	Challenge as a game mechanic induces motivation.
3.	Badges and Achievements (Hamari, 2017; Sailer, 2017)	Badges can be motivated to innovate faster, do more, and work smarter than other competitors.	-Directions Hero -Apple Collector -Best Jumper -Mazes Solver Figure 1
4.	Performance Graphs (Abrams & Walsh, 2014)	Performance graphs are often used in a reward system to encourage students through exercises and activities. They can be used to drive desired behaviors, reward learners, signify status, and even unlock access to new learning stages or rewards.	As in Figure 1
5.	Reward schedules (Abrams & Walsh, 2014)		For every set of completed levels, the child is given a physical simple reward.
6.	Continual and Immediate Feedback (Park & Kim, 2018)	Learners need to be provided with feedback when they are unsuccessful. This does not only help to motivate learners when there is a clear direction for improvement, but it also solidifies the learning.	Assisting children by giving immediate feedback on their movement.
7.	Stories and Characters (Turan et al., 2016)	Creating characters and stories around learning challenges will help to relate to the learners' decisions as the story parts, and how the learning elements fit into the overarching story must be clear.	Each child creates his/her preferred character (with the teacher's assistance) to use it. Also, we designed a forest environment and told children that we will design a way to run from the wild animals (also described in points 5 and 7 in Table 4)
8.	Freedom to Fail (Dicheva et al., 2015; Rahman, Sumpeno, & Zaini, 2018; Wong et al., 2020)	Providing learners with the chance to fail by giving them second chances, multiple lives, or alternative methods to succeed is extremely engaging particularly when a learner is motivated to work through a challenge for points or rewards.	The child can try many times to reach success.

support the application of the learning with tangibles concept that aligns with our proposed approach. These rewards were used by the children to modify and update their main playing avatars. The children also used their customized avatars to play with those rewards such as by imagining and enacting different play scenarios using their avatars and rewards. As presented previously (Abrams & Walsh, 2014, Dicheva et al., 2015; Rahman, Sumpeno, & Zaini, 2018; Wong et al., 2020), a learner is motivated to work through a challenge for points or rewards. The physical rewards included a play dough set, magic

Figure 1.

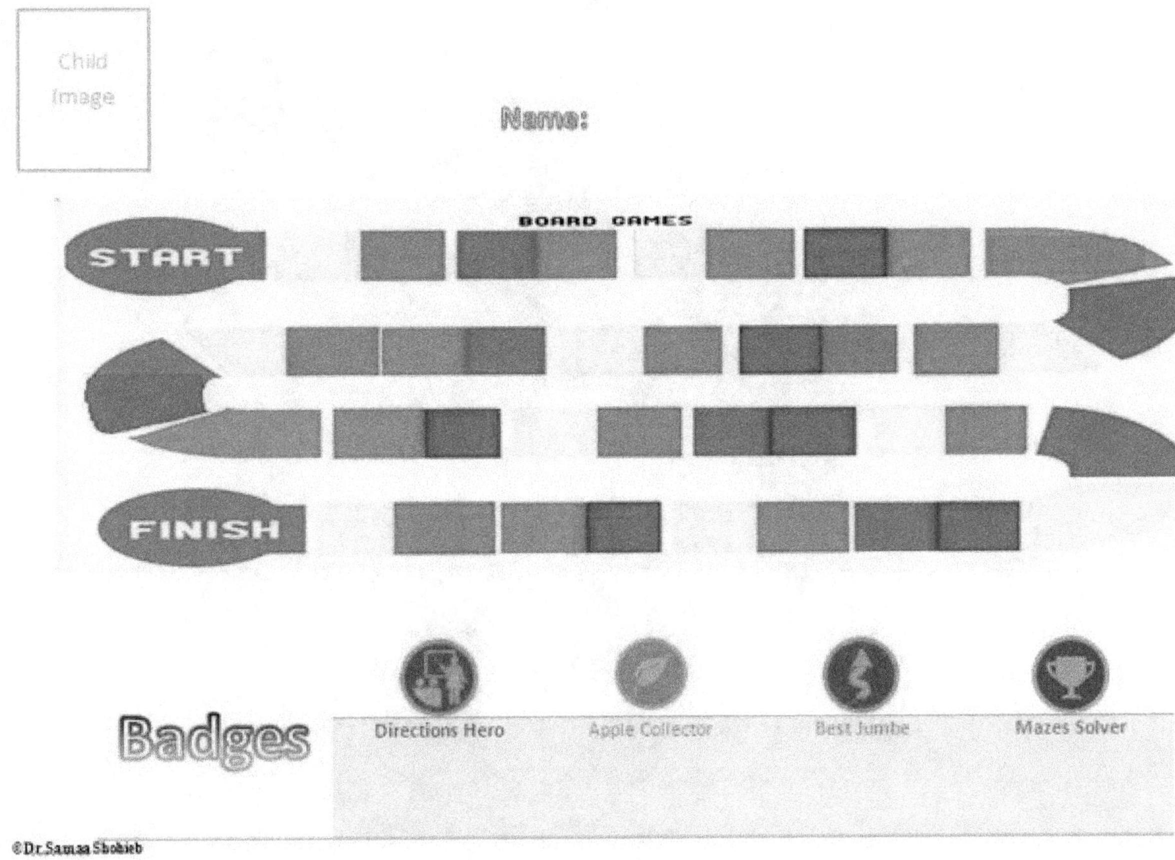

coloring notebook, and a simple toy to decorate their avatars. The full lists of Applying "Design for Kids' Rules" in the Proposed Design are listed in Table 4.

Applying "Gamification Technique" in the Proposed Design

Gamification in teaching takes the data-driven techniques that game designers use to engage players and applies them to non-game experiences to motivate actions that add value to the teaching process (Pausch, Vogtle, & Conway, 1992). Integrating game mechanics with the teaching processes results in motivating the learners and increasing their engagement and participation (Cronk, 2012; Kapp, 2012; Shohieb, 2019). Game mechanics were used in the proposed design, as explained in Table 5. Researchers excluded some mechanics such as leader-boards, as leader-boards are not appropriate for kindergarten children (Abo El-Soud & Shohieb, 2010; Hopfgartner et al., 2015; Rahman, 2018; Riad et al., 2013; Riad et al., 2014; Shohieb et al., 2009; Shohieb et al., 2015; Shohieb, 2016; Wong et al., 2020). The performance graph designed for children is shown in Figure 1.

Figure 2.

Complete Design of All Levels/Sublevels in Each Phase and the Corresponding Intended Learning Outcome

At the introductory session, each child is asked to create his/her preferred character using dough to be used in the execution of the following sessions. This step is performed with the assistance of teachers

Figure 3.

and it aims to create a psychological link between the child and the coding sessions. Teachers also made a demo for the children to show them how to solve problems via the proposed technique and showed what rewards children will get after completing levels and sublevels to motivate them. Afterward, each level/sublevel is presented one by one in the designed order with the commands required to solve it, and then, the children are asked to think. For example, in phase 1_level 1/ sublevel 1, the sublevel is built for a child by the instructor using the tangible blocks, and the left-headed arrows are put aside. Then, a child should think and order a sequence of two left-headed arrows, and move his/her character in these specified steps to reach the target goal or endpoint (as a simulation of running a code after coding). Table 6 presents the complete design of all levels and sublevels in Phase 1.

Phase 2 is similar to Phase 1, but instead of using the sequence of repeated commands, a child should use a single command with a number that indicates the repetition of that command. For example, in phase 2_level 1/ sublevel 1, a child should think and put one left-headed arrow and the number two

Table 6. Complete design of each level and sublevel in Phase 1 and the targeted goal

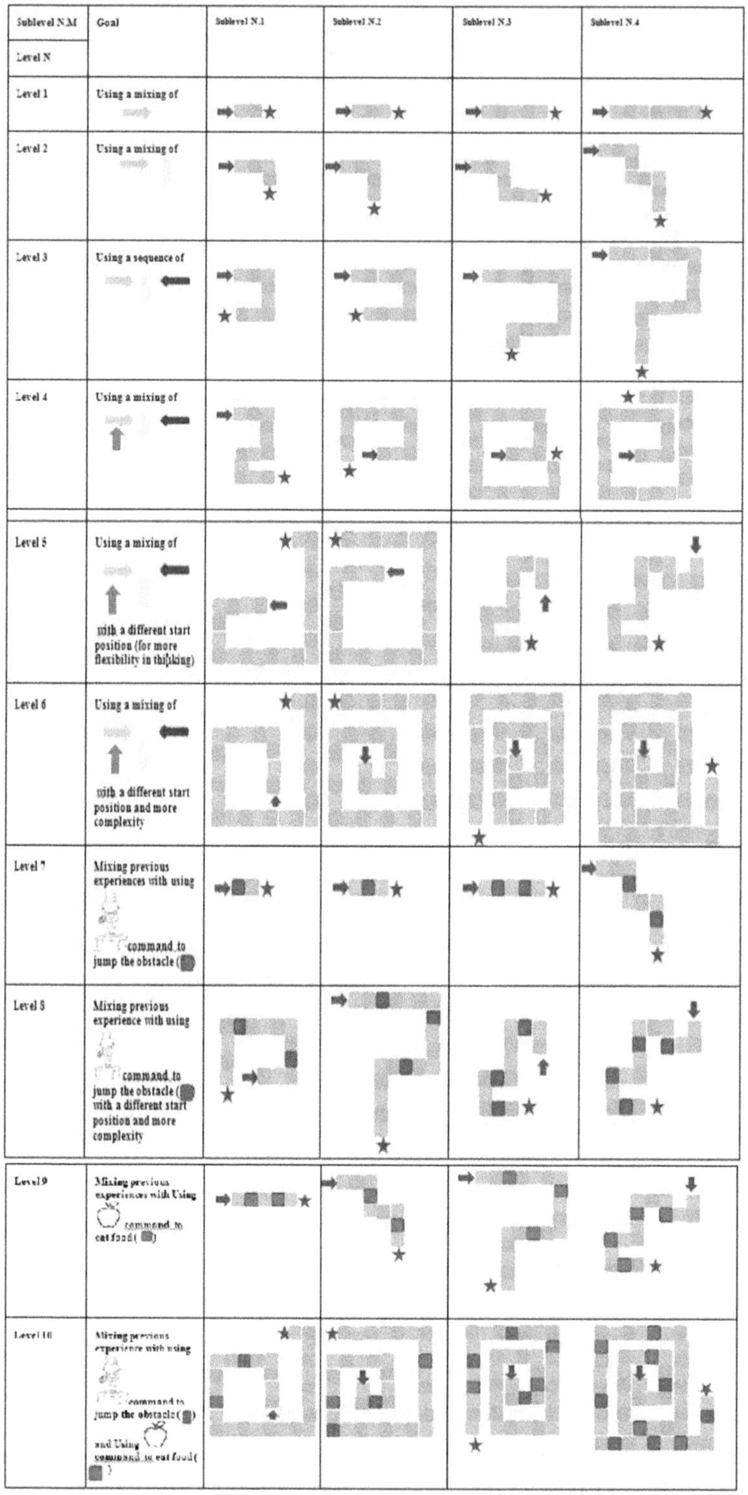

Sublevel N.M / Level N	Goal	Sublevel N.1	Sublevel N.2	Sublevel N.3	Sublevel N.4
Level 1	Using a mixing of				
Level 2	Using a mixing of				
Level 3	Using a sequence of				
Level 4	Using a mixing of				
Level 5	Using a mixing of with a different start position (for more flexibility in thinking)				
Level 6	Using a mixing of with a different start position and more complexity				
Level 7	Mixing previous experiences with using command to jump the obstacle ( )				
Level 8	Mixing previous experience with using command to jump the obstacle (with a different start position and more complexity				
Level 9	Mixing previous experiences with Using command to eat food ( )				
Level 10	Mixing previous experience with using command to jump the obstacle ( ) and Using command to eat food ( )				

beside it, then move his/her character in these specified steps to reach the endpoint. Figure 2 shows a solution for phase 2_level 1/ sublevel 4.

Phase 3 is quite different, as in levels from 1 to 3, the child is asked to solve some predesigned mazes to practice the "if" condition. The mazes are designed by specifying a start point and goal point on the board of Phase 3. Figure 3 shows the board design for the levels in Phase 3. Levels 4 to 6 aim at teaching a child the concepts of building their solutions with simple functions using pre-designed levels. Levels 7 to 10 intend to have the child practice generalizing and applying his/her previous experience to more complex mazes.

Complexity Analysis of Different Levels

The Complexity of Levels **(CoL)** is measured with the following formula: total Number of Blocks at the end of the intended level **(NoB)** * Learning Outcomes in the current level (**LO**) * Number of Commands used in the level **(NoC)**.

CoL = NoB * LO * NoC

For instance; to calculate the Complexity of Phase 1_Level 1, each of the following should be identified:

Total number of blocks (NoB) in Level 1 (at the end of level 1 as shown in Table 6) = 17 blocks
Phase 1LO are 3 (as shown in Table 3) = 3 learning outcomes in level 1

Number of Commands (NoC) used in level 1 = 1 (as shown in the goal column of Table 3, we use only the right arrow i.e.; 1 command)

So, putting these into the formula,

CoL(Phase1_Level1) = 17 * 3 * 1
CoL(Phase1_Level) = 51.

Example 2

To calculate the CoL of Phase 2_Level 4, each of the following should be identified:

NoB in Level 5 (at the end of level 5 as shown in Table 6) = 16 blocks
LO in Phase 2 are 4 (3 LOs in Phase_1 + 1 LO in phase 2 as shown in Table 3) = 4 learning outcomes

NoC= 5 (as shown in the "Goal" column in Table 3, we use the four directions arrows in addition to using a correct number from 1 to 9 to handle the looping concept that is targeted in Phase 2)

CoL(Phase Level5) = 16 * 4 * 5

CoL(Phase Level5) = 51

It should be noted that the CoL decreases in Level 7 and Level 9 as these two levels are just introductory levels for the new commands (apple eating and jumping commands).

METHODOLOGY

Participants

A convenience sampling technique was used for participant recruitment to test Gamirithmic. In this method, the researcher can choose the subjects based on their convenient accessibility and proximity to the researcher (Yıldırım & Şimşek, 2005). The research sample consisted of 36 children aged between 3 and 6 (Mage = 52.55 months (4.37 years) + 8.84) from the two selected national kindergartens. Of the participants, 45% (16) were girls and 55% were boys. A translated and modified version of the General Information Form by the University of Edinburgh[1] was used to collect general information about children and their families. The form included questions about the parents' gender, education, and income. A psychological and behavioral expert has clinically interviewed the selected children. They evaluated the students by criteria of the 4th edition of the Diagnostic and Statistical Manual of Mental Disorders (APA, 2000) (DSM) to detect any mental, visual or auditory dysfunctions and confirmed that the participants did not have any sensory problems.

From the mothers of the participants, 80% were university graduates and 20% were high school graduates. Of the fathers of the participants, 90% were university graduates and 10% were high school graduates. In terms of socioeconomic status (SES), 85% of the families had high SES and 15% had low SES as determined from their reported income.

Ethical Considerations

Ethical approval was obtained from the ethics committee of the Faculty of Computers and Information, Mansoura University. Informed consent was obtained from parents who accepted to participate in the study, after providing a detailed description of the aim, procedure, risks, and benefits of the study. All participants were assured that their participation was voluntary and that refusing to take part in the study would not have any negative consequences. Participant confidentiality has been maintained throughout and after the completion of the study.

Data Collection

Data were collected during 10 to 15-minute sessions (for each child) twice a week for 15 weeks. On the first day, the introductory session (see Complete Design of All Levels/ Sublevel section) was given to all children, which took approximately 120 minutes. Children were not allowed to stop a game until they gave a correct response, i.e., children were requested to try again until they solved the level. The session time was determined based on the average time for which a kindergarten child can focus on a task (McIntosh et. al, 2007). Table 7 decomposes the raw data of the number of tries and errors collected for each level and sublevel during the sessions for each child.

Table 7. Raw data of the number of many tries and errors collected during the sessions for each child

# of the child	Age Year (Y) / Months (M) At the beginning of the experiment Ascendingly	Gender M / F	Grade Pre-KG/ KG1/ KG2	At the start of Phase 1 Errors {E}/ approximated to Minutes{M} respectively (10 steps with 1 commands)	Leve;5 _phase1 Errors{E}/ Time approximated to Minutes{M} respectively (30 steps with 4 commands)	End of phase1 Errors {E}/ Time approximated to Minutes{M} respectively (45 steps with 6 commands	Leve;5 _Phase 2 Errors {E}/ Time approximated to Minutes{M} respectively (30 steps with 8 Loops)	End of phase2 Errors {E}/ Time approximated to Minutes{M} respectively (45 steps with 15 Loops	Practicing in Phase 3 Errors {E}/ Time approximated to Minutes{M} respectively (2 Functions with 6 conditions and 5 Loops)
1.	3Y3M	M	Pre	10E-2M	7E-3M	9E-4M	3E-8M	6E-11M	None
2.	3Y4M	M	Pre	10E-3M	9E-4M	8E-5M	3E-8M	5E-10M	None
3.	3Y5M	F	Pre	9E-2M	7E-2M	6E-5M	2E-7M	4E-9M	None
4.	3Y5M	F	Pre	9E-1M	8E-2M	6E-3M	1E-7M	3E-9M	None
5.	3Y5M	M	Pre	10E-2M	11E-2M	8E-4M	1E-7M	3E-9M	None
6.	3Y6M	F	Pre	9E-1M	7E-2M	2E-4M	2E-6M	3E-8M	None
7.	3Y7M	M	Pre	9E-2M	5E-3M	5E-2M	1E-6M	2E-7M	None
8.	3Y7M	F	Pre	9E-2M	6E-2M	6E-2M	1E-6M	2E-8M	None
9.	3Y8M	M	Pre	9E-1M	6E-2M	2E-4M	1E-5M	2E-8M	None
10.	3Y9M	F	Pre	9E-2M	7E-3M	5E-2M	1E-6M	3E-7M	None
11.	3Y9M	M	Pre	9E-1M	7E-3M	2E-4M	1E-6M	2E-6M	None
12.	3Y9M	M	Pre	8E-2M	5E-2M	3E-2M	2E-6M	1E-7M	None
13.	3Y11M	F	KG1	7E-2M	6E-2M	3E-3M	2E-7M	1E-8M	None
14.	4Y	F	KG1	8E-1M	5E-2M	3E-3M	1E-6M	1E-7M	None
15.	4Y2M	M	KG1	8E-2M	5E-2M	2E-3M	1E-5M	1E-6M	None
16.	4Y4M	F	KG1	8E-2M	4E-2M	3E-2M	1E-6M	0E-5M	None
17.	4Y5M	M	KG1	8E-2M	5E-2M	2E-3M	1E-5M	0E-6M	None
18.	4Y5M	M	KG1	7E-1M	5E-2M	2E-2M	1E-5M	0E-6M	None
19.	4Y6M	M	KG1	8E-2M	4E-2M	1E-3M	1E-4M	0E-6M	None
20.	4Y6M	F	KG1	7E-1M	5E-2M	1E-2M	1E-4M	0E-6M	None
21.	4Y7M	F	KG1	7E-1M	4E-2M	0E-2M	1E-4M	0E-6M	None
22.	4Y8M	M	KG1	8E-2M	3E-2M	2E-3M	1E-3M	0E-5M	None
23.	4Y9M	M	KG1	7E-1M	4E-2M	0E-2M	1E-3M	0E-5M	None
24.	4Y9M	F	KG1	7E-1M	4E-2M	0E-3M	1E-3M	0E-5M	None
25.	4Y9M	F	KG1	7E-1M	3E-2M	0E-2M	1E-3M	0E-5M	None
26.	4Y9M	M	KG1	7E-1M	3E-2M	0E-2M	1E-4M	1E-5M	None
27.	4Y9M	F	KG1	7E-1M	2E-2M	1E-2M	1E-4M	1E-5M	None
28.	4Y10M	F	KG2	5E-1M	2E-2M	1E-2M	1E-4M	0E-5M	2E-12M
29.	5	M	KG2	5E-1M	1E-2M	1E-2M	1E-4M	0E-5M	2E-10M
30.	5Y2M	M	KG2	4E-1M	1E-2M	1E-1M	1E-3M	0E-5M	1E-8M
31.	5Y3M	M	KG2	3E-1M	1E-2M	0E-1M	1E-2M	0E-5M	1E-7M
32.	5Y5M	M	KG2	5E-1M	3E-2M	2E-2M	1E-2M	0E-5M	1E-7M
33.	5Y6M	F	KG2	3E-1M	0E-2M	0E-2M	1E-2M	0E-4M	1E-7M
34.	5Y7M	M	KG2	3E-1M	1E-2M	1E-1M	1E-2M	0E-4M	1E-6M
35.	5Y7M	F	KG2	2E-1M	0E-2M	0E-1M	1E-2M	0E-4M	0E-5M
36.	5Y8M	M	KG2	2E-1M	0E-2M	0E-1M	1E-2M	0E-5M	1E-5M

Data Analysis

The data was coded as the number of errors made and the time taken to complete the task at the start of Phase 1, level 5 of Phase 1, end of Phase 1, level 5 of Phase 2, end of Phase 2, and during Phase 3, where the latter data was not available for all participants since this phase was not tested with KG1 children (children in the first year of kindergarten who were 3-4 years old). Paired sample t-tests were conducted to compare the performance of participants between each consecutive measurement, i.e., the start of Phase 1 and level 5 of Phase 1, level 5 of Phase 1, and the end of Phase 1. Pearson correlations were conducted to investigate the relationship between age and the number of errors made and the time taken to complete the tasks.

RESULTS

Informal interviews revealed that two parents of participating children have tried to use mobile-based games such as "CodeIgniter" with their children who were five years old. The rest of the parents haven't used any technique before to teach algorithmic thinking to their children. After describing the existing tangible games to teach coding for children, parents' opinions about these were asked. Parents reported that these techniques were expensive to purchase and that the available apps were in the English language, which is hard for Arabic children. So, Gamirithmic was designed to address these issues of accessibility, affordability, and provide an engaging educational method of algorithmic thinking and coding techniques for children, even for 3-year-old children who show an ability to comprehend such complicated concepts.

The paired sample t-tests revealed a significant reduction in the errors made between the start of Phase 1 ($M = 7.03$) and Level 5 of Phase 1 ($M = 4.33$), ($t(35) = 13.58$, $p = .00$); a significant reduction in the errors made between Level 5 of Phase 1 and end of Phase 1 ($M = 2.44$), $t(35) = 6.65$, $p = .00$); a significant reduction of errors made between the start of Phase 1 and end of Phase 2 ($M = 1.14$), ($t(35) = 20.74$, $p = .00$); and a significant reduction of errors from the start of Phase 1 and practicing in Phase 3 ($t(8) = 8.32$, $p = .00$) .

For the time taken to complete the different levels, there was a significant increase from the start of Phase 1 ($M = 1.42$) to Level 5 in Phase 1 ($M = 2.17$), ($t(35) = -9.00$, $p = .00$); a significant increase from Level 5 in Phase 1 ($M = 2.167$) to end of Phase 1 ($M = 2.53$), ($t(35) = -2.19$, $p = .035$); a significant increase from the start of Phase 1 to the end of Phase 1 ($t(35) = -7.02$, $p = .00$); a significant increase from Level 5 of Phase 2 ($M = 4.64$) to end of Phase 2 ($M = 6.31$), ($t(35) = -11.60$, $p = .00$); and a significant increase from the start of Phase 1 to the end of Phase 2 ($t(35) = -19.22$, $p = .00$). So, as the complexity increased, the children took more time, yet they made fewer errors. The drop in complexity as new commands are introduced mirrors existing well-established game design techniques (Miyamoto et al., 2008).

CONCLUSION

Currently, there is a lack of gamified training materials designed to develop the logical thinking and coding skills of children aged between 3-6 years. The few available tangible coding games are not accessible for most Arab children because they are too expensive to buy, and similarly for other people in the developing countries. They are also too bulky to be deployed in classroom environments (ANON, 2019; Spin Master - Meccano Meccano, 2019; STEM for Girls, 2019;). In screen-based coding games, learning is limited to visible senses and these games are only available in the English language. The present chapter developed a new technique to address these issues: "Gamirithmic", a cognitive game designed to teach children what today's thinkers need to know to overcome current challenges in design, engineering, and many other fields: coding.

The Gamirithmic technique was able to address the reported problems about existing games as it can stimulate children's tactile experience through different tangible materials targeting different senses; visual sense via the colorful graphical display and set of pictures; and auditory senses through the instructors' motivational and guiding words. This technique is suitable for developing countries as all the materials exist all-around and they cost less than two American dollars.

In Gamirithmic, the interactive learning model uses three senses (touch, vision, and hearing) to teach coding concepts to children. Also, this design overcomes the English language restriction for Arab children by using "Design for Kids" rules (Table 4), based on the gamification technique (Table 5), merged with the feedback received in Arabic language from the researcher.

The analyses showed that children made fewer errors as they progressed in the increasingly complex steps of the game, though they required more time to complete them. Phase 1 contains 10 levels and each level has a new command (the arrows and other objects depicted in the figures above) the complexity of each level (in Phase 1) also increases. The complexity here is represented by increasing the number, type, and directions of the tangible blocks used from the start point to the endpoint. Consequently, the time taken to solve each subsequent level also increased. Phase 2 introduced a new concept in coding, the loops, which increases complexity. Phase 3 also introduced new coding concepts, which are functions and conditions, and as a result, the complexity and the time taken increased in Phase 3. Yet, despite these increases in complexity and time taken, the children made fewer errors as they progressed through the phases, suggesting that they were not only able to understand the earlier coding concepts but to also build on them and successfully grasp the later, increasingly complex coding concepts introduced in the following phases.

The findings suggest that children were able to comprehend and accomplish the increasingly complex demands of the progressing tasks successfully. These results attest to the notion that children are able to successfully play and learn from this game. Based on these findings, this chapter puts forth this newly created game as a possible cognitive development tool that can be implemented in kindergartens or at home as educational entertainment by families to teach algorithmic thinking, a valuable skill for both academics and life, to children starting from an early age.

ACKNOWLEDGMENT

We wish to extend our gratitude to the participants (children and their parents and instructors who helped) in this work for their dedication and time. We also wish to sincerely thank the manager of the school "Mrs. Heba Sultan"; a Montessori specialist who helped in the design process as a domain expert and in conducting the real implementation of this application.

This research received no specific grant from any funding agency in the public, commercial, or not-for-profit sectors.

REFERENCES

Abo El-Soud, M. A., Hassan, A. E., Kandil, M. S., & Shohieb, S. M. (2010). A proposed web based framework e-learning and dictionary system for deaf Arab students. *IJECS*, *2828*, 106401.

Abrams, S. S., & Walsh, S. (2014). Gamified vocabulary. *Journal of Adolescent & Adult Literacy*, *58*(1), 49–58. doi:10.1002/jaal.315

American Psychiatric Association. (2000). *Diagnostic and Statistical Manual of Mental Disorders (DSM-IV-TR)*. American Psychiatric Association Press.

Anzoátegui, L. G. C., Pereira, M. I. A. R., & Jarrín, M. D. C. S. (2017). Cubetto for preschoolers: Computer programming code to code. In *2017 International Symposium on Computers in Education (SIIE)* (pp. 1-5). IEEE. 10.1109/SIIE.2017.8259649

Berkovitz, J. (1994). Graphical interfaces for young children in a software-based math curriculum. In *Conference Companion on Human Factors in Computing Systems* (pp. 247–248). ACM. doi:10.1145/259963.260466

Boeker, M., Andel, P., Vach, W., & Frankenschmidt, A. (2013). Game-based e-learning is more effective than a conventional instructional method: A randomized controlled trial with third-year medical students. *PLoS One*, *8*(12), e82328. doi:10.1371/journal.pone.0082328 PMID:24349257

Bonani, A., Del Fatto, V., Dodero, G., Gennari, R., & Raimato, G. (2018). Participatory Design of Tangibles for Graphs: A Small-Scale Field Study with Children. In Ó. Mealha, M. Divitini, & M. Rehm (Eds.), *Citizen, Territory and Technologies: Smart Learning Contexts and Practices*. Springer. doi:10.1007/978-3-319-61322-2_16

BOOST Creative Toolbox. (2019). Retrieved from https://shop.lego.com/en-GB/Creative-Toolbox-17101

Chawla, K., Chiou, M., Sandes, A., & Blikstein, P. (2013). Dr. Wagon: a 'stretchable' toolkit for tangible computer programming. In *Proceedings of the 12th international conference on interaction design and children* (pp. 561-564). ACM. 10.1145/2485760.2485865

Code Master™ - ThinkFun. (2019). Retrieved from ttps://www.thinkfun.com/products/code-master/1074

codeCampus. (2019). Retrieved from http://codemonkeyplanet.com/

Coding for Beginners. (2019). *STEM for Girls*. Retrieved from https://www.smartgurlz.com/

Cronk, M. (2012). Using Gamification to Increase Student Engagement and Participation in Class Discussion. In T. Amiel & B. Wilson (Eds.), *Proceedings of EdMedia 2012--World Conference on Educational Media and Technology* (pp. 311-315). Association for the Advancement of Computing in Education (AACE).

Cubetto: A toy robot teaching kids code & computer programming. (2019). Retrieved from https://www.primotoys.com

Diamond, A. (2013). Executive functions. *Annual Review of Psychology*, *64*, 135–168.

Dicheva, D., Dichev, C., Christo, G., & Agre, G. (2015). Gamification in Education: A Systematic Mapping Study. *Journal of Educational Technology & Society*, *18*(3), 75–88.

Druin, A. (1999). Children as Our Technology Design Partners. In The Design of Children's Technology. Morgan Kaufmann.

Druin, A., Bederson, B. B., Hourcade, J. P., Sherman, L., Revelle, G., Platner, M., & Weng, S. (2001). Designing a digital library for young children. In *Proceedings of the 1st ACM/IEEE-CS joint conference on Digital libraries* (pp. 398-405). ACM.

Fisher-Price: Baby Toys, Baby Gear, and Parenting Tips. (2019). Retrieved from https://www.fisher-price.com/en_AU/products/Think-and-Learn-Code-a-pillar

Frei, P., Su, V., Mikhak, B., & Ishii, H. (2000). Designing a New Class of Computational Toys. *Proc. ACM CHI 2000*, 129-136.

Futschek, G., & Moschitz, J. (2011). Learning Algorithmic Thinking with Tangible Objects Eases Transition to Computer Programming. In I. Kalaš & R. T. Mittermeir (Eds.), Lecture Notes in Computer Science: Vol. 7013. *Informatics in Schools. Contributing to 21st Century Education. ISSEP 2011*. Springer.

Gelman, D. L. (2014). *Design for kids: digital products for playing and learning*. Rosenfeld Media.

Gordon, M., Ackermann, E., & Breazeal, C. (2015). Social robot toolkit: Tangible programming for young children. In *Proceedings of the Tenth Annual ACM/IEEE International Conference on Human-Robot Interaction Extended Abstracts* (pp. 67-68). ACM.

Goyal, S., Vijay, R., Monga, C., & Kalita, P. (2016). Code Bits: An Inexpensive Tangible Computational Thinking Toolkit For K-12 Curriculum. *Proceedings of the TEI '16: Tenth International Conference on Tangible, Embedded, and Embodied Interaction - TEI '16.*

Hamari, J. (2017). Do badges increase user activity? A field experiment on the effects of gamification. *Computers in Human Behavior*, *71*, 469–478.

Hanna, L., Risden, K., Czerwinski, M., & Alexander, K. J. (1999). The Role of Usability Research in Designing Children's Computer Products. In *The Design of Children's Technology*. ACM.

Hopfgartner, F., Kazai, G., Kruschwitz, U., Meder, M., & Shovman, M. (2015). Second international workshop on gamification for information retrieval (gamifir'15). In *European Conference on Information Retrieval* (pp. 838-840). Springer.

Hurlburt, G. (2018). Thinking Critically about Algorithmic Thinking. *IT Professional*, *20*(2), 5–10.

Jewelbots Friendship Bracelets - STEM for Best Friends. (2019). Retrieved from https://jewelbots.com/

Johnson, M. P., Wilson, A., Blumberg, B., Kline, C., & Bobick, A. (1999). Sympathetic interfaces: using a plush toy to direct synthetic characters. In *Proceedings of the SIGCHI conference on Human Factors in Computing Systems* (pp. 152-158). ACM.

Kano Computer & Coding Kits | Creative Coding For All Ages. (n.d.). Retrieved from https://kano.me/

Kapp, K. M. (2012). *The Gamification of Learning And Instruction: Game-Based Methods And Strategies For Training And Education*. Pfeiffer.

Kovari, A. (2020). Study of algorithmic problem-solving and executive function. *Acta Polytechnica Hungarica*, *17*(9).

Labs, D. (2019). *Digital Dream Labs, LLC | Make Game Time, Brain Time™*. Retrieved from https://www.digitaldreamlabs.com/

Learning Resources. (2019). Retrieved from https://www.learningresources.com/category/category/featured/award-winning.do

Mariappan, M., Sing, J. C., & Nadarajan, M. (2016, December). Design and Development of Tangible Instruction Set for Educational Robotic System. In *Proceedings of the 4th International Conference on Control, Mechatronics and Automation* (pp. 12-15). ACM.

McIntosh, J., Wells, Y., Smyth, B., & Long, C. (2007). Child-focused and child-inclusive divorce mediation: Comparative outcomes from a prospective study of postseparation adjustment. *Family Court Review*, *46*(1), 105–124. doi:10.1111/j.1744-1617.2007.00186.x

McNerney, T. (2004). From turtles to Tangible Programming Bricks: Explorations in physical language design. *Personal and Ubiquitous Computing*, *8*(5), 326–337.

Microduino. (2019). Retrieved from https://microduinoinc.com/

Mikhak, B., Martin, F., Resnick, M., Berg, R., & Silverman, B. (1999). The Children's Wearable Machines: Handheld and Wearable Computers too. *Proc. IEEE HUC 1999*, 31-43.

Miyamoto, T., Noguchi, S., & Yamashita, H. (2008). Selection of an optimal solution for multiobjective electromagnetic apparatus design based on game theory. *IEEE Transactions on Magnetics*, *44*(6), 1026–1029.

Ozobot | Robots to code, create, and connect with. (2019). Retrieved from https://ozobot.com/

Park, S., & Kim, S. (2018). Patterns Among 754 Gamification Cases: Content Analysis for Gamification Development. *JMIR Serious Games, 6*(4).

Patrício, R., Moreira, A. C., & Zurlo, F. (2018). Gamification approaches to the early stage of innovation. *Creativity and Innovation Management*, *27*(4), 499–511.

Patrício, R., Moreira, A. C., & Zurlo, F. (2021). Enhancing design thinking approaches to innovation through gamification. *European Journal of Innovation Management*, *24*(5), 1569–1594. doi:10.1108/EJIM-06-2020-0239

Patrício, R., Moreira, A. C., Zurlo, F., & Melazzini, M. (2020). Co-creation of new solutions through gamification: A collaborative innovation practice. *Creativity and Innovation Management*, *29*(1), 146–160. doi:10.1111/caim.12356

Pausch, R., Pausch, R., Vogtle, L., & Conway, M. (1992). One dimensional motion tailoring for the disabled: A user study. In *Proceedings of the SIGCHI conference on Human factors in computing systems* (pp. 405-411). ACM.

Race to the Treasure Co-operative Game. (2019). Retrieved from https://www.mastermindtoys.com/6009-Race-to-the-Treasure-Co-operative-Game.aspx

Rahman, F. F., Sumpeno, S., & Zaini, A. (2018). Gamification wisata di Museum Mpu Tantular berbasis Augmented Reality. *Jurnal Teknik ITS*, *7*(1), 165–170.

Resnick, M., Martin, F., Berg, R., Borovoy, R., Colella, V., Kramer, K., & Silverman, B. (1998). Digital manipulatives: new toys to think with. In *Proceedings of the SIGCHI conference on Human factors in computing systems*(pp. 281-287). ACM Press/Addison-Wesley Publishing Co.

Riad, A. M., Elminir, H. K., & Shohieb, S. M. (2013). Dynamic Hand Gesture Recognition; Real Time vs. Offline Recognition Using Kinect. *Advances in Computer Science and Engineering*, *11*(1), 39–50.

Riad, A. M., Elminir, H. K., & Shohieb, S. M. (2014). Hand Gesture Recognition System Based on a Geometric Model and Rule Based Classifier. *British Journal of Applied Science and Technology*, *4*(9), 1432–1444.

Riad, A. M., Elminir, H. K., Shohieb, S. M., & Asem, A. S. (2012). SignsWorld: Deeping into the Silence World and Hearing Its Signs (State of the Art). *International Journal of Computer Science and Information Technology*.

Robertson, J., Gray, S., Toye, M., & Booth, J. (2020). The relationship between executive functions and computational thinking. *International Journal of Computer Science Education in Schools*, *3*(4), 35–49.

Robot Kits For Kids | KIBO | KinderLab Robotics. (2019). Retrieved from https://kinderlabrobotics.com/kibo/

Said, N. S. (2004). An engaging multimedia design model. In *Proceedings of the 2004 conference on Interaction design and children: building a community* (pp. 169-172). ACM.

Sailer, M., Hense, J., Mayr, S., & Mandl, H. (2017). How gamification motivates: An experimental study of the effects of specific game design elements on psychological need satisfaction. *Computers in Human Behavior*, *69*, 371–380.

Shaffer, D. W., Squire, K. R., Halverson, R., & Gee, J. P. (2005). Video games and the future of learning. *Phi Delta Kappan*, *87*(2), 105–111.

Shapiro, D. (2019). *Robot Turtles | The Board Game that Teaches Programming to Kids*. Retrieved from http://www.robotturtles.com/

Shohieb, S. M. (2016). *A Benchmark Arabic Sign Language Database: An Atlas for Vision-Based Recognition Processes*. LAP Lambert Academic Publishing.

Shohieb, S. M. (2019). A Gamified e-Learning Framework for Teaching Mathematics to Arab Deaf Students: Supporting an Acting Arabic Sign Language Avatar. *Ubiquitous Learning: An International Journal*, *12*(1), 55–70.

Shohieb, S. M., Elminir, H. K., & Riad, A. M. (2015). Signsworld atlas; a benchmark Arabic sign language database. *Journal of King Saud University-Computer and Information Sciences*, *27*(1), 68–76.

Shohieb, S. M., Hassan, A. E., Abo Elsoud, M., & Kandil, M. S. (2009). Accessibility system for deaf Arab students. In *2009 ITI 7th International Conference on Communications and Information Technology (ICICT)* (pp. 57-60). IEEE.

Sobodić, A., Balaban, I., & Kermek, D. (2018). Usability Metrics for Gamified E-learning Course: A Multilevel Approach. *International Journal of Emerging Technologies in Learning*, *13*(05), 41–55.

Sonia, C., & Carl, G. (2005). *Design principles for children's technology*. Technical Report HCI-TR, Computer Science Department, University of Saskatchewan.

Sphero. (2019). Retrieved from https://www.sphero.com/sprk-plus

Spin Master - Meccano Meccano Erector – M.A.X Robotic Interactive Toy With Artificial Intelligence. (2019). Retrieved from https://www.spinmaster.com/product_detail.php?pid=p21251&bid=

Stanton, D. (2001). Classroom Collaboration in the Design of Tangible Interfaces for Storytelling. *Proc. ACM CHI 2001*, 482-489.

Steiner, K. E., & Moher, T. G. (1992, June). Graphic StoryWriter: An interactive environment for emergent storytelling. In *Proceedings of the SIGCHI conference on Human factors in computing systems* (pp. 357-364). ACM.

Still, J. D., & Dark, V. J. (2013). Cognitively describing and designing affordances. *Design Studies*, *34*(3), 285–301.

Strawhacker, A., & Bers, M. U. (2015). "I want my robot to look for food": Comparing Kindergartner's programming comprehension using tangible, graphic, and hybrid user interfaces. *International Journal of Technology and Design Education*, *25*(3), 293–319.

Sullivan, A., Elkin, M., & Bers, M. U. (2015). KIBO robot demo: engaging young children in programming and engineering. In *Proceedings of the 14th international conference on interaction design and children* (pp. 418-421). ACM.

Torres, R., Gee, J. P., Hayes, E., Games, I. A., Squire, K., & Salen, K. (2008). *Playing to learn game design skills in a game context*. International Society of the Learning Sciences, Inc.

Turan, Z., Avinc, Z., Kara, K., & Goktas, Y. (2016). Gamification and education: Achievements, cognitive loads, and views of students. *International Journal of Emerging Technologies in Learning*, *11*(07), 64–69.

Walz, S. P., & Deterding, S. (Eds.). (2015). *The gameful world: Approaches, issues, applications*. MIT Press.

Wang, D., Zhang, L., Xu, C., Hu, H., & Qi, Y. (2016). A Tangible Embedded Programming System to Convey Event-Handling Concept. In *Proceedings of the TEI '16: Tenth International Conference on Tangible, Embedded, and Embodied Interaction* (pp. 133-140). Academic Press.

Wonder Workshop | Home of Dash, Cue, and Dot – award-winning robots that help kids learn to code. (2019). Retrieved from https://www.makewonder.com/dash/

Wong, C. Y., Wong, C. W., & Boon-itt, S. (2020). Effects of green supply chain integration and green innovation on environmental and cost performance. *International Journal of Production Research*, *58*(15), 4589–4609.

Wyeth, P., & Purchase, H. C. (2003). Using developmental theories to inform the design of technology for children. In *Proceedings of the 2003 conference on Interaction design and children* (pp. 93-100). ACM.

Yildirim, A., & Şimşek, H. (2005). Sosyal bilimlerde nitel araştırma yöntemleri. Ankara: Seçkin Yayıncılık.

ENDNOTE

1 Retrieved from https://www.ed.ac.uk/files/imports/fileManager/ReUse_Video_Recordings.pdf

Compilation of References

Aabakken, L., Adamsen, S., & Kruse, A. (2000). Performance of a colonoscopy simulator: Experience from a hands-on endoscopy course. *Endoscopy*, *32*(11), 911–913. doi:10.1055-2000-8092 PMID:11085483

Aarseth, E., & Grabarczyk, P. (2018, July 25-28). *An ontological meta-model for game research* [Conference presentation]. DiGRA Conference, Turin, Italy. http://www.digra.org/digra-2018-the-game-is-the-message-cfp/

Aarseth, E. (2014). I fought the law: Transgressive play and the implied player. In N. Segal & D. Koleva (Eds.), *From literature to cultural literacy* (pp. 180–188). Palgrave Macmillan. doi:10.1057/9781137429704_13

Ab. Rahman, R., Ahmad, S., & Hashim, U. R. (2018). The effectiveness of gamification technique for higher education students engagement in polytechnic muadzam shah pahang, malaysia. *International Journal of Educational Technology in Higher Education*, *15*(1). Advance online publication. doi:10.118641239-018-0123-0

Abbott, D. (2018, December). Modding tabletop games for education. In *International Conference on Games and Learning Alliance* (pp. 318-329). Springer.

Abdullah, N. L., Hanafiah, M. H., & Hashim, N. A. (2013). Developing Creative Teaching Module: Business Simulation in Teaching Strategic Management. *International Education Studies*, *6*(6), 95–107. doi:10.5539/ies.v6n6p95

Abo El-Soud, M. A., Hassan, A. E., Kandil, M. S., & Shohieb, S. M. (2010). A proposed web based framework e-learning and dictionary system for deaf Arab students. *IJECS*, *2828*, 106401.

Abonyi, A. U., Okafor, M. G., & Okongwu, J. (2020). Law, specialization, teaching and practice. *Chukwuemeka Odumegwu Ojukwu University Law Journal*, *5*(1).

Abramovich, S., Schunn, C., & Higashi, R. M. (2013). Are badges useful in education? It depends upon the type of badge and expertise of learner. *Educational Technology Research and Development*, *61*(2), 217–232. doi:10.100711423-013-9289-2

Abrams, S. S., & Walsh, S. (2014). Gamified vocabulary. *Journal of Adolescent & Adult Literacy*, *58*(1), 49–58. doi:10.1002/jaal.315

Abt, C. C. (1970). *Serious games*. Viking Press.

AbuJarour, S., Krasnova, H., & Hoffmeier, F. (2018). *ICT as an enabler: Understanding the role of online communication in the social inclusion of Syrian refugees in Germany*. Academic Press.

Abu-Jbara, A., Ezra, J., & Radev, D. (2013). Purpose and polarity of citation: Towards nlp-based bibliometrics. *Proceedings of the 2013 Conference of the North American Chapter of the Association for Computational Linguistics: Human Language Technologies*, 596–606.

Adams, A., Lunt, P., & Cairns, P. (2008). A qualitative approach to HCI research. In P. Cairns & A. Cox (Eds.), Research Methods for Human-Computer Interaction (pp. 138–157). Cambridge University Press. doi:10.1017/CBO9780511814570.008

Adams, D. M. (2013). *Exploring the effect of video game playing on static and dynamic spatial cognition skills* (Unpublished doctoral dissertation). University of California.

Adams, D. M., Mayer, R. E., MacNamara, A., Koenig, A., & Wainess, R. (2012). Narrative games for learning: Testing the discovery and narrative hypotheses. *Journal of Educational Psychology*, *104*(1), 235–249. doi:10.1037/a0025595

Adams, E. (2014). *Fundamentals of game design*. Pearson Education.

Adams, E., & Dormans, J. (2012). *Game mechanics: advanced game design*. New Riders.

Adams, T. E., Jones, S. L. H., & Ellis, C. (2015). *Autoethnography*. Series in Understanding Statistics.

Adams, V., Burger, S., Crawford, K., & Setter, R. (2018). Can You Escape? Creating an Escape Room to Facilitate Active Learning. *Journal for Nurses in Professional Development*, *34*(2), E1–E5. doi:10.1097/NND.0000000000000433 PMID:29481471

Admiraal, W., Huizenga, J., Akkerman, S., & Ten Dam, G. (2011). The concept of flow in collaborative game-based learning. *Computers in Human Behavior*, *27*(3), 1185–1194. doi:10.1016/j.chb.2010.12.013

Agency for Toxic Substances and Disease Registry. (2008). *Chromium Toxicity. Clinical Assessment - History, Signs and Symptoms.* https://www.atsdr.cdc.gov/csem/chromium/signs_and_symptoms.html

Agen, F., & Ezquerra, Á. (2021). Analysis of emotions in the work of inquiry: "The Black Box" [Análisis de las emociones en el trabajo de indagación: "La Caja Negra"]. *Investigación en la Escuela*, *3*, 125–138. doi:10.12795/IE.2021.i103.09

Agile alliance. (2018). *Agile glossary*. https://www.agilealliance.org/agile101/agile-glossary/

Agogué, M., Levillain, K., & Hooge, S. (2015). Gamification of creativity: Exploring the usefulness of serious games for ideation. *Creativity and Innovation Management*, *24*(3), 415–429. doi:10.1111/caim.12138

Aguiar-Castillo, L., Hernández-López, L., De Saá-Pérez, P., & Pérez-Jiménez, R. (2020). Gamification as a motivation strategy for higher education students in tourism face-to-face learning. *Journal of Hospitality, Leisure, Sport and Tourism Education*, *27*, 100267. doi:10.1016/j.jhlste.2020.100267

Ahmad, A., Zeshan, F., Khan, M. S., Marriam, R., Ali, A., & Samreen, A. (2020). The impact of gamification on learning outcomes of computer science majors. *ACM Transactions on Computing Education*, *20*(2), 1–25. Advance online publication. doi:10.1145/3383456

Ahmad, I. S., Ahmad, H. K., Aliyu, S. M., & Ahmad, A. M. (2020). Mathefunic: A mobile based game for engaging children with ADHD. *International Journal on Perceptive and Cognitive Computing*, *6*(2), 60–66. doi:10.31436/ijpcc.v6i2.158

Ahmad, T. (2019). *Scenario based approach to re-imagining future of higher education which prepares students for the future of work.* Higher Education, Skills and Work-Based Learning. doi:10.1108/HESWBL-12-2018-0136

Aiken, K. D., Heinze, T. C., Meuter, M. L., & Chapman, K. J. (2016). Innovation through collaborative course development: Theory and practice. *Marketing Education Review*, *26*(1), 57–62. doi:10.1080/10528008.2015.1091679

Airbus Foundation. (2022). *Homepage*. Available at https://www.airbus.com/en/sustainability/airbus-foundation

Akilli, G. K., & Cagiltay, K. (2006). An Instructional Design/Development Model for the Creation of Game-like Learning Environments: The FIDGE Model. In M. Pivec (Ed.), *Affective and emotional aspects of human computer interaction: Game-based and innovative learning approaches* (pp. 93–112). IOS Press.

Akilli, G. K., & Cagiltay, K. (2006). An instructional design/development model for the creation of game-like learning environments: The FIDGE model. In M. Pivec (Ed.), *Affective and emotional aspects of human-computer interaction: Game-based and innovative learning approaches* (pp. 93–112). IOS Press. http://citeseerx.ist.psu.edu/viewdoc/download?doi=10.1.1.465.6601&rep=rep1&type=pdf#page=108

Akl, E. A., Pretorius, R. W., Sackett, K., Erdley, W. S., Bhoopathi, P. S., Alfarah, Z., & Schünemann, H. J. (2010). The effect of educational games on medical students' learning outcomes: A systematic review: BEME Guide No 14. *Medical Teacher*, *32*(1), 16–27. doi:10.3109/01421590903473969 PMID:20095770

Akl, E. A., Sackett, K., Pretorius, R., Erdley, S., Bhoopathi, P. S., Mustafa, R., & Schunemann, H. J. (2013). Educational games for health professionals. *Cochrane Database of Systematic Reviews*, (1), CD006411. doi:10.1002/14651858.CD006411.pub2 PMID:23440807

Aksakal, N. (2015). Theoretical View to The Approach of The Edutainment. *Procedia: Social and Behavioral Sciences*, *186*, 1232–1239. doi:10.1016/j.sbspro.2015.04.081

Alabbasi, D. (2017). Exploring graduate students' perspectives towards using gamification techniques in online learning. *Turkish Online Journal of Distance Education*, *18*(3), 180–196. doi:10.17718/tojde.328951

Alabdulakareem, E., & Jamjoom, M. (2020). Computer-assisted learning for improving ADHD individuals' executive functions through gamified interventions: A review. *Entertainment Computing*, *33*, 100341. doi:10.1016/j.entcom.2020.100341

Al-Azawi, R., Al-Faliti, F., & Al-Blushi, M. (2016). Educational Gamification Vs. Game Based Learning: Comparative Study. *International Journal of Innovation, Management and Technology*, (September), 131–136. doi:10.18178/ijimt.2016.7.4.659

Alda, F. L. (1997). Tratamiento de residuos: Un juego de simulación. *Enseñanza de las Ciencias de la Tierra*, *5*(1), 49–53.

Aleem, S., Capretz, L. F., & Ahmed, F. (2016). Game development software engineering process life cycle: A systematic review. *Journal of Software Engineering Research and Development*, *4*(1), 1–30. doi:10.118640411-016-0032-7

Alessi, S. (1988). Fidelity in the design of instructional simulations. *Journal of Computer-Based Instruction*, *15*(2), 40–47.

Alexander, L. (2012). *GDC 2012: Sid Meier on how to see games as sets of interesting decisions*. Gamasutra. https://www.gamasutra.com/view/news/164869/GDC_2012_Sid_Meier_on_how_to_see_games_as_sets_of_interesting_decisions.php

Alexander, S. (1999). An evaluation of innovative projects involving communication and information technology in higher education. *Higher Education Research & Development*, *18*(2), 173–183. doi:10.1080/0729436990180202

Alexandre-Leclair, L. (2014). Diversity as a motive for entrepreneurship? The case of gender, culture and ethnicity. *Journal of Innovation Economics & Management*, *2*(14), 157–175. doi:10.3917/jie.014.0157

Alexiou, A., Schippers, M. C., Oshri, I., & Angelopoulos, S. (2020). Narrative and aesthetics as antecedents of perceived learning in serious games. *Information Technology & People*, *35*(8), 142–161. Advance online publication. doi:10.1108/ITP-08-2019-0435

Ali, A. Z., & Mahdavi, M. A. (2021). A Gamification Framework for Cognitive Assessment and Cognitive Training: Qualitative Study. *JMIR Serious Games, 9*(2). Https://Games.Jmir.Org/2021/2/E21900 doi:10.2196/21900

Ali, A. M., & Yusof, H. (2011). Quality in qualitative studies: The case of validity, reliability and generalizability. *Issues in Social and Environmental Accounting*, *5*(1), 25–64. doi:10.22164/isea.v5i1.59

Allen, J. F. (2003). Natural language processing. In Encyclopedia of computer science (pp. 1218–1222). Academic Press.

Alliger, G. M., Tannenbaum, S. I., Bennett, W., Traver, H., & Shotland, A. (1997). A meta-analysis of the relations among training criteria. *Personnel Psychology*, *50*(2), 341–358. doi:10.1111/j.1744-6570.1997.tb00911.x

Ally, M., & Prieto-Blázquez, J. (2014). What is the future of mobile learning in education? *International Journal of Educational Technology in Higher Education*, *11*(1), 142–151. doi:10.7238/rusc.v11i1.2033

AlMarshedi, A., Wills, G. B., Wanick, V., & Ranchhod, A. (2014, November). Towards a sustainable gamification impact. In *International Conference on Information Society (i-Society 2014)* (pp. 195-200). 10.1109/i-Society.2014.7009041

Almeida, L., Canabarro, S., & Silva, H. (2017). Ferramenta de Ensino-Aprendizagem na área da saúde: Massive Open Online Courses. *EmRede - Revista de Educação à distância, 4*(1), 130-142. https://www.aunirede.org.br /revista/index.php/emrede/article/view/153

Almeida, F., & Simoes, J. (2019). The role of serious games, gamification and Industry 4.0 tools in the Education 4.0 paradigm. *Contemporary Educational Technology*, *10*(2), 120–136. doi:10.30935/cet.554469

Alomari, I., Al-Samarraie, H., & Yousef, R. (2019). The role of gamification techniques in promoting student learning: A review and synthesis. *Journal of Information Technology Education*, *18*(08), 2019. doi:10.28945/4417

Alqithami, S. (2021). A serious-gamification blueprint towards a normalized attention. *Brain Informatics*, *8*(1), 1–13. doi:10.118640708-021-00127-3 PMID:33856585

Alsawaier, R. S. (2018). The effect of gamification on motivation and engagement. *The International Journal of Information and Learning Technology*, *35*(1), 56–79. doi:10.1108/IJILT-02-2017-0009

Alvares, G. A., Chen, N. T., Notebaert, L., Granich, J., Mitchell, C., & Whitehouse, A. J. (2019). Brief social attention bias modification for children with autism spectrum disorder. *Autism Research*, *12*(3), 527–535. doi:10.1002/aur.2067 PMID:30632321

Alves, F. (2015). *Gamification: Como criar experiências de aprendizagem engajadoras* [Gamification: How to create engaging learning experiences]. DVS Editora.

Alves, F. (2015). *Gamification: how to create engaging learning experiences* [Gamification: como criar experiências de aprendizagem engajadoras] (2nd ed.). DVS Editora.

Alves, L. R. G. (2009). *Educação a distância: O estado da arte* [Online distance learning: The state of art]. Pearson Education do Brasil.

Amad, A. (2015, September 24). *The advantages of Wasabi Waiter Apps in hiring*. The Science Times. Retrieved from https://www.sciencetimes.com/articles/7384/20150924/advantages-wasabi-waiter-apps-hiring.htm

Amado, A., Cortez, P., Rita, P., & Moro, S. (2018). Research trends on Big Data in Marketing: A text mining and topic modeling based literature analysis. *European Research on Management and Business Economics*, *24*(1), 1–7. doi:10.1016/j.iedeen.2017.06.002

American Psychiatric Association. (2000). *Diagnostic and Statistical Manual of Mental Disorders (DSM-IV-TR)*. American Psychiatric Association Press.

Amer, R. S., Denehy, G. E., Cobb, D. S., Dawson, D. V., Cunningham-Ford, M. A., & Bergeron, C. (2011). Development and evaluation of an interactive dental video game to teach dentin bonding. *Journal of Dental Education, 75*(6), 823–831. doi:10.1002/j.0022-0337.2011.75.6.tb05111.x PMID:21642529

Amory, A., Naicker, K., Vincent, J., & Adams, C. (1999). The use of computer games as an educational tool: 1. Identification of appropriate game types and game elements. *British Journal of Educational Technology, 30*(4), 311–322. doi:10.1111/1467-8535.00121

Amory, A., & Seagram, R. (2003). Educational game models: Conceptualization and evaluation. *South African Journal of Higher Education, 17*(2), 206–217. https://eric.ed.gov/?id=EJ832934

Amriani, A., Aji, A., Utomo, A. Y., Wahidah, F., & Junus, K. (2014). Gamified E-learning model based on community of inquiry. *2014 IEEE International Conference on Advanced Computer Science and Information Systems*, 474–480. 10.1109/ICACSIS.2014.7065830

Andaluz, N. (1994). Necesitamos ayuda; ¡sálvanos!: Un juego para enseñar y aprender geología. *Enseñanza de las Ciencias de la Tierra, 2*(1), 278–280.

Anđelković, S., Dedjanski, V., & Pejic, B. (2018). Pedagogical benefits of fieldwork of the students at the Faculty of Geography in the light of the Bologna Process. *Journal of Geography in Higher Education, 42*(1), 110–125. doi:10.1080/03098265.2017.1379058

Anderson, L. W., Krathwohl, D. R., Airasain, P. W., Cruikshank, K. A., Mayer, R. E., Pintrich, P. R., Raths, J., & Wittrock, M. C. (2001). A Taxonomy for Learning, Teaching, and Assessing: A Revision of Bloom's Taxonomy (Abridged). Longman.

Anderson, P. H., & Lawton, L. (2009). Business Simulations and Cognitive Learning: Developments, Desires, and Future Directions. *Simulation & Gaming, 40*(2), 193–216. doi:10.1177/1046878108321624

Andrei, B. A., Casu-Pop, A. C., Gheorghe, S. C., & Boiangiu, C. A. (2019). A study on using waterfall and agile methods in software project management. *Journal Of Information Systems & Operations Management, 13*(1), 125–135.

Andrews, J., & Higson, H. (2008). Graduate Employability, 'Soft Skills' Versus 'Hard' Business Knowledge: A European Study. *Higher Education in Europe, 33*(4), 411–422. doi:10.1080/03797720802522627

Anft, M. (2017). Breaking professional schools out of their silos. *The Chronicle of Higher Education*, (April), 30.

Angeli, C., Valanides, N., & Christodoulou, A. (2016). Theoretical considerations of technological pedagogical content knowledge. In Handbook of technological pedagogical content knowledge (TPACK) for educators (pp. 11-32). Routledge.

Annetta, L. A., Minogue, J., Holmes, S. Y., & Cheng, M.-T. T. (2009). Investigating the impact of video games on high school students' engagement and learning about genetics. *Computers & Education, 53*(1), 74–85. doi:10.1016/j.compedu.2008.12.020

Antonaci, A., Dagnino, F. M., Ott, M., Bellotti, F., Berta, R., De Gloria, A., Lavagnino, E., Romero, M., Usart, M., & Mayer, I. (2015). A gamified collaborative course in entrepreneurship: Focus on objectives and tools. *Computers in Human Behavior, 51*, 1276–1283. doi:10.1016/j.chb.2014.11.082

Antonaci, A., Klemke, R., Kreijns, K., & Specht, M. (2018). Get Gamification of MOOC right! *International Journal of Serious Games, 5*(3), 61–78. doi:10.17083/ijsg.v5i3.255

Antonaci, A., Klemke, R., & Specht, M. (2019, September). The effects of gamification in online learning environments: A systematic literature review. *Informatics (MDPI), 6*(3), 32. doi:10.3390/informatics6030032

Anyaegbu, R., Ting, W., & Li, Y. I. (2012). Serious game motivation in an EFL classroom in Chinese primary school. *The Turkish Online Journal of Educational Technology*, *11*(1), 154–164.

Anzoátegui, L. G. C., Pereira, M. I. A. R., & Jarrín, M. D. C. S. (2017). Cubetto for preschoolers: Computer programming code to code. In *2017 International Symposium on Computers in Education (SIIE)* (pp. 1-5). IEEE. 10.1109/SIIE.2017.8259649

Aparício, M., Oliveira, T., Bacao, F., & Painho, M. (2019). Gamification: A Key Determinant of Massive Open Online Course (MOOC) Success. *Information & Management*, *56*(1), 39–54. Advance online publication. doi:10.1016/j.im.2018.06.003

Apisitniran, L., & Theparat, C. (2018, October 15). Creating the virtuous circle. *The Bangkok Post*. https://www.bangkokpost.com/business/1558130/creating-the-virtuous-circle

Apostol, S., Zaharescu, L., & Alexe, I. (2013). Gamification of learning and educational games. In *Proceedings of the 9th. International Scientific Conference eLearning and Software for Education* (pp. 67-72). Academic Press.

Araujo, E. P. R., & Toledo, M. C. M. (2014). Ciências da Terra em cursos que habilitam ao magistério de Ciências Naturais para o ensino fundamental. *Terræ Didatica*, *10*(3), 319–330. doi:10.20396/td.v10i3.8637347

Arce, N. H., & Valdivia, A. C. (2020). Adapting competitiveness and gamification to a digital platform for foreign language learning. *International Journal of Emerging Technologies in Learning*, *15*(20), 194–209. doi:10.3991/ijet.v15i20.16135

Ardila-Muñoz, J. Y. (2019). Theoretical assumptions for the gamification in the higher education [Supuestos teóricos para la gamificación de la educación superior]. *Magis*, *12*(24), 71–84. doi:10.11144/Javeriana.m12-24.stge

Arjoranta, J. (2014). Game definitions: A Wittgensteinian approach. *International Journal of Computer Game Research*, *14*(1), 1–13. http://gamestudies.org/1401/articles/arjoranta

Arjoranta, J. (2019). How to define games and why we need to. *Computer Games Journal*, *8*(3-4), 109–120. doi:10.100740869-019-00080-6

Armstrong, R. J. (Ed.). (1970). Developing and Writing Behavioral Objectives. Educational Innovaters Press.

Armstrong, M. B., & Landers, R. N. (2014). Reactions to Gamified Training. Poster Presented at the *Old Dominion University 4th Annual Graduate Research Achievement Day*, Norfolk, VA. 10.13140/2.1.2264.3848

Armstrong, M. B., & Landers, R. N. (2017). An Evaluation of Gamified Training: Using Narrative to Improve Reactions and Learning. *Simulation & Gaming*, *48*(4), 513–538. doi:10.1177/1046878117703749

Arnab, S., Lim, T., Carvalho, M. B., Bellotti, F., De Freitas, S., Louchart, S., Suttie, N., Berta, R., & De Gloria, A. (2015). Mapping learning and game mechanics for serious games analysis. *British Journal of Educational Technology*, *46*(2), 391–411. doi:10.1111/bjet.12113

Arsenault, D. (2008). Guitar Hero: "Not like playing guitar at all"? *Loading...*, *2*(2).

Arufe Giráldez, V., & Navarro Patón, R. (2020). Creación de un entorno de aprendizaje gamificado inspirado en la casa de papel. In H. Morente Oria, F. T. González Fernández, & A. S. Sánchez Fernández (Eds.), (pp. 65–83). Ediciones Morata.

Arufe Giráldez, V., Vaquero Cristóbal, R., & Isorna Folgar, M. (2021). Can a didactic proposal for the Physical Education classroom inspired by the Fortnite video game develop the values and various psychological variables in children and adolescents? *Sport Science (Travnik)*, *14*(1), 68–78.

Arufe-Giráldez, V. (2019). Fortnite EF un nuevo juego deportivo para el aula de educación física. propuesta de innovación y gamificación basada en el videojuego fortnite. *Sportis: Revista Técnico-Científica Del Deporte Escolar, Educación Física Y Psicomotricidad, 5*(2), 323-349.

Associassíon Española de Videojuegos - AEVI. (2019). *The Video Game Industry in Spain: Yearbook 2019* [La Industria del Videojuego En España: anuario 2019]. http://www.aevi.org.es/web/wp-content/uploads/2020/04/AEVI-ANUARIO-2019.pdf

Astro-Pi Challenge. (2022). *Homepage*. Available at https://astro-pi.org/

Atanassova, I., Bertin, M., & Mayr, P. (2019). Mining scientific papers: NLP-enhanced bibliometrics. *Frontiers in Research Metrics and Analytics*, *4*, 2. doi:10.3389/frma.2019.00002 PMID:33870034

Atenstaedt, R. (2017). Word cloud analysis of the BJGP: 5 years on. *The British Journal of General Practice*, *67*(658), 231–232. doi:10.3399/bjgp17X690833 PMID:28450341

Attali, Y., & Arieli-Attali, M. (2015). Gamification in assessment: Do points affect test performance? *Computers & Education*, *83*, 57–63. doi:10.1016/j.compedu.2014.12.012

Atwood-Blaine, D., & Huffman, D. (2017). Mobile gaming and student interactions in a science center: The future of gaming in science education. *International Journal of Science and Mathematics Education*, *15*(1), 45–65. doi:10.100710763-017-9801-y

Ausubel, D. P., Novak, J. D., & Hanesian, H. (1980). *Educational psychology* [Psicologia educacional]. Interamericana.

Ausubel, D. P., Novak, J. D., & Hanesian, H. (1968). *Educational psychology: A cognitive view*. Holt McDougal.

Avanzini, F., Baraté, A., Ludovico, L. A., & Mandanici, M. (2019). Metrics for the automatic assessment of music harmony awareness in children. In *Sound & Music Computing Conference* (pp. 372–379). SMC.

Avanzini, F., Baraté, A., Ludovico, L. A., & Mandanici, M. (2021). Songs in Music Education: Design and Early Experimentation of a Web Tool for the Recognition of Harmonic Changes. In *International Conference on Computer Supported Education* (pp. 709-720). SCITEPRESS. 10.5220/0010540407090720

Ávila-Pesántez, D., Rivera, L. A., & Alban, M. S. (2017). Approaches for serious game design: A systematic literature review. *Computers in Education Journal*, *8*(3), 1–11.

Axelsson, A. S., & Regan, T. (2002). *How belonging to an online group affects social behavior – A case study of Asheron's Call* (Technical Report MSR-TR-2002-07). Microsoft Research, Microsoft Corporation.

Aydin, C. H. (2018). MOOCs as change agents. In D. Jansen & L. Konings (Eds.), *The 2018 OpenupEd Trend Report on MOOCs* (pp. 18–21). EADTU.

Ayén, F. (2017). ¿Qué es la gamificación y el ABJ? Iber: Didáctica de las ciencias sociales. *Geografía e Historia*, *1*(86), 7–15.

Ayuso Tapia, G. (2019). *Creation of an Educational Escape Room for Compulsory Secondary Education* [Creación de un Escape Room Educativo para Educación Secundaria Obligatoria]. Universidad de Valladolid, Escuela de Ingeniería Informática de Valladolid. https://uvadoc.uva.es/handle/10324/38983

Azubuike, O. B., Adegboye, O., & Quadri, H. (2021). Who gets to learn in a pandemic? Exploring the digital divide in remote learning during the COVID-19 pandemic in Nigeria. *International Journal of Educational Research Open*, *2*(2), 1–10. doi:10.1016/j.ijedro.2020.100022 PMID:35059664

B., B. M. (1999). *The construction/negotiation of meanings in the initial university course of Differential and Integral Calculus* [Unpublished Doctoral Thesis]. University of São Paulo, São Paulo, Brazil.

Bacea, I. M., Ciupe, A., & Meza, S. N. (2017, July). Interactive Kanban—Blending digital and physical resources for collaborative project based learning. In *2017 IEEE 17th International Conference on Advanced Learning Technologies (ICALT)* (pp. 210-211). IEEE. 10.1109/ICALT.2017.68

Bachen, C. M., Hernández-Ramos, P., Raphael, C., & Waldron, A. (2016). How do presence, flow, and character identification affect players' empathy and interest in learning from a serious computer game? *Computers in Human Behavior*, *64*, 77–87. doi:10.1016/j.chb.2016.06.043

Bacigalupo, M., Kampylis, P., Punie, Y., & Van den Brande, G. (2016). *EntreComp: The entrepreneurship competence framework.* Publication Office of the European Union. https://publications.jrc.ec.europa.eu/repository/handle/JRC101581

Bagozzi, R. P., Yi, Y., & Phillips, L. W. (1991). Assessing construct validity in organizational research. *Administrative Science Quarterly*, 421–458. doi:10.2307/2393203

Bahador, K. M. K., & Haider, A. (2017). Incorporating information technology competencies in accounting curriculum: A case study in Malaysian higher education institutions. *Journal of Engineering and Applied Sciences (Asian Research Publishing Network)*, *12*(21), 5508–5513.

Bailey, K., Bullington, T., & Maclever, L. (2020). *The emergency campaign: Discord, D&D, and distance learning.* Faculty Focus | Higher Ed Teaching & Learning. https://www.facultyfocus.com/articles/online-education/online-course-delivery-and-instruction/the-emergency-campaign-discord-dd-and-distance-learning/

Bai, S., Hew, K. F., & Huang, B. (2020). Does gamification improve student learning outcome? Evidence from a meta-analysis and synthesis of qualitative data in educational contexts. *Educational Research Review*, *30*, 100322. doi:10.1016/j.edurev.2020.100322

Bakar, R., Islam, M. D. A., & Lee, J. (2015). Entrepreneurship education: Experiences in selected countries. *International Education Studies*, *8*(1), 88–99.

Bakhanova, E., Raffe, W. L., Voinov, A., & Marin, J. G. (2019, December 1-6). *Gamification of participatory modeling in the context of sustainable development: Existing and new solutions* [Conference presentation abstract]. 23rd International Congress on Modelling and Simulation, Canberra, Australia. https://opus.lib.uts.edu.au/bitstream/10453/137302/1/bakhanova-3.pdf

Bakker, A. B., Sanz Vergel, A. I., & Kuntze, J. (2015). Student engagement and performance: A weekly diary study on the role of openness. *Motivation and Emotion*, *39*(1), 49–62. doi:10.100711031-014-9422-5

Bandura, A. (1997). *Self-efficacy: The exercise of control.* Macmillan. doi:10.1891/0889-8391.13.2.158

Bandura, A., & Walters, R. (1977). *Soical Learning theory* (Vol. 1). Prentice Hall.

Banfield, J., & Wilkerson, B. (2014). Increasing student intrinsic motivation and self-efficacy through gamification pedagogy. *Contemporary Issues in Education Research*, *7*(4), 291–298. doi:10.19030/cier.v7i4.8843

Baptista, G., & Oliveira, T. (2019). Gamification and serious games: A literature meta-analysis and integrative model. *Computers in Human Behavior*, *92*, 306–315. doi:10.1016/j.chb.2018.11.030

Barata, G., Gama, S., Jorge, J., & Gonçalves, D. (2013). Engaging engineering students with gamification. In *Proceedings of the fifth International Conference on Games and Virtual Worlds for Serious Applications* (pp. 24-31). Academic Press.

Barata, G., Gama, S., Jorge, J., & Gonçalves, D. (2015). Identifying student types in a gamified learning experience. In M. Khosrow-Pour (Ed.), *Gamification: Concepts, methodologies, tools, and applications* (pp. 541–558). IGI Global. doi:10.4018/978-1-4666-8200-9.ch026

Barbosa, M. A. (2004). *Failure in teaching and learning in the discipline of differential and integral calculus* [O insucesso no ensino e aprendizagem na disciplina de cálculo diferencial e integral] [Doctoral dissertation]. Pontifícia Universidade Católica do Paraná.

Barros, C., Carvalho, A. A., & Salgueiro, A. (2020). The effect of the serious game Tempoly on learning arithmetic polynomial operations. *Education and Information Technologies*, *25*(3), 1497–1509. doi:10.100710639-019-09990-4

Barry, I. (2005). Game design. In S. Rabin (Ed.), *Introduction to Game Development* (pp. 99–160). Charles Rive Media, Inc.

Barteit, S., Sié, A., Yé, M., Depoux, A., Louis, V. R., & Sauerborn, R. (2019). Lessons learned on teaching a global audience with massive open online courses (MOOCs) on health impacts of climate change: A commentary. *Globalization and Health*, *15*(1), 52. doi:10.118612992-019-0494-6 PMID:31438984

Bartle, R. (1996). Hearts, clubs, diamonds, spades: Players who suits MUDs. *Journal of MUD Research, 1*(1), 19.

Bartle, R. A. (2015). MMOs from the inside out: The history, design, fun, and art of massively-multiplayer online role-playing games. In MMOs from the inside out: The history, design, fun, and art of massively-multiplayer online role-playing games (pp. 1-735) doi:10.1007/978-1-4842-1724-5

Bartlett, K. A., & Anderson, J. L. (2019). Gaming to learn: Bringing escape rooms to the classroom. In *Handbook of Research on Innovative Digital Practices to Engage Learners* (pp. 1–27). IGI Global. doi:10.4018/978-1-5225-9438-3.ch001

Barton, A. M. (2021). Teaching Lawyers to Think Like Leaders: The Next Big Shift in Legal Education. *Baylor Law Review*, *73*, 115.

Bastian, M., Heymann, S., & Jacomy, M. (2009). Gephi: an open source software for exploring and manipulating networks. *Third International AAAI Conference on Weblogs and Social Media.*

Bateman, J., Allen, M., Samani, D., Kidd, J., & Davies, D. (2013). Virtual patient design: Exploring what works and why. A grounded theory study. *Medical Education*, *47*(6), 595–606. doi:10.1111/medu.12151 PMID:23662877

Battocchi, A., Pianesi, F., Tomasini, D., Zancanaro, M., Esposito, G., Venuti, P., & Weiss, P. L. (2010). Collaborative puzzle game: A tabletop interactive game for fostering collaboration in children with autism spectrum disorders (ASD). *Journal of Assistive Technologies*, *4*(1), 4–13. doi:10.5042/jat.2010.0040

Bauer, K. N., Brusso, R. C., & Orvis, K. A. (2012). Using adaptive difficulty to optimize videogame-based training performance: The moderating role of personality. *Military Psychology*, *24*(2), 148–165. doi:10.1080/08995605.2012.672908

Baydas, O., & Cicek, M. (2019). The examination of the gamification process in undergraduate education: A scale development study. *Technology, Pedagogy and Education*, *28*(3), 269–285. doi:10.1080/1475939X.2019.1580609

Beach, D. (1980). *Personnel: The management of people at work.* Macmillan.

Béchard, J. P., & Grégoire, D. (2005). Entrepreneurship education research revisited: The case of higher education. *Academy of Management Learning & Education*, *4*(1), 22–43. doi:10.5465/amle.2005.16132536

Becker, K. (2021). What's the difference between gamification, serious games, educational games, and game-based learning. *Acad. Lett, 209.*

Bedwell, W. L., Pavlas, D., Heyne, K., Lazzara, E. H., & Salas, E. (2012). Toward a taxonomy linking game attributes to learning: An empirical study. *Simulation & Gaming*, *43*(6), 729–760. doi:10.1177/1046878112439444

Beemer, L. R., Ajibewa, T. A., Dellavecchia, G., & Hasson, R. E. (2019). A pilot intervention using gamification to enhance student participation in classroom activity breaks. *International Journal of Environmental Research and Public Health, 16*(21), 1–11. doi:10.3390/ijerph16214082 PMID:31652885

Begg, M., Dewhurst, D., & Macleod, H. (2005). Game-informed learning: Applying computer game processes to higher education. *Innovate: Journal of Online Education, 1*(6), 1-7. https://www.learntechlib.org/p/107268/

Belchior, P., Marsiske, M., Sisco, S. M., Yam, A., Bavelier, D., Ball, K., & Mann, W. C. (2013). Video game training to improve selective visual attention in older adults. *Computers in Human Behavior, 29*(4), 1318–1324. doi:10.1016/j.chb.2013.01.034 PMID:24003265

Bell, R. (2016). Unpacking the link between entrepreneurialism and employability: An assessment of the relationship between entrepreneurial attitudes and likelihood of graduate employment in a professional field. *Education + Training, 58*(1), 2–17. doi:10.1108/ET-09-2014-0115

Bencsik, A., Mezeiova, A., & Samu, B. O. (2021). Gamification in Higher Education (Case Study on a Management Subject). *International Journal of Learning, Teaching and Educational Research, 20*(5).

Bepicolombo. (2021). *Bepicolombo overview.* Available at https://www.esa.int/Science_Exploration/Space_Science/BepiColombo_overview2

Bereiter, C., & Scardamalia, M. (1993). *Surpassing Ourselves: An Inquiry into the Nature and Implications of Expertise.* Open Court.

Berger, A., Schlager, T., Sprott, D. E., & Herrmann, A. (2017). Gamified interactions: Whether, when, and how games facilitate self–brand connections. *Journal of the Academy of Marketing Science, 81*(2), 1–22.

Berkovitz, J. (1994). Graphical interfaces for young children in a software-based math curriculum. In *Conference Companion on Human Factors in Computing Systems* (pp. 247–248). ACM. doi:10.1145/259963.260466

Berman, A. H., Biguet, G., Stathakarou, N., Westin-Hägglöf, B., Jeding, K., McGrath, C., Zary, N., & Kononowicz, A. A. (2017). Virtual Patients in a Behavioral Medicine Massive Open Online Course (MOOC): A Qualitative and Quantitative Analysis of Participants' Perceptions. *Academic Psychiatry, 41*(5), 631–641. doi:10.100740596-017-0706-4 PMID:28390054

Berman, N. B., Durning, S. J., Fischer, M. R., Huwendiek, S., & Triola, M. M. (2016). The Role for Virtual Patients in the Future of Medical Education. *Academic Medicine, 91*(9), 1217–1222. doi:10.1097/ACM.0000000000001146 PMID:26959224

Bertalero, G., Addebito, P., Bancario, C. C., & Cliente, C. A. L. (2018). *Gamified learning in higher education: A systematic review of the literature.* Academic Press.

Bethke, E. (2003). *Game development and production.* Wordware Publishing, Inc.

Betzner, J. P., & Marek, E. A. (2014). Teacher and Student Perceptions of Earth Science and Its Educational Value in Secondary Schools. *Creative Education, 5*(11), 1019–1031. doi:10.4236/ce.2014.511116

Bezerra, N. J. (2016). *The organization of the Teaching of Differential and Integral Calculus from the perspective of the Theory of Step Formation of Galperin's Mental Actions* [Doctoral thesis]. Federal University of Mato Grosso.

Bhatia, A. K., & Levina, N. (2021) Can Entrepreneurship be taught in a classroom, Business Education. *Harvard Business Review.* https://hbr.org/am/2020/08/can-entrepreneurship-be-taught-in-a-classroom

Bianchi-Berthouze, N., Kim, W. W., & Patel, D. (2007, September). Does body movement engage you more in digital game play? and why? In *International conference on affective computing and intelligent interaction* (pp. 102-113). Springer. 10.1007/978-3-540-74889-2_10

Bicen, H., & Kocakoyun, S. (2018). Perceptions of Students for Gamification Approach: Kahoot as a Case Study. *International Journal of Emerging Technologies in Learning*, *13*(02), 72–93. doi:10.3991/ijet.v13i02.7467

Biddiss, E., & Irwin, J. (2010). Active video games to promote physical activity in children and youth: A systematic review. *Archives of Pediatrics & Adolescent Medicine*, *164*(7), 664–672. doi:10.1001/archpediatrics.2010.104 PMID:20603468

Biggs, J. (1996). Enhancing teaching through constructive alignment. *Higher Education*, *32*(3), 347–364. doi:10.1007/BF00138871

Biggs, W. D. (1987). Functional business games. *Simulation & Gaming*, *18*(2), 242–267. doi:10.1177/104687818701800206

Bilro, R. G., Loureiro, S. M. C., & Angelino, F. J. D. A. (2021). The role of creative communications and gamification in student engagement in higher education: A sentiment analysis approach. *Journal of Creative Communications*. Advance online publication. doi:10.1177/0973258621992644

Bing, W. (2017). The college English teaching reform based on MOOC (Vol. 10, No. 2). Canadian Center of Science and Education. doi:10.5539/elt.v10n2p19

Birchfield, D., & Johnson-Glenberg, M. (2012). A next gen interface for embodied learning: SMALLab and the geological layer cake. In Interdisciplinary Advancements in Gaming, Simulations and Virtual Environments: Emerging Trends (pp. 51-60). IGI Global.

Bíró, G. I. (2014). Didactics 2.0: A pedagogical analysis of gamification theory from a comparative perspective with a special view to the components of learning. *Procedia: Social and Behavioral Sciences*, *141*, 148–151. doi:10.1016/j.sbspro.2014.05.027

Bisquerra, R. (2003). Emotional education and basic life skills [Educación emocional y competencias básicas para la vida]. *Revista de Investigación Educacional*, *21*(1), 7–43.

Bisquerra, R. (2009). *Psychopedagogy of emotions* [Psicopedagogía de las emociones]. Editorial Síntesis.

Bisquerra, R. (2019). Universe of emotions: A didactic material for emotional education [Universo de emociones: un material didáctico para la educación emocional]. *Cuadernos de Pedagogía*, *499*, 105–111.

Bisquerra, R., & Pérez, N. (2007). Socio-emotional competences [Las competencias socioemocionales]. *Educacion XXI*, *10*, 61–82.

Biviano, T. (2017). Practical Lawyering: Intervention in Law School Curriculum Requirements to Prepare New Lawyers for Ethically Competent Practice. *The Georgetown Journal of Legal Ethics*, *30*, 619.

Bjekić, D., Obradović, S., & Bojović, M. (2020). The challenges for teachers: Augmented reality as educational technology for students with dyslexia. *8th International Scientific Conference Technics and Informatics in Education*, *43*(5), 40-49.

Blanco Fernández, J. (2017). *Evaluación de la motivación académica en niños de primer ciclo de educación infantil.* Available from DIALNET.

Blohm, I., & Leimeister, J. M. (2013). Gamification. *Wirtschaftsinformatik*, *55*(4), 275–278. doi:10.100711576-013-0368-0

Blohm, I., & Leimeister, J. M. (2013). Gamification: Design of IT-based enhancing services for motivational support and behavioral change. *Business & Information Systems Engineering*, *5*(4), 275–278. doi:10.100712599-013-0273-5

Blume, B. D., Ford, J. K., Baldwin, T. T., & Huang, J. L. (2010). Transfer of training: A meta-analytic review. *Journal of Management, 36*(4), 1065–1105. doi:10.1177/0149206309352880

BMJ Best Practice. (2020, March 20). *Medical education during the COVID-19 out-break.* The BMJ. https://bestpractice.bmj.com/info/covid-19/

Bobrysheva, N., Frolova, O., Kudryavtseva, V., & Moroz, O. (2021). *While Ashore: coursebook.* Helvetica PH.

Bock, J. G., Haque, Z., & McMahon, K. A. (2020). Displaced and dismayed: How ICTs are helping refugees and migrants, and how we can do better. *Information Technology for Development, 26*(4), 670–691. doi:10.1080/02681102.2020.1727827

Boeker, M., Andel, P., Vach, W., & Frankenschmidt, A. (2013). Game-based e-learning is more effective than a conventional instructional method: A randomized controlled trial with third-year medical students. *PLoS One, 8*(12), e82328. doi:10.1371/journal.pone.0082328 PMID:24349257

Bonani, A., Del Fatto, V., Dodero, G., Gennari, R., & Raimato, G. (2018). Participatory Design of Tangibles for Graphs: A Small-Scale Field Study with Children. In Ó. Mealha, M. Divitini, & M. Rehm (Eds.), *Citizen, Territory and Technologies: Smart Learning Contexts and Practices.* Springer. doi:10.1007/978-3-319-61322-2_16

Bonwell, C. C., & Eison, J. A. (1991). Active Learning: Creating Excitement in the Classroom. 1991 ASHE-ERIC Higher Education Reports. ERIC Clearinghouse on Higher Education, The George Washington University.

Bonwell, C. C., & Eison, J. A. (1991). *Active Learning: Creating Excitement in the Classroom.* ERIC Publications.

Boone, H. N. Jr, & Boone, D. A. (2012, April). Analyzing Likert Data. *Journal of Extension, 50*(2).

BOOST Creative Toolbox. (2019). Retrieved from https://shop.lego.com/en-GB/Creative-Toolbox-17101

Borrachero, A., Brígido, M., Costillo, E., Bermejo, M. L., & Mellado, V. (2013). Relationship between self-efficacy beliefs and emotions of future teachers of Physics in secondary education. *Asia-Pacific Forum on Science Learning and Teaching, 14*(2), 1–11.

Borrego, C., Fernández, C., Blanes, I., & Robles, S. (2017). Room escape at class: Escape games activities to facilitate the motivation and learning in computer science. *Journal of Technology and Science Education, 7*(2), 162. doi:10.3926/jotse.247

Boruchovitch, E., & Gomes, M. A. M. (2019). *Aprendizagem autorregulada: Como promovê-la no contexto educativo?* [Self-regulated learning: How to promote it in the educational context?]. Editora Vozes.

Borys, M., & Laskowski, M. (2013, June 19-21). *Implementing game elements into didactic process: A case study'* [Paper presentation]. Management, Knowledge and Learning International Conference. Zadar, Croatia. http://www.toknowpress.net/ISBN/978-961-6914-02-4/papers/ML13-326.pdf

Botha-Ravyse, C., Lennox, A., & Jordaan, D. (2018). Lessons learned from gamification of a learning experience: A case study. *S.A. Journal for Research in Sport Physical Education and Recreation, 40*(2), 23–40.

Botte, B., Bakkes, S., & Veltkamp, R. (2020). Motivation in Gamification: Constructing a Correlation Between Gamification Achievements and Self-determination Theory. *Lecture Notes in Computer Science, 12517*, 157–166. doi:10.1007/978-3-030-63464-3_15

Bourque, P., & Fairley, R. (2014) *Guide to the Software Engineering Body of Knowledge* (SWEBOK Version 3). IEEE Computer Society. www.swebok.org

Bowen, G. J., Wassenaar, L. I., & Hobson, K. A. (2005). Global application of stable hydrogen and oxygen isotopes to wildlife forensics. *Oecologia, 143*(3), 337–348. doi:10.100700442-004-1813-y PMID:15726429

Boyle, E., Connolly, T. M., & Hainey, T. (2011). The role of psychology in understanding the impact of computer games. *Entertainment Computing*, *2*(2), 69–74. doi:10.1016/j.entcom.2010.12.002

Boysen-Osborn, M., Paradise, S., & Suchard, J. (2018). The toxiscape hunt: An escape room-scavenger hunt for toxicology education. *Journal of Education and Teaching in Emergency Medicine*, *3*(1), 9–19. doi:10.5070/M531037616

Braad, E., Žavcer, G., & Sandovar, A. (2016). Processes and models for serious game design and development. In R. Dörner, S. Göbel, M. Kickmeier-Rust, M. Masuch, & K. Zweig (Eds.), *Entertainment computing and serious games* (pp. 92–118). Springer. doi:10.1007/978-3-319-46152-6_5

Brait, B. (2013). Olhar e ler: Verbo-visualidade em perspectiva dialógica [Looking and reading: verb-visuality in a dialogic perspective]. *Bakhtiniana*, *8*(2), 43–66. doi:10.1590/S2176-45732013000200004

Branch, R. M., & Dousay, T. A. (2015a). Survey of instructional design models. In D. R. Walling (Ed.), *Survey of Instructional Design Models* (5th ed.). Association for Educational Communications and Technology.

Bressoud, D., Carlson, M., Pearson, J. M., & Rasmussen, C. (2012). Preliminary results of the study on characteristics of successful programs in college calculus. *12th International Congress on Mathematics Education*, 8-15.

Breuer, J. S., & Bente, G. (2010). Why so serious? On the relation of serious games and learning. *Journal for Computer Game Culture*, *4*(1), 7–24. doi:10.7557/23.6111

Brezovszky, B., McMullen, J., Veermans, K., Hannula-Sormunen, M. M., Rodríguez-Aflecht, G., Pongsakdi, N., Laakkonen, E., & Lehtinen, E. (2019). Effects of a mathematics game-based learning environment on primary school students' adaptive number knowledge. *Computers & Education*, *128*, 63–74. doi:10.1016/j.compedu.2018.09.011

Bridgstock, R., Grant-Iramu, M., Bilsland, C., Tofa, M., Lloyd, K., & Jackson, D. (2019). Going beyond "getting a job": Graduates' narratives and lived experiences of employability and their career development. In Education for Employability (Volume 2) (pp. 89-104). Brill Sense.

Brígido, M., Borrachero, A. B., Bermejo, M. L., & Mellado, V. (2012). Prospective primary teachers' self-efficacy and emotions in science teaching. *European Journal of Teacher Education*, *1*, 1–18.

Brint, S., & Cantwell, A. M. (2014). Conceptualizing, Measuring, and Analyzing the Characteristics of Academically Disengaged Students: Results From UCUES 2010. *Journal of College Student Development*, *55*(8), 808–823. doi:10.1353/csd.2014.0080

Broadus, R. N. (1987). Toward a definition of "bibliometrics.". *Scientometrics*, *12*(5–6), 373–379. doi:10.1007/BF02016680

Broer, J. (2017). *The gamification inventory: An instrument for the qualitative evaluation of gamification and its application to learning management systems* Retrieved from https://9dok.org/document/6zkewnez-gamification-inventory-instrument-qualitative-evaluation-gamification-application-management.html

Broer, J. (2015). Is this new? Family Resemblances in Gamification in Education. *Bulletin of the Technical Committee on Learning Technology*, *17*(4), 14–17.

Brom, C., Preuss, M., & Klement, D. (2011). Are educational computer micro-games engaging and effective for knowledge acquisition at high-schools? A quasi-experimental study. *Computers & Education*, *57*(3), 1971–1988. doi:10.1016/j.compedu.2011.04.007

Brown, K. G., & Gerhardt, M. W. (2002). Formative evaluation: An integrative practice model and case study. *Personnel Psychology*, *55*(4), 951–983. doi:10.1111/j.1744-6570.2002.tb00137.x

Brown, N., Darby, W., Practitioner, N., Nurse, C., Coronel, H., & Practitioner, N. (2019). An Escape Room as a Simulation Teaching Strategy. *Clinical Simulation in Nursing*, *30*, 1–6. doi:10.1016/j.ecns.2019.02.002

Buasuwan, P. (2018). Rethinking Thai higher education for Thailand 4.0. *Asian Education and Development Studies*, *7*(2), 157–173. doi:10.1108/AEDS-07-2017-0072

Buckley, P., & Doyle, E. (2014). Gamification and student motivation. *Interactive Learning Environments*, *22*(6), 1–14.

Buckley, P., & Doyle, E. (2017). Individualising gamification: An investigation of the impact of learning styles and personality traits on the efficacy of gamification using a prediction market. *Computers & Education*, *106*, 43–55. doi:10.1016/j.compedu.2016.11.009

Bui, P., Rodríguez-Aflecht, G., Brezovszky, B., Hannula-Sormunen, M. M., Laato, S., & Lehtinen, E. (2020). Understanding students' game experiences throughout the developmental process of the number navigation game. *Educational Technology Research and Development*, *68*(5), 2395–2421. doi:10.100711423-020-09755-8

Bukvic, I. I., Cahoon, C., Wyatt, A., Cowden, T., & Dredger, K. (2014). OPERAcraft: Blurring the lines between real and virtual. *2014 ICM/SMC*. https://vtechworks.lib.vt.edu/handle/10919/106442

Bul, K. C., Doove, L. L., Franken, I. H., Oord, S. V. D., Kato, P. M., & Maras, A. (2018). A serious game for children with Attention Deficit Hyperactivity Disorder: Who benefits the most? *PLoS One*, *13*(3), e0193681. doi:10.1371/journal.pone.0193681 PMID:29543891

Bunchball, Inc. (2010). *Gamification 101: An introduction to the use of game dynamics to influence behavior*. Bunchball. Available at: http://jndglobal.com/wp-content/uploads/2011/05/gamification1011.pdf

Burchfield, R. W. (1972). A supplement to the Oxford English dictionary. Academic Press.

Burguillo, J. C. (2010). Using game theory and Competition-based Learning to stimulate student motivation and performance. *Computers & Education*, *55*(2), 566–575. doi:10.1016/j.compedu.2010.02.018

Busenitz, L. W., West, G. P. III, Shepherd, D., Nelson, T., Chandler, G. N., & Zacharakis, A. (2003). Entrepreneurship research in emergence: Past trends and future directions. *Journal of Management*, *29*(3), 285–308. doi:10.1016/S0149-2063(03)00013-8

Buser, T. (2014). *The impact of losing in a competition on the willingness to seek further challenges*. Social Science Research Network. doi:10.2139srn.2479837

Bussarello, R. I. (2016). *Gamification*. Pimenta Cultural.

Butler, Y. G., Someya, Y., & Fukuhara, E. (2014). Online games for young learners' foreign language learning. *ELT Journal*, *68*(3), 265–275. doi:10.1093/elt/ccu008

Buzady, Z. (2017). Flow, leadership and serious games – A pedagogical perspective. *World Journal of Science. Technology and Sustainable Development*, *14*(2–3), 204–217. doi:10.1108/WJSTSD-05-2016-0035

Cadieux, L., & Keenan, M. (2020). Can social communication skills for children diagnosed with autism spectrum disorder rehearsed inside the video game environment of Minecraft generalize to the real world? *JMIR Serious Games*, *8*(2), e14369. doi:10.2196/14369 PMID:32396129

Caillois, R., & Barash, M. (2001). *Man, play, and games*. University of Illinois Press.

Cain, J. (2018). Exploratory implementation of a blended format escape room in a large enrollment pharmacy management class. *Currents in Pharmacy Teaching & Learning*, *11*(1), 44–50. doi:10.1016/j.cptl.2018.09.010 PMID:30527875

Çakıroğlu, Ü., Başıbüyük, B., Güler, M., Atabay, M., & Memiş, B. Y. (2017). Gamifying an ICT course: Influences on engagement and academic performance. *Computers in Human Behavior*, *69*, 98–107. doi:10.1016/j.chb.2016.12.018

Calleja, G., & Callus, I. (2011). Game studies. In B. Clarke & M. Rossini (Eds.), *Routledge companion to literature and science* (pp. 323–334). Routledge. doi:10.4324/9780203848739.ch28

Calonge, A. (2013). Current state of the Geology Teaching, particulary the cristalography, mineralogy and petrology contents. *Seminarios SEM*, *10*, 22–35.

Calvillo-Gámez, E. H., Cairns, P., & Cox, A. L. (2015). Assessing the core elements of the gaming experience. In R. Berhnhaupt (Ed.), *Evaluating user experience in games* (pp. 47–71). doi:10.1007/978-3-319-15985-0_3

Calvo, S., Lafuente, R., Jiménez, J., Bruton, L., Pérez, S., & López-Royo, M. (2018). Room escape a transversal gamification strategy for Physiotherapy students, Edulearn 18. *10th International Conference on Education and New Learning Technology*, 4149-4154.

Cameron, B., & Dwyer, F. (2005). The effect of online gaming, cognition, and feedback type in facilitating delayed achievement of different learning objectives. *Journal of Interactive Learning Research*, *16*, 243–258.

Cameron, J., Banko, K. M., & Pierce, W. D. (2001). Pervasive Negative Effects of Rewards on Intrinsic Motivation: The Myth Continues. *The Behavior Analyst*, *24*(1), 1–44. doi:10.1007/BF03392017 PMID:22478353

Campayo–Munoz, E., & Cabedo–Mas, A. (2017). The role of emotional skills in music education. *British Journal of Music Education*, *34*(3), 243–258. doi:10.1017/S0265051717000067

Campbell, J. (1949). *The Hero with a Thousand Faces*. Princeton University Press.

Campbell, J. (2018). *Sociology & Education*. Scientific e-Resources.

Campbell, P. S. (2010). *Songs in their heads: Music and its meaning in children's lives*. Oxford University Press.

Campillo-Ferrer, J. M., Miralles-Martínez, P., & Sánchez-Ibáñez, R. (2020). Gamification in higher education: Impact on student motivation and the acquisition of social and civic key competencies. *Sustainability*, *12*(12), 4822. doi:10.3390u12124822

Camurri, A., Volpe, G., Canazza, S., Canepa, C., Roda, A., Zanolla, S., & Foresti, G. L. (2010). The 'Stanza Logo–Motoria': an interactive environment for learning and communication. In *Proceedings of SMC Conference* (*Vol. 51*, No. 8). Academic Press.

Cañada-Cañada, F., Hernández-Barco, M. A., Sánchez-Martín, J., & Corbacho-Cuello, I. (2021). Estudo comparativo das diferentes estratégias de aprendizagem baseada em jogos: Rendimento emocional dos professores em formação durante a aprendizagem das ciências. *Revista Internacional de Pesquisa em Didática das Ciências e Matemática*, *2*, 1–25.

CanSat. (2021). *Homepage*. Available at https://www.esa.int/Education/CanSat

Capatina, A., Bleoju, G., Rancati, E., & Hoareau, E. (2018). Tracking precursors of learning analytics over serious game team performance ranking. *Behaviour & Information Technology*, *37*(10/11), 1008–1020. doi:10.1080/0144929X.2018.1474949

Caponetto, I., Earp, J., & Ott, M. (2014, October). Gamification and education: A literature review. In *European Conference on Games Based Learning* (*Vol. 1*, p. 50). Academic Conferences International Limited.

I. Caponetto, J. Earp, M. Ott, & C. Busch (Eds.). (2014). Gamification and Education: a Literature Review. *Proceedings of the 8th European Conference on Games-Based Learning.*

Cardinale Nunes Menezes, C., & De Bortolli, R. (2016). Potential of gamification as assessment tool. *Creative Education, 7*(4), 561–566. doi:10.4236/ce.2016.74058

Carini, R. M., Kuh, G. D., & Klein, S. P. (2006). Student engagement and student learning: Testing the linkages. *Research in Higher Education, 47*(1), 1–32. doi:10.100711162-005-8150-9

Carmona, E., & Cardeñoso, J. M. (2019). Situations based on board games to attend to the elaboration of school mathematical knowledge [Situaciones basadas en juegos de mesa para atender la elaboración del conocimiento matematico escolar]. *Épsilon, 101*, 7–30.

Carmona-Halty, M., Salanova, M., Llorens, S., & Schaufeli, W. B. (2019). Linking positive emotions and academic performance: The mediated role of academic psychological capital and academic engagement. *Current Psychology (New Brunswick, N.J.)*, 1–10.

Carranza, D. B., Negrón, A., & Contreras, M. (2021). Videogame development training approach: A virtual reality and open-source perspective. *Journal of Universal Computer Science, 27*(2), 152–169. doi:10.3897/jucs.65164

Carrillo, L. (1996). Los problemas prácticos en Geología: Problemas, posibilidades y propuestas. *Enseñanza de las Ciencias de la Tierra, 4*(2), 120–123.

Carrillo, L., Luzón, M. A., Mayayo, M. J., Soria, A. R., Yuste, A., & Gil, A. (2018). Resolviendo un asesinato: Una experiencia con la Geología Forense como estrategia de enseñanza-aprendizaje en la Educación Secundaria. *Enseñanza de las Ciencias de la Tierra, 26*(2), 163–175.

Carrion Candel, E. (2019). The use of the game and the cooperative Methodology in Highet Educatio: An alternative for creative teaching. *Artseduca*, (23), 70–97. doi:10.6035/Artseduca.2019.23.4

Carty, E. (2010). Educating Midwives with the World's first simulator: Madame du Coudray's eighteenth century mannequin. *Revue Canadienne de la Recherche et de la Pratique Sage-femme, 9*(1). https://www.cjmrp.com/files/v9n1_carty_ducou dray.pdf

Caruso, J. V. (2019, March). Using Business Simulations to Prepare Students to Think Critically, Make Better Decisions, and Solve Business Problems. In *Developments in Business Simulation and Experiential Learning: Proceedings of the Annual ABSEL conference* (*Vol. 46*). Academic Press.

Carvalho, J. D., Fernandes, S., Lima, R. M., & Mesquita, D. (2018). *Making PBL teams more effective with Scrum.* University of Minho. http://hdl.handle.net/1822/66529

Casanoves, M., Salvadó, Z., González, A., Valls, C., & Novo, M. T. (2017). Learning genetics through a scientific inquiry game. *Journal of Biological Education, 51*(2), 99–106. doi:10.1080/00219266.2016.1177569

Casas, N., Maguregi, G., Zamalloa, T., Echevarría, I., Fernández, M., & Sanz, J. (2016). Las salidas de campo y la Geología. El perfil académico y la actitud del profesorado de la ESO en la CAPV. *Enseñanza de las Ciencias de la Tierra, 24*(2), 213–220.

Castaneda-Vazquez, C., Espejo-Garces, T., Zurita-Ortega, F., & Fernandez-Revelles, A. B. (2019). Physical education's teacher training program through gaming, ict and continuous assessment. *Sport Tk-Revista Euroamericana De Ciencias Del Deporte, 8*(2), 55–63. doi:10.6018portk.391751

Castaño-Muñoz, J., Colucci, E., & Smidt, H. (2018). Free digital learning for inclusion of migrants and refugees in Europe: A qualitative analysis of three types of learning purposes. *International Review of Research in Open and Distributed Learning, 19*(2). Advance online publication. doi:10.19173/irrodl.v19i2.3382

Castillo, E. (1994). El Rocopoly, un recurso didáctico para la enseñanza de la petrología. *Enseñanza de las Ciencias de la Tierra*, *2*(1), 280–281.

Center for Educational Innovation – CEI. (n.d.). *University of Minnesota*. https://cei.umn.edu/active-learning

Cerasoli, C. P., Nicklin, J. M., & Ford, M. T. (2014). Intrinsic motivation and extrinsic incentives jointly predict performance: A 40-year meta-analysis. *Psychological Bulletin*, *140*(4), 980–1008. doi:10.1037/a0035661 PMID:24491020

Ceschin, F., & Gaziulusoy, I. (2016). Evolution of design for sustainability: From product design to design for system innovations and transitions. *Design Studies*, *47*, 118–163. doi:10.1016/j.destud.2016.09.002

Cezar, V., Garcia, P., Botelho, V., & Miletto, E. (2019). Towards an RPG game to teach calculus. In *2019 IEEE 19th International Conference on Advanced Learning Technologies (ICALT)* (pp. 116-118). 10.1109/ICALT.2019.00037

Chacksfield, M. (2009). US army spends $32.8 million on propaganda videogame. *TechRadar*. https://www.techradar.com/news/gaming/us-army-spends-32-8-million-on-propaganda-videogame-657121

Chair, C., & De Lannoy, A. (2018). *Youth, deprivation and the internet in Africa*. Https://researchictafrica.net/after-access-survey-papers/2018/After_Access:_youth_ and_digital_inequality_in_Africa.pdf

Chaitrong, W. (2020, August 3). Clash of old and new values: Is Thailand heading for a big change? *The Nation Thailand*. https://www.nationthailand.com/perspective/30392327

Chamorro-Premuzic, T., & Frankiewicz, B. (2019). Does higher education still prepare people for jobs. *Harvard Business Review*, 7.

Chamoso, J. M., Durán, J., García, J., Martínez, J., & Rodríguez-Sánchez, M. (2004). Analysis and experimentation of games as instruments to teach mathematics [Análisis y experimentación de juegos como instrumentos para enseñar matemáticas]. *Suma, 47*, 47–58. http://revistasuma.es/IMG/pdf/47/047-058.pdf

Chang, C.-C., Lin, C.-Y., Chen, Y.-C., & Chin, Y.-C. (2009). Predicting information-seeking intention in academic digital libraries. *The Electronic Library*, *27*(3), 448–460. doi:10.1108/02640470910966899

Chang, H. (2016). Autoethnography. In *Autoethnography as method* (pp. 43–58). Routledge. doi:10.4324/9781315433370

Chang, H., Ngunjiri, F., & Hernandez, K. A. C. (2016). *Collaborative autoethnography* (Vol. 8). Routledge. doi:10.4324/9781315432137

Chang, J., Lee, M., Ng, K. L., & Moon, K. L. (2003). Business simulation games: The Hong Kong experience. *Simulation & Gaming*, *34*(3), 367–376. doi:10.1177/1046878103255877

Chan, K. H. W., Wan, K., & King, V. (2021). Performance over enjoyment? Effect of game-based learning on learning outcome and flow experience. *Frontiers in Education*, *6*, 1–10. doi:10.3389/feduc.2021.660376

Chau, M., Wong, A., Wang, M., Lai, S., Chan, K. W. Y., Li, T. M. H., Chu, D., Chan, I. K. W., & Sung, W. (2013). Using 3D virtual environments to facilitate students in constructivist learning. *Decision Support Systems*, *56*, 115–121. doi:10.1016/j.dss.2013.05.009

Chawla, K., Chiou, M., Sandes, A., & Blikstein, P. (2013). Dr. Wagon: a 'stretchable' toolkit for tangible computer programming. In *Proceedings of the 12th international conference on interaction design and children* (pp. 561-564). ACM. 10.1145/2485760.2485865

Chen, H. H. (2005). *A formative evaluation of the training effectiveness of a computer game* [Unpublished doctoral dissertation, University of Southern California]. https://www.proquest.com/openview/5126be19de8d9deae152bf5514fcf2bb/1?pq-origsite=gscholar&cbl=18750&diss=y

Cheng, E. W., & Hampson, I. (2008). Transfer of training: A review and new insights. *International Journal of Management Reviews, 10*(4), 327–341. doi:10.1111/j.1468-2370.2007.00230.x

Chen, J. (2007). Flow in games (and everything else). *Communications of the ACM, 50*(4), 31–34. doi:10.1145/1232743.1232769

Chen, M.-B. (2021). The development of a two-level cardboard game tool. *Zhongguo Gongcheng Xuekan, 44*(5), 448–454. doi:10.1080/02533839.2021.1919559

Chen, X., Zou, D., Cheng, G., & Xie, H. (2020). Detecting latent topics and trends in educational technologies over four decades using structural topic modeling: A retrospective of all volumes of Computers & Education. *Computers & Education, 151*, 103855. doi:10.1016/j.compedu.2020.103855

Chen, Z. H. (2014). Learning preferences and motivation of different ability students for social-competition or self-competition. *Journal of Educational Technology & Society, 17*(1), 283–293.

Cheong, C., Cheong, F., & Filippou, J. (2013). Quick quiz: A gamified approach for enhancing learning. In *Proceedings of PACIS 2013* (paper 206). Academic Press.

Cheong, C., Cheong, F., & Filippou, J. (2013). Quick Quiz: A Gamified Approach for Enhancing Learning. *PACIS 2013 Proceedings*, 1–14.

Chernikova, O., Heitzmann, N., Stadler, M., Holzberger, D., Seidel, T., & Fischer, F. (2020). Simulation-based learning in higher education: A meta-analysis. *Review of Educational Research, 90*(4), 499–541. doi:10.3102/0034654320933544

Chia, A., Hung, Y., Zarco, E., Yang, M., Dembicki, D., & Kase, M. (2017). Gamification in the wild: Faculty perspectives on gamifying learning in higher education. *Issues and Trends in Educational Technology*, *5*(2), 4–22.

Choi, H. S., Lee, W. S., & Sohn, S. Y. (2017). Analyzing research trends in personal information privacy using topic modeling. *Computers & Security, 67*, 244–253. doi:10.1016/j.cose.2017.03.007

Chotiratanapinun, T. (2018). *Transformative learning for a shift towards sustainability in Thailand's design education* [Doctoral thesis, Goldsmiths, University of London]. http://research.gold.ac.uk/id/eprint/23309

Chou, Y. (2013). *Explicit vs Implicit Gamification: How to Define Gamified Design.* https://www.gamification.co/2013/04/09/explicit-vs-implicit-gamification/

Chou, Y. (2015). *Learn gamification — The cheat codes to win the game of life.* Retrieved from https://yukaichou.com/

Chou, Y.-K. (2016). Actionable gamification: Beyond points, badges, and leaderboards. Octalysis Media.

Choudaha, R., & Van Rest, E. (2018). *Envisioning Pathways to 2030: Megatrends Shaping the Future of Global Higher Education and International Student Mobility*. ERIC.

Chou, S.-W., & Liu, C.-H. (2005). Learning effectiveness in a Web-based virtual learning environment: A learner control perspective. *Journal of Computer Assisted Learning, 21*(1), 65–76. doi:10.1111/j.1365-2729.2005.00114.x

Chou, Y. (2015). *Actionable gamification: Beyond points, badges, and leaderboards*. Octalysis Group.

Chou, Y. K. (2015). *Actionable Gamification Beyond Points, Badges, and Leaderboards*. Octalysis Media.

Christopher, L., & Waworuntu, A. (2021). Java programming language learning application based on Octalysis gamification framework. *International Journal of New Media Technology, 8*(1), 65–69. doi:10.31937/ijnmt.v8i1.2049

Christy, K. R., & Fox, J. (2014). Leaderboards in a virtual classroom: A test of stereotype threat and social comparison explanations for women's math performance. *Computers & Education, 78*, 66–77. doi:10.1016/j.compedu.2014.05.005

Church, K., & Smyth, B. (2009). Understanding the intent behind mobile information needs. *Proceedings of the 14th International Conference on Intelligent User Interfaces*, 247–256. 10.1145/1502650.1502686

Cilesiz, S. (2009). Educational computer use in leisure contexts: A phenomenological study of adolescents' experiences at internet cafes. *American Educational Research Journal*, *46*(1), 232–274. doi:10.3102/0002831208323938

Ćirić, D., & Gračanin, D. (2017). Agile project management beyond software industry. In *proceedings of the XV international scientific conference on industrial systems* (pp. 332–337). Novi Sad: Faculty of Technical Sciences.

Civil Air Patrol. (2022). https://www.gocivilairpatrol.com/

Clark, R. E. (2001). *Learning from media: Arguments, analysis, and evidence*. Information Age. https://psycnet.apa.org/record/2012-18168-000

Clarke, S., Arnab, S., Morini, L., Wood, O., Green, K., Masters, A., & Bourazeri, A. (2016, October). EscapED: A framework for creating live-action, interactive games for higher/further education learning and soft skills development. In *Proceedings of the 10th European conference on Games Based Learning, ECGBL* (pp. 968-672). Academic Press.

Clarke, S., Peel, D. J., Arnab, S., Morini, L., Keegan, H., & Wood, O. (2017). escapED: A framework for creating educational escape rooms and Interactive Games For Higher/Further Education. *International Journal of Serious Games*, *4*(3), 73–86. doi:10.17083/ijsg.v4i3.180

Clark, R. E. (1983). Reconsidering research on learning from media. *Review of Educational Research*, *53*(4), 445–459. doi:10.3102/00346543053004445

Clark, R. E. (1985). Confounding in educational computing research. *Journal of Educational Computing Research*, *1*(2), 137–148. doi:10.2190/HC3L-G6YD-BAK9-EQB5

Clark, R. E. (1994). Media will never influence learning. *Educational Technology Research and Development*, *42*(2), 21–29. doi:10.1007/BF02299088

Clark, R. E. (2007). Learning from serious games? Arguments, evidence, and research suggestions. *Educational Technology*, *47*(3), 56–59. https://www.jstor.org/stable/44429512

Clauson, A., Hahn, L., Frame, T., Hagan, A., Bynum, L. A., Thompson, M. E., & Kiningham, K. (2019). An innovative escape room activity to assess student readiness for advanced pharmacy practice experiences (APPEs). *Currents in Pharmacy Teaching & Learning*, *11*(7), 723–728. doi:10.1016/j.cptl.2019.03.011 PMID:31227096

Clegg, S., Tan, J., & Saeidi, S. (2010). *Reflecting or Acting? Reflective Practice and Continuing Professional Development in Higher Education.* doi:10.1080/14623940220129924

Clements, D. H. (2000). 'Concrete' Manipulatives, Concrete Ideas. *Contemporary Issues in Early Childhood*, *1*(1), 45–60. doi:10.2304/ciec.2000.1.1.7

Clements, D. H., & Sarama, J. (2014). *Learning and teaching early math: The learning trajectories approach*. Routledge. doi:10.4324/9780203520574

Climate Detectives. (2022). https://climatedetectives.esa.int/

Clouse, V. G. (1990). A controlled experiment relating entrepreneurial education to students' start-up decisions. *Journal of Small Business Management*, *28*(2), 45.

Code Master™ - ThinkFun. (2019). Retrieved from ttps://www.thinkfun.com/products/code-master/1074

codeCampus. (2019). Retrieved from http://codemonkeyplanet.com/

Coding for Beginners. (2019). *STEM for Girls*. Retrieved from https://www.smartgurlz.com/

Codish, D., & Ravid, G. (2014). Academic Course Gamification: The Art of Perceived Playfulness. *Interdisciplinary Journal of E-Learning and Learning Objects*, *10*, 131–151. doi:10.28945/2066

Codish, D., & Ravid, G. (2014). Personality based gamification-Educational gamification for extroverts and introverts. In *Proceedings of the 9th CHAIS Conference for the Study of Innovation and Learning Technologies: Learning in the Technological Era* (Vol. 1, pp. 36-44). Ra'anana: The Open University of Israel.

Cohen, K. J., & Rhenman, E. (1961). The role of management games in education and research. *Management Science*, *7*(2), 101–194. doi:10.1287/mnsc.7.2.131

Colace, F., De Santo, M., & Pietrosanto, A. (2006). Work in Progress: Bayesian Networks for Edutainment. *36th ASEE/IEEE Frontiers in Education Conference*.

Cole, H., & Griffiths, M. D. (2007). Social interactions in massively multiplayer online role-playing gamers. *Cyberpsychology & Behavior*, *10*(4), 575–583. doi:10.1089/cpb.2007.9988 PMID:17711367

Coll, C. (1998). Significado y sentido en el aprendizaje escolar. Reflexiones en torno al concepto de aprendizaje significativo. *Infancia y Aprendizaje*, *11*(41), 131–142. doi:10.1080/02103702.1988.10822196

Coller, B. D., & Shernoff, D. J. (2009). Video game-based education in mechanical engineering: A look at student engagement. *International Journal of Engineering Education*, *25*(2), 308–317. https://www.ijee.ie/contents/c250209.html

Compeau, D., Gravill, J., Haggerty, N., & Kelley, H. (2006). Computer Self-Efficacy: A Review. Human-Computer Interaction in Management Information Systems: Foundations, 225-261.

Connolly, T. M., Boyle, E. A., MacArthur, E., Hainey, T., & Boyle, J. (2012). A systematic literature review of empirical evidence on computer games and serious games. *Computer Education*, *59*(2), 661–686. doi:10.1016/j.compedu.2012.03.004

Conrad, C. E., & Tucker, C. S. (2019). The effects of player type on performance: A gamification case study. *Computers in Human Behavior*, *91*, 333–345. doi:10.1016/j.chb.2018.10.005

Cook, D., Fulton, B., Gonzales, J., Bialoskursky, Y., & Fitch, M. (2016). *Game Design Patterns that Facilitate Strangers Becoming "Friends"* (The Eleventh Annual Game Design Think Tank: Project Horseshoe, 2016). Fat Labs Inc.

Cooper, I. D. (2015). Bibliometrics basics. *Journal of the Medical Library Association: JMLA*, *103*(4), 217–218. doi:10.3163/1536-5050.103.4.013 PMID:26512226

Coorey, J. (2016). Active learning methods and technology: Strategies for design education. *International Journal of Art & Design Education*, *35*(3), 337–347. doi:10.1111/jade.12112

Corbett, S. (2010, September 19). *Learning by playing: Video games in the classroom*. Retrieved from: https://www.nytimes.com/2010/09/19/magazine/19video-t.html

Cordova, D. L., & Lepper, M. R. (1996). Intrinsic motivation and the process of learning: Beneficial effects of contextualization, personalization, and choice. *Journal of Educational Psychology*, *88*(4), 715–730. doi:10.1037/0022-0663.88.4.715

Cornellà, P., Estebanell, M., & Brusi, D. (2020). Gamificación y aprendizaje basado en juegos. Consideraciones generales y algunos ejemplos para la Enseñanza de la Geología. *Enseñanza de las Ciencias de la Tierra*, *28*(1), 5–19.

Cornellà, P., Estebanell, M., & Brusi, D. (2020). Gamification and game-based learning. General considerations and some examples for the Teaching of Geology [Gamificación y aprendizaje basado en juegos. Consideraciones generales y algunos ejemplos para la Enseñanza de la Geología]. *Enseñanza de las Ciencias de la Tierra*, *28*(1), 5–19.

Costello, R., & Lambert, M. (2019). Motivational influences for higher education (HE) students. *International Journal of Online Pedagogy and Course Design*, *9*(1), 38–50. doi:10.4018/IJOPCD.2019010103

Courteille, O., Bergin, R., Courteille, O., Bergin, R., Stockeld, D., Ponzer, S., & Fors, U. (2008). The use of a virtual patient case in an OSCE-based exam–a pilot study. *Medical Teacher*, *30*(3), e66–e76. doi:10.1080/01421590801910216 PMID:18484444

Coutinho, C. P., & Lisbôa, E. S. (2011). Sociedade da informação, do conhecimento e da aprendizagem: Desafios para educação no século XXI [Information, knowledge and learning society: Challenges for education in the 21st century]. *Review of Education*, *18*(1), 5–22.

Cover, J. G. (2014). *The creation of narrative in tabletop role-playing games*. McFarland.

Cowley, B., Moutinho, J. L., Bateman, C., & Oliveira, A. (2011). Learning principles and interaction design for 'Green My Place': A massively multiplayer serious game. *Entertainment Computing*, *2*(2), 103–113. doi:10.1016/j.entcom.2011.01.001

Crawford, C. (2011). *The Art of Computer Game Design*. McGraw Hill Osborne Media.

Crecente-Romero, F., Giménez-Baldazo, M., & Rivera-Galicia, L. F. (2016). Subjective perception of entrepreneurship. Differences among countries. *Journal of Business Research*, *69*(11), 5158–5162. doi:10.1016/j.jbusres.2016.04.097

Crepaldi, M., Colombo, V., Mottura, S., Baldassini, D., Sacco, M., & Antonietti, A. (2020). Antonyms: A computer game to improve inhibitory control of impulsivity in children with attention deficit/hyperactivity disorder (ADHD). *Information (Basel)*, *11*(4), 230. doi:10.3390/info11040230

Cronk, M. (2012). Using Gamification to Increase Student Engagement and Participation in Class Discussion. In T. Amiel & B. Wilson (Eds.), *Proceedings of EdMedia 2012--World Conference on Educational Media and Technology* (pp. 311-315). Association for the Advancement of Computing in Education (AACE).

Crookall, D., & Thorngate, W. (2009). Acting, knowing, learning, simulating, gaming. *Simulation & Gaming*, *40*(1), 8–26. doi:10.1177/1046878108330364

Crujeiras, B. P., & Jiménez, M. P. (2015). Challenges posed by open research activities in the laboratory: Articulation of theoretical and practical knowledge in scientific practices [Desafíos planteados por las actividades abiertas de indagación en el laboratorio: articulación de conocimientos teóricos y prácticos en las prácticas científicas]. *Enseñanza de las Ciencias*, *33*(1), 63–84.

Cruz, C., Hanus, M. D., & Fox, J. (2017). The need to achieve: Players' perceptions and uses of extrinsic meta-game reward systems for video game consoles. *Computers in Human Behavior*, *71*, 516–524. doi:10.1016/j.chb.2015.08.017

Csikszentmihalyi, M. (1990). *Flow: The psychology of optimal experience*. Harper Perennial.

Csikszentmihalyi, M. (1990). *Flow: The Psychology of Optimal Experience*. Herper Perennial.

Csikszentmihalyi, M. (2008). *Flow: the psychology of optimal experience*. Harper & Row.

Csikszentmihalyi, M. (2014). *Flow and the Foundations of Positive Psychology*. Springer. doi:10.1007/978-94-017-9088-8

Csikszentmihalyi, M. (2020). *Finding Flow: The Psychology of Engagement with Everyday Life*. Basic Books.

Cubetto: A toy robot teaching kids code & computer programming. (2019). Retrieved from https://www.primotoys.com

Cunha, M. I. D. (2008). Inovações pedagógicas: O desafio da reconfiguração de saberes na docência universitária [Pedagogical innovations: The challenge of reconfiguration of knowledge in university teaching]. *Cadernos de Pedagogia Universitária*, *6*, 1–41.

Curtin, R., Presser, S., & Singer, E. (2000). The effects of response rate changes on the index of consumer sentiment. *Public Opinion Quarterly*, *64*, 413–428. doi:10.1086/318638 PMID:11171024

Ćwil, M. (2020). *Leaderboards – A motivational tool in the process of business education* (M. Ma, B. Fletcher, S. Gobel, J. Baalsrud Hauge, & T. Marsh, Eds.). Springer Science and Business Media Deutschland GmbH. doi:10.1007/978-3-030-61814-8_15

Cyders, T., & Hilterbran, A. (2016). *Classroom integration of the Slack team collaboration tool*. Academic Press.

Czerwinski, M., Horvitz, E., & Wilhite, S. (2004). A diary study of task switching and interruptions. *Proceedings of the SIGCHI Conference on Human Factors in Computing Systems*, 175–182. 10.1145/985692.985715

da Rocha Seixas, L., Gomes, A. S., & de Melo Filho, I. J. (2016). Effectiveness of gamification in the engagement of students. *Computers in Human Behavior*, *58*, 48–63. doi:10.1016/j.chb.2015.11.021

Daly, S. P. (2001). Student-operated Internet businesses: True experiential learning in entrepreneurship and retail management. *Journal of Marketing Education*, *23*(3), 204–215. doi:10.1177/0273475301233006

Danner, F. W., & Lonky, E. (1981). A Cognitive-Developmental Approach to the Effects of Rewards on Intrinsic Motivation. *Child Development*, *52*(3), 1043–1052. doi:10.2307/1129110

Darejeh, A., & Salim, S. S. (2016). Gamification solutions to enhance software user engagement—A systematic review. *International Journal of Human-Computer Interaction*, *32*(8), 613–642. doi:10.1080/10447318.2016.1183330

Dávila-Acedo, M. A. (2017). Emotions and their causes in the learning of Physics and Chemistry, in the students of Secondary Education [Las emociones y sus causas en el aprendizaje de Física y Química, en el alumnado de Educación Secundaria]. *Revista Eureka Sobre Enseñanza y Divulgación de las Ciencias*, *14*(3), 570–586.

Dávila-Acedo, M. A. (2018). *Emotions in the learning of physics and chemistry in secondary school students. An emotional intervention program* [Las emociones en el aprendizaje de física y química en el alumnado de educación secundaria. Un programa de intervención emocional]. Universidad de Extremadura.

Dávila-Acedo, M. A., Borrachero, A. B., Cañada-Cañada, F., Martínez-Borreguero, G., & Sánchez-Martín, J. (2015). Evolution of the emotions experienced by students of the degree of teacher in primary education, in didactics of the subject and energy [Evolución de las emociones que experimentan los estudiantes del grado de maestro en educación primaria, en didáctica de la materia y la energía]. *Revista Eureka Sobre Enseñanza y Divulgación de Las Ciencias*, *12*(3), 550–564.

Dávila-Acedo, M. A., Cañada-Cañada, F., Sánchez, J., & Mellado, V. (2016). Emotions in learning physics and chemistry in secondary education [Las emociones en el aprendizaje de física y química en educación secundaria]. *Causas relacionadas con el estudiante. Educación en la Química*, *27*(3), 217–225.

Dávila-Acedo, M. A., Cañada-Cañada, F., Sánchez-Martín, J., Airado-Rodríguez, D., & Mellado, V. (2021). Emotional performance on physics and chemistry learning: The case of Spanish K-9 and K-10 students. *International Journal of Science Education*, *43*(6), 1–21. doi:10.1080/09500693.2021.1889069

De Caprariis, P., Barman, C., & Magee, P. (2001). Monitoring the benefits of active learning exercises in introductory survey courses in science: An attempt to improve the education of prospective public school teachers. *The Journal of Scholarship of Teaching and Learning*, *1*(2), 13.

de Castell, S., & Jenson, J. (2003). Serious play. *Journal of Curriculum Studies*, *35*(6), 649–665. doi:10.1080/0022027032000145552

De Freitas, S. (2006). Learning in Immersive worlds A review of game-based learning. *JISC ELearning Innovation*, *3.3*(October), 73. doi:10.1111/j.1467-8535.2009.01024.x de Freitas, S. (2013). *Learning in immersive worlds: A review of game-based learning*. https://www.jisc.ac.uk/media/documents/programmes/elearninginnovation/gamingreport_v3.pdfhttp://curve.coventry.ac.uk/open

de Freitas, S. (2018). Are games effective learning tools? A review of educational games. *Journal of Educational Technology & Society, 21*(2), 74–84.

de Freitas, S., & Jarvis, S. (2007). Serious games engaging training solutions: A research and development project for supporting training needs. *British Journal of Educational Technology, 38*(3), 523–525. doi:10.1111/j.1467-8535.2007.00716.x

De Gloria, A., Bellotti, F., & Berta, R. (2014). Serious games for education and training. *International Journal of Serious Games, 1*(1), 1–15. doi:10.17083/ijsg.v1i1.11

de Klerk, S., & Kato, P. M. (2017). The future value of serious games for assessment: Where do we go now? *Journal of Applied Testing Technology, 18*(S1), 32–37.

De Kort, Y. A., & Ijsselsteijn, W. A. (2008). People, places, and play: Player experience in a socio-spatial context. *Computers in Entertainment, 6*(2), 1–11. doi:10.1145/1371216.1371221

de la Peña, D., Lizcano, D., & Martínez-Álvarez, I. (2021). Learning through play: Gamification model in university-level distance learning. *Entertainment Computing, 39*, 100430. Advance online publication. doi:10.1016/j.entcom.2021.100430

de Oliveira, A. M., & Silva, S. (2020). A boss in higher education: Enunciative look at gamification in the teaching of textual genres [Um chefão no ensino superior: olhar enunciativo sobre a gamificação no ensino de gêneros textuais]. *Revista Docência do Ensino Superior, 10*, 1–20. doi:10.35699/2237-5864.2020.14942

de Sousa Borges, S., Durelli, V. H. S., Macedo Reis, H., & Isotani, S. (2014). A systematic mapping on gamification applied to education. In *Proceedings of the 29th Annual ACM Symposium on Applied Computing* (pp. 216-222). 10.1145/2554850.2554956

De Souza Sombrio, G., Schimmelpfeng, L. E., & Ulbricht, V. R. (2016, October). The production of a gamified learning object accessible to people with visual or hearing disabilities for teaching geometry. In *2016 XI Latin American Conference on Learning Objects and Technology (LACLO)* (pp. 1-10). IEEE. 10.1109/LACLO.2016.7751787

De Souza, A. D., Seabra, R. D., Ribeiro, J. M., & Rodrigues, L. E. D. S. (2017, May). SCRUMI: a board serious virtual game for teaching the SCRUM framework. In *2017 IEEE/ACM 39th International Conference on Software Engineering Companion (ICSE-C)* (pp. 319-321). IEEE. 10.1109/ICSE-C.2017.124

Dec Graduate Exhibition. (2019, May 10). *Board game design for instructing visually-impaired children and peers about Braille blocks*. Facebook. https://www.facebook.com/1090561811128660/photos/a.1111302605721247/1111304399054401/?comment_id=1112929428891898

Deci, E. L., Koestner, R., & Ryan, R. M. (1999). A meta-analytic review of experiments examining the effects of extrinsic rewards on intrinsic motivation. *Psychological Bulletin, 125*(6), 627–668. doi:10.1037/0033-2909.125.6.627 PMID:10589297

Deci, E. L., Koestner, R., & Ryan, R. M. (2001). Extrinsic Rewards and Intrinsic Motivation in Education: Reconsidered Once Again. *Review of Educational Research, 71*(1), 1–27. doi:10.3102/00346543071001001

Deci, E. L., & Ryan, R. M. (1985). *Intrinsic motivation and self-determination in human behavior*. Plenum Press. doi:10.1007/978-1-4899-2271-7

Deci, E. L., & Ryan, R. M. (1985). The general causality orientations scale: Self-determination in personality. *Journal of Research in Personality, 19*(2), 109–134. doi:10.1016/0092-6566(85)90023-6

Deci, E. L., & Ryan, R. M. (2002). Overview of self-determination theory: An organismic dialectical perspective. In E. L. Deci & R. M. Ryan (Eds.), *Handbook of self-determination research* (pp. 3–33). University Rochester Press.

Deci, E. L., & Ryan, R. M. (2004). *Handbook of self-determination research.* University Rochester Press.

Deci, E. L., & Ryan, R. M. (2008). Self-determination theory: A macrotheory of human motivation, development, and health. *Canadian Psychology, 49*(3), 182–185. doi:10.1037/a0012801

Deci, E. L., & Ryan, R. M. (2015). Self-determination theory. In J. D. Wright (Ed.), *International Encyclopedia of the Social & Behavioral Sciences* (2nd ed., Vol. 21, p. 486). Elsevier. doi:10.1016/B978-0-08-097086-8.26036-4

Deci, E. L., Ryan, R. M., Gagné, M., Leone, D. R., Usunov, J., & Kornazheva, B. P. (2001). Need satisfaction, motivation, and well-being in the work organizations of a former eastern bloc country: A cross-cultural study of self-determination. *Personality and Social Psychology Bulletin, 27*(8), 930–942. doi:10.1177/0146167201278002

Delamont, S. (2009). The only honest thing: Autoethnography, reflexivity and small crises in fieldwork. *Ethnography and Education, 4*(1), 51–63. doi:10.1080/17457820802703507

Delany, C., & Golding, C. (2014). Teaching clinical reasoning by making thinking visible: An action research project with allied health clinical educators. *BMC Medical Education, 14*(1), 20. Advance online publication. doi:10.1186/1472-6920-14-20 PMID:24479414

de-Marcos, L., Domínguez, A., Saenz-de-Navarrete, J., & Pagés, C. (2014). An empirical study comparing gamification and social networking on e-learning. *Computers & Education, 75*, 82–91. doi:10.1016/j.compedu.2014.01.012

De-Marcos, L., García-Cabot, A., & García-López, E. (2017). Towards the Social Gamification of e-Learning: A Practical Experiment. *International Journal of Engineering Education, 1*, 1–14. https://portal.uah.es/portal/page/portal/epd2_profesores/prof23288/publicaciones/0PaperSocialGamificationv5.4_IJEE_preprint.pdf

Demkah, M., & Bhargava, D. (2019). Gamification in education: a cognitive psychology approach to cooperative and fun learning. *Proceedings - 2019 Amity International Conference on Artificial Intelligence.* 10.1109/AICAI.2019.8701264

Denden, M., Tlili, A., Essalmi, F., Jemni, M., Chen, N., & Burgos, D. (2021). Effects of gender and personality differences on students' perception of game design elements in educational gamification. *International Journal of Human-Computer Studies, 154*, 102674. Advance online publication. doi:10.1016/j.ijhcs.2021.102674

Denny, P. (2013). The effect of virtual achievements on student engagement. In *Proceedings of the SIGCHI Conference on Human Factors in Computing Systems* (pp. 763-772). ACM. 10.1145/2470654.2470763

Denslow, D. L., & Giunipero, L. C. (2003). *Improving purchasing success through entrepreneurial behaviour.* Paper presented at the ISM's 88th Annual International Supply Management Conference.

Dermeval, D., & Bittencourt, I. I. (2020). Co-designing gamified intelligent tutoring systems with teachers. *Revista Brasileira de Informática Na Educação, 28*, 73–91. doi:10.5753/rbie.2020.28.0.73

Desert Hat. (2009). *Game Design the Miyamoto Way: Flow and Difficulty.* https://deserthat.wordpress.com/2009/11/26/game-design-the-miyamoto-way-flow-and-difficulty/

DeSmet, A., Van Ryckeghem, D., Compernolle, S., Baranowski, T., Thompson, D., Crombez, G., Poels, K., Van Lippevelde, W., Bastiaensen, S., Van Cleemput, K., Vandebosch, H., & De Bourdeaudhuij, I. (2014). A meta-analysis of serious digital games for healthy lifestyle promotion. *Preventive Medicine, 69*, 95–107. doi:10.1016/j.ypmed.2014.08.026 PMID:25172024

Deterding, S. (2011, May). Situated motivational affordances of game elements: A conceptual model. In Gamification: Using game design elements in non-gaming contexts, a workshop at CHI (Vol. 10, No. 1979742.1979575). Academic Press.

Deterding, S., Dixon, D., Khaled, R., & Nacke, L. 2011. From game design elements to gamefulness: Defining "Gamification." *Proceedings of the 2011 Annual Conference Extended Abstracts on Human Factors in Computing Systems - CHI EA '11*, 2425.

Deterding, S., Khaled, R., Nacke, L. E., & Dixon, D. (2011). Gamification: Toward a Definition. Gamification Workshop. *CHI 2011 Gamification Workshop Proceedings,* 12–15.

Deterding, S., Khaled, R., Nacke, L. E., & Dixon, D. (2011). Gamification: toward a definition. In *Proceedings of Gamification Workshop - Conference on Human Factors in Computing Systems (CHI 2011)*. ACM.

Deterding, S. (2011). Situated motivational affordances of game elements: A conceptual model. *CHI Gamification Workshop 2011*, 3–6.

Deterding, S., Dixon, D., Khaled, R., & Nacke, L. (2011). From game design elements to gamefulness: Defining gamification. In *Proceedings of the 15th International Academic MindTrek Conference: Envisioning Future Media Environments* (pp. 9-15). ACM. 10.1145/2181037.2181040

Dewey, J. (1916). *Democracy and Education.* The Free Press.

Di Maggio, R., Donnelly, L., Al Naimi, K., Barone, P., Salvador, F., Dawson, L., Dixon, R., Fitzpatrick, R., Gradusova, O., Nesterina, E., Peleneva, M., Ushacova, O., Molina, C. M., Pirrie, D., Ruffell, A., McKinley, J., Sagripanti, G., Villalba, D., Schneck, B., & Forbes, S. (2017). Global developments in forensic geology. *Episodes*, *40*(2), 120–131. doi:10.18814/epiiugs/2017/v40i2/017014

Diago Nebot, P., & Ventura Campos, N. (2017). Escape Room: educational gamification for learning mathematics [Escape Room: gamificación educativa para el aprendizaje de las matemáticas]. *Suma: Revista sobre Enseñanza y Aprendizaje de las Matemáticas, 85*, 33-40.

Diago Nebot, P. D., & Ventura-Campos, N. (2017). Escape Room: Educational gamification for learning mathematics [Escape Room: gamificación educativa para el aprendizaje de las matemáticas]. *Suma*, *85*, 33–40.

Diahyleva, O. S., Gritsuk, I. V., Kononova, O. Y., & Yurzhenko, A. Y. (2020). Computerized adaptive testing in educational electronic environment of maritime higher education institutions. *CEUR Workshop Proceedings*, *2879*, 411-422.

Diamond, A. (2013). Executive functions. *Annual Review of Psychology*, *64*, 135–168.

Díaz-García, C., Sáez-Martínez, F., & Jiménez-Moreno, J. (2015). Assessing the impact of the "Entrepreneurs" education programme on participants' entrepreneurial intentions. *International Journal of Educational Technology in Higher Education*, *12*(3), 17–31.

Díaz-Ramírez, J. (2020). Gamification in engineering education – An empirical assessment on learning and game performance. *Heliyon*, *6*(9), 1–10. doi:10.1016/j.heliyon.2020.e04972 PMID:32995639

Dicheva, D., Dichev, C., Agre, G., & Angelova, G. (2015). Gamification in education: A systematic mapping study. *Journal of Educational Technology & Society*, *18*(3), 75–88.

Dicheva, D., Dichev, C., Agre, G., & Angelova, G. (2015). Gamification in Education: A Systematic Mapping Study. *Journal of Educational Technology & Society*, *18*(3), 75–88. doi:10.1109/EDUCON.2014.6826129

Dicheva, D., Irwin, K., & Dichev, C. (2018). OneUp: Supporting Practical and Experimental Gamification of Learning. *International Journal of Serious Games*, *5*(3), 5–21. doi:10.17083/ijsg.v5i3.236

Dichev, C., & Dicheva, D. (2017). Gamifying education: What is known, what is believed and what remains uncertain: A critical review. *International Journal of Educational Technology in Higher Education*, *14*(9), 1–36. doi:10.118641239-017-0042-5

Dichev, C., Dicheva, D., Angelova, G., & Agre, G. (2014). From gamification to gameful design and gameful experience in learning. *Cybernetics and Information Technologies*, *14*(4), 80–100. doi:10.1515/cait-2014-0007

Dickey, M. D. (2006). Game design narrative for learning: Appropriating adventure game design narrative devices and techniques for the design of interactive learning environments. *Educational Technology Research and Development*, *54*(3), 245–263. doi:10.100711423-006-8806-y

Dieckmann, P., Friis, S. M., Lippert, A., & Østergaard, D. (2012). Goals, Success Factors, and Barriers for Simulation-Based Learning. *Simulation & Gaming*, *43*(5), 627–647. doi:10.1177/1046878112439649

Digital Media Research Centre. (2020a). *M:EE – Minecraft for Educational Impact*. Available at https://research.qut.edu.au/dmrc/projects/mee-minecraft-for-educational-impact/

Digital Media Research Centre. (2020b). *Project Publication - Minecraft: Education Edition for Educational Impact*. Available at https://research.qut.edu.au/dmrc/wp-content/uploads/sites/5/2019/10/MEE-Research.pdf

Digital.ai. (2021). *15th State of Agile Report*. https://stateofagile.com/#ufh-i-661275008-15th-state-of-agile-report/7027494

Dillenberger, D., & Sandowski, P. (2012). *Subjective learning: Second version* (Report No. 12-007). Penn Institute for Economic Research. https://papers.ssrn.com/sol3/papers.cfm?abstract_id=2017595

Dimitriadou, A., Djafarova, N., Turetken, O., Verkuyl, M., & Ferworn, A. (2021). Challenges in serious game design and development: Educators' experiences. *Simulation & Gaming*, *52*(2), 132–152. doi:10.1177/1046878120944197

Ding, L., Er, E., & Orey, M. (2018). An exploratory study of student engagement in gamified online discussions. *Computers & Education*, *120*, 213–226. doi:10.1016/j.compedu.2018.02.007

Discovery Tour by Ubisoft. (n.d.). *Teacher learning resources*. Ubisoft (UK). https://www.ubisoft.com/en-gb/game/assassins-creed/discovery-tour

Djaouti, D., Alvarez, J., & Jessel, J.-P. (2011). Classifying serious games: The G/P/S model. In Handbook of Research on Improving Learning and Motivation through Educational Games: Multidisciplinary Approaches. IGI Global. doi:10.4018/978-1-60960-495-0.ch006

Dobroskok, I., Rzhevska, N., Ayyildiz, H., Zaimova, D., & Zheliazkov, G. (2020). Game development software tools in higher educational institutions: Experience of Ukraine, Turkey and Bulgaria. *Technologies and Learning Tools*, *78*(4), 90–104. doi:10.33407/itlt.v78i4.3370

Dochy, F., Segers, M., Van den Bossche, P., & Gijbels, D. (2003). Effects of problem-based learning: A meta-analysis. *Learning and Instruction*, *13*(5), 533–568. doi:10.1016/S0959-4752(02)00025-7

Dominguez Alonso, J., & Pino Juste, M. (2014). Motivación intrínseca y extrínseca. análisis en adolescentes gallegos. *International Journal of Developmental and Educational Psychology*, *1*(1), 349–358.

Domínguez, A., Saenz-De-Navarrete, J., De-Marcos, L., Fernández-Sanz, L., Pages, C., & Martinez-Herráiz, J. J. (2013). Gamifying learning experiences: Practical implications and outcomes. *Computers & Education*, *63*, 380–392. doi:10.1016/j.compedu.2012.12.020

Donaldson, M. R., & Cooke, S. J. (2014). Scientific publications: Moving beyond quality and quantity toward influence. *Bioscience*, *64*(1), 12–13. doi:10.1093/biosci/bit007

Donnelly, L. J. (2010). *The role of geoforensics in policing and law enforcement*. Emergency Global Barclay Media Limited.

Dormans, J. (2006). On the Role of the Die: A brief ludologic study of pen-and-paper roleplaying games and their rules. *Game Studies, 6*(1). http://gamestudies.org/0601/articles/dormans

Dorno escape boxes. (2021). https://www.oio-7.top/products.aspx?cid=42&cname=escape+box

Douglas, B. D., & Brauer, M. (2021). Gamification to prevent climate change: A review of games and apps for sustainability. *Current Opinion in Psychology*, *42*, 89–94. Advance online publication. doi:10.1016/j.copsyc.2021.04.008 PMID:34052619

Downes, S. (2005). *An introduction to connective knowledge*. https://www.downes.ca/post/33034

Downes, S. (2007). *What connectivism is*. https://www.downes.ca/post/38653

Downes, S. (2015). The Quality of Massive Open Online Courses. In B. H. Khan & M. Ally (Eds.), *International Handbook of E-Learning: Theoretical Perspectives and Research* (1st ed.). Routledge.

Draper, J., Sobieszczyk, T., Crumpton, C. D., Lefferts, H. L., & Chachavalpongpun, P. (2019). Racial "Othering" in Thailand: Quantitative Evidence, Causes, and Consequences. *Nationalism & Ethnic Politics*, *25*(3), 251–272. doi:10.1080/13537113.2019.1639425

Driskell, J. E., & Dwyer, J. D. (1984). Microcomputer videogame-based training. *Educational Technology*, *24*(2), 11–16. https://www.jstor.org/stable/44427307

Druin, A. (1999). Children as Our Technology Design Partners. In The Design of Children's Technology. Morgan Kaufmann.

Druin, A., Bederson, B. B., Hourcade, J. P., Sherman, L., Revelle, G., Platner, M., & Weng, S. (2001). Designing a digital library for young children. In *Proceedings of the 1st ACM/IEEE-CS joint conference on Digital libraries* (pp. 398-405). ACM.

Duff, P. A. (2006). Beyond generalizability. *Inference and generalizability in applied linguistics: Multiple perspectives, 12*, 65.

Du, H. S., Ke, X., & Wagner, C. (2020). Inducing individuals to engage in a gamified platform for environmental conservation. *Industrial Management & Data Systems*, *120*(4), 692–713. doi:10.1108/IMDS-09-2019-0517

Duolinguo. (2021). https://www.duolingo.com/

Durazzi, N. (2019). The political economy of high skills: Higher education in knowledge-based labour markets. *Journal of European Public Policy*, *26*(12), 1799–1817. doi:10.1080/13501763.2018.1551415

Dweck, C. (2017). Mindset-updated edition: Changing the way you think to fulfil your potential. Hachette UK.

Dweek, C. S. (1986). Motivational processes affecting learning. *The American Psychologist*, *41*(10), 1040–1048. doi:10.1037/0003-066X.41.10.1040

Dworkin, S. L. (2012). Sample size policy for qualitative studies using in-depth interviews. [). Springer.]. *Archives of Sexual Behavior*, *41*(6), 1319–1320. doi:10.100710508-012-0016-6 PMID:22968493

Dyagileva, O., Goridko, N, Popova, H., Voloshynov, S., & Yurzhenko, A. (2020) *Zabezpechennya staloho rozvytku osvity maybutnikh fakhivtsiv mors'koho transportu za dopomohoyu merezhevoyi vzayemodiyi* [Ensuring sustainable development of education of future maritime transport professionals by means of network interaction]. E3S Web of Conferences.

Dymora, P., & Niemiec, K. (2019). Gamification as a supportive tool for school children with dyslexia. *Informatics (MDPI)*, *6*(4), 48. doi:10.3390/informatics6040048

Eccles, J. (2009). Who am I and what am I going to do with my life? Personal and collective identities as motivators of action. *Educational Psychologist*, *44*(2), 78–89. doi:10.1080/00461520902832368

Edge, N., Fitzgerald, E., & Willcoxson, L. (2019). Addressing Key Concerns in Graduate Employability: Changing Our Expectations of Universities. In Education for Employability (Volume 2) (pp. 51-64). Brill Sense.

Edo, M., Baeza, M., Deulofeu, J., & Badillo, E. (2008). Study of the parallelism between the phases of solving a game and the phases of solving a problem [Estudio del paralelismo entre las fases de resolución de un juego y las fases de resolución de un problema]. *Union- Revista Iberoamericana de Educación Matemática, 14*, 61–75.

Eichberg, H. (2018). *Play in Philosophy and Social Thought*. Routledge. https://www.routledge.com/Play-in-Philosophy-and-Social-Thought/Eichberg-Larsen/p/book/9780367519759

Eickhoff, C., Harris, C. G., & de Vries, A. P. (2012). Quality through flow and immersion: Gamifying crowdsourced relevance assessments. *Proceedings of SIGIR'12*. 10.1145/2348283.2348400

Eiland, L. S., & Todd, T. J. (2019). Considerations when incorporating technology into classroom and experiential teaching. *The Journal of Pediatric Pharmacology and Therapeutics: JPPT: the Official Journal of PPAG*, *24*(4), 270–275. doi:10.5863/1551-6776-24.4.270 PMID:31337989

Eleftheria, C. A., Charikleia, P., Iason, C. G., Athanasios, T., & Dimitrios, T. (2013). An innovative augmented reality educational platform using Gamification to enhance lifelong learning and cultural education. *IISA 2013 - 4th International Conference on Information, Intelligence, Systems and Applications*. 10.1109/IISA.2013.6623724

Elena Parra-Gonzalez, M., Segura-Robles, A., & Rosa Gomez-Barajas, E. (2020). Assessing gamified experiences in physical education teachers and students. *Ijeri-International Journal of Educational Research and Innovation*, (13), 166–176.

Eliezer, C. R., Ribeiro, E. A., & Schutz, J. A. (2020). *A educação em tempos de pandemia: desafios e possibilidades* [Education in pandemic times: challenges and possibilities]. Dialética.

Eltegani, N., & Butgereit, L. (2015). Attributes of students engagement in fundamental programming learning. In *2015 International Conference on Computing, Control, Networking, Electronics and Embedded Systems Engineering* (pp. 101-106). IEEE. 10.1109/ICCNEEE.2015.7381438

Emelianenko, A. Y. (2010). Проблематичность однозначного определения феномена игры [The difficulty of a clear definition of "game"]. *RUDN Journal of Philosophy, 4*, 77-81. https://journals.rudn.ru/philosophy/article/viewFile/11684/11114

Endeavor & Sebrae. (2017). *Empreendedorismo nas Universidades Brasileiras 2016*. https://www.sebrae.com.br/Sebrae/Portal%20Sebrae/Anexos/Relatorio%20Endeavor%20impressao.pdf

Enterprise, D. G. (2008). *Entrepreneurship in higher education, especially within non-business studies. Final report of the expert group*. European Commission.

Entertainment Software Association. (2020). 2020 Essential Facts About the Video Game Industry. *Cision*, 1–2. https://www.prnewswire.com/news-releases/new-survey-2020-essential-facts-about-the-video-game-industry-301093972.html

Eppmann, R., Bekk, M., & Klein, K. (2018). Gameful experience in gamification: Construction and validation of a gameful experience scale. *Journal of Interactive Marketing*, *43*, 98–115. doi:10.1016/j.intmar.2018.03.002

Erhel, S., & Jamet, E. (2019). Improving instructions in educational computer games: Exploring the relations between goal specificity, flow experience and learning outcomes. *Computers in Human Behavior*, *91*, 106–114. doi:10.1016/j.chb.2018.09.020

Ermi, L., & Mäyrä, F. (2005, June 16-20). *Fundamental components of the gameplay experience: Analysing immersion* [Paper presentation]. DiGRA 2005: Changing Views – Worlds in Play, Vancouver, Canada. http://www.digra.org/digital-library/publications/fundamental-components-of-the-gameplay-experience-analysing-immersion/

ESA Education Office. (2021). *Education.* Available at https://www.esa.int/Education

ESA Kids. (2021). https://www.esa.int/kids/en/learn

ESA Teach with Space Conference. (2021). https://educationforms.esa.int/booklet.pdf

ESA. (2019). *2019 Essential Facts About the Computer and Video Game Industry*. ESA.

ESA. (2020). *Kerbal includes Ariane 5 and real ESA missions for gamers.* Available at https://www.esa.int/About_Us/Partnerships/Kerbal_includes_Ariane_5_and_real_ESA_missions_for_gamers

ESERO UK. (2021). https://www.stem.org.uk/esero

ESERO UKb. (2021). *Quality assured 3...2...1...lift off! - Building your own paper rock.* Available at https://www.stem.org.uk/resources/elibrary/resource/460411/321lift-building-your-own-paper-rocket

ESERO UKc. (2021). *Resources.* Available at https://www.stem.org.uk/esero/resources

ESERO UKd. (2021). *Cansat.* Available at https://www.stem.org.uk/esero/cansat

ESERO UKe. (2021). *Mission X.* Available at https://www.stem.org.uk/missionx

ESERO. (2021). *European Space Education Resource Office*. Available at https://www.esa.int/Education/Teachers_Corner/European_Space_Education_Resource_Office

Eukel, H. N., Frenzel, J. E., & Cernusca, D. (2017). Educational gaming for pharmacy students–design and evaluation of a diabetes-themed escape room. *American Journal of Pharmaceutical Education*, *81*(7), 6265. doi:10.5688/ajpe8176265 PMID:29109566

European Commission. (2017). *Glossary: Lifelong learning*. EUROSTAT - Statistics Explained. https://ec.europa.eu/Eurostat/statisticsexplained/index.php/Glossary:Lifelong_learning

European Space Agency. (2021). https://www.esa.int/

Eurydice Network. (2012). *Education Information Network in Europe*. https://eacea.ec.europa.eu/national-policies/eurydice/about_en

Fabio, R. A., & Antonietti, A. (2012). Effects of hypermedia instruction on declarative, conditional and procedural knowledge in ADHD students. *Research in Developmental Disabilities*, *33*(6), 2028–2039. doi:10.1016/j.ridd.2012.04.018 PMID:22750359

Faghihi, U., Brautigam, A., Jorgenson, K., Martin, D., Brown, A., Measures, E., & Maldonando-Bouchard, S. (2014). How Gamification Applies for Educational Purpose Specially with College Algebra. *Procedia Computer Science*, *41*, 182–187. doi:10.1016/j.procs.2014.11.102

Faiella, F., & Ricciardi, M. (2015). Gamification and learning: A review of issues and research. *Journal of e-Learning and Knowledge Society, 11*(3), 13-21.

Falah, J., Wedyan, M., Alfalah, S. F. M., Abu-Tarboush, M., Al-Jakheem, A., Al-Faraneh, M., Abuhammad, A., & Charissis, V. (2021). Identifying the characteristics of virtual reality gamification for complex educational topics. *Multimodal Technologies and Interaction*, *5*(9), 53. doi:10.3390/mti5090053

Farbiarz, A., & Farbiarz, J. L. (2008). A educação a distância online: a dicotomia no ciberespaço [Online distance learning: the dichotomy in cyberspace]. *Anais II Simpósio ABCiber - Associação Brasileira de Pesquisadores em Cibercultura*, 1-15. http://cencib.org/simposioabciber/PDFs/CC/Alexandre%20%20Farbiarz%20e%20Jackeline%20%20Farbiarz.pdf

Farbiarz, A., Xavier, G. A., Dias, C. M., & Farbiarz, J. L. (2019). A gamificação como processo metodológico na formação crítica contemporânea: Uma experiência aliando tecnologia, inovação e ludicidade no Ensino Superior [Gamification as a methodological process in contemporary critical education: an experience combining technology, innovation and playfulness in higher education]. *Logos*, *26*, 229–244. https://www.e-publicacoes.uerj.br/index.php/logos/article/view/45676

Fardo, M. L. (2013). Gamification applied in learning environments [A gamificação aplicada em ambientes de aprendizagem]. *Renote*, *11*(1). Advance online publication. doi:10.22456/1679-1916.41629

Faria, A. J., Hutchinson, D., Wellington, W. J., & Gold, S. (2009). Developments in business gaming a review of the past 40 years. *Simulation & Gaming*, *40*(4), 464–487. doi:10.1177/1046878108327585

Fayolle, A., Gailly, B., & Lassas-Clerc, N. (2006). Assessing the impact of entrepreneurship education programmes: A new methodology. *Journal of European Industrial Training*, *30*(9), 701–720. doi:10.1108/03090590610715022

Featherstone, M., & Habgood, J. (2019). UniCraft: Exploring the impact of asynchronous multiplayer game elements in gamification. *International Journal of Human-Computer Studies*, *127*, 150–168. doi:10.1016/j.ijhcs.2018.05.006

Federal Trade Commission. (2016). *Lumosity to pay $2 million to settle FTC deceptive advertising charges for its "brain training" program: Company claimed program would sharpen performance in everyday life and protect against cognitive decline*. https://www.ftc.gov/news-events/press-releases/2016/01/lumosity-pay-2-million-settle-ftc-deceptive-advertising-charges

Feige, D. M. (2012). Computer games as works of art. In J. Fromme & A. Unger (Eds.), *Computer games and new media cultures: A handbook of digital game studies* (pp. 93–106). Springer. doi:10.1007/978-94-007-2777-9_6

Ferguson, K. (2019). *International Escape Room Markets analysis*. The Logic Escapes Me. https://thelogicescapesme.com/news/international-escape-room-markets-analysis

Ferguson, B. R., Gillis, J. M., & Sevlever, M. (2013). A brief group intervention using video games to teach sportsmanship skills to children with autism spectrum disorders. *Child & Family Behavior Therapy*, *35*(4), 293–306. doi:10.1080/07317107.2013.846648

Fernández-Abascal, E., Martín, M., & Domínguez, J. (2001). *Psychological processes* [Procesos psicológicos]. Pirámide.

Fernández-Marchesi, N. (2018). Practical laboratory activities and inquiry in the classroom [Actividades prácticas de laboratorio e indagación en el aula]. *TED: Tecné. Episteme y Didáxis*, *44*, 203–218.

Ferreira, F., & Cavaco, S. (2014, October). Mathematics for all: A game-based learning environment for visually impaired students. In *2014 IEEE Frontiers in Education Conference (FIE) Proceedings* (pp. 1-8). IEEE. 10.1109/FIE.2014.7044493

Ferreira, G. P., Andrade, R., Oliveira, S. T., & Ulbricht, V. R. (2016, July). Learning object design for teaching descriptive geometry: A study from the perspective of gamification and accessibility. *International Conference on Universal Access in Human-Computer Interaction* (pp. 38-48). Springer. 10.1007/978-3-319-40238-3_4

Ferreiro-González, M., Amores-Arrocha, A., Espada-Bellido, E., Aliano-Gonzalez, M. J., Vázquez-Espinosa, M., González-De-Peredo, A., Sancho-Galán, P., Álvarez-Saura, J. Á., Barbero, G. F., & Cejudo-Bastante, C. (2019). Escape ClassRoom: Can You Solve a Crime Using the Analytical Process? *Journal of Chemical Education*, *96*(2), 267–273. doi:10.1021/acs.jchemed.8b00601

Ferriz-Valero, A., Østerlie, O., Martínez, S. G., & García-Jaén, M. (2020). Gamification in physical education: Evaluation of impact on motivation and academic performance within higher education. *International Journal of Environmental Research and Public Health, 17*(12), 1–16. doi:10.3390/ijerph17124465 PMID:32575919

Ferster, C. B., & Skinner, B. F. (1957). *Schedules of reinforcement.* Prentice-Hall, Inc. doi:10.1037/10627-000

Fiet, J. O. (2001). The theoretical side of teaching entrepreneurship. *Journal of Business Venturing, 16*(1), 1–24. doi:10.1016/S0883-9026(99)00041-5

Figueroa Flores, J. F. (2015). Using gamification to enhance second language learning. *Digital Education Review, 27.* Retrieved from https://revistes.ub.edu/index.php/der/article/download/11912/pdf http://education.mit.edu/papers/MovingLearningGamesForward_EdArcade.pdf /

Filatro, A., & Cavalcanti, C. C. (2018). *Metodologias inov-ativas na educação presencial, a distância e corporativa* [Innov-ative methodologies in face-to-face, distance and corporate education]. Saraiva Educação SA.

Filsecker, M., & Hickey, D. T. (2014). A multilevel analysis of the effects of external rewards on elementary students' motivation, engagement, and learning in an educational game. *Computers & Education, 75*, 136–148. doi:10.1016/j.compedu.2014.02.008

Fine, G. A. (1993). Ten lies of ethnography: Moral dilemmas of field research. *Journal of Contemporary Ethnography, 22*(3), 267–294. doi:10.1177/089124193022003001

Fischer, J., Ritchie, E. G., & Hanspach, J. (2012). Academia's obsession with quantity. *Trends in Ecology & Evolution, 27*(9), 473–474. doi:10.1016/j.tree.2012.05.010 PMID:22727015

Fischer, K. W. (2009). Mind, brain, and education: Building a scientific groundwork for learning and teaching. *Mind, Brain and Education: the Official Journal of the International Mind, Brain, and Education Society, 3*(1), 3–16. doi:10.1111/j.1751-228X.2008.01048.x

Fisch, S. M. (2005). Making educational computer games "educational". In M. Eisenberg & A. Eisenberg (Eds.), *IDC '05: Proceedings of the 2005 conference on interaction design and children* (pp. 56–61). Association for Computing Machinery. doi:10.1145/1109540.1109548

Fisher-Price: Baby Toys, Baby Gear, and Parenting Tips. (2019). Retrieved from https://www.fisher-price.com/en_AU/products/Think-and-Learn-Code-a-pillar

Fitsilis, P., & Lekatos, A. (2017, September). Teaching software project management using agile paradigm. In *Proceedings of the 21st Pan-Hellenic Conference on Informatics* (pp. 1–6). 10.1145/3139367.3139413

Fitz-Walter, Z., Johnson, D., Wyeth, P., Tjondronegoro, D., & Scott-Parker, B. (2017). Driven to drive? Investigating the effect of gamification on learner driver behavior, perceived motivation and user experience. *Computers in Human Behavior, 71*, 586–595. doi:10.1016/j.chb.2016.08.050

Fjællingsdal, K. S., & Klöckner, C. A. (2020). Green Across the Board: Board Games as Tools for Dialogue and Simplified Environmental Communication. *Simulation & Gaming, 51*(5), 632–652. Advance online publication. doi:10.1177/1046878120925133

Flavell, J. H. (1979). *Metacognition and Cognitive Monitoring. American Psychological Association.*

Fleming, R. (2013). *Design Education for a Sustainable Future.* Routledge. doi:10.4324/9780203584071

Fletcher, J. D., & Tobias, S. (2006). Using computer games and simulations for instruction: A research review. *Proceedings of the Society for Applied Learning Technology Meeting*, 1–34. https://www.researchgate.net/publication/228511464_Using_computer_games_and_simulations_for_instruction_A_research_review

Fogtmann, M. H., Fritsch, J., & Kortbek, K. J. (2008, December). Kinesthetic interaction: revealing the bodily potential in interaction design. In *Proceedings of the 20th Australasian conference on computer-human interaction: designing for habitus and habitat* (pp. 89-96). 10.1145/1517744.1517770

Foronda, C. L., Fernandez-Burgos, M., Nadeau, C., Kelley, C., & Henry, M. (2020). Virtual simulation in nursing education: A systematic review spanning 1996 to 2018. *Simulation in Healthcare*, *15*(1), 46–54. doi:10.1097/SIH.0000000000000411 PMID:32028447

Fortuna, T. R. (2000). Sala de aula é lugar de brincar? [Is the classroom a place to play?]. In M. L. Xavier & M. I. Dalla Zen (Eds.), *Planejamento em destaque: Análises menos convencionais* [Planning in the spotlight: Less conventional analytics] (pp. 147–164). Mediação.

Fossey, E., Harvey, C., McDermott, F., & Davidson, L. (2002). Understanding and evaluating qualitative research. *The Australian and New Zealand Journal of Psychiatry*, *36*(6), 717–732. doi:10.1046/j.1440-1614.2002.01100.x PMID:12406114

Foster, A. N., Shah, M., & Duvall, M. (2015). Game Network Analysis. In M. Niess & H. Gillow-Wiles (Eds.), *Handbook of Research on Teacher Education in the Digital Age* (pp. 380–411). IGI Global. doi:10.4018/978-1-4666-8403-4.ch015

Frank, P., & Stanszus, L. S. (2019). Transforming consumer behavior: Introducing self-inquiry-based and self-experience-based learning for building personal competencies for sustainable consumption. *Sustainability*, *11*(2550), 1–19. doi:10.3390u11092550

Fredricks, J. A., & McColskey, W. (2012). The Measurement of Student Engagement: A Comparative Analysis of Various Methodsand Student Self-report Instruments. In Handbook of Research on Student Engagement. doi:10.1007/978-1-4614-2018-7_37

Fredricks, J. A., Blumenfeld, P. C., & Paris, A. H. (2004). School engagement: Potential of the concept, state of the evidence. *Review of Educational Research*, *74*(1), 59–109. doi:10.3102/00346543074001059

Freeman, S., Eddy, S. L., McDonough, M., Smith, M. K., Okoroafor, N., Jordt, H., & Wenderoth, M. P. (2014). Active learning increases student performance in science, engineering, and mathematics. *Proceedings of the National Academy of Sciences of the United States of America*, *111*(23), 8410–8415. doi:10.1073/pnas.131903011 PMID:24821756

Frei, P., Su, V., Mikhak, B., & Ishii, H. (2000). Designing a New Class of Computational Toys. *Proc. ACM CHI 2000*, 129-136.

Freire, P. (1970). *Pedagogy of the oppressed.* Seabury Press.

Freire, P. (2003). *Pedagogia da autonomia: Saberes necessários à prática educativa* [Pedagogy of autonomy: Knowledge necessary for educational practice]. Paz e Terra.

Freire, P. (2020). *Pedagogia do oprimido* [Pedagogy of the oppressed] (17th ed.). Paz e Terra.

Freitas, S. A. A., Lacerda, A. R. T., Calado, P. M. R. O., Lima, T. S., & Canedo, E. D. (2017). Gamification in education: A methodology to identify student's profile. *Proceedings - Frontiers in Education Conference,* 1–8. 10.1109/FIE.2017.8190499

Frenzel, A. C., Becker-Kurz, B., Pekrun, R., Goetz, T., & Lüdtke, O. (2018). Emotion transmission in the classroom revisited: A reciprocal effects model of teacher and student enjoyment. *Journal of Educational Psychology*, *110*(5), 628–639. doi:10.1037/edu0000228

Frenzel, A. C., Goetz, T., Lüdtke, O., Pekrun, R., & Sutton, R. E. (2009). Emotional transmission in the classroom: Exploring the relationship between teacher and student enjoyment. *Journal of Educational Psychology, 101*(3), 705–716. doi:10.1037/a0014695

Frenzel, A. C., Pekrun, R., & Goetz, T. (2007). Girls and mathematics – A "hopeless" issue? A control-value approach to gender differences in emotions towards mathematics. *European Journal of Psychology of Education, 22*(4), 497–514. doi:10.1007/BF03173468

Frias, E. R. (2009). *Play of representations (RPG) and aspects of autonomous morality* [Jogo das representações (RPG) e aspectos da moral autônoma] [Master dissertation]. University of São Paulo.

Fu, F. L., Su, R. C., & Yu, S. C. (2009). EGameFlow: A scale to measure learners' enjoyment of e-learning games. *Computers & Education, 52*(1), 101–112. doi:10.1016/j.compedu.2008.07.004

Futschek, G., & Moschitz, J. (2011). Learning Algorithmic Thinking with Tangible Objects Eases Transition to Computer Programming. In I. Kalaš & R. T. Mittermeir (Eds.), Lecture Notes in Computer Science: Vol. 7013. *Informatics in Schools. Contributing to 21st Century Education. ISSEP 2011*. Springer.

Gabdrakhmanov, R. (2020). *Interactive Computer Graphics Models for Distance Courses* [Unpublished master's thesis]. Kazan Federal University, Kazan, Russian Federation.

Gagné, R. M. (1972). Domains of learning. *Interchange, 3*(1), 1–8. doi:10.1007/BF02145939

Galarneau, L., & Zibit, M. (2007). Online games for 21st century skills. *Games and simulations in online learning: Research and development frameworks*, 59-88.

Galbraith, J., & Winterbottom, M. (2011). Peer-tutoring: What's in it for the tutor? *Educational Studies, 37*(3), 321–332. doi:10.1080/03055698.2010.506330

Galeano-Ospino, S., Machuca-Villegas, L., & Gasca-Hurtado, G. P. (2020, October). Knowledge transfer in software development teams using gamification: A systematic literature review. In *International Conference on Software Process Improvement* (pp. 115–130). Springer.

Gallagher, S., & Lindgren, R. (2015). Enactive Metaphors: Learning Through Full-Body Engagement. *Educational Psychology Review, 27*(3), 391–404. doi:10.100710648-015-9327-1

Gallego-Durán, F. J., Villagrá-Arnedo, C. J., Satorre-Cuerda, R., Compañ-Rosique, P., Molina-Carmona, R., & Llorens-Largo, F. (2019). A Guide for Game-Design-Based Gamification. *Informatics (MDPI), 6*(4), 49. doi:10.3390/informatics6040049

Galloway, K. (2017). Getting back to our roots: global law schools in local context. In *Legal Education In The Global Context* (pp. 17–30). Routledge. doi:10.4324/9781315563244-2

Gamology. (n.d.). *Home* [YouTube Channel]. YouTube. Retrieved August 4, 2021, from https://www.youtube.com/c/Gamology

Gandolfi, E., Ferdig, R. E., & Kratcoski, A. (2021). A new educational normal an intersectionality-led exploration of education, learning technologies, and diversity during COVID-19. *Technology in Society, 66*(8), 1–8. doi:10.1016/j.techsoc.2021.101637

Gannaway, D., & Sheppard, K. (2019). Pursuing Employability through Generalist and Specialist Degree Programs: Australian Perspectives. In Education for Employability (Volume 2) (pp. 155-166). Brill Sense.

Garaigordobil, M. (1992). *Juego cooperativo y socialización en el aula*. Seco Olea.

García Tudela, P., Solano Fernández, I., & Sánchez Vera, M. (2020). Analysis of an educational escape room in elementary school mathematics class [Análisis de una escape room educativa en clase de matemáticas de educación primaria]. *Journal for Research in Mathematics Education*, *9*(3), 273–297.

Garcia-Iruela, M., Hijón-Neira, R., & Connolly, C. (2021). Analysis of three methodological approaches in the use of gamification in vocational training. *Information, 12*(8). doi:10.3390/info12080300

García-Peñalvo, F. J., Alarcón, H., & Dominguez, A. (2019). Active learning experiences in engineering education. *International Journal of Engineering Education*, *35*(1), 305–309.

Gargallo, J. B., & Bargalló, C. M. (2011). What experiences do future teachers have about science classes? Implications for their formation [¿Qué experiencias manifiestan los futuros maestros sobre las clases de ciencias? Implicaciones para su formación]. *Review of Education*, *354*, 447–472.

Garris, R., Ahlers, R., & Driskell, J. E. (2002). Games, motivation, and learning: A research and practice model. *Simulation & Gaming*, *33*(4), 441–467. doi:10.1177/1046878102238607

Garris, R., Ahlers, R., & Driskell, J. E. (2017). Games, motivation, and learning: A research and practice model. In *Simulation in Aviation Training* (pp. 475–501). Routledge. doi:10.4324/9781315243092-25

Garritz, A. (2009). Affectivity in the teaching of science [La afectividad en la enseñanza de la ciencia]. *Educación en la Química*, *20*, 212–219.

Garritz, A. (2010). The teaching of science in a society with uncertainty and accelerated change [La enseñanza de la ciencia en una sociedad con incertidumbre y cambios acelerados]. *Enseñanza de las Ciencias*, *28*(3), 315–326. doi:10.5565/rev/ec/v28n3.4

Gasca-Hurtado, G. P., Gómez-Álvarez, M. C., Muñoz, M., & Mejía, J. (2021, September). Gamification Principles to Decrease SPI Change Resistance. In *European Conference on Software Process Improvement* (pp. 241-256). Springer. 10.1007/978-3-030-85521-5_16

Gebran, M. P. (2009). *Tecnologias educacionais* [Educational technologies]. IESDE Brasil S.A.

Gee, J. P. (2008). Learning and games. *The Ecology of Games: Connecting Youth, Games, and Learning*, 21–40. doi:10.1162/dmal.9780262693646.021

Gee, J. P. (2003). *What video games have to teach us about learning and literacy*. Palgrave. doi:10.1145/950566.950595

Gee, J. P. (2005). Learning by Design: Good Video Games as Learning Machines. *E-Learning and Digital Media*, *2*(1), 5–16. doi:10.2304/elea.2005.2.1.5

Gee, J. P. (2015). *Unified discourse analysis: language, reality, virtual worlds, and video games*. Routledge.

Geelan, B., de Salas, K., Lewis, I., King, C., Edwards, D., & O'Mara, A. (2015). Improving learning experiences through gamification: A case study. *Australian Educational Computing, 30*(1).

Gelman, D. L. (2014). *Design for kids: digital products for playing and learning*. Rosenfeld Media.

Genson, G. L. (1992). Teaching entrepreneurship through the classics. *Journal of Applied Business Research*, *8*(4), 135–140. doi:10.19030/jabr.v8i4.6135

Gentry, J. W. (1990). What is experiential learning. *Guide to business gaming and experiential learning, 9*, 20.

Gentry, S., L'Estrade Ehrstrom, B., Gauthier, A., Alvarez, J., Wortley, D., van Rijswijk, J., Car, J., Lilienthal, A., Tudor Car, L., Nikolaou, C. K., & Zary, N. (2018). Serious Gaming and Gamification interventions for health professional education. *Cochrane Database of Systematic Reviews*. Advance online publication. doi:10.1002/14651858.CD012209.pub2

Georgiou, Y., & Kyza, E. A. (2018). Relations between student motivation, immersion and learning outcomes in location-based augmented reality settings. *Computers in Human Behavior, 89*, 173–181. doi:10.1016/j.chb.2018.08.011

Gerstein, M., & Friedman, H. (2016). Rethinking higher education: Focusing on skills and competencies. *Psychosociological Issues in Human Resource Management, 4*(2), 104–121. doi:10.22381/PIHRM4220165

Ghergulescu, I., Moldovan, A. N., Bratu, M., Muntean, C. H., & Muntean, G. M. (2019). A case study in STEM education for learners with special education needs. *Proceedings of the 11th International Conference on Education and New Learning Technologies*, 10152-10157. 10.21125/edulearn.2019.2539

Giannakos, M. N., Jones, D., Crompton, H., & Chrisochoides, N. (2014, June). Designing Playful Games and Applications to Support Science Centers Learning Activities. In *International Conference on Universal Access in Human-Computer Interaction* (pp. 561-570). Springer. 10.1007/978-3-319-07440-5_51

Gibb, A. (2011). Concepts into practice: meeting the challenge of development of entrepreneurship educators around an innovative paradigm: The case of the International Entrepreneurship Educators' Programme (IEEP). *International Journal of Entrepreneurial Behaviour & Research, 17*(2), 146–165. doi:10.1108/13552551111114914

Gibson, D., Ostashewski, N., Flintoff, K., Grant, S., & Knight, E. (2015). Digital badges in education. *Education and Information Technologies, 20*(2), 403–410. doi:10.100710639-013-9291-7

Giddens, A., Appelbaum, R. P., Duneier, M., & Carr, D. (2013). *Essentials of sociology*. W. W. Norton & Company.

Gillett-Swan, J. (2017). The challenges of online learning: Supporting and engaging the isolated learner. *Journal of Learning Design, 10*(1), 20–30. doi:10.5204/jld.v9i3.293

Gil, S. (1996). Los juegos didácticos en la asignatura Paleontología. Un eslabón en el proceso de aprendizaje de los estudiantes. *Enseñanza de las Ciencias de la Tierra, 4*(3), 224–226.

Giraldo, J., Muñoz, J., & Villada, J. (2013). Exergames: A technological tool for physical activity [Exergames: una herramienta tecnológica para la actividad física]. *Revista Medica de Risaralda, 19*(2), 126–130. doi:10.22517/25395203.8527

Giroux, H. A. (2016). Pedagogia crítica, Paulo Freire e a coragem para ser político [Critical pedagogy, Paulo Freire and the courage to be politician]. *Revista e-Curriculum, 14*(1), 296-306. https://revistas.pucsp.br/index.php/curriculum/article/view/27356

Gitlin, L. N., & Hodgson, N. (2016). Online training - can it prepare an eldercare workforce? *Generations (San Francisco, Calif.), 40*(1), 71–81.

Gkikas, K., Nathanael, D., & Marmaras, N. (2007). The evolution of FPS games controllers: How use progressively shaped their present design. *Panhellenic Conference on Informatics (PCI)*, 37–46. http://pci2007.upatras.gr/proceedings/PCI2007_volA/A_037-046_Gkikas.pdf

Glover, I. (2013). Play as you learn : Gamification as a technique for motivating learners. *Proceedings of World Conference on Educational Multimedia, Hypermedia and Telemcommunications, 1*, 1999–2008.

Glover, I. (2013). Play as you learn: gamification as a technique for motivating learners. In J. Herrington, A. Couros, & V. Irvine (Eds.), *Proceedings of World Conference on Educational Multimedia, Hypermedia and Telecommunications 2013* (pp. 1999-2008). AACE.

Gnauk, B., Dannecker, L., & Hahmann, M. (2012, March). Leveraging gamification in demand dispatch systems. In *Proceedings of the 2012 Joint EDBT/ICDT workshops* (pp. 103–110). 10.1145/2320765.2320799

Goi, C. L. (2019). The use of business simulation games in teaching and learning. *Journal of Education for Business, 94*(5), 342–349. doi:10.1080/08832323.2018.1536028

Göksün, D. O., & Gürsoy, G. (2019). Comparing success and engagement in gamified learning experiences via Kahoot and Quizizz. *Computers & Education, 135*, 15–29. doi:10.1016/j.compedu.2019.02.015

Goldshtein, D., Krensky, C., Doshi, S., & Perelman, V. S. (2019). In situ simulation and its effects on patient outcomes: A systematic review. *BMJ Simulation & Technology Enhanced Learning*. Advance online publication. doi:10.1136/bmjstel-2018-000387 PMID:35514456

Goldstein, K. (2014). Why did edutainment become a bad word. *Computers in Entertainment.*

Gómez-Carrasco, C. J., Monteagudo-Fernández, J., Moreno-Vera, J.-R., & Sainz-Gómez, M. (2019). Effects of a gamification and flipped-classroom program for teachers in training on motivation and learning perception. *Education Sciences, 9*(299), 1–15. doi:10.3390/educsci9040299

Gómez, R. L., & Suárez, A. M. (2020). Gaming to succeed in college: Protocol for a scoping review of quantitative studies on the design and use of serious games for enhancing teaching and learning in higher education. *International Journal of Educational Research Open, 2*(2), 1–7. doi:10.1016/j.ijedro.2020.100021

Gomez, T., Moron, C., Ferrandez, D., Saiz, P., & Garrido, R. (2017). Gamification in the education: The benefits of learning through play. *Inted2017: 11th International Technology, Education and Development Conference*, 1051-1060.

González-González, C. S., Toledo-Delgado, P. A., Muñoz-Cruz, V., & Torres-Carrion, P. V. (2019, September). Serious games for rehabilitation: Gestural interaction in personalized gamified exercises through a recommender system. *Journal of Biomedical Informatics, 97*, 103266. doi:10.1016/j.jbi.2019.103266 PMID:31408732

Goodwin, A. L. (2021). Teaching standards, globalisation, and conceptions of teacher professionalism. *European Journal of Teacher Education, 44*(1), 5–19. doi:10.1080/02619768.2020.1833855

Gordon, N. (2014). Flexible pedagogies: Technology-enhanced learning. The Higher Education Academy, 1-24.

Gordon, N. A., & Grey, S. (2018). Approaches to measuring attendance and engagement. *New Directions in the Teaching of Physical Sciences*, (13).

Gordon, A. K. (1970). *Games For Growth.* Educational Games in the Classroom.

Gordon, M., Ackermann, E., & Breazeal, C. (2015). Social robot toolkit: Tangible programming for young children. In *Proceedings of the Tenth Annual ACM/IEEE International Conference on Human-Robot Interaction Extended Abstracts* (pp. 67-68). ACM.

Gordon, N., Brayshaw, M., & Grey, S. (2013). Maximising gain for minimal pain: Utilising natural game mechanics. *Innovation in Teaching and Learning in Information and Computer Sciences, 12*(1), 27–38. doi:10.11120/ital.2013.00004

Gordon, S. K., Trovinger, S., & Delellis, T. (2019). Escape from the usual : Development and implementation of an ' escape room ' activity to assess team dynamics. *Currents in Pharmacy Teaching & Learning, 11*(8), 818–824. doi:10.1016/j.cptl.2019.04.013 PMID:31227197

Goyal, S., Vijay, R., Monga, C., & Kalita, P. (2016). Code Bits: An Inexpensive Tangible Computational Thinking Toolkit For K-12 Curriculum. *Proceedings of the TEI '16: Tenth International Conference on Tangible, Embedded, and Embodied Interaction - TEI '16.*

Grabinger, R. S., & Dunlap, J. C. (1995). Rich environments for active learning: A definition. *ALT-J*, *3*(2), 5–34. doi:10.3402/rlt.v3i2.9606

Graesser, A. C., Singer, M., & Trabasso, T. (1994). Constructing inferences during narrative text comprehension. *Psychological Review*, *101*(3), 371–395. doi:10.1037/0033-295X.101.3.371 PMID:7938337

Graevenitz G.v., Harhoff, D., & Weber, R. (2010) The effects of entrepreneurship education. *Journal of Economic Behaviour and Organisation, 76*(1), 1-39.

Granger, B. P. (2008) *Moderating effect of training content complexity on the relationship between training media and training outcomes* [Master's thesis]. University of South Florida Libraries. https://digitalcommons.usf.edu/etd/1989/

Gredler, M. E. (1996). Educational games and simulations: A technology in search of a (research) paradigm. In D. H. Jonassen (Ed.), *Handbook of research on educational communications and technology* (pp. 521–540). Macmillan. http://citeseerx.ist.psu.edu/viewdoc/download?doi=10.1.1.115.9904&rep=rep1&type=pdf

Greenblat, C. S., & Duke, R. D. (1981). *Principles and practices of gaming-simulation*. Sage. https://catalog.princeton.edu/catalog/309032

Greenblat, C. S. (1973). Teaching with simulation games: A review of claims and evidence. *Teaching Sociology*, *1*(1), 62–83. doi:10.2307/1317334

Gregersen, E. (2019). *The lived experience of a university law clinic supervisor: an autoethnographic inquiry*. University of Northumbria at Newcastle.

Greitemeyer, T., & Mügge, D. O. (2014). Video games do affect social outcomes: A meta-analytic review of the effects of violent and prosocial video game play. *Personality and Social Psychology Bulletin*, *40*(5), 578–589. doi:10.1177/0146167213520459 PMID:24458215

Gressick, J., & Langston, J. B. (2017). The Guilded Classroom: Using Gamification to Engage and Motivate Undergraduates. *The Journal of Scholarship of Teaching and Learning*, *17*(3), 109. doi:10.14434/v17i3.22119

Grey, S., Grey, D., Gordon, N., & Purdy, J. (2017). Using formal game design methods to embed learning outcomes into game mechanics and avoid emergent behaviour. *International Journal of Game-Based Learning*, *7*(3), 63–73. doi:10.4018/IJGBL.2017070106

Grinter, R., & Eldridge, M. (2003). Wan2tlk? Everyday text messaging. *Proceedings of the SIGCHI Conference on Human Factors in Computing Systems*, 441–448. 10.1145/642611.642688

Grivokostopoulou, F., Kovas, K., & Perikos, I. (2019). Examining the impact of a gamified entrepreneurship education framework in higher education. *Sustainability*, *11*(20), 5623. doi:10.3390u11205623

Grodal, T. (2003). Stories for Eye, Ear, and Muscles: Video Games, Media, and Embodied Experiences. In M. Wolff & B. Perron (Eds.), *The Video Game Theory Reader* (pp. 129–156). Routledge.

Groh, F. (2012). Gamification: State of the art definition and utilization. In N. Asaj, B. Konings, M. Poguntke, F. Schaub, & B. Wiedersheim (Eds.), *Proceedings of the 4th seminar on research trends in media informatics* (pp. 39–46). Institute of Media Informatics. https://d-nb.info/1020022604/34#page=39

Grossman, R., Heyne, K., & Salas, E. (2014). Game and simulation-based approaches to training. In K. Kraiger, J. Passmore, N. R. dos Santos, & S. Malvezzi (Eds.), *Handbook of the psychology of training, development, and performance improvement* (pp. 205–224). Wiley Blackwell. doi:10.1002/9781118736982.ch12

GrowthEngineering. (2019, August 29). *The history of gamification: From the beginning to right now.* https://www.growthengineering.co.uk/history-of-gamification/

Grünberg, T. K. (2014). *What's the difference between game mechanics and game dynamics?* Available at: http://www.quora.com/Whats-the-difference-between-game-mechanics-and-game-dynamics

Guillen, G., Hamari, J., & Quist, J. (2021, January 5). Gamification of Sustainable Consumption: a systematic literature review. *Proceedings of the 54th Hawaii International Conference on System Sciences.* 10.24251/HICSS.2021.163

Guillén-Nieto, V., & Aleson-Carbonell, M. (2012). Serious games and learning effectiveness: the case of it's a deal! *Comput. Educ. 58*(1), 435–448. .compedu.2011.07.015 doi:10.1016/j

Gunawan, J. (2016). Understanding culture in higher education in Thailand. In Education for Health: Change in Learning and Practice (Vol. 29, Issue 2, pp. 160–161). Network: Towards Unity for Health. doi:10.4103/1357-6283.188783

Gunawardena, C. N., & Zittle, F. J. (1997). Social presence as a predictor of satisfaction within a computer-mediated conferencing environment. *American Journal of Distance Education, 11*(3), 8–26. doi:10.1080/08923649709526970

Gürol, Y., & Atsan, N. (2006). Entrepreneurial characteristics amongst university students: Some insights for entrepreneurship education and training in Turkey. *Education + Training, 48*(1), 25–38. doi:10.1108/00400910610645716

Gutiérrez Praena, D., Rios Reina, R., Ruiz, R., Talero, E., Callejón, R., Callejón, R., & Sanchez Hidalgo, M. (2019). *The use of an escape room as a teaching resource in the Faculty of Pharmacy* [El uso de una escape room como recurso docente en la Facultad de Farmacia]. https://riunet.upv.es/handle/10251/128803#

Guze, P. A. (2015). Using Technology to Meet the Challenges of Medical Education. *Transactions of the American Clinical and Climatological Association, 126*, 260–270. PMID:26330687

Habgood, M. P. J. (2005). *Zombie division: Intrinsic integration in digital learning games* [Unpublished manuscript]. The Learning Sciences Research Institute, The University of Nottingham. https://www.researchgate.net/publication/242288013_Zombie_Division_Intrinsic_Integration_in_Digital_Learning_Games

Habgood, M. P. J., Ainsworth, S. E., & Benford, S. (2005). Endogenous fantasy and learning in digital games. *Simulation & Gaming, 36*(4), 483–498. doi:10.1177/1046878105282276

Haines, G. H. Jr. (1988). The ombudsman: Teaching entrepreneurship. *Interfaces, 18*(5), 23–30. doi:10.1287/inte.18.5.23

Hair, J. F., Black, W. C., Babin, B. J., & Anderson, R. E. (2010). *Multivariate Data Analysis* (7th ed.). Pearson.

Hair, J. F., Ringle, C. M., & Sarstedt, M. (2011). PLS-SEM: Indeed a silver bullet. *Journal of Marketing Theory and Practice, 19*(2), 139–152. doi:10.2753/MTP1069-6679190202

Hakulinen, L., & Auvinen, T. (2014). The effect of gamification on students with different achievement goal orientations. *Proceedings - 2014 International Conference on Teaching and Learning in Computing and Engineering, LATICE 2014*, 9–16. 10.1109/LaTiCE.2014.10

Hakulinen, L., Auvinen, T., & Korhonen, A. (2013). Empirical study on the effect of achievement badges in TRAKLA2 online learning environment. Learning and Teaching in Computing and Engineering (LaTiCE), 2013. doi:10.1109/LaTiCE.2013.34

Hakulinen, L., Auvinen, T., & Korhonen, A. (2015). The effect of achievement badges on students' behavior: An empirical study in a university-level computer science course. *International Journal of Emerging Technologies in Learning, 10*(1), 18–29. doi:10.3991/ijet.v10i1.4221

Hallford, N., & Hallford, J. (2001a). *Swords and circuitry: A designer's guide to computer role-playing games*. Premier Press.

Hamari, J. (2015). *Gamification - Motivations & Effects*. Academic Press.

Hamari, J., & Koivisto, J. (2013). *Social motivations to use gamification: An empirical study of gamifying exercise* [Paper presentation]. 21st European Conference on Information Systems, Utrecht, The Netherlands.

Hamari, J., & Tuunanen, J. (2014). *Player types: A meta-synthesis*. Academic Press.

Hamari, J., Koivisto, J., & Sarsa, H. (2014). Does gamification work?--a literature review of empirical studies on gamification. In *2014 47th Hawaii international conference on system sciences* (pp. 3025-3034). IEEE.

Hamari, J. (2013). Transforming homo economicus into homo ludens: A field experiment on gamification in a utilitarian P2P trading service. *Electronic Commerce Research and Applications*, *12*(4), 236–245. doi:10.1016/j.elerap.2013.01.004

Hamari, J. (2017). Do badges increase user activity? A field experiment on the effects of gamification. *Computers in Human Behavior*, *71*, 469–478.

Hamari, J., Koivisto, J., & Sarsa, H. (2014). Does gamification work? A literature review of empirical studies on gamification. In *Proceedings of the 47th Hawaii International Conference on System Science* (pp. 3025-3034). 10.1109/HICSS.2014.377

Hamari, J., Shernoff, D. J., Rowe, E., Coller, B., Asbell-Clarke, J., & Edwards, T. (2016). Challenging games help students learn: An empirical study on engagement, flow and immersion in game-based learning. *Computers in Human Behavior*, *54*, 170–179. doi:10.1016/j.chb.2015.07.045

Ham, E. (2016). *Tabletop Game Design for Video Game Designers*. Focal Press.

Hammoud, M. M., Nuthalapaty, F. S., Goepfert, A. R., Casey, P. M., Emmons, S., Espey, E. L., & Peskin, E. G. (2008). To the point: Medical education review of the role of simulators in surgical training. *American Journal of Obstetrics and Gynecology*, *199*(4), 338–343. doi:10.1016/j.ajog.2008.05.002 PMID:18639203

Hanghøj, T. (2013). Game-based teaching: practices, roles, and pedagogies. In S. de Freitas, M. Ott, M. M. Popescu, & I. Stanescu (Eds.), *New Pedagogical Approaches in Game Enhanced Learning: Curriculum Integration* (pp. 81–101). IGI Global. doi:10.4018/978-1-4666-3950-8.ch005

Hanna, L., Risden, K., Czerwinski, M., & Alexander, K. J. (1999). The Role of Usability Research in Designing Children's Computer Products. In *The Design of Children's Technology*. ACM.

Hansch, A., Newman, C., & Schildhauer, T. (2015). *Fostering engagement with gamification: Review of current practices on online learning platforms*. HIIG Discussion Paper Series No. 2015–04, 23. 11.

Hanus, M. D., & Fox, J. (2015). Assessing the effects of gamification in the classroom: A longitudinal study on intrinsic motivation, social comparison, satisfaction, effort, and academic performance. *Computer Education*, *80*, 152–161. doi:10.1016/j.compedu.2014.08.019

Harris, D. (2008). *A comparative study of the effect of collaborative problem-solving in a Massively Multiplayer Online Game (MMOG) on individual achievement* (Publication No. 3317694) [Doctoral dissertation, University of San Francisco]. USF Digital Repository. https://repository.usfca.edu/cgi/viewcontent.cgi?referer=https://www.google.com/&httpsredir=1&article=1259&context=diss

Harrow, A. J. (1972). *Taxonomy of the psychomotor domain : A guide for developing behavioral objectives*. David McKay.

Hartnett, M. (2016). The importance of motivation in online learning. In M. Hartnett (Ed.), *Motivation in online education* (pp. 5–32). Springer. doi:10.1007/978-981-10-0700-2_2

Hartnett, M. (2019). Motivation in distance education. In M. G. Moore & W. C. Diehl (Eds.), *Handbook of Distance Education* (4th ed., pp. 145–157). Routledge.

Harviainen, J. T. (2014). Critical Challenges to Gamifying Education. *Proceedings of the Game On Conference.*

Harwood, T., & Garry, T. (2015). An investigation into gamification as a customer engagement experience environment. *Journal of Services Marketing*, *29*(6–7), 533–546. Advance online publication. doi:10.1108/JSM-01-2015-0045

Hassan, A., Pinkwart, N., & Shafi, M. (2021). Serious games to improve social and emotional intelligence in children with autism. *Entertainment Computing*, *38*, 100417. doi:10.1016/j.entcom.2021.100417

Hassan, M. A., Habiba, U., Majeed, F., & Shoaib, M. (2021). Adaptive gamification in e-learning based on students' learning styles. *Interactive Learning Environments*, *29*(4), 545–565. doi:10.1080/10494820.2019.1588745

Hassenzahl, M. (2018). The thing and I (Summer of '17 remix). In M. Blythe & A. Monk (Eds.), *Funology 2: From usability to enjoyment* (pp. 17–31). Springer. doi:10.1007/978-3-319-68213-6_2

Hattie, J., Biggs, J., & Purdie, N. (1996). Effects of Learning Skills Interventions on Student Learning: A Meta-Analysis. *Review of Educational Research*, *66*(2), 99–136. doi:10.3102/00346543066002099

Hays, R. T. (2005). *The effectiveness of instructional games: A literature review and discussion.* Naval Air Warfare Center Training Systems Division. https://apps.dtic.mil/sti/citations/ADA441935

Healy, M., Brown, J. L., & Ho, C. (2021). Graduate employability as a professional proto-jurisdiction in higher education. *Higher Education*, 1–18.

Heddens, J. W. (1986). Bridging the gap between the concrete and the abstract. *The Arithmetic Teacher*, *33*(6), 14–17. doi:10.5951/AT.33.6.0014

Hegland, P. A., Aarlie, H., Strømme, H., & Jamtvedt, G. (2017). Simulation-based training for nurses: Systematic review and meta-analysis. *Nurse Education Today*, *54*, 6–20. doi:10.1016/j.nedt.2017.04.004 PMID:28456053

Heikkilä, V. T., Paasivaara, M., & Lassenius, C. (2016, May). Teaching university students Kanban with a collaborative board game. In *Proceedings of the 38th international conference on software engineering companion* (pp. 471-480) 10.1145/2889160.2889201

Heim, A. B., & Holt, E. A. (2021). From Bored Games to Board Games: Student-Driven Game Design in the Virtual Classroom. *Journal of Microbiology & Biology Education*, *22*(1), ev22i1.2323. Advance online publication. doi:10.1128/jmbe.v22i1.2323 PMID:33884075

Hemmer, I., Bayrhuber, H., Häußler, P., Hemmer, M., Hlawatsch, S., Hoffmann, L., & Raffelsiefer, M. (2007). Students' interest in geoscience topics, contexts and methods. *Geographie und ihre Didaktik. Journal of Geography Education*, *4*, 185–197.

Heng, K. (2014). The Relationships between Student Engagement and the Academic Achievement of First-Year University Students in Cambodia. *The Asia-Pacific Education Researcher*, *23*(2), 179–189. doi:10.100740299-013-0095-8

Henseler, J., Ringle, C. M., & Sarstedt, M. (2015). A new criterion for assessing discriminant validity in variance-based structural equation modeling. *Journal of the Academy of Marketing Science*, *43*(1), 115–135. doi:10.100711747-014-0403-8

Hermanns, M., Deal, B., Campbell, A. M., Hillhouse, S., Opella, J. B., Faigle, C., & Campbell, R. H. IV. (2018). Using an "Escape Room" toolbox approach to enhance pharmacology education. *Journal of Nursing Education and Practice*, *8*(4), 89. doi:10.5430/jnep.v8n4p89

Hernández-Barco, M., Cañada-Cañada, F., Corbacho-Cuello, I., & Sánchez-Martín, J. (2021a). An Exploratory Study Interrelating Emotion, Self-Efficacy and Multiple Intelligence of Prospective Science Teachers. *Frontiers in Education*, *6*(March), 1–12. doi:10.3389/feduc.2021.604791

Hernández-Barco, M., Sánchez-Martín, J., Blanco-Salas, J., & Ruiz-Téllez, T. (2019). Teaching Down to Earth. Service-Learning methodology for science education and sustainability at University level. A practical approach. *Sustainability*, *12*(542), 1–23.

Hernández-Barco, M., Sánchez-Martín, J., Corbacho-cuello, I., & Cañada-Cañada, F. (2021b). Emotional Performance of a Low-Cost Eco-Friendly Project Based Learning Methodology for Science Education: An Approach in Prospective Teachers. *Sustainability*, *13*(3385), 1–19. doi:10.3390u13063385

Herriott, R. E., & Firestone, W. A. (1983). Multisite qualitative policy research: Optimizing description and generalizability. *Educational Researcher*, *12*(2), 14–19. doi:10.3102/0013189X012002014

Herrman, J. (2019, June 19). Slack Wants to Replace Email. Is That What We Want? *The New York Times*. https://www.nytimes.com/2019/06/19/style/slack-replace-email-ipo-listing.html

Herrmann, K., Hannon, P., Cox, J., Ternouth, P., & Crowley, T. (2008). *Developing entrepreneurial graduates: putting entrepreneurship at the centre of higher education*. NESTA.

HESA. (2021). *Graduates in work | HESA*. Retrieved 5 August 2021, from https://www.hesa.ac.uk/data-and-analysis/graduates/activities/work

Hess, T., & Gunter, G. (2013). Serious game-based and nongame-based online courses: Learning experiences and outcomes. *British Journal of Educational Technology*, *44*(3), 372–385. doi:10.1111/bjet.12024

Hevey, D. (2018). Network analysis: A brief overview and tutorial. *Health Psychology and Behavioral Medicine*, *6*(1), 301–328. doi:10.1080/21642850.2018.1521283 PMID:34040834

High Fliers. (2021). *High Fliers*. Retrieved 8 August 2021, from https://www.highfliers.co.uk/

Higher education sector (for R&D data) | UNESCO UIS. (n.d.). Retrieved July 30, 2021, from http://uis.unesco.org/en/glossary-term/higher-education-sector-rd-data

Hill, D. R., & Brunvand, S. (2018). Gamification. In *The K-12 Educational Technology Handbook*. https://edtechbooks.org/k12handbook/gamification

Hill, D. R., & Brunvand, S. (2017). Gaming the system: Helping students level-up their learning. *International Journal on Teaching and Learning in Higher Education*, *30*(1), 70–79.

Hindle, K. (2002). A grounded theory for teaching entrepreneurship using simulation games. *Simulation & Gaming*, *33*(2), 236–241. doi:10.1177/1046878102332012

Hinds, A. P. (1975). Separating the sirloin from the salami. *Training and Development Journal*, *29*(3), 42–44. https://eric.ed.gov/?id=EJ113779

Ho, A. M. (2018). Unlocking Ideas: Using Escape Room Puzzles in a Cryptography Classroom. *PRIMUS (Terre Haute, Ind.)*, *28*(0), 1–13. doi:10.1080/10511970.2018.1453568

Hoffman, B., & Nadelson, L. (2010). Motivational engagement and video gaming: A mixed methods study. *Educational Technology Research and Development*, *58*(3), 245–270. doi:10.100711423-009-9134-9

Hofstede, G. (1997). *Cultures and Organizations: Software of the Mind*. McGraw-Hill.

Hofstede, G. (2011). Dimensionalizing Cultures: The Hofstede Model in Context. *Online Readings in Psychology and Culture*, *2*(1). Advance online publication. doi:10.9707/2307-0919.1014

Hofstetter, F. T. (1981). *Computer-Based Instruction: Roots*. Origins, Applications, Benefits, Features, Systems, Trends and Issues.

Holcombe, R. G. (1998). Entrepreneurship and economic growth. *Quarterly Journal of Austrian Economics*, *1*(2), 45–62. doi:10.100712113-998-1008-1

Holland, S., Marshall, P., Bird, J., Dalton, S., Morris, R., Pantidi, N., ... Clark, A. (2009, February). Running up Blueberry Hill: Prototyping whole body interaction in harmony space. In *Proceedings of the 3rd international Conference on Tangible and Embedded interaction* (pp. 93-98). 10.1145/1517664.1517690

Holmes, J. (2018). Building confidence in foreign language communication through 'Skilled Use of Interaction Strategies'. *Sciences de l'Homme et Société / Education*. https://dumas.ccsd.cnrs.fr/dumas-01942635

Homer, R., Hew, K. F., & Tan, C. Y. (2018). Comparing digital badges-and-points with classroom token systems: Effects on elementary school ESL students' classroom behavior and English learning. *Journal of Educational Technology & Society*, *21*(1), 137–151.

Hopfgartner, F., Kazai, G., Kruschwitz, U., Meder, M., & Shovman, M. (2015). Second international workshop on gamification for information retrieval (gamifir'15). In *European Conference on Information Retrieval* (pp. 838-840). Springer.

Hoppe, M., Westerberg, M., & Leffler, E. (2017). Educational approaches to entrepreneurship in higher education: A view from the Swedish horizon. *Education + Training*, *59*(7/8), 751–767. doi:10.1108/ET-12-2016-0177

Horváth, I. (2019). MaxWhere 3D capabilities contributing to the enhanced efficiency of the Trello 2D management software. *Acta Polytechnica Hungarica*, *16*(6), 55–71. doi:10.12700/APH.16.6.2019.6.5

Houlfort, N., Koestner, R., Joussemet, M., Nantel-Vivier, A., & Lekes, N. (2002). The impact of performance-contingent rewards on perceived autonomy and competence. *Motivation and Emotion*, *29*(4), 279–295. doi:10.1023/A:1022819120237

Hoyle, R. H. (1995). Structural equation modeling: Concepts, issues, and applications. *Sage (Atlanta, Ga.)*.

Hoysniemi, J. (2006). International survey on the Dance Dance Revolution game. *Computers in Entertainment*, *4*(2), 8. doi:10.1145/1129006.1129019

Hsieh, H. F., & Shannon, S. E. (2005). Three approaches to qualitative content analysis. *Qualitative Health Research*, *15*(9), 1277–1288. doi:10.1177/1049732305276687 PMID:16204405

Hsu, C. L., & Chen, M. C. (2018). How gamification marketing activities motivate desirable consumer behaviors: Focusing on the role of brand love. *Computers in Human Behavior*, *88*(11), 121–133. doi:10.1016/j.chb.2018.06.037

Hsu, E. (1989). Role-event gaming simulation in management education: A conceptual framework and review. *Simulation & Gaming*, *20*(4), 409–438. doi:10.1177/104687818902000402

Huang, W. H. Y., & Soman, D. (2013). *A practitioner's guide to gamification of education. Research reports series, behavioural economics in action*. Academic Press.

Huang, B., & Hew, K. F. (2018). Implementing a theory-driven gamification model in higher education flipped courses: Effects on out-of-class activity completion and quality of artifacts. *Computers & Education, 125*, 254–272. doi:10.1016/j.compedu.2018.06.018

Huang, B., Hwang, G. J., Hew, K. F., & Warning, P. (2019). Effects of gamification on students' online interactive patterns and peer-feedback. *Distance Education, 40*(3), 350–379. doi:10.1080/01587919.2019.1632168

Huang, C. L., Yang, S. C., & Hsieh, L. S. (2019). The cyberbullying behavior of Taiwanese adolescents in an online gaming environment. *Children and Youth Services Review, 106*, 1–10. doi:10.1016/j.childyouth.2019.104461

Huang, R., Ritzhaupt, A. D., Sommer, M., Zhu, J., Stephen, A., Valle, N., Hampton, J., & Li, J. (2020). The impact of gamification in educational settings on student learning outcomes: A meta-analysis. *Educational Technology Research and Development, 68*(4), 1875–1901. doi:10.100711423-020-09807-z

Huang, W. H. Y., & Soman, D. (2013). *A Practitioner's Guide to Gamification of eEducation. Rotman School of Management*. University of Toronto.

Huang, Y., Liu, R., Zhai, S., Ma, X., Zhou, M., & Deng, Q. (2015). A knowledge-intensive serious game for education of traditional chinese medicine: A pilot study. *International Journal of Hybrid Information Technology, 8*(3), 111–120. doi:10.14257/ijhit.2015.8.3.11

Huitt, W., & Hummel, J. (2003). Piagets Theory of Cognitive Development. In *Educational Psychology Interactive: cognitive development*. Valdosta State University. https://www.google.com/url?sa=t&rct=j&q=&esrc=s&source=web&cd=&cad=rja&uact=8&ved=2ahUKEwjijvjfpuLxAhWSHRQKHVJSBHcQgAMoAHoECAIQAg&url=http%3A%2F%2Fscholar.google.es%2Fscholar_url%3Furl%3Dhttps%3A%2F%2Fintranet.newriver.edu%2Fimages%2Fstories%2Flibrary%2Fstennett_psychology_articles%2FPiagets%252520Theory%252520of%252520Cognitive%252520Development.pdf%26hl%3Des%26sa%3DX%26ei%3DsrXuYJrZONzSsQLa-bb4DA%26scisig%3DAAGBfm1v3pK0vg0T8d5QUl1dSac91MMN_g%26nossl%3D1%26oi%3Dscholarr&usg=AOvVaw1_dbqUkiMk_8j2wv5gZCBG

Huizinga, J. (1938). *Homo ludens: A study of the play-element in culture.* Beacon Press.

Huizinga, J. (1971). *Homo ludens: o jogo como elemento da cultura* [Homo ludens: The game as an element of culture]. Editora da Universidade de S. Paulo & Editora Perspectiva.

Huizinga, J. (2007). *Homo ludens: the game as an element of culture* [Homo ludens: o jogo como elemento da cultura]. Perspectiva.

Huizinga, J. (2017). *Homo Ludens: o jogo como elemento da cultura* [Homo Ludens: the game as a cultural element] (8th ed.). Perspectiva.

Huizinga, J. H. L. (2014). *Homo Ludens: the game as an element of culture* [Homo Ludens: o jogo como elemento da cultura]. Perspectiva. doi:10.4324/9781315824161

Hummel, H. G., Nadolski, R. J., Eshuis, J., Slootmaker, A., & Storm, J. (2021). Serious game in introductory psychology for professional awareness: Optimal learner control and authenticity. *British Journal of Educational Technology, 52*(1), 125–141. doi:10.1111/bjet.12960

Hung, A. C. Y. (2017). A Critique and Defense of Gamification. *Journal of Interactive Online Learning, 15*(1).

Hung, A. C. Y. (2018). Gamification as Design Thinking. *International Journal on Teaching and Learning in Higher Education, 30*(3), 549–559.

Hunicke, R., Leblanc, M., & Zubek, R. (2004). MDA: a formal approach to game design and game research. In *Challenges in Games AI Workshop, Nineteenth National Conference of Artificial Intelligence Proceedings*. AAAI Press.

Hunicke, R., LeBlanc, M., & Zubek, R. (2004). MDA: A formal approach to game design and game research. In *Proceedings of the AAAI Workshop on Challenges in Game AI* (*Vol. 4*, No. 1, p. 1722). Academic Press.

Hunicke, R., LeBlanc, M., & Zubek, R. (2004, July). MDA: A formal approach to game design and game research. In *Proceedings of the AAAI Workshop on Challenges in Game AI* (*Vol. 4*, No. 1, p. 1722). Academic Press.

Huotari, K., & Hamari, J. (2012, October). Defining gamification: a service marketing perspective. In *Proceeding of the 16th international academic MindTrek conference* (pp. 17-22). 10.1145/2393132.2393137

Huotari, K., & Hamari, J. (2017). A definition for gamification: Anchoring gamification in the service marketing literature. *Electronic Markets*, *27*(1), 21–31. doi:10.100712525-015-0212-z

Hurlburt, G. (2018). Thinking Critically about Algorithmic Thinking. *IT Professional*, *20*(2), 5–10.

Hursen, C., & Bas, C. (2019). Use of Gamification Applications in Science Education. *International Journal of Emerging Technologies in Learning*, *14*(1), 4–23. doi:10.3991/ijet.v14i01.8894

Hussain, S., Mills, A., & Sanders, A. K. (2018). Use of Slack in the undergraduate classroom as a means of fostering student/faculty engagement. *Qatar Foundation Annual Research Conference Proceedings*. 10.5339/qfarc.2018.SSAHPP995

Iacovides, I., McAndrew, P., Scanlon, E., & Aczel, J. (2014). The gaming involvement and informal learning framework. *Simulation & Gaming*, *45*(4-5), 611–626. doi:10.1177/1046878114554191

Iida, M., Shrout, P. E., Laurenceau, J.-P., & Bolger, N. (2012). Using diary methods in psychological research. In *APA handbook of research methods in psychology* (Vol. 1). American Psychological Association.

Ilardi, B. C., Leone, D., Kasser, T., & Ryan, R. M. (1993). Employee and supervisor ratings of motivation: Main effects and discrepancies associated with job satisfaction and adjustment in a factory setting 1. *Journal of Applied Social Psychology*, *23*(21), 1789–1805. doi:10.1111/j.1559-1816.1993.tb01066.x

Imlig-Iten, N., & Petko, D. (2018). Comparing serious games and educational simulations: Effects on enjoyment, deep thinking, interest and cognitive learning gains. *Simulation & Gaming*, *49*(4), 401–422. doi:10.1177/1046878118779088

Inkpen, K., Booth, K. S., Klawe, M., & Upitis, R. (1995). Playing together beats playing apart, especially for girls [Paper presentation]. The meeting of Computer Support for Collaborative Learning '95, Bloomington, IN.

Instant messaging. (2021). In *Wikipedia*. https://en.wikipedia.org/w/index.php?title=Instant_messaging&oldid=1031867862

International Telecommunication Union (ITU). (2019). *Measuring digital development: Facts and figures 2019*. https://www.itu.int/en/ITU-D/Statistics/Documents/facts/FactsFigures2019.pdf

Iscenco, A., & Li, J. (2014). *The game with impact: Gamification in environmental education and entrepreneurship. Moldovan Environmental Governance Academy*. MEGA.

ISFE. (2020). *Europe Video Game Industry Key Facts 2020*. https://www.isfe.eu/wp-content/uploads/2020/08/ISFE-final-1.pdf

Iten, N., & Petko, D. (2016). Learning with serious games: Is fun playing the game a predictor of learning success? *British Journal of Educational Technology*, *47*(1), 151–163. doi:10.1111/bjet.12226

Ivancheva, M. (2020). Unbundling: A new gendered frontier of exclusion and exploitation in the neoliberal university. *Journal of New Materialist Research*, *1*, 80–109. doi:10.1344/jnmr.v1i1.29204

Izquierdo, M. (2007). Teaching science, a new science [Enseñar ciencias, una nueva ciencia]. *Enseñanza de las Ciencias Sociales*, *6*, 125–138.

Jabbar, A. I. A., & Felicia, P. (2015). Gameplay engagement and learning in game-based learning: A systematic review. *Review of Educational Research*, *85*(4), 740–779. doi:10.3102/0034654315577210

Jacob, M., Kühhirt, M., & Rodrigues, M. (2019). Labour market returns to graduates' international experience: Exploring cross-country variation in Europe. *European Sociological Review*, *35*(4), 491–505. doi:10.1093/esr/jcz022

Jambhekar, K., Pahls, R. P., & Deloney, L. A. (2019). Benefits of an Escape Room as a Novel Educational Activity for Radiology Residents. *Academic Radiology*, 1–8. doi:10.1016/j.acra.2019.04.021 PMID:31160173

Jamieson, I. (1984). Education for enterprise. In *CRAC* (Vol. 19). Ballinger.

Janakiraman, S., Watson, S. L., & Watson, W. R. (2018). Using Game-based Learning to Facilitate Attitude Change for Environmental Sustainability. *Journal of Education for Sustainable Development*, *12*(2), 176–185. doi:10.1177/0973408218783286

Jannicke, B. H., Anna, B., & Klaus-Dieter, T. (2017). Avatars as motivational factors in simulation games. *The International Scientific Conference eLearning and Software for Education*, *1*, 263. 10.12753/2066-026x-17-039

Jaramillo-Alcázar, A., Venegas, E., Criollo-C, S., & Luján-Mora, S. (2021). An approach to accessible serious games for people with dyslexia. *Sustainability*, *13*(5), 2507. doi:10.3390u13052507

Jarvis, P., Holford, J., & Griffin, C. (2003). *The theory & practice of learning*. Routledge. doi:10.4324/9780203465653

JAXA. (2021). https://global.jaxa.jp/.

Jay, J. K., & Johnson, K. L. (2002). Capturing complexity: A typology of reflective practice for teacher education. *Teaching and Teacher Education*, *18*(1), 73–85. doi:10.1016/S0742-051X(01)00051-8

Jelodar, H., Wang, Y., Yuan, C., Feng, X., Jiang, X., Li, Y., & Zhao, L. (2019). Latent Dirichlet allocation (LDA) and topic modeling: Models, applications, a survey. *Multimedia Tools and Applications*, *78*(11), 15169–15211. doi:10.100711042-018-6894-4

Jeong, J. S., González-Gómez, D., & Cañada-Cañada, F. (2016). Students' perceptions and emotions toward learning in a flipped general science classroom. *Journal of Science Education and Technology*, *25*(5), 747–758. doi:10.100710956-016-9630-8

Jeong, K. Y., & Bozkurt, I. (2014). Evaluating a project management simulation training exercise. *Simulation & Gaming*, *45*(2), 183–203. doi:10.1177/1046878113518481

Jerčić, P., Wen, W., Hagelbäck, J., & Sundstedt, V. (2018). The effect of emotions and social behavior on performance in a collaborative serious game between humans and autonomous robots. *International Journal of Social Robotics*, *10*(1), 115–129. doi:10.100712369-017-0437-4

Jewelbots Friendship Bracelets - STEM for Best Friends. (2019). Retrieved from https://jewelbots.com/

Jiménez, C., Lafuente, R., Ortiz, M., Bruton, L., & Luna, V. M. (2017). Room Escape: Proposal of Gamification in the Degree of Physiotherapy [Room Escape: Propuesta de Gamificación en el Grado de Fisioterapia]. *Proc. Congreso Nacional De Innovación Educativa Y De Docencia En Red*, 537–551.

Jimenez-Saez, J. C., Ramirez de la Piscina, S., Castellanos, M., & Palacios, P. (2019). Trends in university teaching in physics: Interaction and gamification. *Edulearn19: 11th International Conference on Education and New Learning Technologies*, 2831-2836. 10.21125/edulearn.2019.0763

Johnson, D., Flagg, A., & Dremsa, T. L. (2010). Effects of using human patient simulator versus a CD-ROM on learning the management of patients exposed to chemical agents. *U.S. Army Medical Department Journal*, 9–16. PMID:21181669

Johnson, L., Adams Becker, S., Cummins, M., Estrada, V., Freeman, A., & Hall, C. (2013). *NMC Horizon report: higher education edition. Report*. The New Media Consortium.

Johnson, L., Adams Becker, S., Estrada, V., & Freeman, A. (2014). *NMC Horizon Report* K-12. The New Media Consortium.

Johnson, M. L., & Larson, S. (2003). Something in the way she moves"-metaphors of musical motion. *Metaphor and Symbol*, *18*(2), 63–84. doi:10.1207/S15327868MS1802_1

Johnson, M. P., Wilson, A., Blumberg, B., Kline, C., & Bobick, A. (1999). Sympathetic interfaces: using a plush toy to direct synthetic characters. In *Proceedings of the SIGCHI conference on Human Factors in Computing Systems* (pp. 152-158). ACM.

Johnson, R. D., & Marakas, G. M. (2000). Research Report: The Role of Behavioral Modeling in Computer Skills Acquisition: Toward Refinement of the Model. *Information Systems Research*, *11*(4), 402–417. doi:10.1287/isre.11.4.402.11869

Johnson, W. L. (2010). Serious use of a serious game for language learning. *International Journal of Artificial Intelligence in Education*, *20*(2), 175–195. doi:10.3233/JAI-2010-0006

Jordan, K. (2014). Initial trends in enrolment and completion of massive open online courses. *The International Review of Research in Open and Distributed Learning.*, *15*(1). Advance online publication. doi:10.19173/irrodl.v15i1.1651

Joy, P. A. (2017). The uneasy history of experiential education in US law schools. *Dickinson Law Review*, *122*, 551.

Juan, A. A., Loch, B., Daradoumis, T., & Ventura, S. (2017). Games and simulation in higher education. *International Journal of Educational Technology in Higher Education*, *14*(1), 1–3. doi:10.118641239-017-0075-9

Juntunen, M. L., & Hyvönen, L. (2004). Embodiment in musical knowing: How body movement facilitates learning within Dalcroze Eurhythmics. *British Journal of Music Education*, *21*(2), 199–214. doi:10.1017/S0265051704005686

Jurado, J. L., Fernandez, A., & Collazos, C. A. (2015, October). Applying gamification in the context of knowledge management. In *Proceedings of the 15th International Conference on Knowledge Technologies and Data-driven Business* (pp. 1–4). 10.1145/2809563.2809606

Jurgelaitis, M., Čeponienė, L., Čeponis, J., & Drungilas, V. (2019). Implementing gamification in a university-level UML modeling course: A case study. *Computer Applications in Engineering Education*, *27*(2), 332–343. doi:10.1002/cae.22077

Jusoff, K., & Khodabandelou, R. (2009). Preliminary study on the role of social presence in blended learning environment in higher education. *International Education Studies*, *2*(4), 79–83. doi:10.5539/ies.v2n4p79

Justice, C., Rice, J., Warry, W., Inglis, S., Miller, S., & Sammon, S. (2007). Inquiry in higher education: Reflections and directions on course design and teaching methods. *Innovative Higher Education*, *31*(4), 201–214. doi:10.100710755-006-9021-9

Kahu, E. R. (2013). Framing Student Engagement in Higher Education. *Studies in Higher Education*, *38*(5), 758–773. doi:10.1080/03075079.2011.598505

Kalogiannakis, M., Papadakis, S., & Zourmpakis, A. I. (2021). Gamification in science education. A systematic review of the literature. *Education Sciences*, *11*(1), 22. Advance online publication. doi:10.3390/educsci11010022

Kalyuga, S., & Plass, J. L. (2009). Evaluating and managing cognitive load in games. In R. Ferdig (Ed.), *Handbook of research on effective electronic gaming in education* (pp. 719–737). IGI Global. doi:10.4018/978-1-59904-808-6.ch041

Kalz, M., Börner, D., Ternier, S., & Specht, M. (2015). Mindergie: A pervasive learning game for pro-environmental behaviour at the workplace. In L. H. Wong, M. Milrad, & M. Specht (Eds.), *Seamless learning in the age of mobile connectivity* (pp. 397–417). Springer. doi:10.1007/978-981-287-113-8_20

Kano Computer & Coding Kits | Creative Coding For All Ages. (n.d.). Retrieved from https://kano.me/

Kappen, D. L., & Nacke, L. E. The kaleidoscope of effective gamification: Deconstructing gamification in business applications. *Conference on Gameful Design*, 119-122. 10.1145/2583008.2583029

Kapp, K. M. (2007). Tools and techniques for transferring know-how from boomers to gamers. *Global Business and Organizational Excellence*, *26*(5), 22–37. doi:10.1002/joe.20162

Kapp, K. M. (2012). *The gamification of learning and instruction: game-based methods and strategies for training and education*. John Wiley & Sons.

Kapp, K. M. (2012). *The gamification of learning and instruction: Game-based methods and strategies for training and education*. Pfeiffer.

Kapp, K. M. (2012). *The Gamification of Learning And Instruction: Game-Based Methods And Strategies For Training And Education*. Pfeiffer.

Kapralos, B. (2021). Learning about serious game design and development at the K-12 level. *International Journal of Information and Learning Technology*, *38*(3), 316–327. doi:10.1108/IJILT-01-2021-0003

Kasser, T., Davey, J., & Ryan, R. M. (1992). Motivation and employee-supervisor discrepancies in a psychiatric vocational rehabilitation setting. *Rehabilitation Psychology*, *37*(3), 175–188. doi:10.1037/h0079104

Kaufmann, D. A. (2018). Reflection: Benefits of Gamification in Online Higher Education. *Journal of Institutional Research*, *7*(1), 125–132. doi:10.9743/JIR.2018.12

Ke, F. (2008). A case study of computer gaming for math: Engaged learning from gameplay? *Computers & Education*, *51*(4), 1609–1620. doi:10.1016/j.compedu.2008.03.003

Ke, F. (2009). A qualitative meta-analysis of computer games as learning tools. In R. E. Ferdig (Ed.), *Effective electronic gaming in education* (pp. 1–32). Information Science Reference. doi:10.4018/978-1-59904-808-6.ch001

Kelley, T. M., & Johnston, E. (2012). Discovering the appropriate role of serious games in the design of open governance platforms. *Public Administration Quarterly*, 504–554.

Kellner, D. (2001). *A cultura da mídia – estudos culturais: Identidade e política entre o moderno e o pós-moderno* [Media culture - cultural studies: Identity and politics between the modern and the postmodern]. EDUSC.

Kelmar, J. H. (1992). Business plans for teaching entrepreneurial behaviour. *Education + Training*, *34*(1). Advance online publication. doi:10.1108/00400919210007511

Kerbal Space Program (KSP). (2021). https://www.kerbalspaceprogram.com/

Kessim, M., & Altinpulluk, H. (2015). A Theoretical Analysis of Moocs Types from a Perspective of Learning Theories. *Procedia: Social and Behavioral Sciences*, *186*, 15–19. doi:10.1016/j.sbspro.2015.04.056

Kessler, M. C., de Paula, C. G., & Lemos, R. S. M. (2011). PROMA: In search of answers to successive repetitions in differential calculus [PROMA: Em busca de respostas para as repetências sucessivas no Cálculo Diferencial]. *Proceeding of XXXIX COBENGE - Congresso Brasileiro de Ensino de Engenharia*, *29*, 1–10.

Keys, B., & Wolfe, J. (1990). The role of management games and simulations in education and research. *Journal of Management*, *16*(2), 307–336. doi:10.1177/014920639001600205

Keys, E., Luctkar-Flude, M., Tyerman, J., Sears, K., & Woo, K. (2020). Developing a Virtual Simulation Game for Nursing Resuscitation Education. *Clinical Simulation in Nursing*, *39*, 51–54. doi:10.1016/j.ecns.2019.10.009

Khaleel, F. L., Sahari Ashaari, N., Tengku Wook, T. S. M., & Ismail, A. (2016). Gamification Elements for Learning Applications. *International Journal on Advanced Science, Engineering and Information Technology*, *6*(6), 868–874. doi:10.18517/ijaseit.6.6.1379

Khaleel, F. L., Siti, T., Tengku, M., Sahari Ashaari, N., & Ismail, A. (2016). The Architecture of Dynamic Gamification Elements Based Learning Content. *Journal of Convergence Information Technology*, *11*(June), 164–177. https://www.researchgate.net/publication/304639660

Khalil, M., Wong, J., de Koning, B., Ebner, M., & Paas, F. (2018). *Gamification in MOOCs: A review of the state of the art* [Paper presentation] IEEE Global Engineering Education Conference (EDUCON2018). 10.1109/EDUCON.2018.8363430

Khalil, M. K., & Elkhider, I. A. (2016). Best Practices Applying learning theories and instructional design models for effective instruction Khalil MK, Elkhider IA. Applying learning theories and instruc-tional design models for effective instruction. *Advances in Physiology Education*, *40*(2), 147–156. doi:10.1152/advan.00138.2015 PMID:27068989

Khaliq, I., & Purkiss, B. (2015). *A study of interaction in idle games & perceptions on the definition of a game. In 2015 IEEE Games Entertainment Media Conference*. IEEE. doi:10.1109/GEM.2015.7377233

Khan, S., Channa, S., Ali, S. A., Khan, M. H., Qazi, A.H., & Mengal, K. (2019). 3d Modeling for Wildlife Encyclopedia Using Blender. *3C Tecnologia*, 133-147. doi:10.17993/3ctecno.2019.specialissue3.133-147

Khoroshko, L. L., Ukhov, P. A., & Keyno, P. P. (2019). Development of massive open online courses based on 3d computer graphics and multimedia. *International Journal of Engineering Pedagogy*, *9*(4), 4–15. doi:10.3991/ijep.v9i4.10193

Khurana, D., Koli, A., Khatter, K., & Singh, S. (2017). *Natural language processing: State of the art, current trends and challenges*. ArXiv Preprint ArXiv:1708.05148.

Kiili, K. (2007). Foundation for problem-based gaming. *British Journal of Educational Technology*, *38*(3), 394–404. doi:10.1111/j.1467-8535.2007.00704.x

Kiili, K., & Lainema, T. (2008). Foundation for measuring engagement in educational games. *Journal of Interactive Learning Research*, *19*(3), 469–488. doi:10.1016/j.iheduc.2004.12.001

Kim, S., Song, K., Lockee, B., & Burton, J. (2018). Gamification cases in education. In Gamification in Learning and Education: Enjoy Learning Like Gaming. (pp. 117–123). Springer International Publishing. doi:10.1007/978-3-319-47283-6_10

Kim, S., Song, K., Lockee, B., & Burton, J. (2018). What is Gamification in Learning and Education? In Gamification in Learning and Education. Advances in Game-Based Learning (pp. 25–38). doi:10.1007/978-3-319-47283-6_4

Kim, B., Park, H., & Baek, Y. (2009). Not just fun, but serious strategies: Using meta-cognitive strategies in game-based learning. *Computers & Education*, *52*(4), 800–810. Advance online publication. doi:10.1016/j.compedu.2008.12.004

Kim, J., & Castelli, D. M. (2021). Effects of gamification on behavioral change in education: A meta-analysis. *International Journal of Environmental Research and Public Health*, *18*(7), 3550. Advance online publication. doi:10.3390/ijerph18073550 PMID:33805530

Kim, S. (2021). How a company's gamification strategy influences corporate learning: A study based on gamified MSLP (mobile social learning platform). *Telematics and Informatics*, *57*, 101505. doi:10.1016/j.tele.2020.101505

Kim, S. B., Kim, K.-T., Kim, O., Seo, E. Y., & Lee, S. J. (2021). A research tool for biomechanics toward sensory-motor manipulation, Unity 3D. *Journal of Biomechanical Science and Engineering*, *16*(2), 1–7. doi:10.1299/jbse.21-00068

Kim, S., Song, K., Lockee, B., & Burton, J. (2018). *Gamification in Learning and education - Enjoy Learning Like Gaming*. Springer International Publishing AG. doi:10.1007/978-3-319-47283-6

Kinio, A. E., Dufresne, L., Brandys, T., & Jetty, P. (2018). Break out of the Classroom : The Use of Escape Rooms as an Alternative Teaching Strategy in Surgical Education. *Journal of Surgical Education*, *76*(1), 134–139. doi:10.1016/j.jsurg.2018.06.030 PMID:30126728

Kirkpatrick, D. L., & Kirkpatrick, J. D. (2006). *Evaluating training programs: The four levels*. Berrett-Koehler. https://www.bkconnection.com/books/title/evaluating-training-programs

Kirkpatrick, D. L., & Kirkpatrick, J. D. (2009). Evaluating: part of a ten-step process. In *Evaluating training programs*. Berrett-Koehler Publishers Inc.

Kirriemuir, J., & McFarlane, A. (2004). *Literature review in games and learning*. Academic Press.

Kiryakova, G., Angelova, N., & Yordanova, L. (2014). *Gamification in education*. Academic Press.

Kiryakova, G., Angelova, N., & Yordanova, L. (2014). *Gamification in Education*. Conference: 9th International Balkan Education and Science Conference, Edirne, Turkey.

Kiryakova, G., Angelova, N., & Yordanova, L. (2014, October). Gamification in education. In *Proceedings of 9th International Balkan Education and Science Conference*.

Kirzner, I. (1979). *Perception, opportunity, and profit: studies in the theory of entrepreneurship. University of Chicago Press*.

Kleiber, I. (2020). (Video) games in the language classroom. HINT. *Heidelberg Inspirations for Innovative Teaching*, 45-59. doi:10.11588/HINT.2020.1.77690

Kline, R. B. (2011). *Principles and practice of structural equation modeling (3. Baskı)*. Guilford.

Klopfer, E., Osterweil, S., & Salen, K. (2009). *Moving learning games forward*. Academic Press.

Kneebone, R. (2005). Evaluating clinical simulations for learning procedural skills: A theory-based approach. *Academic Medicine*, *80*(6), 549–553. doi:10.1097/00001888-200506000-00006 PMID:15917357

Knutas, A., Ikonen, J., Nikula, U., & Porras, J. (2014). Increasing collaborative communications in a programming course with gamification: A case study. *Proceedings of the 15th International Conference on Computer Systems and Technologies - CompSysTech '14,* 370–377. 10.1145/2659532.2659620

Kobes, M., Helsloot, I., de Vries, B., & Post, J. (2010). Exit choice, (pre-)movement time and (pre-)evacuation behaviour in hotel fire evacuation – Behavioural analysis and validation of the use of serious gaming in experimental research. *Procedia Engineering*, *3*, 37–51. doi:10.1016/j.proeng.2010.07.006

Koivisto, J., & Hamari, J. (2014). Demographic differences in perceived benefit from gamification. *Computers in Human Behavior*, *35*, 179–188. doi:10.1016/j.chb.2014.03.007

Koivisto, J., & Hamari, J. (2019). The rise of motivational information systems: A review of gamification research. *International Journal of Information Management*, *45*(4), 191–210. doi:10.1016/j.ijinfomgt.2018.10.013

Kokol, P., Blažun Vošner, H., & Završnik, J. (2020). Application of bibliometrics in medicine: A historical bibliometrics analysis. *Health Information and Libraries Journal*. PMID:31995273

Kolb, D. A. (2014). *Experiential learning: Experience as the source of learning and development*. FT Press.

Komin, S. (1990). Culture and Work-Related Values in Thai Organizations. *International Journal of Psychology, 25*(3–6), 681–704. doi:10.1080/00207599008247921

Koper, R. (2015). How do students want to learn in online distance education? Profiling student preferences. *The International Review of Research in Open and Distributed Learning, 16*(1), 307–329. doi:10.19173/irrodl.v16i1.2000

Koren, M., & Pető, R. (2020). Business disruptions from social distancing. *PLoS One, 15*(9), e0239113. doi:10.1371/journal.pone.0239113 PMID:32946463

Korhonen, H., Montola, M., & Arrasvuori, J. (2009). *Understanding playful user experience through digital games. International Conference on Designing Pleasurable Products and Interfaces*, Compiegne, France.

Koriat, A. (1997). Monitoring one's own knowledge during study: A cue-utilization approach to judgments of learning. *Journal of Experimental Psychology, 126*(4), 349–370. doi:10.1037/0096-3445.126.4.349

Koriat, A., Sheffer, L., & Ma'ayan, H. (2002). Comparing objective and subjective learning curves: Judgments of learning exhibit increased underconfidence with practice. *Journal of Experimental Psychology, 131*(2), 147–162. doi:10.1037/0096-3445.131.2.147 PMID:12049237

Korn, O., & Schmidt, A. (2015). Gamification of Business Processes: Re-designing Work in Production and Service Industry. *Procedia Manufacturing, 3*, 3424–3431. Advance online publication. doi:10.1016/j.promfg.2015.07.616

Kortemeyer, G. (2016). Work habits of students in traditional and online sections of an introductory physics course: A case study. *Journal of Science Education and Technology, 25*(5), 697–703. doi:10.100710956-016-9624-6

Köse, D. B., Morschheuser, B., & Hamari, J. (2019). Is it a tool or a toy? How user's conception of a system's purpose affects their experience and use. *International Journal of Information Management, 49*, 461–474. doi:10.1016/j.ijinfomgt.2019.07.016

Koster. (2004). A theory of fun. Paraglyph Press.

Koster, R. (2010). *A theory of fun for game design*. Paraglyph Press.

Kotler, P., Hermanwan, K., & Iwan, S. (2016). *Marketing 4.0: Moving from traditional to digital*. John Wiley & Sons Inc.

Kotsopoulos, D., Bardaki, C., & Pramatari, K. (2016). Gamification, geolocation and sensors for employee motivation towards energy conservation at the workplace. *MCIS 2016 Proceedings*. https://aisel.aisnet.org/mcis2016/39

Kotsopoulos, D., Bardaki, C., Papaioannou, T. G., Lounis, S., Stamoulis, G. D., & Pramatari, K. (2019). Designing a serious game to motivate energy savings in a museum: Opportunities & challenges. In A. Liapis, G. Yannakakis, M. Gentile, & M. Ninaus (Eds.), Lecture Notes in Computer Science: Vol. 11899. *Games and Learning Alliance* (pp. 572–584). Springer. doi:10.1007/978-3-030-34350-7_55

Kotsopoulos, D., Bardaki, C., Papaioannou, T. G., Pramatari, K., & Stamoulis, G. D. (2020). User-centered gamification: The case of IoT-enabled energy conservation at work. *International Journal of E-Services and Mobile Applications, 12*(2), 15–39. doi:10.4018/IJESMA.2020040102

Koutropoulos, A., Gallagher, M. S., Abajian, S. C., De Waard, I., Hogue, R. J., Keskin, N., & Rodriguez, C. O. (2012). Emotive Vocabulary in MOOCs: Context & Participant Retention. *European Journal of Open, Distance and E-Learning, 1*. https://www.eric.ed.gov/PDFS/EJ979609.pdf

Kovačević, A., Konjović, Z., Milosavljević, B., & Nenadic, G. (2012). Mining methodologies from NLP publications: A case study in automatic terminology recognition. *Computer Speech & Language, 26*(2), 105–126. doi:10.1016/j.csl.2011.09.001

Kovari, A. (2020). Study of algorithmic problem-solving and executive function. *Acta Polytechnica Hungarica*, *17*(9).

Kraiger, K. (2002). Decision-based evaluation. In K. Kraiger (Ed.), *Creating, implementing, and managing effective training and development: State-of-the-art lessons for practice* (pp. 331–375). Jossey-Bass. https://www.researchgate.net/publication/281601028_Decision-based_evaluation

Kraiger, K., & Ford, J. K. (2020). The science of workplace instruction: Learning and development applied to work. *Annual Review of Organizational Psychology and Organizational Behavior*, *8*(1), 45–72. doi:10.1146/annurev-orgpsych-012420-060109

Kraiger, K., Ford, J. K., & Salas, E. (1993). Application of cognitive, skill-based, and affective theories of learning outcomes to new methods of training evaluation. *The Journal of Applied Psychology*, *78*(2), 311–328. doi:10.1037/0021-9010.78.2.311

Krath, J., Schürmann, L., & von Korflesch, H. F. (2021). Revealing the theoretical basis of gamification: A systematic review and analysis of theory in research on gamification, serious games and game-based learning. *Computers in Human Behavior*, *125*, 106963. doi:10.1016/j.chb.2021.106963

Krathwohl, D. R. (2002). A Revision of Bloom's Taxonomy: An Overview. *Theory into Practice*, *41*(4), 212–218. doi:10.120715430421tip4104_2

Krehbiel, T. C., Salzarulo, P. A., Cosmah, M. L., Forren, J., Gannod, G., Havelka, D., Hulshult, A. R., & Merhout, J. (2017). Agile Manifesto for Teaching and Learning. *The Journal of Effective Teaching*, *17*(2), 90–111. https://uncw.edu/jet/articles/vol17_2/krehbiel.html

Krippendorff, K. (2018). *Content analysis: An introduction to its methodology*. Sage publications.

Kropp, M., & Meier, A. (2013, May). Teaching agile software development at university level: Values, management, and craftsmanship. In *2013 26th International Conference on Software Engineering Education and Training (CSEE&T)* (pp. 179–188). IEEE. 10.26041/fhnw-626

Kruglyk, V., Bukreiev, D., Chornyi, P., Kupchak, E., & Sender, A. (2020). Discord platform as an online learning environment for emergencies. *Ukrainian Journal of Educational Studies and Information Technology*, *8*(2), 13–28. doi:10.32919/uesit.2020.02.02

Kuhn, R. (2009). Information literacy for law students: An approach to meeting the challenges of professional training and practice. *Innovation*, *38*(1). Advance online publication. doi:10.4314/innovation.v38i1.46973

Kultima, A., Niemelä, J., Paavilainen, J., & Saarenpää, H. (2008, November). Designing game idea generation games. In *Proceedings of the 2008 conference on future play: Research, play, share* (pp. 137-144). 10.1145/1496984.1497007

Kumar, B., & Khurana, P. (2012). 2012 Gamification in education – learn computer programming with fun International. *Journal of Computers and Distributed Systems*, *2*(1), 46–53.

Kumar, E. (2011). *Natural language processing*. IK International Pvt Ltd.

Kumar, S. (2015). Co-authorship networks: A review of the literature. *Aslib Journal of Information Management*, *67*(1), 55–73. doi:10.1108/AJIM-09-2014-0116

Kuo, M.-S., & Chuang, T.-Y. (2016). How gamification motivates visits and engagement for online academic dissemination – An empirical study. *Computers in Human Behavior*, *55*, 16–27. doi:10.1016/J.CHB.2015.08.025

Kuratko, D. F. (2005). The emergence of entrepreneurship education: Development, trends, and challenges. *Entrepreneurship Theory and Practice*, *29*(5), 577–597. doi:10.1111/j.1540-6520.2005.00099.x

Kush, P., Cudney, E. A., Materla, T., & Antony, J. (2021). Systematic literature review of quality maturity matrix. *Total Quality Management & Business Excellence*, *32*(3-4), 289–297. doi:10.1080/14783363.2018.1552130

Kusuma, G. P., Wigati, E. K., Utomo, Y., & Suryapranata, L. K. P. (2018). Analysis of Gamification Models in Education Using MDA Framework. *Procedia Computer Science*, *135*, 385–392. doi:10.1016/j.procs.2018.08.187

Laabidi, M., Jemni, M., Ayed, L. J. B., Brahim, H. B., & Jemaa, A. B. (2014). Learning technologies for people with disabilities. *Journal of King Saud University-Computer and Information Sciences*, *26*(1), 29–45. doi:10.1016/j.jksuci.2013.10.005

Laas, O. (2017). On game definitions. *Journal of the Philosophy of Sport*, *44*(1), 81–94. doi:10.1080/00948705.2016.1255556

Labs, D. (2019). *Digital Dream Labs, LLC | Make Game Time, Brain Time*™. Retrieved from https://www.digitaldreamlabs.com/

Lacher, L. L., & Biehl, C. (2019). *Investigating team effectiveness using Discord: A case study using a gaming collaboration tool for the CS classroom*. Academic Press.

Lacreu, H. L. (2014). Aciertos, distorsiones y falacias en la enseñanza de las ciencias naturales de la educación secundaria obligatoria de Argentina. *Terræ Didatica*, *10*(3), 217–226. doi:10.20396/td.v10i3.8637323

Lakoff, G., & Johnson, M. (2008). *Metaphors we live by*. University of Chicago press.

Landers, R. N., Armstrong, M. B., & Collmus, A. B. (2017). How to use game elements to enhance learning: Applications of the theory of gamified learning. In M. Ma & A. Oikonomou (Eds.), Serious games and edutainment applications. Springer. doi:10.1007/978-3-319-51645-5_21

Landers, R. N. (2015). Developing a theory of gamified learning: Linking serious games and gamification of learning. *Simulation & Gaming*, *45*(6), 752–768. doi:10.1177/1046878114563660

Landers, R. N. (2019). Gamification misunderstood: How badly executed and rhetorical gamification obscures its transformative potential. *Journal of Management Inquiry*, *28*(2), 137–140. doi:10.1177/1056492618790913

Landers, R. N., & Armstrong, M. B. (2017). Enhancing instructional outcomes with gamification: An empirical test of the Technology-Enhanced Training Effectiveness Model. *Computers in Human Behavior*, *71*, 499–507. doi:10.1016/j.chb.2015.07.031

Landers, R. N., Bauer, K. N., Callan, R. C., & Armstrong, M. B. (2015). Psychological theory and the gamification of learning. In T. Reiners & L. Wood (Eds.), *Gamification in education and business* (pp. 165–186). Springer. doi:10.1007/978-3-319-10208-5_9

Landers, R. N., & Landers, A. K. (2014). An Empirical Test of the Theory of Gamified Learning. *Simulation & Gaming*, *45*(6), 769–785. doi:10.1177/1046878114563662

Laopongharn, W., & Sercombe, P. (2009). What relevance does intercultural communication have to language education in thailand? In ARECLS (Vol. 6, pp. 59–83). Academic Press.

Lao, R. (2015). *A Critical Study of Thailand's Higher Education Reforms: The culture of borrowing*. Routledge.

Lapadat, J. C. (2017). Ethics in autoethnography and collaborative autoethnography. *Qualitative Inquiry*, *23*(8), 589–603. doi:10.1177/1077800417704462

Lapkin, S., Fernandez, R., Levett-Jones, T., & Bellchambers, H. (2010). The effectiveness of using human patient simulation manikins in the teaching of clinical reasoning skills to undergraduate nursing students: A systematic review. *JBI Library of Systematic Reviews*, *8*(16), 661–694. doi:10.11124/01938924-201008160-00001 PMID:27820553

Lasater, K. (2007). Clinical judgment development: Using simulation to create an assessment rubric. *The Journal of Nursing Education*, *46*(11), 496–503. doi:10.3928/01484834-20071101-04 PMID:18019107

Laster, J. (2010). *At Indiana U., A class on game design has students playing to win.* Retrieved from: http://chronicle.com/blogs/wiredcampus/at-indiana-u-a-class-on-game-design-has-students-playing-to-win/21981

Lathwesen, C., & Belova, N. (2021). Escape Rooms in STEM Teaching and Learning—Prospective Field or Declining Trend? A Literature Review. *Education Sciences*, *11*(6), 308. doi:10.3390/educsci11060308

Latulipe, C., Long, N. B., & Seminario, C. E. (2015). Structuring Flipped Classes with Lightweight Teams and Gamification. *Proceedings of the 46th ACM Technical Symposium on Computer Science Education*, 392–397. 10.1145/2676723.2677240

Laurie, R., Nonoyama-Tarumi, Y., Mckeown, R., & Hopkins, C. (2016). Contributions of Education for Sustainable Development (ESD) to Quality Education: A Synthesis of Research. *Journal of Education for Sustainable Development*, *10*(2), 226–242. doi:10.1177/0973408216661442

Lazarides, T. (2015, September 14). *Ex-'Fates Forever' developers making "Discord", a voice comm app for multiplayer mobile games.* TouchArcade. https://toucharcade.com/2015/09/14/ex-fates-forever-developers-making-discord-a-voice-comm-app-for-multiplayer-mobile-games/

Lázaro, I. (2019). Escape Room como propuesta de gamificación en educación. *Revista Educativa Hekademos*, *27*(12), 71–79.

Lázaro, I. G. (2019). Escape Room as a proposal for gamification in education [Escape Room como propuesta de gamificación en educación]. *Revista Educativa Hekademos*, (27), 71–79.

Lazzaro, N. (2004). *Why we play games: Four keys to more emotion without story.* Retrieved from: http://www.xeodesign.com/xeodesign_whyweplaygames.pdf /

Leaning, M. (2015). A study of the use of games and gamification to enhance student engagement, experience and achievement on a theory-based course of an undergraduate media degree. *Journal of Media Practice*, *16*(2), 155–170. doi:10.1080/14682753.2015.1041807

Learning Resources. (2019). Retrieved from https://www.learningresources.com/category/category/featured/award-winning.do

Lee, E., Nakra, T. M., & Borchers, J. (2004, June). You're the conductor: a realistic interactive conducting system for children. In *Proceedings of the 2004 conference on New interfaces for musical expression* (pp. 68-73). Academic Press.

Lee, D., Frey, G. C., Min, A., Kim, B., Cothran, D. J., Bellini, S., Han, K., & Shih, P. C. (2020). Usability inquiry of a gamified behavior change app for increasing physical activity and reducing sedentary behavior in adults with and without autism spectrum disorder. *Health Informatics Journal*, *26*(4), 2992–3008. doi:10.1177/1460458220952909 PMID:32951500

Lee, H., & Doh, Y. Y. (2012, August). A study on the relationship between educational achievement and emotional engagement in a gameful interface for video lecture systems. In *International Symposium on Ubiquitous Virtual Reality* (pp. 34-37). IEEE. 10.1109/ISUVR.2012.21

Lee, J., & Hammer, J. (2011). Gamification in education: What, how, why bother? *Academic Exchange Quarterly*, *15*(2), 3–4.

Leemkuil, H., de Jong, T., & Ootes, S. (2000). *Review of educational use of games and simulations* (No. IST-1999-130). KITS Consortium. https://www.researchgate.net/publication/250740593_Review_of_educational_use_of_games_and_simulations

Legaki, N. Z., Xi, N., Hamari, J., Karpouzis, K., & Assimakopoulos, V. (2020). The effect of challenge-based gamification on learning: An experiment in the context of statistics education. *International Journal of Human-Computer Studies, 144*(12), 1–14. doi:10.1016/j.ijhcs.2020.102496 PMID:32565668

Legerén, B., & Rada, F. (2014). *The rules of the game* [Las reglas del juego]. Avanca Cinema.

Lehtonen, T., Aho, T., Isohanni, E., & Mikkonen, T. (2015). On the role of gamification and localization in an open online learning environment: Javala experiences. In *Proceedings of the 15th Koli Calling Conference on Computing Education Research* (pp. 50-59). ACM. 10.1145/2828959.2828973

Lemke, J. L. (2010). Letramento metamidiático: Transformando significados e mídias [Metamediatic literacy: transforming meanings and media]. *Trabalhos em Lingüística Aplicada, 49*(2), 455–479. doi:10.1590/S0103-18132010000200009

Lennie, J., & Tacchi, J. A. (2013). *Evaluating Communication for Development: A framework for social change*. Routledge. doi:10.4324/9780203078495

Leonard, S., & Oberprieler, K. (2018). Gamifying design education. *Conference Proceedings of the Academy for Design Innovation Management, 1*(1). 10.33114/adim.2017.79

Lepper, M. R. (1985). Microcomputers in education: Motivational and social issues. *The American Psychologist, 40*(1), 1–18. doi:10.1037/0003-066X.40.1.1

Lerdpornkulrat, T., Koul, R., & Poondej, C. (2018). Relationship between perceptions of classroom climate and institutional goal structures and student motivation, engagement and intention to persist in college. *Journal of Further and Higher Education, 42*(1), 102–115. doi:10.1080/0309877X.2016.1206855

Lertchoosakul, K. (2021). The white ribbon movement: High school students in the 2020 Thai youth protests. *Critical Asian Studies, 53*(2), 206–218. doi:10.1080/14672715.2021.1883452

Léste, J. V. (2021). *The Informational Ergonomics of Tabletop Games' Rulebooks. An analysis on informational hierarchy and organization* (1916169/CA) [Masters Dissertation, Pontifical Catholic University of Rio de Janeiro]. Maxwell database.

Leung, A. (2006). A conceptual model of information technology training leading to better outcomes. *International Journal of Business and Information, 1*(1), 74–95. doi:10.6702/IJBI.2006.1.1.4

Levitan, E. P. (2010). *Higher education administrators' perceptions of the use of simulation games for adult learners* (Publication No. 3406153) [Doctoral dissertation, Argosy University]. ProQuest Dissertation Publishing. http://search.proquest.com/docview/275851740

Lewis, Z. H., Swartz, M. C., & Lyons, E. J. (2016). What's the point?: A review of reward systems implemented in gamification interventions. *Games for Health Journal, 5*(2), 93–99. doi:10.1089/g4h.2015.0078 PMID:26812253

Liaw, S. S., & Huang, H. M. (2013). Perceived satisfaction, perceived usefulness and interactive learning environments as predictors to self-regulation in e-learning environments. *Computers & Education, 60*(1), 14–24. doi:10.1016/j.compedu.2012.07.015

Liaw, S. Y., Chan, S. W., Chen, F. G., Hooi, S. C., & Siau, C. (2014). Comparison of virtual patient simulation with mannequin-based simulation for improving clinical performances in assessing and managing clinical deterioration: Randomized controlled trial. *Journal of Medical Internet Research, 16*(9), e214. doi:10.2196/jmir.3322 PMID:25230684

Liaw, S. Y., Wong, L. F., Chan, S. W., Ho, J. T., Mordiffi, S. Z., Ang, S. B., Goh, P. S., & Ang, E. N. (2015). Designing and evaluating an interactive multimedia Web-based simulation for developing nurses' competencies in acute nursing care: Randomized controlled trial. *Journal of Medical Internet Research, 17*(1), e5. doi:10.2196/jmir.3853 PMID:25583029

Liddy, E. D. (2001). *Natural language processing*. Academic Press.

Lieberman, D. A. (2006). What can we learn from playing interactive games? In P. Vorderer & J. Bryant (Eds.), *Playing video games—Motives, responses, and consequences* (pp. 379–397). Lawrence Erlbaum Associates.

Lieberoth, A. (2015). Shallow gamification: Psychological effects of framing an activity as a game. *Games and Culture, 10*(3), 249–268. doi:10.1177/1555412014559978

Lifanova, A., Ngan, H. Y., Okunewitsch, A., Rahman, S., Guzmán, S., Desai, N., . . . Karayel, M. (2016, July). New locals: Overcoming integration barriers with mobile informal and gamified learning. In *Proceedings of the International Conference on Information Communication Technologies in Education (ICICTE)* (pp. 7-9). Academic Press.

Li, K., Hall, M., Bermell-Garcia, P., Alcock, J., Tiwari, A., & González-Franco, M. (2017). Measuring the learning effectiveness of serious gaming for training of complex manufacturing tasks. *Simulation & Gaming, 48*(6), 770–790. doi:10.1177/1046878117739929

Lilley, D., & Lofthouse, V. (2009). Sustainable design education – considering design for behavioural change. *Engineering Education, 4*(1), 29–41. doi:10.11120/ened.2009.04010029

Li, M. C., & Tsai, C. C. (2013). Game-based learning in science education: A review of relevant research. *Journal of Science Education and Technology, 22*(6), 877–898. doi:10.100710956-013-9436-x

Lim, D., & Rubasundram, G. A. (2018). Disruption in teaching & learning: Experiential learning and gamification in practice. *Electronic Journal of Business & Management, 1*, 87–93.

Liñán, F. (2004). Intention-based models of entrepreneurship education. *Piccolla Impresa/Small Business, 3*(1), 11-35.

Lioce, L., Lopreiato, J., Downing, D., Chang, T., Robertson, J., Anderson, M., Diaz, D., & Spain, A. E.Terminology and Concepts Working Group. (2020). *Healthcare Simulation Dictionary* (2nd ed.). Agency for Healthcare Research and Quality. doi:10.23970imulationv2

Lipovetsky, G. (2004). *Os tempos hipermodernos* [Hypermodern times]. Bacarolla.

Lis, S., Baer, N., Franzen, N., Hagenhoff, M., Gerlach, M., Koppe, G., Sammer, G., Gallhofer, B., & Kirsch, P. (2016). Social interaction behavior in ADHD in adults in a virtual trust game. *Journal of Attention Disorders, 20*(4), 335–345. doi:10.1177/1087054713482581 PMID:23564736

Lister, M. (2015). Gamification: The effect on student motivation and performance at the post-secondary level. *Issues and Trends in Educational Technology, 3*(2). Advance online publication. doi:10.2458/azu_itet_v3i2_Lister

Liyanagunawardena, T. R., & Aboshady, O. A. (2018). Massive open online courses: A resource for health education in developing countries. *Global Health Promotion, 25*(3), 74–76. doi:10.1177/1757975916680970 PMID:28134014

Llorens Largo, F., Gallego-Durán, F. J., Villagrá-Arnedo, C.-J., Compañ, P., Satorre Cuerda, R., & Molina-Carmona, R. (2015). Lessons learned by gamifying when it was not yet called gamification [Lecciones aprendidas gamificando cuando aún no se llamaba gamificación]. *La Sociedad Del Aprendizaje. Actas Del III Congreso Internacional Sobre Aprendizaje, Innovación y Competitividad. CINAIC 2015*, 214–219.

Lockee, B., & Song, K. (2021). Three Perspectives to See Students in Gamified Classes. *ISSUU*. https://issuu.com/bainespsa/docs/a76891_isa_journal_issue_24_issuu/s/11678935

Lodi, M. Growth mindset in computational thinking teaching and teacher training. *13th ACM Conference on International Computing Education Research (ICER)*, 281-282. 10.1145/3105726.3105736

Löffler, A., Prifti, L., Levkovskyi, B., Utesch, M., & Krcmar, H. (2018, April). Simulation games for the digital transformation of business processes: Development and application of two prototypes from the automotive and online retail sector. In *2018 IEEE Global Engineering Education Conference (EDUCON)* (pp. 1475-1483). IEEE. 10.1109/EDUCON.2018.8363407

Loganathan, P., Talib, C. A., Thoe, N. K., Aliyu, F., & Zawadski, R. (2019). Implementing technology infused gamification in science classroom: A systematic review and suggestions for future research. *Learning Science and Mathematics Journal, 14*, 60-73. http://recsam.edu.my/sub_lsmjournal/images/docs/2019/2019_5_PL_6073_Final.pdf

Longhini, J., Rossettini, G., & Palese, A. (2021). Massive open online courses for nurses' and healthcare professionals' continuous education: A scoping review. *International Nursing Review*, *68*(1), 108–121. doi:10.1111/inr.12649 PMID:33855697

Long, M. H. (1980). Inside the "black box": Methodological issues in classroom research on language learning. *Language Learning*, *30*(1), 1–42. doi:10.1111/j.1467-1770.1980.tb00149.x

Loon, M., Evans, J., & Kerridge, C. (2015). Learning with a strategic management simulation game: A case study. *International Journal of Management Education*, *13*(3), 227–236. doi:10.1016/j.ijme.2015.06.002

Looyestyn, J., Kernot, J., Boshoff, K., Ryan, J., Edney, S., & Maher, C. (2017). Does gamification increase engagement with online programs? A systematic review. *PLoS One*, *12*(3), e0173403. doi:10.1371/journal.pone.0173403 PMID:28362821

Lopes, A. P., Soler, M., Cana, R., Cortes, L., Bentabol, M., Bentabol, A., ... Luna, M. J. (2019). Gamification in education and active methodologies at higher education. *Edulearn19: 11th International Conference on Education and New Learning Technologies*, 1633-1640. 10.21125/edulearn.2019.0480

López Secanell, I., & Ortega Torres, E. (2020). *Educational Escape Room: Conception of future secondary education teachers in the specialty of physical education and technology on the experience of designing and participating in an educational escape room* [Escape Room Educativa: Concepción de los futuros maestros de educación secundaria en especialidad de educación física y tecnología sobre la experiencia de diseñar y participar en una escape room educativa]. DIDACTICAE, Universitat de Barcelona. https://revistes.ub.edu/index.php/didacticae/article/view/22648/pdf doi:10.1344/did.2020.8.176-192

López, F. R., Arias-Oliva, M., Pelegrín-Borondo, J., & Marín-Vinuesa, L. M. (2021). Serious games in management education: An acceptance analysis. *International Journal of Management Education*, *19*(3), 100517. doi:10.1016/j.ijme.2021.100517

López-Pernas, S., Gordillo, A., Barra, E., & Quemada, J. (2019). Examining the use of an educational escape room for teaching programming in a higher education setting. *IEEE Access: Practical Innovations, Open Solutions*, *7*, 31723–31737. doi:10.1109/ACCESS.2019.2902976

López-Pernas, S., Gordillo, A., Barra, E., & Quemada, J. (2021). Escapp: A Web platform for conducting educational escape rooms. *IEEE Access: Practical Innovations, Open Solutions*, *9*, 38062–38077. doi:10.1109/ACCESS.2021.3063711

López-Quintero, J. L., Pontes-Pedrajas, A., & Varo-Martínez, M. (2019). Las TIC en la enseñanza científico-tecnica hispanoamericana: Una revisión bibliográfica. *Digitital Education Review*, *35*(6), 229–243. doi:10.1344/der.2019.35.229-243

Low, M., Venkataraman, S., & Srivatsan, V. (1994). Developing an entrepreneurship game for teaching and research. *Simulation & Gaming*, *25*(3), 383–401. doi:10.1177/1046878194253006

Lucassen, G., & Jansen, S. (2014). Gamification in consumer marketing-future or fallacy? *Procedia: Social and Behavioral Sciences*, *148*, 194–202. doi:10.1016/j.sbspro.2014.07.034

Lugmayr, A., Sutinen, E., Suhonen, J., Sedano, C. I., Hlavacs, H., & Montero, C. S. (2017). Serious storytelling – a first definition and review. *Multimedia Tools and Applications*, *76*(14), 15707–15733. Advance online publication. doi:10.100711042-016-3865-5

Luria, E., Shalom, M., & Levy, D. A. (2021). Cognitive Neuroscience Perspectives on Motivation and Learning: Revisiting Self-Determination Theory. *Mind, Brain, and Education, 15*(1), 5-17. https:// doi:10.1111/mbe.12275

Lu, W., Janssen, J., Milios, E., Japkowicz, N., & Zhang, Y. (2007). Node similarity in the citation graph. *Knowledge and Information Systems*, *11*(1), 105–129. doi:10.100710115-006-0023-9

Lv, P. H., Wang, G.-F., Wan, Y., Liu, J., Liu, Q., & Ma, F. (2011). Bibliometric trend analysis on global graphene research. *Scientometrics*, *88*(2), 399–419. doi:10.100711192-011-0386-x

Lytvyn, A., Lytvyn, V., Rudenko, L., Pelekh, Y., Didenko, O., Muszkieta, R., & Żukow, W. (2020). Informatization of technical vocational schools: Theoretical foundations and practical approaches. *Education and Information Technologies*, *25*(1), 583–609. doi:10.100710639-019-09966-4

Macauley, K., Brudvig, T. J., Kadakia, M., & Bonneville, M. (2017). Systematic Review of Assessments That Evaluate Clinical Decision Making, Clinical Reasoning, and Critical Thinking Changes After Simulation Participation. *Journal, Physical Therapy Education*, *31*(4), 64–75. doi:10.1097/JTE.0000000000000011

Machajewski, S. T. (2017). *Application of Gamification in a College STEM Introductory Course: A Case Study* [Doctoral Thesis, Northcentral University]. ProQuest Dissertations Publishing.

Madampe, M. A. K. G. (2017). Successful adoption of agile project management in software development industry. *International Journal of Computer Science and Information Technology Research*, *5*(4), 2327.

Maes, P., Darrell, T., Blumberg, B., & Pentland, A. (1997). The ALIVE system: Wireless, full-body interaction with autonomous agents. *Multimedia Systems*, *5*(2), 105–112. doi:10.1007005300050046

Ma, J.-P., Chuang, M.-H., & Lin, R. (2018). An innovated design of ER box by STEAM. In P.-L. P. Rau (Ed.), *Cross-Cultural Design: Applications in Cultural Heritage, Creativity and Social Development* (Vol. 2, pp. 70–79). Springer. doi:10.1007/978-3-319-92252-2_6

Makransky, G., & Petersen, G. B. (2019). Investigating the process of learning with desktop virtual reality: A structural equation modeling approach. *Computers & Education*, *134*, 15–30. doi:10.1016/j.compedu.2019.02.002

Malinverni, L., & Burguès, N. P. (2015, June). The medium matters: the impact of full-body interaction on the socio-affective aspects of collaboration. In *Proceedings of the 14th International Conference on Interaction Design and Children* (pp. 89-98). 10.1145/2771839.2771849

Malinverni, L., Mora-Guiard, J., Padillo, V., Valero, L., Hervás, A., & Pares, N. (2017). An inclusive design approach for developing video games for children with autism spectrum disorder. *Computers in Human Behavior*, *71*, 535–549. doi:10.1016/j.chb.2016.01.018

Malone, T. W., & Lepper, M. R. (1987). Making learning fun: A taxonomy of intrinsic motivations for learning. *Aptitude, learning and Instruction III: Cognitive and affective process analysis.*

Malone, T. W., & Lepper, M. R. (1987). Making learning fun: A taxonomy of intrinsic motivations for learning. In R. Snow & M. J. Farr (Eds.), Aptitude, learning, and instruction volume 3: Conative and affective process analyses (pp. 223–253). Lawrence Erlbaum Associates.

Malone, T. W. (1981). Toward a theory of intrinsically motivating instruction. *Cognitive Science*, *5*(4), 333–369. doi:10.120715516709cog0504_2

Malterud, K., Siersma, V. D., & Guassora, A. D. (2016). Sample size in qualitative interview studies: Guided by information power. *Qualitative Health Research*, *26*(13), 1753–1760. doi:10.1177/1049732315617444 PMID:26613970

Mandanici, M., Rodà, A., & Canazza, S. (2014, September). The "Harmonic Walk": An interactive educational environment to discover musical chords. ICMC.

Mandanici, M., Altieri, F., Pretto, N., Munaro, M., Canazza, S., & Menegatti, E. (2018, November). The "Good or Bad?" Game: Stimulating Listening Skills through Playful Engagement. In *Proceedings of the 4th EAI International Conference on Smart Objects and Technologies for Social Good* (pp. 177-182). 10.1145/3284869.3284917

Mandanici, M., Ludovico, L. A., & Avanzini, F. (2019). A computer-based approach to teach tonal harmony to young students. In *International Conference on Computer Supported Education* (pp. 271-279). SCITEPRESS. 10.5220/0007700402710279

Mandanici, M., Ludovico, L. A., Avanzini, F., & Baratè, A. (2019). Learning tonal harmony through bodily interactions and gamification. In *Music Educators and Researchers of Young Children* (pp. 237–246). Ghent University.

Mandanici, M., Rodà, A., & Canazza, S. (2016). The Harmonic Walk: An interactive physical environment to learn tonal melody accompaniment. *Advances in Multimedia.*

Manoopun, M. (2020). *A design strategy for changing attendee behavior to reduce single-use plastics at EDM festivals in Thailand.* Academic Press.

Manzano-León, A., Camacho-Lazarraga, P., Guerrero, M. A., Guerrero-Puerta, L., Aguilar-Parra, J. M., Trigueros, R., & Alias, A. (2021). Between Level Up and Game Over: A Systematic Literature Review of Gamification in Education. *Sustainability*, *13*(4), 2247. doi:10.3390u13042247

Marcos-Merino, J. M., Esteban Gallego, R., Ochoa De Alda, J. A. G., & Mellado, V. (2020). Effect of practical teaching on the emotions of teachers in training towards Biology: Analysis of the influence of gender [Efecto de la enseñanza práctica en las emociones de los maestros en formación hacia la Biología: análisis de la influencia del género]. *Revista Internacional de Pesquisa em Didática Das Ciências e Matemática*, *1*, 1–22.

Marczewski, A. (2015). User Types. In A. Marczewski (Ed.), Even Ninja Monkeys Like to Play: gamification, game thinking and motivational design (pp. 65-80). CreateSpace independent Publishing Platform.

Marczewski, A. (2018). Even Ninja Monkeys Like to Play: Unicorn Edition. Gamified UK.

Marczewski, A. (2014) User types & player types in gamification. *Proceedings of Gamification World Congress.*

Mariappan, M., Sing, J. C., & Nadarajan, M. (2016, December). Design and Development of Tangible Instruction Set for Educational Robotic System. In *Proceedings of the 4th International Conference on Control, Mechatronics and Automation* (pp. 12-15). ACM.

Marina, J. A. (2004). *Failed intelligence. Theory and practice of stupidity* [La inteligencia fracasada. Teoría y práctica de la estupidez]. Editorial Anagrama S.A.

Marín, V., López, M., & Berea, G. (2015). Can gamification be introduced within primary classes? *Digital Education Review*, *27*, 55–68.

Marques, D. (2017). *Virtual immersive simulation in nursing continuous education: Study developed at a hospital from Minho* [Master's thesis, Nursing School of Porto, Portugal]. RCAAP – Repositório Comum. http://hdl.handle.net/10400.26/22508

Marshall, M. N. (1996). Sampling for qualitative research. *Family Practice, 13*(6), 522–526. doi:10.1093/fampra/13.6.522 PMID:9023528

Martin, C., & Iucu, R. B. (2014). Teaching entrepreneurship to educational sciences students. *Procedia: Social and Behavioral Sciences, 116*, 4397–4400. doi:10.1016/j.sbspro.2014.01.954

Martinengo, L., Yeo, N., Tang, Z. Q., Markandran, K. D., Kyaw, B. M., & Tudor Car, L. (2019). Digital Education for the Management of Chronic Wounds in Health Care Professionals: Protocol for a Systematic Review by the Digital Health Education Collaboration. *JMIR Research Protocols, 8*(3), e12488. doi:10.2196/12488 PMID:30907743

Martínez Felipe, M., & Chivite Pérez, D. (2020). Escape games in education. [Juegos de escape en educación.] Padres y maestros. *Journal of Parents and Teachers, 383*(383), 37–42. doi:10.14422/pym.i383.y2020.006

Martínez-Chico, M., Liso, M. R. J., & Lucio-Villegas, R. L. G. (2015). Effect of a training program to teach science by inquiry based on models, on the didactic conceptions of future teachers [Efecto de un programa formativo para enseñar ciencias por indagación basada en modelos, en las concepciones didácticas de los futuros maestros]. *Revista Eureka Sobre Enseñanza y Divulgación de las Ciencias, 12*(1), 149–166.

Martins, A. M. O., Coimbra, M. N., Oliveira, J. A., & Maturano, A. S. (2019). Metodologias ativas para a inovação e qualidade do ensino e aprendizagem no ensino superior. *Revista EDaPECI, 19*(3), 122-132. doi:10.29276/redapeci.2019.19.312147.122-132

Martí-Parreño, J., Galbis-Córdova, A., & Currás-Pérez, R. (2021). Teachers' beliefs about gamification and competencies development: A concept mapping approach. *Innovations in Education and Teaching International, 58*(1), 84–94. doi:10.1080/14703297.2019.1683464

Martí-Parreño, J., Galbis-Córdova, A., & Miquel-Romero, M. J. (2018). Students' attitude towards the use of educational video games to develop competencies. *Computers in Human Behavior, 81*, 366–377. doi:10.1016/j.chb.2017.12.017

Martí-Parreño, J., Méndez-Ibáñez, E., & Alonso-Arroyo, A. (2016). The use of gamification in education: A bibliometric and text mining analysis. *Journal of Computer Assisted Learning, 32*(6), 663–676. doi:10.1111/jcal.12161

Martí-Parreño, J., Seguí-Mas, D., & Seguí-Mas, E. (2016). Teachers' attitude towards and actual use of gamification. *Procedia: Social and Behavioral Sciences, 228*, 682–688. doi:10.1016/j.sbspro.2016.07.104

Maskeliūnas R., Kulikajevas A., Blažauskas T., Damaševičius R., & Swacha J. (2020). An interactive serious mobile game for supporting the learning of programming in javascript in the context of eco-friendly city management. *Computers, 9*(4), 1–18. doi:10.3390/computers9040102

Mason, C. (2011). Entrepreneurship education and research: Emerging trends and concerns. *Journal of Global Entrepreneurship, 1*(1), 13–25.

Mason, R., & Rennie, F. (2006). *Elearning: The key concepts*. Routledge. doi:10.4324/9780203099483

Masukawa, K. (2016). The Origins of Board Games and Ancient Game Boards. In Simulation and Gaming in the Network Society (pp. 3-11). Springer. doi:10.1007/978-981-10-0575-6_1

Matlay, H., & Carey, C. (2006, October). Entrepreneurship education in the UK: a critical perspective. *ISBE Conference, Cardiff, November*.

Mattar, J. (2009). Interatividade e aprendizagem [Interactivity and learning]. In F. M. Litto & M. Formiga (Eds.), *Educação a distância: o estado da arte* (pp. 112–118). Pearson Prentice Hall.

Mattar, J. (2010). *Games em educação: Como os nativos digitais aprendem* [Games in Education: How digital natives learn]. Pearson Prentice Hall.

Mattar, J. (2010). *Games in education: how digital natives learn* [Games em educação: como os nativos digitais aprendem]. Pearson Prentice Hall.

Maxwell, W. D., Fabel, P. H., Diaz, V., Walkow, J. C., Kwiek, N. C., Kanchanaraksa, S., Wamsley, M., Chen, A., & Bookstaver, P. B. (2018). Massive open online courses in U.S. healthcare education: Practical considerations and lessons learned from implementation. *Currents in Pharmacy Teaching & Learning*, *10*(6), 736–743. doi:10.1016/j.cptl.2018.03.013 PMID:30025774

Mayer, R. E. (2002). Multimedia learning. *Psychology of Learning and Motivation - Advances in Research and Theory*, *41*, 85–139. doi:10.1016/S0079-7421(02)80005-6

Mayer, R. E. (2011). Multimedia learning and games. In S. Tobias & J. D. Fletcher (Eds.), *Computer games and instruction* (pp. 281–305). Information Age Publishing. https://psycnet.apa.org/reMultimedia learning and games.cord/2011-11269-010

Mayer, R. E., & Clark, R. C. (2002). *E-Learning and the Science of Instruction: Proven Guidelines for Consumers and Designers of Multimedia Learning*. Pfeiffer.

Mayer, R. E., Griffith, E., Naftaly, I., & Rothman, D. (2008). Increased interestingness of extraneous details leads to decreased learning. *Journal of Experimental Psychology. Applied*, *14*, 329–339. doi:10.1037/a0013835 PMID:19102616

Mazurek, M. O., Engelhardt, C. R., & Clark, K. E. (2015). Video games from the perspective of adults with autism spectrum disorder. *Computers in Human Behavior*, *51*, 122–130. doi:10.1016/j.chb.2015.04.062

McCartney, R., Boustedt, J., Eckerdal, A., Sanders, K., & Zander, C. (2017). *Folk pedagogy and the geek gene: Geekiness quotient*. Seattle, WA: Assoc Comp Machinery. doi:10.1145/3017680.3017746

McClarty, K. L., Orr, A., Frey, P. M., Dolan, R. P., Vassileva, V., & McVay, A. (2012). A Literature Review of Gaming in Education. *Gaming in Education*, 1–36.

McCoy, L., Lewis, J. H., & Dalton, D. (2016). Gamification and Multimedia for Medical Education: A Landscape Review. *The Journal of the American Osteopathic Association*, *116*(1), 22. doi:10.7556/jaoa.2016.003 PMID:26745561

McCullough, B. (2018). *How the Internet happened: From Netscape to the iPhone* (1st ed.). Liveright Publishing Corporation.

McGaghie, W. C., Issenberg, S. B., Petrusa, E. R., & Scalese, R. J. (2010). A critical review of simulation-based medical education research: 2003-2009. *Medical Education*, *44*(1), 50–63. doi:10.1111/j.1365-2923.2009.03547.x PMID:20078756

McGonigal, J. (2003). This is not a game: Immersive aesthetics and collective play. In *Proceedings of the Melbourne DAC 2003 Streamingworlds Conference*. RMIT University.

McGonigal, J. (2011). *Reality Is Broken: Why Games Make Us Better and How They Can Change the World*. Penguin Press.

McGonigal, J. (2011). *Reality is broken: Why games make us better and how they can change the world*. Penguin.

McGrath, J. E. (1984). *Groups: Interaction and performance*. Prentice-Hall. http://users.ece.utexas.edu/~perry/education/382v-s08/papers/mcgrath84.pdf

McInroy, L. B., & Mishna, F. (2017). Cyberbullying on online gaming platforms for children and youth. *Child & Adolescent Social Work Journal*, *34*(6), 597–607. doi:10.100710560-017-0498-0

McIntosh, J., Wells, Y., Smyth, B., & Long, C. (2007). Child-focused and child-inclusive divorce mediation: Comparative outcomes from a prospective study of postseparation adjustment. *Family Court Review*, *46*(1), 105–124. doi:10.1111/j.1744-1617.2007.00186.x

McMullan, W., Chrisman, J. J., & Vesper, K. H. (2002). Lessons from successful innovations in entrepreneurial support programming. *Innovation and entrepreneurship in Western Canada: From family businesses to multinationals*, 207-223.

McNerney, T. (2004). From turtles to Tangible Programming Bricks: Explorations in physical language design. *Personal and Ubiquitous Computing*, *8*(5), 326–337.

McQuiggan, S., Rowe, J., Lee, S., & Lester, J. (2008). *Story-based learning: The impact of narrative on learning experiences and outcomes*. Springer.

Meakim, C., Boese, T., Decker, S., Franklin, A. E., Gloe, D., Lioce, L., Sando, C. R., & Borum, J. C. (2013). Standards of Best Practice: Simulation Standard I: Terminology. *Clinical Simulation in Nursing*, *9*(6), S3–S11. doi:10.1016/j.ecns.2013.04.001

Medica Ružić, I., & Dumančić, M. (2015). Gamification in education. *Informatologia*, *48*(3–4), 198–204.

MedlinePlus, United States National Library of Medicine. (2021a). *Lead poisoning*. https://medlineplus.gov/ency/article/002473.htm

MedlinePlus, United States National Library of Medicine. (2021b). *Mercury poisoning*. https://medlineplus.gov/ency/article/002476.htm

Mekler, E. D., Birk, M. V., Rank, S., Iacovides, I., & Steinemann, S. T. (2016). Designing for emotional complexity in games: The interplay of positive and negative affect. *CHI PLAY 2016 - Proceedings of the Annual Symposium on Computer-Human Interaction in Play Companion*, 367–371.

Mekler, E. D., Brühlmann, F., Tuch, A. N., & Opwis, K. (2017). Towards understanding the effects of individual gamification elements on intrinsic motivation and performance. *Computers in Human Behavior*, *71*, 525–534. doi:10.1016/j.chb.2015.08.048

Mellado, V., Borrachero, B., Melo, L. V., Dávila-Acedo, M. A., Cañada, F., Conde, M. C., Costillo, E., Cubero, J., Esteban, R., Martínez, G., Ruiz, C., Sánchez, J., Garritz, A., Mellado, L., Vázquez-Bernal, B., Jimenez-Pérez, R., & Bermejo, M. L. (2014). Emotions in science teaching [Las emociones en la enseñanza de las ciencias]. *Enseñanza de las Ciencias*, *32*(3), 11–36.

Mellado, V., Borrachero, B., Melo, L. V., Dávila-Acedo, M. A., Cañada, F., Conde, M. C., Costillo, E., Cubero, J., Esteban, R., Martínez, G., Ruiz, C., Sánchez, J., Garritz, A., Mellado, L., Vázquez-Bernal, B., Jimenez-Pérez, R., & Bermejo, M. L. (2014). Las emociones en la enseñanza de las ciencias. *Enseñanza de las Ciencias*, *32*(3), 11–36. doi:10.5565/rev/ensciencias.1478

Membrive, V., & Armie, M. (2020). *Beyond gamification: Classcraft as an engagement tool in the teaching of english as a second language*. http://end-educationconference.org/wp-content/uploads/2020/06/2020end016.pdf

Mendes, K. B., & Giostri, E. (2008). Teaching calculus I and the reality of engineering and technology students [Ensino de cálculo I e a realidade dos alunos de engenharia e tecnologia]. *XXXVI Congresso Brasileiro De Ensino De Engenharia*, 36.

Menkel-Meadow, C. (2019). Thinking or Acting Like A Lawyer? What We Don't Know About Legal Education and are Afraid to Ask. In *The State of Legal Education Research: Then and Now and Tomorrow*. TaylorFrancis/Routledge.

Merriam, S. B. (2008). Adult learning theory for the twenty-first century. *New Directions for Adult and Continuing Education*, *2008*(119), 93–98. doi:10.1002/ace.309

Mesa, del Carmen, Campos, & Vázquez. (2019). Análisis de la motivación del estudiante de educación superior participante en una propuesta de evaluación formativa. *Sport TK: Revista Euroamericana De Ciencias Del Deporte, 8*(2), 53-58.

Metrôlho, J. C., Ribeiro, F. R., & Passão, P. (2020). Teaching Agile Software Engineering Practices Using Scrum and a Low-Code Development Platform–A Case Study. *ICSEA*, *2020*, 160–165.

Metwally, A. H. S., Nacke, L. E., Chang, M., Wang, Y., & Yousef, A. M. F. (2021). Revealing the hotspots of educational gamification: An umbrella review. *International Journal of Educational Research, 109*. doi:10.1016/j.ijer.2021.101832

Meyer, M. W., & Norman, D. (2020). Changing Design Education for the 21st Century. *She Ji*, *6*(1), 13–49. Advance online publication. doi:10.1016/j.sheji.2019.12.002

Meyer, M., Libaers, D., Thijs, B., Grant, K., Glänzel, W., & Debackere, K. (2014). Origin and emergence of entrepreneurship as a research field. *Scientometrics*, *98*(1), 473–485.

Miau, S., & Yang, J.-M. (2018). Bibliometrics-based evaluation of the Blockchain research trend: 2008–March 2017. *Technology Analysis and Strategic Management*, *30*(9), 1029–1045. doi:10.1080/09537325.2018.1434138

Michael, D., & Chen, S. (2006). *Serious games: Games that educate, train, and inform.* Thomson Course Technology.

Microduino. (2019). Retrieved from https://microduinoinc.com/

Microsoft. (2022). https://www.microsoft.com/it-it

Mikhak, B., Martin, F., Resnick, M., Berg, R., & Silverman, B. (1999). The Children's Wearable Machines: Handheld and Wearable Computers too. *Proc. IEEE HUC 1999*, 31-43.

Miller, C. C. (2021, June 23). Do Chance Meetings at the Office Boost Innovation? There's No Evidence of It. *The New York Times*. https://www.nytimes.com/2021/06/23/upshot/remote-work-innovation-office.html

Mills, S. C. (2006). *Using the internet for active teaching and learning*. Pearson/Merrill/Prentice Hall.

Mina, D., Salah, J., & Abdennadher, S. (2021). ARcode: Programming for Youngsters Through AR. *Lecture Notes in Networks and Systems*, *326*, 65–74. doi:10.1007/978-3-030-86618-1_7

MinecraftEdu. (2022a). https://education.minecraft.net/en-us/homepage

MinecraftEdu. (2022b). *International Space Station.* Available at https://education.minecraft.net/en-us/challenges/a-visit-to-the-international-space-station

MinecraftEdu. (2022c). *Build a Mars rover*. Available at https://education.minecraft.net/en-us/challenges/build-a-mars-rover

MinecraftEdu. (2022d). *Minecraft Teacher Academy*. available at https://education.minecraft.net/en-us/resources/get-trained

MinecraftEdu. (2022e). *New study: understanding the impact of Minecraft in the math classroom.* Available at https://education.minecraft.net/en-us/blog/new-study-understanding-the-impact-of-minecraft-in-the-math-classroom

Minnegalieva, C. B., Galimyanov, A. F., & Khambelov, A. I. (2020). Development of environmental conservation in digital era. *Procedia Environmental Science*, *Engineering and Management*, *7*(3), 469–477.

Minniti, M., & Lévesque, M. (2008). *Recent developments in the economics of entrepreneurship*. Academic Press.

Miri, D. H., & Macke, J. (2021). Gamification, motivation, and engagement at work: A qualitative multiple case study. *European Business Review*. Advance online publication. doi:10.1108/EBR-04-2020-0106

MissionX. (2021). https://www.esa.int/Science_Exploration/Human_and_Robotic_Exploration/Education/Mission_X_-_Train_like_an_astronaut

Miyamoto, T., Noguchi, S., & Yamashita, H. (2008). Selection of an optimal solution for multiobjective electromagnetic apparatus design based on game theory. *IEEE Transactions on Magnetics, 44*(6), 1026–1029.

Mnatsakanyan, O. L. (2012). Organizatsiya kollektivnoy deyatel'nosti shkol'nikov s ispol'zovaniyem servisov sotsial'nykh setey [Organization of collective activities of schoolchildren using social networking services]. *Computer Science Education.*

Mogli, M., & Papadopoulou, M. (2018). "If I stay here, I will learn the language": Reflections from a case study of Afghan refugees learning Greek as a Second Language. *Research Papers in Language Teaching & Learning, 9*(1).

Mohd, C. K. N. C. K., & Shahbodin, F. (2015). Personalized learning environment: Alpha testing, Beta Testing & user acceptance test. *Procedia: Social and Behavioral Sciences, 195*, 837–843. doi:10.1016/j.sbspro.2015.06.319

Moita, F. (2007). *Game on: Jogos eletrônicos na escola e na vida da geração* [Game on: Electronic games at school and in the life of the generation @]. Alínea.

Moizer, J., Lean, J., Dell'Aquila, E., Walsh, P., Keary, A. A., O'Byrne, D., Di Ferdinando, A., Miglino, O., Friedrich, R., Asperges, R., & Sica, L. S. (2019). An approach to evaluating the user experience of serious games. *Computers & Education, 136*, 141–151. doi:10.1016/j.compedu.2019.04.006

Molina, J. J., Ortiz, A., & Agreda, M. (2017). Analisis de la integracion de procesos gamificados en Educacion Primaria. In Innovacion docente y uso de las TIC en eduacion. Universidad de Malaga (UMA).

Mollick, E. R., & Rothbard, N. (2014). *Mandatory fun: Consent, gamification, and the impact of games at work.* The Wharton School Research Paper Series.

Monaghan, S. R., & Nicholson, S. (2017). Bringing Escape Room Concepts to Pathophysiology Case Studies. *HAPS Educator, 21*(2), 49–65. doi:10.21692/haps.2017.015

Monterrat, B., Lavoué, É., & George, S. (2017). Adaptation of gaming features for motivating learners. *Simulation & Gaming, 48*(5), 625–656. doi:10.1177/1046878117712632

Montessori, M. (1916). *The Montessori Method.* Schocken Books.

Moon Camp. (2022). https://mooncampchallenge.org/

Moore, D. L., & Tarnai, J. (2002). Evaluating nonresponse error in mail surveys. In R. M. Groves, D. A. Dillman, J. L. Eltinge, & R. J. A. Little (Eds.), *Survey Nonresponse* (pp. 197–211). John Wiley & Sons.

Moore, L., & Campbell, N. (2021). Effectiveness of an escape room for undergraduate interprofessional learning: A mixed methods single group pre-post evaluation. *BMC Medical Education, 21*(1), 1–8. doi:10.118612909-021-02666-z PMID:33879150

Moore, M., & Kearsley, G. (2007). *Distance education: an integrated vision* [Educação a distância: uma visão integrada]. Thomson Learning.

Moore, T., & Morton, J. (2017). The myth of job readiness? Written communication, employability, and the 'skills gap' in higher education. *Studies in Higher Education, 42*(3), 591–609. doi:10.1080/03075079.2015.1067602

Mora, F. (2012). What are emotions? [¿Qué son las emociones?]. In R. Bisquerra (Ed.), *Cómo educar las emociones? La inteligencia emocional en la infancia y la adolescencia* (pp. 14–24). FAROS.

Mora, F. (2017). *Neuroeducation: you can only learn what you love* [Neuroeducación: sólo se puede aprender aquello que se ama]. Alianza Editorial.

Morales Moreno, N. (2020). *Teaching-learning of Physics and Chemistry Through Play: Didactic Proposal based on an Escape-Room* [Enseñanza-aprendizaje de la Física y la Química Mediante el Juego: Propuesta Didáctica basada en un Escape-Room]. Universidad de Granada. https://digibug.ugr.es/bitstream/handle/10481/62767/TFM%20Noelia%20Morales%20Moreno.pdf?sequence=1&isAllowed=y

Moreira, M. A., & Mansini, E. A. (2011). *Meaningful Learning: David Ausubel's Theory* [Aprendizagem Significativa: A Teoria de David Ausubel]. Centauro.

Moreno Fuentes, E. (2019). Breakoutedu as a key tool for gamification in the initial training of teachers [El Breakoutedu como herramienta clave para la gamificación en la formación inicial de maestros/as]. *Revista electrónica de Tecnología Educativa, 67*, 66–79. https://www.edutec.es/revista/index.php/edutec-e/article/view/1247/665

Morford, Z. H., Witts, B. N., Killingsworth, K. J., & Alavosius, M. P. (2014). Gamification: The intersection between behavior analysis and game design technologies. *The Behavior Analyst, 37*(1), 25–40. doi:10.100740614-014-0006-1 PMID:27274957

Morgan, J. (2013, December 17). *Want to work here? Play this game first!* Forbes. https://www.forbes.com/sites/jacobmorgan/2013/12/17/want-to-work-here-play-this-game-first/#73827d254249

Morganti, L., Pallavicini, F., Cadel, E., Candelieri, A., Archetti, F., & Mantovani, F. (2017). Gaming for Earth: Serious games and gamification to engage consumers in pro-environmental behaviours for energy efficiency. In Energy Research and Social Science (Vol. 29, pp. 95–102). Elsevier Ltd. doi:10.1016/j.erss.2017.05.001

Morris, B. J., Croker, S., Zimmerman, C., Gill, D., & Romig, C. (2013). Gaming science: The "Gamification" of scientific thinking. *Developmental Psychology, 4*, 1–16. PMID:24058354

Morschheuser, B., Hamari, J., Koivisto, J., & Maedche, A. (2017). Gamified crowdsourcing: Conceptualization, literature review, and future agenda. *International Journal of Human-Computer Studies, 106*, 26–43. doi:10.1016/j.ijhcs.2017.04.005

Morschheuser, B., Hassan, L., Werder, K., & Hamari, J. (2018). How to design gamification? A method for engineering gamified software. *Information and Software Technology, 95*, 219–237. doi:10.1016/j.infsof.2017.10.015

Morshead, R. W. (1965). Taxonomy of Educational Objectives Handbook II: Affective Domain. *Studies in Philosophy and Education, 4*(1), 164–170. doi:10.1007/BF00373956

Mostafa, M., & Faragallah, O. S. (2019). Development of Serious Games for Teaching Information Security Courses. *IEEE Access: Practical Innovations, Open Solutions, 7*, 169293–169305. doi:10.1109/ACCESS.2019.2955639

Mounier, A., & Tangchuang, P. (2010). *Education and Knowledge in Thailand: The Quality Controversy*. Silkworm Books.

Mullins, J. K., & Sabherwal, R. (2020). Gamification: A cognitive-emotional view. *Journal of Business Research, 106*, 304–314. doi:10.1016/j.jbusres.2018.09.023

Munaro, M., Basso, F., & Menegatti, E. (2016). OpenPTrack: Open source multi-camera calibration and people tracking for RGB-D camera networks. *Robotics and Autonomous Systems, 75*, 525–538. doi:10.1016/j.robot.2015.10.004

Muñoz, J. (1994). Ludolitos. *Enseñanza de las Ciencias de la Tierra, 2*(1), 282–284.

Muñoz, M., Peña Pérez Negrón, A., & Hernández, L. (2020). Gamification in Virtual reality Environments for the integration of Highly Effective Teams. In *Virtual Reality Designs* (pp. 151–175). CRC Press. doi:10.1201/9781003019589-7

Muntean, C. I. (2011). Raising engagement in e-learning through gamification. In *Proceedings of the 6th International Conference on Virtual Learning* (pp. 323-329). Academic Press.

Murga-Menoyo, M. Á. (2015). Competences for sustainable development: The capacities, attitudes and target values of education within the framework of the post-2015 Global Agenda [Competencias para el desarrollo sostenible: las capacidades, actitudes y valores meta de la educación en el marco de la Agenda global post-2015]. *Foro de Educación, 13*, 55–83. doi:10.14516/fde.2015.013.019.004

Murillo-Zamorano, L. R., Lopez Sanchez, J. A., Godoy-Caballero, A. L., & Bueno Munoz, C. (2021). Gamification and active learning in higher education: Is it possible to match digital society, academia and students' interests? *International Journal of Educational Technology in Higher Education, 18*(1), 1–27. doi:10.118641239-021-00249-y

Murphy, K. R. (2008). Explaining the weak relationship between job performance and ratings of job performance. *Industrial and Organizational Psychology: Perspectives on Science and Practice, 1*(2), 148–160. doi:10.1111/j.1754-9434.2008.00030.x

Murray, J. (2018). The play's the thing. In International Journal of Early Years Education (Vol. 26, Issue 4). doi:10.1080/09669760.2018.1527278

Murray, J. H. (2003). *Hamlet no Holodeck* [Hamlet on the Holodeck]. Itaú Cultural, UNESP.

Murray, L. (2019). Solving crimes with geology. *Engineering & Technology, 14*(5), 54–57. doi:10.1049/et.2019.0506

Murray, R. C. (2004). *Evidence from the Earth: Forensic Geology and Criminal Investigation*. Mountain Press Publishing.

Murty, V. P., & Adcock, R. A. (2017). Distinct medial temporal lobe network states as neural contexts for motivated memory formation. In D. E. Hannula & M. C. Duff (Eds.), *The hippocampus from cells to systems* (pp. 467–501). Springer. doi:10.1007/978-3-319-50406-3_15

Music for children: Orff-Schulwerk. (1991). (American edition). Schott.

Myers, M. (2000). Qualitative research and the generalizability question: Standing firm with Proteus. *Qualitative Report, 4*(3), 9. doi:10.46743/2160-3715/2000.2925

Mykhailyshyn, H., Kondur, O., & Serman, L. (2018). Innovation of education and educational innovations in conditions of modern higher education institution. *Journal of Vasyl Stefanyk Precarpathian National University, 5*(1), 9–16. doi:10.15330/jpnu.5.1.9-16

Nabi, G., Holden, R., & Walmsley, A. (2010). Entrepreneurial intentions among students: Towards a re-focused research agenda. *Journal of Small Business and Enterprise Development, 17*(4), 537–551. doi:10.1108/14626001011088714

Nabi, G., Walmsley, A., Liñán, F., Akhtar, I., & Neame, C. (2018). Does entrepreneurship education in the first year of higher education develop entrepreneurial intentions? The role of learning and inspiration. *Studies in Higher Education, 43*(3), 452–467. doi:10.1080/03075079.2016.1177716

Nacke, L. E., & Deterding, C. S. (2017). The maturing of gamification research. *Computers in Human Behaviour*, 450-454.

Nah, F. F., Venkata, R. T., Shashank, R., & Pavani, R. (2013). Gamification of Education Using Computer Games. In Human Interface and the Management of Information. Information and Interaction for Learning, Culture, Collaboration and Business. Springer Berlin Heidelberg. doi:10.1007/978-3-642-39226-9_12

NASA. (2016). *Gamers Tackle Virtual Asteroid Sampling Mission*. Available at https://www.nasa.gov/feature/goddard/2016/gamers-tackle-virtual-asteroid-sampling-mission

NASA. (2021). https://www.nasa.gov/

Nasirzadeh, E., & Fathian, M. (2020). Investigating the effect of gamification elements on bank customers to personalize gamified systems. *International Journal of Human-Computer Studies*, *143*, 102469. Advance online publication. doi:10.1016/j.ijhcs.2020.102469

National Center for Education Statistics. (n.d.). *Fast facts: Back to school statistics.* https://nces.ed.gov/fastfacts/display.asp?id=372

Naudé, W. (2010). Entrepreneurship, developing countries, and development economics: New approaches and insights. *Small Business Economics*, *34*(1), 1–12. doi:10.100711187-009-9198-2

Navan, A. A., & Khaleghi, A. (2020). Using gamification to improve the education quality of children with autism. *Revista Científica (Maracaibo)*, *1*(37), 90–106. doi:10.14483/23448350.15431

Navarro Mateos, C., Pérez López, I., & Marzo, P. (2021). La gamificación en el ámbito educativo español: revisión sistemática (Gamification in the Spanish educational field: a systematic review). *Retos*, *42*, 507–516. doi:10.47197/retos.v42i0.87384

Navarro, E. O., Baker, A., & Van der Hoek, A. (2004, January 18-21). *Teaching software engineering using simulation games* [Paper presentation]. International Conference on Simulation in Education, San Diego, CA. http://isr.uci.edu/content/teaching-software-engineering-using-simulation-games

Nawawi, R. (2016). *The formation of the value of Thai society in the context of national security.* National Defence College of Thailand.

Nazry, N. N. M., & Romano, D. M. (2017). Mood and learning in navigation-based serious games. *Computers in Human Behavior*, *73*, 596–604. doi:10.1016/j.chb.2017.03.040

Nebel, S., Schneider, S., & Rey, G. D. (2016). From duels to classroom competition: Social competition and learning in educational videogames within different group sizes. *Computers in Human Behavior*, *55*, 384–398. doi:10.1016/j.chb.2015.09.035

Negre, C. (2017). *"BreakoutEdu", microgamification and meaningful learning* [«BreakoutEdu», microgamificación y aprendizaje significativo]. https://www.educaweb.com/noticia/2017/07/26/breakoutedumicrogamificacion-aprendizaje-significativo-15068

Neto, L. V., Fontoura, P. H. Jr, Bordini, R. A., Otsuka, J. L., & Beder, D. M. (2020). Design and implementation of an educational game considering issues for visually impaired people inclusion. *Smart Learning Environments*, *7*(1), 1–16. doi:10.118640561-019-0103-4

Newell, W. H. (2007). *13 Decision Making in Interdisciplinary Studies.* Academic Press.

Ngammuk, P. (2001). *An analysis of Thai cultural characteristics of students in higher education institutions under the Ministry of University Affairs* [Doctoral thesis]. Chulalongkorn University.

Ngammuk, P. (2016). A Comparison of the Twelve Core Values of Thai people defined by the Head of the National Council for Peace and Order (NCPO) found in Thai private and public university students. *Hawaii International Conference on Education.*

Ngan, V. (2013). *Thallium poisoning*. https://dermnetnz.org/topics/thallium-poisoning/

Ngan, H. Y., Lifanova, A., Jarke, J., & Broer, J. (2016, September). Refugees welcome: Supporting informal language learning and integration with a gamified mobile application. In *European Conference on Technology Enhanced Learning* (pp. 521-524). 10.1007/978-3-319-45153-4_54

Ngunjiri, F. W., Hernandez, K. A. C., & Chang, H. (2010). Living autoethnography: Connecting life and research. *Journal of Research Practice*, *6*(1), E1–E1.

Nguyen, C. T. (2017). Philosophy of games. *Philosophy Compass*, *12*(8), e12426. doi:10.1111/phc3.12426

Nicholson, S. (2015). *Peeking behind the locked door: A survey of escape room facilities*. Academic Press.

Nicholson, S. (2015). *Peeking Behind the Locked Door: A Survey of Escape Room Facilities*. https://scottnicholson.com/pubs/erfacwhite.pdf

Nicholson, S. (2016a). Ask Why: Creating a Better Player Experience through Environmental Storytelling and Consistency in Escape Room Design. *Meaningful Play 2016*, 1–17. https://scottnicholson.com/pubs/askwhy.pdf

Nicholson, S. (2016b). The State of Escape: Escape Room Design and Facilities. *Meaningful Play 2016*, 20. https://scottnicholson.com/pubs/stateofescape.pdf

Nicholson, S. (2018). Creating engaging escape rooms for the classroom. *Childhood Education*, *94*(1), 44–49. doi:10.1080/00094056.2018.1420363

Nicholson, S. A. (2015). A Recipe for Meaningful Gamification. T. In L. C. W. Reiners (Ed.), *Gamification in Education and Business*. Springer. doi:10.1007/978-3-319-10208-5_1

Nijs, L., & Leman, M. (2014). Interactive technologies in the instrumental music classroom: A longitudinal study with the Music Paint Machine. *Computers & Education*, *73*, 40–59. doi:10.1016/j.compedu.2013.11.008

Nobre, H., & Ferreira, A. (2017). Gamification as a platform for brand co-creation experiences. *Journal of Brand Management*, *24*(4), 349–361. doi:10.105741262-017-0055-3

Noe, R. A., Tews, M. J., & McConnell Dachner, A. (2010). Learner engagement: A new perspective for enhancing our understanding of learner motivation and workplace learning. *The Academy of Management Annals*, *4*(1), 279–315. doi:10.5465/19416520.2010.493286

Nordby, A., Øygardslia, K., Sverdrup, U., & Sverdrup, H. (2016). The art of gamification; teaching sustainability and system thinking by pervasive game development. *Electronic Journal of e-Learning, 14*(3), 152-168.

Nørgård, R. T., Whitton, N. J., & Toft-Nielsen, C. (2016). *Playful teaching between freedom and control: exploring the magic circle in higher education.* https://www.srhe.ac.uk/conference2016/abstracts/0175. pdf

Nørgård, R. T., Toft-Nielsen, C., & Whitton, N. (2017). Playful learning in higher education: Developing a signature pedagogy. *International Journal of Play*, *6*(3), 272–282. doi:10.1080/21594937.2017.1382997

Norman, G. (2009). Teaching basic science to optimize transfer. *Medical Teacher*, *31*(9), 807–811. doi:10.1080/01421590903049814 PMID:19811185

Novak, J., Lozos, J. C., & Spear, S. E. (2019). Development of an Interactive Escape Room Intervention to Educate College Students about Earthquake Preparedness. *Natural Hazards Review*, *20*(1), 06018001. doi:10.1061/(ASCE)NH.1527-6996.0000322

Nowell, L. S., Norris, J. M., White, D. E., & Moules, N. J. (2017). Thematic analysis: Striving to meet the trustworthiness criteria. *International Journal of Qualitative Methods*, *16*(1). doi:10.1177/1609406917733847

O'Brien, N. B., & Yebra, J. M. (2019). *Design of an Educational Escape Room as a Gamifying and Motivating Tool for learning English in Primary* [Diseño de una Escape Room Educativa como Herramienta Gamificadora y Motivadora para el Aprendizaje del Inglés en Primaria]. Universidad de Zaragoza, Facultad de Ciencias Humanas y de la Educación. https://core.ac.uk/download/pdf/290000125.pdf

O'Brien, K., & Pitera, J. (2019). Gamifying instruction and engaging students with Breakout EDU. *Journal of Educational Technology Systems*, *48*(2), 192–212. doi:10.1177/0047239519877165

O'callaghan, D., Greene, D., Carthy, J., & Cunningham, P. (2015). An analysis of the coherence of descriptors in topic modeling. *Expert Systems with Applications*, *42*(13), 5645–5657. doi:10.1016/j.eswa.2015.02.055

O'Neil, H. F., & Perez, R. S. (2008). *Computer games and team and individual learning*. Elsevier. https://www.semanticscholar.org/paper/Computer-Games-and-Team-and-Individual-Learning-O'Neil-Perez/e7cda4b404d149e70c-6675c6ed01efbbff29a54b

O'Neil, H. F., Wainess, R., & Baker, E. L. (2005). Classification of learning outcomes: Evidence from the games literature. *Curriculum Journal*, *16*(4), 455–474. doi:10.1080/09585170500384529

Obando Zapata, G., & Muñera Córdoba, J. J. (2003). Problem situations as a strategy for mathematical conceptualization [Las situaciones problema como estrategia para la conceptualización matemática]. *Revista Educación y Pedagogía*, *15*(35), 183–199.

Ohn, K. M., Yusof, S., Urban, D., & Arifin, Z. (2018). ID NO. UMS001 TOPIC: Gamified Online Learning Design: GOLD for score in medical education. *University Carnival on e-Learning (IUCEL)*, 274.

Ohn, M. H., & Ohn, K. M. (2020). An evaluation study on gamified online learning experiences and its acceptance among medical students. *Tzu-Chi Medical Journal*, *32*(2), 211. PMID:32269957

Ohn, M. H., Ohn, K. M., Souza, U. D., Yusof, S., & Ariffin, Z. (2019). Effectiveness of innovative gamified learning among undergraduate medical students. *Journal of Physics: Conference Series*, *1358*(1), 012060.

Oikarinen, J., & Reed, D. (1993). *"Internet Relay Chat Protocol." Request for Comment:1459*. Network Working Group.

Okada, A., Rocha, A. K. L. T., Fuchter, S. K., Zucchi, S., & Wortley, D. (2019). Formative assessment of inquiry skills for responsible research and innovation using 3D virtual reality glasses and face recognition. In S. Draaijer, D. Joosten-ten Brinke, & E. Ras, (Eds.), *Technology Enhanced Assessment Conference: Revised selected papers* (pp. 91– 101). Springer. 10.1007/978-3-030-25264-9_7

Oksanen, K. (2013). Subjective experience and sociability in a collaborative serious game. *Simulation & Gaming*, *44*(6), 767–793. doi:10.1177/1046878113513079

Oksanen, K., & Hämäläinen, R. (2014). Game mechanics in the design of a collaborative 3D serious game. *Simulation & Gaming*, *45*(2), 255–278. doi:10.1177/1046878114530799

Oliva, J. M. O., & Acevedo, J. A. D. (2005). Science teaching in primary and secondary today. Some proposals for the future [La enseñanza de las ciencias en primaria y secundaria hoy. Algunas propuestas de futuro]. *Revista Eureka Sobre Enseñanza y Divulgación de las Ciencias*, *2*(2), 241–250.

Oliveira, S., & Cruz, M. (2018). The gamification Octalysis framework within the primary English teaching process: The quest for a transformative classroom. *Revista Lusófona de Educação*, *41*(41), 63–82. doi:10.24140/issn.1645-7250.rle41.04

Olson, R. E., McKenzie, J., Mills, K. A., Patulny, R., Bellocchi, A., & Caristo, F. (2019). Gendered emotion management and teacher outcomes in secondary school teaching: A review. *Teaching and Teacher Education*, *80*, 128–144. doi:10.1016/j.tate.2019.01.010

Olszewski, A. E., & Wolbrink, T. A. (2017). Serious Gaming in Medical Education: A Proposed Structured Framework for Game Development. *Simulation in Healthcare: Journal of the Society for Simulation in Healthcare*, *12*(4), 240–253. doi:10.1097/SIH.0000000000000212

Onrubia, J. (2016). Learning and teaching in virtual environments: Joint activity, teacher assistance and knowledge construction. *Red-Revista de Educacion a Distancia,* (50).

Onrubia, J., & Engel, A. (2012). The role of teacher assistance on the effects of a macro-script in collaborative writing tasks. *International Journal of Computer-Supported Collaborative Learning*, *7*(1), 161–186. doi:10.100711412-011-9125-9

Oosterbeek, H., Van Praag, M., & Ijsselstein, A. (2010). The impact of entrepreneurship education on entrepreneurship skills and motivation. *European Economic Review*, *54*(3), 442–454. doi:10.1016/j.euroecorev.2009.08.002

Opdal, P. A. (2020). Inside the black box: On the concepts "teaching" and "learning" and the connections between them. *Scandinavian Journal of Educational Research*, *64*(3), 457–470. doi:10.1080/00313831.2019.1577752

Oprescu, F., Jones, C., & Katsikitis, M. (2014). I PLAY AT WORK-ten principles for transforming work processes through gamification. *Frontiers in Psychology*, *5*(JAN), 1–5. doi:10.3389/fpsyg.2014.00014 PMID:24523704

Oravec, J. A. (2015). Gamification and multigamification in the workplace: Expanding the ludic dimensions of work and challenging the work/play dichotomy. *Cyberpsychology (Brno)*, *9*(3). Advance online publication. doi:10.5817/CP2015-3-6

Organisation for Economic Co-operation and Development. (2008). *The Looming Crisis in the Health Workforce: How can OECD countries respond?* OECD Publishing.https://www.who.int/hrh/migration/looming_crisis_health_workforce.pdf?ua=1

Organisation for Economic Co-operation and Development. (2016). *Innovating Education and Educating for Innovation: The Power of Digital Technologies and Skills*. OECD Publishing. https://www.oecd.org/education/ceri/GEIS2016-Background-document.pdf

Organisation for Economic Co-operation and Development. (2019). *Health at a Glance 2019: OECD Indicators.* OECD Publishing. c09-en doi:10.1787/4dd50

Orion, N. (2017). The relevance of earth science for informed citizenship: Its potential and fulfillment. In L. Leite, L. Dourado, A. Afonso, & S. Morgado (Eds.), *Contextualizing Teaching to Improving Learning: The Case of Science and Geograph* (pp. 41–56). Nova Science Publishers.

Orion, N. (2019). The future challenge of Earth science education research. *Disciplinary and Interdisciplinary Science Education Research*, *1*(3), 1–8. doi:10.118643031-019-0003-z

Ortiz-Colón, M. A., Jordán, J., & Agredal, M. (2018). Gamification in education: An overview on the state of the art. *Educação e Pesquisa*, *44*, 1–17.

Ortiz-Rojas, M., Chiluiza, K., & Valcke, M. (2017). Gamification in Computer Programming: Effects on Learning, Engagement, Self-Efficacy and Intrinsic Motivation. *The 11th European Conference on Game-Based Learning ECGBL 2017*, 507–514. 10.1109/EDUCON.2017.7943073

OSIRIS-REx. (2021). https://www.nasa.gov/osiris-rex

Ouariachi, T., Li, C. Y., & Elving, W. J. L. (2020). Gamification approaches for education and engagement on pro-environmental behaviors: Searching for best practices. *Sustainability*, *12*(11), 4565. Advance online publication. doi:10.3390u12114565

Owens, D., & Shekhar, G. (2018). Using SCRUM principles to transform the classroom. *AMCIS 2018 Proceedings*, 85. https://aisel.aisnet.org/amcis2018/TREOsPDS/Presentations/85

Özdener, N. (2018). Gamification for enhancing Web 2.0 based educational activities: The case of pre-service grade school teachers using educational Wiki pages. *Telematics and Informatics*, *35*(3), 564–578. doi:10.1016/j.tele.2017.04.003

Ozobot | Robots to code, create, and connect with. (2019). Retrieved from https://ozobot.com/

Paas, F., Tuovinen, J. E., van Merriënboer, J. J. G., & Aubteen Darabi, A. (2005). A motivational perspective on the relation between mental effort and performance: Optimizing learner involvement in instruction. *Educational Technology Research and Development*, *53*(3), 25–34. doi:10.1007/BF02504795

Paddock, M., & Biggers, A. (2018). *What is arsenic poisoning?* https://www.medicalnewstoday.com/articles/241860

Padilha, J. M., Machado, P. P., Ribeiro, A. L., Ribeiro, R., Vieira, F., & Costa, P. (2021). Easiness, usefulness and intention to use a MOOC in nursing. *Nurse Education Today*, *97*, 104705. doi:10.1016/j.nedt.2020.104705

Padilha, J., Machado, P., Ribeiro, A., & Ramos, J. (2018). Clinical virtual simulation in nursing education. *Clinical Simulation in Nursing*, *15*(C), 13–18. doi:10.1016/j.ecns.2017.09.005

Padilha, J., Machado, P., Ribeiro, A., Ramos, J., & Costa, P. (2019). Clinical virtual simulation in nursing education: Randomized controlled trial. *Journal of Medical Internet Research*, *21*(3), e11529. doi:10.2196/11529 PMID:30882355

Padilha, J., Ribeiro, A., Rosa, J., Marques, D., & Machado, P. (2020). Clinical Virtual Simulation as Lifelong Learning Strategy—Nurse's Verdict. *Clinical Simulation in Nursing*, *47*, 1–5. doi:10.1016/j.ecns.2020.06.012

Pakinee, A., & Puritat, K. (2021). Designing a gamified e-learning environment for teaching undergraduate ERP course based on big five personality traits. *Education and Information Technologies*, *26*(4), 4049–4067. doi:10.100710639-021-10456-9 PMID:33613080

Palfrey, J., & Gasser, U. (2008). *Born Digital: Understanding the First Generation of Digital Natives*. Basic Books.

Palomino, P., & del Carmen, M. (2021). Implications of gamification in Higher Education: A systematic review of student perception. *Rie-Revista De Investigacion Educativa*, *39*(1), 169–188. doi:10.6018/rie.419481

Palomino, P., Toda, A., Oliveira, W., Rodrigues, L., Cristea, A., & Isotani, S. (2019, November). Exploring content game elements to support gamification design in educational systems: narrative and storytelling. In *Brazilian Symposium on Computers in Education (Simpósio Brasileiro de Informática na Educação-SBIE)* (Vol. 30, No. 1, p. 773). 10.5753/cbie.sbie.2019.773

Palomo Blázquez, A. (2019). *Escape room in the classroom: Learning through challenge* [Escape room en el aula: Aprender a través del desafío]. Revista Digital Docente.

Pan, R., Lo, H., & Neustaedter, C. (2017). Collaboration, Awareness, and Communication in Real-Life Escape Rooms. *Proceedings of the 2017 Conference on Designing Interactive Systems - DIS '17*, 1353–1364. 10.1145/3064663.3064767

Papastergiou, M. (2009). Digital game-based learning in high school computer science education: Impact on educational effectiveness and student motivation. *Computers & Education*, *52*(1), 1–12. doi:10.1016/j.compedu.2008.06.004

Pappas, C. (2017). What are the most effective uses of gamification in learning? *How Gamification Reshapes Learning*.

Parapanos, D., & Michopoulou, E. (2021). Gamification, Game Mechanics, Game Thinking and Players' Profile and Life Cycle. In X. Feifei & D. Buhalis (Eds.), *Gamification for Tourism* (pp. 13–34). Channel View Publications. doi:10.21832/9781845418236-004

Park, S., & Kim, S. (2018). Patterns Among 754 Gamification Cases: Content Analysis for Gamification Development. *JMIR Serious Games, 6*(4).

Park, K. C., & Lee, C. H. (2019). A study on the research trends for smart city using topic modeling. *Journal of Internet Computing and Services*, *20*(3), 119–128.

Parra González, M. E., Segura Robles, A., & Gómez Barajas, E. R. (2020). Assessing gamified experiences in physical education teachers and students. *IJERI: International Journal of Educational Research and Innovation*, (13), 166–176.

Parra-González, E., López-Belmonte, J., Segura-Robles, A., & Moreno-Guerrero, A.-J. (2021). Gamification and flipped learning and their influence on aspects related to the teaching-learning process. *Heliyon*, *7*(2), 1–10. doi:10.1016/j.heliyon.2021.e06254 PMID:33659757

Parsons, D., Thorn, R., Inkila, M., & MacCallum, K. (2018, December). Using Trello to support agile and lean learning with Scrum and Kanban in teacher professional development. In *2018 IEEE International Conference on Teaching, Assessment, and Learning for Engineering (TALE)* (pp. 720-724). IEEE. 10.1109/TALE.2018.8615399

Pasupa, S. (2016). *Sustainable Development in Thailand Supported by Industrial Design Education* [Doctoral thesis, Loughborough University]. https://repository.lboro.ac.uk/articles/thesis/Sustainable_development_in_Thailand_supported_by_industrial_design_education/9355721

Patel, J. K., & Sakadasariya, A. (2018). Survey on virtual reality in social network. In *Proceedings of the 2nd International Conference on Inventive Systems and Control*. ICISC.

Patrício, R., Moreira, A. C., & Zurlo, F. (2018). Gamification approaches to the early stage of innovation. *Creativity and Innovation Management*, *27*(4), 499–511.

Patrício, R., Moreira, A. C., & Zurlo, F. (2018). Gamification approaches to the early stage of innovation. *Creativity and Innovation Management*, *27*(4), 499–511. doi:10.1111/caim.12284

Patrício, R., Moreira, A. C., & Zurlo, F. (2021). Enhancing design thinking approaches to innovation through gamification. *European Journal of Innovation Management*, *24*(5), 1569–1594. doi:10.1108/EJIM-06-2020-0239

Patrício, R., Moreira, A., Zurlo, F., & Melazzini, M. (2020). Co-Creation of New Solutions Through Gamification: A Collaborative Innovation Practice. *Creativity and Innovation Management*, *29*(1), 146–160. doi:10.1111/caim.12356

Pausch, R., Pausch, R., Vogtle, L., & Conway, M. (1992). One dimensional motion tailoring for the disabled: A user study. In *Proceedings of the SIGCHI conference on Human factors in computing systems* (pp. 405-411). ACM.

Paxi Facebook. (2022). https://www.facebook.com/PaxiESAKids

Paxi Twitter. (2022). https://twitter.com/Paxi_ESAKids

Paxi. (2021). *About Paxi*. Available at https://www.esa.int/kids/en/about_Paxi/Paxi

Paz, I. (2019). *eMDAx Tool Proposed game design framework for educational games* [Ferramenta eMDAx Proposta de framework de game design para jogos educacionais] [Master Thesis]. Universidade da Beira Interior, Portugal.

Paz, D. P., Franco, M. H., & Bertagnolli, S. d. (2017). Educational digital game for the development of intercultural competence of Spanish-speaking learners [Jogo digital educacional para o desenvolvimento da competência intercultural de aprendizes de língua espanhola]. *Proceedings of SBGames 2017*.

Pedaste, M., Mäeots, M., Siiman, L. A., de Jong, T., van Riesen, S. A. N., Kamp, E. T., Manoli, C. C., Zacharia, Z. C., & Tsourlidaki, E. (2015). Phases of inquiry-based learning: Definitions and the inquiry cycle. *Educational Research Review*, *14*, 47–61. doi:10.1016/j.edurev.2015.02.003

Pedersen, R. E. (2003). *Game design foundations*. Wordware Publishing, Inc.

Pedreira, O., García, F., Piattini, M., Cortiñas, A., & Cerdeira-Pena, A. (2020). An architecture for software engineering gamification. *Tsinghua Science and Technology*, *25*(6), 776–797. doi:10.26599/TST.2020.9010004

Pedro, L. Z., Lopes, A. M. Z., Prates, B. G., Vassileva, J., & Isotani, S. (2015). Does gamification work for boys and girls? An exploratory study with a virtual learning environment. In *Proceedings of the 30th Annual ACM Symposium on Applied Computing* (pp. 214-219). 10.1145/2695664.2695752

Pedroli, E., Pallavinci, F., Serino, S., Cipresso, P., Chicchi Giglioli, A., & Riva, G. (2016). The use of virtual reality tools for the assessment of executive functions and unilateral spatial neglect. In F. Hu, J. Lu, & T. Zhang (Eds.), *Virtual reality enhanced robotic systems for disability rehabilitation, edition* (pp. 115–140). Advances in medical technologies and clinical practice. IGI Global. doi:10.4018/978-1-4666-9740-9.ch007

Pekrun, R. (2014). Emotions and Learning. In UNESCO (Ed.), Emotions and Learning (pp. 6–30). Gonnet Imprimeur.

Pekrun, R., & Stephens, E. J. (2010). Achievement Emotions: A Control-Value Approach. *Social and Personality Psychology Compass*, *4*(4), 238–255. doi:10.1111/j.1751-9004.2010.00259.x

Peleg, R., Yayon, M., Katchevich, D., Moria-shipony, M., & Blonder, R. (2019). *A Lab-Based Chemical Escape Room: Educational, Mobile, and Fun!* doi:10.1021/acs.jchemed.8b00406

Pellas, N. (2017). An exploration of interrelationships among presence indicators of a community of inquiry in a 3D game-like environment for high school programming courses. *Interactive Learning Environments*, *25*(3), 343–360. doi:10.1080/10494820.2015.1127819

Penaluna, K., Penaluna, A., & Jones, C. (2012). The context of enterprise education: Insights into current practices. *Industry and Higher Education*, *26*(3), 163–175. doi:10.5367/ihe.2012.0098

Peng, W., Lin, J.-H., Pfeiffer, K. A., & Winn, B. (2012). Need satisfaction supportive game features as motivational determinants: An experimental study of a self-determination theory guided Exergame. *Media Psychology*, *15*(2), 192. doi:10.1080/15213269.2012.673850

Peñuelas-Calvo, I., Jiang-Lin, L. K., Girela-Serrano, B., Delgado-Gomez, D., Navarro-Jimenez, R., Baca-Garcia, E., & Porras-Segovia, A. (2020). Video games for the assessment and treatment of attention-deficit/hyperactivity disorder: A systematic review. *European Child & Adolescent Psychiatry*, 1–16. doi:10.100700787-020-01557-w PMID:32424511

Percival, F., & Ellington, H. I. (1980). The place of case studies in the simulation/gaming field. In P. Race & D. Brook (Eds.), *Perspectives on academic gaming & simulation 5: Simulation and Gaming for the 1980s*. Kogan Pages.

Perez Lopez, I., Rivera Garcia, E., & Trigueros Cervantes, C. (2019). 12+1. feelings of physical education college students towards a gamification proposal: "Game of thrones: The anger of the dragons. *Movimento*, *25*, e25038. doi:10.22456/1982-8918.88031

Pérez-Castillo, R., Caballero, I., & Rodríguez, M. (2018, April). Improving the experience of teaching Scrum. In *2018 IEEE Global Engineering Education Conference (EDUCON)* (pp. 1598–1605). IEEE. 10.1109/EDUCON.2018.8363426

Perez-Lopez, I. J., Rivera Garcia, E., & Trigueros Cervantes, C. (2017). "The prophecy of the chosen ones": An example of gamification applied to university teaching. *Revista Internacional de Medicina y Ciencias de la Actividad Física y del Deporte*, *17*(66), 243–260. doi:10.15366/rimcafd2017.66.003

Pérez, M. C. (2011). Board games in early childhood education [Los juegos de mesa en la educación infantil]. *Pedagogía Magna*, *11*, 354–359.

Perkins, G. (2007). Simulation in resuscitation training. *Resuscitation*, *73*(2), 202–211. doi:10.1016/j.resuscitation.2007.01.005 PMID:17379380

Pernelle, P., Carron, T., Talbot, S., & Wayntal, D. (2021). Fast gamification approach: Increase of the motivation in remote classes. *Proceedings of the 13th International Conference on Computer Supported Education*, 282–287. 10.5220/0010461702820287

Perrotta, C., Featherstone, G., Aston, H., & Houghton, E. (2013). *Game-based learning: Latest evidence and future directions*. NFER. https://www.nfer.ac.uk/publications/game01/game01.pdf

Perrotta, C., Featherstone, G., Aston, H., & Houghton, E. (2013). *Game-based learning: Latest evidence and future directions*. NFER.

Perttula, A., Kiili, K., Lindstedt, A., & Tuomi, P. (2017). Flow experience in game based learning–a systematic literature review. *International Journal of Serious Games*, *4*(1), 57–72. doi:10.17083/ijsg.v4i1.151

Pessini, A., Kemczinski, A., & Hounsell, M. d. (2015). An Authoring Tool for the development of Serious RPG Games [Uma Ferramenta de Autoria para o desenvolvimento de Jogos Sérios do Gênero RPG]. *Computer on the Beach 2015*, 71-80.

Peter Beck. (2021). *Rocket Lab CEO Peter Beck & Kerbal Space Program*. Available at https://www.youtube.com/watch?v=FWKLiJu7EtA

Peters, M. A. (2005). The new prudentialism in education: Actuarial rationality and the entrepreneurial self. *Educational Theory*, *55*(2), 123–137. doi:10.1111/j.0013-2004.2005.00002.x

Peterson, R. A. (1994). A meta-analysis of Cronbach's coefficient alpha. *The Journal of Consumer Research*, *21*(2), 381–391. doi:10.1086/209405

Petkov, S., & Savishchenko, M., V., Semenyshyna-Fihol, B., A. Poda, T., & M. Chaika, I. (2020). Application of Mock-Court as an Interdisciplinary Model for Consolidation of Professional Training of Law Students. *Journal Of Education And E-Learning Research*, *7*(2), 122–129. doi:10.20448/journal.509.2020.72.122.129

Pettit, R. K., McCoy, L., Kinney, M., & Schwartz, F. N. (2014). A multimedia audience response game show for medical education. *Medical Science Educator*, *24*(2), 181–187. doi:10.100740670-014-0038-x

Pham, T. (2021). Communication competencies and international graduates' employability outcomes: Strategies to navigate the host labour market. *Journal of International Migration and Integration*, 1–17.

Phelps, E. A. (2006). Emotion and Cognition: Insights from Studies of the Human Amygdala. *Annual Review of Psychology*, *57*(1), 27–53. doi:10.1146/annurev.psych.56.091103.070234 PMID:16318588

Philbin, S. P. (2017). Investigating the scope for agile project management to be adopted by higher education institutions. In *Software Project Management for Distributed Computing* (pp. 345–366). Springer. doi:10.1007/978-3-319-54325-3_14

Phillips, C., Johnson, D., Klarkowski, M., White, M., & Hides, L. (2018). The impact of rewards and trait reward responsiveness on player motivation. *CHI PLAY 2018 - Proceedings of the 2018 Annual Symposium on Computer-Human Interaction in Play*. 10.1145/3242671.3242713

Phillips, C., Johnson, D., Wyeth, P., Hides, L., & Klarkowski, M. (2015). Redefining videogame reward types. *OzCHI 2015: Being Human - Conference Proceedings*, 83–91. 10.1145/2838739.2838782

Phillips, C., Johnson, D., & Wyeth, P. (2013). Videogame reward types. *ACM International Conference Proceeding Series*, 103–106. 10.1145/2583008.2583025

Phillips, J. J., & Phillips, P. P. (2016). *Handbook of training evaluation and measurement methods*. Routledge. doi:10.4324/9781315757230

Phillips, R. S., Horstman, T., Vye, N., & Bransford, J. (2014). Engagement and Games for Learning: Expanding Definitions and Methodologies. *Simulation & Gaming*, *45*(4-5), 548–568. doi:10.1177/1046878114553576

Piaget, J. (1945). *Play, Dreams, and Imitation in Childhood.* Norton.

Piaget, J. (1999). *Play, dreams and imitation in child-hood.* Psychology Press.

Pidkasisty, P. I., Friedman, L. M., & Garunov, M.G. (1999). Psikhologo-didakticheskiy spravochnik prepodavatelya vysshey shkoly [Psychological and didactic reference book of a teacher of higher education]. Moscow: Pedagogical Society of Russia.

Pierfy, D. A. (1977). Comparative simulation game research: Stumbling blocks and stepping. *Simulation & Games*, *8*(2), 255–268. doi:10.1177/003755007782006

Pietroszek, K., Agraraharja, Z., & Eckhardt, C. (2021, March). The Royal Game of Ur: Virtual Reality Prototype of the Board Game Played in Ancient Mesopotamia. In *2021 IEEE Conference on Virtual Reality and 3D User Interfaces Abstracts and Workshops (VRW)* (pp. 647-648). IEEE.

Pimentel, F. S. C. (2013). *Online Interaction: A challenge of mentoring* [Interação On-line: um desafio da tutoria]. Edufal.

Pimentel, F. S. C. (2018). Gamification in education, coining a concept [Gamificação na educação, cunhando um conceito]. In E. Fofonca, G. S. Brito, M. Estevam, & N. P. V. Camas (Eds.), *Metodologias pedagógicas inovadoras: contextos da educação básica e da educação superior* (pp. 76–87). Editora IFPR.

Pimentel, F. S. C., & Mercado, L. P. L. (2019). The policy of expansion of higher education through the UAB in Alagoas [A política de expansão do ensino superior por meio da UAB em Alagoas]. *EDUCAÇÃO*, *7*(3), 127–138. doi:10.17564/2316-3828.2019v7n3p127-138

Piñero Charlo, J. C. (2020). Educational Escape Rooms as a Tool for Horizontal Mathematization: Learning Process Evidence. *Education in Science*, *10*(9), 213. doi:10.3390/educsci10090213

Piñero Charlo, J. C., Ortega García, P., & Román García, S. (2021). Formative Potential of the Development and Assessment of an Educational Escape Room Designed to Integrate. *Education in Science*, *11*(3), 131. doi:10.3390/educsci11030131

Piñero, J. C. (2019). Análisis sistemático del uso de salas de escape educativas: estado del arte y perspectivas de futuro. *Espacios, 40*(44), 9. http://www.revistaespacios.com/a19v40n44/19404409.html

Pingdom. (2012). *IRC is dead, long live IRC.* Pingdom.Com. https://www.pingdom.com/blog/irc-is-dead-long-live-irc/

Pink, D. H. (2011). *Drive: The surprising truth about what motivates us.* Penguin.

Pinter, R., Čisar, S. M., Balogh, Z., & Manojlović, H. (2020). Enhancing higher education student class attendance through gamification. *Acta Polytechnica Hungarica*, *17*(2), 13–33. doi:10.12700/APH.17.2.2020.2.2

Pipitone, C., Guitart, J., Agudelo, C., & García, À. (2019). Favoring the positive emotional change towards the sciences in the initial training of teachers [Favoreciendo el cambio emocional positivo hacia las ciencias en la formación inicial del profesorado]. *Ápice. Revista de Educación Científica*, *3*(1), 41–54.

Pirrie, D. (2009). Forensic geology in serious crime investigation. *Geology Today*, *25*(5), 188–192. doi:10.1111/j.1365-2451.2009.00729.x

Pirrie, D., Donnelly, L., Rollinson, G. K., Butcher, A. R., Dawson, L. A., & Pirrie, H. A. (2013). Forensic geology at the International School Science Fair 2013. *Geology Today*, *29*(6), 222–228. doi:10.1111/gto.12028

Piscicelli, L., Cooper, T., & Fisher, T. (2015). The role of values in collaborative consumption: Insights from a product-service system for lending and borrowing in the UK. *Journal of Cleaner Production, 97*, 21–29. doi:10.1016/j.jclepro.2014.07.032

Pitan, O. S. (2017). *Graduate employees' generic skills and training needs.* Higher Education, Skills and Work-Based Learning. doi:10.1108/HESWBL-04-2017-0026

Piteira, M., Costa, C. J., & Aparicio, M. (2017). A conceptual framework to implement gamification on online courses of computer programming learning: implementation. In *10th International Conference of Education, Research and Innovation (ICERI2017)* (pp. 7022-7031). 10.21125/iceri.2017.1865

Pivec, M., Dziabenko, O., & Schinnerl, I. (2003). *Aspects of Game-Based Learning.* Academic Press.

Platt, L. (2004). Accepting Risk-Daring Greatness. *Vital Speeches of the Day, 70*(17), 541.

Plisson, J., Lavrac, N., & Mladenic, D. (2004). A rule based approach to word lemmatization. *Proceedings of IS, 3*, 83–86.

Podsakoff, P. M., & Organ, D. W. (1986). Self-reports in organizational research: Problems and prospects. *Journal of Management, 12*(4), 531–544. doi:10.1177/014920638601200408

Polat, E. S. (Ed.). (2004). Teoriya i praktika distantsionnogo obucheniya: Uchebnik. razresheniye [Theory and practice of distance learning: Textbook. allowance]. Center "Academy".

Polczyk, P. (2012). *Autoethnography as an accessible method of research.* Academic Press.

Politis, Y., Robb, N., Yakkundi, A., Dillenburger, K., Herbertson, N., Charlesworth, B., & Goodman, L. (2017). People with disabilities leading the design of serious games and virtual worlds. *International Journal of Serious Games, 4*(2), 63–73. doi:10.17083/ijsg.v4i2.160

Politowski, C., Petrillo, F., Montandon, J. E., Valente, M. T., & Guéhéneuc, Y.-G. (2021). Are game engines software frameworks? A three-perspective study. *Journal of Systems and Software, 171*, 110846. doi:10.1016/j.jss.2020.110846

Polo-Peña, A. I., Frías-Jamilena, D. M., & Fernández-Ruano, M. L. (2020). Influence of gamification on perceived self-efficacy: Gender and age moderator effect. *International Journal of Sports Marketing & Sponsorship.* Advance online publication. doi:10.1108/IJSMS-02-2020-0020

Polya, G. (1945). *How To Solve It.* Academic Press.

Ponto, J. (2015). Understanding and Evaluating Survey Research. *Journal of the Advanced Practitioner in Oncology, 6*(2), 168.

Poon, C. Y. S., Hui, V. K. Y., Yuen, G. W. C., Kwong, V. W. Y., & Chan, C. S. (2019). A well-slept teacher is a better teacher: A multi-respondent experience-sampling study on sleep, stress, and emotional transmission in the classroom. *PsyCh Journal, 8*(3), 280–292. doi:10.1002/pchj.282 PMID:30983162

Poondej, C., & Lerdpornkulrat, T. (2016). Relationship between motivational goal orientations, perceptions of general education classroom learning environment, and deep approaches to learning. *Kasetsart Journal of Social Sciences, 37*(2), 100–103. doi:10.1016/J.KJSS.2015.01.001

Pope, D. (2003). *Doing school: How we are creating a generation of stressed-out, materialistic, and miseducated students.* Yale University Press.

Popovych, I. S., Blynova, O. Y., Aleksieieva, M. I., Nosov, P. S., Zavatska, N. Y., & Smyrnova, O. O. (2019). Research of the relationship between the social expectations and professional training of lyceum students studying in the field of shipbuilding. *Espacios, 40*(33).

Porter, L. W. (1994). The relation of entrepreneurship education to business education. *Simulation & Gaming*, *25*(3), 416–419. doi:10.1177/1046878194253008

Pottle, J. (2019). Virtual reality and the transformation of medical education. *Future Healthcare Journal*, *6*(3), 181–185. doi:10.7861/fhj.2019-0036 PMID:31660522

Poza García, M. (2018). *Educational escape room as a motivating and innovative resource in early childhood education* [Escape room educativa como recurso motivador e innovador en educación infantil]. Universidad de Valladolid. Facultad de Educación de Soria. https://uvadoc.uva.es/handle/10324/34270

Pratt, M. A., & Hahn, S. (2015). Effects of simulation on student satisfaction with a capstone course. *Journal of Hospitality & Tourism Education*, *27*(1), 39–46. doi:10.1080/10963758.2015.998911

Preece, J., Rogers, Y., & Sharp, H. (2002). *Interaction design: Beyond human computer interaction.* John Wiley & Sons. https://www.wiley.com/en-us/Interaction+Design%3A+Beyond+Human+Computer+Interaction%2C+4th+Edition-p-9781119088790

Prensky, M. (2012). Learning based on digital games [Aprendizagem baseada em jogos digitais]. São Paulo: SENAC.

Prensky, M. (2001). Fun, play and games: What makes games engaging. In M. Prensky (Ed.), *Digital game-based learning* (pp. 106–145). McGraw-Hill.

Prensky, M. (2001a). True believers: Digital game-based learning in the military. In M. Prensky (Ed.), *Digital game-based learning*. McGraw-Hill.

Prensky, M. (2001b). Fun, play and games: What makes games engaging. In M. Prensky (Ed.), *Digital game-based learning*. McGraw-Hill.

Prensky, M. (2003). *Don't Bother Me Mom: I'm learning. How computer and video games are preparing your kids for 21st Century success and how you can help*. Paragon House.

Prensky, M. (2012). *Digital Game-Based Learning* [Aprendizagem Baseada em Jogos Digitais]. Senac São Paulo.

Prensky, M. R. (2010). *Teaching digital natives: Partnering for real learning*. Corwin Press.

Pressman, R., & Maxim, B. (2016). *Software Engineering* [Engenharia de Software] (8th ed.). McGraw Hill Brasil.

Prieto Andreu, J. M. (2020). A systematic review about gamification, motivation and learning in high school [Una revisiÓn sistemÁtica sobre gamificaciÓn, motivaciÓn y aprendizaje en universitarios]. *Teoría de la Educación*, *32*(1), 73–99. doi:10.14201/teri.20625

Prieto, L. M., Trevisan, M. D. C. B., Danesi, M. I., & Falkembach, G. A. M. (2005). Uso das tecnologias digitais em atividades didáticas nas séries iniciais [Use of digital technologies in didactic activities in the initial grades]. *Renote: revista novas tecnologias na educação, 3*(1), 1-11.

Prince, M. (2004). Does active learning work? A review of the research. *Journal of Engineering Education*, *93*(3), 223–231. doi:10.1002/j.2168-9830.2004.tb00809.x

Private Division. (2021). https://www.privatedivision.com/

Protasio, A., & Dias, C. M. (2016). Narrativa nos jogos: uma oportunidade para autoria coletiva na escola [Narrative in games: an opportunity for collective authorship in schools]. In J. L. Farbiarz, A. Farbiarz, & B. J. W. Hemais (Eds.), *Design para uma educação inclusiva* (pp. 117–128). Blucher. Blucher.openaccess.blucher.com.br/article-details/narrativa-dos-jogos-uma-oportunidade-para-autoria-coletiva-na-escola-20195

Quality Assurance Agency for Higher Education. (2012). *Enterprise and entrepreneurship education: guidance for UK higher education providers*. QAA.

Quaye, S. J., Harper, S. R., & Pendakur, S. L. (Eds.). (2019). *Student engagement in higher education: Theoretical perspectives and practical approaches for diverse populations*. Routledge. doi:10.4324/9780429400698

Quiñones, M. A., Ford, J. K., & Teachout, M. S. (1995). The relationship between work experience and job performance: A conceptual and meta-analytic review. *Personnel Psychology*, *48*(4), 887–910. doi:10.1111/j.1744-6570.1995.tb01785.x

Quora. (2022). https://www.quora.com/Why-should-Kerbal-Space-Program-be-played-in-schools

Race to the Treasure Co-operative Game. (2019). Retrieved from https://www.mastermindtoys.com/6009-Race-to-the-Treasure-Co-operative-Game.aspx

Radujković, M., & Sjekavica, M. (2017). Project management success factors. *Procedia Engineering*, *196*, 607–615. doi:10.1016/j.proeng.2017.08.048

Raessens, J. F. F. (2006). Playful Identities, or the Ludification of Culture. *Games and Culture*, *1*(1), 52–57. doi:10.1177/1555412005281779

Raessens, J. F. F. (2012). *Homo Ludens 2.0: The ludic turn in media theory* (A. G. Fokkema, Trans.). Universiteit Utrecht, Faculteit Geesteswetenschappen.

Rafael, R. C. (2017). *Differential and Integral Calculus: a study on strategies to reduce the percentage of non-approval* [Cálculo Diferencial e Integral: um estudo sobre estratégias para redução do percentual de não aprovação] [[Master Dissertation]. Federal University of Juiz de Fora.

Rahman, F. F., Sumpeno, S., & Zaini, A. (2018). Gamification wisata di Museum Mpu Tantular berbasis Augmented Reality. *Jurnal Teknik ITS*, *7*(1), 165–170.

Raina, V. (2011). *Between behaviourism and constructivism*. doi:10.1080/09502386.2011.534578

Rajanen, D., & Rajanen, M. (2019). Climate change gamification: A literature review. In J. Koivisto & J. Hamari (Eds.), *GamiFIN Conference 2019* (pp. 253–264). GamiFIN Conference. http://ceur-ws.org/Vol-2359/

Rajani, N. B., Mastellos, N., & Filippidis, F. T. (2021). Impact of gamification on the self-efficacy and motivation to quit of smokers: Observational study of two gamified smoking cessation mobile apps. *JMIR Serious Games*, *9*(2), e27290. PMID:33904824

Rajbanshi, R., & Chandra Luitel, B. (2020). Transformative Learning: An Approach to Understand Participatory Action Research. *Transformations, 6*(1). https://nsuworks.nova.edu/transformations

Raksaseri, K. (2020, April 25). 19 Thai unis list on "THE Impact" ranks. *Bangkok Post*. https://www.bangkokpost.com/thailand/general/1906975/19-thai-unis-list-on-the-impact-ranks

Raktham, C. (2008). *Cultures and Learner Behaviours: A Qualitative Investigation of a Thai Classroom*. Academic Press.

Ramirez, M. (2007). *Sustainability integration in industrial design education: A world wide survey Sustainability integration in industrial design education: a worldwide survey*. www.ulsf.org

Ramirez, D., & Squire, K. (2015). Gamification and learning. In S. P. Walz & S. Deterding (Eds.), *The gameful world: Approaches, issues, applications* (pp. 629–652). The MIT Press.

Ramos, M. N. (2002). A educação profissional pela pedagogia das competências e a superfície dos documentos oficiais [Professional education through the pedagogy of competences and the surface of official documents]. *Educação & Sociedade*, *23*(80), 401–422. doi:10.1590/S0101-73302002008000020

Raposo, L. (2012). *Design of educational game design document and development of a prototype educational game for mobile devices* [Conceção do educational game design document e desenvolvimento de um protótipo de jogo educativo para dispositivos móveis] [Master Thesis]. Faculdade de Engenharia da Universidade do Porto. Portugal.

Raposo, L., & Garcia, P. (2016). *Bike a Planet: Educating through a healthy video game* [Bike a Planet: Educando através de um videojogo saudável] [Poster communication]. 4° Congresso de Comunicação de Ciência, SciCom PT 2016, Lisboa, Portugal.

Raposo, L., Morais, C., & Paiva, J. (2012). "GEO-GO" – a geographical adventure in the form of educational game: description of the project and its development ["GEO-GO" – uma aventura geográfica sob a forma de jogo educativo: descrição do projeto e seu desenvolvimento]. In *Proceedings of Encontro sobre Jogos e Mobile Learning*. Universidade de Coimbra.

Rapp, A. (2015). A qualitative investigation of gamification: Motivational factors in online gamified services and applications. *International Journal of Technology and Human Interaction*, *11*(1), 67–82. doi:10.4018/ijthi.2015010105

Rapp, A. (2017). Designing interactive systems through a game lens: An ethnographic approach. *Computers in Human Behavior*, *71*, 455–468. doi:10.1016/j.chb.2015.02.048

Rapp, A. (2017). From Games to Gamification: A Classification of Rewards in World of Warcraft for the Design of Gamified Systems. *Simulation & Gaming*, *48*(3), 381–401. doi:10.1177/1046878117697147

Rapp, A., Cena, F., Hopfgartner, F., Hamari, J., & Linehan, C. (2016, October). Fictional game elements: Critical perspectives on gamification design. In *Proceedings of the 2016 Annual Symposium on Computer-Human Interaction in Play Companion Extended Abstracts* (pp. 373-377). 10.1145/2968120.2968125

Rasheed Hasan, L. (2020). Is It Possible to Use Facebook instead of MOODLE Learning Management Systems (LMS) to Support the Learning Process? *ACM International Conference Proceeding Series*. 10.1145/3421682.3421695

Rashid, S., & Yadav, S. S. (2020). Impact of Covid-19 pandemic on higher education and research. *Indian Journal of Human Development*, *14*(2), 340–343. doi:10.1177/0973703020946700

Raspberry Pi Foundation. (2022). https://www.raspberrypi.org/

Ratcliffe, R. (2020, December 24). "We want a true democracy": students lead Thailand's protest movement. *The Guardian*. https://www.theguardian.com/world/2020/aug/24/we-want-a-true-democracy-students-lead-thailands-protest-movement

Reddit. (2022a). https://www.reddit.com/r/KerbalSpaceProgram/comments/ac7dyi/do_schools_use_ksp_to_teach_students/

Reddit. (2022b). https://www.reddit.com/r/KerbalAcademy/comments/k6p9qx/kerbaledu_2/

Reeve, J., & Sickenius, B. (1994). Development and validation of a brief measure of the three psychological needs underlying intrinsic motivation: The AFS scales. *Educational and Psychological Measurement*, *54*(2), 506–515. doi:10.1177/0013164494054002025

Rego, P., Moreira, P. M., & Reis, L. P. (2010). Serious games for rehabilitation: A survey and a classification towards a taxonomy. In *5th Iberian conference on information systems and technologies* (pp. 1-6). IEEE.

Rehkopf, M. (2021). *¿Qué es un tablero Kanban?* Atlassian. https://www.atlassian.com/es/agile/kanban/boards

Řehůřek, R., & Sojka, P. (2011). *Gensim—statistical semantics in python*. Retrieved from Genism. Org.

Reigeluth, C. M. (1987). *Instructional theories in action : Lessons illustrating selected theories and models*. Academic Press.

Reiners, T., Wood, L. C., Chang, V., Guetl, C., Herrington, J., Teräs, H., & Gregory, S. (2012). *Operationalising gamification in an educational authentic environment* [Paper presentation]. International Conference on Internet Technologies & Society 2012. https://researchrepository.murdoch.edu.au/id/ eprint/13958/1/reiners_et_al_2012PostprintOperationalising_gamification_in_an_educati onal_authentic_environment.pdf

Reiners, T., Wood, L. C., Chang, V., Gütl, C., Herrington, J., Teräs, H., & Gregory, S. (2012). *Operationalising gamification in an educational authentic environment*. Academic Press.

Reio, T. G., Rocco, T. S., Smith, D. H., & Chang, E. (2017). A Critique of Kirkpatrick's Evaluation Model. *New Horizons in Adult Education and Human Resource Development*, *29*(2), 35–53. doi:10.1002/nha3.20178

Reiser, R. (2001). A history of instructional design and technology: Part i: A history of instructional media. *Educational Technology Research and Development*, *49*(1), 53–64. doi:10.1007/BF02504506

Remote Adventures. (2021). https://theescapegame.com/blog/remote-adventures-our-answer-to-friendly-family-competition-over-the-holidays/

Reñe Bru, M. (2020). *Escape room in 3rd year of ESO for meaningful learning of chemistry* [Sala de escape en 3° de ESO para el aprendizaje significativo de la química]. Re-UNIR. https://reunir.unir.net/handle/123456789/10572

Resnick, M., Martin, F., Berg, R., Borovoy, R., Colella, V., Kramer, K., & Silverman, B. (1998). Digital manipulatives: new toys to think with. In *Proceedings of the SIGCHI conference on Human factors in computing systems*(pp. 281-287). ACM Press/Addison-Wesley Publishing Co.

Retana-Alvarado, D. A., De las Heras-Pérez, M. Á., Vázquez-Bernal, B., & Jiménez-Pérez, R. (2018). The change in the emotions of teachers in initial training towards the classroom climate in an intervention based on school research [El cambio en las emociones de maestros en formación inicial hacia el clima de aula en una intervención basada en investigación escolar]. *Revista Eureka Sobre Enseñanza y Divulgación de las Ciencias*, *15*(2), 2602.

Rhodes, M. G., & Tauber, S. K. (2011). The influence of delaying judgments of learning on metacognitive accuracy: A meta-analytic review. *Psychological Bulletin*, *137*(1), 131–148. doi:10.1037/a0021705 PMID:21219059

Riad, A. M., Elminir, H. K., Shohieb, S. M., & Asem, A. S. (2012). SignsWorld: Deeping into the Silence World and Hearing Its Signs (State of the Art). *International Journal of Computer Science and Information Technology*.

Riad, A. M., Elminir, H. K., & Shohieb, S. M. (2013). Dynamic Hand Gesture Recognition; Real Time vs. Offline Recognition Using Kinect. *Advances in Computer Science and Engineering*, *11*(1), 39–50.

Riad, A. M., Elminir, H. K., & Shohieb, S. M. (2014). Hand Gesture Recognition System Based on a Geometric Model and Rule Based Classifier. *British Journal of Applied Science and Technology*, *4*(9), 1432–1444.

Ribeiro, L., Leal da Silva, T., & Quadrado Mussi, A. (2018). Gamification: A methodology to motivate engagement and participation in a higher education environment. *International Journal of Education and Research*, *6*(4), 249–264.

Richter, G., Raban, D. R., & Rafaeli, S. (2015). Studying gamification: The effect of rewards and incentives on motivation. In Gamification in Education and Business (pp. 21–46). doi:10.1007/978-3-319-10208-5_2

Richter, N. F., Cepeda, G., Roldán, J. L., & Ringle, C. M. (2015). European management research using partial least squares structural equation modeling (PLS-SEM). *European Management Journal*, *33*(1), 1–3. doi:10.2196/27290

Rieber, L. P. (1996). Seriously considering play: Designing interactive learning environments based on the blending of microworlds, simulations, and games. *Educational Technology Research and Development*, *44*(2), 43–58. doi:10.1007/BF02300540

Rieckmann, M. (2018). Learning to transform the world: key competencies. In Issues and trends in Education for Sustainable Development in Issues and trends in education for sustainable development (1st ed., pp. 39–59). United Nations Educational, Scientific and Cultural Organization.

Riemann, H. (2016). *Harmony simplified, or the theory of the tonal functions of chords (classic reprint)*. Academic Press.

Rigby, S., & Ryan, R. M. (2011). *Glued to games: How video games draw us in and hold us spellbound*. Praeger.

Rincon-Flores, E. G., López-Camacho, E., & López, O. O. (2020). Engaging a Calculus Course with Telepresence through Gamification. *2020 IEEE Global Engineering Education Conference (EDUCON)*, 1055-1059. 10.1109/EDUCON45650.2020.9125163

Ritterfeld, U., & Weber, R. (2006). Video games for entertainment and education. In P. Vorderer & J. Bryant (Eds.), *Playing video games. Motives, responses, and consequences* (pp. 399–413). Lawrence Erlbaum Associates.

Rivera, E. S., & Garden, C. L. P. (2021). Gamification for student engagement: A framework. *Journal of Further and Higher Education*, *45*(7), 999–1012. Advance online publication. doi:10.1080/0309877X.2021.1875201

Rivera-Trigueros, I., & Sánchez-Pérez, M. D. M. (2020). Conquering the iron throne: Using classcraft to foster students'motivation in the efl classroom. *Teaching English with Technology*, *20*(4), 3–22.

Robertson, M., Collins, A., Medeira, N., & Slater, J. (2003). Barriers to Start-Ups and Their Effect on Aspirant Entrepreneurs. *Education and Training*, *45*(6), 308-316. Available: www.lmu.ac.uk/business-start-up

Robertson, J., Gray, S., Toye, M., & Booth, J. (2020). The relationship between executive functions and computational thinking. *International Journal of Computer Science Education in Schools*, *3*(4), 35–49.

Robertson, M., & Collins, A. (2003). The video role model as an enterprise teaching aid. *Education + Training*, *45*(6), 331–340. doi:10.1108/00400910310495987

Roberts, T. L., Lowry, P. B., & Sweeney, P. D. (2006). An evaluation of the impact of social presence through group size and the use of collaborative software on group member"voice" in face-to-face and computer-mediated task groups. *IEEE Transactions on Professional Communication*, *49*(1), 28–43. doi:10.1109/TPC.2006.870460

Robot Kits For Kids | KIBO | KinderLab Robotics. (2019). Retrieved from https://kinderlabrobotics.com/kibo/

Robson, K., Plangger, K., Kietzmann, J., McCarthy, I., & Pitt, L. (2015). Is it all a game? Understanding the principles of gamification. *Business Horizons*, *58*(4), 411–420. doi:10.1016/j.bushor.2015.03.006

Rocket Lab. (2021). https://www.rocketlabusa.com/

Rode, J., Blythe, M., & Nardi, B. (2012). Qualitative research in HCI. In CHI'12 Extended Abstracts on Human Factors in Computing Systems (pp. 2803–2806). doi:10.1145/2212776.2212725

Röder, M., Both, A., & Hinneburg, A. (2015). Exploring the space of topic coherence measures. *Proceedings of the Eighth ACM International Conference on Web Search and Data Mining*, 399–408. 10.1145/2684822.2685324

Rodrigues, L. F., Oliveira, A., & Costa, C. J. (2016). Does ease-of-use contributes to the perception of enjoyment? A case of gamification in e-banking. *Computers in Human Behavior*, *61*, 114–126. doi:10.1016/j.chb.2016.03.015

Rodríguez, A., Boada, I., Thió-Henestrosa, S., & Sbert, M. (2018). CPRforblind: A video game to introduce cardiopulmonary resuscitation protocol to blind people. *British Journal of Educational Technology*, *49*(4), 636–645. doi:10.1111/bjet.12627

Rogers, C. B., El-Mounaryi, H., Wasfy, T., & Satterwhite, J. (2017). *Assessment of STEM e-learning in an immersive virtual reality (VR) environment* [Paper presentation]. 2016 ASEE Annual conference & exposition, New Orleans, LA, United States. 10.18260/p.26336

Rogers, Y., Sharp, H., & Preece, J. (2013). *Interaction design: beyond human-computer interaction* [Design de interação: além da interação humano-computador] (3rd ed.). Bookman Editora.

Roh, Y. S., Lee, W. S., Chung, H. S., & Park, Y. M. (2013). The effects of simulation-based resuscitation training on nurses' self-efficacy and satisfaction. *Nurse Education Today*, *33*(2), 123–128. doi:10.1016/j.nedt.2011.11.008 PMID:22153054

Rojas, D., Kapralos, B., & Dubrowski, A. (2013). The missing piece in the gamification puzzle. In *Proceedings of the First International Conference on Gameful Design, Research, and Applications* (pp. 135-138). ACM. 10.1145/2583008.2583033

Ro, M., Brauer, M., Kuntz, K., Shukla, R., & Bensch, I. (2017). Making Cool Choices for sustainability: Testing the effectiveness of a game-based approach to promoting pro-environmental behaviors. *Journal of Environmental Psychology*, *53*, 20–30. doi:10.1016/j.jenvp.2017.06.007

Rosa, J. (2017). *Virtual immersive simulation in nursing continuous education: Study developed at a hospital from Douro Litoral* [Master's thesis, Nursing School of Porto, Portugal]. RCAAP – Repositório Comum. http://hdl.handle.net/1040 0.26/22506

Rosen, E. F., & Petty, L. C. (1992). Computer-aided instruction in a physiological psychology course. *Behavior Research Methods, Instruments, & Computers*, *24*(2), 169–171. doi:10.3758/BF03203492

Rosetta. (2021). https://www.esa.int/Enabling_Support/Operations/Rosetta

Rosli, K., Khairudin, N., & Saat, R. M. (2019). Gamification in entrepreneurship and accounting education. *Academy of Entrepreneurship Journal*, *25*(3), 1–6.

Ross & Bennett. (2020). Increasing Engagement with Engineering Escape Rooms. *IEEE Transactions on Games*. . doi:10.1109/TG.2020.3025003

Ross, R., & de Souza-Daw, A. (2021, June). Educational Escape Rooms as an Active Learning Tool for Teaching Telecommunications Engineering. In Telecom (Vol. 2, No. 2, pp. 155-166). Multidisciplinary Digital Publishing Institute. doi:10.3390/telecom2020010

Rossini, T. S. S., do Amaral, M. M., & Santos, E. (2021). The viralization of online education: Learning beyond the time of the coronavirus. *Prospects*, *51*(1-3), 285–297. doi:10.100711125-021-09559-5 PMID:33967347

Ross, R. (2019). Design of an open-source decoder for educational escape rooms. *IEEE Access: Practical Innovations, Open Solutions*, *7*, 145777–145783. doi:10.1109/ACCESS.2019.2945289

Ross, R., & Bell, C. (2019, August). Turning the classroom into an escape room with decoder hardware to increase student engagement. In *2019 IEEE Conference on Games (CoG)* (pp. 1-4). IEEE. 10.1109/CIG.2019.8848020

Ross, R., & Hall, R. (2021). Towards Teaching Digital Electronics Using Escape Rooms. *Advances in Engineering Education*, *9*(2), 1–19.

Ross, R., & Kurtz, R. (1993). Making Manipulatives Work: A Strategy for Success. *The Arithmetic Teacher*, *40*(5), 254–257. doi:10.5951/AT.40.5.0254

Roundy, P. T., Bradshaw, M., & Brockman, B. K. (2018). The emergence of entrepreneurial ecosystems: A complex adaptive systems approach. *Journal of Business Research*, *86*, 1–10. doi:10.1016/j.jbusres.2018.01.032

Rowley, J. (2014). Data analysis. In D. Coghlan & M. Brydon-Miller (Eds.), *The SAGE encyclopedia of action research* (pp. 239–242). Sage.

Rozendaal, M. C., & Schifferstein, H. N. (2010). Pleasantness in bodily experience: A phenomenological inquiry. *International Journal of Design*, *4*(2), 55–63.

Ruffel, A. (2010). Forensic pedology, forensic geology, forensic geoscience, geoforensics and soil forensics. *Forensic Science International*, *202*(1-3), 9–12. doi:10.1016/j.forsciint.2010.03.044 PMID:20430544

Ruffel, A., Pirrie, D., & Power, M. R. (2013). Issues and opportunities in urban forensic geology. *Geological Society of London, Special Publications*, *384*(1), 147–161. doi:10.1144/SP384.19

Ruipérez-Valiente, J. A., Gomez, M. J., Martínez, P. A., & Kim, Y. J. (2021). Ideating and Developing a Visualization Dashboard to Support Teachers Using Educational Games in the Classroom. *IEEE Access: Practical Innovations, Open Solutions*, *9*, 83467–83481. doi:10.1109/ACCESS.2021.3086703

Ruiz, L. (1992). Pasatiempos y Geología: posibilidades didácticas. In Actas de VII Simposio sobre Enseñanza de la Geología (pp. 313-351). Instituto de Ciencias de la Educación, Universidade de Santiago de Compostela.

Ruiz, F. J. (2007). Modelos didácticos para la enseñanza de las ciencias naturales. *Revista Latinoamericana de Estudios Educativos*, *3*, 41–60.

Rush, D. E., & Connolly, A. J. (2020). An agile framework for teaching with scrum in the IT project management classroom. *Journal of Information Systems Education*, *31*(3), 196–207. https://aisel.aisnet.org/jise/vol31/iss3/4

Rutten, N., van Joolingen, W. R., & van der Veen, J. T. (2012). The learning effects of computer simulations in science education. *Computers & Education*, *58*(1), 136–153. doi:10.1016/j.compedu.2011.07.017

Ryan, R. M. (1982). Control and information in the intrapersonal sphere: An extension of cognitive evaluation theory. *Journal of Personality and Social Psychology*, *43*(3), 450–461. doi:10.1037/0022-3514.43.3.450

Ryan, R. M., & Deci, E. L. (1987). The support of autonomy and the control of behavior. *Journal of Personnel Psychology*, *53*(6), 1024–1037. doi:10.1037/0022-3514.53.6.1024 PMID:3320334

Ryan, R. M., & Deci, E. L. (2000). Intrinsic and Extrinsic Motivations: Classic Definitions and New Directions. *Contemporary Educational Psychology*, *25*(1), 54–67. doi:10.1006/ceps.1999.1020 PMID:10620381

Ryan, R. M., & Deci, E. L. (2000). Self-determination theory and the facilitation of intrinsic motivation, social development, and well-being. *The American Psychologist*, *55*(1), 68–78. doi:10.1037/0003-066X.55.1.68 PMID:11392867

Ryan, R. M., & Deci, E. L. (2009). Promoting self-determined school engagement, motivation, learning, and well-being. In K. Wentzel, A. Wigfield, & D. Miele (Eds.), *Handbook of motivation at school* (pp. 171–196). Routledge.

Ryan, R. M., & Deci, E. L. (2020). Intrinsic and extrinsic motivation from a self-determination theory perspective: Definitions, theory, practices, and future directions. *Contemporary Educational Psychology*, *61*, 101860. doi:10.1016/j.cedpsych.2020.101860

Ryan, R. M., Rigby, C. S., & Przybylski, A. (2006). The motivational pull of video games: A self-determination theory approach. *Motivation and Emotion*, *30*(4), 347–365. doi:10.100711031-006-9051-8

Sabri, H., Cowan, B., Kapralos, B., Porte, M., Backstein, D., & Dubrowskie, A. (2010). Serious games for knee replacement surgery procedure education and training. *Procedia: Social and Behavioral Sciences*, *2*(2), 3483–3488. doi:10.1016/j.sbspro.2010.03.539

Sackett, P. R., & Mullen, E. J. (1993). Beyond formal experimental design: Towards an expanded view of the training evaluation process. *Personnel Psychology*, *46*(3), 613–627. doi:10.1111/j.1744-6570.1993.tb00887.x

Said, N. S. (2004). An engaging multimedia design model. In *Proceedings of the 2004 conference on Interaction design and children: building a community* (pp. 169-172). ACM.

Sailer, M., & Homner, L. (2020). *The gamification of learning: A meta-analysis.* https://link.springer.com/article/10.1007/s10648-019-09498-w

Sailer, M., Hense, J. U., Mayr, S. K., & Mandl, H. (2017). How gamification motivates: An experimental study of the effects of specific game design elements on psychological need satisfaction. *Computers in Human Behavior*, *69*, 371–380. doi:10.1016/J.CHB.2016.12.033

Sailer, M., & Homner, L. (2020). The Gamification of Learning: A Meta-analysis. *Educational Psychology Review*, *32*(1), 77–112. doi:10.100710648-019-09498-w

Sajjadi, P., Hoffmann, L., Cimiano, P., & Kopp, S. (2019). A personality-based emotional model for embodied conversational agents: Effects on perceived social presence and game experience of users. *Entertainment Computing*, *32*, 1–10. doi:10.1016/j.entcom.2019.100313

Sakunprasert, T. (2018). *The application of gamification in Thai organization.* Academic Press.

Salam, M., Awang Iskandar, D. N., Ibrahim, D. H. A., & Farooq, M. S. (2019). Service learning in higher education: a systematic literature review. *Asia Pacific Education Review, 20*(4), 573-593. doi:10.1007/s12564-019-09580-6

Salas, E., Tannenbaum, S. I., Kraiger, K., & Smith-Jentsch, K. A. (2012). The science of training and development in organizations: What matters in practice. *Psychological Science in the Public Interest*, *13*(2), 74–101. doi:10.1177/1529100612436661 PMID:26173283

Salen, K., Tekinbaş, K. S., & Zimmerman, E. (2004). *Rules of play: Game design fundamentals.* MIT Press. https://mitpress.mit.edu/books/rules-play

Salen, K., & Zimmerman, E. (2003). This is not a game: play in cultural environments. In *Level Up Conference Proceedings*. DIGRA.

Salen, K., & Zimmerman, E. (2012). *Regras do jogo: Fundamentos do design de jogos* [Rules of play: Game design fundamentals]. Blucher.

Salza, P., Musmarra, P., & Ferrucci, F. (2019). *Agile methodologies in education: A review. Agile and lean concepts for teaching and learning.* Springer. doi:10.1007/978-981-13-2751-3_2

Samonte, M. J. C. (2020, June). An assistive technology using FSL, speech recognition, gamification and online handwritten character recognition in learning statistics for students with hearing and speech impairment. In *Proceedings of the 2020 The 6th International Conference on Frontiers of Educational Technologies* (pp. 92-97). 10.1145/3404709.3404746

Sampayo-Vargas, S., Cope, C. J., He, Z., & Byrne, G. J. (2013). The effectiveness of adaptive difficulty adjustments on students' motivation and learning in an educational computer game. *Computers & Education*, *69*, 452–462. doi:10.1016/j.compedu.2013.07.004

Sánchez Lamas, A. (2018). *Educational Escape Rooms: practical example and guide for its design* [Escape Rooms educativas: ejemplo práctico y guía para su diseño]. Universitat Oberta de Catalunya.

Sanchez, D. R., & Langer, M. (2020). Video game pursuit (VGPu) scale development: Designing and validating a scale with implications for game-based learning and assessment. *Simulation & Gaming*, *51*(1), 55–86. doi:10.1177/1046878119882710

Sanchez, D. R., Langer, M., & Kaur, R. (2019). Gamification in the classroom: Examining the impact of gamified quizzes on student learning. *Computers & Education*, *144*, 103666. doi:10.1016/j.compedu.2019.103666

Sanchez, E., Young, S., & Jouneau-Sion, C. (2017). Classcraft: From gamification to ludicization of classroom management. *Education and Information Technologies*, *22*(2), 497–513. doi:10.100710639-016-9489-6

Sanchez-Martín, J., Cañada-Cañada, F., & Dávila-Acedo, A. (2018). Emotional responses to innovative science teaching methods: Acquiring emotional data in a general science teacher education class. *Journal of Technology and Science Education JOTSE*, *8*(4), 346–359. doi:10.3926/jotse.408

Sánchez-Martín, J., Cañada-Cañada, F., & Dávila-Acedo, M. A. (2017). Just a game? Gamifying a general science class at university: Collaborative and competitive work implications. *Thinking Skills and Creativity*, *26*, 51–59. doi:10.1016/j.tsc.2017.05.003

Sánchez-Martín, J., Corrales-Serrano, M., Luque-Sendra, A., & Zamora-Polo, F. (2020). Exit for success. Gamifying science and technology for university students using escape-room. A preliminary approach. *Heliyon*, *6*(7), e04340. doi:10.1016/j.heliyon.2020.e04340 PMID:32671257

Sanmugam, M., Zaid, N. M., Abdullah, Z., Aris, B., Mohamed, H., & van der Meijden, H. (2016). The impacts of infusing game elements and gamification in learning. In *2016 IEEE 8th international conference on engineering education (ICEED)* (pp. 131-136). IEEE. 10.1109/ICEED.2016.7856058

Sanmugam, M., Abdullah, Z., Mohamed, H., Aris, B., Zaid, N. M., & Suhadi, S. M. (2016). The Affiliation between Student Achievement and Elements of Gamification in Learning Science. In *Proceedings of the 2016 4th International Conference on Information and Communication Technology* (pp. 1-4). 10.1109/ICoICT.2016.7571962

Santana Astronomical Observatory of Azores - OASA. (n.d.). http://oasa.centrosciencia.azores.gov.pt

Santos, E. O., & Weber, A. (2013). Educação e cibercultura: Aprendizagem ubíqua no currículo da disciplina didática [Education and cyberculture: ubiquitous learning in the didactic subject curriculum]. *Revista Diálogo Educacional*, *13*(38), 285–303. doi:10.7213/dialogo.educ.7646

Saputra, M. R. U., & Risqi, M. (2015). Lexipal: Design, implementation and evaluation of gamification on learning application for dyslexia. *International Journal of Computers and Applications*, *131*(7), 37–43. doi:10.5120/ijca2015907416

Sarfraz, I., Rajendran, D., Hewege, C., & Mohan, M. D. (2018). An exploration of global employability skills: A systematic research review. *International Journal of Work Organisation and Emotion*, *9*(1), 63–88. doi:10.1504/IJWOE.2018.091339

Saslaw, J. (1996). Forces, containers, and paths: The role of body-derived image schemas in the conceptualization of music. *Journal of Music Therapy*, *40*(2), 217–243. doi:10.2307/843889

Sato, A. K. (2010). Game design and prototyping: Concepts and applications throughout the design process [Game design e prototipagem: conceitos e aplicações ao longo do processo projetual]. *Proceedings of SBGames*, *2010*, 74–84.

Savage, D. D., & Bales, R. (2017). Video games in job interviews: Using algorithms to minimize discrimination and unconscious bias. *ABA Journal of Labor & Employment Law*, *32*(2), 211–228. https://heinonline.org/HOL/LandingPage?handle=hein.journals/lablaw32&div=18&id=&page=

Savi, R. (2011). *Evaluation of games aimed at the dissemination of knowledge* [Avaliação de jogos voltados para a disseminação do conhecimento] [Doctoral dissertation]. Federal University of Santa Catarina, Brazil.

Savi, R., & Ulbricht, V. R. (2008). Jogos digitais educacionais: Benefícios e desafios. *Renote: revista novas tecnologias na educação, 6*(2), 1-10.

Sawyer, B., & Smith, P. (2008). *Serious games taxonomy*. Serious Games Initiative.

Scaife, M., & Rogers, Y. (1999). Kids as informants: Telling us what we didn't know or confirming what we knew already. In A. Druin (Ed.), *The design of children's technology* (pp. 29–50). Morgan Kaufmann.

Schäfer, A., Holz, J., Leonhardt, T., Schroeder, U., Brauner, P., & Ziefle, M. (2013). From boring to scoring–a collaborative serious game for learning and practicing mathematical logic for computer science education. *Computer Science Education, 23*(2), 87–111. doi:10.1080/08993408.2013.778040

Schäfer, U. (2017, April). Training scrum with gamification: Lessons learned after two teaching periods. In *2017 IEEE Global Engineering Education Conference (EDUCON)* (pp. 754–761). IEEE. 10.1109/EDUCON.2017.7942932

Schaufeli, W. B., Martínez, I. M., Pinto, A. M., Salanova, M., & Barker, A. B. (2002). Burnout and engagement in university students a cross-national study. *Journal of Cross-Cultural Psychology, 33*(5), 464–481. doi:10.1177/0022022102033005003

Schell, J. (2008). *The art of game design: A book of lenses*. CRC Press. https://www.schellgames.com/art-of-game-design/

Schellenberg, E. G., Bigand, E., Poulin-Charronnat, B., Garnier, C., & Stevens, C. (2005). Children's implicit knowledge of harmony in Western music. *Developmental Science, 8*(6), 551–566. doi:10.1111/j.1467-7687.2005.00447.x PMID:16246247

Schell, J. (2008). *The Art of Game Design: A Book of Lenses*. Morgan Kaufmann Publishers. doi:10.1201/9780080919171

Schlemmer, E. (2016) Hybridism, Multimodality and Nomadism: co-determination and coexistence for an Education in the context of ubiquity [Hibridismo, Multimodalidade e Nomadismo: codeterminação e coexistência para uma Educação em contexto de ubiquidade]. In Educação a distância, qualidade e convergências: sujeitos, conhecimentos, práticas e tecnologias. São Carlos: EdUFSCar.

Schlemmer, E. (2015). *Gamificação em contexto de hibridismo e multimodalidade na educação corporativa* (Vol. 5). Revista FGV Online.

Schmidt-Kraepelin, M., Thiebes, S., Baumsteiger, D., & Sunyaev, A. (2018). *State of play: A citation network analysis of healthcare gamification studies*. Academic Press.

Schmitt, V. G. H., & Cequea, M. M. (2020). Flipped classroom: A change in paradigms in higher education [Aula invertida: Uma mudança nos paradigmas no ensino superior; Clase invertida: Un cambio de paradigmas en la educación superior]. *Interciencia, 45*(11), 501–507.

Schofield, M. (2021). Gamification Tools to Facilitate Student Learning Engagement in Higher Education: A Burden or Blessing? In Fostering Communication and Learning With Underutilized Technologies in Higher Education (pp. 21-35). IGI Global. doi:10.4018/978-1-7998-4846-2.ch002

Schön, D. A. (1983). *The reflective practitioner: How professionals think in action*. Basic Books.

Schumpeter, J. A. (1926). *Theorie der wirtschaftlichen Entwicklung* (2nd ed.). Duncker & Humboldt.

Schuytema, P. (2008). *Game Design. A Practical Approach*. Charles River Media.

Schwaber, K., Sutherland, J., & Beedle, M. (2013). *The definitive guide to Scrum: The rules of the game*. Scrum.org. http://www.scrumguides.org/docs/scrumguide/v1/Scrum-guide-us.pdf

Schwartz, D. (2021). *Using Discord to facilitate student engagement*. https://digitalscholarship.unlv.edu/btp_expo/122

Sciamarelli, M. (2015). *11 – Teaching children with mascot-inspired projects*. Available at https://www.teachingenglish.org.uk/sites/teacheng/files/pub_F004_ELT_Creativity_FINAL_v2%20WEB.pdf#page=108

Scott, W. (2002). *Education and Sustainable Development: challenges, responsibilities, and frames of mind*. The Trumpeter. https://trumpeter.athabascau.ca/index.php/trumpet/article/view/123/134

Scott, J. (1988). Social network analysis. *Sociology*, *22*(1), 109–127. doi:10.1177/0038038588022001007

Seaborn, K., & Fels, D. I. (2015). Gamification in theory and action: A survey. *International Journal of Human-Computer Studies*, *74*, 14–31. doi:10.1016/j.ijhcs.2014.09.006

Selevko, G. K. (2006). Entsiklopediya obrazovatel'nykh tekhnologiy [Encyclopedia of educational technologies] (Vol. 2). Research Institute of School Technologies.

Sempere Pla, S. (2020). Gamification project based on the escape room applied to a bilingual classroom of primary education with CLIL approach [Proyecto de gamificación basado en el escape room aplicado a un aula bilingüe de educación primaria con enfoque AICLE]. *Tecnología. Ciência & Educação (Bauru)*, *16*, 5–40.

Senderek, R., Brenken, B., & Stich, V. (2015). The implementation of game based learning as part of the corporate competence development. In A. Pester, V. Alexandrov, J. J Noguez, & L. J. Neri (Eds.), *Proceedings of the 2015 international conference on interactive collaborative and blended learning* (pp. 44-51). IEEE. 10.1109/ICBL.2015.7387632

Sergi, B. S., Popkova, E. G., Bogoviz, A. V., & Ragulina, J. V. (2019). Entrepreneurship and Economic Growth: The Experience of Developed and Developing Countries. In Entrepreneurship and Development in the 21st Century (Lab for Entrepreneurship and Development). Emerald Publishing Limited. doi:10.1108/978-1-78973-233-720191002

Sexton, D. L., & Upton, N. B. (1987). Evaluation of an innovative approach to teaching entrepreneurship. *Journal of Small Business Management*, *25*(1), 35.

Shaffer, D. W., & Gee, J. P. (2006). *How computer games help children learn*. Palgrave Macmillan. doi:10.1057/9780230601994

Shaffer, D. W., Squire, K. D., Halverson, R., & Gee, J. P. (2005). Video games and the future of learning. *Phi Delta Kappan*, *87*(2), 104–111. doi:10.1177/003172170508700205

Shalar, O., Huzar, V., Strykalenko, Y., Yuskiv, S., Homenko, V., & Novokshanova, A. (2019). Psycho-pedagogical aspects of interaction between personality traits and physical qualities of the young gymnasts of the variety and circus studio. *Journal of Physical Education and Sport*, *19*(6), 2283–2288. doi:10.7752/jpes.2019.s6344

Shapiro, D. (2019). *Robot Turtles | The Board Game that Teaches Programming to Kids*. Retrieved from http://www.robotturtles.com/

Sharma, S., & Somani, A. (2019). Gamification in Entertainment Industry: Glimpses From Indian Film Industry. In P. Mishra & S. Dham (Eds.), *Application of Gaming in New Media Marketing* (pp. 236–243). IGI Global. doi:10.4018/978-1-5225-6064-7.ch014

Shawyun, T. (2005). *Values of Thai Undergraduate and Graduate Students: A Case Study of Assumption University*. doi:10.13140/RG.2.2.30591.71848

Sheldon, J. P. (2004). Gender stereotypes in educational software for young children. *Sex Roles*, *51*(7), 433–444. doi:10.1023/B:SERS.0000049232.90715.d9

Sheldon, L. (2020). *The Multiplayer Classroom: Designing coursework as a game*. CRC Press. doi:10.1201/9780429285035

Shen, Y. S., Choi, H. C., Joppe, M., & Yi, S. (2020). What motivates visitors to participate in a gamified trip? A player typology using Q methodology. *Tourism Management*, *78*(6), 1–14. doi:10.1016/j.tourman.2019.104074

Shepel, E. V. (2013). *Razvitiye poznavatel'noy samostoyatel'nosti studentov-ekonomistov v strukture individual'noy trayektorii professional'noy podgotovki* [Development of the cognitive independence of economics students in the structure of the individual trajectory of vocational training]. Academic Press.

Sherman, M., Chernikova, V. (2013) *Inozemna kompetentnist' yak faktor rozvytku tvorchykh zdibnostey maybutnikh sudnovodiiv* [Foreign language competence as a factor in the development of creative abilities of future navigators]. Kherson State Technical University.

Sherman-Morris, K., & McNeal, K. S. (2016). Understanding Perceptions of the Geosciences Among Minority and Nonminority Undergraduate Students. *Journal of Geoscience Education*, *64*(2), 147–156. doi:10.5408/15-112.1

Shi, L., & Cristea, A. I. (2016). Motivational Gamification Strategies Rooted in Self-Determination Theory for Social Adaptive E-Learning. In A. Micarelli, J. Stamper, & K. Panourgia (Eds.), *Intelligent Tutoring Systems* (Vol. 9684, pp. 294–300). Springer International Publishing. doi:10.1007/978-3-319-39583-8_32

Shin, N., Sutherland, L. M., Norris, C. A., & Soloway, E. (2012). Effects of game technology on elementary student learning in mathematics. *British Journal of Educational Technology*, *43*(4), 540–560. doi:10.1111/j.1467-8535.2011.01197.x

Shi, Y. R., & Shih, J. L. (2015). Game factors and game-based learning design model. *International Journal of Computer Games Technology*, *2015*, 1–11. doi:10.1155/2015/549684

Shohieb, S. M., Hassan, A. E., Abo Elsoud, M., & Kandil, M. S. (2009). Accessibility system for deaf Arab students. In *2009 ITI 7th International Conference on Communications and Information Technology (ICICT)* (pp. 57-60). IEEE.

Shohieb, S. M. (2016). *A Benchmark Arabic Sign Language Database: An Atlas for Vision-Based Recognition Processes*. LAP Lambert Academic Publishing.

Shohieb, S. M. (2019). A Gamified e-Learning Framework for Teaching Mathematics to Arab Deaf Students: Supporting an Acting Arabic Sign Language Avatar. *Ubiquitous Learning: An International Journal*, *12*(1), 55–70.

Shohieb, S. M., Elminir, H. K., & Riad, A. M. (2015). Signsworld atlas; a benchmark Arabic sign language database. *Journal of King Saud University-Computer and Information Sciences*, *27*(1), 68–76.

Shorey, S., & Ng, E. D. (2020). The use of virtual reality simulation among nursing students and registered nurses: A systematic review. *Nurse Education Today*, *104662*. Advance online publication. doi:10.1016/j.nedt.2020.104662 PMID:33203545

Shura, R., Siders, R. A., & Dannefer, D. (2011). Culture Change in Long-term Care: Participatory Action Research and the Role of the Resident. *The Gerontologist*, *51*(2), 212–225. Advance online publication. doi:10.1093/geront/gnq099 PMID:21163911

Shute, V. J., Ventura, M., & Ke, F. (2015). The power of play: The effects of Portal 2 and Lumosity on cognitive and noncognitive skills. *Computers & Education*, *80*, 58–67. doi:10.1016/j.compedu.2014.08.013

Siemens, G. (2010). *Knowing knowledge* [Conociendo el conocimiento]. Ediciones Nodos Ele. https://archive.org/details/2010ConociendoElConocimiento

Siemens, G. (2005). Connectivism: A learning theory for the digital age. *International Journal of Instructional Technology & Distance Learning, 2*(1), 3–10. http://www.itdl.org/Journal/Jan_05/article01.htm

Siemens, G. (2012). Connectivism: a theory of learning for the digital age [Conectivismo: uma teoria da aprendizagem para a era digital]. In *Conectados no ciberespaço. Paulinas.*

Sierra, M. C., & Fernández-Sánchez, M. R. (2019). Gamificando el aula universitaria. Análisis de una experiencia de Escape Room en educación superior. *Revista de Estudios y Experiencias en Educación, 18*(36), 105–115. doi:10.21703/rexe.20191836sierra15

Sierra, M. C., & Fernández-Sánchez, M. R. (2019). Gamifying the university classroom. Analysis of an Escape Room experience in higher education [Gamificando el aula universitaria. Análisis de una experiencia de Escape Room en educación superior]. *Revista de Estudios y Experiencias en Educación, 18*(36), 105–115.

Sigala, M. (2015). The application and impact of gamification funware on trip planning and experiences: The case of TripAdvisor's funware. *Electronic Markets, 25*(3), 189–209. doi:10.100712525-014-0179-1

Signori, G. G., De Guimarães, J. C. F., Severo, E. A., & Rotta, C. (2018). Gamification as an innovative method in the processes of learning in higher education institutions. *International Journal of Innovation and Learning, 24*(2), 115–137. doi:10.1504/IJIL.2018.094066

Silraungwilai, U. (2016). The Twelve Thai National Core Values : The Intersection Between Thai Identities and Thai Cultural Competences. *APHEIT Journal, 22*(1), 134–140.

Silva-Calpa, G. F. M., Raposo, A. B., & Suplino, M. (2018, May). CoASD: A tabletop game to support the collaborative work of users with autism spectrum disorder. In *2018 IEEE 6th International Conference on Serious Games and Applications for Health (SeGAH)* (pp. 1-8). IEEE. 10.1109/SeGAH.2018.8401358

Silva, E. (2009). Measuring skills for 21st-century learning. *Phi Delta Kappan, 90*(9), 630–634. doi:10.1177/003172170909000905

Silva, J. B. D., Sales, G. L., & Castro, J. B. D. (2019). Gamificação como estratégia de aprendizagem ativa no ensino de Física [Gamification as an active learning strategy in the Physics education]. *Revista Brasileira de Ensino de Física, 41*(4), 1–9. doi:10.1590/1806-9126-rbef-2018-0309

Silva, T., Melo, J., & Tedesco, P. (2016). A model to promote student engagement in programming learning using gamification [Um Modelo para Promover o Engajamento Estudantil no Aprendizado de Programação Utilizando Gamification]. *Brazilian Journal of Computers in Education, 26*(3), 120–138. doi:10.5753/rbie.2018.26.03.120

Simões, J., Redondo, R. D., & Vilas, A. F. (2013). A social gamification framework for a K-6 learning platform. *Computers in Human Behavior, 29*(2), 345–353. doi:10.1016/j.chb.2012.06.007

Simon, R. L., Torres, C. R., & Hager, P. F. (2014). *Fair play: The ethics of sport.* Westview Press.

Simpson, O. (2003). *Student retention in online, open, and distance learning.* Psychology Press. doi:10.4324/9780203416563

Singer, E., van Hoewyk, J., & Maher, M. P. (2000). Experiments with incentives in telephone surveys. *Public Opinion Quarterly, 64*, 171–188. doi:10.1086/317761 PMID:10984332

Singer, M. (1990). *Psychology of language: An introduction to sentence and discourse processing.* Lawrence Erlbaum.

Sioux Group & Go Gamers (2021). *Game Brasil 2021 Search* [Pesquisa Game Brasil 2021]. https://www.pesquisagamebrasil.com.br/pt/ebooks/

Sipiyaruk, K., Hatzipanagos, S., Reynolds, P. A., & Gallagher, J. E. (2021). Serious games and the COVID-19 pandemic in dental education: An integrative review of the literature. *Computers*, *10*(4), 1–15. doi:10.3390/computers10040042

Sitzmann, T. (2011). A meta-analytic examination of the instructional effectiveness of computer-based simulation games. *Personnel Psychology*, *64*(2), 489–528. doi:10.1111/j.1744-6570.2011.01190.x

Sitzmann, T., Ely, K., Brown, K. G., & Bauer, K. N. (2010). Self-assessment of knowledge: A cognitive learning or affective measure? *Academy of Management Learning & Education*, *9*(2), 169–191. doi:10.5465/amle.9.2.zqr169

Skinner, B. F. (1953). *Science and human behavior*. Macmillan.

Smiderle, R., Rigo, S. J., Marques, L. B., Peçanha de Miranda Coelho, J. A., & Jaques, P. A. (2020). The impact of gamification on students' learning, engagement and behavior based on their personality traits. *Smart Learn. Environ.*, *7*(1), 3. doi:10.118640561-019-0098-x

Smith, K., & Abrams, S. S. (2019). Gamification and accessibility. *The International Journal of Information and Learning Technology*, *36*(2), 104–123. doi:10.1108/IJILT-06-2018-0061

Smith, M. W., Sharit, J., & Czaja, S. J. (1999). Aging, motor control, and the performance of computer mouse tasks. *Human Factors*, *41*(3), 389–396. doi:10.1518/001872099779611102 PMID:10665207

Smith, P. K., Mahdavi, J., Carvalho, M., Fisher, S., Russell, S., & Tippett, N. (2008). Cyberbullying: Its nature and impact in secondary school pupils. *Journal of Child Psychology and Psychiatry, and Allied Disciplines*, *49*(4), 376–385. doi:10.1111/j.1469-7610.2007.01846.x PMID:18363945

Soares, A., Gazzinelli, M., Souza, V. D., & Araújo, L. H. (2015). The Role Playing Game (RPG) as a pedagogical strategy in the training of the nurse: An experience report on the creation of a game. *Texto & Contexto Enfermagem*, *24*(2), 600–608. doi:10.1590/0104-07072015001072014

Sobodić, A., Balaban, I., & Kermek, D. (2018). Usability Metrics for Gamified E-learning Course: A Multilevel Approach. *International Journal of Emerging Technologies in Learning*, *13*(05), 41–55.

Soboleva, E. V., Sabirova, E. G., Babieva, N. S., Sergeeva, M. G., & Torkunova, J. V. (2021). Formation of Computational Thinking Skills Using Computer Games in Teaching Mathematics. *Eurasia Journal of Mathematics, Science and Technology Education*, *17*(10), 1–16. doi:10.29333/ejmste/11177

Sohn, T., Li, K. A., Griswold, W. G., & Hollan, J. D. (2008). A diary study of mobile information needs. *Proceedings of the Sigchi Conference on Human Factors in Computing Systems*, 433–442. 10.1145/1357054.1357125

Solicitors Regulation Authority. (2014). *Academic Stage Handbook*. Solicitors Regulation Authority.

Solicitors Regulation Authority. (2021). *SQE2 assessment specification | SQE | Solicitors Regulation Authority*. SQEWebsite. Retrieved 5 August 2021, from https://sqe.sra.org.uk/exam-arrangements/assessment-information/sqe2-assessment-specification

Solís-Espallargas, C., Colomar, I. E., & García, A. R. (2015). A research-based learning experience with Black Boxes in initial teacher training [Una experiencia de aprendizaje por investigación con Cajas negras en formación inicial de maestros]. *Revista Eureka*, *12*(1), 167–177.

Songer, R. W., & Miyata, K. (2014). A playful affordances model for gameful learning. In *Proceedings of the TEEM '14 2nd International Conference on Technological Ecosystems for Enhancing Multiculturality* (pp. 205-213). 10.1145/2669711.2669901

Sonia, C., & Carl, G. (2005). *Design principles for children's technology*. Technical Report HCI-TR, Computer Science Department, University of Saskatchewan.

Souitaris, V., Zerbinati, S., & Al-Laham, A. (2007). Do entrepreneurship programmes raise entrepreneurial intention of science and engineering students? The effect of learning, inspiration and resources. *Journal of Business Venturing*, *22*(4), 566–591. doi:10.1016/j.jbusvent.2006.05.002

Sousa-Vieira, M. E., Ferreira-Pires, O., López-Ardao, J. C., & Fernández-Veiga, M. (2021). *Effectiveness of Gamification in Undergraduate Education*. doi:10.5220/0010495603760385

Span, P. (2016, January 19). After the F.T.C.'s failing grade for Lumosity. *The New York Times*. https://www.nytimes.com/2016/01/19/health/ftcs-lumosity-penalty-doesnt-end-brain-training-debate.html?_r=0

Sphero. (2019). Retrieved from https://www.sphero.com/sprk-plus

Spiegel, M., & Marxt, C. (2011). Defining Technology Entrepreneurship. *2011 IEEE International Conference on Industrial Engineering and Engineering Management*, 1623-1627. 10.1109/IEEM.2011.6118191

Spin Master - Meccano Meccano Erector – M.A.X Robotic Interactive Toy With Artificial Intelligence. (2019). Retrieved from https://www.spinmaster.com/product_detail.php?pid=p21251&bid=

Squad. (2021). https://squad.com.mx/

Squire, K. (2003). Video games in education. *International Journal of Intelligent Simulations and Gaming*, *2*(1), 49–62.

Squire, K. (2011). *Video Games and Learning: Teaching and participatory culture in the digital age*. Teachers College Press.

Srirejeki, K., & Faturokhman, A. (2020). An Experimental Study on the Effectiveness of Entrepreneurship Education. *Economy Transdisciplinarity Cognition, 23*(1).

Stanton, D. (2001). Classroom Collaboration in the Design of Tangible Interfaces for Storytelling. *Proc. ACM CHI 2001*, 482-489.

Stark, M. (2003, September 1). Derek Bok: Business lessons for education leaders. *Harvard Business School Working Knowledge*. Retrieved from http://hbswk.hbs.edu/ archive /3646.html

Steegh, A. M., Höffler, T. N., Keller, M. M., & Parchmann, I. (2019). Gender differences in mathematics and science competitions: A systematic review. *Journal of Research in Science Teaching*, *56*(10), 1431–1460. doi:10.1002/tea.21580

Steegh, N. (2005). Using Externships to Introduce Family Law Students to New Professional Roles. *Family Court Review*, *43*(1), 137–148. doi:10.1111/j.1744-1617.2005.00013.x

Stefaniak, J. (2019). The Utility of Design Thinking to Promote Systemic Instructional Design Practices in the Workplace. *TechTrends*, *64*(2), 202–210. doi:10.100711528-019-00453-8

Stefaniak, J., & Xu, M. (2020). An Examination of the Systemic Reach of Instructional Design Models: A Systematic Review. *TechTrends*, *64*(5), 710–719. doi:10.100711528-020-00539-8

Steghöfer, J. P., Burden, H., Alahyari, H., & Haneberg, D. (2017). No silver brick: Opportunities and limitations of teaching Scrum with Lego workshops. *Journal of Systems and Software*, *131*, 230–247. doi:10.1016/j.jss.2017.06.019

Steiner, K. E., & Moher, T. G. (1992, June). Graphic StoryWriter: An interactive environment for emergent storytelling. In *Proceedings of the SIGCHI conference on Human factors in computing systems* (pp. 357-364). ACM.

Steinkuehler, C., & Duncan, S. (2008). Scientific habits of mind in virtual worlds. *Journal of Science Education and Technology*, *17*(6), 530–543. doi:10.100710956-008-9120-8

Stein, M. K., & Bovalino, J. W. (2001). Manipulatives: One Piece of the Puzzle. *Mathematics Teaching in the Middle School*, *6*(6), 356–359. doi:10.5951/MTMS.6.6.0356

Stenros, J. (2015). *Playfulness, play, and games: A constructionist ludology approach* [Doctoral dissertation]. Tampere University Press. https://trepo.tuni.fi/handle/10024/96986

Stenros, J. (2017). The game definition game: A review. *Games and Culture*, *12*(6), 499–520. doi:10.1177/1555412016655679

Stewart, J., & Knowles, V. (2003). Mentoring in undergraduate business management programmes. *Journal of European Industrial Training*, *27*(2/3/4), 147–159. doi:10.1108/03090590310468967

Still, J. D., & Dark, V. J. (2013). Cognitively describing and designing affordances. *Design Studies*, *34*(3), 285–301.

Stott, A., & Neustaedter, C. (2013). Analysis of gamification in education. Academic Press.

Stott, A., & Neustaedter, C. (2013). Analysis of Gamification in Education. Academic Press.

Strawhacker, A., & Bers, M. U. (2015). "I want my robot to look for food": Comparing Kindergartner's programming comprehension using tangible, graphic, and hybrid user interfaces. *International Journal of Technology and Design Education*, *25*(3), 293–319.

Strzalkowski, T., & Symborski, C. (2017). Lessons learned about serious game design and development. *Games and Culture*, *12*(3), 292–298. doi:10.1177/1555412016673524

Styhre, A. (2020). Governing Innovation-Led Economies: The Role of Business Creation and Creativity. In Indie Video Game Development Work (pp. 37-77). Palgrave Macmillan.

Sua, C. H., & Cheng, C. H. (2013). A mobile game-based insect learning system for improving the learning achievements. *Procedia: Social and Behavioral Sciences*, *103*, 42–50. doi:10.1016/j.sbspro.2013.10.305

Suarta, I. M., Suwintana, I. K., Sudhana, I. F. P., & Hariyanti, N. K. D. (2017). Employability skills required by the 21st-century workplace: A literature review of labour market demand. *Advances in Social Science, Education and Humanities Research*, *102*(58), 337–342. doi:10.2991/ictvt-17.2017.58

Subhash, S., & Cudney, E. A. (2018). Gamified learning in higher education: A systematic review of the literature. *Computers in Human Behavior*, *87*, 192–206. doi:10.1016/j.chb.2018.05.028

Sugrue, B., & Rivera, R. J. (2005). *State of the industry: ASTD's annual review of trends in workplace learning and performance*. ASTD. https://www.td.org/research-reports/2005-state-of-the-industry-report

Suleman, F. (2018). The employability skills of higher education graduates: Insights into conceptual frameworks and methodological options. *Higher Education*, *76*(2), 263–278. doi:10.100710734-017-0207-0

Sullivan, A., Elkin, M., & Bers, M. U. (2015). KIBO robot demo: engaging young children in programming and engineering. In *Proceedings of the 14th international conference on interaction design and children* (pp. 418-421). ACM.

Sun, L., & Yin, Y. (2017). Discovering themes and trends in transportation research using topic modeling. *Transportation Research Part C, Emerging Technologies*, *77*, 49–66. doi:10.1016/j.trc.2017.01.013

Sun, P.-C. C., Tsai, R. J., Finger, G., Chen, Y.-Y. Y., & Yeh, D. (2008). What drives a successful e-Learning? An empirical investigation of the critical factors influencing learner satisfaction. *Computers & Education*, *50*(4), 1183–1202. doi:10.1016/j.compedu.2006.11.007

Suppipat, S., Hu, A. H., & Chotiratanapinun, T. (2021). Gamifying Sustainable Design to Enhance Environmental Consciousness of Industrial Design Students. In Y. Kishita, M. Matsumoto, M. Inoue, & S. Fukushige (Eds.), EcoDesign and Sustainability II (pp. 291–310). Springer. doi:10.1007/978-981-15-6775-9_19

Supriana, I., Agustin, R. D., Bakar, M. A., & Zin, N. A. M. (2017). Serious games for effective learning. In *2017 6th International Conference on Electrical Engineering and Informatics (ICEEI)* (pp. 1-6). IEEE. 10.1109/ICEEI.2017.8312466

Surendeleg, G., Murwa, V., Yun, H. K., & Kim, Y. S. (2014). The Role of Gamification in Education – A Literature Review. *Contemporary Engineering Sciences*, *7*(29), 1609–1616. doi:10.12988/ces.2014.411217

Susaeta, H., Jimenez, F., Nussbaum, M., Gajardo, I., Andreu, J. J., & Villalta, M. (2010). From MMORPG to a classroom multiplayer presential role playing game. *Journal of Educational Technology & Society*, *13*(3), 257–269.

Susi, T., Johannesson, M., & Backlund, P. (2007). *Serious games, an overview* (Technical report HIS-IKI-TR-07-001). University of Skvde.

Susi, T., Johannesson, M., & Backlund, P. (2007). *Serious Games*. Academic Press.

Suwankarjank, V., & Rugwongwan, Y. (2021). Design Thinking Model in Design Education for Thai Product Design Student. *Review of International Geographical Education Online*, *11*(3). Advance online publication. doi:10.33403/rigeo.800453

Swacha, J. (2021). State of Research on Gamification in Education: A Bibliometric Survey. *Education Sciences, 11*, 69.

Swacha, J. (2021). State of research on gamification in education: A bibliometric survey. *Education Sciences*, *11*(2), 69. doi:10.3390/educsci11020069

Sweller, J. (2011). Cognitive Load Theory. *Psychology of Learning and Motivation - Advances in Research and Theory, 55*, 37–76. doi:10.1016/B978-0-12-387691-1.00002-8

Syed, S., & Spruit, M. (2017). Full-text or abstract? examining topic coherence scores using latent dirichlet allocation. *2017 IEEE International Conference on Data Science and Advanced Analytics (DSAA)*, 165–174. 10.1109/DSAA.2017.61

Symonenko, S. V., Zaitseva, N. V., Osadchyi, V. V., Osadcha, K. P., & Shmeltser, E. O. (2019) *Virtual'na real'nist' u navchanni inozemnykh mov u vyshchykh navchal'nykh zakladakh* [Virtual reality in foreign language training at higher educational institutions]. *2nd International Workshop on Augmented Reality in Education.*

Tabachnik, B. G., & Fidell, L. S. (2007). *Using multivariate statistics* (5th ed.). Allyn and Bacon.

Tabatabai, S. (2020). Simulations and Virtual Learning Supporting Clinical Education During the COVID 19 Pandemic. *Advances in Medical Education and Practice*, *11*, 513–516. doi:10.2147/AMEP.S257750 PMID:32821192

Tanaka, J. W., Wolf, J. M., Klaiman, C., Koenig, K., Cockburn, J., Herlihy, L., Brown, C., Stahl, S., Kaiser, M. S., & Schultz, R. T. (2010). Using computerized games to teach face recognition skills to children with autism spectrum disorder: The Let's Face It! program. *Journal of Child Psychology and Psychiatry, and Allied Disciplines*, *51*(8), 944–952. doi:10.1111/j.1469-7610.2010.02258.x PMID:20646129

Tan, J. A., Hall, R. J., & Boyce, C. (2003). The role of employee reactions in predicting training effectiveness. *Human Resource Development Quarterly*, *14*(4), 397–411. doi:10.1002/hrdq.1076

Tankovska, H. (2021). *Most popular messaging apps.* Statista. https://www.statista.com/statistics/258749/most-popular-global-mobile-messenger-apps/

Tarouco, L. M., Roland, L. C., Fabre, M. C., & Konrath, M. L. (2004). Educational games [Jogos educacionais]. *RENOTE: Revista Novas Tecnologias Na Educação,* 1-7.

Tarud, J. (2021, March). *The Evolution of Chat Apps—Koombea Weekly Blogpost*. Koombea. https://www.koombea.com/blog/chat-apps-evolving/

Tavares, B. L. (2017). Changing the construct: Promoting cross-cultural conversations in the law school classroom. *Journal of Legal Education*, *67*(1), 211–241.

Tay, L. (2010). Employers: Look to gaming to motivate staff. *IT News for Australian Business*.

Taylor, G., Jungert, T., Mageau, G. A., Schattke, K., Dedic, H., Rosenfield, S., & Koestner, R. (2014). A self-determination theory approach to predicting school achievement over time: The unique role of intrinsic motivation. *Contemporary Educational Psychology*, *39*(4), 342–358. doi:10.1016/j.cedpsych.2014.08.002

TeachCrunch. (2018). *TeacherGaming, a startup from MinecraftEdu team, raises $1.6M to put games into the classroom*. Available at https://techcrunch.com/2018/01/24/teachergaming/?guccounter=1&guce_referrer=aHR0cHM6Ly93d3cuZ29vZ2xlLmNvbS8&guce_referrer_sig=AQAAAJuibv_w-QUMmS72W-ktDoG9dgmmOdYBwhxgM5o7g-yajidgZ7YsY3ESOfYyzR6c2RlcR5Cj1uSAPuCwxlyxHRLF-uMXDpOFxjiKtw980eNOJQWa0gP5wAT1K81FG3b-kK9x7zE0qv7_8TplZ8iF9bo52Th9AItNy4J1pd01v4unBU

TeacherGaming. (2021). https://teachergaming.com/

Tekinbas, K. S., & Zimmerman, E. (2003). *Rules of play: Game design fundamentals*. MIT press.

Terlutter, R., & Capella, M. L. (2013). The gamification of advertising: Analysis and research directions of in-game advertising, advergames, and advertising in social network games. *Journal of Advertising*, *42*(2-3), 95–112. doi:10.1080/00913367.2013.774610

Thailand Sustainability Expo. (2021). *Thailand Sustainability Expo 2021*. https://tsx2021.thailandsustainabilityexpo.com/index.php

The economic impact of universities in 2014–15. (n.d.). Retrieved July 30, 2021, from https://www.universitiesuk.ac.uk/economic-impact

The Economist Intelligence Unit. (2017, November 16). Thailand 4.0: in sight but not in reach. *The Economist*. http://www.eiu.com/industry/article/786131662/thailand-40-in-sight-but-not-in-reach/2017-11-16

The National Council of Teachers of Mathematics. (Ed.). (2000). *Principles and Standards for School Mathematics*. https://www.nctm.org/Standards-and-Positions/Principles-and-Standards/Principles,-Standards,-and-Expectations/

The Risk Assessment Information System. (1997). *Formal Toxicity Summary for Antimony*. https://rais.ornl.gov/tox/profiles/antimony.html

Tholen, G., & Brown, P. (2017). *Higher education and the myths of graduate employability*. Academic Press.

Thomae, H. (1999). The nomothetic-idiographic issue: Some roots and recent trends. *International Journal of Group Tensions*, *28*(1), 187–215. doi:10.1023/A:1021891506378

Thomas, R., Cahill, J., & Santilli, L. (1997). Using an interactive computer game to increase skill and self-efficacy regarding safer sex. *Health Education & Behavior*, *24*(1), 71–86. doi:10.1177/109019819702400108 PMID:9112099

Tilbury, D., & Wortman, D. (2004). *Engaging People in Sustainability*. Commission on Education and Communication, IUCN. https://www.researchgate.net/publication/255964013

Times Higher Education. (2021). *Impact Rankings 2021*. Times Higher Education. www.timeshighereducation.com/impactrankings

Tisza, G., & Markopoulos, P. (2021). Understanding the role of fun in learning to code. *International Journal of Child-Computer Interaction*, *28*, 100270. doi:10.1016/j.ijcci.2021.100270

Tobias, S., & Fletcher, J. D. (2011). *Computer games and instruction*. Information Age. https://eric.ed.gov/?id=ED529495

Toda, A. M., Valle, P. H. D., & Isotani, S. (2017). The Dark Side of Gamification: An Overview of Negative Effects of Gamification in Education. In Higher Education for All. From Challenges to Novel Technology-Enhanced Solutions. Springer. doi:10.1007/978-3-319-97934-2_9

Toda, A. M., Valle, P. H., & Isotani, S. (2017, March). The dark side of gamification: An overview of negative effects of gamification in education. In Researcher links workshop: higher education for all (pp. 143-156). Academic Press.

Toda, A. M., do Carmo, R. M. C., da Silva, A. P., Bittencourt, I. I., & Isotani, S. (2019). An approach for planning and deploying gamification concepts with social networks within educational contexts. *International Journal of Information Management*, *46*, 294–303. doi:10.1016/j.ijinfomgt.2018.10.001

Toda, A. M., Klock, A. C. T., Oliveira, W., Palomino, P. T., Rodrigues, L. R., Shi, L., Bittencourt, I., Gasparini, I., Isotani, S., & Cristea, A. I. (2019). Analysing gamification elements in educational environments using an existing Gamification taxonomy. *Smart Learning Environments*, *6*(16), 1–14. doi:10.118640561-019-0106-1

Tohidi, H., & Jabbari, M. M. (2012). The effects of motivation in education. *Procedia: Social and Behavioral Sciences*, *31*, 820–824. doi:10.1016/j.sbspro.2011.12.148

Toh, W., & Kirschner, D. (2020). Self-Directed Learning in Video Games, Affordances and Pedagogical Implications for Teaching and Learning. *Computers & Education*, *154*, 103912. doi:10.1016/j.compedu.2020.103912

Tokareva, E. A., Smirnova, Y. V., & Orchakova, L. G. (2019). Innovation and communication technologies: Analysis of the effectiveness of their use and implementation in higher education. *Education and Information Technologies*, *24*(5), 3219–3234. doi:10.100710639-019-09922-2

Tolkien, J. R. (2012). *The Lord of the Rings: one volume*. Houghton Mifflin Harcourt.

Tomaselli, F., Sanchez, O., & Brown, S. (2015). How to engage users through gamification: The prevalent effects of playing and mastering over competing. In *Proceedings of the Thirty Sixth International Conference on Information Systems* (pp. 1-16). Academic Press.

Tomas, L., Rigano, D., & Ritchie, S. M. (2016). Students' regulation of their emotions in a science classroom. *Journal of Research in Science Teaching*, *53*(2), 234–260. doi:10.1002/tea.21304

Torres, M. (2010). La enseñanza tradicional de las ciencias versus las nuevas tendencias educativas. *Revista Electrónica Educare*, *14*(1), 131–142. doi:10.15359/ree.14-1.11

Torres, R., Gee, J. P., Hayes, E., Games, I. A., Squire, K., & Salen, K. (2008). *Playing to learn game design skills in a game context*. International Society of the Learning Sciences, Inc.

Tovey, M. (2015). *Design Pedagogy: Developments in Art and Design Education* (M. Tovey, Ed.). Gower Applied Research.

Towsend, R. (2003). *The Internet and the History Classroom: Introduction*. American Historical Association. https://www.historians.org/publications-and-directories/perspectives-on-history/may-2003/the-internet-and-the-history-classroom

Training Industry Report. (2020, November/December). *Training Magazine, 57*(5), 22-37. https://pubs.royle.com/publication/?m=20617&i=678873&p=24

Trainor, L. J., & Trehub, S. E. (1994). Key membership and implied harmony in Western tonal music: Developmental perspectives. *Perception & Psychophysics*, *56*(2), 125–132. doi:10.3758/BF03213891 PMID:7971113

Tran, T. T. (2016). Enhancing graduate employability and the need for universityenterprise collaboration. *Journal of Teaching and Learning for Graduate Employability*, *7*(1), 58–71. doi:10.21153/jtlge2016vol7no1art598

Trinidad, M., Ruiz, M., & Calderón, A. (2021). A bibliometric analysis of gamification research. *IEEE Access: Practical Innovations, Open Solutions*, *9*, 46505–46544. doi:10.1109/ACCESS.2021.3063986

Trowler, V. (2010). Student Engagement Literature Review. The Higher Education Academy. doi:10.1037/0022-0663.85.4.571

Trujillo, F. (2017). Del juego a la gamificación. Mitos y leyendas de las TIC. *Aula de innovación educativa, 267*, 38-40.

Tsai, S. L., Chai, S. K., Hsieh, L. F., Lin, S., Taur, F. M., Sung, W. H., & Doong, J. L. (2008). The use of virtual reality computer simulation in learning Port-A cath injection. *Advances in Health Sciences Education: Theory and Practice*, *13*(1), 71–87. doi:10.100710459-006-9025-3 PMID:16944000

Tsay, C. H. H., Kofinas, A., & Luo, J. (2018). Enhancing student learning experience with technology-mediated gamification: An empirical study. *Computers & Education*, *121*, 1–17. doi:10.1016/j.compedu.2018.01.009

Tuan, L., & Doan, N. (2010). Teaching English Grammar through Games. *Studies in Literature & Language*, *1*(7), 61–75. cscanada.net/index.php/sll/article/ download/j.sll.1923156320100107.006/1463

Tu, C.-H. (2000). On-line learning migration: From social learning theory to social presence theory in a CMC environment. *Journal of Network and Computer Applications*, *23*(1), 27–37. doi:10.1006/jnca.1999.0099

Tudge, J. R. H., & Winterhoff, P. A. (1993). Vygotsky, Piaget, and Bandura: Perspectives on the Relations between the Social World and Cognitive Development. *Human Development*, *36*(2), 61–81. doi:10.1159/000277297

Tulloch, K., & Pammer, K. (2019). Tablet computer games to measure dorsal stream performance in good and poor readers. *Neuropsychologia*, *130*, 92–99. doi:10.1016/j.neuropsychologia.2018.07.019 PMID:30030193

Tulloch, R. (2014). Reconceptualising gamification: Play and pedagogy. *Digital Culture & Education*, *6*(4), 317–333.

Turan, Z., Avinc, Z., Kara, K., & Goktas, Y. (2016). Gamification and education: Achievements, cognitive loads, and views of students. *International Journal of Emerging Technologies in Learning*, *11*(07), 64–69.

Tweney, D. (2009). Sept. 24, 1979: First Online Service for Consumers Debuts. *Wired*. https://www.wired.com/2009/09/0924compuserve-launches/

Tzima, S., Styliaras, G., & Bassounas, A. (2021). Revealing hidden local cultural heritage through a serious escape game in outdoor settings. *Information (Switzerland)*, *12*(1), 1–17. doi:10.3390/info12010010

Uhlemann, J., Costa, R., & Charpentier, J. C. (2020). Product design and engineering—Past, present, future trends in teaching, research and practices: Academic and industry points of view. *Current Opinion in Chemical Engineering*, *27*, 10–21. doi:10.1016/j.coche.2019.10.003

Ulijn, J. M., Duill, M. O., & Robertson, S. A. (2004). Teaching business plan negotiation: Fostering entrepreneurship among business and engineering students. *Business Communication Quarterly*, *67*(1), 41–57. doi:10.1177/1080569903262040

UNESCO. (2020). *Education for sustainable development: A roadmap*. https://unesdoc.unesco.org/ark:/48223/pf0000374802

UNHCR. (2020, September 3). *Coming together for Refugee Education*. https://www.unhcr.org/media-page-coming-together-for-refugee-education.html

United Nations Department of Global Communications. (2018, April 21). *The 17 Goals - Sustainable Development Goals*. United Nations. https://sdgs.un.org/goals

United Nations. (2020). *Policy Brief: Education during COVID-19 and beyond*. https://www.un.org/development/desa/dspd/wp-content/uploads/sites/22/2020/ 08/sg_policy_brief_covid-19_and_education_august_2020.pdf

Universidade Federal Fluminense. (2016). *Curso de Jornalismo - Projeto Pedagógico de Curso (PPC): Formulário nº 02 - Princípios Norteadores* [Journalism Course - Pedagogical Course Project (PPC): Form nº 02 - Guiding Principles]. Journalism Course.

Uribe, R. V., Alicia, S., & Cobos, U. (2014). *Board Games as Tool for Teaching Basic Sustainability Concepts to Design Students*. The European Conference on Sustainability, Energy and the Environment 2014.

Uribe, R. V., Santamaría Ortega, A., Alicia, S., & Cobos, U. (2017). *Sustainability Should Be Fun. Designing Boardgames to Teach Sustainability*. The Asian Conference on Sustainability, Energy & the Environment 2017.

Urquidi, A., & Tamarit, C. (2015). Serious games as a facilitating instrument of learning: Empirical evidence [Juegos serios como instrumento facilitador del aprendizaje: evidencia empírica]. *Opción*, *31*(3), 1201–1220.

Vahed, A. (2008, October). *The tooth morphology board game: An innovative strategy in tutoring dental technology learners in combating rote learning* [Conference Paper]. European Conference on Games-Based Learning, Barcelona, Spain. https://www.researchgate.net/publication/268925737_The_Tooth_Morphology_Board_Game_An_Innovative_Strategy_in_Tutoring_Dental_Technology_Learners_in_Combating_Rote_Learning

Valkanos, E., & Fragoulis, I. (2007). Experiential learning–its place in in-house education and training. *Development and Learning in Organizations*, *21*(5), 21–23. doi:10.1108/14777280710779454

Vallerand, R. J., Blais, M. R., Brière, N. M., & Pelletier, L. G. (1989). Construction et validation de l'échelle de motivation en éducation (EME). *Canadian Journal of Behavioural Science/Revue Canadienne Des Sciences Du Comportement*, *21*(3), 323.

van Aalderen-Smeets, S. I., van der Molen, J. H., & Asma, L. J. F. (2012). Primary teachers' attitudes toward science: A new theoretical framework. *Science Education*, *96*(1), 158–182. doi:10.1002ce.20467

van Berlo, Z. M., van Reijmersdal, E. A., & Eisend, M. (2021). The gamification of branded content: A meta-analysis of advergame effects. *Journal of Advertising*, *50*(2), 179–196. doi:10.1080/00913367.2020.1858462

van de Walle, J. A., Karp, K. S., Williams, B., & Jennifer, M. (2013). Elementary and Middle School Mathematics: Teaching Developmentally (8th ed.). Pearson.

van der Meij, H., Albers, E., & Leemkuil, H. (2011). Learning from games: Does collaboration help? *British Journal of Educational Technology*, *42*(4), 655–664. doi:10.1111/j.1467-8535.2010.01067.x

van der Spek, E. D. (2011). *Experiments in serious game design: A cognitive approach* [Unpublished doctoral dissertation]. Universiteit Utrecht, The Netherlands.

Van Dijk, J. (2020). *Digital Divide*. Polity Press.

Van Dooren, M. M., Siriaraya, P., Visch, V., Spijkerman, R., & Bijkerk, L. (2019). Reflections on the design, implementation, and adoption of a gamified eHealth application in youth mental healthcare. *Entertainment Computing*, *31*, 100305. doi:10.1016/j.entcom.2019.100305

Van Eck, R. (2006). Digital game-based learning: It's not just the digital natives who are restless. *EDUCAUSE Review*, *41*(2), 16.

Van Eck, R. (2015). Digital game-based learning: Still restless, after all these years. *EDUCAUSE Review*, *50*(6), 13.

van Gaalen, A., Brouwer, J., Schönrock-Adema, J., Bouwkamp-Timmer, T., Jaarsma, A., & Georgiadis, J. R. (2021). Gamification of health professions education: A systematic review. *Advances in Health Sciences Education: Theory and Practice*, *26*(2), 683–711. doi:10.100710459-020-10000-3 PMID:33128662

van Roy, R., & Zaman, B. (2017). Why gamification fails in education and how to make it successful: Introducing nine gamification heuristics based on self-determination theory. In M. Ma & A. Oikonomou (Eds.), Serious games and edutainment applications, volume II (pp. 485-509). Springer International Publishing AG.

van Roy, R., & Zaman, B. (2015). Moving beyond the effectiveness of gamification. In *Proceeding of CHI 2015 Workshop Gamifying Research*. ACM.

van Roy, R., & Zaman, B. (2019). Unravelling the ambivalent motivational power of gamification: A basic psychological needs perspective. *International Journal of Human-Computer Studies*, *127*, 38–50. doi:10.1016/j.ijhcs.2018.04.009

VandeWalle, D. (1997). Development and validation of a work domain goal orientation instrument. *Educational and Psychological Measurement*, *57*(6), 995–1015. doi:10.1177/0013164497057006009

Vanevenhoven, J., & Drago, W. A. (2015). The structure and scope of entrepreneurship programs in higher education around the world. In *Entrepreneurial Learning* (pp. 117–133). Routledge. doi:10.4324/9781315857817-6

Vartanian, O., & Beatty, E. (2015). Cognitive brain training, video games, and creativity. *Video Games and Creativity*, *2015*, 185–198. doi:10.1016/B978-0-12-801462-2.00009-6

Vasconcellos, M., Dias, C. M., Ribeiro, D., & Carvalho, F. G. (in press). Gamificação para o mundo real: Repensando práticas [Gamification for the real world: rethinking practices]. In Educação para Práticas Inovadoras, Lúdicas e Inclusivas: Contribuições para o ensino de graduação. Editora da UFF.

Vasquez, V. M. (2019). Game on. *Curriculum Inquiry*, *49*(2), 173–190. doi:10.1080/03626784.2019.1593789

Vázquez, A., & Manassero, M. A. (2007). En defensa de las actitudes y emociones en la educación científica (II): Evidencias empíricas derivadas de la investigación. *Revista Eureka Sobre Enseñanza y Divulgación de las Ciencias*, *4*(3), 417–441. doi:10.25267/Rev_Eureka_ensen_divulg_cienc.2007.v4.i3.03

Vázquez, A., & Manassero, M. A. (2007). In defense of attitudes and emotions in scientific education (II): Empirical evidence derived from research [En defensa de las actitudes y emociones en la educación científica (II): evidencias empíricas derivadas de la investigación]. *Revista Eureka Sobre Enseñanza y Divulgación de las Ciencias*, *4*(3), 417–441.

Vázquez, A., & Manassero, M. A. (2008). The decline in students' attitudes towards science: A disturbing indicator for science education [El declive de las actitudes hacia la ciencia de los estudiantes: un indicador inquietante para la educación científica]. *Revista Eureka Sobre Enseñanza y Divulgación de las Ciencias*, *8*(3), 274–292.

Veldkamp, A., Daemen, J., Teekens, S., Koelewijn, S., Knippels, M. C. P. J., & van Joolingen, W. R. (2020). Escape boxes: Bringing escape room experience into the classroom. *British Journal of Educational Technology*, *51*(4), 1220–1239. doi:10.1111/bjet.12935

Veldkamp, A., van de Grint, L., Knippels, M. C., & van Joolingen, W. (2020a). Escape education: A systematic review on escape rooms in education. *Educational Research Review*, *31*, 100364. doi:10.1016/j.edurev.2020.100364

Vellutino, F. R., Fletcher, J. M., Snowling, M. J., & Scanlon, D. M. (2004). Specific reading disability (dyslexia): What have we learned in the past four decades? *Journal of Child Psychology and Psychiatry, and Allied Disciplines*, *45*(1), 2–40. doi:10.1046/j.0021-9630.2003.00305.x PMID:14959801

Vergara, D., Paredes-Velasco, M., Chivite, C., & Fernandez-Arias, P. (2020). The challenge of increasing the effectiveness of learning by using active methodologies. *Sustainability*, *12*(20), 8702. doi:10.3390u12208702

Vergne, M. J., Simmons, J. D., & Bowen, R. S. (2019). Escape the Lab: An Interactive Escape-Room Game as a Laboratory Experiment. *Journal of Chemical Education*, *96*(5), 985–991. doi:10.1021/acs.jchemed.8b01023

Villagrasa, S., Fonseca, D., Redondo, E., & Duran, J. (2014). Teaching case of gamification and visual technologies for education. *Journal of Cases on Information Technology*, *16*(4), 38–57. doi:10.4018/jcit.2014100104

Virtual Heroes. (2007). *Zero Hour: America's Medic*. www.virtualheroes.biz/VHFree/Content/ReferenceMaterials/RefMaterialZeroHour.zip

Visvizi, A., Lytras, M. D., Damiani, E., & Mathkour, H. (2018). Policy making for smart cities: Innovation and social inclusive economic growth for sustainability. *Journal of Science and Technology Policy Management.*

Vittersø, J., & Csikszentmihalyi, M. (2000). Finding Flow. The Psychology of Engagement with Everyday Life. *Journal of Happiness Studies*, *1*(1), 121–123. Advance online publication. doi:10.1023/A:1010032312178

Vlachopoulos, D., & Makri, A. (2017). The effect of games and simulations on higher education: A systematic literature review. *International Journal of Educational Technology in Higher Education*, *14*(1), 1–33. doi:10.118641239-017-0062-1

Vladoiu, M., & Constantinescu, Z. (2020). Learning during Covid-19 pandemic: Online education community, based on discord. *2020 19th RoEduNet Conference: Networking in Education and Research (RoEduNet),* 1–6. 10.1109/RoEduNet51892.2020.9324863

Vogel, C., Hochberg, J., Hackstein, S., Bockshecker, A., Bastiaens, T. J., & Baumöl, U. (2018). Dropout in distance education and how to prevent it. In *Proceedings of EdMedia: World Conference on Educational Media and Technology* (pp. 1788-1799). Association for the Advancement of Computing in Education (AACE).

Vogel, J. J., Vogel, D. S., Cannon-Bowers, J., Bowers, C. A., Muse, K., & Wright, M. (2006). Computer gaming and interactive simulations for learning: A meta-analysis. *Journal of Educational Computing Research*, *34*(3), 229–243. doi:10.2190/FLHV-K4WA-WPVQ-H0YM

Vogelzang, J., Admiraal, W. F., & Van Driel, J. H. (2020). A teacher perspective on Scrum methodology in secondary chemistry education. *Chemistry Education Research and Practice*, *21*(1), 237–249. doi:10.1039/C9RP00111E

Voice Online Editorial Division. (2021, April 15). วิจัย 'คนรุ่นใหม่' ทำความเข้าใจม็อบเพดานสูง – คำตอบการเปลี่ยนแปลงอยู่ที่รุ่นกลาง! [Research 'the new generation' to understand the high ceiling mob – the answer to the change lies in the middle generation!]. *Voice Online*. https://www.voicetv.co.th/read/nW0ygLK3U?fbclid=IwAR07HcQjqbB2UZTH0yLilcf-in0sK3CyxliHZiLAxJvb6wy9eae1GF71lI4

Volkswagen. (2009). *The Fun Theory*. Retrieved from Thefuntheory.com: http://www.thefuntheory.com/

Volkswagen. (2010). *The Speed Camera Lottery*. http://www.thefuntheory.com/speed-camera-lottery-0

Volpe, G., & Camurri, A. (2011). A system for embodied social active listening to sound and music content. *Journal on Computing and Cultural Heritage*, *4*(1), 1–23. doi:10.1145/2001416.2001418

Von Ehren, S. (2020, June 11). Why do people love games? *The New York Times*. https://www.nytimes.com/2020/06/11/style/why-people-love-games.html

Von Wangenheim, C. G., Rausis, B., Soares, G. M., Savi, R., & Borgatto, A. F. (2015). Project detective – A game for teaching earned value management. *International Journal of Teaching and Case Studies*, *5*(3-4), 216–234.

Von Wangenheim, C. G., Savi, R., & Borgatto, A. F. (2013). SCRUMIA— An educational game for teaching SCRUM in computing courses. *Journal of Systems and Software*, *86*(10), 2675–2687. doi:10.1016/j.jss.2013.05.030

Voogt, J., & Roblin, N. P. (2012). A comparative analysis of international frameworks for 21st century competences: Implications for national curriculum policies. *Journal of Curriculum Studies*, *44*(3), 299–321. doi:10.1080/00220272.2012.668938

Vorderer, P., Hartmann, T., & Klimmt, C. (2003). Explaining the enjoyment of playing video games: The role of competition. In *Proceedings of the Second International Conference on Entertainment Computing* (pp. 1-9). Carnegie Mellon University.

Vörös, A. I. V., & Sárközi, Z. (2017, December). Physics escape room as an educational tool. In AIP Conference Proceedings (Vol. 1916, No. 1, p. 050002). AIP Publishing LLC.

Vos, L., & Brennan, R. (2010). Marketing simulation games: Student and lecturer perspectives. *Marketing Intelligence & Planning*, *28*(7), 882–897. doi:10.1108/02634501011086472

Vuorikari, R., Punie, Y., Carretero Gomez, S., & Van Den Brande, G. (2016). *DigComp 2.0: The Digital Competence Framework for Citizens. Update Phase 1: the Conceptual Reference Model.* Publications Office of the European Union. https://publications.jrc.ec.europa.eu/repository/handle/JRC101254

Vygotsky, L. (1978). *Mind in Society*. Harvard University Press.

Vygotsky, L. S. (1978). *Mind and Society: The Development of Higher Mental Processes*. Harvard University Press.

Vygotsky, L. S. (1978). *Mind in society: The development of higher psychological processes*. Harvard University Press.

Waern, A. (2012, June). Framing games. *Proceedings of DiGRA Nordic 2012 Conference: Local and Global – Games in Culture and Society, 10,* 1-14. http://www.digra.org/wp-content/uploads/digital-library/12168.20295.pdf

Wahyuningsih, E., & Baidi, B. (2021). Scrutinizing the potential use of Discord application as a digital platform amidst emergency remote learning. *Journal of Educational Management and Instruction*, *1*(1), 9–18. doi:10.22515/jemin.v1i1.3448

Walsh, A. (2017). *Making Escape Rooms for Educational Purposes: A Workbook*. Academic Press.

Walz, S. P., & Deterding, S. (2014). An Introduction to the Gameful World. In S. P. Walz & S. Deterding (Eds.), *The gameful world. Approaches, issues, applications* (pp. 1–13). The MIT Press.

Walz, S. P., & Deterding, S. (Eds.). (2015). *The gameful world: Approaches, issues, applications*. MIT Press.

Wan Tahir, W. M. M., Mohd Noor, I. H., Daud, D., & Hussin, A. H. (2018). Towards interactive learning style in accounting: The game approach. *Academic Journal of Business and Social Sciences*, *2*, 1–8.

Wang, D., Zhang, L., Xu, C., Hu, H., & Qi, Y. (2016). A Tangible Embedded Programming System to Convey Event-Handling Concept. In *Proceedings of the TEI '16: Tenth International Conference on Tangible, Embedded, and Embodied Interaction* (pp. 133-140). Academic Press.

Wang, H., & Sun, C.-T. (2011). Game reward systems: Gaming experiences and social meanings. *DiGRA Conference, 114.*

Wang, J., Song, Q., Gao, S., & Tao, Y. (2020). *A systematic review of game learning research in China*. Retrieved from https://www.scopus.com/inward/record.uri?eid=2-s2.0-85088751792&doi=10.1007%2f978-3-030-50164-8_36&partnerID=40&md5=8eaa111998a526f90927667bbab3443a doi:10.1007/978-3-030-50164-8_36

Wang, C. H., Wu, K. C., & Tsau, S. Y. (2019). Flow learning experience: Applying marketing theory to serious game design. *Journal of Educational Computing Research*, *57*(2), 417–447. doi:10.1177/0735633117752454

Wang, M.-T., & Eccles, J. S. (2013). School context, achievement motivation, and academic engagement: A longitudinal study of school engagement using a multidimensional perspective. *Learning and Instruction*, *28*, 12–23. doi:10.1016/J.LEARNINSTRUC.2013.04.002

Wang, Q., Woo, H. L., & Zhao, J. (2009). Investigating critical thinking and knowledge construction in an interactive learning environment. *Interactive Learning Environments*, *17*(1), 95–104. doi:10.1080/10494820701706320

Wang, R., DeMaria, S., Goldberg, A., & Katz, D. (2016). A Systematic Review of Serious Games in Training Health Care Professionals. *Simulation in Healthcare: The Journal of the Society for Simulation in Healthcare*, *11*(1), 41–51. doi:10.1097/SIH.0000000000000118 PMID:26536340

Wang, W. (2004). *Steal this file sharing book: What they won't tell you about file sharing*. No Starch Press.

Wang, W., Guo, L., He, L., & Wu, Y. J. (2019). Effects of social-interactive engagement on the dropout ratio in online learning: Insights from MOOC. *Behaviour & Information Technology*, *38*(6), 621–636. doi:10.1080/0144929X.2018.1549595

Warmelink, H., Mayer, I., Weber, J., Heijligers, B., Haggis, M., Peters, E., & Louwerse, M. (2017). AMELIO: Evaluating the Team-building Potential of a Mixed Reality Escape Room Game. *Extended Abstracts Publication of the Annual Symposium on Computer-Human Interaction in Play - CHI PLAY '17 Extended Abstracts*. 10.1145/3130859.3131436

Washbush, J., & Gosen, J. (2001). An exploration of game-derived learning in total enterprise simulations. *Simulation & Gaming*, *32*(3), 281–296. doi:10.1177/104687810103200301

Watkins, M., Casamayor, J. L., Ramirez, M., Moreno, M., Faludi, J., & Pigosso, D. C. A. (2021). Sustainable Product Design Education: Current Practice. *She Ji: The Journal of Design, Economics, and Innovation*, *7*(4), 611–637. doi:10.1016/j.sheji.2021.11.003

Wattanasoontorn, V., Boada, I., García, R., & Sbert, M. (2013). Serious games for health. *Entertainment Computing*, *4*(4), 231–247. doi:10.1016/j.entcom.2013.09.002

Waytz, A., & Gray, K. (2018). Does Online Technology Make Us More or Less Sociable? A Preliminary Review and Call for Research. *Perspectives on Psychological Science*, *13*(4), 473–491. doi:10.1177/1745691617746509 PMID:29758166

Weber, R. P. (1990). Basic content analysis (2nd ed.). Sage Publications. doi:10.4135/9781412983488

Weiner, E. J., & Sanchez, D. R. (2020). Cognitive ability in virtual reality: Validity evidence for VR game-based assessments. *International Journal of Selection and Assessment*, *28*(3), 215–235. doi:10.1111/ijsa.12295

Werbach, K., & Hunter, D. (2012). *For the win: How game thinking can revolutionize your business*. Wharton Digital Press.

Werbach, K. (2014). (Re) defining gamification: A process approach. In *International conference on persuasive technology* (pp. 266–272). Springer. 10.1007/978-3-319-07127-5_23

Werbach, K., & Hunter, D. (2012). *For the win: How game thinking can revolutionize your business*. Wharton Digital Press.

Wertsch, J. V. (1984). The zone of proximal development: Some conceptual issues. *New Directions for Child and Adolescent Development*, *1984*(23), 7–18. doi:10.1002/cd.23219842303

Westera, W. (2019). Why and how serious games can become far more effective: Accommodating productive learning experiences, learner motivation and the monitoring of learning gains. *Journal of Educational Technology & Society*, *22*(1), 59–69.

Whalen, C., Moss, D., Ilan, A. B., Vaupel, M., Fielding, P., Macdonald, K., Cernich, S., & Symon, J. (2010). Efficacy of TeachTown: Basics computer-assisted intervention for the intensive comprehensive autism program in Los Angeles unified school district. *Autism*, *14*(3), 179–197. doi:10.1177/1362361310363282 PMID:20484002

Whitson, C., & Consoli, J. (2009). Flow Theory and Student Engagement. *Journal of Cross-Disciplinary Perspective In Education, 2*(1), 40–49.

Whitton, N. (2010). *Learning with digital games: A practical guide to engaging students in higher education*. Routledge.

Whitton, N. (2018). Playful learning: Tools, techniques, and tactics. *Research in Learning Technology*, 26.

Whitton, N., & Langan, M. (2018). Fun and games in higher education: An analysis of UK student perspectives. *Teaching in Higher Education.*

Whitton, N., & Moseley, A. (2014). Deconstructing Engagement. *Simulation & Gaming, 45*(4–5), 433–449. doi:10.1177/1046878114554755

Wiemker, M., Elumir, E., & Clare, A. (2015). Escape room games. *Game Based Learning, 55*, 55–75.

Wiggins, B. E. (2016). An overview and study on the use of games, simulations, and gamification in higher education. *International Journal of Game-Based Learning, 6*(1), 18–29. doi:10.4018/IJGBL.2016010102

Wijman, T. (2021). *Global Games Market to Generate $175.8 Billion in 2021; Despite a Slight Decline, the Market Is on Track to Surpass $200 Billion in 2023.* Newzoo. https://newzoo.com/insights/articles/global-games-market-to-generate-175-8-billion-in-2021-despite-a-slight-decline-the-market-is-on-track-to-surpass-200-billion-in-2023/

Williams, P. (2018). Using escape room-like puzzles to teach undergraduate students effective and efficient group process skills. *ISEC 2018 - Proceedings of the 8th IEEE Integrated STEM Education Conference,* 254–257. 10.1109/ISECon.2018.8340495

Wilson, R. A., Foglia, L., Shapiro, L., & Spaulding, S. (2019). Embodied Cognition. In *The Stanford Encyclopedia of Philosophy.* https://plato.stanford.edu/archives/win2019/entries/embodied-cognition/

Wilson, K. A., Bedwell, W. L., Lazzara, E., Salas, E., Burke, S. C., Estock, J. L., Orvis, K. L., & Conkey, C. (2009). Relationships between game attributes and learning outcomes: Review and research proposals. *Simulation & Gaming, 40*(2), 217–266. doi:10.1177/1046878108321866

Wilson, R. D. (2011). *External validation of an instructional design model for high fidelity simulation: model application in a hospital setting*. Arizona State University.

Wilson-Sands, C., Brahn, P., & Graves, K. (2015). The Effect of Instructional Method on Cardiopulmonary Resuscitation Skill Performance: A Comparison Between Instructor-Led Basic Life Support and Computer-Based Basic Life Support With Voice-Activated Manikin. *Journal for Nurses in Professional Development, 31*(5), E1–E7. doi:10.1097/NND.0000000000000203 PMID:26381346

Winarno, A., & Wijijayanti, T. (2018). Does Entrepreneurial Literacy Correlate to the Small-Medium Enterprises Performance in Batu East Java? *Academy of Entrepreneurship Journal, 24*(1), 1–13.

Wiratraman, H. P. (2019). The Challenges of Teaching Comparative Law and Socio-Legal Studies at Indonesia's Law Schools. *Asian Journal of Comparative Law, 14*(S1), S229–S244. doi:10.1017/asjcl.2019.15

Wired. (2021). *Kerbal Space Program: dieci anni di voli spaziali insegnati da un videogioco*. Available at https://www-wired-it.cdn.ampproject.org/c/s/www.wired.it/amp/308408/gadget/videogiochi/2021/06/24/kerbal-space-program-anniversario/

Wittayasin, S., & Wittayasin, S. (2017). Education Challenges to Thailand 4.0. *Int. J. Integr. Educ. Dev, 2*(2), 29–35.

Wohlin, C., Höst, M., & Henningsson, K. (2003). Empirical research methods in software engineering. In *Empirical methods and studies in software engineering* (pp. 7–23). Springer. doi:10.1007/978-3-540-45143-3_2

Wolfson, A. J., Rowland, S. L., Lawrie, G. A., & Wright, A. H. (2014). Student conceptions about energy transformations: Progression from general chemistry to biochemistry. *Chemistry Education Research and Practice*, *15*(2), 168–183. doi:10.1039/C3RP00132F

Wonder Workshop | Home of Dash, Cue, and Dot – award-winning robots that help kids learn to code. (2019). Retrieved from https://www.makewonder.com/dash/

Wong, C. Y., Wong, C. W., & Boon-itt, S. (2020). Effects of green supply chain integration and green innovation on environmental and cost performance. *International Journal of Production Research*, *58*(15), 4589–4609.

Wong, C., & Kasari, C. (2012). Play and joint attention of children with autism in the preschool special education classroom. *Journal of Autism and Developmental Disorders*, *42*(10), 2152–2161. doi:10.100710803-012-1467-2 PMID:22350340

Wongcha-um, P. (2020, August 18). Thai school "Hunger Games" salute protests spread. *Reuters*. https://www.reuters.com/article/us-thailand-protests-idUSKCN25E1AT

Wong, P. K., Ho, Y. P., & Autio, E. (2005). Entrepreneurship, innovation and economic growth: Evidence from GEM data. *Small Business Economics*, *24*(3), 335–350. doi:10.100711187-005-2000-1

Wong, W. L., Shen, C., Nocera, L., Carriazo, E., Tang, F., Bugga, S., Narayanan, H., Wang, H., & Ritterfeld, U. (2007). Serious video game effectiveness. In R. Bernhaupt, & M. Tscheligi (Eds.), *Proceedings of the international conference on advances in computer entertainment technology* (pp. 49-55). Association for Computing Machinery. 10.1145/1255047.1255057

Woodfield, R. (2014). Undergraduate retention and attainment across the disciplines. *Higher Education Academy*, *27*, 1–77.

World Commission on Environment and Development. (1987). *Our Common Future*. Oxford University Press.

World Government Summit. (2016). *Gamification and the future of education*. Oxford Analytica. http://www.oxan.com

World Health Organization & WHO Patient Safety. (2011a). *Patient safety curriculum guide: multi-professional edition.* World Health Organization. https://apps.who.int/iris/handle/10665/44641

World Health Organization. (2011b). *Global Health and Aging*. World Health Organization. https://www.who.int/ageing/publications/global_health.pdf

World Health Organization. (2013). *Transforming and scaling up health professionals' education and training: World Health Guidelines 2013*. World Health Organization. https://apps.who.int/iris/bitstream/handle/10665/ 93635/9789241506502_eng.pdf

World Health Organization. (2019). *WHO guideline: Recommendations on digital interventions for health system strengthening*. World Health Organization. https://apps.who.int/iris/rest/bitstreams/1238054/retrieve

World Health Organization. (2020a). *WHO Global Code of Practice on the International Recruitment of Health Personnel*. World Health Organization. https://apps.who.int/gb/ebwha/pdf_files/WHA73/A73_9-en.pdf

World Health Organization. (2020b). *Digital education for building health workforce capacity*. World Health Organization. https://apps.who.int/iris/ bitstream/handle/10665/331524/9789240000476-eng.pdf?sequence=1&isAllowed=y

Wortley, D. J. (2016). The Education Game Using Gamification in the Classroom. *ThaiSim Journal: Learning Development*, *1*(1), 18–24.

Wouters, P., Paas, F., & van Merriënboer, J. J. M. (2008). How to optimize learning from animated models: A review of guidelines base on cognitive load. *Review of Educational Research*, *78*(3), 645–675. doi:10.3102/0034654308320320

Wouters, P., van der Spek, E. D., & van Oostendorp, H. (2009). Current Practices in Serious Game Research. In L. Boyle, M. Stansfield, & T. Connolly (Eds.), *Games-Based Learning Advancements for Multi-Sensory Human Computer Interfaces* (pp. 232–250). doi:10.4018/978-1-60566-360-9.ch014

Wouters, P., van Nimwegen, C., van Oostendorp, H., & van der Spek, E. D. (2013). A meta-analysis of the cognitive and motivational effects of serious games. *Journal of Educational Psychology*, *105*(2), 249–265. doi:10.1037/a0031311

Wouters, P., van Oostendorp, H., Boonekamp, R., & van der Spek, E. D. (2011). The role of game discourse analysis and curiosity in creating engaging and effective serious games by implementing a back story and foreshadowing. *Interacting with Computers*, *23*(4), 329–336. doi:10.1016/j.intcom.2011.05.001

Wozniak, J. (2020). Gamification for sales incentives. *Contemporary Economics*, *14*(2), 144–161. doi:10.5709/ce.1897-9254.337

Wu, C., Wagenschutz, H., & Hein, J. (2018). Promoting leadership and teamwork development through Escape Rooms. *Medical Education*, *52*(5), 561–562. doi:10.1111/medu.13557 PMID:29508433

Wu, T. (2016). *The attention merchants: The epic scramble to get inside our heads* (1st ed.). Alfred A. Knopf.

Wu, W. H., Yan, W.-C., Kao, H.-Y., Wang, W.-Y., & Wu, Y.-C. J. (2016). Integration of RPG use and ELC foundation to examine students' learning for practice. *Computers in Human Behavior*, *55*, 1179–1184. doi:10.1016/j.chb.2014.10.023

Wu, Y.-J., Kiefer, S. M., & Chen, Y.-H. (2019). Relationships between learning strategies and self-efficacy: A cross-cultural comparison between Taiwan and the United States using latent class analysis. *International Journal of School & Educational Psychology*, 1–13.

Wyeth, P., & Purchase, H. C. (2003). Using developmental theories to inform the design of technology for children. In *Proceedings of the 2003 conference on Interaction design and children* (pp. 93-100). ACM.

Xi, N., & Hamari, J. (2019). Does gamification satisfy needs? A study on the relationship between gamification features and intrinsic need satisfaction. *International Journal of Information Management*, *46*, 210–221. doi:10.1016/j.ijinfomgt.2018.12.002

Xi, N., & Hamari, J. (2020). Does gamification affect brand engagement and equity? A study in online brand communities. *Journal of Business Research*, *109*(3), 449–460. doi:10.1016/j.jbusres.2019.11.058

Xu, Y., & Hi, H. (2011). *Literature review on web application gamification and analytics* (CSDL Technical Report 11-05). University of Hawaii.

Yang, Y., Asaad, Y., & Dwivedi, Y. (2017). Examining the impact of gamification on intention of engagement and brand attitude in the marketing context. *Computers in Human Behavior*, *73*, 459–469. doi:10.1016/j.chb.2017.03.066

Yao, L., Mimno, D., & McCallum, A. (2009). Efficient methods for topic model inference on streaming document collections. *Proceedings of the 15th ACM SIGKDD International Conference on Knowledge Discovery and Data Mining*, 937–946. 10.1145/1557019.1557121

Yee, N. (2006). Motivations for play in online games. *Cyberpsychology & Behavior*, *9*(6), 772–775. doi:10.1089/cpb.2006.9.772 PMID:17201605

Yee, N. (2006). The demographics, motivations, and derived experiences of users of massively multi-user online graphical environments. *Presence (Cambridge, Mass.)*, *15*(3), 309–329. doi:10.1162/pres.15.3.309

Yildirim, A., & Şimşek, H. (2005). Sosyal bilimlerde nitel araştırma yöntemleri. Ankara: Seçkin Yayıncılık.

Yi, M. Y., & Davis, F. D. (2003). Developing and Validating an Observational Learning Model of Computer Software Training and Skill Acquisition. *Information Systems Research*, *14*(2), 146–169. doi:10.1287/isre.14.2.146.16016

Yin, R. K. (2003). *Estudo de Caso: Planejamento e métodos* [Case Study: Planning and methods]. Bookman Editora.

Yllana-Prieto, F., Jeong, J. S., & González-Gómez, D. (2021). An online-based edu-escape room: A comparison study of a multidimensional domain of psts with flipped sustainability-stem contents. *Sustainability*, *13*(3), 1–18. doi:10.3390u13031032 PMID:34676112

Young, M. F., Slota, S., Cutter, A. B., Jalette, G., Mullin, G., Lai, B., Simeoni, Z., Tran, M., & Yukhymenko, M. (2012). Our Princess Is in Another Castle: A Review of Trends in Serious Gaming for Education. *Review of Educational Research*, *82*(1), 61–89. doi:10.3102/0034654312436980

Zagalo, N. (2013). *Video games in Portugal: History, Technology and Art* [Videojogos em Portugal: História, Tecnologia e Arte]. FCA Editora.

Zain, N. H. M. (2021). Learning through games: An approach for children with autism spectrum disorder during COVID-19 pandemic. *Turkish Journal of Computer and Mathematics Education*, *12*(5), 1820–1829. doi:10.17762/turcomat.v12i5.2196

Zainuddin, Z., Chu, S. K. W., Shujahat, M., & Perera, C. J. (2020). The impact of gamification on learning and instruction: A systematic review of empirical evidence. *Educational Research Review*, *30*, 1–23. doi:10.1016/j.edurev.2020.100326

Zainuddin, Z., Shujahat, M., Haruna, H., & Chu, S. K. W. (2020). The role of gamified e-quizzes on student learning and engagement: An interactive gamification solution for a formative assessment system. *Computers & Education*, *145*, 103729. Advance online publication. doi:10.1016/j.compedu.2019.103729

Zaman, M. (2013). Entrepreneurial characteristics among university students: Implications for entrepreneurship education and training in Pakistan. *African Journal of Business Management*, *7*(39), 4053–4058.

Zamora-Polo, F., Sánchez-Cortés, M. M., Reyes-Rodríguez, A. M., & Sanz-Calcedo, J. G. (2019). Developing project managers' transversal competences using building information modeling. *Applied Sciences (Basel, Switzerland)*, *9*(4006), 1–17. doi:10.3390/app9194006

Zarco Claudio, N., Machancoses, M., & Fernández Piqueras, R. (2019). The effectiveness of the Escape Room as a strategy for motivation, cohesion and learning mathematics in sixth grade [La eficacia de la Escape Room como estrategia de motivación, cohesión y aprendizaje de matemáticas en sexto de educación primaria]. *Edetania*, *56*, 23–42.

Zaug, P., Gros, C. I., Wagner, D., Pilavyan, E., Meyer, F., Offner, D., & Strub, M. (2021). Development of an innovative educational escape game to promote teamwork in dentistry. *European Journal of Dental Education*, *26*(1), 116–122. doi:10.1111/eje.12678 PMID:33561894

Zhang, J., Luxton-Reilly, A., Denny, P., & Whalley, J. (2021). Scientific Collaboration Network Analysis for Computing Education Conferences. *Proceedings of the 26th ACM Conference on Innovation and Technology in Computer Science Education*, 1, 582–588. 10.1145/3430665.3456385

Zhao, C.-M., & Kuh, G. D. (2004). Adding Value: Learning Communities and Student Engagement. *Research in Higher Education*, *45*(2), 115–138. doi:10.1023/B:RIHE.0000015692.88534.de

Zhonggen, Y. (2019). A meta-analysis of use of serious games in education over a decade. *International Journal of Computer Games Technology*. doi:10.1155/2019/4797032

Zichermann, G., & Cunningham, C. (2011). *Gamification by design. Implementing game mechanics in web and mobile apps*. O'Reilly.

Zichermann, G., & Cunningham, C. (2011). *Gamification by design: Implementing game mechanics in web and mobile apps*. O'Reilly Media, Inc.

Zichermann, G., & Cunningham, C. (2011). *Gamification by design: Implementing game mecha-nics in web and mobile apps*. O'Reilly Media.

Zichermann, G., & Cunningham, C. (2011). *Gamification by Design: Implementing Game Mechanics in Web and Mobile Apps*. O'Reilly.

Zin, N. A. M., Jaafar, A., & Yue, W. S. (2009). Digital game-based learning (DGBL) model and development methodology for teaching history. *WSEAS Transactions on Computers*, *8*(2), 322–333.

Zolkina, A. V., Lomonosova, N. V., & Petrusevich, D. A. (2020). Gamification as a tool of enhancing teaching and learning effectiveness in higher education: Needs analysis [Оценка востребованности применения геймификации как инструмента повышения эффективности образовательного процесса]. *Science for Education Today*, *10*(3), 127–143. doi:10.15293/2658-6762.2003.07

Zwikael, O., & Gonen, A. (2007). Project execution game: Training towards managing unexpected events. *Journal of European Industrial Training*, *31*(6), 495–512. doi:10.1108/03090590710772668

Zyda, M. (2005). From visual simulation to virtual reality to games. *IEEE Computer*, *38*(9), 25–32. doi:10.1109/MC.2005.297

About the Contributors

Oscar Bernardes holds a Ph.D. in management, since 2013. He worked as management consultant for several years, in several organizations (social, profitable, and governmental). He is Invited Professor at Polytechnic Institute of Porto (P.Porto), Portugal, where he has been lecturing courses in the following areas: entrepreneurship, innovation, marketing and general management. His research interests include entrepreneurship, gamification, innovation, and marketing.

Vanessa Amorim is a Business and Economics Ph.D. student at the University of Aveiro - Portugal. She has a master's in Organizational Management - Specialization: Business Management and a Post-Graduation in Management Tools for Business Competitiveness from Institute Polytechnic of Porto - Portugal. Her main research interests are Innovation, Entrepreneurship, Marketing, and Business Management.

António Carrizo Moreira obtained a Bachelor's degree in Electrical Engineering and a Master's degree in Management, both from the University of Porto, Portugal. He received his Ph.D. in Management from the University of Manchester, England. He has a solid international background in industry leveraged working for a multinational company in Germany as well as in Portugal. He has also been involved in consultancy projects and research activities. He is an Associate Professor at the Department of Economics, Management, Industrial Engineering, and Tourism, University of Aveiro, Portugal, where he is the Director of the PhD program in Economics and Management Studies. He is member of GOVCOPP research unit.

* * *

Luis Aimacaña-Espinosa studied Educational Sciences with a Mention in Biology and Chemistry at the Central University of Ecuador. He studied for a master's in Innovation and Educational Leadership from the Indoamérica Technological University. He has educational experience for more than 14 years, of which he was a Computer Teacher at the Ciudad de Ibarra School for two years, was also a Chemistry teacher at the San Francisco de Quito Municipal Educational Unit for two years, and a Current Chemistry Teacher at the Guayllabamba Educational Institution for ten years. He has written book chapters and research articles on teaching methodologies. He has participated in international scientific conferences.

Waleed Al-Adrousy works in the Computer Science Department, Mansoura University: BSc 2004; MSC 2010; Ph.D. 2015. Interested in game development, mobile application, and software engineering fields.

Irene Alcoceba Herrero has a degree in Nursing from the University of Valladolid and a Master's Degree in Critical Care and Emergency Nursing from the University of León. Pre-doctoral researcher and nurse in the Cardiac Critical Care Unit. Oral communication at the VIII Conference of CyL researchers and three articles published in high-impact journals.

Juan Arenillas Lara is the Head of the Neurology Department at the University Hospital and Associate Professor of Neurology at the Faculty of Medicine at the University of Valladolid. He is a senior researcher that has experience in the area of innovative learning based on more than 25 years of expertise, providing opportunities to demonstrate knowledge and understanding of innovative learning, promoting health and good habits through his clinical practice, and engaging in activities that clarify and enhance understanding of innovative learning, utilizing project management skills to plan and implement activities. Notably, he is in the top 2% of the most widely cited scientists worldwide and those with the highest research output until 2019, according to the Ranking of the World Scientists: Worlds Top 2% Scientists, published by Stanford University.

Víctor Arufe Giráldez is a professor at the Faculty of Education of the University of A Coruña, editor-in-chief of the scientific journal Sportis, director of the UNIDEF Research Unit, author of the successful blog Education, Innovation and Entrepreneurship www.victorarufe.com with more than 700,000 annual visits, author of numerous books and scientific articles, awarded numerous awards for innovation and gamification in education and invited speaker at more than 50 national and international conferences.

Daniel Barros is a professor at the Faculty of the City of Maceió, FACIMA/FAA/IESA, and a member of the Structuring Teaching Nucleus (NDE) of the Advertising and Advertising course. He has a degree in Social Communication and Public Relations from the Federal University of Alagoas - UFAL (2010) and an Information Systems degree from UFAL (2017). He is a Specialist (MBA) in Marketing and Advertising by Faculty Maurício de Nassau (2011), a Master in Education by the Post-Graduate Program (stricto sensu) in Education - PPGE, at the Federal University of Alagoas (2018), and a member of the Research Group Virtual Communities - UFAL.

Lucas Bastos is a Doctor and Master in Media and Everyday Life at Universidade Federal Fluminense (PPGMC). Bachelor in Social Communication at Universidade Federal Fluminense (UFF). Professor of Social Communication at Faculdade Católica Salesiana develops studies about games as cultural artifacts and application in educational contexts as tools for media literacy development projects.

Julia Bevzenko graduated from Kherson State University, Ukraine. She teaches General English, Maritime English, and English for a particular purpose at Maritime Applied college of Kherson State Maritime Academy.

Gabriela Birnfeld Kurtz has a Ph.D. in Communication and Information at the Federal University of Rio Grande do Sul (2020). Master in Social Communication from the Pontifical Catholic University of Rio Grande do Sul (2013-2015). Graduated in Advertising and Propaganda from the Pontifical Catholic University of Rio Grande do Sul (2012). Her academic work mainly focuses on cyberculture and games. She is currently a professor in the Advertising and Propaganda course at PUCRS and a member of IDEAR (PUCRS Entrepreneurship and Innovation Laboratory).

Katerini Bizota is a special educator working in the public sector in Athens, Greece. She studied Education and Social Policy (University of Macedonia, Thessaloniki). She demonstrated a genuine interest in volunteering in organizations and camps with children with special needs throughout her studies. She worked as an intern at Berlin British School and was involved in the EAL department working closely with small groups. She holds an MA entitled 'Language Education for Refugees and Migrants' (Hellenic Open University), navigating her expertise to Second Language Acquisition. Since then, she has worked voluntarily as a Greek Language teacher in NGOs in Athens. She is particularly interested in innovation and educational technology through a critical pedagogy lens.

José Luis David Bonilla Carranza is PhD. Student in Electronics and Computer Science. Currently working as a Professor in the Department of Information and Knowledge-Based Innovation at CUCEI of the University of Guadalajara, Mexico, where he teaches subjects such as video game development, computer graphics, Internet programming, and computer simulation, among others. He is the author or co-author of several national and international articles and conferences related to the world of video games. Creator of communities such as creavideojuegos.org being an enthusiast in videogame programming, he is currently working on the Johnny Tequila project.

Viviane Botelho graduated in Chemical Engineering in 2009 from the Federal University of Rio Grande (FURG). She holds a master's degree (2012) and a doctorate (2015) in Chemical Engineering from the Federal University of Rio Grande do Sul (UFRGS). She is currently a professor at the Department of Exact, Social and Applied Sciences at the Federal University of Sciences of Health of Porto Alegre (UFCSPA), working in mathematics and scientific computing. She is a permanent professor in the Graduate Program in Information Technology and Health Management at UFCSPA. She is a member of the Intelligent Systems Applied to Health research group. He is currently working on research in mathematical computational modeling, machine learning, simulation, and optimization, with a focus on healthcare applications.

Brunella Botte graduated in Sciences of Communication at the Sapienza University of Rome with a major in Digital Communication. She is a Researcher at Link Campus University, Department of Science of Life & Health, and currently PhD student at Utrecht University. Her field of scientific interests is game design for digital game-based learning, with particular focus on gamification and serious games and on how rewards can support players' motivation. She was also a founder at Nutgames s.r.l., a company specialized in mobile games and applications. She is also a certified LEGO® Serious Play™ Facilitator.

Suzanne Brown-McBride is currently a Ph.D. student in the Learning Design and Technology program at the University of Hawai'i at Mānoa.

Stein Brunvand, before earning his doctorate degree in Learning Technologies at the University of Michigan, was an elementary school teacher. He taught third grade for three years in the Marshall Islands at George Seitz Elementary school and fifth grade for three years here in Michigan at Greyhound Intermediate in a town called Eaton Rapids. When not teaching or conducting research, he enjoys spending time with his wife and two daughters. Stein is very interested in the enhancement of learning environments through the integration of technology and enjoys working with preservice and practicing teachers to learn how this can be done more effectively. In his dissertation, he looked at how scaffolds impact what preservice teachers learn and notice from videos of classroom practice. While at UM-Dearborn, he has investigated the impact of research-based professional development on integrating technology in K-12 classrooms. Stein has also explored the use of e-portfolios in teaching and learning with undergraduate and graduate students.

Florentina Cañada is an associate professor of science education in the Department of Science and Mathematics Education at the University of Extremadura, Spain. Her research area includes Science teaching, pre-service teacher, instructional design and development, and emotion regulation. She has published over 50 refereed journal papers and book chapters in Science education. Since 2013, she has been the head of the research group Professional development of science and mathematics teachers.

Marcos Castro studied a Bachelor of Mathematics at the Universidad Industrial de Santander. He studied for a master's degree in Education at the Autonomous University of Bucaramanga. He has educational experience in the field of Mathematics for more than seven years. In addition, he has researched active learning methodologies using technological tools, being part of the Genially Latam ambassadors, a member of the Latin American group of online teachers, and a Colombian delegate of the network of mathematics circles and festivals (Cyfemat). She is an active participant in the Fields research group at the Research and Development University and a professor in the computer engineering program at the University of La Rioja (Colombia).

Vinicius Cezar is a Business Administration with Emphasis in Systems Analysis (2007/PUCRS), receiving an academic distinction award as the best student given by the Rio Grande do Sul Regional Council of Administration (CRA/RS). MBA in Project Management with an emphasis on Information Technology (2011/PUCRS). Master in Informatics in Education (2019/IFRS). He is a student for a Ph.D. in the Informatics in Education Graduate Program (PPGIE) at UFRGS. He currently works as Ombudsman, Data Processing Officer (DPO), and Information and Communication Security Manager at the Federal University of Health Sciences of Porto Alegre (UFCSPA).

Treechada Chotiratanapinun holds a Ph.D. in Design from Goldsmiths, University of London, and is a Lecturer in Product Design at Silpakorn University in Thailand. Her research interests center around the intersection of sustainable design, design education, and education for sustainable development (ESD). She is a pioneer in developing a transformative sustainability pedagogy for Thai design learners. With an interdisciplinary background in Communication Arts, Marketing, Product Design, Educational Studies, and Sustainability, she also works as a consultant for organizations aiming to reduce environmental impact and enhance social benefits.

María Coco Martín is a Senior Researcher in the Neurology department at the Faculty of Medicine at the University of Valladolid. She is President of the European Society for Low Vision Research and Rehabilitation. Exclusive Spanish Partner of ENVITER Network (European Network For Vision

Impairment Training Education & Research). She has more than 18 years of teaching experience in visual rehabilitation and learning design courses at public and private universities at the Faculty of Medicine, School of Optometry, and School of Physiotherapy. She has promoted the first online course of the Public University of Valladolid, Spain designing the Moodle platform, learning model, teaching materials, and assessment tools for more than 25 different subjects. She has received two granted projects at the University to implement new resources for e-learning.

António Fernando Coelho is an Associate Professor with Habilitation at the Department of Informatics Engineering of the Faculty of Engineering, University of Porto. He is also a senior researcher at INESC TEC since 1995, coordinating the Computer Graphics and Virtual environments area at the Information Systems and Computer Graphics center. His research activity focuses on Computer Graphics and Digital Media, in research lines on Procedural Modeling, Virtual and Augmented Reality, Digital Games, Gamification, Procedural content generation, Pervasive Games, Game-based Learning, and Geospatial Systems. He has coordinated and participated in several research projects, including European, national, and specialized consulting projects. He was involved in organizing scientific events such as EuroVis 2019, which was held in Porto, and was also one of the local chairs of Eurographics 2016, held in Lisbon, and of SGAMES 2016, in Porto. Since 2012 he has been leading the Informatics Engineering Department's strategic and multidisciplinary project in the Digital Media area, having been the Director of the Master's Degree in Multimedia from 2012 to 2015 and the Director of the Doctoral Program in Digital Media from 2015. The project is included in the national program UT Austin | Portugal; being the Researcher Responsible for this program at UP from 2014 to 2017, and has participated in creating the UP Digital Media competency center, the Media Innovation Labs (MIL). He is a member of the MIL Advisory Board and is the coordinator of one of the MIL's Laboratories, the Digital Media Learning Lab (DMLL). He is also an evaluator of A3ES in the External Evaluation Committee (CAE) for the Multimedia area.

Débora Conforto is a Ph.D. in Education, Federal University of Rio Grande do Sul. Specialist in Informatics in Education and Educational Software Modeling, from the Pontifical Catholic University of Rio Grande, do Sul. Graduated in Biological Sciences from the Pontifical Catholic University of Rio Grande do Sul. Researcher at the Federal University of Rio Grande do Sul, research projects funded by the National Council for Scientific and Technological Development (CNPq). She acted as supervisor of Educational Technologies of the Marist Network and, currently, as coordinator of the Online Education sector, Coordinator of Online Graduation of the Pontifical Catholic University of Rio Grande do Sul. Publications in Mobile Learning, Learning Designer, Virtual Learning Environments, Digital Inclusion, Usability, and Web Accessibility.

Isaac Corbacho-Cuello is a Professor in the Faculty of Education, University of Extremadura. His research areas include science teaching, training primary education teachers, and instructional design.

Daniel José Nunes Madureira da Cunha has attended the Doctoral Programme in Nursing Science at the University of Porto - Biomedical Sciences Institute Abel Salazar since 2016. He has a Specialist Title in Nursing, Master in Nursing, Specialist Nurse in Medical-Surgical Nursing, and Licentiate in Nursing. He is a Nurse at Oporto Hospital Center and an Adjunct Professor at the Nursing School of Santa Maria. He operates in the area(s) of Medical and Health Sciences with a special focus on Health

Sciences with special reference to Nursing. He has participated in scientific events with oral communications or Poster presentations and received one award. Participate as a researcher in some projects.

Alicia Danielsson is an assistant teaching professor in law at the University of Bolton. Her interests and expertise are in Human Rights Law, EU law, International Business and Trade Law, Jurisprudence, Legal Research Methods, International Criminal Justice, and Comparative Law. Alicia joined the university in 2017, having previously worked at Abertay University in Dundee. She is the program leader for the postgraduate courses within the School of Law and manages the Centre for Contemporary Coronial Law. Other responsibilities include teaching several core subjects in the Bachelor of Laws (LLB) and Master of Laws (LLM) programs, supervising postgraduate and undergraduate research projects, acting as an Enhanced Personal Tutor, and running the School of Law's Social Media Platforms. Her subject-specific research interests lie in comparative and EU law, with a specific focus on freedom, security, and justice, as well as EU labor law and human rights protection. Alicia's research interests and focus also include exploring law teaching methods and inclusive practices within legal education, particularly about experiences of law students with specific learning difficulties (SpLDs), to develop more inclusive teaching practices within law education.

Cynthia Dias graduated in Journalism and Cinema from PUC-Rio, Master and Doctor in Design from the same university. She coordinates and works as a professor-researcher at the Center for Educational Technologies in Health (NUTED) of the Joaquim Venâncio Polytechnic School of Health (EPSJV / FIOCRUZ). She is part of the LINC-Design laboratory (PUC-Rio), where she oversees the "Design for a Multimodal Education" Axis. She is part of the research group Jogos e Saúde (FIOCRUZ) and the Ludus Magisterium group. She has experience in Audiovisual Education and develops applied analog games and game design processes with students in Professional Education in Health. She coordinated the development of the game "Sowing Care," part of the "Popular Education and Medicinal Plants in Primary Health Care" project.

Ceymi Doenyas did Ph.D. studies and subsequent work focuses on understanding the gut-brain axis-related, neural, and genetic mechanisms underlying autism spectrum disorder (ASD), creating technology-based interventions to make ASD education more affordable, and formulating social living models to foster communities where individuals with ASD and their families are accepted and included. Also, study the executive functions and theory of mind abilities of children typically developing (TD). The academic endeavors follow my mission to help advance the scientific understanding of ASD and improve the living conditions of individuals with ASD and their families locally and globally, as well as to generate fun educational methods to improve the executive functions of TD children starting from an early age.

Alexandre Farbiarz holds a Ph.D. in Design from PUC-Rio, a Master in Education and Language from USP, and a Master in Design from PUC-Rio. He is an Associate Professor in the Department of Social Communication at the Institute of Art and Social Communication (IACS) at the Fluminense Federal University (UFF), Brazil. He is a permanent professor at the Graduate Program in Media and Everyday Life (PPGMC). He is the Coordinator of the research group Education for the Media in Communication (educ@mídias.com/PPGMC/UFF) and the research group Design in the Reading of Subjects and Supports in Interaction (DeSSIn/PPG Design/PUC-Rio). He researched in the areas of Communication,

Design, and Education, with an emphasis on discursive relationships, media, and teaching-learning; acting mainly on the themes: Critical Education for the Media, Media-Education, Media Literacy, Educommunication, Online Education, Games, and Education, Gamification, Visual Communication, Discourse, and Language.

Jackeline Farbiarz holds a Ph.D. in Education and Language from the University of São Paulo (USP) and a Master in Language from Pontifical University Catholic of Rio de Janeiro (PUC-Rio), Brazil. She serves as Director of the Department of Arts and Design at PUC-Rio. She is also Associate Professor and Researcher in the graduate Program in Design (PPGDesign – DAD/PUC-Rio). She coordinates the Laboratory of Language, Interaction, and Construction of Meanings / Design and is the leader of the Research Groups in Design in the Reading of Disciplines and Supports in Interaction (LINC-Design). She researched in the areas of Design, Language, and Education, emphasizing discursive relationships, inclusive design, design and partnership, multimodality, and new technologies in teaching-learning contexts. As activities result of her work at LINC-Design / PUC-Rio, she is the general coordinator of the Technology, Teaching-Learning, Inclusion, Sustainability Congress (TEIAS), an interinstitutional and interdisciplinary event.

Annalisa Galeone achieved her Ph.D. in Management and Innovation with a specialization in Marketing in April 2020 at the Catholic University of the Sacred Heart in Milan, Italy. From time to time, she still collaborates with Centrimark – the Center for Marketing and Research of the Catholic University. She is interested in carrying out research in Services Marketing, focusing her attention on the tourism and hospitality industry. Her research interests include and are not limited to Gamification, Edutainment, Transformative Service Research (TSR), value co-creation, sustainable tourism, eco-tourism, hospitality, individual and collective well-being, neuromarketing, and international marketing. Currently, she works within the space industry as Change and Adoption Officer for ATG Europe B.V. at the European Space Agency (ESA) in the Netherlands.

Claire Garden is an Associate Professor and Head of Teaching and Learning at Edinburgh Napier University School of Applied Sciences. She holds a Ph.D. in Molecular Neuroscience and currently undertakes scholarship and pedagogical research in the following areas: 1. Novel learning and teaching methods to improve student engagement. 2. Skills development and routes to employment for Biomedical Sciences graduates. 3. Inclusive teaching and learning approaches. She is a Senior Fellow of the Higher Education Academy and Member of the Royal Society of Biology.

Eloisa Gonçalves is a professor at the Municipal Education Foundation of Niterói - Rio de Janeiro, working since 2010 in the Coordination of Education, Media and Digital Technologies, responsible for training teachers in Educational Technology. She holds a Master's in Education from the State University of Rio de Janeiro (2018). She is also a doctoral candidate in the Graduate Program in Media and Daily Life, linked to the Fluminense Federal University, since 2019.

Neil Gordon is a senior lecturer in the Department of Computer Science & Technology at the University of Hull, where he is the program leader for the Computer Science family of degrees. His doctorate was in applied mathematics, considering the use of computer algebra, and provided the basis of later work at the interface of mathematics to computing. As a lecturer in computer science, his teaching duties range from first-year core modules to specialist masters' level computing courses, including software engineering. As well to his published research, he has produced several national reports on Higher Education, including issues of retention and attainment in computer science.

Simon Grey is a lecturer in the Department of Computer Science & Technology at the University of Hull. He is the program leader for the Computer Science with Games Programming family of degrees. He is a fellow of the Higher Education Academy and a committee member of the Playful Learning Association.

Hélia Guerra is an Auxiliary Professor at the Faculty of Sciences and Technology of the University of Azores, Ponta Delgada, Portugal, where she has been since 1993. She holds a Ph.D. in Computer Science (2004), an MSc in Informatics (1997), and a BSc in Mathematics/Informatics (1992). She is a researcher at the Algoritmi Centre (Computer Science and Technologies R&D line) of the University of Minho and a founding member and the coordinator of the eHealth R&D unit of the University of Azores. Her research interests span the domain of information systems, software engineering, artificial intelligence, and health informatics. She has been involved in several organizations of international conferences and has several publications in conference proceedings, chapter books, and journals.

Richard Hall is a Director of RAMPS Laboratory and has a Ph.D. in Computer Science. Richard has worked as a University Lecturer, Technical Program Manager, and Software Engineer across private industry, state government, and university sectors.

Miriam Hernández is a Ph.D. student at the University of Extremadura, Spain. She has been carrying out her doctoral research in Science Education for four years (2018-2022) at the Department of Science and Mathematics Education, University of Extremadura, Spain. Her research area includes Science teaching, training primary education teachers, instructional design and development, and emotion regulation.

Joaquín Herrera Medina is a Technician in the integral rehabilitation of visually impaired and blind people and an associate professor at the University of Valladolid. He has a long professional career with experience in caring for visually impaired people. He has great dedication and personal motivation to continue to make achievements in this field and publish prestigious publications in high-impact journals.

David R. Hill earned a Ph.D. in Special Education from the University of Pittsburgh (Pitt) and an M.S.L. from the University of Pittsburgh School of Law. Before earning his Ph.D. at Pitt, David spent 11 years in K-12 education as an Administrator and a National Board Certified Teacher, serving students with various disabilities, including intellectual disability, autism, emotional behavior disabilities, and specific learning disabilities. His research interests include Developing effective inclusive, evidence-based practices for students with disabilities to enhance teacher instruction. The integration of various technologies to improve pedagogic methods for teachers. He examined legal issues in special education and holdings from litigation to see how they may impact school districts.

Denis Hyams-Ssekasi joined the University in April 2015 following 12 years of experience delivering Business and Management courses in undergraduate and postgraduate programs in the UK Higher Education. Before this, Denis worked as a senior lecturer, module leader, and course-coordinator of Management and Leadership programs at the University of Huddersfield. Denis holds undergraduate honors and postgraduate qualifications in Human Resource Management, Management, Business Administration, Education, and a teaching qualification. Denis Completed his Doctorate in 2012. He is a member of the Chartered Institute of Personnel Development and a Senior Fellow of the Higher Academy. Denis has a proven and sustained record of accomplishment of contribution to students' learning and development. Denis has been involved in student research related to flexible working, employee engagement, and behavior in the workplace and has successfully led several teaching and learning initiatives, including personal development planning, employability, and mentoring projects. His research interests include Strategic Management and Leadership, Entrepreneurship, High-Performance Work Systems, Employee Performance, Internationalisation, Outsourcing, International Transitions, Intercultural communications, and social impacts.

Janio Jadán-Guerrero studied Systems Engineering at the Central University of Ecuador, a Master's Degree in Computer Security at the University of Costa Rica, and a Master's Degree in Business Administration and Marketing at the Indoamérica Technological University, and a PhD. in Computer Science from the University of Costa Rica. Her line of research is based on Human-Computer Interaction. He has written books and research articles in high-impact scientific journals from various parts of the world. He has participated in important national and international scientific conferences. He has been a research leader and professor at various higher education institutions: Pontificia Universidad Católica del Ecuador, Sede Ambato, the Technical University of Ambato, and Indoamérica Technological University. He is a lead professor in various masters and doctoral programs. He has also developed technology for children with different abilities, including Kiteracy, a literacy kit for children with intellectual disabilities, AINIDIU, a virtual assistant for children with visual disabilities, and Qínqu, an inclusive board game. He is currently the Institutional Director of Research and researcher at the Center for Research in Mechatronics and Interactive Systems (MIST) of the Indoamerican Technological University. He is also a professor at the Faculty of Engineering and Information and Communication Technologies (FITIC); he as well a Master's degree in Education, a mention in Innovation and Educational Leadership (MEILE), and a Master's in Education, mention Pedagogy in Digital Environments (MEPED).

Manu Melwin Joy is currently working as Assistant Professor at the School of Management Studies, Cochin University of Science and Technology, Kochi, India. His research focus includes Gamification, Design Thinking, HR Analytics, and Talent Retention. He has completed certification in Gamification from the University of Pennsylvania and Design Thinking from the University of Virginia. Apart from publishing articles in accredited journals, he has authored many books, with the most recent one titled "Fun is future- A collection of compelling gamification success stories." He has handled sessions on gamification across the country for corporates such as The Hindu Group, The Federal Bank, Apollo Tyres, The Popular Group, etc., and educational institutions like G L Bajaj Institute of Technology and Management (Greater Noida), Bapuji Group of Institutions(Davangere), Kerala Veterinary and Animal Sciences University (KVASU) to name a few.

Adriana Kampff is a Doctorate in Informatics in Education and Master in Computer Science from UFRGS. Specialization in Curriculum Management and Graduation in Informatics from PUCRS. Main research areas: Educational Technologies (digital educational technologies in education and teaching mediated by digital technologies), Teacher Education (active methodologies and digital resources in education), and Educational Management (curriculum innovation).

Nuri Kara works as an Assistant Professor in the department of Digital Game Design at Istanbul Bilgi University in Turkey. He earned a Ph.D. in Computer Education and Instructional Technology from the Middle East Technical University. His research interests focus on serious games, smart toys, human-computer interaction, instructional technologies, and gamification.

(Olena Kononova - Contributing Author) She teaches General English, Maritime English, and English for a particular purpose.

Asha S. Kutty is working as Assistant Professor at the Department of Management Studies of Mar Dionysius College. She has completed an MBA from DCMS, University of Calicut and has ten years of teaching experience (UG and PG) in various colleges. She is doing her research in CUSAT. She completed a Diploma in Applied Psychology and certification in Gamification from the University of Pennsylvania. She is a member of the Board of Studies (Management Studies) of the University of Calicut. She has more than ten articles in various national and international accredited journals and has authored a book titled "G 4 Games & L 4 Learning". She has attended/presented more than 25 papers in both national and international conferences and has attended 20 MDP/FDPs. She has received an appreciation letter from KSHEC. She is the recipient of the Dr. B. R. Ambedkar National Award 2020-21 award under the category of Education. She is also the recipient of the prestigious award by the Global Research Foundation as "Excellent and Dedicated Professional Achiever." Her areas of interest are Game-Based Learning, Gamification for Learning & Development.

Luis Leal Vega is a Graduate of Nursing from the University of Valladolid with a Masters's Degree in Ophthalmological Nursing. He is currently studying for his Ph.D. in the Health Sciences Research Program at the University of Valladolid and has extensive research experience in various clinical trials and innovative research projects both at the national and European levels.

Clifton Lee is currently an Industrial/Organizational Psychology master's student at SFSU. Before joining the I/O Psychology program at SFSU, Mr. Lee graduated from California State Polytechnic University, Pomona, where he was a McNair Scholar and an active member of the University's Psi Chi chapter. His current interests include working with virtual teams of people in organizations. He has worked on several research projects as part of the WorkTech lab. He is also currently working on an internship in talent management and training with a start-up organization based out of California.

Peter Leong is an Associate Professor with the Department of Learning Design & Technology, University of Hawaii-Manoa. He has extensive experience in developing and delivering online courses and distance education. Dr. Leong was the President of the Pan-Pacific Distance Learning Association and served as the President of the International Division of the Association for Educational Communications and on the Executive Board of the International Council of Educational Media. His research interests include student satisfaction with online learning, faculty support for technology integration, technologies for distance education, gamification, and teaching & learning in virtual worlds.

Naira Libermann is a Dr. in Educational Sciences UTAD Portugal, Master in Administration at UFRGS (2001), graduated in Administration at PUCRS (1993), graduated in Pedagogy (Full Degree) at PUCRS (1988). She was Executive Director of the Brazilian Small Business Service, is currently Coordinator of the IDEAR Interdisciplinary Laboratory of Entrepreneurship and Innovation at PUCRS, the Coordinator of the Entrepreneur Nucleus at PUCRS, and is a professor at the School of Business at PUCRS, and Director of CRIARE Consultoria Empresarial. He has experience in Administration and Adult Education, acting on the following topics: small businesses, entrepreneurship, Business Management strategy, Business Networks, and Innovation Management.

Katerina Makri is a Senior researcher with a Ph.D. in the field of Educational Technology with interests focusing on teachers' professional development through e-learning, blended learning, and content authoring with participatory web technologies (Web 2.0), curriculum design, professional communities of practice, digital literacies, and creativity in learning and teaching. She has extended experience in educational research with students and teachers through state-funded (Hellenic) and EU projects, using qualitative methods and content analysis. She is also a certified adult educator and vocational trainer in several disciplines: language learning (Greek as a second language), ICT (basic skills), educational technology (pedagogical use of digital tools), and in different educational settings: tertiary education (under and post graduate), professional - vocational education (in-service and pre-service), corporate training and technological education. She has taught for four years in blended, and distance learning courses and has worked as an e-learning course designer and consultant. She has produced and published various digital educational materials for blended and online / f2f settings.

Marcella Mandanici is a professor of Music Education Technologies at the Music Conservatory "L.Marenzio" in Brescia (Italy). She is a composer of instrumental and electronic music and holds a Ph.D. in Information Engineering at the University of Padova. Her main research areas are computer-supported music education; sound and music computing; interfaces for music production, education, and rehabilitation. She has been a PC member of SMC, CSME/CSEDU, and Ubimus 2020 and 2021 and revised papers for international journals and conferences. Since 2016 she has been teaching acoustics and psychoacoustics, and computer music. Since 2019 she has been the manager of a master's course in "Technologies for Music Education" and is the organizer of various music technology workshops and conferences for music teachers. She has authored over 25 scientific works in sound and music computing, multimedia, and music education.

Giada Marinensi graduated in Sciences of Communication at the Sapienza University of Rome. She is a researcher at Link Campus University, Department of Human Sciences, and she coordinates the research team specializing in e-learning methods and technologies. Her fields of scientific interest are e-learning and new technologies and methods in the teaching/learning process, such as social learning, mobile learning, and digital game-based learning, with a particular focus on gamification and serious games. Before that, she was for seven years team leader at an Italian ICT company, and as an Instructional System Designer, she was responsible for the design of many e-learning projects.

Margarida Marques is a researcher at the University of Aveiro (UA) is an integrated member of CIDTFF - Research Centre on Didactics and Technology in the Education of Trainers, where she has been studying technology-supported game-based learning in science education (REF-182-97-ARH/2018). She is a member of the EduPARK (http://edupark.web.ua.pt/?lang=en), LoCALL (http://bit.ly/2OZEeNn), and NaLoC (https://www.ua.pt/pt/cidtff/naloc) projects, LCD - Laboratory of Digital Contents, and CIDTFF Group 2 | Science, Technology and Innovation. She is also a member of the coordination team of the CIDTFF Programmatic Funding project (2020-2023) "SKG - Smart Knowledge Garden" and "OESC - Open Education Smart Campus" (https://www.ua.pt/pt/cidtff/page/26651). Finally, she is a member of the DEP - Department of Education and Psychology, where she has taught curricular units of High Degrees and Master's Courses since 2019. Margarida co-authored several scientific publications (books, book chapters, journal papers, and conference papers) and contributed to several other scientific communications about i) innovation in science education: digital game-based learning and other technology-supported education; ii) scientific literacy (e.g., climate literacy); and iii) teacher professional development. Her 5-year h-index is 6 in Scopus (https://goo.gl/ynTnrP) and 9 in Google Scholar (https://goo.gl/3af4WR), revealing relevant knowledge production with an impact on the academic community. She completed her Ph.D. in Didactics and Training, a branch of Didactics and Curricular Development (https://ria.ua.pt/handle/10773/13142) in 2014. Previously, she concluded her Master in Curricular Management (https://ria.ua.pt/handle/10773/1022) in 2008 and her Graduation in Teaching of Biology and Geology in 2004. All her academic courses were by UA.

Adrián Martín Gutiérrez is a degree in Marketing and Market Research from the University of Valladolid and a master's degree in business administration (MBA). He currently performs the researcher's functions, providing a multidisciplinary approach between the health field and business field, considering public-private collaboration to carry out innovative national and European projects.

Evandro Manara Miletto is an Associate Professor at the Federal Institute of Education, Science and Technologiy of Rio Grande do Sul (IFRS), Porto Alegre Campus, Brazil, where he works as Research Director. Prof Miletto received his Master's and PhD degrees in Computer Science at the Federal University of Rio Grande do Sul (UFRGS), in 2005 and 2009, respectively. He developed a doctoral internship at the Université Paris-Sud 11 in Paris in 2009. Since 2002 he has conducted multidisciplinary research on topics such as Computers in Education, Computer Music, HCI, and CSCW. His research is currently based on Computers in Education including topics such as ITC and networked music, with focus on novice users. Other academic activities involved international experiences with CAPES-GRICES (UNL, Portugal) and CAPES-COFECUB (Paris-Sud, France), and currently an ongoing international cooperation project with the CEGEP de Sherbrooke, which explores computing technology applied to environmental education with several published papers as result.

Chulpan Minnegalieva graduated from the Mechanics and Mathematics Faculty of Kazan State University. She worked as a teacher at a school and pedagogical institute. Since 2011 she has worked at the Institute of Computational Mathematics and Information Technologies of Kazan Federal University. She is an Associate Professor. Research interests: computer algebra systems, digitalization of education, multimedia technology in education, gamification.

Jan Miškov deals with the topics of e-learning, educational games, media effects, and teaching models. Besides the educational potential of digital games, he is fascinated by their visual culture, functioning, structure and shared traits with previous media types. He is currently completing his dissertation at the Faculty of Education of Masaryk University, where he teaches gamification in education. He previously received a master's degree in the field of media studies and journalism at the Faculty of Social Studies. He had published findings on utilizing game principles in online teaching from educators' and students' perspectives and outlined his approach to the simulation of an editorial content management system as part of the education model for his game journalism course. In accordance with his professional interest in play culture and aesthetics, he contributed to a collection of essays on contemporary Japanese pop culture of video games and an article on the genealogy of interactive drama. He helped to organize international conferences on game studies.

Carla Morais has a degree in Chemistry, a Master's in Multimedia Education, and a Ph.D. in Teaching and Dissemination of Sciences from the Faculty of Science of the University of Porto (FCUP). She is an Assistant Professor and member of the Science Education Unit at the same Faculty. She is also a member of the Centre for Research in Chemistry at the University of Porto (CIQUP – RG5: Education, Science Communication, and Society). She is engaged, as a trainer, in developing courses on Continuing Education for teachers. She has published articles in national and international journals. She has presented lectures in schools, conferences, and scientific meetings, in the field of Chemistry Education and Communication and the use of educational technologies. She is co-author of textbooks, popular science books, and educational software for Chemistry and Physics teaching. Her areas of interest include professional development and pedagogic practices for Physics and Chemistry teachers, dissemination models and processes for scientific knowledge, and the involvement and participation of citizens in Science, technological and digital ecologies in Science Education and Communication.

Mirna Muñoz has a Ph.D. in Computer Languages, Informatics Systems, and Software Engineering from the Polytechnic University of Madrid. She has a postdoctoral stay at the University of Carlos III of Madrid. She works as a Software Engineering researcher at the Software Engineering Unit of CIMAT in México. She is a member of the Software Engineering research group at CIMAT, Computer Science Mexican Society, and Computer Science Mexican Academy and participates Actively in the WG24 of ISO/IEC. She is a National Researchers System of Mexico member in Level I. She has participated in the Spanish Translation of CMMI-Dev model v1.2 and v1.3. Her current research interest is on software process and its assets definition in software and different domains, project management, software process improvements focusing on the human factor, multi-model environments, the implementation of quality models and standards as well as methodologies and agile methods, gamification and serious games, the integration of highly effective teams. Her contribution will be given by collaborating in identifying soft skills for engineers, performing systematic literature reviews, and using gamification within teamwork. Besides, she is an expert in project management.

Rubén Navarro Patón has a degree in Physical Activity and Sports Sciences and a Ph.D. from the University of Vigo. Among his lines of research are the training of teachers in all their fields and educational stages. Associate Professor, Faculty of Teacher Education, University of Santiago de Compostela (Spain).

Pey Ng is a junior clinical fellow doctor with an interest in academics and innovation.

Ana Cecilia Nunes is academic head of IDEAR – The Interdisciplinary Lab for Entrepreneurship and Innovation at the Pontifical Catholic University of Rio Grande do Sul – PUCRS. Adjunct Professor at PUCRS. Her Ph.D. was a joint degree Ph.D. between PUCRS (Brazil) and the University of Beira Interior (Portugal), partially financed by Capes/PDSE. Her research spans interdisciplinary entrepreneurship education and media management discussions.

Khin Maung Ohn is an orthopedic professor in the faculty of medicine and health sciences. He has more than 15 years of teaching experience for undergraduate and postgraduate medical students. His special interest is in medical education.

Sonia Osorio Angel has a degree in Computer Science obtained in 1998. Master of Education in 2010. Ph.D. student in Computer Science and Electronics. Associate Professor in the Computational Sciences Department of the Universidad de Guadalajara since 2000. Serving students in Programming, Data Structures, Software Engineering, and Project Management.

Miguel Padilha has been a nurse since 1997 and a specialized rehabilitation nurse. Furthermore, he is a medical-surgical nursing specialist in the care branch for people with chronic conditions. He has a Ph.D. in Nursing and is a Coordinator Professor at the Nursing School of Porto in Portugal. Miguel is the coordinator of specialization and Master's degree in Rehabilitation Nursing. Miguel is the Principal Investigator of the Tech4EduSim group (Technologies for Education and Simulation in Healthcare) in CINTESIS. His main research interests are COPD self-management and simulation in nursing education.

Adriana Peña Pérez Negrón received her Ph.D. in Computer Science in 2009 from the Universidad Politécnica de Madrid, Spain. Her main research interest is the user's avatar display of nonverbal communication in Collaborative Virtual Environments. She is a research professor in the Computer Science Department at the CUCEI of the Universidad de Guadalajara, Mexico.

Fernando Pimentel has a degree in Pedagogy from Cesmac University Centre (2005), a specialist in Teaching in Higher Education from Castelo Branco University (2007) and specialist in Technologies in Education from PUC/RJ (2010). Master (2010) and Ph.D. (2015) in Education from the Federal University of Alagoas. Did post-doctoral training in Education and Psychology on the theme of digital games and learning at the University of Aveiro, Portugal (2021). I was a teacher of Basic Education in public schools, a tutor in the continuing education program of the Distance Education Secretariat (MEC), a tutor at Tiradentes University, and a teacher in the Government of Alagoas State. He has experience in the area of Education in dialogue with the assumptions of teaching-learning, especially in the following topics: learning, digital games in education, gamification, active methodologies, online education, Webquest, tutoring, and evaluation. He was vice-coordinator of the Institutional Coordination of Distance Education and Deputy Coordinator of UAB / UFAL. He was the coordinator of the Graduate Program in Education (PPGE/Cedu/Ufal). He is currently part of the INEP's bank of institutional evaluators, an adjunct professor at the Federal University of Alagoas, and leader of the Virtual Communities Research Group - Ufal.

José Carlos Piñero Charlo is an assistant professor in the department of didactic (section of mathematics). Research interest: educational gamification for learning mathematics. Professional interest in flipped and blended learning, experimented with new technologies for team group learning in university education. A professional researcher with a vast experience in electron microscopy techniques (scanning and transmission). Deep knowledge in physics, highlighting electronics and quantum optics. Experience in designing laboratory equipment.

Lázaro Raposo has a Bachelor's degree in Computer Sciences (University of Azores) and a Master's Degree in Multimedia (FEUP), with a thesis about educational games. In 2014 he founded Cereal Games, an Azorean development studio focused on Serious Games, where he plays the roles of educational game designer and producer, developing educational games for museums, science centers, and schools. Since 2009, invited teacher at the University of Azores, to lecture on agile software development methodologies, among others.

Errol Scott Rivera is the Curriculum Design Officer focusing on Inclusivity at Cardiff University. His role involves using pedagogic theory to improve the effectiveness and inclusivity of university teaching practice. Currently, he is transitioning to an Academic Developer role at the University of Glasgow in Scotland. His doctoral work in education at Edinburgh Napier University reconciles theories of the psychology of learning design and engagement to measure the effectiveness of teaching interventions such as gamification. As an educational developer, he receives Advance HE's Collaborative Award for Teaching Excellence. As a Creative Writing MA lecturer, he has earned a commendation from the Scottish Government for his work engaging young people in arts, education, and citizenship.

João Frias Rosa has the title of Specialist in Nursing, professional title of Specialist Nurse in Medical-Surgical Nursing, and Master Degree in Medical-Surgical Nursing from the Porto Nursing School. Professionally collaborated at the University Hospital Center of Porto, reaching 13 years of performance dedicated to caring for people in emergency and critical status. Currently is Adjunct Professor at ISAVE - Health Superior Institute. In the research field, cooperates with the research group Tech4edusim / CINTESIS - Technologies for Education and Simulation in Health, as a Non-Doctoral Researcher associated with the R&D Unit. Finally, he is a Ph.D. Student in Nursing Sciences, from ICBAS - School of Medicine and Biomedical Sciences, with scientific production in communication and information technologies linked with emergency nurses' training and skills development.

Robert Ross is the Head of Electronics and Robotics Engineering at La Trobe University and the Director of the RAMPS research laboratory. He is an educational escape room pioneer, having published six peer-reviewed papers about educational escape rooms, a book on creating educational escape rooms (Inescapable Learning: Unlock the power of educational escape rooms), and with his wife, Sarah, founded the company Escape Room Education (www.escaperoomeducation.com). His teaching has been highly awarded the 2021 Provost Teaching Excellence Award, the 2019 School of Engineering Mathematical Sciences Teaching Excellence Award, and the 2017 Pro Vice-Chancellors Teaching Excellence Award.

Sarah Lynne Ross is the director and owner of Escape Escape Room Education (www.escaperoomeducation.com), a company that designs and distributes educational escape room games and decoders.

José A. Ruipérez-Valiente received the B.Eng. degree in telecommunications from Universidad Católica de San Antonio de Murcia, and the M.Eng. degree in telecommunications and the M.Sc. and Ph.D. degrees in telematics from Universidad Carlos III of Madrid while conducting research with Institute IMDEA Networks in the area of learning analytics and educational data mining. He was a postdoctoral associate with MIT. He has received more than 20 academic/research awards and fellowships, has published more than 90 scientific publications in high impact venues, and participated in over 18 funded projects. He is currently an Assistant Professor within the Information and Communications Engineering Department of the University of Murcia.

Diana R. Sanchez is an Assistant Professor in the Industrial/Organizational Psychology program in the College of Science and Engineering at San Francisco State University beginning Fall 2017. She received her undergraduate degree in Industrial/Organizational Psychology from Portland State University and her master's degree from the University of Baltimore in Industrial/Organizational Psychology. She continued her educational training at Colorado State University, completing her Ph.D. in Industrial/Organizational Psychology. Before joining the staff at SFSU, her applied experience included over 12 years of experience in Human Resources and I/O Psychology. Dr. Sanchez runs the Workplace Technology Research Lab, where graduate and undergraduate students examine various workplace technology forms' development, application, and effectiveness. The primary purpose of this lab is to provide students with guidance and information on how to produce high-quality research and disseminate this information via conference and academic paper submissions. The lab aims to improve the effectiveness of technology innovation and implementation at work.

Alberto Sanmiguel-Rodríguez is professor and research at the Antonio de Nebrija University and University Camilo José Cela. State permanent staff as full professor. He has participated in several national and international seminars and congresses, from which the 9th National Congress of Physical Activity and Sports Science and the 15th IARTEM International Conference held at the Odense - UCL University College (Denmark) stand out. He has participated in the organization and scientific committee in the 2nd and 3rd Global Education Congresses, EDUCA 2019 and 2020, respectively, and in the 15th Sports and Health Sciences International Congress, 2019. He is the author of numerous scientific articles.

Samaa Shohieb is an associate professor at the Information Systems Department, Computers and Information Sciences faculty, Mansoura University, Egypt. She's interested in Human-computer Interaction integrated with E-society, Gaming, and Gamification as solutions for diverse users, especially those with specified capabilities.

Emerson Silva graduated in Physical Education (Full Licentiate) from Estácio de Alagoas College in 2021. In 2021, he started a specialization course in Exercise Physiology at the Physical Education and Sports Institute - IEFE from the Federal University of Alagoas - UFAL. Also, in the same year, she started her master's degree in Education at the Education Center - CEDU from the Federal University of Alagoas - UFAL, developing her research on teaching competencies for developing educational escape rooms. This research is carried out in partnership with the research group Virtual Communities - UFAL and researchers from the University of Aveiro - PT Unlock project. He has experience in the following research areas: Education, Learning, Game-based Learning, Gamification, Physical Education, and digital games focused on health and quality of life.

Janaina Silva graduated in Pedagogy from the Federal University of Alagoas - Ufal (2021); Participant in the Institutional Program of Scholarships for Scientific Initiation-PIBIC (2017/2018, 2018/2019, and 2019/2020); Master's student in the Information and Communication Technologies in Education research line of the Graduate Program in Education (PPGE/Cedu/Ufal) and member of the Virtual Communities Research Group - Ufal.

Suphichaya Suppipat is a Ph.D. candidate at the Institute of Environmental Engineering and Management, National Taipei University of Technology in Taiwan, and a Lecturer in Industrial Design at Chulalongkorn University in Thailand. She obtained a Master of Science in Industrial Ecology from the Norwegian University of Science and Technology, Norway. Over her decade of working experience in the product design industry and academia, she has dedicated most of her teaching hours to disseminating the concept of life cycle assessment in design and integrating various LCA-based tools in the product design process in Thailand.

Guilherme Xavier is a Master's and Doctor in Design from the Pontifical Catholic University of Rio de Janeiro. He is a researcher linked to LINC (Language, Interaction and Construction of Meanings/Design Laboratory), the supervisor at NINJA (Interdisciplinary Nucleus of Applied Games), and a member of the Structuring Teaching Nucleus of Digital Media at the Department of Arts & Design in the same university. He is interested in studying games in their productive, interactive, social, and historical dimensions, working as a teacher of academic disciplines related to design, imagery, and interactive digital media. He also presents himself as a ludologist and consultant for integrating entertainment and educational activities.

Alona Yurzhenko was born on November 18, 1989. She graduated from Kherson State University in 2012 with the specialty "Humanities. Language and Literature (English)" and was qualified as a lecturer of English Language and Foreign Literature. Since 2020 - Ph.D. in the specialty 13.00.04 "Theory and Methodology of Professional Education." Since 2019 - Assistant of English Language Department for Maritime Officers (abridged program). She teaches the discipline "English Language (for professional purposes)." Teaching experience in higher education institutions - 2 years. Alona Yurzhenko is the author/co-author of more than 60 scientific articles published in collections included in the list of professional publications of Ukraine, 4 of which are indexed in Scopus and WOS, as well as publications in collections of abstracts of 20 international conferences in the specialty. Research interests: gamification, AR, ICT in teaching of English, development of communicative competence, sustainable development of education, e-courses, LMS MOODLE. Orcid: https://orcid.org/0000-0002-6560-4601. Google Scholar: https://scholar.google.com.ua/citations?user=ZZMeUyMAAAAJ&hl=ru. Publons: https://publons.com/researcher/1768320/alona-yurzhenko/. Scopus: https://www.scopus.com/authid/detail.uri?authorId=57209800663.

Index

D

E

F

G

H

I

K

L

M

N

O

P

Q

R

S

T

U

V

www.ingramcontent.com/pod-product-compliance
Lightning Source LLC
LaVergne TN
LVHW080616300926
849162LV00005B/1182